CHILD PSYCHOLOGY

A Canadian Perspective

THIRD EDITION

Alastair J. Younger
University of Ottawa

Scott A. Adler
York University

Ross Vasta

John Wiley & Sons Canada, Ltd.

Library and Archives Canada Cataloguing in Publication

Child psychology: a Canadian perspective/Alastair Younger, Scott Adler, Ross Vasta.—3rd ed.

Includes bibliographical references and index.

ISBN 978-1-11-803391-3

1. Child psychology—Textbooks.

I. Adler, Scott II. Vasta, Ross III. Title.

BF721.Y65 2012 155.4 C2010-907597-8

Production Credits

Acquisitions Editor: Rodney Burke
Vice President & Publisher: Veronica Visentin
Marketing Manager: Patty Maher
Editorial Manager: Karen Staudinger
Production Manager: Tegan Wallace
Developmental Editor: Gail Brown
Media Editor: Channade Fenandoe
Editorial Assistant: Laura Hwee
Interior Design: Adrian So
Cover Design: Joanna Vieira
Cover Image: © Tara Moore/Corbis
Typesetting: Aptara
Printing & Binding: Quad/Graphics

Printed and bound in the United States of America
1 2 3 4 5 QG 16 15 14 13 12

John Wiley & Sons Canada, Ltd.
6045 Freemont Blvd.
Mississauga, Ontario L5R 4J3
Visit our website at: www.wiley.ca

ABOUT THE AUTHORS

ALASTAIR J. YOUNGER

Alastair Younger is Full Professor of Psychology at the University of Ottawa, Canada's largest bilingual university. He received his B.A. in Psychology from Carleton University in Ottawa in 1976, after which he completed graduate studies in clinical and developmental psychology at Concordia University in Montreal. He completed his M.A. in 1979 and his Ph.D. in 1984. While at Concordia, he became involved in the Concordia Risk Study from its inception in 1976. He is registered as a clinical psychologist with the College of Psychologists of Ontario, and is a member of the Canadian Psychological Association and the Society for Research in Child Development. He is co-author of the previous two editions of *Child Psychology*, as well as the Canadian edition of *Visualizing Psychology*, all published by Wiley Canada. In addition, he has authored more than 15 student study guides for courses in introductory psychology, child psychology, and abnormal psychology, which have been used widely across Canada and the United States, as well as in Australia and New Zealand. He has been a professor at the University of Ottawa for more than 25 years and is currently Director of Undergraduate Programs in Psychology. He has taught courses in child psychology, theories of development, social development, and research methods and ethics. His research focuses on children's peer relations, especially shyness/withdrawal and aggression in children.

SCOTT A. ADLER

Scott Adler is Associate Professor in the Department of Psychology and the Centre for Vision Research at York University in Toronto. He received his B.S. in Psychology with honours in 1990 from Brooklyn College of the City University of New York. He then attended Rutgers University, where he completed his M.S. in 1992 and his Ph.D. in 1995, studying the development of infant memory. He was awarded the Master's thesis of the year award from the New Jersey Psychological Association in 1992, the Dissertation Award from the International Society of Infant Studies, and the Shahin Hastroudi Memorial Prize from the American Psychological Society in 1996. He then was awarded a National Institute for Mental Health Postdoctoral Fellowship at the University of Denver in 1995. In 1998, he became a Neurobiology Research Associate at the Salk Institute for Biological Studies in San Diego, before moving to York University in 2000. His research program, funded by the U.S. National Institutes of Health, aims to understand the development of attentional, perceptual, and cognitive capacities in infancy, and is undertaken from a neuroscience perspective. In particular, his research has focused on infants' eye movements, selective attention, object recognition, memory processes, and future-oriented thinking. He has authored over 20 research papers and book chapters, and is co-author of the previous edition of *Child Psychology*. He has taught courses in developmental psychology, infancy, cognitive developmental theory, and developing the visual brain.

ROSS VASTA

Ross Vasta was Distinguished Professor of Psychology at the State University of New York at Brockport. He received his undergraduate degree from Dartmouth College in 1969 and his Ph.D. in clinical and developmental psychology from the State University of New York at Stony Brook in 1974. He was a Fellow in the American Psychological Society and the American Psychological Association (Division 7). In 1987 he was awarded the SUNY Chancellor's Award for Excellence in Teaching. His previous books include *Studying Children: An Introduction to Research Methods*, *Strategies and Techniques of Child Study*, and *Six Theories of Child Development*. He also edited the annual series, *Annals of Child Development*. Ross Vasta passed away in 2000.

Dedications

To my parents, Alan and Catherine, who nurtured my own development as a child, cognitively, academically, and spiritually. Your tireless encouragement contributed so much to who I am now. To my children, Melanie and Daniel, who provided me with first-hand knowledge of child development as they grew up, and whose childhoods have furnished so many delightful anecdotes for my child psychology classes. To my wife, Manal. Your inspiration and support has contributed in such a major way to the writing of this book. I couldn't have completed it without you.

—Alastair J. Younger

I want to especially dedicate this edition to my mother, Estelle Adler, who passed away during the writing of this edition. One of the most important qualities that she instilled in me was perseverance. On so many levels my mother's passing required much perseverance on my part to complete this edition. So much of this book details the importance of our parents, particularly our mother, in our development. My mother epitomized these qualities and I would not be where I am as a person, as a husband and father, as a researcher, and as an educator without her parenting. For this I will be forever grateful and I miss her greatly. Love you, Mom.

—Scott A. Adler

PREFACE

Child Psychology has long been praised as a text that reflects the principles of child psychology in a relevant and engaging manner. This scientifically-oriented text has always combined a thorough level of coverage of the best research in child psychology with an engaging, reader-friendly tone. Our goal in writing the third edition was to build on these strengths, particularly from a Canadian perspective. Thus, while writing this book, we strove to produce a book that continues to be truly Canadian in its focus, that highlights Canadian issues and content, that emphasizes Canadian statistics and social policies, and that focuses on the high-quality contributions of Canadian researchers.

NEW TO THIS EDITION

A key feature of this edition is the addition of a new chapter on neural and brain development (Chapter 6). Over the last 10 to 15 years, we have witnessed a major shift in how psychological processes are studied and understood. Researchers are not only trying to understand mental and behavioural processes, but also the brain structures and mechanisms responsible for those processes. Developmental researchers are increasingly trying to link the development of cognitive, language, social, and behavioural processes to the underlying neural and brain development. In recognition of the growing importance of neural and brain development in understanding the developing psychology of the child, and consequently the importance for students to have a thorough grounding in this topic, we have included a distinct chapter dedicated to neural and brain development. Though other child psychology textbooks, including previous editions of this text, have included some basic information about brain development in chapters on physical development, this textbook is unique in that it is the only one to include a chapter dedicated solely to this topic.

Preparation for the revisions of the other chapters began with a thorough evaluation of the contents of the previous edition by a number of expert reviewers, including current users of the text. We have been responsive to their insightful and invaluable feedback, while at the same time maintaining the approach and framework used historically by *Child Psychology.* The main suggestions were to incorporate new research developments, to include features on emerging "hot topics" in the field of child psychology, and to reorganize some textual material to increase readability. Key additions and changes to the book are as follows.

CONTEMPORARY FOCUS

We have thoroughly revised, rewritten, and updated this edition. A major focus was to ensure that the material presented in this book reflects the most recent findings of Canadian and international research in developmental psychology. As a consequence, we have added almost 1,000 new references to this edition.

Extensive chapter changes based on research have improved topic coverage. The most noteworthy and extensive changes can be found in Chapter 3 "Genetics: The Biological Context of Development," Chapter 4 "Prenatal Development," Chapter 8 "Cognitive Development: The Piagetian and Vygotskian Approaches," Chapter 12 "Early Social and Emotional Development," Chapter 14 "Moral Development," Chapter 15 "Families and Peers," and Chapter 16 "Gender Role Development and Sex Differences."

CONTENT REVISION

Content areas have been significantly strengthened. For example, we have updated our discussion of genetic disorders in Chapter 3 with even newer information on Tay Sachs disease in Québécois populations and current Canadian research on fragile X syndrome. We have also included in this chapter a new feature on gene therapy and its uses and limitations. In Chapter 4, we have considerably developed our coverage of the effects of teratogens. We have included the most recent Canadian data on the prenatal effects of diseases, cigarette smoking, and the use of both prescription medication and illicit drugs. In addition, we have substantially increased our discussion of Fetal Alcohol Spectrum Disorder (FASD) and its cognitive and social consequences.

We have substantially expanded our coverage of infant development on many fronts. Particularly, as mentioned, Chapter 6 is dedicated to up-to-date theories, knowledge, and data concerning the structure and function of the neuron and brain and their development. In this new chapter, we have reviewed the most up-to-date techniques for recording and imaging the brain and their applicability to the study of development; we have discussed the neuron and its developmental course; and we have thoroughly described the most recent data on the different brain structures, their functions, and their development, including brain plasticity. In Chapter 7, new material has been added on visual development, including recent data concerning the developmental timeline for depth perception and new data from eye movement, visual search, and negative priming studies on the development of selective attention. A considerable amount of new material on language development in infancy has been added to Chapter 11, including a discussion of the use of baby sign language.

In our discussion of cognitive development, we have combined the separate chapters on Piaget's theory and Vygotsky's theory from the previous edition into a single chapter where we compare and contrast each approach. In Chapter 9, we have expanded and updated the material on infant memory and categorization, the usage of memory strategies by children, preschoolers' number processing, and the development of executive functions and reasoning skills.

In Chapter 12, we have expanded our discussion of both the development and the socialization of emotions. As well, in this chapter we expand our discussion of the phases of the development of attachment and the characteristics of parental care related to attachment. We conclude Chapter 12 with a new Canadian feature on persistent infant crying in the first months of life, and the PURPLE crying program developed by Ronald Barr of the University of British Columbia. In Chapter 13, we have further developed our discussion of the emergence of self-control and discuss the classic Canadian research of Donald Meichenbaum on the use of private speech as a means of gaining self-control in impulsive children.

We have made considerable changes to Chapter 14. We include an example of Kohlberg's moral dilemmas, and discuss in detail findings related to the criticism that Kohlberg's dilemmas may reflect a gender bias. In our discussion of the topics of empathy and sympathy, we present Martin Hoffman's six-stage model of the development of empathy in children. In our discussion of aggression, we distinguish between function (*proactive* and *reactive* aggression) and form (*physical*, *verbal*, *relational*). We have also significantly updated our material on families and aggression, as well as our discussion of television and video-game violence. In addition, we have included a detailed discussion of social-information-processing models of aggression. Our discussion of bullying has been revised and updated. We discuss recent Canadian anti-bullying strategies, including the WITS anti-victimization program developed at the University of Victoria, as well as the Canadian PREVnet anti-bullying initiative. We have also added a new feature on cyber bullying to this material.

Our discussion of the family, in Chapter 15, contains an extensive amount of new material. We have substantially expanded our discussion of sibling relationships. We have also increased our coverage of divorce and its effects on children, and our discussion of post-divorce custody arrangements common in Canada. We include recent Canadian statistics on post-divorce contact with the father and a discussion of factors related to father contact. In our discussion of alternative family compositions, we have added a discussion of factors that can promote resiliency among teenage mothers. In our discussion of peer relationships in Chapter 15, we have expanded our coverage of contextual differences between boys' and girls' friendship groups. We also discuss in greater detail the differences between *sociometric* popularity and *perceived* popularity, an area of research that has gained much attention in recent years.

In Chapter 16, we have updated our sections on gender differences in quantitative and spatial abilities, as well as our discussion of research on interventions to increase spatial abilities in children and adults. We have also considerably updated our section on sexual relationships and behaviour.

A central aim in revising the content was to provide expanded descriptions of current "hot topics" in child psychology. We further explore those topics already included in the previous edition, and also add emerging issues. These hot topics include gene therapy; prenatal cigarette, alcohol, and drug use; recent Canadian data on the prenatal effects of maternal HIV infection; sudden infant death syndrome (SIDS); kangaroo care for premature infants; ethnicity and IQ testing; bilingualism and French immersion; the burgeoning phenomenon of baby sign language; shaken baby syndrome; bullying and victimization, including the increasing problem of cyber bullying; video-game violence and aggression; divorce, remarriage, and alternative family structures; children's use of the Internet; and the effectiveness of training in spatial abilities.

We strove to write a truly Canadian text. Consequently, Canadian data are paramount in every chapter. For example, throughout the book we feature data from a number of very recent surveys by the Public Health Agency of Canada, very recent Canadian data on factors influencing prenatal development, current statistics on infant mortality rates from across Canada, census data on the family recently released by Statistics Canada, current data concerning international adoptions in Canada released by the Adoption Council of Canada, recent data on rates of French immersion released by Canadian Parents for French, and much more.

HALLMARK FEATURES

Several important features have characterized *Child Psychology* throughout each of its editions. These include an emphasis on psychology as a science, the importance of a contextualist view of human development, a balanced theoretical framework for interpretation of findings and on the methods through which knowledge is obtained, and a concern with cultural context and cultural diversity. In addition, *Child Psychology* has always featured a topical organization, state-of-the-art coverage, and a focus on readability and accessibility to students.

SCIENTIFIC ORIENTATION

In this text, we treat child psychology as a natural science and present it in a way that reflects its scientific underpinnings. In addition to providing a full chapter on research methods (Chapter 2), we discuss specific methodological issues throughout the textbook, such as comparing research designs for examining genetic influences on development in Chapter 3, consideration of brain recording and imaging techniques for studying development in Chapter 6, discussing methods of studying infant perception in Chapter 7, describing computer simulations in Chapter 9, and considering contrasting approaches to assessing infant–caregiver attachment in Chapter 12.

A CONTEXTUALIST APPROACH

The most important and distinctive feature of *Child Psychology* remains its emphasis on the contextualist view of human development. Inspired by Urie Bronfenbrenner's seminal work and fuelled by the rediscovery of Lev Vygotsky's writings, modern child psychology has increasingly adopted a contextualist perspective. The child is not viewed as a passive recipient of environmental influences, but rather as an active producer of those influences. From the very beginning, the infant engages in a transactional "dance" with the caregiver, each regulating the behaviour of the other. As the child grows, development interacts in critical ways with the social contexts in which it occurs, the most important being the family system, the peer group, the school, and the cultural environment.

As in previous editions, *Child Psychology* integrates relevant contextual material throughout the text. Thus, in addition to discussing the effects of schools, families, and peers in separate chapters, we consider such effects in relation to each of the relevant topics. For example, Chapter 12 examines the contribution of maternal caregiving to the development of attachment, Chapter 13 discusses the ways in which schools can affect self-esteem, and Chapter 14 considers the influences of both parents and peers on moral development. This approach allows the course to move from one area of development to another in a topical manner, while including the broad tapestry of variables that affect each area.

BALANCED THEORETICAL PRESENTATION

Rather than emphasizing any single theoretical orientation, *Child Psychology* examines topics from the perspectives of the principal theoretical traditions that characterize the discipline: the cognitive-developmental approach, the environmental/learning approach, the ethological/evolutionary approach, and the sociocultural approach.

The fundamental tenets of the four general approaches are first presented in Chapter 1. Many of the remaining chapters begin by examining how the four traditions address the particular chapter's topic area, and go on to consider relevant research findings and applications. As a result, the student can approach the substantive material in these chapters with a conceptual structure that facilitates interpretation, comparison, and critical analysis. For example, Chapter 12 on early social development includes an account of Bowlby's influential evolutionary model, and the subsequent discussion of attachment then considers the evidence in support of this position. Similarly, Chapter 14, on moral development, begins by outlining the theoretical models of Piaget, Kohlberg, and Turiel, each of which is revisited in the later discussion of research on moral reasoning.

CULTURAL DIVERSITY

Each edition of this book has seen expanded coverage of research in diverse communities and cultures around the world. Discussions of development in different cultures are woven throughout the text. For example, we describe how different cultures affect cognitive development (Chapter 8) and foster different approaches to language learning (Chapter 11), we discuss different conceptions of the self and morality across different cultures (Chapters 13 and 14), and we consider cultural variations in child-rearing practices (Chapter 15).

TOPICAL ORGANIZATION

We have chosen to organize the book topically. By considering each topic area in its own chapter, we believe we can most effectively present and critique the full body of research and theorizing relevant to that area. The 16 chapters can be grouped into four general parts:

Chapters 1 and 2 provide the foundation of the discipline, covering history, theory, and research methods. In keeping with the scientific orientation of the text, both theories and research methods are presented in some detail.

Chapters 3 to 6 focus on biological and physical development, including genetics, prenatal development, birth, growth, motor development, and brain development.

Chapters 7 to 11 cover sensory and perceptual development, three approaches to cognitive development, intelligence and schooling, and language.

Chapters 12 to 16 describe social and personality development, including emotional development, attachment, the self-system, moral reasoning, prosocial and antisocial behaviour, family relations, peer relations, and gender-role development.

Although the overall organization is topical, the internal presentation of chapters 6 to 16 is developmental. The topic area—be it language, gender roles, or another topic—begins with the newborn and describes development through adolescence. This approach helps students to appreciate the continuity of growth within each area, and also to understand the ongoing interactions between biological processes and contextual influences.

STATE-OF-THE-ART COVERAGE

The field of child psychology is generating information at a staggering rate. To prepare a textbook of manageable proportions, authors must make some tough decisions. We have chosen to present a state-of-the-art treatment of child psychology that focuses on the latest issues and findings. To this end, we have incorporated hundreds of new references from the last three or four years into this new edition.

READABILITY AND ACCESSIBILITY

Above all, we have worked hard to make our text interesting and accessible to the student reader. We believe that the text's comfortable writing style and the clarity with which concepts are introduced, discussed, and interrelated will enable students to read and understand a rigorous treatment of the issues. Users of previous editions have consistently praised the accessibility of the text, and we believe that we have produced a text that simply and effectively communicates the essence and excitement of child psychology.

PEDAGOGICAL FEATURES

Throughout the text, we have integrated several new pedagogical features as well as new Canadian research, issues, and data to make this text more relevant and more engaging to Canadian students. The text was extensively redesigned to ensure that the content of this new edition is presented in a user-friendly and appealing fashion, without affecting its rigour. Throughout each chapter, a variety of pedagogical features help the reader learn the content and context of this dynamic discipline.

LEARNING OBJECTIVES

Each major section in a chapter opens with a learning objective and ends with a series of short-answer questions. These questions are intended to help students fulfill the learning objective by guiding their learning and testing their mastery of the material. Answers to these questions are found at the end of each chapter. The answers serve not only as a way for students to check their knowledge and understanding, but also as a convenient review of the key points in the chapter.

Learning Objective 12.2

Understand the development of early communication between the infant and caregiver.

CHAPTER-OPENING VIGNETTES

Each chapter begins with a brief discussion designed to capture the student's interest by introducing the topic under consideration and to show the practical applications of that topic.

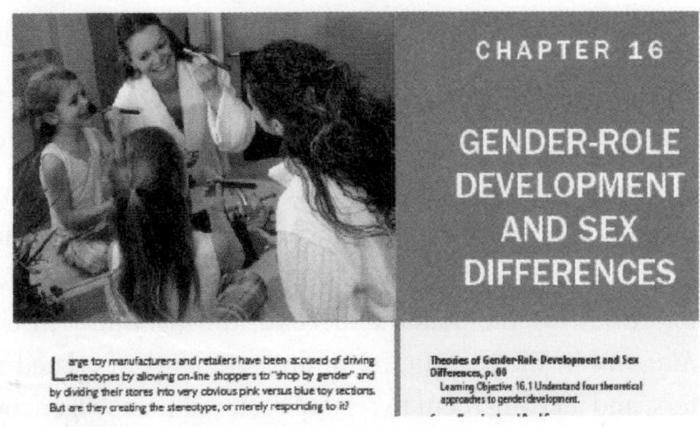

CHAPTER 16
GENDER-ROLE DEVELOPMENT AND SEX DIFFERENCES
Large toy manufacturers and retailers have been accused of driving stereotypes by allowing on-line shoppers to "shop by gender" and by dividing their stores into very obvious pink versus blue toy sections. But are they creating the stereotype, or merely responding to it?
Theories of Gender-Role Development and Sex Differences, p. 00
Learning Objective 16.1 Understand four theoretical approaches to gender development.

FOCUS ON RESEARCH

Canadian researchers figure prominently in the field of child psychology. Throughout each chapter, we have integrated research conducted at Canadian institutions into the discussion. Consequently, students are able to see how Canadian research fits into the science of child psychology. In addition, we have featured research conducted by Canadian researchers that fits well within the theme of the chapter. This provides students with more in-depth examination of Canadian research within a specific domain. Examples include research on the effects of prenatal marijuana use (Chapter 4), research on French immersion programs (Chapter 11), and research on shyness (Chapter 15).

FOCUS ON RESEARCH 2.1
THE CONCORDIA RISK STUDY: A CANADIAN LONGITUDINAL INVESTIGATION OF AGGRESSIVE AND WITHDRAWN CHILDREN

Longitudinal research is frequently costly and time-consuming. It also suffers from the disadvantage of attrition—the loss of individuals under study—often because participants move away. Nevertheless, longitudinal research is valuable as it really is the only way to investigate the stability or persistence of behaviour and the effects of early experience on later development.

One well-known Canadian longitudinal investigation has been underway for more than 30 years at Concordia University in Montreal. Begun in 1976 by Jane Ledingham and Alex Schwartzman (Ledingham, 1981; Schwartzman, Ledingham, & with higher levels of adolescent sexual behaviour and higher-than-average rates of teenage pregnancies (Serbin, Peters, McAffer, & Schwartzman, 1991). Moreover, for both boys and girls, aggression in combination with withdrawal is associated with even more negative consequences, predicting a greater number of social and behavioural problems than does aggression alone (Moskowitz & Schwartzman, 1989).

What about social withdrawal? Does it, too, predict later problems? Although we tend to think of shy, withdrawn children as not being at risk for later problems, the Concordia Risk Study

ON THE CUTTING EDGE

On the Cutting Edge features are designed to make students aware of recent and exciting research findings. Among the topics singled out for such coverage are gene therapy (Chapter 3), the ability of newborns to recognize their mother's face (Chapter 7), theory of mind in infancy (Chapter 8), and persistent infant crying and the risk of shaken baby syndrome (Chapter 12).

ON THE CUTTING EDGE 7.1
CAN NEWBORNS RECOGNIZE THEIR MOTHERS' FACES?

One of the important tasks of infancy is to learn to recognize and to prefer the primary caregiver, who, in most instances, is the baby's mother. We have seen that a preference for the mother's voice or the mother's odour appears in the first few days of life. Might a preference for the mother's face also be present this early?

There are numerous reasons to think that the answer to this question will be no. In both the auditory and the olfactory realms, babies receive stimulation from the mother during the prenatal of a stranger (Walton, Bower, & Bower, 1992). The investigators who conducted these studies have been careful to control for other possible bases for recognition of the mother, such as auditory or olfactory cues. Thus, the response really does seem to be the mother's face.

How could a baby with such a limited visual system and such limited visual experience recognize the mother? The study by Pascalis and colleagues (1995) suggests an answer. After demonstrating the preference for the mother's face, the re-

RESEARCH CLASSIC

Research Classic presents studies of enduring historical value. Examples include Arnold Gesell's research on motor development in twins (Chapter 5), Rosenthal and Jacobson's research on teacher expectations (Chapter 10), Harry Harlow's work with attachment in infant monkeys (Chapter 12), and Diana Baumrind's initial studies of parenting styles (Chapter 15).

RESEARCH CLASSIC 10.1
PYGMALION IN THE CLASSROOM

Teachers naturally welcome information about their students that might help them to teach more effectively. For many, results from standardized assessment tests—such as IQ and academic achievement measures—are useful sources of information. Normally, of course, such tests are designed to be as accurate as possible. One of the most famous experiments in child psychology, however, was built around the provision of deliberately inaccurate test information to teachers.

Robert Rosenthal and Lenore Jacobson (1968) informed on an IQ test given at the end of the year. By the end of the year, the bloomers were also earning better grades in reading and arithmetic. Apparently the teachers' expectancies acted as *self-fulfilling prophecies*: children who were expected to perform well did perform well.

The Rosenthal and Jacobson study is not only one of the most famous, but also one of the most controversial experiments in child psychology. The original study has been subjected to a number of criticisms, and its results have not always been

APPLICATION

This feature presents examples of research programs and findings that have been applied to solve practical problems in schools, homes, hospitals, and other real-world settings. Examples include prevention of sudden infant death syndrome (SIDS) (Chapter 5), improving children's eyewitness testimony (Chapter 9), and reducing stereotype threat in minority populations (Chapter 10).

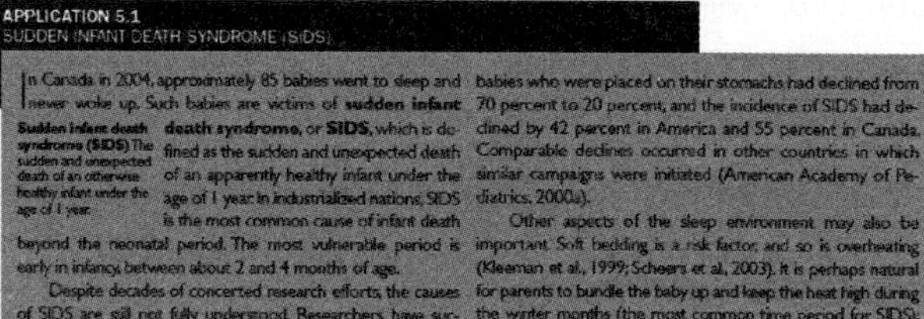
APPLICATION 5.1
SUDDEN INFANT DEATH SYNDROME (SIDS)

In Canada in 2004, approximately 85 babies went to sleep and never woke up. Such babies are victims of **sudden infant death syndrome**, or **SIDS**, which is defined as the sudden and unexpected death of an apparently healthy infant under the age of 1 year. In industrialized nations, SIDS is the most common cause of infant death beyond the neonatal period. The most vulnerable period is early in infancy, between about 2 and 4 months of age.

Sudden infant death syndrome (SIDS) The sudden and unexpected death of an otherwise healthy infant under the age of 1 year.

Despite decades of concerted research efforts, the causes of SIDS are still not fully understood. Researchers have suc- babies who were placed on their stomachs had declined from 70 percent to 20 percent, and the incidence of SIDS had declined by 42 percent in America and 55 percent in Canada. Comparable declines occurred in other countries in which similar campaigns were initiated (American Academy of Pediatrics, 2000a).

Other aspects of the sleep environment may also be important. Soft bedding is a risk factor, and so is overheating (Kleeman et al., 1999; Scheers et al., 2003). It is perhaps natural for parents to bundle the baby up and keep the heat high during the winter months (the most common time period for SIDS);

MARGIN MATERIAL (KEY TERM GLOSSARY, LINKS TO RELATED MATERIAL, FOR THOUGHT AND DISCUSSION)

Identical or monozygotic (MZ) twins Twins who develop from a single fertilized ovum and thus inherit identical genetic material.

Links to Related Material

In Chapter 10, you will learn more about how the genetic foundations of intelligence interact with environment to influence children's cognitive development.

For Thought and Discussion

Are you aware of "niche-picking" during your childhood or in your life now? To what extent do you seek out environments that best fit your genetic predispositions?

A number of pedagogical features are found in the margins as students read through the chapter. First, boldfaced *key terms* in the text highlight terms of importance to students. These items are defined in the margin on the same page, as well as at the end of the book, providing a convenient guide for reviewing the material. Second, throughout each chapter we have presented *Links to Related Material* in the margin, reminding students of related material they have read in previous chapters, and alerting them to related material they will encounter in later chapters. These links connect similar subject matter and methods discussed in other chapters, thereby allowing students access to a bigger picture of the field of child psychology. Third, we have inserted comments and questions about the material students are reading throughout each chapter. This material, labelled *For Thought and Discussion,* is designed to stimulate thinking and can serve as the basis for in-class discussion.

RESOURCES

A full package of materials accompanies the text to support student learning and instructor teaching. The textbook's companion website (www.wiley.com/go/younger) offers a wealth of resources for both students and instructors. The student companion website includes practice quizzes, as well as links to interesting and relevant websites for the content of each chapter. The instructor website includes resources such as an instructor's manual, PowerPoint slides, test bank files, and videos.

ACKNOWLEDGEMENTS

A project of this size requires the participation of many people, and we acknowledge all the colleagues who provided feedback and suggestions for each edition of this textbook. In particular, we thank those who provided feedback for this edition; their insights and feedback were invaluable and constructive, and helped to shape the textbook you have in your hands.

Brenda Baird, *University of Ottawa*
Annie Bernier, *Université de Montréal*
Jessey Bernstein, *McGill University*
Angela R. Birt, *Mount Saint Vincent University*
Jeremy Carpendale, *Simon Fraser University*
Jason Daniels, *University of Alberta*
Nukte Edguer, *Brandon University*
Elizabeth Kelley, *Queen's University*
Trudy Kwong, *Grant MacEwan University*
Sarah Lippé, *Université de Montréal*
Mowei Liu, *Trent University*
Sandra Martin-Chang, *Concordia University*
Laura Melnyk, *University of Western Ontario*
Ulrich Müller, *University of Victoria*
Geoff Navara, *Trent University*
Caroline Sullivan, *University of Ottawa*
Lindie Synnott, *Bishop's University*
Maggie Toplak, *York University*

We thank especially Christopher Fennell (University of Ottawa) for his expert contributions to Chapter 11, Language Development. We are grateful to Jocelyn Wentland for her valuable input into the discussion of sexual development in Chapter 16, and Laura Doey for her contribution to the discussion of cyber bullying in Chapter 14. We are also grateful to Pierre Gosselin (University of Ottawa) for his many contributions to the first edition of the text, to Robin Harwood (University of Connecticut) for her contributions to this edition, and to Marshall Haith, Scott Miller, and Sheri Ellis for their contributions to earlier editions of this book. We thank also the contributors who revised the textbook's various ancillaries: Jason Daniels (University of Alberta), Sandra Martin-Chang (Concordia University), Ulrich Müller (University of Victoria), and Lindie Synnott (Bishop's University).

We thank our Acquisitions Editor, Rodney Burke. We owe special thanks to our Developmental Editor, Gail Brown; this book could not have been completed without her assistance, incredible patience, enthusiasm, and expertise at every step in the process. The editorial and proofreading contributions of Janice Dyer, Laurel Hyatt, and Barbara Tomlin are also greatly appreciated.

Finally, we want to express very special appreciation to our respective spouses, Manal Guirguis-Younger and Laura Adler, for their endless support during our work on this book, as well as for spending countless hours reading and providing feedback. Without their help and patient encouragement, this book would not be what it is.

Alastair J. Younger, Ottawa, Ontario
Scott A. Adler, Toronto, Ontario
March 2012

BRIEF CONTENTS

CONTENTS

CHAPTER 1

BACKGROUND AND THEORIES

A popular nursery rhyme says that boys are made of "snips and snails and puppy-dogs' tails" and girls are made of "sugar and spice and everything nice." Researchers in child psychology have long tried to find out what boys and girls are actually made of and what might account for any differences between the sexes. Developmental psychologists systematically study how children's brains, personalities, and behaviour develop alongside their bodies.

Studying children, especially those who can't talk, requires devising creative ways of observing them scientifically and developing theories to explain what psychologists observe. For example, some 50 years ago, Robert Fantz noticed that newly hatched chicks started pecking for food right away. Wondering if newborn humans could also perceive their world, he devised a simple but groundbreaking experiment. He placed disks with various shapes and images on them in front of babies aged 1 to 15 weeks. He recorded how long they stared at each shape, and found that they stared longer at some shapes than others. Fantz deduced that newborns can perceive and discriminate among various objects. Fantz's preferential-looking method for studying babies is still used today.

Older children can be observed in constructed scenarios as well. In a recent experiment testing emotions, children aged 4 to 7 visiting a museum were told they would receive "very cool stickers" from a child in another city in a sealed envelope. One third did receive the stickers, one third got a note saying "I used all the stickers before I mailed this," and one third received the same note but with "I am really sorry" added. The children who received the apology were far more likely to rate the sender as "nice" but also "sad."

In this chapter, we will introduce you to the science of child psychology, discuss a number of theorists who have played a prominent role in the history of this science, and discuss the major concepts that underlie the field of developmental psychology.

Source: Fagan, Joseph F. III, "Visual perception and experience in early infancy: A look at the hidden side of behavior development." In H. Hayne and J. W. Fagen (Eds.), *Progress in infancy research: Volume 3*, Mahwah, NJ: Lawrence Erlbaum Associates, 2003, pp. 28–31.

Lopez-Duran, Nestor, "An apology is more than a word: Effects of apologies on children's emotions," Child-Psych Blog, May 28, 2009; retrieved from http://www.child-psych.org/2009/05/effects-of-apologies-on-childrens-emotions.html. ■

Learning Objective 1.1

Understand the philosophical and historical roots of child psychology.

DEVELOPMENTAL PSYCHOLOGY AND ITS ROOTS

This book presents the modern science of child psychology. In it, we trace the growing child's development from the embryo's earliest beginnings in the mother's womb to the child's eventual ascent into adolescence. We describe the many factors that affect children's development, as well as how researchers go about the work of identifying them.

Attempts to explain children's development go as far back as history can trace. But child psychology as a science is only a little more than 100 years old. What distinguishes our efforts during this past century is psychologists' use of the scientific method. This approach involves rules that specify how research evidence should be gathered, how it may be analyzed, and what sorts of conclusions researchers may draw from their findings. Scientists have used this method to study an endless number of phenomena, from stars to starfish. In this book, we examine how they use it to study children.

At first glance, understanding child development may not appear to be very difficult. Certainly the typical behaviours of infants and young children—including their physical abilities, their interactions with others, and even the ways they think—are simpler than those same behaviours in adults. But it is a mistake to conclude that the processes involved are simple. Psychologists have learned that human development is a complex and intricate puzzle, and unravelling its mysteries has proven to be a major challenge. We have learned a great deal since the methods of science were first applied to the study of children around 100 years ago. Yet the more we learn, the more apparent it becomes that we have only scratched the surface.

WHAT IS DEVELOPMENTAL PSYCHOLOGY?

To begin, it is important to understand exactly what psychology is and what psychologists study. Psychology is the scientific study of behaviour. The behaviour that most psychologists study is human behaviour. But any species—from mice to mynah birds to monkeys—can be examined legitimately from a psychological (and developmental) perspective.

Developmental psychology The branch of psychology devoted to the study of changes in behaviour and abilities over the course of development.

Developmental psychology, one of the largest of psychology's many subfields, is concerned with *the changes in behaviour and abilities that occur as development proceeds.* Developmental researchers examine what these changes are and why they occur. To put it another way, developmental research has two basic goals. One is *description*—to identify children's behaviour at each point in their development. This involves questions such as: When do babies begin to detect colours? What do 5-year-olds understand about the mind? How do adolescents usually resolve conflicts with their peers? The second goal is *explanation*—determining the causes and processes that produce changes in behaviour from one point to the next. This involves examining the effects of such factors as the genes children inherit from their parents, the biological characteristics of the human brain, the physical and social environment in which children live, and the types of experiences they encounter.

Developmental psychologists study behaviour changes at all phases of the life cycle (Overton, 2010). Most, though, have focused on the childhood period, ending at adolescence. For this reason, *developmental psychology* and *child psychology* have traditionally referred to the same body of scientific knowledge. That situation has changed somewhat in recent years as research is increasingly being directed toward issues of adulthood and old age. This book, however, focuses on the traditional early period (and so we have chosen the title *Child Psychology*).

WHY STUDY CHILDREN?

For Thought and Discussion

What aspects of children's development are you particularly interested in learning about in this course?

If developmental psychologists can study any species of animal and any period in the life cycle, why has so much research traditionally concentrated on humans during the childhood years? We have at least five answers to this question.

PERIOD OF RAPID DEVELOPMENT Because developmental researchers are interested in studying change, it makes sense for them to focus on a period when much change occurs. More developmental changes take place during the first part of the life of most species than during any other period. In humans, changes involving physical growth, social interactions, acquisition of language, memory abilities, and virtually all other areas of development are greatest during childhood.

LONG-TERM INFLUENCES Another important reason for studying children is that the events and experiences of the early years strongly affect an individual's later development. As the poet William Wordsworth once noted (and many psychologists have since reiterated), "The child is father to the man." Almost all psychological theories suggest that who we are today depends very much on our development and experiences as children.

INSIGHT INTO COMPLEX ADULT PROCESSES Not all psychologists are primarily concerned with early development. But even researchers who attempt to understand complex adult behaviours often find it useful to examine those behaviours during periods when they are not so complex. For example, humans are capable of sophisticated communication because languages follow systems of rules. Determining these rules, however, has proven to be very difficult.

One approach to this problem is to study our language system as it is being acquired. Thus, in language development, as well as in many other areas, the growing child is a showcase of developing skills and abilities, and researchers interested in different aspects of human development have taken advantage of this fact to help them understand adult behaviour.

REAL-WORLD APPLICATIONS Developmental psychologists often conduct their research in laboratory settings where they investigate theoretical questions regarding basic psychological processes. Nevertheless, the products of this research benefit children with real-world problems, such as poverty, illiteracy, drugs, and crime. Legislators and other policy makers often turn to psychologists to provide them with usable knowledge regarding the effects of these problems on children and possible ways to treat them (Aber, Bishop-Josef, Jones, McLearn, & Phillips, 2006; McLoyd, Aikens, & Burton, 2006). Developmental research also touches such areas as the effects of daycare, classroom teaching methods, and parental disciplinary techniques, among others. Simply put, one reason we study children is to make their lives better.

Research in child psychology often addresses issues of applied importance. One such issue is the possible effects of daycare on children's development. (*Banana Stock*)

INTERESTING SUBJECT MATTER A final and important reason why so many developmental psychologists have directed their efforts toward understanding children is that the human child is an intriguing and wondrous creature. When we consider that children have attracted the attention of artists, writers, and scholars in many other fields of study, it is perhaps not surprising that psychologists, too, have found this subject matter appealing. Our own interest in pursuing this area of science reflects our personal love of children and our fascination with their behaviour and development.

HISTORICAL VIEWS OF CHILDHOOD

Have you ever wondered why children are treated so specially? Have you thought about why we have laws designed to protect children from dangerous toys, dangerous activities, dangerous substances, and even dangerous parents? Why we consider it important that all children receive a free public education—and why they must remain in school until they reach a certain age?

It is likely that you have taken these matters for granted. It may seem obvious that children need special attention, care, and protection. The value of educating children, too, may seem self-evident. But these attitudes reflect a certain understanding of childhood and of how children develop. You might be surprised to learn that this understanding is a relatively recent development in Western culture.

ANCIENT GREECE AND ROME Consider, for example, the status of children in the Greek and Roman civilizations, which extended from about 600 B.C.E. to about 400 C.E. Although great Greek thinkers such as Plato and Aristotle wrote of the importance of education, they also defended practices that today would seem unthinkable. *Infanticide*, the killing of newborns, was routine and viewed as an appropriate way to deal with babies who were illegitimate, unhealthy, or simply unwanted (Breiner, 1990; Langer, 1974). Severe punishment and exploitation of children were neither uncommon nor considered wrong or cruel. The ancient Romans, for example, bought and sold children for various purposes, including domestic work and service in brothels for the sexual pleasure of adults (Mounteer, 1987). So although the ancient world recognized the importance of the childhood years, it did not display the caring and protective attitudes toward children that exist today.

THE MEDIEVAL AND RENAISSANCE PERIODS Following the collapse of the Roman Empire, the Catholic Church attempted to improve the lives of children by promoting an image of them as pure and innocent. The church took a strong stand against infanticide and offered parents of unwanted children the alternative of shipping them away to convents and monasteries—an arrangement that benefitted both parties. Although educational training during this period reached one of its lowest levels in recorded history, the Church did provide simple reading and writing instruction to children involved in religious studies (Sommerville, 1982). Unfortunately, however, abuse and exploitation of children remained commonplace throughout the Middle Ages.

The Renaissance began early in the 14th century and extended into the 17th century. This era brought increased concern for the welfare of children. In Florence, Italy—generally considered the birthplace of the Renaissance—charitable institutions known as foundling homes were set up by wealthy individuals to take in sick, lost, and unwanted children. Foundling homes, which eventually spread throughout Western Europe, were significant in that they represented a new and growing belief that society had some responsibility for the care and protection of its youngsters (Trexler, 1973).

The Renaissance also saw the re-emergence of scientific investigation in such fields as astronomy, medicine, and physics. The science of psychology did not yet exist, however, so the study of human development was primarily the concern of philosophers and religious scholars. As you will see in this chapter, the science of child psychology emerged around the beginning of the 20th century. But before that, philosophers discussed and debated various ideas about human nature and human development. We find the roots of our modern scientific understanding of child development in these debates, and in this chapter we discuss important early theorists who contributed to this understanding, as well as pioneers in the science of psychology.

John Locke (above top left) proposed the notion of tabula rasa; Jean-Jacques Rousseau (above top right) described his views of human development in his novel *Émile*; Johann Gottfried von Herder (bottom right) developed ideas regarding culture and socialization; Charles Darwin (bottom left) laid the foundation for the modern fields of ethology and sociobiology with his theory of evolution. (*Top left, NYPL; top right, Corbis-Bettman; bottom right, Corbis-Bettman; bottom left, Getty Images*)

EARLY THEORISTS

Before there was a field called child psychology, children were topics of interest for philosophers and scientists. Four early scholars—John Locke, Jean-Jacques Rousseau, Johann Gottfried von Herder, and Charles Darwin—offered theories of human behaviour that are the direct ancestors of the major theoretical traditions found in child psychology today. These modern traditions include one model that focuses on the influence of the child's environment, a second that emphasizes the role of the child's cognitive development, a third that argues that development is shaped by and embedded in a sociocultural context, and a fourth that is most concerned with the evolutionary origins of behaviour.

JOHN LOCKE (1632–1704) One of the most famous of early English philosophers was John Locke, a physician and a leading political figure of the time. According to Locke, all children are created (born) equal, and the mind of a newborn infant is like a **tabula rasa**—literally a "blank slate" (think of a blank computer screen with nothing written on it). All knowledge comes to the child only through experience and learning. Children are therefore neither innately good nor innately evil; they are simply the products of their environment and upbringing. This environmentalist point of view also means that any child is theoretically capable of becoming anything—a surgeon, an actor, a skilled artisan—if given the proper rearing and training. Similarly, the wrong environment can produce a scoundrel (Crain, 2011).

Tabula rasa Latin phrase meaning "blank slate," used to describe the newborn's mind as entirely empty of innate abilities, interests, or ideas.

Locke's writings were not all scholarly. He also offered advice to parents on the best methods for rearing their children. Although he stressed the use of rewards and punishments, Locke did not favour material rewards (e.g., candy and toys) or physical punishment. Discipline, he believed, should involve praise for appropriate behaviours and scolding for inappropriate behaviours. Locke also discussed the importance of stimulating children to begin learning at a very early age (Crain, 2011). Locke's ideas gained wide acceptance among British and European scholars as well as the general public. But within less than a century, this strong environmentalist model was replaced by a very different conception of the child.

JEAN-JACQUES ROUSSEAU (1712–1778) Jean-Jacques Rousseau was born in Switzerland, but spent most of his life in France, where he became a leading philosopher of his day. He is considered the father of French romanticism, a movement that emphasized themes of sentimentality, naturalness, and innocence. These ideas were reflected in Rousseau's conception of the child.

Rousseau's views on development were presented in his novel *Émile* (1762), in which he described the care and tutoring of a male child from infancy to young adulthood. Using this literary vehicle, Rousseau outlined his views of human development and offered suggestions on the most appropriate methods of child rearing and education (Crain, 2011; Mitzenheim, 1985).

In contrast to Locke, Rousseau believed that children are born with knowledge and ideas that unfold naturally with age. In this view, development follows a predictable series of stages that are guided by an inborn timetable. Rousseau also believed that whatever knowledge the child does not possess innately is acquired gradually from interactions with the environment, guided by the child's own interests and level of development. Thus, the wisest approach to child rearing is not to instruct children formally, but to have them learn through exploration and discovery. By emphasizing innate processes as the driving forces in human development, Rousseau's theory contrasted with the environmentalism of Locke and would today be referred to as **nativism**.

For Thought and Discussion

One theme that has interested philosophers is whether children are born with a tendency to be good, bad, or neither. What do you think? Is this a question that would be worth studying by psychologists?

Nativism The theory that human development results principally from inborn processes that guide the emergence of behaviours in a predictable manner.

Rousseau's ideas had a major impact in Europe, and his nativistic view of development was hailed by both scientific and political writers. As we will see, they reappeared some 200 years later in the work of another Swiss theorist, Jean Piaget.

JOHANN GOTTFRIED VON HERDER (1744–1803) Another thinker whose writings anticipated modern ideas about development was Johann Gottfried von Herder, a leader in German romanticism. Von Herder's theory of development is essentially an account of socialization into a group or community (Jahoda, 1993). According to von Herder, everyone is born into a specific cultural community with a shared language and historical traditions. These shared practices in turn shape the minds of the members of the community. Von Herder was perhaps most revolutionary in his appreciation for cultural diversity; he opposed attempts to impose one culture's values on another. Instead, he argued for **cultural relativism**, the idea that each culture must be examined and evaluated on its own terms.

Cultural relativism The belief that each culture should be examined and evaluated on its own terms.

Von Herder placed special emphasis on language, the means by which cultural practices and values are transmitted from generation to generation. He argued that studying the diversity of the world's languages offers insights into the history of humankind. He also emphasized the dynamic nature of both language and culture. He believed that language and culture are not passively absorbed by children, but are continually reinterpreted and changed by the members of the community: "We live in a world we create."

As we will see, von Herder's views on the relationship between thought and language, the dynamic nature of culture, and the importance of a historical perspective foreshadow those of the Russian theorist Lev Vygotsky and modern adherents to the sociocultural approach.

CHARLES DARWIN (1809–1882) A fourth major ancestor of modern developmental thought was the English biologist Charles Darwin. His theory of evolution, presented in *On the Origin of Species* (1859), was the forerunner of the modern ethological approach. More generally, Darwin's ideas have influenced almost every major theory of development (Dixon & Lerner, 1999).

Darwin's evolutionary theory begins with the assumption that individual members of a species vary in many characteristics: some are faster, some are stronger, some weigh less, and so on. A further assumption is that some of this variation is biological in origin; that is, it results from inborn, hereditary differences rather than from differences in experience. It can thus be passed on from parent to offspring. A third assumption is that most species produce more offspring than their environment can support, which means that the individual members must compete for survival. Depending on the environment, some variations may increase the chances for survival, such as providing better ways of avoiding danger or acquiring food. If so, individuals possessing these traits are more likely to survive and pass the traits along to future generations. Through this process, which Darwin called **natural selection**, the species evolves to more adaptive forms. The evolutionary model thus suggests that some of the present-day behaviours of humans (or any other organism) had their origins countless years ago, when they somehow contributed to the survival of an earlier form of a species.

Natural selection An evolutionary process proposed by Charles Darwin, in which characteristics of an individual that increase its chances of survival are more likely to be passed along to future generations.

Darwin's theory of evolution did not directly address the issue of child development, but his views led other biologists of the time to propose the principle of **recapitulation** (Haeckel, 1906/1977). According to this notion, the development of the individual proceeds through stages that parallel the development of the entire species. As applied to our species, it means that human development follows a progression similar to that which evolved through the various prehuman species (Wertheimer, 1985).

Recapitulation An early biological notion, later adopted by psychologist G. Stanley Hall, that the development of the individual repeats the development of the species.

Although recapitulation theory is no longer scientifically supported, the idea that children's development repeats the development of the species had great appeal for some early developmentalists. Furthermore, by providing a theory that both explained the developing behaviours observed by Rousseau and others and served as a framework for future research on human development, Darwin's writings helped launch the scientific study of the child (Charlesworth, 1992).

Darwin was also a keen observer of child development. Indeed, his detailed record of the growth and behaviour of his infant son, "Doddy," was one of the first developmental studies (Darwin, 1877). The intensive study of one's own child's development—a method known as the **baby biography** approach—was an important early method in the attempt to develop a scientific approach to the study of childhood.

Baby biography Method of study in which a parent studies the development of his or her own child.

PIONEERS OF CHILD PSYCHOLOGY

The belief that the development of the child is related to the evolution of the species gave birth to the science of developmental psychology. But the evolutionary perspective was soon joined by other theoretical models, as child development quickly became the focus of increasing scientific debate and research. Only a few of the individuals who contributed to the rise of this movement are discussed here. Our purpose is not to provide a detailed history of child study, but to point out the origins of some important ideas and controversies that remain a part of modern developmental science.

G. STANLEY HALL (1846–1924) Referred to as the father of child psychology, G. Stanley Hall is credited with founding the field of developmental psychology (Appley, 1986). He conducted and published the first systematic studies of children in North America. Although neither his research nor his theoretical ideas—which favoured the theory of recapitulation—ultimately had much impact, Hall did make lasting contributions to the field (Hilgard, 1987; Ross, 1972). As an educator at Clark University in Worcester, Massachusetts, Hall trained the first generation of developmental researchers. He also established several scientific journals for reporting the findings of child development research, and he founded and became the first president of the American Psychological Association. Finally, a more indirect contribution was his invitation to Sigmund Freud to present a series of lectures in the United States—an event that, as we will see later, led to the introduction of psychoanalytic theory into North American psychology.

Some of the pioneers of psychology invited by G. Stanley Hall to Clark University in 1909. Hall is seated front centre, and Sigmund Freud is seated front left. (*Culver Pictures Inc*).

JAMES MARK BALDWIN (1861–1934) James Mark Baldwin was the first academic psychologist in Canada. In 1899, Baldwin, a graduate of Princeton, was invited to take up a faculty position at the University of Toronto where he set up the first psychology laboratory in Canada (Hoff, 1992; Wright, 1999, 2002). Although initially interested in psychophysical research, Baldwin's interests moved toward the study of children. He began a research program studying infant development, employing the baby biography approach described above to present his observations of the development of his own infants (Hoff, 1992, Wright, 2002). He published articles examining such topics as the origins of handedness, colour vision, and suggestibility and imitation in infancy (Cairns & Cairns, 2006; Hoff, 1992). Baldwin had a strong inclination toward theory, and published many books and articles in the area of mental development. He argued that development progresses through a sequence of stages, and stressed the interaction of heredity and environment. These notions influenced Jean Piaget's theorizing about development (Cairns & Cairns, 2006; Grusec & Lytton, 1988).

JOHN B. WATSON (1878–1958) The theoretical idea that is generally shared by the scientists of a given period is referred to as its **zeitgeist**—a German term meaning "the spirit of the times." When a science is very young, the zeitgeist can change dramatically from one time to the next. Major shifts in thinking regarding one of the most basic issues of human development—what causes changes in behaviour in growing children—had already occurred several times in the centuries before the science of developmental psychology emerged in the mid-1800s. We saw that the zeitgeist of the 17th century was Locke's environmentalist view of human development. This model was replaced first by Rousseau's nativistic explanation, and then by the evolutionary theories of Darwin and Hall. As the 20th century dawned, the pendulum began to swing away from biological interpretations of development and back toward the environmentalist position.

Zeitgeist The spirit of the times, or the ideas shared by most scientists during a given period.

John B. Watson was the first major psychologist to adopt Locke's belief that human behaviour can be understood principally in terms of experiences and learning. His new approach, which he called **behaviourism**, also differed radically regarding what psychologists should study and which methods of investigation they should use (Horowitz, 1992).

Behaviourism A theory of psychology, first advanced by John B. Watson, that human development results primarily from conditioning and learning processes.

Watson's early career was devoted to the study of animal psychology. Psychologists then (as now) were divided in terms of what they studied and how they studied it. Some, like Watson, concentrated on the physiological workings of the body. But many were exclusively concerned with the psychological functioning of the human mind and, in particular, with consciousness and such issues as how individual perceptions are combined to form ideas and thoughts. The most common research method was *introspection*, which involved engaging research participants in a task and then having them try to look inward and report on the processes occurring in their minds.

Watson found this approach unsatisfactory for a number of reasons. First, little agreement was ever found across participants' descriptions of their internal experiences. Further, Watson felt strongly that psychology should follow the example of the other natural sciences and deal only with objective, observable subject matter—in this case, observable behaviour. Finally, his interest in animal psychology led him to reject any method that could not also be used to study other species. These ideas were radical for the time, but Watson's persuasiveness soon propelled behaviourism into the forefront of psychological theory (Cohen, 1979).

The basic tenet of behaviourism is that changes in behaviour result primarily from conditioning processes. Watson argued that learning occurs through the process of association, as described in the work of the Russian physiologist Ivan Pavlov (1849–1936). Pavlov had shown that any simple reflex can be conditioned to many different stimuli—for example, he conditioned dogs to salivate at the sound of a bell.

Watson believed that this simple conditioning process explained how human behaviour changes over time. All human behaviour, he argued, begins as simple reflexes. Then, through an association process like that described by Pavlov, various combinations of simple behaviours become conditioned to many stimuli in the environment. For example, language ("verbal behaviour," to Watson) begins as simple infant sounds that grow in complexity as they continue to be conditioned to objects and events in the surrounding environment. Furthermore, as speech grows more sophisticated, it gradually develops a silent form, which we know as thinking, reasoning, and problem solving. Watson, therefore, believed that it was crucial for psychologists to study infants and young children—not simply to observe early physical changes, but to study the first steps in the conditioning process that produces complex human behaviour.

The Pavlovian conditioning process that formed the core of Watson's behaviouristic theory was straightforward and easy to understand. It was this simplicity, along with Watson's demand for strict experimental methods, that led North American psychologists of the time to embrace behaviourism as a major advance in scientific thinking. By the second decade of the 20th century, a new zeitgeist had emerged.

Today, Watson's strict environmentalist views and the major role he assigned to conditioned reflexes are no longer supported by most developmental psychologists. However, his contributions to psychology were nevertheless significant. His call for objective methods of study, in particular, brought early experimental psychology in line with the other natural sciences. Virtually all modern experimental psychology is based on the methods argued for by Watson, including precise specification of experimental procedures and emphasis on observable and measurable behaviours.

ARNOLD GESELL (1880–1961) Just as scientists begin to accept a particular way of looking at things, someone seems to come along with an important criticism of that view or with new evidence supporting some earlier position. So when the zeitgeist swings back toward a prior point of view, it is usually because of new research findings or a more complete theoretical explanation of the facts. Accordingly, developmentalists began returning to the biological model of child development in the 1930s, but not because they once again accepted recapitulation theory. Rather, they were persuaded to reconsider the nativistic viewpoint by the research and ideas of one of G. Stanley Hall's most successful students, Arnold Gesell.

Gesell established the Yale Clinic of Child Development in 1911 and spent almost 50 years there studying and describing the development of the typical child. Although Gesell did not agree that human development mirrors the evolution of the species, he did believe that development is guided primarily by biological processes. He therefore felt that growth and the emergence of motor skills (crawling and sitting, for example) should follow very predictable patterns. In his scheme, the environment plays only a minor role—perhaps affecting the age at which certain skills appear—but never affecting the sequence or pattern of development. Gesell described the complex of biological mechanisms that guide development simply as **maturation**. The resulting patterns of growth and development were as yet unknown, and Gesell set about to identify them.

Maturation The biological processes assumed by some theorists to be primarily responsible for human development.

Using observational methods and hundreds of children of many different ages as research participants, Gesell conducted the first large-scale study to examine children's behaviour in great detail. This research revealed a high degree of uniformity in children's development. They did not all develop at the same rate—some walked earlier and others later—but the pattern of development was very consistent. For example, almost all children walked before they ran, ran before they skipped, and skipped before they hopped. From his work, Gesell established statistical **norms**—a sort of developmental timetable that describes the usual order in which children display various early behaviours and the age range within which each behaviour normally appears (Gesell & Thompson, 1938). These norms proved very valuable to physicians and parents as general guidelines for evaluating developmental progress—so much so that they continue to be revised and used today.

Norms A timetable of age ranges indicating when normal growth and developmental milestones are typically reached.

Among Arnold Gesell's most important contributions to developmental psychology were his innovative research techniques, including an observation dome that permitted photographing the child unobtrusively from any angle. (*Herbert Gehr/Time & Life Pictures/Getty Images*)

Gesell did not rely on the outdated research methods of the past when acquiring this sort of descriptive information. In fact, the sophisticated research techniques he developed for observing and recording children's behaviour are among his most important contributions to psychology (Thelen & Adolph, 1992). Gesell pioneered the use of film cameras to record children's behaviour. He also developed one-way viewing screens, and he constructed a photographic dome that allowed observations from all angles without disturbing the child under study.

Gesell's innovative methods of study and his establishment of developmental norms greatly expanded our knowledge of children's everyday skills and behaviour. But his strongly biological philosophy, like most extreme viewpoints, was an oversimplification because it largely neglected the crucial role of environmental factors. His emphasis on patterns of unfolding behaviour and his focus on similarities in children's development, however, may have helped prepare North American psychologists to accept the more influential views of another of Rousseau's theoretical descendants, Jean Piaget, whose work we discuss throughout this book.

SIGMUND FREUD (1856–1939) We backtrack now to 1909, when, as Watson was introducing behaviourism to the scientific world, another important event took place. G. Stanley Hall invited some of the most eminent psychologists of the day, including Sigmund Freud of Vienna, to Clark University to celebrate the institution's 20th anniversary (Hall and Freud are seen seated together in the photograph on page 7). On this occasion, Freud first outlined his grand theory of psychological development. American psychologists were not immediately receptive to Freud's model, and it proved to be no obstacle to Watson's emerging behavioural movement. But the seeds of psychoanalytic thought had been planted in North American soil, and in time Freud's views would attract a good deal of attention both inside and outside of psychology.

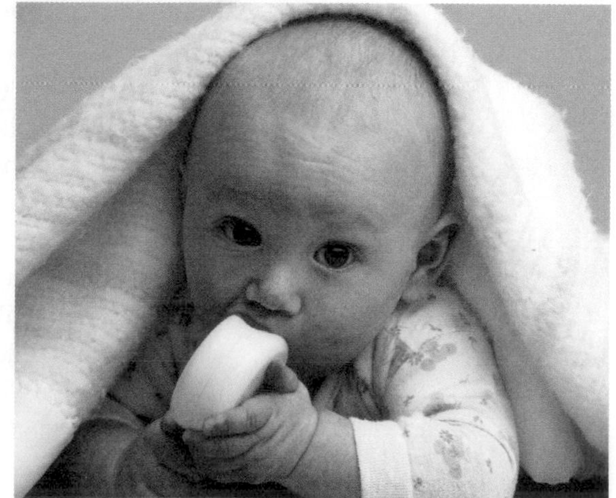

The first of Freud's psychosexual stages is the oral stage. (*PhotoDisc, Inc.*)

Freud made two major contributions to psychology. His greatest impact was in the area of clinical psychology, where his model of personality and techniques of psychoanalysis continue to represent a major school of thought in psychotherapy. His contribution to developmental psychology was his stage theory of psychosexual development. Although he spent little time observing children directly, he used his patients' and his own recollections of childhood experiences to construct a comprehensive model of child development.

The central theme of Freudian developmental theory is that each child is born with a certain amount of sexual energy, called *libido*, which is biologically guided to certain locations on the body, called the *erogenous zones*, as the child grows. In this model, *sexual energy* refers simply to the ability to experience physical pleasure. The arrival of the libido at each erogenous zone marks a new stage in the child's psychosexual development, and during that stage the child receives the greatest physical pleasure in that bodily location. Freud identified five stages, beginning at birth and ending in late adolescence (see Table 1.1). Successful movement from stage to stage requires that the child receive the proper amount of physical pleasure from each erogenous zone.

Freud's theory of child development is actually a theory of personality formation. It assumes that many aspects of adult personality result from events during childhood psychosexual stages. If a child's experiences during a stage are not what they should be, some portion of the libido will remain *fixated* in that erogenous zone, rather than moving on to the next one. For example, if a child is not given the appropriate amount of oral gratification during the first stage, the libido will remain partially fixated at the mouth. Later in life, this fixation will be manifest in the adult's continually seeking physical pleasure in this erogenous zone—perhaps by smoking, chewing on pencils, or having an unusual interest in kissing.

Repression Freud's term for the process through which desires or motivations are driven into the unconscious, as typically occurs during the phallic stage.

Identification The Freudian process through which the child adopts the characteristics of the same-sex parent during the phallic stage.

The most complex of the psychosexual stages is the phallic stage. During this stage, according to Freud, children become sexually attracted to the parent of the opposite sex, a situation referred to as the *Oedipus complex*. But they soon experience feelings of conflict as they realize that the same-sex parent is a powerful rival. Children purportedly resolve this conflict in two ways. First, they force their desires into the unconscious, a process called **repression**, which also wipes out their memory of these feelings. Then, they compensate for this loss by making a determined effort to adopt the characteristics of the same-sex parent, a process called **identification**.

Although Freud's theory had some influence on North American developmentalists, they never fully accepted it, for several reasons. First, it is vague, and its key elements cannot be scientifically verified or disproven. Furthermore, Freud's heavy reliance on unobservable mechanisms, such as unconscious motives, is not consistent with North American psychology's belief that science should be based on measurable and verifiable observations.

Interactionist perspective The theory that human development results from the combination of inborn processes and environmental factors.

Nevertheless, in spite of its failings, Freud's theory of child development includes two fundamental concepts that are generally accepted today. The first is the rejection of both a purely nativistic and a strictly environmentalist explanation of human behaviour. Freud was the first major developmentalist to argue for an **interactionist perspective**, which views both inborn processes and environmental factors as significant contributors to the child's development. Today, almost all child psychologists subscribe to an interactionist position. The second fundamental concept is Freud's suggestion that early experiences can have important effects on behaviour in later life. Most contemporary developmentalists agree with this idea, although few would explain these effects in terms of unresolved childhood conflicts hidden in the adult's unconscious (Beier, 1991; Emde, 1992).

Perhaps a third positive outcome of Freud's theory is that it inspired a number of related models of development that have achieved somewhat greater acceptance in developmental psychology. One of these, proposed by Erik Erikson, is described next.

ERIK ERIKSON (1902–1994) Erik Erikson grew up in Germany just after the turn of the century, but practised primarily in the United States. His comprehensive model of human development continues to be of interest to many psychologists today.

Erikson's model, although based on Freud's theory, differed in some major ways. For one, Erikson believed that development continues throughout life. He thus replaced Freud's five stages of development with an eight-stage model that continues into old age. Erikson also believed that we cannot understand personality development without considering the environment in which it occurs. After studying a number of diverse cultures—including Native American tribes in California and South Dakota, inner-city youth, and the people of India—Erikson developed a psycho*social* model (in contrast to Freud's psycho*sexual* model) of personality that included a major role for social and cultural influences. Finally, Erikson's model was based on the study of normal individuals and emphasized the positive, healthy aspects of personality, whereas Freud's drew heavily on his work with patients in psychoanalysis.

Like Freud, Erikson believed that all children progress through a predictable series of stages. This progression, he argued, is not random, but follows a blueprint or timetable built into our genes. According to Erikson, each individual's ultimate goal is the quest for **identity**, which develops gradually across the eight stages. But at each stage, a positive personality characteristic associated with the search for identity conflicts with a negative characteristic resulting from interaction with the social world. For example, in Erikson's second stage, a toddler's new-found physical abilities—such as walking and controlling bladder and bowel functions—lead to positive feelings of *autonomy* as the child begins to exert more control over his or her life. But these new abilities also tend to cause conflict in the child's social world—with parents, for instance—leading to feelings of *shame* and *doubt*. According to Erikson, the best resolution of these conflicts would have the child leaving the stage with a strong sense of the positive personality characteristic, but also with a small degree of the negative characteristic. The eight stages are presented in Table 1.1, which includes a comparison with the stages proposed by Freud.

Identity In Erikson's theory, the component of personality that develops across the eight stages of life and that motivates progress through the stages.

TABLE 1.1 STAGES OF DEVELOPMENT: ERIKSON AND FREUD

	Erikson's Psychosocial Stages		Freud's Psychosexual Stages	
Ages (yrs)	**Name**	**Characteristics**	**Name**	**Characteristics**
Birth–1.5	Basic Trust vs. Mistrust	Infants must form trusting relationships with caregivers. If care is inadequate, mistrust develops instead.	Oral	Libido is located at the mouth; principal source of physical pleasure is sucking.
1.5–3	Autonomy vs. Shame	As they master various skills—walking, toileting, and so forth—children begin to develop feelings of autonomy and self-control. Failure to meet expectations can lead to shame and doubt.	Anal	Child attains physical pleasure first from having bowel movements and later from withholding them.
3–6	Initiative vs. Guilt	Children take more initiative in dealing with their environment, but may experience guilt as a result of conflicts with caregivers.	Phallic	Libido moves to the genital area. Children become sexually attracted to the parent of the opposite sex, but experience conflict as they realize the same-sex parent is a powerful rival. Resolving this conflict involves forcing the libido into the unconscious and trying to adopt the characteristics of the same-sex parent.
6–12	Industry vs. Inferiority	School-age children develop industry by successfully dealing with demands to learn new skills; failure leads to feelings of inferiority.	Latency	Libido remains repressed and inactive.
12–18	Identity vs. Role Confusion	Teenagers must develop a sense of identity in various areas, such as occupation and gender, or risk role confusion in adulthood.	Genital	Libido re-emerges in the genital area; child again develops attraction toward opposite sex—this time directed toward peers.
Young Adult	Intimacy vs. Isolation	Young adults must form intimate relationships or suffer from loneliness and isolation.		
Adult	Generativity vs. Stagnation	Adults must find ways to support future generations, through child rearing or other productive activities, or come to a standstill in their lives.		
Older Adult	Ego Integrity vs. Despair	Older adults must come to feel a sense of fulfillment in life or experience despair as they face death.		

Erikson's theory is thus also interactionist, combining both inborn and environmental factors. Each person is guided through the psychosocial stages by genetic processes, but the individual's social and cultural surroundings help determine how the conflicts are resolved at each stage and so also contribute heavily to personality development.

LEARNING OBJECTIVE 1.1

Understand the philosophical and historical roots of child psychology.

1. What are two basic goals of research in developmental psychology?
2. What contributions were made by John Locke, Jean-Jacques Rousseau, Johann Gottfried von Herder, and Charles Darwin?
3. How did G. Stanley Hall and James Mark Baldwin contribute to the study of development?
4. How did John B. Watson help make child psychology a natural science?
5. What were Arnold Gesell's major contributions to the study of development?
6. How are Freud's and Erikson's views of development similar?

Learning Objective 1.2

Explain the influences of nature and nurture, stability and change, and uniformity and variation on child development.

ISSUES IN DEVELOPMENTAL PSYCHOLOGY

As we described the views of some of the pioneers of developmental psychology, a number of issues repeatedly arose. Three issues in particular have run through scientific thinking about development almost from the very beginning, and they remain a source of debate today. These issues revolve around the questions of nature versus nurture, continuity versus discontinuity, and normative versus idiographic development.

Nature versus nurture debate The scientific controversy regarding whether the primary source of developmental change rests in biological (nature) factors or in environmental and experiential (nurture) factors.

NATURE VERSUS NURTURE

The most basic and long-standing issue in child psychology (and perhaps in all of psychology) involves the relative influence of inborn, biological **nature** factors and environmental, experiential **nurture** factors. This debate has existed at least since Locke and Rousseau first proposed their rather pure environmental and nativistic models of child development. The nurture view was later taken up by Watson and other learning theorists, whereas the nature position formed the basis of the theories of Hall and Gesell. The modern debate, however, is far more complex than it was in the early days of psychology (Elman et al., 1996; Rutter, 2002; Spelke & Newport, 1998).

Amanda Dunbar was a child artist prodigy. Her accomplishments are a result of both nature (the favourable genes with which she was born) and nurture (the supportive environment in which she has developed). *(Courtesy of Amanda Dunbar, www.amandadunbar.com)*

We noted earlier that virtually all child researchers today subscribe to some form of interactionist position, in which both nature and nurture are assumed to contribute to human development. Nevertheless, the nature–nurture debate has not ended. Most psychologists continue to emphasize the importance of either nature or nurture in their accounts of development. For example, when a child demonstrates an unusual gift for languages or athletics, some psychologists believe the talent is due to a fortuitous combination of genes from parents who are probably gifted in similar ways. Others point to environmental factors, such as the opportunities children are provided with to acquire and practise the necessary skills and the rewards they receive for high levels of achievement.

Another example can be found in the development of aggressive behaviour. Some psychologists explain aggressive behaviour in terms of environmental factors, such as exposure to violent models or ineffective parenting that rewards aggression. Others might offer a biological account that focuses on an inherited disposition that makes it difficult for the child to regulate his or her emotions, or perhaps neurological problems that interfere with the processing of social cues.

In reality, of course, both high levels of achievement and aggressive behaviour are best understood in terms of a combination of biological and experiential factors. Children who excel in languages or in sports are probably born with a unique combination of characteristics that increases their likelihood of success in those domains. In turn, their early success often leads to increased opportunities and rewards. Similarly, some antisocial children may well have a biologically based propensity to respond with aggression to frustrating situations. Nonetheless, the fact that they act on their aggressive impulses is the result of learning.

The processes by which biological and environmental factors work together over the course of development are as yet far from understood. Recent advances in the fields of behavioural genetics and the brain sciences suggest that these processes may be even more complex than psychologists initially believed. For example, we now know that biological entities such as genes and basic brain chemistry, once thought to be unchanging, are themselves responsive to environmental influence (Plomin & Rutter, 1998; Shonkoff & Phillips, 2000). Several theoretical models describing how our genes and environment may work together to guide our behaviour are discussed in Chapter 3.

Links to Related Material

In Chapter 3 we explore the interaction of biology and environment more fully.

Nature versus nurture questions arise in almost every topic considered in this text. At times, however, they appear under different labels, such as heredity versus environment, maturation versus learning, or emergent abilities versus acquired skills. Whatever the name, these debates tend to involve the same fundamental issue.

CONTINUITY VERSUS DISCONTINUITY

A second long-standing issue in child psychology is whether development displays **continuity** or **discontinuity**. This debate actually has two components (Emde & Harmon, 1984). One involves the pattern of development. Is development smooth and stable, with new abilities, skills, and knowledge gradually added at a relatively uniform pace (continuous)? Or does development occur at different rates, alternating between periods of little change and periods of abrupt, rapid change (discontinuous)? The second component involves the connectedness of development. Continuity theorists contend that many of the behaviours and abilities we see in adolescents and adults can be traced directly back to development early in life. Discontinuity theorists, in contrast, suggest that some aspects of development emerge relatively independently of what has come before and cannot be predicted from the child's previous behaviour (Clarke & Clarke, 1976).

Continuity versus discontinuity debate The scientific controversy regarding whether development is constant and connected (continuous) or uneven and disconnected (discontinuous).

For Thought and Discussion

How predictable are you? Which aspects of your personality have remained the same since you were a young child, and which have changed?

The continuity model is often associated with the belief that human behaviour consists of many individual skills that are added one at a time, usually through learning and experience. As children acquire more and more of these skills, they combine and recombine them to produce increasingly complex abilities. This approach emphasizes quantitative change—the simpler elements are essentially added together to produce the more advanced capabilities—and tends to characterize environmentalist models of development. In contrast, psychologists who favour the discontinuity model usually hold that development is guided primarily by internal biological factors. Stage theorists, for example, argue that the unevenness of children's development—relatively stable periods followed by abrupt changes—reflects the discontinuous nature of the changes taking place in the underlying structures of the body and brain. Thus, development is thought to involve qualitative changes in previous abilities or behaviours.

Like the nature versus nurture issue, the question of continuity versus discontinuity is not all-or-nothing. Psychologists on both sides of the debate agree that some developmental processes are more accurately described by one model, others by the competing model (Bjorklund, 1997; Rutter, 1987), while some involve both (Scher, Epstein, & Tirosh, 2004).

NORMATIVE VERSUS IDIOGRAPHIC DEVELOPMENT

A third issue that commonly arises in child psychology is not a matter of debate so much as a description of a researcher's focus of study. Some psychologists are concerned with **normative** development, meaning what children have in common or how development is similar for all children. Others focus on **idiographic** development, meaning the differences in development from one child to the next.

Normative versus idiographic development The question of whether research should focus on identifying commonalities in human development (normative development) or on the causes of individual differences (idiographic development).

Normative research focuses on the "average" child, with the primary goal of identifying and describing how normal development proceeds from step to step. A related issue involves the search for **universals of development**—behaviours or patterns of development that characterize all children everywhere. Idiographic research, in contrast, centres on the individual child and the factors that produce human diversity.

Universals of development
Aspects of development or behaviour that are common to children everywhere.

Normative research attempts to identify commonalities among children, whereas idiographic research is concerned with why one child is different from the next. *(Photodisc/Getty Images)*

Research on language development illustrates these two approaches. Researchers interested in normative development search for common patterns of linguistic development, both in children who speak the same language and in those who speak different languages. Theorists who adopt an idiographic perspective are more concerned with identifying and explaining the individual differences that are evident as children master language. Such individual differences might result from differences in experience, such as the type of speech adults use when talking with children, or from biological factors, such as brain trauma or inheritance of a particular genetic disorder.

Historically, the normative approach was associated with biological theories of development, such as Gesell's, whereas the idiographic approach was associated with researchers who emphasized environmental and experiential processes. This distinction is no longer tenable. Today it is clear that individual differences in development can be due to biological factors, and universals of development can be due to common experiences.

LEARNING OBJECTIVE 1.2

Explain the influences of nature and nurture, stability and change, and uniformity and variation on child development.

1. How do nature and nurture jointly contribute to child development?
2. Why might some researchers focus on stability or continuity in development, while others focus on discontinuity or change?
3. Why might some researchers focus on typical or normal development, while others focus on individual variation?

Learning Objective 1.3

Describe the cognitive-developmental approach and the two major theories of cognitive development.

THEORIES OF DEVELOPMENT: COGNITIVE-DEVELOPMENTAL APPROACHES

Most psychologists characterize themselves in terms of a particular theoretical orientation; that is, their view of how development occurs and which factors are most responsible for changes in children's behaviour. Today, the majority of child psychologists identify themselves with one of four general theoretical views: the cognitive-developmental approach, the sociocultural approach, the environmental/learning approach, or the evolutionary approach. In the remainder of this chapter, we outline the principal ideas and underlying assumptions of these four theories. Then, as we discuss various topics throughout the rest of the book, we will compare and contrast the approaches taken by these theories, including the types of questions they ask and the research methods they prefer.

We begin with the cognitive-developmental approach. As we have seen, the roots of this tradition lie in the 18th-century writings of Rousseau. The modern version of the approach includes several related theories. For years, it was most closely associated with the work of Jean Piaget. Since the 1970s, however, several other cognitively oriented models have become popular among psychologists.

An important characteristic of this approach is its emphasis on cognition. According to these theories, the changes we witness in children's behaviours and abilities arise largely from changes in their knowledge and intellectual skills. The major goals for psychologists of this tradition, therefore, are to specify what children know, how this knowledge is organized, and how it changes or develops.

PIAGET'S THEORY

If we had to select one psychologist whose work has had the greatest influence on the study of child development, we would have to consider Jean Piaget (1896–1980) as a very strong candidate. His ideas have inspired more research than those of any other theorist, and his conception of human development revolutionized thinking about children and their behaviour.

Jean Piaget was a pioneer of child psychology whose early ideas remain largely accepted today by many researchers. (© *Farrell Grehan/Corbis*)

Piaget was born and raised in Switzerland. From boyhood he was interested in science, particularly biology and animal behaviour. Although he eventually left this area of study, his background in biology is reflected in his theory of child development. Piaget had always been drawn to the study of psychology, and after earning his doctorate in 1918, he moved from Switzerland to Paris where he became involved in the development of intelligence tests for children.

Intelligence testing was a new field at this time. Two of its founders, Alfred Binet and Theodore Simon, were attempting to develop tests that could predict children's success in school. Simon hired Piaget to administer the tests, which gave him his first real experience with developmental work. But unlike his employers, Piaget was less interested in the number of test items children answered correctly than in the reasons for their incorrect responses. Children of different ages, he observed, not only knew different amounts of information, but also looked at the world in very different ways. Their answers revealed *qualitative* (style-related) differences in thinking beyond the *quantitative* (amount-related) differences in factual information.

After two years in Paris, Piaget returned to Switzerland and began his own research on the development of children's knowledge. Piaget called his area of interest **genetic epistemology**, by which he meant the study of the nature of knowledge in young children, its origins (i.e., *genesis*), and how it changes as they grow older. Piaget was interested not in the precise knowledge and facts that children possess—for example, *what* children know when they enter school—but rather in how they go about acquiring and using that knowledge—*how* children think.

Genetic epistemology Piaget's term for the study of children's knowledge and how it changes with development.

To investigate children's knowledge, Piaget developed his own research technique. Whereas Gesell's methods involved observing children without interfering with them, Piaget challenged children with simple tasks and verbal problems that required solutions and explanations. His technique, known as the **clinical method**, involved a loosely structured interview in which he asked a question or posed a problem and then, depending on the child's response, followed up with other questions intended to reveal the child's reasoning or problem-solving approach.

Clinical method Piaget's principal research method, which involved a semi-structured interview with questions designed to probe children's understanding of various concepts.

Piaget's research initially attracted some attention in North America during the 1920s and 1930s. But his writings were difficult for scholars to understand because they contained many terms and concepts that differed from the scientific language North Americans were using. Piaget's somewhat informal methods of investigation were also viewed as a problem by more rigorous experimental researchers. During the 1940s and 1950s, North American child psychology once again turned toward environmental and conditioning models, and interest in Piaget's theory disappeared.

Beginning in the late 1950s, however, North American psychologists began to rediscover Piaget's work. His theoretical writings were translated into more familiar concepts, and his studies were replicated under controlled experimental conditions (Flavell, 1963). In addition, his theory generated many new questions that psychologists felt could and should be investigated, such as questions about children's understanding of time, logic, and causality. Piaget's many books on child psychology remain the greatest contribution to the field by a single scholar (Beilin, 1992a).

According to Piaget's theory, human development can be described in terms of *functions* and *cognitive structures*. The functions are inborn biological processes that are the same for everyone and remain unchanged throughout our lives. Their purpose is to construct internal cognitive structures. The structures, in contrast, change repeatedly as the child grows.

COGNITIVE STRUCTURES The most fundamental aspect of Piaget's theory, and often the most difficult to understand, is the belief that intelligence is a process—not something that a child *has* but something that a child *does*. Piaget's child does not possess knowledge passively, but understands the world by acting or operating on it.

Links to Related Material

Piaget's influence on our understanding of cognitive development is examined in more depth in Chapter 8.

For example, Piaget would describe an infant's knowledge of a ball in terms of the various actions the infant can perform with it—pushing the ball, throwing it, mouthing it, and so on. These actions are a reflection of the cognitive structures of infancy, which are called **schemes**. A scheme involves two elements: an object in the environment (such as a ball), and the child's reactions to the object. A scheme is therefore not a physical structure but a psychological one. Early on, the infant has comparatively few of these schemes, and they are related to one another in very simple ways. As development proceeds, however, schemes increase in both number and complexity of organization. These two characteristics of children's cognitive structures—number and complexity—define the child's intelligence at any point in development.

Schemes Piaget's term for the cognitive structures of infancy. A scheme consists of a set of skilled, flexible action patterns through which the child understands the world.

Schemes and other cognitive structures also display certain flexibilities. An infant does not perform exactly the same behaviour with every ball she encounters—some may produce more squeezing, others more rolling—nor are the infant's reactions the same with every object. The way a ball is grasped may be somewhat different from the way a rattle is grasped, and the way either of these objects is sucked may be different from the way a nipple is sucked. Cognitive structures are flexible in another sense—they change over time. A particular scheme, such as grasping, reflects more and more skill as the infant applies it to more and more objects. In this way, schemes eventually become more individualized, or *differentiated*, so that a ball becomes primarily an object to be thrown, a rattle primarily an object to be shaken, and a nipple primarily an object to be sucked.

In Piaget's theory, children act upon the world at every stage of development. The schemes with which they do so, however, change as the child develops. (*Creatas/Media Bakery*)

Beyond these simple schemes of infancy, new and higher-level cognitive structures gradually emerge. An 8-year-old confronted with a ball, for example, still has all the earlier schemes available (although sucking is not a very likely response), but the older child can also understand a ball by acting on it using mental operations, such as assigning it certain properties (colour, size), actions (bouncing, hitting), or capabilities (being a member of the category of "round things").

For Piaget, *development* referred to this continual reorganization of knowledge into new and more complex structures. Much of our discussion in Chapter 8 concerns what these structures are and how they change with development.

FUNCTIONS The functions that guide cognitive development are also central to Piaget's theory. Piaget stressed two general functions, both of which reflect his training in biology. One is **organization**. Because an individual's cognitive structures are interrelated, any new knowledge must be fit into the existing system. According to Piaget, this need to integrate new information, rather than simply to add it on, forces our cognitive structures to become ever more elaborately organized.

Organization The tendency to integrate knowledge into interrelated cognitive structures. One of the two biologically based functions stressed in Piaget's theory.

The second function is **adaptation**, which in general terms refers to an organism's attempt to fit with its environment in ways that promote survival. In Piaget's model, cognitive adaptation involves two processes. **Assimilation** entails trying to make sense of new experiences in terms of our existing cognitive structures. The infant who brings everything to his mouth to suck is demonstrating assimilation, as is the toddler who calls all men "Daddy." Note that assimilation may require some distortion of the new information to make it fit into the child's existing schemes. But trying to fit new things into what we already know is a necessary part of adapting to the world.

Adaptation The tendency to fit with the environment in ways that promote survival. One of the two biologically based functions stressed in Piaget's theory.

Assimilation Interpreting new experiences in terms of existing cognitive structures. One of the two components of adaptation in Piaget's theory.

When new information is too different or too complex, **accommodation** occurs. Here, our cognitive structures change in order to integrate the new experiences. For example, the infant eventually learns that not all objects are to be sucked, just as the toddler learns that different labels or names need to be applied to different men. It is primarily through accommodation that the number and complexity of children's cognitive structures increase; that is, intelligence grows.

Accommodation Changing existing cognitive structures to fit with new experiences. One of the two components of adaptation in Piaget's theory.

Piaget assumed that assimilation and accommodation operate closely together. A growing child is continually making slight distortions of information to assimilate it into existing structures, while also making slight modifications in these structures to accommodate new objects or events. The interplay of these two functions illustrates another important aspect of Piaget's theory, the concept of **constructivism**. Children's knowledge of events in their environment is not an exact reproduction of those events; it is not like a perfect photograph of what they have seen or a precise recording of what they have heard. Children take information from the environment and bend, shape, or distort it until it fits comfortably into their existing cognitive organization. As we said earlier, they *operate* on it. Even when they accommodate structures to allow for new experiences, the accommodation is seldom complete, and some distortion of the information remains. Thus, when 6-, 8-, and 10-year-old children watch a movie or hear a lecture, they come away with somewhat different messages, even though they may have seen or heard the same input. Each child acts on the information somewhat differently, fitting it into his or her own existing set of structures. In this sense, the child constructs knowledge about the world, rather than simply receiving it.

For Thought and Discussion

Both Piaget and Freud noted how infants bring everything to their mouths to suck. How did their views differ in terms of why infants do this?

Constructivism Piaget's belief that children actively create knowledge, rather than passively receive it from the environment.

The processes of assimilation, accommodation, and construction make the child's cognitive system increasingly more powerful and adaptive. However, these processes produce only small-scale changes. At certain points in development, Piaget argued, more major adjustments are required. At these points, the cognitive system, because of both biological maturation and past experiences, has completely mastered one level of functioning and is ready for new, qualitatively different challenges—challenges that go beyond what the current set of structures can handle. At such points, the child moves to a new stage of development.

STAGES OF DEVELOPMENT Piaget was a stage theorist. In his view, all children move through the same stages of cognitive development in the same order. At each stage, the child's cognitive functioning is qualitatively different and affects the child's performance in a wide range of situations.

There are four such general stages, or **periods**, in Piaget's model.

Periods Piaget's term for the four general stages into which his theory divides development. Each period is a qualitatively distinct form of functioning that characterizes a wide range of cognitive activities.

- The **sensorimotor** period represents the first two years of life. The infant's initial schemes are simple reflexes, and knowledge of the world is limited to physical interactions with people and objects.
- During the **preoperational** period, from roughly 2 to 6 years, the child begins to use symbols, such as words and numbers, to represent the world cognitively.

Sensorimotor Form of intelligence in which knowledge is based on physical interactions with people and objects. The first of Piaget's periods, extending from birth to about 2 years.

Preoperational Form of intelligence in which symbols and mental actions begin to replace objects and overt behaviours. The second of Piaget's periods, extending from about 2 to about 6 years old.

An important accomplishment of the preoperational period is the ability to use symbols, such as numbers, to represent the world. (*Blend Images/Media Bakery*)

- The period of **concrete operations** lasts from approximately age 6 to age 11. Children in this stage are able to perform mental operations on the pieces of knowledge they possess, permitting a kind of logical problem solving that was not possible during the preoperational period.
- The final stage, the period of **formal operations**, extends from about age 12 through adulthood. This period includes all the higher-level abstract operations, enabling the child to deal with events or relations that are only possible, as opposed to those that actually exist.

The accuracy of Piaget's theory has been studied extensively over the years. In Chapter 8 we consider the four stages in detail and describe the evidence psychologists have gathered that both supports and questions various aspects of this theory.

Concrete operations Form of intelligence in which mental operations make logical problem solving with concrete objects possible. The third of Piaget's periods, extending from about 6 to 11 years of age.

Formal operations Form of intelligence in which higher-level mental operations make possible logical reasoning with respect to abstract and hypothetical events and not merely concrete objects. The fourth of Piaget's periods, beginning at about 12 years of age.

For Thought and Discussion

What are some advantages and disadvantages of conceptualizing the mind in terms of computer operations?

INFORMATION-PROCESSING MODELS

A second type of cognitive-developmental model is the information-processing approach, which we describe in detail in Chapter 9. Information-processing theorists view cognition as a system composed of three parts.

1. Information in the world provides the input to the system. Stimulation enters our senses in the form of sights, sounds, tastes, and so on.
2. Processes in the brain act on and transform the information in a variety of ways, including encoding it into symbolic forms, comparing it with previously acquired information, storing it in memory, and retrieving it when necessary. Most psychologists working in the information-processing tradition have concentrated on this middle part of the system, designing their studies to reveal the nature of these internal processes and how they interact with one another.
3. The third part of the system is the output, which is our behaviour—speech, social interactions, writing, and so on.

As you have probably noticed, there is an inescapable connection between the information-processing approach to cognition and the functioning of a computer. Some psychologists make this connection very strongly. Their goal is to construct computer programs that simulate human behaviour so that ultimately we will be able to specify our cognitive processes in precise mathematical and logical terms. More often, however, researchers use the *computer analogy* simply as a way of thinking about information flowing through a system where it is processed and then re-emerges in a different form.

In recent years, the information-processing view has emerged as one of the leading approaches to the study of human cognition. Its popularity reflects in part the growing interest in *cognitive science*, an interdisciplinary field in which researchers in biology, mathematics, philosophy, and neuroscience, among other disciplines, are attempting to understand the workings of the human brain and its mental capacities (e.g., Johnson & De Haan, 2010; Keil, 2006).

Like Piaget's theory, information-processing theories fall within the cognitive-developmental approach. In addition to sharing Piaget's emphasis on underlying rules or structures, information-processing researchers study many of the same phenomena as Piaget. Indeed, some information-processing researchers have proposed stage theories that have ties to Piaget's stages. Most information-processing theorists, however, do not subscribe to the kinds of broad, general stages offered by Piaget. Their models are more domain-specific, and they attempt to construct models that are more precise, more complete, and more testable than those proposed by Piaget. Recently, however, some these domain-specific models, such as the *Dynamic Systems Approach*

(Courage & Howe, 2002; Lewis, 2000a; Thelen & Smith, 2006) are being broadened to become more general models of development.

Information-processing researchers are interested in development in such domains as attention, memory, problem solving, reading, arithmetic, and other cognitive processes. Information-processing theory is concerned not just with *what* changes occur with age in cognitive ability, but also with *why* such improvement takes place. Researchers from this approach have studied how physical maturation affects children's cognitive abilities. Investigators have also examined the development of the *strategies* children use, their understanding of *rules*, and the development of their *expertise* in particular areas (Demetrick, Mouyl, & Spanoudis, 2010; Munakata, 2006; Ornstein & Light, 2010).

Not all information-processing research has been concerned with children, and much of it has not been directed toward developmental issues. Nevertheless, the approach has infused many areas of child psychology, and it will turn up throughout this text in topics as diverse as perception, language, gender roles, and aggression.

Links to Related Material

The influence of information-processing models on our understanding of children's cognitive development will be discussed in further detail in Chapter 9.

LEARNING OBJECTIVE 1.3

Describe the cognitive-developmental approach and the two major theories of cognitive development.

1. What is the key view of the cognitive-developmental approach?
2. How did Piaget describe human development?
3. How do information-processing models view cognition?

THEORIES OF DEVELOPMENT: THE SOCIOCULTURAL APPROACH

Learning Objective 1.4

Describe the sociocultural approach to development.

The theories discussed in the preceding section differ in important ways. Nevertheless, they share a focus on the child functioning largely on his or her own. Cognitive-developmental researchers typically investigate children's thinking by asking them to reason about problems alone, in settings far removed from the daily situations in which children usually apply their cognitive skills. Furthermore, cognitive-developmental theories locate the sources of cognitive change—be it reorganization of cognitive structures, faster processing of information, or growth in general knowledge—primarily in the heads of individual children.

The sociocultural approach, which we describe in detail in Chapter 8, offers a very different perspective. As von Herder observed nearly 200 years ago, development occurs in a social, cultural, and historical context. This context includes other people, such as parents and teachers, who support and guide children's cognitive activities. It also includes cultural tools and traditions that shape mental processes. Defining features of the sociocultural approach, then, include an emphasis on social processes, cultural practices, and the everyday contexts of development.

Links to Related Material

The influence of the sociocultural approach on our understanding of children's cognitive development will be discussed in greater depth in Chapter 8.

VYGOTSKY'S THEORY

The most influential contemporary theory in the sociocultural tradition is that of Soviet psychologist Lev Vygotsky. Vygotsky was born in Russia in the same year as Piaget, and their early work occupied the same period. Their backgrounds were very different, however. For example, Vygotsky was trained not in science, like Piaget, but in law, literature, and linguistics. The differences between these two contemporary theorists are reflected in the contrasting models of human development they constructed (Glassman, 1994; Kozulin, 1990).

A similarity between the two scholars, however, is that both received little attention from Western scientists until the 1960s, when their work was translated into English and their theories began to be tested experimentally. Piaget was still active at this time, and continued to contribute to the scientific advances brought about by his theory. Vygotsky, however, died at age 37 and never saw his ideas pursued by other researchers. Initially, his writings were misunderstood, and they were banned in the former Soviet Union for over 20 years. Thus, his work remained unknown even to many of his contemporary Soviet psychologists.

To understand Vygotsky's theory, it is important to appreciate the political environment of the time. Vygotsky began working in psychology shortly after the Russian Revolution, which replaced the rule of the czar with Marxism. The new philosophy stressed socialism and collectivism; individuals were expected to sacrifice their personal goals and achievements for the betterment of the larger society. Sharing and cooperation were encouraged, and the success of any individual was seen as reflecting the success of the culture. Marxists also placed a heavy emphasis on history, believing that any culture could be understood only through examination of the ideas and events that shaped it.

Vygotsky's model of human development incorporated these elements—hence the label *sociocultural* approach. The model holds that the individual's development is a product of his or her culture. In this theory, *development* refers largely to mental development, such as thought, language, and reasoning processes. Vygotsky assumed that these abilities develop through social interactions with others (especially parents), and thus represent the shared knowledge of the culture. Whereas Piaget believed that all children's cognitive development follows a very similar pattern of stages, Vygotsky saw intellectual abilities as much more specific to the culture in which the child was reared.

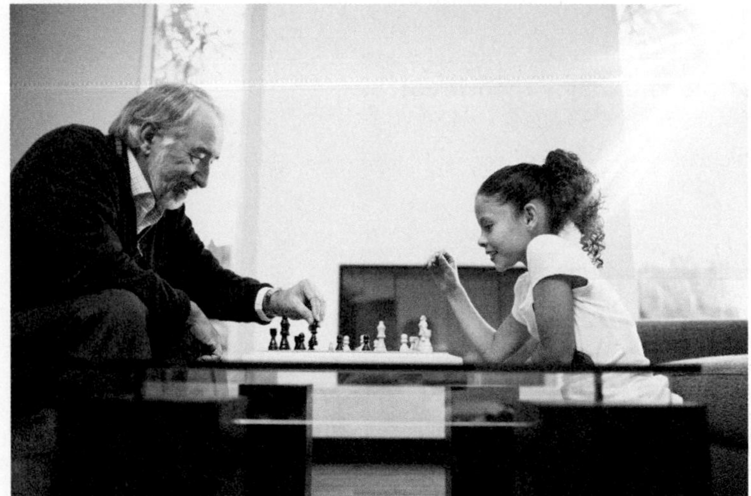

Vygotsky believed that children acquire cognition through shared experiences with others in their culture who are more knowledgeable. (© *Hello Lovely/Corbis*)

Vygotsky's theory emphasizes a number of related elements (Kozulin, 1990; Wertsch & Tulviste, 1992). Most important, it holds that culture is a major determinant of individual development. Humans are the only species that has created cultures, and every human child develops in the context of a culture. Culture makes two sorts of contributions to the child's intellectual development.

1. Children acquire much of the content of their thinking—that is, their knowledge—from the culture around them.
2. Children acquire their thinking and reasoning processes—what Vygotskians call the **tools of intellectual adaptation**—from their culture.

Tools of intellectual adaptation Vygotsky's term for the of thinking and problem-solving techniques that children internalize from their culture.

In short, culture teaches children both what to think and how to think.

How does culture exert its influences? Vygotsky believed that cognitive development results from a **dialectical process** in which the child learns through shared problem-solving experiences with someone else, usually a parent or teacher (Rogoff, 1998). Initially the adult assumes most of the responsibility for guiding the problem solving. Gradually, however, the responsibility shifts partly and then completely to the child. Language plays a central role in this process in two ways. First, it describes and transmits to children the rich body of knowledge that exists in the culture. Second, it provides the means, or method, of problem solving, which is demonstrated by the adult and then adopted by the child.

Dialectical process The process in Vygotsky's theory whereby children learn through problem-solving experiences shared with others.

This transfer of control from adult to child reflects a final Vygotskian theme: development as a process of **internalization** (Cox & Lightfoot, 1997). Bodies of knowledge and thinking tools at first exist outside the child, in the surrounding culture. Development, according to Vygotsky, consists of gradually internalizing them. This is what Vygotskians mean when they say that children's cognitive abilities grow directly out of their cultural experiences.

Internalization Vygotsky's term for the child's incorporation, primarily through language, of bodies of knowledge and tools of thought from the culture.

BRONFENBRENNER'S ECOLOGICAL MODEL

Vygotsky's theorizing is not the only basis for the modern sociocultural approach. Another important contributor is the **ecological perspective**, developed most fully by Urie Bronfenbrenner (1979, 1992; Bronfenbrenner & Morris, 2006).

Ecological perspective An approach to studying development that focuses on individuals within their environmental contexts.

The ecological perspective is not really a new theoretical model, but instead represents a different way of thinking about and studying human development (Moen, Elder, & Luscher, 1995). Traditionally, scientific research on children's development has taken place in laboratory settings. There are good reasons for this. The most important is that scientific investigation demands careful experimental control and, until recently, the laboratory has afforded the only setting in which such control could be achieved.

Urie Bronfenbrenner's work has revitalized interest in the ecological approach to studying human development. (*Courtesy of Cornell University*)

The starting point for the ecological perspective is an obvious fact: Children's development does not generally take place in laboratories. It takes place at home, with the family; at school, with classmates and teachers; in the park, with neighbours and peers; and, more generally, within a larger social and cultural environment. In short, *development always occurs in a context*. More important, the context often influences the course of that development.

The ecological approach is based on the notion that, to completely understand development, we must consider how the unique characteristics of a child interact with that child's surroundings. The child possesses a variety of personal characteristics. The most important of these are described by Bronfenbrenner as *developmentally generative*—capable of influencing other people in ways that are important to the child—and *developmentally disruptive*—capable of causing problems in the environment with corresponding negative effects on the child.

By instigating various responses and reactions from others, children in a sense become "producers" of their own environments—a concept we will come across again at various points. Examples of these characteristics include personality traits that are positive (sociability, cooperativeness, curiosity) or negative (impulsiveness, explosiveness, distractibility), physical appearance, and intellectual abilities.

Bronfenbrenner's theory contends that the child and the environment continually influence one another in a bidirectional, or **transactional**, manner. For example, suppose a child has the developmentally generative characteristics of being bright and articulate. These may affect the child's environment by resulting in the parents' sending her to a better school, which in turn may influence the child by resulting in improved academic skills, which again may affect her environment by attracting friends who have high career aspirations, and so forth, in an ongoing cycle of interaction and development. These sorts of interactions, Bronfenbrenner argued, are very difficult to study if the child is removed from the natural environment in which they occur.

Transactional influence A bidirectional, or reciprocal, relationship in which individuals influence one another's behaviours.

Figure 1.1 shows Bronfenbrenner's ecological model of development. At the centre is the child and his or her physical and personal attributes. Around the child is the environment, viewed as a series of interrelated layers, with those closest to the child having the most direct impact and those farther away influencing the child more indirectly.

For Thought and Discussion

In your development, how have you influenced the environment that influences you? What desirable and undesirable aspects of your environment have you produced?

Nearest to the child is the **microsystem**, which for most children includes the family, the school, the church, the playground, and so forth, along with the relationships the child forms within these settings. The microsystem possesses physical characteristics such as the size of the child's house, the amount of nearby playground equipment, and the number of books in the child's daycare centre. It also consists of people, including family members, the other children on the block, the child's teacher, and so on. These people in turn possess characteristics that may be relevant to the child's development, such as the socioeconomic status of the peer group, the educational background of the parents, and the political attitudes of the teacher. The microsystem is not constant, but changes as the child grows.

Microsystem The environmental system closest to the child, such as the family or school. The first of Bronfenbrenner's layers of context.

FIGURE 1.1

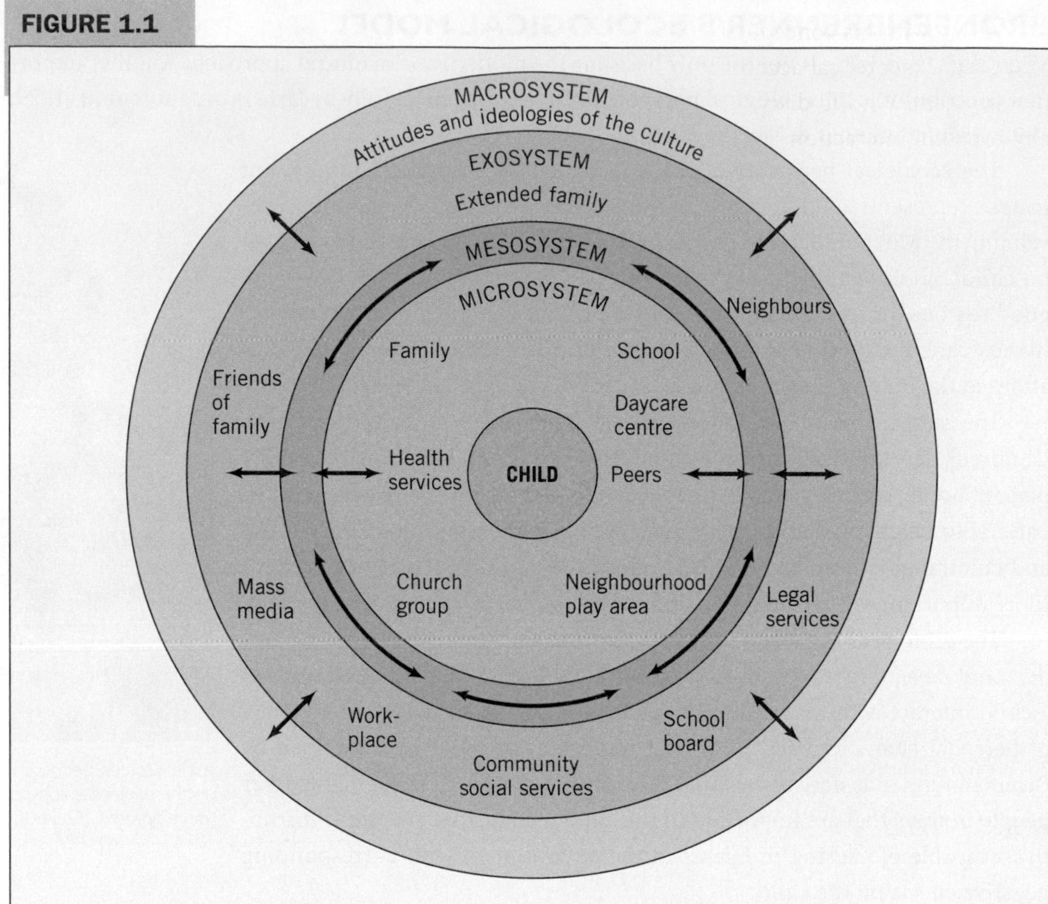

Bronfenbrenner's ecological model of the environment.
From Kopp, Claire B./Krakow, Joanne B., The Child: Development in a Social Context, 1982, Figure 12.1, p. 648. Reprinted by permission of Pearson Education, Inc. Upper Saddle River, New Jersey.

Mesosystem The interrelationships among the child's microsystems. The second of Bronfenbrenner's layers of context.

Exosystem Social systems that can affect children but in which they do not participate directly. Bronfenbrenner's third layer of context.

Macrosystem The culture or subculture in which the child lives. Bronfenbrenner's fourth layer of context.

Chronosystem Bronfenbrenner's term for the passage of time as a context for studying human development.

The **mesosystem** refers to the system of relationships among the child's microsystems. This might include the parents' relationship with the child's teacher and the relationship between the child's siblings and neighbourhood friends. In general, the more interconnected these systems are, the more the child's development is likely to be supported in a clear and consistent way.

The **exosystem** refers to social settings that can affect the child but in which the child does not directly participate. Some examples are the local government, which decides how strictly air pollution standards will be enforced or which families will be eligible for welfare payments; the school board, which sets teachers' salaries and recommends the budget for new textbooks and equipment; and the parents' places of employment, which determine work hours and health care benefits.

Finally, the **macrosystem** involves the culture and subculture in which the child lives. The macrosystem affects the child through its beliefs, attitudes, and traditions. Children living in Canada may be influenced, for example, by beliefs regarding democracy and equality, and perhaps human rights. In certain parts of the country, children may also be affected by regional attitudes regarding, say, the importance of rugged individualism, or perhaps a strong sense of community. If a child lives in an ethnic or racially concentrated neighbourhood, the values and cultural traditions of that group may add yet another source of influence. The macrosystem is generally more stable than the other systems, but it can also change as a society evolves—for example, from a liberal political era to a conservative one, from economic prosperity to depression, or from peace to war (Elder & Caspi, 1988).

Not shown in the diagram is an additional factor that must be considered when studying human development: the passage of time. The interactions that take place among the various systems in the child's world gradually change over time and as the child grows. This source of influence, which Bronfenbrenner termed the **chronosystem**, adds even more complexity and richness to the challenge of analyzing children's development.

Along with his conceptual model for studying development in context, Bronfenbrenner also proposed a theoretical account of how genes and environment operate together to guide human development. We will discuss that theory in Chapter 3, along with several other models of gene–environment interaction.

In Bronfenbrenner's ecological systems theory, development may vary depending on the context in which it occurs. (*Left, CP Photo/Tom Hanson; right, © Yungshu Chao/iStock*)

LEARNING OBJECTIVE 1.4

Describe the sociocultural approach to development.

1. How do sociocultural approaches differ from cognitive-developmental approaches?
2. What does Vygotsky's theory stress?
3. What is the focus of the ecological model?

THEORIES OF DEVELOPMENT: ENVIRONMENTAL/LEARNING APPROACHES

Learning Objective 1.5

Describe the environmental/learning approaches to development.

Just as Rousseau was the ancestor of the cognitive-developmental approach, so Locke was the great-grandfather of the learning tradition. Locke's belief that environment and experiences are the keys to understanding human behaviour—a view that Watson translated into behaviourism early in the 20th century—continues to be the guiding principle for many child psychologists today.

The essence of the environmental/learning view is that a great deal of human behaviour, especially social behaviour, is acquired rather than inborn. Of course, modern behavioural psychologists, like all contemporary psychologists, are interactionists. They accept that biological and cognitive factors make important contributions to human development. But they do not share the belief that biology and evolutionary history largely dictate human development (a view discussed later in this chapter). Nor do they accept the idea that cognition is the fundamental process in psychological development and that changes in behaviour always reflect or require advances in cognitive abilities.

DEFINING LEARNING

Behavioural psychologists believe that the changes in behaviour that occur as children develop are often *learned*, meaning they result from conditioning and learning principles. When psychologists use the term **learning**, they are not referring simply to what goes on in a classroom (although, one

Learning A relatively permanent change in behaviour that results from practice or experience.

hopes, a good deal of it takes place there as well). Instead, they view learning much more generally, defining it as *a relatively permanent change in behaviour that results from practice or experience*. This definition has three distinct elements.

1. The first part of the definition, *relatively permanent*, distinguishes learned changes in behaviour from changes that are only temporary and that often reflect physiological processes—such as when behaviour changes as a result of sleep, illness, or fatigue.
2. The second part, *change in behaviour*, means that learning must always be demonstrated through changes in observable behaviour. If a psychologist were interested in determining whether a child had learned a list of words, for example, the child would need to demonstrate this learning through some aspect of behaviour, such as writing, reciting, or recognizing the words.
3. The final part of the definition, *results from practice or experience*, is meant to separate learned changes in behaviour from changes caused by more general biological processes, such as growth, pregnancy, or even death.

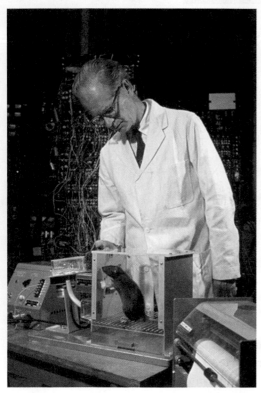

B. F. Skinner's revision of Watson's early behaviouristic views introduced principles of operant conditioning. (*Nina Leen/ Time Life Pictures/Getty Images*)

B. F. SKINNER

We saw earlier that Watson attempted to build a comprehensive theory of child development based on the conditioning of reflexes. His attempt failed in part because human behaviour was too complex to be completely explained by Pavlovian conditioning. Except in very young infants, reflexes account for only a small part of human behaviour. How, then, can a learning theory attempt to explain the whole range of typical child behaviours? One answer emerged in the work of another pioneer of behaviourism, B. F. Skinner (Gewirtz & PelaezNogueras, 1992a).

Skinner accepted the role of Pavlovian conditioning of reflexes, but he added a second type of behaviour to learning theory and, correspondingly, a second type of learning. According to his model, all behaviour falls into one of two categories: respondent behaviour or operant behaviour.

The first category of behaviour involves reflexes. A **reflex** is composed of a stimulus that reliably elicits a response. This relation is biological and inborn. The salivation response of Pavlov's dogs is an example. Skinner called these responses **respondent behaviours**. The most important characteristic of a respondent behaviour is that it is completely controlled by the stimulus that elicits it. Quite simply, the response occurs when the stimulus is present and does not occur when the stimulus is absent. In humans, respondent behaviours are particularly obvious during infancy, and include such reflexive behaviours as sucking in response to a nipple being placed in the mouth and grasping in response to an object touching the palm of the hand. Older children and adults also display a few respondent behaviours, usually in the form of simple physiological responses (e.g., blinking and sneezing) and emotional responses (e.g., some aspects of fear, anger, and sexual arousal).

Operant behaviours are very different. We can think of them roughly as voluntary responses, and they include the vast majority of all human behaviours. Operant behaviours are controlled by their effects; that is, by the consequences they produce. In general, pleasant consequences make the behaviours more likely to occur again, whereas unpleasant consequences have the opposite effect (Skinner, 1953).

Reflex A biological reaction in which a specific stimulus reliably elicits a specific response.

Respondent behaviours Responses based on reflexes, which are controlled by specific eliciting stimuli. The smaller category of human behaviours.

Operant behaviours Voluntary behaviour controlled by its consequences. The larger category of human behaviours.

TYPES OF LEARNING

To understand environmental/learning accounts of child development, we must consider the various types of conditioning and learning that operate on the child. In this section, we examine three forms of learning: habituation, classical conditioning, and operant learning.

HABITUATION You may have observed how infants can learn to sleep through routine household noises. If given enough exposure, babies very quickly get used to slamming doors, ringing phones, and similar sounds that might otherwise wake them. Unfortunately, many parents, unaware of this fact, try to keep everyone very quiet during nap times. The absence of typical household sounds, however, may prevent the infant from becoming accustomed to them and make her more likely to awaken at the first bark of the family dog.

The infant's change in behaviour in this example illustrates the simplest form of learning, called **habituation**. Imagine that we clap our hands loudly near an infant. Initially, the infant will display a full-body startle reflex. If we continue to clap our hands at frequent intervals (say, every 15 seconds), the size of the startle response will decrease steadily until it may be difficult to detect at all. This simple change in behaviour caused by repeatedly presenting a stimulus illustrates learning through habituation.

How do we know that habituation really represents some form of learning? Maybe the infant's muscles have simply become too fatigued to produce the response any longer—a change in behaviour that, according to our earlier definition, we could not consider to be learned. To demonstrate that fatigue is not the reason for the decreased response, we need only change the stimulus. Assume, for instance, that the repeated hand clapping has reduced the startle to a very low level. Now, after waiting 15 seconds, we sound a loud buzzer instead of clapping our hands. With great reliability, the startle response will reappear at the same high level it showed when we first clapped our hands. The recovery of a habituated response that occurs as a result of a change in the eliciting stimulus is known as **dishabituation**.

Although habituation does not account for a great deal of children's development, psychologists have discovered that it can be a very useful technique for studying infants' perceptual and cognitive abilities.

CLASSICAL CONDITIONING **Classical conditioning**—sometimes called **respondent conditioning**—was discovered by Pavlov. It involves reflexes or respondent behaviours. In this type of learning, the stimulus is termed the **unconditioned stimulus (UCS)** and the elicited response is called the **unconditioned response (UCR)**. Classical conditioning involves having another stimulus, which previously did not elicit the UCR, acquire the power to do so. The neutral (new) stimulus is paired or associated with the UCS. After a number of such pairings, it elicits the UCR (or a response very similar to it), at which point the previously neutral stimulus is now termed a **conditioned stimulus (CS)**.

We can illustrate this process with an example involving children's emotional responses, the aspect of human development in which classical conditioning plays its largest role. Fear responses, for instance, can be naturally elicited by a number of stimuli, a very common one being pain. Suppose a child visits the dentist for the first time. The stimuli in that environment—the dentist, the office, the instruments, and so forth—are neutral to the child and so have no particular emotional effect on his behaviour. During the visit, however, suppose the child experiences pain (UCS), which elicits fear (UCR). The various neutral stimuli become associated with the UCS because they are paired with it, and thus may become conditioned stimuli (CS) for the fear response. After that, the sight of the dentist or sound of the drill, for example, will also elicit the fear response. In the same way, many common fears of childhood can be learned responses to places or objects that previously were not frightening. (See *Research Classic 1.1* for a classic demonstration of the conditioning of fear.)

Classical conditioning often produces **stimulus generalization**, which means that stimuli similar to the CS also become conditioned. In our example, the child may come to fear not only his own dentist, but all dentists, and perhaps even anyone wearing a similar medical coat. Fortunately, the conditioned association can

Habituation The decline or disappearance of a response as a result of repeated presentation of the eliciting stimulus. The simplest type of learning.

Dishabituation The recovery of a habituated response that results from a change in the eliciting stimulus.

Links to Related Material

In Chapter 6, we explain how researchers have used habituation (and dishabituation) as a technique for studying the abilities of newborn infants.

Classical (respondent) conditioning A form of learning, involving reflexes, in which a neutral stimulus acquires the power to elicit a reflexive response (UCR) as a result of being associated (paired) with the naturally eliciting stimulus (UCS). The neutral stimulus then becomes a conditioned stimulus (CS).

Unconditioned stimulus (UCS) The stimulus portion of a reflex, which reliably elicits a respondent behaviour (UCR).

Unconditioned response (UCR) The response portion of a reflex, which is reliably elicited by a stimulus (UCS).

Conditioned stimulus (CS) A neutral stimulus that comes to elicit a response through a conditioning process in which it is consistently paired with another stimulus (UCS) that naturally evokes the response.

Stimulus generalization A process related to classical conditioning in which stimuli that are similar to the conditioned stimulus (CS) also acquire the power to elicit the response.

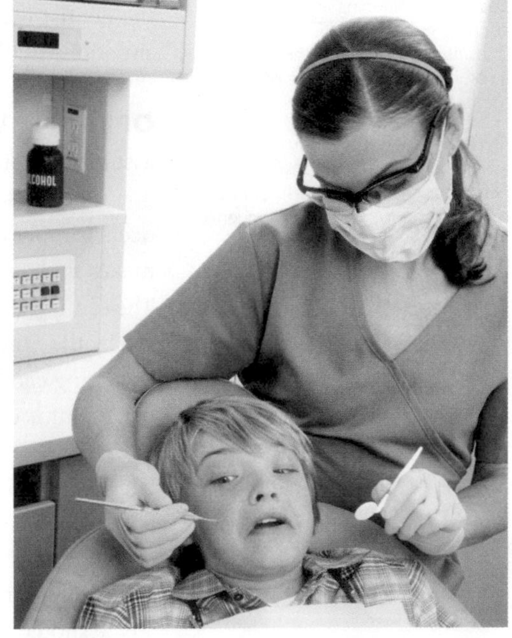

A child's subsequent visits to the dentist may elicit fear responses if he experiences pain during the first visit. *(Upper Cut Images/SuperStock, Inc.)*

RESEARCH CLASSIC 1.1
LITTLE ALBERT AND LITTLE PETER: CONDITIONING AND COUNTER-CONDITIONING FEAR

Perhaps the most famous research conducted by John B. Watson involved the conditioning of a fear response in an 11-month-old child named Albert B. (Watson & Rayner, 1920). The study was designed to show that fear is an unconditioned response that can be easily conditioned to a variety of common stimuli.

Watson believed that children fear dogs, dentists, and the like because they associate these objects or persons with an unconditioned stimulus for fear, such as pain or a sudden loud noise. To illustrate this process, Watson first exposed Albert to a tame white laboratory rat, which produced only mild interest in the child. On several later occasions, Watson presented the rat to Albert and then made a loud noise (UCS) behind Albert. The noise elicited a pronounced fear response (UCR) in the form of crying and trembling. Very soon, the sight of the rat alone was enough to make Albert cry in fear—it had become a conditioned stimulus (CS) for that response.

Watson demonstrated stimulus generalization by showing that objects similar to the rat, such as cotton or a white fur coat, also elicited the fear response. A few years later, Watson and his associate Mary Cover Jones applied the fear-conditioning process in reverse (Jones, 1924). A 3-year-old named Peter was brought to them with an intense fear of rabbits and other furry creatures. The researchers reasoned that if this fear had been learned (conditioned), it could be unlearned. They called their method for eliminating the fear response to the rabbit *counter-conditioning*. It involved presenting the conditioned stimulus in such a way that it would not elicit the fear response, but would instead elicit a competing emotional response—in this case, pleasure derived from eating.

On the first day of treatment, Peter was placed in a high chair and fed his lunch. At the same time, a caged rabbit was displayed on the other side of the room, far enough away so that the fear response did not occur. Each day, while Peter ate, the rabbit was moved slightly closer. In the end, Peter was not at all disturbed at having the rabbit sit next to him while he ate his lunch. The rabbit was no longer a conditioned stimulus for fear and had, instead, become associated with pleasure.

Of course, an experiment of the sort conducted with Little Albert would not be permitted today because psychologists now have strict ethical guidelines for research that prohibit exposing a child to this type of fear experience (see Chapter 2). The experiment with Little Peter, however, is very similar to the type of fear-reduction therapy used today by clinical psychologists, and would be considered a form of behaviour modification.

Extinction A process related to classical conditioning in which the conditioned stimulus (CS) gradually loses its power to elicit the response as a result of no longer being paired with the unconditioned stimulus (UCS).

Operant learning A form of learning in which the likelihood of an operant behaviour changes as a result of its reinforcing or punishing consequences.

also be unlearned, a process called **extinction**. Suppose the child in our example often returns to the dentist without experiencing any more pain. The dentist and other conditioned stimuli in the situation will then gradually cease to elicit fear and return to being neutral.

OPERANT LEARNING A third type of learning is called **operant learning**. Learning theorists assume operant learning is very important for understanding the typical behaviour of children.

Operant behaviours are influenced by their effects, and many of children's everyday behaviours occur simply because they resulted in desirable consequences in the past. Any consequence that makes a response more likely to occur again is called a *reinforcer*. Consider the following examples. The same child may (1) share her toys with a friend because doing so often produces similar sharing by the other child, (2) throw a temper tantrum in the supermarket because this usually results in getting candy from her parent, (3) twist and shake the knob of the playroom door because this behaviour is effective in getting it open, (4) work hard at skating lessons because the coach praises her when she performs well, and (5) put a pillow over her head when her baby brother is crying because this behaviour helps reduce the unpleasant sound.

For Thought and Discussion

What are some examples of processes of classical and operant conditioning in your own childhood development?

It should be obvious from this list that reinforcers can take many forms. Nevertheless, they all fall into one of two categories: Those that involve getting something good are called **positive reinforcers**, and those that involve getting rid of something bad are called **negative reinforcers**.

Positive reinforcer A consequence that makes the behaviour it follows more likely through the presentation of something pleasant.

Negative reinforcer A consequence that makes the behaviour it follows more likely through the removal of something unpleasant.

It should also be apparent from our list of examples that the reinforcement process does not work only on desirable or beneficial responses. Reinforcement increases the likelihood of any behaviour that leads to a pleasant consequence, whether we would typically view that behaviour as appropriate (sharing toys), inappropriate (throwing a tantrum in a supermarket), or neutral (opening a door).

Not all consequences are reinforcing, however. Behaviour sometimes produces effects that are unpleasant, and these *reduce* the likelihood that the behaviour will occur again. Such unpleasant consequences are called **punishers**. We usually think of punishment as something that is delivered by parents or teachers for misbehaviour, but the principle of punishment, like the principle of reinforcement, is simply part of nature's learning process. Punishment teaches organisms which responses are wise to repeat and which are better to avoid. Punishment, too, can entail either getting something bad (such as a spanking, a failing grade, or a scraped knee) or losing something good (such as a favourite toy, a chance to sit by a friend at lunch, or TV privileges for a week). Either way, behaviours that lead to punishing consequences become less likely to occur again.

Punisher A consequence that makes the behaviour it follows less likely, either through the presentation of something unpleasant or the removal of something desirable.

SOCIAL-LEARNING THEORY

Another major approach that has developed within the environmental/learning tradition is **social-learning theory**. The leading spokesperson for this approach has been Canadian-born Albert Bandura (1986, 2001, 2006). Like other behavioural psychologists, Bandura believes that cognitive development alone does not explain childhood changes in behaviour, and that learning processes are responsible for much of children's development. However, he also feels that some learning processes are affected by the child's cognitive abilities. This is especially true for the more complex types of learning that Bandura believes are involved in children's development beyond the infant years. We turn next to one of these types, observational learning.

Social-learning theory A form of environmental/learning theory that adds observational learning to classical and operant learning as a process through which children's behaviours change.

CANADIAN CONTRIBUTIONS 1.1
ALBERT BANDURA

Albert Bandura, 1973. (*Jon Brenneis/Time & Life Pictures/Getty Images*)

Albert Bandura was born and raised in the small town of Mundare, Alberta, not far from Edmonton. Although his parents' formal education was limited, they placed great value on academic achievement and encouraged him throughout his educational career (Bandura, 2007). He attended the University of British Columbia and was attracted by chance to the field of psychology—an Introduction to Psychology course happened to fit his schedule, so he registered for it (Bandura, 2007). He went on to major in psychology and received his B.A. in psychology from UBC in 1949. He did his graduate studies at the University of Iowa, a university known for its behavioural emphasis. While there, he developed an interest in human social learning, an interest that has since dominated his work. After obtaining his Ph.D. in 1952, he began a career as professor at Stanford University, where he has remained until present. His initial work on observational learning (Bandura & Walters, 1963) was published with another Canadian, Richard Walters, who was Bandura's first graduate student at Stanford University (Davison, Blankstein, Flett, & Neale, 2011). Bandura's research and theory have greatly influenced our understanding of child development and of human behaviour in general. His work has received international acclaim, resulting in many awards and honours, including awards from a number of Canadian universities. In 2000, the Canadian Psychological Association honoured his contributions to psychology by making him its honorary president. In 2004, the American Psychological Association awarded Bandura the Award for Lifetime Contributions to Psychology.

For Thought and Discussion

What three persons or characters most influenced your behaviour through observational learning during childhood?

OBSERVATIONAL LEARNING Skinner's addition of operant learning to Watson's Pavlovian conditioning greatly expanded learning theory's ability to explain children's behaviour. Nevertheless, some problems remained. One was that children sometimes acquire new behaviours simply by seeing someone else perform them. A second was that children sometimes become more or less likely to perform a behaviour after seeing another person experience reinforcing or punishing consequences for that behaviour. Neither of these facts is easily explained by a type of learning in which changes in behaviour occur only when children experience direct consequences for their actions.

Observational learning A form of learning in which an observer's behaviour changes as a result of observing a model.

Bandura solved this problem by proposing that as children grow, their development is increasingly based on a fourth type of learning—**observational learning**. Learning by observation occurs when an observer's behaviour is affected by witnessing a model's behaviour (and often the consequences of the model's behaviour). In developmental psychology, the observers are children and the models include parents, teachers, siblings, classmates, sports celebrities, TV personalities, and even cartoon characters—in short, just about anyone in the child's world.

Vicarious reinforcement Reinforcing consequences experienced when viewing a model that affect the observer.

Vicarious punishment Punishing consequences experienced when viewing a model that affect the observer.

Bandura and other researchers have studied three important questions regarding the modelling process:

1. Which models are most likely to influence a child's behaviour?
2. Under what circumstances is this influence most likely to occur?
3. How does a child's behaviour change as a result of observational learning?

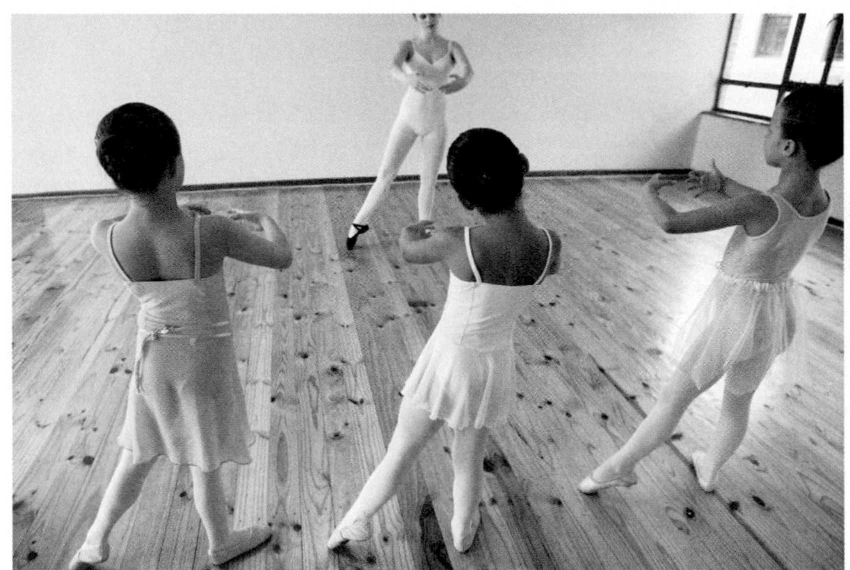

Imitation is an important process by which children acquire new skills and behaviours. *(Ant Strack/Corbis)*

The simple answer to the first question is that a model who possesses a characteristic that the child finds attractive or desirable—such as talent, intelligence, power, good looks, or popularity—is most likely to be imitated. Other issues can sometimes come into play, however, including the child's level of development and the types of behaviours being modelled.

The circumstances under which modelling is most effective can also vary, but one of the most important factors is whether the model receives reinforcing or punishing consequences for the behaviour. One of Bandura's most significant contributions to social-learning theory is his demonstration that the consequences of a model's behaviour can affect the behaviour of an observer. When an observer sees a model receive reinforcement for a response, the observer receives **vicarious reinforcement** and, like the model, becomes more likely to produce that same response. The opposite is also true when the observer receives **vicarious punishment** as a result of witnessing a model being punished. In some sense, then, observational learning is the same as operant learning, except that the child experiences the consequences vicariously rather than directly.

Imitation Behaviour of an observer that results from and is similar to the behaviour of a model.

The most obvious and perhaps the most important result of modelling is **imitation**, which occurs when children copy what they have seen. Imitation can take such varied forms as climbing on a chair to steal a cookie from the shelf after seeing an older sibling do it, adopting the clothing style of a popular professional athlete, or copying the problems a teacher writes on the chalkboard.

Response inhibition Not displaying a particular behaviour that has just been modelled; often as a result of vicarious punishment.

A second result of modelling occurs when the observer becomes less likely to perform a behaviour that has just been modelled. This effect, known as **response inhibition**, is a common result of vicarious punishment. The teacher who publicly disciplines an unruly child to set an example for the rest of the class is counting on observational learning to inhibit similar behaviours in the other children.

One of Bandura's early studies provides a clear illustration of the effects of vicarious reinforcement and vicarious punishment. In this study, one group of youngsters observed a model rewarded for displaying new aggressive behaviours toward an inflated toy clown, whereas a second group saw those same behaviours punished. When given an opportunity to play with the doll themselves, the children who witnessed the reinforcement imitated many of the model's aggressive acts toward the doll, whereas the group who observed punishment did not. But when later offered rewards for reproducing the aggressive behaviours, both groups were able to perform them quite accurately (Bandura, 1965). Obviously, all of the children had acquired (learned) the new behaviours, even though the vicariously experienced punishment had inhibited some children from performing them. This distinction between acquisition and performance has been of particular interest to researchers studying the potential effects of viewing television violence on children's aggressive behaviour, which we discuss in Chapter 14.

The acquisition–performance distinction is evident in Bandura's theoretical formulation of observational learning, shown in Figure 1.2. Bandura believes that learning by observation involves four separate processes. The first two account for the acquisition, or learning, of a model's behaviour, and the other two control the performance, or production, of these behaviours (Bandura, 1977).

Links to Related Material

Bandura's social learning theory has been of particular interest to researchers studying the potential effects of viewing television violence on children's aggressive behaviour; see Chapter 14.

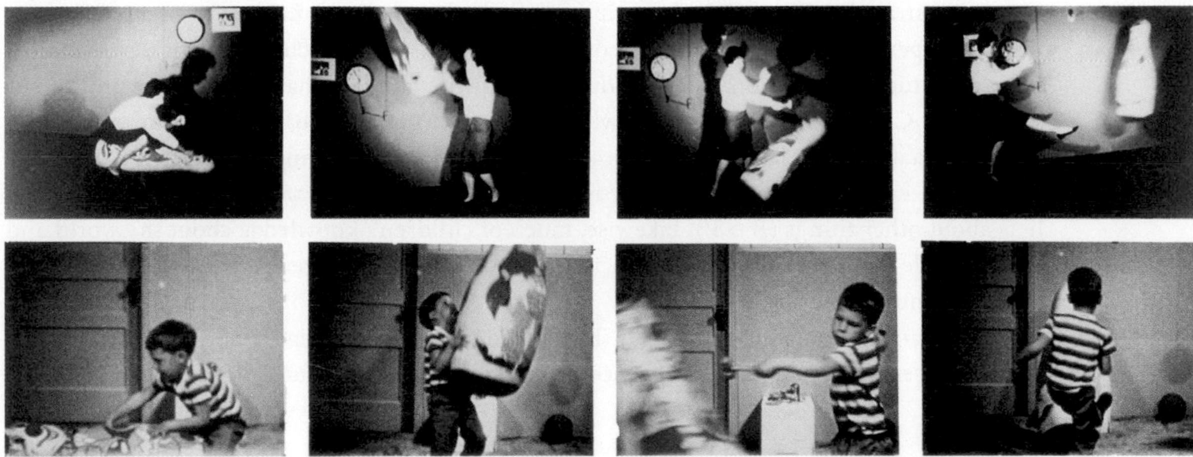

Albert Bandura's early research showed that children exposed to filmed violence were capable of very accurately imitating the model's aggressive acts when given the opportunity to reproduce them. (*Stanford University*)

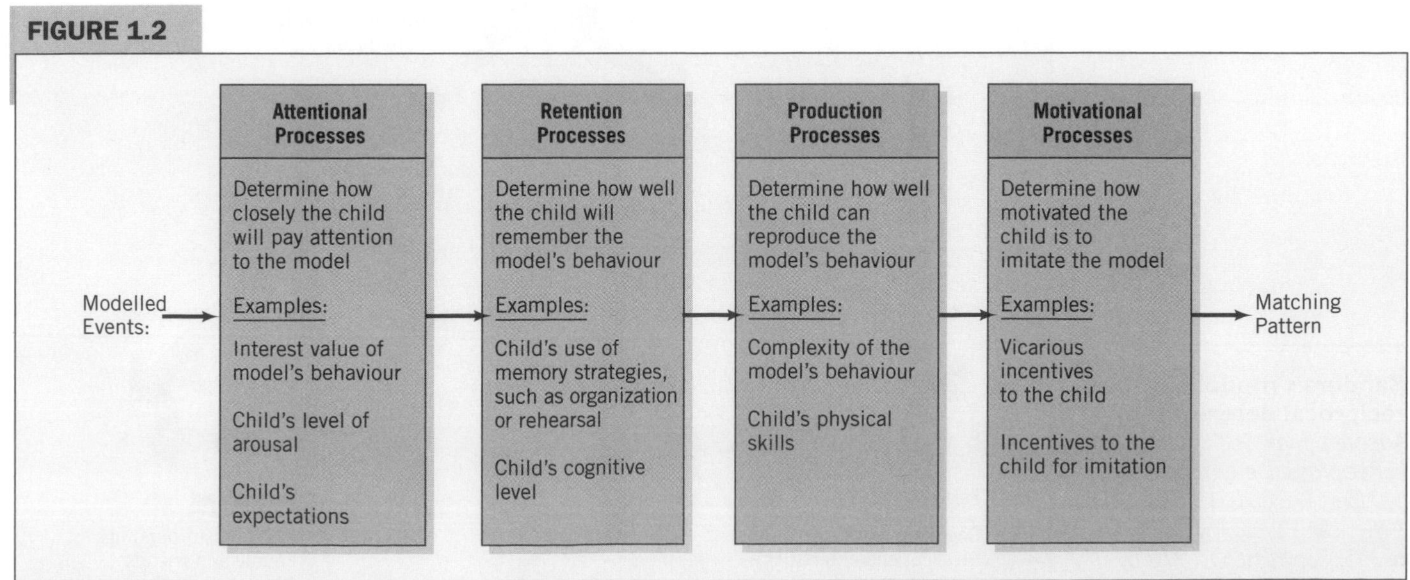
FIGURE 1.2
Modelled Events:
Attentional Processes
Determine how closely the child will pay attention to the model
Examples:
Interest value of model's behaviour
Child's level of arousal
Child's expectations
Retention Processes
Determine how well the child will remember the model's behaviour
Examples:
Child's use of memory strategies, such as organization or rehearsal
Child's cognitive level
Production Processes
Determine how well the child can reproduce the model's behaviour
Examples:
Complexity of the model's behaviour
Child's physical skills
Motivational Processes
Determine how motivated the child is to imitate the model
Examples:
Vicarious incentives to the child
Incentives to the child for imitation
Matching Pattern

Bandura's model of observational learning. *Adapted from Albert Bandura,* Social Learning Theory, First Edition, © *1977, p. 23. Reprinted by permission of Pearson Education, Inc., Upper Saddle River, New Jersey.*

- *Attentional processes* determine how closely the child pays attention to what the model is doing.
- *Retention processes* refer to how well the child can store the modelled information in memory for later use.
- *Production processes* control how well the child can reproduce the model's responses.
- *Motivational processes* determine who and what a child chooses to imitate.

Bandura's theory thus suggests four important reasons why children do not imitate everything they see in everyday life. A child may fail to imitate an observed behaviour because she did not pay attention to what the model was doing, does not recall the model's responses, does not possess the physical skills to repeat the model's behaviour, or simply feels little motivation to do what the model did.

RECIPROCAL DETERMINISM Bandura's social-learning analysis is truly interactionist. It is based on his view that human development reflects the interaction of the person (P), the person's behaviour (B), and the environment (E). Bandura describes this process of interaction as **reciprocal determinism** (Bandura, 1978).

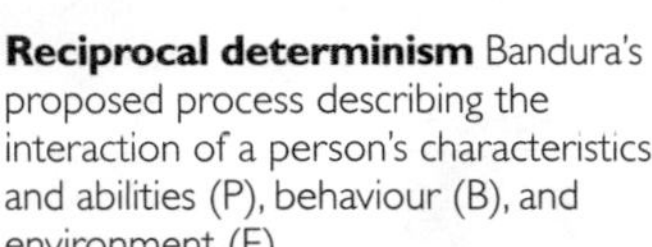

Reciprocal determinism Bandura's proposed process describing the interaction of a person's characteristics and abilities (P), behaviour (B), and environment (E).

As illustrated in Figure 1.3, the reciprocal determinism model forms a triangle of interactions. The person includes the child's cognitive abilities, physical characteristics, personality, beliefs, attitudes, and so on, which influence both the child's behaviour and the child's environment. Children choose not only what they want to do (P → B) but also where and with whom to do it (P → E). These influences are reciprocal, however. Children's behaviour (and the reactions it engenders) can affect their feelings about themselves and their attitudes and beliefs about other things (B → P). Likewise, much of children's knowledge about the world and other people results from information they receive from TV, parents, textbooks, and other environmental sources (E → P).

Environment also affects behaviour. The consequences of children's behaviour and the models they observe can powerfully influence what they do (E → B). But children's behaviour also

FIGURE 1.3

Behaviour
Motor responses
Social interactions
Language

B

P

E

Person
Cognitive abilities
Physical characteristics
Personality
Beliefs, attitudes, etc.

Environment
Physical surroundings
Family and friends
Other social influences

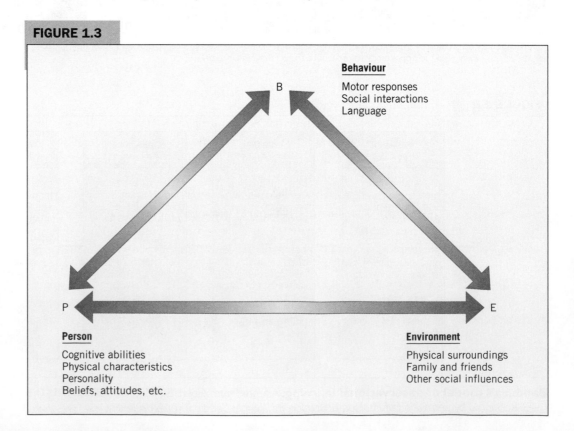

Bandura's model of reciprocal determinism. *Adapted from "Self System in Reciprocal Determinism" by Albert Bandura, 1978,* American Psychologist, 33, *p. 345. Copyright © 1978 by the American Psychological Association.* Adapted by permission.

contributes to creating their environment. A child who shares and cooperates with classmates is likely to attract many friends, whereas the opposite may be the case for a child who behaves selfishly or aggressively (B → E).

Bandura's addition of observational learning to the environmental/learning tradition, along with his willingness to incorporate cognitive aspects of development, has greatly increased the explanatory power of social-learning theory and has made it the most important learning-based approach. We consider the role of this model in many aspects of children's development throughout this text.

LEARNING OBJECTIVE 1.5

Describe the environmental/learning approaches to development.

1. What basic assumption underlies environmental/learning approaches?
2. What three types of conditioning are stressed in traditional learning theories?
3. How does social learning theory differ from earlier models?
4. Why can we call Bandura's theory interactionist?

THEORIES OF DEVELOPMENT: EVOLUTIONARY AND BIOLOGICAL APPROACHES

Learning Objective 1.6

Describe the evolutionary and biological approaches to development.

The fourth major theoretical approach in modern child psychology is the evolutionary/biological approach. We can trace the historical roots of this tradition to the work of Darwin. The modern version of the approach begins with a discipline referred to as **ethology**: the study of development from an evolutionary perspective.

Ethology The study of development from an evolutionary perspective.

BEHAVIOUR AND EVOLUTION

When trying to understand the ethological approach, it is important to keep in mind that from an evolutionary perspective, our species is the product of millions of years of change. What we are today represents a small part of an enormous process. Human beings are only one of the 5 million or so species that presently inhabit the earth, and ethology considers human development within the context of the entire animal kingdom. It should not be surprising, then, that much of the research conducted within this tradition involves non-human species.

Like the other theoretical models, ethology attempts to explain changes in behaviour that occur across development. According to ethological theorists, these changes have two kinds of determinants, or causes—immediate and evolutionary. The immediate determinants are the more obvious, and include the environment in which the behaviour occurs, the animal's recent experiences, and the state or condition of the animal—whether it is hungry, tired, or angry, for example. The evolutionary determinants of behaviour are less clear. Not all present-day behaviours or characteristics were necessarily selected for in evolution. Some, however, are presumed to have contributed to the animal's chances of survival, and thus to have been passed along to future generations through the natural selection process. To explain such behaviours as hunting for prey or constructing a dam, ethologists consider both the immediate circumstances, such as the availability of prey or of appropriate building materials, and factors in the animal's evolutionary past, such as the climate and terrain in which the behaviours evolved.

CLASSICAL ETHOLOGY

Ethology first gained scientific recognition in the 1930s with the work of two pioneers in animal study, Konrad Lorenz and Niko Tinbergen. Both were zoologists by training, and their early investigations focused exclusively on non-human animals. Nevertheless, their research laid the groundwork for the growing trend toward the application of ethological principles to child development, and in 1973 they were jointly awarded a Nobel Prize for their pioneering research.

INNATE MECHANISMS Ethologists have identified four qualities that characterize virtually all innate, or inborn, behaviours (Eibl-Eibesfeldt, 1989).

1. They are *universal* to all members of the species.
2. Because they are usually biologically programmed responses to very specific stimuli, they *require no learning or experience.*
3. They are normally *stereotyped*, meaning they occur in precisely the same way every time they are displayed.
4. They are only *minimally affected by environmental influences* (in the short run, that is; natural selection pressures affect them across generations).

Countless examples of such behaviours have been identified in virtually every known species, ranging from the nest-building behaviours of ants to the pecking responses of chickens to the herding behaviours of antelope. In humans, such innate behaviours are most evident during infancy. An inborn response such as sucking, for example, is found in all babies, does not need to be learned, occurs in a stereotyped pattern, and is influenced very little by the environment (at least during the first weeks of life). The idea of a stimulus that elicits a simple, reflexive, biological response, such as sucking, is neither new nor of interest only to ethologists (as the work of Pavlov and Watson clearly demonstrates). But ethologists have typically been interested in more complex sequences of innate behaviours, which they call **modal action patterns**. These are the chains of responses that we see, for example, when spiders spin webs, birds build nests, or bears care for newborn cubs. A modal action pattern is triggered by a specific stimulus in the animal's environment, what Lorenz called an **innate releasing mechanism**. A classic example of such a mechanism was demonstrated by Tinbergen (1973) in his work with the stickleback.

Modal action pattern A sequence of behaviours elicited by a specific stimulus.

Innate releasing mechanism A stimulus that triggers an innate sequence or pattern of behaviours.

The stickleback is a freshwater fish with three sharp spines. In winter, the males stay in schools and are relatively inactive. In spring, the rising water temperature sets off a distinctive pattern of mating behaviours. Each stickleback leaves the school and builds a tunnel-like nest in the sand, which he defends as his own territory against other males. When a female approaches the area above the nest, the male begins his courtship by stabbing her with one of his spines. He then swims down to the nest in an unusual zigzag pattern. The stabbing and swimming motion apparently excite the female, who follows him to his nest. When she enters it, the male places his face against her tail and begins to quiver. This stimulates the female to release her eggs, which the male fertilizes by releasing his sperm. He then chases her away and waits for another female to approach. This ritual continues until five or so females have released eggs in the nest. The male subsequently cares for the developing eggs, driving away intruders and fanning the water with his tail to provide the eggs with sufficient oxygen.

In addition to observing this mating process in the wild, Tinbergen studied sticklebacks in the laboratory. There he exposed the fish to wooden models of other sticklebacks of various colours and shapes to determine experimentally which stimuli are necessary to trigger and maintain the chain of behaviours. The details of these experiments are not crucial for our purposes, but the work does raise several important issues.

One issue concerns the relevance of these sorts of modal action patterns for human development. Although the mating rituals of humans are (fortunately) very different from those of sticklebacks, ethologists believe that many response patterns in humans are also triggered by very specific stimuli. These may include, for example, maternal responses to newborn babies or certain forms of aggression. A related issue concerns the nature versus nurture question. The stickleback

For Thought and Discussion

What kinds of human behaviours do you think would have aided survival or reproductive advantage?

does not need to learn the complex courtship responses; they are elicited biologically by stimuli in the environment. This does not mean, however, that other aspects of the stickleback's behaviour do not change in response to experiences or consequences. From the opposite perspective, even though many aspects of human behaviour clearly result from learning processes, ethologists contend that this does not rule out the possibility that other aspects of human behaviour—perhaps even complex behaviour patterns—are controlled by innate evolutionary processes. Thus, modern ethologists, too, are interactionists, assuming important roles for both nature and nurture processes.

Tinbergen's research strategy also illustrates how ethologists combine naturalistic and laboratory methods. The great majority of their investigations involve observing behaviours in the natural settings where they evolved. In this way, the researcher can examine how an animal's responses typically occur. But the behaviours are also studied in more structured settings, where the researcher can control the conditions under which events take place and can subject an animal's rituals and routines to various experimental tests.

SENSITIVE PERIODS An important issue in psychology concerns how an animal's genetic or biological makeup can influence the learning process; that is, how nature and nurture work together to change behaviour. Ethologists argue that animals are biologically programmed so that some things are learned most easily during certain periods of development. A dramatic example of this is illustrated by Lorenz's research on **imprinting**, the process by which newborns of some species form an emotional bond with their mothers.

Imprinting A biological process of some species in which the young acquire an emotional attachment to the mother through following.

In many bird species whose young can walk almost immediately after hatching, baby birds soon begin to follow the mother as she moves about. Lorenz guessed that this simple act of following was responsible for the strong social bond that developed between the newborn and the parent. To confirm his suspicion, Lorenz removed just-hatched goslings from their mother and had them follow another animal, or various non-living objects that he pulled along, or even himself. As he predicted, the young birds quickly imprinted to whatever they followed and thereafter treated it as their mother (Lorenz, 1937).

Konrad Lorenz found that newly-hatched goslings, when permitted to follow him around for a short time, would imprint to him and thereafter treat him as their mother. *(Nina Leen/Getty Images/Time Life Pictures)*

Lorenz further discovered that one of the most important influences on imprinting was the age of the chicks. If the act of following occurred during a period that began several hours after birth and lasted until sometime the next day, the attachment bond reliably developed. When the following occurred only before or after this period, however, little or no imprinting resulted. Ethologists now use the term **sensitive periods** to describe points in development when learning is much easier than it is at earlier or later points. Sensitive periods are not restricted to imprinting or even to the area of mother–infant attachment. Child researchers have applied the concept to areas as diverse as language acquisition (Newport, 1991) and gender-role development (Money & Annecillo, 1987), as we will see in later chapters.

Sensitive period A period of development during which certain behaviours are more easily learned.

APPLICATIONS TO HUMAN DEVELOPMENT

Our main interest in ethological theory is its application to child development. Modern researchers are finding many areas of development in which evolutionary processes may be important (Beaulieu & Bugental, 2007; Geary & Bjorklund, 2000; Scarr, 1993).

JOHN BOWLBY'S WORK As early as the 1940s, Lorenz suggested that physical characteristics of babies, such as the shapes of their heads and the sounds of their cries, might serve as stimuli to trigger caregiving by mothers (Lorenz, 1950). Developmental psychologists likewise interpreted infants' early reflexive behaviours in terms of their evolutionary value to the species. Nevertheless, the scientific application of the ethological model to child development is usually considered to have begun in 1969, when John Bowlby published the first of his three volumes on the subject (Bowlby, 1969/1982, 1973, 1980).

Bowlby, an English physician and psychoanalyst, was the first to attract child psychologists to an evolutionary interpretation of human development. As a clinician, Bowlby had witnessed the emotional problems of children who had been reared in institutions. Such children often had difficulty forming and maintaining close relationships. Bowlby attributed this problem to the children's lack of a strong attachment to their mothers during infancy. His interest in this area eventually led him to an ethological explanation of how and why the mother–infant bond is established (Bretherton, 1995).

Bowlby's theory is an interesting mix of ethology and Freudian theory (Holmes, 1995; Sroufe, 1986). As did Freud, Bowlby believed that the quality of the early relationship (between baby and mother) is critical to later development, and these first experiences are carried forward by processes in the unconscious. Bowlby's theory also reflects a fundamental principle of classical ethology: a close mother–infant bond is crucial in humans (and in most higher-level species) for the survival of the young. Infants who remain near the mother can be fed, protected, trained, and transported more effectively than can infants who stray from her side. The behaviours used by the mother and infant to keep the pair in close contact must therefore be innate and controlled by a variety of releasing stimuli (we discuss these behaviours in Chapter 12). Bowlby further maintains that the attachment bond develops easily during a sensitive period, but after this time it may become impossible for the child to ever achieve a truly intimate emotional relationship (Bowlby, 1988).

Bowlby's work has encouraged a great deal of additional research on attachment and bonding processes in humans. More importantly for this tradition, it began a general movement toward examining other aspects of child development within an evolutionary context. Psychologists have since investigated children's aggression, peer interactions, cognitive development, and many other topics.

Ethologists have also influenced developmental research methods. Observational methods have always been used by child researchers, but there has been a renewed interest in studying children in their natural environments. Observational techniques that do not influence or intrude on children's normal social interactions are increasingly being added to more experimental approaches to studying these behaviours.

Sociobiology A branch of biology that attempts to discover the evolutionary origins of social behaviour.

SOCIOBIOLOGY One offshoot of classical ethology involves an attempt to apply evolutionary principles to human social behaviour. This area of research, called **sociobiology**, began rather dramatically in 1975 with the publication of a book by Harvard biologist E. O. Wilson, entitled *Sociobiology: The New Synthesis*. According to Wilson's radical and somewhat controversial theory, genes are very selfish structures whose only interest is to ensure their own survival from generation to generation.

Many specific physical characteristics (colour of fur, size of ears, and so on) are carried in an animal's genes. When a characteristic is valuable for survival or reproduction, the genes that produce it are more likely to be passed along to the next generation—Darwin's natural selection process. Sociobiologists believe that genes influence not only physical traits, but also social behaviours. Social behaviours that are more adaptive for survival are thus assumed to undergo the same natural selection process as physical traits.

The sociobiological view can be illustrated by a frequently cited example. Consider a mother who risks her life to save her child from danger. According to the traditional ethological model, this response by the mother should not have an evolutionary basis because natural selection would not favour behaviours that reduce an individual's chances of survival. Sociobiologists contend, however, that the mother's genes have in some way programmed her to do whatever she can to ensure her genes are passed on to future generations. Because her child carries many of those same genes, and because he would have many reproductive years ahead, evolutionary mechanisms drive the mother to sacrifice her life to save that of her child (Dawkins, 1976).

Wilson suggests that genetic effects on social behaviour are better understood at the level of the culture or society, rather than of the individual. He claims, for example, that many cultural practices, such as taboos against incest and laws against murder, reflect an evolutionary process that favours individuals whose social behaviours are in line with what is best for the survival of the species. This theory has been both praised and criticized (Lerner & von Eye, 1992). But it has sparked a great deal of debate and has drawn additional attention to the evolutionary perspective.

EVOLUTIONARY DEVELOPMENTAL PSYCHOLOGY A more recent development is the emergence of **evolutionary developmental psychology** (Bjorklund, 2006; Bjorklund & Pellegrini, 2000, 2002b; Ellis & Bjorklund, 2005; Geary, 2005; Grotuss, Bjorklund, & Csinady, 2007), a subdivision of *evolutionary psychology* (Buss, 1999). Evolutionary developmental psychology shares the general ethological emphasis on evolution and the selection of adaptive behaviour, as well as the sociobiologists' specific concern with explaining the origins of human behaviour patterns. Its scope, however, is broader than that of sociobiology; in particular, it encompasses the evolutionary origins of contemporary cognitive abilities, as well as those that underlie social relations and social interactions. This emphasis is reflected in the titles or subtitles of several books devoted to the approach: *Origins of the Social Mind: Evolutionary Psychology and Child Development* (Ellis & Bjorklund, 2005), *The Origins of Human Nature: Evolutionary Developmental Psychology* (Bjorklund & Pellegrini, 2002b), and *The Evolution of Cognition* (Heyes & Huber, 2000).

Evolutionary developmental psychology A branch of evolutionary psychology that encompasses the evolutionary origins of contemporary cognitive abilities, as well as those that underlie social relations and social interactions.

Two themes help characterize evolutionary developmental psychology. One concerns the fit between the adaptational challenges faced by our ancestors across the millennia during which our present characteristics were selected, and those that confront contemporary humans. In some instances, the challenges are similar, and thus characteristics that evolved thousands of years ago still serve us well today. The formation of an attachment bond in infancy is one example; mastery of the culture's language system is another. In other instances, however, new challenges have arisen since the last significant evolutionary change in our species; learning to read is an example in this category, as are many of the other skills transmitted in school. Evolutionary psychologists predict that skills such as reading, which evolution has not prepared us for, will be more difficult to attain and more variable across children than are developments like attachment or language—and as we will see, this is in fact the case.

A second theme central to the *developmental* part of evolutionary developmental psychology is the argument that the attributes that are adaptive and promote survival will vary with the developmental level of the organism. Discussions of natural selection tend to stress the characteristics of adults that lead to successful mate selection and reproduction. Such characteristics are important; however, they can operate only for individuals who also possess the characteristics that allowed them to survive infancy and childhood. Thus, this approach provides an evolutionary framework for making sense of the attributes and developmental tasks that characterize different phases of childhood.

For Thought and Discussion

Which approach to explaining human development fits best with your own thinking regarding how we develop—cognitive, sociocultural, environmental, or evolutionary? Why?

As we saw, Lorenz provided an early version of this argument with his contention that certain characteristics of babies promote caregiving and thus survival. Bjorklund and Pellegrini (2002a) offer another example. They suggest that the rough-and-tumble play that is common among boys may help them learn forms of social signalling that will be beneficial for later social behaviour, as well as provide exercise that is important for skeletal and muscular development.

LEARNING OBJECTIVE 1.6

Describe the evolutionary and biological approaches to development.

1. How does ethology explain development?
2. What are four characteristics of innate behaviour?
3. What are three applications of evolutionary theory to human development?

CONCLUSION

Although child study is still young compared with other physical and biological sciences, our understanding of developmental processes is progressing so rapidly that it is difficult to keep up with the information being generated by researchers. The remainder of this text, therefore, focuses on the current state of the field rather than on historical issues and research. Yet, as we proceed from topic to topic, you may be struck by how familiar some of the recurring controversies sound, reminiscent of the fundamental differences that arose between Locke and Rousseau or Watson and Gesell.

Indeed, it may seem that ideas regarding child development have not changed very much in the past few hundred years. Locke, Rousseau, and Darwin offered explanations of human behaviour that are, in essence, still with us today. Modern theories of development, however, are different from these early models in several important ways.

The first is that today's viewpoints are much less extreme. There are no longer pure nature or nurture theories, for example. Thus, although each of the major developmental theories described in this chapter has its own ideas, philosophy, and methods, each also accepts many of the ideas of the other models. As psychologists continue to add to our knowledge of child development, the overlap among the approaches will undoubtedly grow.

A second difference is that today's psychologists no longer attempt to explain human development with only a few principles or processes. We have come to realize that behaviour has many causes and the mechanisms through which they operate are intricate and often interrelated. Modern theoretical explanations reflect this increasing complexity, and this trend is also likely to continue.

The final difference is that today's models are based on a great deal of scientific data. Early theories of human development were mostly the products of philosophical debates and logical deductions. Modern explanations, in contrast, have grown out of research findings, and they are continually being modified and revised in response to new observations and experimental data. A particular child psychologist may prefer one theoretical approach over another. In the final analysis, however, the evidence provided by research will determine which theories will survive and which will be abandoned.

SUMMARY

KEY TERMS

accommodation, p. 17
adaptation, p. 17
assimilation, p. 17
baby biography, p. 6
behaviourism, p. 7
chronosystem, p. 22
classical (respondent) conditioning, p. 25
clinical method, p. 15
concrete operations, p. 18
conditioned stimulus (CS), p. 25
constructivism, p. 17
continuity versus discontinuity debate, p. 13
cultural relativism, p. 5
developmental psychology, p. 2
dialectical process, p. 20
dishabituation, p. 25
ecological perspective, p. 21
ethology, p. 31
evolutionary developmental psychology, p. 35
exosystem, p. 22
extinction, p.26
formal operations, p. 18
genetic epistemology, p. 15
habituation, p. 25
identification, p. 10
identity, p. 11
imitation, p. 28
imprinting, p. 33
innate releasing mechanism, p. 32
interactionist perspective, p. 10

internalization, p. 20
learning, p. 23
macrosystem, p. 22
maturation, p. 8
mesosystem, p. 22
microsystem, p. 21
modal action pattern, p. 32
nativism, p. 5
natural selection, p. 6
nature versus nurture debate, p. 12
negative reinforcer, p. 26
normative versus idiographic development, p. 13
norms, p. 9
observational learning, p. 28
operant behaviours, p. 24
operant learning, p. 26
organization, p. 17
periods, p. 17
positive reinforcer, p. 26
preoperational, p. 17
punisher, p. 27
recapitulation, p. 6
reciprocal determinism, p. 30
reflex, p. 24
repression, p. 10
respondent behaviours, p. 24
response inhibition, p. 28
schemes, p. 16
sensitive period, p. 33
sensorimotor, p. 17
social-learning theory, p. 27
sociobiology, p. 34
stimulus generalization, p. 25
tabula rasa, p. 5
tools of intellectual adaptation, p. 20
transactional influence, p. 21
unconditioned response (UCR), p. 25
unconditioned stimulus (UCS), p. 25
universals of development, p. 14
vicarious punishment, p. 28
vicarious reinforcement, p. 28
zeitgeist, p. 7

LEARNING OBJECTIVES

LEARNING OBJECTIVE 1.1 Understand the philosophical and historical roots of child psychology.

1. *What are two basic goals of research in developmental psychology?*
   The two basic goals of research in developmental psychology are to describe behaviours at each point in development and to explain the changes that occur from one point to the next.

2. *What contributions were made by John Locke, Jean-Jacques Rousseau, Johann Gottfried von Herder, and Charles Darwin?*
   John Locke based his approach on the strict environmentalist position that all knowledge is acquired through experience, viewing the newborn as a tabula rasa. Jean-Jacques Rousseau proposed a nativistic model in which development unfolds according to inborn processes. Johann Gottfried von Herder argued for the notion of cultural relativism, believing that shared cultural symbol systems and practices shape development. Charles Darwin's theory of evolution stressed the principle of natural selection, and suggested that many human behaviours have their origins in the past, when they were valuable for our ancestors' survival.

3. *How did G. Stanley Hall and James Mark Baldwin contribute to the study of development?*
   The scientific study of children began with the research of G. Stanley Hall, who trained the first generation of developmental psychologists. James Mark Baldwin established the first psychological laboratory in Canada, and investigated infant development using the baby biography method.

4. *How did John B. Watson help make child psychology a natural science?*
   John B. Watson helped make child psychology a natural science by introducing objective research methods based on observable and measurable behaviours. His behaviourist theory of development held that the conditioned reflex was the fundamental unit of development.

5. *What were Arnold Gesell's major contributions to the study of development?*
   Arnold Gesell's research with children renewed interest in the biological perspective by offering evidence that inborn maturational processes account for developmental changes. His observational studies produced age-related norms of behaviour.

6. *How are Freud's and Erikson's views of development similar?*
   Both Sigmund Freud and Erik Erikson proposed stage theories of child development that took an interactionist view. Freud's psychosexual stages are based on the notion that sexual energy, termed libido, is biologically guided to certain erogenous zones of the body as the child grows. Erikson's psychosocial stages parallel Freud's psychosexual stages, but continue beyond adolescence into adulthood and emphasize social and cultural influences.

LEARNING OBJECTIVE 1.2 Explain the influences of nature and nurture, stability and change, and uniformity and variation on child development.

1. *How do nature and nurture jointly contribute to child development?*
   Researchers generally agree that both nature and nurture play a role in development. However, the exact relationship is cause for continued debate. Some researchers believe that biological factors (nature) play a primary role, with the environment modifying inherent characteristics. Others believe that while biology lays a foundation for development, significant differences in outcomes are determined by experience (nature).

2. *Why might some researchers focus on stability or continuity in development, while others focus on discontinuity or change?*
   A particular focus of a researcher is related to a belief about how development occurs. The continuity model assumes that human behaviour consists of many individual skills that are added one at a time, producing increasingly complex behaviours indicative of quantitative change. According to the discontinuity model, development occurs in stages, with relatively stable periods of development interrupted by abrupt changes. According to this model, development involves qualitative changes in previous abilities and behaviours. Researchers agree that some developmental processes are described more accurately by one model and others by the competing model.

3. *Why might some researchers focus on typical or normal development, while others focus on individual variation?*
   Normative research focuses on the statistically "average" child, with the goal of identifying and describing how normal development proceeds. A related notion is the search for universals of development that characterize all children everywhere. Research on ideographic development centres on the individual child and the factors that produce human diversity, such as cultural differences.

LEARNING OBJECTIVE 1.3 Describe the cognitive-developmental approach and the two major theories of cognitive development.

1. *What is the key view of the cognitive-developmental approach?*
   The cognitive-developmental approach is based on the belief that cognitive abilities are fundamental and that they guide children's behaviour. The key to understanding changes across development, then, lies in understanding what children know and how this knowledge is organized.

2. *How did Piaget describe human development?*
   Piaget described human development in terms of inborn functions and changing cognitive structures. With development, the structures increase in number and complexity. Changes

in structures are guided by two functions—organization and adaptation. Adaptation, in turn, consists of assimilation and accommodation. These processes reflect Piaget's constructivist view of development—the belief that children construct their understanding of the world rather than passively receive it from the environment. As children do this, they pass through four stages, or periods, of development: the sensori-motor period, the preoperational period, the period of concrete operations, and the period of formal operations.

3. *How do information-processing models view cognition?*
Information-processing models conceptualize cognition as a computer-like system with three parts. Stimulation from the outside world makes up input, the first part; mental processes act on that information and represent the second part; and behaviour of various sorts makes up the output of the system, the third part. Information-processing models are concerned with how maturation, along with children's use of strategies and rules, influence the development of cognitive abilities.

LEARNING OBJECTIVE 1.4 Describe the sociocultural approach to development.

1. *How do sociocultural approaches differ from cognitive-developmental approaches?*
Cognitive-developmental approaches are concerned primarily with changes that take place within individual children, often examining thinking in situations far removed from children's daily lives. Sociocultural approaches emphasize social processes, cultural practices, and the everyday contexts of development, contending that social processes are crucial in the development of children's cognitive abilities.

2. *What does Vygotsky's theory stress?*
Vygotsky's theory stresses the role of culture. Development involves the child's gradual internalization of bodies of knowledge and tools of thought, primarily through shared experiences with parents and teachers.

3. *What is the focus of the ecological model?*
Bronfenbrenner's ecological model focuses on the contexts in which development occurs. The model includes a series of four contextual layers: the microsystem, which is closest to the child; the mesosystem; the exosystem; and the macrosystem.

LEARNING OBJECTIVE 1.5 Describe the environmental/learning approaches to development.

1. *What basic assumption underlies environmental/learning approaches?*
Environmental/learning theories begin with the assumption that much of children's typical behaviour is acquired through conditioning and learning principles. Learned behaviours are distinguished from behaviours that are temporary, unobservable, or based solely on biological processes.

2. *What three types of conditioning are stressed in traditional learning theories?*
The three types of conditioning and learning stressed in traditional learning accounts are habituation (and dishabituation), classical conditioning, and operant learning. Habituation involves a decline in response to a repeated stimulus. In classical conditioning, an originally reflexive response comes under the control of a new stimulus. Operant learning is controlled by the consequences of behaviour. Consequences that make behaviour more probable are called reinforcers; those that make behaviour less probable are called punishers.

3. *How does social learning theory differ from earlier models?*
Social-learning theory, based largely on the ideas of Bandura, proposes a greater role for cognitive factors than did earlier learning models. According to this theory, observational learning

occurs when an observer's behaviour changes as a result of viewing the behaviour of a model and perhaps the consequences of that behaviour. The most important result of modelling is imitation. Conversely, response inhibition occurs when imitation of an observed behaviour becomes less likely—usually because the model has received punishment for it. Acquisition of a modelled behaviour is determined by the observer's attentional and retentional processes, whereas performance of the behaviour is controlled by the observer's production and motivational processes.

4. *Why can we call Bandura's theory interactionist?*
   Bandura's theoretical model, reciprocal determinism, holds that human development results from the complex interaction of characteristics of the person, the person's behaviour, and the environment. All three factors operate to influence one another.

LEARNING OBJECTIVE 1.6 Describe the evolutionary and biological approaches to development.

1. *How does ethology explain development?*
   Ethology is based on the principles of evolution as first proposed by Darwin. Ethologists believe that behaviours have both immediate and evolutionary determinants. These scientists are primarily concerned with innate behaviours, and they attempt to explain complex response patterns in terms of their survival value for the species.

2. *What are four characteristics of innate behaviour?*
   Lorenz and Tinbergen, two founders of the ethological movement, identified four characteristics of innate behaviour: it is universal; it is stereotyped; it requires no learning; and it is minimally affected by the environment. Ethologists have described how complex sequences of inherited responses (modal action patterns) are triggered by stimuli in the environment and how innate mechanisms, such as imprinting, influence the learning process.

3. *What are three applications of evolutionary theory to human development?*
   Human ethology emerged largely as a result of Bowlby's research on the attachment process. Sociobiology is a recent attempt to explain social behaviour in terms of an evolutionary model in which the survival of the genes supersedes any other goal. This mechanism is believed to be principally expressed in cultural and social structures. Evolutionary developmental psychology emphasizes the fit between our evolutionary history and our current adaptational challenges, as well as the variation in adaptive qualities across different phases of development.

CHAPTER 2

RESEARCH METHODS

Sometimes things that we know to be true turn out not to be true—or at least not true in any simple or automatic way. Consider the effects of rewards on children's behaviour. Long before there was a science of psychology to verify the phenomenon, parents and teachers knew that they could promote desirable behaviour in children by providing positive consequences for the behaviour. And indeed, the principle of reinforcement is one of the most solidly established findings in psychology. But are rewards always a good way to promote desired behaviour? The following study by Mark Lepper, David Greene, and Richard Nisbett suggests that they may not be.

Preschool children were first given a chance to draw with coloured markers during the free-play portion of the school day. This "baseline" period indicated to researchers how interested each child was in the activity. Then each child participated individually in an experimental session, during which he or she was asked to produce marker drawings for an adult "who's come to the nursery school for a few days to see what kinds of pictures boys and girls like to draw." For some of the children, these were the only instructions. Some children, however, were also promised an attractive reward for producing the drawings: a "Good Player Award" with a gold star and red ribbon and a place for the child's name.

All the children in the study churned out a large number of drawings. However, a surprising result occurred across the following days, when the children were again back in the classroom and had a choice of whether to play with the markers. The children who had been rewarded for drawing spent considerably less time drawing with the markers than did the other children—and considerably less time than they themselves had spent during the baseline period. The reward, the researchers argued, had undercut the children's intrinsic interest in the activity. Drawing had become something to do in order to get a prize. When the prize was no longer there, drawing was no longer very attractive.

Note the message that this finding carries for parents. Using strong rewards to elicit desired behaviour (or strong threats to discourage undesired behaviour) may well be effective in the short term—at the cost, however, of making children believe that they are responding only to the reward or punishment. Long-term compliance with parental wishes might be better fostered by techniques that help children to value certain actions in themselves and not simply as a way to get something good or avoid something bad. ■

The developing child may seem quite different from atoms fusing to produce nuclear energy or leaf cells using light and carbon dioxide to make food. Yet the research methods used by developmental psychologists to study children share many features with those used by physicists, biologists, and other researchers in the natural sciences. In this chapter, we examine some of these methods and the ways child psychologists can use them to unlock the mysteries of human development.

We saw in Chapter 1 that the study of the child became scientific in the 19th century, when G. Stanley Hall and other pioneers attempted the first systematic studies of child development. Since then, the research methods used by child psychologists have advanced in many ways. These advances have contributed importantly to the enormous growth in our knowledge and understanding of developmental processes (Miller, 2007).

We begin by outlining some of the ideas and concepts that are basic to all scientific research. We then consider the principal research methods used in developmental psychology. Last, we discuss the sometimes thorny issue of research ethics.

Learning Objective 2.1

Understand how researchers use the scientific method to study child development.

SCIENTIFIC RESEARCH

Scientific method The system of rules used by scientists to conduct and evaluate their research.

The approach scientists use to study any problem or issue is known as the **scientific method**. The method is really a system of rules that scientists use to design and conduct their research, evaluate their results, and communicate their findings to other scientists. These rules have evolved over hundreds of years, and they can be applied to the study of virtually anything.

THE ROLE OF THEORY

Theory A broad set of statements describing the relation between a phenomenon and the factors assumed to affect it.

Law (principle) A predicted relation between a phenomenon and a factor assumed to affect it that is supported by a good deal of scientific evidence.

Hypothesis A predicted relation between a phenomenon and a factor assumed to affect it that is not yet supported by a great deal of evidence. Hypotheses are tested in experimental investigations.

In Chapter 1 we presented four major *theories*, but we did not actually define the term. In psychology, a **theory** is a set of statements describing the relation between behaviour and the factors that influence it.

A specific statement that is well supported by research evidence is called a **law** or **principle**—the principle of reinforcement is a good example. A statement that simply postulates, or proposes, a relation is called a **hypothesis**. Any individual study is usually designed to test a researcher's hypothesis regarding how some aspect of children's behaviour is affected by some factor in their world.

Theories have two important roles in scientific research. The first is to *organize research findings*. As investigators acquire knowledge, they use theories to fit the information together into a coherent explanation of the behaviours and processes being studied. Once the knowledge is organized, it is sometimes obvious that certain questions remain to be answered or that specific relations probably exist even though they do not yet have substantial supporting evidence. A second role of theories, then, is to *guide new research* by indicating to investigators which hypotheses should be tested next.

Psychologists do not investigate children's development by randomly studying any question that pops into their heads. Instead, research is typically guided by an underlying theory and theoretical orientation. Thus, cognitive-developmentalists tend to investigate characteristics of children's knowledge, whereas environmental/learning theorists are more likely to study ways in which behaviour is acquired through experience. Similarly, sociocultural theorists focus on the social and cultural bases for development, and ethologists are more likely to search for various innate patterns of response.

OBJECTIVITY AND MEASUREMENT

Objectivity A characteristic of scientific research; it requires that the procedures and subject matter of investigations be formulated so that they could, in principle, be agreed on by everyone.

Children are not of interest only to psychologists, of course. Scholars in literature, music, and art, for example, have devoted much attention to the developing child. But in these fields, the emphasis is frequently on individual tastes, personal opinions, and other subjective judgments. In psychology and the other natural sciences, the emphasis is on **objectivity**.

The primary goal of objective methods of study is to permit any other scientist, at least in principle, to conduct the same research in the same manner (and presumably arrive at the same results). In addition, objectivity helps reduce potential sources of bias that may enter into the research, such as the experimenter's personal beliefs or preferences regarding what the results should be. These goals are achieved in a number of ways.

One is through a focus on *observable* behaviours. Recall that our two primary goals in child psychology concern behaviour—to describe children's behaviour at each point in their development and to identify the causes and processes that produce changes in behaviour from one point to the next. Even developmentalists who are primarily concerned with cognition observe the effects of internal cognitive processes on some aspect of behaviour. For example, we study assimilation and accommodation by observing a child's reactions to new experiences; we study intelligence by calculating a child's performance on an IQ test; and we study social skills by observing how a child interacts with peers.

An important characteristic of psychological research is the focus on objective definitions and measurable behaviours. (© *Steve Debenport/iStock*)

A second requirement for ensuring objectivity is that the behaviours under study must be *measurable*. It is not enough that we can observe behaviour; we must also feel confident as to when the behaviour did or did not occur, when one behaviour ended and the next one began, and so forth. Such confidence is achieved by defining and describing the behaviour very precisely so that independent observers would have no trouble agreeing on what happened in a given situation. For example, suppose we are interested in studying children's altruism—their willingness to help someone else. We might first define altruism in terms of sharing behaviours, and then develop a procedure that entails observing the number of nickels just won in a game that a child donates to a charity. Or suppose we want to investigate an infant's attachment to his or her mother. We could define attachment in terms of specific behaviours, such as crying, smiling, and searching, and then measure the amount of time that elapses before the infant displays each of these behaviours after the mother has left the room. In this way, abstract concepts such as "altruism" and "attachment" become measurable in an objective, scientific way.

A third way to achieve objectivity—and a further important aspect of measurement—is to make everything in the research study *quantifiable*; that is, able to be counted. The researcher must quantify not only the children's behaviours, but also the factors that the researcher hypothesizes may be affecting the behaviours. Often such factors are physical. The number of children in a classroom, the length of time a child spends reading, or the amount of alcohol that a pregnant mother has consumed, for example, are relatively easy to define in this way. Factors that involve the behaviours of others—social approval, peer interactions, or modelling, for instance—are more difficult to deal with, but they, too, must be carefully defined so they can be measured and counted.

For Thought and Discussion

Can we use the scientific method to study everything about child development? Are there aspects of children's lives that we might not be able to study using methods that are objective and quantifiable?

Deciding how to define the constructs of interest is important, but it is just one step in the measurement process. Researchers must also decide how to collect the relevant data. Suppose, for example, that a researcher has decided to measure attachment by studying the behaviours that infants show when interacting with their mother. How can the researcher determine which behaviours a particular baby in fact shows? One way would be by observing the baby and mother in their natural setting at home. Another way might be to bring them into a laboratory setting to observe their behaviour. The researcher might also gather the information from someone who is knowledgeable about the baby's typical behaviour, and so on. There are many ways, each with its own advantages and shortcomings.

LEARNING OBJECTIVE 2.1

Understand how researchers use the scientific method to study child development.

1. What is the scientific method?
2. What two roles do theories play in the research process?
3. How do researchers ensure objectivity in their study of children?

Learning Objective 2.2

Compare and contrast the research methods commonly used to study children.

TYPES OF RESEARCH

Research in psychology generally falls into one of three categories: descriptive, correlational, or experimental. Here we discuss each of these approaches as they apply to the study of children. Table 2.1 later in the chapter summarizes the various descriptive, correlational, and experimental methods used in the study of children.

DESCRIPTIVE RESEARCH

Descriptive research Research based solely on observations, with no attempt to determine systematic relations among the variables.

The first major type of psychological research is the purely descriptive approach. When applied to children, **descriptive research** consists of simply observing or interviewing children or other significant people in their lives and recording information of interest. The researcher typically makes no attempt to manipulate things and observe consequences, but rather describes things the way they are. Early baby biographies, such as those in which Charles Darwin and James Mark Baldwin kept daily records of the behaviours of their infants, provided the first systematic descriptive data on human development. Gesell's norms, which described the typical skills and abilities of children of various ages, also used the descriptive method.

More recently, psychologists have used descriptive research to document the amount of time children of different ages devote to TV viewing and other leisure activities, the content of children's disputes with friends and family, and how adolescents distribute their time among friends, family, and peers. Descriptive methods take various forms, such as observation, interviews, and in-depth case studies.

Naturalistic observation Systematic observation of behaviour in natural settings.

OBSERVATIONAL METHODS One descriptive method employed in the study of children is **naturalistic observation**, which entails carefully observing children's behaviour in natural settings. Researchers watch children interacting, playing, solving problems, and so on. Many people enjoy watching children at play or at work and may spend periods of time simply observing them. What differentiates naturalistic observation as a method for studying children from such casual observations is that, like the other research methods described, observational methods employed by researchers stress objectivity and are purposefully designed to answer certain research questions about children.

Observing behaviour and recording the observations has a very real risk of being influenced by the observer's expectations, beliefs, ideas, and so on. Consequently, researchers take steps to minimize these potential sources of bias. Consider the following example. Two children are playing together. One slaps the other on the back with a smile on his face. The behaviour is noted by two different observers. One observer writes, "playfully and affectionately

Naturalistic observation allows researchers to study the behaviour of children in real-life settings, such as a playground. What could be some drawbacks of observing in such naturalistic settings? (© *Christopher Futcher/iStock*)

pats another child on the back." The other writes, "aggressively slaps the other child on the back." Both observations are of the same behaviour, yet both are clearly very different. How do we know which is correct? Although both individuals were observing the same behaviour, each observer added information that was not observable—specifically, information about the motives of the children.

For Thought and Discussion

What are some examples of research questions that you think could be studied using naturalistic observation? How would you go about studying them?

Researchers employing observational methods follow a number of steps to minimize the influence of observers' expectations and interpretations (Goodwin, 2011). First, they clearly identify what behaviours are to be recorded and define precisely what constitutes an instance of the behaviour. Then, observers are given training using this *observational protocol.* Finally, the accuracy of the observations is assessed by having two observers watch the same episode of behaviour and independently record their observations. If there is good agreement between observers in their independent observations, researchers can be confident in the accuracy of the observations. Most observational studies are video recorded, thus the recordings can be viewed repeatedly to test the accuracy of observers' data.

Simply knowing that you are being observed can affect your behaviour. Many of us have had the opportunity in the local shopping mall to pass by an electronics store that has a camera and monitor in the window. When children see themselves on the screen, how do they behave? Similarly, what do you think is likely to happen to children's behaviour if you place a camera in a classroom or playground?

Observer influences The effects of knowing that you are being observed.

It is important to minimize such **observer influences**—the effects of knowing that you are being observed—so that researchers may have confidence in the soundness of their observations. The best way is to make the observer's presence as inconspicuous as possible. The camera may be placed discreetly in a corner of the playground or classroom, or perhaps behind a window overlooking the playground. Also, participants can be habituated to the presence of the camera for a few days before the study begins. Although children's behaviour may be initially influenced by the camera's presence, such pre-exposure ensures that they forget the camera is there and their behaviour returns to normal.

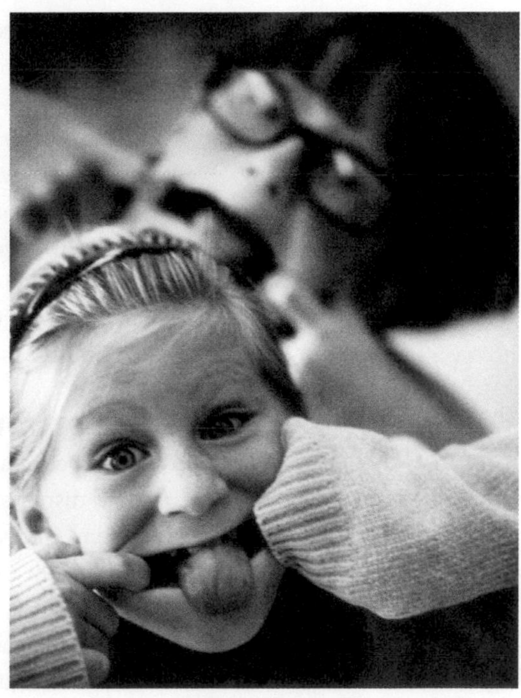

The presence of a camera can actually affect children's behaviour. How do researchers attempt to minimize observer effects? (*Purestock/Media Bakery*)

Sometimes researchers using an observational approach find that the behaviours in which they are interested do not occur frequently or consistently in the naturalistic setting, and may therefore be difficult to study. Moreover, because the investigator has no control over what takes place in the naturalistic setting, the situation itself may not be identical for each child, making it difficult to compare one child's behaviour to that of another. To deal with such concerns, children's behaviour is sometimes observed in settings that are controlled by the investigator. Such **structured observation** may take place in a laboratory setting, where researchers can control the physical aspects of the environment in which the child is being observed, such as the presence of certain toys or certain individuals. In such a setting, researchers can also control the events that occur.

A good example of a structured observation is the Strange Situation procedure discussed in Chapter 12. This procedure assesses infant–mother attachment by exposing the infant to a series of events that includes a separation from the mother, the presence of an unfamiliar adult, and the return of the mother after her absence. By observing infants' reactions to these events, researchers can evaluate the security of their attachment relationships. Standardization of the setting allows the study of children's reactions to experiences that might occur only rarely in the natural environment. In addition, researchers can compare children in terms of how each responds to the same event. However, because the structured setting of the lab differs from real-life settings, observations made in the lab may not be completely generalizable to other settings.

Structured observation Observation of behaviour in settings that are controlled by the investigator.

Links to Related Material

In Chapter 12, you will read more about how attachment in infancy is assessed.

INTERVIEW METHODS Another descriptive method that is often used in the study of children is the **interview method**, where researchers talk with children, asking them about aspects of their lives. Interviews can be *open-ended*, with children responding freely and in a conversational way on a given

Interview method Collecting information through verbal reports, such as interviews or questionnaires.

Interviews can provide a rich source of information about children. What kinds of questions would be interesting to ask children? In what ways could the responses of other informants, such as teachers or parents, be important? (*Creatas/Media Bakery*)

topic, or they can be *structured*, with the interviewer asking a specific set of questions. Open-ended interviews can gather a wealth of information about children's knowledge, opinions, feelings, beliefs, and values, and that information can be used to generate hypotheses for further study. Open-ended interviews can be studied *qualitatively* for themes that emerge (Goodwin, 2011; Jackson & Verberg, 2007), thus increasing our understanding of particular meanings that children themselves may give to events or activities. Alternatively, many researchers create a standardized *interview protocol*, or *questionnaire*, in which every child is asked the exact same questions in the same order. This facilitates quantification of the information gathered.

The interview method is not restricted to children; researchers often ask questions of other knowledgeable informants. Parents or teachers, for example, are often good sources of information about children and are frequently asked about children's behaviour and performance. In studies of children's social relationships, classmates or other peers may be knowledgeable informants who can offer insights on behaviour.

Interviews and questionnaires can be valuable sources of information about how the person being interviewed feels and thinks. However, interviews rely on the informant's knowledge, memory, and ability or willingness to communicate information. As such, they may not always accurately reflect actual behaviour. For example, asking children why it is important not to hit other children can yield interesting information on their perceptions of morality. However, asking them how many times in the past week they have actually hit another child may provide a different picture than would observing their behaviour in the school playground.

For Thought and Discussion

Why might interviews and observations concerning children's behaviour yield contradictory data? What questions might be interesting to ask children and other knowledgeable informants in their lives?

CASE STUDIES Sometimes descriptive research involves only a single individual who becomes the subject of a **case study**. Often these studies are concerned with clinical issues, such as when a child displays a rare disorder or when a new treatment approach is applied to a developmental problem. Occasionally a child has encountered experiences so unusual that psychologists become interested for theoretical reasons.

Case study A research method that involves only a single individual, often with a focus on a clinical issue.

A dramatic example of such a situation is the case of "Genie," a child who was kept isolated by her parents and never spoken to until she was 13 years old (Curtiss, 1977; Rymer, 1994). Genie presented language researchers with a unique opportunity to investigate whether being deprived of exposure to language early on can affect a child's ability to acquire verbal skills at an advanced age. Such a question, of course, could never have been studied in any conventional experimental way.

The major limitation of using only a single research participant is that the researcher must be very cautious about drawing conclusions from the case. Genie, for example, was not only deprived of language, but also experienced an extremely harsh and unusual childhood because of her parents. Whether the data regarding her language abilities can be generalized to other children thus remains unclear.

Despite limitations, case studies can be valuable in the research process. They may raise new questions or issues that can be studied using more carefully controlled research methods.

CORRELATIONAL RESEARCH

The step beyond observing and describing behaviours involves identifying any systematic relations in the observations. Specifically, researchers attempt to identify correlations among variables. A **variable** is any factor that can take on different values along some dimension. Common examples include human physical characteristics—height, weight, age, and so on—and aspects of the environment—temperature, room size, distance to the nearest library, and number of people in a family. Behaviours, if properly defined, can also be variables and can vary along several dimensions, such

Variable Any factor that can take on different values along a dimension.

as how many times a child asks the teacher for help (*frequency*), how loudly a baby cries (*intensity*), or how long a child practises the piano (*duration*).

A **correlation** is a statement that describes how two variables are related. Perhaps a psychologist would like to know whether children's ages are correlated with—that is, systematically related to—their heights. The researcher might observe and record the heights of 100 children, aged 2 to 12, and examine whether changes in the one variable correspond to changes in the other. In this case, the psychologist could expect to find a clear relation between the variables of age and height: as children increase in age, they generally increase in height as well. This type of relation, in which two variables change in the same direction, is described as a **positive correlation**.

Correlation The relation between two variables, described in terms of direction and strength.

Positive correlation A correlation in which two variables change in the same direction.

What about the relation between a child's age and the number of hours each day that the child spends at home? Here we would also discover a systematic relation, but the variables involved would move in opposite directions—as a child's age increases, the amount of time spent at home generally decreases. This sort of relation is called a **negative correlation**.

Negative correlation A correlation in which two variables change in opposite directions.

Finally, we might investigate the relation between a child's height and the number of children in the child's classroom. In this case, we would likely find that the two variables are not related to one another at all and so have no correlation.

Correlations can be described not only in terms of their direction (positive or negative), but also in terms of their strength. A strong correlation means that two variables are closely related. In such cases, knowing the value of one gives us a good indication of the value of the second. As a correlation grows weaker, the amount of predictability between the two variables decreases. When the variables are completely unrelated, knowledge of the value of one gives us no clue as to the value of the other.

The direction of a correlation is indicated by a plus or minus sign, and its strength is indicated by a numerical value that can be calculated from a simple statistical formula. The result is called the **correlation coefficient (*r*)**, which can range between +1.00 and –1.00. A correlation coefficient of +.86 indicates a strong positive correlation, while +.17 indicates a weak positive correlation. Similarly, –.93, –.41, and –.08 denote, respectively, a strong, moderate, and weak negative correlation. A coefficient of 0 means there is absolutely no correlation between two variables. Correlations can also be presented visually with a **scatter diagram**, where one variable is plotted on the vertical axis and the other on the horizontal axis. Each dot represents one child and shows the child's values for the two variables. Examples of scatter diagrams are shown in Figure 2.1.

Correlation coefficient (*r*) A number between +1.00 and –1.00 that indicates the direction and strength of a correlation between two variables.

Scatter diagram A graphic illustration of a correlation between two variables.

To illustrate both the usefulness and the limitations of correlational research, let us consider a hypothetical example. Suppose a research team is interested in learning whether a relation exists between the amount of time children watch the educational TV program *Sesame Street* and their readiness to learn to read. To begin, the researchers randomly select a number of children and measure each child's values on the reading-ability variable (perhaps by giving the children a reading readiness test on which they can score between 0 and 100) and on the viewing variable (perhaps by having parents record the number of hours each week that the child watches *Sesame Street*). Then the researchers calculate the correlation between the two sets of scores and discover the variables have a correlation coefficient of +.78, as shown in Figure 2.2. What can the research team conclude from these findings?

Because the two variables display a strong positive correlation, we know that as one increases the other increases, and knowing a child's value on one of the variables allows us to predict fairly well the child's value on the other variable. We therefore might be tempted to believe that the study shows that viewing *Sesame Street* promotes the skills children need to learn to read, or, in more general terms, that a change in one of the variables causes change in the other. Herein lies a major limitation of correlational research—*a correlation cannot be used to show causality between the variables*. The correlation in the example may accurately reveal the pattern and strength of the reading–viewing relation, but it cannot reveal cause and effect between the variables. Why not?

For Thought and Discussion

What are some aspects of children's behaviour that might correlate with their viewing of violence on TV? What are some possible explanations for these correlations?

If we think carefully about the findings, we realize that some other conclusions cannot be ruled out. For example, rather than TV viewing having an effect on reading readiness, the reverse is equally plausible. That is, children whose prereading skills are relatively advanced may watch *Sesame Street* more often than do children whose skills are less advanced (possibly because they enjoy it more). Another possibility is that the two variables are both influenced by some third variable

FIGURE 2.1

Correlations
+.17
Number of siblings
Child's sociability

Correlations
−.11
Parent's education
Number of children

+.86
Child's height
Child's weight

−.42
Contact with mother
Child's age

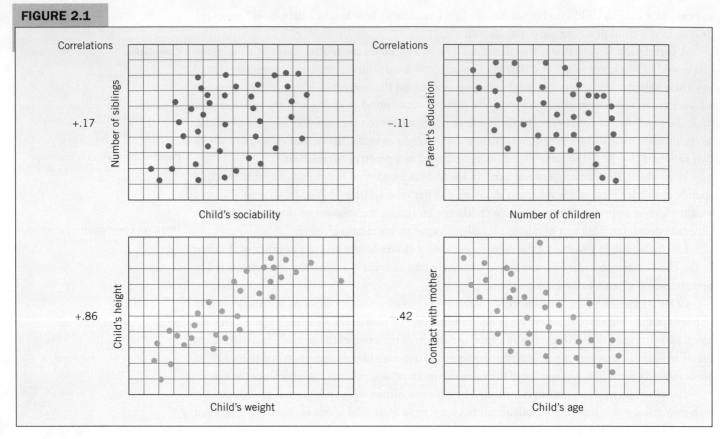

Scatter diagrams illustrating correlations between two variables. Each dot represents one child and shows the child's values for the two variables. One value is plotted from the vertical axis and the other from the horizontal axis. The left two graphs show positive correlations, and the right two graphs show negative correlations.

FIGURE 2.2

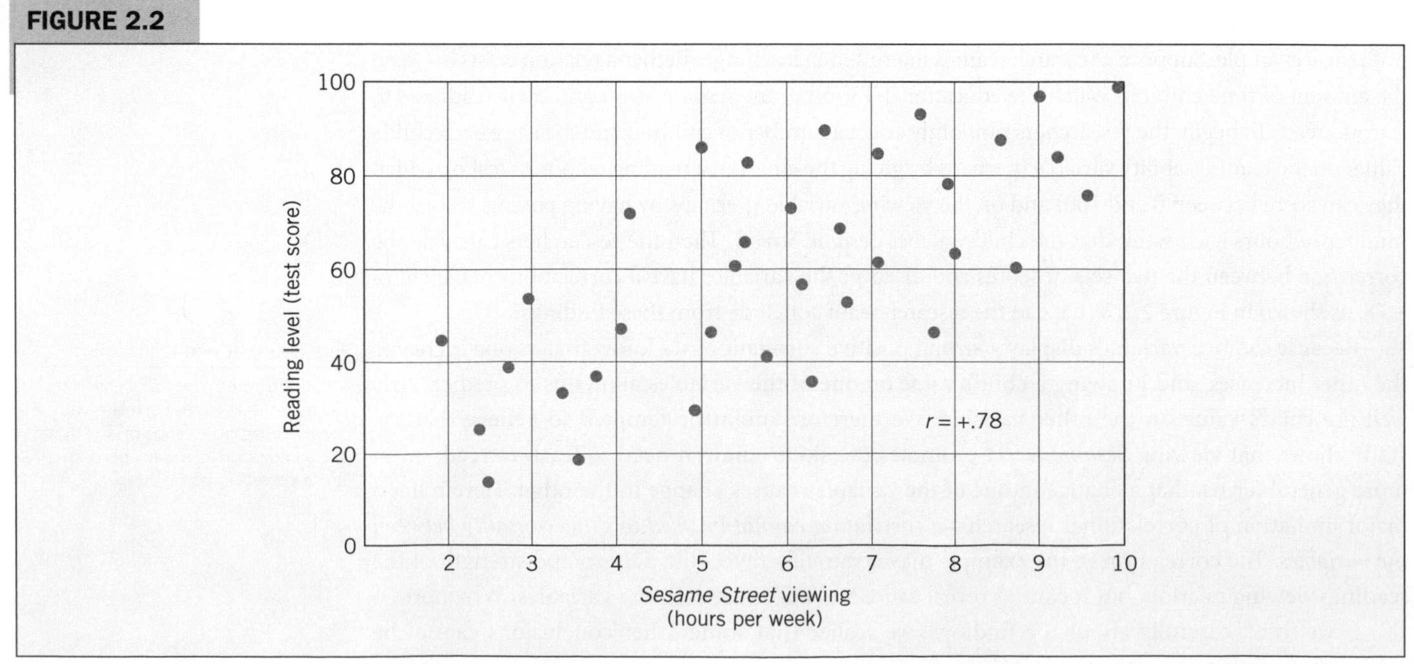

A scatter diagram of a hypothetical correlation between children's viewing of *Sesame Street* and their reading level. The correlation coefficient (*r*) shows a strong positive relation between the two variables.

that we have not measured. For instance, both might be affected by the educational background of the child's parents. Indeed, there is a good chance that the better educated a child's parents are, the more likely they are to engage in other activities that promote prereading skills, such as reading books with their children, as well as encouraging their children to view educational television. Thus, although correlational research is a valuable tool for identifying and measuring systematic relations, it cannot be used to explain them; explanation requires further research.

Nevertheless, like descriptive research, correlational research can play an important role in the scientific research process, and can raise interesting and provocative questions. Investigators may then form these questions into specific research hypotheses that they can examine using more rigorous methods of research.

EXPERIMENTAL RESEARCH

A powerful type of research in developmental psychology is the experiment. A simple experiment often involves investigating the relation between just two variables; but, unlike correlational research, experimentation permits us to draw *cause-and-effect* conclusions about the variables.

The most important difference between a correlational study and an experimental study lies in how the information is gathered. Correlational research is based on measurement alone. The two variables of interest are observed and recorded without any intrusion or interference by the researcher. In an experiment, however, the researcher systematically *manipulates*—alters or changes—one variable and then looks for any effects (changes) in the second variable. The variable that is systematically manipulated is called the **independent variable**. The variable affected (at least potentially) by the manipulation is called the **dependent variable**. In psychological research, the dependent variable is typically some aspect of behaviour, whereas the independent variable is a factor the researcher suspects may influence that behaviour.

Independent variable The variable in an experiment that is systematically manipulated.

Dependent variable The variable that is predicted to be affected by an experimental manipulation. In psychology, usually some aspect of behaviour.

Let us return to the previous example and consider how researchers might use the experimental method to address the question of whether watching *Sesame Street* affects reading level. First, the researchers need a hypothesis that clearly identifies the independent and dependent variables. If the hypothesis is that viewing the program causes improvements in reading ability, then the independent variable is the amount of viewing and the dependent variable is the child's reading level. The next step involves systematically manipulating the independent variable. As in the correlational approach, the researchers select a number of children, but in this case they randomly divide the children into several groups. Randomly dividing the participants into groups minimizes the possibility that there might be differences between the groups that could affect their results. Let's say the children were randomly divided into four groups. The researchers then require the children in the first group to watch two hours of *Sesame Street* each week; the second group, four hours; the third group, eight hours; and the fourth group, ten hours. After perhaps six months, the researchers administer the reading test to all the children and examine how the different groups perform. Figure 2.3 shows possible results. If the differences in performance among groups are sufficiently large (as determined by the appropriate statistical tests), not only can the researchers conclude that the two variables are systematically related, but they can also make the causal statement that viewing *Sesame Street* improves children's reading ability. That is, the researcher's hypothesis now has been supported by experimental data.

ADDITIONAL CONSIDERATIONS Experimental research is a powerful scientific tool, not only because it can reveal cause-and-effect relations, but also because it can be applied to a wide variety of problems and settings. Much of the experimentation conducted by child psychologists takes place in laboratories, where researchers can exert considerable control over testing conditions. But experimental studies can also be conducted in field settings—playgrounds, classrooms, or children's homes, for example—where the effects of manipulating a variable can be studied in a more natural setting. What defines experimental research is not *where* the research takes place, but rather *how* the research is conducted. As we mentioned earlier, the defining characteristic of an experiment is the systematic manipulation of the independent variable by the researcher.

FIGURE 2.3

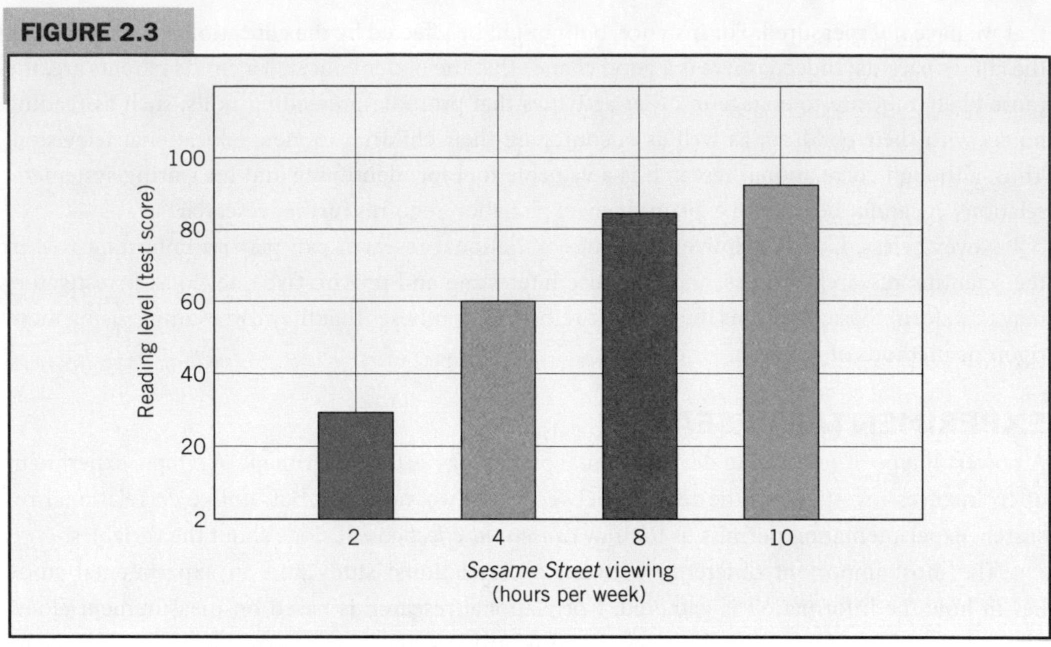

***Sesame Street* Viewing and Reading Test Performance.** Each bar shows the average test score for all the children in that experimental group. What do these results indicate about the relation between *Sesame Street* viewing and reading ability? Why can we say from these findings that viewing *Sesame Street* improves reading ability?

The experimental approach is extremely important in the study of child development, and examples of experiments are frequently described in the pages that follow. We have outlined here the most basic concepts involved in this method, but many detailed procedures not discussed must be followed before researchers can be confident that an experiment is scientifically sound. These involve such matters as how the research participants are selected and assigned to groups, under what conditions the data are gathered, which statistical tests are conducted, and so forth. Furthermore, experimental studies—as well as correlational studies—are typically more complex than we have indicated. For one thing, a single study often involves a number of variables rather than just two, and sometimes several hypotheses are tested at once.

Not all variables, however, can be experimentally manipulated. Some independent variables may actually be characteristics of the participants themselves. For example, researchers interested in how children react to divorce cannot realistically conduct experimental research. Imagine the ethical implications if a researcher were to assign families randomly to two groups and require the parents in one to divorce while keeping those in the other group together. How many parents would go along with such a manipulation, even in the interests of science?

Moreover, some independent variables simply cannot be manipulated, even if there are no ethical implications of doing so. Suppose a researcher wanted to compare children of different linguistic backgrounds, or to compare boys and girls. Variables such as these cannot be experimentally manipulated—rather, researchers are forced to study participants as they find them. Although such **quasi-experimental studies** allow researchers to make comparisons between groups, they differ from true experiments in a significant way. Unlike experimental research, where the investigator randomly assigns participants to groups and then applies the independent variable, in quasi-experimental research the groups are determined on the basis of an existing characteristic of the participants. A study looking at divorce might compare groups of parents who are divorced and non-divorced. A study looking at gender differences might compare boys and girls. In such studies, in contrast to those involving experimental manipulation, the investigator has considerably less control over the independent variable. Because researchers are unable to apply the independent variable to the groups they are studying, the conclusions that can be drawn are limited. Although

Quasi-experimental studies
Comparison of groups differing on some important characteristic.

researchers can talk about differences between groups, with quasi-experimental research they cannot make cause–effect conclusions.

Finally, perhaps the major caution with respect to conclusions from experimental research concerns generalizability. The imposition of experimental control, whether in the laboratory or in the natural environment, can sometimes create situations that are far removed from the real-life situations to which we hope to generalize; if so, the researcher must be cautious in concluding that the effects demonstrated would hold under more natural circumstances. As we will detail, the issue of experimental control is a particular challenge for psychologists interested in studying child development in diverse cultures. Discussions of generalizability, as well as the other issues that we have just briefly mentioned, can be found in chapters and texts devoted to methodology in psychology (e.g., Goodwin, 2011; Miller, 2007). Table 2.1 outlines various descriptive, correlational, and experimental methods used in the study of children.

TABLE 2.1 TYPES OF RESEARCH USED IN THE STUDY OF CHILDREN

Type of Research	Method	Description	Usefulness	Drawbacks
Descriptive	*Naturalistic Observation*	Children's behaviour is observed in real-life settings.	Direct source of information for how children behave in the natural setting.	Presence of observers may alter the setting and thus the behaviour. Some behaviours may be difficult to observe in the natural setting. Setting may not be the same for all children, making it difficult to compare between participants.
	Structured Observation	Children's behaviour is observed in a structured laboratory environment.	Controlled laboratory environment ensures that the behaviours of interest will occur. Allows for comparisons across participants.	Setting is not real-life, which can reduce the generalizability of the findings.
	Interview	Children or other knowledgeable informants are asked to provide verbal reports via interview or questionnaire.	Can provide valuable information about what informants think or feel.	Not all behaviours are accessible to verbal report. Concerns about what the interviewer wants to hear or about portraying oneself positively may influence the accuracy of reports.
	Case Study	Detailed descriptive study of a single individual.	Allows the study of specific or unusual situations, thus aiding clinical intervention. Can raise questions for further study using other research methods.	Because only one child is studied, findings may not be generalizable to other children.
Correlational	*Correlational Study*	Examines how two or more variables are related.	Allows researchers to quantify relationships between variables and make predictions about one variable based on the other.	Cannot be used to show causality.
Experimental	*Experiment*	Researcher manipulates independent variable and looks for corresponding changes in dependent variable.	Allows researchers to assess the effects of one variable on another.	It is not always possible or ethical to manipulate certain types of variables. Results may not be generalizable to real-life settings.
	Quasi-Experimental	Groups that differ on some important characteristic are compared.	Allows researchers to examine variables that cannot be experimentally manipulated.	Cannot be used to show cause-and-effect relationships.

LEARNING OBJECTIVE 2.2

Compare and contrast the research methods commonly used to study children.

1. What are observational research, the interview method, and the case study method? What are advantages and disadvantages of each of these methods?
2. What is correlational research? What does it tell us about causal relations between variables?
3. What elements comprise an experiment? What are advantages and disadvantages of the experimental method in research with children?

Learning Objective 2.3

Analyze the strengths and limitations of the four basic methods for studying child development as a process.

STUDYING DEVELOPMENT

As we have seen, development involves changes in behaviour over time. Many of the issues of interest to developmental researchers, therefore, focus on how children's behaviour at one age differs from their behaviour at another age. Sometimes these issues are mainly descriptive, such as how a child's speech progresses from the one-word utterances of the toddler, to the ill-formed sentences of the preschooler, to the reasonably accurate sentences of the preadolescent. At other times, the issues concern the causes of behaviour, such as the possible effects of daycare programs on children's later social adjustment to school. For either type of question, however, the psychologist needs a research method that will allow the comparison of behaviours at different ages. Four methods are available for this purpose: the longitudinal design, the cross-sectional design, a method that combines the two, and the microgenetic technique. These methods are summarized in Table 2.2 later in the chapter.

LONGITUDINAL RESEARCH

Longitudinal design A research method in which researchers study the same individuals repeatedly over time.

One approach to studying children's behaviour at different ages is the **longitudinal design**. The logic of this approach is quite simple. Researchers first measure the behaviours of interest at some early point in development, and then measure them again at various intervals as the child grows. The main advantage of this method is that it allows the researcher to study directly how each behaviour changes as the child gets older (Menard, 2002).

The amount of time required for a longitudinal study can vary considerably. Some questions can be explored within a relatively brief time frame. For example, determining whether different techniques of caring for premature infants have different effects on the age at which the babies begin to walk and talk should take only 18 months to 2 years of observation. Other questions, such as whether a child's early disciplinary experiences influence his or her own use of punishment as a parent, may need to extend over decades.

Longitudinal studies can be either correlational or experimental. If we measure behaviours at one age and then again at a later age, we can determine the consistency of the behaviours by calculating the correlation between the two sets of measurements. Experimental longitudinal studies usually involve introducing a manipulation at one point in development and then examining its effects on the dependent variables of interest at some later point or points in development. For example, researchers at the University of Montreal (Vitaro, Brendgen, & Tremblay, 2001) used an experimental longitudinal study to assess the effectiveness of an intervention to reduce delinquency. Aggressive boys were randomly assigned at age 13 to a group that received the intervention or to a control group that did not, and their subsequent delinquent behaviour was examined longitudinally at ages 14, 15, and 16. Results of the study were promising and suggested further factors to be considered in future interventions.

Links to Related Material

We discuss interventions to reduce aggression in children in Chapter 14.

The longitudinal approach allows us to examine age-related changes by repeatedly observing the same children as they develop. Two types of research questions are particularly well-suited to the longitudinal approach (Magnusson et al., 1994). Both are forms of the continuity–discontinuity issue introduced in Chapter 1. The first concerns the *stability*, or persistence, of behaviours. For instance, if we wish to determine the extent to which a child's temperament (an aspect of personality) remains constant throughout life, the best approach is to periodically measure this characteristic in the same children and examine the correlations among the sets of scores. (*Focus on Research 2.1* describes a major Canadian longitudinal study of aggressive and withdrawn children conducted over more than 30 years.)

The second type of question that works well with the longitudinal method involves the *effects of early experiences* on later behaviour. If we wish to determine whether certain events or conditions that occur during a child's early years—divorce, an infant stimulation program, or the quality of diet, for instance—produce long-term effects, the clearest answers will be obtained with

FOCUS ON RESEARCH 2.1
THE CONCORDIA RISK STUDY: A CANADIAN LONGITUDINAL INVESTIGATION OF AGGRESSIVE AND WITHDRAWN CHILDREN

Longitudinal research is frequently costly and time-consuming. It also suffers from the disadvantage of attrition—the loss of individuals under study—often because participants move away. Nevertheless, longitudinal research is valuable as it really is the only way to investigate the stability or persistence of behaviour and the effects of early experience on later development.

One well-known Canadian longitudinal investigation has been underway for more than 30 years at Concordia University in Montreal. Begun in 1976 by Jane Ledingham and Alex Schwartzman (Ledingham, 1981; Schwartzman, Ledingham, & Serbin, 1985; Ledingham, Younger, Schwartzman, & Bergeron, 1982), this study examined over 4,000 children from grades 1, 4, and 7. The investigation identified groups of children who were highly aggressive, highly withdrawn, or both highly aggressive and withdrawn at the same time. These groups were followed longitudinally to see the outcomes of these patterns of social maladjustment. The project focused on francophone children because Statistics Canada had reported that francophones in Montreal constituted one of the most geographically stable groups in urban Canada. Such stability is an important consideration in view of the disadvantage of attrition in longitudinal research that we discuss in this chapter, and has allowed these researchers to follow their participants for many years.

The Concordia Risk Study is unique; although there are other studies of highly aggressive or highly withdrawn children, it was the first to study children displaying both types of maladjustment. Its methodology allowed the researchers to map out the developmental course of aggression and withdrawal in both boys and girls.

So, what can the Concordia study tell us about aggressive, withdrawn, and aggressive-withdrawn children? First, aggressiveness in childhood is associated with a number of problems in later childhood and adolescence. Aggression in childhood predicted later school failure, as well as increased need for later psychiatric intervention in adolescence for both boys and girls (Moskowitz & Schwartzman, 1989). In addition, looking at girls in particular, the researchers found that aggression is associated with higher levels of adolescent sexual behaviour and higher-than-average rates of teenage pregnancies (Serbin, Peters, McAffer, & Schwartzman, 1991). Moreover, for both boys and girls, aggression in combination with withdrawal is associated with even more negative consequences, predicting a greater number of social and behavioural problems than does aggression alone (Moskowitz & Schwartzman, 1989).

What about social withdrawal? Does it, too, predict later problems? Although we tend to think of shy, withdrawn children as not being at risk for later problems, the Concordia Risk Study shows that high levels of social withdrawal may indeed be associated with maladjustment. Social withdrawal in childhood was found to be related to poor school achievement and negative self-perceptions in later childhood and adolescence, for both boys and girls (Moscowitz & Schwartzman, 1989).

Recently, these investigators have extended their follow-up study into adulthood, examining how childhood aggression and withdrawal in girls may impact their own families when they become mothers (DeGenna, Stack, Serbin, Ledingham, & Schwartzman, 2007; Stack, Serbin, Enns, Ruttle, & Barrieau, 2010; Stack, Serbin, Schwartzman, & Ledingham, 2005; Temcheff et al., 2008). The findings indicate that childhood aggression continues to be associated with problems into adulthood, predicting family difficulties for women identified as aggressive many years earlier. Mothers who were aggressive as children reported higher parenting stress and poorer mental health, and were found to provide a poorer home environment for their children than non-aggressive mothers. Childhood withdrawal was also found to be related to later family life. Women who were identified as withdrawn in childhood reported poorer educational attainment, poorer family income, and greater parenting stress than non-withdrawn women.

The Concordia Risk Study continues to follow this sample, and will continue to provide valuable information about the long-term consequences of childhood aggression and withdrawal—information that could only be gained using a longitudinal procedure.

Links to Related Material

We discuss two Canadian early stimulation programs—Better Beginnings, Better Futures and Aboriginal Head Start—in Chapter 10.

an experimental longitudinal approach. For example, we might identify children who have participated in an early stimulation program and children who have not, and then follow both groups for a number of years to see whether differences emerge in their success in school.

Despite the obvious value of the longitudinal approach, the method does have certain disadvantages. One is the problem of *attrition*, the loss of individuals in the study, which can occur for a variety of reasons. Families may move away, children may become ill or develop other problems that interfere with participation in the study, or parents may simply lose interest and withdraw from the project. Other problems may develop because of the repeated testing. For example, a study concerned with the stability of a child's intelligence requires that IQ tests be administered at regular intervals. But repeated experience with tests themselves may make a child "test-wise" to the expected types of responses, and may thus artificially improve the child's performance.

In longitudinal research the same individuals are studied over a period of time. What are some reasons why researchers use the longitudinal approach to study development? (*Copyright 2008 L'Image Photography*)

For Thought and Discussion

Why is longitudinal research used to study development?

A third disadvantage relates directly to the fact that longitudinal studies are often designed to last for many years. There is a very real possibility that the issues involved or the instruments used at the beginning of the study may become outdated. For example, the experimental questions posed at the outset of the project may become less important as the years pass and other research findings are published. Similarly, the tests and instruments used may become obsolete. Finally, there is a major practical disadvantage. Because it often requires a large research staff and many hours of observation or testing, longitudinal research can be very expensive.

CROSS-SECTIONAL RESEARCH

Cross-sectional design A research method in which people of different ages are studied simultaneously to examine age-related differences in some aspect of behaviour.

An alternative to longitudinal research is the **cross-sectional design**, which allows researchers to examine developmental differences in behaviour by studying children of different ages at the same point in time. In this type of research, the age of the children becomes an independent variable in the research design. The major advantage of this approach is that it is much less time-consuming than the longitudinal method. Rather than waiting five years to determine, say, how memory processes in 3-year-olds differ from memory processes in 8-year-olds, we can simply study a group of 3-year-olds and a group of 8-year-olds at the same time. The relatively short time required also means that such experiments are rarely plagued by the problems of attrition, repeated testing, outdated issues and instruments, and high cost.

Still, the cross-sectional approach has two significant disadvantages. First, this method cannot be used to investigate questions of behaviour stability and early experience. It is impossible to determine persistence of an early trait or the impact of an early event by examining those behaviours in *different* older children.

Cohort effect A problem sometimes found in cross-sectional research in which people of a given age are affected by factors unique to their generation.

Second is a problem known as the **cohort effect**, which occurs because certain aspects of people's behaviour are influenced by the unique events and conditions experienced by their particular generation or cohort. For example, suppose we were investigating the cognitive skills of individuals at ages 50, 60, and 70 and found that the 60-year-olds performed better on our reasoning and problem-solving tests than did the younger or older groups. Would these results allow us to conclude that cognitive development improves across part of the adult age span and then declines as people grow older?

People of a given age may be affected by factors unique to their generation, such as growing up in the Saskatchewan Dustbowl during the Great Depression. (*Photo courtesy of Saskatchewan Archives Board, R-A26140-1.*)

Although such an interpretation is certainly consistent with our data, another explanation arises when we consider the educational backgrounds of the three groups of participants. People in their 50s, 60s, and 70s had different educational experiences, which might affect their performance on tests of cognitive ability. Those currently in their 70s were in school during World War II, when progressive ideas and nationalistic ideals shaped the curriculum. People in their 60s started school after 1950, when sweeping post-war changes stimulated an emphasis on teaching science, mathematics, and technology. And those in their 50s started school in the early 1960s, when greater emphasis began to be placed on children's social and emotional development. The different experiences of these three cohorts might affect their cognitive performance independently of the differences in their ages alone. The performance differences we observe, therefore, may not reflect the differences in their ages so much as their different life experiences.

For Thought and Discussion

What are some events that have affected the life course of people your age? How might your life have been different if those events had not occurred?

It is worth noting that the cohort effect can also be important in a longitudinal study. Most longitudinal studies examine a single cohort; that is, individuals who are the same age at the start of the study and thus were born at about the same time. Although differences between ages in a longitudinal study cannot therefore be attributed to the cohort effect, given that it is the same cohort being studied over time, the applicability of its findings to other groups may be affected. It is possible, therefore, that whatever patterns we find across different ages reflect experiences specific to the particular cohort studied. Imagine, for example, that we were to carry out a longitudinal study with people born in 1920. We are interested in stability or change as our sample progresses through various phases in the developmental span. All we know for certain, however, is what happens for a sample of people who experienced the Great Depression in childhood and adolescence, a world war in young adulthood, another war shortly thereafter, and so forth.

Cross-sequential design A research method combining longitudinal and cross-sectional designs.

COMBINING LONGITUDINAL AND CROSS-SECTIONAL RESEARCH

To obtain the best features of the longitudinal and cross-sectional designs, researchers sometimes combine the two methods into a **cross-sequential design**. The combined approach begins with a simple cross-sectional investigation, during which groups of children of different ages are studied simultaneously. The same groups are then studied again at one or more later points in time to provide a longitudinal perspective on the question.

For instance, an investigator might begin by measuring the amount of competitiveness displayed by 4-year-olds, 7-year-olds, and 10-year-olds playing a game. Three years later, the investigator retests the children, who are now 7, 10, and 13 (see Figure 2.4). This procedure makes a number of data comparisons possible. For example, cross-sectional comparisons among the children can be made at both the initial testing and the later testing to see whether children of different ages show different levels of competitiveness. In addition, the researcher can examine the stability of each child's competitiveness by comparing the child's scores at the two ages.

The combined design also permits the investigator to check directly for two of the common problems associated with the individual designs. If the data for the groups at ages 7 and 10 during the first testing differ from the data for these

FIGURE 2.4

Year	Time 1 (2012)	Time 2 (2015)
Cohort 1	Age 4	Age 7
Cohort 2	Age 7	Age 10
Cohort 3	Age 10	Age 13

A Cross-Sequential Design. Children aged 4, 7, and 10 years (Cohorts 1, 2, and 3) are compared cross-sectionally at Time 1 to reveal age differences. Three years later, at Time 2, another cross-sectional study is conducted comparing these three groups of children who are now aged 7, 10, and 13. How might cohort effects play a role in any differences found?

To examine the stability of competitiveness, the researcher examines each of the three groups longitudinally, comparing their scores at Time 2 to those at Time 1. How could repeated testing affect the results?

Comparing the groups who were ages 7 and 10 at Time 1 with those who are ages 7 and 10 at Time 2 allows the researcher to examine for a cohort effect or for a repeated-testing effect.

groups during the second testing, then these differences are very likely the result of either a cohort effect (a cross-sectional design problem) or a repeated-testing effect (a longitudinal design problem). In either case, the investigator will need to exercise caution in drawing conclusions regarding age-related differences in competitiveness or the stability of the behaviour over time. But if the data from these corresponding groups are very similar, the researcher can have considerable confidence in the results of the study.

Although combined designs are potentially very informative, they also are time-consuming and costly, and their use has therefore been limited.

MICROGENETIC STUDIES

Microgenetic method A research method in which a small number of individuals are observed repeatedly in order to study an expected change in a developmental process.

A different approach to the study of developmental change involves the intensive study of a small number of children over a brief period of time. The purpose of this **microgenetic method** is to investigate changes in important developmental processes as they are occurring (Flynn, Pine, & Lewis, 2007; Flynn & Siegler, 2007; Siegler, 2006).

As we discussed in Chapter 1, some aspects of human development are thought to be discontinuous—they are relatively stable for a period of time, but then move abruptly to a higher level. Investigators attempting to understand the nature of such changes have used the microgenetic approach in the hope of examining the particular developmental process as it goes from one level to the next. Much of the research using this approach has been concerned with children's cognitive abilities, probably because the concept of discontinuous change is consistent with the view of development held by Piaget and many other cognitive-developmental psychologists.

A microgenetic study begins with several children who are about the age at which a developmental change is expected to occur. The researcher repeatedly observes and measures the behaviour of interest in these children. For example, if the research is concerned with children's use of a particular cognitive strategy for solving a certain type of problem (a common focus of such research), the children may be asked to complete many such problems over a period of weeks. In such a study, the researcher not only notes the correctness of the children's solutions, but also examines precisely how they approach each problem, perhaps by asking them to describe what they are doing. In this way, the investigator attempts to identify when a child moves from the use of a simpler cognitive strategy to a more sophisticated one. By examining this process very carefully, the researcher may acquire a better understanding of exactly how it works.

TABLE 2.2 METHODS USED TO STUDY THE PROCESS OF DEVELOPMENT

Method	Description	Usefulness	Drawbacks
Longitudinal	The same group of children is studied repeatedly at different ages.	Allows the researcher to study changes as children age. Can be used to examine stability of behaviour as well as effects of early experiences.	Attrition. Repeated testing can influence results. Issues and instruments may become outdated. Time-consuming and expensive.
Cross-Sectional	Groups of children of different ages are compared at one point in time.	Relatively quick and low cost. No problems of attrition or repeated testing.	Cannot be used to examine stability and change. Cohort effects can influence findings.
Cross-Sequential	Combines cross-sectional and longitudinal research. Children of different age groups are followed longitudinally.	Allows both cross-sectional and longitudinal comparisons to be made. Allows researchers to examine for cohort effects.	Time-consuming and costly.
Microgenetic	Intensive study of a small number of children over a brief period of time.	Allows examination of developmental changes that are discontinuous.	Repeated testing can influence results.

Although the microgenetic method can yield a great deal of new information about a developmental process, it, too, has drawbacks (Miller, 2007). One practical problem is that making many observations over a compressed period of time can be expensive. Another consideration is that great care must be taken to ensure the repeated assessment of the child's abilities does not itself cause changes in the behaviour of interest. Table 2.2 summarizes the various methods used to study the process of development.

LEARNING OBJECTIVE 2.3

Analyze the strengths and limitations of the four basic methods for studying child development as a process.

1. What are the strengths and limitations of longitudinal research?
2. What are the strengths and limitations of cross-sectional research design?
3. What are the strengths and limitations of cross-sequential research design?
4. What are the strengths and limitations of microgenetic research?

OTHER RESEARCH TACTICS

Learning Objective 2.4

Understand the uses of cultural research, comparative research, and psychophysiological methods.

Developmental psychologists use many additional research methods. In this section we describe cultural research, comparative research, and psychophysiological methods, three popular approaches to investigating various developmental issues.

CULTURAL RESEARCH

Cross-cultural studies Research designed to determine the influence of culture on some aspect of development and in which culture typically serves as an independent variable.

We saw in Chapter 1 that an emphasis on the social and cultural contexts for development is a defining feature of the sociocultural approach to children's development. How can we determine the role culture plays in a particular aspect of behaviour or development?

The most common approach is to study the same behaviour in different cultures. In **cross-cultural studies**, researchers use culture as an independent variable and examine its effects on the dependent variable(s) of interest. Though we often associate the terms *independent variable* and *dependent variable* with carefully controlled manipulations, it would be a mistake to assume that all cross-cultural research involves standardized psychological procedures. Cross-cultural psychologists actually use a variety of methods, including interviews, observations of everyday activities, and archived reports of early travellers and anthropologists, as well as laboratory tasks and psychological tests.

Links to Related Material

As you read in Chapter 1, an emphasis on the social and cultural contexts for development is a defining feature of the sociocultural approach to children's development. How can researchers determine the role that culture plays in particular aspects of behaviour or development?

One important use of cross-cultural studies is to test the universality of a phenomenon. Motor development serves as a good example. Although there are significant individual differences in the ages at which infants acquire motor skills, such as crawling and walking, differences between cultures are far smaller than one might expect given the large variations in the amount of time and encouragement children are given to practise those skills from culture to culture. Cross-cultural studies are also useful for documenting variations in child development across cultures. As we will see throughout this text, cross-cultural studies have revealed impressive variability across a wide range of behaviours and abilities, including parenting, peer relationships, moral reasoning, mathematical reasoning, and memory (Berry, 2002; Chen & French, 2008; Monzo & Rueda, 2006).

Cross-cultural studies can sometimes help to determine whether patterns of behaviour are universal to humans or result from factors specific to a particular culture. (*John Eastcott and Yva Momatiuk/National Geographic Stock*)

Cross-cultural psychologists face a number of methodological challenges. One in particular bears mentioning here: the difficulty of devising studies that measure the "same" behaviour in different cultural contexts. Experimental tasks and situations that are common or sensible in one culture often seem strange to children living elsewhere. When experimental procedures differ markedly from a child's everyday experience, it is hard to know whether psychologists are tapping into the same behaviour observed under conditions that more closely resemble the child's daily life.

Cultural psychology Study of a single culture from the perspective of members of that culture, the goal being to identify the values and practices important to the culture.

A second approach to the study of culture and development has emerged, partly in response to the methodological problems of cross-cultural research. This approach, known as **cultural psychology**, favours studying a single or small number of cultures in depth. The aim of this approach is to understand as fully as possible the different aspects of culture and how they are interrelated (Cole & Packer, 2010; Shweder et al., 2006). The starting point, therefore, is not some set of measures developed by Western researchers (as is true in most cross-cultural research), but rather lengthy immersion in the culture or cultures of interest. Researchers might live for months or even years as members of a culture, during which time they will use various **ethnographic methods** (observations, informal conversations, structured interviews) to gather as much information as possible about cultural practices and values (Hammersley, 2006; Miller, 2007). Cultural psychologists may use standardized psychological instruments, but they derive these procedures from practices in the cultures under study instead of importing established instruments from outside.

Ethnographic methods Methods of study employed in cultural psychology in which the researcher lives as a member of a culture and gathers information about the culture through various techniques (e.g., observations, interviews) over an extended period of time.

Cultural psychologists sometimes do compare cultures. In fact, cultural psychologists study many of the same issues as cross-cultural psychologists, including child rearing, reasoning, and basic cognitive processes. However, both their methods and their goals differ from researchers who employ traditional cross-cultural techniques. Specifically, cross-cultural psychologists make a concerted effort to test all groups under similar conditions, ideally using identical tasks and procedures. Cultural psychologists, in contrast, may vary their methods from culture to culture, adapting their methods to existing cultural practices. Cultural psychologists believe this approach is best suited to understanding development within cultural context. Cross-cultural psychologists have a different goal—to integrate the results of studies from a variety of cultures to create a more universal theory of human development.

COMPARATIVE RESEARCH

Comparative research Research conducted with non-human species to provide information relevant to human development.

Psychologists also study behaviours across species. Although **comparative research** of this sort has served many different purposes, developmentalists typically conduct research with animals for one of two reasons. First, researchers of the ethological tradition study animal behaviour for clues to the evolutionary origins of similar human behaviours. For instance, determining how the imprinting process causes newborn birds to develop social attachments to their mothers may help child researchers understand the mechanisms involved in the development of attachment between human infants and their mothers. Similarly, studying the play-fighting that commonly occurs among pups of many species may provide insights into the rough-and-tumble social interactions of young children.

More frequently, however, comparative research permits developmental psychologists to conduct studies that would be prohibited with humans for ethical reasons. What happens, for instance, to an infant who is reared for six months without a mother? Does the visual system develop normally in an infant raised in total darkness? Do high levels of stress early in life shape brain structure and function, and do such changes increase the risk for emotional disturbance? These, as well as many other questions, would be impossible to address experimentally with humans. However, researchers have studied each of these issues in the laboratory using other species.

PSYCHOPHYSIOLOGICAL METHODS

Most of the research methods discussed throughout this chapter have involved assessing some form of voluntary behaviour displayed by children or significant others in their lives. In some situations, however, researchers must use more specialized techniques in their research. A variety of psychophysiological indices have been used. For example, infancy researchers have investigated the sensory and perceptual abilities of newborns and young infants, including whether they display

Links to Related Material

See chapters 5 and 7 for a more in-depth discussion on the various research methods used when studying infants.

built-in preferences for certain stimuli such as their mother's voice or music. How would you assess such preferences? You cannot interview newborns to ask about their preferences. But you can look for changes in physiological activity upon presentation of stimuli. Researchers have used measures such as change in heart rate, breathing rate, and even sucking rate to assess perceptual abilities and preferences in infants (e.g., Groome et al., 1999; Saffran, Werker, & Werner, 2006). Other researchers are interested in topics such as children's responses to stress or perception of pain. Reactivity to stress in children can involve assessing levels of the stress hormone cortisol in a child's saliva (Fisher et al., 2007; Gunnar & Quevedo, 2007). Pain perception can be measured by asking children how much pain they're experiencing; however, it can be difficult for them to quantify the feeling. Researchers at Dalhousie University and the University of British Columbia have, however, developed a means to quantify pain in young children using their facial expressions (Gilbert et al., 1999). These and other specific methods are discussed at various points throughout the text.

Measures of brain activity have also been used in research with children. The *electroencephalograph* (EEG) allows researchers to measure electrical activity in the brain, and can be useful in indicating what regions of the brain are activated by specific stimuli (Saffran et al., 2006). For example, infants show sensitivity to speech sounds from birth. EEG recordings have been used to show that their brain activity is greater in the left hemisphere when listening to speech than to non-speech sounds (Molfese & Molfese, 1979). *Neuroimaging techniques* use computer programs to convert data taken from brain-scanning devices into visual images of the brain. One such technique, *functional magnetic resonance imaging* (fMRI), allows researchers to watch the brain as an individual carries out various tasks (for example, solving mathematical problems) (Rickard et al., 2000). This technique has also shed light on brain abnormalities that may be involved in disorders such as childhood schizophrenia (Crow, 2004; Phares, 2008). We discuss these and related techniques in more detail in Chapter 6. Such measures of brain activity are intriguing and open new avenues for research with children, although they are costly, require a high degree of training, and are not applicable to all topics of research.

Links to Related Material

In Chapter 6, you will read more about these and other techniques used to study brain development and brain functioning.

LEARNING OBJECTIVE 2.4

Understand the uses of cultural research, comparative research, and psychophysiological methods.

1. What is the goal of cross-cultural research?
2. How do the questions asked and methods used by cultural psychologists and cross-cultural psychologists differ?
3. What are two reasons developmental psychologists might conduct research with animals?
4. What are the reasons for using psychophysiological methods in developmental research?

ETHICAL ISSUES

Learning Objective 2.5

Explain the ethical guidelines for human research that developmental researchers must follow.

No one would question the fact that psychological research often produces findings that benefit children, adults, and society as a whole. Nevertheless, almost any research involving humans can pose a variety of risks. Investigators have an obligation to determine exactly what potentially negative effects may result from their research and to consider whether these risks outweigh the potential value of the research findings (Fisher & Tryon, 1990; Kodish, 2005; Thompson, 1990).

Links to Related Material

In Chapter 1, you read about early investigations, such as Watson's conditioning of Little Albert, which would not be permitted today. Researchers today focus on safeguarding children's rights and well-being in the procedures they use.

Concern over ethical issues has not always been as great as it is today. Early investigators had few restrictions on their research, as evidenced by such questionable experiments as Watson's conditioning of 11-month-old Little Albert. Today, however, attention is increasingly focused on safeguarding children's rights and well-being (Sieber, 1992).

POTENTIAL RISKS

An obvious concern in any experiment is the possibility of physical injury to the child, although this problem is relatively rare in developmental research. A more common, and often more subtle, issue involves potential psychological harm to the child. Some experimental hypotheses may require, for example, observing how children respond when they cannot solve a problem, are prohibited from playing with an attractive toy, or are exposed to violent behaviour. These procedures may produce various negative emotions, such as feelings of failure, frustration, or stress. The concern is that the children may continue to experience these emotions for some time after leaving the experimental situation.

A less obvious category of problems involves violations of privacy. If a researcher secretly gains access to a child's school records, if observations are conducted without a child's knowledge, or if data regarding a child or a family become public knowledge, the legal and ethical rights of these individuals may be violated.

SAFEGUARDS

The concern for ethical research practices has led to the development of safeguards designed to avoid or eliminate potential risks. These safeguards have become a routine part of modern research procedures. In addition, professional scientific organizations have developed codes of ethical standards to guide their members. *Canadian Code of Ethics for Psychologists* (2001), published by the Canadian Psychological Association, *Ethical Principles of Psychologists and Code of Conduct* (2002), published by the American Psychological Association, and *SRCD Ethical Standards for Research with Children* (2007), published by the Society for Research in Child Development and reproduced in part in Table 2.3, are three important examples.

TABLE 2.3 *ETHICAL STANDARDS FOR RESEARCH WITH CHILDREN*, SOCIETY FOR RESEARCH IN CHILD DEVELOPMENT

Children as research participants present ethical problems for the investigator that are different from those presented by adult participants. Children are more vulnerable to stress than adults and, having less experience and knowledge than adults, are less able to evaluate the social value of the research and less able to comprehend the meaning of the research procedures themselves. In all cases, therefore, the child's consent or assent to participate in the research, as well as the consent of the child's parents or guardians, must be obtained. In general, no matter how young children are, they have rights that supersede the rights of the investigator. The investigator is therefore obligated to evaluate each proposed research operation in terms of these rights, and before proceeding with the investigation, should obtain the approval of an appropriate Institutional Review Board. The principles listed below are to be subscribed to by all members of the Society for Research in Child Development. These principles are not intended to infringe on the right and obligation of researchers to conduct scientific research.
Principle 1. Nonharmful Procedures The investigator should use no research operation that may harm the child either physically or psychologically. The investigator is also obligated at all times to use the least stressful research operation whenever possible. Psychological harm in particular instances may be difficult to define; nevertheless its definition and means for reducing or eliminating it remain the responsibility of the investigator. When the investigator is in doubt about the possible harmful effects of the research operations, consultation should be sought from others. When harm seems inevitable, the investigator is obligated to find other means of obtaining the information or to abandon the research.
Principle 2. Informed Consent Before seeking consent or assent from the child, the investigator should inform the child of all features of the research that may affect his or her willingness to participate and should answer the child's questions in terms appropriate to the child's comprehension. The investigator should respect the child's freedom to choose to participate in the research or not by giving the child the opportunity to give or not give assent to participation as well as to choose to discontinue participation at any time. Assent means that the child shows some form of agreement to participate without necessarily comprehending the full significance of the research necessary to give informed consent. Investigators working with infants should take special effort to explain the research procedures to the parents and be especially sensitive to any indicators of discomfort in the infant. In spite of the paramount importance of obtaining consent, instances can arise in which consent or any kind of contact with the participant would make the research impossible to carry out. Nonintrusive field research is a common example. Conceivably, such research can be carried out ethically if it is conducted in public places, participants' anonymity is totally protected, and there are no foreseeable negative consequences to the participant.

TABLE 2.3 *ETHICAL STANDARDS FOR RESEARCH WITH CHILDREN,*
SOCIETY FOR RESEARCH IN CHILD DEVELOPMENT (*continued*)

Principle 3. Parental Consent The informed consent of parents, legal guardians or those who act in loco parentis (e.g., teachers, superintendents of institutions) similarly should be obtained, preferably in writing. Informed consent requires that parents or other responsible adults be informed of all the features of the research that may affect their willingness to allow the child to participate. Not only should the right of the responsible adults to refuse consent be respected, but they should be informed that they may refuse to participate without incurring any penalty to them or to the child.
Principle 4. Additional Consent The informed consent of any persons, such as school teachers for example, whose interaction with the child is the subject of the study, should also be obtained. As with the child and parents or guardians, informed consent requires that the persons interacting with the child during the study be informed of all features of the research which may affect their willingness to participate.
Principle 5. Incentives Incentives to participate in a research project must be fair and must not unduly exceed the range of incentives that the child normally experiences. Whatever incentives are used, the investigator should always keep in mind that the greater the possible effects of the investigation on the child, the greater is the obligation to protect the child's welfare and freedom.
Principle 6. Deception Although full disclosure of information during the procedure of obtaining consent is the ethical ideal, a particular study may necessitate withholding certain information or deception. Whenever withholding information or deception is judged to be essential to the conduct of the study, the investigator should satisfy research colleagues that such judgment is correct. If withholding information or deception is practiced, and there is reason to believe that the research participants will be negatively affected by it, adequate measures should be taken after the study to ensure the participant's understanding of the reasons for the deception.
Principle 7. Anonymity To gain access to institutional records, the investigator should obtain permission from responsible authorities in charge of records. Anonymity of the information should be preserved and no information used other than that for which permission was obtained.
Principle 8. Mutual Responsibilities From the beginning of each research investigation, there should be clear agreement between the investigator and the parents, guardians or those who act in loco parentis, and the child, when appropriate, that defines the responsibilities of each. The investigator has the obligation to honor all promises and commitments of the agreement.
Principle 9. Jeopardy When, in the course of research, information comes to the investigator's attention that may jeopardize the child's well-being, the investigator has a responsibility to discuss the information with the parents or guardians and with those expert in the field in order that they may arrange the necessary assistance for the child.
Principle 10. Unforeseen Consequences When research procedures result in undesirable consequences for the participant that were previously unforeseen, the investigator should immediately employ appropriate measures to correct these consequences, and should redesign the procedures if they are to be included in subsequent studies.
Principle 11. Confidentiality The investigator should keep in confidence all information obtained about research participants. The participants' identities should be concealed in written and verbal reports of the results, as well as in informal discussion with students and colleagues.
Principle 12. Informing Participants Immediately after the data are collected, the investigator should clarify for the research participant any misconceptions that may have arisen. The investigator also recognizes a duty to report general findings to participants in terms appropriate to their understanding.
Principle 13. Reporting Results Because the investigator's words may carry unintended weight with parents and children, caution should be exercised in reporting results, making evaluative statements, or giving advice.
Principle 14. Implications of Findings Investigators should be mindful of the social, political and human implications of their research and should be especially careful in the presentation of findings from the research. This principle, however, in no way denies investigators the right to pursue any area of research or the right to observe proper standards of scientific reporting.

Source: Excerpted from *SRCD Ethical Standards for Research with Children, 1990. SRDC Newsletter (Winter), pp. 5-6.*

Perhaps the most important measure used to ensure that research is conducted ethically is *peer review*. Before beginning a research study, investigators are required to submit the research plan to the *institutional review board* of the university, hospital, school board, or other setting where the research will be conducted for comments and approval. This practice permits an objective examination of the procedures by knowledgeable individuals, including both scientists and community members who are not personally involved in the research. Institutional review boards weigh the possible value of the research findings against potential risks. Sometimes they offer suggestions as to how negative effects might be prevented or minimized. All research carried out in institutional settings must first be carefully evaluated by the institution's review board. Virtually all government agencies that provide funding for research require such ethical compliance, as do the scientific and professional journals that publish the research.

For Thought and Discussion

Do you think 3-year-olds can give informed consent for research participation? How can the principle of informed consent be satisfied in research with young children?

An important component of such ethical compliance is the requirement that researchers obtain the *informed consent* of the participants in the study. When children are the participants, researchers must first obtain the written permission of the child's parents. In addition, each child must be made aware of the general procedures of the study. Most important, the child has the right to refuse to participate or to withdraw from the study at any time, even though the parents have given their permission. Assuring that children understand their rights as research participants can be an especially challenging task (Abramovitch et al., 1991; Hurley & Underwood, 2002).

If the research procedures may produce negative feelings in the child, the investigator must provide some means of reducing those feelings before the child leaves. For example, if a child is participating in an experiment in which he or she experiences failure, the investigator might end the research session by having the child perform a relatively easy task that will ensure success. Also, to whatever extent seems reasonable, the investigator should at some point explain to the child the purpose of the study and the child's role in it, a procedure called *debriefing*.

Maintaining *confidentiality* is also a crucial aspect of ethical research. Whenever possible, the identities of the participants and information about their individual performance should be concealed from anyone not directly connected with the research. Anonymity is often achieved by assigning numbers to the participants and then using these numbers instead of names during the analysis of the data.

For Thought and Discussion

Does research with animals violate the spirit of informed consent? Should ethical standards for research with animals differ from those for research with humans?

Research conducted with animals must also carefully follow ethical guidelines. Canadian researchers must adhere to standards prescribed by the Canadian Council on Animal Care (2005) for the humane care and treatment of animals, which address issues such as justification for the research, housing, and treatment of the animals, providing veterinary care, and so on. The majority of institutions where such research is carried out have an animal care committee that evaluates research to be conducted and ensures compliance with these guidelines. Similar guidelines can be found in the American Psychological Association's *Guidelines for Ethical Conduct in the Care and Use of Animals* (2005).

Finally, all research psychologists have some ethical responsibilities that go beyond the protection of the individuals participating in the research. For example, scientists who report data that may be controversial or that may affect social policy decisions have an obligation to describe the limitations and degree of confidence they have in their findings. In addition, investigators should normally provide their research participants with some general information about the final results of the research, as an acknowledgment of the importance of their contribution to the overall research process.

LEARNING OBJECTIVE 2.5

Explain the ethical guidelines for human research that developmental researchers must follow.

1. What are the most common categories of risk in research with children?
2. What safeguards are routinely used to minimize risk?

CONCLUSION

Our purpose in devoting an entire chapter to research methods is to emphasize the fact that effective methods are crucial for advancing scientific knowledge. Unlocking the secrets of child development requires several elements. It begins, of course, with the perceptive insights of an astute researcher. Even the brightest researcher, however, cannot answer important theoretical questions without the necessary research techniques. For example, researchers suspected the existence of atoms and genes many years ago. But it was not until the advent of the particle accelerator and the electron microscope that scientists could confirm these suspicions. In the same way, psychologists have long debated the capabilities of the newborn. Only since the 1960s, however, have research techniques been developed that permit the scientific study of many related questions.

Another reason for including this chapter is that the remainder of the text presents a good deal of research evidence regarding developmental progress and processes. This evidence, for the most part, has been gathered through the methods described here, so it is helpful to approach it with an understanding of the differences between the correlational and experimental designs, longitudinal and cross-sectional experiments, and so on. These basics will also pave the way for the many more specific techniques and procedures used in various areas, which we describe as they come into play.

SUMMARY

KEY TERMS

case study, p. 46
cohort effect, p. 54
comparative research, p. 58
correlation, p. 47
correlation coefficient (r), p. 47
cross-cultural studies, p. 57
cross-sectional design, p. 54
cross-sequential design, p. 55
cultural psychology, p. 58
dependent variable, p. 49
descriptive research, p. 44
ethnographic methods, p. 58
hypothesis, p. 42
independent variable, p. 49
interview method, p. 45
law (principle), p. 42
longitudinal design, p. 52
microgenetic method, p. 56
naturalistic observation, p. 44
negative correlation, p. 47
objectivity, p. 42
observer influences, p. 45
positive correlation, p. 47
quasi-experimental studies, p. 50
scatter diagram, p. 47
scientific method, p. 42
structured observation, p. 45
theory, p. 42
variable, p. 46

LEARNING OBJECTIVES

LEARNING OBJECTIVE 2.1 Understand how researchers use the scientific method to study child development.

1. *What is the scientific method?*
   The scientific method consists of the rules that researchers use to conduct and describe their investigations.

2. *What two roles do theories play in the research process?*
   Theories help organize the information gathered from scientific studies. They also guide researchers to the important questions that need to be examined next.

3. *How do researchers ensure objectivity in their study of children?*
   Objectivity is achieved in a number of ways. First, researchers focus on behaviours that are directly observable. Second, researchers must be able to measure what is observed. Confidence is gained by precisely defining and describing what is being studied, so that independent observers would have no trouble agreeing on what happened in a given situation. Third, to ensure objectivity, everything in the study must be quantifiable. That is, everything must be able to be counted, including the behaviours and the factors that affect the behaviours.

LEARNING OBJECTIVE 2.2 Compare and contrast the research methods commonly used to study children.

1. *What are observational research, the interview method, and the case study method? What are advantages and disadvantages of each of these methods?*
   Observational research may occur in naturalistic settings or in those structured by the researchers. *Naturalistic observation* takes place in children's natural environments, such as their homes or schools, and provides a direct source of information for how children behave in the natural setting. However, the procedure has some drawbacks. The presence of observers may alter the setting and thus the behaviour. As well, some behaviours may be difficult to observe in the natural setting. Finally, because the setting may not be the same for all children, it may be difficult to compare between participants. *Structured observation* entails observing children's behaviour in a structured laboratory environment. This standardization of the setting allows the study of children's reactions to experiences that might not occur in a natural environment. However, observations made in the lab may not be generalizable to other settings.

   The interview method involves talking with children or knowledgeable others about aspects of the child's life, via interview or questionnaire. Interviews can provide valuable information about how a person thinks and feels. However, because interviews rely on the informant's knowledge, memory, and ability or willingness to communicate information, they may not always accurately reflect actual behaviour.

   The case study method involves only a single individual. Often these studies are concerned with clinical issues, or are undertaken if a child has experienced something so unusual that it attracts the interest of psychologists for theoretical reasons. In these instances case studies are a valuable research tool. Caution must be exercised, however, when drawing conclusions based on a single research participant.

2. *What is correlational research? What does it tell us about causal relations between variables?*
   Correlational research identifies systematic relationships between variables. A correlation is a statement that describes how two variables are related. A positive correlation indicates that the two variables change together in the same direction, while a negative correlation indicates that the variables change in opposite directions. Correlations can also be described in terms of their strength. A strong correlation indicates that the variables are closely related, whereas a weak correlation indicates less of a relationship. A major limitation is that correlations cannot be used to infer cause–effect relationships between variables.

3. *What elements comprise an experiment? What are advantages and disadvantages of the experimental method in research with children?*
   An experiment involves systematically manipulating the independent variable and observing its effect on the dependent variable. This procedure allows researchers to determine cause–effect relationships between the two variables. However, it may not always be possible or ethical to manipulate certain independent variables. In such situations, researchers may use a quasi-experimental study, where groups that differ on some important characteristic are compared. Nevertheless, because the researcher does not manipulate the independent variable, quasi-experimental studies cannot be used to show causality.

LEARNING OBJECTIVE 2.3 Analyze the strengths and limitations of the four basic methods for studying child development as a process.

1. *What are the strengths and limitations of longitudinal research?*
   In longitudinal research, the same group of children is studied repeatedly at different ages. Longitudinal research allows researchers to study changes as children age, examining the stability of behaviour over time and the effects of early experiences. Limitations of the longitudinal approach include attrition, the effects of repeated testing, the possibility that the research issues and instruments may become outdated, and the fact that the method is time-consuming and expensive.

2. *What are the strengths and limitations of cross-sectional research design?*
   In cross-sectional research groups of children of different ages are compared at one point in time. The method is a relatively quick and low-cost way to examine for age differences, and there are no problems with attrition or repeated testing. The drawback of this approach is that it cannot be used to examine stability and change. Additionally, *cohort effects* (unique events experienced by a particular generation) can influence the findings.

3. *What are the strengths and limitations of cross-sequential research design?*
   Cross-sequential research combines cross-sectional and longitudinal research. Children of different age groups are followed longitudinally, allowing both cross-sectional and longitudinal comparisons to be made. It also allows researchers to examine cohort effects. However, it can be a time-consuming and costly procedure.

4. *What are the strengths and limitations of microgenetic research?*
   Microgenetic research is an intensive study of a small number of children over a brief period of time. The strength of this design is that it allows examination of developmental changes that are discontinuous, in which abrupt change occurs from one level of development to another. The limitation of this type of research is that repeated testing can influence results.

LEARNING OBJECTIVE 2.4 Understand the uses of cultural research, comparative research, and psychophysiological methods.

1. *What is the goal of cross-cultural research?*
   One important goal of cross-cultural research is to test the universality of a phenomenon, such as motor development. Although there are significant individual differences in the ages at which infants crawl and walk, differences between cultures are far smaller than you might expect. Another goal of cross-cultural psychologists is to integrate the results of studies from a variety of cultures to create a more universal theory of human development.

2. *How do the questions asked and methods used by cultural psychologists and cross-cultural psychologists differ?*
   Cross-cultural psychologists attempt to test all groups under similar conditions, ideally using identical tasks and procedures. Cultural psychologists study a single or small number of cultures in depth. The aim of this approach is to understand as fully as possible the different aspects of culture and how they are interrelated. Cultural psychologists use ethnographic methods to gather as much information as possible about cultural practices and values.

3. *What are two reasons developmental psychologists might conduct research with animals?*
   Developmental researchers of the ethological tradition study animal behaviour for clues to the evolutionary origins of similar human behaviours. Other researchers use animal studies to examine questions that could not be experimentally conducted with humans because of ethical concerns.

4. *What are the reasons for using psychophysiological methods in developmental research?*
Researchers have used psychophysiological methods to study perceptual abilities and preferences in infants, where interview methods are not useful. They have also used these methods as objective measures of stress and pain in young children. Measures of brain activity allow researchers to assess the functioning of regions of the brain in response to certain types of stimulation or while the child undertakes a specific task.

LEARNING OBJECTIVE 2.5 Explain the ethical guidelines for human research that developmental researchers must follow.

1. *What are the most common categories of risk in research with children?*
Physical injury to the child is a concern in any research; however, this problem is relatively rare in developmental research. Investigators must consider potential psychological harm, such as producing feelings of failure, frustration, or stress. Similarly, they must consider a child's privacy when conducting research that involves children.

2. *What safeguards are routinely used to minimize risk?*
Researchers routinely use certain safeguards to minimize risk, including the following: prior reviewing of research plans by an institutional review board; obtaining the informed consent of parents, teachers, and children involved in a research study; eliminating any experimentally produced negative feelings through extra procedures; debriefing participants in terms of the purpose of the research; and strictly maintaining confidentiality. Additional ethical requirements include taking some responsibility for the social ramifications of research findings and providing feedback to participants about the outcome of the research project.

CHAPTER 3

GENETICS: THE BIOLOGICAL CONTEXT OF DEVELOPMENT

Rarely have two hockey line-mates had the same on-ice bond as top-scoring Vancouver Canucks Daniel and Henrik Sedin. Each always seems to always know where the other is and what he will do, both translating apparent "telepathy" and obvious skill into more pucks in the net than almost anyone else in the NHL. Can we attribute this chemistry to the fact that as identical twins they share 100 percent of their genetic make-up? Possibly. "If I know he's having a tough time, I'll go through the same feelings even though I don't have the same problem," Daniel says.

While psychologists love to study twins to test theories of nature versus nurture, the Sedins themselves credit their success not to their twinness but to the fact that they spend so much time together—both on and off the ice—they know each other well enough to anticipate what the other is thinking. "If you put all the hours we've been together playing soccer or other sports, it's every day since we were six," says Henrik. "Being twins helps, but it's more than that." So strong is their bond that the twins refuse to ever be traded to separate teams.

The possible advantages of being twins can apparently be mimicked in sports. When synchronized swimmers Carolyn Waldo and Michelle Cameron competed for Canada in the 1988 Olympics, they saw stiff competition from American identical twins Karen and Sarah Josephson. Waldo and Cameron pretended to act like twins, warming up at the same pace, aligning their movements, trying to guess what the other was thinking, even synchronizing their heart rates. They won gold.

In this chapter we will look at what studies of twins can tell us about how our genes contribute to behaviour and aptitudes. We will examine the science of genetic inheritance and the ways in which genes interact with the environment, as well as a number of genetic and chromosomal abnormalities and their effects.

Source: Albergotti, Reed, "The NHL's telepathic twins," *The Wall Street Journal*, April 21, 2011.

Farber, Michael, "Freaky good," *Sports Illustrated*, May 4, 2009.

McGran, Kevin, "Double trouble awaits in Sedin twins," *The Toronto Star*, May 29, 2011.

We saw in chapter 1 that one of the enduring issues in developmental psychology concerns the relative importance of biological (nature) factors and environmental (nurture) factors. We saw, too, that most child researchers today favour an interactionist perspective. Environmental effects played out at the chromosomal level offer an insight into how complex and subtle these interactions can be. In this chapter, we delve more deeply into the fascinating world of genetics.

Now that we have presented some history, theory, and methodology of child development, it is time to turn to the development of the individual child. Where do we begin? People often think of birth as the beginning of life. We will see in the next chapter, however, that by the time a baby comes into the world, a good deal of development has already taken place inside the mother's womb. Perhaps, then, we should consider that development begins when the father's sperm fertilizes the mother's egg at conception. But even this event is a continuation, rather than the start, of the developmental process. To understand the development of the child, we must begin with genetic processes inside the child's parents that determine how they pass their heredity on to the next generation.

But this starting point is just that. Our genes guide, regulate, and influence development throughout our lives. Precisely how they do so, and exactly how much of our behaviour is affected by our genes, are two exciting and controversial issues in modern child psychology.

Unlike most of the other topics in this book, genetics will take us briefly into the fields of biology and biochemistry. Our primary emphasis, however, will remain on the psychological perspective and how behaviour is influenced by genetic processes. First, we discuss the basic concepts surrounding genes and their functions. Then we consider genetic disorders and why they occur. Next we examine the methods psychologists use to study gene–environment interactions and some of what they have learned. Finally, we present several models that attempt to explain how genes and environment interact to produce behaviour.

Links to Related Material

As you saw in Chapter 1, the interaction of nature and nurture is an enduring issue in developmental psychology. This chapter delves more deeply into how genes and the environment interact to influence child development.

Learning Objective 3.1

Identify and describe the mechanisms and processes by which physical and behavioural characteristics are inherited.

MECHANISMS OF INHERITANCE

How does a baby inherit the characteristics of his or her parents—black or white skin, red or brown hair? How does a fertilized human egg know to develop into a person rather than a chimpanzee? How does a single cell give rise to trillions of other cells that become different parts of the body—the fingers, the heart, the brain, and so on? Such questions lie at the heart of the puzzle of inheritance, a mystery that scientists are now slowly beginning to solve.

CELL DIVISION

All living things are composed of cells. Adult humans, on average, possess about 10 trillion of them. Cells have three major subdivisions: the nucleus; the cytoplasm, which surrounds the nucleus; and the cell membrane, which encases the cell.

Inside the nucleus lies the body's genetic material, DNA, which is organized into chemical strands called **chromosomes**. In humans, each cell nucleus contains 23 pairs of chromosomes, 46 in all. For each pair, one chromosome came from the father, the other from the mother. Twenty-two of the pairs are called **autosomes**. The two members of each of these 22 pairs are similar to one another and carry the same genes in the same locations. The 23rd pair makes up the **sex chromosomes**, which come in two varieties. The X chromosome is of about average size and carries a good deal of genetic material, whereas the Y chromosome is much smaller and has many fewer genes. When the pair consists of two X chromosomes (XX), the person is female; when the pair consists of one of each type (XY), the person is male.

Chromosomes Chemical strands in the cell nucleus that contain the genes. The nucleus of each human cell has 46 chromosomes, with the exception of the gametes, which have 23.

Autosomes The 22 pairs of human chromosomes, other than the sex chromosomes.

Sex chromosomes The pair of human chromosomes that determines one's sex. Females have two X chromosomes; males have an X and a Y.

Although there are many specialized cells, they can be divided into two broad types—*body cells* and *germ cells*. These cells are principally distinguished by how they reproduce and the roles they play in hereditary transmission.

Cells constantly reproduce; their reproduction is probably the most fundamental genetic process that takes place in our bodies. In the time it takes you to read this sentence, more than 100 million cells in your body will have reproduced. Body cells, by far the larger category, reproduce by a process called mitosis, whereas germ cells reproduce by a process called meiosis.

In **mitosis**, diagrammed on the left-hand side of Figure 3.1, each parent cell produces two identical child cells through a series of three phases. In the first phase (Figure 3.1*a*), each of the 46 chromosomes in the cell duplicates itself, producing two identical strands connected near their centres, like an X. Next, these joined strands line up at the cell's midline (Figure 3.1*b*). Each X splits and the two identical chromosomal strands move to opposite sides of the cell, a nucleus forms around each set of chromosomes, and the cell itself divides in two (Figure 3.1*c*). With mitosis complete, each new cell contains 46 chromosomes and is genetically identical to the parent cell.

Mitosis The process by which body cells reproduce, resulting in two identical cells.

FIGURE 3.1

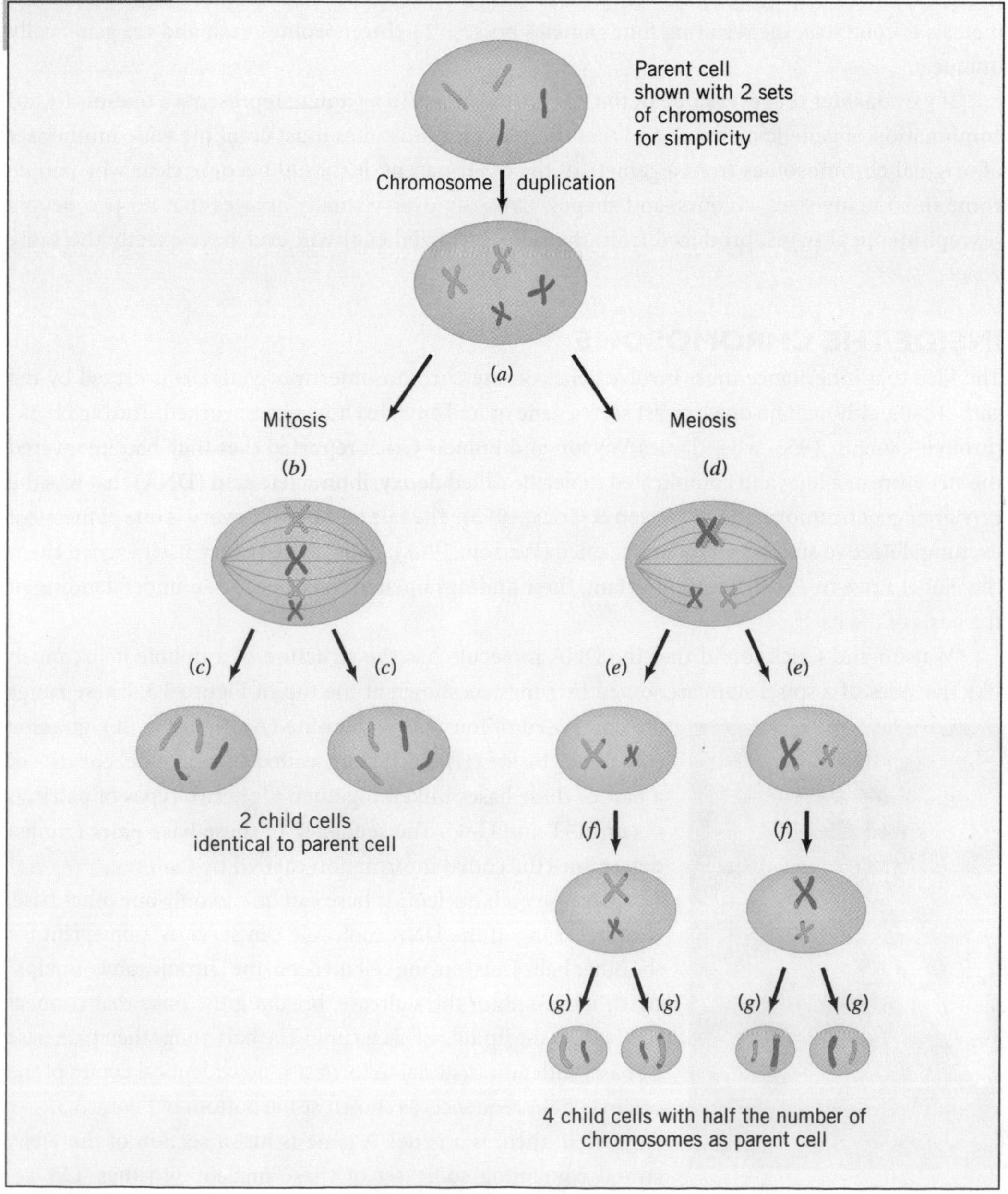

Parent cell shown with 2 sets of chromosomes for simplicity

Chromosome duplication

(*a*)

Mitosis

(*b*)

(*c*) (*c*)

2 child cells identical to parent cell

Meiosis

(*d*)

(*e*) (*e*)

(*f*) (*f*)

(*g*) (*g*) (*g*) (*g*)

4 child cells with half the number of chromosomes as parent cell

Mitosis and Meiosis. Mitosis results in two cells identical to the parent and to each other. Meiosis results in four cells different from the parent cell and from each other. *Adapted from* Biology: Exploring Life *(p. 152) by G. D. Brum & L. K. McKane, 1989, New York: John Wiley & Sons. Adapted by permission of the authors.*

Meiosis The process by which germ cells produce four gametes (sperm or ova), each with half the number of chromosomes of the parent cell.

Crossing over The exchange of genetic material between pairs of chromosomes during meiosis.

In **meiosis**, the process by which germ cells reproduce, four child cells are produced that are all different from one another and that contain only 23 chromosomes each. These child cells, called gametes, are the sperm or the ova that will combine at conception to form a new individual with the full complement of 46 chromosomes. Meiosis, diagrammed on the right side of Figure 3.1, requires several additional phases. The 46 chromosomes of the cell similarly duplicate themselves into two identical strands that remain attached like an X (Figure 3.1*a*). Then an important new process occurs. The X-shaped chromosomes pair up with their partners (remember, the 46 chromosomes are arranged in 23 pairs) and the strands of one X exchange pieces with the strands of the partner X (Figure 3.1*d*). This process, called **crossing over,** means that the two strands that form each X are no longer identical. (Figure 3.2 offers a greatly simplified representation of such an exchange.) The Xs then line up at the midline of the cell. One X from each pair moves to one end of the cell, a nucleus forms around each half, and the cell divides (Figure 3.1*e*). This process is then repeated (figures 3.1*f* and 3.1*g*). Thus, when meiosis is complete, the resulting four gametes possess 23 chromosomes each and are genetically unique.

FIGURE 3.2

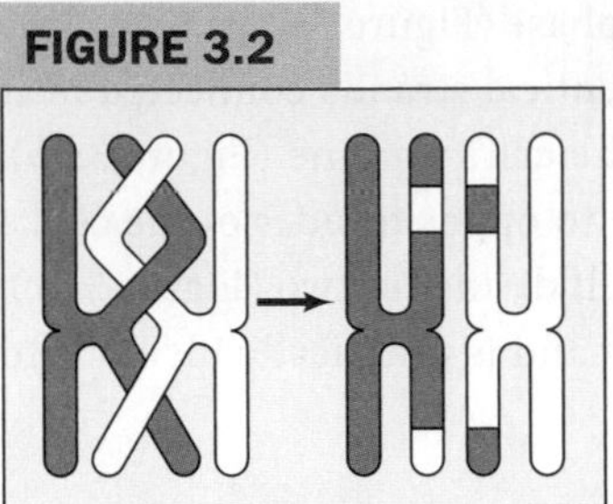

Crossing over results in the exchange of genetic material. After the cross-over, all four strands are different. *Adapted from* Biology: Exploring Life *(p. 44) by G. D. Brum & L. K. McKane, 1989, New York: John Wiley & Sons. Adapted by permission of the authors.*

For Thought and Discussion

If crossing over did not occur, would children look more similar or less similar to their siblings and parents? Why?

If we consider that every one of the 23 chromosomes in a gamete represents a one-of-a-kind combination of genetic material, and that these 23 chromosomes must combine with another set of original chromosomes from a gamete of the other parent, it should become clear why people come in so many sizes, colours, and shapes. Crossing over virtually assures that no two people (except identical twins, produced from the same fertilized egg) will ever have exactly the same genes.

INSIDE THE CHROMOSOME

Gene A segment of DNA on the chromosome that codes for the production of proteins. The basic unit of inheritance.

Deoxyribonucleic acid (DNA) A stair-like, double-helix molecule that carries genetic information on chromosomes.

Base pair The unit of length of the double-stranded DNA molecule.

The idea that inheritance must involve genes on the chromosomes was generally accepted by the early 1940s, although no one had yet seen a **gene** or had any idea how genes worked. The big breakthrough came in 1953, when James Watson and Francis Crick reported that they had uncovered the structure of a long and complicated molecule called **deoxyribonucleic acid (DNA)** that was the carrier of genetic information (Watson & Crick, 1953). The tale of their discovery is one of the most exciting detective stories in modern science (Watson, 1968), and the discovery itself earned them the Nobel Prize in 1962. Most important, their findings opened the door for an understanding of the basis of life itself.

Watson and Crick found that the DNA molecule has the structure of a double helix, much like the sides of a spiral staircase joined by rungs, as shown at the top of Figure 3.3. These rungs are composed of four bases: adenine (A), thymine (T), guanine (G), and cytosine (C). Each rung, called a nucleotide, consists of a pair of these bases linked together. Only two types of pairings occur, A–T and G–C. The sequence of these **base pairs** (rungs) determines the coded information carried by the gene.

James Watson received the Nobel Prize with Francis Crick for discovering the structure of the DNA molecule. (© *Karen Kasmauski/Corbis*)

Because each nucleotide base can link to only one other base, each half-rung of the DNA molecule can serve as a blueprint for the other half. Thus, during cell division, the chromosome "unzips" down the length of the staircase, breaking the links that connect the bases at the middle of each rung. The half-rungs then pair, base by base, with new material to form two new identical copies of the original DNA sequence, as shown at the bottom of Figure 3.3.

What, then, is a gene? A gene is just a section of the DNA strand containing some set of these nucleotide rungs. On average, a gene contains about 1,000 nucleotides, although some contain as many as 2 million. Again, when we consider that the chromosomes in a human body cell together contain about 20,000 to 25,000 genes, and that each chromosome underwent the crossing-over process during meiosis, it is easy to understand why each individual person is unique.

The number and precise sequence of nucleotides in the genes answers the question posed earlier about how the cell knows to develop into a human rather than a chimpanzee. The sequence is especially critical here because approximately 98 percent of human DNA is also found in the DNA of the chimpanzee (Biological Systems, 1988).

The location of genes on the chromosome is likewise very important. For each pair of chromosomes, the genes for the same trait (e.g., eye colour or nose shape) are in the same locations and are called **alleles**. We will see shortly that both genes are involved in how the trait is expressed, but because the two alleles are not always the same, many different combinations of characteristics can result. In recent years, scientists have made remarkable progress in mapping the precise locations of various genes on the human chromosomes. This will give them a clearer picture of the human genome, as well as make it possible to alter a person's hereditary code through genetic engineering (discussed in Chapter 4).

FIGURE 3.3

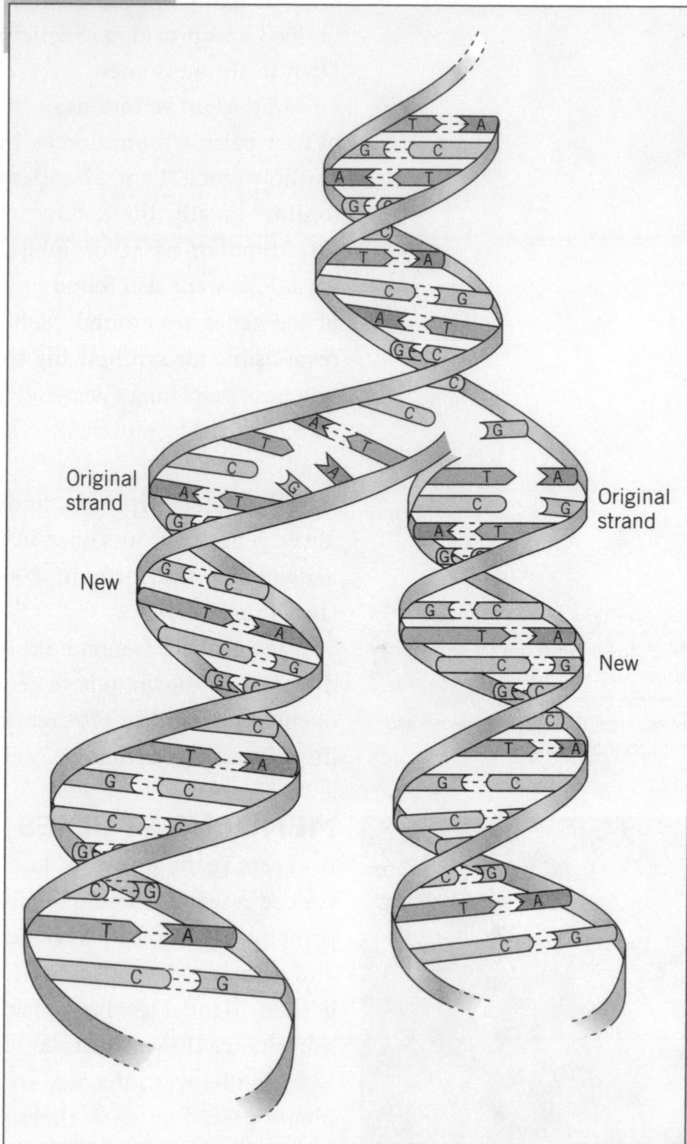

Structure and replication of DNA.

How do genes affect behaviour? The answer to this question is complex and not yet entirely understood. It begins with the fact that there are two kinds of genes—structural genes and regulator genes. The job of the *structural genes* is to guide the production of proteins, which serve many different functions in various parts of the body. Indeed, one researcher has written that "the human cell can be viewed as a protein factory" (Brown, 1999, p. 37). The job of the *regulator genes* is to control the activities of the structural genes. The regulator genes can thus selectively suppress the production of protein so that the cells in a particular organ, such as the heart, liver, or brain, produce only proteins that are appropriate for that organ. The regulator genes also turn structural genes on and off at different points in development—for example, initiating and controlling the many changes that take place during puberty. They apparently do this in response to what is going on in their environment—meaning the cells around them—demonstrating that even at this molecular level, nature and nurture always operate together.

Alleles Genes for the same trait located in the same place on a pair of chromosomes.

Through these as yet incompletely understood processes, our genes can affect our sensory abilities, our nervous system, our muscles and bones, and so on, thus influencing our behaviour and development in a reasonably direct manner. Later in the chapter we will see how genes also appear to affect human behaviour through more indirect processes.

THE HUMAN GENOME PROJECT

In 1989, the Human Genome Project was launched, headed by James Watson, one of the discoverers of the structure of DNA. The main purpose of the project was to determine the sequence of the 3 billion base pairs that make up human DNA and to identify human genes. About 18 countries participated in the project, including Canada, the United States, Japan, the United Kingdom, Australia, Germany, France, Denmark, Italy, and China. Sequencing the 3 billion chemical base pairs was a task of daunting magnitude, but the development of new technologies allowed geneticists to rapidly and automatically sequence large amounts of DNA. The sequencing was completed in 2003 and provided geneticists with detailed information about the structure and function of DNA in chromosomes.

Important variations in size between chromosomes were found with respect to the number of base pairs. Chromosomes 1 and 2, for example, are almost 250 million base pairs long, while chromosomes 21 and 22 are less than 50 million pairs long. The sex chromosomes were also found to differ greatly: the X chromosome is 153 million base pairs long, while the Y chromosome is just 51 million base pairs long (National Center for Biotechnology Information, 2003). Important variations were also found in the size of genes, the functional part of our DNA. Although most of the genes are around 28,000 base pairs long, some are much larger. For example, the gene responsible for synthesizing the protein dystrophin, located on the X chromosome, is 2.4 million base pairs long (Venter et al., 2001). Duchenne muscular dystrophy, a severe genetic disease characterized by muscle weakness and wasting, is the consequence of a faulty version of this gene (Kelly, 2007).

The most surprising finding of the Human Genome Project was that we actually have fewer genes than was once believed—around 20,000 to 25,000 (International Human Genome Sequencing Consortium, 2004)—in contrast to earlier estimates of as many as 140,000 (Baltimore, 2001).

For Thought and Discussion

What do you think are some possible future outcomes of the Human Genome Project? What ethical issues might the new knowledge and associated technology raise?

The Human Genome Project has great implications for the medical field because numerous diseases are known to have genetic origins. Identifying genes that are responsible for diseases has opened the door for research into genetic treatments for inherited disorders. We discuss genetic disorders and *gene therapy* later in the chapter.

MENDEL'S STUDIES

In recent years, scientists' knowledge of genetic processes has relied on the development of advanced research techniques and powerful laboratory instruments. Yet some of the fundamental principles of heredity have been understood since the mid-1800s, when they were discovered and described by an Austrian monk named Gregor Mendel (1822–1884). Working alone in his garden, Mendel used pea plants, careful observations, and brilliant logic to develop a theory of inheritance that remains largely correct today.

Gregor Mendel, whose pioneering work with pea plants paved the way for the modern science of genetics. (*James King-Holmes//Photo Researchers, Inc.*)

Mendel was intrigued by the process of hereditary transmission. He wondered how pea plants passed on such characteristics as flower colour to the next generation. To study this process, Mendel mated purple-flowered and white-flowered plants. People believed at the time that when a mother and father had different traits, the traits blend in the child. But Mendel believed that the process must work in some other way. He knew that parent plants with purple and white flowers did not produce offspring with lavender flowers. In fact, all the offspring of the purple- and white-flowered plants that he mated had purple flowers. Had the white trait disappeared entirely? Apparently not, because when Mendel next mated the new purple-flowered plants with each other, one out of every four of the second-generation offspring was white.

Phenotype The characteristic of a trait that is expressed or observable. The phenotype results from an interaction of genotype and environment.

Genotype The arrangement of genes underlying a trait.

Through many experiments involving colour and other characteristics, Mendel developed a theory to account for his observations. He correctly deduced that each observable trait, such as colour, requires two elements, which we now know are a pair of genes (alleles), one inherited from each parent. Today, we call the expressed or observable trait the **phenotype**, and the underlying genes the **genotype**.

PRINCIPLES OF GENETIC TRANSMISSION Mendel's theory involved several new principles, the most important of which was the *principle of dominance*: The alleles of a trait (purple-flower gene and white-flower gene) are not equal, and one usually dominates the other. As it turns out, the gene for purple flowers in pea plants is a **dominant gene** and the gene for white flowers is a **recessive gene**. Mendel discovered that when either gene is dominant, that characteristic is expressed; only when both genes are recessive is the other characteristic expressed. For example, if we think of the colour trait in the pea plant as involving purple (P) or white (w) genes, then plants with the genotype PP, Pw, or wP will have purple flowers, and only those with the genotype ww will have white flowers. Plants thus can have the same phenotype (purple flowers) with different genotypes (PP, Pw, or wP).

Dominant gene A relatively powerful allele whose characteristics are expressed in the phenotype, regardless of the allele with which it is paired.

Recessive gene A relatively weak allele whose characteristics are expressed in the phenotype only when it is paired with another recessive gene.

Mendel's theory included several other principles. The *principle of segregation* states that each inheritable trait is passed on to the offspring as a separate unit (the alleles that produce flower colour are separate from one another and passed on that way, which is why the blending idea was incorrect). The *principle of independent assortment* asserts that traits are passed on independently of one another (for example, which flower-colour trait is passed on has no bearing on which stem-length trait is passed on).

Mendel's principles have proven to be surprisingly accurate, not just for pea plants, but throughout the huge variety of life forms. Indeed, his discovery of dominant and recessive traits applies to many human characteristics, as shown in Table 3.1. One commonly cited example is eye colour: the gene for brown eye colour is dominant, and that for blue eye colour is recessive. Thus, a mother and father who both possess brown–blue gene combinations for eye colour have brown eyes themselves and are three times as likely to produce a brown-eyed child as a blue-eyed child.

TABLE 3.1 SOME COMMON DOMINANT AND RECESSIVE TRAITS

Dominant	Recessive
Brown eyes	Blue, grey, or green eyes
Normal hair	Baldness (in men)
Dark hair	Blond hair
Normal colour vision	Colour blindness
Freckles	No freckles
Dimples	No dimples
Free earlobes	Attached earlobes
Double-jointed thumbs	Tight thumb ligaments

REVISIONS OF MENDEL'S PRINCIPLES Years of research have supported Mendel's basic ideas, but have also uncovered other processes involved in hereditary transmission. For instance, single traits are often the product of more than one pair of genes—a process known as **polygenic inheritance.** In humans, height, weight, and skin colour are all the product of polygenic inheritance. More critically for our purposes, most behavioural traits of interest—for example, temperament and intelligence—are also affected by multiple genes.

Polygenic inheritance The case in which a trait is determined by a number of genes.

A second modification is that some traits result from genes that display **incomplete dominance**; that is, they are neither entirely dominant nor entirely recessive. For example, sickle-cell anemia is passed on through a recessive gene. However, the blood of people who have this recessive gene along with a dominant normal gene will show some mild characteristics of the disease (this differs from the early idea of blending, however, because the two genes remain separate and are passed on that way to future generations).

Incomplete dominance The case in which a dominant gene does not completely suppress the effect of a recessive gene, which is then somewhat expressed in the phenotype.

A third addition to Mendel's principles involves **codominance**, in which both genes of a trait are dominant and so both characteristics are expressed completely. For example, the genes for A and B blood types are codominant, so a person who inherits one from each parent will have blood type AB.

Codominance The case in which both alleles are dominant and each is completely expressed in the phenotype.

The impetus for a fourth and relatively recent revision was a puzzling finding. In some instances, a trait does not follow any of the usual laws of inheritance; rather, it matters whether the mother or father provides a particular gene. For example, diabetes is more likely to be inherited from the father, whereas the mother is a more likely source of asthma. What occurs in such cases is **genomic imprinting**: The relevant alleles are biochemically marked such that one of them is

Genomic imprinting The case in which the allele from one parent is biochemically silenced and only the allele from the other parent affects the phenotype.

"imprinted" or silenced (for example, the allele for diabetes in the mother) and only the other allele finds expression in the phenotype (Sack, 2008). It is estimated that the human genome contains between 100 and 200 imprinted genes (Davies, Isles, & Wilkinson, 2001).

Mendel's principles must be revised in one more important way. Scientists now know that the environment can play a crucial role in the expression of genes. One example is that the fur colour of the Arctic fox changes with temperature from white in winter to brown in summer. In this way, the fox is camouflaged in both the winter snow and the brown underbrush of summer. A human example is that medical students taking exams show reduced activity of messenger RNA (the molecules responsible for protein synthesis) in the immune system, and thus a modification of the activity of the genes in response to environmental stress. Genes always operate within an environmental context, and the immediate context can affect the way in which they are expressed (Gottlieb, 1998).

LEARNING OBJECTIVE 3.1

Identify and describe the mechanisms and processes by which physical and behavioural characteristics are inherited.

1. What are chromosomes, where are they in the body, and what do they do?
2. How do cells reproduce in a way that makes every individual genetically unique?
3. What is DNA and how does it combine to create genes?
4. What facts and principles of inheritance did Mendel discover?
5. What are some principles of inheritance that researchers have uncovered since Mendel?

Learning Objective 3.2

Describe different types of genetic disorders and their impact on child development.

GENETIC AND CHROMOSOMAL DISORDERS

Given the billions of sperm cells generated by the male and the 2 million or so ova generated by the female, we should not be surprised that genetic imperfections sometimes occur. These variations, or *mutations*, are the driving force behind evolution. When the "errors" turn out to be adaptive, they result in improvements in the species. The overwhelming majority of mutations, however, are maladaptive. Through a natural screening process in humans, about 90 percent of all genetic abnormalities result in miscarriage rather than live births. The problems that we consider now are therefore the exception to the general rule.

Some human disorders are entirely hereditary and are passed along according to the same principles of inheritance that determine eye colour and nose shape. Other genetic disorders are not inherited, but may result from errors during cell division in meiosis. Chromosomes and the genes they carry can also be made abnormal by radiation, drugs, viruses, chemicals, and perhaps even the aging process. In this section, we examine the various kinds of genetic disorders and discuss some examples of each. Table 3.2 summarizes both the disorders discussed in the text and several other important examples.

HEREDITARY DISORDERS

According to Mendel's principles, just as a child may inherit genes for brown or blue eyes, abnormal genes can also be passed along to offspring. Whether defective genes are expressed in the phenotype depends on whether they are dominant or recessive. If a defective gene inherited from one parent is recessive, the dominant (and usually normal) allele from the other parent can prevent the problem. Of course, the problem gene still exists in the genotype and will be passed on to half the person's offspring. Most of the offspring will themselves be unaffected; those who receive the defective gene from both parents, however, will develop the disorder.

TABLE 3.2 EXAMPLES OF GENETIC DISORDERS

Disorder	Cause	Incidence (North America)	Description
Huntington's disease	Dominant gene on chromosome 4	1 in 18,000 to 25,000	Deterioration of the nervous system, uncontrollable muscular movements, disordered brain function, death
Neurofibromatosis (Type 1)	Dominant gene on chromosome 17	1 in 3,000	Discoloration and tumours of the skin, heightened probability of learning difficulties, and mild intellectual disability
Tay-Sachs disease	Recessive gene on chromosome 15	1 in 360,000 for general population 1 in 3,600 for Ashkenazi Jews and Québécois	Nervous system deterioration, blindness, paralysis, early death
Phenylketonuria	Recessive gene on chromosome 12	1 in 10,000	If untreated, severe intellectual disability, hyperactivity, convulsions
Sickle-cell anemia	Recessive gene on chromosome 11	1 in 600 for African Americans	Oxygen deprivation, severe pain, tissue damage, early death
Cystic fibrosis	Recessive gene on chromosome 7	1 in 2,500 for Caucasians 1 in 17,000 for African Americans 1 in 90,000 for Asians	Breathing and digestive problems, infection of lungs, early death
Down syndrome	Extra chromosome at pair 21	1 in 1,000 (incidence increases with age of mother)	Moderate to severe intellectual disability, distinctive physical features, immune deficiencies, heart defects
Fragile X syndrome	Gene on X chromosome	1 in 4,000 for males 1 in 8,000 for females	Intellectual disability, language difficulties, distinctive physical features
Turner's syndrome	Absence of one of the X chromosomes	1 in 2,500 for females	Short stature, incomplete development of sex characteristics, below-average spatial intelligence
Klinefelter's syndrome	Extra X chromosome	1 in 750 male births	Somewhat feminine appearance, incomplete development of sex characteristics, below-average verbal intelligence

DOMINANT TRAITS Dominant genes that cause severe problems typically disappear from the species because the affected people usually do not live to reproduce. In a few cases, however, severely disabling dominant genes are passed on because they do not become active until relatively late in life. People with these genes may reproduce before they know that they have inherited the disease.

An example is *Huntington's disease*. The age of onset of this disease varies, but it typically strikes people between about 30 and 40 years of age. Quite suddenly, the nervous system begins to deteriorate, resulting in uncontrollable muscular movements and disordered brain function. The disease became familiar to many people when it took the life of American folk singer Woody Guthrie, famous for writing the song "This Land" (you may remember sitting by a campfire singing "This land is your land, This land is my land…").

Until recently, the children of a person stricken with Huntington's had no way of knowing whether they also carried the gene and could pass it on to their offspring. Late in 1983, scientists discovered which chromosome carries the gene for Huntington's. Ten years later, they located the exact gene responsible for the disease and learned how to tell whether a person has inherited it (Morell, 1993; Taylor, 2004, 2005).

RECESSIVE TRAITS Like Mendel's purple flowers, which did not reveal the white-flower gene they carried, parents can carry problem recessive genes that have no effect on them. If both parents carry such a recessive gene, they can combine in the offspring to produce the disorder (just as two brown-eyed parents can produce a blue-eyed child). It has been estimated that on average, each of us carries four potentially lethal genes as recessive traits (Scarr & Kidd, 1983), but because most of these dangerous genes are rare, it is unlikely that we will mate with someone who has a matching recessive gene. Even then, the probability that a child will receive both recessive genes is only one in four.

Some diseases carried by recessive genes produce errors of metabolism, which cause the body to mismanage sugars, fats, proteins, or carbohydrates. For example, with *Tay-Sachs disease* the nervous system disintegrates because of the lack of an enzyme that breaks down fats in brain cells. The fatty deposits swell, and the brain cells die. Tay-Sachs disease is rare in the general population, with an incidence of 1 in 300,000 births. However, among Ashkenazi Jews, who account for most of the North American Jewish population, 1 in 25–30 people is a carrier of the gene (in contrast to 1 in 200–300 in the general population) and the incidence is greatly increased (Wailoo & Pemberton, 2006). The disease also occurs at elevated rates in the Québécois population (Portail Québécois des Maladies Génétiques Orphelines, 2010; Wailoo & Pemberton, 2006), especially in the Bas St-Laurent and Gaspésie regions of Quebec where as many as 1 in 13 people may be carriers of the gene (Laberge et al., 2005). The incidence is also elevated among the Cajuns in Louisiana, although its origins differ from those identified in the Québécois population. Infants afflicted with this disease appear normal at birth and through their first half-year. Then, at about 8 months of age, they usually become extremely listless, and they are often blind by the end of their first year. Most stricken children die by the age of 4. At present there is no treatment for the disorder; however, its incidence has been reduced dramatically through carrier screening programs, such as those instituted in high schools in Montreal, Quebec (Laberge et al., 2005; Mitchell, Capua, Clow, & Scriver, 1996; Scriver, 2001).

Another metabolic disorder that results from a recessive gene is *phenylketonuria* (PKU), a problem involving the body's management of protein. This disease occurs when the body fails to produce an enzyme that breaks down phenylalanine, an amino acid. As a result, abnormal amounts of the substance accumulate in the blood and harm the developing brain cells. Infants with PKU are typically healthy at birth but, if untreated, begin to deteriorate after a few months of life as the blood's phenylalanine level mounts. Periodic convulsions and seizures may occur, and the victims usually suffer from **intellectual disability** (Chen, 2006; Sack, 2008).

Intellectual disability A disorder characterized by limited intellectual and adaptive functioning (also sometimes referred to as mental retardation).

Our understanding of how PKU disrupts normal metabolism has resulted in one of the early victories of science over genetic abnormalities. Discovery of the mechanism of the disease led to the development of special diets that are low in phenylalanine and thus prevent its accumulation in the bloodstream. Although children placed on these special diets shortly after birth remain at risk for some cognitive deficits (American Academy of Pediatrics, 2008; Diamond et al., 1997), most achieve at least close to normal intellectual functioning, in marked contrast to the devastating effects in the absence of treatment. Because of the dramatic results of timely intervention in this disease, newborn babies in Canada are now routinely tested for PKU through a simple blood test procedure (Canadian Paediatric Society, 2010). A similar program is in effect in the United States (American Academy of Pediatrics, 2008). The lesson in the PKU story is that genes are not necessarily destiny—how or whether a gene's influence is played out can depend on interactions with the environment.

For Thought and Discussion

Who should have access to or control genetic information about individuals? Families, physicians, employers, insurance companies? To what uses should genetic information be put? Do you think there should be limits to those uses?

A recessive genetic abnormality that does not involve metabolism is *sickle-cell anemia* (SCA). People who have inherited a gene for this recessive trait from both parents have red blood cells that do not contain normal hemoglobin, a protein that carries oxygen throughout the body. Instead, abnormal hemoglobin causes their red blood cells to become sickled, as shown in Figure 3.4. These sickled cells tend to clog small blood vessels instead of easily passing through them as normal cells do, thus preventing blood from reaching parts of the body. An unusual oxygen demand, such as that brought on by physical exertion, may cause the sufferer to experience severe pain, tissue damage, and even death because of the inadequate supply of oxygen (Chen, 2006; Wailoo & Pemberton, 2006).

FIGURE 3.4

Scanning electron micrographs of red blood cells from normal individuals (left) and individuals with sickle-cell anemia (right).
(Bill Longcore/Photo Researchers, Inc.)

About 8 percent of African Americans carry the recessive gene for SCA (Sack, 2008). Among the Bamba, a tribe in Africa, the incidence has been reported to be as high as 39 percent. Such a high rate of occurrence seems surprising from a Darwinian perspective—in which non-adaptive traits are weeded out through natural selection—because individuals who have two genes for SCA frequently die young and produce few children. How, then, could such a characteristic be preserved through the process of natural selection? The answer reveals a rare instance in which a gene is maladaptive in one environment but adaptive in another.

Scientists have noted that the Bamba live in areas where the incidence of malaria is high, but Bamba children who carry the SCA gene are about half as likely to have malarial parasites as those who do not. Although it is unclear how this gene offers resistance to malaria, its presence appears to permit more carriers to grow up and have children, even though one in four will have SCA. Apparently the negative effects of malarial parasites on reproduction are greater than the effects of carrying the SCA gene.

X-LINKED TRAITS As we mentioned earlier, there are important differences between the two sex chromosomes. The Y chromosome is much smaller and carries many fewer genes than the X chromosome. Indeed, in comparison to the more than 1,000 genes located on the X chromosome, there are only 307 genes on the Y chromosome (Snustad & Simmons, 2009). These differences have implications for the transmission of certain kinds of disorders called **X-linked disorders**. Some genes found on the X chromosome do not have a corresponding allele on the Y chromosome. In a female, if there is a recessive allele on one X chromosome, there is a good chance that the corresponding dominant allele on her other X chromosome will override its expression, although she will be a carrier of the recessive gene and will pass it on to half her children. Males have no such protection, and are thus more vulnerable than females to recessive disorders that travel only on the X chromosome (Kelly, 2007). X-linked disorders, therefore, occur more frequently in males, and the gene is passed to them from their mothers.

X-linked disorders Disorders that result from recessive genes located on the X chromosome, leaving males more vulnerable to them.

An example of an X-linked disorder is *hemophilia*, a serious bleeding disorder caused by low levels or complete absence of a blood protein essential for clotting. The disorder results from a recessive allele on the X chromosome (Sack, 2008; Snustad & Simmons, 2009). Females, who are likely to have a normal version of this allele on their other X chromosome, are less likely to have the disorder. They can, however, be carriers who can pass the defective allele on to their own children. Males, who do not have a second protective allele, will have the disorder if they inherit the recessive allele from their mother. Other well-known X-linked disorders include *Duchenne muscular dystrophy*, *red-green colour blindness*, and *fragile X syndrome* (Kelly, 2007; Passarge, 2007). (See Focus on Research 3.1 for further discussion of fragile X syndrome.)

Whether we are talking about X-linked disorders, or disorders resulting from faulty genes located on the autosomes, it is clear that many new findings are on the horizon of genetic research. For example, *cystic fibrosis*, an autosomal recessive disorder, is a serious and potentially deadly disorder characterized by an accumulation of mucus in the lungs and digestive tract. The gene responsible for this disease was identified in 1989 by Lap-Chee Tsui, who at the time was head of the Genetics and Genomic Biology Program at the Hospital for Sick Children in Toronto, in collaboration with Francis Collins at the University of Michigan. Within the last few years, investigators have also discovered the gene for a type of *Alzheimer's disease* that runs in families and for *amyotrophic lateral sclerosis* (*ALS*), also known as Lou Gehrig's disease. In addition, researchers at McGill University in Montreal (Kibar et al., 2007) have recently discovered a gene that may be responsible for neural tube defects in children, including anencephaly and spina bifida (discussed further in Chapter 4). The genetic locus of many other diseases may soon be discovered as part of the Human Genome Project, discussed earlier. Identifying the gene responsible for disorders often leads to research aimed at correcting the genetic defect. We discuss such gene therapy in *On the Cutting Edge 3.1*.

ON THE CUTTING EDGE 3.1
GENE THERAPY

One of the most promising outcomes of the Human Genome Project is the discovery of specific genes responsible for many inherited disorders. Identification of these genes brings with it the possibility of treating genetic disorders by repairing or replacing genes. *Gene therapy* is a recent approach, having its beginnings in the 1990s. Most gene therapy involves *somatic gene therapy*, in which the gene is inserted into the tissue of an individual with the goal of treating a disorder in that particular person. A less common, and more controversial form of gene therapy is *germ line therapy*, in which the gene is inserted into the reproductive cells, with the goal of preventing a disorder in future generations (Kelly, 2007; Kimmelman, 2008).

Despite some early setbacks, gene therapy has become an area of intense recent research. In order for gene therapy to be effective, researchers must first identify the faulty gene responsible for a disorder. They must also understand how the gene is involved in the disorder, so that they may know how to alter the gene and where in the body to insert cells containing the healthy gene to maximize the effects. Finally, they must be able to copy the healthy gene in the laboratory, for insertion into the cells of the affected individual (Health Canada, 2005).

How do researchers get something as small as a gene into an individual's cells? Researchers frequently use viruses as *vectors*—a means of inserting a new gene into a cell. Viruses typically reproduce by inserting their own genetic material into the cells of a host, thereby producing copies of themselves. However, viruses usually produce negative consequences when they infect a cell. In order to use a virus as a non-harmful vector, researchers must modify the virus in the laboratory, inserting into it the altered gene while at the same time blocking its ability to reproduce its own genetic material (Kelly, 2007). Once this phase is successfully completed, the virus is then used to introduce the new gene into the individual's cells, where the new gene replaces the faulty gene. This insertion can take place in the laboratory, in cells that have been removed from the individual's body. These cells that now contain the new, healthy gene are then grown in the laboratory, and when enough of the altered cells have been produced, they are then inserted back into the individual. Alternatively, the insertion can take place directly into target cells in the person's body (Health Canada, 2005; Kelly, 2007). When gene therapy produces successful results, it is usually necessary to repeat the process multiple times to maintain the effect (Snustad & Simmons, 2009).

Gene therapy was first successfully used in 1990 to treat a 4-year-old girl named Ashanti who suffered from severe combined immunodeficiency disease (SCID). SCID is a serious and incurable disease of the immune system resulting from the lack of an enzyme called adenosine deaminase (ADA). Cells were extracted from the girl and the ADA-producing gene was inserted into the cells. The cells—a billion or so—were then reinjected into Ashanti's bloodstream, where they produced the needed ADA. Ashanti's treatment was successful; however, the procedure must be repeated periodically to maintain its effectiveness.

Gene therapy has been successfully used to treat a handful of other children with SCID (Snustad & Simmons, 2009). The favourable results opened the door to human trials using gene therapy for other inherited diseases. Not all gene therapy trials have been similar success stories, however. In 1998, an experimental human trial using gene therapy to treat a genetic liver disease resulted in the death of an 18-year-old male (Kelly, 2007). This tragic event led to the development of stringent guidelines and safety regulations for gene therapy, which stipulate that risks of the therapy must be carefully evaluated and must be minimal, the disease must not be treatable by any other means, and data on its safety and effectiveness must be available from experiments with animals or human cells (Snustad & Simmons, 2009). With these regulations in effect, gene therapy research continues,

(*continued*)

On the Cutting Edge 3.1 Gene Therapy *(continued)*

and promising preliminary experimental results have been found for a number of genetic disorders, including Huntington's disease (Johnson & Davidson, 2010; Southwell, Ko, & Patterson, 2009), cystic fibrosis (Copreni, Penzo, Carrabino, & Conese, 2004; Machado-Aranda et al., 2005), hemophilia (Nienhuis, 2008), PKU (Chen & Woo, 2007), Tay-Sachs disease (Cachón-González, et al. 2006; Martino et al., 2005), and many others.

In 2010, there were 1,644 human clinical trials of gene therapy taking place around the world, of which 22 were in Canada (see Figure 3.5). Most major hospitals and universities across Canada have research teams involved in developing or testing experimental gene therapy treatments. McMaster University in Hamilton, Ontario, is an excellent example. Its Centre for Gene Therapeutics was established in 1999 to engage in cutting-edge research in gene therapy interventions for cancer, inflammatory diseases, and infectious diseases. It is quite likely that the future will see effective gene therapy treatments for many disorders.

FIGURE 3.5

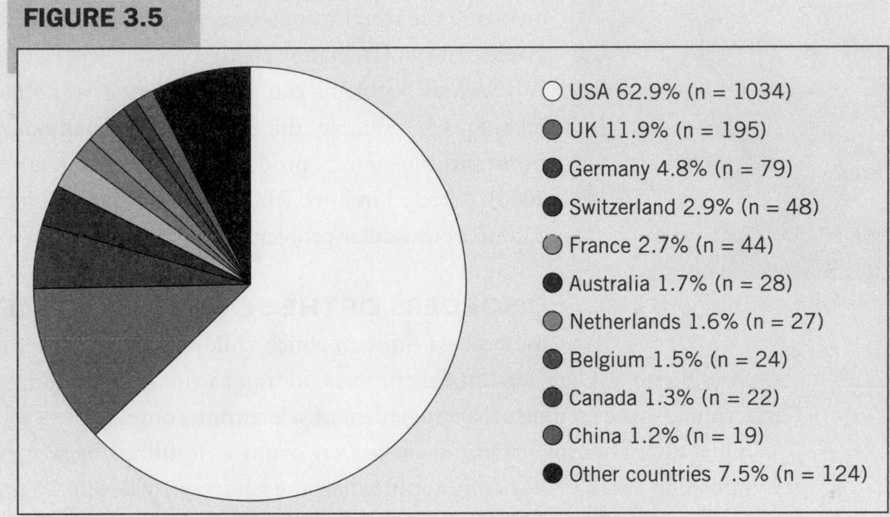

Geographical Distribution of Gene Therapy Clinical Trials (by country). From *Journal of Gene Medicine*, © 2010 John Wiley & Sons Canada, Ltd. Source: www.wiley.com//legacy/wileychi/genmed/clinical/

STRUCTURAL DEFECTS IN THE CHROMOSOME

The genetic abnormalities we have discussed thus far are all passed along according to the regular principles of inheritance. But genetically based problems may also result from physical changes in chromosomes. These changes can occur during meiosis in one of the parents, and they can involve the sex chromosomes or certain of the 22 autosomes. As mentioned, environmental hazards can also damage chromosomes. About 1 percent of human babies are born with a chromosomal abnormality. The actual occurrence of chromosomal anomalies may be as frequent as 25 percent of all conceptions; however, the large majority of these zygotes fail to develop, and the pregnancy does not continue (Delhanty, 2006).

AUTOSOMAL DISORDERS One of the most frequently observed effects of structural abnormality is *Down syndrome*, named after John Langdon H. Down, the physician who first described it. Down syndrome is also known as trisomy-21 because the 21st pair of chromosomes has a third member (Snustad & Simmons, 2009). Children born with this disorder typically have cheerful dispositions and are friendly and outgoing. However, they suffer from moderate to severe intellectual disability; they tend to have poor muscle tone and problems with expressive language; and they have a distinctive appearance that includes a flattened face and folded eyelids. The cause of Down

Children with Down syndrome have distinctive facial features. (*Bill Aaron/PhotoEdit*)

syndrome was identified in 1957, marking the first time a human disease had been directly linked to a chromosomal disorder.

The likelihood that a couple will produce a child with Down syndrome increases dramatically with the age of the mother (Health Canada, 2002). Fewer than 1 in 1,000 babies of mothers under age 30 have Down syndrome, whereas the incidence is 70 times greater for women between the ages of 45 and 49. Still, only a small proportion of births to older mothers involve Down syndrome. In addition, the mother is not always the source of the problem; in 20 to 30 percent of the cases, it is the father who contributes the extra chromosome (Behrman, Kliegman, & Jenson, 2000).

Trisomies may affect other chromosomes as well. However, only those involving the sex chromosomes or the autosomes 13, 18, and 21 result in a viable embryo (Delhanty, 2006).

Serious problems can also be caused when part of a chromosome is missing. For example, the deletion of a small amount of genetic material from chromosome 5 produces *cri du chat* (cat's cry) syndrome (Chen, 2006). Affected infants, who have a cat-like cry, have intellectual disability and neuromuscular problems.

DISORDERS OF THE SEX CHROMOSOMES Earlier, we described the process through which children receive either two X chromosomes or one X and one Y. Occasionally, this process does not work as it should. When this happens, the embryo may have an unusual arrangement of sex chromosomes.

One such abnormality occurs when an ovum is fertilized by a sperm that carries no sex chromosome at all, or less commonly, when the sperm provides an X and the ovum has no sex chromosome (Wodrich, 2006). In either case, the result is a monosomy of the sex chromosomes, in which an embryo has only an X and is designated 45,XO. Most of these embryos fail to develop in the uterus and are spontaneously aborted by the mother without her even being aware that conception had occurred (Chen, 2006; Wodrich, 2006). However, in the few cases in which the fetus develops completely, the child displays a variety of abnormalities referred to as *Turner's syndrome*. At birth, the baby is female in appearance, but the ovaries have already begun to disappear and do not produce the hormones necessary for the sex differentiation process to continue (Gardner & Sutherland, 2004). As a result, women with Turner's syndrome do not develop breasts or menstruate unless they are given hormone therapy. Physically, they are typically short and have an unusual neck and chest structure. Behaviourally, they demonstrate deficiencies in spatial skills, mathematics, attention, and social interaction (El Abd, Turk, & Hill, 1995; Ross, Zinn, & McCauley, 2000; Wodrich, 2006).

Another chromosomal problem is a trisomy that occurs when a male inherits an extra X chromosome. This extra X chromosome, which may come from either parent (Chen, 2006; Wodrich, 2006), results in a 47,XXY child with characteristics referred to as *Klinefelter's syndrome*. The child has a normal male appearance, and the effects of the extra X chromosome may be undetected until puberty, when secondary sex characteristics develop (Blachford, 2002; Wodrich, 2006). Men with Klinefelter's syndrome have long arms, very little body hair, an underdeveloped penis, and sometimes overdeveloped breasts. They are often somewhat timid and unassertive in their interpersonal interactions (Mandoki et al., 1991). Testosterone injections, beginning at puberty, have been found to help development in some cases (Blachford, 2002).

A third chromosomal abnormality is a trisomy that occurs when the sperm provides two Y chromosomes. The 47,XYY males produced when this occurs have large body builds and masculine personality characteristics (Blachford, 2002; Owen, 1979). These males may exhibit poor frustration tolerance, an increased risk for learning difficulties, and poor physical coordination. It was once thought that these men were more likely than others to become criminals or to display aggressive and antisocial behaviour; however, more recent research has not supported this contention (Blachford, 2002; Chen, 2006; Ike, 2000).

One important application of our rapidly accumulating knowledge about genetic disorders involves genetic counselling for couples and prospective parents. We discuss this topic in Chapter 4.

Links to Related Material

In Chapter 4, you will learn more about genetic counselling and other methods of preventing birth defects.

FOCUS ON RESEARCH 3.1
FRAGILE X SYNDROME

A relatively common disorder of the sex chromosomes is fragile X syndrome, a condition caused by an abnormality in a gene on the X chromosome (Hagerman, 1996). Fragile X syndrome is second only to Down syndrome as a genetically based cause of intellectual disability. Because it is an X-linked disorder, boys are more likely to be affected than girls. The vast majority of boys who inherit the gene display intellectual disability, spatial difficulties, and problems with visual-motor coordination (Kogan, Boutet, et al., 2004), as well as a variety of other symptoms, including facial dysmorphia (elongated face, large ears, prominent forehead and jaw), hyperactivity, attention deficit, and anxiety (Chen, 2006; Pozdnyakova & Regan, 2005). In contrast, only about 30 percent of girls who carry the gene on one of their X chromosomes show clear evidence of the syndrome. The syndrome results from the absence of a protein called FMRP (Fragile X Mental Retardation Protein). This protein is normally present in all the cells of the human body, but its concentration is particularly high in neurons—about 100 times higher. The protein is not synthesized in children with the syndrome because the sequence of the bases on their X chromosome is altered.

One of the leading Canadian research teams studying the physiological bases of fragile X disorder is the Research Centre at Saint-François d'Assise Hospital, affiliated with Laval University in Quebec City. Researchers from this group, directed by Edward Khandjian, have reported that FMRP plays a crucial role in transporting RNA (ribonucleic acid—the molecule that provides instructions for protein synthesis) from the nucleus to the cytoplasm in neurons (Huot et al., 2005; Mazroui et al., 2002).

Other Canadian researchers are examining the cognitive deficits associated with fragile X syndrome. For example, Kim Cornish of McGill University, and Cary Kogan and Isabelle Boutet of the University of Ottawa study attentional problems and visual-motor difficulties in children with fragile X syndrome. Dr. Cornish is conducting longitudinal research charting the visual and attentional development of boys with fragile X beginning at age 5. Drs. Kogan, Boutet, and Cornish have collaborated in the study of visual and spatial learning abilities in boys affected by fragile X syndrome (Kogan, Boutet, Cornish, et al., 2009). These researchers have successfully used operant conditioning procedures derived from research with non-human primates to assess cognitive deficits in boys whose poor language abilities, anxiety, and attention deficits would otherwise seriously detract from their test performance.

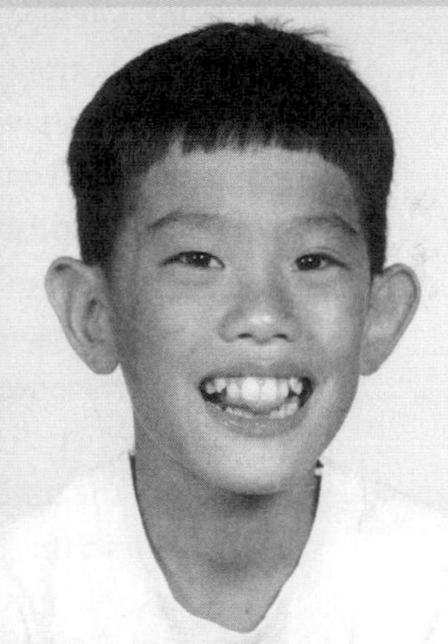

Boys with fragile X syndrome display symptoms, such as facial dysmorphia (elongated face, large ears, prominent forehead and jaw). Photograph from Jorde, L. B., Carey, J. C., Bamshad, M. J., *Medical Genetics*, Fourth Edition, Figure 5-15b, p. 96. © Copyright Elsevier 2010. Reprinted by permission.

LEARNING OBJECTIVE 3.2

Describe different types of genetic disorders and their impact on child development.

1. How are genetic disorders transmitted?
2. What are some examples of dominant and recessive genetic disorders?
3. How are X-linked disorders transmitted, and why do they affect males more than females?
4. What are some examples of X-linked disorders?
5. What are some examples of disorders caused by defects of the autosomes?
6. What are some examples of disorders caused by defects of the sex chromosomes?

Learning Objective 3.3

Describe the influence that genes have on the development of psychological abilities and traits.

STUDYING THE EFFECTS OF GENES ON BEHAVIOUR

How do researchers study the influences of genes on behaviour? People are not pea plants, and scientists are not free to mate humans of their choice to see how the offspring will turn out. Researchers have to rely on observation, experiments by nature, and careful analyses of their data. Fortunately, scientists' statistical methods and their access to large populations of research participants have come a long way since Mendel's time (Lemery & Goldsmith, 1999; Pennington, 2001).

The effects of genes on human behaviour and development in three principal areas have been studied extensively over the years: intellectual abilities, psychiatric disorders (including children's behaviour problems), and aspects of personality (including infant temperament). In this section, we present some of what psychologists have learned about genetic contributions to these areas as we examine the four major methods that have been used in their investigation: family studies, adoption studies, twin studies, and combinations of these approaches.

FAMILY STUDIES

Children inherit 50 percent of their genes from each parent. Siblings, on average, share 50 percent of their genes. Grandparent and grandchild share 25 percent, as do aunts and uncles with their nieces and nephews. The family-study approach asks whether the phenotypic similarity on some trait follows from the genotypic similarity among the people being compared. If it does, then you should be more similar to your parents or siblings than you are to an uncle or cousin, and more similar to your uncle or cousin than you are to people with whom you share no genes.

One of the earliest family studies demonstrates both the potential and the limitations of this approach. In 1912, Henry Goddard published a report that claimed to demonstrate a genetic basis for intelligence. The subject of Goddard's study was the Kallikak family. During the American Revolution, a soldier whom Goddard called Martin Kallikak (a pseudonym) had an illegitimate son by a tavern maid with intellectual disability. Later, Kallikak married a woman of normal intelligence from a respected family.

Goddard traced five generations of Kallikak's offspring from these two lines. Of the 480 or so descendants of the tavern maid, he identified many as criminal, alcoholic, or "immoral," and 25 percent as suffering from intellectual disability. In contrast, the 496 descendants from Kallikak's marriage were all intellectually normal, according to Goddard, and most occupied respected positions in their communities. Because Kallikak was the father to both family lines, Goddard concluded that the differences between them must be due to the genetic differences between his two mates. Of course, this conclusion ignored the vastly different environments and upbringing of the two lines of descendants. Distinguishing between hereditary and environmental influences is a major limitation of the family-study method. As scientists have pointed out, lots of things run in families—names, photo albums, and cake recipes, for example. Not all of these are determined by our genes.

Links to Related Material

In Chapter 10, you will learn more about how the genetic foundations of intelligence interact with environment to influence children's cognitive development.

Family studies can be of value, however. Sometimes they point out characteristics that might have a genetic component and so encourage more definitive research using one of the more rigorous methods that we discuss next. For example, family studies have shown that a number of traits, including measures of intelligence, *do* follow the pattern we would expect if genes are important; that is, close relatives are most similar, and the degree of similarity drops off as the degree of genetic overlap drops. Similarly, family studies have shown that children of mothers who have schizophrenia are about 13 times as likely as children of normal mothers to develop the disorder, and children who have siblings with schizophrenia are nine times as likely as children in general (Plomin et al., 1997a). Do findings such as these indicate an important role for the genes? Research using more sophisticated methods provides some answers.

ADOPTION STUDIES

As we have just seen, the difficulty in interpreting family studies is that either genes or environment could account for the patterns we find. The adoption-study method is designed to address this issue. Children who are living in adoptive homes are compared with their biological parents (who share their genes but not their environments) and with their adoptive parents (who share their environments but not their genes). If the correlation with one set of parents is stronger than with the other, we have a good idea of which factor makes a greater contribution to individual differences in the trait we are measuring.

Sometimes the method includes siblings, because many adoptive families go on to adopt a second child. These two children share a similar environment but none of the same genes. Their similarity in terms of whatever behaviours we choose to study can thus be compared with the similarity of biological siblings in families used for comparison. Again, differences in the correlations between the two sets of siblings could shed light on whether environment or heredity has more influence on the behaviours of interest.

A major study that employed this approach is the Colorado Adoption Project. This research, begun in 1975, is a longitudinal study of about 250 families with adopted children and, for comparison, 250 families with biological children. The children were first studied when they were infants and preschoolers, and they have been followed and studied ever since (Alarcon et al., 1999; DeFries, Plomin, & Fulker, 1994; Petrill, Plomin, DeFries, & Hewitt, 2003; Wadsworth et al., 2006).

One focus of this project has been intelligence (we discuss methods of studying intelligence again in Chapter 10). The children have been tested using a variety of different instruments on both general intellectual ability and specific cognitive skills (such as memory, vocabulary, spatial relations, and reading). The findings clearly support a role for genetic processes. Stronger correlations have been found between the scores of biological siblings than between those of adoptive siblings, and between the scores of adoptive children and their biological parents, than between the children and their adoptive parents. These findings indicate that, at least to some degree, children inherit their intellectual abilities (Cherny & Cardon, 1994; Petrill et al., 2004; Wadsworth et al., 2001, 2002, 2006).

Adoption studies also provide evidence about the origins of problems in development. For example, one study sought to explain the hostile and antisocial behaviours of a group of adolescents who had been adopted at birth (Ge et al., 1996). The hypothesis was that these behaviours could be connected to both the biological and the adoptive parents, but that both connections involved the children's genes. The researchers first showed that these adolescents were more likely to have biological parents with psychiatric disorders than were a comparison group of adopted adolescents who showed no such problems. This finding suggests, as does much other research, that some problem behaviours can be inherited (Rutter & Caesar, 1991). The researchers next showed that the troubled adolescents were also more likely to have adoptive parents who used harsh and inconsistent punishment. This apparent environmental influence also has been found many times before (Patterson, Reid, & Dishion, 1992).

Links to Related Material

In Chapter 14, you will read more about the contributions of both heredity and the family environment to the development of antisocial, aggressive behaviour in children.

What makes the study important is a third finding: a positive relation between the adoptive parents' disciplinary practices and the biological parents' history of psychiatric problems. Thus, children of parents with psychiatric problems were more likely to encounter harsh discipline from their adoptive parents. It is worth thinking for a moment about how this relation could come about. The two sets of parents, after all, have never met; why should the behaviours of one group be related to the psychological characteristics of the other? The critical link, the researchers hypothesized, was the child. Specifically, the researchers speculated that:

1. The children initially inherited their behaviour problems from their biological parents.
2. These problems then evoked responses (harsh discipline) from their adoptive parents.
3. The adoptive parents' disciplinary practices then served to maintain the children's problem behaviours.

Adoption studies have also addressed the issue of schizophrenia, described earlier. Children of schizophrenic mothers who are placed in adoptive homes are around 10 times as likely to develop schizophrenia as are either the biological children of the adoptive parents or adopted children of normal mothers (Plomin et al., 1997b). This finding suggests a major role for heredity in the development of the disease and is consistent with other research showing that psychological disorders can be inherited (Plomin & McGuffin, 2003; Rutter et al., 1990).

TWIN STUDIES

Identical or monozygotic (MZ) twins Twins who develop from a single fertilized ovum and thus inherit identical genetic material.

Fraternal or dizygotic (DZ) twins Twins who develop from separately fertilized ova and who thus are no more genetically similar than are other siblings.

Approximately 1 of every 85 births yields twins, providing investigators with an interesting opportunity to study the role of genetic similarity. Twins come in two varieties (see Figure 3.6). **Identical twins** develop from the same fertilized egg and are called monozygotic twins (MZ) (mono, "one"; zygote, "fertilized egg"). They have exactly the same genes. **Fraternal twins** develop from two different eggs and are called dizygotic twins (DZ) (di, "two"). Their genetic makeup is no more similar than that of any two children who have the same parents; on average, 50 percent of the genes of dizygotic twins are the same.

Because identical twins have exactly the same genes, comparing how similar they are allows researchers to see the contribution of heredity to a variety of traits or behaviours. However, because identical twins have been together since birth (indeed, since conception), they also tend to share an extremely similar environment. As a result, if they are similar in a particular characteristic, it is difficult to know if the similarity is due to their identical genetic make-up, their very similar

FIGURE 3.6

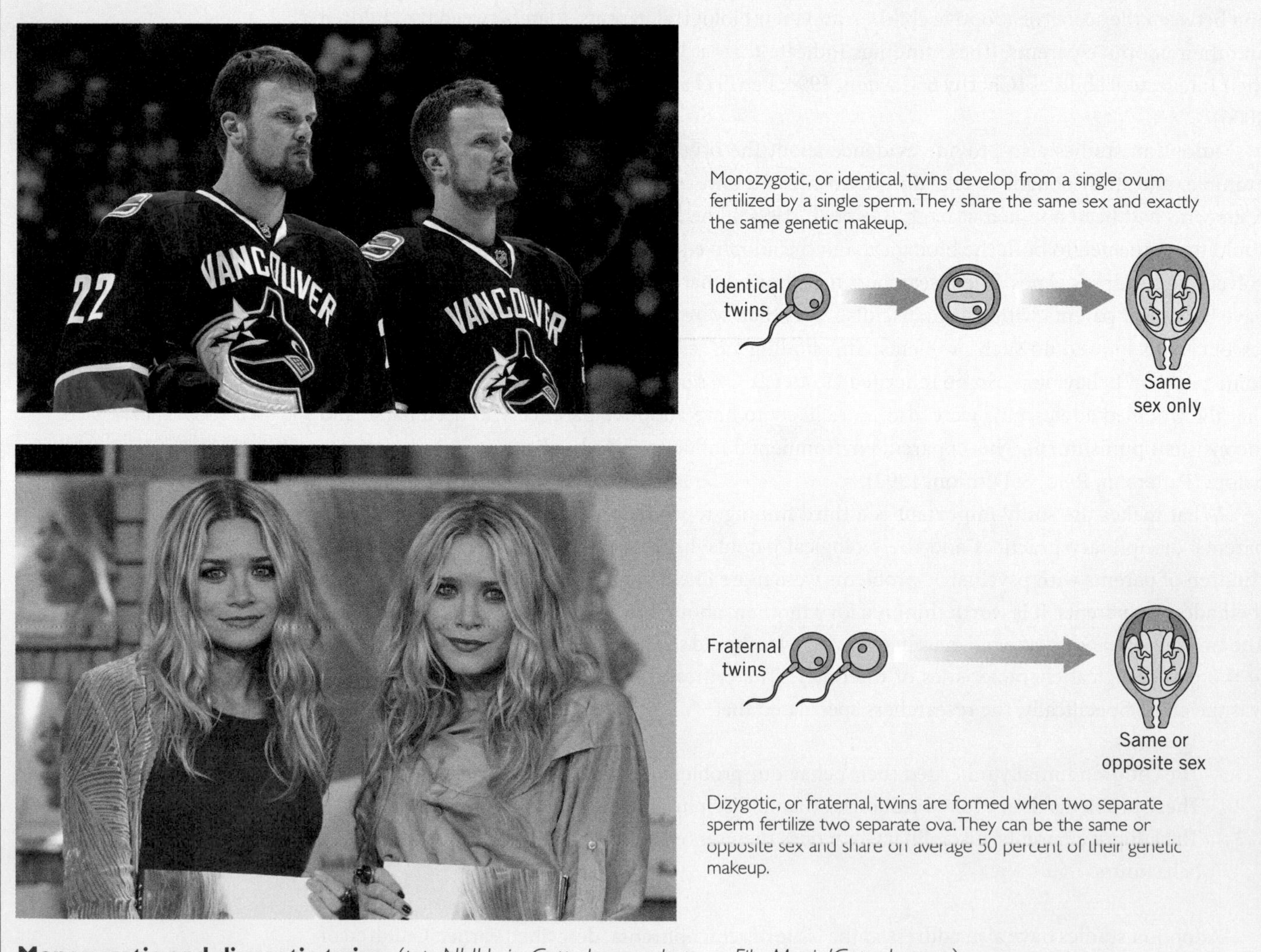
22
VANCOUVER
VANCOUVER
Monozygotic, or identical, twins develop from a single ovum fertilized by a single sperm. They share the same sex and exactly the same genetic makeup.
Identical twins
Same sex only
Fraternal twins
Same or opposite sex
Dizygotic, or fraternal, twins are formed when two separate sperm fertilize two separate ova. They can be the same or opposite sex and share on average 50 percent of their genetic makeup.

Monozygotic and dizygotic twins. *(top, NHLI via Getty Images; bottom, FilmMagic/Getty Images)*

environments, or both. Fraternal twins provide a good comparison group. The logic of the twin-study approach begins with the assumption that fraternal twins share an environment that is as similar as the environment shared by identical twins. Researchers then look at a particular trait or behaviour displayed by the sets of twins. If the trait is more similar in the identical twins than in the fraternal twins, we should be able to conclude that the greater similarity results from the greater similarity of their genes (Gregory, Ball, & Button, 2011).

Many twin studies have specifically targeted intelligence and its heritability. As shown in Table 3.3, hundreds of studies have been conducted, with virtually every one finding higher correlations between the IQ scores of MZ twins than between those of DZ twins (Bouchard & McGue, 1981; McGue et al., 1993). Clearly, intelligence—at least when measured by IQ tests—has a genetic component. In recent work with infants, whose intelligence is assessed using instruments that rely less on language and verbal abilities and more on simple motor and perceptual responses, MZ twins also showed higher correlations than did DZ twins (Cherny et al., 1994b; Wilson et al., 2001).

For Thought and Discussion

Do genes or environmental factors play the larger role in musical ability? What about athletic skill? Interpersonal skills? Why do you think so? How could you study these questions?

Twin studies have also been used to address a variety of personality issues. Many such studies have been conducted with adults and have produced some unusual findings. For example, if one identical twin experiences divorce, the chance that the other twin will experience divorce is six times that of the general population; the likelihood falls to two times the population average for a fraternal twin. Of course, there is no such thing as a divorce gene; the increase in risk for divorce is probably related to personality characteristics affected by genetic inheritance (McGue & Lykken, 1992).

An important personality area in children involves their *temperament*. Babies come into the world with a particular style of responding. Some are irritable and cry frequently; some are easy-going and smile a lot; some are active; some are cuddly; and so forth. Aspects of temperament sometimes persist well into the early school years and may eventually form the basis for some aspects of adult personality (Bates et al., 2010; Caspi & Shiner, 2006). Do genes influence temperament? Apparently they do, at least to some extent (Kagan & Fox, 2006; Rothbart & Bates, 2008). As early as 3 months of age, and throughout the first years of life, identical twins are more similar than fraternal twins on a variety of measures, including attention, activity, and involvement in testing (Braungart et al., 1992b; Emde et al., 1992; Manke, Saudino, & Grant, 2001). Researchers have looked at the trait of shyness, testing twin babies at 14 and 20 months in both the laboratory and at home. Results indicate that genes are strongly involved in this aspect of temperament at both ages and in both locations (Cherny et al., 1994a, 2001).

Links to Related Material

In Chapter 12, you will learn more about temperament, a genetically based dimension of personality evident in infancy.

TABLE 3.3 AVERAGE CORRELATIONS OF VARIOUS ABILITIES FROM SEVERAL TWIN STUDIES

		Average Correlation	
	Number of Studies	Identical Twins	Fraternal Twins
Ability			
General intelligence	30	.82	.59
Verbal comprehension	27	.78	.59
Number and mathematics	27	.78	.59
Spatial visualization	31	.65	.41
Memory	16	.52	.36
Reasoning	16	.74	.50
Clerical speed and accuracy	15	.70	.47
Verbal fluency	12	.67	.52
Divergent thinking	10	.61	.50
Language achievement	28	.81	.58
Social studies achievement	7	.85	.61
Natural science achievement	14	.79	.64
All abilities	211	.74	.54

Source: Reprinted from *Homo, 29*, R. C. Nichols, "Heredity and Environment: Major Findings from Twin Studies of Ability, Personality and Interests," Table 1, p. 163, 1978.

FIGURE 3.7

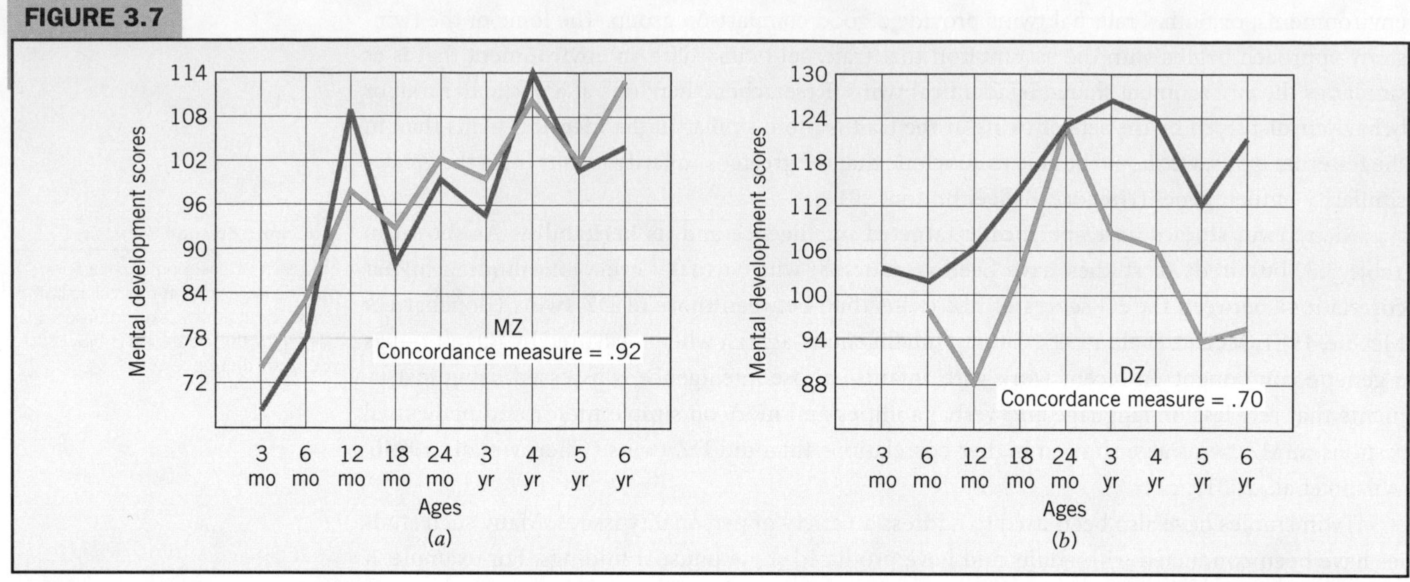

Concordance in IQ changes in (a) identical, or monozygotic (MZ), twins and (b) fraternal, or dizygotic (DZ), twins from 3 months to 6 years of age. The scales are different to accommodate different ranges of scores. The important point is that changes in performance are more similar for monozygotic twins. *Adapted from "The Louisville Twin Study: Developmental Synchronies in Behavior" by R. S. Wilson, 1983,* Child Development*, 54, p. 301. Copyright © 1983 by The Society for Research in Child Development, Inc. Adapted by permission.*

Developmental pacing The rate at which spurts and plateaus occur in an individual's physical and mental development.

Finally, behaviour geneticists have used twins to examine whether genetic influences underlie certain changes we see in children's development and behaviour. Physical development (such as height and weight) tends to occur in spurts and plateaus. The rhythm of these life events is called **developmental pacing**. Psychologists assume that developmental pacing is guided by the regulator genes, which turn the structural genes on and off at different points in development and thus control protein production. But what about similar sorts of changes in behavioural traits, such as intellectual abilities? Are they also controlled by genes? One way to address this question is to see whether identical twins show more concordance (similarity) in these changes than do fraternal twins. The evidence suggests that they do. Figure 3.7 shows the results of a study comparing the intellectual development of almost 500 pairs of identical and fraternal twins, followed from the age of 3 months to 15 years. The MZ twins clearly showed greater concordance in their shifts in performance than did the DZ twins, supporting the notion that genes direct the pacing of these abilities (Wilson, 1983, 1986).

COMBINED TWIN-STUDY AND ADOPTION-STUDY APPROACHES

There is one major problem with the twin-study approach: How do we know that a family treats a set of fraternal twins as similarly as a set of identical twins? Because identical twins look more alike, and perhaps because they know they are identical, parents and others may expect them to act the same. These expectations may influence how people behave toward the children and, as a result, may affect how the children themselves behave (Gregory et al., 2011). A method that avoids these problems involves twins who are separated early in life and raised in different adoptive homes. If genes play a role in creating individual differences in behaviour, then identical twins raised apart should still be more alike than fraternal twins raised apart. Although this combined approach is the most desirable, it also is the most difficult to use because so few twins are raised apart.

The best-known research project of this type is the Minnesota Study of Twins Reared Apart (Bouchard, 1997; Bouchard et al., 1990; Segal, 1999). The study involves 135 pairs of twins who are currently in their 50s. As with the handful of separated-twin studies that preceded it, the Minnesota Study provides strong evidence for a genetic contribution to differences in IQ. Even when reared apart, identical twins correlate substantially in IQ (Johnson, Bouchard, McGue, et al., 2007)—in fact, their average similarity is greater than that for fraternal twins growing up in the same home.

Identical twins who have been reared apart are also similar on a variety of personality characteristics, such as extroversion and neuroticism (Bouchard, 2004; Loehlin, 1992). Indeed, their similarity extends to some outcomes (for example, religious attitudes and beliefs) that we might have thought were unlikely to be affected by genes (Bouchard, 2004, 2008; Bouchard & McGue, 2003; Waller et al., 1990).

Researchers have noted one important limitation regarding combined twin and adoption studies as a means of determining the heritability of psychological abilities and traits. The major limitation is that, because of the selective placement practices followed by most agencies, the homes in which adopted children are placed tend to be relatively homogeneous (Gregory et al., 2011). For example, adopted children are generally placed in middle- or high-income families, and so the environmental effects associated with being reared in poverty are not typically included in adoption studies of twins reared apart. This fact suggests that adoption studies may underestimate environmental influences, simply by holding socioeconomic factors relatively constant across adoptive homes (Bouchard & McGue, 2003).

LEARNING OBJECTIVE 3.3

Describe the influence that genes have on the development of psychological abilities and traits.

1. How are family, adoption, and twin studies used to study the effects of genes on behaviour?
2. What do these types of studies tell us about the heritability of psychological abilities and traits?
3. What are some temperamental characteristics that are influenced by genes?

MODELS OF GENE–ENVIRONMENT INTERACTION

Learning Objective 3.4

Understand four models of how genes and environment interact to influence the development of behaviour.

When thinking about the role of genes in development, we must keep in mind an important distinction that we first discussed in Chapter 1. Recall that some psychologists focus on normative development—they are concerned with the ways in which humans are alike. Other psychologists are more interested in idiographic processes—they focus on what makes us different from one another. We can look at this issue in another way. Humans are different from other species, which are in turn different from one another. What gives a species its identity are the characteristics that all members *share*; that is, how they are alike. There is no doubt that genes are responsible for making each species unique; psychologists who study normative development are really trying to learn about humans as a species. But humans (and all other animals) also differ among themselves—not just in physical characteristics, but in behaviour and development as well. These are the individual differences of interest to psychologists who take an idiographic approach. How much of a role do genes play in these sorts of differences? This is the main question being asked today by researchers in the field of **behaviour genetics**.

Behaviour genetics The field of study that explores the role of genes in producing individual differences in behaviour and development.

All contemporary psychologists believe that genes (nature) and environment (nurture) interact to determine human behaviour, but they differ as to which factor they feel has more influence. A related and perhaps even more useful question concerns *how* genes and environment exert their effects; that is, by what processes do these factors operate and how do they interact with one another?

In this section, we examine four theoretical models that attempt to explain how genes and environment work together to determine any child's behaviour and development. Because the models are complex, we will present only their fundamental ideas. But they illustrate the increasing role that psychologists are ascribing to genetic processes as this area is becoming better understood.

GOTTESMAN'S LIMIT-SETTING MODEL

Reaction range In Gottesman's model, the term for the range of ability or skill that is set by the genes. The value achieved within this range is determined by the environment.

An early model proposed by Irving Gottesman (1974) suggested that genes interact with the environment by setting the upper and lower limits of our development. Our environment and experiences then determine where we end up in this genetically determined **reaction range.**

An example of this model drawn from the lives of people might be athletic prowess. Figure 3.8 shows the ranges of possible basketball skills that might exist for groups of children born with different genotypes representing different heights. Group A consists of children who carry a gene that makes them unusually short. Groups B and C represent typical girls and boys, respectively, who are of average height for their gender. Group D represents children who have inherited genes that make them unusually tall. Note that the reaction range (RR) of the groups varies, with the tallest individuals having the widest potential range of basketball abilities and the shortest having the narrowest. The graph also includes three levels of environment: restricted (where perhaps the child has no exposure to basketball at all), natural (the environment of a youngster growing up in a typical North American town), and enriched (such as when the child's father is a basketball coach).

Note how genes and environment interact in this model. Genes have set the limits on potential basketball skills, such that very short children (Group A) will not become proficient at these skills regardless of their environment, whereas very tall children (Group D) have the greatest opportunity to benefit from a more supportive environment. But it is important to note also that the reaction ranges overlap. This means that either poor genes or a poor environment can be somewhat overcome by strength in the other. This model, of course, could be applied to many other behaviours and abilities, such as mathematics performance, musical ability, or any number of traits or skills.

SCARR'S NICHE-PICKING MODEL

Behavioural geneticist Sandra Scarr has proposed that genes play a much more active role in development than simply setting limits within which the environment can operate (Scarr, 1992, 1993; Scarr & McCartney, 1983). In Scarr's model, genes actually play a role in determining the kind of environment the child experiences.

The traditional view in psychology has been that different family environments cause children to develop in different ways. For example, we know that children whose parents provide books,

FIGURE 3.8

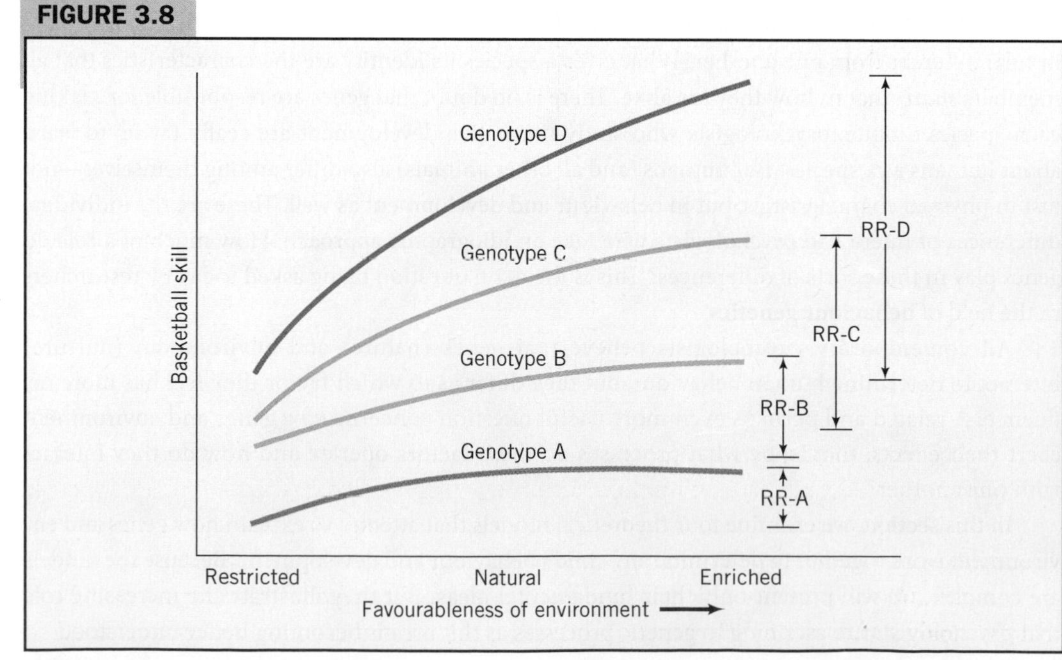

The reaction range concept, showing the simultaneous influences of genes and environment. *Adapted from "Developmental Genetics and Ontogenetic Psychology: Overdue Détente and Propositions from a Matchmaker" by I. I. Gottesman, 1974. In A. D. Pick (Ed.),* Minnesota Symposia on Child Psychology, *vol. 8, p. 60, University of Minnesota Press. Copyright © 1974 by the University of Minnesota. Adapted by permission.*

educational activities, and encouragement to succeed tend to perform well in school, and children whose parents are harsh and punitive are more likely to be aggressive and to display various other behaviour problems. The child's developmental outcome, therefore, was assumed to be rather directly determined by the child's family environment.

FIGURE 3.9

Genotype parent → Genotype child
Genotype parent → Environment child
Genotype child → Environment child
Genotype child → Phenotype child
Environment child ⇄ Phenotype child

Scarr's model of the reciprocal influence between environments and genes. The child's genotype is important not only as a direct contributor to the child's phenotype; it is also one determinant of the environment the child experiences. *Adapted from "How People Make Their Own Environments: A Theory of Genotype-Environment Effects" by S. Scarr & K. McCartney,* Child Development, 54, *p. 425. Copyright © 1983 by the Society for Research in Child Development. Adapted by permission.*

Scarr disagrees with this view. Her model invokes an important idea discussed in Chapter 1, namely that children play a role in producing their own environments. This, she proposes, occurs through the genes. (Figure 3.9 provides a schematic summary of the model.) Consider the family example again. Although parents do provide children with their family environment, they also provide them with their genes. The child's genes, in turn, operate to produce a correlation between the child's genotype and the child's environment; that is, they ensure that both genes and environment push development in the same direction. They do so in three different ways, which Scarr believes change in relative importance as the child grows from infancy to adolescence.

During infancy, genes exert their influence principally through a **passive gene–environment correlation**. The baby's environment is almost entirely dictated by the parents, but because the parents and child share so many of the same genes, the environment they create is usually very consistent with, and supportive of, the child's genotype. For example, musically inclined parents are likely both to give birth to musically inclined children and to provide a musical home environment for them.

Passive gene–environment correlation Situation in which genes and environment affect development similarly because the genes the child receives from the parents are compatible with the environment the parents provide.

As children get older, their genes become more likely to produce an **evocative gene–environment correlation**. Children now do things that evoke certain responses from their parents and others (recall Bronfenbrenner's notion of developmentally generative and developmentally disruptive behaviours, presented in Chapter 1). For example, a child who speaks and reads early—behaviours that likely have some genetic basis—may prompt parents to provide a rich language environment, including books, storytelling, and educational games. In this way, the child's genes help create an environment that is compatible with the child's genetically set predispositions.

Evocative gene–environment correlation Situation in which genes and environment affect development similarly because genetically set predispositions of the child elicit compatible experiences from the environment.

According to Scarr and McCartney's model, niche picking occurs when children choose environments that reflect and support their genetic predispositions. (*left © JoseGirarte/iStock; right © Carmen Martínez Banús/iStock*)

For Thought and Discussion

Are you aware of "niche-picking" during your childhood or in your life now? To what extent do you seek out environments that best fit your genetic predispositions?

Finally, as children gain more independence, their genes can operate through a more **active gene–environment correlation** to produce environments that suit them. Children, on their own, can seek out the particular environments, or *niches*, that best fit their interests and talents—such as the library, gym, or rock concert.

Active gene–environment correlation Situation in which genes and environment affect development similarly because children seek out experiences that are compatible with their genetic predispositions.

Scarr's model of gene–environment interaction does not ignore the importance of the child's family environment. However, it views the environment less as a direct cause of the child's development and more as a vehicle that enables the genes to guide the child along a particular developmental path. Scarr contends that genetic influences actually grow stronger with age, as children become better able to actively recruit the environments their genes bias them toward. This prediction runs counter to the traditional view that genes start us off in a particular direction and then our environment more or less takes over. As we will see shortly, there is some striking evidence in support of Scarr's prediction.

PLOMIN'S ENVIRONMENTAL GENETICS MODEL

A third model of gene–environment interaction has been presented by Robert Plomin (2000, 2004; Plomin & Asbury, 2005; Plomin, DeFries, McLearn, & McGuffin, 2008). His approach shares many of the same ideas as Scarr's model. He believes that children's developmental outcomes are related to their family environments for two reasons:

1. Children share many genes with their parents, who in turn provide the environment for their children.
2. Children evoke from their parents the sorts of responses and surroundings that suit their genes.

Plomin has gone so far as to refer to his work as *environmental genetics*, which means the study of how our genes influence our environments. Further, his model is not limited to parent–child interactions, but also extends to other family members (Plomin et al., 1994).

Non-shared environment A concept used in behaviour genetics to refer to presumed aspects of the environment that children experience differently.

The most important addition in Plomin's model is the concept of **non-shared environment** (Plomin, 2004; Plomin & Asbury, 2005; Plomin et al., 2001; Reiss et al., 2000). This idea is most easily understood in terms of siblings. We know that children reared in the same family have many similarities. Psychologists have not been surprised to find that intelligence, physical abilities, personality, and other characteristics are generally more similar between brothers and sisters than they are between unrelated children. These similarities have always been assumed to result from siblings' sharing both many of the same genes (around 50 percent) and the same family environment. Given these two major sources of similarity, a more interesting question becomes: Why do many siblings behave and develop so differently from one another?

For Thought and Discussion

In what ways did you and your siblings live in a non-shared environment? How do you think your experiences and your siblings' experiences contributed to differences in your development? How might the experiences you provide your children lead them down different life paths?

Plomin's answer is that although these children live in the same family, they do not necessarily experience the same environments. Rather, parents often treat children differently from one another, and children frequently react to the same family events and experiences in different ways. Moreover, the source of both these differences, Plomin believes, is genetic. His argument is that although 50 percent of siblings' genes are the same, 50 percent are also different. These different genes, Plomin contends, lead siblings to evoke different treatment from their parents and to respond in different ways to the same events. In short, the aspects of the family environment that they experience differently—the non-shared aspects—are what make siblings different from one another.

What about siblings' similarities? Perhaps the most controversial aspect of this model is that, like Scarr and other behaviour geneticists, Plomin believes that the similarities we see in siblings result mostly from their genetic similarity (the 50 percent of the genes they share). Their common family environment, by contrast, is thought to contribute very little to explaining why they are alike.

What sort of evidence might support such a position? Two findings from adoption studies provide the strongest support (Plomin & Asbury, 2005; Turkheimer & Waldron, 2000). First, adoptive siblings (that is, unrelated children growing up in the same home) are considerably less similar across a range of measures than are biologically related siblings. This finding suggests that sharing a common environment is not enough to make siblings alike; rather, the typical similarity between siblings apparently results from their shared genes. Second, adoptive siblings are more similar to one another in early childhood than they are by the time they reach adolescence, even though by adolescence they have had many more years of living together in the same home. Thus, the family environment apparently operates to make siblings different, not the same.

A further finding from adoption studies is relevant to both Scarr's and Plomin's models. With age, the psychological characteristics of an adopted child become increasingly similar to those of the biological mother and less similar to those of the adoptive mother. We might, of course, have expected the reverse: that the influence of the adoptive mother would grow with the years that she and the child spend together. Instead, it is the genes that grow in importance as children get older. This finding does not mean that the environment has become unimportant. Rather, the pattern presumably occurs because parents generally control children's environments at younger ages, but as children grow older they are increasingly able to choose their own environments and experiences—Scarr's niche picking—thus permitting their genes to operate in a more active way to influence their development (Plomin, 2004; Plomin et al., 1997b).

BRONFENBRENNER AND CECI'S BIOECOLOGICAL MODEL

The most recent and perhaps most complex of the models we will consider is that of Urie Bronfenbrenner and Stephen Ceci (Bronfenbrenner, 1999; Bronfenbrenner & Ceci, 1994; Bronfenbrenner & Morris, 2006). This model derives from Bronfenbrenner's ecological approach described in Chapter 1. We will see shortly why the researchers call it a *bioecological model.*

Bronfenbrenner and Ceci assign much more importance to the environment than do many behaviour geneticists. They agree with the idea that children's genes influence their development and that, to some degree, they do so by steering the environment in the right direction. But the bioecological model adds a more explicit description of how and when this occurs.

According to this analysis, genes can only exert their influence when certain experiences activate them. These experiences, called **proximal processes**, are interactions between the child and the child's direct-contact (microsystem) world—parents, siblings, toys, books, pets, and anything else of significance in the child's immediate environment—that have a positive effect on the child's psychological functioning. Such interactions may involve, for example, play with siblings, social activities with friends, reading and problem solving with parents, and other sorts of stimulating experiences. An additional requirement is that these interactions must take place fairly regularly and must continue for some time. When these requirements hold, the child's genes are able to use the experiences to achieve their ends, and, as a result, the child reaches his or her maximum genetic potential. But if proximal processes are weak or missing in the child's life, the genes cannot fully express themselves, and so the child's development will remain below what it could have been.

Proximal processes Bronfenbrenner and Ceci's term for interactions between the child and aspects of the microsystem that have positive effects on psychological functioning and that help maximize expression of the child's genetic potential.

Bronfenbrenner and Ceci also believe that proximal processes are valuable to the child in both high- and lower-quality environments, but in different ways. When the environment is stable and rich with resources—as is the case in many middle-income households—these interactions have the best opportunity to help children develop their fullest abilities (such as the example of musical talent described earlier). When the child's environment is disorganized and disadvantaged—as in many poor neighbourhoods—proximal processes can help prevent undesirable outcomes that might otherwise have occurred (such as aggression, violence, or other problem behaviours to which genes may have predisposed the child).

Note how the child's biology (genes) and ecology (immediate environment) contribute more equally and in greater interaction in this model than in either the more strongly genetic or strongly environmental approaches. Perhaps for this reason, Bronfenbrenner and Ceci use the term *bioecological* to describe it.

LEARNING OBJECTIVE 3.4

Understand four models of how genes and environment interact to influence the development of behaviour.

1. What is meant by the range of reaction? What does it tell us about the interaction of genes and environment?
2. What are three types of gene–environment correlations?
3. What is meant by non-shared environment?
4. What role do proximal processes play in development?

CONCLUSION

There is probably no topic in this book for which the recent gains in knowledge have been as great as for genetics. Much of what we have presented in this chapter is very new. There seems little doubt that many additional discoveries will soon be forthcoming. What conclusions can be taken away from all this work?

A first conclusion is that genetic processes reach into many more areas of development than we once believed. One researcher summarizes this conclusion succinctly: "Everything is heritable" (Turkheimer, 2000, p. 160). This does not mean, of course, that any human psychological trait is totally genetic in origin. But it does mean that genes have been shown to play some role for virtually every psychological outcome of interest that has been the subject of behaviour genetics research—whether the domain be cognitive abilities, personality attributes, or psychiatric problems.

A second conclusion concerns the question of greatest interest to the psychologist: *How* do genes exert their effects? Until recently, knowledge of specific genes and specific genetic mechanisms was limited to the case of disorders—identifying the gene for Huntington's disease, for example, or the chromosomal abnormality in the case of Down syndrome. This is no longer the case. Recent years have seen reports of specific genes that contribute to a wide range of important outcomes in human development; a partial list includes intelligence, language, aggression, neuroticism, dyslexia, and sensation seeking. With the success of the Human Genome Project, knowledge of specific genes for specific outcomes seems certain to grow.

A third conclusion is perhaps the most important, and it is that genes will never be the whole story. The same data from behaviour genetics studies that tell us that genes are important also tell us that genes are not all-important—at best, genes account for about half the variation in particular outcomes, meaning that environment accounts for at least half. Furthermore, a grounding in the genetics of disorders can be misleading when we think about how specific genes contribute to psychological outcomes. As Plomin (2000, p. 235) puts it, "If you inherit the Huntington's disease allele, you will die from the disease regardless of your other genes or your environment." Outcomes such as language or aggression, however, are not determined by a single gene; rather, there are multiple genes (perhaps thousands in the case of a complex trait like intelligence) that are relevant. The effect of any gene depends on the genotype as a whole, and the expression of the genes depends on an environmental context. The eventual phenotype—whether it be height, weight, intelligence, or personality—always depends on the environment as well as the genes.

This last point can serve as a conclusion not just for this chapter, but for the book as a whole. If there is one message that you should take away from this course, it is this: At every point in development, genes and environment work together to determine each and every aspect of our behaviour.

SUMMARY

KEY TERMS

active gene–environment correlation, p. 89
alleles, p. 71
autosomes, p. 68
base pairs, p. 70
behaviour genetics, p. 87
chromosomes, p. 68
codominance, p. 73
crossing over, p. 70
deoxyribonucleic acid (DNA), p. 70
intellectual disability, p. 76
developmental pacing, p. 86
dominant gene, p. 73
evocative gene–environment correlation, p. 89
fraternal or dizygotic (DZ) twins, p. 84
gene, p. 70

genomic imprinting, p. 73
genotype, p. 72
identical or monozygotic (MZ) twins, p. 84
incomplete dominance, p. 73
meiosis, p. 70
mitosis, p. 69
non-shared environment, p. 90
passive gene–environment correlation, p. 89
phenotype, p. 72
polygenic inheritance, p. 73
proximal processes, p. 91
reaction range, p. 88
recessive gene, p. 73
sex chromosomes, p. 68
X-linked disorders, p. 77

LEARNING OBJECTIVES

LEARNING OBJECTIVE 3.1 Identify and describe the mechanisms and processes by which physical and behavioural characteristics are inherited.

1. *What are chromosomes, where are they in the body, and what do they do?*
   Inside the cell's nucleus, the body's genetic material (DNA) is organized into chemical strands called chromosomes. In humans, each cell nucleus contains 23 pairs of chromosomes, one from the father and the other from the mother. The members of these pairs are similar to one another and carry the same genes in the same location. The 23rd pair makes up the sex chromosomes. When the pair consists of two X chromosomes (XX), the person is female. When it consists of one of each type (XY), the person is male.

2. *How do cells reproduce in a way that makes every individual genetically unique?*
   Cell reproduction is the most fundamental genetic process that takes place in our bodies. Through a process called meiosis, cells divide to form gametes—the sperm or ova that will combine at conception to form a new individual. In an additional process called crossing over, the chromosome partners share genetic material. When the entire process is complete, the resulting four gametes each possess 23 chromosomes and are genetically unique. The gamete now represents a one-of-a-kind combination of genetic material. When a gamete containing 23 chromosomes from one parent combines with a gamete containing 23 chromosomes from the other parent, the result is a genetically unique individual.

3. *What is DNA and how does it combine to create genes?*
   Deoxyribonucleic acid (DNA) is the carrier of genetic information inside the chromosome. The DNA molecule has the structure of a double helix, much like the sides of a spiral staircase joined by rungs. The rungs consist of four bases (nucleotides): adenine (A), thymine (T), guanine (G), and cytosine (C). The sequence of how these rungs link together determines the coded information carried by the gene.

4. *What facts and principles of inheritance did Mendel discover?*
   From experimenting with pea plants, Mendel developed a theory that each observable trait, such as colour of flowers, requires two elements—one inherited from each parent. These two elements are a pair of genes (alleles). The expressed or observable trait is called the phenotype, and the underlying genes, the genotype. The principle of dominance states that when either gene is dominant, the dominant characteristic is expressed. Only when both genes are recessive are recessive characteristics expressed. The principle of segregation states that each inheritable trait is passed on to the offspring as a separate unit. The principle of independent assortment states that traits are passed on independently of one another.

5. *What are some principles of inheritance that researchers have uncovered since Mendel?*
   First, single traits, including behavioural traits, are often the product of more than one pair of genes, a process known as polygenic inheritance. Second, some traits result from genes

that display incomplete dominance; they are neither entirely dominant nor entirely recessive. Third, in some cases both genes of a trait are dominant, referred to as codominance; therefore, both characteristics are expressed completely. Fourth, genomic imprinting describes instances in which a trait does not follow the usual laws of inheritance. The alleles for the trait are biochemically marked such that one of them is imprinted or silenced, and only the other allele affects the phenotype.

LEARNING OBJECTIVE 3.2 Describe different types of genetic disorders and their impact on child development.

1. *How are genetic disorders transmitted?*
   Whether or not defective genes are expressed in the phenotype depends on whether they are dominant or recessive. If a defective gene inherited from the parent is recessive, the dominant (and usually normal) allele from the other parent can prevent the problem. However, the problem gene still exists in the genotype and will be transmitted to half the person's offspring. Most of the offspring will be unaffected, but those who receive the defective gene from both parents will develop the disorder.

2. *What are some examples of dominant and recessive genetic disorders?*
   Dominant genes that cause severe problems typically disappear from the species, because the people affected do not live to reproduce. In some cases, severely disabling dominant genes are passed on because they do not become active until relatively late in life; people with these genes may reproduce before they know that they have inherited the disease. Huntington's disease and neurofibromatosis are examples of dominant genetic disorders. It is also possible to carry potentially lethal genes as recessive traits, but because most of these dangerous genes are rare, it is unlikely that we will mate with someone who has a matching recessive gene. Even then, the possibility that a child will receive both recessive genes is only one in four. Examples of disorders caused by recessive genes are Tay-Sachs disease, phenylketonuria, and sickle-cell anemia.

3. *How are X-linked disorders transmitted, and why do they affect males more than females?*
   The Y chromosome is much smaller than the X chromosome and carries much less genetic information. Some genes found on the X chromosome do not have a corresponding allele on the Y chromosome. For a female, if there is a recessive allele on one X chromosome, the corresponding allele on the other X chromosome may override its expression. Males have no such protection, and are therefore more vulnerable than females to recessive disorders that travel only on the X chromosome.

4. *What are some examples of X-linked disorders?*
   Hemophilia, Duchenne muscular dystrophy, red-green colour blindness, and fragile X syndrome are examples of X-linked disorders.

5. *What are some examples of disorders caused by defects of the autosomes?*
   Genetically based problems may result from defects in the chromosomes. These defects often occur during meiosis in one of the parents and can involve certain of the 22 autosomes. Down syndrome (trisomy-21) is the result of an extra chromosome at the 21st pair. Cri du chat syndrome is the result of the deletion of material from chromosome 5.

6. *What are some examples of disorders caused by defects of the sex chromosomes?*
   In Turner's syndrome the child has only one X chromosome. Although the child is female, her ovaries will not produce the hormones necessary for the sex differentiation process

to continue. Klinefelter's syndrome occurs when a male inherits an extra X chromosome (XXY). The presence of the Y chromosome causes the child to be male; however, male hormone levels are low and the child is somewhat feminized. A third chromosomal abnormality occurs when the sperm provides two Y chromosomes. The XYY males produced when this occurs have large body builds and masculine personality characteristics. The most common disorder of the sex chromosomes is fragile X syndrome, caused by an abnormal gene on the X chromosome, causing intellectual disability. Boys are more often affected than girls.

LEARNING OBJECTIVE 3.3 Describe the influence that genes have on the development of psychological abilities and traits.

1. *How are family, adoption, and twin studies used to study the effects of genes on behaviour?*
   The family-study approach asks whether the phenotypic similarity on some trait follows from the genotypic similarity among the people being compared. Close relatives should be most similar, and the degree of similarity declines as the degree of genetic similarity decreases. Therefore, you should be more similar to your parents or siblings than to an uncle or cousin. In adoption studies, children who live in adoptive homes are compared with their biological parents (who share their genes but not their environments) and their adoptive parents (who share their environments but not their genes). Adoption studies help separate the contributions of genes and environment to individual differences in the trait we are measuring. Sometimes this method includes siblings as well; differences between adoptive and biological siblings can shed light on the influence of heredity and the environment. Identical twins share 100 percent of their genes, while fraternal twins share 50 percent. If a trait is more similar in identical than in fraternal twins, the similarity results from their more similar genes. Twin studies also examine identical and fraternal twins reared apart.

2. *What do these types of studies tell us about the heritability of psychological abilities and traits?*
   In three areas in particular—intellectual performance, personality, and psychiatric disorders—genetic processes have been shown to play a significant (although never all-important) role. The relevant evidence includes the similarity of adoptive children to their biological parents and the strong similarity between pairs of identical twins, even when the twins have been separated and reared in different environments.

3. *What are some temperamental characteristics that are influenced by genes?*
   Twin studies suggest that aspects of temperament such as attention, activity, involvement in testing, extroversion, and shyness are genetically influenced.

LEARNING OBJECTIVE 3.4 Understand four models of how genes and environment interact to influence the development of behaviour.

1. *What is meant by the range of reaction? What does it tell us about the interaction of genes and environment?*
   Gottesman's limit-setting model suggests that genes interact with the environment by setting the upper and lower limits of our development. Our environment and experiences then determine where we fall within this reaction range.

2. *What are three types of gene–environment correlations?*
   Scarr's niche-picking model describes the reciprocal influence between environments and genes. During infancy, genes exert their influence principally through a passive gene–environment correlation, where the baby's environment is almost entirely dictated by the parents. As children get older, they do things that evoke certain responses from their parents and others: an evocative

gene–environment correlation. Finally, as children gain more independence they can seek out niches that best fit their abilities: an active gene–environment correlation.

3. *What is meant by non-shared environment?*
   The non-shared environment is an important component of Plomin's environmental genetics model. The notion emphasizes how the environment operates to make the children within a family different. Although 50 percent of siblings' genes are the same, 50 percent are also different. These different genes can evoke different treatment from parents and can also lead children to experience their environment differently—non-shared aspects of the environment that can make siblings different from one another.

4. *What role do proximal processes play in development?*
   According to Bronfenbrenner and Ceci's bioecological model, genes can only exert their influence when certain experiences activate them. These experiences are referred to as proximal processes and reflect the child's direct and continued contact with things of significance in the immediate environment.

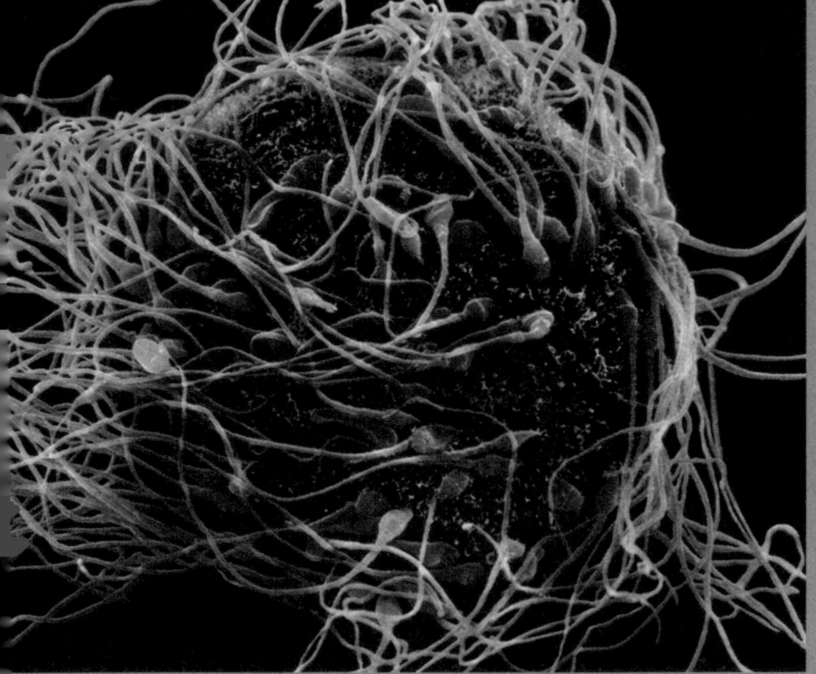

CHAPTER 4

PRENATAL DEVELOPMENT

Thankfully, most babies are born healthy, but their complex development in the womb can sometimes go wrong. A fetus can be affected by myriad factors, including the mother's consumption of alcohol, which could cause her baby to be born with fetal alcohol syndrome (FAS). FAS children show unique facial characteristics, such as a short nose and thin upper lip. More problematic, however, are the cognitive problems that FAS children can have, such as poor memory, disorganization, and being easily distracted.

FAS children can also exhibit behavioural problems, which if left undiagnosed and untreated can have disastrous consequences. As teens and adults, they can get into trouble with the law. A Canadian study estimated that young people with fetal alcohol spectrum disorder or FASD (showing some but not necessarily all of the FAS symptoms) are 19 times more likely to be in jail or prison than youths without FASD. The researchers, with the Centre for Addiction and Mental Health in Toronto, point out that there is an even higher estimated number of prisoners who have FAS but remain undiagnosed.

The Canadian legal community is responding by training more police officers, lawyers, social workers, corrections officers, court workers, and judges to recognize signs of FASD. "Law enforcement officers must be aware of FASD, its characteristics and behaviours," says former RCMP Commissioner Giuliano Zaccardelli. "This is necessary so they can identify and deal effectively and appropriately with clients who come into contact with the law as victims, suspects or witnesses."

In this chapter we will look at the stages of prenatal development, some of the factors that can adversely affect this development, and promising advances in treatment and prevention of the causes of developmental damage.

Source: Public Health Agency of Canada, *An inventory of education and training programs: FASD and the judicial/criminal justice system*, Ottawa: Author, 2011.

Royal Canadian Mounted Police, *Fetal alcohol spectrum disorder: FASD guidebook for police officers*, Ottawa: Author, no date.

Popova, S., Lange, S., Bekmuradov, D., Mihic, A., and Rehm, J., "Fetal alcohol spectrum disorder prevalence estimates in correctional systems: a systematic literature review," *Canadian Journal of Public Health*, September-October 2011, pp. 336–40. ■

FIGURE 4.1

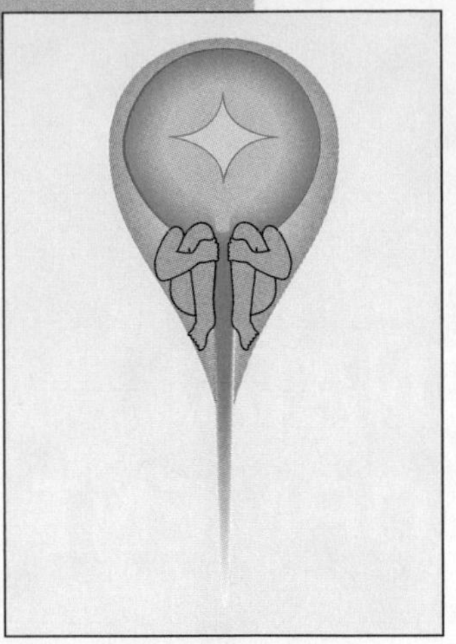

Copy of a 17th-century drawing of a sperm. The miniature human was thought to enlarge after entering the ovum.

WHEN WE CONSIDER the course of a child's life, the nine months between conception and birth may be the most unappreciated period of development. This is probably because the events that occur during this time are largely hidden from view. Yet during these nine months, what begins as a microscopic fertilized egg undergoes a series of dramatic changes and eventually emerges as a living, breathing baby.

You can probably imagine how people from ancient cultures must have struggled to explain how a fully-formed creature could appear at birth. As late as the 18th century, some believed that people were completely formed even before conception. One theory, preformationism, proposed that each sperm cell contained a tiny individual (called a homunculus), like the one shown in Figure 4.1, who would grow when deposited in a woman's womb. Another version of the theory held that the fully formed baby resided instead in the ovum (Needham, 1959).

More than 100 years ago, a Swiss zoologist peering through a microscope became the first person to see a sperm enter an egg, fertilize it, and produce the cell for a new embryo. Such discoveries led to our current understanding of fertilization and prenatal development (Touchette, 1990). This understanding also includes knowledge about factors that impair development, such as genetic defects, infections, drugs, and environmental poisons.

Learning Objective 4.1

Trace the changes that occur in the three stages of prenatal development.

STAGES OF PRENATAL DEVELOPMENT

Even though it is the largest cell in the body, the ovum is no larger than the period at the end of this sentence, and the sperm cell that fertilizes it weighs less than 1/30,000 as much. Nevertheless, in only nine months this tiny genetic package grows into a baby whose mass is billions of times greater.

Every stage of development along the journey from conception to birth represents a mix of the influences of nature and nurture. Even the genetic material that the mother and father contribute to the offspring can be affected by environmental factors, such as radiation. Other environmental factors, such as nutrition, infections, and drugs, can also influence development. In this section, we follow the baby's prenatal development through three stages, or periods: the period of the zygote, the period of the embryo, and the period of the fetus. First we consider the starting point of development—conception.

CONCEPTION

Conception The combining of the genetic material from a male gamete (sperm) and a female gamete (ovum); fertilization.

Zygote A fertilized ovum.

Prenatal development begins at **conception**, or fertilization, when a sperm unites with an ovum (egg) to form a single cell, called a **zygote**. The zygote receives 23 chromosomes from the mother and 23 from the father, to form a new and genetically unique person.

Once every 28 or so days, about halfway through a woman's menstrual cycle, an ovum is produced by either her left or right ovary (they alternate each month) and begins to travel through the fallopian tube toward the uterus, which at this point is only about the size of a plum. For the next 24 hours, the ovum is capable of being fertilized. Sperm from the male, which are deposited in the vagina, remain viable for two to three days. This time is crucial because their longer journey takes them through the cervix and the uterus before entering the fallopian tube, where the ovum is located. Of the several million sperm that are typically deposited, only 100 to 200 of the strongest and healthiest make it all the way to the ovum, and only one actually penetrates the wall to fertilize the ovum. Within about an hour of penetration, the genetic material from the sperm and the ovum have completely merged to form a zygote, and development of the baby begins.

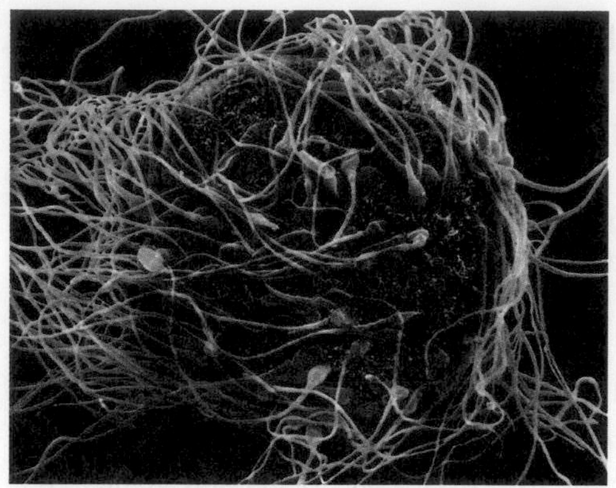

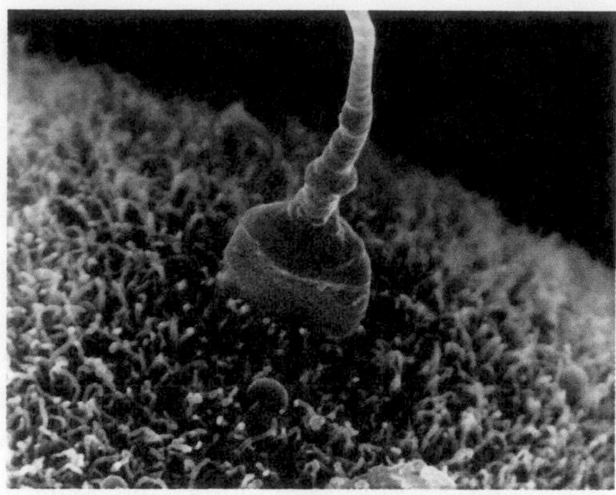

Although hundreds of sperm reach the ovum, only one actually penetrates its wall and fertilizes it. Once fertilized, rapid chemical changes make the outer layer of the egg cell impenetrable to other sperm cells. (*David M. Phillips/Photo Researchers, Inc.*)

THE PERIOD OF THE ZYGOTE (CONCEPTION TO SECOND WEEK)

The zygote multiplies rapidly as it continues its four-day, 10-centimetre journey through the fallopian tube to the uterus. At first the zygote is a solid mass of cells, but it gradually changes into a hollow sphere as it prepares to implant into the wall of the uterus. Now the cells begin to specialize, some forming an inner cell mass that will become the embryo, and some forming important structures that will support the embryo's development. Figure 4.2 illustrates the events of the first week of human development.

Implantation takes about a week. During this time, the zygote settles into the blood-enriched lining of the uterus, where it will remain attached for the duration of the pregnancy. The period of the zygote ends about two weeks after fertilization, which corresponds to the first missed menstrual period. By the time a woman suspects she may be pregnant, prenatal development is well underway.

FIGURE 4.2

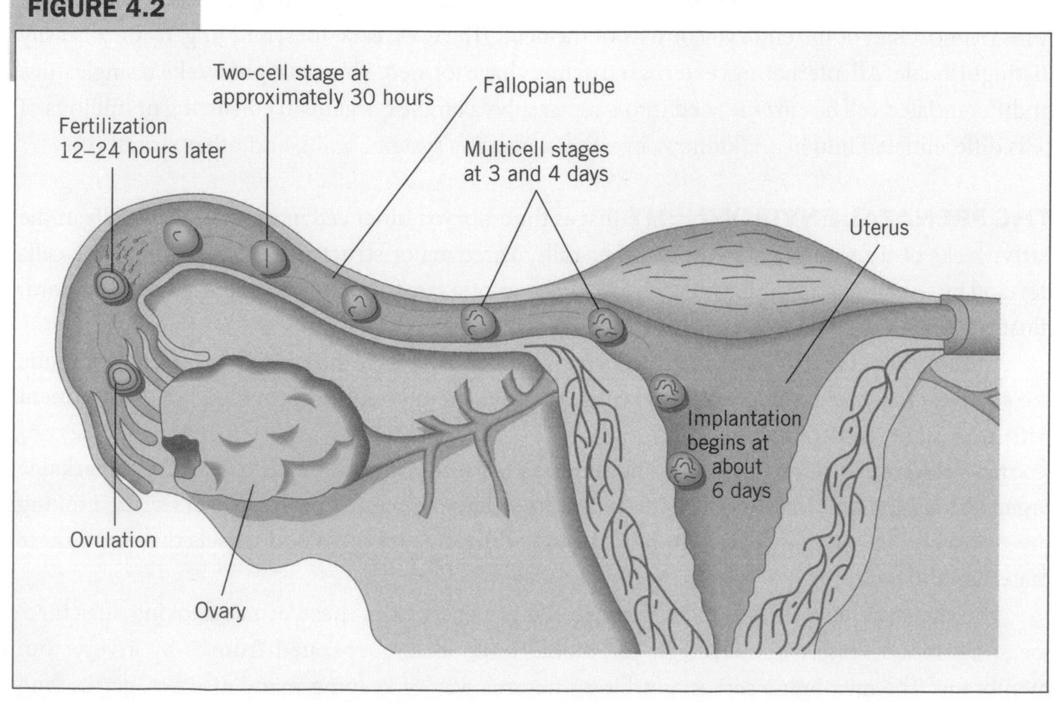

Schematic representation of the events of the first week of human development.

THE PERIOD OF THE EMBRYO (THIRD TO EIGHTH WEEK)

Embryo The developing organism from the third week, when implantation is complete, through the eighth week after conception.

The period of the **embryo** begins when implantation is complete and lasts for around six weeks. Although the embryo at first is only the size of an apple seed, all major internal and external structures form during this period. For that reason, these weeks are the most delicate of the pregnancy and the time when the growing embryo is most vulnerable to threats from both the internal and external environments (which will be discussed shortly).

FIGURE 4.3

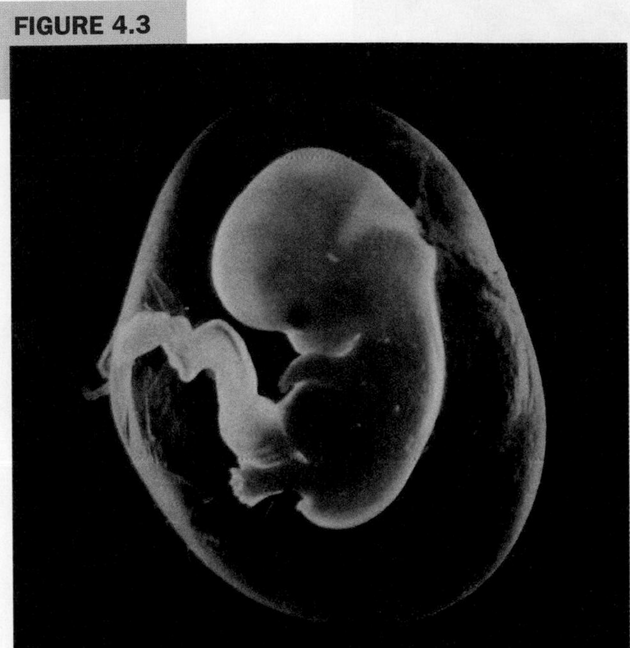

By the time the embryo has reached eight weeks, its mass has increased a staggering 2 million percent. *(Dr. M.A. Ansary/Photo Researchers, Inc.)*

In the third week, the inner cell mass differentiates into three layers from which all body structures will emerge. Two layers form first—the *endodermal* layer and the *ectodermal* layer. The endodermal cells will develop into internal organs and glands. The ectodermal cells become the parts of the body that maintain contact with the outside world—the nervous system; the sensory parts of the eyes, nose, and ears; skin; and hair. The third cell layer then appears between the endodermal and ectodermal layers. This is the *mesodermal* layer, which will give rise to muscles, cartilage, bone, sex organs, and the heart. The heart is beating by the end of the third week.

Around the beginning of the fourth week, the embryo looks something like a tiny tube. The shape of the embryo gradually changes, however, because cell multiplication is more rapid in some locations than in others. By the end of the fourth week, the embryo assumes a curved form. We can distinguish a bump below the head, which is the primitive heart, and the upper and lower limbs, which have just begun to form as tiny buds.

The embryo's body changes less in the fifth week, but the head and brain develop rapidly. The upper limbs form, and the lower limbs appear and look like small paddles. In the sixth week, the head continues to grow rapidly and differentiation of the limbs occurs, as elbows, fingers, and wrists become recognizable. It is now possible to discern the ears and eyes. The limbs develop rapidly in the seventh week, and stumps appear that will form fingers and toes.

For Thought and Discussion

The embryo stage is the most vulnerable time for prenatal development, but this is three to eight weeks after conception when women often do not realize they are pregnant. What are the implications of this fact for sexually active women?

By the end of the eighth week, as shown in Figure 4.3, the embryo has distinctly human features. Almost half of the embryo consists of the head. The eyes, ears, toes, and fingers are all easily distinguishable. All internal and external structures have formed. Thus, in eight weeks, a single, tiny, undifferentiated cell has proliferated into a remarkably complex organism consisting of millions of cells differentiated into heart, kidneys, eyes, ears, nervous system, brain, and other structures.

THE PRENATAL ENVIRONMENT Just as the embryo's inner cell mass changes rapidly in the early weeks of development, so do its other cells. Three major structures arising from these cells develop by the end of the embryonic period: the amniotic sac, the placenta, and the umbilical cord, illustrated in Figure 4.4.

Amniotic sac A fluid-containing watertight membrane that surrounds and protects the embryo or fetus.

Placenta An organ that forms where the embryo attaches to the uterus. This organ exchanges nutrients, oxygen, and wastes between the embryo or fetus and the mother, through a very thin membrane that does not allow the passage of blood.

Umbilical cord A soft cable of tissue and blood vessels that connects the fetus to the placenta.

The **amniotic sac** is a watertight membrane filled with fluid. As the embryo grows, the amniotic sac surrounds it, cushioning and supporting it within the uterus, and providing an environment with a constant temperature.

The **placenta**, formed from both the mother's tissue and the embryo's tissue, is a remarkable organ through which the mother and the embryo (later the fetus) exchange materials. Linking the embryo to the placenta is the **umbilical cord**, which houses the blood vessels that carry these materials.

The exchange of materials takes place in the placental villi. These ornate-looking structures are small blood vessels immersed in the mother's blood but separated from it by a very thin membrane. The membrane serves as a filter—nature's way of keeping many diseases, germs, and

FIGURE 4.4

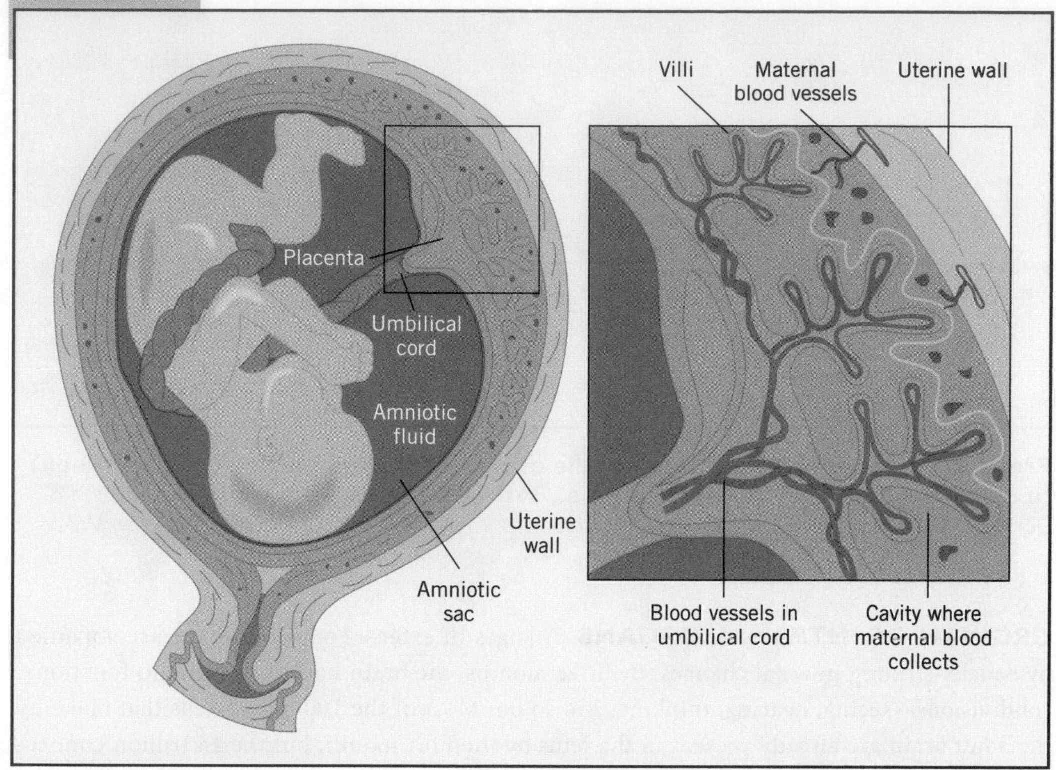

Maternal structures that support the embryo and fetus include the placental villi, amniotic sac, placenta, and umbilical cord.

impurities in the mother's blood from reaching the baby. Unfortunately, as we will see shortly, it is not a perfect filter. Blood itself does not pass between the mother and the fetus (which is why the mother and baby can have different blood types); however, oxygen and nutrients do pass from the mother's blood through the placenta to the fetus, and waste products of the fetus pass into the mother's blood to be carried away and excreted.

THE PERIOD OF THE FETUS (NINTH TO 38TH WEEK)

At the end of the eighth week, the period of the **fetus** begins. The principal changes for the fetus include further development of the organ structures already formed and increases in size and weight. Beginning its third month weighing less than 30 grams and measuring 5 centimetres in length, the average fetus will be born 266 days after conception, weighing about 3 to 3.5 kilograms and measuring about 51 centimetres in length. Fetal growth begins to slow around the eighth month—which is good for both the mother and the fetus because if it did not, the fetus would weigh over 90 kilograms at birth!

Fetus The developing organism from the 9th week to the 38th week after conception.

EXTERNAL CHANGES During this period, the appearance of the fetus changes drastically. The head grows less than do other parts of the body, so that its ratio decreases from 50 percent of the body mass at 12 weeks to 25 percent at birth. The skin, which has been transparent, begins to thicken during the third month. Facial features, which appeared almost extraterrestrial at six weeks, become more human looking, as the eyes move from the sides of the head to the front.

The eyelids seal shut near the beginning of the third month and remain that way for the next three months. Nails appear on fingers and toes by the fourth month, and pads appear at the ends of the fingers that will uniquely identify the individual for life. Head hair also begins to grow. A bone structure begins to support a more erect posture by six months. These changes can be seen in Figure 4.5, which illustrates the development of the embryo at 4 and 8 weeks and the fetus from 12 to 38 weeks.

FIGURE 4.5

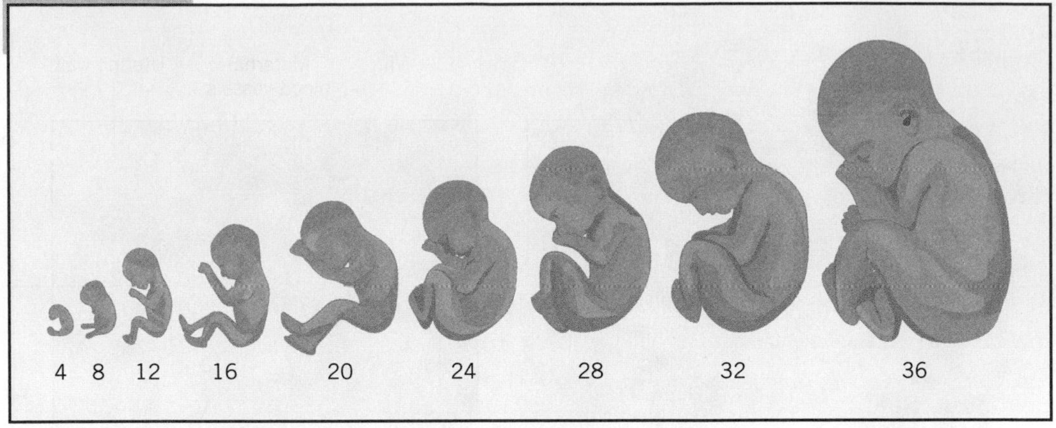

Prenatal development from the middle of the embryonic period (i.e., 4th week) to near the end of the fetal period (i.e., 36th week). *Adapted from G. J. Tortora and B. Derrickson,* Anatomy and Physiology, *12th Edition, p. 1151, Table 29.2. © 2009. Hoboken: Wiley.*

GROWTH OF INTERNAL ORGANS Changes in external appearance are accompanied by equally striking internal changes. By three months, the brain has organized into functional subdivisions—seeing, hearing, thinking, and so on. Most of the 100 billion cells that make up the adult brain are already present in the fetus by the fifth month, but the 14 trillion connections they will make between themselves and incoming and outgoing nerve cells will not be completed until well after birth. Other nerve cells grow and establish connections throughout fetal development.

A major mystery facing scientists is how the single, undifferentiated zygote cell can give rise to billions of fibres that properly connect eyes, ears, touch sensors, muscles, and the parts of the brain. We discussed part of the answer to this question in Chapter 3: from the moment of conception, the subset of genes known as *regulator genes* direct the activity of other genes, causing some to form arms, some legs, and so forth. It is also clear, however, that environmental factors and interactions between nerve cells play a role, as no two brains are wired identically—not even those of identical twins, who have exactly the same genetic material (Edelman, 1993; Rakic, 1988).

Other internal organs continue to develop. Sexual development becomes apparent in males by the end of the third month with the appearance of external sexual organs. In females, the precursors of ova, or *oocytes*, form on the outer covering of the ovaries; all the oocytes the female will ever possess will be present at birth. The fallopian tubes, uterus, and vagina develop, and the external labia become discernible.

Links to Related Material

In Chapter 16, you will learn more about how gender differentiation occurs prenatally, and the effects that prenatal exposure to hormones has on gender development.

EARLY SIGNS OF BEHAVIOUR Fetal activity begins in the third month, when the fetus is capable of forming a fist and wiggling toes; the mother, however, feels none of this. The fetus also appears to become sensitive to environmental stimulation, moving its whole body in response to a touch stimulus.

By the fourth month the eyes are sensitive to light through the lids, and by the fifth month a loud noise may activate the fetus. During this same month, the fetus swims effortlessly, a luxury gradually lost as quarters later become increasingly cramped. The fetus is now capable of kicking and turning and may begin to display rhythms of sleep and activity. By the seventh month, brain connections are sufficient for the fetus to exhibit a sucking reflex when the lips are touched.

TOWARD INDEPENDENCE The later stages of prenatal development ready the fetus to live outside the mother's body. Although separate from the mother in many ways during development, the fetus is nevertheless completely dependent on her for survival during most of the prenatal period. Recall that the support system in the uterus provides oxygen, nutrients, waste disposal, and a constant temperature for the fetus. Although physicians have made marked progress in saving premature babies, they have been unable to lower the **age of viability** below 23 to 24 weeks of fetal age.

Age of viability The age (presently 23 or 24 weeks) at which the infant has a chance to survive if born prematurely.

The major obstacle to independent life for a fetus born prematurely is the immaturity of the air sacs of the lungs, which have to exchange carbon dioxide for oxygen. The inability of the fetus to digest food or control body temperature is also a problem, and fat has not yet formed under the skin to assist in temperature regulation.

ON THE CUTTING EDGE 4.1
FAMILIES CREATED BY ALTERNATIVE METHODS OF CONCEPTION

Infertility can be a frustrating problem for couples hoping to start a family. Sometimes the difficulty involves the woman's ova (or lack of them); other times, the problem lies in the quantity or quality of the male sperm. Fortunately, medical science today offers couples several alternative methods for conceiving a child.

When the problem involves the sperm, the most common solution is donor insemination in which sperm donated from another male is inserted into the female, which initiates a pregnancy. Another popular method is *in vitro fertilization* (IVF). In this process, an egg and sperm (donated from either a third party or from one or both members of the couple) are combined in a laboratory procedure; then the fertilized egg is implanted in the woman's uterus, where, if all goes well, it begins to develop. These new reproductive technologies have provided a solution for a long-standing problem of biology. But what are the psychological implications of these procedures? What impact do they have on the children who are products of this technology and on their parents?

Researchers have investigated this issue by comparing families with a child conceived by these methods with families whose children were conceived naturally, and also with families whose children were adopted (Golombok et al., 1995; Golombok, MacCallum, & Goodman, 2001; Owen & Golombok, 2009). The focus of the research was social-emotional development and family functioning. Parents and children were interviewed, observed interacting with one another, and given a battery of tests. The first assessments were made when the children were between 4 and 8 years of age, and the sample was followed up longitudinally when they entered adolescence (at around 12 years), and again in late adolescence (at around 18 years).

The researchers wondered whether families formed with the help of new technologies might experience more difficulties than the natural-conception families, for several possible reasons. For one, the child, in most cases, is genetically unrelated to one or both of the parents. (Interestingly, the child was informed of this in only one family.) Would the non-genetic parent have difficulty relating to the child? Would the absence of a biological connection among all family members interfere with the establishment of the normal social and emotional bonds? Among other concerns were whether the parents would feel unduly stressed by the unusual situation, and whether the parents' relationship with one another would suffer if only one parent were genetically related to the child.

The results of the study are quite interesting. At the time of the first assessments, parents of children conceived by the two alternative reproductive methods were found to be similar to the adoptive parents, and superior to parents in the natural-conception families in a number of areas. Mothers in these families were rated as warmer and more emotionally involved with their children, and both mothers and fathers were found to interact more with their children. By the time of the follow-up at 12 years, the differences in parental involvement seemed to no longer be apparent. However, at the follow-up at 18 years, mothers in the two alternative reproductive groups were again found to be warmer than those in natural-conception families (and also than those in the adoptive families). Importantly, at no time period were there any differences among the children from the different family types. Thus, the children whose conception stemmed from the new reproductive technologies showed no ill effects as a result of their unusual beginnings.

(continued)

On the Cutting Edge 4.1 Families Created by Alternative Methods of Conception *continued*

Their feelings about themselves, their relations with their parents and with other children, and their overall psychological adjustment were no different from those of the children in the two comparison groups. The researchers point out that involvement of a sperm donor does not appear to have an adverse effect on mother–child relations, even during the potentially difficult period of adolescence. No differences were observed between fathers of the four groups (Owen & Golombok, 2009).

Other studies of IVF samples support these conclusions (MacCallum, Golombok, & Brinsden, 2007; Colpin, 2002; Hahn & DiPietro, 2001; Van Balen, 1998). Differences between IVF and natural-conception families are infrequent; and when they do occur, they tend to favour the parents or children in the IVF group, as in the studies described above. Research on the new reproductive technologies is still very new, and any conclusions must therefore be tentative. To date, however, there is no evidence to suggest that the new technologies pose a threat to family functioning or harmony. It seems likely that parents who must seek special methods of conception will have heavily invested in the job of parenting. Genetic ties between parents and children may not be as important as the parents' strong commitment to parenthood.

By 6 to 7 months of age, the fetus has a chance of survival outside the mother's body. The brain is sufficiently developed to provide at least partial regulation of breathing, swallowing, and body temperature. However, a baby born after only seven months of development will need to be provided with extra oxygen, will have to take food in very small amounts, and will have to live for several weeks in an incubator for temperature control.

In the eighth month, fat appears under the skin, and although the digestive system is still too immature to adequately extract nutrients from food, the fetus begins to store maternal nutrients in its body. Even a baby born at eight months, however, is susceptible to infection. Beginning in the eighth month, the mother's body contributes disease-fighting antibodies, which she has developed through her own exposure to foreign bodies, to the fetus. This process is not complete until 9 months of fetal age. It is an important process because the antibodies help protect babies from infection until they are around 6 months of age, when they can produce their own antibodies in substantial amounts.

Some precursors of later individual differences among children become evident during the last weeks of prenatal life. Fetuses differ, for example, in how much they move around in the womb (DiPietro, 2005), and these differences show some relation to individual differences in both activity level and temperament at 2 years of age (DiPietro et al., 2002). Similarly, fetuses vary in their patterns of heart rate change (DiPietro, 2005), and these variations have been shown to correlate with some aspects of both temperament and cognitive development in early childhood (Bornstein et al., 2002; DiPietro et al., 1996b). We hasten to add, however, that the relations are modest, and neither temperament nor anything else can be predicted with certainty from measures available during the prenatal period. Thus, parents should not anticipate a challenging toddler just because their fetus seems to kick more than the average baby.

LEARNING OBJECTIVE 4.1

Trace the changes that occur in the three stages of prenatal development.

1. What changes occur during the period of the zygote between conception and the end of the second week of development?
2. What changes occur during the period of the embryo between weeks 3 and 8?
3. What changes occur during the period of the fetus between the 9th week and birth?
4. Describe two alternative methods of conception.

TERATOLOGY

Learning Objective 4.2

Describe the impact of teratogens on prenatal development.

It is natural to think that prenatal development depends only on genes and that the environment begins to affect the baby only after birth. Yet although the uterus may not seem like an environment in the usual sense, it is the only home the embryo and fetus know. We will see that a number of factors affect the quality of this home and determine whether development is normal or abnormal—indeed, whether development can occur at all.

Approximately 3 to 5 percent of all live-born babies are identified as malformed at birth. Some malformations are difficult to detect at first, but become apparent with age. Thus, by the early school years, approximately 6 to 7 percent of children are identified as having congenital malformations—malformations that existed at birth. Many more babies would be born with malformations, were it not for a natural prenatal process that results in miscarriage or spontaneous abortion. It is estimated that 90 percent of some kinds of malformations end in spontaneous abortions, and that without this natural screening process, the observed incidence of congenital malformation would be 12 percent or higher (Shepard, 1986).

We have already seen that some abnormalities are caused by genetic defects. Malformations may also be caused by infectious diseases, drugs, and other environmental hazards. Non-genetic agents that can cause malformation in the embryo and fetus are referred to as **teratogens** (*teratos* is a Greek base meaning "monster"). The term **teratology** refers to the study of the effect of teratogens on development.

Teratogen An agent that can cause abnormal development in the fetus.

Teratology The study of the effects of teratogens on development.

Much of our discussion of teratogens will focus on their physical effects. Indeed, teratogens are defined in terms of their creation of physical malformations. However, psychologists have increasingly noted that teratogens can have psychological and behavioural effects as well. This realization has given rise to a new field, called *psychoteratology*. Researchers in this field use behaviour rather than physical outcomes to study the potentially damaging effects of teratogens, and have found that behavioural effects may show up even when physical effects do not. Thus, in many cases, behavioural measures may be more sensitive than physical measures.

HISTORICAL IDEAS

Although the field of teratology only recently achieved scientific status, it has had an interesting history. The birth of malformed babies probably gave rise to at least some of the creatures of Greek mythology, such as the one-eyed Cyclops and various creatures that are part human and part beast (Warkany, 1977). But although monsters were sometimes idolized in ancient times, people in the medieval period believed that the birth of malformed babies portended catastrophe, and malformed infants and children were often put to death. Some believed these babies were produced through the mating of humans with animals, and it was not unusual for mothers and midwives who delivered malformed babies to be put on trial for witchcraft.

Such practices gradually gave way to the more benign belief that maternal fright, thoughts, and impressions could create a monster birth (Warkany, 1981). Running parallel to these theories were ancient beliefs that the food and drink a pregnant woman ingested could affect the fetus. In the Bible, an angel admonishes the mother of Samson that when she conceives, she should not "drink wine or similar drink, nor eat anything unclean" (Judges 13:14).

Despite the apparent fact that people of biblical times believed that maternal nourishment could affect the development of the fetus, a great deal of time elapsed before people fully realized the potential effects of the external world on the fetus. People generally believed that the embryo and fetus lived in a privileged environment, protected against harm by the placenta and its amniotic world.

By 1930, however, there was general recognition that X-rays could produce intrauterine growth retardation, microcephaly (an abnormally small head and brain), and small eyes. By the mid-1940s, it was obvious that a pregnant mother who contracted rubella (German measles) during the early months of pregnancy had a relatively high chance of producing a baby with congenital abnormalities of the eye, ear, heart, and brain.

Still, these events were seen as exceptional. A major disaster finally shook people's faith in the privileged-environment belief, but only as recently as the early 1960s. A mild and seemingly harmless sedative, thalidomide, was developed in the late 1950s, and many pregnant women took it for morning sickness. Physicians soon noticed a sharp increase in the number of babies born with defective limbs. Careful questioning of mothers, analysis of doctors' prescriptions, and epidemiological research implicated thalidomide as the culprit. The field of teratology experienced a dramatic surge as a result of this event, and has been expanding rapidly ever since.

GENERAL PRINCIPLES

Many teratogens have been identified as causing defects in humans. Evaluating an agent for teratogenic effects, however, is fraught with problems. For obvious reasons, animals must be the "guinea pigs" for substance testing, but the potential teratogen may not have the same effect on animal and human fetuses. Furthermore, people often take more than one drug, and a particular drug may do damage only in combination with another drug, with a disease, or with stress. (Some common teratogens and their effects are listed in Table 4.1.)

Several principles capture important features of how teratogens act (Hogge, 1990).

1. *A teratogen's effect depends on the genetic makeup of the organism exposed to it.* A prime example is thalidomide. The human fetus is extremely sensitive to this substance, but rabbits and rats are not. One reason why thalidomide was not initially suspected to be a teratogen was that testing on these animals revealed no ill effects. The principle of genetic differences in sensitivity also applies to individuals within a species. Some babies are severely affected because their mothers drank alcohol during pregnancy, but others are apparently not affected by this practice.
2. *The effect of a teratogen on development depends partly on timing.* Even before conception, teratogens can affect the formation of the parents' germ cells. Formation of female germ cells begins during fetal life, and formation of sperm can occur up to 64 days before the sperm are expelled. Thus, a fetus can be affected by drugs that the pregnant grandmother took decades earlier, or by X-ray exposure that the father experienced many weeks before conception.

   For two to three weeks after conception, the zygote's fluids do not mix with those of the mother, so the zygote is relatively impervious to some teratogens. After the zygote has become implanted into the wall of the uterus, however, many substances in the mother's bloodstream can pass through the placental barrier and into the blood of the embryo. Thus after implantation, the embryo enters a particularly sensitive period. Teratogens can produce organ malformation from two to eight weeks post-conception because this is a time when organs are forming. After the organs have formed, teratogens primarily produce growth retardation or tissue damage (Goldman, 1980).

   Which organ is affected by a teratogen depends in part on which organ is forming. Rubella is an example of how crucial timing can be. Rubella affects only 2 to 3 percent of the offspring of mothers infected within two weeks after their last period, whereas it affects 50 percent of offspring when infection occurs during the first month following conception, 22 percent when it occurs during the second month, and 6 to 8 percent when it occurs during the third month. The incidence falls to very low levels thereafter. Whether ear, eye, heart, or brain damage occurs depends on the stage of the formation of each organ when the mother is infected (Murata et al., 1992; Whitley & Goldenberg, 1990). Figure 4.6 presents a schematic illustration of the sensitive or critical periods in prenatal development.
3. *The effect of a teratogen may be unique.* Although there are some common birth defects (such as deafness, eye damage, or intellectual disability) that result from exposure to a

FIGURE 4.6

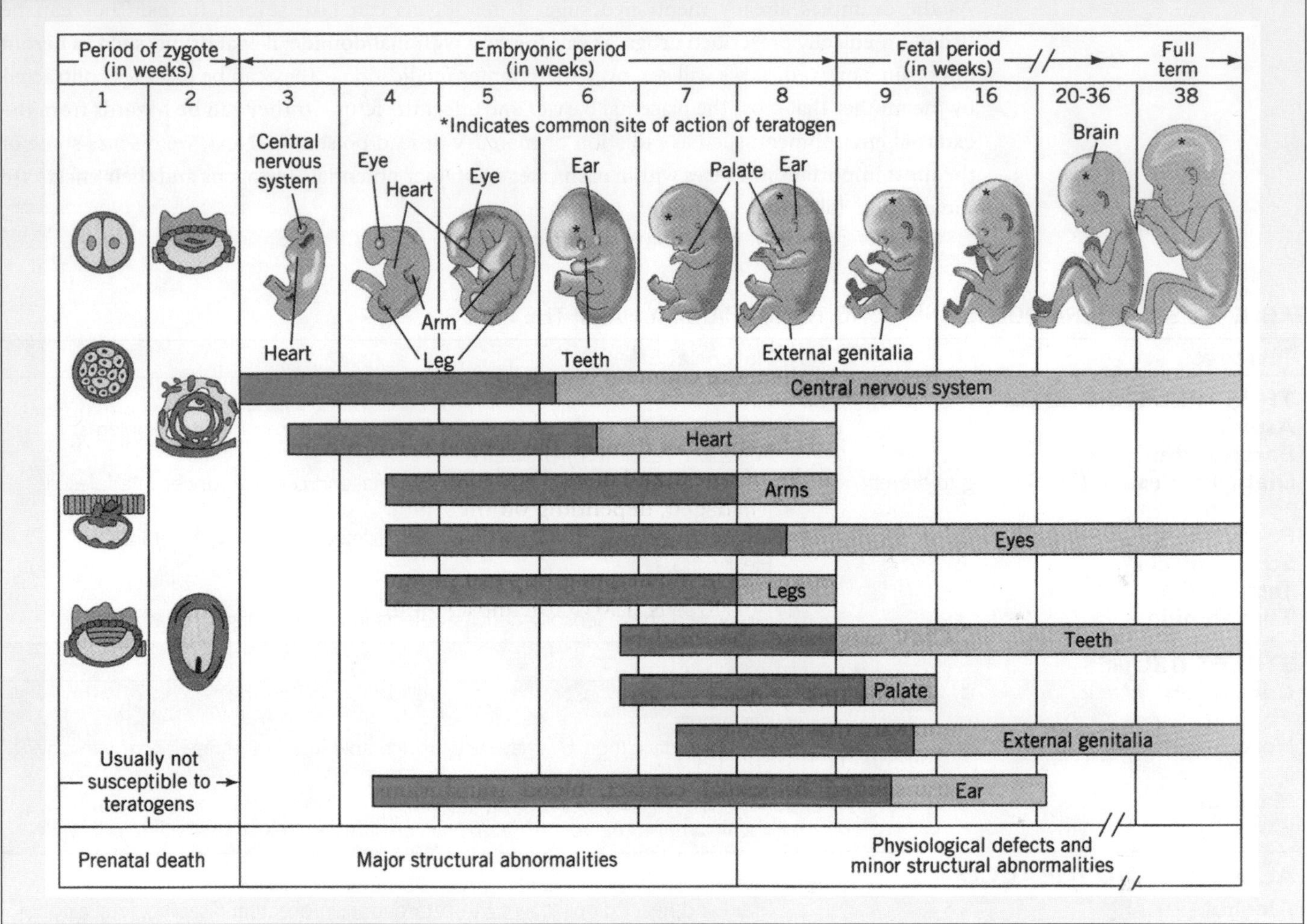

A schematic illustration of the sensitive or critical periods in prenatal development. Sensitivity to teratogens is greatest from three to nine weeks after conception, the period when organ formation occurs. The most critical age period of vulnerability for each organ is shown in green, and continuing periods where the likelihood of damage declines is shown in orange. *Adapted from* Before We Are Born, *3rd ed. (p. 118) by K. L. Moore, 1989, Philadelphia: Saunders. Copyright 1989 by W. B. Saunders Company.*

variety of teratogens (see Table 4.1), many birth defects are the unique result of exposure to a particular teratogen. For example, thalidomide produces gross limb defects, whereas rubella primarily affects sensory and internal organs.

4. *The abnormal development caused by teratogens may be severe.* Teratogenic effects may include malformation of limbs or other parts of the body, growth retardation, functional and behavioural disorders, or even death.
5. *Teratogens differ in how they gain access to the fetus.* Radiation passes to the fetus directly through the mother's body. Chemicals, on the other hand, usually travel to the fetus through the blood and across the placental membrane. The mother's blood may be able to filter some potentially harmful chemicals to protect the fetus. The placenta serves as a filter, but not as a complete barrier; materials may be slowed by this filter, but will not necessarily be stopped. In addition, some teratogens move past this filter faster than others.
6. *The likelihood and degree of abnormal development increase with the level of exposure to the harmful agent.* Depending on the amount of the teratogen the fetus is exposed to and the duration of the exposure, the outcome can range from no effect at all to death.

TYPES OF TERATOGENS

As the examples already mentioned suggest, teratogens can take several forms. They can be drugs—medically prescribed drugs, as was the case with thalidomide; illegal drugs, such as heroin or cocaine; or even, as we will see, over-the-counter medications. They can be diseases contracted by the mother that cross the placental barrier and affect the fetus. Or they can be hazards from the external environment, such as radiation or mercury or lead poisoning. Next, we discuss some of the most important instances within each category. Other potential teratogens and their effects are indicated in Table 4.1.

TABLE 4.1 SOME TERATOGENS AND CONDITIONS THAT MAY HARM THE FETUS

Teratogen	Potential Effect
THERAPEUTIC DRUGS	
Aspirin	In large quantities, miscarriage, bleeding, newborn respiratory problems
Barbiturates	Newborn respiratory problems
Diethylstilbestrol (DES) *(drug to prevent miscarriage)*	Genital abnormalities in both sexes; vaginal and cervical cancer in adolescent females
Phenytoin *(an anticonvulsant drug)*	Threefold increase in likelihood of heart defects and growth retardation
Streptomycin	Hearing loss
Tetracycline	Most commonly, staining of teeth; can also affect bone growth
Thalidomide	Deformed limbs, sensory deficits, defects in internal organs, death
STREET DRUGS	
Cocaine and crack	Growth retardation, premature birth, irritableness in the newborn, withdrawal symptoms
Heroin and methadone	Growth retardation, premature birth, irritableness in the newborn, withdrawal symptoms, SIDS
Marijuana	Exaggerated startle response, fine motor tremors, and poor habituation to visual stimuli in newborns; later problems in the area of executive function
ALCOHOL AND TOBACCO	
Alcohol	Brain and heart damage, growth retardation, intellectual disability, fetal alcohol syndrome
Smoking	Growth retardation, prematurity
INFECTIONS	
HIV	Facial malformations; can result in AIDS in the infant
Cytomegalovirus	Deafness, blindness, abnormal head and brain growth, intellectual disability
Herpes simplex	Intellectual disability, eye damage, central nervous system damage
Rubella	Intellectual disability, eye damage, deafness, heart defects
Syphilis	Central nervous system damage, deformities of the teeth and skeleton, possible fetal death
Toxoplasmosis	Abnormalities in brain and head growth
ENVIRONMENTAL HAZARDS	
Lead	Miscarriage, neuromuscular problems, intellectual disability
Mercury	Neurological problems, abnormal head and brain growth, intellectual disability
PCBs	Growth retardation, skin pigmentation
Radiation	Leukemia, abnormal brain and body growth, cancer, genetic alterations, miscarriage, stillbirth

DRUGS "The desire to take medicine is, perhaps, the greatest feature which distinguishes us from animals." So said Sir William Osler, a medical historian (Finnegan & Fehr, 1980). People in our culture today consume chemicals not only as medicines to treat specific conditions, but as means to induce various mental states. Many such substances—alcohol, caffeine, and nicotine—have become so much a part of daily life that we often do not think of them as drugs. A drug, however, can be defined as any substance other than food intended to affect the body. The average pregnant woman takes four to ten drugs of some sort during pregnancy, and up to 80 percent of the drugs are not prescribed by a physician. Indeed, use of over-the-counter medications, such as analgesics, antihistamines, and decongestants, is quite common during pregnancy (Werler et al., 2005), as is the use of a variety of herbal products for which there is very little information concerning safety in pregnancy (Marcus & Snodgrass, 2005). In the following section, we look at some drugs, prescription and otherwise, which have documented adverse effects on the fetus.

THALIDOMIDE We mentioned earlier that the effects of thalidomide dramatically increased awareness of the potential damage that chemicals can do to the fetus. Thalidomide was sold as an over-the-counter tranquilizer that was marketed as a non-addictive sleep aid. Its mild tranquilizing properties were said to help counter the symptoms of *morning sickness*. Morning sickness is the nausea experienced by about 80 percent of pregnant women, which peaks at eight to twelve weeks into the pregnancy and then gradually fades away (Smolin & Grosvenor, 2010). Thalidomide was developed in the late 1950s and first licensed for use in Canada in early 1961. It was sold as well in at least 46 other countries. However, because the Food and Drug Administration (FDA) was skeptical of the data on its safety, thalidomide was not approved for use in the United States and very few American babies were affected (Benderly, 2007).

For Thought and Discussion

Thalidomide has been used in some countries to treat leprosy and certain forms of cancer. However, its use is severely restricted. Under what circumstances should the use of thalidomide be allowed? What precautions should be taken if it is used?

The tragic consequences of the sedative became apparent in Europe later that year. Depending on when a mother took the drug, her baby was born with malformations of the eyes and ears, deformation of the internal organs, or fused fingers and toes. Some babies were born with a defect called *phocomelia*, a condition in which the limbs are drastically shortened and the hands and feet are connected to the torso like flippers. When these defects were reported, the drug was banned in Germany and Britain, but remained available for another three to six months in several other countries, including Canada (CBC Archives, 2006). It is estimated that more than 10,000 babies worldwide and approximately 125 babies in Canada were born disabled as a result of thalidomide use (Thalidomide Victims Association of Canada, 2006).

The teratogenic effects of thalidomide were especially surprising because doctors considered it to be a mild drug. The women who took it experienced no apparent side effects, and the drug produced no harmful effects in the offspring of pregnant animals on which it was tested. Clearly, we had a lot to learn about how chemicals affect the fetus, and we still do. This incomplete knowledge makes it all the more unwise for pregnant women to ingest drugs that they can avoid.

OTHER THERAPEUTIC DRUGS Many pregnant women take prescribed drugs as part of a continuing regimen of health care—for example, to treat diabetes or blood-clotting tendencies—or as treatments for health problems brought on by the pregnancy. Some of these drugs may increase the risk of fetal problems, creating the need to weigh the risk to the fetus from taking the drug against the risk to the mother from not taking it.

Some anticoagulants, anticonvulsants, antibiotics, and a variety of other prescription medications have been implicated in the increased likelihood of harm to the fetus (Wilson, 2007). The action of these drugs is often not straightforward. Indeed, drugs may interact with other substances. For example, aspirin, which is not teratogenic at a particular dosage in rats, can have teratogenic effects if administered in combination with benzoic acid, a widely used food preservative. Nevertheless, it is important to keep in mind that the danger from most prescribed medications is fairly low, and that by far the majority of mothers taking them have healthy infants, especially when the medication is administered by a physician who is aware of the pregnancy.

Several sex hormones, too, can produce teratogenic effects. These hormones are sometimes used to treat various gynecological conditions in women or to reduce the likelihood of miscarriage. The use of certain sex hormones in early pregnancy has been associated with masculinization of the external genitalia of females (Wilson, 2007).

Some pregnant women took a particularly damaging synthetic female hormone, diethylstilbestrol (DES), in the 1950s and early 1960s to reduce the likelihood of miscarriage. Harmful effects were not observed in their offspring until much later when they reached adolescence. Physicians discovered that a high percentage of the female children of these women later developed vaginal and cervical problems, and some of these offspring developed cervical cancer (Giusti, Iwamoto, & Hatch, 1995). The male offspring of mothers who took DES were also later found to be affected, being more likely to develop testicular cancer and to have a lowered sperm count (Sharpe & Skakkebaek, 1993; Wilcox et al., 1995). The studies of sex hormones illustrate yet another problem in detecting teratogenic agents—the possible delay by many years of any observable effect.

STREET DRUGS The increasing availability of powerful mood- and mind-altering illegal drugs since the 1960s has been a major health concern in Canada and the United States. Unfortunately, it has also provided substantial evidence about the dangers of drug in-take by pregnant women, both to themselves and to their fetuses. Addictive drugs have attracted the most attention.

Heroin addicts, for example, are more likely to have medical complications during pregnancy and labour. Their newborn babies are also likely to experience drug-withdrawal symptoms, referred to as neonatal abstinence syndrome (NAS), characterized by irritability, tremors, and gastrointestinal distress (Briggs et al., 2008; Cunningham et al., 2010; Gabbe et al., 2007). Frequently, addiction to heroin is compounded by poor nutrition and inadequate health care; almost 75 percent of addicts do not see a physician during pregnancy. Medical complications, including anemia, cardiac disease, hepatitis, tuberculosis, hypertension, and urinary infections, occur in 40 to 50 percent of heroin-dependent women who are observed during the prenatal period. These women are more likely to miscarry or to give birth prematurely. Their babies are usually lighter than normal (Briggs et al., 2008) and are more likely to have brain bleeding, low blood sugar, and jaundice. They are also more at risk for *sudden infant death syndrome*, or *SIDS* (in which the baby unexpectedly stops breathing and dies) (Hans, 1992; Rosen & Johnson, 1988).

Links to Related Material

In Chapter 5, you will read more about sudden infant death syndrome (SIDS). You will read about factors that place infants at risk for SIDS, as well as programs designed to reduce its occurrence.

Heroin-dependent expectant mothers may use methadone, a synthetic drug designed to help break the heroin habit. Methadone, however, is also addictive, and it too is associated with neonatal abstinence syndrome (Jansson, DiPietro, Elko, & Velez, 2010).

Cocaine is a readily-available drug, especially in the much cheaper form of crack, which has increased use of the drug to epidemic proportions. Cocaine affects the fetus indirectly through reduced maternal blood flow to the uterus, limiting the fetus' supply of nutrients and oxygen. Additionally, cocaine passes through the placenta and enters the fetus' bloodstream, where it gains direct access to the brain in as little as three minutes. In the brain, cocaine affects chemical nerve transmitters in addition to increasing heart rate and blood pressure.

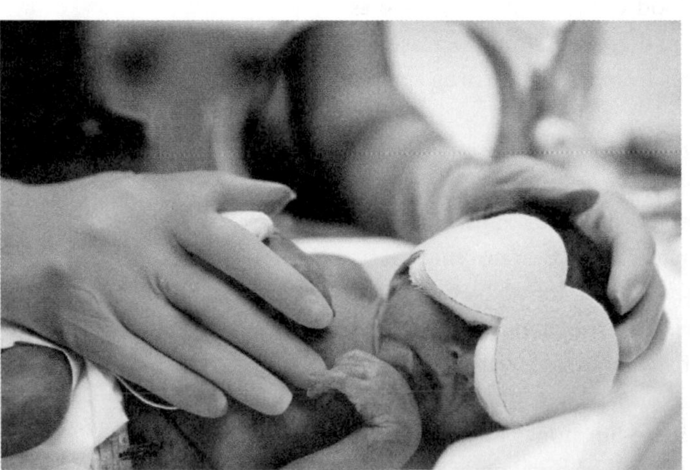

Newborn babies who have been exposed to cocaine as fetuses are more likely to be premature and irritable, and to have disruptive sleep patterns. (*Corbis/Media Bakery*)

Cocaine-exposed babies are more likely to be miscarried or stillborn. If they are born alive, they are more likely to be premature, undersized, or to suffer retarded growth (Briggs et al., 2008). They also are more likely to have difficulty regulating their level of alertness, their emotional reactivity, and their sleep patterns, and they may be hard to handle (DiPietro et al., 1995; Gabbe et al., 2007; Phillips et al., 1996).

Despite these problems, studies have turned up conflicting findings as to how babies exposed to cocaine turn out. Some studies have reported that exposed babies are later more impulsive than non-exposed babies, and have greater difficulty regulating their attention. Other studies report few or no long-term effects that can be attributed to cocaine exposure alone. Cocaine research shares the same difficulties as research on many other teratogens. Mothers who use cocaine are more likely to use other drugs and to smoke and drink. They are also more likely to live in poverty and chaos, to be undernourished and in poor health, and to be depressed. Given this complex of factors, which often exists both before and after a child is born, it is difficult to pinpoint the role of prenatal cocaine exposure in the child's development (Gabbe et al., 2007; Lester, 2000; Mayes & Fahy, 2001; Stanwood & Levitt, 2001).

Investigators are becoming more aware of the effects of the postnatal environment on the cocaine-exposed child. Given an irritable baby who has difficulty falling into regular sleep patterns and a mother who is depressed, has few resources, and continues her drug habit, there is little likelihood that a healthy mother–infant interaction will develop. Many investigators believe that the quality of this relationship and the postnatal environment may be major contributors to the child's outcome (Frank et al., 2005; Gabbe et al., 2007).

The use of marijuana and hallucinogens accelerated rapidly in the 1960s and 1970s, and marijuana remains the most often used illicit drug. As with other drugs, the effects of marijuana are difficult to separate from other environmental and health care practices. Research suggests that heavy use of marijuana may cause newborns to be jittery and to habituate poorly to visual stimuli (Fried, 2002b). Research also suggests, however, that negative effects of marijuana are less likely if the users otherwise engage in good health practices (Fried, O'Connell, & Watkinson, 1992). Follow-up studies reveal certain cognitive effects of prenatal marijuana exposure that continue into young adulthood (Fried, 2002a, 2002b; Fried, Watkinson, & Gray, 2003; Smith, Fried, Hogan, & Cameron, 2004, 2006). Focus on Research 4.1 describes a long-term Canadian investigation of the effects of prenatal marijuana exposure.

CAFFEINE Caffeine is the drug most commonly consumed during pregnancy. However, until recently the effect of caffeine on the fetus had received relatively little attention. As is often the case, one of the difficulties in determining the effect of caffeine has been separating its effects from those of other drugs, such as nicotine and alcohol. Notwithstanding these challenges, several recent studies have found that caffeine is associated with an increased risk of premature birth and lower birth weight infants (Bech et al., 2005; CARE Study Group, 2008; Weng et al., 2008). Although the likelihood of negative effects is much reduced when the daily intake of caffeine is 100 mg or less (about one cup of brewed coffee), the risk increases as the amount of caffeine ingested daily increases (CARE Study Group, 2008; Weng et al., 2008). Caffeine is present not only in coffee, but also in energy drinks, and to a lesser extent in tea, colas, and even chocolate.

NICOTINE Approximately 18 percent of the Canadian population aged 15 and over smoke tobacco (Health Canada, 2011). Although the number who smoke while pregnant has declined substantially in recent years, almost 10 percent of Canadian women continue to smoke throughout their pregnancy (Health Canada, 2007). Adolescent mothers, those with less than a high-school education, and those living in low-income households are at higher risk to smoke during their pregnancies (Public Health Agency of Canada, 2009).

The effects of nicotine and cigarette smoke on the fetus have been well documented (Cornelius & Day, 2000). Smoking is known to impair the functioning of the placenta, especially oxygen exchange. On average, babies of mothers who smoke while pregnant are smaller (Breslau et al., 2005; Cowperthwaite et al., 2007; Huijbregts et al., 2006), and the likelihood of premature delivery and complications increases with the number of cigarettes smoked per day (Cornelius et al., 1995; Gabbe et al., 2007; Health Canada, 2003). In addition, the risk of SIDS is elevated in babies exposed prenatally to cigarette smoke: as many as one-third of all SIDS deaths may be attributable to prenatal smoking (Dietz et al., 2010: Mitchell & Milerad, 2006).

As children, babies whose mothers smoked are at heightened risk for social and behavioural problems (Batstra et al., 2003; Day et al., 2000; Fried et al., 2003; Wasserman et al., 2000). They also are at elevated risk for relatively poor performance on measures of language and cognitive development (Batstra et al., 2003; Cornelius et al., 2001; Fried et al., 2003; Gabbe et al., 2007). To reduce

FOCUS ON RESEARCH 4.1
THE OTTAWA PRENATAL PROSPECTIVE STUDY: A CANADIAN LONGITUDINAL INVESTIGATION OF THE EFFECTS OF PRENATAL MARIJUANA EXPOSURE

Researchers have been aware of the negative consequences of prenatal exposure to alcohol and cigarette smoke for many years. Indeed, there has been a concerted effort by Canadian health authorities to educate the public, making them aware of the harmful effects of such prenatal drug use. Much less is known, however, about the effects of marijuana use while pregnant. Yet, as Fried (2002b) points out, marijuana is the most popular illegal drug used by young women, and a number of studies indicate that the percentage of women who report having used marijuana while pregnant may be fairly high, ranging from 10 to 16 percent in middle-income populations to 23 to 30 percent in inner city populations (Fried, 2002b). Clearly, research into the consequences of prenatal marijuana use is needed.

Beginning in 1978, Peter Fried and his colleagues at Carleton University in Ottawa followed longitudinally a group of children who were exposed prenatally to marijuana smoke (Fried, 1989). The Ottawa Prenatal Prospective Study is valuable as it is one of a small number of longitudinal studies that have addressed the question of whether there are harmful effects of prenatal marijuana use, by looking at such effects on children as they grow up into adolescence.

Participants were informed of the study by their obstetricians or by notices in prenatal clinics. Participating mothers-to-be were interviewed once during each trimester of their pregnancy, where information was collected about their backgrounds, diet, health, and their cigarette, alcohol, and marijuana use. The study initially involved 682 women in the Ottawa region. A subsample of 180 children was selected for follow-up into childhood and adolescence (Fried, 2002b).

Interestingly, Dr. Fried observed that many mothers, upon becoming aware of their pregnancy, reduced or stopped their use of alcohol and cigarettes. It seemed that the message from health authorities concerning the harmful effects of prenatal alcohol and tobacco use was getting across. However, a similar reduction was not seen for marijuana use. Fried suggested that lack of information about marijuana may have been responsible, leading some mothers to conclude there were no harmful consequences.

So, are there negative consequences of prenatal marijuana exposure? Dr. Fried and his colleagues examined the newborn infants of mothers who had smoked marijuana, looking for a number of birth defects commonly seen as a result of teratogen exposure. Overall, no patterns of minor physical birth defects were observed in such infants, with the exception of certain abnormalities in the spacing of the eyes and in the shape of the eyelids of infants whose mothers had been heavy users (i.e., those who smoked more than six times per week) (Fried, 1989, 2002b). However, several neurological consequences were found. Newborns exposed prenatally to marijuana tended to display increased fine motor tremors, exaggerated and prolonged startle responses, and poorer habituation to visual stimuli (Fried, 1989, 2002b).

Are the effects of prenatal marijuana exposure long-lasting? Dr. Fried and colleagues followed up with their sample, repeatedly testing them throughout childhood, adolescence, and into young adulthood. The researchers report that the effects beyond infancy are subtle (Fried, 2002b). Indeed, there seemed to be little evidence for any effects during the toddler period. Yet, as the children grew, signs of mild cognitive effects became apparent, signs that continued from the preschool period all the way into young adulthood. Although prenatal marijuana exposure seemed to have no effect on children's overall IQ, other aspects of intellectual functioning did seem affected. In particular, there appeared to be effects on children's *executive function*—cognitive abilities and behaviours that are crucial in effortful, goal-oriented situations (see Chapter 8 for a more detailed discussion of executive function). Children who were exposed to marijuana showed problems in such aspects of executive function as attention and impulsivity, problem-solving, and the manipulation and integration of visuoperceptual skills (Fried, 2002a, 2002b; Fried et al., 2003; Smith et al., 2004, 2006). Moreover, prenatal marijuana exposure was also associated with increased risk for later cigarette and marijuana use in adolescence (Porath & Fried, 2005). Dr. Fried concluded that there does indeed seem to be evidence for long-term negative consequences of prenatal exposure to marijuana, but emphasized the need for further, well-controlled investigations in this area.

The Ottawa Prenatal Prospective Study highlights the importance of studies investigating the effects of prenatal drug use, and provides an excellent example of how longitudinal studies can reveal the long-term effects of early experience—in this case, experience before birth.

such risks, the Public Health Agency of Canada (2008) advises expectant mothers to quit smoking completely—the sooner the better. Mothers who smoke are strongly advised to discuss methods of smoking cessation with their physician and to implement them as soon into the pregnancy as possible (Osadchy, Kazmin, & Koren, 2009).

Unfortunately, pregnant women cannot necessarily escape all of these consequences by refraining from smoking. Even passive exposure to others' smoke has been shown to affect the growth of the fetus (Dejin-Karlsson et al., 1998; Eskenazi et al., 1995; Public Health Agency of Canada, 2008).

As research has furthered our knowledge of factors that can harm the fetus, agencies have become increasingly effective in alerting expectant mothers. (*Licensed under Health Canada copyright*)

ALCOHOL In Canada and the United States, alcohol is the most widely used drug that is known to harm the fetus. Prenatal alcohol exposure is the leading non-genetic cause of intellectual disability (also referred to as mental retardation) among Canadian children and in the Western world (Public Health Agency of Canada, 2004b, 2006a).

Although the effects of alcohol on the fetus were suspected in the 18th century, a clear picture of the consequences of chronic maternal alcoholism for the fetus did not emerge until 1973. At this time, investigators described **fetal alcohol syndrome (FAS)**, a unique set of problems in the fetus caused by the mother's alcohol consumption (Jones et al., 1973).

Links to Related Material

In Chapter 3, you learned about a number of genetic causes of intellectual disability. In this chapter we discuss some prenatal environmental causes.

Fetal alcohol syndrome (FAS) A set of problems in the infant and child caused by the mother's use of alcohol during pregnancy; typically includes facial malformations and other physical and mental disabilities.

Among the defining characteristics of FAS are a set of facial anomalies, especially thinning of the upper lip, flattening of the philtrum (the cleft above the upper lip) and of the nasal bridge, and anomalies in the shape of the corners of the eyelids (see Figure 4.7 for an illustration of the facial features associated with FAS). Other characteristics of FAS include growth retardation, intellectual disability, and learning disabilities. Behaviour problems compound these difficulties, as infants with FAS are irritable, sleep less well, and are difficult to feed (Wekselman et al., 1995). By school age, these children are more likely to have difficulty sustaining effort and attention and to have language problems and motor-performance deficits (Schonfeld et al., 2001; Streissguth & Connor, 2001). It is not uncommon for adults with FAS to experience mental health problems and to have difficulty holding a job (Chudley et al., 2005). Later problems with the law are not unusual, and incarceration does not appear effective in reducing such problems. Indeed, the Canadian Bar Association recently passed a resolution calling for an alternative to prison for offenders coping with the effects of FAS (Tibbetts, 2010).

The incidence of FAS in North America is estimated to be 1 to 3 per 1,000 live births (Chudley et al., 2005). The incidence is much higher, however, among children whose mothers habitually engage in binge drinking (Mayes & Fahy, 2001; Pacey, 2009). In some Canadian Aboriginal communities, the incidence may be as high as 2.5 to 10 percent (Chudley et al., 2005), and in one isolated community in northern British Columbia, it was reported to be 19 percent (Robinson, Conry, & Conry, 1987).

A number of children exposed prenatally to alcohol demonstrate some, but not all, of the characteristics of FAS. They may lack some of the facial features that characterize FAS children, and their growth retardation and neurological dysfunction may be less severe. These children are said to have *fetal alcohol spectrum disorder (FASD)*. The term FASD is used to refer to the differing degrees of effects that may result from prenatal alcohol exposure, ranging from little or no obvious effects at one end of the spectrum to the full-blown symptoms of FAS at the other extreme (Chudley et al., 2005; Stade, Stevens, Unger, Beyene, & Koren, 2006). FASD is more common than FAS, occurring in about 10 in 1,000 births (Carson, Cox, Crane, et al., 2010; Streissguth & Connor, 2001). An estimated 300,000 Canadians of all ages are affected by FASD (Public Health Agency of Canada, 2007).

FIGURE 4.7

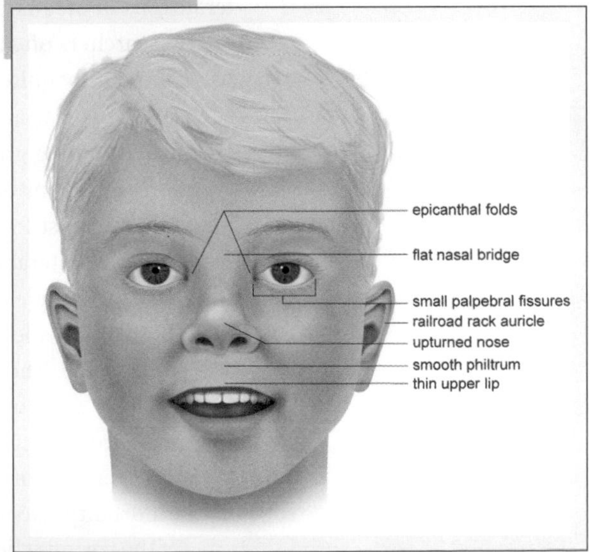

Characteristic facial features associated with fetal alcohol syndrome. *From "Alcohol Spectrum Disorders" by D. J. Wattendorf and M. Muenke, M.D., National Human Genome Research Institute.* American Family Physician, 72(2), *2005, p. 279–285. http://www.aafp.org/afp/2005/0715/p 279.html.*

Because their physical anomalies may be less pronounced, it may not be readily apparent that some children with mild degrees of FASD are coping with the cognitive, attentional, and learning problems associated with prenatal alcohol exposure. However, recent Canadian research suggests that because of these neurological problems and the difficulties in social relations that often ensue, children with FASD may be stigmatized as "bad kids." They may be difficult for parents to deal with, may be taken advantage of by other children, or may get involved in negative peer relationships (Sanders & Buck, 2010). Children with FASD frequently struggle with depression and anxiety, and often report a poorer quality of life than do their peers (Stade et al., 2006). Professionals who work with these children stress the importance of early identification so that appropriate intervention can take place. Although FASD is a life-long disability, some of its secondary effects, such as problems at home, at school, and with peers, may be reduced through the creation of stable and supportive home and school environments (Koren, Fantus, & Nulman, 2010; Sanders & Buck, 2010).

The majority of Canadians are aware that alcohol use can be harmful to the fetus (Public Health Agency of Canada, 2006a). As a consequence, most Canadian women who drink alcohol reduce or stop their intake upon realizing they are pregnant, especially those whose pregnancies are followed by a physician (Thanh & Jonsson, 2010). However, many women are unsure whether there is a "safe" amount of alcohol that can be ingested while pregnant (Public Health Agency of Canada, 2006a). Indeed, 6 to 10 percent of Canadian mothers report consuming some alcohol during their pregnancies (Public Health Agency of Canada, 2009; Thanh & Jonsson, 2010). Is there a safe amount? This is a topic of debate in the medical community (Pacey, 2009), and the answer is that we simply do not know for sure. The Public Health Agency of Canada (2007) advises that there is no safe amount and no safe time to drink alcohol during pregnancy. The Canadian Paediatric Society (2007) likewise cautions that the more alcohol consumed while pregnant, the greater the risk, and advises that it is best to have none.

For Thought and Discussion

Should pregnant mothers who knowingly ingest teratogens be prosecuted for child abuse? What might be some drawbacks of such a public policy?

ENVIRONMENTAL CHEMICALS The number and amount of chemicals in our environment have increased explosively since the beginning of the Industrial Revolution. Insecticides, herbicides, fungicides, solvents, detergents, food additives, and miscellaneous other chemicals have become common in our daily existence. Approximately 70,000 chemicals are presently in use (Bellinger & Adams, 2001). Only a small fraction of these chemicals have been tested as potential teratogens in pregnant laboratory animals.

Researchers often find that chemicals are potentially teratogenic in animals, but the doses they use are typically quite large. People generally experience comparable doses only in rare instances, such as industrial accidents or concentrated dumping (for example, in Love Canal, a former chemical dumping ground near Niagara Falls, NY). The rates of defective births and spontaneous abortions are monitored routinely in many hospitals in North America, providing a measure of protection against long-term chronic exposure of undiscovered teratogens. However, as we have seen, complex interactions among chemicals and delayed effects can often make detection difficult.

A clear example of the effects of environmental chemicals comes from Cubatão, a small town in an industrial valley in Brazil. Cubatão was slowly choking through pollution of its streams, air, and countryside. Thousands of tons of particulate matter were being discharged into the air from smokestacks, and huge amounts of organic matter and heavy metals were being dumped into the streams. Through an ambitious cleanup program, the town reduced discharges of particulate matter by 72 percent, organic waste into rivers by 93 percent, and heavy metals by 97 percent. The infant mortality rate in Cubatão dropped to one-half the 1984 rate (Brooke, 1991).

Of the various chemicals present in the environment, metals have come under special scrutiny. Mercury and lead have been suspected teratogens for many years. A disaster comparable to that caused by thalidomide occurred in Japan between 1954 and 1960, when people ate fish from a bay that had been contaminated with mercury from industrial dumping. Soon after the contamination, the proportion of miscarriages and stillbirths rose to 43 percent (Bellinger & Adams, 2001). Many mothers who ate the fish gave birth to infants with intellectual disability and neurological symptoms resembling cerebral palsy. Autopsies of those who died revealed severe brain damage (Dietrich, 1999).

Prenatal exposure to lead from automobile exhausts and lead-based paints has been implicated in miscarriages, neuromuscular problems, and intellectual disability (Bellinger et al., 1986). Follow-ups of children who experienced high lead exposure as babies reveal negative effects on vocabulary, motor coordination, reading ability, and higher-level thinking, even after 11 years (Needleman et al., 1990).

Another group of environmental chemicals that can harm fetuses consists of polychlorinated biphenyls (PCBs), widely used as lubricants, insulators, and ingredients in paints, varnishes, and waxes. Cooking oil used in Japan in 1968 and in Taiwan in 1979 was accidentally contaminated by PCBs, and pregnant women who used the oil were more likely to have stillborn infants and infants with darkly pigmented skin.

In the United States, PCB levels were relatively high in fish taken from Lake Michigan. Offspring of mothers who ate these fish were smaller at birth, had somewhat smaller heads, and were more likely to startle and be irritable. Babies who had detectable PCB levels in their blood at birth performed more poorly on various visual measures at both 7 months and 4 years of age (Jacobson & Jacobson, 1988; Jacobson et al., 1992). Partly for these reasons, PCBs are no longer produced in the United States. PCBs were never produced in Canada; however, they were widely used here in the past. In 1977, the Canadian government made it illegal to import, manufacture, or sell PCBs (Environment Canada, 2003).

MATERNAL INFECTIOUS DISEASES Several viral and bacterial infections in the mother can harm the fetus. We discuss some of the more common ones here.

RUBELLA Rubella (also known as German measles) is a mild disease of limited duration (Cunningham et al., 2010). However, if contracted early in pregnancy, it can damage the central nervous system of the fetus, resulting in blindness, deafness, and intellectual disability. The heart, liver, and bone structure may also be damaged, depending on the timing of infection. Fortunately, childhood immunization programs instituted in the early 1970s have dramatically reduced the incidence of rubella in the Canadian population, and, as a consequence, the incidence of congenital rubella syndrome (Dontigny, Arsenault, & Martel, 2008; Public Health Agency of Canada, 2006b).

HERPES Two viruses in the herpes group can produce central nervous system damage. Cytomegalovirus (CMV), the most common intrauterine viral infection, may cause abnormal brain and head growth, encephalitis, blindness, deafness, and intellectual disability. An estimated 0.2 to 2.2 percent of neonates are born with CMV each year, but only 5 to 15 percent of them are seriously affected (Yinon, Farline, & Yudin, 2010).

Because pregnant mothers are often unaware that they have been infected by CMV, doctors have made little progress in discovering the specific effects of fetal exposure at particular ages. CMV can be transmitted through contact with infected saliva or urine, or through blood or sexual contact (Gabbe et al., 2007).

Another herpes virus, herpes simplex, can infect the genitals of adults. This virus reached epidemic levels in the United States by the early 1980s. Physicians in Canada are not required to report cases of herpes simplex to the Public Health Agency of Canada. As a result, detailed statistics on the frequency of its occurrence in Canada are not readily available; however, its prevalence is estimated to be similar to that in the United States (Steben & Sacks, 1997). In the infant, herpes simplex can cause encephalitis, central nervous system damage, and eye damage. Most herpes simplex infections of infants occur following direct contamination by the mother's infected birth canal during the birth process, especially if there are active herpes lesions present at the time of birth. Antiviral medication is frequently used to control outbreaks of herpes lesions, allowing for vaginal delivery.

When active lesions are present at the time of birth, Canadian guidelines recommend caesarean delivery (Money & Steben, 2008; Paquet & Steben, 2010).

HIV Another virus that reached epidemic levels in the 1980s is the human immunodeficiency virus (HIV), which causes acquired immunodeficiency syndrome (AIDS). By the end of 2007, there had been 64,800 positive tests for HIV reported in Canada. Each year, about 600 new positive tests for HIV are reported for Canadian women, 90 percent of whom are of child-bearing age (Raboud et al., 2010). The prevalence of HIV among Canadian women who are pregnant is 3 to 4 in 10,000. The prevalence may be three or more times higher in certain major cities (Public Health Agency of Canada, 2003), and it has been increasing over the past five years (Raboud et al., 2010). The virus is transmitted from one person to another through body fluids. It can be transmitted from mother to fetus through the placenta prior to birth, and can also be transmitted from mother to infant through breast milk following birth.

In addition to causing AIDS, HIV can act as a teratogen. Some infected babies are born with facial deformities—larger-than-normal eye separation, boxlike foreheads, flattened nose bridges, and misshapen eye openings. Until recently, approximately 25 percent of infants with HIV-infected mothers acquired the virus, and most died in early childhood. Fortunately, the recent development of highly active forms of antiviral treatment has substantially reduced the prenatal transmission of HIV. In fact, the latest Canadian treatment guidelines for prenatal care of HIV-infected mothers have reduced the incidence of HIV transmission to the infant to around 1 percent (Raboud et al., 2010).

SYPHILIS AND GONORRHEA Syphilis and gonorrhea are sexually transmitted diseases. After declining for several years, the incidence of syphilis began to increase in 2001. This disease is caused by a spirochete, a type of bacteria, which can infect the fetus and cause central nervous system damage, deformities of the teeth and skeleton, and even death. The fetus is relatively resistant to infection from the syphilis spirochete until about 18 weeks into the pregnancy (Cunningham et al., 2010).

Gonorrhea is also caused by a bacterial agent. Its incidence has been reported to be as high as 30 percent in some populations. Premature birth, premature rupture of membranes, and spontaneous abortion are associated with gonorrhea. The fetus is affected in about 30 percent of cases. The most common problem is eye infection, which can lead to blindness if untreated. Fortunately, almost all newborns are treated with antibiotic eye drops at birth to prevent this problem (Cunningham et al., 2010).

LEARNING OBJECTIVE 4.2

Describe the impact of teratogens on prenatal development.

1. What are teratogens?
2. How do teratogens act?
3. What are some examples of teratogens?

Learning Objective 4.3

Describe the natural challenges that can affect fetal development.

NATURAL CHALLENGES

Much current media attention focuses on potential teratogens that mothers voluntarily consume or to which mothers are exposed in the modern industrial environment. Yet mothers and fetuses have always faced natural challenges from the environment. The quality of the mother's nutrition is an important determinant of how the fetus develops. Parental age and even maternal experiences and stress may also have an effect.

NUTRITION

Most Canadians are aware of the importance of nutrition during pregnancy: eating well/good nutrition was the top answer—mentioned by 86 percent of respondents—in a 2006 Public Health Agency of Canada survey on what women should do to have a healthy baby. But why is nutrition so important?

The original fertilized egg must multiply into trillions of cells to form a fully developed fetus. During prenatal development, cells increase not only in number, but also in size. As Figure 4.8 illustrates, the baby and its accompanying support system will weigh 11 to 16 kilograms (25 to 35 pounds) by the ninth month of pregnancy, billions of times the weight of the fertilized egg.

Where does all of this mass come from? The answer is obvious—from the mother. Thinking about the issue this way brings home the importance of maternal nutrition. The quality of the cells of the fetus can be no better than that of the nutrients the mother supplies through the placental circulation system. Earlier we said that, at least in the early stages of development, the functioning of cells depends on the environment they are in. The quality of the mother's nutrition is probably the most important environmental influence on the fetus and newborn baby (Morgane et al., 1993).

FIGURE 4.8

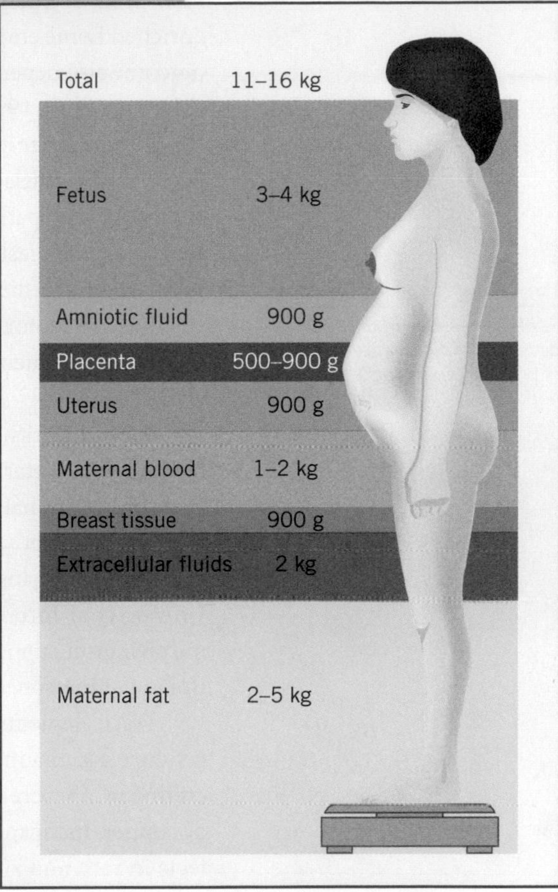

Weight gained during pregnancy is due to increases in the weight of the mother's tissues, as well as the weight of the fetus, placenta, and amniotic fluid. *Adapted from Figure 14.4, p. 587 in* Nutrition: Science and Applications, *Second Edition, Lori A. Smolin and Mary B. Grosvenor, John Wiley & Sons, Inc, 2010.*

The prospective mother, then, must supply nutrients for the fetus and its support system. In part, her ability to do this depends on her nutrition during pregnancy. But it also depends to a great extent on her nutritional status *before* pregnancy. Both mothers and their fetuses fare more poorly when the mother has had long-term malnutrition than when the mother has good pre-pregnancy nutrition (Smolin & Grosvenor, 2010; Whitney & Rolfes, 2011). Moreover, even the mother's ability to conceive can be affected by poor pre-pregnancy nutrition. Starvation, and even over-dieting, anorexia, and excessive exercise have the potential to interfere with ovulation, thereby reducing fertility (Smolin & Grosvenor, 2010).

Maternal malnutrition can have devastating effects on the fetus. Autopsies of severely malnourished stillborn infants from developing countries reveal that their brains weighed up to one-third less than expected. In the United States, deficits of between 6 to 25 percent in the size of major internal organs have been found in infants born to urban poor families (Naeye, Diener, & Dellinger, 1969; Parekh et al., 1970). Malnutrition is associated with increased rates of spontaneous abortion, infant death, and congenital defects. Malnutrition also interferes with the development of the placenta, thereby reducing the amount of nutrients available to the fetus. Pregnant women who have inadequate diets are thus more likely to have small and premature babies (Smolin & Grosvenor, 2010; Whitney & Rolfes, 2011). (Problems associated with low birth weight are discussed in Chapter 5.)

As is sometimes the case with teratogens, however, it can be difficult to isolate the effects of malnourishment from other factors. Malnutrition is often accompanied by inadequate housing and sanitation, and inferior education and health care, as well as the daily stress of poverty. Catastrophic events sometimes provide a means for separating out the influences of at least some of these factors. During World War II, for example, the entire populations of many countries had severe limitations imposed on their food supplies, limitations that were not associated with the other factors mentioned above. Food supplies in the Netherlands were especially scarce. There was a notable decline in conceptions associated with the inadequate nutrition, as well as a substantial increase in miscarriages, stillbirths, and congenital malformations. Thus, many effects of malnutrition were seen, even in the absence of the effects of poverty and poor education.

What about the intellectual abilities of babies who were malnourished during fetal life? The outcome depends, to a large extent, on their childhood environments. Children who were malnourished as fetuses because of World War II, but who had adequate diet and stimulation as infants and children, showed no long-term intellectual deficit. Similarly, many Korean children suffered malnutrition during the Korean War, but were later adopted by families who provided them with good nutrition and education. These children later performed as well on intellectual and achievement tests as children who had not suffered early malnutrition. The general conclusion is that an enriched home environment may compensate for many of the effects of early malnutrition, but the outcome also depends on when during pregnancy the malnutrition occurred and how severe it was (Morgane et al., 1993; Vietze & Vaughan, 1988; Zeskind & Ramey, 1981).

On the other hand, babies who are malnourished both as fetuses and also after birth are more likely to show delayed motor and social development. They become relatively inattentive, unresponsive, and apathetic (Bauerfeld & Lachenmeyer, 1992). Health organizations worldwide have recognized the lasting consequences of early nutritional deficits and have initiated attempts to supplement the diets of pregnant women and infants. Babies with supplemented diets are more advanced in motor development and more socially interactive and energetic, an encouraging sign that the consequences of bad nutrition may be avoided (Grantham-McGregor et al., 2001; Joos et al., 1983).

For Thought and Discussion

How might problems of impoverished developing nations relate to problems of prenatal development in their populations?

Food quantity is not the only issue in maternal nutrition. A pregnant woman and her fetus have special dietary needs. Proteins, essential fatty acids, vitamins, and minerals are especially important. Animal studies reveal that protein deficits produce damage to the kidneys and intestines and disrupt skeletal growth in the fetus. Low intake of certain vitamins can affect the eyes and internal organs and increase the number of malformations (Rosso, 1990). Researchers at the University of Toronto and the University of Western Ontario report, however, that using a prenatal multivitamin supplement may provide protection against a number of such birth defects (Goh, Bollano, Einarson, & Koren, 2006).

Trace elements in the diet are also important. An absence of iron in the mother's blood can produce anemia in her baby. Diets lacking iodine are associated with an increased likelihood of cretinism, a severe thyroid deficiency that causes physical stunting and mental deficiency. Deficits of copper, manganese, and zinc produce central nervous system damage and other negative effects in rats, and zinc deficiency has been implicated in the occurrence of anencephaly (absence of the cortex of the brain). Deficits of folic acid in pregnant mothers have been associated with neural tube defects—anencephaly and no closure of the spinal cord (spina bifida)—in babies (Goh et al., 2006; Grantham-McGregor, Ani, & Fernald, 2001; Van Allen, McCourt, & Lee, 2002).

Excesses of nutrients can also be damaging. Excessive amounts of the sugar galactose in diabetic mothers may cause cataracts and other physical problems, even death, in fetuses; the babies at birth are more likely to have passive muscle tone and to be less attentive (Langer, 1990). Just as deficits in iodine can cause problems, excess iodine can have a detrimental effect on thyroid function. Excesses of vitamin A can cause damage to the eyes and face, as well as the central nervous system of the developing fetus (Katz & Friedman, 2008; Wilson, 2007).

MATERNAL EXPERIENCES AND STRESS

Of all the factors that might influence the fetus, none has generated more speculation than that of the mother's own experiences. The belief that the mother's mental impressions could affect the fetus is quite old. We may chuckle when we hear that a pregnant woman's child will favour classical music if the mother listens to Beethoven. Yet surveys conducted not that long ago reveal that some people still believe that birthmarks are caused by maternal frights or unsatisfied food cravings; for example, that an unsatisfied craving for strawberries may produce a strawberry-coloured birthmark (Ferriera, 1969).

Modern investigators have dismissed beliefs in magical influences on the fetus and have focused on psychological factors that have fairly well-documented influences on the body. For example, psychological stress increases the activity of the adrenal glands. The secretions from these glands enter the mother's blood and can be transmitted to the fetus through the placenta. Additionally, hormones released during stress can reduce the blood flow and oxygen available to the fetus. Thus, identifiable physical pathways exist by which maternal emotional states could affect the fetus.

Research reveals that there are, in fact, relations between maternal anxiety during pregnancy and some later child outcomes. For example, high levels of anxiety have been associated with newborn irritability, feeding and sleep problems during infancy, and behavioural problems at 4 years of age (O'Connor et al., 2002; Van Den Bergh, 1992). They have also been associated with a heightened probability of congenital physical anomalies, such as heart defects and cleft palate (Carmichael & Shaw, 2000).

As with many of the other factors we have discussed in this chapter, there are problems in interpreting these relations because of limitations in researchers' ability to control all the potentially important variables (DiPietro, 2004). Often mothers' reports of anxiety were obtained after their babies were born. These reports of anxiety might have been influenced by the babies' malformation or irritability rather than the other way around—the cause-and-effect problem of correlational research mentioned in Chapter 2. Further, there is often no way to separate prenatal and postnatal influences on the infant. A mother who has reported a great deal of prenatal anxiety may handle her infant differently, for example, and it may be this handling that makes her baby irritable. Finally, the genetic relation between the mother and her baby, rather than the prenatal experience, may be the operative factor. A mother who is genetically predisposed to anxiety, which might reflect abnormal hormonal activity, could pass this genetic predisposition on to her fetus.

Although factors such as these probably contribute to the predictive power of prenatal anxiety, it is unlikely that they account for all the effects. One kind of evidence in support of this conclusion is the fact that some effects of maternal stress are evident during the prenatal period and at birth—and thus before postnatal influences or characteristics of the child could be playing a role. For example, high levels of prenatal stress increase the probability of preterm birth, as well as low birth weight and problems during delivery (Lobel, Dunkel-Schetter, & Scrimshaw, 1992; Paarlberg et al., 1995).

Another type of evidence for the effects of prenatal stress comes from studies of environmental disasters that have produced high levels of stress in random groups of people. One such disaster study was conducted by researchers in Montreal. In the winter of 1998, a severe ice storm hit eastern Canada. Power was cut for thousands of residents for periods as long as several weeks during the coldest time of the year, particularly in eastern Ontario, the Eastern Townships region of Quebec, and the northern portions of several New England states. Television viewers were shocked to see images of hydro towers in Quebec bent over to the ground under the weight of the ice. Many people, especially those living in rural regions, were forced to leave their homes or do without power and, in some cases, water. Not surprisingly, this was a time of extreme stress for many residents. Researchers from McGill University and the University of Montreal (King & Laplante, 2005; Laplante et al., 2004) interviewed expectant mothers who had lived through the ice storm in the most severely hit region, and found that many had indeed experienced high levels of stress during this environmental calamity. Children born to mothers who had experienced high levels of prenatal stress were found, at 2 and later at 5½ years of age, to show poorer intellectual and language abilities (King & Laplante, 2005).

We should add, however, that the negative effects are by no means inevitable, nor is all prenatal stress negative. Maternal anxiety and stress within normal limits, especially in women who are well-nourished, financially stable, and carrying wanted pregnancies, do not seem predictive of negative outcomes (DiPietro et al., 2006). As well, an important determinant is the degree of social support available to the mother during pregnancy. When support is available—for example, a supportive spouse or readily available family members—then negative outcomes are a good deal less likely (Feldman et al., 2000).

PARENTAL AGE

Traditionally, the optimal time for childbearing has been thought to fall between the ages of 20 and 34, with ages 25 to 29 being the best time within this optimal range. There has been concern, therefore, with departures in either direction from this supposed optimal period—births to mothers who are age 35 or older, and births to mothers who are still in their teens.

The typical age at which a woman gives birth to her first child has risen dramatically in both Canada and the United States since the 1970s. Between 1991 and 2000, the rate of births to Canadian mothers between the ages of 35 and 39 rose by over 63 percent and the rate for mothers 40 or older more than doubled (Health Canada, 2003). Similar increases have been reported in the United States (Martin, Park, & Sutton, 2002). In contrast, births to teenagers in both Canada and the United States have declined significantly over the last 25 years (Dryburgh, 2000; Martin et al., 2002). Nevertheless, in 2005, over 14,000 Canadian teenagers gave birth (Statistics Canada, 2007b). Table 4.2 shows the number of Canadian births by age of the mother for the year 2005.

TABLE 4.2 NUMBER OF CANADIAN BIRTHS IN 2005 BY AGE OF THE MOTHER

Age (years)	Number of Births
Under 15	118
15–19	13,895
20–24	55,318
25–29	105,566
30–34	107,524
35–39	49,526
40–44	9,728
45–49	396
Not specified	105
Total	342,176

Source: Adapted from Statistics Canada (2007). *Births: 2005*. Catalogue no. 84F0210XIE. Ottawa, Ontario: Ministry of Industry.

We have already discussed one risk of motherhood at a relatively advanced age. As we saw in Chapter 3, increased maternal age is associated with an increased likelihood of giving birth to a baby with Down syndrome. The father's age also carries a risk for the fetus, because the relative frequency of mutation in the father's sperm increases with age. A genetic disorder related to the father's age is *achondroplasia*, a mutation that becomes dominant in the child who inherits it and causes bone deformities (Chen, 2006). The most obvious characteristics are dwarfism and a large head with a prominent forehead and a depressed bridge of the nose. As shown in Figure 4.9, the relative likelihood that a child will inherit achondroplasia increases with the father's age, much as the relative likelihood of Down syndrome increases with the mother's age (Friedman, 1981; Giudicelli et al., 2008). Recent findings suggest the father's age may also be important as a contributor to *autistic disorder* (Croen et al., 2007; Reichenberg et al., 2006).

Genetic disorders are not the only risk that older parents face. In some samples, older mothers have been found to be more at risk for preterm birth, difficulties during delivery, and both infant and maternal mortality (Gilbert, Nesbitt, & Danielsen, 1999; Lisonkova et al., 2010). Such problems, however, are less common in births to older women today than they were 20 or 30 years ago. Women who defer birth until a later age are better educated today than were their counterparts decades ago, and they are more likely to seek early prenatal care and to be in good health. When the mother's health is good, motherhood at a relatively advanced age appears to carry only minimal risks.

In general, babies who are born to mothers in their teens are also at greater than average risk for complications during pregnancy, preterm birth, and low birth weight (Moore & Brooks-Gunn, 2002). Here, too, however, factors associated with pregnancy during a particular age period appear to be more important than maternal age per se. In particular, teenage mothers are less likely than mothers in general to receive adequate prenatal care and nutrition, and more likely to engage in behaviours that pose risks for both their own and their fetuses' health, such as smoking or use of illegal drugs during pregnancy. When these factors are controlled, the problems associated with teenage pregnancy are greatly reduced.

Links to Related Material

In Chapter 15, you will learn more about the difficulties faced by teenage mothers and their children.

FIGURE 4.9

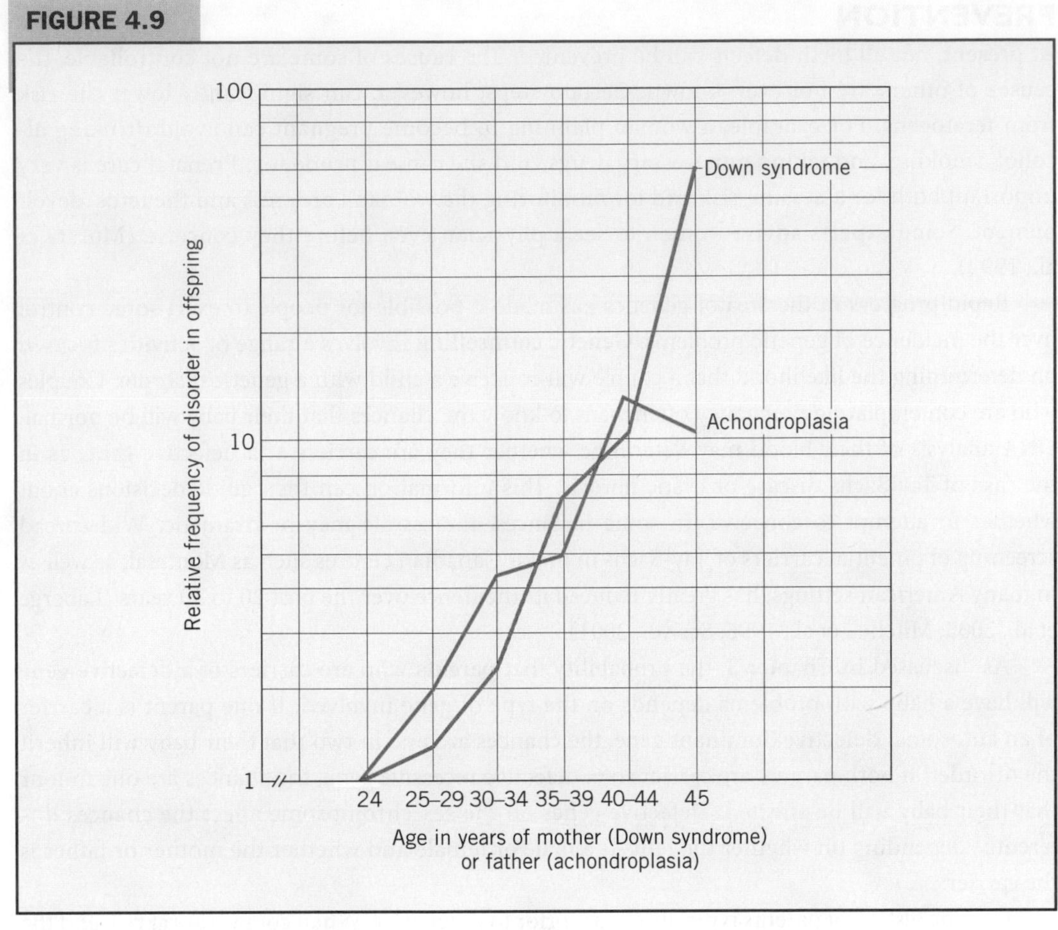

Relative frequency of Down syndrome and achondroplasia in the offspring of mothers (Down syndrome) and fathers (achondroplasia) of various ages. *From "Genetic Disease in the Offspring of Older Fathers" by J. M. Friedman.* Obstetrics and Gynecology, 57, 1981, *p. 746. Reprinted with permission from the American College of Obstetricians and Gynecologists. .*

LEARNING OBJECTIVE 4.3

Describe the natural challenges that can affect fetal development.

1. How is nutrition important for fetal development?
2. What are the consequences of maternal stress?
3. What effect does parental age have on prenatal development?

PREVENTING, DETECTING, AND TREATING BIRTH DEFECTS

Learning Objective 4.4

Discuss the various methods of preventing, identifying, and treating birth defects prenatally.

We noted earlier that spontaneous abortion ends fetal development in most cases in which the fetus has severe genetic abnormalities or a problem exists in the uterine environment. Although there are thousands of genetic abnormalities and challenges to the fetus, it is important to view these risks in perspective. More than 90 percent of infants are born healthy and normal, and the large majority of the remaining infants have minor problems that can be corrected or will be outgrown. Still, small percentages can translate to large numbers of people, and statistics provide little comfort to those affected. In a single year, between 7,000 and 10,000 babies are born with birth defects in Canada (Health Canada, 2002).

Can anything be done to prevent birth defects? How can a mother be sure the baby she is carrying is healthy? And how can birth defects be treated?

PREVENTION

At present, not all birth defects can be prevented. The causes of some are not controllable; the causes of others are not even known. Certain steps, however, can significantly lower the risk from teratogens. For example, a woman planning to become pregnant can avoid drinking alcohol, smoking, and taking unnecessary drugs, and she can eat prudently. Prenatal care is very important both for assessing risk and for monitoring the woman's progress and the fetus' development. Some experts advise women to see a physician even before they conceive (Murata et al., 1992).

Genetic counselling The practice of advising prospective parents about genetic diseases and the likelihood that they might pass on defective genetic traits to their offspring.

Rapid progress in the area of genetics has made it possible for people to exert some control over the incidence of genetic problems. **Genetic counselling** involves a range of activities focused on determining the likelihood that a couple will conceive a child with a genetic disorder. Couples who are contemplating pregnancy often want to know the chances that their baby will be normal. DNA analysis of their blood may determine whether they are carriers of a defective gene, as in the case of Tay-Sachs disease or cystic fibrosis. This information can then guide decisions about whether to attempt to conceive. In some instances, the results may be dramatic. Widespread screening of potential carriers of Tay-Sachs in major Canadian centres such as Montreal, as well as in many American settings, has greatly reduced its incidence over the past 20 to 30 years (Laberge et al., 2005; Mitchell et al., 1996; Scriver, 2001).

As discussed in Chapter 3, the probability that parents who are carriers of a defective gene will have a baby with problems depends on the type of gene involved. If one parent is a carrier of an autosomal defective dominant gene, the chances are one in two that their baby will inherit the disorder. If both parents are carriers of a defective recessive gene, the chances are one in four that their baby will be affected. Defective genes on the sex chromosome affect the chances differently, depending on whether the fetus is a male or female and whether the mother or father is the carrier.

Genetic testing of parents typically occurs prior to pregnancy. When couples are at risk and the woman has become pregnant, parents often consider procedures for testing the fetus.

SCREENING FOR ABNORMALITIES

Significant progress has been made in detecting problems in newborn infants, which opens up the possibility for early treatment. Phenylketonuria (PKU), the genetic disorder of metabolism discussed in Chapter 3, serves as an example. Although scientists understood at the beginning of the 1960s what caused PKU and how to treat it through diet, they had no method for determining which newborn infants had PKU. By the time they discovered the defect in a child, irreversible damage had occurred. Then, in 1961 a blood test was developed to detect excess phenylalanine in the blood. Infants with PKU were put on a special diet, which was maintained throughout childhood, to prevent the severe intellectual disability and neurological consequences of untreated PKU. Today, all infants born in Canada and the United States are given a blood test for PKU, and, as a consequence, PKU is no longer a major health problem.

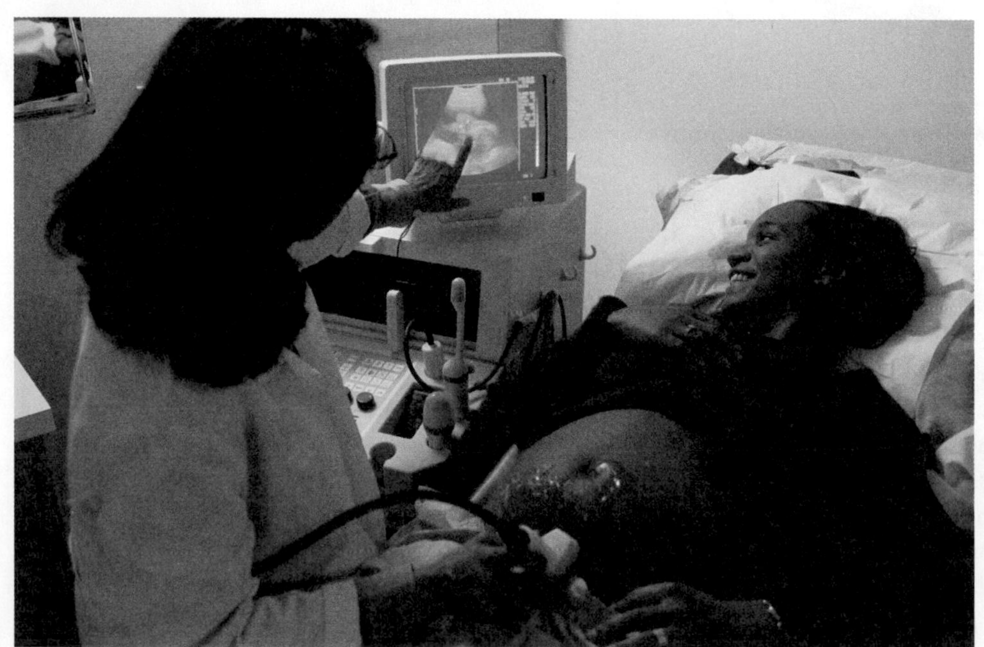

Although ultrasound imaging helps to identify the sex of a fetus, and can reveal some disorders, there are many problems it cannot detect. (*PhotoDisc, Inc.*)

Even more dramatic advances permit parents to learn about the status of the fetus as early as 9 weeks into a pregnancy and, as we shall see, sometimes in the first days following conception.

ULTRASOUND IMAGING **Ultrasound imaging** uses sound-like waves to provide a continuous picture of the fetus and its environment. The level of detail in this image permits an assessment of fetal age, as well as identification of the sex of the fetus by 16 to 20 weeks. The ultrasound image can also determine whether there is more than one fetus. Although many potential problems are not detectable with ultrasound, the procedure can reveal some disorders, including: abnormal head growth; defects of the heart, bladder, and kidneys; some chromosomal anomalies; and neural tube defects (Cohen, 2006). Ultrasound imaging is also helpful for diagnostic procedures that require collection of amniotic fluid or tissue, such as the methods we consider next: amniocentesis and chorionic villus sampling.

Ultrasound imaging A non-invasive procedure for detecting physical defects in the fetus. A device that produces sound-like waves of energy is moved over the pregnant woman's abdomen, and reflections of these waves form an image of the fetus.

AMNIOCENTESIS An especially important tool for assessment is **amniocentesis**, because it provides samples of both the amniotic fluid and the fetal cells in it. A needle is passed through the mother's abdomen and into the amniotic cavity to collect the fluid (Goldberg & Musci, 2006). Analysis of the fluid can reveal abnormalities. For example, alpha-feto protein (FEP), a substance the fetus produces, circulates in the amniotic fluid. Abnormally high levels of FEP occur when the fetus has certain types of damage to the brain, the central nervous system, or the liver and kidneys. Chromosomal analysis of the fetal cells can also detect a number of problems, such as Down syndrome. With the success of the Human Genome Project, the list of detectable diseases has grown dramatically in recent years. Fetal cells can be tested for many genetic defects, including achondroplasia, cystic fibrosis, Duchenne muscular dystrophy, sickle-cell anemia, Tay-Sachs, and so on.

Amniocentesis A procedure for collecting cells that lie in the amniotic fluid surrounding the fetus. A needle is passed through the mother's abdominal wall into the amniotic sac to gather discarded fetal cells. These cells can be examined for chromosomal and genetic defects.

CHORIONIC VILLUS SAMPLING Amniocentesis cannot usually be conducted until after the 14th week of pregnancy. **Chorionic villus sampling** (CVS) can make information available about the fetus several weeks earlier. In this procedure, cells are collected from the chorion, a part of the placenta. A small tube is inserted through either the abdomen or the cervix and into the fetal placenta to collect a sample of fetal cells (Goldberg & Musci, 2006). These cells reveal large-scale defects of the chromosomes, as well as more minute defects in the DNA. CVS is possible as early as 10 weeks. Both amniocentesis and CVS carry a slight risk (ranging from 1 to 2 percent) of miscarriage following the procedure (Cavallotti et al., 2004; Scott et al., 2002).

Chorionic villus sampling (CVS) A procedure for gathering fetal cells earlier in pregnancy than is possible through amniocentesis. A tube is passed through the abdomen or the cervix so that fetal cells can be gathered at the site of the developing placenta.

ENDOSCOPIC FETOSCOPY A relatively new procedure available for prenatal screening is endoscopic fetoscopy. In this procedure, a fibre-optic endoscope is inserted into the uterus either through the abdomen or the cervix (Deprest et al., 2006). The endoscope allows the physician to visualize the fetus, obtain fetal tissue samples, or even perform fetal surgery. Diagnosing and treating defects prenatally can prevent serious complications that might arise during and following birth.

IN VITRO SCREENING Scientists have succeeded in screening embryos in the test tube before they are implanted in the mother's uterus. Egg cells are collected from the mother and then fertilized in a petri dish through *in vitro* fertilization. One or two cells are removed from each embryo when it reaches the six- to ten-cell stage, at about three days post-fertilization (Ginsberg, 2006). From these cells, the sex of the embryo can be determined, and, within a few hours, the DNA of the cell can be checked for suspected anomalies.

It is possible to detect several hundred disorders through in vitro screening techniques. However, only a small minority of women who have at-risk pregnancies participate in this prenatal screening. Pre-implantation in vitro screening may be recommended when parents are carriers of a genetic or chromosomal disorder, when mothers have a history of unexplained miscarriages, or when they are outside the optimal childbearing age range (Audibert, 2009). Such pre-implantation embryo screening is available at some fertility clinics in Canada. The procedure is costly, however, and is not covered by provincial medical insurance programs. Moreover, only about 20 to 30 percent of implanted embryos result in a successful pregnancy (Audibert, 2009).

TREATMENT

The growing sophistication of diagnostic procedures has made early detection of developmental abnormalities more likely. But what happens when a fetus is found to be developing abnormally? The parents may decide to terminate the pregnancy, but there may be treatment alternatives. Developments in the medical treatment of fetuses parallel the rapid advances in early diagnosis. Current approaches to prenatal treatment fall into three categories: medical therapy, surgery, and genetic manipulation.

MEDICAL THERAPY Medical therapy is currently the most widely available of the three methods. An example is providing extra vitamins to the mother when inborn errors of metabolism result in deficiencies in the fetus (Bringman & Phillips, 2006). Likewise, dietary interventions are sometimes prescribed. For example, we have discussed how dietary restrictions in children with PKU can greatly reduce the damaging effects of excess phenylalanine. Adults who have PKU often abandon the diet when they reach maturity. Although the excess phenylalanine that results has little harmful effect on the fully mature adult, if a woman with PKU is pregnant, the excess can have serious negative effects on the fetus she is carrying. Prenatal restriction of phenylalanine in the diet of mothers with PKU, beginning as early in the pregnancy as possible, can mitigate the harmful effects on the fetus of the phenylalanine build-up in the mother's blood (Bringman & Phillips, 2006; Chen, 2006).

Other medical interventions may involve treating illnesses in the mother and thereby benefitting the fetus. Earlier in the chapter, for example, we discussed how drug treatment of pregnant women with HIV has markedly reduced the incidence of babies who are born infected with the virus (Raboud et al., 2010). Similarly, treatment of maternal infections such as syphilis and toxoplasmosis has been successful in reducing harmful effects on the fetus (Bringman & Phillips, 2006).

Finally, it is also possible to provide therapy directly to the fetus. Pharmacological interventions have been used to directly treat a number of fetal disorders, including cardiac and thyroid disorders (Bringman & Philips, 2006).

FETAL SURGERY The use of fetal surgery is illustrated by the experience of a pregnant woman who had earlier given birth to an infant with hydrocephaly, an abnormal accumulation of fluid inside the skull that results in brain damage. An ultrasound diagnosis indicated that the fetus she was currently carrying was also accumulating fluid on the brain and would likely suffer brain damage if treatment were delayed until birth. Surgeons, working through a fibre-optic endoscope (described earlier), inserted a small valve in the back of the fetus' head to permit the excess fluid to drain, thereby relieving pressure on the brain.

Physicians are now able to carry out surgery on fetuses to address a variety of problems that are either life-threatening or will result in severe damage if not corrected early in development. Among the conditions for which fetal surgery is an option are blockage of the urinary tract, congenital diaphragmatic hernia (a condition in which the diaphragm does not fully form, allowing organs to enter the chest cavity and affect lung growth), and spina bifida and other neural tube defects (Bebbington, Johnson, Wilson, & Adzick, 2006).

FETAL GENE THERAPY Probably the greatest promise for prenatal treatment lies in the field of gene therapy. Suppose we could detect, say, the lack of an enzyme in a fetus' blood and could identify the specific gene that caused the defect. Working in the laboratory with a blood sample from the fetus, we would clip out the defective gene and insert a synthetic gene. After producing many copies of the blood cells containing the repaired chromosome, we would inject them into the fetus where they would survive, replicate, and provide sufficient amounts of the enzyme for normal development.

As we discussed in Chapter 3, such gene therapy is largely an experimental treatment. Most applications of the procedure involve treating disorders in children, or even adults. Research into uses of gene therapy with fetuses has thus far been limited to studies with animals (David & Rodeck, 2006). In addition, applications to date have been limited to the somatic or body cells and have not encompassed the germ cells involved in reproduction. In *germ-line therapy*, characteristics of the germ or sex cells are altered, which means that any changes affect not only the treated individual, but also the genes the individual passes on to his or her offspring. At present, germ-line therapy remains a prospect for the future (Snustad & Simmons, 2009). Notwithstanding these limitations, fetal applications of gene therapy remain exciting prospects for the future.

Links to Related Material

In Chapter 3, we discussed gene therapy and its potential uses as a treatment for genetic disorders.

For Thought and Discussion

Do you think it should be public policy for a population to be genetically screened? What might be some potential dangers in such a policy?

ETHICAL CONSIDERATIONS

The ability to diagnose abnormal development raises innumerable ethical questions—questions that people may find difficult to answer. Today's fetal-screening techniques can detect the presence of sickle-cell anemia, Huntington's disease, Down syndrome, cystic fibrosis, and numerous other maladies. What are the consequences of this knowledge? If no treatment is possible, the options are to terminate the pregnancy or to bring a child with a serious disorder into the world. Should damaged fetuses be aborted? If so, how disabling must the genetic defect be? If a child is diagnosed as genetically damaged as a fetus, should insurance companies be able to deny the child insurance, given that the companies know that health expenses will be exorbitant compared with those of other children?

The treatment of disorders while babies are still in the womb also raises difficult ethical questions. Procedures such as fetal surgery and gene repair are expensive, and not all families have the resources to benefit from them. In addition, most such procedures are still in the experimental phase, and they carry risks for both the baby and the mother. Surgery for urinary tract defects, for example, results in fetal death in 5 to 10 percent of the cases (Yankowitz, 1996).

Decisions regarding the health and life of a fetus or infant are intensely emotional and deeply embedded in social, ethical, and moral convictions. They are also very personal. As new technologies are developed, the fine line that separates these personal beliefs and feelings on the one side, and the government's role in protecting the rights of fetuses and infants on the other, may become increasingly blurred.

LEARNING OBJECTIVE 4.4

Discuss the various methods of preventing, identifying, and treating birth defects prenatally.

1. What is genetic counselling?
2. Discuss the available methods of screening prenatally for abnormalities.
3. What methods are used for prenatally treating abnormalities?
4. What ethical questions are associated with prenatal screening?

CONCLUSION

We live in a time when knowledge and technology in many fields are expanding at a dizzying pace. Nowhere are the effects of progress more dramatic than in biology and health-related fields. The field of prenatal development has benefited enormously from these advances.

Only relatively recently have we developed an understanding of the processes of conception and embryological development. It has been especially important for us to learn that differentiation of body parts and limbs occurs in the first eight weeks or so after conception. With this knowledge, we have been better able to understand why infections and certain drugs have more devastating effects on the organism during the early prenatal period than later.

Our awareness that the placenta does not always filter out chemicals and toxins from the mother's blood, and that these substances thus enter the bloodstream of the fetus, has had profound effects. Scientists actively look for causes of abnormal development that were previously ignored. Environmental pollutants, drugs, and other chemicals are suspect, and it is now routine to test new chemicals for toxic effects on the fetus. The new field of psychoteratology may provide even more sensitive indicators of harmful substances. Although we may not always know how or why these substances affect the fetus, at least we are learning when they do. Partly because of this knowledge, the ratio of stillbirths to live births in Canada and the United States has reached an all-time low.

An important message from this information is that the baby is in an environment from the moment of conception. By the time of birth, interactions between genes and the environment have been at play during the full nine months of development.

One might come away from this chapter fearful about all the things that threaten a baby's prenatal development. Keep in mind, though, that the very large majority of babies are born healthy and whole. Fortunately, as we learn about the dangers the fetus faces, we are increasingly able to take precautions to increase the likelihood that the newborn will get a healthy start.

SUMMARY

KEY TERMS

age of viability, p. 103
amniocentesis, p. 123
amniotic sac, p. 100
chorionic villus sampling (CVS), p. 123
conception, p. 98
embryo, p. 100
fetal alcohol syndrome (FAS), p. 113
fetus, p. 101
genetic counselling, p. 122
placenta, p. 100
teratogen, p. 105
teratology, p. 105
ultrasound imaging, p. 123
umbilical cord, p. 100
zygote, p. 98

LEARNING OBJECTIVES

LEARNING OBJECTIVE 4.1 Trace the changes that occur in the three stages of prenatal development.

1. *What changes occur during the period of the zygote between conception and the end of the second week of development?*
   Prenatal development begins with conception and proceeds through the period of the zygote, the period of the embryo, and the period of the fetus. At conception, a sperm cell penetrates an egg cell to form a zygote. The zygote multiplies rapidly during its four-day, 10-centimetre journey through the fallopian tube to the uterus, where it becomes fully implanted by the end of the second week.

2. *What changes occur during the period of the embryo between weeks three and eight?*
   Now an embryo, the cell mass rapidly differentiates into organs (heart, kidneys, eyes, ears, nervous system, and brain) and support structures (the amniotic sac, placenta, and umbilical

cord). In the six weeks that make up the period of the embryo, a cluster of cells is transformed into a complex and differentiated organism.

3. *What changes occur during the period of the fetus between the ninth week and birth?*
   At the end of the eighth week, the fetal period begins. The primary task for the fetus is growth and further development of organ systems. Behaviour begins in the third month. The fetus grows toward increasing independence, but is unable to survive before about 23 to 24 weeks of fetal age. By nine months following conception, the normal fetus is ready to face the external world.

4. *Describe two alternative methods of conception.*
   Two methods of conception are often used when infertility is a problem. When the problem involves the male, the most common solution is donor insemination, in which sperm donated from another male is inserted into the female. Another method is in vitro fertilization. In this process, an egg and sperm (donated from either a third party or from one or both members of the couple) are combined in a laboratory procedure; then the fertilized egg is implanted in the female's uterus.

LEARNING OBJECTIVE 4.2 Describe the impact of teratogens on prenatal development.

1. *What are teratogens?*
   Teratogens are agents that interfere with normal prenatal development. Teratology is the study of such agents. Psychoteratology focuses on the behavioural effects of teratogens. These effects may not always be obvious at birth and do not always include physical problems.

2. *How do teratogens act?*
   Six principles describe how teratogens act: (1) the effect depends on the genetic makeup of the organism; (2) the effect depends on timing; (3) the effect may be unique to the teratogen; (4) the abnormal development caused by teratogens may be severe; (5) teratogens gain access to the fetus in different ways; and (6) the effect increases with the level of exposure.

3. *What are some examples of teratogens?*
   Drugs are one category of teratogen. Street drugs, although illegal, have become increasingly available and can have highly negative effects on the fetus. Babies of drug-addicted mothers may be born addicted, and they are likely to have many developmental problems. Therapeutic drugs may also be harmful, as was the case with thalidomide.

   Some substances are so common in our daily lives that we may fail to think of them as drugs. Caffeine, nicotine, and alcohol are examples. Smoking has consistently been shown to affect growth and also to increase the risk of premature delivery, birth complications, and sudden infant death syndrome (SIDS). Alcohol consumption can produce a range of physical malformations and intellectual consequences, including fetal alcohol syndrome (FAS) and fetal alcohol spectrum disorder (FASD).

   Exposure to harmful chemicals can also occur when we take in the chemical by-products of industry through the food we eat and the air we breathe. Mercury and lead have been documented as particularly teratogenic, and PCBs also appear to be harmful.

   Diseases contracted by a pregnant woman can also affect the fetus. Among the conditions that can be transmitted to the fetus and produce damage are rubella, herpes, and HIV, which is the cause of AIDS.

LEARNING OBJECTIVE 4.3 Describe the natural challenges that can affect fetal development.

1. *How is nutrition important for fetal development?*
   The quality of the mother's nutrition is probably the most important environmental influence on the fetus. Maternal malnutrition can have devastating effects on the fetus, including

increased rates of spontaneous abortion, infant death, and congenital defects. The ultimate effect of fetal malnutrition depends in part on postnatal nutrition and on the level of stimulation in the environment.

2. *What are the consequences of maternal stress?*
   Although it can be difficult to isolate the effects of prenatal stress from other factors, maternal stress during pregnancy does seem to have potential negative effects on both the development of the fetus and later child outcomes. High levels of maternal stress increase the probability of preterm birth, low birth weight, and problems during delivery. Intellectual and language abilities may also be affected. Maternal anxiety and stress within normal limits, however, does not seem harmful. Social support can help reduce the potential harmful effects of stress.

3. *What effect does parental age have on prenatal development?*
   Parental age can also be a risk factor. As the parents' age increases, there is increased risk of Down syndrome and achondroplasia. On average, both older mothers and teenage mothers are more likely to have problems during pregnancy or birth than are women in the optimal childbearing age range. In both cases, however, factors associated with age (e.g., the mother's health) appear to be more important than age per se.

LEARNING OBJECTIVE 4.4 Discuss the various methods of preventing, identifying, and treating birth defects prenatally.

1. *What is genetic counselling?*
   Genetic counselling involves a range of activities focused on determining the likelihood that a couple will give birth to a child with a genetic disorder. Couples may seek genetic counselling if there is a family history of some genetic disease. Other risk factors are membership in an ethnic group that is known to have a heightened probability of inheriting a specific disorder (Tay-Sachs, sickle-cell anemia) or advanced age of the parents.

2. *Discuss the available methods of screening prenatally for abnormalities.*
   During pregnancy, diagnostic procedures provide a window on prenatal development that was unknown only a few decades ago. Ultrasound imaging can detect growth anomalies, such as abnormal head growth; heart, bladder, and kidney problems; and neural tube defects. Amniocentesis and chorionic villus sampling provide fetal cells that can be analyzed for chromosomal defects and genetic problems, as well as some other disorders. Endoscopic fetoscopy allows the fetus to be visually examined, and sometimes surgically treated, using a fibre-optic endoscope. Screening has even been carried out on embryos in test tubes.

3. *What methods are used for prenatally treating abnormalities?*
   When problems are detected, treatment can sometimes proceed even while the fetus is still in the uterus. Medical therapy, such as drug treatment, providing extra vitamins or other nutrients, and so on, is one possibility. Surgery is a second possibility, sometimes using the endoscopic fetoscopy procedure described previously. Gene therapy is increasingly becoming a third possibility.

4. *What ethical questions are associated with prenatal screening?*
   The ability to diagnose abnormal prenatal development raises numerous ethical questions concerning treatment, terminating pregnancies, prolonging life, and so on. These questions are intensely emotional and deeply personal, and have no easy answers.

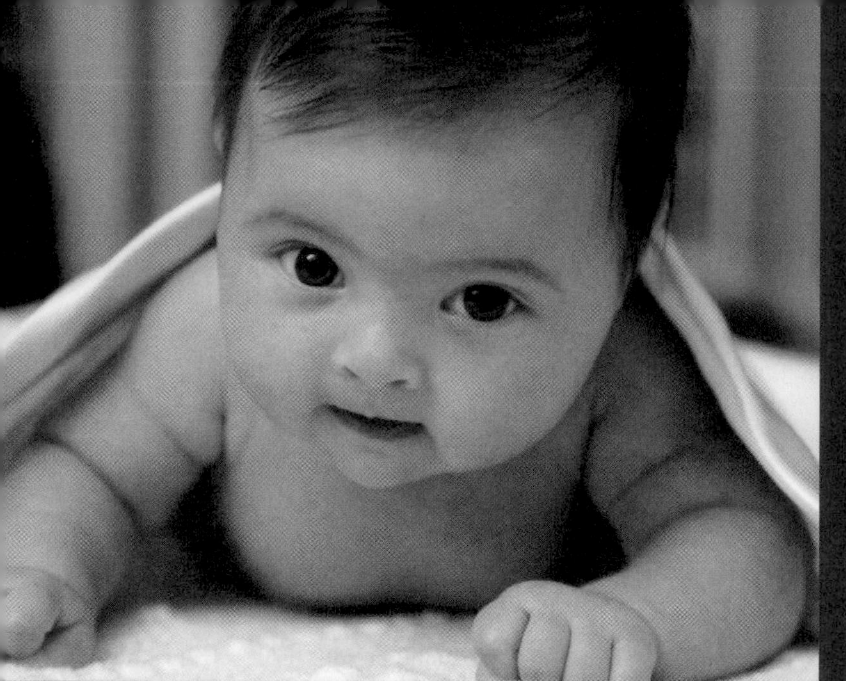

CHAPTER 5

PHYSICAL DEVELOPMENT: BIRTH, MOTOR SKILLS, AND GROWTH

By all indications, Tavin Roe is a normal and healthy 6-year-old. However, his early infancy was by no means typical or easy. Indeed, Tavin has overcome obstacles that few children have ever had to face. Tavin weighed only three pounds, 12 ounces when he was born at Royal Columbian Hospital in Burnaby, British Columbia in 2002.

Until recently, babies as young and as tiny as Tavin often did not survive without severe disabilities. When Tavin was born, he was taken immediately to the neonatal intensive care unit, where he needed oxygen and was placed in an incubator. "He wasn't able to coordinate breathing and eating at the same time," Tavin's mom, Kim Robinson said, adding that, while she was worried about Tavin, the hospital staff made her feel that her son was in good hands.

Each time Tavin was taken off oxygen he turned blue, so staff had to repeatedly place him back on oxygen. "It's terrifying. You don't know what's going to happen," Robinson said. Tavin, who was born nine weeks early, spent the first two months of his life in the hospital. Some babies may need to be kept in the unit for a few hours after birth, while others stay for up to three months.

Depending on each infant's needs, doctors may hook up incubators to monitor the babies' progress and ensure they have a speedy and safe recovery. Other premature babies need to be placed on a ventilator because their underdeveloped lungs cannot function on their own. Still others have to undergo intestinal, hernia, or other surgery.

Robinson was worried that her son would have developmental problems as a result of being born so early. However, after eight weeks in the unit, he was finally completely healthy and able to go home.

Clearly, tiny premature babies are a triumph of modern medical science. It is also a testimony to the strength that even the tiniest babies—and their families—can summon in the face of adversity. In this chapter we examine children's physical development and growth. We begin by examining the birth process, considering both the challenges that all newborns face—and the special challenges that sometimes arise—and how medical science has learned to deal with these challenges.

Source: Hitchcock, Erin, "Unit offers big help for the tiniest babies," *Burnaby Now*, February 9, 2008. ■

THIS CHAPTER FOCUSES ON the child's physical development, beginning at birth and continuing through adolescence. What happens during birth or the perinatal period can affect the child for years to come, and so we discuss the nature of the birth process and the factors, such as prematurity, that put children at risk for developmental problems. Physical development involves more than just growth, although that is certainly an important part of it. We will also see how a baby acquires the motor skills to manipulate objects and to explore the environment, skills that have enormous psychological impact on development. Finally, we examine the physical changes during adolescence that prepare the body for reproduction but that also can affect the individual's self-image and identity.

Learning Objective 5.1

Discuss the stages of labour, the social and cultural factors that influence childbirth, and the assessment of factors affecting newborn health.

Perinatal period The events and environment surrounding the birth process.

BIRTH AND THE PERINATAL PERIOD

Our story starts with birth and its surrounding events—the **perinatal period.** Birth is truly a momentous event, as the child moves from a relatively sheltered and protected environment to the busy and much less predictable outside world, where the remainder of development will occur.

Typically, the birth process proceeds smoothly. In this technological age, we sometimes forget that humans have accomplished this feat over millions of years without hospitals, doctors, or elaborate equipment. Occasionally, however, modern technology is crucial for making the process work and even for saving the baby's life. After briefly describing the physical aspects of birth, we consider some problems that can arise and the notion of infants at risk.

LABOUR AND DELIVERY

Typically around 38 weeks after fertilization and sometimes earlier, a pregnant woman will go into labour, the first step in the birth process. Labour at full-term and at preterm appears to be initiated by changes in the fetal brain (Smith, 1999), and has even been linked to specific genes (Wu, Ma, Zhang, Chakrabarty, & Nathanielsz, 2003). Chemicals are released that signal the muscles of the mother's uterus to start contracting rhythmically, initially every 15 to 20 minutes and then at shorter intervals. The complete birth process requires, on average, about 8 to 16 hours for the first baby and about half as much time for later babies.

Labour consists of three stages, as shown in Figure 5.1. The first and longest stage begins when the early contractions start to narrow the uterus and dilate (widen) the cervical opening through which the baby will pass. This stage ends when the cervix is fully dilated, usually about 10 cm. By the end of this stage, the contractions are very intense, occurring every two to three minutes. The second stage begins when the fetus starts to pass through the cervix and ends when the baby has been completely delivered into the world. During this stage the contractions are long and closely

FIGURE 5.1

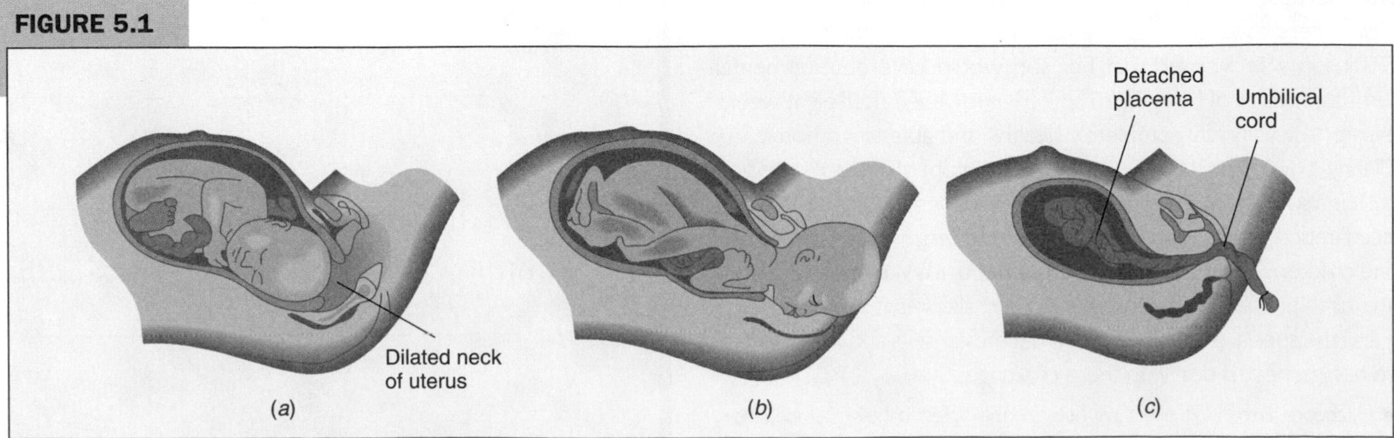

The three stages of labour: (a) the neck of the uterus dilates; (b) the baby is delivered; and (c) the placenta is expelled.

spaced, and the mother is encouraged to assist the process by pushing with each contraction. The third stage, which often lasts only minutes, involves the delivery of the placenta and related other membranes, referred to as the *afterbirth.*

Technological advances permit the monitoring of the fetus' state during birth. Physicians can visualize the fetus, the umbilical cord, and the placenta by ultrasound to determine, for example, whether there is a danger that the umbilical cord will wrap around the fetus' neck (which can cause strangulation). They also can electronically record the heart rate and activity of the fetus through the mother's abdomen to determine whether there are signs of **fetal distress,** which would be indicated by an abnormally high or low heart rate (Galazios et al., 2010).

Fetal distress A condition of abnormal stress on the fetus, reflected during the birth process in an abnormal fetal heart rate.

Sometimes birth cannot proceed according to nature's plan because, for example, the baby is lying in an unusual position in the uterus (such as sideways or buttocks down), delivery is proceeding too slowly, or the baby's head is too large to pass through the cervical opening. In such cases, the doctor often elects to perform a **caesarean section**, in which the baby is surgically removed directly from the uterus. The rate of caesarean deliveries has fluctuated markedly across the last several decades. In Canada, caesarean births have increased 40 percent since 1997 to over 26 percent of all births in 2005. A similar trend occurred in the United States, where the percentage of caesarean births skyrocketed from 5 percent in 1969 to 25 percent in 1988 and to 31 percent in 2007. Some critics were alarmed by this increase, charging that many of these procedures were performed for unjustifiable reasons, such as greater convenience for doctors, reduced risk of malpractice suits, maternal requests to avoid labour, and perhaps due to the increased use of epidurals (Klein, 2005; Menacker, Declercq, & Macdorman, 2006; Robson, Tan, Adeyemi, & Dear, 2009). Perhaps because of such criticisms, the rate of caesarean births declined across the first half of the 1990s, only to begin to move upward again in 1997. Why might there be concern about a increased rate of caesarean deliveries? Such deliveries pose greater risks of infection for the mother than do vaginal births, and they also expose the newborn to higher levels of pain-relieving medication (Trevathen, 1987). Yet, in developing countries that tend to have high maternal, infant, and neonatal mortality rates, increased access to caesarean deliveries are likely to produce lower levels of mortality (Betrán et al., 2007). At present, however, there is no clear evidence that caesarean birth has any long-term negative effects on children's development.

Caesarean section Surgical delivery of the fetus directly from the uterus; performed when normal delivery is prohibited.

CULTURAL ATTITUDES TOWARD BIRTH

Although the stages of birth are the same in all cultures, there are many variations in how cultures think about and deal with birth.

It has been said that in most Western countries, pregnancy, labour, and delivery have typically been treated as if they were the symptoms of an illness. Pregnant women have been encouraged to visit the doctor regularly. Most have given birth in a hospital lying down (some say for the convenience of the doctor) and have been given drugs to block pain. Often, after the baby's birth, doctors and nurses, not the baby's mother, have taken over the baby's care, at least for a while.

Is Western civilization unique in looking at pregnancy as a sort of disability and birth as a process requiring medical intervention? Not entirely. Among the Cuna Indians of Panama, for example, a pregnant woman must visit the medicine man daily for herbal medicines, and women are given medication throughout labour. Various interventions during labour are practised in many cultures: the pregnant woman's abdomen may be massaged, perhaps with masticated roots or melted butter, or even constricted to help push out the baby. For difficult cases, midwives of Myanmar (formerly Burma) tread on the woman's abdomen with their feet.

Nevertheless, the attitude of the West is often contrasted with that of cultures in which birth is seen as an everyday occurrence. Among the Jarara of South America, for example, labour and birth are so much a part

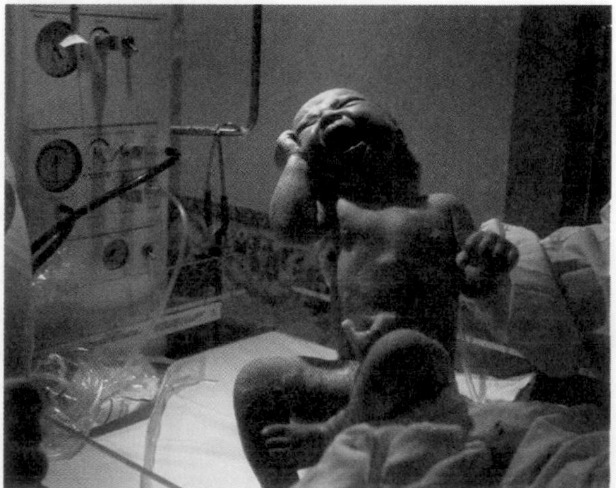

In many societies, doctors and nurses take over the baby's care, at least for a little while after birth. (*Jeff McIntosh/The Canadian Press*)

of daily life that a woman may give birth in a passageway or shelter in view of everyone. In many cultures, women give birth alone. And some non-Western women deliver in an upright position—kneeling, sitting, squatting, and even standing—rather than lying down.

Practices have changed fairly rapidly in North America, where there has been a trend toward making birth more "natural." An English obstetrician, Grantly Dick-Read, wrote a book, *Natural Childbirth,* in 1933 and a second, *Childbirth without Fear,* in 1944 to put forth the view that Western societies had created an association between childbirth and pain. Fear of pain, he said, actually created tension and muscle cramping that produced pain unnecessarily. These ideas were reinforced by Dr. F. Lamaze in *Painless Childbirth* (1970). Lamaze's popular method of preparation for childbirth is based on conditioning through breathing and muscle exercises and on educating the mother about pregnancy and labour.

Other related obstetric practices have emerged in recent years. One involves having the father present during the birth process, sometimes serving as the mother's breathing coach. Another is a return to giving birth at home, often with the assistance of a trained midwife rather than a doctor.

Is the naturalist trend right? Although more research is needed, to date no negative effects have been shown for practices that depart from the medicated, hospital-birth model that has been the norm in Canada and the United States. Maybe the truly remarkable fact is that mothers and newborns usually survive the birth process just fine, whatever the rituals are within their respective cultures.

Culture also affects the likelihood that the mother will survive pregnancy and childbirth. In the United States, because of improved health care, maternal deaths per 100,000 pregnant women have fallen from approximately 660 in 1931 to approximately 7 today. In Canada, there were 12 maternal deaths per 100,000 pregnant women in 2008. In some African countries, however, the death rate is still as high as 1,200 per 100,000 pregnancies. Around the world even today, more than 350,000 women each year lose their lives from complications of pregnancy and labour (World Health Organization, 2010).

Babies face hazards during the birth process as well, and some do not survive. Scientists and physicians have devoted enormous efforts to addressing these problems and are making good progress. In 1901, there were 134 deaths for every 1,000 infants under the age of 1 year in Canada. In 2007, the rate was 5.1, about 26 times lower. However, as shown in Table 5.1, there are some disparities across Canada. In 2007, the highest infant mortality rate occurred in Nunavut, with 15.1 deaths per 1,000 infants. Infant mortality rates in the Northwest Territories, however, have decreased faster than those of other parts of the country over the past 40 years. The gap between the richest and the poorest neighbourhoods has also declined since the 1970s. In 1996, even the poorest neighbourhoods in Canada had infant mortality rates lower than those of the United States (6.4 and 7.8, respectively). Nevertheless, in 2008, 22 countries had infant mortality rates lower than Canada's rate.

THE CONCEPT OF RISK

Parents worry about whether their baby will be normal. In more than nine out of ten cases, the baby is born on time and healthy. But some parents and their babies are not so fortunate. Approximately 3 percent of all babies born in Canada each year—10,000 or so infants—are born with major physical malformations.

At risk Describes babies who have a higher likelihood of experiencing developmental problems.

Whereas some babies have immediately obvious physical problems, other babies are considered **at risk** for cognitive and social problems and developmental delays. Psychologists believe that the earlier they can identify these babies, the earlier they can intervene to help. Thus, over the past few decades, hundreds of studies have attempted to discover what factors put infants in the highest category of risk. Three indicators seem to be most important: maternal and family characteristics, the physical compromise of the newborn, and the performance of the newborn on behavioural assessments.

MATERNAL AND FAMILY CHARACTERISTICS A baby's chances of developing problems can be predicted, in part, from the family context in which the child is born. Around 85 percent

TABLE 5.1 INFANT MORTALITY RATES IN CANADA FROM 2003 TO 2007 (DEATHS IN THE FIRST YEAR PER 1,000 LIVE BIRTHS)

	2003	2004	2005	2006	2007
Canada	**5.3**	**5.3**	**5.4**	**5.0**	**5.1**
Newfoundland	5.0	5.1	6.2	5.3	7.5
Prince Edward Island	4.9	4.3	2.2	2.1	5.0
Nova Scotia	5.7	4.6	4.0	4.0	3.3
New Brunswick	4.1	4.3	4.1	4.0	4.3
Quebec	4.4	4.6	4.6	5.1	4.5
Ontario	5.3	5.5	5.6	5.0	5.2
Manitoba	8.0	7.0	6.6	6.0	7.3
Saskatchewan	6.3	6.2	8.3	6.1	5.8
Alberta	6.6	5.8	6.8	5.3	6.0
British Columbia	4.2	4.3	4.5	4.1	4.0
Yukon Territory	6.0	11.0	0.0	8.2	8.5
Northwest Territories	5.7	0.0	4.2	10.2	4.1
Nunavut	19.8	16.1	10.0	13.4	15.1

Source: "Infant Mortality Rates in Canada from 2003 to 2007," adapted from the Statistics Canada publication "Deaths," June 29, 2010. Catalogue No. 84F0211X, available at: http://www.statcan.gc.ca/daily-quotidien/100223/dq100223a-eng.htm

of the risk of severe developmental problems can be attributed to what happens in the prenatal period. As mentioned in the preceding chapter, several maternal factors increase risk for the fetus, including the mother's use of drugs or alcohol, exposure to viral infections during pregnancy, smoking, and poor nutrition. In addition, living in conditions of poverty increases the probability of almost every early threat to the well-being of mother and child. Both preterm birth and low birth weight are almost twice as likely for low-income families as for the general population, and inadequate prenatal care is close to three times more common (Children's Defense Fund, 2008). Over time, babies born in families who have strained financial resources, poor social support, and little education are at greater risk for a number of negative outcomes than are those born in more advantaged families (Bradley & Corwyn, 2002; Conger & Donnellan, 2007).

In Canada, it is estimated that 10 percent of babies are at risk due to the poor health, nutritional status, and economic and social conditions of their mothers (Health Canada, 2000). In order to develop or enhance programs for vulnerable pregnant woman and to give babies a healthier start in life, the government of Canada has launched the Canada Prenatal Nutrition Program (CPNP) in partnership with community groups. Around 350 projects serving over 2,000 communities across Canada are funded by this program. Inuit and on-reserve First Nations communities are served by 450 other projects. Most of the projects offer food and vitamin supplements, breastfeeding support, nutrition counselling, counselling on lifestyle issues, food preparation training, child care, and referral to other services. In 2001, over 50,000 women participated in the program, 6,000 of whom were living in Inuit and on-reserve First Nations communities (Public Health Agency of Canada, 2008).

PHYSICAL COMPROMISE OF THE NEWBORN A second general indicator of risk is evidence of physical problems in the newborn, most frequently, low birth weight. Around 5 to 6 percent of the babies born in Canada each year (around 18,000) have a low birth weight, below 2,500 g (about 5.5 lb). Low-birth-weight babies are about 25 times more likely to die in the first month of life than are babies with normal birth weight (Mathews, Menacker, & MacDorman, 2004), though trends indicate that mortality is decreasing in low-birth-weight babies due to improved health care treatments (Meadow, Lee, Lin, & Lantos, 2004). They are also at greater risk for many problems, large and small (Hack, Klein, & Taylor, 1995). Why is this so?

The newborn must make a number of adaptations to the outside world. Temperature control and nutrition are no longer provided by the mother's body, but these needs are rather easily met by the parents or other providers. Breathing, however, is a different story. After living in a water world for almost nine months, the baby must draw the first breath of air within seconds after birth. Babies with low birth weight are more likely to have difficulty initiating or maintaining breathing. Failure to breathe prevents the delivery of oxygen to cells—a condition called **anoxia**—which can cause the cells to die. The brain cells are especially sensitive to oxygen deficits. Severe anoxia, for example, may damage the brain area that controls movement of the limbs, resulting in a spastic-type movement referred to as cerebral palsy (Behrman, Kliegman, & Jenson, 2000).

Anoxia A deficit of oxygen to the cells that can produce brain or other tissue damage.

Low-birth-weight babies may be placed in two groups. One comprises babies whose birth weights are low because they were born **preterm**, meaning before the end of the normal 38 weeks of pregnancy. Preterm babies often have the breathing problems just described. In many, tiny blood vessels in the brain burst, causing bleeding and contributing to the infant's risk.

Preterm Describes babies born before the end of the normal gestation period.

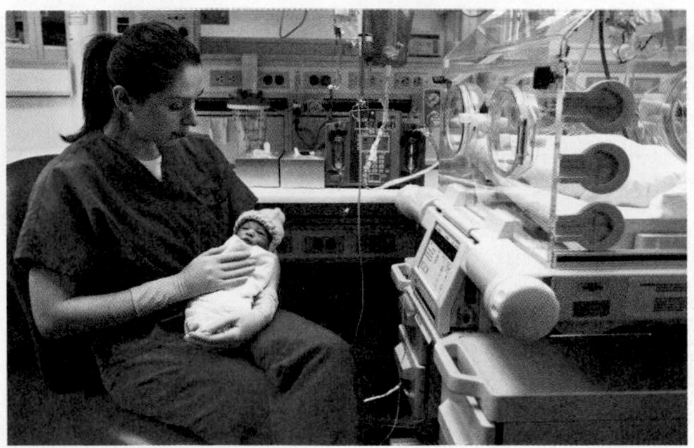

Babies born with low birth weight are at greater risk for many problems. (*Corbis/Media Bakery*)

Even disregarding these physical challenges, development in a preterm baby may lag behind that in a full-term baby, at least for a time. Although we would expect the preterm infant, who is comparable to a fetus still in the womb, to be less advanced than the full-term baby, even when matched for the number of days following fertilization, the preterm infant usually has less mature brain patterns and is more disorganized and difficult to soothe (Anderson & Doyle, 2003; Duffy, Als, & McAnulty, 1990). In the long term, these babies can be expected to have more frequent problems with growth and overall health issues (Saigal et al., 2000). They also are at greater risk for cognitive and behavioural problems in later childhood and adolescence (Saigal, 2004; Taylor et al., 2000).

The other group of babies born with a low birth weight are those whose fetal growth was retarded. These babies are considered **small for gestational age** (SGA). They may be born at the expected gestational age of 9 months, or they may be born earlier (and so are both SGA and preterm), but they are in this category because their weight places them among the bottom 10 percent of babies born at that particular gestational age. Although the cause is frequently unknown, several factors including chromosomal abnormalities, infections, poor maternal nutrition, and maternal substance abuse appear to increase the likelihood that a baby's prenatal growth will be delayed.

Small for gestational age (SGA) Describes babies born at a weight in the bottom 10 percent of babies of a particular gestational age.

SGA babies also face developmental risks (Goldenberg, 1995). For example, these infants are not aroused easily, and they tend to have poor muscle tone, appearing limp when held. They also are disadvantaged beyond the newborn period; for example, they show poorer recognition memory than do babies born at normal weight (Gotlieb, Baisini, & Bray, 1988). SGA babies who are preterm perform more poorly on verbal tests of IQ as preschoolers than do preterm babies whose weights were appropriate for their ages, although their eventual developmental course depends heavily on the quality of their post-birth environment (Dowling & Bendell, 1988; Gorman & Pollitt, 1992).

Recent research suggests that being born even as little as one week premature confers a slightly greater need for special education remedies for various learning disabilities (MacKay, Smith, Dobbie, & Pell, 2010). This likely results from a higher risk for neurodevelopmental problems in preterm infants, which may affect cognitive functioning into adolescence (Stephens & Vohr, 2009). However, recent use of various drugs, such as perinatal steroids and inhaled nitric oxide, have been shown to mitigate any neurodevelopmental impairments in low-birth-weight babies (Barrington & Finer,

2010; Jobe, 2004). Additionally, a major concern for preterm infants is the various conditions, such as bleeding in the brain and excessive fluids, that cause the brain to swell and that cause injury to the immature brain, resulting in cerebral palsy as well as serious learning deficiencies. A promising new treatment has been devised, however, to drain any excess fluids in a premature baby's brain, thereby reducing potential disabilities (Whitelaw et al., 2010).

Steady improvement in technology has produced a dramatic decline in deaths resulting from low birth weight, according to Klaus Minde of McGill University. Although a birth weight below 2,500 g (5.5 lb) is classified as low, babies weighing only 500 g (a little more than 1 lb) have at least a 25 percent chance of surviving, and the odds rise to more than 90 percent for babies who weigh at least 1,000 g (about 2.2 lb) (Minde, 1993). The tiniest babies—those who weigh less than 1,000 g—are 50 to 60 times more likely to survive today than was the case 35 years ago (Minde, 2000). Much of this progress can be attributed to the development of neonatal intensive care units (NICUs). In these facilities, low-birth-weight babies receive various forms of stimulation—rocking, sound recordings of the mother's heartbeat, high-contrast mobiles, gentle massage, and the like—which appear to help their early development (Field, 2001; Mueller, 1996). In addition to NICUs, advances in drug treatments have led to nearly a 50 percent increase since the early 1980s in survivability, and a 50 percent decrease in the incidence of cerebral palsy and neurological impairments (Wilson-Costello et al., 2007).

One consequence of these interventions is that very tiny babies who would once have died at birth are now kept alive and have more positive developmental outcomes. These babies, however, face strong challenges in life and to their well-being; the lighter the baby, the higher these risks.

PHYSICAL AND BEHAVIOURAL ASSESSMENT A third indicator of risk is poor performance on standard assessments. Perhaps as a sign of things to come, almost all babies born in Canada and the United States begin life with a test. Tests are used to screen babies for disorders, to determine whether a baby's nervous system is intact, and to characterize how a newborn responds to social and physical stimuli. Even though newborns are new to the external world, they possess a surprising range of behaviours and functions. Newborn tests can assess more than 85 percent of such behaviours and functions (Francis, Self, & Horowitz, 1987). Here, we consider the two most-often used tests: the Apgar exam and the Brazelton Neonatal Behavioral Assessment Scale.

In 1953, Dr. Virginia Apgar introduced a test that permitted obstetricians to objectively record the status of the newborn. This test has become the standard for the baby's first assessment. The **Apgar exam** focuses on five of the newborn's vital functions, which are measured by heart rate, respiration, muscle tone, response to a mildly painful stimulus, and skin colour. The newborn receives a score from 0 to 2 on each of these items. Table 5.2 presents each of the five functions. For example, the baby earns a 2 for the heart-rate category if the heart beats 100 to 140 times per minute; a 1 if the rate is less than 100; and a 0 if no beat is detectable. Babies are typically assessed on the five categories almost immediately after birth and then again five minutes later. The highest possible score is 10. On average, about 77 percent of newborns receive a score of 8 to 10, 17 percent a score of 3 to 7, and 6 percent a score of 0 to 2 (Apgar, 1953).

Apgar exam An exam administered immediately after birth that assesses vital functions, such as heart rate and respiration.

Investigators use the Apgar test to identify babies who may need special monitoring and attention through early infancy. Several factors tend to lower the Apgar score, including maternal depression, anxiety, smoking, drinking, and labour medication. Psychologists have examined the relation between a newborn's Apgar score and intellectual functioning later in infancy and early childhood. The results have been mixed. Some investigators have reported a positive relation. For example, a recent assessment of the relation between Apgar scores and IQ found that the lower the Apgar score for a newborn, the lower the IQ is as a teenager (Odd, Rasmussen, Gunnell, Lewis, & Whitelaw, 2008). However, others report no relation when socio-economic status, race, and gender are taken into consideration (Francis et al., 1987; Malacova et al., 2009).

TABLE 5.2 THE FIVE VITAL FUNCTIONS ASSESSED AND SCORING SYSTEM FOR THE APGAR TEST

Function	0 Point	1 Point	2 Point
Activity (Muscle Tone)	Absent	Arms and Legs Flexed	Active Movement
Pulse	Absent	< 100 bpm	> 100 bpm
Grimace (Reflex Irritability)	No response	Grimace	Sneeze, cough, pulls away
Appearance (Skin Colour)	Blue-grey, pale all over	Normal, except for extremities	Normal over entire body
Respiration	Absent	Slow, irregular	Good, crying

The Apgar exam assesses vital life processes and can be quickly administered, but the results provide only limited information. The newborn possesses a wealth of behavioural tools that cannot be captured in a brief exam that focuses on physiological functioning. Moreover, newborn babies differ substantially in how they behave, and these differences may affect how parents and others treat them. For these reasons, investigators have focused increasingly on tests of how well the newborn's behaviour is organized.

Brazelton Neonatal Behavioral Assessment Scale The most comprehensive of newborn assessment instruments; assesses attention and social responsiveness, muscle tone and physical movement, control of alertness, and physiological response to stress.

The **Brazelton Neonatal Behavioral Assessment Scale** (Brazelton & Nugent, 1995) is the most comprehensive of the newborn tests. The main idea underlying this scale is that the seemingly helpless newborn actually possesses organized behaviours for dealing with both attractive stimuli—such as pleasant sights, sounds, and tastes—and offensive stimuli—such as loud noises and pinpricks. Assessors observe the baby in a number of states, or levels of alertness, to obtain a sense of the baby's style and temperament. An important feature of the exam is that it evaluates the newborn's ability to habituate. Recall from Chapter 1 that habituation is a simple form of learning in which a reflex response to a stimulus declines or disappears when the stimulus occurs repeatedly.

The exam includes items in four categories: attention and social responsiveness; muscle tone and physical movement; control of alertness (habituation, irritability, and excitability); and physiological response to stress. The baby's performance on these measures provides indicators of well-being and risk. For example, a baby who is unable to habituate to a repeated stimulus or remain alert may fall into a higher risk category. Table 5.3 provides some sample items from the Brazelton Scale.

Dr. T. Berry Brazelton developed a widely used scale for assessing the newborn. (*Courtesy of Dr. T. Berry Brazelton*)

The Brazelton Scale does a fairly good job of characterizing how a baby is doing in the early period. It is helpful, for example, in identifying problems in babies who have been subjected to conditions that put them at risk, such as low birth weight or prenatal drug exposure. Because the Brazelton Scale is so helpful in identifying babies potentially at risk, it is now used worldwide (Nugent, Petrauskas, & Brazelton, 2009). It is not a good predictor, however, of development beyond the early infancy period (Lester & Tronick, 2001). The same conclusion applies to other early assessment instruments, as well as to each of the risk factors discussed when considered in isolation. This fact may seem surprising to anyone who has seen a very-low-weight baby in the newborn intensive care nursery. A 907-g (2-lb) baby who is little more than tubes, able to breathe only with a respirator, and perhaps suffering internal brain bleeding, may seem to be on the verge of death.

TABLE 5.3 EXAMPLES OF ITEMS FROM THE BRAZELTON NEONATAL BEHAVIORAL ASSESSMENT SCALE

Item	Description
Response decrement to light	While infant is asleep, shine light in eyes and observe response; after response disappears, wait 5 seconds and re-present; continue for either 10 trials or until habituation occurs.
Response decrement to rattle	While infant is asleep, shake rattle near ear and observe response; continue for either 10 trials or until habituation occurs.
Inanimate visual orientation	Slowly move a red ball across the infant's field of vision; record ability to track both horizontally and vertically.
Animate visual orientation	Have examiner slowly move his or her face across the infant's field of vision; record ability to track both horizontally and vertically.
Animate auditory orientation	While out of the infant's line of sight, have examiner speak softly into baby's ear; record ability to localize on each side.
Defensive movement	With infant in supine position, hold cloth over eyes for 30 seconds; record defensive responses (e.g., swipes at cloth).

Source: From Brazelton, Berry, T. and Nugent, Kevin, J. (2011). *Neonatal Behavioral Assessment* Scale, 4th Edition. (Part of the Clinics in Developmental Medicine Series.) London: Mac Keith Press. Used with permission.

Amazingly, this baby is more than likely to turn out fine. The best predictor of developmental difficulties is the number of risk factors to which an infant is subjected; the greater the number, the more likely that the infant will have problems (Walker, Wachs, Gardner, Lozoff, Wasserman, Pollitt, & Carter, 2007).

THE ROLE OF THE LATER ENVIRONMENT Some babies who are born at risk have suffered brain or central nervous system damage that affects their functioning throughout life. However, in many cases, whether babies born at risk achieve normal development appears to depend largely on the context in which they are reared. Because most of the research supporting this finding has been carried out with preterm infants, we focus on that work, but many of these factors play a role in determining the outcome of any baby at risk.

One factor in a baby's developmental progress is the quality of the relationship that forms between the parents and the baby (Mangelsdorf et al., 1996; Gianni et al., 2006). At-risk babies often pose special challenges to this relationship. For example, a preterm baby may spend weeks in a plastic enclosure in a special-care hospital nursery that affords the parents little opportunity to hold and cuddle the baby. When finally at home, the baby is likely to have an irritating cry, be difficult to soothe, and have irregular patterns of sleep and wakefulness (Hughes et al., 2002). Such babies also smile less when interacting with adults and are more likely to turn away and avoid eye-to-eye contact (Eckerman et al., 1999). Unfortunately, the nature of the parent–baby interaction may play an important role in very preterm babies' cognitive and motor development (Treyvaud et al., 2009).

These real problems are aggravated by people's reactions to preterm babies. In one study, several sets of parents were shown a film of a 5-month-old baby after they had been told that the baby was normal, difficult, or premature (a term the researchers used for both SGA and preterm babies). Those who were told that the baby was premature judged the crying segments of the film more negatively than did other parents, and physiological measures indicated that they experienced the baby's cries as more stressful (Frodi et al., 1978).

Other investigators have observed that parents treat their preterm children differently, even after apparent differences between them and full-term babies have disappeared (Strathearn, 2003; Beckwith & Parmelee, 1986). The tendency to expect negative behaviour from premature infants is referred to as *prematurity stereotyping* (Stern et al., 2006). Such stereotypes increase the possibility that a negative cycle between parent and infant will be set in motion. Of course, the degree to which this occurs depends, in part, on the tolerance and flexibility of the caregivers, which is often related to their accurate understanding of the infant's needs (Benasich & Brooks-Gunn, 1996). The resources available to the family can also be important. By 2 to 3 years of age, preterm children born into families that have strong financial resources seem indistinguishable from children born at term. Conversely, the presence of financial and other stresses reduces the emotional availability of the parents, and makes it less likely that they will adapt successfully to the challenges of the preterm infant (Berlin et al., 1988).

A contributor to disruption of the parent–infant relationship in the past was the hospital policy of not permitting the parents to hold or touch their infant in the special-care nursery because of the fear of infection. We can easily imagine how a mother's confidence in caring for her newborn might be jeopardized after being limited for six to eight weeks to watching the baby through a transparent incubator shield. As investigators began to recognize the importance of the very earliest social interactions between mother and infant, the situation changed. A group at Stanford University took the daring step of permitting parents to handle their infants in the special-care nursery, and demonstrated that no increased danger of infection resulted (Barnett et al., 1970). Subsequent work demonstrated that handling enhanced mothers' self-confidence in responding to their babies (Leiderman & Seashore, 1975; Seashore et al., 1973).

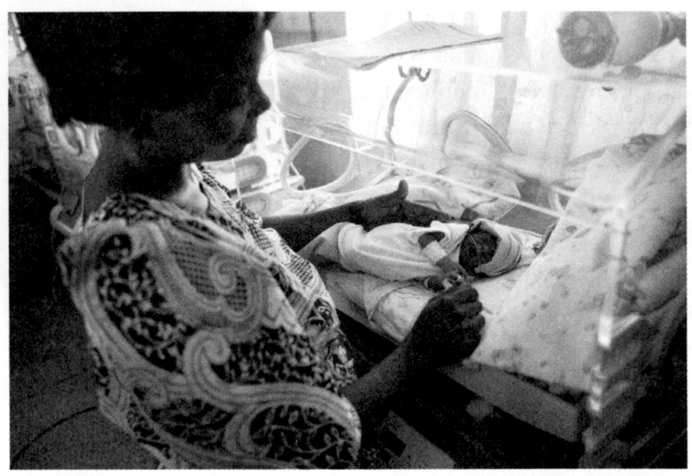
Modern hospital practice recognizes that the opportunity for parents to touch and to stimulate their preterm infants can be valuable—for both infant and parent. (© *Jake Lyell/Alamy*)

As mentioned earlier, NICUs have become important facilities for improving the survivability and early development of low-birth-weight infants. One of the side effects of NICUs, however, is that because the babies are secluded in an incubator, the amount of direct skin-to-skin contact between parents and their newborn babies is severely limited. Recently, a new intervention called *kangaroo care* has been introduced, which helps parents to increase the amount and duration of their skin-to-skin contact. The kangaroo care intervention has three components: (1) the infant is positioned upright on the mother's or father's chest (i.e., kangaroo position) and is maintained in this position for 24 hours a day until he reaches full-term gestational age; (2) the infant receives kangaroo nutrition, including breastfeeding and vitamin supplements; and (3) the baby is clinically monitored every day until it is gaining at minimum 20 g per day, after which it is monitored on a weekly basis until it reaches full-term gestational age (Tessier et al., 2009). Research by Rejean Tessier of Laval University in Quebec and his colleagues has shown that kangaroo care not only facilitates the rate of growth and development of preterm infants to a greater extent than traditional NICU care, but it also increases mothers' confidence in their preterm infants' development and protects against developmental delay (Tessier, Cristo, Velez, Giron, de Calume, et al., 2003; Tessier, Cristo, Velez, Giron, Nadeau, et al., 2003; Tessier et al., 1998). Furthermore, the extent of the beneficial effects of kangaroo care are related to how much the father is involved in providing the care, and the effects seem to provide a greater benefit for male infants (Tessier et al., 2009). In terms of mothers' self-confidence, kangaroo care has been shown to provide a beneficial boost there as well (Johnson, 2007). The importance of skin-to-skin contact for infants, and premature infants in particular, has led not only to encouraging mothers to handle their babies, but also to giving their premature babies massage therapy. This massage therapy not only enhances mothers' self-confidence, but also has positive effects on preterm infants' development, including improving weight gain (Field, Diego, & Hernandez-Reif, 2010). A factor related to skin-to-skin contact is the lack of stimulation that infants often experience when they must spend time in the hospital. The temperature-controlled, patternless plastic chambers in which they are placed deprive them not only of human physical contact, but of sensory input as well. As we have seen, intervention procedures introduced in NICUs have begun to address this problem.

There is concern, however, that for some premature babies, added stimulation becomes overstimulation and has a negative rather than positive effect. One creative idea is to provide stimulation that the babies themselves can decide to experience or avoid. For example, one investigator placed a "breathing" teddy bear in the baby's bed, which the baby could either contact or avoid. Premature babies who had the breathing bear tended to stay near it more than those who had a non-breathing bear, and they spent a longer amount of time in quiet sleep (Thoman, 1993).

LEARNING OBJECTIVE 5.1

Discuss the stages of labour, the social and cultural factors that influence childbirth, and the assessment of factors affecting newborn health.

1. What happens during the three stages of childbirth?
2. What societal attitudes influence the experience of childbirth in Canada today?
3. How does culture affect the survival rate of mother and newborn?
4. What are some indicators of babies at risk?
5. What are some common birth complications?
6. What are the common tests for assessing newborns' behavioural and physical health?
7. Discuss the reasons for low birth weight in infants.
8. What are some environmental factors that affect at-risk infants' development?

THE ORGANIZED NEWBORN

Learning Objective 5.2

Describe ways in which the infant's behaviour appears to be organized at birth.

Look at a newborn baby and you will see that the baby's face, if he is awake, changes expression rapidly for no apparent reason, and his legs and arms often flail around with no seeming purpose or pattern. A sleeping baby is less active, but her sleep is punctuated by twists, turns, startles, and grunts—a fairly unorganized picture. Seeing these behaviours, you can understand why, during most of the history of child psychology, people considered the newborn a passive and helpless creature whose activity was essentially random. Any organized behaviour was thought to depend on external stimulation. Is it true that the newborn comes into the world with no organized patterns of behaviour for sleeping, eating, getting the caregiver's attention, or even moving? Must caregivers teach the baby all these things?

Research on newborn behaviour since the 1960s has drastically changed these views. Certainly, the newborn is not as coordinated or predictable as the 2-year-old, but the behaviour of the newborn is neither random nor disorganized. The newborn possesses natural rhythms of activity that generate patterns of sleeping and wakefulness, eating, and motion. Moreover, the newborn is equipped with many reflexive responses to external stimulation and a few organized behavioural patterns for investigating and controlling the environment through looking, sucking, and crying.

STATES OF ALERTNESS

Often the first question grandparents and friends ask the nurse about the new baby is, "Is the baby asleep or awake?" But there are other possibilities. Over 40 years ago, Peter Wolff, at the Harvard Medical School, carefully watched several newborn babies for many hours and was struck by

TABLE 5.4 STATES OF INFANT ALERTNESS

State	Characteristics
Deep sleep	Regular breathing; eyes closed with no eye movements; no activity except for occasional jerky movements
Light sleep	Eyes closed but rapid eye movements can be observed; activity level low; movements are smoother than in deep sleep; breathing may be irregular
Drowsiness	Eyes may open and close but look dull when open; responses to stimulation are delayed, but stimulation may cause state to change; activity level varies
Alert inactivity	Eyes open and bright; attention focused on stimuli; activity level relatively low
Alert activity	Eyes open; activity level high; may show brief fussiness; reacts to stimulation with increases in startles and motor activity
Crying	Intense crying that is difficult to stop; high level of motor activity

how much their levels of alertness varied and yet how similar these levels were from one baby to another (Wolff, 1959, 1966). He captured these observations by defining six states of infant alertness: (1) quiet, or deep, sleep; (2) active, or light, sleep; (3) drowsiness; (4) alert inactivity; (5) alert activity; and (6) crying. These states are described in Table 5.4.

Several aspects of these states and how they change with age make them useful for understanding early development, for assessing the effects of various factors—such as teratogens—on development, and for comparing one infant with another. Recordings of brain activity by an **electroencephalograph (EEG)** reveal that states become increasingly distinct with age. Investigators believe this change reflects how the baby's brain matures (Colombo, 2001). Similar information can also be obtained by examining the ease with which babies move from one state to the next (Halpern, MacLean, & Baumeister, 1995).

Electroencephalograph (EEG)
An instrument that measures brain activity by sensing minute electrical changes at the top of the skull.

Links to Related Material

In this chapter we introduce the role of EEG brain recording in understanding the development of states. In Chapter 6, we consider the role of EEG in furthering our understanding of brain development.

The time distribution of sleep states changes rapidly with age (Groome et al., 1997; Holditch-Davis, Scher, Schwartz, & Hudson-Barr, 2004). Whereas the fetus of 25 weeks gestational age engages almost exclusively in active sleep, the newborn spends only about half the time in active sleep and half in quiet sleep (see Figure 5.2). By 3 months, quiet sleep occurs twice as much as active sleep (Berg & Berg, 1987), and this trend continues into the second year of life with increasing

FIGURE 5.2

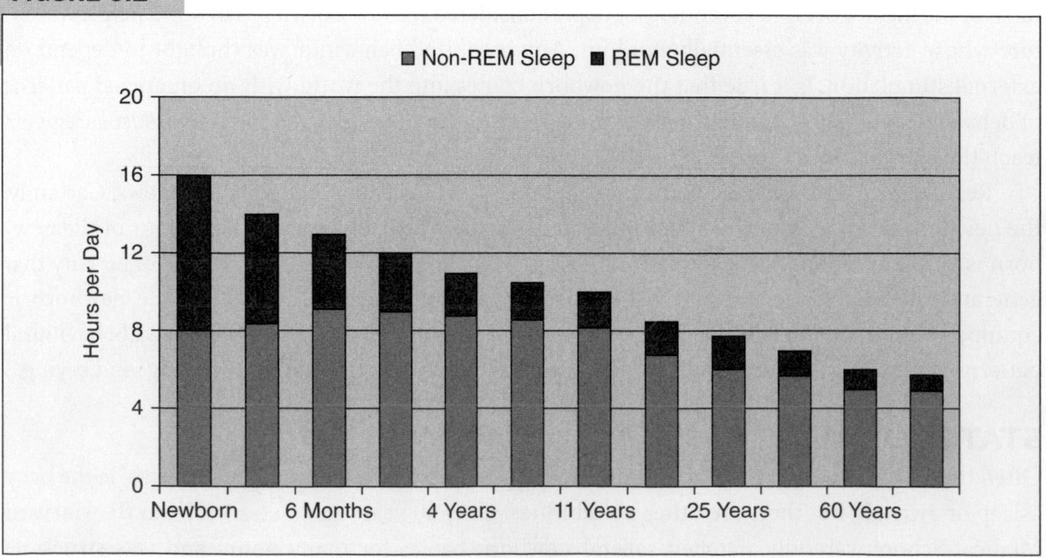

Number of hours of non-REM and REM sleep, and total number of hours of sleep at different ages from the newborn through the aging adult. Total number of hours sleeping shows a steady decline with age. Further, the percentage of the time in REM sleep declines from about half in the newborn to about 20 percent in the adult. *Adapted from "Ontogenic development of the human sleep-dream cycle" by H. P. Roffwarg, J. N. Muzio, and W. C. Dement, 1966,* Science, *152, 604–619, Figure 1.*

time in quiet sleep and less time in active sleep (Staunton, 2005). In active sleep, babies periodically move and breathe irregularly, but the most notable feature is that they frequently move their eyes back and forth with their eyelids closed (as do adults), and so this sleep state is often called **rapid eye movement (REM) sleep**.

Rapid eye movement (REM) sleep A stage of light sleep in which the eyes move rapidly while the eyelids are closed.

The shift from dominantly active (REM) sleep to dominantly quiet sleep has aroused considerable speculation about the function of REM sleep. In the adult, REM sleep constitutes only about 20 percent of total sleep time and is associated with dreaming. Research suggests that the high rate of REM activity in early development reflects a kind of internal motor that keeps nerve pathways active until the baby receives enough stimulation from the external world (Kandel & O'Dell, 1992). Consistent with this idea is the finding that babies who have longer awake periods, which presumably provide the needed stimulation, have shorter REM periods during sleep (Denenberg & Thoman, 1981; Garcia-Rill, Kobayashi, & Good, 2003; Peirano, Algarin, & Uauy, 2003).

Because the organization of sleep states—how well they are differentiated and their time distribution—reflects brain maturation, we might expect at-risk babies to be less organized than other infants. Indeed, state organization is affected in babies of alcoholic and drug-addicted mothers, and babies who are unstable in their time distribution across various states between 2 and 5 weeks of life are more likely to have later medical and behavioural problems than are relatively stable babies (Halpern et al., 1995; Tuladhar, Harding, Adamson, & Horne, 2005). Similarly, later cognitive, motor, and psychosocial outcomes of preterm children are related to the pattern of their sleep states in infancy (Holditch-Davis, 2005; Holditch-Davis, Belyea, & Edwards, 2005).

APPLICATION 5.1
SUDDEN INFANT DEATH SYNDROME (SIDS)

In Canada in 2004, approximately 85 babies went to sleep and never woke up. Such babies are victims of **sudden infant death syndrome**, or **SIDS**, which is defined as the sudden and unexpected death of an apparently healthy infant under the age of 1 year. In industrialized nations, SIDS is the most common cause of infant death beyond the neonatal period. The most vulnerable period is early in infancy, between about 2 and 4 months of age.

Sudden infant death syndrome (SIDS) The sudden and unexpected death of an otherwise healthy infant under the age of 1 year.

Despite decades of concerted research efforts, the causes of SIDS are still not fully understood. Researchers have succeeded, however, in identifying a number of risk factors; that is, factors whose presence increases the likelihood of SIDS. Fortunately, many of these factors are conditions that are under the parents' control.

One clearly important factor is the position in which the baby is placed for sleep. Sleeping in the prone, or on-the-stomach, position is associated with a heightened probability of SIDS (Hunt & Hauck, 2006). Discovery of this association led to a Back to Sleep campaign in the United States and Canada, a campaign that encouraged parents to place babies on their backs for sleeping rather than on their stomachs. Within five years, the percentage of American and Canadian babies who were placed on their stomachs had declined from 70 percent to 20 percent, and the incidence of SIDS had declined by 42 percent in America and 55 percent in Canada. Comparable declines occurred in other countries in which similar campaigns were initiated (American Academy of Pediatrics, 2000a).

Other aspects of the sleep environment may also be important. Soft bedding is a risk factor, and so is overheating (Kleeman et al., 1999; Scheers et al., 2003). It is perhaps natural for parents to bundle the baby up and keep the heat high during the winter months (the most common time period for SIDS); too much confinement and warmth, however, may be dangerous rather than beneficial.

Another risk factor that is clearly under parental control is maternal smoking. Both smoking while pregnant and smoking in the vicinity of the infant are associated with an increased probability of SIDS (Horne et al., 2004; Shah et al., 2006). In addition, maternal drinking during pregnancy has been associated with increased risk of SIDS (Duncan et al., 2008; Iyasu et al., 2002). With the success of the Back to Sleep campaign, the association of maternal smoking and drinking with SIDS may in part be the basis for the socio-economic and racial differences recently found in the incidence of SIDS (Chang et al., 2008;

(continued)

Application 5.1 Sudden Infant Death Syndrome (SIDS) *continued*

Mathews, & MacDorman, 2006). The association with SIDS, however, is hardly the only reason to stop these practices—parental smoking and drinking have been linked to a number of health problems in infancy (Mannino et al., 2001).

Some of the predictors of SIDS reside more in the infant than in the immediate environment. Babies who are born preterm, at low birth weight, are exposed to drugs prenatally, or have low Apgar scores are at heightened risk for SIDS. More immediately, babies who suffer from respiratory infections are more vulnerable to SIDS. There is also evidence that some victims of SIDS may have abnormalities in the portion of the brain that controls breathing and waking from sleep (Panigrahy et al., 1997). Apparently, particularly when other risk factors are operating (e.g., overheating, a respiratory infection), these babies may simply be unable to rouse themselves from the sleep state. Finally, the practice of co-sleeping (mother and baby sharing a bed) as opposed to sleeping alone has been associated with an increased risk of SIDS, though this may be mediated by the presence of other risk factors (Ruys et al., 2007; Vennemann et al., 2009).

Having noted these various risk factors, we should reiterate that scientists still do not fully understand the causes of SIDS, and at present there is no certain prescription for guarding against SIDS. Nevertheless, it clearly makes sense for parents to do all that is under their control to try to prevent this most heartbreaking of family tragedies.

Links to Related Material

In Chapter 4 you read how prenatal exposure to drugs and cigarette smoke can increase the incidence of SIDS. Here you read more about the causes of SIDS, as well as about programs designed to reduce its incidence.

Arousal states also play an important role in infants' interactions with the environment. When babies are in states of alertness—rather than crying, asleep, or drowsy—they are more receptive to stimuli and learn more readily, and are better prepared for social interaction (Berg & Berg, 1987; Feldman, 2007; Thoman, 1990). Thus, states affect the impact of external events. External events, in turn, can affect an infant's state. As David Pederson and Dick Ter Vrugt (1973) of the University of Western Ontario point out, a crying baby will often shift to a quiet, alert state if picked up by an adult and gently rocked up and down on the adult's shoulder (Karp, 2002). Swaddling, or wrapping an infant tightly, can also soothe an infant's cries and improve the quality of sleep (Franco et al., 2005).

Another external factor is where the baby sleeps. Although sleep and its various states have a strong biological basis, it is not clear where nature intended babies to sleep. In North America, most middle-income families have babies sleep by themselves in their own beds. Among many lower-income families and some ethnic groups, babies are more likely to sleep with their parents. The most common reason given by middle-income mothers for the separate sleeping arrangements is the desire to build the infant's independence (Goldberg & Keller, 2007). The most common reasons given by mothers who prefer sharing a bed are the desire to develop a closeness with the infant, as well as the ease of feeding and caregiving (Goldberg & Keller, 2007; Kawasaki et al., 1994; Morelli et al., 1992). Having the infant share a bed, or at least a room, with the parents is a common practice across many of the world's cultures (Nelson, Schiefenhoevel, & Haimerl, 2000).

RHYTHMS

Most children and adults have regular patterns of daily activity. For the most part, they sleep at night, are awake during the day, and eat at fairly predictable times. We can say that their daily patterns follow a repeating rhythm. This regular and predictable pattern of daily activity is called a *circadian rhythm*, which follows a roughly 24-hour cycle. On the other hand, one need only look at the red, tired eyes of a new parent to know that the newborn baby's habits are not so regular. Can we conclude, then, that the baby enters the world with no rhythms at all and must be taught by the parents when to eat, when to sleep, and when to wake? Not at all. Newborn babies are rhythmic creatures. The newborn's biological clock just seems to tick at a different rate than ours, and it gradually shifts into synchrony with ours as the baby develops.

The newborn's states, like the adult's, occur as rhythms cycling within other rhythms. The baby engages in a cycle of active and quiet sleep that repeats each 50 to 60 minutes. This cycle is coordinated with a cycle of wakefulness that occurs once every three to four hours (Parmelee & Sigman, 1983; Scher, Epstein, & Tirosh, 2004). What produces this behaviour? We might suspect that the sleep–wake cycle reflects a cycle of hunger or of external disruption by caregivers. However, the cycle seems to be controlled by internal mechanisms related to brain maturation, particularly the hypothalamus, and is even evident prenatally (Mirmiran, Maas, & Ariagno, 2003; Rivkees, 2007). Much to the relief of their parents, infants gradually adapt to the 24-hour light–dark cycle. Sleep periods become longer at night, usually at around 5 or 6 weeks of age, as awake periods lengthen during the day. By 12 to 16 weeks of age, the pattern of sleeping at night and being awake during the day is fairly well established, even though the baby still sleeps about the same amount as the newborn (Berg & Berg, 1987).

Although the rhythms of the newborn seem to be biologically programmed, they are not free from environmental influences. For example, newborn babies who stay in their mothers' rooms in the hospital begin to display day–night differences in their sleep cycles earlier than babies who stay in the hospital nursery. These rooming-in babies also spend more time in quiet sleep and less time crying than do babies in nursery groups (Keefe, 1987). Establishing babies' healthy circadian rhythms can also be facilitated by exposing them to low-intensity cycled lighting (Rivkees, 2007). Furthermore, prenatal experience can also affect rhythmic activity, for example, by disrupting the neurons in the hypothalamus that are responsible for circadian functions (Chen, Kuhn, Advis, & Sarkar, 2006). Newborns who have alcoholic or drug-dependent mothers have more difficulty synchronizing their various sleep–wake rhythms and adapting to the night–day cycle than do other babies (Parmelee & Sigman, 1983; Sander et al., 1977).

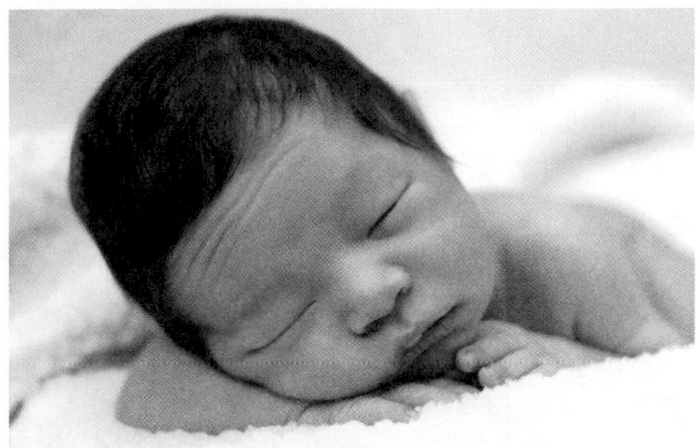

The newborn's sleep–wake cycle seems to be internally controlled. The newborn begins to adapt to the 24-hour light–dark cycle by 5 or 6 weeks of age. (© *Julie Fairman/iStock*)

REFLEXES

We have seen that the newborn baby has identifiable states of alertness, and that these states fit into overall rhythms. Newborns are also equipped with a number of behaviours and behaviour patterns. Some of these, called **reflexes**, are highly stereotyped and occur as brief responses to specific stimuli. As we discussed in Chapter 1, some theorists believe reflexes have evolved in humans over millions of years because they serve (or served at one time) an important survival function.

Reflex An automatic and stereotyped response to a specific stimulus.

Reflexes are of interest not only to psychologists trying to understand early development; they can have applied value as well because their presence or absence provides information about the baby's brain and nervous system. For example, an infant should reflexively bend to the left side when the doctor runs a thumb along the left side of the baby's spinal column. If this reflex occurs on the left side but not on the right side, it may indicate damage to the nerves on the right side.

Some reflexes last throughout life, but the reflexes of most interest here are those that disappear in the first year of life because their disappearance indicates the development of more advanced brain functions. Table 5.5 lists some of the more common reflexes, as well as the stimuli that produce them and their developmental course. We discuss only a few of these reflexes here.

The *rooting reflex* is the first to appear. If we stroke a newborn's cheek next to the mouth, the baby will turn its head to that side and search with the mouth. This reflex is adaptive in an evolutionary sense because it helps the baby find the nipple of the mother's breast for feeding. This reflex appears as early as 2 to 3 months gestational age and represents the first indication that the fetus can respond to touch. Rooting generally disappears in infants around 3 to 4 months of age (Peiper, 1963).

The *palmar reflex* is elicited by pressure against the palm of a newborn's hand, such as with a finger. The baby responds by grasping the finger tightly. Newborns are capable of supporting their own weight in this manner—a potentially important ability for babies of our evolutionary ancestors, who needed to cling tightly to their mothers as they moved around. This reflex disappears at 3 to 4 months of age, and children are not again able to support their own weight until around 4 or 5 years of age (McGraw, 1940).

TABLE 5.5 NEWBORN REFLEXES

Name	Testing Method	Response	Developmental Course	Significance
Blink	Flash a light in infant's eyes	Closes both eyes	Permanent	Protects eyes from strong stimuli
Biceps reflex	Tap on the tendon of the biceps muscle	Contracts the biceps muscle	Brisker in the first few days than later	Absent in depressed infants or those with congenital muscular disease
Knee jerk or patellar tendon reflex	Tap on the tendon below the patella or kneecap	Quickly extends or kicks the knee	More pronounced in the first 2 days than later	Absent or difficult to obtain in depressed infants or infants with muscular disease; exaggerated in hyperexcitable infants
Babinski	Gently stroke the side of the infant's foot from heel to toes	Flexes the big toe dorsally; fans out the other toes; twists foot inward	Usually disappears near the end of the first year; replaced by plantar flexion of big toe in the normal adult	Absent in infants with defects of the lower spine; retention important in diagnosing poor myelination of motor tracts of the brainstem in older children and adults
Withdrawal reflex	Prick the sole of the infant's foot with a pin	Flexes leg	Constantly present during the first 10 days; present but less intense later	Absent with sciatic nerve damage
Plantar or toe grasp	Press finger against the ball of the infant's foot	Curls all toes under	Disappears between 8 and 12 months	Absent in infants with defects of the lower spinal cord
Tonic neck reflex	Lay baby down on back	Turns head to one side; baby assumes fencing position, extending arm and leg on this side, bending opposite limbs, and arching body away from direction faced	Found as early as 28th prenatal week; frequently present in first weeks, disappears by 3 or 4 months	Paves way for eye–hand coordination
Palmar or hand grasp	Press rod or finger against the infant's palm	Grasps the object with fingers; can suspend own weight for brief period of time	Increases during the first month and then gradually declines and is gone by 3 or 4 months	Weak or absent in depressed babies
Moro reflex (embracing reflex)	Make a sudden loud sound; let the baby's head drop back a few inches; or suspend horizontally, then lower hands rapidly about six inches and stop abruptly	Extends arms and legs and then brings arms toward each other in a convulsive manner; fans hands out at first, clenches them slightly	Begins to decline in third month, generally gone by fifth month	Absent or constantly weak Moro indicates serious disturbance of the central nervous system; may have originated with primate clinging
Stepping or Automatic walking reflex	Support baby in upright position with bare feet on flat surface; move the infant forward and tilt him slightly from side to side	Makes rhythmic stepping movements	Disappears in 2 to 3 months	Absent in depressed infants
Swimming reflex	Hold baby horizontally on stomach in water	Alternates arm and leg movements, exhaling through the mouth	Disappears at 6 months	Demonstrates coordination of arms and legs
Rooting reflex	Stroke cheek of infant lightly with finger or nipple	Turns head toward finger, opens mouth, and tries to suck finger	Disappears at approximately 3 to 4 months	Absent in depressed infants; appears in adults with severe cerebral palsy
Babkin or Palmarmental reflex	Apply pressure on both of baby's palms when baby is lying on back	Opens mouth, closes eyes, and turns head to midline	Disappears in 3 to 4 months	Inhibited by general depression on central nervous system

Source: Excerpted from *Child Psychology: A Contemporary Viewpoint*, 2nd ed. (Table 4.1), by E.M. Hetherington and R.D. Parke, 1979, New York; McGraw-Hill.

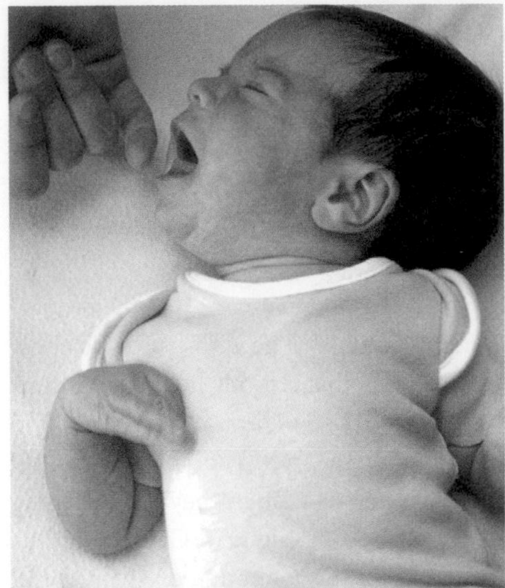

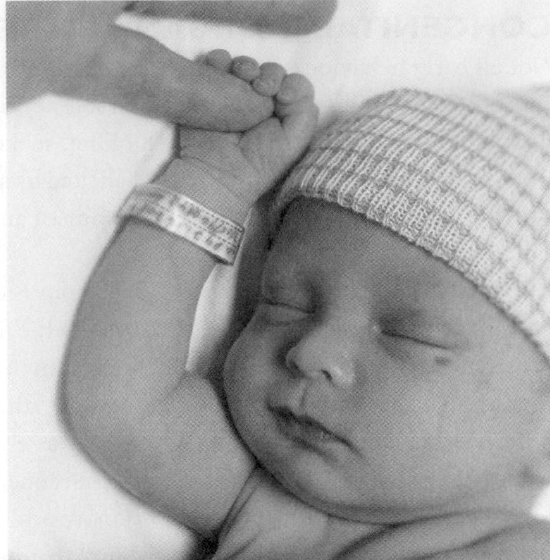

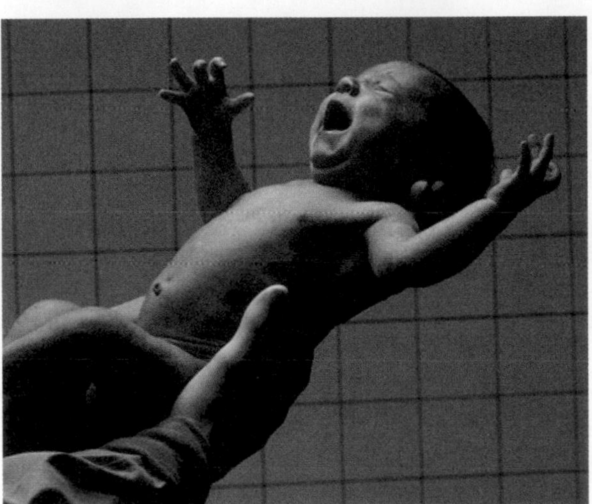

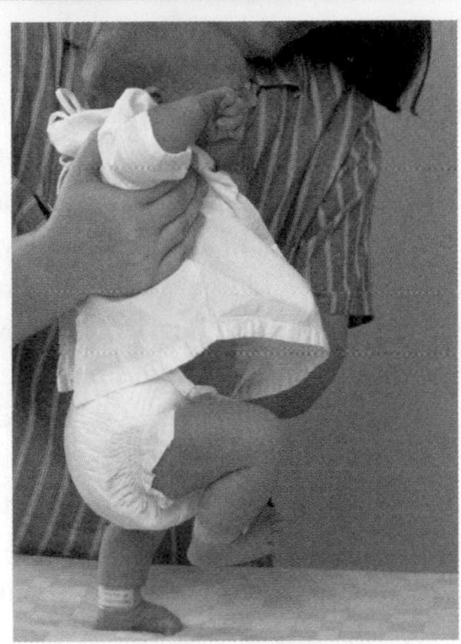

Some newborn reflexes, clockwise from top left: *rooting reflex*—baby attempts to suck when cheek is stroked; *palmar reflex*—baby reflexively grasps a finger or other object placed in the palm of the hand; *stepping reflex*—when held upright with feet touching a flat surface, the newborn makes stepping movements as if walking; *Moro reflex*—in reaction to sudden light, sound, or loss of head support, the baby thrusts out its arms and arches its back. (*clockwise from top left: Elizabeth Crews/The Image Works; Comstock/Jupiter Images; Jennie Woodcock/Reflections Photolibrary/Corbis; Comstock/Media Bakery*)

The *Moro reflex* consists of a series of reactions to sudden sound or the loss of head support. The infant first thrusts her arms outward, opens her hands, arches her back, and stretches her legs outward, then she brings her arms inward in an embracing motion with fingers formed into fists. The absence of a Moro reflex is a sign of brain damage, and its failure to disappear after 6 or 7 months of age is also cause for concern. Moro, who first described the reflex (Moro, 1918), argued that it is a relic of an adaptive reaction by primates to grab for support while falling. However, others have disputed this argument (e.g., Peiper, 1963). As with many newborn reflexes, the evolutionary roots of the Moro reflex are not certain.

When pressure is applied to the soles of the feet, the baby will flex his legs up and down in the *stepping reflex*. This reflex usually disappears by around 3 months of age. The disappearance of the reflex at this time seems to result from a faster increase in the baby's weight relative to a slower increase in his muscle strength; thus, his muscles are increasingly unable to support his weight (Thelen, Fisher, & Ridley-Johnson, 2002). Research has shown that if the legs are supported in water, the reflex can be demonstrated in older infants (Thelen & Fisher, 1983). Similarly, if the reflex is practised, it can become stronger (Zelazo et al., 1993).

Although there is an automatic quality to reflexes, environmental factors do affect them. For example, a baby who has just nursed may not show a rooting response, and most other reflexes are also somewhat sensitive to the baby's biological state. Still, reflexes are generally tied to specific stimuli and are rarely seen in their absence. This is not the case for the behaviours we refer to as congenitally organized behaviours.

For Thought and Discussion

What might have been the benefits of some of the reflexes for our ancient ancestors? Can you think of any other explanations for these inborn reflexes?

CONGENITALLY ORGANIZED BEHAVIOURS

Congenitally organized behaviours Early behaviours of newborns that do not require specific external stimulation and that show more adaptability than simple reflexes.

Not all early behaviours are responses to stimulation. The newborn also initiates activities and is capable of sustaining them over considerable periods of time. Such activities are called **congenitally organized behaviours**. Specifically, looking, sucking, and crying are three well-organized behaviours that, unlike reflexes, are often not elicited by a discrete, identifiable stimulus. These behaviours provide infants with means to get nourishment and to control and explore their environments.

LOOKING The newborn's looking behaviour is often unexpected (Crouchman, 1985). New parents may be amazed when their baby, even in the first moments of life, will lie with eyes wide open, seemingly examining them and other objects in the room. In a room that is dimly lit, the light coming through the window may be an especially attractive target. And babies do not simply respond reflexively to light when they look. As early as eight hours after birth, and in complete darkness, babies open their eyes wide and engage in frequent eye movements, as though they are searching for something to explore (Haith, 1991). We will discuss perception in depth in Chapter 7. Our point now is that looking behaviour shows that newborns possess tools for acting on their world, not just for reacting to it.

SUCKING In some respects, sucking seems to fit the definition of a reflex because it is easily elicited by oral stimulation, at least when the newborn is hungry. In other respects, though, it is not reflex-like. Babies may suck spontaneously, even during sleep. The sucking act is also not stereotyped, but instead adapts to a variety of conditions, such as how much fluid can be obtained with each suck. In addition, sucking is sensitive to sensory events. Babies who are sucking tend to stop when they see something start to move or when they hear a voice (Haith, 1966). These characteristics set sucking apart from simpler reflexes.

Sucking is a marvellously coordinated act. Babies suck one to two times each second, and each suck requires an orchestration of actions. Milk is extracted from the nipple both by suction (as with a straw) and by a squeezing action, and these actions must be coordinated with both breathing and swallowing. Some babies show excellent sucking coordination and pressure accuracy within a day after birth, whereas others may require a week or so of practice (Craig & Lee, 1999; Peiper, 1963).

No other newborn behaviour seems to serve quite as many purposes as sucking. It is, of course, a way to get nourishment, but it is also a primary means by which babies begin to explore the world. Even at birth, many babies suck their fingers and thumbs, and it appears that some newborns have even practised this as fetuses. Later, they continue to explore with their mouths as they become better able to grasp and find new objects (Rochat, 1989).

Sucking also seems to buffer the infant against pain and overstimulation. Agitated babies quiet when they suck on a pacifier, especially when it contains a sweet substance (Smith & Blass, 1996). One study found that crying during circumcision was reduced by about 40 percent when babies were permitted to suck on a pacifier (Gunnar, Fisch, & Malone, 1984). This finding confirms experimentally what civilizations have known for some time; for thousands of years, Jewish babies have been encouraged to suck on wine-soaked cotton during circumcision. Additionally, sucking plays a social role in the process of emotional attachment between infant and mother (Bowlby, 1969).

Finally, infants can also learn to modify their sucking, as demonstrated by its use in the high-amplitude, non-nutritive sucking paradigm (Eimas et al., 1971; Jusczyk, 1985). In this paradigm, infants learn that the presentation of a stimulus depends on maintaining sucking at a particular rate on a pacifier. Furthermore, they change their rate of sucking when the stimulus changes. Studies that use high-amplitude sucking have shown babies' remarkable capacities for perceiving speech information; for example, babies prefer to listen to speech than non-speech sounds (Vouloumanos & Werker, 2007) and are sensitive to aspects of word order before they understand words (Christophe et al., 2003).

CRYING A third organized behaviour of the newborn is crying. Like sucking, crying coordinates various components of behaviour, such as breathing, vocalizing, and muscular tensing, in a rhythmic pattern. Psychologists are interested in crying both as a diagnostic tool and for its social role.

Wolff (1969) distinguished among three types of cries in the very young infant: a hungry, or basic, cry; a mad, or angry, cry; and a pain cry. The first two are similar in pitch but different in that the mad cry forces more air through the vocal cords, producing more variation. The pain cry has a more sudden onset, with a much longer initial burst and a longer period of breath-holding between cries. Other researchers have identified the types as expressing hunger, fear, or pain (Wasz-Hockert, Michelsson, & Lind, 1985). Although it was once believed that parents could reliably distinguish among different types of cries, more recent research calls this idea into question (Gustafson, Wood, & Green, 2000) and suggests that the different cries may primarily act as indicators of the baby's behavioural state rather than as a signal (Barr, 2004). What seems clear is that parents—and adults in general—can distinguish among cries based on intensity, and are more likely to respond as the cry becomes more intense (Soltis, 2004). Incredibly, the theory that the differentiation of infants' cries is likely based on the acoustic properties of the cries is supported by the recent demonstration that a computer system can distinguish between different types of cries (Abdulaziz & Ahmad, 2010). Contextual cues then aid in determining the meaning of the cry. However, as recent Canadian research has shown, teen mothers may not be as responsive to the infants' cries as adult mothers (Giardino, Gonzalez, Steiner, & Fleming, 2008).

The crying of healthy newborn infants is fairly characteristic in both pitch and rhythm. An unusual cry, therefore, can signal problems. Babies who are immature or brain damaged produce higher-frequency cries with abnormal timing patterns (Zeskind & Lester, 2001). Babies who show evidence of malnutrition at birth or are preterm often also have higher-pitched cries. Infants who have genetic anomalies, such as *cri du chat* syndrome (in which the infant's cry sounds like that of a cat) or Down syndrome, have atypical cries as well.

Some investigators have speculated that babies influence early social relationships with their caregivers by the nature of their cries (Lester, 1984). Cries of at-risk babies are perceived as more grating, piercing, and aversive than the cries of other babies, "difficult" babies seem to have more aversive cries than "easy" babies (Soltis, 2004), and babies with colic have cries that are more intense and persistent (Barr et al., 2005). In fact, mothers who perceived their infants as problematic criers ended up having children who increased their crying during toddlerhood and then also scored higher on problem behaviour assessments when they were preschoolers (McKenzie & McDonough, 2009). Thus, as noted earlier, cries experienced as aversive may set in motion a negative cycle between baby and caregiver.

More broadly, crying is a major factor in early social interaction because it is one of the infant's basic tools for getting the caregiver to come closer (for a further discussion of the social quality of infants' cries, see Chapter 12). Because adults dislike hearing babies cry, they typically do something to quiet the crying baby. Parents may try various techniques for soothing a baby who fusses for no apparent reason. Picking the baby up is an effective method to quiet the baby. Swaddling (wrapping a baby snugly in a blanket) and pacifiers are also sometimes effective, as is continuous or rhythmic sound (Brackbill et al., 1966; Campos, 1989; Karp, 2007). Even in the first month of life, crying may be controlled by events other than feeding or pain relief; infants often stop crying if they have interesting things to watch or sounds to listen to (Wolff, 1969).

Links to Related Material

Here, you read about crying in terms of infants' physical development. In Chapter 12, you will read about the role of crying in infants' social and emotional development.

The three congenitally organized behaviours of looking, sucking, and crying are gradually fine-tuned by the infant to more effectively explore and control the physical and social world. Other skills, such as reaching, grasping, and walking, also play a role, and elaborate emotional behaviours, such as smiling and laughing, enrich the social interactions of the developing infant. We will leave the more social components of early development to Chapter 12 and consider next some other physical accomplishments of the infant.

LEARNING OBJECTIVE 5.2

Describe ways in which the infant's behaviour appears to be organized at birth.

1. What states of alertness does the infant demonstrate?
2. How does the newborn's sleep–wake cycle change in the early months of life?
3. What factors might be related to the occurrence of SIDS?
4. What is a reflex? What are some of the newborn's reflexes?
5. How are congenitally organized behaviours different from reflexes?
6. What roles do looking, sucking, and crying play in an infant's development?

Learning Objective 5.3

Trace the development of motor skills in infancy and childhood.

MOTOR DEVELOPMENT

Looking, crying, and sucking are limited in their ability to control the environment. Imagine for a moment that you cannot move around or grasp and manipulate objects, so you must depend on others to provide interesting things for you to inspect. This is the state of the newborn baby. Before long, however, these limitations disappear and the infant is a go-for-everything, grab-anything 9-month-old.

The acquisition of motor skills is a key feature of development in human infancy, in effect giving the baby powerful tools for acquiring knowledge and gaining a sense of competence and self-control. These skills continue to develop well into the childhood years, when they play important roles in other aspects of development.

Postural development The increasing ability of the baby to control parts of its body, especially the head and trunk.

Locomotion The movement of a person through space, such as walking and crawling.

Prehension The ability to grasp and manipulate objects with the hands.

Motor development can be divided into two general categories. The first comprises **postural development** and **locomotion**, which involve control of the trunk of the body and coordination of the arms and legs for moving around. The second category is **prehension**, the ability to use the hands as tools for such purposes as eating, building, and exploring.

PRINCIPLES AND SEQUENCES

Proximodistal Literally, near to far. This principle of development refers to the tendency of body parts to develop in a trunk-to-extremities direction.

The progression of motor skills tends to follow two general principles. The first principle is that development proceeds in a **proximodistal** direction; that is, body parts closest to the centre of the body come under control before parts farther out.

The acquisition of early prehensile skills provides a good example. In the first weeks, the newborn can position himself toward an object but cannot reach it. Although his arm movements seem random, the infant does direct some movements toward the object. In the second month of life, the baby sweeps his hand more deliberately near the object and begins to contact it more consistently. By 4 months of age, the infant can often grab at objects in a way that looks convincingly deliberate, but he uses the whole hand with as yet little individual finger control. Gradually the baby coordinates his fingers so that at 6 months of age, he may reach for a cube with one hand and all fingers extended. Once the object is in hand, the baby may transfer the cube from hand to hand and rotate his wrist to see it from various perspectives. By 9 months, the baby can grasp a small pellet neatly between forefinger and thumb, and the 1-year-old can hold a crayon to make marks on paper.

Cephalocaudal Literally, head to tail. This principle of development refers to the tendency of body parts to mature in a head-to-foot progression.

The second principle is that control over the body develops in a **cephalocaudal**, or head-to-foot, direction. The progression of early postural and locomotor skills illustrates this principle.

The newborn who is placed on her stomach can move her head from side to side, although her head must be supported when she is lifted to someone's shoulder. A 3-month-old infant first holds her head erect and steady in the vertical position, and then pushes off the mattress with her hands to lift her head and shoulders to look around. At 6 months, the baby can pull herself to a sitting position, and may even be able to drag herself around a bit by her arms (crawling). But only at around 8 months can the baby use her legs to move herself forward with her belly off the floor (creeping).

FIGURE 5.3

Rolling over → Pivoting → Crawling on stomach → Crawling on hands and knees → Crawling on hands and feet — 87% →
1%
6% →
2% →
1% →
Sitting up — Shuffling — 2% →
Rolling — <1% →
"Bridging" — <1%
Snake-like movements — <1% →
Standing up
Walking

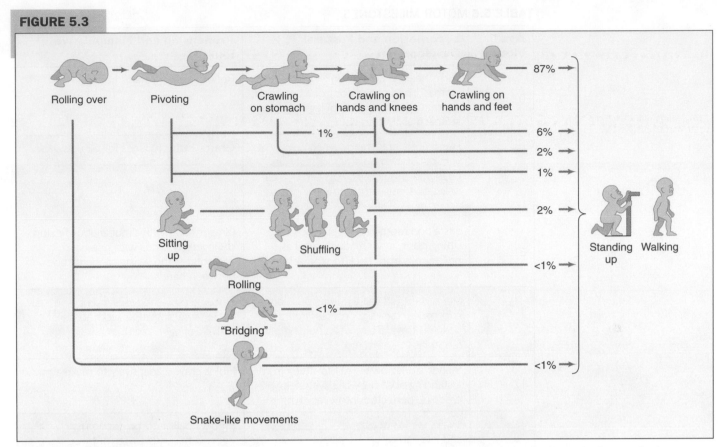

A baby's self-produced locomtion. Most babies follow a fairly regular sequence in learning to walk, gradually transferring responsibility for movement from the arms to the feet. But some skip certain stages of crawling, and others never crawl at all. *Adapted from "Early Development of Locomotion: Significance of Prematurity, Cerebral Palsy and Sex" by R. H. Largo, L. Molinari, M. Weber, L. C. Pinto, and G. Duc, 1985,* Developmental Medicine and Child Neurology, *27, 183–191, Figure 2. Copyright © 1985 by MacKeith Press. Adapted by permission.*

By the time the infant is 1 year old, the parents are likely to find her standing in the crib, rattling the side bars, and perhaps distressed at being unable to figure out how to sit down again! Typically, soon after her first birthday, the baby is able to control her legs sufficiently to begin walking without support.

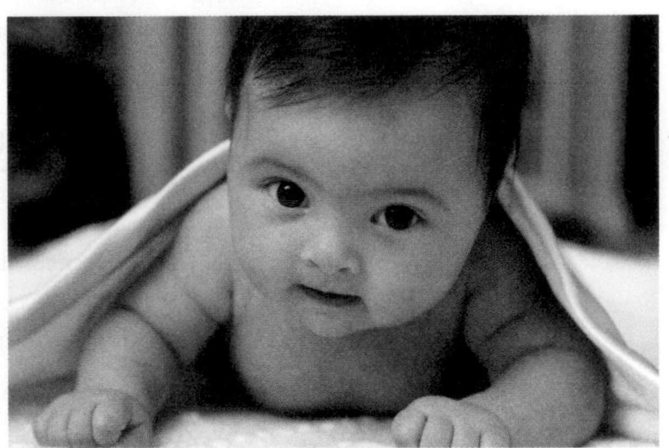

At around 3 months, infants can elevate their head and shoulders by arms, hands, or elbows, when lying on their stomachs. (© *Nathan Maxfield/ iStock*)

The top portion of Figure 5.3 shows a typical baby's stages of progression toward self-produced locomotion. The cephalocaudal progression just described is clearly evident, with the hands most active early on and responsibility for movement gradually transferring down to the legs. The lower portion of Figure 5.3 illustrates how babies can reach the same goal by following different routes. Some babies, for example, never crawl before walking. Psychologists now know that infants do not all develop a given motor skill (such as walking or standing) in the same way—a point to which we return in a moment.

Table 5.6 presents some of the milestones of motor-skill acquisition; again, the proximodistal and cephalocaudal principles described earlier are apparent. The majority of babies follow these general sequences. It is important to note, however, that the ages given in the table are only approximate; some infants master these skills earlier, and others master them later. This variation in when motor skills are developed has taken on new significance since the recent discovery that infants also vary in how they develop specific skills. The result is that psychologists are now thinking about motor development very differently.

TABLE 5.6 MOTOR MILESTONES

Age in Months	Locomotion and Postural Development	Prehension and Manipulative Skills
0	Turns head to side when lying on stomach; poor head control when lifted; alternating movements of legs when on stomach as if to crawl	Reflex grasp—retains hold on ring
3	Head erect and steady when held vertically; when on stomach, elevates head and shoulders by arms or hands or elbows; sits with support; anticipates adjustment of lifting	Grasps rattle; reaches for objects with two hands
6	Sits alone momentarily; pulls self to sitting position with adult's hand as puller; rolls from back to stomach	Grasps cube with simultaneous flexion of fingers; reaches with one hand and rotates the wrist; transfers cube between hands
9	Sits alone; pulls self to sitting position in crib; makes forward progress in prone position toward toy; walks holding on to furniture	Pincer grasp—opposes thumb and finger in seizing cube; picks up pellet with forefinger and thumb
12	Stands alone; lowers self to sitting from a standing position; walks with help; creeping perfected; into everything	Holds crayon adaptively to make a mark
18	Walks well (since about 15 months) and falls rarely; climbs stairs or chair	Throws balls into box; scribbles vigorously; builds tower of three or more blocks
24	Walks up and down stairs; walks backward; runs	Places square in form board; imitates folding of paper; piles tower of six blocks; puts blocks in a row to form a train

Source: Based on information from *Manual for the Bayley Scales of Infant Development* by N. Bayley, 1969, New York: Psychological Corporation and "The Denver Developmental Screening Test" by W. K. Frankenburg and J. Dodds, 1967, *Journal of Pediatrics*, 71, 181–191. Reprinted with permission from Elsevier.

THE NATURE AND NURTURE OF MOTOR-SKILLS DEVELOPMENT

Motor skills appear in a fairly predictable sequence and at similar times from one infant to another. Does this mean that sitting, crawling, reaching, and so forth are genetically programmed and simply emerge according to a biological set of instructions within the child? More and more, psychologists are answering no to this question.

For one thing, different child-rearing experiences—often associated with different cultural practices—can clearly affect the timing of motor-skill development. For example, African infants generally sit, stand, and walk from one to several months earlier than do North American infants (Konner, 1976; Super, 1981). But how the infants are dealt with, not heredity, seems to account for much of the difference.

One investigator reported that the Kipsigis in western Kenya believe their infants will not sit, stand, or walk without practice. Thus, they energetically provide practice for their infants in these skills. For example, they dig a special hole in the ground using sand to reinforce their infants' sitting skills. Kenyan babies do not differ from North American babies in the development of skills that are not encouraged in this way, such as crawling and rolling over (Super, 1981). Mothers in Jamaica provide their babies with similar types of early physical stimulation, and these babies, too, develop motor skills earlier than do Caucasian infants in other cultures (Hopkins, 1991).

A glance back at Figure 5.3 shows a second reason that genetics cannot rigidly control motor development: not all babies get to the same place by following the same path. Using the microgenetic method described in Chapter 2, researchers have carefully charted the development of motor skills in many individual infants. One study examined the development of reaching and grasping in four infants from ages 3 weeks to 1 year. Although all four eventually were able to reach out and grasp a toy, the manner in which they achieved this goal varied considerably from one child to the next (Thelen, Corbetta, & Spencer, 1996). In fact, as we will see in Chapter 7, the development of reaching and locomotion may play a significant role in the assessment of the development of depth perception.

For Thought and Discussion

How have cultural expectations affected your motor development and motor skills?

A DYNAMIC SYSTEMS APPROACH These sorts of findings have prompted researchers to think about motor development in a new way. The **dynamic systems approach** was developed within the science of physics, but in developmental psychology it has been applied to children's motor development most extensively by Esther Thelen (Thelen, 2000; Thelen & Corbetta, 2002; Thelen & Smith, 2006).

Dynamic systems approach Thelen's model of the development of motor skills in which infants who are motivated to accomplish a task create a new motor behaviour from their available physical abilities.

Thelen proposes that both nature and nurture contribute to the development of motor skills. Given that the emergence of these skills follows a predictable sequence for most babies, biological factors would seem to be strongly involved. Because practice and experience can affect motor-skills development and because children seem to acquire specific skills somewhat differently, environmental factors must be involved as well. Thelen argues that developmentalists need a model to help them understand the combined contributions of these two factors.

According to her dynamic systems analysis, the crucial element that unites the nature and nurture contributions and, more importantly, that stimulates the development of any particular skill, is the infant's "task" or "goal." As babies mature biologically and cognitively, they become motivated to accomplish more things in the world around them. They seek to reach things, to grasp things, to move or shake things, to move themselves closer to things, and so on. These are the tasks of infancy.

RESEARCH CLASSIC 5.1
DOES MOTOR DEVELOPMENT DEPEND ON PRACTICE OR ON MATURATION?

The nature–nurture debate regarding motor development is very old. During the 1920s and 1930s, the zeitgeist in developmental psychology leaned heavily toward biological explanations of children's development. We saw in Chapter 1 that G. Stanley Hall's early evolutionary views were revised and resurrected during this period by his student, Arnold Gesell, at Yale University.

One major theoretical issue of the time concerned children's motor-skills acquisition. Learning-oriented psychologists, such as John B. Watson, argued that the crawling, climbing, and walking displayed by all normal infants represented reflexes conditioned through experience and practice. But Gesell and other biologically oriented theorists believed that these behaviours emerged according to a genetic timetable. Simple biological maturation, not conditioning and learning principles, guides their appearance.

To compare these two theories, Gesell developed a research method called the co-twin control, using identical twins so that biological factors would be the same for the two infants. Gesell then selected one infant, whom he termed twin T, to receive training and extra practice each day at climbing stairs and related motor skills. The control infant, twin C, received no extra practice. After six weeks of training, twin T had become a very accomplished climber—but so had twin C. Gesell interpreted these findings to mean that the climbing skill must have been a result only of the children's biological development and not of their practice or experience (Gesell & Thompson, 1929). Studies of the same sort by other researchers appeared to confirm this conclusion (McGraw, 1935).

Later research, however, demonstrated that Gesell's conclusions had been a bit simplistic. Whereas extra training may not accelerate children's motor development, some amount of experience appears necessary for development to occur normally. Infants deprived of physical stimulation or the opportunity to move about were found to have delayed motor development (Dennis, 1960; Dennis & Najarian, 1957). When such infants were then given extra stimulation, their motor skills improved rapidly (Sayegh & Dennis, 1965).

The method of the co-twin control was a useful technique for comparing the effects of maturation and learning (which is, of course, a specific case of nature versus nurture). But as psychologists now agree, both these processes are essential for normal motor development.

To accomplish such tasks, babies learn that various motor behaviours—such as those involving the arms, fingers, head, shoulders, and so on—can be useful.

Sometimes, though, the task requires a behaviour that the child does not possess, and so the infant must create such a behaviour. To do this, the infant draws on the physical responses and abilities already available to her—what the baby can already do with her arms, legs, hands, and fingers; muscle strength; balance and coordination; and so on. These abilities, of course, depend largely on age and biological maturation, but they also depend on the abilities the baby has created up to that point. A 9-month-old, therefore, should have many more physical responses and abilities on which to draw than would, say, a 4-month-old. As a result, even when faced with the same task, the two children will likely create different new motor behaviours and so accomplish the task in different ways. Note that this is true not just for babies of different ages; any two children, even of the same age, will have different physical resources available to them as a result of both genetic differences and different experiences up to that point.

Thelen has found that infants go through two stages as they try to assemble a new motor behaviour from the abilities currently available to them. The first stage involves exploration, as the baby tries many different responses in a relatively random and uncoordinated fashion. In the second stage, selection, the baby learns exactly what works and what does not work and fine-tunes the many responses into an efficient package.

In short, the dynamic systems approach predicts that the motor skill a particular child develops at any given time will depend on (a) the task at hand, including how difficult it is and how motivated the child is to accomplish it, and (b) the physical abilities the child already possesses that form the starting point for creating the new behaviour. The first of these (the task) is obviously very much influenced by the baby's environment and experiences; the second (the infant's physical abilities) is strongly influenced by the baby's biological maturation, as well as prior experiences.

FIGURE 5.4

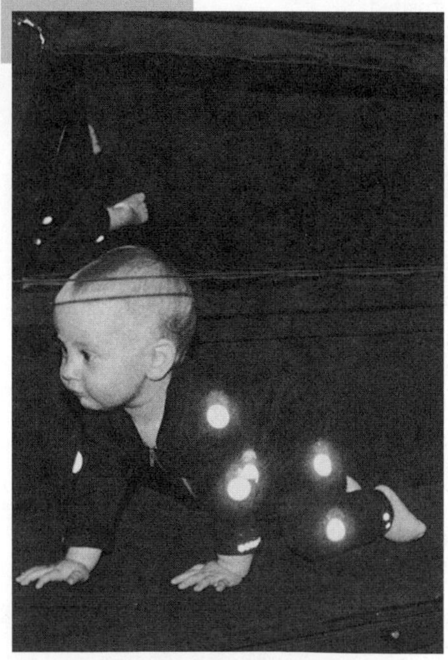

Tracking a baby's movements. Scientists use computerized techniques to track light reflections on babies' joints to study how babies acquire skill in crawling. *(Janette B. Benson, University of Denver)*

RESEARCH EXAMPLES Thelen demonstrated these principles in a clever laboratory study. Three-month-old infants were placed on their backs in cribs, where they could see a mobile suspended above them. The babies' feet were individually attached with cords to the mobile in such a way that either single kicks or alternating kicking movements were effective in making the mobile move. At first, the babies explored different leg movements, but after a short while, they learned to produce the necessary kicking behaviours, presumably because they were motivated to accomplish the task of moving the mobile. Thelen next tied each baby's feet loosely together so that the motor behaviour that would best move the mobile was a combined two-foot kick. Again the infants explored various leg movements before finally selecting a coordinated leg action that was effective in achieving their purpose (Thelen, 1994).

Another example involves locomotion. Researchers at the University of Denver videotaped the motions of babies' body parts as they learned to creep across the floor to reach an object. As shown in Figure 5.4, the babies wore black bodysuits that had small reflective markers (the kind bicyclists wear at night) at the shoulder, elbow, and other joints. Reflections from these markers were read by a computer and analyzed to determine the path, velocity, and timing of the children's movements.

The researchers found that once babies have the physical strength to move along with their bodies held above the floor, they begin to explore different patterns of arm-and-leg coordination. They eventually settle on a diagonal pattern (right hand and left leg, then left hand and right leg) as the most efficient and stable way of locomotoring along, and thus reaching the object (Benson, 1990; Freedland & Bertenthal, 1994).

The essence of the dynamic systems approach, then, is that an infant does not simply wake up one morning with a new motor skill that has emerged spontaneously from his or her genetic code. Instead, a new skill is developed only when the infant is motivated to accomplish a task and has sufficient physical abilities to assemble into the necessary motor behaviour.

Why, then, do most babies follow the same general sequence of motor development? The answer is probably simply that the physical resources of infants at the same points in development are reasonably similar, and infants' tasks in any given culture tend also to be reasonably similar. On the other hand, Thelen's dynamic systems analysis shows why it also should not be surprising that babies differ in the timing of their motor-skill development and in the manner in which they acquire these skills. Nature provides most of the raw material of motor development, but nurture determines the timing and direction development will take.

THE PSYCHOLOGICAL IMPLICATIONS OF MOTOR DEVELOPMENT

Learning to move around is not only a motor accomplishment for babies; it also helps them organize their world (Adolph & Berger, 2006; Bertenthal, Campos, & Kermoian, 1994). For example, babies' self-produced locomotion seems to contribute to their perception of the world and to their spatial understanding (discussed in more detail in Chapter 7). In one study, the level of infants' experience with sitting and their motor skills at exploring objects predicted their ability to perceive objects in three dimensions (Soska, Adolph, & Johnson, 2010). In another study, a toy was hidden in one of two coloured containers placed in front of an infant. Infants with crawling experience were better able to find the toy under a variety of conditions—such as when the babies were placed on the opposite side of the table (thereby reversing the left or right location of the toy from the baby's perspective)—than were babies of the same age who had not yet mastered crawling (Benson & Uzgiris, 1985). Similarly, infants with little crawling experience were unable to correctly locomote to their mother calling them from behind one of eight possible curtains in a maze, whereas infants with more extensive crawling experience could (Clearfield, 2004). In addition, infants with little locomotor experience were more likely to incorrectly solve new spatial locomotor problems with the same response that correctly solved a previous problem (termed a perseverative error) than infants with locomotor expertise (Berger, 2010).

Links to Related Material

Here, you read about the implications of motor development for making perseverative errors. In Chapter 8, you will read about infants' perseverative errors in the A-not-B task.

A baby's control over body movement also helps her understand the meaning of distance and heights. Crawling seems to be related to infants' learning to fear heights (Campos, Bertenthal, & Kermoian, 1992). Later, when babies can control their distance from their mothers or other caregivers, they use their motor skills to venture off (when they feel safe) or to return for comfort (when they feel insecure), as we will see again in Chapter 12.

MOTOR DEVELOPMENT IN CHILDHOOD

Motor development has attracted the most attention from infant researchers, but motor skills continue to develop during the childhood years (Gallahue & Ozmun, 1995).

An infant's first steps are a major milestone of development. (*Camille Tokerud/Getty Images*)

By their second birthday, most children have overcome their battle with gravity and balance and are able to move about and handle objects fairly efficiently. Their early abilities form the basis for skills that appear between 2 and 7 years of age. Three sets of fundamental movement skills emerge: locomotor movements, manipulative movements, and stability movements.

Locomotor movements include walking, running, jumping, hopping, skipping, and climbing. Manipulative movements include throwing, catching, kicking, striking, and dribbling. Stability movements involve body control relative to gravity, and include bending, turning, swinging, rolling, head standing, and beam walking. These fundamental skills typically appear in all children and can be further refined by adolescents, who may develop exceptional skills as skaters, dancers, and gymnasts.

The refinement of motor skills depends a great deal on the development of the muscles and the nerve pathways that control them, but other factors are important as well. Motor skills depend in part on sensory and perceptual skills, for example, and children acquire many of their motor skills in play, which involves social and physical interactions.

Links to Related Material

The specifics of the prefrontal cortex maturation, mentioned here as underlying reaction time improvement, will be discussed in Chapter 6.

One important aspect of motor skills is reaction time—the time required for the external stimulus to trigger the ingoing nerve pathways, for the individual to make a decision, and for the brain to activate the muscles through the outgoing nerve pathways. Reaction time improves substantially through the preschool and elementary school years, even for simple motor movements (Bard, Hay, & Fleury, 1990; Dougherty & Haith, 1993). In particular, maturation of the prefrontal cortex in the brain that supports decision and cognitive processes seems to underlie the improvement in reaction time (Tsujimoto, 2008).

LEARNING OBJECTIVE 5.3

Trace the development of motor skills in infancy and childhood.

1. What general principles of sequences do most infants follow in their acquisition of motor skills?
2. What are examples of milestones in the sequence of motor development?
3. How does cultural context shape early motor development?
4. What is the dynamic systems approach to motor development?
5. How do motor skills continue to develop in childhood?

Learning Objective 5.4

Describe the patterns of growth and maturation in development and the factors that influence them.

PHYSICAL GROWTH

Growth is perhaps the most fundamental aspect of child development. It is continuous throughout childhood, but it does not happen uniformly. Rather, the overall rate of growth fluctuates during the growth years, with different body parts growing at different rates. In this section, we discuss the unfolding of whole-body growth, adolescent sex differentiation, and factors that affect physical growth and development.

FIGURE 5.5

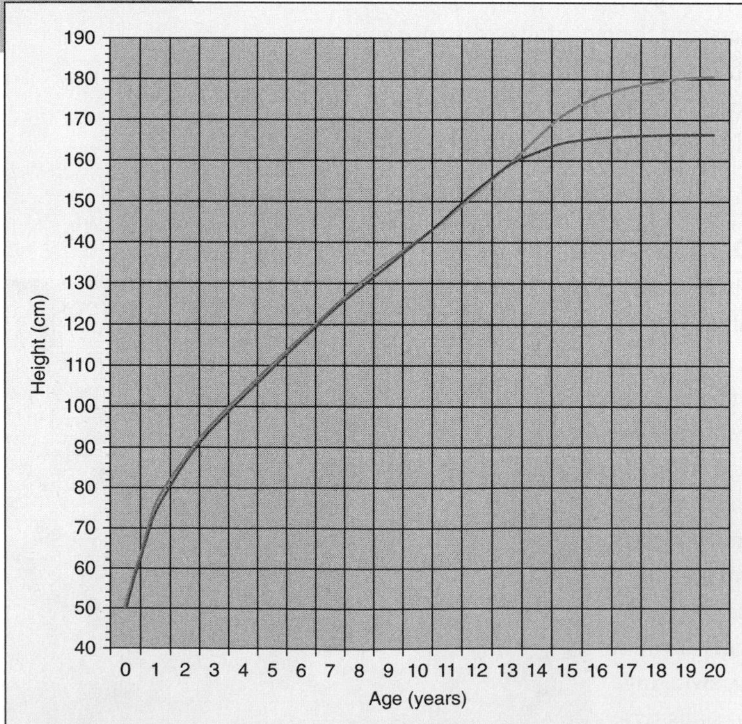

Typical male and female growth curves. Birth length doubles by around the 4th year, but growth slows, and length increases by only around 50 percent by the 13th year. Adult height can be estimated by doubling the height of males at 3 years and of females at 30 months. *Data from "References for growth and pubertal development from birth to 21 years in Flanders, Belgium" by M. Roelants, R. Hauspie, and K. Hoppenbrouwers, 2009,* Annals of Human Biology, 36, *680-694, Table V.*

GROWTH IN SIZE

We saw in Chapter 4 that the fetus' growth rate is dramatically high, although it necessarily slows as birth approaches. This general slowing trend characterizes growth up to adolescence.

Figure 5.5 shows an average growth curve for males and females. Boys and girls are approximately the same height until around 10 years of age. A growth spurt typically occurs between 10 and 12 years of age for girls and between 12 and 14 years of age for boys. This age difference accounts for the common observation that girls, on average, are taller than boys in grades 7 and 8, a relation that permanently reverses a couple of years later. In North America and northern and western Europe, where good records have been kept, we know that height increases are just about completed by 15.5 years of age in girls and 17.5 years in boys; less than 2 percent of growth is added afterward (Malina, 1990; Tanner, 1990).

There is evidence that growth rates have changed over recent history in some parts of the world. In Europe and North America, after about 1900, the average height of 5- to 7-year-olds increased 1 to 2 cm per decade, and the average height of 10- to 14- year-olds increased 2 to 3 cm per decade. Adult height, however, increased only 0.6 cm per decade between 1880 and 1960. In recent decades, however, height

FIGURE 5.6

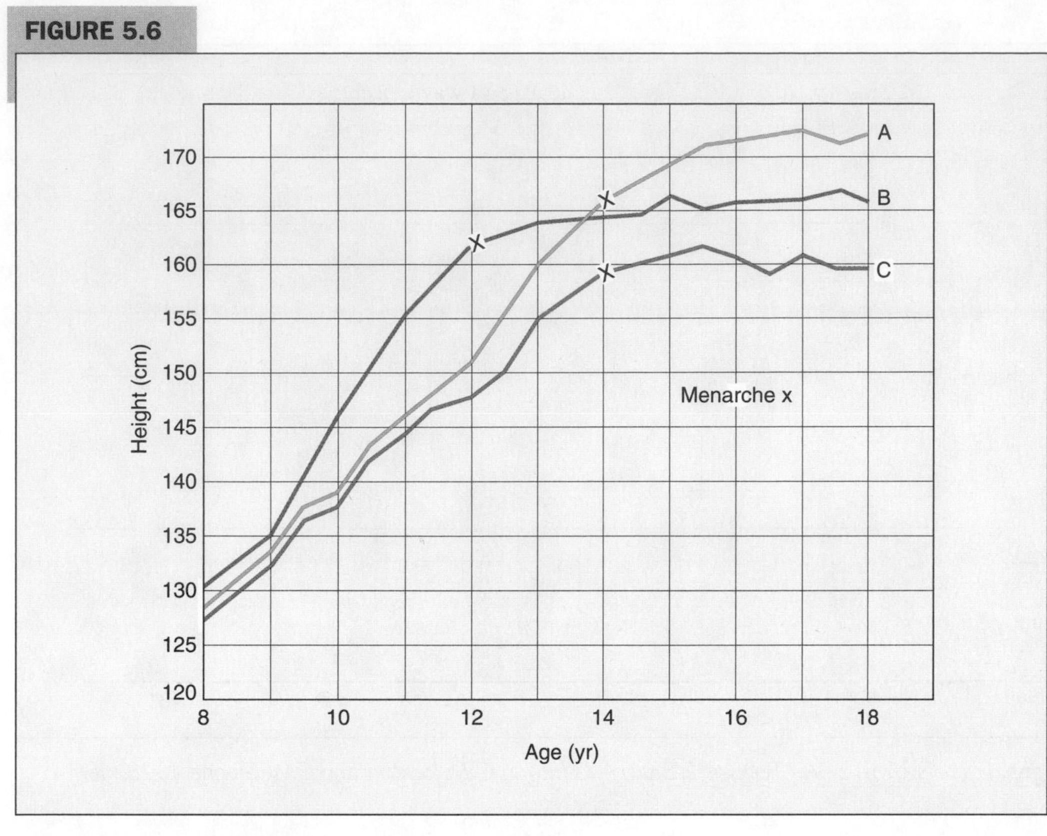

Curves showing the heights of three girls over time. Age of menarche is indicated by an X. *Adapted from "Individual Patterns of Development" by N. Bayley, 1956,* Child Development, *27, 52. Copyright © 1956 by The Society for Research in Child Development, Inc.*

has increased by 1.2 cm per decade in boys and 0.8 cm in girls (Roelants, Hauspie, & Hoppenbrouwers, 2009). Thus, the increase in children's heights apparently reflected a trend toward faster maturation more than a trend toward greater ultimate stature. Before this century, it was fairly typical for people to grow until age 25 or so, whereas today growth usually continues only until about age 18 or 19.

Charts like the one in Figure 5.5 may give the impression that there is (or should be) a normal growth rate. But few children exactly fit the averages on these charts. Although it is obvious that individuals reach different ultimate heights and weights, it may be less apparent that their rates of growth may also differ. To illustrate, Figure 5.6 shows a growth curve for three girls. Girl B reached menarche, the onset of menstruation, before girls A and C. She was taller than both at age 12, but was ultimately shorter than girl A. Such differences in the age of onset of the growth spurt are likely to accompany differences in the age of puberty. They may also have long-term implications for personality development, a topic to which we return later.

Links to Related Material

Environmental resources that promote good nutrition and lack of illness are important for optimal growth throughout childhood, just as they were in the prenatal period, as you read in Chapter 4.

Factors that may produce individual differences in growth rates include malnutrition and disease. For example, researchers recorded the growth rate of a child who suffered from two episodes of inadequate nutrition (Prader, Tanner, & von Harnack, 1963). The child's growth was severely affected. After the episodes were over, the child did not simply return to his normal rate of growth. Rather, he experienced a remarkable acceleration in growth, which returned him to his expected growth path. This **catch-up growth** is relatively common as an aftermath of disease or limited malnutrition (Tanner, 1992). However, limited catch-up growth has been found among children who are born small for gestational age, particularly the very preterm (Knops et al., 2005).

Catch-up growth Accelerated growth that follows a period of delayed or stunting growth resulting from disease or malnutrition.

How might we distinguish a child whose rate of maturation is slow from a child who is genetically targeted for a small adult stature? A technique for making this distinction uses the child's **skeletal maturity**, or **bone age**, which may differ from the child's chronological age. Bones develop from the centre and extend outward toward the bone ends, called the *epiphyses.* As a bone reaches its ultimate length, the epiphyses close, and no further growth is possible. Scientists can use X-rays to determine how a child's bone development compares with that of his or her peers, and approximately how much more growth remains to occur (Tanner, 1990).

Skeletal maturity (bone age) The degree of maturation of an individual as indicated by the extent of hardening of the bones.

FIGURE 5.7

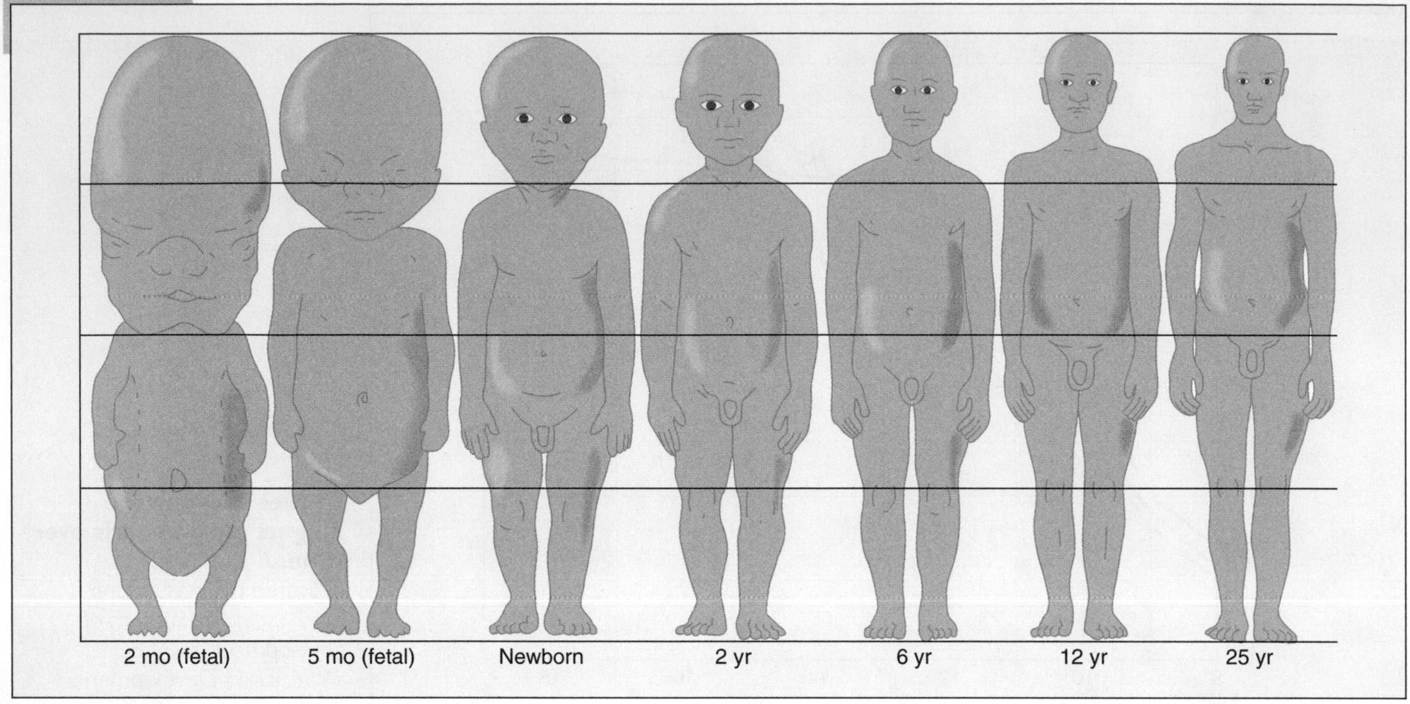

2 mo (fetal) 5 mo (fetal) Newborn 2 yr 6 yr 12 yr 25 yr

Body proportions at several ages. *From* Growth *by W. J. Robbins, S. Brady, A. G. Hogan, C. M. Jackson, and C. W. Greene, 1928, New Haven: Yale University Press, 118.*

CHANGES IN BODY PROPORTION AND COMPOSITION

Another aspect of growth rate concerns the rates at which different parts of the body develop. Figure 5.7 shows a graph of proportional growth of the body. Most noticeably, the relative size of the head changes from 50 percent of total body length at 2 months fetal age, to 25 percent at birth, and to only about 10 percent by adulthood. This shift reflects the cephalocaudal, or top-down, sequence of development described earlier.

We have seen that a spurt in height accompanies adolescence. More of this height comes from trunk growth than from leg growth. However, in one of the few violations of the cephalocaudal and proximodistal principles, leg growth occurs earlier than trunk growth by six to nine months. Parents often wonder whether children at this stage will always be all hands and feet (Tanner, 1990).

Internal organs also follow individual paths of growth. Up to about 8 years of age, the brain grows much faster than the body in general, and the reproductive organs grow much more slowly. Then, the rate of brain growth slows to a gradual halt, whereas the reproductive system reaches a plateau between 5 and 12 years of age and surges at around 14 years of age.

The proportion of fat to muscle also changes with age and differs between boys and girls. The fetus begins to accumulate fat in the weeks before birth. This process continues until around nine months after birth. After that, fat gradually declines until around 6 to 8 years of age. Girls have a bit more fat than boys at birth. This difference increases gradually through childhood until about 8 years of age, and then increases more rapidly (Siervogel et al., 2000).

During the adolescent growth spurt, girls continue to gain fat faster than males. Muscle growth also occurs during adolescence, more strikingly for boys than for girls (Malina, 1990). However, because girls reach their growth spurt before males, there is a two-year period in which girls, on average, have more muscle than boys. Changes in body proportions that occur in adolescence result in greater shoulder width and muscular development in males and broader hips and more fat in females.

PUBERTY

We have seen that gender affects body size and composition. Now, we look more closely at the physical aspects of gender in the growth years, especially in adolescence.

CHANGES DURING PUBERTY After the fetal period, adolescence produces the greatest surge of differentiation between the two sexes. These changes occur when certain chemicals—hormones—provided by various endocrine glands are released into the bloodstream. Especially important glands for growth and sexual differentiation in adolescence are the gonads, the adrenals, and the thyroid. In addition, growth hormone, secreted by the pituitary gland, helps stimulate bone growth (Kulin, 1991; Paikoff & Brooks-Gunn, 1990).

The most significant aspect of development during adolescence is **puberty**—the series of changes that culminate in sexual maturity and the ability to reproduce. Some changes involve development of the reproductive organs—the vagina, uterus, and ovaries in girls, and the penis, scrotum, and testes in boys (known as *primary sexual characteristics*). Other changes involve related body proportions, such as breast development in girls, voice change in boys, and the development of pubic hair in both sexes (known as *secondary sexual characteristics*). Puberty usually begins between the ages of 10 and 14, typically earlier for girls than for boys.

Puberty The period in which chemical and physical changes in the body occur that enable sexual reproduction.

In males, the first sign of puberty, which occurs at around age 11 on average, is an enlargement of the testes and a change in the texture and colour of the scrotum. Later, the penis enlarges, pubic hair appears, and sperm production begins, followed by the appearance of hair under the arms and on the face. Near the end of puberty, the larynx lengthens, causing the male voice to become deeper. This lengthening is sometimes evident in a breaking of the voice.

For females, the first sign of puberty is breast budding, which may occur as early as 8 years of age and as late as 13 years, followed by the appearance of pubic hair. Menarche occurs relatively late in puberty. In northern and central Europe and North America, 95 percent of girls begin menarche between 11 and 15 years of age. On average, girls of African descent begin slightly earlier than Caucasian girls (Biro et al., 2001). Usually ovulation follows the onset of menarche by one or two years. The trend toward faster maturation has also been reflected in the age of menarche, which has decreased over the last century (Meredith, 1963; Tanner, 1987). Earlier maturation can be explained by better living conditions—better nourishment, better health care, and lowered incidence of disease.

Variations among adolescents in the timing of puberty can have a number of sources. Genes are clearly important, as are nutrition and general physical health. Even conditions in the home can affect the timing. In one study, girls whose home lives were characterized by high levels of stress (for example, discord between parents, absence of the father) were earlier to enter puberty than were girls who lived in less stressful home environments (Ellis & Garber, 2000).

How quickly adolescents move through puberty varies as widely as when they start. For example, it may take a girl as few as one-and-a-half years or as many as five years to complete puberty. If we were to study a single class of boys and girls in an elementary school, beginning when the first student began puberty and following the group until the last student finished puberty, chances are we would have to follow the group for a full ten years (Petersen, 1987). Imagine how much variation in maturation there would be in the middle years and how it might play out in social relations, self-image, and confidence.

ATTITUDES TOWARD PUBERTY Psychologists studying adolescence used to focus on physical changes. As investigators have learned more about the dynamics of adolescent change, however, they have increasingly emphasized social and cultural factors. More and more, investigators talk about biosocial or psychobiological factors in adolescence, rather than only about biological factors (Graber, Brooks-Gunn, & Petersen, 1996).

Consider, for example, how girls react to the onset of menarche. This event usually heightens a girl's self-esteem and her prestige among peers. However, girls who are psychologically unprepared for menarche, perhaps because they lack information about it, have more negative feelings about its onset. Later in life, these girls are also more negative about menstruation, report more severe symptoms, and are more self-conscious about it than are other girls (Brooks-Gunn, 1987, 1991).

Links to Related Material

In Chapter 13 you will read more about self-esteem and how it is related to gender and age.

Social factors also influence how adolescents feel about the changes in their bodies and when they occur. In much of North America, the ideal female is thin. But as we have seen, females add fat during puberty, and their hips broaden. In contrast, males add muscle and shoulder width,

Social factors influence how adolescents feel about changes in their bodies and when they occur. (© *Peter Banos/Alamy*)

characteristics that better fit the preferred cultural image of males. Not surprisingly then, early-maturing females tend to be more dissatisfied with their bodies during puberty than late-maturing females, whereas the opposite is true for males (Crockett & Petersen, 1987; Graber et al., 1994; Ohring, Graber, & Brooks-Gunn, 2002).

A negative body image is not the only outcome linked to early or late maturity. Early maturity in girls is associated with a heightened probability of a number of problems, including lower physical activity, depression, eating disorders, and substance abuse (Baker, Birch, Trost, & Davison, 2007; Dick et al., 2000; Ge, Conger, & Elder, 2001a; Mendle, Harden, Brooks-Gunn, & Graber, 2010; Stice, Presnell, & Bearman, 2001). We should add, of course, that these are simply on-the-average relations; most early-maturing girls escape such outcomes. For boys, late maturity tends to carry problems, including heightened anxiety and lower popularity among peers (Jones, 1965; Petersen, 1988). There is some evidence, however, that early maturity for boys may increase the probability of depression, just as is true for early-maturing girls (Ge, Conger, & Elder, 2001b; Mendle et al., 2010).

Only limited research exists on how early and late maturers succeed later in life. One longitudinal study indicates that the difficulties encountered by early-maturing girls are not necessarily lasting ones; by early adulthood, the girls who matured early were indistinguishable on most measures from their late-maturing peers. They did, however, lag behind in educational attainment (Cavanagh, Riegle-Crumb, & Crosnoe, 2007). Another study reported that adolescent boys who had matured early had more stable careers than did late maturers, and that they scored higher on tests of sociability, dominance, self-control, and responsibility. On the positive side, late-maturing boys were more nurturing and seemed better able than earlier maturers to face their emotions and feelings (Brooks-Gunn & Reiter, 1990; Jones, 1965). However, late-maturing boys are at greater risk for exhibiting disruptive behaviour and substance abuse problems as they transition into adulthood (Graber, Seeley, Brooks-Gunn, & Lewinsohn, 2004).

FACTORS THAT AFFECT GROWTH AND MATURATION

Our genes play a major role in our growth and physical maturation. Thus, children tend to resemble their parents—tall parents, for example, usually have taller children than do short parents. But like every other aspect of human development, growth and maturation are also influenced by the context of development.

HEREDITY Recall from Chapter 3 that investigators sometimes compare similarities in identical twins with similarities in fraternal twins to determine how much genetic factors influence particular behaviours. A similar strategy yields information about the role of heredity in the onset and pace of puberty and body structure.

One study of twins has been underway in Louisville, Kentucky, for over 40 years, and more than 500 pairs of twins have been studied. Identical twins have been found to become increasingly close in height up to around 4 years of age and to stabilize at a very high correlation of around .94. Fraternal twins of the same sex do the opposite. At birth, their correlation in height is about .77, but it drops to .59 at 2 years and to .49 at 9 years, at which point it stabilizes. A similar pattern exists for weight (Wilson, 1986). Identical twins are also more similar than fraternal twins in their spurts and lags in growth (Mueller, 1986).

FIGURE 5.8

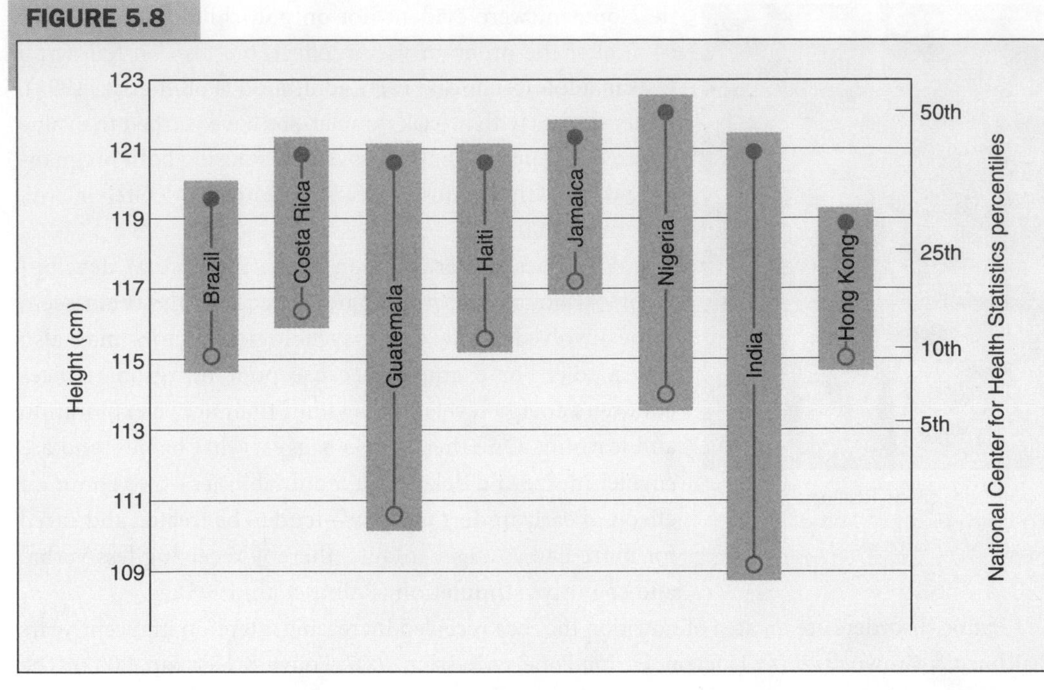

Average heights of 7-year-old boys in several countries. The solid circles at the top indicate the heights of boys from higher socio-economic classes, and the open circles at the bottom indicate the heights of boys from lower socio-economic classes. *Adapted from "Genetics, Environment, and Growth: Issues in the Assessment of Nutritional Status" by R. Martorell, 1984. In A. Velasquez and H. Bourges (Eds.),* Genetic Factors in Nutrition *(p. 382), Orlando, FL: Academic Press. Copyright © 1984. Reprinted with permission of the author.*

Several other measures support the role of heredity in the rate of maturation. Identical twins display much greater similarity in the age of eruption of their teeth than do fraternal twins, and they are more similar in the pace of bone development, as well as in breast development in girls and testicular development in boys. The age of onset of menarche differs by less than four months in identical twins. One study revealed that even when identical twins were reared apart, the onset of menarche differed by an average of only 2.8 months. In contrast, fraternal twins reared together typically differ by 6 to 12 months in the age of onset of menarche. Such findings imply that genes play a substantial role in maturation, a conclusion also supported by similarities in the age of onset of menarche between mothers and daughters (Bailey & Garn, 1986).

If genetic factors influence maturation and eventual stature, we might expect to find maturational differences among genetic groups. In fact, we do. Asians reach puberty faster than do Europeans and move through it more quickly (but achieve a smaller stature). Africans proceed through adolescence at about the same pace as Europeans and Americans, but when they have equivalent quality of life, they reach a taller stature (see Figure 5.8) (Evelyth, 1986).

NUTRITION It should come as no surprise that relations have been found between the adequacy of a child's nutrition and various measures of that child's growth and development. Considering that about 40 percent of the world's children below age 5 are underweight, this is not a minor issue (Pollitt et al., 1996).

Even mild to moderate malnutrition can cause problems in children (Ricciuti, 1993). A major research project investigated the diets of children in Kenya, Egypt, and Mexico. The report concluded that even when children were consuming ample quantities of food, the quality of their diets affected their scores on various tests of cognitive and intellectual development. Deficiencies in certain vitamins (principally vitamins A, B12, and D) and minerals (especially calcium, iron, and zinc) seemed to be most clearly involved (Sigman, 1995).

Recent studies indicate, however, that the effects of early malnutrition are not as irreversible as was once thought. Dietary correction and stimulating environments can have remarkable recuperative effects, although prevention is clearly better than treatment. One team of researchers, for example, provided nutritional supplements to pregnant women in Guatemalan villages where food resources were scarce and many villagers were underfed. Supplements were also given to the children during the first two years of life. Beneficial effects on various aspects of cognitive

Malnutrition, especially early in life, can have devastating effects. Treatment, where available, can have beneficial results. Central Hospital in Lilongwe, Malawi, has one such pediatric malnutrition ward. *(Obed Zilwa/AP/The Canadian Press)*

development were evident not only in childhood, and thus soon after the program was in effect, but also on follow-up tests in adolescence and early adulthood (Pollitt et al., 1993). Other studies with at-risk populations have verified the value of providing nutritional improvements during both pregnancy and the early childhood years (Grantham-McGregor, Ani, & Fernald, 2001).

Why does undernutrition affect intellectual development? Although direct biological effects on the brain seem to be involved, social and psychological factors may also play a role. For example, because poor nutrition reduces children's energy levels, it may limit their active exploration and learning. One theory also suggests that babies who are smaller in size and delayed in motor abilities—two common effects of early undernutrition—tend to be treated and cared for more like younger infants, thereby receiving less verbal and cognitive stimulation (Pollitt et al., 1993).

Eating disorders are an area of nutrition that has received increasing attention in recent years (Fairburn & Brownell, 2002; Hudson, Hiripi, Pope, & Kessler, 2007; Polivy & Herman, 2002). The causes of eating disorders are not completely understood. Researchers have examined a variety of influences, including genetically-related biochemistry, personality factors related to self-esteem and stress management, and social pressure from family and/or friends to be thin and to control weight. In addition, researchers have noted the significant role played by society, which idealizes thinness, provides women with unrealistic standards of physical beauty, and places too much emphasis on women's appearances as opposed to their ideas or accomplishments.

Anorexia nervosa A severe eating disorder, usually involving excessive weight loss through self-starvation; most often found in teenage girls.

With one such disorder, **anorexia nervosa**, the individual—most often a young female—voluntarily engages in severe dietary restriction to maintain a physique that is extremely thin. Adolescent anorexics often have a distorted concept of nourishment and body image. The damaging effects of this self-starvation include muscle wasting, dry skin and hair, constipation, dehydration, and sleep disturbance. Sometimes growth and development are impaired, menstruation ceases, and breast development is permanently affected. Between 5 and 8 percent of individuals with anorexia die from starvation or suicide (Herzog et al., 2000; Schmidt, 2000). Even if treated, long-term consequences may include irregular heart rhythms and possibly heart failure.

Links to Related Material

Exposure to media messages regarding unattainable standards of feminine beauty appear linked to the greater incidence of eating disorders in young women. In Chapter 16, you will learn more about societal influences on how we construct "feminine" and "masculine" behaviour.

Another eating disorder is **bulimia nervosa**, which involves binging on large quantities of food and then inducing vomiting to purge the excess calories and maintain a normal weight level. This disorder often results in damage to teeth and gums, cracked and damaged lips, and serious imbalances in body fluids. Bulimics, like anorexics, also frequently have distorted concepts of food and body image, and they often have guilt, anxiety, and depression. Although they are typically more aware that they have a problem than are anorexics, this knowledge does not easily translate into behaviour; indeed, impulsivity and lack of control are characteristics of the disorder (Leon, 1991; Polivy & Herman, 2002).

Bulimia nervosa A disorder of food binging and sometimes purging by self-induced vomiting; typically observed in teenage girls.

Obesity A condition of excess fat storage; often defined as weight more than 20 percent over a standardized ideal weight.

Obesity, or excess fat storage, is one of the most common disorders in Canada today. Obesity is usually defined as weight 20 percent or more over a standard weight for height. Around 37 percent of Canadian children aged 2 to 17 are overweight, and nearly 17 percent can be considered obese (Statistics Canada, 2004). Among the factors contributing to obesity are genetic predisposition, low levels of physical activity, and low family income. For example, more obese children are inactive (38 percent) compared with non-obese children (30 percent). In some instances, parents may inadvertently contribute to the problem by their feeding practices—for example, by frequent admonitions to "clean your plate," or by making approval or rewards contingent on eating behaviour (Fisher & Birch, 2001).

For Thought and Discussion

What is your BMI (body mass index)? Divide your weight in pounds by your height in inches squared, and multiply by 703. A BMI of 25.0 to 29.9 is considered overweight and above 30.0 is considered obese.

Obesity has several effects on development. Obese females tend to begin puberty earlier than do non-obese females, for example, and obese males hit their growth spurt earlier than do their counterparts. Obesity has psychological consequences as well. Obese children typically have poor bodily self-esteem, a finding that is evident as early as age 5 (Davison & Birch, 2002). Many obese children feel insecure and are overprotected by their parents. They frequently experience school difficulties, neuroses, and social problems. A vicious circle may become established in which social and psychological problems induce eating, and weight gain further contributes to the problems.

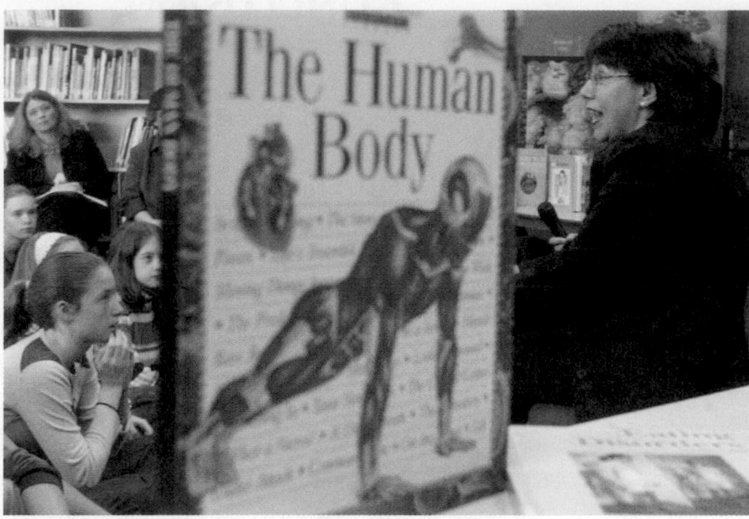

In 2002, then Health Minister Anne McLellan announced that the federal government would be investing in research on obesity and healthy body weight. (*The Canadian Press*)

Binge-eating disorder is a more recently recognized condition that is characterized by episodes of uncontrolled eating. Unlike anorexia and bulimia, however, binge-eating disorder typically occurs without compensatory activities, such as vomiting or laxative abuse, to avoid weight gain. Though binge eating is typically associated with obesity (Decaluwe & Braet, 2003), being obese is not a requirement for having this disorder (Dingemans, Bruna, & van Furth, 2002).

ABUSE AND PSYCHOLOGICAL TRAUMA Up to now we have focused on the physical aspects of the context of growth and development; however, psychological trauma can also impair growth. A failure-to-thrive syndrome has been described in infants who fail to gain weight for no obvious reasons other than psychological disturbances or maltreatment and abuse by parents. Diane Benoit (1993), of the Hospital for Sick Children in Toronto, notes that these babies tend to gain weight readily when their care is transferred to hospital personnel (Drotar et al., 1990).

A report on 13 children between the ages of 3 and 11 years provides an example of how psychological trauma can affect growth. These children lived in homes that were unusually stressful as a result of marital problems or alcohol abuse, and there were several cases of child abuse. The children appeared to have abnormally low pituitary gland activity and their growth rates were substantially impaired. Shortly after they were removed from their homes, the circulation of growth hormone from the pituitary increased and the growth of most of the children accelerated (Powell, Brasel, & Blizzard, 1967). Thus, there is at least some environmental control over a characteristic that was once thought to be controlled almost exclusively by genetics.

LEARNING OBJECTIVE 5.4

Describe the patterns of growth and maturation in development and the factors that influence them.

1. How can growth change over time in different populations?
2. What factors affect individual differences in growth rate?
3. How do growth rates and body proportions change across childhood?
4. What physical changes occur with puberty for girls and boys?
5. How do cultural practices and social attitudes affect the experience of puberty?
6. Why is childhood obesity a growing health concern, and what factors place a child at risk for it?
7. What are some causes and consequences of the two leading eating disorders?

CONCLUSION

This chapter concludes a set of three chapters that concern the more biological aspects of human development. In Chapters 3 and 4, we focused on genetics and prenatal development. In this chapter, we discussed the behaviours and physical equipment the baby brings to the world and how this basic equipment develops through infancy, childhood, and adolescence.

Until recently, psychologists have not been very open to considering the physical and biological bases of behaviour. Rather, a tension existed between the more physically-based and the more psychologically based disciplines, with psychologists more focused on demonstrating that social and environmental factors influence behaviour. However, the mood seems to be changing. As we have seen, biological influences that we might at first imagine would act on their own are found, on closer examination, to cooperate with environmental factors to produce their ultimate effect. We have seen many examples of this interdependence—for instance, the effects of health care on birth mortality, the family setting on the outcome of infants at risk, prenatal exposure to cocaine on the newborn's state organization and rhythms, practice on motor development, and psychological trauma on growth. For this reason, many of the tensions that once existed between psychologists and biologists have largely disappeared, and the search is on to understand how biological factors and experience collaborate to influence human development. We will mention numerous instances of such collaboration as we move through the remaining topics in the book.

SUMMARY

KEY TERMS

anorexia nervosa, p. 160
anoxia, p. 134
Apgar exam, p. 135
at risk, p. 132
Brazelton Neonatal Behavioral Assessment Scale, p. 136
bulimia nervosa, p. 160
caesarean section, p. 131
catch-up growth, p. 155
cephalocaudal, p. 148
congenitally organized behaviours, p. 146
dynamic systems approach, p. 151
electroencephalograph (EEG), p. 140
fetal distress, p. 131
locomotion, p. 148
obesity, p. 160
perinatal period, p. 130
postural development, p. 148
prehension, p. 148
preterm, p. 134
proximodistal, p. 148
puberty, p. 157
rapid eye movement (REM) sleep, p. 141
reflex, p. 143
skeletal maturity (bone age), p. 155
small for gestational age (SGA), p. 134
sudden infant death syndrome (SIDS), p. 141

LEARNING OBJECTIVES

LEARNING OBJECTIVE 5.1 Discuss the stages of labour, the social and cultural factors that influence childbirth, and the assessment of factors affecting newborn health.

1. *What happens during the three stages of childbirth?*
   The first and longest stage of labour begins when the early contractions start to dilate or widen the cervical opening. This stage ends when the cervix is fully dilated to about 10 cm or four inches. By the end of this stage, the contractions are very intense, occurring every two to three minutes. The second stage begins when the fetus starts to pass through the cervix and ends when the baby is completely delivered. During this stage, the contractions are long and closely spaced, and the mother is encouraged to push with each contraction. The third stage lasts only a few minutes, and involves the delivery of the placenta and related membranes, referred to as the afterbirth.

2. *What societal attitudes influence the experience of childbirth in Canada today?*
In Western societies, including Canada, childbirth has been treated as if it were an illness. Most women give birth in a hospital and are given drugs to block pain. Recent societal trends have been toward making birth more "natural." For example, in an attempt to overcome the fear of childbirth, Lamaze developed a method of preparation for childbirth through breathing and muscle exercises and educating the mother about the birth process. Additional practices recently undertaken as a result of a change in societal attitudes toward childbirth include involving the father in the birth process, giving birth at home, and using a midwife rather than a doctor.

3. *How does culture affect the survival rate of mother and newborn?*
In the United States, because of improved health care, maternal deaths decreased from 660 per 100,000 pregnancies to 7 over the last 75 years. Similarly, in Canada, there were only 7.8 maternal deaths per 100,000 pregnancies in 2001. In some African countries, however, where health care is not as readily available, the maternal death rate is still as high as 1,300 per 100,000 pregnancies.
Infant mortality has been the focus for health care and has led to progress in its decrease in Canada. In 1901, there were 134 deaths for every 1,000 infants under the age of 1 year, whereas in 2004, the rate was 5.3, about 25 times lower. Yet, there is still progress to be made; there were 15 countries with infant mortality rates lower than Canada's as of 2004.

4. *What are some indicators of babies at risk?*
A baby's chances of developing problems can be predicted, in part, from the family context in which the child is born. Around 85 percent of the risk of severe developmental problems can be attributed to what happens in the prenatal period. Several maternal factors increase the risk for the fetus, including the mother's use of drugs or alcohol, exposure to viral infections during pregnancy, smoking, and poor nutrition. In addition, living in conditions of poverty increases the probability of developing problems. A second general indicator of risk is evidence of physical problems in the newborn, most frequently, low birth weight. A third indicator of risk is poor performance on standard assessments, such as the Apgar exam and the Brazelton Neonatal Behavioral Assessment Scale.

5. *What are some common birth complications?*
Common complications include the umbilical cord wrapping around the fetus' neck, fetal distress, which is indicated by an abnormally high or low heart rate, and the baby lying in an unusual position such as buttocks down (breech).

6. *What are the common tests for assessing newborns' behavioural and physical health?*
The Apgar exam has become the standard for the baby's first assessment, and it is typically administered one minute and five minutes following birth. This exam focuses on five vital physiological functions: heart rate, respiration, muscle tone, response to a mildly painful stimulus, and skin colour. The Brazelton Neonatal Behavioral Assessment Scale evaluates the newborn's ability to habituate. The exam includes items in four categories: attention and social responsiveness; muscle tone and physical movement; control of alertness; and physiological response to stress.

7. *Discuss the reasons for low birth weight in infants.*
Low-birth-weight babies may be placed in two groups. One consists of babies whose birth weights are low because they were born preterm (before 38 weeks gestation). The other group consists of those whose fetal growth was retarded. These babies are considered small for gestational age (SGA). They may be born at the expected gestational age of 40 weeks, or they may be born earlier, but they are in this category because their weight places them among the bottom 10 percent of babies born at that particular gestational age. The cause is frequently unknown;

however, chromosomal abnormalities, infections, poor maternal nutrition, and maternal substance abuse are factors that appear to be an influence.

8. *What are some environmental factors that affect at-risk infants' development?*
Some babies who are born at risk have suffered brain or central nervous system damage that affects their functioning throughout life. However, whether babies born at risk achieve normal development appears to depend largely on the environment in which they are reared. One factor in a baby's developmental progress is the quality of the relationship that forms between the parents and the baby. At-risk babies often pose special challenges to this relationship because they are likely to have an irritating cry, be difficult to soothe, have irregular patterns of sleep and wakefulness, smile less, and avoid eye-to-eye contact. These problems are aggravated by parent's reactions to preterm babies, typically expecting negative behaviour from premature infants (called prematurity stereotyping) and thereby setting in motion a negative cycle between infant and parent.

A related factor is the lack of stimulation that infants often experience when they must spend time in the hospital. The temperature-controlled, patternless plastic chambers in which they are placed deprive them not only of human physical contact, but of sensory input as well. Intervention procedures introduced in NICUs have begun to address this problem. However, for some premature babies, the added stimulation becomes overstimulation and has a negative effect.

LEARNING OBJECTIVE 5.2 Describe ways in which the infant's behaviour appears to be organized at birth.

1. *What states of alertness does the infant demonstrate?*
There are six states of infant arousal or alertness: 1) quiet or deep sleep, 2) active or light sleep, 3) drowsiness, 4) alert inactivity, 5) alert activity, and 6) crying.

2. *How does the newborn's sleep–wake cycle change in the early months of life?*
Infants gradually adapt to the 24-hour light–dark cycle. Sleep periods become longer at night at around 5 or 6 weeks of age, as awake periods lengthen during the day. By 12 to 16 weeks, the pattern of sleeping at night and being awake during the day is fully established.

3. *What factors might be related to the occurrence of SIDS?*
One factor that might be related to the occurrence of SIDS is the position in which the baby is placed to sleep. Sleeping on the stomach or in the prone position is associated with a high probability of SIDS. Soft bedding and overheating are also considered to be risk factors. Maternal smoking during pregnancy and smoking in the vicinity of the infant after birth are associated with an increased probability of SIDS. Some predictors of SIDS lie with the infant rather than the environment. Preterm and low-birth-weight babies, along with babies who suffer from respiratory infections, are more vulnerable to SIDS. Finally, co-sleeping (mother and baby sharing a bed) has also been associated with increased risk of SIDS, though this may be mediated by the presence of other risk factors.

4. *What is a reflex? What are some of the newborn's reflexes?*
A reflex is an innate behaviour or behaviour pattern. Reflexes like breathing and blinking are essential to survival, while others may have served important survival functions sometime in our evolutionary past. For example, the rooting reflex, in which the baby turns the head to the side when the corresponding cheek is stroked, usually disappears around 3 to 4 months of age. Similarly, the palmar reflex, which causes the baby to grasp the source of pressure placed on the hand, was adaptive for babies of our evolutionary ancestors who needed to cling tightly to their mothers as they moved around. This reflex disappears at 3 to 4 months of age as well. The Moro reflex consists of a series of reactions to sudden sound or the loss of head support. The

infant first thrusts her arms outward, opens her hands, arches her back, and stretches her legs outward, then she brings her arms inward in an embracing motion with fingers formed into fists. This reflex disappears by 6 to 7 months of age. Finally, the stepping reflex occurs when pressure is applied to the soles of the feet and the baby flexes her legs up and down. This also disappears by 3 months of age.

5. *How are congenitally organized behaviours different from reflexes?*
   A reflex is a response to stimulation, whereas activities that are initiated by the newborn and sustained over a considerable period of time are congenitally organized behaviours. Examples of congenitally organized behaviours include looking, sucking, and crying—all of which are well-organized and are often not elicited by a discrete identifiable stimulus.

6. *What roles do looking, sucking, and crying play in an infant's development?*
   In the first moments of life, the newborn will lie with eyes wide open, seemingly examining objects in the room. As early as 8 hours after birth, and in the dark, babies open their eyes wide and explore their surroundings. The keenness of their gaze is often unexpected. However, this demonstrates that newborns have the tools for acting on their world, not just reacting to it. Sucking is an incredibly coordinated act. Babies suck one to two times each second, with each one requiring an orchestration of suction and squeezing to express milk. These actions must be coordinated with breathing and swallowing. Sucking is one of the primary ways that infants explore their world, especially as they become better able to grasp and find new objects. Sucking also acts as a buffer against pain and over stimulation. Infants can learn to modify their sucking as demonstrated by its use in the high-amplitude, non-nutritive sucking paradigm. Crying coordinates breathing, vocalizing, and muscular tension in a rhythmic pattern. It is a critically important form of communication for the newborn. Different types of crying communicate different messages. Babies have separate cries for fear, hunger, and pain. The crying of healthy newborns is fairly characteristic in both pitch and rhythm. An unusual cry, therefore, can signal problems. Crying is a major factor in early social interaction because it is one of the infant's basic tools for getting the caregiver to come closer.

LEARNING OBJECTIVE 5.3 Trace the development of motor skills in infancy and childhood.

1. *What general principles of sequences do most infants follow in their acquisition of motor skills?*
   Motor development concerns both postural development and locomotion, which involve control of the trunk of the body and coordination of arms and legs for moving around. It also involves the ability to use the hands as tools for eating, building, and exploring. Two principles guide our understanding of the development of motor skills. First, control over the body develops in a head-to-foot direction (cephalocaudal). Second, development proceeds in a proximodistal fashion; that is, body parts closest to the centre of the body come under control before parts further away from the body.

2. *What are examples of milestones in the sequence of motor development?*
   A milestone is an average age for attaining a particular developmental skill. In voluntary reaching, developmental milestones are prereaching, using the reflex grasp, transferring an object from hand to hand, and using the pincer grasp. In locomotion, the milestones are holding the head up, sitting, creeping, crawling, standing while holding on, and then walking without support.

3. *How does cultural context shape early motor development?*
   Different childrearing experiences, often associated with different cultural practices, can clearly affect the timing of motor development. For example, African infants generally sit stand and walk from one to several weeks earlier than do North American infants. This may be the result of African parents designing ways in which the infant can "practise" these developmental skills.

Jamaican mothers provide similar types of early physical stimulation. Further, motor development cannot be rigidly controlled, and the cultural and environmental context must exert an effect because not all babies get to the same place (walking) by following the same path.

4. *What is the dynamic systems approach to motor development?*
The dynamic systems approach proposes that both nature and nurture contribute to the development of motor skills. According to this approach, the crucial element that unites the nature and nurture contributions, and that stimulates the development of any particular skill, is the nature and goal of the infant's "task." To accomplish the tasks of infancy (for example seeking to reach, grasp, move, or shake things), babies learn that various motor behaviours are useful. Skills are accomplished depending on the task at hand, including how difficult it is and how motivated the child is to accomplish it, and the physical abilities the child already possesses that form the starting point for creating the new behaviours. Infants are thought to go through two stages, according to this approach, as they try to assemble a new motor behaviour from the abilities currently available to them. The first stage involves exploration, as the baby tries many different responses in a relatively random and uncoordinated fashion. In the second stage, selection, the baby learns exactly what works and what does not work and fine-tunes the many responses into an efficient package.

5. *How do motor skills continue to develop in childhood?*
A child's early abilities, such as learning to walk and handle objects fairly efficiently, form the basis for skills that appear between 2 and 7 years of age. Three sets of fundamental movement skills emerge: locomotor movements, manipulative movements, and stability movements. Locomotor movements include walking, running, jumping, hopping, skipping, and climbing. Manipulative movements include throwing, catching, kicking, striking, and dribbling. Stability movements involve body control relative to gravity and include bending, turning, swinging, rolling, head standing, and beam walking.
The refinement of motor skills depends a great deal on the development of the muscles and nerve pathways that control them, along with sensory and perceptual skills.

LEARNING OBJECTIVE 5.4 Describe the patterns of growth and maturation in development and the factors that influence them.

1. *How can growth change over time in different populations?*
Growth is perhaps the most fundamental aspect of child development. It is continuous throughout childhood, but it does not happen uniformly. Rather, the overall rate of growth fluctuates during the growth years, with different body parts growing at different rates. Boys and girls are approximately the same height until around 10 years of age. A growth spurt typically occurs between 10 and 12 years of age for girls and between 12 and 14 years of age for boys. This age difference accounts for the common observation that girls, on average, are taller than boys in grades 7 and 8, a relation that permanently reverses a few years later. In North America and northern and western Europe, where good records have been kept, we know that height increases are just about completed by 15.5 years of age in girls and 17.5 years in boys.

2. *What factors affect individual differences in growth rate?*
Many factors influence growth and maturation: genetics, gender, nutrition, disease, and health processes play an important role.

3. *How do growth rates and body proportions change across childhood?*
Growth is continuous throughout childhood, but does not proceed uniformly. The rate of growth gradually slows, then experiences a spurt at adolescence, and stops soon afterward.

Growth rates vary widely among children, as do the heights ultimately reached. Different parts of the body develop at different rates, following a cephalocaudal progression. Body organs also vary in rates of maturation; the brain, for example, develops very early. A spurt in height accompanies adolescence, with more of this height coming from trunk growth than from leg growth.

Internal organs also follow individual paths of growth. Up to about 8 years of age, the brain grows much faster than the body in general, and the reproductive organs grow much more slowly. Then, the rate of brain growth slows to a gradual halt, whereas the reproductive system reaches a plateau between 5 and 12 years of age and surges at around 14 years of age.

4. *What physical changes occur with puberty for girls and boys?*
Boys and girls grow fairly similarly until adolescence. Girls typically experience the adolescent growth spurt and puberty earlier than do boys. Boys add more height once their growth spurt has begun, as well as more muscle mass and shoulder width. Girls experience relatively more fat and hip width.

5. *How do cultural practices and social attitudes affect the experience of puberty?*
The adolescent's attitude toward these changes may reflect social and cultural factors, such as the amount of information he or she has about the changes and the body image that society considers ideal. On average, relatively early pubertal onset is a risk factor for girls, whereas relatively late onset is a risk factor for boys. Girls react to the onset of menarche with a heightening of their self-esteem and their prestige among peers. However, girls who are psychologically unprepared for menarche, perhaps because they lack information about it, have more negative feelings about its onset. Social factors, such as the ideal female in North America being thin, also influence how adolescents feel about the changes in their bodies and when they occur. Early-maturing females tend to be more dissatisfied with their bodies during puberty than late-maturing females, whereas the opposite is true for males.

6. *Why is childhood obesity a growing health concern, and what factors place a child at risk for it?*
Adolescents who were overweight or obese had significantly worse self-reported physical health, and also were more likely to experience functional limitations based on their weight. Interestingly, researchers only found an association between being overweight or obese and experiencing poorer emotional, school, or social functioning among young adolescents (ages 12 to 14 years). Racial differences exist in measures of self-perception and perceived social acceptance based on weight. In the United States in particular, Caucasian American girls appear more likely than African American girls to be dissatisfied with their weight and body shape, despite the fact that African American girls are more likely to be identified as overweight or obese.

7. *What are some causes and consequences of the two leading eating disorders?*
Anorexia nervosa is characterized by excessive weight loss, fear of body fat and weight gain, and an inaccurate perception of one's own body weight or shape. People with anorexia experience face many of the same consequences that victims of starvation do, such as brittle hair and nails, cold intolerance, and loss of menstrual cycle in females. Long-term consequences of anorexia, even when treated, may include irregular heart rhythms and heart failure. Bulimia nervosa is characterized by binge eating (ingesting large amounts of food within a short period of time), followed by purging or other behaviours to rid the body of the food that was eaten. Purging may be accomplished through self-induced vomiting, laxatives, diet pills, diuretics (pills that rid the body of water), strenuous exercise, or fasting. Bulimia has long-term health consequences after binging and purging behaviours have ceased. Repeated

vomiting can cause inflammation of the esophagus and erosion of tooth enamel. The loss of potassium associated with repeated vomiting can damage the heart muscle and increase the risk for cardiac arrest.

The causes of eating disorders are not completely understood. Researchers have examined a variety of influences, including genetically related biochemistry, personality factors related to self-esteem and stress management, and social pressure from family and/or friends to be thin and to control weight. In addition, researchers have noted the significant role played by society, which idealizes thinness, provides women with unrealistic standards of physical beauty, and places too much emphasis on women's appearances as opposed to their ideas or accomplishments.

CHAPTER 6

NEURAL AND BRAIN DEVELOPMENT

In August 2002, Monica Tomasone, a 6-month-old baby from Richmond Hill, Ontario, woke up crying. Her mother, Annemaria, went into her room to check on her, thinking that she was crying because of a high fever. Upon entering the room, Annemaria noticed that Monica was twitching. Realizing that her daughter was convulsing and having a seizure, she took Monica to the hospital. After numerous CAT scans and MRIs, no problems were found in Monica's brain.

At age 2, after numerous tests, Monica was diagnosed with autism spectrum disorder and entered into a special treatment program and school. Autistic spectrum disorder is one of the most debilitating developmental disabilities. The child with autism typically lacks the communication and social interaction skills that are so vital for a child's development. What is particularly frustrating is that Autistic Spectrum Disorder is typically not diagnosed until 7 years of age when the child enters school. Monica was lucky, having been diagnosed at 2. Earlier diagnosis means earlier intervention and, consequently, better outcomes.

What would be helpful in diagnosing this and other disorders is a detectable brain marker. As with Monica, scans of young children's brains typically do not reveal clear diagnostic features. Recently, however, researchers in the United Kingdom have designed a brain scanning methodology that may identify just such a brain marker at an early age. The potential for such a brain scanning tool is unprecedented and exciting!

It is important to understand the structure and development of the brain not only because of autism or other developmental disorders, but because the brain is central to every aspect of development and human behaviour and function.

In this chapter, we will examine the structure and development of the neural system and the brain. We will first summarize the methodologies used to scan and record the structure and functioning of the brain and their developmental relevance. Next, we will consider the structure of neurons and their development. We will conclude with a discussion of the structure of the brain and its development. ■

Learning Objective 6.1

Describe the different methodologies used to study how the brain works and develops.

METHODOLOGICAL ISSUES

Notwithstanding behaviourism and its influence on developmental theories, the importance of the brain in behavioural and cognitive functioning has been well accepted. Historically, the problem has been how to actually measure the brain's activity during an individual's completion of a task, and then link that activity to specific behaviours and cognitive functions. Add to this the need to determine how to do this in a way that is age-appropriate in order to study development issues. Over the last couple of decades, new technologies and methodologies have emerged that permit scientists to glimpse inside the brain and gain an understanding of how it works. These techniques reveal information not only about the anatomy of the brain, but also about brain activity—that is, the changes that occur in the course of processing a stimulus or carrying out a task. These new tools revolve around **neuroimaging techniques**—technologies and methodologies that enable scientists to generate "structural" and "functional" maps of brain activity through measurements of changes in the brain's metabolism, blood flow, or electrical activity (Johnson & de Haan, 2011; Lenroot & Giedd, 2006). There have also been some exciting advances in recent years in using the neuroimaging techniques to study brain development and brain functioning (Casey & de Haan, 2002; Johnson & de Haan, 2011; Nelson & Luciana, 2008).

Neuroimaging techniques The technologies and methodologies that enable scientists to generate "structural" and "functional" maps of brain activity through measurements of changes in the brain's metabolism, blood flow, or electrical activity.

The neuroimaging techniques, in conjunction with more behavioural paradigms, have consequently led to a much clearer picture of the neural system and brain, and their behavioural and cognitive functioning, throughout development. To fully understand what we know about brain structure, functioning, and development, a discussion of the neuroimaging methodologies and technologies is necessary. Neuroimaging techniques fall into three categories: those that measure the electrical activity of the brain, those that distinguish between the different physical structures of the brain, and those that assess the functional and metabolic activity of the brain. We will consider the techniques used in each of these categories, and the advantages and disadvantages of each.

For Thought and Discussion

Advances in neuroimaging technology have led to a better understanding of the brain and its functioning. How has other technology—such as the advent of the computer—clarified our understanding of mental activity?

MEASURING THE BRAIN'S ELECTRICAL ACTIVITY

When signals are sent along neurons, an electrical field is generated that can then be measured. To measure this electrical activity, sensitive electrodes are gently placed at particular points on the scalp. The electrodes can detect small changes in electrical voltage on the scalp as a result of the underlying neural activity. Consequently, this technique generates maps of neural activity on the surface of the brain (see Figure 6.1). For example, a study assessing the electrical brain activity of individuals preparing to make gestures or use tools with their hands produced maps showing similar activity over time (Wheaton, Nolte, Bohlhalter, Fridman, & Hallett, 2005). The accuracy and precision of these maps depends on the number of electrodes placed on the scalp, with more electrodes (up to 256) providing greater precision (de Haan, 2007).

FIGURE 6.1

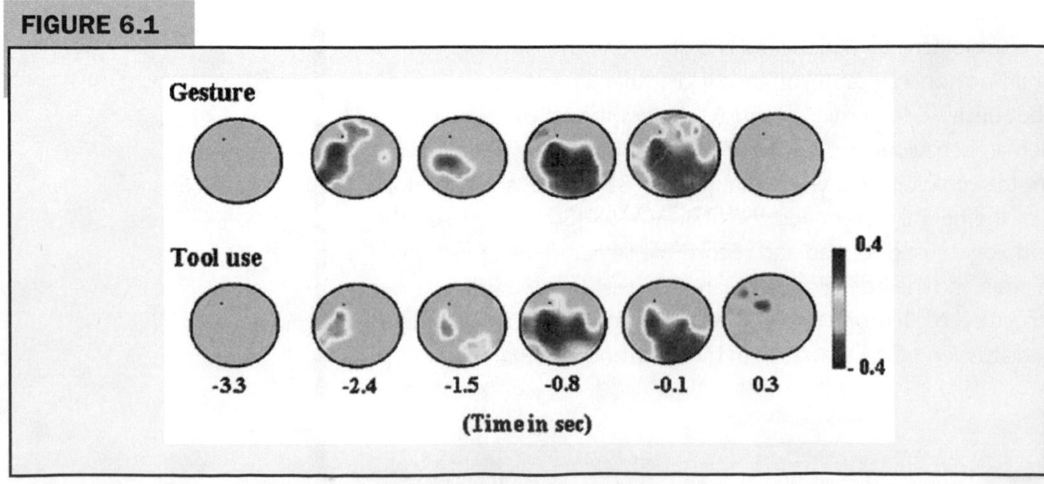

Maps of the brain's electrical activity over time recorded by electrodes on the scalp as individuals prepare to make a gesture or use a tool with their hands. The red colour represents greater activity, whereas the blue colour represents less activity. The front of the brain is at top of each circle. *From Morrison, F. J., Smith, L. & DowEhrensberger, M. (1995). Education and cognitive development: A natural experiment.* Developmental Psychology, *31, 794.*

Recording of the brain's electrical activity using electrodes on the scalp falls into two general types. The first, **spontaneous electroencephalography (EEG)**, measures the rhythms of electrical activity of groups of neurons as a person is exposed to a variety of stimulus conditions. Typically, this type of measure is used for assessing brain activity when different types of stimuli are presented during different levels of sleep/wake states (e.g., Hangya et al., 2011). Some recent studies have even suggested a relationship between patterns of spontaneous EEG recordings and visual attention and perception (Busch, Dubois, & Van Rullen, 2009; Busch & Van Rullen, 2010). Developmentally, spontaneous EEG recordings can be used to assess the nature of neural and brain maturation and, potentially, determine those who are at risk for neurological problems. For example, EEG has been used to assess the neural status of newborn infants who have suffered loss of oxygen during childbirth. In this case, a procedure is used to cool their brain and then rewarm their brain to maintain their neural metabolism and prevent significant long-term damage (Ancora, Maranella, Locatelli, Pieratoni, & Faldella, 2009). Recently, in work conducted by researchers at the University of Toronto and McGill University in Montreal, EEG measurements with the eyes open versus closed has been used to determine whether there are differences in the rates of brain maturation between the sexes in late childhood (Cragg et al., 2011). These studies demonstrate the breadth of usefulness of spontaneous EEG in assessing both typical and potentially atypical neural and brain development.

Spontaneous electroencephalography (EEG)
A technique for measuring the spontaneous electrical activity of groups of neurons across the brain to different stimulation conditions using electrodes placed on the scalp.

For Thought and Discussion

Just as APGAR scores, for example, are used to assess at risk infants, how might using EEGs with newborns help identify infants at risk and construct intervention programs?

Similar to EEG, the second type of technique measures the brain's electrical activity by placing electrodes on the scalp. But, instead of measuring spontaneous activity across the brain, this technique measures the activity of specific brain areas following presentation of a particular stimulus or action, averaged over many trials. This technique is called **event-related potentials (ERPs)** (Picton & Taylor, 2007) and has been used to investigate neural and brain connections for all kinds of functioning, from the processing of emotions, to visual information, to language, and pretty much everything in between (e.g., Kotz, 2009; Olofsson, Nordin, Sequeira, & Polich, 2008; Zhang & Luck, 2008). Researchers, for example, have been using ERPs to examine the neural mechanisms of various aspects of face processing (Rossignol, Philippot, Doulliez, Crommelinck, & Campanella, 2005; Schyns et al., 2003; Willis et al., 2010). ERPs provide detailed pictures of which regions of the brain respond to a particular type of information.

Event-related potentials (ERPs)
A technique for measuring the electrical activity of specific brain areas in response to the presentation of a particular stimulus or action.

Links to Related Material

In this chapter, we discuss the use of ERPs for measuring and localizing brain activity during face processing in infancy. In Chapter 7, we discuss the perceptual development in processing and recognizing faces.

The ERP technique has gained popularity for use in early development because it can be used with people of any age, even infants (de Haan, 2007; Picton & Taylor, 2007). Additionally, the technique is essentially the same at all ages—the same type of measure can be taken of brain activity at different ages, thereby providing the opportunity for continuous assessment across development. Figure 6.2 shows electrodes being used in a study measuring neuronal activity in infants through ERPs. ERPs have been measured in studies assessing the development of a wide range of capacities, including auditory and language processing (Picton, 2007; Trainor, Shahin, & Roberts, 2003), memory (Czernochowski, Mecklinger, & Johansson, 2009), and visual perception (Grossmann, Gliga, Johnson, & Mareschal, 2009; Lippé et al., 2007), just to name a few. Just as ERPs have been used to assess the mechanisms responsible for face processing in adults, they have also been used to assess the development of the face processing neural mechanism. Leppänen, Moulson, Vogel-Farley, and Nelson (2007), for example, recorded ERPs from 7-month-old infants and adults as they viewed fearful, happy, and emotionally-neutral faces. Both the infants and adults exhibited greater activity at the same scalp location for fearful than for either happy or neutral faces, suggesting that the same brain areas are responsible for face processing throughout development. With such obvious usefulness and the age-range compatibility of this technique, ERPs have become the technique of choice for understanding brain functioning in early development and beyond.

FIGURE 6.2

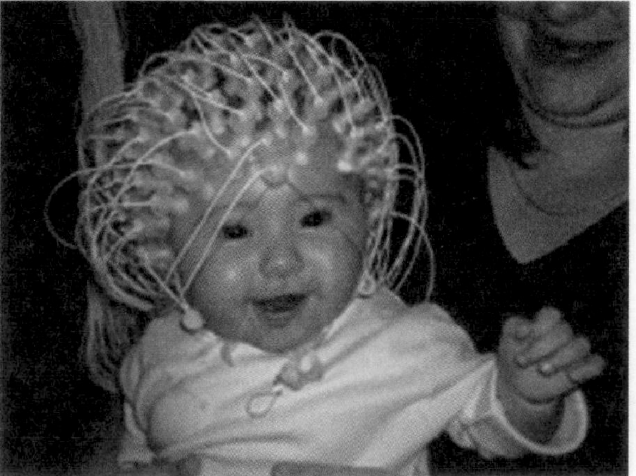

Electrodes being used in a study measuring neuronal activity in infants through event related potentials (ERPs). Source: Laurel Trainor, McMaster University http://www.psychology.mcmaster.ca/ljt/.

Magnetoencephalography (MEG) A technique in which the magnetic field generated by the electrical activity of the brain is measured by sensors placed on the scalp.

Other techniques have emerged that also measure aspects of the brain's electrical activity in relation to particular stimulation. In **magnetoencephalography (MEG)**, the magnetic field generated by the electrical currents in the brain is detected by sensors on the scalp. Though MEG has much in common with EEG and ERP, this technique has advantages over both. In particular, the skull and scalp can distort the electrical signals, leading to inaccurate EEG and ERP recordings. For the magnetic fields recorded by MEG, the skull and scalp are transparent, allowing MEG to "see" the activity of neurons directly. As with ERPs, MEG has been used to investigate the neural mechanisms of a large range of behavioural and cognitive functioning, including visual processing (Parkkonen, Andersson, Hämäläinen, & Hari, 2008), motor behaviour (Caetano, Jousmäki, & Hari, 2007), and even speech perception (Kazanina, Phillips, & Idsardi, 2006). MEG has been used to study many of the same types of processing at different ages (Batty & Taylor, 2006; Kylliäinen et al., 2006), even with fetuses (Sheridan, Matuz, Draganova, Eswaran, & Preissi, 2010). Though not as popular as ERPs, MEG studies of processing development are increasing in number. However, MEG does suffer from the drawback that it is more sensitive than ERP to movement of the individual, producing more blur in the activity data and making it more difficult to get clean results. Since infants have a tendency to move—a lot—and they cannot be told to remain still, MEG is at a disadvantage relative to ERP, which explains ERP's greater popularity.

ASSESSING THE BRAIN'S ANATOMICAL STRUCTURE

While the previously discussed techniques measure the brain's activity under various conditions and generally provide a reasonable indication of where in the brain that activity has occurred, they do not provide any information about the brain's actual anatomical structure. Modern technology has provided two techniques for assessing the anatomical structure of the brain. Neither technique measures brain structure directly, but both infer the brain's structure from their metabolic properties.

Structural magnetic resonance imaging (MRI) A technique that images the anatomical structure of the brain by creating a magnetic field that interacts with molecules in the body. When the magnetic field is removed, the molecules emit energy that is detected and from which images of the structures being scanned are produced.

The more commonly used technique that has both research as well as diagnostic applications is **structural magnetic resonance imaging (MRI)**. In structural MRI, individuals lie in a scanner that contains a large and powerful magnet (Figure 6.3a). The magnet produces a magnetic field that interacts with molecules, such as water, in the body. When the magnetic field is turned off, the affected molecules release energy that is then detected by the scanner and converted to images of brain structure (Figure 6.3b). Structural MRIs, though less detailed than microscopic analysis of

FIGURE 6.3

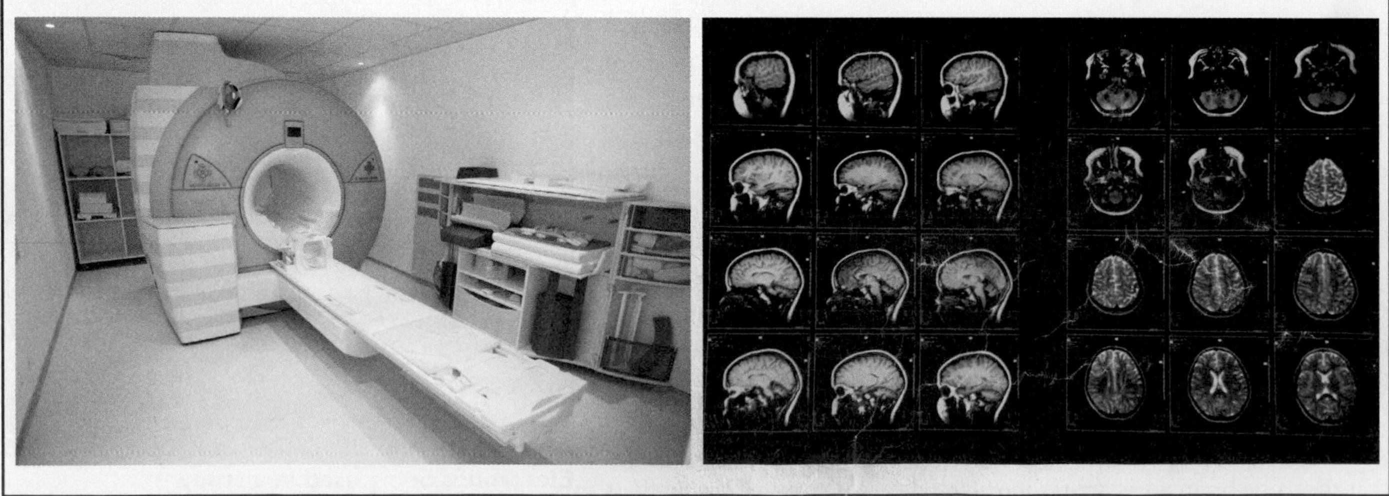

(Left) An MRI scanner. The MRI scanner contains a magnet that surrounds the person being scanned, producing a magnetic field that interacts with molecules in the brain. When the magnetic field is removed, the molecules emit energy that is then used to produce images of the brain. **(Right) Sample of brain images produced by MRI.** Allows scientists or doctors to specify which particular vertical or horizontal slice should be imaged. *(© mayo5/iStock; © Corbis Premium RF/Alamy)*

post-mortem tissue samples, are superior because they are non-invasive, emit no radiation, and are harmless. Furthermore, MRI has the capacity to distinguish between different types of tissue, leading to extensive maps of the structural relations among these tissues. For example, in the brain, structural MRIs can differentiate between grey (groups of neurons) and white (bundles of connecting fibres) matter.

Structural MRIs have been used extensively for diagnostic purposes, assessing the underlying brain damage that occurs with disease (e.g., Li & Wahlund, 2011) and traumatic injuries (e.g., Marino, Ciurleo, Bramanti, Federico, & De Stefano, 2011). But, at the same time, MRI also has significant research applications. Structural MRI of an autistic individual's brain, for example, provides valuable information about the brain regions that show differences relative to a typical person's brain. Anagnostou and Taylor (2011), from the University of Toronto, have reviewed much of the structural MRI research on autism. They have identified a number of differences, including the suggestion that the brains of autistic individuals overgrow early in development, leading to differences in the volume and connectivity of particular regions. Similarly, structural MRI studies of individuals with prosopagnosia, a deficiency in processing and recognizing faces, have shown that there are differences in their brains relative to individuals who have no difficulty in processing and recognizing faces (Pitcher, Walsh, & Duchaine, 2011). Clearly, structural MRIs have become a critical diagnostic and research tool for determining and mapping brain damage and deficiencies in clinical populations, as well as providing some important clues about the function of various brain structures. But what is the role of structural MRIs in the study of developmental processes?

For Thought and Discussion

If we could use MRI techniques on infants to identify those with autism or other developmental disabilities, what would this do for the identification, classification, treatments, and outcomes for those diagnosed with a developmentally disabled brain?

In fact, structural MRI has been used extensively to map the anatomy of the brain across development (Giedd & Rapoport, 2010). Because the person needs to remain still during the scan to ensure clear and accurate images, scans of young children and particularly infants are done while they are sleeping. As a result, a wealth of data has been gleaned from structural MRIs with infants and children—much of which will be discussed in other sections of this chapter. In fact, structural MRI has been used with all ages, from newborns and young infants (Brain Development Cooperative Group & Evans, 2006; Knickmeyer et al., 2008), to children and adolescents (Lenroot & Giedd, 2006; Ostby et al., 2009). Structural MRI has even been used to assess the maturation of the fetal brain (Prayer et al., 2006; Rados, Judas, & Kostovic, 2006), showing a general increase in the size and volume of the brain and a steady maturation and differentiation of the various distinct brain structures with age. In addition, studies using this technique have demonstrated that after showing an initial increase in volume, the grey matter in the brain then decreases throughout development, whereas the white matter shows a steady increase in volume throughout development. We will see later that this finding is due to the developmental processes related to the growth of neurons and their synaptic connections in the brain.

A more recent technique for imaging the anatomical structure of the brain has been developed as a modification of MRI. This new technique is called **diffusion tensor imaging (DTI)**, and is sometimes referred to as diffusion MRI. Though structural MRI provides detailed information about the different structures in the brain, it does not provide information about how those structures are connected. In other words, we need to understand how the different parts of the brain talk to each other and thereby enable the coordination of function between structures that leads to some behaviour. DTI is capable of imaging those connections rather than just the structures. As a variation of MRI, DTI also measures the interaction between a magnetic field and water molecules. However, DTI specifically measures those water molecules as they move along tissue, such as neural tracts consisting of axons that serve as the "wire" through which neuronal signals are sent from one structure to another. DTI is also capable of determining the direction of movement and hence the direction of the signal—an important piece of information in determining how different structures are related and interact. In all, DTI can produce images of the brain's white matter, consisting of the neural tract connections and directions, such as shown in Figure 6.4. Studies using DTI have examined the connections between structures responsible for memory across the lifespan (Charlton, Barrick, & Markus, 2010; Fuentemilla, Camara, & Munte, 2009),

Diffusion tensor imaging (DTI) An imaging technique that measures the diffusion or movement of water molecules through neural tracts that connect brain structures.

Links to Related Material

Here we indicate the importance of increases with age in the level of white matter and myelination of axons for development in some psychological processes, such as attention, motor skills, and memory. In Chapter 5, we discussed the behavioural development of motor skills such as walking. In Chapter 7, we discuss how attention and the allocation of attentional resources develop. In Chapter 9, we discuss the development of different types of memory and memory skills on a variety of behavioural tasks.

FIGURE 6.4

An image produced from DTI of the neural tract connections throughout all brain-related structures. *(Simon Fraser/Photo Researchers, Inc.)*

visual processing (Lanyon et al., 2009; Bennett, Motes, Rao, & Rypma, 2011; Wilcke, O'Shea, & Watts, 2009), and language (Elmer, Hanggi, Meyer, & Jancke, 2010). Though DTI is a relatively new brain imaging technique, its usefulness extends across a wide range of domains.

The imaging technique of DTI has also been used to investigate the development of white matter and the neural tracts connecting brain structures. Since DTI is a derivation of MRI, it has the same requirement that the individual being scanned remain still. But, as we saw with structural MRI, this requirement is fulfilled in infants and young children by conducting the scans while they are sleeping. DTI studies have been conducted with adolescents (Asato, Terwilliger, Woo, & Luna, 2010), young infants (Provenzale, Isaacson, Chen, Stinnett, & Liu, 2010), and even newborns (Oishi et al., 2011), and comparing children to adults (Loenneker et al., 2011). One of the main observations from many of these developmental studies is that the diffusion of water through white matter decreases with age, likely reflecting the developmental maturation of axons and their myelination (we will describe and discuss axons and myelination in a later section). Furthermore, it has been found that white matter increases with age in regions of the brain responsible for attention, motor skills, memory, and cognitive ability (Barnea-Goraly et al., 2005). These increases are likely related to the development in the child's ability to focus attention for fine motor skills such as walking, jumping, and catching; to remember more items for longer periods of time; and to perform more complex thinking.

MAPPING THE FUNCTIONAL STRUCTURE OF THE BRAIN

Though techniques for measuring brain activity and for mapping the anatomical structure of the brain continue to provide invaluable information, including information about the brain's development, they all are limited in their capacity to answer the ultimate question about the relation between brain structure, brain function, and behaviour. ERPs provide incredible pictures of the relation between behaviour and brain activity, particularly in terms of its temporal resolution. That is, ERPs provide very precise timing on small millisecond time scales of brain activity events in relation to the observable behaviour. This allows for accurate descriptions of the relation between particular brain activity events and a specific aspect of the behaviour in question. However, ERPs are less able to determine specific brain structures responsible for that activity, providing evidence of only gross surface brain areas without an indication of which specific brain structure lying underneath the electrode(s) is responsible. In contrast, while structural MRIs and DTIs provide fairly detailed maps of the brain's structure and connections, they do not measure the activity of those structures relative to an individual's behaviour on particular tasks. To overcome these limitations, techniques have been developed that image the activity of brain structures over time as individuals perform different types of tasks.

Positron emission tomography (PET) An imaging technique that measures the activity of brain areas by detecting the radiation emitted by an injected glucose-like isotope that has been taken up by cells in the brain that are doing work.

The first technique is called **positron emission tomography (PET)**. The PET procedure measures metabolic activity in the brain through the injection of a radioactive positron-emitting isotope into the bloodstream. Typically, the isotope resembles glucose so that it is taken up by cells (including neurons) needing energy because they are doing work. Brain areas that are especially active as the individual completes some task "light up" as the gamma ray radiation is emitted. The PET scanner (similar in look to MRI scanners) detects the radiation and its concentration, which are then converted to pictures of the activation (see Figure 6.5). From these images, the relative activity of different brain areas can be deduced; that is, which brain areas are more or less engaged. PET has been used to research the brain mechanisms involved during working memory and long-term memory tasks (Braskie et al., 2011; LaMontagne & Habib, 2010), visual processing (Corbetta & Shulman, 1998; Ganis, Thompson, & Kosslyn, 2003), and speech perception (Grèzes & Decety, 2002; Watkins & Paus, 2004). Developmentally, PET has been used to examine how the functioning of some of the brain mechanisms related to these psychological processes change as we age (Chugani, 1998). However, because the procedure requires the injection of a radioactive substance, studies with children and infants have been limited to clinical cases in which diagnostic needs have justified its use.

FIGURE 6.5

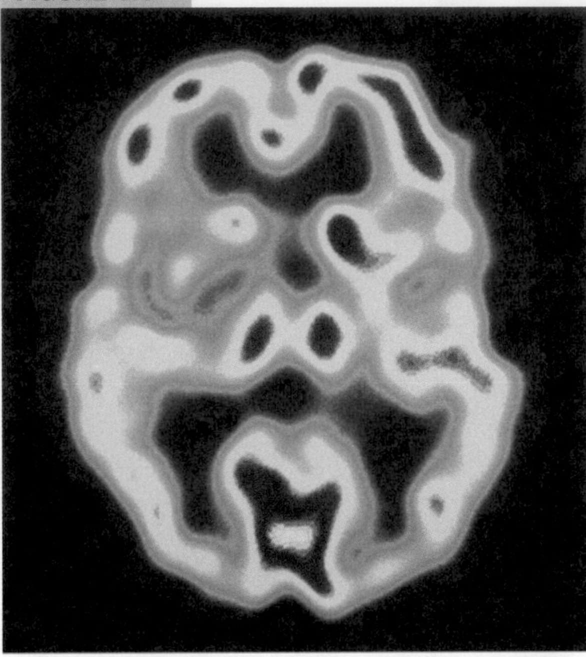

An image produced from a PET scan of the activity in different brain areas. Red indicates the most activity and deep blue indicates the least activity. *(Department of Nuclear Medicine, Charing Cross Hospital/Photo Researchers, Inc.)*

A more widely applicable technique is **functional magnetic resonance imaging**, or **fMRI**, which has essentially become the technique of choice for determining the functionality of brain structures because it does not require the injection of a radioactive substance. fMRI has also become popular because of one of its main advantages over other techniques: its high spatial resolution images show activity on the order of every 2 to 3 millimetres. This technique is essentially a modification of structural MRI and also uses a scanner with a powerful magnet inside. Functional magnetic resonance imaging takes advantage of the physiological fact that when a brain area is active, the cells in that area need oxygen. That oxygen is transported by the blood molecule of hemoglobin. Thus, there is an increase in blood flow and oxygenated hemoglobin in that area, and the oxygenated blood is more magnetized than non-oxygenated blood. The change in the blood oxygen level dependent (BOLD signal) response across the brain is what is detected and imaged in fMRI. Figure 6.6 shows a sample image from a functional magnetic resonance imaging procedure.

Functional magnetic resonance imaging (fMRI) The imaging technique that measures the level of oxygenated blood taken up by active brain areas. Oxygenated blood is more magnetized than non-oxygenated blood, leading to higher measurement of the blood oxygen level dependent (BOLD signal) in areas that are active.

FIGURE 6.6

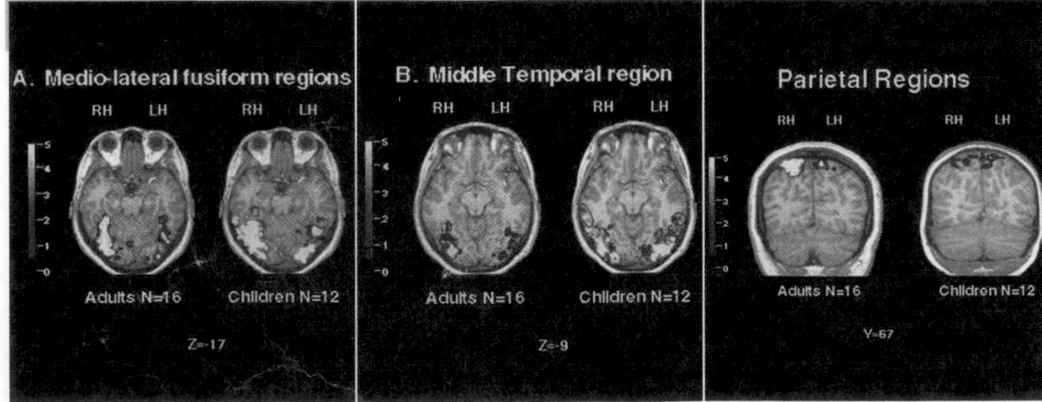

Examples of functional magnetic resonance imaging. Radio waves and a strong magnetic field are used to provide pictures of blood flow and chemical changes in the brain as different cognitive tasks are performed. In both children and adults, different regions of the brain are activated for different tasks. (*Note:* RH = right hemisphere and LH = left hemisphere.). *From Passarotti, A. M., Paul, B. M., Bussiere, J. R., Buxton, R. B., Wong, E. C., & Stiles, J. (2003). The development of face and location processing: An fMRI study.* Developmental Science, *6, 108, 109. Copyright © 2003 by Blackwell Publishers. Reprinted by permission.*

Use of fMRI to research and map the function of a wide variety of brain areas has been extensive and is ongoing. For example, studies with fMRI have been conducted to identify functional regions that are active during attention (Bouvier & Engel, 2011), object perception (Straube & Fahle, 2011), working memory (Scalf, Dux, & Marois, 2011), speech and language processing (Vaden, Piquado, & Hickok, 2011), and even during social interactions (Radke, de Lange, Ullsperger, & de Bruijn, 2011). Thus, using fMRI is strongly suited to advance the understanding of the connection between behaviour and brain function. Consequently, being able to use fMRI to study the behaviour–brain function relation during development has immense advantages over other techniques to illuminate the relation between brain development and behavioural development. Figure 6.6 shows fMRI brain scan images of just such a developmental study. Passarotti and colleagues (2003) compared 10- to 12-year-olds and adults on a task during which they had to match faces presented consecutively. They found that the selectivity of brain areas for processing faces narrows as we get older. Unfortunately, fMRI is not particularly usable with children younger than age 5 or 6. This is because fMRI requires the participant to remain very still for an extended period (typically around 45 minutes), which is difficult for young children and infants to do. Studying infants with fMRI is possible if the infant is sleepy or sleeping and he/she is listening to auditory stimuli such as speech or music; however, this significantly limits what psychological process can be studied.

Near infra-red spectroscopy (NIRS) An imaging technique in which infrared light is beamed through the skull and brain, and its absorption and scatter by blood oxygen in the brain is measured.

A fairly new procedure has been designed that does not suffer the same movement limitation as fMRI. This procedure is called **near infra-red spectroscopy (NIRS)**. It has a certain similarity to fMRI in that it too measures the BOLD signal. However, rather than measuring the blood oxygen level by magnetizing it as in fMRI, the NIRS procedure beams near infra-red light, which passes through the skull and brain, and measures the absorption and scatter of the light by blood oxygen. If there is an increase of blood oxygen level in a particular area of the brain, then the infra-red light exhibits greater absorption and scatter when passing through that area. The infra-red light emitters and detectors are housed in a cap that is placed on the head, similar to the electrodes for ERP. Because emitters and detectors are on the scalp, rather than in a scanning machine as with fMRI, the NIRS procedure is less sensitive to motion and does not require the participant to remain still for extended periods. As a consequence, even the brain activity and functions of babies can be studied.

Links to Related Material

Here we discuss one example of the use of NIRS for studying the neural basis for the development of processing object information. In Chapter 7, we discuss development of the capacity to perceive objects.

Brain areas that are working harder take up more blood oxygen, absorbing and scattering more of the infrared light. Though not many studies using the NIRS procedure have been conducted with infants as of yet, one study provides a good illustration of its potential. Wilcox and colleagues (2009) examined the functional development of brain areas that in adults are specialized for processing feature information of objects versus the objects' spatial information. Using NIRS, they found that similar to adults, 6.5-month-old infants exhibit greater activity in the temporal cortex when objects' features differ than when their spatial information differs. This suggests that the functional specialization of different brain areas in processing different information about objects develops relatively early. The study by Wilcox and colleagues demonstrates the potential for the NIRS procedure to be used in the future to help us better understand the functional development of brain areas and structures, even in infants.

We have outlined here the main techniques and procedures that have been and continue to be used to map and measure the structure of the brain, its activity and function, and its development. None of these procedures by themselves provide the entire picture of the brain. However, the combination of findings from studies using different procedures provides a much more complete portrait of brain structures and function and their development. In fact, combinations of techniques (e.g., fMRI and DTI, fMRI and EEG) have recently been used in a single study to complement each technique's specific qualities to provide more complete and accurate functional maps of brain structures. In the next sections, we consider and describe the structures that make up the brain, including the neuron and larger brain areas, and their development.

LEARNING OBJECTIVE 6.1

Describe the different methodologies used to study how the brain works and develops.

1. What are the goal and purpose of neuroimaging techniques?
2. What are the different techniques for assessing the brain's electrical activity?
3. How useful are the techniques that measure the brain's electrical activity for assessing brain development?
4. What are the techniques for imaging the anatomical structure of the brain?
5. How useful are the techniques that image the brain's anatomical structure for determining the development of the brain's anatomical structure?
6. What techniques have been devised for determining the function of different brain structures?
7. To what extent can the techniques for determining brain function be used to assess the development of those brain functions?

THE NEURON: THE BUILDING BLOCK OF THE BRAIN

Learning Objective 6.2

Describe the structures and functions of the neurons, and trace the development of the neural system during childhood.

It is hardly necessary to say that the brain is central to every aspect of development and every sort of human function. We have already reviewed the methodologies that have been used to assess and map the structure and function of the brain. In this section, we look at the building block of brain structure—the neuron.

STRUCTURE OF THE NEURON

The brain consists of two general types of cells: the neurons and the glial cells. Though glial cells are generally thought not to play a direct role in the brain's computations, they do play a role in the development of the brain, as we will see later. The brain contains approximately 100 billion nerve cells, or **neurons**; each of these cells has around 3,000 connections with other cells, which add up to several quadrillion message paths. No one completely understands how all these communication paths work, but we do know quite a bit.

Neuron A nerve cell, consisting of a cell body, axon, and dendrites. Neurons transmit activity from one part of the nervous system to another.

Dendrite One of a net of short fibres extending out from the cell body in a neuron; receives activity from nearby cells and conducts that activity to the cell body.

Axon A long fibre extending from the cell body in a neuron; conducts activity from the cell to other cells.

Like every other cell, each neuron has a nucleus and a cell body. But neurons are unique among cells in that they develop extensions on opposite sides, as shown in Figure 6.7. On the incoming side, the extensions, called **dendrites**, often form a tangle of strands that look like the roots of plants. By the incoming side, what is meant is that the dendrites receive electrical impulses or signals that code various types of information from other neurons. The dentrites then pass the signal along to the soma or cell body. The outgoing extension, called an **axon**, is more like a single strand. The axon conducts a signal away from the cell body and toward another neuron. The signal being conducted down the axon of one neuron is transmitted to the dendrites of the next neuron. No neuron has more than a single axon, but that single axon can branch quite extensively, resulting in the thousands of connections that a single neuron can make with other cells. Axons usually extend farther from the cell than do dendrites and may be quite long. In fact, some axons can be as much as 1 metre long. They are often covered by a sheath

FIGURE 6.7

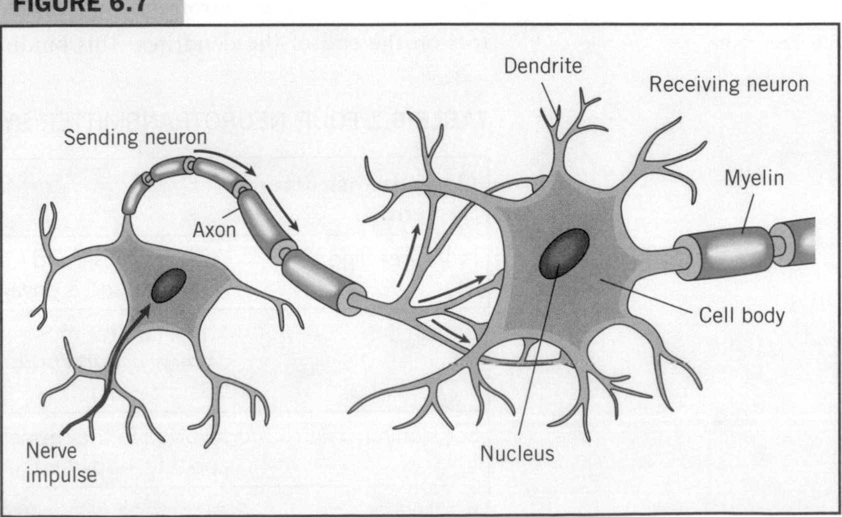

Nerve cells, or neurons.

FIGURE 6.8

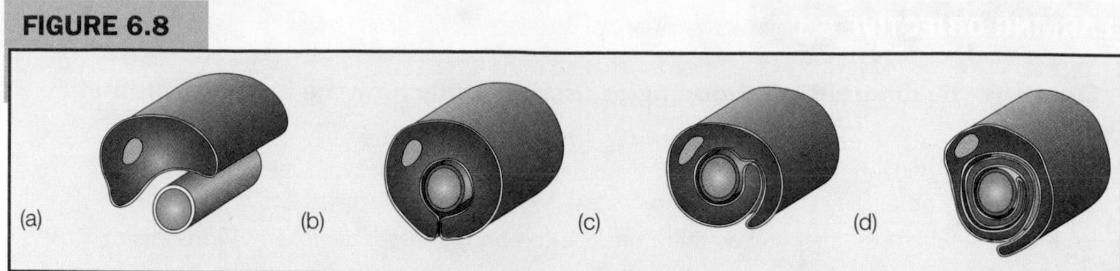

The general sequence, as illustrated in cross-section, by which a glial cell myelinates an axon. First, the glial cell makes contact with the axon (a), then engulfs the axon (b). The glial cell wraps around the axon (c), and finally surrounds the axon multiple times to form the myelin (d). *From Johnson, M. H. & de Haan, M. (2011),* Developmental cognitive neuroscience *(3rd ed., Figure 4.6, p. 53). Oxford: Wiley-Blackwell.*

Myelin A sheath of fatty material that surrounds and insulates the axon, resulting in speedier transmission of neural activity.

Glial cell A cell that wraps itself around the axon.

Synapse The small space between neurons, across which neural activity is communicated from one cell to another.

Neurotransmitter A chemical that transmits electrical activity from one neuron across the synapse to another neuron.

Synaptic vesicles Structures near the end of the axon in which neurotransmitters are stored. When encountering an electrical signal coming down the axon, the vesicle moves to the end of the axon and releases its neurotransmitter molecules into the synapse.

of a fatty substance, **myelin**, which insulates them and speeds up message transmission. Myelin can be thought of as similar to the rubber sheath that surrounds wires, in that it prevents electrical current from leaving the axon, thereby increasing the efficiency at which information is relayed. Myelin and myelination of axons is derived from outgrowths from **glial cells** that wrap themselves around the axon, as shown in Figure 6.8. It takes a number of glial cells to completely myelinate an axon. The gaps between the myelin sheaths of the different glial cells are called nodes of Ranvier.

Once the signal travels down the axon to reach its end or axon terminals, the signal must pass to the dendrites of the next cell. However, the axons and their terminals do not touch the dendrites of the other neuron, but are separated by fluid-filled gaps called **synapses**. There are two types of synapses—chemical and electrical—which are in large part distinguished by the distance between the presynaptic axon and the postsynaptic dendrite. When the synaptic gap is small, an electrical signal can jump from one neuron to the next. However, when the gap is larger, the electrical signal cannot jump and so the information signal crosses by the flow of chemicals called **neurotransmitters**. Neurons expressing these neurotransmitters are grouped into four major systems, with each somewhat localized in distinct brain areas and with somewhat distinct functions and effects (Table 6.1). The four systems are: *noradrenaline*—with effects on arousal and reward; *dopamine*—with effects on motor behaviours and cognition; *serotonin*—with effects on mood, satiety, body temperature, and sleep; and *cholinergic*—with effects on learning and short-term memory. Certain diseases may be related to problems with a specific neurotransmitter system; for example, Parkinson's disease and even schizophrenia have been linked to failure of neurons in the dopamine system. This is not an exhaustive list of the effects for each system, but represents their main effects. Further, there is some overlap between systems. For example, except for the serotonin system, all of the other systems play a role in reward effects.

How do neurotransmitters act to transmit signals across a synapse? Figure 6.9 provides an illustration of how neurotransmitters work. Neurotransmitters are contained within **synaptic vesicles** near the axon terminal. When a signal travels down the axon and reaches the axon terminal, the synaptic vesicle moves to the end of the axon and releases its neurotransmitter molecules into the synapse. The neurotransmitter then crosses the synaptic gap and attaches to the receptors on the end of the dendrites. This binding of neurotransmitter to receptors initiates a new

TABLE 6.1 FOUR NEUROTRANSMITTER SYSTEMS AND THEIR FUNCTIONS

Neurotransmitter System	Function
Noradrenaline	Affects arousal and feelings of reward, mediates the fight-or-flight response, and is engaged in the allocation of attention
Dopamine	Important for motor control, aspects of higher-order cognition such as memory and problem solving, and learning new responses through reinforcement
Serotonin	Involved in the regulation of many basic metabolic functions such as appetite, body temperature, sleep/wake cycle, and mood
Cholinergic	Associated with learning mechanisms and the storage of information in short-term memory

signal in the next neuron, which travels down the dendrite and starts the process all over again. This structure and mechanism for signal transmission forms the basis for the neuronal structure and organization of the brain, which we will consider next.

FIGURE 6.9

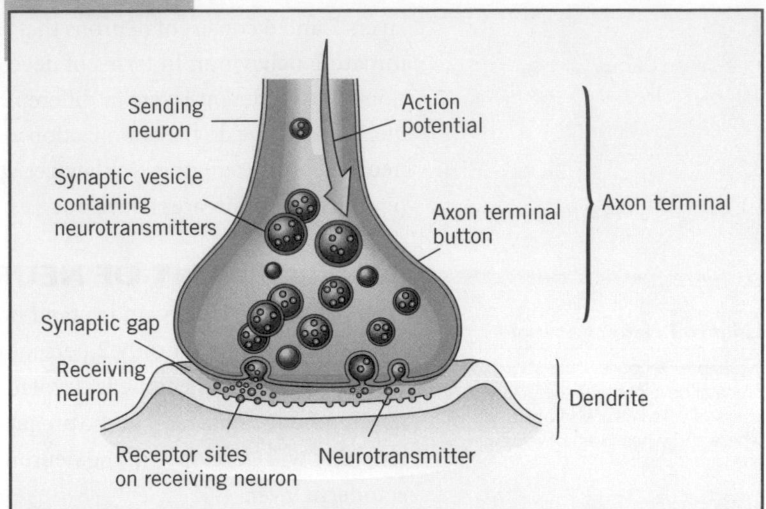

The transmission of a signal across a synapse. Neurotransmitters are released from synaptic vesicles on the presynaptic axon terminal. The neurotransmitters cross the synapse and bind to receptors on the dendrite, initiating the signal in the next neuron.

ORGANIZATIONAL STRUCTURE OF NEURONS IN THE BRAIN

The organization of neurons in the brain forms a well-defined structure. The neurons in the cortex (grey cell covering) of the brain are organized into a flat sheet with six layers (see Figure 6.10), sometimes called the laminar structure (Johnson & de Haan, 2011). The most superficial or outer layer is labelled layer 1, whereas the most inner layer is labelled layer 6. As the brain expanded through evolution, this sheet folded on itself, forming indentations and lobes that have come to define the brain. There are many different types of neurons spread through the layers of the brain—up to 25 different types—with many being restricted to particular layers. Classification of the different types of neurons is based on shape, function, and location. The most common type, making up approximately 80 percent of the cortex, is pyramidal cells. They are called pyramidal cells because the cell body is shaped like a pyramid. The axons of these cells are relatively long, feeding into other cortical and subcortical regions of the brain, and so are responsible for enabling and coordinating the communication of the different areas of the brain. Another major type of neuron is called Purkinje cells, which are located in the cerebellum. They have an extensive tree-like network of dendrites, which suits their main function of serving as the sole output from the cerebellum for coordinating motor behaviour. This specificity of neuronal organization is further illustrated in part (c) of Figure 6.10, which shows that the axons and dendrites of cells in different layers have different patterns of projections compared to other layers.

As we have already seen, each layer of cortex seems to be defined by particular characteristics. There are not many cell bodies in layer 1; instead, it consists mostly of long white axon fibres running horizontally. These fibres serve to link different regions of the cortex that are some distance apart from each other. Although layers 2 and 3 also consist of primarily horizontal connecting fibres, these connections are of a much shorter variety, providing communication of signals between adjacent areas of the cortex. Layer 4 is the layer where most signals coming out of the brain,

FIGURE 6.10

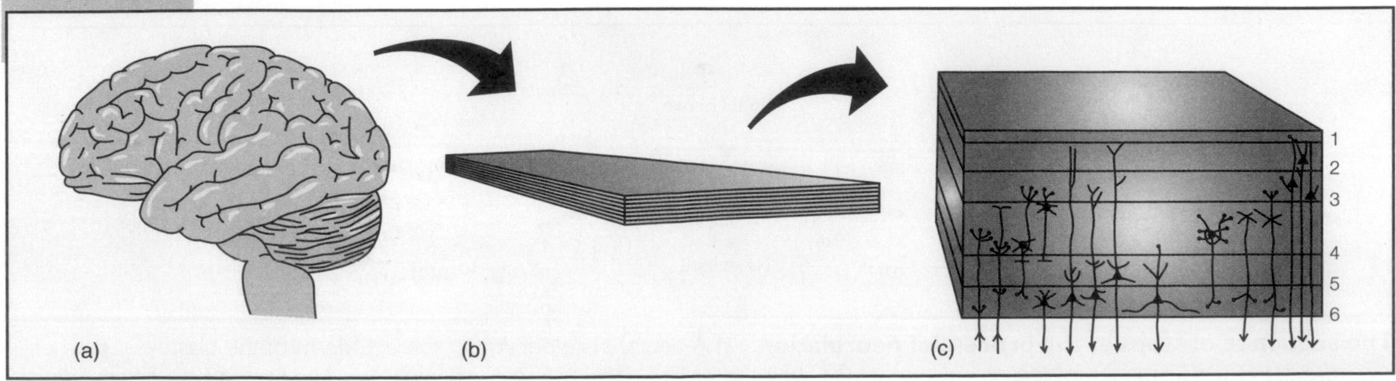

Schematic that graphically represents that the cortex's convoluted appearance (a), when laid out flat is made up of a thin sheet of six layers (b), each layer of which has a distinct neural makeup (c). *From Johnson, M. H. & de Haan, M. (2011),* Developmental cognitive neuroscience *(3rd ed., Figure 4.1, p. 44). Oxford: Wiley-Blackwell.*

such as from the eyes, or muscles in legs, or smells from the nose, input into the cortex. Finally, layers 5 and 6 consist of neurons that send output from the brain to other areas that are involved in initiating behaviour. In terms of development, there are differences in the timing of the organization of the different layers in different regions, as we will touch on a bit later. This brings us to the question of how do the organization and structure of neurons in the brain develop? That is, how are neurons produced, how do they get where they need to be, and how do the connections between neurons and brain areas develop?

DEVELOPMENT OF NEURONAL STRUCTURE IN THE BRAIN

Links to Related Material

In Chapter 4, you learned about prenatal development, the different layers of cells in the blastocyst, and where and when brain development begins.

Scientists only partially understand how the brain, in its amazing complexity, develops. Although the brain accounts for only 2 percent of adult body weight, estimates suggest that at least 50 percent of the human genome is devoted to making the brain (Pennington, 2001). Brain and neuron development begin early in the prenatal period, soon after conception. The initial differentiation of cells that will develop into the neuronal structure of the brain occurs in the blastocyst, within the ectoderm layer.

The brain begins its development during weeks 3 and 4 after conception through a process called *neurulation* (White & Hilgetag, 2008). As illustrated in Figure 6.11, during neurulation, a section of the ectoderm begins to pinch inward; this section is known as the neural plate, and the pinching is known as the neural groove. As the pinching continues and the neural groove becomes deeper, two portions of ectoderm on either of the neural plate come together. The joining of the two portions of ectoderm results in the pinching off and closing of the neural plate, and the forming the hollow neural tube. The neural tube will further differentiate along its length: the top end will become the various parts of the brain and the bottom end will become the spinal cord. The neurons are generated along the inner walls of this tube within what are called proliferative zones. There are two of these zones, with one likely being evolutionarily older and producing neurons for the older parts of the brain, such as the brain stem. The other zone produces neurons for the neocortex or the "new" cortex, such as in the frontal lobe of the brain.

Links to Related Material

In Chapter 3, you learned about the process of mitosis for cell division. Here, we see how such a process is important for the development of the brain.

CELL PRODUCTION Both neurons and glial cells are produced in the proliferative zones during what scientists have identified as the first of four stages in the process of neuronal and brain development. This first stage is called *cell production.* The production of cells is so prolific that the fetal brain generates cells at a rate of 250,000 per minute! The cells are produced by the division of precursor cells, with *neuroblasts* giving rise to neurons and *glioblasts* giving rise to glial cells. Each neuroblast in the proliferation zone only produces a limited number of neurons. Some neuroblasts give rise to particular types of neurons; for example, about a couple of handfuls of precursor cells in the proliferation zone produce all of the Purkinje cells in the cerebellum (Nowakowski, 1987). All of this cell production is done during the fetal period, with the generally held assertion that all the neurons we will ever have are produced by birth (Nowakowski,

FIGURE 6.11

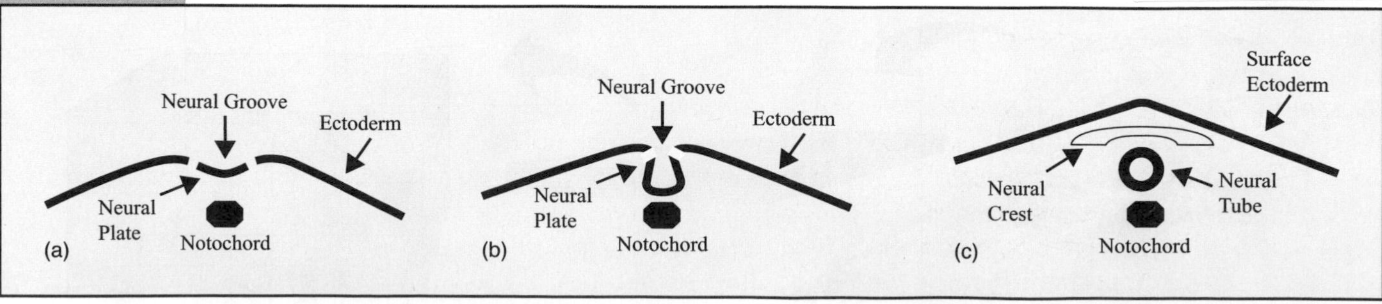

The sequence of steps in the process of neurulation. (a) A neural plate portion of the ectoderm of the blastocyst pinches inward, starting the formation of the neural groove. (b) The neural plate continues to pinch inward as two sections on either side of the neural plate come together. (c) The neural groove completely closes off as the neural plate becomes the neural tube. *Adapted from Nowakowski, R. S. & Hayes, N. L. (2002). Principles of CNS development (Figure 5.2, p. 62). In M. H. Johnson, Y. Munakata, & R. O. Gilmore (Eds.),* Brain development and cognition. *Oxford: Blackwell.*

2006). It is a sobering thought that we will never again have as many brain cells as when we were a newborn! Though the estimates vary, by the time cell production is complete, there are approximately 100 billion neurons in the brain (Azevedo et al., 2009). However, research suggests that though no new neurons are produced in most areas of the brain, in other areas—especially those involved in learning and memory, such as the hippocampus—new neurons continue to be produced through a process of mitosis called *neurogenesis* (Neves, Cooke, & Bliss, 2008), even as older neurons are dying off.

As cells continue to be produced, the top end of the neural tube expands and differentiates into three vesicles: the *proencephalon* (forebrain), *mesencephalon* (midbrain), and *rhombencephalon* (hindbrain). Further cell production gives rise to further differentiation of these vesicles. In the end, the proencephalon develops into the recognizable cerebral hemispheres of the brain, the thalamus and hypothalamus; the mesencephalon develops into the midbrain; and the rhombencephalon develops into the cerebellum and the medulla. We will discuss these brain areas, their function, and their development a little bit later. What should be clear here is that much of the early development and differentiation is a direct result of cell production.

As was discussed in Chapter 4, the early prenatal period is a very sensitive time for the beginning of brain development. In particular, teratogens such as HIV, rubella, and alcohol are shown to have an adverse effect on brain development. One important manner in which these teratogens have their effect is by disrupting cell production during the 6th to 18th weeks after conception. The disruption takes the form of fewer cells being produced in the proliferating zones than is typical, resulting in the condition of a small brain or microencephaly (Volpe, 2000). Overproduction of cells can also occur, resulting in macroencephaly or large brain, but this is usually attributed to a mutation in the genes that control cell proliferation. Regardless, both conditions typically lead to mental retardation and physical impairment. In fact, these conditions have been related to particular developmental disorders. Underproduction of neurons or *microencephaly* has been linked to fetal-alcohol syndrome (Niccols, 2007), and overproduction of neurons or *macroencephaly* has been linked to autism (Barnard-Brak, Sulak, & Ivey, 2011). Thus, cell production is a critical phase in typical brain development. Disruption of this production for any reason can and likely will lead to serious developmental problems.

Though the number of cells reaches its peak by the time we are born, more cells are produced prenatally than we need postnatally. Consequently, there is a process of *cell death* or apoptosis to get rid of the extra neurons. During this process, neurons that are not being stimulated and onto which synaptic connections are not being made die off from lack of use. Essentially, since these neurons are not needed or necessary, they are trimmed from the system (Rakic, 2005). The dramatic nature of cell death that occurs before birth is illustrated by studies looking at the number of neurons in the visual cortex. At 28 weeks after conception, there are approximately 142 million neurons, but by the time of birth there are only 88 million—a reduction in number of over 35 percent in just 10 weeks of gestation (Huttenlocher, 2002). Other estimates indicate that between 40 to 60 percent of all neurons die (Oppenheim & Johnson, 2003). Regardless of which value is correct, it should be clear that cell death is a widespread phenomenon.

CELL MIGRATION Since the neurons are produced in the proliferation zones rather than in the specific areas of the developing brain, they must make their way to their proper locations (Kolb, 1989). That is, after the cells have been produced near the centre of the brain, they must migrate outward to their proper and intended locations. This *cell migration* is the second stage of neural development and early brain development. How do the neurons know where to go? Two processes seem to be involved: *passive displacement* and *active cell migration* (Nowakowski & Hayes, 2002). During passive displacement, which is the more common of the two, newly produced cells push out previously produced cells farther from the proliferative zones. This type of migration results in what is called an "outside-in" neural pattern. That is, the cells that are older are pushed out toward the surface of the brain, whereas the younger and more recently produced cells remain closer to

FIGURE 6.12

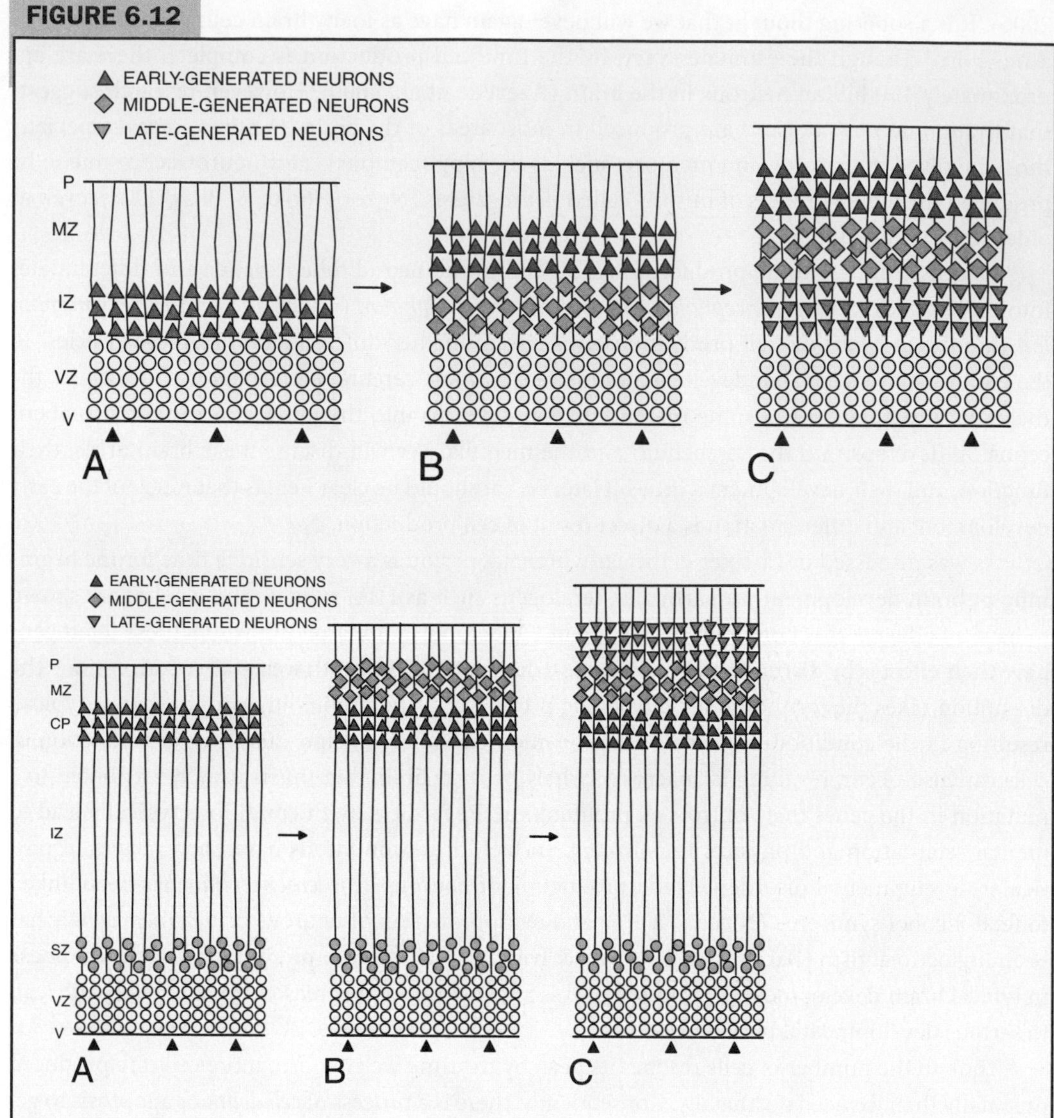

Schematics of neural migration. Top: Passive cell migration, where newly produced neurons push out neurons that were produced earlier. Bottom: Active cell migration, where newly produced neurons actively pass to migrate farther away than neurons that were produced earlier. *From Nowakowski, R. S. & Hayes, N. L. (2002). Principles of CNS development (Figure 5.7, p. 71 and Figure 5.8, p. 72). In M. H. Johnson, Y. Munakata, & R. O. Gilmore (Eds.),* Brain development and cognition. *Oxford: Blackwell.*

where they were produced (see Figure 6.12 top). Brain structures that are created and populated in this manner include the thalamus, the hippocampus, and much of the brain stem.

During active cell migration, cells move much greater distances than those that move by passive displacement. Newly produced neurons use glial cells as guides to move past previously produced cells. These glial cells direct the newly produced cells toward their final location. The final location of the migrating cells is determined by a chemical attraction between the target location and the migrating cell. This type of migration results in what is called an "inside-out" neural pattern. So, cells that are younger and more recently produced move past previously produced cells and closer to the surface (see the bottom part of Figure 6.12). Active migration is responsible for the development and population of the cerebral cortex, and the cerebellum as well. Furthermore, active migration seeding the cerebral cortex in an inside-out pattern is likely what gives the cortex the layered structure that we discussed earlier. Migration of neurons to their final locations is complete by 7 months of gestation (Huttenlocher, 1990).

That migration occurs and is completed during gestation, as with cell production, makes the processes of migration and proper formation of the brain structures sensitive to disruption. Though there are no clear environmental causes of disorders of cell migration, except a suggestion that prenatal exposure to alcohol causes disruption of migration of cells to the cortex (Miller, 1986), there are clear genetic causes (Liu, 2011). The effect of disruption in cell migration has even been implicated in developmental disorders. Wegiel and colleagues (2010) looked at the nature of the alterations to brain areas associated with autism by comparing the brains of 4- to 6-year-old children with autism to the brains of typically developing individuals. They found that areas such as subcortical regions, the hippocampus, and the cerebellum in autistic children all showed patterns indicating disrupted cell migration. Whether disorders of cell migration might be involved in other developmental disorders remains an open question at this point. Regardless, cell migration is clearly an important stage in brain development, with far reaching consequences for behavioural and psychological development.

CELL ELABORATION AND DIFFERENTIATION When the neuron has found its home, it then follows one of two paths: either it will differentiate and elaborate its axons and dendrites, or it will die as discussed earlier. When the cells take the first path, the third stage of neuronal development, *cell elaboration*, begins. In this process, an extensive network of axons and dendrites form synapses with hundreds, if not thousands, of other cells. How do axons know where to go? They detect molecules in their neural environment that either attract them toward neighbouring neurons or, in other instances, repel them from neighbouring neurons (Tessier-Lavigne & Goodman, 1996). By using the molecular cues, axons extend themselves micrometre by micrometre. Often, the axon is required to extend over fairly long distances before reaching its target area. Then, not only does it need to select the appropriate cell, the axon also needs to select the appropriate part of the dendritic tree on that cell.

One of the most important and dramatic features of cell elaboration is the increase in size and complexity of the dendritic tree (see Figure 6.13). Initially, dendrites appear as thick protuberances (bulges) from the cell body with few spines. As the dendrites develop, spines begin to appear on the protuberances and their number and density increase. The growth of the dendritic tree occurs in conjunction with the extension of axons. That is, the sprouting of dendrites is first seen at approximately 15 weeks of gestation, around the same time axons begin to reach their target areas. The combination of axon expansion and dendritic sprouting provides the ingredients for the formation of synapses, also called *synaptogenesis*.

FIGURE 6.13

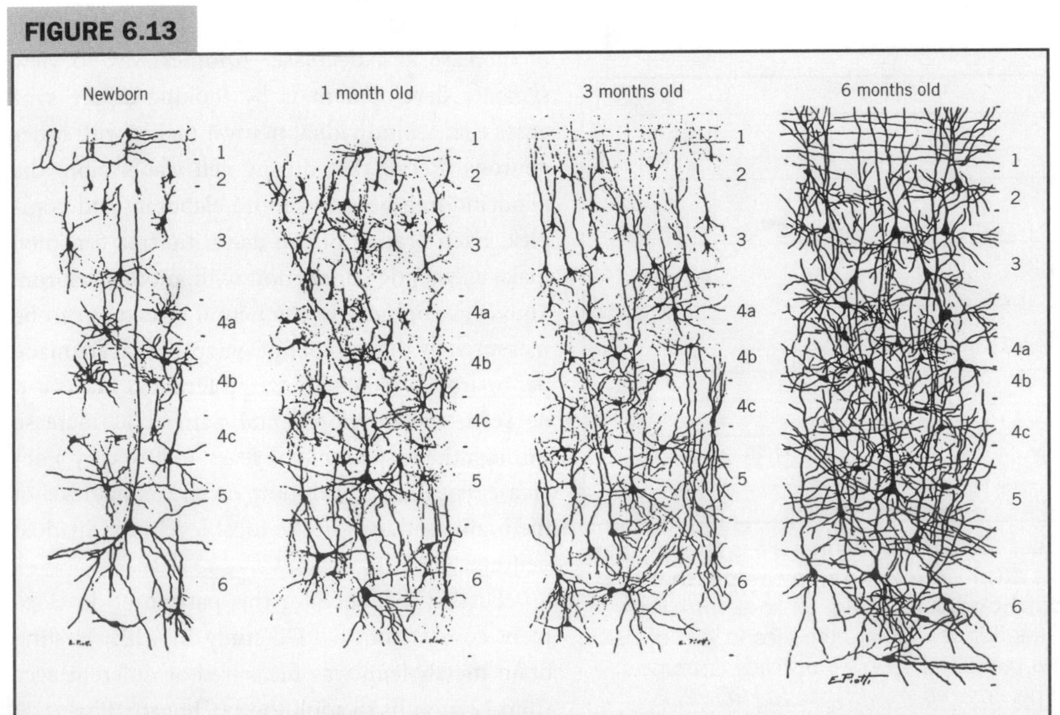

The change in the number, density, and complexity of the dendritic tree. *From Johnson, M. H. & de Haan, M. (2011),* Developmental cognitive neuroscience *(3rd ed., Figure 4.5, p. 52). Oxford: Wiley-Blackwell. Based on Golgi stain preparations from Conel (1939–1967). The Postnatal Development of the Human Cerebral Cortex, Vols. I -VIII. Cambridge, MA: Harvard University Press.*

As we have seen with the other aspects of neuronal development, disruption can occur in the developmental process, and cell elaboration is no different. Environmental agents such as toxins, malnutrition, and oxygen deprivation can cause errors in axon extension and dendritic sprouting. Furthermore, genetic disorders, including autism and muscular dystrophy, seem to specifically cause disruption in the development of dendrites (Webb, Monk, & Nelson, 2001). Because these errors and disruptions occur early in the developmental sequence, they have a much larger impact on the final neural product. Fewer synaptic connections are likely made or are not properly positioned, thereby affect normal functioning. And, since information processing in the brain and the resulting behaviour are due to a network of neural events, abnormality in one region will not be localized but will have a cascade effect on other brain areas and, consequently, on a multitude of behaviours (Nowakowski & Hayes, 2002).

Cell elaboration continues for years after birth, with some dendritic expansion occurring in the cortex through the 24th postnatal month (Mrzljak, Uylings, Kostovic, & VanEden, 1990). The first synapses appear around the 23rd week of gestation (Nelson, Thomas, & de Haan, 2006), with the peak synaptic production not occurring until around 8 months after birth (Webb et al., 2001). This peak synaptogenesis results from an overproduction of both axons and dendrites, producing as many as 40 percent more synapses than will eventually exist in the adult (Levitt, 2003). Though synaptic production reaches its peak at different times depending on the brain area, all areas have reached their peak by 2 years of age (Huttenlocher & Dabholkar, 1997). After reaching peak production, the number of synapses then declines, presumably due to a cutting back or pruning process. Although when the final level is reached varies according to brain area, by adolescence it seems to level off for all areas (Nelson et al., 2006). Which synapses are pruned seems to follow a "use it or lose it" rule. That is, synapses that are used more and are more active are strengthened, whereas those that are used less and are less active are weakened and eliminated (Greenough & Black, 1999; Johnson, 2001). Thus, experience plays an important role in the eventual sculpting of the connections of the brain through the cutting back process. Neurons and their connections compete for survival; the ones that are used appear to survive, whereas those that are not used disappear.

For Thought and Discussion

Why do you think humans have evolved this way, rather than with all of the connections already established? How would development be different if they were?

The developmental course of synaptic production or overproduction and the subsequent pruning is evident in a number of ways. In addition to the number of synapses discussed, the density of those synapses (measured as the number of synapses per cubic millimetre of brain volume) shows the same developmental pattern of increase and decrease. Another way to view synaptic development is by looking at the synapses that an individual neuron makes with other neurons. Recall that during cell elaboration, the dendritic tree becomes more elaborate and complex. Each branch of the dendritic tree can then make a synaptic connection with another neuron. Thus, development in the neural structure can be measured by the number of synapses that are made per neuron, which is shown in Figure 6.14. As can be seen, the developmental pattern of increase through the first couple of years, followed by a decrease, is exhibited not only on the global level of the brain, but also on the local level of individual neurons.

Further evidence for this pattern of development comes from a PET study in which resting brain metabolism was measured at different ages from 12 months to adulthood (Chugani, Phelps, &

FIGURE 6.14

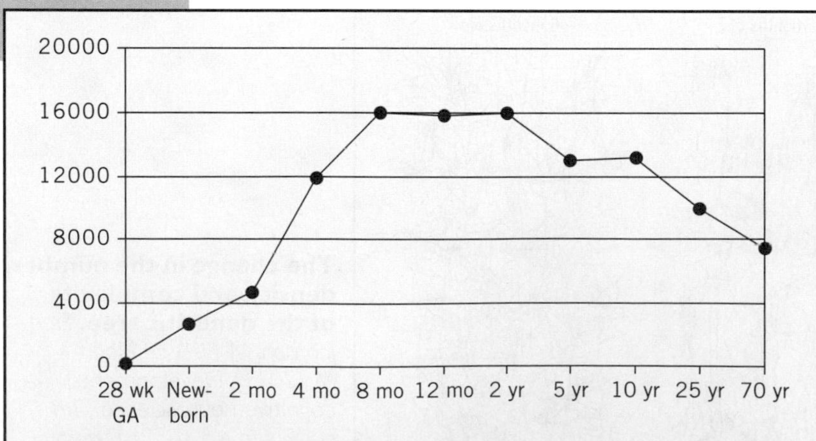

The average number of synapses for each neuron across the lifespan, starting prenatally at 28 weeks after conception, to the postnatal infant, and then childhood, adulthood, and aging. Synapses increase early, reaching a peak at the end of the first year or into the second year of life. Cutting back of synapses then begins, resulting in a slow but steady decrease in the number of synapses per neuron. *Adapted from Johnson M. H. (1997).* Developmental cognitive neuroscience *(Ch. 2, Building a brain). Oxford: Blackwell.*

Mazziota, 2002). Resting brain metabolism is based on the uptake of glucose that is needed for basic cell functioning in the absence of a specific task. Its level is thought to reflect the number of synapses. The resting brain metabolism exhibits the same developmental pattern, with an increase in the early years of life to levels above that of an adult (i.e., overproduction) and then a decrease to adult levels by the adolescent years. These findings suggest that this developmental pattern is programmed by genetics, affecting many aspects of neuronal and brain development. All of the varied brain areas, regardless of whether you look at the level of individual neurons or at large brain areas, exhibit the rise and fall pattern of development, which strongly suggests that this pattern is determined by a genetic program. Experience then directs the specific nature of how this pattern is implemented; for example, its time course.

MYELINATION The last stage of neural development is myelin formation, or *myelination.* Recall that myelin is produced by extensions from glial cells that wrap themselves around axons, thereby increasing the speed and efficiency with which signals are transmitted. Consequently, myelination is thought to play a significant role in behavioural and cognitive development (Durston & Casey, 2006). In fact, the developmental course for the myelination of various brain areas seems to mirror the behavioural onset of a number of capacities. For example, a combined DTI and fMRI study of temporal cortex areas in children and adults that are involved in language processing found that as age increased, so too did the level of myelination (Brauer, Anwander, & Friederici, 2011). Further, as age and myelination increased, so too did language processing abilities. Similar relations have been found between parietal-temporal areas and reading (Klinberg et al., 2000), as well as between frontal areas and broad measures of cognitive function such as IQ (Schmithorst et al., 2005). Thus, the more myelinated neurons an area has, the more mature that area is, and the more efficient and sophisticated the behavioural manifestation of that area's functioning. This, of course, should not be taken to mean that unmyelinated neurons and brain areas are not functioning and producing cognitive and behavioural consequences, because even unmyelinated areas process information and transmit signals. Thus, areas can be functionally immature and unmyelinated but still be affecting behaviour.

Overall, grey matter in the brain—consisting primarily of cell bodies, dendrites, and synaptic connections—shows the increase then decrease pattern that we have previously discussed. In contrast, white matter in the brain—consisting of myelinated axons—shows a steady increase from early childhood through early adulthood (Casey, Tottenham, Liston, & Durston, 2005). Figure 6.15 shows structural MRI images of the increase in myelinated axons in early development. The particular sequence of myelination shows a very regular pattern. Myelination begins during the prenatal period in the peripheral nervous system, then axons involved in motor behaviour begin to myelinate, followed by those involved in sensory systems. During the first year of life, myelination occurs in the brain stem and cerebellum. Cortical areas start myelinating before birth, but continue well after the first year and into early adulthood. Sensorimotor areas that control fine-motor movement are the first cortical areas to myelinate, with completion occurring around age 4. Parietal and temporal cortical areas, which are concerned with language, attention, memory, and consciousness, continue to myelinate up to puberty (Tanner, 1990). Prefrontal and frontal areas that control higher-order cognitive processes such as working memory, reasoning, planning, and decision-making continue to myelinate into early adulthood (Huttenlocher et al., 1982). As we will see in chapters to come, this developmental course for the myelination of these areas and the functions they serve closely mirrors the developmental course of those behavioural functions.

FIGURE 6.15

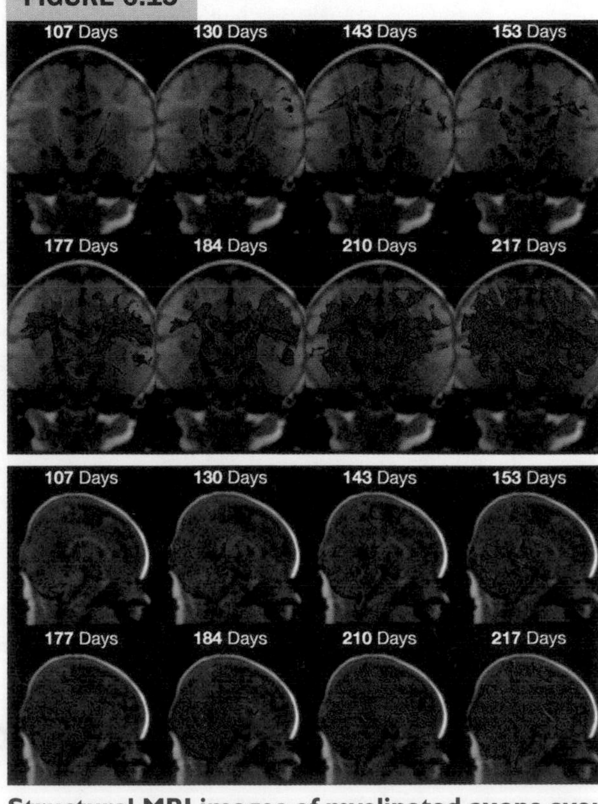

Structural MRI images of myelinated axons over the early part of postnatal development. *From* Johnson, *M. H. & de Haan, M. (2011).* Developmental cognitive neuroscience *(3rd ed., Figure 2.4 colour plates). Oxford: Wiley-Blackwell.*

FIGURE 6.16

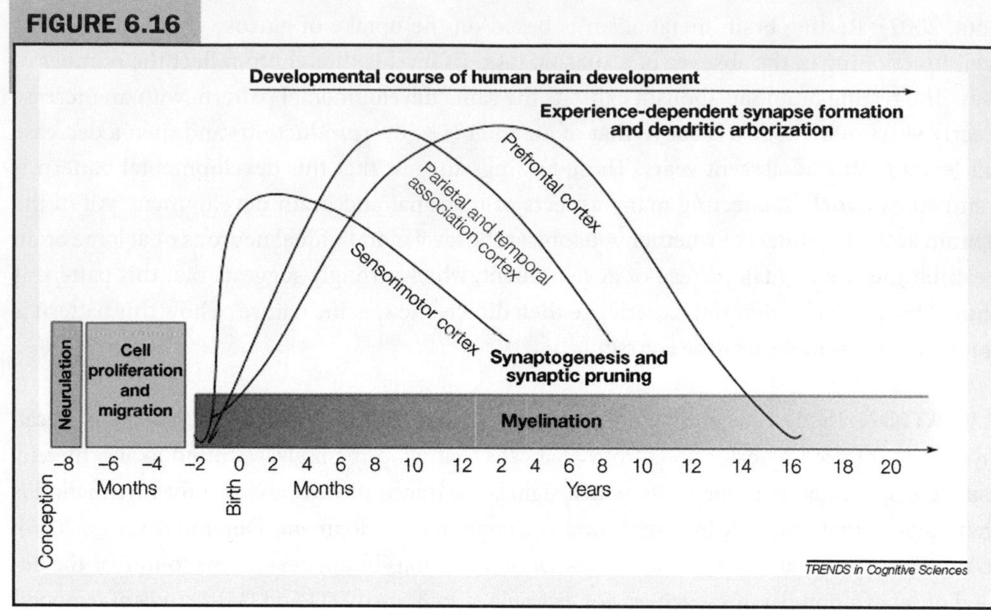

The approximate timeline for the stages of neuronal development. *From Johnson, M. H. (1997).* Developmental cognitive neuroscience *(Figure 4.8 on colour plates, Ch. 2, Building a brain). Oxford: Blackwell.*

Overall, the development of neurons and neuronal structure begins within a few weeks after conception and continues through adolescence and into early adulthood. Figure 6.16 provides a graphic summary of this timeline. The basic building blocks of the functional brain are laid down during the first two trimesters of fetal life. This timing makes the early phase of neural and brain development very sensitive to disruption by environmental and genetic factors, leading to potentially significant consequences. The last trimester and the first years after birth see the building blocks elaborated by the growth of axons and the dendritic tree. Further, especially during the first few years of life, the building blocks are connected by the formation of synapses. These phases show an increase-decrease pattern of development: first there is overproduction, followed by the cutting back or pruning of the unused, unneeded, and unnecessary. Finally, the most prolonged developmental change, lasting through early adulthood, occurs in increasing the efficiency and functionality of those connections by way of myelination.

LEARNING OBJECTIVE 6.2

Describe the structures and functions of the neurons, and trace the development of the neural system during childhood.

1. What are the different parts of the neuron?
2. What are the four main neurotransmitter systems and their functions?
3. Describe the process of neurulation.
4. The development of the neural structure of the brain has four stages. What are these four stages?
5. What are the developmental timelines of the four stages of development of the neural structure of the brain and how do they compare?

Learning Objective 6.3

Describe the structures of the brain and their functions.

BRAIN STRUCTURES

The neurons and neural structures that we have discussed in the preceding sections do not act on their own, but are grouped into larger structures and areas. The brain has four major parts—the brainstem, midbrain, cerebellum, and cerebrum. These four parts are organized in such a way that they interact with each other in a hierarchical manner.

ORGANIZATION AND FUNCTION OF BRAIN STRUCTURES

The first and the evolutionarily oldest part is the **brainstem**. This structure adjoins and is continuous with the spinal cord and includes the medulla, pons, and midbrain. The brainstem has evolved into a relay station for information transfer between the body and other major structures of the brain. As such, the brainstem is involved in controlling many of our basic functions, including hunger and feeding, sleep cycle, temperature, respiration, pain sensitivity, and sexual behaviour. Because of the role the brainstem plays in vital functioning, damage to any part of the brainstem can, and likely will, have very serious effects, including inducing coma (Parvizi & Damasio, 2003) and breathing difficulties (Kumar et al., 2008), if not death.

Brainstem The lower part of the brain, closest to the spinal cord, which is important for controlling basic bodily functions; includes the medulla, pons, and cerebellum.

The **midbrain** part of the brainstem not only serves as a relay station for controlling breathing and swallowing, it also plays a reflexive role in visual and auditory processing. In fact, the occulomotor nerve that controls eye movements, pupil constriction and dilation, and keeps the eyelid open, is contained within the midbrain. In addition, two structures in the midbrain play important roles in processing and relaying of information: the *inferior colliculus* for hearing and the *superior colliculus* for vision (Morgan, 2005). In describing the superior colliculus, researchers have shown that it consists of a map representing spatial locations in the world (Krauzlis, 2009; Marino, Rodgers, Levy, & Munoz, 2008). With this map as a basis, the superior colliculus is involved in providing input for guiding visual attention and controlling eye movements. That is, the superior colliculus relays sensory input from the retina to higher cortical systems about where information is located, and receives signals for initiating eye movements to those locations. A study by Shen and Paré (2007) of Queen's University found that neural activity in the superior colliculus was greatest when the stimulus target and its location were being selectively attended to and when an eye movement was made to that target's location. This finding illustrates the role of the superior colliculus in particular and the midbrain in general in relaying and integrating information.

Midbrain A part of the brain stem that serves as a relay station and as a control area for breathing and swallowing; also houses the reflexive part of the auditory and visual systems.

Directly behind the brainstem and tucked underneath the cerebral hemispheres (which we will discuss next) is the **cerebellum**. The cerebellum has the appearance of a separate structure from the rest of the brain, consisting of parallel grooves. These grooves are created by a thin, continuous layer of neural tissue that is folded in a manner resembling an accordion. There are a number of different types of neurons within the cerebellum, but perhaps the most important and numerous are the Purkinje cells with their dense, extensive, and complex dendritic trees, which we mentioned earlier. Control over motor behaviour is the main function of the cerebellum, affecting equilibrium, posture, and motor learning. Tomassini and colleagues (2011) investigated the relation between motor learning and the cerebellum with structural and functional MRI by having individuals learn to squeeze their right hand with a particular sequence of intensity. Individuals repeated the sequence of intensity and the researchers assessed activity in the cerebellum across the repetitions. They found that functional activation in the cerebellum increased with each additional repetition of the motor sequence, and was related to how well individuals were able to learn the motor sequence. These findings demonstrate that the cerebellum is involved in motor learning, increasing activation as the motor task is learned. Additional functions of the cerebellum include involvement in attention and language. In addition, the cerebellum seems to have emotional functions as well, regulating one's responses on the basis of fear and pleasure (Wolf, Rapoport, & Schweizer, 2009).

Cerebellum Situated behind the brainstem and under the cerebral hemispheres, this distinct and unique looking structure is involved in motor control and learning, attention, language, and regulating emotional responses.

The last major structure is the **cerebrum**, which is the highest brain centre and includes the left and right hemispheres and the bundle of nerves called the **corpus collosum** that connect them. Of most interest to psychologists is the relatively thin shell of grey matter that covers the cerebrum, called the **cerebral cortex**. As we mentioned earlier, the grey matter consists mostly of neuron cell bodies and dendrites, whereas the white matter situated under the grey matter consists mostly of myelinated axons. The cerebral cortex appears to be the most recently evolved part of the brain and is sometimes referred to as the *neocortex* ("neo" for new). It is crucial for the functioning of the senses, language, memory, thought, and decision-making, and the control of voluntary actions.

Cerebrum The highest brain centre; includes both hemispheres of the brain and the interconnections between them.

Corpus collosum The bundle of nerves that connect the left and right hemispheres of the brain.

Cerebral cortex The thin sheet of grey matter that covers the brain.

FIGURE 6.17

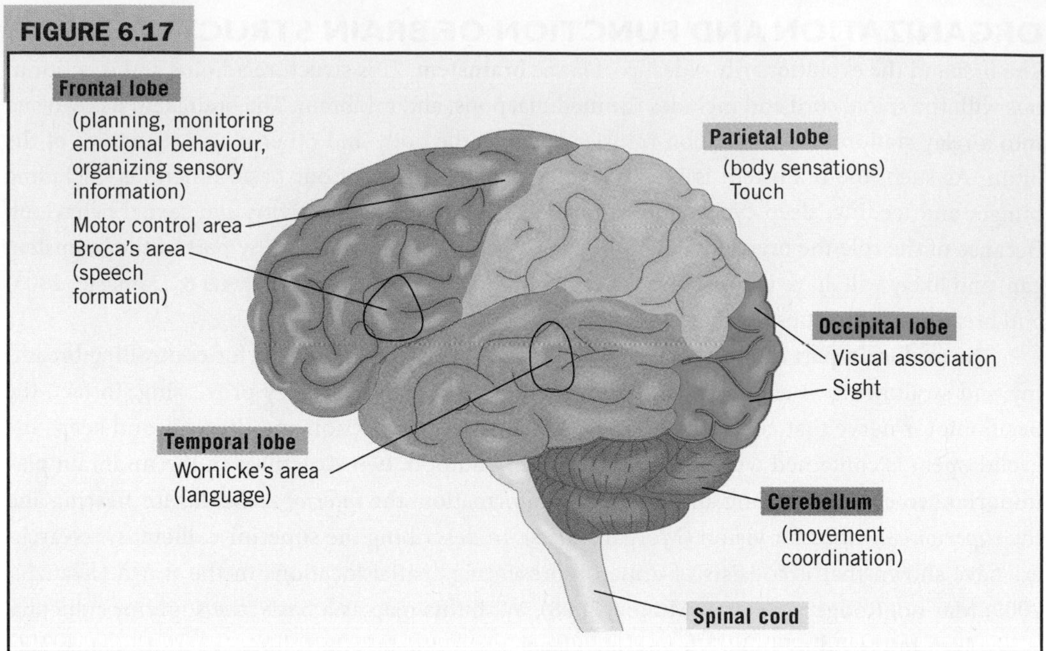

Some areas of the cerebral cortex are specialized for particular functions; this diagram shows a few of them.

Particular areas of the cerebral cortex, typically referred to as lobes, have specific responsibilities and psychological functions, although some areas are more specialized than others. Some of the specialized functions of the different lobes are identified in Figure 6.17.

HEMISPHERIC SPECIALIZATION

The two hemispheres of the cerebrum are not perfectly symmetrical but are *lateralized*—meaning that the left brain and the right brain are somewhat specialized. In general, the left side of the brain manages sensory input and motor movements on the right side of the body, while the right side of the brain controls input and movements on the left side. The left side of the brain is also usually more specialized for language performance, verbal memory, and decision-making. The right side, in contrast, is more specialized for spatial and mathematical tasks. Another way to think about this distinction is that the left side is more oriented to words and concepts, and the right side is more oriented to images.

One kind of evidence for hemispheric specialization comes from cases of brain injury. Damage to the left hemisphere is more likely to result in language impairments than is damage to the right hemisphere (Bates & Roe, 2001). Another kind of evidence comes from PET imaging studies. These studies reveal that the left side of the brain is typically more active during language tasks and the right side is more active during mathematical tasks. In one study, researchers imaged individuals' brains as they were listening to a story or were at rest (Josse, Mazoyer, Crivello, & Tzourio-Mazoyer, 2003). It was found that the areas in the left hemisphere were disproportionately active relative to the similar areas in the right hemisphere when listening to a story. Further, significantly larger portions of those areas in the left hemisphere were devoted to processing the story than in the right hemisphere. That language shows specialization in the left hemisphere highlights that the left hemisphere serves more linguistic, verbal, and non-spatial functions, whereas the right hemisphere serves more spatial and reasoning functions. fMRI studies bear this out by showing that there is greater activation in the left hemisphere for verbal math problems and greater activation in the right hemisphere for spatial and deductive reasoning tasks (Colvin, Funnell, & Gazzaniga, 2005; Kroger, Nystrom, Cohen, & Johnson-Laird, 2008).

Consistent with the studies just mentioned that show that both hemispheres can process mathematical information, other studies show that other brain functions are also not completely specialized; most tasks, including language processing, reading, and listening, involve areas on both sides of the brain (Corina, Vaid, & Bellugi, 1992; Scott & Wise, 2003). Hemispheric specialization also shows individual differences. That is, not everyone shows the typical left-hemisphere dominance for language. Some people have right-hemisphere dominance for language and some people have mixed dominance. Left-handers more frequently have right-hemisphere or mixed dominance.

CEREBRAL LOBES AND FUNCTION

As indicated earlier and shown in Figure 6.17, the cerebral cortex can be separated into distinct areas that are distinguished by their functional specialization. There are four functionally distinct lobes: occipital, parietal, temporal, and frontal. We will discuss each in turn, starting with the **occipital lobe**. The occipital lobe is the smallest of the lobes and is located in the rearmost location of the brain. Its main function is to process visual information and, therefore, it is sometimes referred to as the *visual cortex*. The occipital lobe can itself be subdivided into a number of functional sections, differentiated by the type and complexity of the visual information that they process. Once basic visual information, such as simple features and orientation, is processed by the initial section (the primary visual cortex, also sometimes referred to as V1), that information is sent on for further processing along one of two pathways depending on the type of information (Milner & Goodale, 2008). Figure 6.18 provides a representation of the direction and location of the two pathways. The dorsal (the upperside) stream pathway, sometimes called the "where" stream, is associated with motion and object location information, as well as information that provides control of eye movements and reaching (Cohen, Cross, Tunik, Grafton, & Culham, 2009; Pisella, Sergio, Blangero, Torchin, Vighetto, & Rossetti, 2009). The dorsal stream is thought to be "blind" to identity and function. A recent study shows that the dorsal stream is involved in the determination of the appropriate motor response in grasping a tool, for example, and is indifferent to identifying what type of tool it is (Almeida, Mahon, & Caramazza, 2010).

Occipital lobe Located in the rearmost location of the brain, its main function is the processing of visual information; can be subdivided into a number of functional sections, differentiated by the type and complexity of the visual information being processed.

In contrast, the ventral (the underside) stream pathway, sometimes called the "what" stream, is generally associated with information, such as shape and colour, for representing, identifying, and recognizing different types of forms and objects (Reddy & Kanwisher, 2006). To represent and recognize objects over significant time spans, that information needs to be encoded in long-term memory, which consequently is associated with ventral stream processing (Meeuwissen, Takashima, Fernandez, & Jensen, 2011). The distinction between the dorsal and ventral streams is thought to have developmental relevance, as each has a different maturational timeline, as we will see shortly.

Parietal lobe Located above and forward from the occipital lobe; receives information from different senses, particularly touch; integrates multisensory information from different parts of the body; maps perceived objects relative to one's body; is involved in number processing.

The **parietal lobe** is situated above and forward from the occipital lobe. Neurons in the parietal lobe are sensitive to receiving information from different senses, particularly touch, and from different parts of the body. The parietal lobe then integrates the multisensory information from different body parts, thereby enabling us to interact with the objects and world around us and navigate through it. By virtue of being part of the dorsal stream pathway, another main function of the parietal lobe is to map visually perceived objects to locations relative to one's body (Medendorp, Goltz, Vilis, & Crawford, 2003; Postma, Kessels, & van Asselen, 2008). For example, as the author sits at his desk and writes this, his parietal lobe is mapping the visually perceived tea cup to a position down and to the right of where the author is looking and about half a metre to the right of his right hand. This map of body-related locations can then be used to determine where to look and where and how to grasp (Goldberg, Bisley, Powell, & Gottlieb, 2006; Murata et al., 2000). The parietal lobe also seems to be involved in number processing, as indicated by heightened activity in the parietal cortex during the processing of number quantities (Ischebeck, Schocke, & Delazer, 2009; Santens, Roggeman, Fias, & Verguts, 2010).

FIGURE 6.18

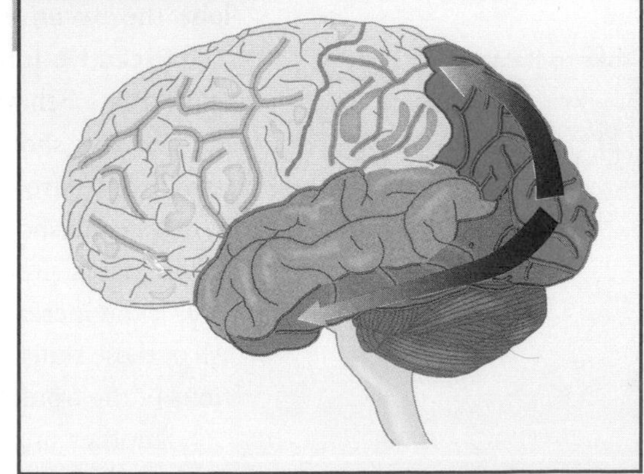

An illustration of the dorsal processing pathway, shown by the green-highlighted area of cortex, and the ventral processing pathway, shown by the purple-highlighted area of cortex.

Temporal lobe Located below the parietal lobe and forward of the occipital lobe; has as its main function the processing of auditory information; functions to process speech and language; involved in object perception and recognition; transfers information from short-term memory, encoding it in long-term memory.

The third lobe, the **temporal lobe**, is located forward from the occipital lobe and below the parietal lobe. One of the main functions of the temporal lobe is the perception of auditory information. This function makes the temporal lobe particularly specialized for the processing of speech and language. In fact, contained within the temporal lobe is an area called *Wernicke's area*, which plays a significant role in processing and understanding written and spoken language, including comprehension and naming of objects. Damage to this area causes deficits in language comprehension but seems to leave speech production intact (Dronkers, Redfern, & Knight, 2000). As part of the ventral stream pathway, the temporal lobe is also involved in the perception of objects and their recognition. In one recent fMRI study, Bell and colleagues (2008) showed subjects images of faces, body parts (both animate types of stimuli), objects, and places (both inanimate types of stimuli) while imaging their temporal cortex. Within the temporal cortex, discrete areas showed heightened activity for animate versus inanimate stimuli. This indicates that the temporal lobe is highly specialized for object perception and recognition.

The temporal lobe is also thought to be involved in long-term memory. Deep within the temporal is the *hippocampus*, a structure known to be involved in transferring information from short-term to long-term memory (Eichenbaum, Yonelinas, & Ranganath, 2007; Squire & Schachter, 2002). Damage to the hippocampus will cause anterograde amnesia (loss of memory for new events). For example, in the case of H.M., his hippocampus was surgically destroyed to alleviate severe epileptic seizures. A consequence of this surgery was that H.M. had significant difficulty in forming new memories (Squire, 2009). Yet, H.M. was still able to recall in vivid detail events that had happened years earlier, including events from his childhood. Considering that language and verbal capacities are related to remembering and recognizing objects and events, it should not be a surprise that these functions are encompassed together in the temporal lobe.

Frontal lobe Located at the very front of the brain; functions include working memory, planning, and decision-making; involved in executive functions that monitor and choose appropriate behaviours in a given situation or task; also plays a role in associating information in long-term memory.

The last but most evolutionarily recent lobe is the **frontal lobe**. The frontal lobe is located at the very front of the brain, hence its name. Functions of the frontal lobe include attention, short-term and working memory, planning, decision-making, and behavioural regulation. The role of the frontal lobe in working memory was recently demonstrated in a study in which magnetic stimulation was administered to the frontal lobe as a working memory task was completed. Individuals needed to complete a prospective memory-verbal task that required them to respond each time a word that had been presented before the task began appeared (Basso, Ferrari, & Palladino, 2010). At the same time, individuals were exposed to a secondary task that either required high working memory demands or low demands. Only when stimulation was administered to the frontal lobe during the high working memory demand task did performance on the main task suffer. This indicates that prospective memory (remembering for the future) and working memory are both functions of the frontal lobe, though they distinctly use limited processing resources. What decides where processing resources are allocated? This is done by another critical function of the frontal lobe, the *executive function*.

Links to Related Material

Here we discuss the frontal lobe involvement in executive functions. In Chapter 9, we discuss how the psychological mechanisms of executive function develop.

Executive functions monitor the expected consequences of current behaviours, choose the appropriate behaviour in a given situation or task, and moderate responses in social situations. Studies have shown, for example, that damage to the frontal lobe can result in alterations in the executive control of a number of different behaviours, including the ability to recognize emotions in others and show empathy (Bramham, Morris, Hornak, Bullock, & Polkey, 2009); solve problem-solving tasks (Roca et al., 2010); plan and apply strategies (Gouvela, Brucki, Malheiros, & Bueno, 2007); and increase impulsive and risky behaviour (Floden, Alexander, Kubu, Katz, & Stuss, 2008). All of these skills rely on the control and inhibitory processes that are central to the executive functions of the frontal lobe (Teuber, 2009).

Another important function of the frontal lobe is that it is involved in long-term memories (Blumenfeld & Ranganath, 2007). The area termed the prefrontal cortex is particularly involved in binding distinct information from an event or task into a single memory, even across time. For example, one recent fMRI study showed that the prefrontal cortex was involved during the initial encoding and binding of pairs of words to remember, where each item in a pair was separated by a delay (Hales & Brewer, 2011). Additionally, the frontal lobe is involved in the formation of long-term memories for items and events that help to form expectations and direct the planning of behaviour for future goals and events (Bollinger, Rubens, Zanto, & Gazzaley, 2010). This is another example of the frontal lobe involvement in control processes for various functions.

Though we have outlined distinct specializations and functions for the different hemispheres and various lobes and structures of the brain, often there is much overlap between structures for a given function. Further, for any given capacity or behaviour, multiple structures in the brain are involved. The functions outlined are the preferential and primary tendencies for those areas. Yet, how do these structural specializations come to be? That is, how do the functional distinctions that we have outlined develop?

LEARNING OBJECTIVE 6.3

Describe the structures of the brain and their functions.

1. What are the four major brain structures and their functions?
2. How are the two hemispheres differentially specialized?
3. What are the four distinct lobes of the cerebral cortex and their functions?

DEVELOPMENT OF THE MAJOR STRUCTURES AND FUNCTION OF THE BRAIN

Learning Objective 6.4

Describe the development of the structures and function of the brain.

The fetus' brain grows faster than any other organ (except perhaps the eye), and this pace continues in infancy. At birth, the baby's body weight is only 5 percent of adult weight, whereas the brain weighs 25 percent of its adult value. By 3 years of age, the brain has attained 80 percent of its ultimate weight, compared with 20 percent for body weight, and by 6 years it has reached 90 percent (Kolb & Whishaw, 2009; Paus et al., 2001). However, the brain does not mature uniformly, and in fact, there may be sensitive periods at particular ages for the functional development of brain areas governing everything from sensory processing to higher-level cognitive processes (Thomas & Johnson, 2008). In this section, we will discuss the developmental sequence for the various brain structures and areas that were outlined in the previous section.

DEVELOPMENT OF HEMISPHERIC SPECIALIZATION

As noted earlier, the two hemispheres of the brain are not perfectly symmetrical but are *lateralized.* In other words, the left and right hemispheres, though overlapping in function, do show certain distinct specializations. The left side of the brain, while dealing with sensory input and motor movements on the right side of the body, seems to preferentially process words, language, and verbal memory. The right side of the brain, while controlling input and movements on the left side of the body, seems more specialized for images, and spatial and mathematical tasks. How do these hemispheric specializations come to be? That is, how and when do they develop?

Early on, most thought that the lateralization of the hemispheres was a gradual process of development through childhood and reaching completion some time in adolescence (Lenneberg, 1967). Now, however, many believe that some amount of lateralization and specialization is prespecified, meaning that it occurs prenatally and is present from birth (Johnson & de Haan, 2011). Much of the debate over how much of lateralization is prespecified and how much develops later, after birth, centres around the extent to which there is a relation between specialization of cognitive function and lateralization of motor attributes such as handedness—a relation that has not been unequivocally established. Thus, this debate plays a central role in the discussion of how much of brain development is predetermined by genetics and maturation, leading to commonality of brain functioning, cognition, and behaviour across individuals. Alternatively, the issue involves how much of brain development is determined by each individual's experiences. This latter alternative will be important in our discussion of brain plasticity at the end of the chapter.

Regardless, there is general agreement that some hemispheric specialization appears quite early, being present shortly after birth. For example, newborn babies have a tendency, when lying on their backs, to turn their heads either to the right or left. These same babies, when reaching for objects, tend to reach with the hand on the same side to which they turned their head (Kinsbourne, 1989). This would seem to show that the lateralization for the side preference of handedness is in place at birth. Additionally, ERP recordings in newborn infants reveal more activity in response to speech sounds on the left than on the right side (Molfese & Molfese, 1979), and some physical differences in size and shape between the hemispheres are already present at birth (Kosslyn et al., 1999). Recent structural MRI studies have suggested that the physical differences between the hemispheres are even observable in utero in the fetus (Kasprian et al., 2011). Nevertheless, newborns and infants do not show all the forms of lateralization that will eventually develop (Werker & Vouloumanos, 2001).

In adults, the right hemisphere tends to show a lateralized advantage for face processing. A number of studies have demonstrated that this lateralization is in place by 4 to 5 months of age (Deruelle & de Schonen, 1998), after receiving some visual input. For example, Le Grand, Mondloch, Maurer, and Brent (2003) from McMaster University studied babies who were deprived of visual input to either the left or right hemisphere early in life due to a congenital cataract in either their right or left eye. Those individuals who had deprivation to the right hemisphere showed severe impairment in developing expertise in face processing, whereas those with left hemisphere deprivation did not. These findings indicate that the two hemispheres are not equivalent in their capacity to use the appropriate input to develop the function of face processing, with the right hemisphere showing dominance.

For language, also lateralized to the left hemisphere, such specialization seems to occur relatively early, within a couple of months after birth. In an fMRI study in which speech information is presented to sleeping 2- to 3-month-old infants, those left hemisphere areas that serve language processing in adults were found to already be active in the infants (Dehaene-Lambertz, Dehaene, & Hertz-Pannier, 2002). In a more recent MEG and structural MRI study, words and their related objects were presented to 12- to 18-month-old infants. Similar to adults, brain response to the word-object events was localized to the left hemisphere, in the frontal and temporal cortices (Travis et al., 2011).

The issue that is still unresolved is how the lateralization and specialization of the hemispheres comes to be. There are a number of different theories, all based on the idea that at birth there is an inherent inequality or bias in hemispheres that disposes them to the exhibited lateralization and specialization (Johnson & de Haan, 2011). See Table 6.2 for an overview of these models. There is some support for this general concept, as we noted earlier; a recent study showed structural differences between the hemispheres even in the fetus. These theories suggest that we are set up at birth for processing language in the left hemisphere and for functions such as face and spatial processing in the right hemisphere because we inherit genes (*biased gene* model), we have neuroanatomical differences at birth (*biased brain* model), or as newborns we turned our heads to the right (*biased head* model). Thus, because of whichever bias accounts for initial hemispheric differences, the differences result in asynchronous development of the hemispheres that yield specialized processing of particular types of inputs in the two hemispheres. Perhaps, for example, early structural development of the left hemisphere in utero might make it more susceptible to the speech and language experience received by the fetus, resulting in the left hemisphere's preference for language processing. Each model has problems, from accounting for gender differences in lateralization and hemispheric specialization (see *On the Cutting Edge 6.1*), to how neuroanatomical differences arise in the first place, to what is the effect of left-handedness. Yet, it is clear that there is lateralization of the hemispheres at birth and functional specialization soon after, during the first few months of life.

ON THE CUTTING EDGE 6.1
CAUSE OF SEX DIFFERENCES IN CEREBRAL LATERALIZATION

Many of us are familiar with the statement that females are left-brained and males are right-brained. Others are more familiar with the statement that females are more verbal whereas males are more spatial and mathematical. These points of view are widespread in our society, affecting parents' expectations of their children's abilities and influencing how teachers view and interact with girls and boys when teaching different subjects (see Halpern, 2012). Is there any basis for this viewpoint?

Links to Related Material

In Chapter 16 you will learn more about the influences of parents and teachers in the development of sex differences and gender roles.

Much research has documented that the brains of females and males are structurally different. For example, fMRI research has indicated that areas of the temporal lobe associated with speech and language are larger on the left than the right hemisphere, and that this asymmetry is larger in males than females (e.g., Kulynych et al., 1994). Furthermore, specific areas such as Wernicke's and Broca's in the temporal and frontal lobes are larger and have greater dendritic trees in females than males (Harasty et al., 1997; Jacobs, Schall, & Scheibel, 1993). Recent fMRI studies have been consistent with these findings. For example, one study showed that during language/verbal tasks, neural activity in males tends to be more lateralized to the left hemisphere, whereas females exhibit more bilateral activity. On visuospatial tasks, in contrast, the opposite pattern emerges, with males showing bilateral activity and females exhibiting activity lateralized to the right hemisphere (Clements et al., 2006). What causes these sex differences in cerebral lateralization to develop?

One particular theory suggests that there is a direct relationship between the level of hormones in the uterus during gestation and the construction of lateralization in the cortex during development (Geschwind & Galaburda, 1987). In particular, this theory holds that the level of testosterone in utero influences the migration of the neurons into the cortex. Higher levels of testosterone, typically found in males, are thought to delay migration of neurons to the left hemisphere and consequently more lateralization to the right hemisphere. That is, higher levels of testosterone during gestation are thought to delay the growth of areas in the left hemisphere (McManus & Bryden, 1991). Though problems have been raised with this theory, particularly since lateralization and handedness are related (e.g., how would this mechanism work in those who are not right-handed [Previc, 1994]), recent research supports this theory.

Recent work has established that males tend to have higher levels of prenatal exposure to testosterone than females (Manning et al., 2007). These higher levels of testosterone exposure are associated, for example, with asymmetry in hand skills, consistent with the relation between handedness and lateralization (Fink, Manning, Neave, & Tan, 2004). A link between higher levels of testosterone and greater degree of lateralization has also been found in females on a chimeric face test (Bourne & Gray, 2009; Bourne & Maxwell, 2009). In the chimeric face test, images of faces are split vertically and one half is shown displaying either a positive emotion or a negative emotion, whereas the other half is shown displaying a neutral expression. Then, two faces are presented, one with the emotion on left and the other with the emotion on the right, and the individual is asked to decide which of the two faces looks happier or sadder. Which of the two faces is chosen depends on the nature of lateralization of the cerebral cortex for emotional processing (Indersmitten & Gur, 2003). Bourne and Gray found that even for females, higher prenatal exposure to testosterone resulted in stronger right hemisphere lateralization for processing emotion. Thus, these research findings indicate that prenatal testosterone exposure is associated with greater amount of cerebral lateralization, even in females.

Links to Related Material

Here you read about the influence of prenatal sex hormones on cerebral lateralization. In Chapter 16 you will learn about how exposure to prenatal sex hormones can also influence behaviour.

Recent research thus supports the notion that cerebral lateralization might well be the result of hormonal levels experienced prenatally during the initial stages of brain development.

TABLE 6.2 THREE MODELS FOR DESCRIBING THE DEVELOPMENT OF HEMISPHERIC LATERALIZATION

Model	Description
Biased Gene	The lateralization of the brain and its functions is produced from a bias or inequality in the hemispheres at birth due to genes that are inherited.
Biased Brain	The brain shows neuroanatomical differences between the hemispheres at birth, which in turn biases those hemispheres to distinct types of processing.
Biased Head	Infants' tendency to shift their heads to one side limits the range of stimulation each hemisphere receives, thereby biasing the type of processing that each hemisphere does.

Links to Related Material

Here you learned about the protracted development of hemispheric specialization for language processing. In Chapter 11, you will learn about the development of language, including syntactical principles and grammatical rules.

However, we should not consider the early hemispheric specialization and lateralization to be either the end of development or set in stone. Hemispheric specialization continues to develop and be refined during childhood. Research with children 7 to 16 years of age, for example, has shown that the left hemispheric areas that are specialized for language processing (e.g., syntactic processing) continue to mature and become refined throughout childhood and even into adolescence (Nuñez et al., 2011). This protracted development may help account for the relative long development period of language skills, especially learning grammatical rules. Nevertheless, much lateralization and specialization is evident early on due to a combination of differences in the physical structure of the hemispheres and their development and the input that the hemispheres receive.

In Chapter 16, we will see that hemispheric specialization may also play a role in the development of gender differences.

DEVELOPMENT OF CORTICAL FUNCTION

With the advent of many of the techniques described earlier, there has been a tremendous explosion in the amount of research into the nature of the cortical areas that serve many behavioural functions. This growth in research has also extended to the development of cortical functions and the relation between brain development and the development of children's behavioural and cognitive abilities (Nelson et al., 2006). Throughout the rest of the chapters of this book, we will relate many of children's abilities and their development to specific instances of development in cortical functions. Here we will discuss development in cortical functions more generally.

Earlier, we outlined the large cortical areas and their functions. Before delving into when these different areas become functionally mature, we need to ask how the distinctions between these areas first occur. From a neurobiological perspective, the different areas often can be determined by differences in the laminar structure in different regions, such as differences in the thickness of the layers. These differences arise prenatally by way of the neural developmental process of neuronal migration. However, although general structural differences between the areas do exist, they are not completely distinct. There is much overlap in the neuroanatomical structure of these areas, so the different areas have come to be defined by their functionality. How do these functional divisions arise?

Two possibilities have been proposed to account for the development of divisions in cortical functionality. The first proposal is that development occurs on the basis of a *protomap* (Rakic, 1988). This idea suggests that the cortex is intrinsically structured as distinct areas. As a consequence, each area has specific features that are appropriate for mapping the particular input it will receive and the functions it will be required to serve onto it. Studies that support a protomap show that even after knocking out the gene or genes that code for sensory connections to the cortex, well-defined cortical areas are still exhibited (Miyashita-Lin, Hevner, Wassarman, Martinez, & Rubenstein, 1999). This would seem to suggest that definition of the cortical areas does not rely on sensory input, but instead is already there based on intrinsic factors. Alternatively, the second proposal suggests that the cortical divisions spring from an undifferentiated *protocortex* (O'Leary, 2005). This view suggests that the differentiation of cortical areas occurs as a response to external factors such as input from other areas of the brain and from the outside world through the sensory systems. Here, studies show evidence that cortical areas can be rewired and their features and functions changed on the basis of experience (Bystrom, Blakemore, & Rakic, 2008). Thus, the specification of cortical functions is affected by the experiential input provided. In actuality, the reality is likely somewhere between these two proposals: there is some initial and intrinsic specification of the cortical area distinctions without external input. But, these distinctions are poorly defined with much overlap, requiring experience and extrinsic input to help further define the cortical areas, their interactions, and even change their functioning (Kingsbury & Finlay, 2001).

For functional development, this all means that each cortical area has its own initial specialization that limits the type of input that can initially be processed by the infant. Then, as these areas receive input through experiences as the child ages, there is further differentiation of the cortical areas. The increased differentiation of the cortical areas then further modifies the type of input that the infant and child can process. With the varied initial states of maturity and differentiation, and the changes in the type of inputs that experiences at different ages can provide, there is a resulting differential development of the different cortical areas. As illustrated by Huttenlocher and Dabholkar (1997), for example, the visual cortex reaches developmental landmarks such as peak synaptic density earlier than does the frontal cortex (see Figure 6.19). Next, we will look at the functional development of each of the cortical areas previously outlined, starting with the occipital lobe and visual cortex. However, as explained in the discussion of methodologies, many of the techniques used to study the function of cortical areas are not useable in early development. As a consequence, our knowledge of the functional development of much of the cortex is still quite limited. The areas about which the most is known are the visual and frontal cortices.

OCCIPITAL LOBE Many models of development propose that a newborn's initial visual behaviour is controlled by subcortical units such as the superior colliculus, as well as other midbrain and cerebellar structures (Atkinson, 2000; Johnson & de Haan, 2011). These subcortical systems allow for infants to orient their eyes and head reactively to changing events in their world. There is also likely some basic face processing occurring subcortically, particularly in the hippocampus, allowing for vital social interactions and attachment processes to begin as infants need to recognize their mother's and father's faces (de Haan, 2008).

Links to Related Material

Here, we relate orienting and face recognition in newborns to particular subcortical pathways. In Chapter 7, you will read more about the specifics of the development of orienting and face recognition behaviour. In Chapter 12, you will focus on the development of social interactions and attachment.

Soon after birth, the occipital lobe or visual cortex shows significant development, with synaptic density reaching its peak very early (see Figure 6.19). As outlined earlier, the main function of the visual cortex is to process visual information about objects and events. This visual information has different characteristics, each processed by distinct populations of neurons in the visual cortex and distinct pathways emanating from within the visual cortex. Some of these characteristics are colour, orientation, depth or binocular, size, and motion information. Most of the modules in the visual cortex become functional, affecting behaviour, by 3 months of age, in line with the rapid growth of synaptic connections in this area. For the processing of orientation—a necessary feature for the perception of objects, for example—studies have measured the visually evoked potentials of the visual cortex (similar to ERPs in that brain activity is measured with EEGs) as the infant views a black and white striped stimulus that either changes its stripes from black to white (or vice versa) or changes in the orientation of the stripes. Activity in the visual cortex in response to the change in orientation was exhibited by 6 to 8 weeks of age (Braddick et al., 1986) and perhaps even as early as 3 weeks of age (Braddick, 1993). In either case, the responses are similar to those of an adult by 3 months of age (Baker, Norcia, & Candy, 2011). Furthermore, sensitivity to the degree of orientation shows a clear developmental trend of increasing sensitivity to smaller orientation changes over the first 3 months (Atkinson, Wattam-Bell, & Braddick, 2002; see Figure 6.20).

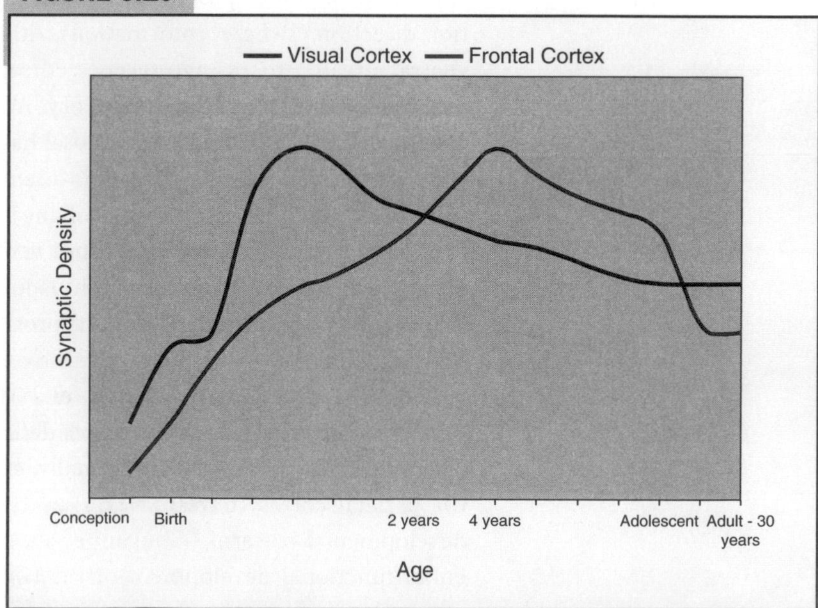

The change in synaptic density of the visual cortex relative to the frontal cortex from conception to adult. Visual cortex synaptic density reaches its peak earlier than the frontal cortex, indicating a more protracted development of the frontal cortex. *Adapted from Nelson, Thomas, & de Haan (2006). Neural bases of cognitive development (Figure 1.2, p. 11). In D. Kuhn & R.S. Siegler (Eds.),* Handbook of child psychology: *Vol. 2: Cognition, perception, and language. Hoboken, NJ: Wiley.*

FIGURE 6.20

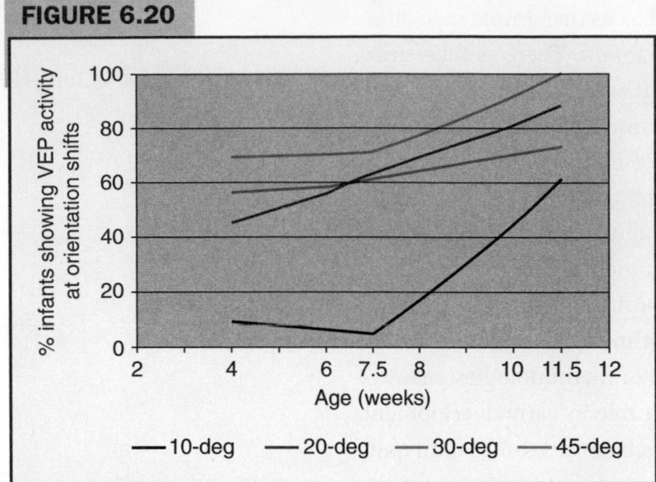

Percentage of infants at different ages who exhibit visual cortex activity to stimuli whose orientations changed by 10, 20, 30, and 45 degrees. Results show that sensitivity by a significant portion of the infants to the smallest orientation change does not occur until almost 3 months of age. *Adapted from Atkinson, J. (2000).* The Developing Visual Brain *(Figure 6.3, p. 73). Oxford: Oxford University Press.*

The processing of colour in the visual cortex, also important for object identification and recognition, shows a similar developmental trend to that of orientation. These studies are conducted in a similar fashion to the orientation studies in that ERPs are measured, but instead of changing the orientation, the colours in the stripe pattern change. Using this design, Morrone and colleagues (1993) demonstrated that activity in the visual cortex is relatively weak for red–green discriminations until about 6 weeks of age. Further research suggests that the full colour system does not show functionality until 3 months of age, consistent with the findings for orientation, and that there is continued development for the first year (Atkinson et al., 2002).

Interestingly, the processing of other visual features that are served by the visual cortex seems to show a slightly extended developmental pattern. Neural responses in the visual cortex to motion coherence and direction and to binocular disparity (depth from seeing with both eyes) seem to emerge between 7 and 12 weeks of age (Atkinson & Braddick, 2003; Braddick, Atkinson, & Wattam-Bell, 2003), slightly later than the onset for orientation and colour. This differential onset of neural sensitivity to the various visual features has fuelled proposals that there is differential development of the ventral and dorsal pathways emanating from the visual cortex. Recall that the dorsal pathway is involved in processing information related to where items are, such as motion and object location, as well as information that provides control of actions that enable us to interact with those items, such as eye movements and reaching. The ventral pathway, in contrast, is involved in processing information related to what the items are, such as shape and colour—information that is necessary for identifying and recognizing different types of forms and objects. Based on the differential development of the neural apparatus for colour processing ("what" information), for example, versus processing of motion direction ("where" information), Atkinson (1998) has proposed that the development of ventral stream processing precedes dorsal stream processing, which has a protracted course of development (also see Gunn, Cory, Atkinson, Braddick, Wattam-Bell, Guzzetta, & Cioni, 2002; Coch et al., 2005). This proposal has been supported by studies indicating that children treated with congenital cataracts in their eyes exhibit more difficulty in perceiving motion (dorsal stream) than they do perceiving form (ventral stream) (Ellenberg et al., 2002; Lewis et al., 2002). Because development of ventral stream processing precedes dorsal stream processing, ventral stream development is less susceptible to the effects of or lack of experience. Dorsal stream development, with its protracted time course, is more susceptible to the effects of development.

More recently, Maurer, Lewis, and Mondloch (2005) at McMaster University, however, have reported that cataracts produce deficits of similar strength in functions of both the ventral and dorsal pathways. Additionally, structural neuroanatomy studies have indicated that the parietal cortex (dorsal stream) and the temporal cortex (ventral stream) show similar developmental patterns (Chugani et al., 2002). This suggests that there might not be differential functional development of the two pathways. Unfortunately, answering the question of whether these two pathways show differential functional development is complicated by two issues. First, the structural neuroanatomical findings do not provide any evidence for functional development. In fact, though there are findings showing that neurons in the ventral pathway are activated by form stimuli such as faces by 6 weeks of age (Rodman, Skelly, & Gross, 1991), there are no equivalent studies for dorsal pathway functions. Thus, there is no direct evidence to answer the question of whether the two pathways have different time courses for their development (Iliescu & Dannemiller, 2008). Second, the two streams may not be well segregated or particularly distinct in infancy and only become so with age (Dobkins, 2005). In adults, colour information (ventral) has little to no bearing on the perception of motion (dorsal), but in infants there is an effect of colour. Thus, the structural apparatus for the two streams seem to show differential development, leading perhaps to differential functional development. There is little evidence, however, for distinct developmental timelines for the functions of the two pathways downstream in parietal and temporal cortices—areas that we will consider next.

PARIETAL LOBE PET scan studies of the activity of the parietal cortex have demonstrated that this area matures later than the visual cortex. Though there is a slight increase in activity by 4 weeks of age, substantial increases in activity indicating maturation do not occur until approximately 3 months of age (Chugani et al., 2002). As part of the dorsal processing pathway, this developmental pattern suggests that functions served by the parietal cortex will also not show maturity until approximately 3 months. One important function served by the parietal cortex is the planning of eye movements in response to the location of stimuli relative to one's own body. Gilmore and Johnson (1997) have explored the issue that development of eye movement planning is consistent with the maturation in parietal cortex activity. They presented infants 6 months and younger with two briefly flashed targets and then assessed their eye movements to these targets. At earlier ages, infants either make an eye movement in between the two targets or first to one target and then to the second target, based on where that target was before they made the first eye movement. Only by 3 to 6 months of age do infants shift their eye movements to take into account the fact that the relative location of the second target has changed due to their making an eye movement to the first target. Infants are then able to plan their second eye movement in relation to where that stimulus is relative to where the eye is after the first eye movement. ERP studies have similarly shown that saccade-related (a rapid intermittent eye movement) activity in the parietal area is exhibited after 6 months of age but not before for planned saccades, such as eye movements that anticipate the appearance of a stimulus (Johnson, Mareschal, & Csibra, 2008).

As noted earlier, the dorsal pathway, which includes the parietal cortex, is thought to have a protracted developmental time course. Other parietal cortex functions show a consistent developmental pattern of not reaching adult-like levels until much later. One such function is mental rotation—the ability to represent and imagine the rotation and movement of an object through space (Ark, 2002). Activation of parietal areas during mental rotation tasks, such as having to mentally rotate either a letter or number from one of four possible orientations to their upright position and then having to determine whether it was backwards or not, does not reach adult levels until between 8 and 12 years of age (Nelson et al., 2006). In a similar vein, the ability to integrate parts of a pattern, object, or event into a cohesive whole does not show parietal activation until relatively late. fMRI studies indicate that activity in parietal areas for spatial integration tasks does not reach adult levels until children are between 12 and 14 years old (Moses et al., 2002). Additionally, a similar pattern of parietal functional development has been shown in memory tasks in which children and adults watched a series of pictures that are repeated after presentation of 10–15 intervening items, and had to indicate whether repeated pictures were old or new. ERPs indicated significant maturation between 10 and 12 years with continued development into adolescence (Czernochowski, Mecklinger, & Johansson, 2009). Thus, though the parietal cortex shows some functionality early in infancy, the functional development of parietal areas continues to mature through early adolescence.

TEMPORAL LOBE In contrast to parietal areas that are part of the dorsal processing stream, temporal areas are part of the ventral processing stream. As such, a major function of the temporal cortex is the perception and recognition of objects (Bell, Hadj-Bouziane, Frihauf, Tootell, & Ungerleider, 2009). In

Links to Related Material

In Chapter 8, you will read about Piaget's cognitive theory and the assessment of one major milestone, object permanence. You will also be introduced to more recent work suggesting an earlier emergence of the capacity for object permanence, in line with the functional brain development outlined here.

line with this role, recent research shows that the infant's temporal cortex is similarly specialized for processing object or shape information. As we will discuss in Chapter 8, a major milestone of infancy is the capacity to represent objects when they are not currently visible (called *object permanence*), such as when they go behind another object. When activity in the temporal cortex is assessed by an EEG, 6-month-old babies seem to show activity during the period when the object is hidden from view (Southgate, Csibra, Kaufman, & Johnson, 2008). Figure 6.21 shows an EEG map of activation when an object is hidden. Wilcox, Haslup, and Boas (2010) used NIRS to measure infants' brain activity as they completed tasks that required more specific processing such as its shape or its speed, rather than just whether there was activity when an object was hidden. In this study, 5- to 7-month-old infants either saw an object (e.g., green ball) go behind a screen and then when it emerged from the other side the object had changed (e.g., green square), or saw the object go behind the screen at one speed and emerge at a different speed. Results indicated that areas of the temporal cortex associated with the ventral stream show more activity to the shape change than the speed change. These findings indicate that the object processing component of the temporal cortex and ventral processing stream shows consistent initial development to that of the parietal cortex and the dorsal processing, exhibiting initial functional development by 6 months of age.

FIGURE 6.21

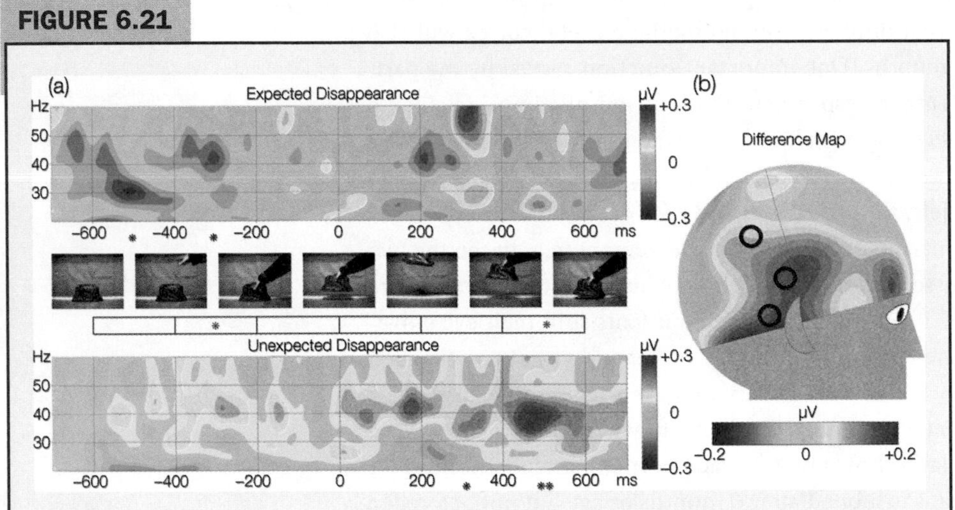

An EEG activity map of infants viewing an object hidden by a screen. Red indicates more activity and blue indicates less activity. The greatest concentration of activity is in the temporal areas. *From Johnson, M. H. & de Haan, M. (2011).* Developmental cognitive neuroscience *(3rd ed., Ch. 6, Perceiving and acting on the physical world, Figure 6.3 colour plates). Oxford: Wiley-Blackwell.*

As mentioned earlier in this chapter, fMRI studies with adults have indicated distinct areas within the temporal cortex for processing faces. As we will see in Chapter 7, the perception of faces seems to show preferential development relative to the perception of other objects. Consistent with this, PET studies have indicated that the areas in the temporal cortex associated with face processing (e.g., fusiform face area) are activated more by a human face than by other sorts of visual information at 2 months of age (Tzourio-Mazoyer et al., 2002). ERP studies have shown a similar developmental trend, with temporal area activation in response to faces exhibited by 3 months of age, and increased specialization of the face areas throughout the first year (Halit, de Haan, & Johnson, 2003). fMRI studies have suggested that further developmental specialization of the face areas continues into middle childhood (Cohen-Kadosh & Johnson, 2007). Consistent with the view that the dorsal and ventral processing streams show a similar early developmental timeline, these findings seem to show an early functionality but a protracted developmental course.

The temporal cortex is also heavily involved in the processing of language. It includes parts like Wernicke's areas that play a significant role in the processing and understanding of both written and spoken language. Although there is little research on the functional development of the specific language areas within the temporal cortex, there are a handful of studies on the development of temporal cortical activation during language processing tasks. Both ERP and fMRI studies have demonstrated temporal cortical activation to speech sounds in 3-month-old infants (Dehaene-Lambertz & Dehaene, 1994; Dehaene-Lambertz, Dehaene, & Hertz-Pannier, 2002), which again is consistent with structural maturation of the temporal lobe (Chugani et al., 2002). For example, Dehaene and colleagues (2002) used fMRI to measure brain activation as 3-month-olds heard French speech presented forwards and backwards. Though both forwards and backwards speech were associated with activity in the temporal cortex, only forward speech was associated with activity in areas typically considered speech processing areas in adults. In another MEG study, Imada and colleagues (2006) examined temporal area activity in response to the presentation of syllables in newborns, 6-month-olds, and 12-month-olds. They found that speech-related activity was exhibited by 6 months of age, but not younger, and continued strengthening through the first year. This pattern is likely due to the need for speech perception experience. Speech processing areas in the temporal cortex, therefore, seem to become functional between 3 and 6 months of age, with continued development through the first year or so, a timeline consistent with the developmental pattern exhibited for speech development.

Long-term memory is the other critical and major function in which the temporal cortex is involved. As pointed out earlier, the structure within the temporal cortex that seems to play a significant role in the encoding of information in long-term memory is the hippocampus. As already indicated, the temporal cortex shows some early development that supports some basic functions, but it has a fairly protracted time course to reach full functional maturity—the hippocampus is no different. Certain parts of the hippocampus in the medial temporal lobe mature early during the first few months (Seress, 2001), which allows for the learning and memory of associations between, for example, objects and consequences (Johnson & de Haan, 2011). Many modern infant toys take advantage of these types of associations: if the infant pulls on, hits, or kicks a certain part of a toy, a particular light or sound is presented, while interacting with another part of the toy causes a different light and sound to go off. Over time, the young infant learns to associate that object on the toy with a particular consequence and then remembers this association over days and weeks.

Links to Related Material

Here, we consider the issue of the development of areas in the temporal cortex that are related to language and speech processing. In Chapter 11, you will learn how the ability to detect speech sounds, understand language, and produce language develops.

As the temporal cortex and hippocampus continue to mature, significant functional changes occur over the first 2 years of life. This period of development provides functionality for supporting more sophisticated types of long-term memory that seem to emerge. Such functionality includes improvement in encoding information in long-term memory. In fact, ERP studies show stronger temporal area activity to familiar information in 10-month-olds as compared to 9-month-olds, whereas there was no difference between the ages for novel information (Bauer et al., 2006).

Improvements in storing information in long-term memory that affect how much and how long information is remembered, related to temporal cortical activity, also are evident. In another ERP study, changes in how much and how long infants remember modelled sequences of actions (such as putting a pencil through the bottom of a styrofoam cup and then putting a play dough ball on the point of the pencil) were related to the level of activity in the temporal cortex through 20 months of age (Bauer, 2007). These findings are consistent with structural development of the hippocampus, which shows a peak in the number of synapses between 20 and 24 months (Huttenlocher & Dabholkar, 1997). The hippocampus continues to develop throughout the preschool years until it reaches an adult level of maturity as indicated by an equivalent number of synapses. Similarly, encoding and storage functions show a similar timeline, with continued improvement through the preschool years (Bauer, 2007). Unfortunately, there do not appear to be any studies with this age group that allow for a direct connection of memory function to specific temporal cortical and hippocampal activity.

Across different functions, the parietal cortex—like the temporal cortex—shows early functionality, but the development of these functions is protracted over extended periods of time. For some functions, development can extend well into adolescence. What might be the reason for the protracted development? The likely cause is the need for experiential input that helps guide the development of the function as well as the cortical areas that are related to those functions (Johnson & de Haan, 2011).

Links to Related Material

Here you read about the role of the temporal cortex in the development of long-term memory. In Chapter 9, you will read more about the development of long-term memory capacities.

FRONTAL LOBE As stated earlier, one of the last areas to mature is the frontal cortex, which controls much of the higher cognitive functioning such as memory and decision-making. Since these areas were the last to evolve, they are the most highly evolved in humans. The prefrontal cortex (PFC) is one of the most studied areas from a developmental perspective within the frontal cortex, which plays a role in the functional emergence of working memory. This area accounts

CANADIAN CONTRIBUTIONS 6.1
ADELE DIAMOND

Dr. Adele Diamond. Photo courtesy of Martin Dee, University Photographer, Public Affairs, The University of British Columbia.

Dr. Adele Diamond is one of the major figures in the field of cognitive development, and is one of the initial proponents of the research area of developmental cognitive neuroscience. Dr. Diamond is a professor at the University of British Columbia, holds a Canada Research Chair in developmental cognitive neuroscience, and is a fellow of the Royal Society of Canada.

As should be clear from what we have written in this chapter, Dr. Diamond is at the forefront of research into the development of higher-order cognitive functions and the brain areas responsible for these functions. In particular, since 1980, she has focused on the functioning and development of one specific area of the frontal cortex, namely, the prefrontal cortex (PFC) (Diamond, 2002). The functions served by the prefrontal cortex include the core components of executive functions, particularly inhibitory control, cognitive flexibility, and working memory. Though the PFC has a protracted development, Dr. Diamond (1990a) has examined its functioning in infancy with the use of Piaget's A-not-B task, as discussed on the next page. In this task, the child must keep in mind for a short period of time where an object was hidden before the child can go and search for it. On any given trial, the child must update his or her memory with information about the object's most recent hiding location to correctly search the most immediate hiding location rather than where the object had been found before. This task, therefore, taps into a number of functions associated with the PFC, particularly working memory and inhibitory control. Changes in EEG patterns with development have been observed over the PFC area during performance of the A-not-B task (Bell & Fox, 1992). Furthermore, Dr. Diamond has demonstrated that lesions to the PFC are associated with disruption in performance on the A-not-B task in not only infants, but also adults (Diamond, 1990b; Diamond & Goldman-Rakic, 1989). Thus, this work was among the first to demonstrate a strong link between brain functioning and cognitive development, particularly the PFC and executive functions (Diamond, 2006b).

Dr. Diamond's research into the development of the PFC and its associated involvement in executive functions, working memory and inhibitory control, has led to a number of other breakthrough findings. Among these findings are those related to ADD and ADHD (attention deficit disorder and attention deficit/hyperactivity disorder), and to the genetic disorder of PKU (phenylketonuria). She has shown that ADHD and ADD (or inattentive-type ADHD) are not likely the same disorder, with differences in the underlying cognitive as well as brain deficits (Diamond, 2005). According to Dr. Diamond, children with ADD have problems in the area of the PFC as their core deficit, resulting in issues with working memory, whereas ADHD children seem to show deficits in a different area of the brain, called the striatum. That these may be different disorders rather than different subtypes of the same disorder has important clinical applications that are still being explored.

PKU is a genetic disorder that results in children being born without the enzyme that turns phenylalanine into the useful amino acid called tyrosine (Chen, 2006; Sack, 2008). Without the enzyme, phenylalanine builds up in the newborn infant's blood system, poisoning the brain, and causing mental retardation (Diamond et al., 1997). These newborns are put on diets that restrict foods with phenylalanine, thereby lowering phenylalanine levels in their blood. When the diet is not strictly followed, the PFC is particularly sensitive to even small amounts of excess of phenylalanine. The consequential small reduction in the amount of tyrosine reaching the PFC leads to deficits in inhibitory control and working memory, among other disruptions. Medical experts had previously thought that maintaining blood phenylalanine levels of 10 mg per decilitre of blood was benign. Dr. Diamond's work indicated that levels needed to be lower than 6 mg of phenylalanine per decilitre for deficits in cognitive functions related to the PFC not to be exhibited (Diamond et al., 1997). Furthermore, Dr. Diamond showed that the timing of when newborns are put on the phenylalanine restricted diet is important, with a significant delay after birth resulting in greater deficits in the visual system that also last longer (Diamond, 2001). As a direct result of her research, numerous countries in North America and Europe have lowered the acceptable blood phenylalanine levels to 2 to 6 mg per decilitre and have required that the phenylalanine restricted diet be initiated within a week after birth.

Links to Related Material

In Chapter 3 you learned how the harmful effects of the genetic disorder PKU can be reduced through a diet low in phenylalanine. Here, you learn about Dr. Diamond's research into the actual blood levels of phenylalanine necessary to minimize the harmful effects.

We have outlined just a few of the areas in which Dr. Diamond has made crucial contributions as a Canadian researcher. Dr. Diamond has demonstrated that the prefrontal cortex and the cognitive functions it serves are critical components in understanding both typical and atypical cognitive development. More generally, she has shown that documenting the relation between that development and brain function is critical to construct a fuller understanding of cognitive development.

for nearly one-third of the total surface area of the cortex (Brodmann, 1912). Adele Diamond at the University of British Columbia has been at the forefront of documenting the development of the PFC (Diamond, 2000, 2006a; Rennie, Bull, & Diamond, 2004) and its role in the development of the functions of not only working memory, but also object permanence (see *Canadian Contributions 6.1*). Though we will discuss object permanence in more depth in Chapter 8, this cognitive function refers to the capacity to know that an object exists even when not physically and perceptually available. Piaget designed the A-not-B task to behaviourally assess the development of object permanence. Research has consistently found that successful performance on this task does not occur until the second half of the first year of life. In the A-not-B task, infants are shown a toy hidden a few times at location A. After each time, the infant is given the opportunity to retrieve the toy from location A. Subsequently, the toy is hidden at a second location, B. Until near the end of the first year, infants typically will incorrectly search back at location A.

Diamond and others have found that infants' capability to successfully find the toy at location B in the A-not-B task is related to the development in functioning of the PFC (Baird et al., 2002; Bell, Wolfe, & Adkins, 2007; Diamond, 2001). That is, various studies of brain-damaged infants and imaging have shown that the PFC shows significant maturation between 5 and 12 months of age, and this maturation is consistent with the development of successful performance on the A-not-B task (Bell & Fox, 1992; Diamond & Goldman-Rakic, 1989). For example, a NIRS study showed that level of success on the object permanence task was related to the level of blood oxygenation in the PFC (Baird et al., 2002). The relation between the PFC and performance on object permanence tasks likely stems from the fact that successful completion of these tasks requires the capacity of memory for the recent location and inhibition of searching at the previous location. Numerous studies, such as those looking at the effects of lesions to the PFC (Johnson & de Haan, 2011), have indicated that the PFC is involved in spatial working memory and the inhibition of inappropriate responses.

The PFC has a particularly protracted period of maturation, showing some involvement in cognitive development in infancy and then again in preschool years, but not reaching full maturity until adulthood (Casey et al., 2005; Diamond, 2006b; Klingberg, 2006). As represented in Figure 6.16, the PFC shows a much more protracted period of synapse creation and pruning, with the peak occurring during the preschool years. The preschool years, therefore, seem to be of great importance in the development of the PFC and its functions (Diamond, 2002). Numerous behavioural studies have demonstrated that performance on various types of spatial working memory tasks and tasks that require the inhibition of inappropriate responses increases between approximately 4 and 8 years (for review, see Tsujimoto, 2008). To examine the relation of the development of children's performance to PFC maturation, Tsujimoto and colleagues (2004) conducted a NIRS study where children between 4 and 7 years old performed a spatial working memory/recognition task (see Figure 6.22) in which they had to remember whether the test square was in the same location as one of the two squares previously presented. Activation in the PFC and correct performance on this spatial working memory task were associated mainly with the age of children. That is, as children got older, they performed better on the task, and activation in the PFC increased. Thus, though working memory and the PFC are functional by some time near the end of the first year of

Links to Related Material

In Chapter 8, you will learn about object permanence and Piaget's A-not-B task. Here you have read about the development of the prefrontal cortex that may function to support performance in object permanence and the A-not-B task.

When an infant pulls on, hits, or kicks a certain part of a toy, and a particular light or sound is presented, over time the young infant learns to associate that part of the toy with a particular consequence and remembers this association. *(Waldemar Dabrowski/iStock)*

FIGURE 6.22

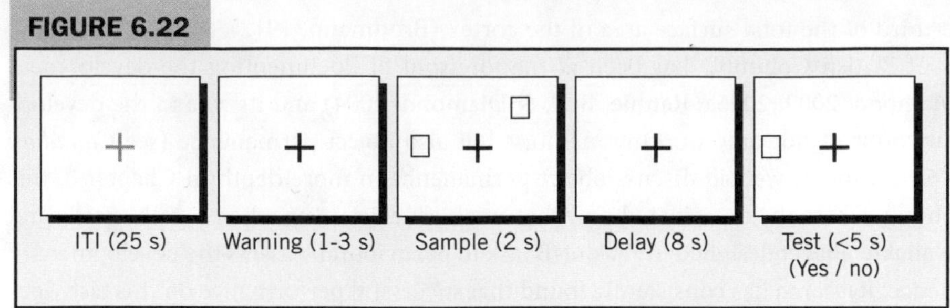

The sequence for the spatial working memory task used in Tsujimoto et al. (2004). During the interval between trials (ITI), a fixation cross was presented. This cross darkened as a warning that the trial was to begin. Then two sample square cues were presented at distinct locations. After a delay, one square cue was presented and the children had to indicate whether or not it was in the same location as one of the sample cues. *Adapted from Tsujimoto, S. (2008). The prefrontal cortex: Functional neural development during early childhood (Figure 4, p. 352).* The Neuroscientist, *14, 345 -358.*

life, the PFC and its functions continue to develop into childhood, reaching their peak during the preschool years. Yet, the PFC and its functionality do not reach adult levels until well in adolescence, if not early adulthood (Johnson & de Haan, 2011; Klingberg, 2006).

Another important capability of the frontal cortex is the mechanism of executive function, which is involved in choosing which response and behaviour is appropriate for a given situation or task. Executive function, consequently, is involved in recognizing emotions and showing empathy, decision-making, problem solving, and planning, among other behaviours. As executive function has been shown to be involved in mediating developmental tasks such as the A-not-B, mainly due to its response inhibition component (Diamond, 2002), there is meaningful development in performance on executive function tasks and associated frontal cortical activity between 3 and 6 years of age (Swingler, Willoughby, & Calkins, 2011). On other executive function tasks, such as decision-making tasks, development shows a slower course. In a recent study, Crone and colleagues (2008) tested children, adolescents, and young adults in a computer simulated decision-making task in which they had to help a dog find its way home by choosing which of four doors across two houses (two doors per house) to open. After choosing a door, they received feedback of either a plus or minus sign, depending on whether they successfully got the dog home. The rules that led to successful completion of the task changed randomly, but could be deduced via the feedback given, leading to changes in decision-making. fMRI data indicated that activation in some frontal areas was evident and adult-like in children 8 to 11 years of age, showing more activation to negative feedback (due to wrong responses) than positive feedback. Broader activation of frontal areas, however, showed continued development after 14 to 15 years into the young adult group of 18- to 24-year-olds. Similar patterns of these behaviours and regions of brain activation, but different levels of intensity of activation, have been found across children, adolescents, and young adults (Bechara, Damasio, Tranel, & Damasio, 1997; Crone & van der Molen, 2008; Crone & Westenberg, 2009), clearly showing that development of the frontal cortex has the longest timeline for reaching full maturity.

Cortical areas, from visual to temporal and parietal to frontal, show ever-increasing protracted timelines in structure and function, which seems to indicate that experience and learning are important factors for their full development. Such experiential development in the brain and its functions is termed *plasticity*, a topic that we will examine next.

BRAIN PLASTICITY

Up to this point, our discussion of neural and brain development seemingly gives the impression that the different structures and components mature on their own, at their own schedule, without any influence from the world with which the child interacts. While this is for the most part true prenatally (see discussion of prenatal learning in Chapter 7), such a picture certainly is not an accurate representation of how experience influences brain development. Clearly, we know that experience affects how our brains work; we learn new things and we remember particular events in our lives—all requiring changes in the brain where the learning and the remembering are occurring. The changes that occur in the brain as a result of particular experiences are referred to as **plasticity**.

Plasticity Changes in brain structure and function as a result of experience.

The classic example of plasticity is that after an injury and damage to portions of the brain, other areas of the brain rewire themselves to take over the lost functions. For example, a person who sustains damage to the portion of the brain that serves language processing and production is often eventually able to recover language capacities as a result of therapeutic experiences. The therapy helps rewire the brain so other areas take over the language functions that were previously served by the damaged areas. This illustrates a basic principle of plasticity: experiential stimulation is necessary for neurons to rewire themselves and form new connections.

But, plasticity is not just a property of a damaged brain; it is likely fundamental to the course of brain development. As we will see in chapters to come, experience and learning have profound effects on the development of everything from perception to social interactions. Consequently, these experiences change the functioning of the brain areas involved in those behaviours. How experience influences neural and brain development can readily be seen through the central process of generating synapses. During the process of synaptogenesis, synapses are produced and synapses that are used as we have various experiences are strengthened. Those synapses that are not used during our experiences are pruned away. Thus, the development of the brain is heavily influenced by the day-to-day experiences that infants and children have as they look around, as they hear the sounds in their environment, and as they interact socially with caregivers, siblings, and peers—generally, as they experience life.

The effect of experience on synaptogenesis and brain development comes in two forms: **experience-expectant** and **experience-dependent** (Black et al., 1998; also see Johnson, 2007). Experience-expectant synaptogenesis is the manner in which synapses are formed, maintained, and pruned based on experiences that are typical (in other words, expected) for that species. These experiences are expected because through evolutionary mechanisms, previous generations received particular stimulation that resulted in their brains evolving down through the generations to process that stimulation. Those particular experiences then become expected and necessary for typical development to proceed. Consequently, all members of a given species will develop similar capacities assuming the same species-expected environment. In humans, for example, certain types of visual and auditory experiences are expected by our sensory systems for those cortical areas to develop properly. Thus, to see and hear properly, we need to have the experience of particular types of stimulation during early development. Further, this type of plasticity accounts for the common course of brain and psychological development across all individuals of a species.

Experience-expectant synaptogenesis The mechanism by which synapses are formed, maintained, and pruned based on experiences that are typical for that species. Given the same species-expected environment, all members' brains will develop the same capabilities.

Experience-dependent synaptogenesis Changes in brain structure and function as a result of experience.

Experience-expectant mechanisms are clearly a necessary process for that species that allows development to proceed properly. But what happens when those expected experiences are not available in early development, as is the case when babies are born with cataracts in their eyes? Previously, we described research with babies who had cataracts by Daphne Maurer and her colleagues that provided evidence related to the development of the dorsal and ventral processing streams. This research also addresses the issue of brain plasticity and experience-expectant mechanisms by comparing the visual development of babies who had those cataracts removed fairly soon after birth and those who did not have them removed for several years (Maurer, Mondloch, & Lewis, 2007; Mondloch, Le Grand, & Maurer, 2003; also see Putzar et al., 2007). When these babies were tested years later, their visual abilities were directly related to the timing of cataract removal and consequently the onset of expected visual experience: the longer the delay in removing the cataracts, the poorer their visual abilities. Yet, even with early removal of the cataracts within a few months after birth, babies do not fully develop certain visual capacities such as acuity and the recognition of faces (Le Grand, Mondloch, Maurer, & Brent, 2004; Maurer, Ellemberg, & Lewis, 2006). Some visual abilities recover completely after early removal of cataracts but other abilities do not, which suggests that plasticity of different brain areas and their functions do not show the same sensitive periods to expected experiences. We will return to this concept a little later.

Alternatively, whereas the experience-expectant mechanisms are engaged in the synaptogenesis and brain development across a species, experience-dependent synaptogenesis mechanisms function as a result of unique experiences for the individual. That is, each one of us, as we grow and mature, has experiences that are unique in some way to us and are not experienced at all or not experienced in the same way by others, including our own parents, brothers, or sisters. As a result of that unique experience, the synapses in our brain that process that experience are strengthened, and those that do not process the information contained in that unique experience are weakened. Over time, those weakened synapses are pruned because they fail to be useful in processing that experience-dependent information. In other words, this type of plasticity follows the "use it or lose it" principle and, consequently, is responsible for individual differences in brain and psychological development.

One example of the experience dependent mechanism and the use it or lose it principle comes from the development of phonemic discrimination (phonemes are the smallest unit of sound that conveys meaning in language). Not all possible phonemes are used in all languages, so native speakers of a particular language will have difficulty discriminating phonemes that are not part of their language. For example, in Japanese there are no /r/ or /l/ phonemes, so native Japanese speakers have difficulty discriminating these phonemes. However, before we are born, our brain does not know which language and which phonemes it will need to process, so the neurons and synaptic connections in our brain exist to process any phonemic information that we might encounter. Through experience-dependent mechanisms, the neurons and synapses that are not used because the native language heard after birth does not contain those phonemes are likely pruned over time, leading to an inability to discriminate those phonemes. Janet Werker of the University of British Columbia has studied just such a mechanism in the ability of English-speaking infants to discriminate phonemes from Native American languages (Werker & Tees, 2002, 2005). She has found that these infants are quite capable of discriminating the Native American phonemes before approximately 6 months of age, but that this capacity seems to be lost somewhere between 6 and 12 months. Interestingly, such findings are consistent with the timeline for development of language areas in the temporal lobe that we discussed earlier. Thus, depending on an individual's specific experiences, his or her brain and its psychological and behavioural functions will develop accordingly.

Links to Related Material

In Chapter 11, you will learn about the development of phonemic discrimination and language. Here you have learned about the experience-dependent mechanism that is involved in that development.

These experience-mediated changes in the brain and functions do not show the same timeline across the different brain areas. That is, when and for how long there is sensitivity to plasticity varies across the brain areas. Since plasticity is likely a main driving force behind brain and functional development, the differential time course of development of the brain areas is likely reflected in the sensitive period that those areas exhibit for plasticity (Neville, 2007). The brain stem, for example, which matures rather quickly, is less plastic than cortical areas that show a more protracted developmental pattern (Aylward, 1997). Similarly, differential patterns of plasticity emerge across the cortical areas, and even within functional cortical areas, that shadow the developmental timing of those areas. For example, the sensitive period for plasticity of the occipital lobe is earlier than either the parietal or temporal lobe or the frontal lobe (Nelson et al., 2006). Plasticity and experience, therefore, is intimately involved in development of brain structures and their function. In the chapters to follow, we will explore various psychological and behavioural domains where experience plays a crucial role in development—likely through yet undiscovered mechanisms of brain plasticity!

For Thought and Discussion

Can you think of experiences that were either expectant or dependent that would have resulted in changes in your brain and its function?

LEARNING OBJECTIVE 6.4

Describe the development of the structures and function of the brain.

1. When do the hemispheres become lateralized and specialized?
2. What are the different theories that attempt to explain the development of hemispheric specialization?
3. What are the two possible accounts for the development of the cortical functional divisions?
4. What is the developmental timeline for the four cortical divisions?
5. What are the experience-expectant and experience-dependent mechanisms of synaptogenesis and brain plasticity?

CONCLUSION

Though the use of techniques for recording and imaging brain activity has expanded by leaps and bounds over the last 20 years, their use in the investigation of development has only recently taken off. We now have the capability of not only unravelling one the greatest scientific mysteries, the brain, but also of beginning to divulge how this complex instrument develops and is affected by our experiences.

We have learned from this research that the brain is more complex and functional at an earlier age than previously assumed. Development in the specificity and functionality of the brain, particularly of cortical areas, has been shown to follow a fairly regular pattern across individuals. Such regularity might intuitively appeal to a maturational or a purely nature view of brain development. This regularity has also led to the view that there is a tight linkage between neural and brain development and cognitive development based on the age of onset. Unfortunately, both of these conceptions are simplistic. Throughout development, our brains are highly sensitive to the nurturing quality of experiences. The development of our brains, therefore, is determined not only by biological and genetic mechanisms, but also as a result of individualistic experiences. Furthermore, though the time course of brain development, particularly cortical development, and cognitive development are clearly related, the role of experience brings up the question of the direction of that relation. That is, does development in certain brain structures enable the capacity for certain cognitive experiences, or does having certain cognitive experiences stimulate development of the appropriate brain structures? This is one of the great mysteries of development, though the answer is likely not to be as simple as we might think.

With additional research and knowledge of the typical course of neural and brain development, there might soon come a time when we will be able to diagnose when typical brain development is disrupted and under what circumstances. Such a capacity would likely not only increase our understanding of the underlying brain factors for various developmental disabilities, but would also facilitate the diagnosis of the resulting developmental disabilities before behavioural symptoms are evident. Early diagnosis on the basis of the evaluation of the nature of neural and brain development would likely lead to earlier interventions and treatment, and more positive outcomes.

For any further advances in understanding brain development, its role in cognitive and behavioural development, and how its disruption leads to developmental disorders, a couple of issues need to be resolved. First, further advances need to be made in methodology as some of the current techniques are not useable with infants and children. To get a complete picture of the development of brain structure and its function, the entire age range needs to be examined by the same methodologies. Second, there currently does not exist a complete theoretical framework for understanding the relation between the brain and its functioning with observable behaviour. Consequently, our understanding of how brain structural and functional development are related to cognitive and behavioural development is at its very early stages. The future will clearly see an exponential growth in research in brain development and its implications, both positive and negative.

SUMMARY

KEY TERMS

axon, p. 177
brainstem, p. 187
cerebellum, p. 187
cerebral cortex, p. 187
cerebrum, p. 187
corpus collosum, p. 187
dendrite, p. 177
diffusion tensor imaging (DTI), p. 173
event-related potentials (ERPs), p. 171
experience-dependent synaptogenesis, p. 203
experience-expectant synaptogenesis, p. 203
frontal lobe, p. 190
functional magnetic resonance imaging (fMRI), p. 175
glial cell, p. 178
magnetoencephalography (MEG), p. 172
midbrain, p. 187
myelin, p. 178
near infra-red spectroscopy (NIRS), p. 176
neuroimaging techniques, p. 170
neuron, p. 177
neurotransmitter, p. 178
occipital lobe, p. 189
parietal lobe, p. 189
plasticity, p. 203
positron emission tomography (PET), p. 174
spontaneous electroencephalography (EEG), p. 171
structural magnetic resonance imaging (MRI), p. 172
synapse, p. 178
synaptic vesicles, p. 178
temporal lobe, p. 190

LEARNING OBJECTIVES

LEARNING OBJECTIVE 6.1 Describe the different methodologies used to study how the brain works and develops.

1. *What are the goal and purpose of neuroimaging techniques?*
   Until relatively recently, there has been no way to link brain activity to specific behaviours and cognitive functions, or to determine how this link is affected by development. Neuroimaging techniques provide a means of looking inside the brain and revealing its anatomical structure and the changes that occur in its activity during the processing of a stimulus or completion of a task. Furthermore, some of these techniques can be used to study the development of the anatomical structure of the brain and the development of its functioning during stimulus processing.

2. *What are the different techniques for assessing the brain's electrical activity?*
   There are a number of techniques used for measuring the brain's electrical activity. All take advantage of the fact that as signals travel through neurons in the brain, electrical and magnetic fields are generated. These fields can then be detected and measured by electrodes and sensors that are placed on the scalp. Electroencephalography (EEG) measures spontaneous electrical activity of groups of neurons across the brain during stimulus events via electrodes on the scalp. Event-related potentials (ERPs) are similar to EEGs in that they measure brain electrical activity via electrodes on the scalp, but differ in terms of the nature of the electrical activity that is measured. Instead of measuring spontaneous activity across the whole brain to stimulus events, ERPs measure the electrical activity of specific brain areas in response to the presentation of a specific stimulus or to the generation of a specific action. The last technique, magnetoencephalography (MEG), measures the magnetic field rather than the electrical activity that is generated by signal transmission. The magnetic field is also detected by sensors on the scalp. MEG has an advantage over EEG and ERPs in that electrical signals can be distorted by passage through the skull and scalp, but these are transparent to magnetic fields. Thus, MEG can record the activity of the neurons directly. MEG is at a disadvantage, however, because it is more sensitive to movement of the individual whose activity is being recorded.

3. *How useful are the techniques that measure the brain's electrical activity for assessing brain development?*
Both EEG and ERPs have become quite popular for use in developmental studies. This is mainly because they are non-invasive, requiring only that a cap with sensors be put on the head, and can be used across the entire lifespan, even with newborns. Thus these techniques, particularly ERPs, are easy to use across the developmental spectrum, providing meaningful data across a wide range of capacities. MEG, which has methodological advantages over EEG and ERPs due to the finer detail that it provides of brain activity, has seen an increase in usage in developmental studies. However, the sensitivity of MEG to movement of the individual is a distinct disadvantage for using this technique with infants and young children. It is much more difficult for infants and young children to remain as still as possible during recording as it is for adults. As a result, the data at the younger ages will not be as clean and clear, likely increasing the inaccuracy of the data and perhaps the interpretations. For this reason, ERPs remain the popular choice for measuring brain activity across the developmental range.

4. *What are the techniques for imaging the anatomical structure of the brain?*
Two techniques are typically used to assess the anatomical structure of the brain. The first, structural magnetic resonance imaging (MRI), is a technique in which a magnetic field generated by powerful magnets interact with water molecules in the brain. When the magnetic field is turned off, the molecules release energy that is then detected by the scanner and converted to images of brain structure. MRI has the capacity to distinguish between different tissues, such as grey and white brain matter, and the relations among these tissues. Structural MRI, consequently, has become critical for identifying distinct brain structures and when those structures are atypical. More recently, a second technique has been devised called diffusion tensor imaging (DTI). As a modification of MRI, it is also sometimes termed diffusion MRI. The unique aspect of DTI is that though structural MRI provides detail maps of the structures of the brain, it does not provide information about how those structures are connected to one another. DTI measures the interaction between a magnetic field and water molecules as those water molecules move along neural tracts consisting of axons. DTI is also capable of determining the direction of the movement of the water molecules and hence the direction of the signal, thereby providing information for how different brain structures are related, interact, and communicate with each other.

5. *How useful are the techniques that image the brain's anatomical structure for determining the development of the brain's anatomical structure?*
Structural MRI has been used extensively to map the structural components of the brain across development. With structural MRI, the individual is required to remain still during the imaging process to ensure a clear, sharp, and accurate image. Young children and infants, therefore, are usually scanned while they are sleeping to minimize movement. As a result, a wealth of data has been obtained about the development of brain structures from newborns and infants through childhood and adolescence, as well as from adults. Recently, structural MRI has even been used to examine the brain structure and maturation of the brain in a fetus. DTI, because of its similarity to MRI, also requires that the individual remains still during scanning. So, similar to MRI, DTI studies with young children and infants are done while they are sleeping. Since DTI is a relatively recent advance, not many development studies have been done with this technique. However, those that have been done have provided substantial information about the development and maturation of axons and their myelination from infancy through childhood and adolescence.

6. *What techniques have been devised for determining the function of different brain structures?*
Imaging of the functional structure of the brain has seen an incredible explosion over the last 10 years or so. Three techniques have fuelled this explosion. Positron emission tomography (PET) measures the metabolic activity in the brain by detecting the gamma ray radiation from

a positron-emitting isotope that has been injected into the bloodstream. This isotope resembles glucose, which is the fuel for cells that is taken up by neurons when they need energy to do some work. As brain areas become active because the individual is completing some specific type of task, they light up as a scanner detects the gamma ray radiation. Consequently, images of the relative activation of different brain areas can be analyzed, indicating the relative level of work being done by those areas. Depending on the nature of the task (i.e., perception, memory, or language), different patterns of activation will be seen. A second, but likely the most widely used technique, is functional magnetic resonance imaging (fMRI). fMRI is similar to structural MRI and takes advantage of the fact that neurons and brain areas that are active require oxygen. That oxygen is transported to the brain areas in the blood by hemoglobin. Blood that contains oxygen is more magnetized than non-oxygenated blood. As brain areas become active due to the active performance of some task, there is an increase in oxygenated blood flow to those areas. The blood oxygen level dependent (BOLD) response across different brain areas is then imaged by the MRI scanner. fMRI has been and continues to be used extensively to identify the functional brain areas for a wide range of tasks, from attention and perception to memory, speech, and language processing, and even social interactions. The final functional imaging technique is fairly new and shares similarities with fMRI. This new procedure, called near infra-red spectroscopy (NIRS), also measure the BOLD signal. However, instead of measuring the magnetization of the blood as in fMRI, NIRS beams infra-red light through the skull and brain and then measures the absorption and scatter of the light by the blood oxygen. Where there is an increase in blood oxygen indicating those brain areas are doing more work, there is greater absorption and scatter of the infra-red light.

7. *To what extent can the techniques for determining brain function be used to assess the development of these brain functions?*
   Neither PET nor fMRI are particularly applicable for use to study the development of brain function in children or infants, but for different reasons. Because PET requires the injection of a radioactive substance into the bloodstream, parents and researchers are hesitant to consider using this technique with young people. PET studies with children and infants have been limited to clinical cases for which diagnostic needs have justified its use. fMRI, although it does not require the injection of a radioactive substance, is not particularly usable with children younger than age 5 or 6. fMRI not only requires individuals to remain completely still, but that requirement lasts for an extended period of time, typically around 45 minutes. While staying still would be difficult enough for children and infants, staying still for that long would be impossible. Furthermore, fMRI cannot be used when children are sleeping because it would severely limit the range of tasks and functions that could be studied. The purpose of fMRI is to map which areas are active and functioning during the completion of particular tasks. If the individual is asleep, the child cannot complete any task and, hence, the purpose of fMRI would not be met. NIRS, however, is gaining a lot of attention from developmental researchers because it does not have the disadvantages of PET and fMRI. There is no radioactive isotope, nor does the individual need to remain absolutely still. Because the emitters and detectors of the infra-red light are housed in a cap that is placed on the scalp, NIRS is less sensitive to the movement of the individual. As a consequence, NIRS can be used to assess the functional activity of even young infants' brains. Though NIRS has not been used extensively yet to study functional brain development mainly because of its newness, some recent studies have used it to examine the functional development of brain areas responsible for object perception in 6.5-month-olds.

LEARNING OBJECTIVE 6.2 Describe the structures and functions of the neurons, and trace the development of the neural system during childhood.

1. *What are the different parts of the neuron?*
   Besides a nucleus and cell body like every other cell, the neuron consists of the following unique parts: dendrites, axon, myelin, nodes of Ranvier, synapses, and synaptic vesicles.

Dendrites are a network of short fibres that extend out from the neuron's cell body, receive activity and signals from nearby cells, and conduct those signals to the cell body. Axons are long fibres that also extend out from the cell body and transmit activity and signals from the cell body to other cells. Myelin is a sheath of fatty material that surrounds and insulates the axon, enabling faster transmission of neural signals down the axon; the myelin sheath is generated by extensions from supporting glial cells. Nodes of Ranvier are gaps in the myelin sheath that form because a number of glial cells are required to completely myelinate an axon. Synapses are the small fluid-filled spaces in between the axon of one neuron and the dendrites of other neurons across which neural activity and signals are transmitted. They occur because the neurons do not make direct contact with each other. Synaptic vesicles are structures near the end of the axon within which neurotransmitters (chemicals that transfer signals across synapses) are stored.

2. *What are the four main neurotransmitter systems and their functions?*
   Synapses can come in two types: chemical or electrical. When the synaptic gap is small, then an electrical signal can jump from the axon of one neuron to the dendrite of another. When the gap is large, however, the neural signal crosses from axon to dendrite by the flow of chemicals called neurotransmitters. There are four major systems of neurotransmitters: noradrenaline, dopamine, serotonin, and cholinergic. The noradrenaline system affects arousal, including the fight-or-flight response, feelings of reward, and is also involved in the allocation of attentional resources. The dopamine system plays an important role in controlling motor behaviour, learning, and aspects of higher-order cognition such as memory and problem solving. The serotonin system is involved in the regulation of basic metabolic functions such as appetite, body temperature, hunger, mood, and the sleep/wake cycle. Finally, the cholinergic system is associated with learning and short-term memory storage.

3. *Describe the process of neurulation.*
   The brain begins its development during weeks 3 and 4 after conception through the process of neurulation. Weeks 3 and 4 after conception are part of the embryo stage, during which the three layers of cells of the zygote begin to differentiate. During neurulation, a section of the ectoderm (the outermost layer) begins to pinch inward. This section is termed the neural plate and the pinching is termed the neural groove. As the pinching continues, the neural groove becomes deeper and the two ends of the neural plate come closer together. Eventually, the two ends of the neural plate join, closing the neural plate and pinching completely off to form the hollow neural tube. The neural tube will further differentiate over time, with its top end becoming the various parts of the brain and the bottom part becoming the spinal cord.

4. *The development of the neural structure of the brain has four stages. What are these four stages?*
   After neurulation, there are four stages in the process of neuronal and brain development. The first stage is called cell production, during which the cells that make up the brain are produced along the inner walls of the neural tube in specialized proliferative zones. One zone produces evolutionarily older neurons for the older parts of the brain such as the brainstem. The other zone produces cells for the newer part of the brain, such as the frontal lobe. Neurons are produced from neuroblasts in the proliferative zones. At its peak in the fetus, approximately 250,000 neurons are produced every minute. Once the neurons are produced in the proliferative zones, they then need to make their way to their proper location in the brain. This is the second stage and is called cell migration. There are two processes for cells to get to their intended location. During passive displacement, newly produced cells push out previously produced cells, generating an "outside-in" neural pattern of older cells more to the outside of the brain and newer cells toward the inside of the brain. Passive displacement is the typical process for populating the thalamus, hippocampus, and brain stem structures. The other process, called active cell migration, consists of cells moving much greater distances. Newly produced neurons use

glial cells as guides to move past previously produced cells. The final location for these actively migrating cells is determined by a chemical attraction between neurons already at the target location and the migrating cell. This type of migration produces an "inside-out" neural pattern. Active cell migration is typically responsible for populating much of the cerebral cortex. The third stage of neural and brain development is cell elaboration and differentiation, which occurs once the neuron has found its final location. During this stage, the extensive network of axons and dendrites form synapses with thousands of other cells. Axons are attracted to or repelled from other neurons by detecting molecules in the neural environment. The dendritic tree also increases in size and complexity during cell elaboration and differentiation. The combination of axon expansion and dendritic sprouting enables the production of synapses, which is called synaptogenesis. The last stage of neural development is the formation of myelin around the axons. Myelination occurs by glial cells producing extensions that wrap themselves around axons.

5. *What are the developmental timelines of the four stages of development of the neural structure of the brain and how do they compare?*
   The stages of neural development show a fairly regular or orderly timeline. Cell production begins as soon as neurulation is complete, around 4 weeks after conception. All of the 100 billion neurons in the brain are produced by the time cell production is complete during the fetal period. Though no new neurons are produced in most parts of the brain after birth, certain areas involved in learning and memory can continue to produce new cells throughout life. Furthermore, while the most cells we will ever have are there before we are born, more cells are produced than we need postnatally. Consequently, there is cell death to get rid of the extra neurons, the ones that are not stimulated and used. The peak number of cells occurs by 28 weeks of conception, after which the number decreases substantially. Cell migration coincides with cell production and is also complete by the end of gestation. In fact, cell migration is completed by 7 months (or 28 weeks) after conception, about the time of the peak number of cells and before cell death begins to take its toll. Cell elaboration and differentiation has been seen as early as 15 weeks after conception, with the sprouting of dendrites and the extension of axons to their targets. This stage is more prolonged than either cell production or migration, as dendritic expansion is seen as late as 2 years after birth. Synapses first appear around 23 weeks after conception, reaching peak production between 8 months and 24 months after birth, depending on the brain area. As with cell production, more synapses are produced than are needed, and after about 2 years of age, synapses that are not being used begin to be pruned away. By adolescence, the number of synapses seems to level off for all brain areas. Finally, myelination is the most prolonged stage of neural development. Myelination sequence seems to exhibit a regular pattern. The myelination of axons in the peripheral system, then the motor behaviour areas, followed by sensory systems begin during the prenatal period and are completely myelinated by age 4. During the first year of life, the brain stem and cerebellum myelinate. Cortical areas start myelinating before birth, but continue to myelinate into early adulthood.

   In summary, the building blocks of the brain are laid down during the first two trimesters of pregnancy. During the last trimester of pregnancy and the first years after birth, the building blocks are elaborated by the growth of axons and the dendritic tree. Also during the first years of life, the building blocks are connected by synapses. These processes all show an increase-decrease pattern in which there is overproduction followed by the cutting back of unused and unneeded neurons and synaptic connections. Finally, the most prolonged phase, lasting until early adulthood, is the increase in the efficiency and functionality of the connections by way of myelination.

LEARNING OBJECTIVE 6.3 Describe the structures of the brain and their functions.

1. *What are the four major brain structures and their functions?*
   The four major brain structures are the brainstem, midbrain, cerebellum, and cerebrum. The brainstem is the evolutionarily oldest part of the brain and it adjoins and is continuous

with the spinal cord. This structure includes the medulla, pons, and the midbrain. As the oldest structure, the brainstem plays a crucial role in basic functioning, relaying information between the brain and the rest of the body. It controls hunger and feeding, the sleep cycle, body temperature, breathing, sensitivity to pain, and sexual behaviour. The midbrain, as part of the brainstem, also relays information. In the case of the midbrain, it controls breathing and swallowing, as well as reflexive control of visual and auditory processing. This reflexive control of visual processing includes that of eye movements, pupil constriction, and dilation. Within the midbrain are two structures, the inferior colliculus and superior colliculus, that play important roles in representing and relaying auditory and visual information. The third structure, the cerebellum, is situated behind the brainstem and underneath the cerebral hemispheres. The cerebellum has a distinct appearance relative to the rest of the brain, consisting of neural tissues with parallel grooves. Control over motor behaviour is the main function of the cerebellum, affecting equilibrium, posture, and motor learning. Additional functions of the cerebellum include attention, language, and the regulating emotional responses. The last structure, the cerebrum, is the evolutionarily newest brain structure and consists of the left and right hemispheres and a nerve bundle called the corpus collosum that connects them. Of particular interest is the thin sheet of grey matter that covers the cerebrum, called the cerebral cortex. The rest of the cerebrum consists mostly of white matter. Grey matter is made up of cell bodies and the dendrites of the neurons, whereas white matter contains the myelinated axons. The cerebral cortex is further divided into lobes, with each lobe generally having specific functionality. Crucial functions of the cerebral cortex include processing sensory information, language, memory, higher-order thinking, decision-making, as well as the control of voluntary actions.

2. *How are the two hemispheres differentially specialized?*
The two hemispheres of the cerebrum are not perfectly symmetrical but are lateralized, which means that the left brain and the right brain are somewhat specialized. In general, the left side of the brain manages sensory input and motor movements on the right side of the body, while the right side of the brain controls input and movements on the left side. The left side of the brain is also usually more specialized for language performance, verbal memory, and decision-making. The right side, in contrast, is more specialized for spatial and mathematical tasks. Another way to think about this distinction is that the left side is more oriented to words and concepts, and the right side is more oriented to images. Hemispheric specialization also shows individual differences. That is, not everyone shows the typical left-hemisphere dominance for language. Some people have right-hemisphere dominance for language and some people have mixed dominance. Left-handers more frequently have right-hemisphere or mixed dominance.

3. *What are the four distinct lobes of the cerebral cortex and their functions?*
There are four functionally distinct lobes: occipital, parietal, temporal, and frontal. The occipital lobe is the smallest of the lobes and is located in the rearmost location of the brain. Its main function is to process visual information. The occipital lobe can be further divided into a number of functional sections, differentiated by the type and complexity of the visual information that they process. Once basic visual information is processed, that information is sent on for further processing along one of two pathways, depending on the type of information. The dorsal or upperside "where" stream pathway is associated with processing motion and object location information, as well as information that provides control of eye movements and reaching. The ventral or underside "what" stream pathway is generally associated with processing information, such as shape and colour. This information is necessary for representing, identifying, and recognizing different types of forms and objects. The ventral stream, because it is involved in the representation and recognition of objects, is also associated with the encoding of that information in long-term memory. The parietal lobe is situated above

and forward from the occipital lobe. Neurons in the parietal lobe are sensitive to receiving information from different senses, particularly touch, and from different parts of the body. The parietal lobe then integrates the multisensory information from different body parts, thereby enabling us to interact with the objects and world around us and navigate through it. As a part of the dorsal stream, the parietal lobe is also involved in mapping visually perceived objects to locations relative to one's body. The third lobe, the temporal lobe, is located forward from the occipital lobe and below the parietal lobe. The main function of the temporal lobe is the perception of auditory information, making the temporal lobe particularly specialized for the processing of speech and language. To this end, the parietal lobe contains Wernicke's area, which plays a significant role in processing and understanding written and spoken language, including comprehension and naming of objects. The temporal lobe also contains the hippocampus, a structure known to be involved in transferring information from short-term to long-term memory. The last but most evolutionary recent lobe is the frontal lobe, which is located at the very front of the brain. Functions of the frontal lobe include attention, short-term and working memory, planning, decision-making, and behavioural regulation. The frontal lobe is also involved in long-term memories, as the prefrontal cortex has been shown to be associated with the formation of long-term memories that are used in producing expectations and directing behaviour planning to future events.

LEARNING OBJECTIVE 6.4 Describe the development of the structures and function of the brain.

1. *When do the hemispheres become lateralized and specialized?*
   Some amount of lateralization and specialization is prespecified, meaning that it occurs prenatally and is present from birth, as evidenced by newborn babies having the tendency, when lying on their backs, to turn their heads preferentially either to the right or left. But much of lateralization and specialization seems to rely on receiving input from experiences. As result, lateralization of different functions occurs at different ages. Face processing, for example, is in place by 4 or 5 months of age. For language, specialization seems to occur earlier, by 2 to 3 months after birth.

2. *What are the different theories that attempt to explain the development of hemispheric specialization?*
   There are a number of different theories for explaining the development of hemispheric specialization, all based on the idea that at birth there is an inherent inequality or bias in hemispheres that disposes them to the exhibited lateralization and specialization. These theories suggest that we are set up at birth for processing language in the left hemisphere and for functions such as face and spatial processing in the right hemisphere. The biased gene model suggests that lateralization of the brain and its functions are due to bias set up in the hemispheres by our genes. The biased brain model proposes that there are neuroanatomical differences between the hemispheres at birth, which then bias the type of information each hemisphere processes. Finally, the biased head model suggests that the tendency of infants to shift their heads to one side biases the range of stimulation each hemisphere receives and consequently the type of processing each hemisphere can do.

3. *What are the two possible accounts for the development of the cortical functional divisions?*
   Two possibilities have been proposed to account for the development of divisions in cortical functionality. The first proposal is that development occurs on the basis of a protomap. This idea suggests that the cortex is intrinsically structured as distinct areas such that each area has specific features that are appropriate for mapping onto it the particular input it will receive and the functions it will be required to serve. This would seem to suggest that definitions of the cortical areas do not rely on sensory input, but instead are already there based on intrinsic

factors. The second proposal suggests that the cortical divisions spring from an undifferentiated protocortex. This idea proposes that differentiation of cortical areas occurs as a response to external factors such as input from other areas of the brain and from the outside world through the sensory systems. Thus, the specification of cortical functions is affected by the experiential input provided. The reality is likely somewhere between these two proposals, with some initial and intrinsic (without external input) specification of the cortical area distinctions. But, these distinctions are poorly defined with much overlap, requiring experience and extrinsic input to help further define the cortical areas.

4. *What is the developmental timeline for the four cortical divisions?*
With the varied initial states of maturity and differentiation of the different areas at birth, and the changes in the type of inputs that experiences at different ages can provide, there is a resulting differential development of the different cortical areas. For example, the visual cortex shows earlier timing of reaching developmental landmarks such as peak synaptic density than does the frontal cortex. Soon after birth, the occipital lobe shows significant development, with synaptic density reaching its peak very early. Activity in response to certain aspects of visual information, such as orientation, motion, and colour, is evident at 6 to 8 weeks of age, with full functionality by 3 months of age. The actual age of onset for processing the different types of visual information differs, with motion showing a later onset than orientation or colour. This differential onset of neural sensitivity to the various visual features suggests that there is differential development of the ventral and dorsal pathways emanating from visual cortex. The development of ventral stream processing is therefore thought to precede dorsal stream processing, which has a protracted course of development. The parietal lobe is the next cortical division to mature. Though there is a slight increase in activity by 4 weeks of age, substantial increases in activity indicating maturation do not occur until approximately 3 months of age, with full functionality likely not before 6 months. Though this timeline is consistent for certain parietal functions, such as the planning of eye movements, other functions show a much more protracted development. As part of the dorsal pathway, this is to be expected. The capacity for mental rotation, for example, does not seem to reach full functionality in the parietal lobe until between 8 and 12 years of age. A similar pattern is seen for memory functioning, with functional development not being achieved until 10 to 12 years of age, with continued development into adolescence.

The temporal lobe seems to show much the same pattern of development as the parietal lobe, with some functions developing early and others showing a more protracted development time course. Object perception seems to show functional development by 6 months of age. Face perception exhibits early functioning in the temporal lobe by 3 months of age, with continuing development throughout the first year of life and further specialization of face processing areas reaching into middle childhood. The language function of the temporal lobe shows some development at 3 months of age with activation to speech sounds, but no responses to speech until about 6 months and continued strengthening through the first year. Finally, the functioning of the temporal lobe in association with long-term memory shows significant development during the first 2 years of life, with continued improvement through the preschool years.

The frontal lobe, which is involved in much of higher-order cognition, shows the most protracted developmental trend. Though the prefrontal cortex, which plays a role in the functional emergence of working memory, shows significant maturation between 5 and 12 months of age, it continues to show development through the preschool and early school years. Development of the prefrontal cortex seems to peak around 7 to 8 years of age, after which it levels off. But, it does not reach adult levels of functionality until adolescence. Another function of the frontal lobe, executive function, shows an even more protracted developmental timeline. Functioning of the frontal lobe on executive function tasks only shows meaningful development by 3 to

6 years of age. Adult-like functioning is not seen until about 8 to 11 years of age, with continued development and more consistent functioning not evident until adulthood.

Because cortical areas, from visual to temporal and parietal to frontal, show ever-increasing protracted timelines in structure and function, this seems to indicate that experience and learning are important factors for their full development.

5. *What are the experience-expectant and experience-dependent mechanisms of synaptogenesis and brain plasticity?*
Experience-expectant mechanisms of synaptogenesis and brain plasticity are those in which experiences that are typical or expected for that species influence which synapses are formed, maintained, and pruned. These experiences are expected because through evolutionary mechanisms, previous generations received particular stimulation that resulted in their brains evolving down through the generations to process that stimulation. Those particular experiences then become expected and necessary for typical development to proceed. Given those expected experiences, all members of that species will develop similar brain capacities. In contrast, experience-expectant mechanisms are engaged in the synaptogenesis and brain plasticity across a species as a result of unique experiences for the individual member. Each one of us, as we grow and mature, has experiences that are unique in some way to us that are not experienced at all or not experienced in the same way by others. These unique experiences then strengthen the synapses and areas in our brain that process that experience and weaken those that do not process the information contained in that unique experience. In other words, this type of plasticity follows the "use it or lose it" principle and, consequently, is responsible for the individual differences in brain and psychological development.

CHAPTER 7

SENSORY AND PERCEPTUAL DEVELOPMENT

Until not that long ago, it was believed that babies were blind at birth. But a curious psychologist refuted that notion with a simple experiment in the early 1980s.

Andrew Meltzoff and his colleagues observed 40 newborns under three days old to see whether they could imitate two facial gestures: tongue protrusion, and mouth opening. When Meltzoff stuck his tongue out at the youngest of the babies, just 42 minutes old, he was astounded to see a tongue sticking back at him. The researchers reported that the experiment could weed out random oral movements and confirm true imitation.

Today, researchers still use simple observation to discover how babies can sense and perceive their world, but they have additional sophisticated techniques to help reveal that babies have far more sensory and perceptual abilities than we ever thought. At the Laboratory for Developmental Studies at Harvard University's Department of Psychology, a team of researchers, led by Elizabeth Spelke, places sensor nets with electrodes over babies' scalps to measure their brains' electrical activity and nerve signals sent to muscles. Devices record a baby's sucking to indicate their excitement level and infrared laser beams measure blood flow in the brain.

Among the Harvard findings are that six-month-olds can see a ball rolling and know that it will keep doing so, and can expect a ball to pop out the other side of a screen when it rolls behind it. They can also do baby math, staring longer—and thus seeming to be more perplexed or bothered—at a screen showing 4 dots plus 4 dots equals 16 than when they correctly equal 8.

What about babies' sense of hearing and ability to process sounds? A colleague of Spelke's, Katherine Kinzler, found that babies' understanding of language can be quite sophisticated. "Five-month-old babies will look longer at somebody who spoke to them in their language. Older infants want to accept a toy from someone who has spoken their language," she says.

In this chapter we look at the fascinating process of children learning to use their senses to make sense of their environment.

Source: Meltzoff, Andrew, and Moore, M. Keith, "Newborn infants imitate adult facial gestures," *Child Development*, *53*, 1983, pp. 702–209.

Highfield, Roger, "Harvard's baby brain research lab," *The Telegraph*, April 30, 2008.

Learning Objective 7.1

Explain the issues for understanding perceptual development.

Sensation The experience resulting from the stimulation of a sense organ.

Perception The interpretation of sensory stimulation based on experience.

Attention The selection of particular sensory input for perceptual and cognitive processing and the exclusion of competing input.

ISSUES IN THE STUDY OF PERCEPTUAL DEVELOPMENT

To talk about perceptual development, we must first distinguish among three processes: sensation, perception, and attention. **Sensation** refers to the detection and discrimination of sensory information—for example, hearing and distinguishing high and low tones. **Perception** refers to the interpretation of sensations and includes recognition ("I've heard that song before") and identification ("That was thunder"). **Attention** refers to the selectivity of perception, as when a child fails to hear his parent calling because he is watching television.

Whether the focus is on sensation, perception, or attention, research on perceptual development addresses the same two general questions that underlie all research in child psychology: what are the most important changes that occur across the course of development, and how can we explain these changes? As we will see, answering the first question requires that we begin our examination very early in life. All of the sensory systems are operative from birth, and all achieve close to adult-level functioning by the end of infancy. It is for this reason that most of this chapter concentrates on the infant period. Infancy, in the words of Bornstein and Arterberry (1999), is where "most of the 'action'... takes place" (p. 244).

The question of how to explain perceptual development is a particular form of the nature versus nurture issue. The empiricist or nurture position views the child as beginning life with only minimal ability to take in and make sense of sensory information. The emphasis, rather, is on the role of experience in perceptual development. According to this view, a child builds perceptual impressions through associations. For example, a baby seeing a face for the first time sees no relation among the eyes, eyebrows, nose, mouth, ears, and hairline. It is only through experience that the baby comes to see all of these elements as belonging together and can eventually recognize a familiar face or distinguish one face from another.

Links to Related Material

In Chapter 1, you learned about the nature versus nurture debate regarding development. Here, you learn how this debate is related to explaining perceptual development.

Through experience, according to the empiricist position, babies also learn to connect sights with sounds, touch with vision, and so on. The sound of a human voice seems at first no more likely to accompany the sight of a face than does the sound of a horn. Only experience makes the combination of face and voice more natural than that of face and horn.

As we will see, a strong version of the environmental/learning view of infant perception is not tenable. Nevertheless, modern research makes it clear that experience does contribute to perceptual development, and it does so from very early in life. Research on the central nervous system illustrates how experience can affect even single sensory cells—both their survival and the connections that form among them. Experience produces a kind of Darwinian survival-of-the-fittest battle among brain cells (Edelman, 2003; Seth & Baars, 2005). As we noted in Chapter 6, many of the neurons we are born with die early in life. Researchers believe that visual experience activates some cells, which survive, but that other cells are not activated, and these die or their synapses are consequently trimmed back (Markham & Greenough, 2004).

For Thought and Discussion

Is this plasticity of perceptual abilities due to experience-expectant or experience-dependent mechanisms?

For example, each cell (neuron) in the occipital cortex or visual area of the brain is stimulated by one type of visual element, such as vertical edges, but not by other elements, such as horizontal edges. Other brain cells respond to horizontal edges, but are insensitive to vertical edges. Still other cells "like" angles, or diagonal lines, or the ends of lines, or other visual elements. Researchers believe that when a stimulus repeatedly activates combinations of such cells—as when a baby looks at a square—the connections among these cells grow stronger (Singer, 2007). Eventually, the cells fire in synchrony and a person sees a whole square rather than a combination of lines and intersections (Hebb, 1949). The important point here is that these cells are sensitive to experience at a very early age (Knudsen, 2004).

Other theorists believe (with, as we will see, a good deal of empirical support) that the biological contribution to perceptual development is considerably greater than the environmental/learning position allows (Spelke & Kinzler, 2007). Such theorists emphasize the natural equipment that animals and humans have evolved for gathering information from their world, equipment that is either present from the start of life or that emerges in the course of biological maturation.

A particularly influential position in this regard is the theory developed by James and Eleanor Gibson (Gibson, 1966; Gibson, 1969; Gibson & Pick, 2000). The Gibsons do not believe that perception involves combining pieces of input through experience, as in the traditional learning view. Instead, they argue that objects in the world give off physical energy that is already organized and can be perceived in its entirety. Perceptual development, they suggest, consists of a child's increasing sensitivity to the organization of this energy and to which properties of objects and people remain stable and which properties change.

In general, theorists such as the Gibsons assume that natural relations exist between the senses. For example, the Gibsonian analysis suggests that even infants should be sensitive to the synchrony of visual and auditory events, and this appears to be the case. When young babies watch people speak, they can detect when speakers' lip movements are not synchronized with the sounds that they hear (Bahrick, Hernandez-Reif, & Flom, 2005). (We discuss this research more fully later.) This ability is difficult to account for by traditional learning theories, which emphasize the need for certain sound–vision experiences. Such experiences are fairly limited for very young infants. Note that theorists generally assume that the earlier in development a perceptual skill emerges, the less likely it is that it has been acquired by experience.

Although the Gibsonian approach stresses the biological basis for perceptual development, the emphasis is not solely on nature. As the title of one of Eleanor Gibson's major works—*Principles of Perceptual Learning* (1969)—indicates, nurture plays an important role as well. With experience, infants and children become increasingly skilled at detecting the information available in sensory stimulation and thus at perceiving the world accurately. The approach is therefore definitely interactionist—as, indeed, are all contemporary approaches to the study of perceptual development.

For Thought and Discussion

Why is it important to distinguish between behaviours that mainly result from nurture and those that mainly result from nature?

The other two general issues introduced in Chapter 1 are also represented in research on perceptual development. Although departures from the norm (for example, visual or auditory impairments) can certainly be of great pragmatic importance, most work on perceptual development is toward the normative end of the normative–idiographic continuum. The developments of interest (for example, perception of depth, perception of size constancy) are not ones that typically show important individual differences; rather, these are basic accomplishments demonstrated by virtually every member of the species. The focus, then, is on when and how they emerge in almost all children, not on individual differences among children.

The normative emphasis of most work on perceptual development sets the form taken by the third general issue: continuity–discontinuity. Because individual differences are seldom a focus of research, relatively few studies have examined the stability or predictability of individual differences over time (we will see some exceptions to this statement in Chapter 10). Instead, the challenge (still far from fully met, as we will see) has been to trace the gradual evolution of particular perceptual competencies as the child develops. For example, how—that is, through what phases and what processes—does a rudimentary form of size constancy present early in infancy evolve into the mature constancy of the older child or adult?

A baby's ability to perceive interesting objects, such as Dad's face, is a result of both nature and nurture. (© *Cultura Creative/Alamy*)

We will see these points frequently illustrated as we discuss major findings from the study of perceptual development. In what follows, we first examine the capacities that babies have for learning about the objects and people in their world and how these capacities develop. After we consider the perceptual modes (vision, touch, and so on) separately, we see how children coordinate information from these modes. We then discuss how the child integrates perception and attention with action in the smooth flow of behaviour.

LEARNING OBJECTIVE 7.1

Explain the issues for understanding perceptual development.

1. What is the difference between sensation, perception, and attention?
2. How do environmental/learning theories explain perceptual development?
3. What is the Gibsonian explanation of perceptual development?
4. How does the continuity–discontinuity issue of development relate to perceptual development?

Learning Objective 7.2

Outline the development of the basic sensory capacities such as touch, smell, taste, and vestibular sensitivity.

TOUCH AND PAIN, SMELL AND TASTE, MOTION AND BALANCE

Now we turn to an examination of what young babies actually perceive. We have much less information about the sensory modes of touch, smell, taste, and body balance and motion than about hearing or vision. Nevertheless, these sensory capacities are vitally important to the survival of young organisms. In most animals, these capacities develop earlier than hearing and vision, and so we consider them first.

TOUCH AND PAIN

Anyone who wonders whether the newborn baby senses touch or experiences pain should watch the baby's reaction to a heel prick for a blood sample or to circumcision (Shah & Ohlsson, 2007). The angry cry that follows the prick of the needle is a clear sign that the baby can feel pain, as are the physiological changes—for example, changes in blood cortisol level—that follow a medical procedure such as circumcision (Gunnar et al., 1985). Furthermore, the effects of early exposure to pain are not necessarily short-lived, with research at the University of British Columbia demonstrating possible long-term consequences, including possible effects on brain development (Grunau, Holsti, & Peters, 2006). That is, because the newborns' neurons are still in such an early stage of development, any insult such as exposure to pain results in damage to the development of those neurons (Anand & Scalzo, 2000). These neuronal changes have behavioural consequences, including potential increases in the incidence of ADHD (attention deficit and hyperactivity disorder) and increases in sensitivity to pain. For example, newborns who receive repeated needle pricks as part of a screening test for diabetes react more strongly to subsequent blood tests than do other newborns (Taddio et al., 2002). Male babies who are circumcised without anaesthesia are more sensitive during vaccinations four to six months later (Taddio et al., 1997).

For years, standard medical practice was to perform neonatal surgical procedures without anaesthesia, both because of doubts about whether newborns experience pain and because of concerns about the safety of anaesthesia for the tiny neonate. Fortunately, advances in knowledge about the newborn period have spurred the search for effective forms of pain relief for this age group (Zempsky & Cravero, 2004).

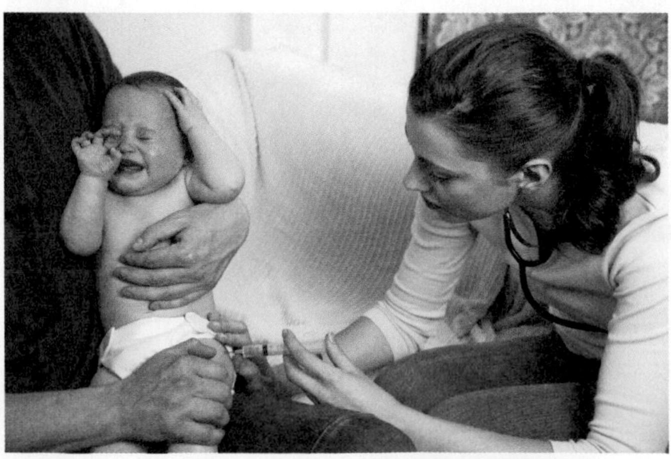

The angry cry in response to the prick of a needle is an indication that babies can feel pain. (*Emma Innocenti/The Image Bank/Getty Images*)

Newborn babies also show touch reflexes, such as those described in Chapter 5. In fact, the fetus displays the first sign of sensitivity to external stimulation through reactions to touch. As early as the second month following conception, the fetus responds to stroking at the side of the mouth. Touch sensitivity increases over the first several days of life (Haith, 1986).

Touching is important for relations between children and adults. A hand placed on the newborn's chest can quiet a crying episode, and gentle stroking can soothe even premature babies

FOCUS ON RESEARCH 7.1
MEASURING PAIN IN YOUNG CHILDREN FROM FACIAL BEHAVIOUR

Assessing pain is an important component of medical intervention. To develop less painful medical procedures for people or to reduce pain associated with disease, health professionals need to know the levels of pain people are experiencing.

In older children and adults, pain is usually assessed by verbal self-reports. For example, patients may be asked to rate their pain on a 10-point scale. Such ratings are part of the information used by medical staff to administer the right amount of pain reliever to their patients. However, this technique does not work with young children and children who are developmentally delayed because of their limited cognitive and verbal abilities. To overcome this problem, Canadian researchers at Dalhousie University and the University of British Columbia (Chambers, Cassidy, McGrath, Gilbert, & Craig, 1996) developed the Child Facial Coding System. This system describes 13 facial actions that account for both gross and subtle movements observed in the preschooler's facial pain displays. Pain expressions are described in terms of combinations of these action units. The appearance changes produced by some of these action units are indicated in Table 7.1.

Figure 7.1 shows a pictorial representation of a face with persistent pain. The facial pattern is quite complex, and includes the lowering of the brows, the squeezing of the eyes, the deepening of the nasolabial furrow, the raising of the cheek, the opening of the mouth, and the stretching of the mouth in a horizontal direction. The Child Facial Coding System has been found to be useful in assessing acute pain as well as persistent pain, and has been applied to a variety of medical procedures, including immunization, venipuncture, and finger lancing.

TABLE 7.1 SOME ACTION UNITS THAT MAY BE PART OF PAIN EXPRESSIONS

Facial Action	Description of Appearance Changes
Brow lower	Eyebrows are lowered and pulled together
Eye squeeze	Eyelids are tensed and there is a bulging in the lower eyelid
Eye squint	Eye opening is narrowed, eyelids appear tense, and there is bagging of the lower eyelid
Nasolabial furrow	The line adjacent to the nostril is deepened and pulled upward
Nose wrinkle	Skin around the nose is drawn upward and horizontal puckers appear across the nose
Cheek raise	Cheeks are raised toward the eyes and bulging appears under the eyes
Horizontal mouth stretch	Lips, lip corners, and surrounding skin are stretched laterally
Vertical mouth stretch	Lips are parted and jaw is lowered

Source: Adapted from "Postoperative pain expression in preschool children: Validation of the Child Facial Coding System" by C. A. Gilbert, C. M. Lilley, K. D. Craig, P. J. McGrath, C. A. Court, S. M. Bennett, & C. J. Montgomery (*Clinical Journal of Pain, 15*, 1999, p. 192–200). Copyright 1999 by Lippincott, Williams, & Wilkins, Inc. Adapted by permission.

FIGURE 7.1

Pictorial representation of a face with persistent pain. *Source: From "Postoperative pain expression in preschool children: Validation of the Child Facial Coding System" by C. A. Gilbert, C. M. Lilley, K. D. Craig, P. J. McGrath, C. A. Court, S. M. Bennett, and C. J. Montgomery* (Clinical Journal of Pain, *15, 1999, p. 192–200). Copyright 1999 by Lippincott, Williams, & Wilkins, Inc. Reproduced by permission.*

(Oehler & Eckerman, 1988). For older infants, touching increases positive emotion and visual attention during interactions between infant and caregiver (Stack & Muir, 1992). It is interesting to note that parents can usually recognize their infant by touch alone within the first few days of life (Kaitz et al., 1993).

Haptic perception The perceptual experience that results from active exploration of objects by touch.

Psychologists refer to the active, exploratory use of touch as **haptic perception**. Even neonates have some ability to acquire information about objects through touch, as shown by the fact that they habituate when the same object is placed repeatedly in their hand and dishabituate when the shape of the object is changed (Streri & Féron, 2005). With age, infants assume an increasingly active role in acquiring information through touch, and they become increasingly skilled in

FIGURE 7.2

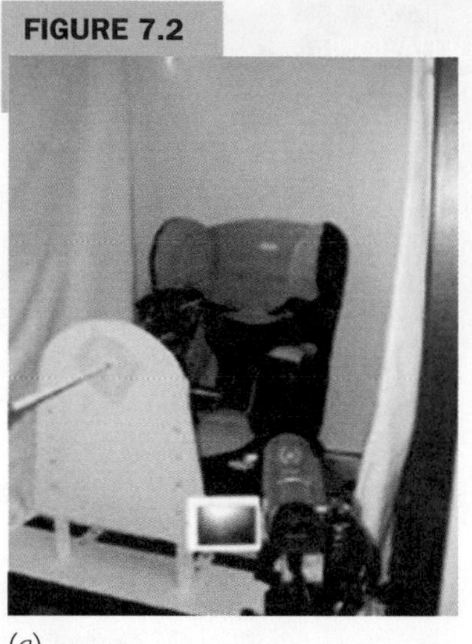

(a)

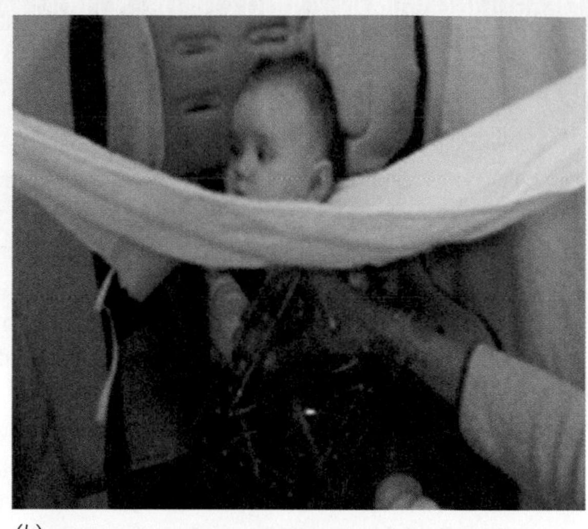

(b)

The experimental setup used to determine infants' haptic preference for orientation of an object without any visual information. Here the object is a rod, which is shown in the vertical orientation. *From Kerzerho, S., Gentaz, E., and Streri, A. (2009). "Factors influencing manual discrimination of orientations in 5-month-old infants," (Figure 1).* Perception, *38, 44–51. London: Pion Ltd. London.*

FIGURE 7.3

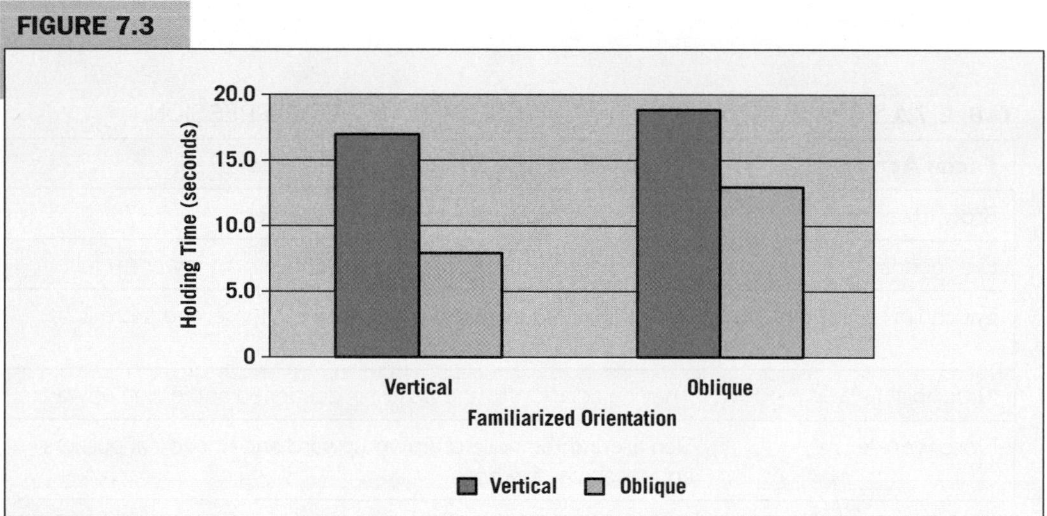

Test Orientation. Five-month-old infants were familiarized by touch to a rod in either a vertical or oblique orientation, and then tested with both of these orientations. Results indicate that regardless of which orientation infants were familiarized to, they always preferred to hold a rod in the vertical orientation. *Adapted from Kerzerho, S., Gentaz, E., and Streri, A. (2009). "Factors influencing manual discrimination of orientations in 5-month-old infants," (Table 1).* Perception, *38, 48. London: Pion Ltd. London.*

doing so. By the end of the first year of life, infants can recognize a familiar object by exploration with the hand alone (Rose, Gottfried, & Bridger, 1981). Infants can also use touch to discriminate features of those objects. See Figure 7.2 for an example of the setup for assessing infants' haptic perception. For example, infants exhibit a haptic preference for objects oriented vertically rather than those oriented on a slant, most likely due to the reaction, including that of the hand, to gravity (Kerzerho, Gentaz, & Streri, 2009; see Figure 7.3). Haptic perception continues to improve, as Barbara Morrongiello of the University of Guelph and her collaborators report, throughout the childhood years (Morrongiello et al., 1994b).

SMELL AND TASTE

When can babies smell odours? How might we be able to tell? Researchers have explored these questions by observing whether babies make a face, turn their heads, or do nothing at all when presented with a smell. Even newborns turn their heads away from a cotton swab that smells bad (Rieser, Yonas, & Wikner, 1976). Babies produce positive facial expressions in response to banana, strawberry, and vanilla smells, and negative expressions in response to smells of rotten eggs and fish (Crook, 1979; Steiner, 1979). Furthermore, newborn infants can differentiate and prefer human milk over formula (Marlier & Schaal, 2005). Sensitivity to odours may even be evident prenatally, as exposure to certain odours as a fetus may affect behaviour after birth (Beauchamp & Menella,

2009). Thus, the newborn's sense of smell is keen, and it improves over the first few days of life (Lipsitt, Engen, & Kaye, 1963).

The infant uses this ability as early as the first week of life to distinguish the mother's smell. Three-day-old infants orient more toward a pad moistened with the mother's amniotic fluid than to a pad moistened with the fluid of another woman (Marlier, Schaal, & Soussingham, 1998). Six-day-olds turn more frequently toward the mother's breast pad than toward the pad of another woman (MacFarlane, 1975). In fact, the capacity to recognize their mother's odour is likely evident even prenatally (Porter, Raimbault, Henrot, & Saliba, 2008). Parents make use of olfactory cues as well. As with the sense of touch, parents can recognize their infant from smell alone within the first few days of life (Porter, Balogh, & Makin, 1988).

Babies are also sensitive to taste at birth, and likely before. As the fluid that a baby sucks is sweetened, the baby sucks harder, consumes more, and tends to quiet faster from crying episodes (Blass & Camp, 2003; Blass & Smith, 1992). The type of formula, namely, bitter or sweet, that babies were exposed to prior to starting on solid foods affected their subsequent preferences for and how much they ate of similarly flavoured cereals (Menella, Forestell, Morgan, & Beauchamp, 2009). Even neonates who are born preterm prefer a sweetened solution, a finding that demonstrates that the relevant taste receptors are functioning before the normal term for birth (Smith & Blass, 1996). Additional support for the functioning of taste receptors before birth comes from evidence that exposure to flavours prenatally will affect taste preferences after birth (Mennella et al., 2001).

As illustrated in Figure 7.4, newborn babies can distinguish among different tastes. At 2 hours of age, babies make different facial expressions when they taste sweet and non-sweet solutions, and they also differentiate sour, bitter, and salty tastes (Rosenstein & Oster, 1997). At around 4 months of age, they begin to prefer salty tastes, which they found aversive as newborns (Beauchamp et al., 1994). These reactions to tastes are thought to be fundamentally controlled by the brainstem (Berridge, 2000)—the more evolutionarily primitive part of the brain. Thus, infants' reactions and differentiation of tastes may reflect primitive, innate sensitivities that were evolutionarily programmed to support survival. However, these innate taste preferences might be alterable by early exposure, prenatally and postnatally, to particular flavours (Faith, 2010).

The fact that newborns reject certain fluids and grimace in response to negative odours and tastes indicates that they come into the world with likes and dislikes. Within months, it can be a challenge to find the older infant's mouth with a spoon that contains something the infant has decided he dislikes just by looking at it.

FIGURE 7.4

(a) (b) (c)

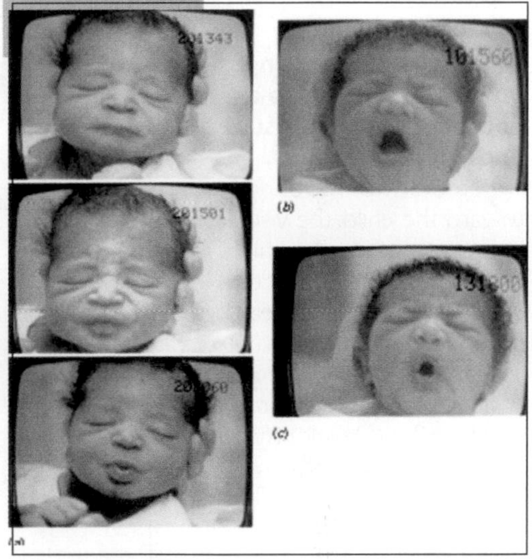

A newborn tasting (a) a sweet solution, (b) a bitter solution, and (c) a sour solution. *From "Differential Facial Responses to Four Basic Tastes in Newborns" by D. Rosenstein and H. Oster* (Child Development, *59, 1988, P. 1561–1563). Copyright © 1988 by the Society for Research in Child Development, Inc. Reprinted by permission.*

VESTIBULAR SENSITIVITY

Vestibular sensitivity refers to our ability to detect gravity and the motion of our bodies, which helps us maintain body posture. In adults, disturbance of the vestibular sense causes dizziness and an inability to remain standing in the dark.

Vestibular sensitivity The perceptual experience that results from motion of the body and the pull of gravity.

Newborns are sensitive to vestibular stimulation along all three axes of motion—front to back, up and down, and side to side (Reisman, 1987). The soothing properties of rocking and jiggling for crying babies clearly demonstrate this sensitivity. Postural adjustments can also affect a baby's alertness. For instance, babies are often more alert when in a vertical than when in a horizontal position (Korner & Thoman, 1970).

Posture and balance are not ends in themselves; rather, they are necessary for allowing the infant to look around, manipulate objects, and even locomote (Adolph & Berger, 2006). For example, the development trends in infants' capacity to reach and grasp accurately for objects rely on the development of the capacity to balance themselves and maintain their posture (Gibson & Pick, 2000; Spencer et al., 2000). Thus, the development in vestibular sensitivity and posture are a necessary scaffold for the development of motor skills.

Several investigators have examined the relation between vestibular and visual perception in providing the infant with a sense of self-motion. Visual cues and vestibular cues are usually consistent in telling us whether we are moving or stationary. However, sometimes conflict between these cues produces confusing effects, with visual cues usually winning out, at least initially. For example, if you are seated in a stopped train next to another stopped train, and then the other train begins to move forward, it may seem to you that your train is moving backward.

Figure 7.5 shows an apparatus used to test the relation between visual and vestibular cues in infancy. Infants who have begun to walk (typically when they are a year to a year and a half old) are placed in a room with walls that can move as the floor remains stationary. When the front and side walls move, visual cues tell the infant that she is moving forward, but vestibular cues indicate she is not moving at all. Apparently the visual cues win out, as babies often fall backward in this situation (Lee & Aronson, 1974). A similar phenomenon occurs in babies who are old enough to only sit up (Bertenthal & Bai, 1989). Indeed, even newborns show some adjustment of their heads in response to visual cues that signal movement (Bertenthal & Clifton, 1998).

FIGURE 7.5

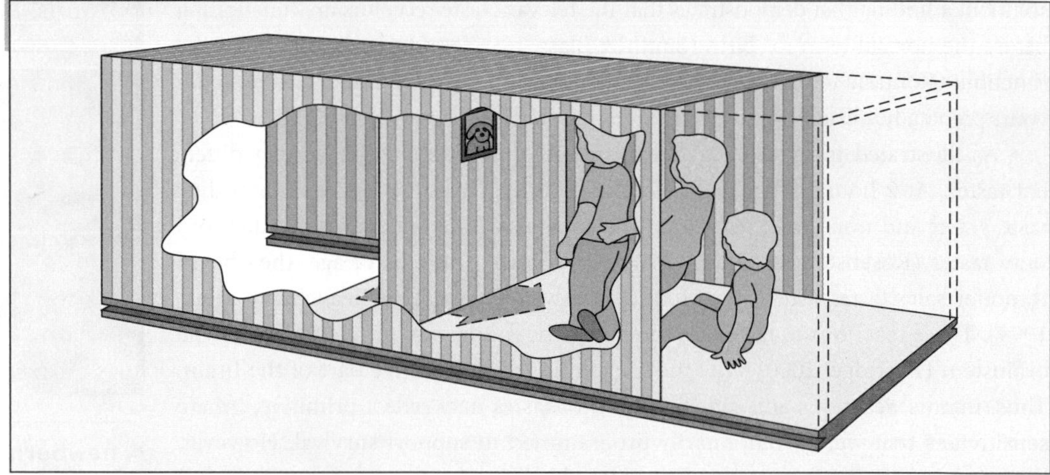

Apparatus for testing infants' response to a conflict between visual and vestibular cues. When the wall moves toward the child, the visual cues suggest that the child is swaying forward, and the child compensates by leaning back. *From "Infants' Sensitivity to Optical Flow for Controlling Posture" by B. I. Bertenthal and D. L. Bai* (Developmental Psychology, *25, 1989, p. 939). Copyright © 1989 by the American Psychological Association.*

LEARNING OBJECTIVE 7.2

Outline the development of the basic sensory capacities such as touch, smell, taste, and vestibular sensitivity.

1. What is infants' sensitivity to pain and what is the effect of early pain exposure?
2. How early do infants show a sensitivity to touch and how does this sensitivity develop?
3. In what ways does touch have social and perceptual consequences for infants?
4. What odours and tastes do infants prefer and how soon do these preferences develop?
5. What is a newborn's sensitivity to vestibular stimulation and what is its effect on infants?
6. What is the relation between vestibular sensitivity, such as posture, and the development of motor skills?
7. What is the relation between vestibular and visual cues in providing infants with a sense of self-motion?

Learning Objective 7.3

Describe the development of infants' sensitivity to auditory information.

HEARING

Hearing is one of our most important senses; a great deal of information about the world comes to us from sounds alone. Cars approaching from behind, a ringing phone, music from a computer or MP3 player, and, most important, human speech—all are perceived through the sense of hearing.

How do we know that a newborn baby can hear? As with smell and taste, we can exploit babies' naturally occurring responses to changes in stimulation. The baby may tighten his eyelids, for example, in response to a sound, turn his head and eyes toward the source of the sound, or perhaps become quiet. Changes in the baby's heart rate and breathing also occur in response to sounds (Aslin, Pisoni, & Jusczyk, 1983; Groome et al., 1999).

Imagine that we are interested not just in whether babies can detect sounds, but also in their ability to discriminate among different sounds. Here, the habituation–dishabituation procedure described in Chapter 1 can be especially informative. We might first present a particular sound (sound A) repeatedly until the baby habituates to it; that is, no longer shows much (if any) response. Then, we present sound B. If the baby dishabituates in response to this change in stimulus, then we have good evidence that she can hear the difference between A and B.

The habituation technique is a general methodology that can be applied to any of the sensory modes. It provided the basis for several of the conclusions about touch and smell summarized in the preceding section. As we will see, it has also been important in the study of vision.

PRENATAL HEARING

Even the fetus can hear. Electrical recordings of brain responses demonstrate sound reception in fetuses as early as the 25th week after conception, about 3.5 months before full-term birth (Lecanuet, 1998; Sheridan, Draganova, Ware, Murphy, Govindan, Siegel, Eswaran, & Preissl, 2010). These findings indicate that fetuses receive sound impulses. But how do they respond to sounds?

Two investigators used ultrasound imaging to answer this question. (Ultrasound techniques, as mentioned in Chapter 4, create a picture of the fetus.) The images showed that although fetuses did not respond to auditory stimuli before 24 weeks after conception, after 28 weeks, virtually all fetuses clamped their eyelids in response to sound. All the fetuses who did not respond (1 to 2 percent) were born with hearing deficits or serious impairments (Birnholz & Benacerraf, 1983).

But, we might ask, how good is the sound quality available to the fetus? One curious mother decided to answer this question by swallowing a microphone (she "drank the microphone," as she described it) and recording her own voice and other sounds. Although the stomach recording was muffled, various sounds could be discerned (Fukahara, Shimura, & Yamanouchi, 1988). As we might expect, the mother's speech was more audible than were sounds originating from outside, a finding that has emerged in other studies as well (Richards et al., 1992).

If some aspects of maternal speech are perceptible in the womb, might babies be affected by what they hear prenatally? A fascinating program of research by DeCasper, Fifer, and associates (DeCasper & Fifer, 1980; DeCasper & Spence, 1986; Fifer & Moon, 1995) suggests that the answer is yes. The initial study in the series (DeCasper & Fifer, 1980) reported a surprising finding: babies less than 4 days old could discriminate their mothers' voices from strangers' voices (discrimination was shown by the fact that the babies altered their sucking rhythms more readily when their own mother's voice served as a reinforcer than they did when the reinforcer was the voice of a stranger).

One possible explanation for such early discrimination and preference for the mother is that the babies had become familiar with their mothers' voices in the womb (DeCasper et al., 1994). If this explanation is correct, we would expect no early preference for the father's voice, despite the fact that babies often hear the father in the days following birth. This, in fact, is the case: 4-day-old babies show no preference for their father's voice over that of a male stranger (DeCasper & Prescott, 1984).

The case for familiarity coming from fetal experience would be strengthened further if the infant could recognize a particular event that was only experienced before birth. DeCasper and Spence (1986) asked pregnant women to read aloud one of three stories each day in the last six weeks of pregnancy. When tested at 3 days of age, their babies showed a preference for the familiar story over a new story, whether it was the mother's voice reading the story or that of a stranger. This finding demonstrates a clear effect of prenatal experience, and it tells us as well that the fetus can become familiar not only with the mother's voice, but also with some of the specific sound patterns that the mother produces.

Indeed, Barbara Kisilevsky of Queen's University and her associates (Kisilevsky et al., 2003) report that the fetus may even show signs of recognizing the mother's voice. Examining 60 term fetuses, these researchers found heart rate increases in response to a recording of the mother's voice, but not to a similar recording of a stranger's voice. Furthermore, in a study of 104 fetuses, the Kisilevsky group showed that not only does heart rate show evidence of a discrimination between the mother's and a female stranger's voice, but also shows a discrimination between the mother's and father's voices (Kisilevsky et al., 2009).

Other research suggests that fetuses may also pick up more general aspects of their own native languages. Newborn French babies can discriminate a woman speaking French from the same woman speaking Russian; babies of non-French-speaking mothers, however, do not make this discrimination (Mehler et al., 1988). Finally, another study from the DeCasper group (DeCasper et al., 1994) reports heart rate change in response to a familiar passage in third trimester fetuses—and thus provides evidence of the effects of auditory experience even prior to birth.

Research on prenatal hearing and learning is an ongoing enterprise, and most investigators are cautious in drawing conclusions. Nevertheless, it seems clear that fetuses can hear more than was once believed. However, research has recently shown that the ability of the fetus to process and recognize its mother's voice is attenuated by conditions that delay maturation of the fetus' auditory system, such as maternal hypertension (Lee et al., 2007) or smoking (Key et al., 2007). This suggests that the effect of prenatal exposure to sounds is related to the relative development of the central nervous system.

Links to Related Material

In Chapter 4, you learned about the detrimental effects of exposure to smoke and nicotine on the development of the fetus.

SENSITIVITY TO SOUND

Newborn babies appear to be less sensitive to sound than are adults (Aslin & Hunt, 2001). An adult, for example, can easily hear a whisper at a distance of about 1.4 metres (4.5 feet); a newborn, however, requires a stimulus closer to normal conversational level to be able to hear at that distance. Fluid in the middle ear may be part of the problem.

How well a sound can be heard depends on its pitch. Adults can hear sounds of intermediate pitch better than sounds of high or low pitch. According to a study by Sandra Trehub, of the University of Toronto, and her collaborators (1983), newborn babies hear relatively better at low frequencies, but by 6 months of age their high-frequency sensitivity is as good as that of adults (see also Werner & Bargones, 1992). Sensitivity to sound increases until around 10 years of age. Sensitivity to higher frequencies, however, peaks earlier and does not improve beyond about 4 or 5 years of age (Trehub et al., 1988).

These behavioural findings are mirrored by those from electrophysiological studies. Measures of infants' brainstem-evoked potentials have similarly indicated that infants initially show sensitivity at low frequencies (Abdala & Folsom, 1995; Kushnerenko et al., 2007). By 6 months of age, these measures show mature resolution sensitivity across the frequency range, including high frequencies. The parallel findings for frequency sensitivity exhibited by behavioural and electrophysiological measures suggest development is the result of the neural basis of auditory processing rather than maturation of the structures in the inner ear. Recent brain research at McMaster University provides support for the development of neural structures as key in the auditory processing of pitch. In particular, this research suggests that the shift in infant's sensitivity to pitch occurs in the 3 to 4 month age range due to the functional emergence of certain cortical mechanisms around this time (He & Trainor, 2009).

Sensitivity measurements determine how loud a sound must be for the infant to detect it (Saffran, Werker, & Werner, 2006). However, infants, as well as adults, are normally exposed to sounds that are much louder than this threshold level. For a full understanding of infants' hearing capacity, we must also know how well they can discriminate sounds that differ in various characteristics, such as intensity, frequency, and duration.

For Thought and Discussion

What kinds of sounds might you present to encourage an infant's development of auditory skills, and why?

DISCRIMINATING SOUNDS

Infants are able to distinguish differences in intensity, or loudness, at an early age. For example, after a 6-month-old becomes familiar with a sound approximately as loud as an ordinary conversation at a distance of about 1 metre (3 feet), a small increase in intensity produces a noticeable change in heart rate (Moffitt, 1973). Twelve-month-olds can detect even very slight shifts in intensity (Trehub & Schneider, 1983).

How well do infants distinguish among sound frequencies? Newborn infants' discrimination abilities are still immature, as they have been shown to distinguish a 20 percent difference, but not a 5 percent difference, in the frequency of a sound (Novitski et al, 2007). However, that they respond differently to sounds of different frequencies at all provides one kind of evidence of their ability to discriminate. In fact, low-frequency tones are generally effective in quieting babies, whereas higher tones tend to distress them (Eisenberg, 1976). By 5 months of age, infants are almost as good as adults at distinguishing among high-frequency tones that vary only slightly (Werner & Bargones, 1992).

Babies are better at discriminating complex sounds than we might suspect. Infants as young as 4 months are sensitive to various properties of music, such as contour and rhythm, and they (like most adults) prefer consonant musical inputs to dissonant ones (Trainor, Tsang, & Cheung, 2002; Zentner & Kagan, 1998). By the middle of the first year, babies can pick out melodies, even when the key changes (Trehub & Schellenberg, 1995) or the tempo changes (Trehub, 2000). Recent work at McMaster University suggests that the capacity to discriminate melodies on the basis of key changes is evident even earlier, in 2-month-olds (Plantinga & Trainor, 2009). This means that they can perceive the relations among the frequencies, even when the frequencies themselves change.

Babies can also tell the difference between a lullaby and an adult-directed song, even when the song and lullaby are from a foreign culture (Trehub & Henderson, 1994). Indeed, from birth, infants show a preference for lullaby-type input over adult songs (Masataka, 1999). There is no indication, however, that prenatal exposure to music enhances infants' musical sensitivity (Trehub, 2003). However, though the effects of postnatal music exposure on the sensitivity to culture-specific scales and harmonies of musical structure do not seemingly emerge until between 5 and 7 years of age (Trainor, 2005), effects on sensitivity to culture-specific rhythms seems to emerge much earlier, at 7 months of age (Gerry, Faux, & Trainor, 2010).

Links to Related Material

Newborn infants are particularly sensitive to speech sounds. In Chapter 11, we will learn about infants' ability to discriminate speech sounds at a very early age, as a foundation for the development in language acquisition.

Babies are especially sensitive to the characteristics of sound that will be important for language perception. Young infants prefer to listen to sounds that fall within the frequency range of the human voice, and they can distinguish different speech sounds from as early as 1 month of age (Aslin, Jusczyk, & Pisoni, 1998). We consider the issue of perception of speech more fully in Chapter 11.

SOUND LOCALIZATION

An important property of sounds is the direction from which they come. Even newborns distinguish very general sound location (Morrongiello et al., 1994a). They turn their eyes and heads toward a sound source to the left or right if the sound is relatively continuous. In one experiment, carried out in the delivery room by a scientist-parent, some evidence of ability to localize sounds was evident within 10 minutes of birth (Wertheimer, 1961).

Research indicates that the localization response disappears around the second month of life and reappears in a more vigorous form in the third or fourth month. When the response reemerges, it is faster and more skilled, suggesting that a different brain centre has taken control of this ability (Muir & Clifton, 1985). Localization is one of several behavioural systems that show such a U-shaped pattern of development in early infancy (Bever, 1982). Darwin Muir of Queen's University suggests that the basis for the U-shaped function for sound localization is neural maturation, in which early localization is reflexive and then comes under cortical control (Muir & Hains, 2004).

Over the first year and a half of life, babies make increasingly fine distinctions of auditory space (Ashmead et al., 1991; Morrongiello, 1988). To accomplish this feat, they must solve an interesting and very general problem for growing organisms, one of appropriate *recalibration*, or readjustment.

The problem is that accurate sound localization depends, in large part, on the detection of the time difference between when a sound arrives at the two ears. For example, a sound on the right produces energy that reaches the right ear before it reaches the left ear. With age, the head grows larger so that the distance between the two ears increases. Therefore, a sound that comes from the same off-centre location produces a greater time difference in an older child than in a younger child.

Because even newborns display some accuracy in locating sounds, babies must perform a recalibration to accommodate growth at an older age, continually adjusting the relation between sound cues and what these cues mean for the location of the sound-producing object (Clifton et al., 1988; Morrongiello et al., 1994a). The need for readjustment presents a general problem for babies in many action systems—eye movements, head movements, reaching, and walking, to name a few. And researchers still do not know how it happens.

LEARNING OBJECTIVE 7.3

Describe the development of infants' sensitivity to auditory information.

1. What sounds do fetuses hear and discriminate?
2. What effect does prenatal auditory experience have on infants after birth?
3. To which sounds are infants sensitive and how does this sensitivity develop?
4. What types of sounds do infants discriminate?
5. What is the nature of the development in infants' ability to localize sounds?

VISION

Learning Objective 7.4

Outline infants' capacity for processing visual information.

Take a moment to look around and appreciate the richness and complexity of your visual environment. You can see variations in brightness and colour and texture, and you can tell which surfaces are hard and which are soft. You can see dozens of objects and many items of function—light switches that can be flicked, containers that hold objects, shelves that contain books, chairs that support people. Vision provides an immense amount of information about the world, and you know how to easily interpret this information.

Now, consider what this world must look like to a newborn baby. First, can the newborn see? If so, how well? When the baby can see well enough to differentiate objects, how does he know that one object is in front of another, that an object can serve as a container, or even that the container—say, a cup—is separate from the table on which it rests? How does the baby know that a tree seen through a window is outside the room, rather than part of the glass? From this small sample of questions, you can see how much the baby must come to understand. In the past three decades, we have discovered a great deal about how this understanding develops. Here, we first consider two basic questions: how good is the newborn baby's vision, and how quickly does it improve?

SENSORY CAPABILITIES

We have known for some time that newborn babies can see something. New parents notice their baby often turns her head toward a source of light, such as a window. In the first days of life, awake babies also distinguish light intensity. They open their eyes widely in darkness and close them in bright light; typically, they choose to look at moderate light levels (Haith, 1980). Babies find visual movement especially attractive even at birth, and they become increasingly sensitive to movement over the first several months of life (Aslin & Shea, 1990; von Hofsten, Kellman, & Putaansuu, 1992).

How do we know what babies see? That is, what procedure can we use to determine what babies see? Determining what babies see is difficult because we cannot easily communicate with infants: they do not talk, so they cannot provide verbal responses; they cannot take instructions, because they do not understand verbal commands; and their motor control is underdeveloped (as we saw in Chapter 5), so they cannot make motor responses such as pressing a key on a keyboard.

However, researcher Robert Fantz observed that babies look at different things for different periods of time (Fantz, 1961). He suggested that we could measure the amount of time babies look at one display rather than at another to determine what babies can see and discriminate.

The procedure for measuring where babies look is straightforward. The researcher shows the baby two displays, side by side. With properly adjusted lighting, the researcher can see the reflection of these displays on the surface of the baby's eye, much as you can see the reflection of a window in daylight in the eyes of a person to whom you are talking. When the baby looks at one of the displays, that display is reflected from the surface of the eye. The researcher, using two stopwatches or the equivalent on a computer, can record how long the baby looks at each display. This is the **preference method**, because it shows if the infant has a preference; that is, looks longer at one stimulus than at the other. If the infant does show a preference, we conclude that she can discriminate between the stimuli. *Research Classic 7.1* describes this technique in more detail.

Preference method A research method for the study of visual ability in infancy. Two visual stimuli are presented simultaneously, and the amount of time the infant looks at each is measured.

Links to Related Material

In Chapter 16 you will learn how the preference method is used to assess infants' awareness of gender stereotypes.

RESEARCH CLASSIC 7.1
WHAT DO BABIES SEE? THE WORK OF ROBERT FANTZ

The key problem in understanding perceptual development is that we cannot easily communicate with infants. People have wondered since the beginning of time what the newborn baby can see and when the baby can tell one colour or face or shape from another.

Through much of the modern era of psychology, researchers have approached these questions somewhat indirectly. For example, an investigator might measure the heart rate or respiration of a baby looking at a picture of a face, and then see whether changes occur when the baby looks at a picture of the facial features (mouth, eyes, nose) scrambled up in a different pattern. If so, the investigator might conclude that there is something special about the face for the infant. Other indirect approaches use learning procedures. If a baby can learn to turn her head right when a red stimulus appears and left for a blue stimulus, presumably the baby can discriminate between red and blue.

Robert Fantz made a discovery that profoundly affected research on infant vision (Fantz, 1961). Fantz observed that babies look at different things for different periods of time. He suggested simply measuring the amount of time babies look at one display in relation to another to determine what babies can see and discriminate in the displays. This direct approach eliminated the need to use cumbersome electrodes to measure physiological changes or the tedium of training and learning procedures.

The procedure for measuring where babies look is straightforward. The researcher shows the baby two displays, side by side. With properly adjusted lighting, the researcher can see the reflection of a window in daylight in the eyes of the baby. When the baby looks at one of the displays, the display is reflected from the surface of the eye over the black pupil opening. The researcher, using two stopwatches, can record how long the baby looks at each display. Figure 7.6 shows an early version of the Fantz apparatus.

This approach is labelled the preference method, because what we are interested in is whether the infant will show a preference; that is, look longer at one stimulus than at another. If the infant does show a preference, we conclude that she can discriminate between the stimuli.

Researchers have used this powerful technique to study a host of issues concerning infant vision, including visual acuity, colour perception, form perception, face recognition, and picture perception. Because an infant's interest in a particular visual display declines over time and recovers for novel stimuli, investigators have also been able to use this technique to study how an infant's memory develops and how various types of developmental problems (such as Down syndrome and prematurity) affect perceptual processing and memory (Bornstein & Sigman, 1986).

A remarkable fact about the Fantz discovery is how obvious it seems after the fact. Many great contributors to science have been able to see the obvious among the complex and to find significance in what others have overlooked.

FIGURE 7.6

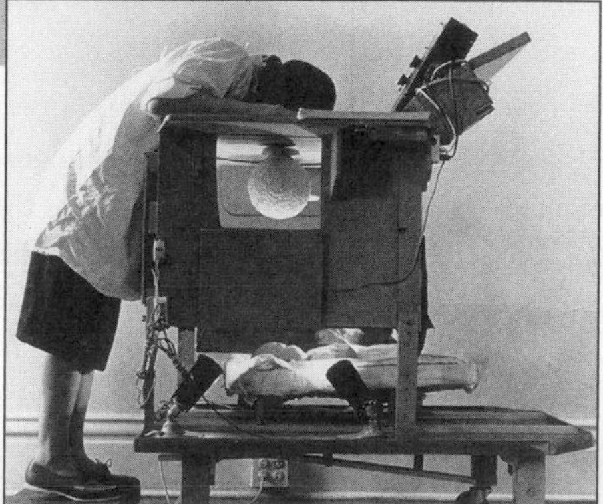

Apparatus used in the Fantz preference method to study infants' visual abilities. *From "The Origin of Form Perception" by R. L. Fantz* (Scientific American, *204, 1961, p. 66). Copyright © by Scientific American, Inc. Photograph by David Linton.*

Visual acuity The clarity with which visual images can be perceived.

VISUAL ACUITY Newborn babies look more at patterned than at unpatterned displays. For example, if we show a baby a picture of a black-and-white bull's eye and a grey card that are equally bright, the baby will look more at the pattern than at the plain card (Fantz, 1961). We can use the preference method and the infants' preferential tendency to look at patterns to measure the baby's **visual acuity**, or how sharply he can see things. To measure visual acuity, therefore, we show the baby a grey picture next to a second picture that contains vertical, black-and-white stripes. Ordinarily, the baby looks longer at the striped picture. Over repeated presentations, we make the stripes more narrow and compressed, which makes them more difficult to distinguish from the grey picture. Eventually, the baby no longer looks more at the striped pattern, presumably because he can no longer tell the difference between the two pictures.

Infants find patterned stimuli interesting in early life. *(Creatas/Media Bakery)*

Using this approach, Daphne Maurer and Terri Lewis (2001), of McMaster University, have estimated that the newborn's acuity is about 20/400 to 20/800 (meaning that a normal-vision adult sees at 400 to 800 feet what the newborn sees at 20 feet), compared with normal adult acuity of 20/20 (see also Kellman & Banks, 1998). By 3 months of age, acuity improves to around 20/100; by 12 months, it approximates that of adults (Hainline, 1998), though there is continued development into childhood (Skoczenski & Norcia, 2002). Figure 7.7 shows how a picture of a face might look to infants at 1, 2, and 3 months of age from a distance of about 15 centimetres (6 inches).

FIGURE 7.7

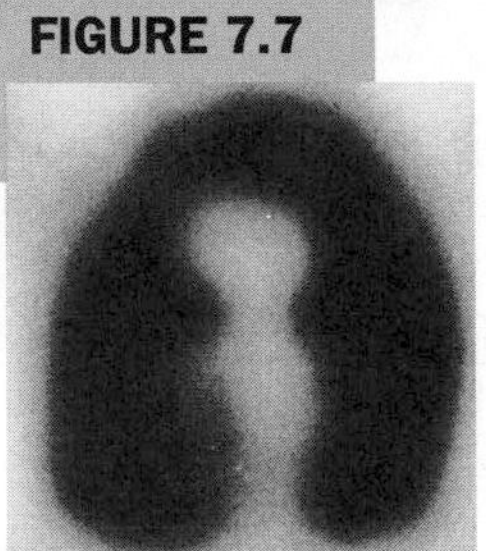
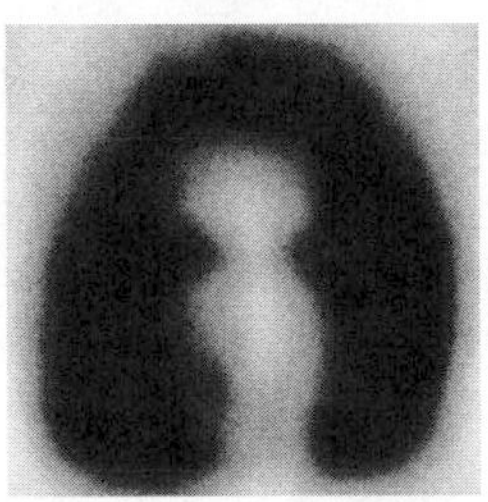
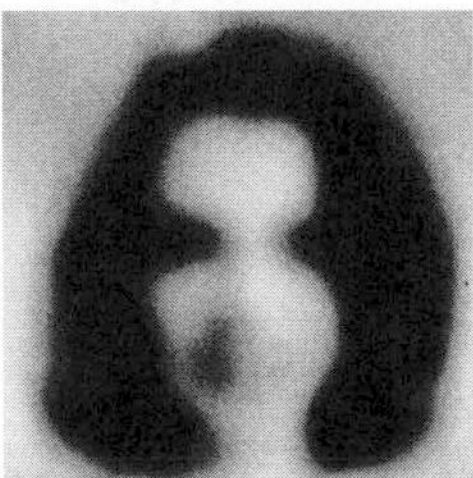

Visual acuity improves dramatically during the first months of life, as illustrated in computer estimations of what a picture of a face looks like to 1-, 2-, and 3-month-olds at a distance of about 15 centimetres (6 inches). All estimations were taken from the original, which illustrates adult acuity (seen on the far right). *From "The Recognition of Facial Expressions in the First Two Years of Life: Mechanisms of Development" by Charles A. Nelson* (Child Development, *58, Figure 1, p. 892). Copyright © 1987 by the Society for Research in Child Development, Inc. Reprinted by permission. These photos were made available by Martin Banks and Arthur Ginsburg.*

Visual accommodation The automatic adjustment of the lens of the eye to produce a focused image of an object on the light-sensitive tissue at the back of the eye.

Why do younger infants have poorer vision? Early studies of infants younger than 1 month of age suggested that the lens of the eye did not vary its focus with distance, a process called **visual accommodation** (Haynes, White, & Held, 1965). Rather, the lens seemed to be fixed for optimal focus at a distance of about 18 to 20 centimetres (7 to 8 inches). Because this is the typical distance of the mother's face from the baby's eyes during feeding, ethologists constructed a nice story about why evolution might use such a trick to ensure that the baby would be attracted to the mother's face.

Evolutionary explanations are often very seductive, but they can also be wrong, as this one was. In fact, the baby's lens is not fixed, but it does not vary with distance as the adult's does. At birth, the brain circuits that are responsible for accommodation are simply not sufficiently mature to pick up minor differences in the precision of focus. Thus, variations for focal distance in the early weeks of life are relatively useless. It appears to be only by chance that the lens has a relatively fixed focus at around 18 to 20 centimetres (7 to 8 inches). Accommodation improves between 1 and 3 months of age and is almost adult-like by 6 months of age (Bobier et al., 2000; Hainline & Abramov, 1992).

COLOUR VISION When can babies see colour? The answer is: in a limited way, from birth, but much better by 4 months of age.

Babies tend to look at coloured objects, and that tendency has helped psychologists answer this question. According to Russell Adams and Mary Courage (1998) of Memorial University of Newfoundland, given optimal circumstances, newborns can make some colour discriminations—red from green, for example, and both red and green from white (see also Adams, 1989). In most respects, however, early colour perception is limited. Aspects of the visual system that mediate colour perception are not mature at birth, and newborns are unable to see many of the contrasts that are available to adults (Adams, 1995).

Like many forms of perception, however, colour perception improves rapidly in the early months, and by 4 months, infants' ability to perceive colour appears equivalent to that of an adult (Teller & Bornstein, 1987). The basis for this pattern of development is thought to be related to the differential maturation of the colour receptor cells in the retina (Adams & Courage, 2002; Suttle, Banks, & Graf, 2002). There are three types of colour receptors called cones: one that is sensitive to red, one that is sensitive to green, and a third that is sensitive to blue. Though the red and green receptor cells seem to be functional early in infancy, the blue receptor cell does not seem to become functional until 3 to 4 months of age (Suttle et al., 2002). This pattern of colour receptor cell maturation is consistent with the developmental trend in infants' perception of colours.

VISUAL PATTERN AND CONTRAST

For years, many people believed that newborn babies were blind, or at best capable merely of reflexively looking at a source of light. As suggested in the discussion of visual acuity, Robert Fantz proved them wrong. Even newborn babies looked longer at a patterned display than at a non-patterned display, as shown in Figure 7.8.

Investigators later developed the techniques shown in Figure 7.9 to measure what parts of displays newborns look at. They discovered that newborns look primarily at high-contrast edges—for example, where black and white meet—and move their eyes back and forth over those contrast edges (Haith, 1980, 1991). In classic research, for example, Peter Salapatek demonstrated that newborns visually scan only the edges of triangles and other geometric figures (Salapatek, 1968; Salapatek & Kessen, 1973) and the outline edge of faces (Maurer & Salapatek, 1976). An example of this visual scanning pattern is shown in Figure 7.10.

As babies get older, they prefer patterns that are more densely packed. Whereas 3-week-olds look longer at a 6-by-6 checkerboard than at a 12-by-12 or a 24-by-24 checkerboard, 6-week-olds are more likely to look longest at the intermediately complex display and 3-month-olds at the most complex display (Karmel & Maisel, 1975).

An early theory held that babies prefer increased complexity (that is, more checks) as they get older and become more complex themselves. However, several investigators have pointed out that as the number of checks increases, so does the amount of black–white edges in the display. Most investigators now believe that babies are attracted to the displays that offer the most edge contrasts that they can see at a particular age (Banks & Ginsburg, 1985; Brown, Adusumilli, & Lindsey, 2005). Why? Perhaps these findings suggest what babies are trying to accomplish with their visual behaviour.

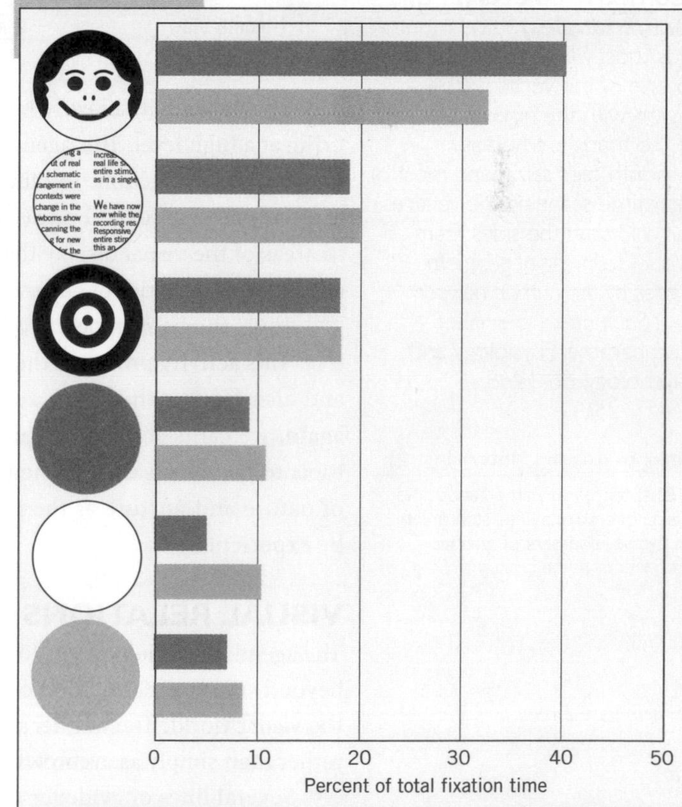

Stimuli that Robert Fantz showed to infants. The length of the blue bars indicates the average time that 2- to 3-month-olds looked at the stimulus, and the length of the green bars indicates the looking time for 3- to 6-month-olds. *From "The origin of form perception" by R. Fantz (Scientific American, 204, 1961, p. 72). Reproduced with permission. Copyright © 1961 Scientific American, Inc. All rights reserved.*

FIGURE 7.9

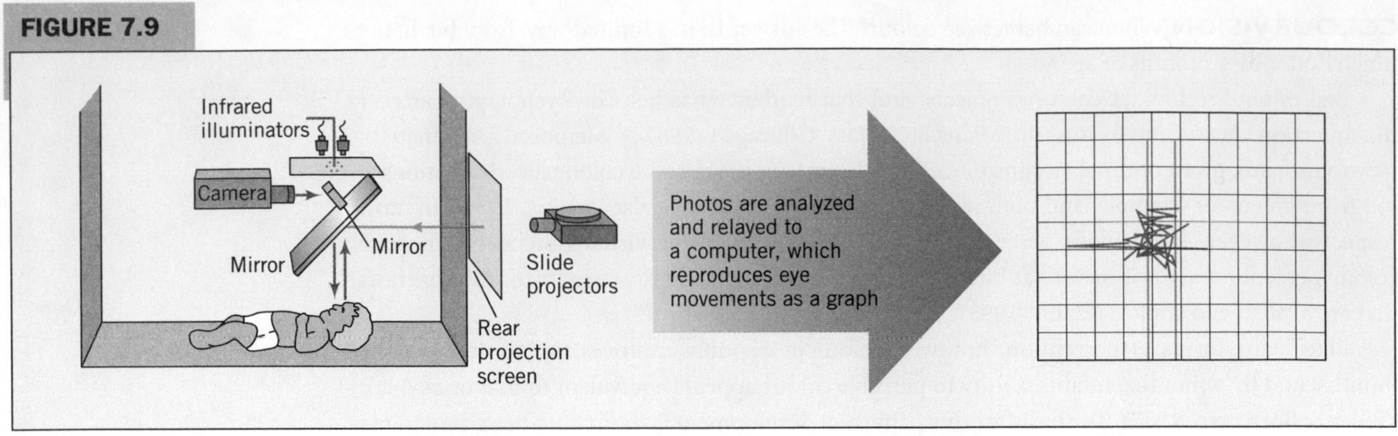

Studying how babies look at stimuli. A camera records the baby's eye movements as he looks at a reflected image. Pictures of the eye are then analyzed. Measurements of the positions of the centre of the pupil and the reflected infrared light spots identify where the baby's eye fixated when the picture was taken. This information is relayed to a computer that reconstructs the baby's eye movements in graphic form. Shown is a reconstruction of a newborn's fixations on a vertical bar.

FIGURE 7.10

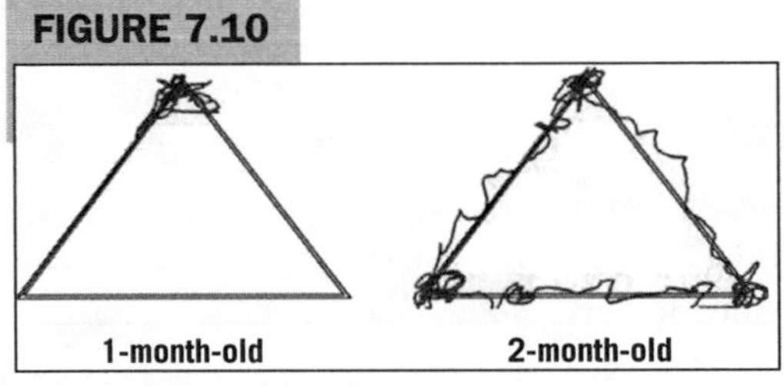

Assessment of visual scanning patterns demonstrates the development of where infants look on simple geometric objects (in this case, triangles). One-month-olds mostly limit their scanning to one of the vertices (the region with the highest contrast) of the triangle, whereas 2-month-olds still spend most of their time scanning the vertices, but also scan the sides. *From "Visual scanning of geometric figures by the human newborn" by P. Salapatek* (Journal of Comparative Physiology and Psychology, *66, 1968, p. 247–258*).

Links to Related Material

In Chapter 5, you learned about the effects of environmental stimulation on the development of synaptic connections in the brain.

When babies move their eyes over edges, they activate the cells of the visual areas of the brain. The strongest brain activity occurs when the baby adjusts the eye so that images of the edges fall near the centre of the eye—that is, when the baby looks straight at the edges. Also, the more detail the baby can see, the stronger the activation. Haith (1980) has suggested that the baby's visual activity in early infancy reflects a biological "agenda" for the baby to keep brain-cells firing at a high level. This agenda makes sense because, as we have seen, cells in the brain compete to establish connections to other cells. Activity tends to stabilize the required connections, while inactive pathways deteriorate (Greenough & Black, 1999). Fortunately, this agenda brings the baby to areas of the visual display that are also psychologically meaningful. Edges provide information about the boundaries of objects, their relation in depth, and where they can be grasped.

Thus, the baby appears to be "programmed" to engage in visual activity that is very adaptive. This activity produces the sensory input needed to maintain and tune the neural apparatus, and also focuses the baby's attention on the most informative parts of the visual world. Once again, we can see that the young infant is anything but passive. Even the newborn possesses tools to get necessary experience for normal development. And we can see again the interplay of nature and nurture as the potential routes for development provided by biology are shaped by experience.

VISUAL RELATIONS

The agenda that biology sets for the newborn makes sense initially, but growing babies must move beyond simply exciting their own brains and begin to appreciate the organization among parts of the visual world. The mother's face, for example, needs to be seen as a whole, meaningful object rather than simply as eyebrows, eyes, ears, a nose, and so on.

Several lines of evidence suggest that, although newborns are sensitive to very simple relations among stimuli, babies really begin to "put things together" between 1 and 3 months of age (Cohen, 1998; Haith, 1990). One example of the kind of research from which this conclusion is drawn is pictured in Figure 7.11. Infants were shown an arrangement of bars that formed a circular or square pattern. In some patterns, one bar was misaligned. To adults, the one misaligned bar seems strange because they see all the other bars as going together. The misalignment had no effect on the visual fixations of 1-month-olds, but 3-month-olds looked longer around the

FIGURE 7.11

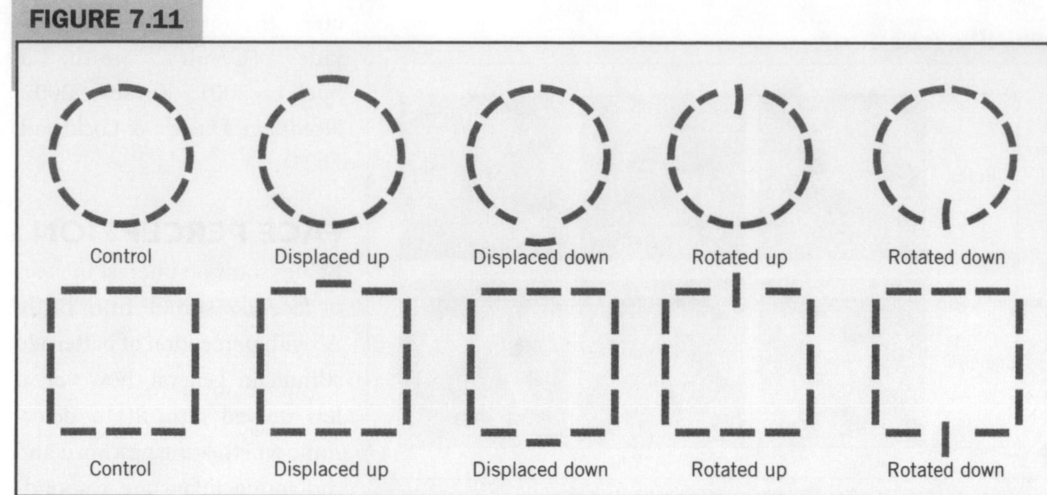

Stimuli used in the study by Van Giffen and Haith. Babies were shown the control stimulus three times, in alternation with one of the experimental figures. *From "Infant Visual Response to Gestalt Geometric Forms" by K. Van Giffen and M. M. Haith* (Infant Behavior and Development, *7, Figure 1, 1984, p. 338). Copyright © 1984 Elsevier. Reprinted with permission.*

displaced bar than around the properly aligned ones (Van Giffen & Haith, 1984). Thus, between 1 and 3 months of age, babies begin to see the organization in visual displays rather than only the details.

Of course, babies do not appreciate all possible visual relations by 3 months of age. As you can demonstrate to yourself by walking into a modern art gallery, the perception of organization takes time and effort and knowledge. Consider the display shown in Figure 7.12*a*. Adults report perceiving a square that overlays full circles at each of the corners in this display. They also report faint edges that connect the corners of the square, even though no such edges exist. Adults, of course, have considerable knowledge about such things as squares and how a square might block the view of circles behind it.

Babies looked at the arrangement in Figure 7.12*b* (the same elements, with some rotated to destroy the illusion) until their looking habituated. They then were tested for dishabituation with either the illusion stimulus in Figure 7.12*a* or the second non-illusion stimulus shown in Figure 7.12*c*. Both test stimuli involved a change in two corner elements, and hence we might expect them to be equally easy to discriminate. Five-month-old infants did not consistently detect either of these changes; however, 7-month-olds were able to detect the change when it involved the illusion in Figure 7.12*a*, indicating that they were able to group its elements perceptually in a way that the younger infants were not yet able to do (Bertenthal, Campos, & Haith, 1980). Recent research, however, suggests that the ability to perceive this illusion may be evident as young as 4 months of age (Kavsek, 2002).

The capacity for the perception of visual organization continues to show improvement beyond infancy into childhood and even adolescence (Hadad, Maurer, & Lewis, 2010; Kovács, Kozma, Fehér & Benedek, 1999). In particular, improvement occurs in the ability to group individual elements in the perception of an organized stimulus like a square or circle, such as the stimuli shown in Figure 7.13, while in the presence of similar background elements. Using these types of stimuli, infants show very little improvement in the ability to group the individual elements and perceive the shapes. In contrast, 5- to 6-year-old children show some improvement, and this ability becomes adult-like in adolescence (Baker, Tse, Gerhardstein, & Adler, 2008; Hadad et al., 2010; Kovács et al., 1999). Slow maturation of the primary visual cortex may be responsible for this delayed visual organization ability (Burkhalter et al., 1993; Kovács, 1996), with full functionality requiring the proper visual input experience (Kovács, Polat, Norcia, Pennefather, & Chandna, 2000).

These studies and others like them demonstrate an important point: the perception of visual organization, like most developmental phenomena, is not something that happens all at once for all displays. The ability to appreciate visual organization begins between 1 and 3 months of age, but this ability continues to improve and is affected by both knowledge and the

FIGURE 7.12

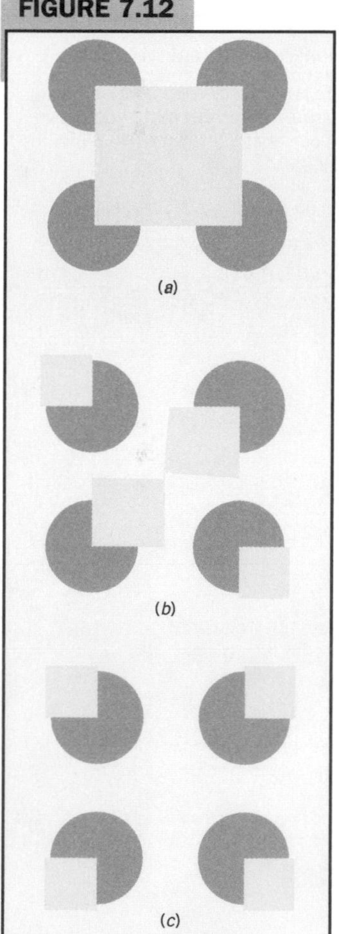

Stimuli used in studies by Bertenthal (all three stimuli) and Shapiro (*a* and *b* only). *From "Development of Visual Organization: The Perception of Subjective Contours" by B. I. Bertenthal, J. J. Campos, and M. M. Haith* (Child Development, *51, Figure 1, 1980, p. 1073). Copyright © 1980 by the Society for Research in Child Development, Inc. Reprinted by permission.*

FIGURE 7.13

Examples of the circle and square contours in the presence of randomly oriented background elements used in the Baker et al. (2008) study to examine the development in the perception of visual organization. *From "Contour integration by 6-month-olds: Discrimination of distinct contour shapes" by* (Vision Research, *Figure 7, 48, 2008, p. 136–148*).

cues the environment provides (Condry, Smith, & Spelke, 2001; Kavsek, 2002; Needham, Dueker, & Lockhead, 2005).

FACE PERCEPTION

Babies show an interest in faces or face-like stimuli from birth. As with perception of patterned stimuli in general, however, it has proved difficult to determine whether the newborn and the young infant are responding to the face per se, or simply to the interesting parts that make up the face. As Figure 7.14 shows, young infants' processing of faces is limited—they tend to look near the high-contrast borders of the face, and they pay relatively little attention to interior detail. In addition, a number of studies with infants in the first 2 or 3 months of life have failed to find a preference for faces over comparable non-face stimuli; that is, stimuli that are matched on such dimensions as contrast, brightness, and curvature (Maurer, 1985). (*Focus on Research 7.2* describes Canadian research on infants' face perception.)

For Thought and Discussion

To stimulate development of the visual system, how might you design a nursery for an infant 1 to 6 months of age?

Despite these cautions, recent evidence suggests that even newborns may be responsive to faces under some conditions. Figure 7.15 shows a set of stimuli used in this research. The stimuli were presented not statically, but in motion across the infant's visual field, and the researcher measured whether the babies moved their eyes or head to track the stimuli. The question was whether the face-like pattern would prove more interesting than the other targets. The answer was yes: newborn babies, including some just a few minutes old, tracked the face more than they did the other stimuli (Johnson et al., 1991; Valenza et al., 1996).

Since the research by Johnson and colleagues, there have been several other demonstrations that newborn babies respond differentially to faces. For instance, Catherine Mondloch of Brock University and her collaborators (1999) used the Fantz preference method and thus measured attention to static faces, rather than tracking of moving faces (see also Cassia, Simion, & Umilta, 2001). There is also increasing evidence that it is really faceness, and not other aspects of the stimulation, that attracts newborn attention (de Haan, 2001). Furthermore, there is evidence that infants just a few hours old can discriminate their mother's face from a stranger's (Bushnell, 2001). On the other hand,

FIGURE 7.14

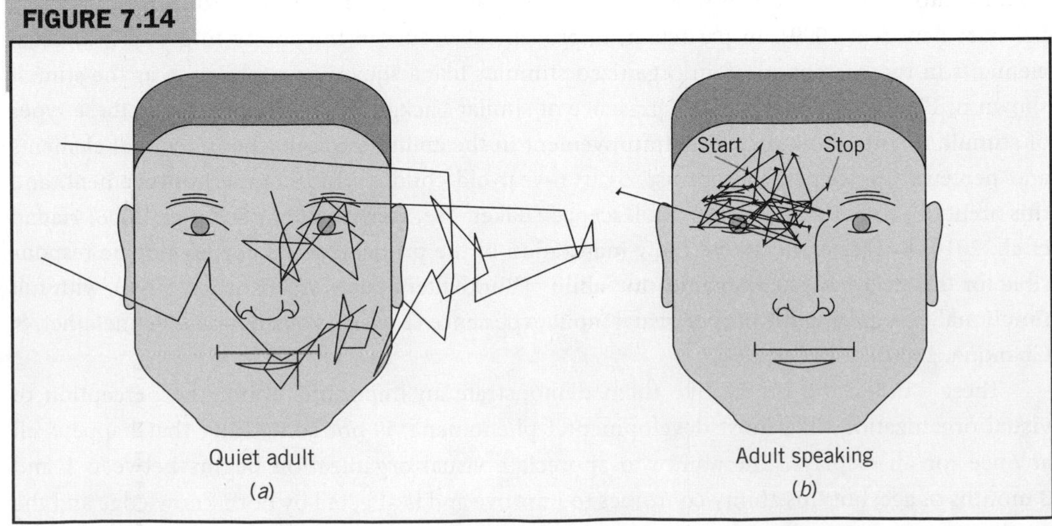

An apparatus similar to that shown in Figure 7.9 recorded a baby's fixations on a face. A computer reconstructed the baby's fixations on a face when (*a*) the adult was quiet and (*b*) the adult talked. A rotating arrow (*b*) shows the sequence of fixations and where the baby began and ended looking.

it is important to note that the response to faces in the early weeks of life, even if genuine, is fragile and limited in comparison with what it will eventually be. Indeed, the evidence suggests that different brain centres may underlie early and later response to faces (Halit, de Haan, & Johnson, 2003). In fact, full cortical specialization for face processing seems to emerge slowly over approximately the first 10 years of life (Kadosh & Johnson, 2007).

By about 3 months of age, the preference for faces over comparable non-face stimuli is clearly established (Dannemiller & Stephens, 1988). By this age, most babies also show a preference for a familiar face (typically mother's) over an unfamiliar one (Barrera & Maurer, 1981b). Interestingly, babies also show a preference for relatively attractive faces (as determined by adult ratings) over relatively unattractive ones (Langlois et al., 1987); in fact, this preference is evident even in the newborn period (Bartrip, Morton, & de Schonen, 2001). One possible explanation for this finding is that attractive faces are really a kind of average or composite of faces in general, a melding together and evening out of the range of human features. As such, they fit babies' developing image of the face better than do examples that deviate from the average, and for this reason they elicit more attention (Rubenstein, Kalakanis, & Langlois, 1999).

FIGURE 7.15

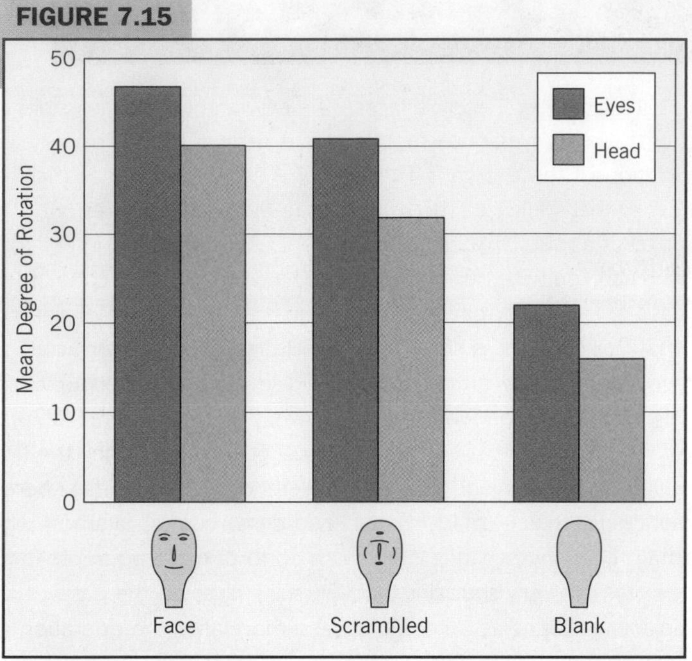

Stimuli and results from the Johnson et al. study of newborns' tendency to track moving objects. The babies moved their eyes and heads more in response to the face than in the response to the other two stimuli. *From "Newborns' Preferential Tracking of Facelike Stimuli and Its Subsequent Decline" by M. H. Johnson, S. Dziurawiec, H. Ellis, and J. Morton* (Cognition, *40(6), 1991). Copyright © 1991 by Elsevier Science Publishers. Reprinted by permission.*

For Thought and Discussion

What criteria would you use to identify an "attractive" face? Which of those criteria might an infant possess innately? Why do you think infants prefer "attractive" faces?

Several further developments in face perception are evident by the second half of the first year. Infants become capable of recognizing a face as the same despite changes in expression or orientation (Cohen & Strauss, 1979). They show an ability to classify faces on the basis of sex; for example, they habituate if shown a series of male faces, but dishabituate if a female face appears (Quinn et al., 2002). By 9 months of age (but not at 6 months), infants can distinguish between own-race faces and other-race faces, as they not only look longer at a face from one race after being familiarized to face from a different race, but also look longer at novel individual faces from their own race but not from other races (Anzures, Quinn, Pascalis, Slater, & Lee, 2009). They can even differentiate their own face from those of others, and appear to recognize it as a familiar stimulus. In addition, by 6 months of age, infants (like older children and adults) show different forms of brain activity when processing faces than when responding to other sorts of stimuli (de Haan & Nelson, 1999).

Faces are not only interesting stimuli to view; they are also sources of social information. The sensitivity of babies to emotional expressions in faces grows slowly over the first two years of life (Bornstein & Arterberry, 2003; de Haan & Nelson, 1998). Even 3-month-olds, however, may look longer at faces as the intensity of the smile increases. This tendency appears to depend on experience. Babies whose mothers call attention to themselves and smile when their babies look at them show the strongest preferences for smiling faces (Kuchuk, Vibbert, & Bornstein, 1986). Further, 7-month-old babies will initially look longer to a fearful than a happy face, and this differentiation is exhibited in ERP (event-related potentials) recordings as well. This finding suggests that the neural mechanisms for processing affective facial expressions are functional in early infancy (Leppänen, Moulson, Vogel-Farley, & Nelson, 2007). We will see in Chapter 12 that by the end of the first year, babies can differentiate a number of other expressions of emotion.

FOCUS ON RESEARCH 7.2
FACE PERCEPTION DURING EARLY INFANCY

The human face is a complex visual object. People's faces differ in terms of the shapes of the head, eyes, nose, mouth, and so on, and in the relative position of these organs. These differences are subtle, and it is amazing that adults can recognize thousands of faces at a glance. It takes about 10 years of expertise with faces before children reach adult-like performance in distinguishing people on the basis of facial information alone (Mondloch, LeGrand, & Maurer, 2002). Younger children can distinguish faces, but their judgment relies heavily on non-facial information, like hairstyle, clothing accessories, or whether or not the person is wearing glasses.

For several years now, Dr. Daphne Maurer and Dr. Terri Lewis, professors at the Department of Psychology of McMaster University, in Hamilton, Ontario, have been investigating infants' face perception. What makes their research very special is that, among other things, they study infants as young as 1 hour old, providing information on their visual abilities before a significant amount of experience with faces is acquired. In one article, they reported that infants pay more attention to schematic human faces than to other stimuli, even when the stimuli are comparable in terms of other dimensions, such as levels of contrast and complexity (Mondloch, Lewis, Budreau, Maurer, et al., 1999). Their findings suggest that there may be a mechanism predisposing newborns to look toward faces, a mechanism likely to be innate and that may involve brain structures that are primarily subcortical. Their data also suggest that this primitive mechanism wanes by 6 weeks and is replaced by another mechanism involving the cortical structures of the brain.

Another interesting question examined by Dr. Maurer and Dr. Lewis concerns the importance of early visual experience for the development of vision. Infancy is a period when the neural architecture of the brain undergoes most of its development. Since it is likely that the development of neural networks responsible for vision is triggered by stimulation from the environment, it is possible that deprivation of normal visual input early in life will have deleterious long-term effects on vision. The researchers at McMaster University investigated this issue by testing children who were deprived of normal visual input until they had surgery to remove dense central cataracts and were fitted with contact lenses (see Figure 7.16). Their research shows that visual deprivation during the first 6 months of life results in poorer acuity and in constriction of the visual field several years later (Bowering, Maurer, Lewis, & Brent, 1997; Lewis, Maurer, & Brent, 1995). Their results also indicate that visual deprivation during the first 6 months has permanent and deleterious effects on face perception. Specifically, children who had dense central cataracts when they were infants continued to perform more poorly than did normal children when distinguishing faces on the basis of configural information nine years and more after the operation (Le Grand, Mondloch, Maurer, & Brent, 2004).

FIGURE 7.16

Assessing vision in infants with dense central cataract. © Terry Lewis. Reprinted with permission.

As with the study of infant vision in general, research on face perception reveals some surprising early competencies, coupled with definite advances across the course of infancy. In *On the Cutting Edge 7.1*, we consider some recent research that adds to the early competency part of the picture.

OBJECTS AND THEIR PROPERTIES

The ability of babies to appreciate the relations among visual elements—for example, lines, angles, and edges—is important for their perception of the objects that populate the world. But knowledge of objects involves more than the ability to perceive how the parts fit together to make a whole. In this section, we discuss some further aspects of object perception that emerge during infancy.

THE CONSTANCIES As an object moves farther away from us, its image on the eye shrinks. Yet the object continues to appear the same size, at least up to a point. For example, a child standing

ON THE CUTTING EDGE 7.1
CAN NEWBORNS RECOGNIZE THEIR MOTHERS' FACES?

One of the important tasks of infancy is to learn to recognize and to prefer the primary caregiver, who, in most instances, is the baby's mother. We have seen that a preference for the mother's voice or the mother's odour appears in the first few days of life. Might a preference for the mother's face also be present this early?

There are numerous reasons to think that the answer to this question will be no. In both the auditory and the olfactory realms, babies receive stimulation from the mother during the prenatal period, and thus they have a chance to acquire some familiarity with her characteristics prior to birth. In contrast, learning of the mother's face must clearly depend on experience following birth. As we have seen, newborns and young infants typically attend to only certain aspects of the face and ignore other aspects, especially the inner detail (recall Figure 7.14). Furthermore, they do not see at all clearly what they do attend to; on the most optimistic estimate, newborn visual activity is only about one-tenth that of the 20/20 optimal adult level (recall Figure 7.7).

Given this catalogue of reasons to doubt early visual recognition of the mother, you have probably guessed by now that recent research suggests that newborns do recognize their mothers' faces. Babies as young as 2 days old have been shown to look more at their mothers' faces than at the face of a stranger (Bushnell, Sai, & Mullin, 1989; Pascalis et al., 1995). Furthermore, there is evidence that infants just a few hours old might be able to discriminate their mother from a stranger (Bushnell, 2001). Newborn babies also alter their sucking patterns more readily to produce a view of their mother's face than to view the face of a stranger (Walton, Bower, & Bower, 1992). The investigators who conducted these studies have been careful to control for other possible bases for recognition of the mother, such as auditory or olfactory cues. Thus, the response really does seem to be the mother's face.

How could a baby with such a limited visual system and such limited visual experience recognize the mother? The study by Pascalis and colleagues (1995) suggests an answer. After demonstrating the preference for the mother's face, the researchers redid the experiment, but with one difference: now the women wore scarves that covered their hair and part of their foreheads. With the scarves in place, newborns could no longer distinguish their mother from a stranger. A subsequent study demonstrated that it is not until about 5 weeks of age that infants can recognize the mother when she is wearing a scarf (Bartrip, Morton, & de Schonen, 2001).

What this research suggests is that newborn recognition of the mother is not based on attention to the inner details of her face. Newborns seem to rely instead on peripheral information, such as hairline and the shape of head. Early recognition of the mother, like the early interest in face-like stimuli, is therefore crude and limited in comparison with the face perception of the older infant. Nevertheless, recent research on response to the mother's face, like research on face perception in general, suggests that newborn infants are more responsive to faces than psychologists once believed. And this early responsiveness seems clearly conducive to the important task of forming emotional ties with others.

in front of you seems shorter than an adult standing across the street, even though the child casts a larger image on your eyes than does the adult. This phenomenon is called **size constancy**.

Objects also change apparent shape as they rotate or as we move around them. **Shape constancy** refers to the stability of our perception despite changes in the shape of the image on the eye. Objects in the world continually change in brightness as well. Still, a dark dress continues to look dark whether it is dimly lit in a shop or brightly illuminated by direct sunlight. This is the phenomenon of **brightness constancy**. Finally, **colour constancy** refers to the perception of a colour as the same despite changes in the hue of light (for example, the fluorescent light of a department store versus sunlight).

Size constancy The experience that the physical size of an object remains the same, even though the size of its projected image on the eye varies.

Shape constancy The experience that the physical shape of an object remains the same, even though the shape of its projected image on the eye varies.

Brightness constancy The experience that the brightness of an object remains the same, even though the amount of light it reflects back to the eye changes (because of shadows or changes in the illuminating light).

Colour constancy The experience that the colour of an object remains the same, even though the wavelengths it reflects back to the eye change (because of changes in the colour of the illuminating light).

Visual constancies are important because they address the fundamental question of how stable the world is for the infant. After all, without such constancies, each time a baby saw an object at a different distance, in a different orientation, or in a different light, it would appear to be a different object. Instead of seeing only one mother, the infant would experience a different mother every time he saw her from a different angle. Fortunately for both baby and mother, the baby's visual world, as we will see, appears to be a good deal less chaotic than this.

Let us first consider size constancy. Figure 7.17 shows one approach to testing size constancy in very young infants (Slater, Mattock, & Brown, 1990). The stimuli are two cubes, one twice as large as the other. The baby first receives a series of familiarization trials in which one of the cubes is presented at different distances. For example, a baby might see the small cube at a distance of 23 cm

FIGURE 7.17

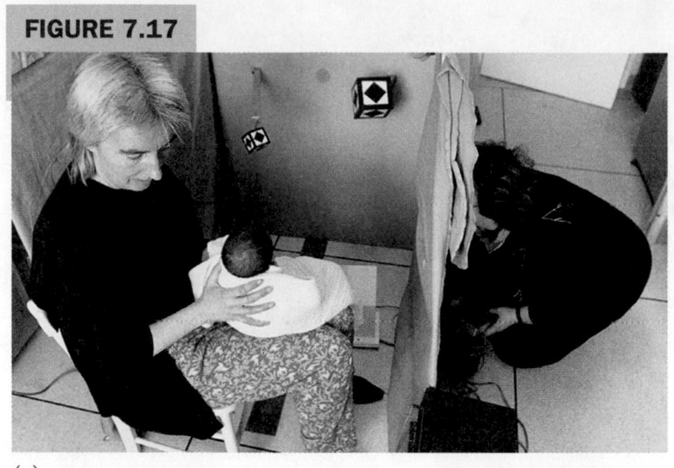

(a)

(b)

Procedure for testing size constancy in newborn babies. The top (*a*) shows the experimental arrangement, and the bottom (*b*) shows the stimuli for the critical test trial. *From "Size Constancy at Birth: Newborn Infants' Responses to Retinal and Real Size" by A. Slater, A. Mattock, and E. Brown* (Journal of Experimental Child Psychology, *49, 1990, p. 317, 318). Copyright © 1990 by Academic Press. Reprinted by permission.*

(9 in.), then at 53 cm (22 in.), then at 38 cm (15 in.), and so forth. Because both the distance and the size of the retinal image vary from trial to trial, the only constant element is the actual size of the cube. The test trials follow the familiarization phase. Now both cubes are presented simultaneously, but at different distances, with the larger cube twice as far away as the smaller one. The question of interest is whether the baby will show a preference by looking longer at one of the two cubes.

Before we describe the findings, it is worth taking a moment to think through the logic of the experiment. Why might the baby show a preference? The retinal image cannot be the basis for a preference because the two cubes—as Figure 7.17*b* illustrates—project the same-size image. The baby has not encountered the viewing distances before; thus, there is no reason to think that distance will be important. On the other hand, one of the cubes is familiar and the other is novel, and hence we might see a preference based on relative familiarity. Note, however, that the small cube will be familiar only if the baby has been able to perceive its constant size during the familiarization trials. If, instead, size is perceived as changing every time distance changes, then both cubes will appear new on the test trials.

In fact, all of the newborn babies tested looked significantly longer at the larger cube. This finding tells us that they could see a difference between the two cubes despite the equivalent retinal images. And the preference for the novel stimulus suggests that they did, indeed, find the small cube familiar and therefore less interesting. As noted, they could do so only if they perceived the constant size across presentations.

This study suggests, then, that some size constancy is present at birth. There is also evidence, based on a similar methodology, for some degree of shape constancy at birth (Slater & Morison, 1985). It is important to note, though, that "some constancy" is not complete constancy. Both size constancy and shape constancy are stronger and more easily demonstrated by 3 or 4 months of age than they are in the newborn (Granrud, 2006). Indeed, the ability to judge the size of objects with changing distance improves up to at least 10 or 11 years of age (Day, 1987). Thus, constancy, like other perceptual accomplishments, is not an all-or-nothing affair.

To date, there have been no demonstrations that the other forms of constancy we identified—brightness constancy and colour constancy—are present from birth. Brightness constancy, however, is evident as early as 7 weeks for objects that are not too small (Dannemiller, 1985), and some degree of colour constancy is available by 4 months of age (Dannemiller & Hanko, 1987).

OBJECT CONTINUITY Our knowledge of objects extends beyond the various constancies. Because we understand principles of solidity and continuity, we see objects as continuous and whole, even when our view is partially blocked. For example, when a person stands in front of a table, blocking the midsection of the table from our view, we naturally infer that the two ends of the table are connected. In a sense, we perceive a whole table. Do young infants also perceive objects as continuous and whole when they are partially blocked by other objects?

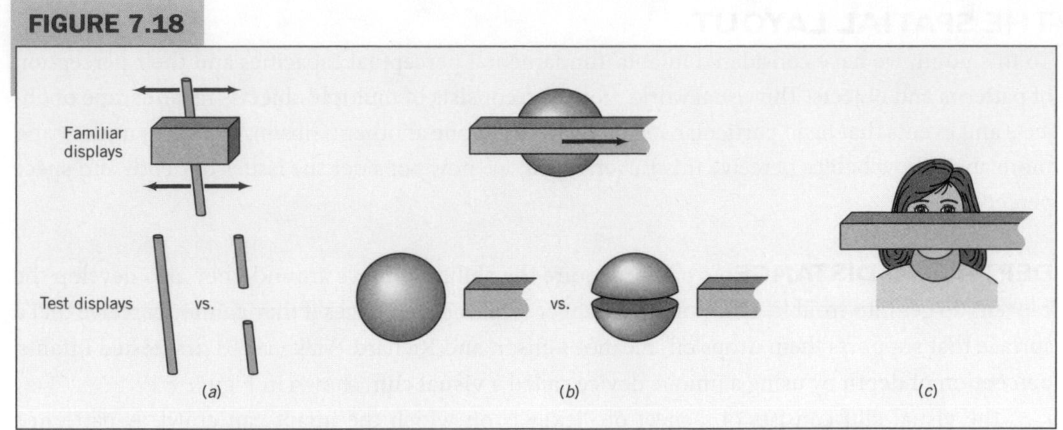

Some pictures used to study object perception in infants. *From "Perception of Unity, Persistence, and Identity: Thoughts on Infants' Conceptions of Objects" by E. S. Spelke (in J. Mehler and R. Fox (Eds.),* Neonate Cognition: Beyond the Blooming Buzzing Confusion, *Figures 6.1, 6.2, and 6.3, p. 91–93, Hillsdale, NJ: Erlbaum. Reprinted by permission of the author.*

In one set of experiments, 4-month-old babies looked at a partially blocked object—for example, a long rod partly hidden by a block but moving left and right behind it, as shown in the top of Figure 7.18*a*—until their interest declined. They then were shown the two stimuli at the bottom of Figure 7.18*a*: a continuous rod, paired with two rod pieces. Note that the latter stimulus is identical to what they were able to see with the block in place. Presumably, if the babies had perceived earlier that the rod was continuous, they should have looked longer at the two separated rods than at the more typical and familiar continuous rod. They did not, suggesting that they had not perceived a single whole rod behind the block (Spelke, 1985).

In a variation of this procedure, babies saw a bar move out from in front of a sphere that it had partially blocked, as illustrated in the top of Figure 7.18*b*. The movement of the bar revealed either a whole sphere or two separated sphere parts (bottom of Figure 7.18*b*). Again, the babies paid no special attention to the separated parts. The researchers tried several displays—including a face, as shown in Figure 7.18*c*—but had no success in demonstrating that infants could infer more about the objects than what they could see (Kellman & Spelke, 1983).

These findings seem amazing. Is it possible that babies see people as cut into pieces when they stand behind a table? Probably not. In all these studies, the partially hidden object was stationary, and so was the baby. In the real world, when we see one object partially blocked by another, our own movement produces more displacement of the closer object than of the "pieces" of the farther object. This is a clue that the blocked object is continuous. Furthermore, the blocked object itself may move, providing another clue. For example, infants who saw a sphere move behind a blocking rod (that is, the two parts of the sphere moved simultaneously) later looked at the separated sphere parts as though they had not seen them before. Under these conditions, infants apparently perceived the moving sphere as whole (Kellman, 1996; Spelke, 1988). Given movement and other optimal cues (for example, use of a highly textured object), infants as young as 1 month can perceive the continuity of partially visible objects (Johnson, 1997; Johnson & Aslin, 1995; Kawabata et al., 1999). Newborns, however, cannot, which suggests that some experience may be necessary for this accomplishment (Slater et al., 1994, 1996).

Based on several experiments of the kind just described, Spelke has argued that infants in the early months of life understand object continuity, along with several other basic properties of objects. Some other properties, however (such as the effects of gravity), are not understood until the second year of life (Spelke, 1991; Spelke & Hermer, 1996; Spelke et al., 1992), though the basis for this object "understanding" is debatable (Haith, 1998; Johnson, et al., 2003). We return to the question of what infants know about objects in Chapter 8. What is interesting about the findings of the continuity studies described is that they suggest that the perception of the spatial layout of objects, particularly their relative depths such as "in front" and "behind," is exhibited early in infancy.

THE SPATIAL LAYOUT

To this point, we have considered infants' fundamental perceptual capacities and their perception of patterns and objects. The visual world, however, consists of multiple objects—a landscape of objects and events that lie in particular spatial relations to one another (Gibson, 1988). To understand more about how babies perceive this richer world, we now consider the issues of depth and space perception.

Visual cliff A research method for the study of depth perception in infancy. The infant is placed on a glass-covered table near an apparent drop-off, and perception of depth is inferred if the infant avoids the drop.

DEPTH AND DISTANCE As babies acquire the ability to move around, they also develop the capacity to get into trouble. One potential danger is falling over edges if they cannot perceive that a surface that supports them drops off. Eleanor Gibson and Richard Walk (1960) first tested infants' perception of depth by using a unique device called a **visual cliff**, shown in Figure 7.19.

The visual cliff consists of a sheet of Plexiglas on which the infant can crawl. A patterned cloth lies just beneath the clear surface on one side. Under the other side is the same cloth pattern, but it lies several feet below the clear surface. Infants able to crawl were placed on a small platform just at the edge of the boundary between "safe" and "deep." Although their mothers called to them from across the deep side, most infants were unwilling to cross, apparently because they perceived the depth and danger. Subsequent research has confirmed the pattern identified by Gibson and Walk. Most babies old enough to be tested avoid the deep side of the cliff, and by 9 or 10 months, this avoidance response is quite strong (Bertenthal, Campos, & Kermoian, 1994).

FIGURE 7.19

Around the time that babies develop skill in crawling, they become fearful of heights in the absence of support, as they display in their reluctance to cross a visual cliff. *(Mark Richards/Photo Edit)*

When does the ability to perceive the depth of the deep side develop? An ingenious approach to this question, one that can be used with infants too young to crawl, involves measuring infants' heart rates as the experimenter lowers them to the clear surface of the visual cliff on both the deep and the safe sides. The heart rates of infants as young as 2 months of age slow when they are lowered to the deep side. This finding tells us that the babies notice the difference and are interested in it; there is no evidence, however, that they fear the depth. By 9 months, the response is quite different. Now the heart rate increases over the drop-off, suggesting that babies are afraid, and now most infants are also unwilling to cross over to the deep side (Campos, Bertenthal, & Kermoian, 1992; Campos et al., 1978).

The shift from interest to fear in response to drop-offs occurs after about 7 months of age. This is also the time when babies begin to take responsibility for their own movements—for instance, by crawling or by pushing themselves around in walkers. Might the two developments be related? Various kinds of evidence suggest that they are (Campos, Bertenthal, & Kermoian, 1992). For example, there is a correlation between crawling experience and fear of depth: babies who have been crawling the longest are most likely to show the fear response on the visual cliff. There is also experimental evidence for a relationship: babies who have been provided with walkers in which they can move themselves around show the fear response earlier. Apparently, moving about on one's own furnishes information about drop-offs and falls that is less readily available to the non-mobile infant. (We should add, however, that we are not advocating the use of walkers. Walkers have been linked to a heightened risk of injury in infancy, and the Consumer Product Safety Bureau of Canada therefore called for a ban on their use in 2004.)

Moving around independently requires new perceptual learning. This is so because babies in the first year of life have difficulty separating their perception of space from the actions they perform. For example, babies who are able to reach around a barrier for a hidden object have to relearn the task when they are required to crawl around the barrier to get it (Lockman & Adams, 2001). Similarly, infants who can perceive and avoid a drop-off while in a sitting posture may respond differently when put in the posture for crawling (Adolph, 2000). It should be pointed out that the critical issue is the new perceptual learning required by self-produced locomotion rather than posture, because once the avoidance of the deep side is established when crawling, it is maintained when shifting to walking (Witherington et al., 2005). Thus, what seem like very similar tasks to an adult do not at first seem similar to the baby. Furthermore, self-produced movement may produce increased sensitivity to **optic flow**—the visual sensation that when we move, the objects around us apparently move (even if they actually do not). As a consequence of the increased sensitivity to optic flow, development in the sensory and motor areas of the brain are likely facilitated, thereby enabling improved motor behaviour and perception of their spatial environment (Schmuckler & Tsang-Tong, 2000). Thus, as infants gain more experience with the effects of their own movements, they gradually develop a more unified understanding of space.

Optic flow The sensation that objects are apparently moving as a result of self-produced movement.

How are babies able to perceive depth? They might use a number of different types of perceptual cues for depth. (Indeed, two researchers of the topic have written that "God must have loved depth cues, for He made so many of them"—Yonas & Granrud, 1985, p. 45). Some cues are referred to as **pictorial cues** because they are the kind of information that can be conveyed in a picture (Figure 7.20). For example, railroad tracks appear to converge at a distant point, and this apparent non-parallelism creates an impression of depth. Objects that are nearer may hide objects that are farther along the same line of sight (a dime, held in the right position, can block an object as large as the moon). Finally, the relative size of objects provides a cue about their distance. If we see a picture in which a dog is larger than a car, we assume the car is farther away, and we can even judge their relative distance from one another because we know how big cars and dogs are (remember size constancy).

Pictorial cues Visual cues that indicate the relative distances of objects through static, picture-like information—for example, interposition of one object in front of another.

Another class of cues is **kinetic cues**—cues produced by movement, either of the observer or of the objects. Probably the most important kinetic cue is **motion parallax**. When we move, nearer objects appear to change position faster than do farther objects; similarly, when two objects move within our visual field, the nearer object appears to move faster. (You can verify this phenomenon by moving your head from side to side and noting the appearance of near and far objects.) Such differences in apparent movement furnish information about relative depth.

Kinetic cues Visual cues that indicate the relative distances of objects through movement of the objects or of the observer.

Motion parallax An observer's experience that a closer object moves across the field of view faster than a more distant object when both objects are moving at the same speed or when the objects are stationary and the observer moves.

Moving objects provide additional cues when their movement puts them on a collision course with the observer. In this situation, as the size of the object in the eye increases, it blocks more and more of the background, and all the parts of the object get larger. You blink when an object approaches in this way, and so, it turns out, do babies as young as 1 month of age (Yonas, 1981).

Sensitivity to different depth cues develops at different ages (Yonas & Owsley, 1987). Babies can make some use of kinetic depth cues between 1 and 3 months of age. Responses to static pictorial cues, though appearing at slightly later ages, also show differential development. Some cues apparently induce depth at 5 months (e.g., texture gradients), whereas others do not induce

FIGURE 7.20

Examples of some pictorial depth cues. From left to right: interposition—objects that are closer block or occlude parts of objects that are farther and behind; relative size—if two objects are the same size, the object that casts a smaller retinal image is perceived as farther than the object that casts a larger retinal image; texture gradient—the density of surface texture appears to increase as the surface recedes; and linear perspective—parallel lines seem to converge in the distance. If infants are sensitive to these cues, they will reach for the nearer object or part of the stimulus containing these cues. (*iStock; © Stephen Strathdee/iStock; © Walter Galloway/iStock; © Ziutograf/iStock*)

depth until 7 months (e.g., relative size) (Hemker, Granrud, Yonas, & Kavsek, 2010). Some recent studies suggest that even infants as young as 3 months might be able to use certain pictorial cues (Bertin & Bhatt, 2006). Similarly, by some behavioural measures (e.g., the blink response to an approaching object), perception of depth is present quite early; by others (e.g., fear on the visual cliff), it emerges considerably later. We can see again that there is no single answer to the "when" question for most developmental phenomena of interest. Perception of depth is a gradual, rather than instantaneous, achievement.

KEEPING TRACK OF LOCATIONS IN SPACE We will see in Chapter 13 that the young infant only gradually learns the distinction between the self and the external world of objects. There exist essentially two types of coding of location in space (Liben & Christensen, 2010). The first is termed *egocentric coding*, which means the understanding of space and objects is tied to one's own actions and body. The second is termed *allocentric coding*, which means the understanding of space and objects is tied to other objects and landmarks in the environment. Early in development, babies understand the world egocentrically; that is, they use egocentric coding. Thus, babies who find an object to their right expect to find that object on their right again, even if they rotate their body. Gradually, babies shift to an allocentric coding and learn to use stable landmarks in the environment to find objects, because these provide reliable cues that do not change as babies move around (Piaget, 1954).

A clever study by Linda Acredolo (1978) examined this developmental shift in spatial coding for infants at 6, 11, and 16 months of age. The wall to each side of the infant had a window. Infants learned to turn and look at one window—say, the one on the left—to make an interesting visual display appear. For half the infants, a coloured star around the window where the display would appear served as a landmark. The remaining infants had no landmark.

After the infants learned the left-turn response, their chair was rotated 180 degrees so that the correct response was now a right turn. If the babies were responding with reference only to their own body, they would continue to look to the left. If they could use the landmark or if they could compensate for the rotation of their body, they would look to the right. Whether or not the landmark was present, 6-month-olds turned to the left side; that is, they used their bodies, rather than the landmark, as the frame of reference. The 11-month-olds also tended to turn left when no landmark was present, but were able to use the landmark to respond when it was present. Finally, the oldest group responded correctly whether the landmark was present or not. Thus, there was a clear progression with age in the ability to use external referents to judge spatial location.

We have seen that one factor that affects how infants respond to depth is the opportunity to move themselves around. It seems plausible that moving on their own might also help infants keep track of spatial locations. In contrast, like passengers in a car, passively moved babies might not understand how they got from one place to another or the spatial consequences of the move.

It turns out that self-produced movement does facilitate understanding of locations. Performance on tasks, such as those used by Acredolo (1978), is better when infants move on their own than when they are carried around the display (Benson & Uzgiris, 1985). And infants who have begun to crawl do better on such measures than do infants who are not yet crawling (Bertenthal, Campos, & Barrett, 1984).

The effects of self-produced movement extend to a number of other early developments in addition to the tasks considered here (Campos et al., 2000). One such effect may be its role in cortical brain maturation. Infants with more crawling experience, for example, have been shown to have more mature activation profiles in the frontal and occipital lobes (Bell & Fox, 1996)—areas related to various types of spatial processing. Thus, babies' control over their own movement through space apparently plays an important role in their mastery of the spatial world.

LEARNING OBJECTIVE 7.4

Outline infants' capacity for processing visual information.

1. What visual information can newborn infants see? And, how well?
2. What is the development of infants' ability to see faces?
3. What are the properties of objects that infants develop the capacity to appreciate?
4. When do infants develop the capability to perceive distance and depth, and why?
5. How do infants perceive the spatial layout of objects?

INTERMODAL PERCEPTION

Learning Objective 7.5

Gain an understanding of how infants integrate the information from different senses that come from a single event.

Up to this point, we have discussed the various perceptual modes separately. But, of course, we actually perceive most objects, people, and events in our world through more than one mode. A dog, for example, provides a great deal of visual information. It also supplies auditory information by barking, panting, and moving around. Touch may provide another cue as the dog sidles up against your leg. Unfortunately, the dog may stimulate yet another perceptual mode, smell, from a distance of several feet. Although these perceptual cues may sometimes be available simultaneously, you probably can tell that the dog is nearby with only a few of the cues, maybe even with one alone.

How the child comes to realize that cues from different senses "go together" has puzzled psychologists and philosophers for some time (Lewkowicz, 2000; Bahrick & Lickliter, 2002). As we will see in Chapter 8, Piaget (1952) argued that the sensory modes are largely separate at birth and that the baby integrates them only through experience. For example, the baby can relate touch and vision only when he learns to look at objects as his hand grasps them. In contrast, other theorists, such as the Gibsons (e.g., Gibson & Pick, 2000), have argued that some coordination of the senses is present from the start. There is, as we will see, some truth to both positions.

Researchers generally have approached infants' understanding of intermodal relations in one of two ways (Rose & Ruff, 1987). Many studies focus on how exploring in one mode triggers exploration in a different mode. Other studies focus on how input from different senses comes to indicate a single mental representation—how we know, for example, that a particular sight, touch, and smell all come from the same dog.

EXPLORATORY INTERMODAL RELATIONS

We appreciate the spatial location of objects through many sensory modes—vision, audition, touch, and sometimes even smell. Investigators have asked whether infants are born with knowledge of space that is used by all the different sensory modes. If so, this shared knowledge could provide a basis for the intercoordination of the senses. For example, you know where to look when a person calls your name from behind or from the side. Will a newborn baby, who has had no opportunity to associate sound location and visual location, do the same?

As we mentioned earlier, the answer is yes. The newborn turns her eyes and head toward the sound of a voice or a rattle if the sound continues for several seconds (Ennouri & Bloch, 1996; Morrongiello et al., 1994a). And the interrelation among sensory modes is not limited to sound and vision. You will remember that one of the infant's earliest reflexes involves turning the head toward the cheek being stroked, an exploratory action that helps the newborn find the nipple. Similar relations exist between smell and vision—as noted, a 6-day-old baby will turn toward a breast pad that exudes the odour of the mother's milk (MacFarlane, 1975; Marlier & Schaal, 2005).

Babies explore novel objects with multiple modalities, including vision and touch. (*Brand X Pictures*)

An important form of exploratory relations among perceptual modes is the relation between vision and reaching. Infants' reaching for a rattle that they see illustrates how vision can trigger tactile exploration. Babies do not reach and grasp objects accurately before 4 or 5 months of age, but they move their arms in the right direction much earlier, perhaps as early as during birth (von Hofsten, 1982; White, Castle, & Held, 1964). In fact, the exploratory relation between vision and reaching may be sufficiently coordinated in newborns that they will work at keeping their hands in view. If weights are attached to each wrist of a newborn, he will allow those weights to pull his arm down when he cannot see that arm, but will resist the weight when his arm is in front of his face (van der Meer, van der Weel, & Lee, 1996).

Such relations among the sensory modes are present at birth, presumably because they have evolutionary value. We call these *prepared relations*—relations for which the baby is predisposed by biology but that are also modifiable by experience. Some degree of modifiability is clearly necessary so that the initially crude connections among perceptual modes can be sharpened by experience. Recall the notion of recalibration introduced earlier. If relations among the senses were fixed at birth, children would have no means by which they could adapt to such physical changes as the distance between their eyes and ears or the changing length of their arms and legs. In fact, all of the prepared relations evident in the newborn show substantial improvement across the course of infancy. Infants' localization of sounds, for example, is much more precise and flexible by 5 or 6 months of age than at birth (Morrongiello, 1994). Similarly, visually directed reaching becomes increasingly skilled and effective as infants gain more and more experience in acting on the world (Adolph & Berger, 2006; Wentworth, Benson, & Haith, 2000).

The examples of exploratory activity described here support the idea that relations among the sensory modes exist quite early. Next, however, we must ask whether babies realize they are exploring the same object in the two modes. This question raises the issue of mental representation.

INTERMODAL REPRESENTATION

How can we determine whether infants can use different perceptual modes to form a single mental representation of an object? Two kinds of evidence are informative. The first examines whether babies can transfer the benefit of experience from one mode to another. The second examines whether babies know that the same object is stimulating two modes. Psychologists have used these approaches to examine relations between haptic and visual perceptions and between vision and audition.

HAPTIC–VISUAL RELATIONS As noted earlier, haptic perception refers to active exploration by means of touch, as when a baby handles a rattle. Sucking can also be an important form of haptic exploration, especially for young infants.

Several researchers have investigated whether infants can transfer information gained from sucking to visual perception of the same object. Meltzoff and Borton (1979) provided 1-month-old infants with an opportunity to suck on either a nubby (bumpy) nipple or a smooth nipple. They then presented the infants pictures of the nubby and smooth nipples, side by side. Infants looked longer at the nipple they had sucked. This finding suggests that cross-modal cues can specify the same object for infants at an amazingly early age, but we should be careful in reaching conclusions. Although some experimenters have reported similar findings (Gibson & Walker, 1984; Pecheux, Lepecq, & Salzarulo, 1988), others have been unable to replicate the results (Brown & Gottfried, 1986; Maurer, Stager, & Mondloch, 1999), and thus at present, it is not clear how early such oral–visual matching is possible.

Infants have also been tested for the ability to recognize objects visually that they have previously explored only by hand. Recent studies have suggested that this capacity is available to the newborn (Streri, 2003). However, this ability is fragile: newborns could successfully visually recognize an object that they had previously explored with their right hand, but not when they had explored that object with their left hand (Streri & Gentaz, 2004). Thus, this ability, if present in the first half-year of life, is relatively weak. However, babies between 6 and 12 months of age clearly demonstrate that they can make the match (Rose & Orlian, 1991; Ruff & Kohler, 1978). Babies are also able to learn about an object visually and then recognize that object by touch, but the vision-to-touch connection is more difficult to make than is the touch-to-vision connection. Infants typically succeed only if they are allowed more time to explore the object or if they are already somewhat familiar with it (Bushnell, 1994; Rose, 1994).

An ingenious study examined whether babies can detect differences between what they feel and what they see. Babies were given the impression that they were reaching for an object reflected in a mirror, but they were actually reaching for an object hidden behind the mirror. On trick trials, babies felt a furry object while viewing a smooth object or vice versa. On non-trick trials, the objects matched. Whereas 8-month-olds did not show different facial expressions for trick and non-trick trials, 9.5- and 11-month-olds showed more surprise during the trick trials, indicating that they perceived the mismatch (Bushnell, 1982). However, research by Mark Schmuckler of the University of Toronto, using preferential looking, suggests that infants as young as 5 months of age can match and detect differences between what they feel and what they see (Figure 7.21). In these studies, infants matched visual information about their leg movements with the movement that they felt their legs are making, and they also discriminated visual information that indicated another child's leg movements that did not match their actual movements (Schmuckler & Fairhall, 2001; Schmuckler & Jewell, 2007).

FIGURE 7.21

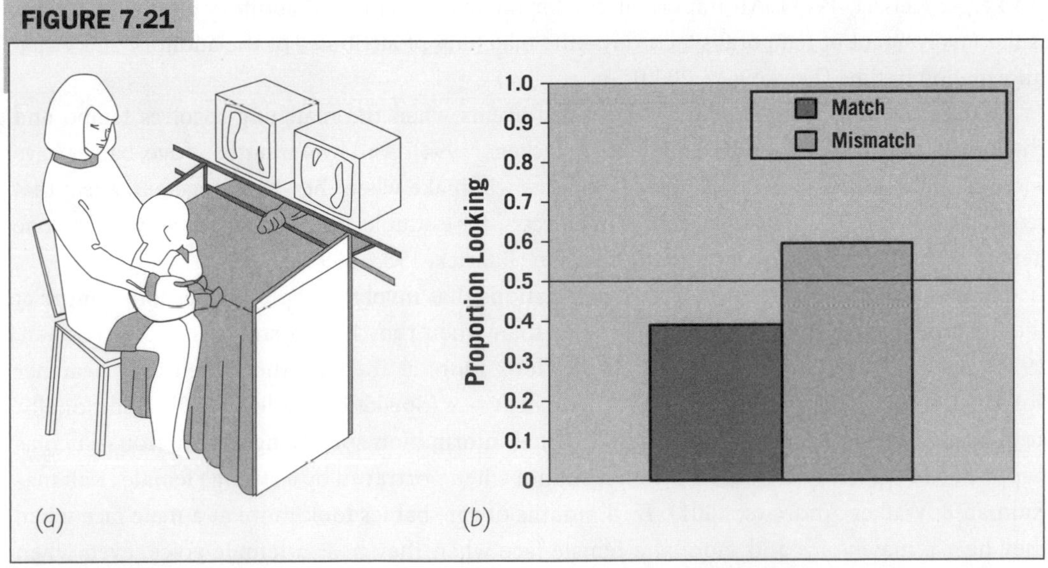

(*a*) **Setup used by Schmuckler and colleagues to assess infants' ability to perceive haptic–visual relations.** Note that the infant's legs are underneath a tabletop and behind a curtain such that they could only feel the movement of their legs. A camera, mounted underneath, records the infant's leg movements. On the screens in front of them, one displayed the infant's own leg movements, whereas the other displayed another infant's leg movements—thus, what infants see of leg movements and what they feel of their own legs moving can be dissociated, and their ability to relate haptic and visual information can be examined. (*b*) Results of Schmuckler's experiment of infants' perception of haptic–visual relations. Infants looked for a greater proportion of the time at the leg movements that did not match their felt movements. *From "Infants' Visual-Proprioceptive Intermodal Perception With Imperfect Contingency Information" by M.A. Schmuckler and D.T. Jewell* (Developmental Psychobiology, *49, 2007, p. 391–392*). *Copyright © 2007 by Wiley. Reprinted by permission.*

AUDITORY–VISUAL RELATIONS Can babies detect a correspondence between a sound and a visual event? Interestingly, babies naturally look at visual events that correspond to the sounds they hear. Researchers have capitalized on this tendency to explore the kinds of auditory–visual relations that babies appreciate.

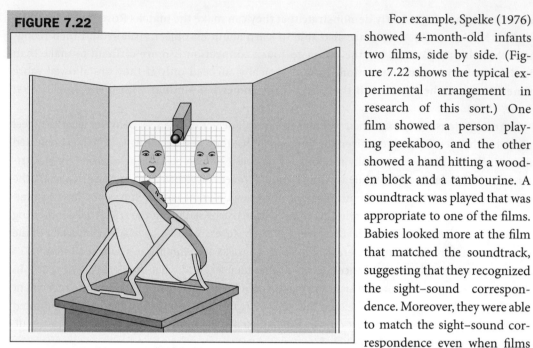

FIGURE 7.22

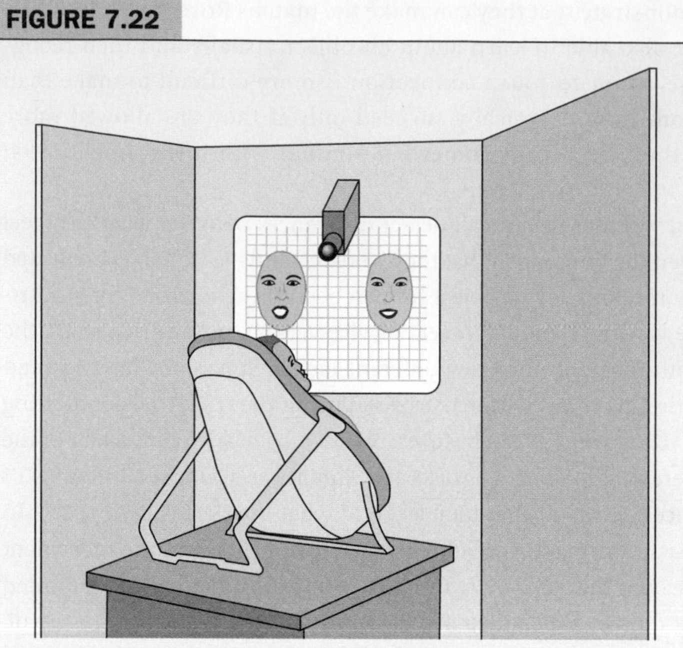

Experimental arrangement used to study intermodal perception in infants. In the example shown, both faces are talking, but the soundtrack corresponds to the lip movements of only one of the speakers. *From "The Bimodal Perception of Speech in Infancy" by P. K. Kuhl and A. N. Meltzoff (Science, 218, 1982, p. 1139). Copyright © 1982 by the AAAS. Reprinted by permission.*

For example, Spelke (1976) showed 4-month-old infants two films, side by side. (Figure 7.22 shows the typical experimental arrangement in research of this sort.) One film showed a person playing peekaboo, and the other showed a hand hitting a wooden block and a tambourine. A soundtrack was played that was appropriate to one of the films. Babies looked more at the film that matched the soundtrack, suggesting that they recognized the sight–sound correspondence. Moreover, they were able to match the sight–sound correspondence even when films were superimposed (Bahrick, Walker, & Neisser, 1981). An important cue for infants' matching of auditory and visual events is the involvement of temporal synchrony—the matching of attributes of the auditory and visual information in time (Lewkowicz, 2000).

Babies can also match auditory and visual events when the matching involves tempo and rhythm (Bahrick & Lickliter, 2000; Bahrick & Pickens, 1994). And by 4 months of age, babies have some idea about the types of sounds new objects will make when they bang together, a feat that requires knowledge of several properties of objects—for example, their hardness and whether one item or several items are involved in the collision (Bahrick, 1983, 1992).

Babies also appreciate auditory–visual relations that involve people. Babies look longer at their mother's face when they hear her voice than when they hear a stranger's voice (Cohen, 1974). As early as 3.5 months of age, babies look more at their mother when they hear her voice and more at their father when they hear his voice (Spelke & Owsley, 1979). Additionally, at this age infants can match auditory and visual information specifying an emotion—such as happy or sad—portrayed by their mother, but not when portrayed by a strange female (Kahana-Kalman & Walker-Andrews, 2001). By 4 months of age, babies look more at a male face when they hear a male voice and more at a female face when they hear a female voice, even when both faces and voices are unfamiliar (Walker-Andrews et al., 1991). By 4 months, they can also match on the basis of age, directing attention to either an adult or a child speaker, depending on whether the voice they hear is adult-like or child-like (Bahrick, Netto, & Hernandez-Reif, 1998). As with matching auditory and visual information of events involving objects, temporal synchrony, which is always available in the matching of faces and voices, is an important cue (Lewkowicz, 2010).

Some sensitivities seem to be even more subtle. Spelke and Cortelyou (1981) showed 4-month-old infants two films with adult female strangers as speakers; in only one of the two films did the movement of the speaker's lips correspond to the soundtrack the babies heard. The infants looked more at the speaker whose lip movements were in synchrony with the sound. A series of studies by Kuhl and Meltzoff (1982, 1984, 1988) posed an even more challenging matching task. In this case, the two speakers repeatedly pronounced two words that differed by just a single vowel—for example, one said *pop* and the other said *pep*. To match face and voice in this case, the infant had to engage in a kind of lip reading, mapping particular mouth movements onto particular sounds.

Four-month-olds were able to do so: they looked longer at the speaker whose word was heard on the soundtrack. Indeed, even *newborns* may be capable of such matching (Aldridge et al., 1999). This is not that surprising, as the auditory–visual matching cue of temporal synchrony is likely available at birth (Lewkowicz, 2000). Infants, then, are surprisingly good at picking up the commonality in cues from different senses.

The baby's awareness that different cues from the same objects are coordinated greatly simplifies the task of organizing the overwhelming number of stimuli in the world into more manageable chunks. It is important to remember, though, that intermodal capabilities emerge at different times. At first, for example, infants simply appreciate that synchrony exists between visual and auditory events. More subtle forms of intermodal perception appear in steps as the baby matures (Lewkowicz, 2000).

We have discussed two basic approaches to the study of intermodal perception. Research on intermodal exploration has shown that babies come into the world with a number of inborn relations among sensory modes. Yet it also seems that forming mental representations of objects from the inputs of many perceptual modes requires some experience. As always, nature and nurture work together to guide development.

LEARNING OBJECTIVE 7.5

Gain an understanding of how infants integrate the information from different senses that come from a single event.

1. What are the different theories for how the child comes to realize that cues from different senses go together?
2. How do infants use exploratory behaviour to coordinate information from the different modalities?
3. What is the basis for early exploratory behaviour?
4. What is the nature of infants' capacity to integrate haptic and visual information, and auditory and visual information?

ATTENTION AND ACTION

Learning Objective 7.6

Sketch the development of infants' ability to allocate their attention and to use that attention to guide their behaviour.

Because sensory and perceptual processes are triggered by external stimuli, it may seem that these processes are passive and simply activated by events in the world. However, the perceptual modes are the mind's tools for gathering information about the environment, and the mind uses these tools actively. This is what we mean by *attention*: the active, selective taking in of some but not all of the potentially available information in a situation. Furthermore, perception is typically not an end in itself, but a means toward the goal of operating on the world effectively: "We perceive in order to act, and we act to perceive" (Pick, 1992, p. 791). In this final section of the chapter, we examine the dynamic aspect of perception, considering both how action affects perception and how perception guides action. We begin with infancy and then move on to older children.

For Thought and Discussion

Research suggests that we perceive in order to act. Does this generalization apply to you in your daily activities? How might it apply to the life of an infant?

INFANCY

ATTENTION Even newborn infants attend to mild sounds and sights. Their bodies become quieter, they stop what they are doing (such as sucking), they widen their eyes, and their heart rates slow down (see Figure 7.23). These changes in behaviour appear designed to optimize the baby's readiness to receive stimuli. First described by Sokolov (1960) as the **orienting reflex**, these changes can be observed, for example, when newborns attend to moving lights, to sounds that change gradually, or to sounds of low frequency (Haith, 1966). However, if the physical stimuli

Orienting reflex A natural reaction to novel stimuli that enhances stimulus processing and includes orientation of the eyes and ears to optimize stimulus reception, inhibition of ongoing activity, and a variety of physiological changes.

FIGURE 7.23

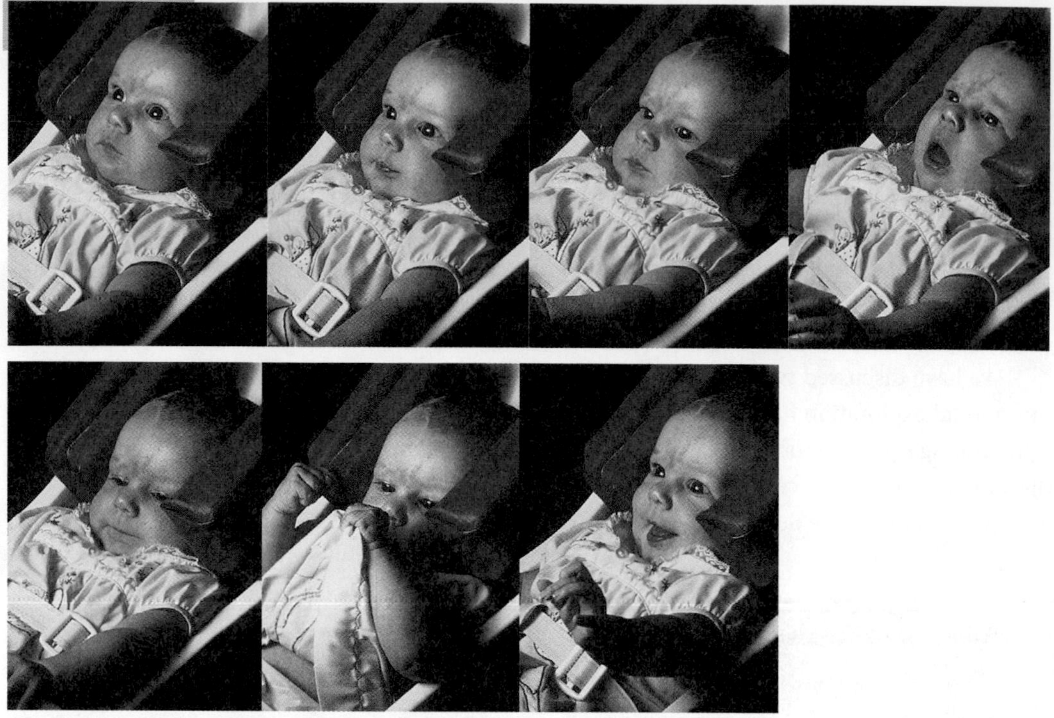

Examples of the orienting reflex in a young infant. Attention is high when a new stimulus first appears (pictures 1 and 2), then declines as the stimulus becomes familiar (pictures 4–6), and then peaks again when the stimulus changes (picture 7). *From* The World of the Newborn *by D. Maurer and C. Maurer (New York: Basic Books, 1988, pp. 128–129). Copyright © 1988 by Daphne Maurer and Charles Maurer.*

Defensive reflex A natural reaction to novel stimuli that tends to protect the organism from further stimulation, and that may include orientation of the stimulus receptors away from the stimulus source and a variety of physiological changes.

Selective attention Concentration on a stimulus or event with attendant disregard for other simultaneously available stimuli or events.

are too intense or the changes too abrupt, infants close their eyes and become agitated and their heart rates increase—a protective reaction called the **defensive reflex** (Graham & Clifton, 1966). The orienting and defensive reflexes appear to be the baby's earliest forms of positive and negative attention.

We have already discussed other indicators of newborns' attention, such as the tendency to look toward the location of a sound and to turn the head toward cheek stimulation or an attractive odour. Typically, however, investigators are more interested in the development of **selective attention**, the infant's ability to focus on one stimulus rather than another. Even newborns have the capacity for at least a simple form of selective attention, choosing to look at displays of intermediate levels of brightness over extreme levels (Lewkowicz & Turkewitz, 1981) and at patterned over non-patterned displays (Fantz, 1963). Newborns also adjust their sucking activity to hear their mother's voice, rather than the voice of a woman unknown to them (DeCasper & Fifer, 1980). This capacity for selective attention provides a powerful tool for investigating infant perception, as we have already seen.

Attending selectively, however, does not consist just of focusing on one stimulus rather than another. Rather, it consists of a number of different components that have been demonstrated in adults. These include: the attentional pop-out and visual search of a distinctive item from among a set of many items; the inhibition of returning to attend to an item one has already searched; the shifting of attention from one item to another; the disengagement of attention from one item in order to shift to another; and the active inhibition of the item not originally selected. These components are critical for effective perceptual processing and preventing overload of the perceptual system, because we are constrained in the amount of visual information that can be perceptually processed at any particular moment. Though these components have been demonstrated in adults, do infants exhibit them as well? For infants, these selective attention components would seem to be crucial for filtering and making sense of their environment, with which they have little or no experience, as they pursue the construction of a knowledge base.

Researchers have found evidence of many of these selective attention components in infancy. First, let us consider pop-out and visual search. Imagine it is raining and you are searching for a friend's coat, which happens to be red. You enter the coat room and all the coats but your friend's are grey—what happens? Your attention is consequently almost automatically captured by your friend's coat—this is pop-out. Now imagine that the other coats are of all different colours so that your friend's is not distinctive, and you have to visually search through the coats until you find your friend's. Consequently, the time it takes to find your friend's coat by way of pop-out does not change as the number of grey coats increases, but detection time does increase as the number of different coloured coats increases.

In a study by Scott Adler at York University, using eye movements as a measure, 3-month-old infants were shown to exhibit this exact pattern when searching for a '+' among '*Ls*'. The time it takes infants to initiate an eye movement to the '+' does not increase as the number of '*Ls*' increases (Adler & Orprecio, 2006), similar to adults. However, when the '+' was not present, then the time it took to initiate an eye movement to one of the '*Ls*' increased as the number of '*Ls*' increased, as it did with adults (see Figure 7.24). This suggests that the same attentional mechanisms that are responsible for the pop-out and visual search components for selectively attending to one out of many items in adults are functioning in early infancy.

Another phenomenon of selective attention is that when searching for a particular item among many, we inhibit attention from going back to items or locations to which we have previously attended and searched—this is termed *inhibition of return*. This ensures that attention is allocated efficiently to locations that have not yet been searched, and thereby increases the likelihood and speed that the item of interest will be found. Numerous studies have documented the exhibition of this aspect of selective attention in infants by 6 months of age (Clohessy & Posner, 1991; Hood, 1993) and perhaps in newborns (Valenza, Simion, & Umilta, 1994). Research has suggested that in infants, as in adults, this capacity is mediated by the functioning of the frontal cortex (Richards, 2001).

To shift attention from one item to another, we must first remove or *disengage* attention from the item to which it is currently deployed. Studies have indicated that younger infants are slower to disengage their attention than are older infants, but become adult-like during the first year of life (Blaga & Colombo, 2006; Hood & Atkinson, 1993). Finally, when we select a particular item for our attention, at the same time we inhibit attention to the item or items that are not selected. Though

FIGURE 7.24

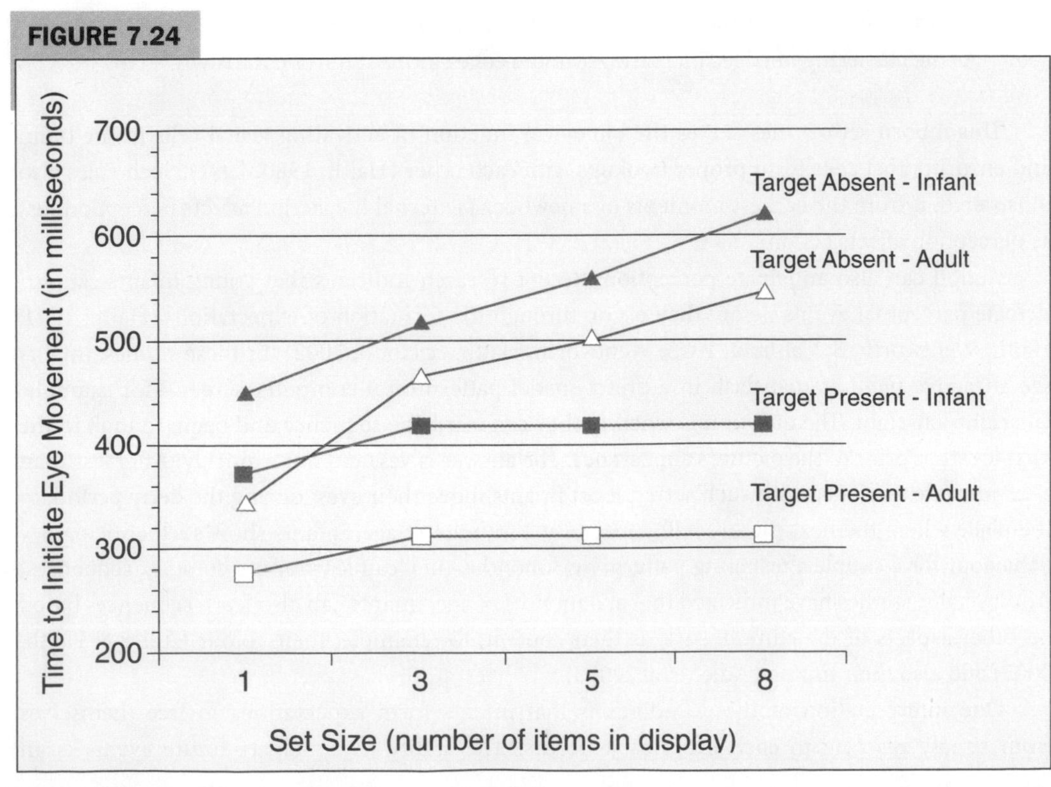

Infants' and adults' times to make an eye movement to an item in Target Present (i.e., + among *Ls*) and Target Absent displays (i.e., all *Ls*). *Adapted from "The eyes have it: Visual pop-out in infants and adults" by Adler and Orprecio* (Developmental Science, *9, 2006, p. 189–206*). Reprinted by permission of Wiley-Blackwell.

this aspect of selective attention has not been systematically studied in infants, a recent study suggests that it might be functioning in early infancy as well (Amso & Johnson, 2005). Together, these demonstrations indicate that the structures for filtering one's world and focusing attention on items of interest is already present and functioning early in infancy, and the time course of their development may reflect maturation of the underlying neural systems (Johnson, 1990).

What controls these characteristics of selective attention? It is thought that in early infancy, attention is controlled by aspects of stimulation, such as the distinctiveness of the stimulus that controls pop-out and visual search. Some properties of stimulation that control and guide attention are *absolute*, in the sense that they can be specified independently of the perceiver. Movement is an example; so, in the visual realm, are contrast and curvature. In the early weeks of life, it is primarily dimensions of this sort that seem to compel infant attention. Other properties of stimulation are *relative*, in the sense that they must be defined with respect to a particular perceiver. Novelty is an example—a particular stimulus is not novel in an absolute sense; rather, it is novel to someone who has never encountered it before. Surprise is another example—events are not surprising in themselves but rather *to* someone, given their fit with that person's expectations. From approximately 3 months on, it is primarily events in this second category—in particular, events that are in some way new or discrepant or surprising—that are most interesting. Indeed, this is true not just during infancy, but for children and adults as well (Kagan, 2002).

ACTION We turn now to the relation between perception and action. The looking activity of young infants is a good example of the role that action plays in perception. When alert and active, young infants make new visual fixations two or three times each second. Newborn infants even search actively with their eyes in darkness, indicating their perceptual system is active even when there is no stimulus to produce a reaction. They continue to search when a light is turned on until they find light–dark edges. When they do, they cross back and forth over those edges, adjusting their visual scanning as necessary. They seem to come into the world with a set of rules for acting:

1. If awake and the light is not too bright, open eyes.
2. If in darkness, search around.
3. If find light, search for contrasting edges.
4. If find edges, stay near them and cross back and forth over them.
5. As the clustering of edges increases, scan the edges more and more narrowly.

This inborn set of rules serves the biological function of activating visual cells in the brain and ensuring that cells form proper hookups with each other (Haith, 1980, 1991). Such rules also illustrate that from the earliest moments of a newborn's external life, action affects perception just as perception affects action.

Action can also anticipate perception. Recent research indicates that young infants can anticipate perceptual events before they occur, through the formation of expectations (Haith, 1994; Haith, Wentworth, & Canfield, 1993; Wentworth, Haith, & Hood, 2002). In these studies, infants see attractive pictures that flash in a preset spatial pattern on a computer screen—for example, left-right-left-right. The question is whether they can learn the sequence and begin to look to the next location prior to the picture's appearance. The answer is yes, and quite quickly: After less than a minute of experience with such series, most infants move their eyes, during the delay period, to the place where the next picture will appear. By 2 months of age, infants show such anticipatory behaviour for a simple alternating pattern; by 3 months, they can learn more complex sequences. Additionally, studies have indicated that at 3 months of age, infants can also learn sequences based on other aspects of the stimuli, such as their content; for example, their colour (Adler & Haith, 2003) and also their timing (Adler et al., 2008).

One interpretation of these findings is that infants form expectations to free themselves from simply reacting to each event as it occurs. The ability to anticipate future events is an important component of many kinds of cognitive activity throughout the lifespan (Haith et al., 1994). Apparently, such "future-oriented processing" begins very early.

Most of our discussion so far has concerned vision. Babies also use other action tools to investigate objects; for example, they use their mouths and tongues (Rochat, 1993), and, most obviously, their hands. We have seen that infants begin to use vision to direct their hands toward objects by about 4 months. From the onset of visually directed reaching, babies show success at grasping not only stationary objects, but also moving objects. This achievement requires that they reach not to the present location, but to an anticipated future site (Bertenthal, 1996; Spelke & von Hofsten, 2001). Thus reaching, like eye movements, is *prospective*—directed not just to current reality, but also to anticipated future reality.

When infants begin to move around by themselves, links between perception and action become even stronger. As we have seen, self-produced movement produces new experiences and sometimes new understandings—such as the onset of fear of heights (Campos et al., 1992). Moving around independently also requires new perceptual learning. This is so because babies in the first year of life have difficulty separating their perception of space from the actions they perform. For example, babies who are able to reach around a barrier for a hidden object have to relearn the task when they are required to crawl around the barrier to get it (Lockman & Adams, 2001). Similarly, infants who can perceive and avoid a drop-off while in a sitting posture may respond differently when put in the posture for crawling (Adolph, 2000). Thus, as infants gain more experience with the effects of their own movements, they gradually develop a more unified understanding of space.

OLDER CHILDREN

ATTENTION Although infants are capable of selective attention, there is a general shift with age from control of attention by external stimuli to stronger self-regulation based on the individual's own goals and intentions. Flavell (1985) identified four important aspects of attention that develop with age.

1. *Control* of attention improves with age as attention span increases and distractibility decreases. For example, children younger than 2.5 years of age are easily distracted from watching television programs by toys in the room and other events in the house. Soon enough, however, it may become difficult to pull them away from the set (Anderson et al., 1986; Ruff, Capozzoli, & Weissberg, 1998).
2. *Adaptability* of attention to the task also changes. When an experimenter tells children to pay attention to a particular task, older children do so and disregard things that are not central to it. Younger children, however, focus on many more of the irrelevant aspects and so do not perform as well on the main task (Hagen & Hale, 1973; Miller, 1990).
3. Another feature of attentional change is *planfulness.* When an experimenter asks children to judge whether two complex pictures are the same, younger children often use a haphazard comparison strategy, not examining all the details before making a judgment. Older children are more systematic, comparing each detail across pictures, one by one (Vurpillot, 1968).
4. Finally, children become better at *adjusting* their attentional strategies as they gather information from a task. For example, experienced readers change their reading speed as the difficulty of the text changes, whereas younger readers tend to maintain a fairly regular reading speed, regardless of difficulty (Day, 1975).

We saw that the study of children's eye movements demonstrates selective attention and the interplay of action and perception very early in life. Eye movements are also informative in the study of older children. In one experiment, children were shown pairs of houses, such as those in Figure 7.25, and were asked to judge whether the houses in each pair were identical

FIGURE 7.25

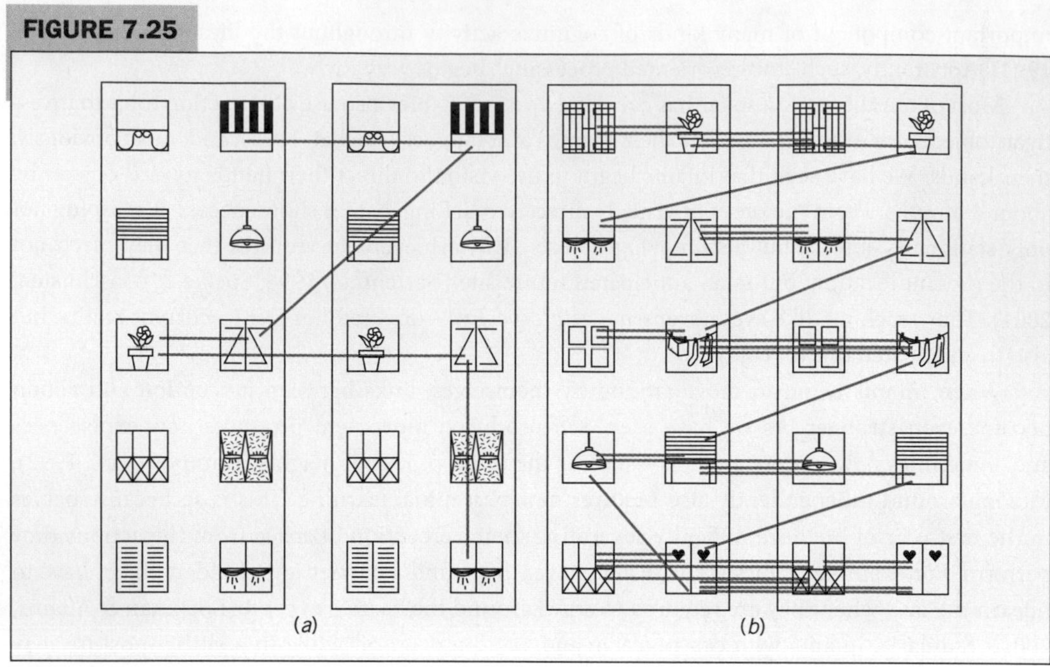

Reconstruction of a fixation sequence by (*a*) an inefficient child, and (*b*) an efficient child. Their task was to judge whether the windows in two houses were identical or different. *From "Extent of Visual Exploration and Number of Elements Present around the Stimulus in a Perceptual Differentiation Task" by E. Vurpillot, R. Castelo, and C. Renard (Année Psychologique, 75, 1975, Figure 2, p. 362–363). Reprinted by permission of Presses Universitaires de France.*

or different. The experimenter recorded the children's eye fixations and movements as they looked at the two houses. Each house had several windows of varying shapes with varying decorations. A thorough examination of the houses required comparing the windows of the houses one by one.

Striking differences were found between children at 4 and 9 years of age. The younger children appeared to have little or no plan for the task. Rather than comparing the corresponding windows in the pair of houses, the younger children often looked at windows in different locations in a haphazard order, and did not check all windows before deciding the houses were the same. Older children, in contrast, scanned comparable windows, systematically checking each pair of windows before making a "same" decision. They were also more efficient, ending their inspection as soon as a difference between windows permitted them to say "different" (Vurpillot & Ball, 1979).

In general, studies of scanning and other forms of perceptual activity reveal increased carefulness in gathering information, more flexibility in search, and lowered distractibility as children move from the preschool to the middle-elementary school years (Ruff & Rothbart, 1996). Such studies also reveal clear links between attention and learning and problem solving. Developmental improvements in attention are one source of differences between younger and older children in problem-solving prowess. Individual differences in attention at any age are one reason some children learn more effectively than others. Unfortunately, not every child's attentional skills and control develops properly, as is the case of children dealing with attention deficit and hyperactivity disorder (ADHD). See *Application 7.1* for a discussion of ADHD attentional problems.

Developmental level is not the only contributor to how children deploy their attention. Barbara Rogoff and colleagues (Chavajay & Rogoff, 1999; Rogoff et al., 1993) observed toddlers (children 12 to 24 months old) in the United States and Mayan toddlers in Guatemala in situations in which there were potentially many stimuli and events to attend to. The Mayan toddlers were more likely than their American counterparts to attend simultaneously to two or three ongoing events, as opposed to focusing on a single thing at a time. One 12-month-old, for example, "skillfully closed things in a jar with his older sister, whistled on his toy whistle that his mother had mischievously slipped into his mouth, and at the same time watched a passing truck with interest"(Chavajay & Rogoff, 1999, p. 1080). The basis for the differences among the toddlers became evident from observations of the mothers' behaviour: Mayan mothers, like their children, were more likely than the

APPLICATION 7.1
ADHD: HELPING CHILDREN WITH ATTENTIONAL PROBLEMS

An important developmental achievement is the capacity to control and direct attention effectively. Not all children, however, master the challenges of attentional control as quickly or as fully as others. Anyone who has spent much time in elementary school classrooms is familiar with children who constantly fidget and talk out inappropriately, who seem unable to stay in their seat or to concentrate for more than brief periods of time, and whose uncontrolled behaviour distracts not only from their own but also their classmates' learning.

Attention deficit hyperactivity disorder (ADHD) is a relatively new label for what is almost certainly a very old problem. The term refers to a clinical syndrome characterized by the kinds of behaviour patterns just described. Children with ADHD have great difficulty maintaining attention, they are often hyperactive, and their behaviour has a generally uncontrolled and impulsive quality. These children perform poorly in school, and they often have difficulties in interpersonal relations as well. ADHD emerges early in childhood and can be a lifelong condition (American Psychiatric Association, 2000; Wender, 2000).

Attention deficit hyperactivity disorder (ADHD) A developmental disorder characterized by difficulty in sustaining attention, hyperactivity, and impulsive and uncontrolled behaviour.

The diagnosis of ADHD has become increasingly common. Current estimates of the proportion of school-age children in Canada range from 3.8 to 9.8 percent (Breton, et al., 1999). Boys are diagnosed with the disorder more often than are girls; it is unclear, however, whether this disparity reflects a genuine difference between the sexes or simply the fact that boys are more likely to show the disruptive behaviours that lead to clinical evaluation (Barkley, 2006). The latter possibility is supported by the fact that gender differences are especially marked when teacher reports are the basis for identifying children for evaluation (Campbell, 2000).

The precise cause of ADHD remains a source of controversy (Faraone & Biedermann, 2000; Joseph, 2000). The evidence suggests that in most cases, both nature and nurture contribute. The fact that ADHD tends to run in families suggests a biological component. Approximately 50 percent of children with ADHD have a relative with ADHD, usually a parent or sibling (Silver, 1999). In one study, 51 percent of identical twin pairs were concordant for ADHD; that is, if one twin had the disorder, the other did as well (Goodman & Stevenson, 1989). Further evidence for the importance of biological factors comes from the studies of brain structure and functioning. Individuals with ADHD often show abnormalities in the prefrontal cortex—the region of the brain responsible for attention and inhibition of behaviour (Barkley, 2006).

Experience can also be important. The home lives of children with ADHD tend to be characterized by high levels of stress and parental punitiveness (Bernier & Siegel, 1994; Hammerness, 2009). The relationship between child and environment in most such cases is almost certainly transactional (Chapter 1): aspects of parenting may contribute to the child's problems, but the presence of a difficult child also creates stress for the parents, whose attempts to cope may then make the child's problems even greater (Campbell, 2000). In some instances, ADHD may have its origins even earlier in development—in the prenatal environment and the exposure of the fetus to teratogens, such as alcohol and drugs (Barkley, 2006; Hammerness, 2009).

Just as both nature and nurture may contribute to the emergence of ADHD, attempts to help children with ADHD may take both biological and environmental routes. One of the most common and effective treatments for these children is a biological one. Administration of stimulant drugs, such as Ritalin, has been used to treat ADHD since the 1930s. This treatment leads to improvement in approximately 75 percent of cases (Barkley, 2006; Hammerness, 2009). Ritalin and similar drugs tend to decrease activity level and heighten attention—which, of course, is precisely the sort of change that children with ADHD need (Hammerness, 2009; Wender, 2000).

Although drug treatment can be an important part of a therapy program for ADHD, medication does not cure the condition, and medication alone is unlikely to give children with ADHD all the help they need. The most effective treatment programs combine medication with changes in the child's environment. Environmental interventions can take many forms. Among the approaches that have proved beneficial are operant conditioning of appropriate behaviours, modelling, and family-oriented forms of therapy (Barkley, 2006). As we would expect, interventions that involve both the school and the home tend to be most effective.

At present, there is no known cure for ADHD, and not even the best treatment programs can guarantee long-term success. Still, recent years have seen important advances in our ability to help children and families cope with one of the most common and debilitating of childhood disorders.

American sample to attend simultaneously to multiple events. The children's attentional patterns, then, reflected those of their mothers. We can see a theme from the sociocultural approach in this work: children are socialized for forms of activity—in this case, patterns of attention—that are valued in the culture in which they are developing.

ACTION We turn finally to some research that examines the relation between perception and various forms of skilled motor behaviour. Action skills—behaviours that require physical coordination, such as reaching, walking, and catching—involve a complex interplay between perception and various parts of the motor system (Bertenthal & Clifton, 1998). The development of these skills is made more complicated by the fact that the growing body and limbs change in size, weight, and proportion. Perception plays a key role in the continuing adjustment required for skill development, providing feedback about the relative accuracy of performance. Feedback indicates the difference between reaching a goal (such as catching a ball) and not reaching it (missed it by 15 cm [6 inches]).

One study examined how children of different ages adjust action to perception in the development of skill (Hay, 1984). Glass wedges placed in front of the eyes of 5- to 11-year-old children created a shift in the apparent location of visual objects (much like the apparent shift of underwater objects seen from above). If the child did not watch his arm as it moved toward the object, but simply reached directly for the object where it appeared to be, he would reach too far to one side and miss.

The 5-year-olds tended to make more direct reaches, correcting their hand position only after the hand had reached the apparent position of the object. The 7-year-olds made slower or more hesitant reaches, with starts and stops followed by small corrections near the end. Children 9 and 11 years of age were more likely to begin with a direct movement, gradually slowing their reach as they approached the object, and making corrective movements near the end. Apparently the 5-year-olds paid little attention to feedback, whereas the 7-year-olds overemphasized it, much as an unpractised driver oversteers a sliding car. By 9 years of age, children used feedback more effectively.

Children's playing of video games provides an opportunity for examining the development of perceptual-motor coordination. (*Stanislav Solntsev/Digital Vision/ Getty Images*)

This study reveals an expected improvement with age in the coordination between perception and action. In some contexts, however, the perceptual-action skills of the young child seem to outshine those of the adult. Watching children play video games will convince any doubter that children are capable of highly sophisticated forms of perceptual-motor coordination. In fact, it is commonly assumed that children are more competent in such skills than are adults. However, we should not forget that children have more practice and are more motivated to engage in such activities.

One research team developed a technology for exploring this issue. Adults and 4-, 7-, and 12-year-olds played the video game Asteroids over several sessions in the laboratory so that the researchers could observe them as the players evolved from novices to intermediates. The tasks in the game are to manoeuvre a spaceship so that it is not hit by flying rocks and to try to shoot down the rocks. The fast movement of the game makes it perceptually demanding, and the player uses several buttons to control turning and flying the spaceship and shooting its gun. A computer recorded all the game displays and all the players' actions, including eye movements, for later analysis.

Links to Related Material

Here we discussed the relation between playing video games and perceptual-motor coordination. In Chapter 14, you will learn about the relation between video game playing and anti-social, aggressive behaviour.

People in all age groups initially simplified the task by using as few controls as possible—for example, pressing only the spaceship's right-turn and fire buttons. The younger groups maintained this strategy throughout and therefore never got much better. The older groups, however, tried new strategies with time, learning to move or fly the spaceship around the screen. The shift to new strategies had a short-term cost because new flyers tended to run into things and destroy the spaceship. Ultimately, however, the ability to fly produced better performance.

We can see similarities with the earlier discussion of attention and eye-movement strategies. Here, too, development consists of increasing flexibility in the use of skills and increasing use of strategies. There is hope beyond elementary school, after all!

For Thought and Discussion

Do you use certain strategies for paying attention? Are the same strategies generally available to infants and young children? Why, or why not?

LEARNING OBJECTIVE 7.6

Sketch the development of infants' ability to allocate their attention and to use that attention to guide their behaviour.

1. What are the two behavioural tools that newborns have that are early forms of attention?
2. Which aspects of selective attention are functional in infancy?
3. In early infancy, what controls selective attention?
4. How does action, with vision and the hands, anticipate perception?
5. What aspects of attention develop in older children?
6. How do sociocultural influences affect the development of attention?
7. What is the relation between the development of action or motor skill and perception in older children?
8. What are some causes and consequences of attentional disorders, such as ADHD?

CONCLUSION

The issues that we have addressed in this chapter are long-standing. What is new in the modern era is not the questions, but rather the method of answering them. The last three decades have seen the development of powerful scientific methods for addressing what were once matters for purely philosophical speculation.

This research has taught us that many earlier ideas about infants were wrong. Many experts thought babies were blind and deaf at birth, an idea that lent support to the empiricist view that perceptual capacities were based solely on experience and learning. We now know that all the perceptual systems function even before the fetus has reached the age of normal-term birth. We live in the age of the "competent infant," in which many new capabilities have been discovered and infancy seems much less a period of perceptual disability than was once believed.

At the same time, we must be careful not to attribute too much skill to the infant. A recent "superbaby" craze (reinforced by articles in such widely read publications as *Time* and *Newsweek*) has led many people to think that babies can do almost anything. However, even in terms of very basic sensory processes—in detecting and discriminating the physical energies that stimulate the receptors—it is clear that a newborn baby has a great deal left to accomplish. And as we have seen, perceptual skills must be increasingly refined.

It is useful to think of babies as coming into the world with the essential tools for taking in and seeking out perceptual information. This is most obviously the case with eye movements. Other tools will soon mature, such as grasping, reaching, crawling, and walking. These tools are present at birth or mature during infancy in babies of every culture. However, the *content* of perception, the actual information gathered, is highly dependent on experience. Whether babies become familiar with faces that are brown, yellow, or white, or learn to understand French, Chinese, or English, depends on the culture in which they are reared.

As in most cases, then, the diametrically opposed nature and nurture views are both correct. Evolution has provided a creature with all the tools necessary to collect information about the world. Experience determines exactly what that information will be.

SUMMARY

KEY TERMS

attention, p. 216
attention deficit hyperactivity disorder (ADHD), p. 251
brightness constancy, p. 235
colour constancy, p. 235
defensive reflex, p. 246
haptic perception, p. 219
kinetic cues, p. 239
motion parallax, p. 239
optic flow, p. 239
orienting reflex, p. 245
perception, p. 216
pictorial cues, p. 239
preference method, p. 227
selective attention, p. 246
sensation, p. 216
shape constancy, p. 235
size constancy, p. 235
vestibular sensitivity, p. 221
visual accommodation, p. 228
visual acuity, p. 228
visual cliff, p. 238

LEARNING OBJECTIVES

LEARNING OBJECTIVE 7.1 Explain the issues for understanding perceptual development.

1. *What is the difference between sensation, perception, and attention?*
   Sensation is the detection of sensory information from the environment. Perception is the interpretation of that information. Attention is the mechanism that determines what information in the environment is selected for processing.

2. *How do environmental/learning theories explain perceptual development?*
   Environmental/learning theories emphasize the role of experience in guiding development. Development occurs as babies learn through experience to construct increasingly complex perceptions from the separate input of the senses. Through experience, infants combine information from different senses, such as sights with sounds, into a unitary perception.

3. *What is the Gibsonian explanation of perceptual development?*
   Gibsonians do not believe that perceptual development involves the successive combining of information through experience. Instead, Gibsonians believe in a biological approach to perceptual development, and that objects in the world emit an energy that is already organized and includes the natural relations between the senses (for example, the temporal synchrony between visual and auditory components of the same event). So the connections between sensory information do not need to be made through experience, as they already exist. Development, consequently, consists of increasing sensitivity to the organization of the energy, and which perceptual properties remain stable and which change.

4. *How does the continuity–discontinuity issue of development relate to perceptual development?*
   Most research on perceptual development has focused on normative development. As a result, individual differences have seldom been a focus and few studies have examined the stability of individual differences. Instead, research has focused on an attempt to trace the gradual or continuous evolution of particular perceptual skills through development.

LEARNING OBJECTIVE 7.2 Outline the development of the basic sensory capacities such as touch, smell, taste, and vestibular sensitivity.

1. *What is infants' sensitivity to pain and what is the effect of early pain exposure?*
   Newborn babies sense pain, as is evident by their reaction to a heel prick or circumcision. They exhibit an angry cry, as well as physiological changes, indicative of feeling pain. Further, the

effect of a baby feeling pain is not short-lived—newborns who receive a painful needle prick react more strongly to subsequent needle pricks. Also, circumcised males are more sensitive to vaccinations four to six months later.

2. *How early do infants show a sensitivity to touch and how does this sensitivity develop?*
Newborn babies show touch reflexes. Even fetuses are sensitive to touch, as shown by their response to the stroking of the side of the mouth. Touch sensitivity increases over the first several days of life. The active, exploratory use of touch is called haptic perception. By the end of the first year of life, infants can recognize a familiar object through exploration with the hand alone.

3. *In what ways does touch have social and perceptual consequences for infants?*
Touching is important for relations between children and adults. A hand placed on the newborn's chest can quiet a crying episode, and gentle stroking can soothe even premature babies. For older infants, touching increases positive emotion and visual attention during interactions between infant and caregiver. Parents can usually recognize their infant by touch alone within the first few days of life. Infants use touch to explore and acquire information about objects. Infants learn to recognize a familiar object by exploration with the hand alone and to discriminate features of those objects, as well.

4. *What odours and tastes do infants prefer and how soon do these preferences develop?*
Newborns will turn their heads away from and make negative expressions to bad smells and produce positive facial expressions to nice smells. Newborns can also differentiate human milk from formula. Odour sensitivity may even be evident prenatally. Within the first week, an infant can distinguish its mother's smell from another woman's. Babies are also sensitive to taste at birth, preferring sweet solutions. Taste sensitivity is also present prenatally. Newborn babies can distinguish among different tastes, making different facial expressions for sweet, sour, bitter, and salty tastes.

5. *What is a newborn's sensitivity to vestibular stimulation and what is its effect on infants?*
Vestibular sensitivity refers to the ability to detect gravity and the motion of our bodies, which helps us maintain body posture and balance. Newborns are sensitive to motions along three axes: front to back, up and down, and side to side. The soothing properties of rocking and jiggling for crying babies clearly demonstrate this sensitivity.

6. *What is the relation between vestibular sensitivity, such as posture, and the development of motor skills?*
Posture and balance are necessary for allowing the infant to look around, manipulate objects, and even locomote. Development in infants' capacity to reach and grasp accurately for objects relies on the development of its vestibular sensitivity and in the capacity to balance itself and maintain its posture.

7. *What is the relation between vestibular and visual cues in providing infants with a sense of self-motion?*
Visual cues and vestibular cues are usually consistent in telling us whether we are moving or stationary. Sometimes, however, conflict between these cues produces confusing effects, with visual cues usually winning out.

LEARNING OBJECTIVE 7.3 Describe the development of infants' sensitivity to auditory information.

1. *What sounds do fetuses hear and discriminate?*
Fetuses exhibit brain responses indicating sound reception as early as the 25th week after conception. By 28 weeks, fetuses close their eyelids in response to sound, indicating that they

respond to sounds they hear. Their mother's speech is more audible to the fetus than sounds from outside.

2. *What effect does prenatal auditory experience have on infants after birth?*
   Based on the auditory experience prenatally, newborn babies can discriminate their mothers' voices from strangers' voices. Newborns can recognize stories that they experienced prenatally. Newborns may even pick up aspects of their native language prenatally. Thus, the fetus can become familiar not only with the mother's voice but also with some of the specific sound patterns that the mother produces.

3. *To which sounds are infants sensitive and how does this sensitivity develop?*
   Newborn babies appear to be less sensitive to sound than are adults—adults can easily hear a whisper but a newborn requires normal conversational level to hear. Newborn babies hear better at low frequencies, but by 6 months of age, their high-frequency sensitivity is as good as an adult's. Sensitivity increases until about 10 years of age, though sensitivity to high frequency does not improve after 4 or 5 years of age.

4. *What types of sounds do infants discriminate?*
   Infants are able to distinguish differences in intensity, or loudness, at an early age. That infants respond differently to sounds of different frequencies provides one kind of evidence of their ability to discriminate. Babies can discriminate complex sounds, such as the properties of music, and types of music. Finally, babies within the first month can distinguish different speech sounds.

5. *What is the nature of the development in infants' ability to localize sounds?*
   Newborns can distinguish general sound location, turning their eyes and head toward the direction of a sound source. This localization capacity disappears around the second month of life, only to reappear in the third or fourth month. When it re-emerges, it is faster and more skilled, suggesting a shift in brain control. Over the first year and a half of life, babies make increasingly fine distinctions of auditory space, requiring recalibration because of growth of the head and distance of the ears with age.

LEARNING OBJECTIVE 7.4 Outline infants' capacity for processing visual information.

1. *What visual information can newborn infants see? And, how well?*
   It is hard to know what babies see, because we cannot easily communicate with infants; however, by measuring the amount of time babies look at one display rather than another, researchers are able to record how long babies look at each display. If the infant shows a preference, we conclude that he or she can discriminate between the stimuli. Using this technique, newborn visual acuity has been estimated to be about 20/400 compared with normal adult acuity of 20/20. The ability to focus improves between 1 and 3 months of age, and is almost adult-like by 6 months of age. Though newborns can see some colours—discriminating red from green—colour perception is equivalent to an adult's by 4 months of age. Babies prefer to look primarily at high-contrast edges (where black and white meet) because this stimulates the visual areas of the brain. Initially, newborns prefer simple stimuli, but as they get older they prefer increasing complexity in the stimulus. Between 1 and 3 months, babies begin to "put things together," perceiving the relations and organization of visual objects.

2. *What is the development of infants' ability to see faces?*
   Newborns show an interest in and respond differentially to faces, but they tend to look near the high-contrast borders of the face and pay little attention to the interior details. However,

newborns can discriminate their mother's face from a stranger's, indicating that they can appreciate "faceness." By 3 months, infants' face perception is clearly established, allowing them to discriminate between a familiar and unfamiliar face and an attractive and unattractive one. By the second half of the first year, they can recognize faces that have a change in expression or orientation. Infants at this age can also discriminate faces on the basis of gender and can discriminate their own face from those of others. Infants also view faces as social stimuli, with sensitivity to emotional expressions in faces growing slowly over the first two years of life.

3. *What are the properties of objects that infants develop the capacity to appreciate?*
   Infants are able to perceive size constancy among objects in their visual world, with some evidence that newborns possess this capacity. This means that the infant is able to recognize the difference in objects, even when researchers manipulate the objects so that they produce the identical retinal images on the infant's eyes. Similarly, newborns have been shown to possess some capacity for shape constancy. Shape constancy is the ability to recognize that a shape is the same even when seen from different perspectives. Though not evident at birth, brightness constancy has been shown at 7 weeks of age and colour constancy at 4 months. Infants 4 months of age are also able to perceive objects as continuous and whole even if the object is partially blocked from view.

4. *When do infants develop the capability to perceive distance and depth, and why?*
   Infants' perception of depth was first tested by using a unique device called a visual cliff. The visual cliff has a deep and a shallow end, both covered by Plexiglas. The infant is placed in between the two ends and is called by his mother from one of the ends; the researcher assesses whether he crosses the deep end to go to his mother. By 9 months, infants avoid the deep end, while infants as young as 2 months seem to notice the depth but do not show fear of the depth until 9 months. The timing of their fear and avoidance of the deep side is related to when they start to locomote on their own. Infants perceive depth by use of pictorial cues, such as near objects hiding parts of farther objects and closer objects appearing bigger than farther objects. Kinetic cues include motion parallax, in which when moving, nearer objects appear to change position faster than farther objects. In addition, objects get bigger as they move toward us and get smaller as they move away. Some use of kinetic cues is evident between 1 and 3 months of age, but response to pictorial cues is not evident until 6 or 7 months.

5. *How do infants perceive the spatial layout of objects?*
   There exist essentially two types of coding of location in space. The first is *egocentric coding*, which is the understanding that space and objects are tied to one's own actions and body. The second is *allocentric coding*, which is the understanding that space and objects are tied to other objects and landmarks in the environment. Early in development, the baby understands the world through the use of egocentric coding. In the first half of the second year of life, infants shift to using allocentric coding. Understanding of spatial locations is facilitated by self-produced movement.

LEARNING OBJECTIVE 7.5 Gain an understanding of how infants integrate the information from different senses that come from a single event.

1. *What are the different theories for how the child comes to realize that cues from different senses go together?*
   Piaget argued that the sensory modes are largely separate at birth and that the baby integrates them only through experience. Gibsonians, in contrast, argued that some coordination of the senses is present from birth.

2. *How do infants use exploratory behaviour to coordinate information from the different modalities?*
   Newborns, for example, will turn their eyes and head toward a sound. Thus the interrelation among sensory modes is detected through exploration of the event. An important form of exploratory relations among perceptual modes is the relation between vision and reaching. Infants' reaching for an object that they see illustrates how vision can trigger tactile exploration. In fact, the exploratory relation between vision and reaching may be sufficiently coordinated in newborns that they will work at keeping their hands in view.

3. *What is the basis for early exploratory behaviour?*
   Relations among the sensory modes are present at birth because of prepared relations, which are relations for which the baby is predisposed by biology but that are modifiable by experience.

4. *What is the nature of infants' capacity to integrate haptic and visual information, and auditory and visual information?*
   Several researchers have investigated whether infants can transfer information gained from sucking to visual perception of the same object. One-month-old infants, given an opportunity to suck on either a nubby (bumpy) nipple or a smooth nipple and then presented with pictures of the nubby and smooth nipples, looked longer at the nipple they had sucked. This suggests that cross-modal cues can specify the same object for infants at an amazingly early age. Similar findings apply to recognizing objects visually that they have previously explored only by hand. This ability is relatively weak in infants in the first half-year of life, but improves in strength between 6 and 12 months of age. Babies are also able to learn about an object visually and then recognize that object by touch. This is evident by examining whether infants can detect differences between what they feel and what they see. Studies have suggested that this capacity might be available as early as 5 months of age.

   In terms of integrating auditory and visual information, 4-month-olds look more to a film that matches a concurrent soundtrack than to a film that does not, suggesting they detect the sight–sound correspondence. Babies can also match auditory and visual events when the matching involves tempo and rhythm. Babies also appreciate auditory–visual relations that involve people by 3.5 months of age, looking longer at the mother's face when they hear her voice than when they hear a stranger's voice. They can also match auditory and visual information on the basis of emotion and age. Infants, then, are surprisingly good at picking up the commonality in cues from different senses.

LEARNING OBJECTIVE 7.6 Sketch the development of infants' ability to allocate their attention and to use that attention to guide their behaviour.

1. *What are the two behavioural tools that newborns have that are early forms of attention?*
   The two tools that newborns have are the orienting reflex and the defensive reflex. The orienting reflex includes the changes in heart rates, quieting of bodies, and widening of eyes that occurs when the newborn is attending to a stimulus. If the stimuli are too intense, then infants close their eyes, become agitated, and their heart rates increase, indicative of the defensive reflex.

2. *Which aspects of selective attention are functional in infancy?*
   Selective attention is the capacity to focus on one stimulus rather than another. There are many aspects or components that are part of selective attention. Researchers have found evidence of many selective attention components in infancy. These components include pop-out and visual search for a distinctive item from among a set of many items, the inhibition of returning to attend to an item one has already attended to, the shifting of attention from one item to another, the disengagement of attention from one item to shift to another, and the active inhibition of the item not originally selected.

3. *In early infancy, what controls selective attention?*
   It is thought that in early infancy attention is controlled by aspects of stimulation. Some properties of stimulation that control and guide attention are absolute, in the sense that they can be specified independently of the perceiver, such as movement. Other properties of stimulation are relative, in the sense that they must be defined with respect to a particular perceiver; for example, novelty. Initially, attention is controlled by absolute properties, and then at around 3 months of age, relative properties are available to the infant to control his attention.

4. *How does action, with vision and the hands, anticipate perception?*
   Recent research indicates that young infants can anticipate perceptual events before they occur, through the formation of expectations. This is shown by infants making eye movements in anticipation of a forthcoming stimulus in a predictable sequence. Presumably, infants form expectations to free themselves from simply reacting to each event as it occurs. In reaching for moving objects, babies need not reach to the present location to show success, but to an anticipated future location.

5. *What aspects of attention develop in older children?*
   Control of attention improves with age as attention span increases and distractibility decreases. Adaptability of attention to the task also changes, with increasing ability to disregard things that are not central to the task. Planfuless of attention improves as older children are more systematic, comparing each detail of a task, whereas younger children are more haphazard in comparing details. Finally, children become better at adjusting their attentional strategies as they gather information from a task.

6. *How do sociocultural influences affect the development of attention?*
   Children are socialized for forms of activity—in this case, patterns of attention—that are valued in the culture in which they are developing. For example, observing toddlers in the United States and Mayan toddlers in Guatemala in situations in which there were potentially many stimuli and events to attend to demonstrated that Mayan toddlers were more likely than their American counterparts to attend simultaneously to two or three ongoing events, as opposed to focusing on a single thing at a time. The basis for the differences among the toddlers became evident from observations of the mothers' behaviour: Mayan mothers, like their children, were more likely than the American sample to attend simultaneously to multiple events.

7. *What is the relation between the development of action or motor skill and perception in older children?*
   Action skills—behaviours that require physical coordination, such as reaching, walking, and catching—involve a complex interplay between perception and various parts of the motor system. The development of these skills is made more complicated by the growing body and limbs. Perception plays a key role in the continuing adjustment required for skill development, providing feedback about the relative accuracy of performance. Development in the coordination of action skills and perception through a feedback system continues well into the school years.

8. *What are some causes and consequences of attentional disorders such as ADHD?*
   The precise cause of attentional disorders like ADHD remains a source of controversy. The evidence suggests that in most cases both nature and nurture contribute. ADHD tends to run in families, therefore suggesting a biological component. Experiences can also be important.

Children may be exposed to teratogens such as alcohol or drugs, which may mimic or exacerbate the characteristics of ADHD. Children with attentional disorders have great difficulty maintaining attention and are often hyperactive and impulsive in their behaviour. Children with untreated ADHD are likely to perform poorly in school and may have difficulties in interpersonal relations as well.

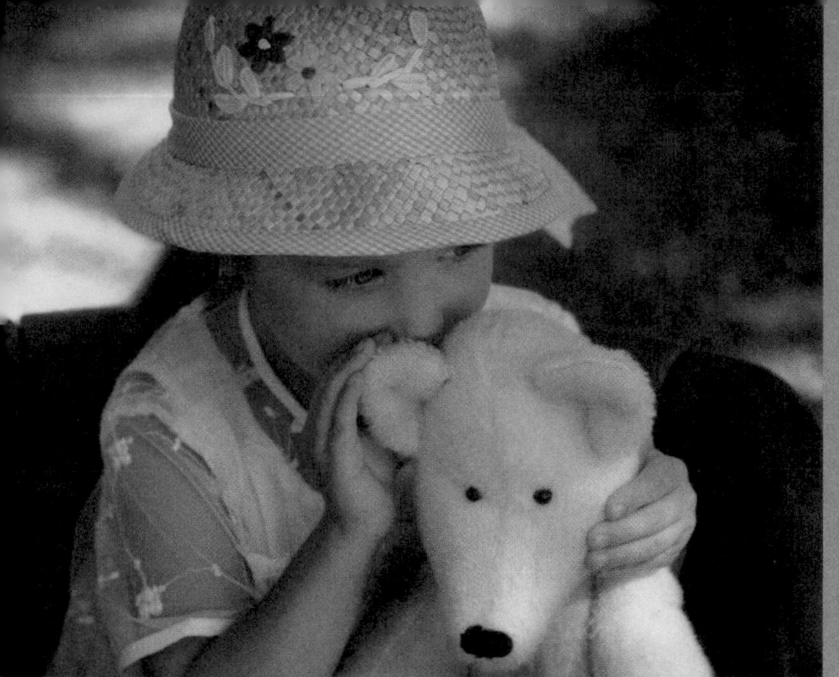

CHAPTER 8

COGNITIVE DEVELOPMENT: PIAGETIAN AND VYGOTSKIAN APPROACHES

"Why can I put my hand through water and not through soap?"
"Why doesn't butter stay on top of hot toast?"
"When I mix red and orange, it makes brown. Why?"
"Where was I before I was born?"
"When are all the days going to end?"

As any parent knows, question-asking is one of the most frequent activities of childhood. Child psychologists have long known this as well; in fact, some of the field's earliest scientific efforts were examinations of children's spontaneous questions. The examples above, collected by Paul Harris (2000), come from several of these pioneering studies, including some of the first work with children by Jean Piaget.

As these examples make clear, children's questions come in many forms. Some concern mundane matters; others address issues of deep personal or scientific significance. Some questions are easily answerable; others raise issues that continue to challenge philosophers or scientists. The constant element is the search for understanding: the attempt to make sense of the many (thousands!) topics that children must somehow come to understand. In the next several chapters, we consider how psychologists have attempted to make sense of children's sense-making efforts. ■

In the last chapter, we saw that the infant's perceptual abilities are considerably more impressive than psychologists once believed. But we saw as well that even the modern "superbaby" is not equivalent to an adult, and that major improvements in perceptual ability occur within the short span of infancy. The same applies—perhaps even more so—to children's cognitive development.

Cognition Higher-order mental processes, such as reasoning and problem solving, through which humans attempt to understand the world.

Gaining an understanding of how children make sense of the world has long been the focus of research into cognitive development. **Cognition** refers to higher-order mental processes—processes such as *thinking*, *reasoning*, *learning*, and *problem solving*—by which humans attempt to understand and adapt to their world. As with perceptual development, recent research has taught us that infants and young children are often far more cognitively competent than we used to believe. Yet the child's thinking may differ from that of the adult in many ways, and these differences continue to intrigue and baffle researchers and parents alike. Discovering the mixture of competence and limitations that characterizes thought at different points in childhood is one of the two great challenges faced by cognitive development researchers. The second challenge is to discover how children overcome these limitations and how new forms of competence emerge.

In the next two chapters, we consider three general approaches to these questions. In this chapter, we first focus on the cognitive-developmental approach, as represented by the work of Jean Piaget. We examine both Piaget's original theory and research and more recent studies that challenge, modify, or extend the Piagetian position. Then we consider the sociocultural approach, represented by the work of Lev Vygotsky. Finally, in the next chapter, we shift our attention to the current major representative of the cognitive-developmental approach—the information-processing perspective. Although these perspectives overlap in certain areas, they differ in significant ways in their approach to cognitive development.

Learning Objective 8.1

Define the concepts from biology that Piaget used to explain cognitive development and evaluate his theory of stages.

PIAGET'S THEORY

As we saw in Chapter 1, Piaget's training included heavy doses of both biology and philosophy. From philosophy came much of the content of his work. Piaget's goal throughout his career was to use the study of children to answer basic philosophical questions about the nature and origins of knowledge. His research thus shows a consistent focus on what have long been central topics in philosophy: the child's understanding of space, time, and causality; of number and quantity; of classes and relations; and of invariance and change. Undoubtedly one reason Piaget's studies have attracted so much attention is that they identify such basic and important forms of knowledge. Another reason is Piaget's surprising, and controversial, claim that these basic forms of knowledge often take a long time to develop.

Jean Piaget remains the field's most influential theorist of cognitive development. Many of his most important insights derived from his skill as an observer of children's behaviour. (© *Bettmann/Corbis*)

From biology, Piaget took ideas about both the structure and the function of intelligence. A basic principle in biology is that of *organization*. An organism is never simply a random collection of cells, tissues, and organs; rather, organisms are always highly organized systems. One job of the biologist is to discover the underlying organization. Piaget maintained that the same principle applies to human intelligence. For Piaget, the essence of intelligence does not lie in individually learned responses or isolated memories; the essence lies instead in the underlying organization. This organization takes the form of the various cognitive structures that the developing child constructs. *Cognitive structures* are ways to organize information to understand and remember it more effectively. The job of the psychologist is to discover what these structures are and how they change.

MECHANISMS OF CHANGE

Biology also contributed to the functional side of Piaget's theory. Another basic biological principle is that of *adaptation*. All organisms adapt to the environment in which they must survive, often by means of very complex mechanisms. The biologist tries to discover what these mechanisms of adaptation are. Human intelligence, according to Piaget, is an adaptive phenomenon—indeed, it may be the primary means by which humans adapt to the environmental challenges they face.

Adaptation occurs through the complementary processes of *assimilation* and *accommodation.* Whenever we interact with the environment, we assimilate the environment to our current cognitive structures; that is, we fit it in or interpret it in terms of what we already understand. When children assimilate, they may distort reality to fit with the understanding they already possess. For example, a preschooler who is familiar with the category "fish" may insist that dolphins and whales are also fish—she is assimilating these aquatic animals into her current understanding of what "fish" are. Yet at the same time, we are continually accommodating our cognitive structures to fit with the environment; that is, altering our understanding to take new things into account. So, as a child learns more about the characteristics of fish and mammals, she changes her understanding of whales and dolphins to reflect their status as mammals. It is through innumerable instances of assimilation and accommodation that cognitive development occurs.

Links to Related Material

Chapter 1 introduced Piaget's concepts of schemes, constructivism, and adaptation processes. In this chapter, we expand on these concepts.

The term *development* reflects one final influence from biology: organisms are not static. Rather, they change both across the lifetime of the individual and across the history of the species. One more task for the biologist, therefore, is to describe and explain the changes that occur. Intelligence, too, changes as the child develops, and the child psychologist must describe and explain these changes. For Piaget, there is no single organization or set of cognitive structures that defines childhood intelligence. As children develop, they construct qualitatively different structures, structures that allow a progressively better understanding of the world. These qualitatively different structures define the Piagetian *stages of development.* Thus, Piaget can be considered a stage theorist.

Piaget divided development into four general stages, or periods: sensorimotor, preoperational, concrete operational, and formal operational. These periods were introduced in Chapter 1 and are summarized in Table 8.1.

For Thought and Discussion

The biological concepts that Piaget used apply throughout the lifespan. What are some examples from your life in which you responded to new experiences using assimilation and accommodation?

TABLE 8.1 PIAGET'S FOUR PERIODS OF DEVELOPMENT

Period	Age (years)	Description
Sensorimotor	0 to 2	Infants understand the world through the overt actions performed on it. These actions reflect the sensorimotor schemes. Across infancy, the schemes become progressively more complex and interrelated. Decentering occurs, and the infant comes to understand object permanence.
Preoperational	2 to 6	The child can now use representations, rather than overt actions, to solve problems. Thinking is consequently faster, more efficient, more mobile, and more socially shareable. The child's initial attempts at representational functioning also show limitations, including egocentrism and centration.
Concrete operational	6 to 12	The advent of operations allows the child to overcome the limitations of preoperational thought. Operations are a system of internal mental actions that underlie logical problem solving. The child comes to understand various forms of conservation, as well as classification and relational reasoning.
Formal operational	12 to adult	The further development of operations leads to a capacity for hypothetical–deductive reasoning. Thought begins with possibility and works systematically and logically back to reality. The prototype for such logical reasoning is scientific problem solving.

LEARNING OBJECTIVE 8.1

Define the concepts from biology that Piaget used to explain cognitive development and evaluate his theory of stages.

1. What is the role of organization in the development of cognitive structures?
2. What processes of adaptation are essential for cognitive change and how do they work?
3. What four periods of cognitive development did Piaget propose and how do they differ?

Learning Objective 8.2

Trace the substages and benchmarks of the sensorimotor period in child development.

COGNITION DURING INFANCY: THE SENSORIMOTOR PERIOD

The first of Piaget's periods is the sensorimotor period. It is the period of infancy, extending from birth until about 2 years of age.

You can gain some idea of the magnitude of cognitive advance during this period by imagining the following two scenes: bringing a newborn home from the hospital, and planning a 2-year-old's birthday party. Only two years separate the two events, yet how different are the sorts of things that one can do with, say to, and expect of the two children!

STUDYING INFANT INTELLIGENCE

Piaget's conclusions about infant development were based on the study of his own three children from birth through the end of infancy (Piaget, 1951, 1952, 1954). His method of investigation combined naturalistic observation with experimental manipulation. Both Piaget and his wife Valentine (herself a trained psychologist) spent many hours simply watching the everyday behaviour of their babies. But these naturalistic observations were supplemented by frequent, small-scale experiments. If, for example, Piaget was interested in his daughter's ability to cope with obstacles, he would not necessarily wait until an obstacle happened along. Instead, he might interpose a barrier between his daughter and her favourite toy and then record her response to this challenge.

Piaget's method has both strengths and weaknesses. On the positive side, the method combined the observation of behaviour in the natural setting and the longitudinal study of the same children as they develop. This approach permitted insight into forms and sequences of development that could not have been gained solely from controlled laboratory study.

Perhaps the most obvious limitation of Piaget's method was his sample. A sample of three is a shaky basis for drawing conclusions about universals of human development—especially when all three are from the same family and are being observed by their own parents! However, many studies have replicated Piaget's findings with larger and more representative samples and more objective techniques of data collection. So despite its limitations and inaccuracies, Piaget's general picture of infancy was reasonably representative of major developmental milestones (Müller, Carpendale, & Smith, 2009).

THE SIX SUBSTAGES

Piaget divided the sensorimotor period into six substages. In the descriptions that follow, the ages should be taken simply as rough averages. What is important in a stage theory is not the age but the *sequence*—the order in which the stages come—which is assumed to be the same for all children.

SUBSTAGE 1: EXERCISING REFLEXES (BIRTH TO 1 MONTH) In Piaget's view, the newborn's adaptive repertoire is limited to simple, biologically provided *reflexes*. Thus, the newborn sucks when a nipple rubs against the lips, grasps when an object grazes the palm, and orients when an appropriate visual stimulus appears. These behaviours are seen as automatic responses to particular environmental stimuli, and they show only slight change during the first month of life.

It should be clear from Chapter 5 that Piaget underestimated the newborn's behavioural competence. Indeed, most of what he labelled reflexes we would today refer to as congenitally organized

Links to Related Material

In Chapter 5, you learned about some of the basic reflexes that infants are born with. Here, you read how Piaget's theory treats these reflexes as the first step in the infant's ability to understand the world.

behaviours, a term that reflects the complexity and the coordination that behaviours, such as sucking and looking, may show. However, these behaviours are important in Piaget's view because they represent the building blocks from which all future development proceeds. Development occurs as the behaviours are applied to more objects and events—in Piaget's terms, as babies assimilate more things—and as their behaviours begin to change in response to these new experiences—in Piaget's terms, as they begin to accommodate. As the initially inflexible behaviours begin to be modified by experience, the infant is entering the second of the sensorimotor substages.

SUBSTAGE 2: DEVELOPING SCHEMES (1 TO 4 MONTHS) As the infants' behaviours adapt, their *reflexes* become *sensorimotor schemes*. **Sensorimotor schemes** are the skilled and generalizable action patterns with which the infant acts on and makes sense of the world. The sucking scheme, for example, is the infant's organized action pattern of sucking that can be applied to innumerable stimuli; not only nipples, but rattles, stuffed toys, and fingers as well.

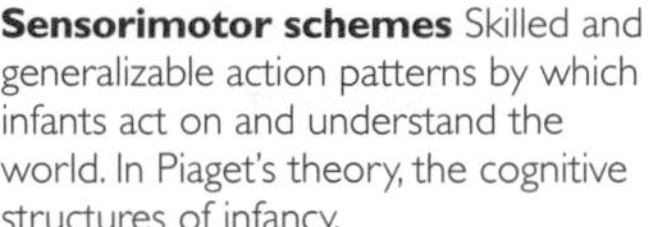

Sensorimotor schemes Skilled and generalizable action patterns by which infants act on and understand the world. In Piaget's theory, the cognitive structures of infancy.

The notion of schemes captures a central aspect of Piaget's theory, namely, the role of action in intelligence. For Piaget, intelligence at every period of development involves some form of action on the world. During infancy, actions are literal and overt. The infant knows the world through behaviours such as sucking, grasping, and manipulating.

Schemes undergo two sorts of development during the second substage. First, individual schemes become progressively refined. A 1-month-old will grasp a hard, thin rattle and a soft, fat stuffed toy in essentially the same way. A 4-month-old, in contrast, is considerably more skilled and has accommodated the grasping scheme to a variety of environmental stimuli. Particular schemes may continue to evolve throughout infancy.

The second change involves the coordination of initially independent schemes. Rather than being performed in isolation, the schemes are now combined into larger units. Of particular importance is the fact that schemes involving the different sensory modes—vision, hearing, touch, taste, smell—begin to be brought together. Thus, the infant hears a sound and turns toward the source of the sound, a coordination of hearing and vision. Or the infant looks at an object and then reaches out to grasp and manipulate it, a coordination of vision and touch.

Recent studies indicate that Piaget underestimated the degree of early coordination between the senses (Rochat, 2001). As we saw in Chapter 7, even newborns show a tendency to turn toward the source of a sound (Ennouri & Bloch, 1996). Other studies have suggested that the rudiments of visually directed reaching may be present quite early (Spelke & von Hofsten, 2001), as may be the ability to achieve a primitive matching of tactile and visual inputs (Streri, 2003). The competencies identified in these studies are limited, and they certainly do not negate Piaget's claim that intermodal coordination improves across the early months. But they do suggest that the beginnings of such coordination are present earlier than he believed.

SUBSTAGE 3: DISCOVERING PROCEDURES (4 TO 8 MONTHS) Although infants act on the environment from birth, their behaviour in the first few months has an inner-directed quality. When a young baby manipulates a stuffed toy, for example, the baby's interest seems to lie more in the various finger movements being performed than in the toy itself. Thus, the substage 2 infant uses schemes for the pure pleasure of using them—grasping for the sake of grasping, sucking for the sake of sucking, and so on. In substage 3, the infant begins to show a clearer interest in the outer world. The schemes begin to be directed away from the baby's own body and toward exploration of the environment. Thus, the substage 3 infant who manipulates a toy does so because of a real interest in exploring that object.

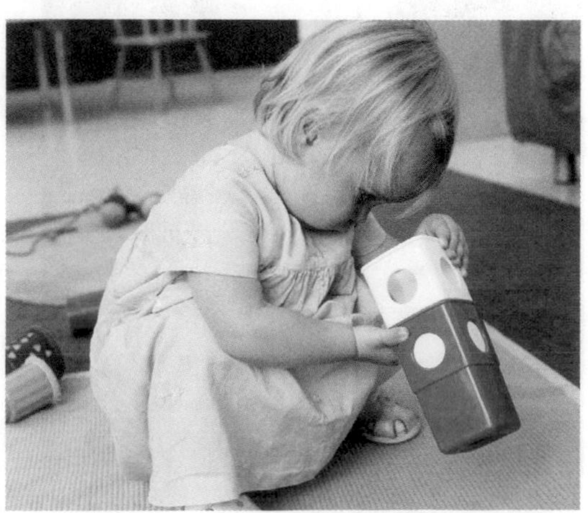

Exploration of objects is part of Piaget's substage 3. (*Banana Stock*)

One manifestation of this greater awareness of the environment is that the infant discovers *procedures* for reproducing interesting events. For example, the infant might accidentally kick a doll suspended above the crib, making the doll jump, and then spend the next 10 minutes happily kicking and laughing. Or the infant might happen to create an interesting sound by rubbing a toy against the bassinet hood and then repeat the procedure to hear the sound again. The infant is beginning to develop knowledge of what he can do to produce desirable outcomes. That this knowledge is still far from perfectly developed is implied by the term *accidentally.* The substage 3 infant shows a kind of after-the-fact grasp of causality. Once the infant has accidentally hit on some interesting outcome, he may be able to reproduce it. What the infant cannot yet do is figure out in advance how to produce interesting outcomes.

SUBSTAGE 4: INTENTIONAL BEHAVIOUR (8 TO 12 MONTHS) During substage 4, this after-the-fact restriction disappears. Now the infant first perceives some desirable goal and then figures out how to achieve it. In so doing, the infant demonstrates the first genuinely intentional behaviour.

Intentional behaviour In Piaget's theory, behaviour in which the goal exists prior to the action selected to achieve it; made possible by the ability to separate means and end.

In Piaget's analysis, **intentional behaviour** involves an ability to separate *means* and *end.* The infant uses one scheme as a means to lead to some other scheme, which then becomes the goal, or end. The typical situation for studying intentional behaviour involves response to obstacles. Suppose the baby is about to reach for a toy and we drop a pillow between her hand and toy. How does the baby respond? Simple though this problem may seem, before stage 4 the infant cannot solve it. The younger infant may storm ineffectually at the pillow or may immediately activate the goal scheme; that is, do to the pillow what she would have done to the toy. What the substage 3 infant does not do—and the substage 4 infant does—is first intentionally push the pillow aside and then reach for the toy. This sort of adaptive problem solving requires a separation of means and end. The infant must use the push-aside scheme as a means to get to the reach-and-play scheme, the desired end.

Links to Related Material

In Chapter 5, we discussed the infant's increasing motor skills. How do you think these motor skills influence the kind of physical actions upon objects that Piaget's theory maintains is the hallmark of the sensorimotor period?

Recent research, however, has suggested that infants as young as 6 months, and perhaps even 3 months, may exhibit intentional behaviour. Maria Legerstee of York University has shown that when 6-month-olds are faced with a situation in which their mothers remain unresponsive to their interactions—called the *still-face paradigm*—they will attempt to intentionally regulate the interaction by increasing their vocalizations and smiles (Legerstee & Markova, 2007). Additionally, eye movement studies with 3-month-olds have suggested that an early form of intentional behaviour is evident. When viewing a predictable picture sequence (e.g., left-right-left-right), these infants will make anticipatory eye movements to the location of the next picture before it appears (Adler & Haith, 2003). Since these anticipatory eye movements occur when no picture is on the screen, the initiation of the eye movement must come from the infant rather than being elicited by the environment, indicating that infants intended to make the eye movement. Together, these findings suggest that Piaget yet again underestimated the age at which the infant is capable of a particular cognitive behaviour, in this case intentional behaviour.

Links to Related Material

We will return to the still-face paradigm in Chapter 12 when we discuss face-to-face interactions between infants and their mothers.

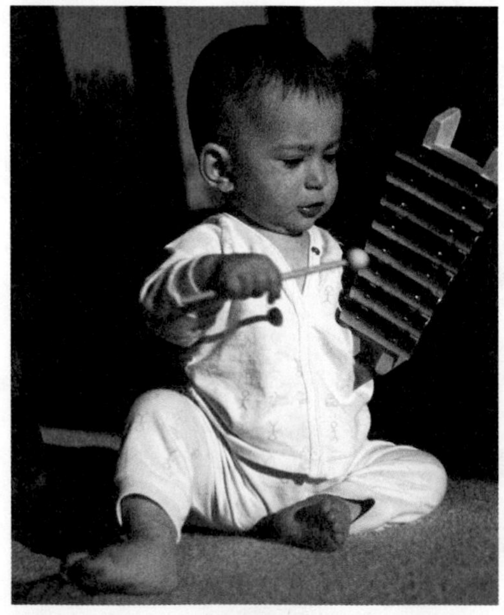

A hallmark of substage 5 is the ability to explore and experiment in new ways to produce novel effects. (*Peter Byron/PhotoEdit*)

SUBSTAGE 5: NOVELTY AND EXPLORATION (12 TO 18 MONTHS) Piaget's name for substage 5 is "the discovery of *new* means through active exploration." The word *new* differentiates between substage 4 and substage 5. The substage 4 infant tends to use mostly familiar schemes to produce a small range of mostly familiar effects. The substage 5 infant, in contrast, begins deliberately and systematically to vary her behaviours, thus creating both new schemes and new effects.

The advances of substage 5 are evident when the infant has some problem to solve. The infant now is not limited to reproducing previously successful solutions or slight variants of them. Instead, the infant can discover completely new solutions through an active process of trial and error. Piaget documented, for example, how infants at this stage discover that a faraway goal can be retrieved by means of a string, and that a stick can be used to push, pull, or otherwise act on some distant object. These behaviours can be considered as the first instances of the important human ability to use tools (Flavell, Miller, & Miller, 2002).

The substage 5 infant also experiments for the pure pleasure of experimentation. An example familiar to many parents is the "high-chair behaviour" of the 1-year-old. The baby leans over the edge of her high chair and drops her spoon to the floor, carefully noting how it bounces. The parent retrieves and returns the spoon, whereupon the baby leans over the other side of the chair and drops the spoon again, perhaps with a bit more force this time. The parent again returns the spoon, and this time the baby flings it across the room—whereupon the exasperated parent gives up and removes either baby or spoon from the situation. It is through such active experimentation that infants learn about the world.

SUBSTAGE 6: MENTAL REPRESENTATION (18 TO 24 MONTHS) The first five sensorimotor substages are a time of remarkable cognitive progress. Yet there is still one more advance to be made. During the first five substages, the infant's adaptation to the world occurs through overt behaviour. Even the substage 5 infant's problem solving is based on trying one behaviour after another until a solution is reached. At substage 6, the infant now becomes capable of **mental representation**—of thinking about and acting on the world internally and not merely externally. It is this advance that will bring the sensorimotor period to an end.

Mental representation The use of symbols to picture and act on the world internally.

An example of mental representation can be seen in the following story about Piaget's daughter Jacqueline at age 20 months. Jacqueline is carrying some blades of grass through the house.

> Jacqueline... arrives at a closed door—with a blade of grass in each hand. She stretches out her right hand toward the knob but sees that she cannot turn it without letting go of the grass. She puts the grass on the floor, opens the door, picks up the grass again and enters. But when she wants to leave the room things become complicated. She puts the grass on the floor and grasps the doorknob. But then she perceives that in pulling the door toward her she will simultaneously chase away the grass which she placed between the door and the threshold. She therefore picks it up in order to put it outside the door's zone of movement. (Piaget, 1952, p. 339)

As infants progress through the sensorimotor substages, they become increasingly skilled at acting on the environment to produce interesting outcomes. (*Elizabeth Crews/The Image Works*)

When Jacqueline pauses with her hand on the doorknob the second time, she is apparently doing two things. She is imagining the problem—the door sweeping over the grass. She is also imagining the solution—moving the grass beyond the sweep of the door. She is thus engaged in a kind of mental problem solving, based on an internal use of representations or symbols, which is not possible earlier in infancy.

For Piaget, the onset of representation defines the movement from the sensorimotor period to the next period of development, the preoperational period. Table 8.2 summarizes the six sensorimotor substages.

TABLE 8.2 THE SIX SENSORIMOTOR SUBSTAGES

Stage	Age (months)	Description
1. Exercising reflexes	0 to 1	The infant is limited to exercising inborn reflexes—for example, sucking and grasping.
2. Developing schemes	1 to 4	The reflexes evolve into adaptive schemes. The schemes begin to be refined and coordinated.
3. Discovering procedures	4 to 8	Behaviour becomes more outwardly oriented. The infant develops procedures for reproducing interesting events.
4. Intentional behaviour	8 to 12	The first truly intentional behaviour emerges. The infant can separate means and end in pursuit of a goal.
5. Novelty and exploration	12 to 18	The infant begins to vary the schemes systematically to produce new effects. Problems are solved through an active process of trial and error.
6. Mental representation	18 to 24	The capacity for representational or symbolic functioning emerges. Mental problem solving begins to replace overt trial and error.

OBJECT PERMANENCE

Object permanence The knowledge that objects have a permanent existence that is independent of our perceptual contact with them. In Piaget's theory, a major achievement of the sensorimotor period.

One important aspect of infant development during the sensorimotor stage, both because of its importance in Piaget's theory and because it has been the target of dozens of follow-up studies, is the phenomenon of object permanence. **Object permanence** refers to our knowledge that objects continue to exist independent of our perception of them (Figure 8.1). That is, a toy does not cease to exist just because you can no longer feel it, a rattle just because you can no longer hear it, or Mommy just because you can no longer see her. It is hard to imagine more basic knowledge than this. Yet Piaget's research suggests that this understanding develops only gradually across the entire span of infancy.

Piaget described the development of object permanence in terms of the same six-stage progression that he used for the sensorimotor period as a whole. During the first two substages—that is, the first 3 or 4 months—babies do not realize that objects exist apart from their own actions on them. Should a toy drop out of sight, for example, the 3-month-old acts as though it no longer exists. The young infant will not search for a vanished object, and is likely instead to turn fairly quickly to some other activity. At most, the baby may follow an object with his eyes or stare for a while at the place where an object has just disappeared.

It is only during the third substage, at about 4 to 8 months, that babies begin to search for vanished objects. At first, however, the search shows a number of curious limitations. The infant may search, for example, if the object is partially hidden, but not if it is totally hidden. The search may even depend on how much of the object is hidden. If only a corner of a sought-after toy is visible, the baby may sit perplexed. As soon as a bit more is revealed, however, the baby may happily reach out and retrieve the toy. Search may also depend on whether the infant's own action or something else makes the object disappear. The baby who pushes a toy over the edge of the high chair may look down at the floor to find it. If you do the pushing, however, search is less likely. For Piaget, this observation is evidence that the infant's knowledge of the object still depends on his action on it.

Substage 4 marks an important step forward with regard to object permanence. The infant now (at about 8 to 12 months) can search systematically and intelligently for hidden objects. The substage 4 infant searches even when the object is completely gone and even when it was not her own actions that made it disappear. Infants' understanding of permanence, however, is still limited, especially when they must cope with more than one hiding place. Piaget might, for example, hide a toy under a pillow two or three times to his daughter's left, each time allowing her to retrieve it successfully. Then, with his daughter watching, he might hide the same toy under a blanket to her right. The baby would watch the toy disappear under the blanket and then turn and search under the pillow! What seemed to define the object was not its objective location, but the baby's previous success at finding it—it became "the thing that I found under the pillow." For Piaget, this behaviour (labelled the **A-not-B error**) is evidence that even at this substage, the baby's knowledge of objects is not freed from her own actions on them.

A-not-B error Infants' tendency to search in the original location in which an object was found, rather than in its most recent hiding place; a characteristic of stage 4 of object permanence.

FIGURE 8.1

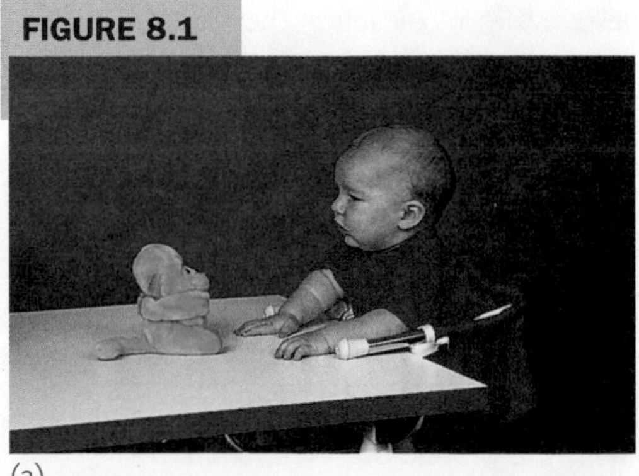

(a)

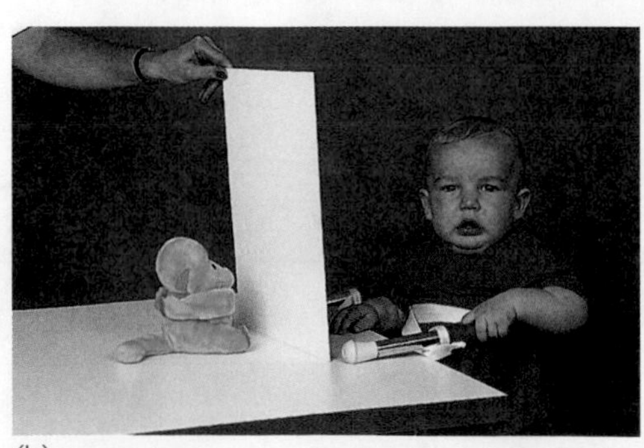

(b)

At birth and for the next three or four months, children do not show signs of object permanence. They do not seem to realize that objects continue to exist when they cannot be seen, heard, or touched—out of sight is truly out of mind. (*Doug Goodman/ Photo Researchers*)

The infant does, of course, eventually overcome this limitation. The substage 5 infant (about 12 to 18 months) can handle the multiple-hiding-place problems that baffle a younger baby. But there is still one more limitation. The infant can handle such problems only if he can see the object as it is moved from one hiding place to another. Suppose, however, that the movements are not visible—that the task involves what Piaget labelled *invisible displacements*. Piaget might hide a toy in his fist, for example, and then move the fist in succession through hiding places A, B, and C before bringing it out empty. To infer the movements of a hidden object, the infant must be able to represent the object when it is not visible. Solution of this problem is found only at substage 6, when the capacity for symbolic functioning emerges.

The work on object permanence illustrates two general themes in Piaget's approach to development. One is the notion of development as a process of **progressive decentering**. According to Piaget, the infant begins life in a state of profound **egocentrism**; that is, she literally cannot distinguish between herself and the outer world. The young infant simply does not know what is specific to the self (one's own perceptions, actions, wishes, and so on) and what exists apart from the self. This egocentrism is reflected most obviously in the absence of object permanence. For the young infant, objects exist only to the extent that she is acting on them. Only gradually, across infancy, does the infant decenter and grow more aware of both self and world.

Progressive decentering Piaget's term for the gradual decline in egocentrism that occurs across development.

Egocentrism In infancy, an inability to distinguish the self (e.g., one's actions or perceptions) from the outer world. In later childhood, an inability to distinguish one's own perspective (e.g., visual experience, thoughts, feelings) from that of others.

The second theme is the importance of **invariants** in development. We live in a world of constant flux, a world in which all sorts of things (what we can or cannot see, how things look, etc.) change from one moment to the next. Piaget maintained that one important kind of knowledge that the child must acquire is a knowledge of what it is that stays the same—remains invariant—in the face of constant change. The first and most basic cognitive invariant is object permanence, the realization that the existence of objects is invariant despite changes in our perceptual experience of them.

Invariants Aspects of the world that remain the same, even though other aspects have changed. In Piaget's theory, different forms of invariants are understood at different stages of development.

TESTING PIAGET'S CLAIMS: MORE RECENT WORK ON INFANT COGNITION

Piaget's studies continue to inspire contemporary research on infant intelligence. Object permanence has been the most popular focus for such research.

OBJECT PERMANENCE Replication studies have amply confirmed Piaget's claims about the kinds of errors infants make when they must search for hidden objects (Harris, 1989). Nevertheless, many researchers have wondered whether the infant's understanding is really as limited as Piaget believed. A particular concern has been Piaget's emphasis on motor search behaviours in assessing object permanence; that is, behaviours such as lifting a cloth or pushing aside a screen. An infant may know that an object still exists, but simply fail to show the kinds of active search behaviours that Piaget required. How else might we assess what infants know about objects? The most informative approach has made use of the habituation phenomenon described in Chapter 1. *Habituation*, you may recall, refers to a decline in response to a repeated stimulus; conversely, *dishabituation* refers to the recovery of response when the stimulus changes. Researchers have probed infants' understanding of objects by seeing what sorts of changes in objects they are likely to notice and dishabituate to. Of particular interest are infants' responses to changes that seem to violate the laws of object permanence.

Mastery of object permanence is a major achievement of infant cognitive development. The infant's search for vanished objects provides the clearest evidence that such knowledge is developing. *(Courtesy of CJW)*

Canadian-born researcher Renée Baillargeon devised some intriguing experiments to examine this issue (Baillargeon et al., 2011). In one study (Baillargeon, 1987), babies were first shown a screen that rotated, like a drawbridge, though a 180-degree arc (see Figure 8.2*a*). Although this event was initially quite interesting, after a number of repetitions the babies' attention dropped off, showing that they had habituated to the rotation. At this point a wooden box was placed directly

FIGURE 8.2

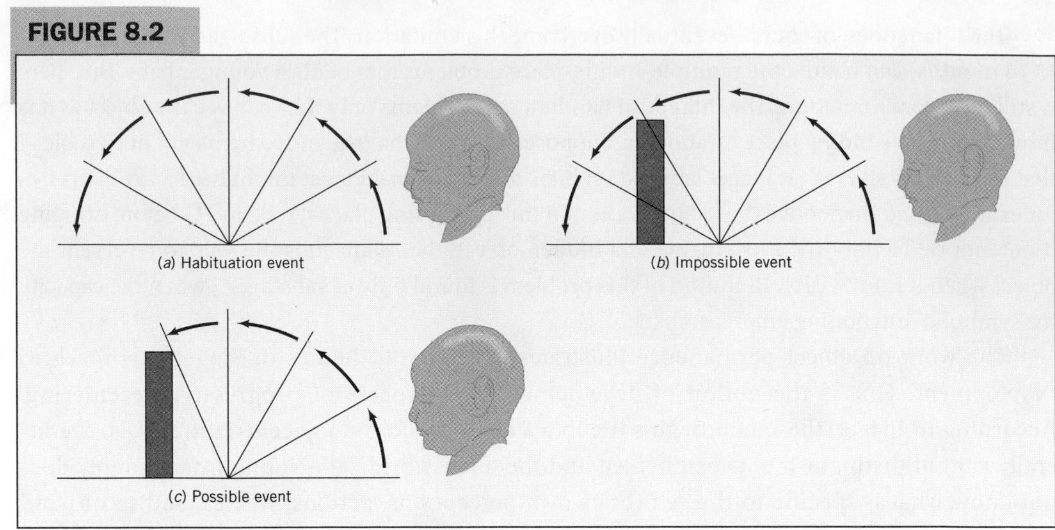

The Baillargeon test of object permanence. Infants were first habituated to the event shown in (a). Response was then measured to either the possible event in (c), in which the screen rotates to point of contact with the box and stops, or the impossible event in (b), in which the screen continues to move through the area occupied by the box. *Adapted from "Object Permanence in 31/2- and 41/2-Month-Old Infants," by R. Baillargeon, 1987,* Developmental Psychology, 23, *656. Copyright © 1987 by the American Psychological Association.* Adapted by permission.

in the path of the screen (see Figure 8.2*b*). Note that the baby could see the box at the start of a trial, but the box disappeared from view once the screen had reached its full height. In one experimental condition, labelled the "possible event" in the figure (see Figure 8.2*c*), the screen rotated to the point at which it reached the box and then stopped—as indeed it should with a solid object in its path. In the other condition, labelled the "impossible event," the screen rotated to the point of contact with the box and then kept going through its full 180-degree arc! (This outcome was made possible by a hidden platform that dropped the box out of the way.)

Adults confronted with such an event would probably be quite surprised because they would know that the box still existed behind the screen, even though it could no longer be seen. Infants as young as 4.5 months apparently possess the same knowledge. Their attention did not increase when they viewed the possible event; looking times shot up, however, when the screen appeared to pass magically through a solid object. The most obvious explanation for such recovery of interest is that the infants knew that the box must still exist and therefore expected the screen to stop.

Young infants know something not only about the existence of hidden objects, but also about the properties of these objects. In a further experiment, Baillargeon replaced the hard and rigid box with a soft and compressible ball of gauze. Infants' attention was not increased due to the continued rotation of the screen in the soft-object case, indicating that they retained information about the presence and also the compressibility of the hidden object.

Recent research has even suggested the existence of brain correlates for the capacity of object permanence. Studies have indicated, for example, that there is a surge of neural activity in the infant's temporal lobe when an object moves behind another object that prevents the infant from seeing it and is set to reappear on the other side (Kaufman, Csibra, & Johnson, 2003, 2005). These findings suggest that brain activity exists that is related to the representation of the permanence of objects, and that might be responsible for infants' behavioural exhibition of object permanence.

Having emphasized the positive picture that emerges from these studies, we should add two cautionary notes. The first is that the procedural innovations do not always result in successful performance. Baillargeon, for example, reports that young infants know that *some* object is still there, but have little ability to remember or reason about its quantitative properties once they can no longer see it. This means, for example, that they do not increase attention if the drawbridge rotates somewhat farther than it should given the height of the concealed box, as long as it stops eventually; nor do they increase attention if a large toy emerges from under a small cover, as long as *something* emerges (Baillargeon, 1994). Findings such as these confirm a general tenet of Piaget's approach to infant intelligence—new knowledge does not emerge full-blown, but only gradually and through a series of progressively more mature forms.

The second caution is that not all researchers are persuaded that studies such as Baillargeon's really demonstrate object permanence months earlier than Piaget believed (Bogartz et al., 2000; Cashon & Cohen, 2000; Schilling, 2000). Some researchers have argued that correct responses do not really reflect knowledge of the hidden object. In the drawbridge study, for example, infants may prefer to look at familiar objects and events (because they were not sufficiently habituated) and thus look longer at the familiar 180-degree rotation event for this reason, irrespective of what happens with the box behind (Cashon & Cohen, 2000). Others have agreed that correct responses can be explained through simpler processes than substage 4 object permanence. Infants may, for example, retain a mental image of the vanished object that persists for a few seconds after its disappearance; their increased attention then results from the mismatch between the perceptual image and the test event the infant is currently viewing, not from a violation of object permanence (Meltzoff & Moore, 1999a). Finally, studies of infants' predictive tracking of an object that is hidden from view behind another object indicate that the capacity to represent the object during its time when hidden from view emerges between 3 and 5 months of age (Bertenthal et al., 2007; Johnson, Amso, & Slemmer, 2003; Rosander & von Hofsten, 2004). Everyone, it seems fair to say, agrees that there is an underestimation in Piaget's account; at present, however, there is no agreement as to how much. Furthermore, no study to date has contradicted Piaget's claim that active search behaviours for hidden objects are absent prior to about 8 or 9 months. Why babies' ability to organize intelligent behaviours lags so far behind their initial knowledge is one of the most intriguing questions in modern infancy research (Bertenthal, 1996; Munakata et al., 1997).

PHYSICAL KNOWLEDGE Object permanence is one important kind of physical knowledge. In this section, we review several other kinds that also emerge, at least in their initial forms, during infancy.

Understanding of causality is a classic philosophical issue to which Piaget devoted much attention. His conclusions about infants' knowledge of cause and effect were based largely on their ability to act effectively to produce desired outcomes—for example, to push aside an obstacle to attain a goal. As with object permanence, later studies that have reduced the response demands on the infant present a more positive picture of infant knowledge. The most common strategy has been to habituate the infant to an event with a particular causal structure (for example, a red ball that strikes and propels a green ball) and then test for dishabituation to events that either preserve or violate that structure (for example, a green ball that propels a red ball). Infants as young as 6 or 7 months have been found to be sensitive to the causal relations (Cohen & Amsel, 1998; Newman et al., 2008).

IMITATION Among the many topics that Piaget explored in his sensorimotor studies was the development of imitation. He reported that imitation, like other sensorimotor accomplishments, begins with rudimentary and limited forms early in life and slowly progresses toward the skilled behavioural system of the toddler or preschool child. Infants' ability at 6 to 8 months of age, according to Piaget, is limited in that they imitate only those behaviours that they already produce spontaneously and that they can see and hear themselves perform. Thus, the infant might imitate a movement, such as finger wiggling, for which there is perceptible feedback. But we would not expect a young baby to be able to imitate a facial expression, such as opening the mouth or sticking out the tongue.

Some research evidence has provided a strong challenge to this view. Across a series of studies, Meltzoff and Moore (1977, 1983, 1989, 1994, 1999b; for reviews see Meltzoff, 2002, 2011) have examined infants' ability to imitate facial expressions of a variety of sorts. Their procedure involves videotaping the infant's face as an adult model performs the target behaviours (see Figure 8.3). Meltzoff and Moore report that even newborns can imitate both mouth opening and tongue

FIGURE 8.3

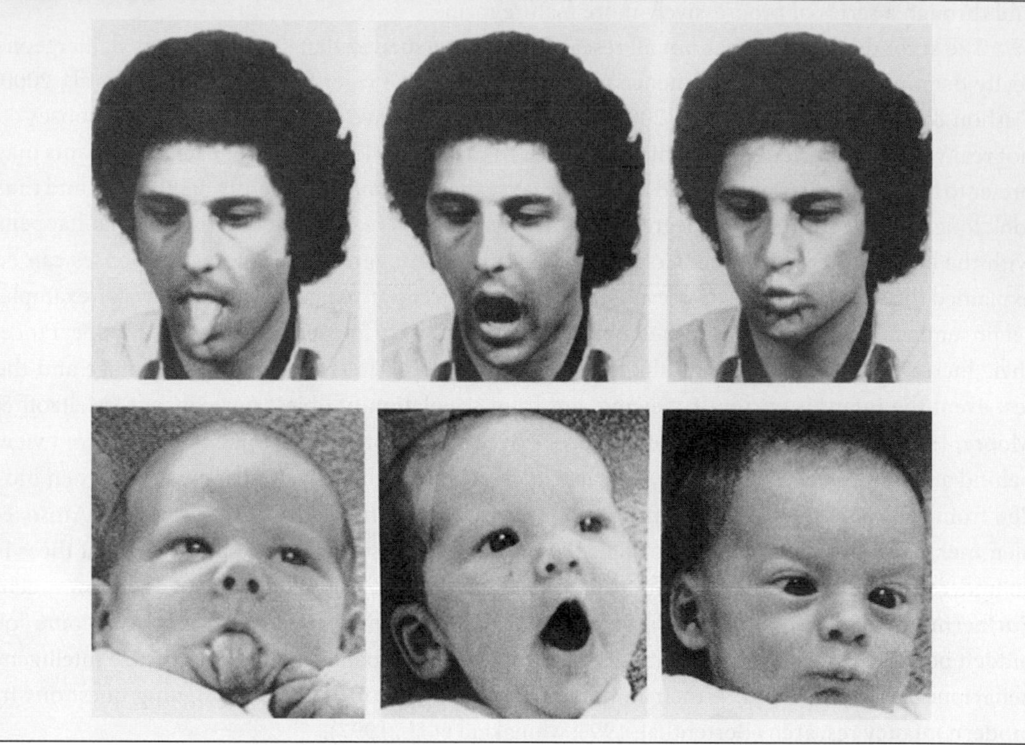

Adult model and infant response in Meltzoff and Moore's study of neonatal imitation. Even very young infants appear to imitate the adult's facial expressions. *From "Imitation of Facial and Manual Gestures by Human Neonates" by A. N. Meltzoff and M. K. Moore, 1977, Science, 198, 75. Copyright © 1977 American Association for the Advancement of Science. Reprinted by permission.*

protrusion, reliably producing these behaviours more often in response to the model than in the model's absence.

That modern research techniques often reveal greater competence than was evident to Piaget should be a familiar conclusion by now. The discrepancy in the Meltzoff and Moore studies, however, is especially striking—not just success far earlier than reported by Piaget, but the presence at birth of behavioural competencies that Piaget thought required many months of slow construction. In light of such a strong claim, it is not surprising that neonatal imitation has been the subject of dozens of recent studies. Some of this work provides support for Meltzoff and Moore's claims (e.g., Chen, Striano, & Rakoczy, 2004; Nagy & Molner, 2004); other investigators, however, have reported difficulties in replication or caution about the genuineness of the phenomenon (e.g., Anisfeld, 1996; Anisfeld et al., 2001; Jones, 2009). At present, therefore, the status of newborn imitation remains controversial. If valid, however, Meltzoff and Moore's findings would constitute perhaps the most dramatic example of competence that exists earlier than Piaget claimed.

LEARNING OBJECTIVE 8.2

Trace the substages and benchmarks of the sensorimotor period in child development.

1. What distinguishes the first two substages of Piaget's sensorimotor period of cognitive development?
2. What role do schemes and procedures play in cognitive development?
3. When during infancy does intentional behaviour develop?
4. What is object permanence, and how do infants develop this knowledge?
5. How do contemporary studies inform Piaget's classic work on cognitive development in infancy?

THOUGHT IN THE PRESCHOOLER: THE PREOPERATIONAL PERIOD

Learning Objective 8.3

Identify some strengths and limitations of preoperational thought in children's cognitive development.

The preoperational period extends from about age 2 to about age 6 years. Remember that Piagetian age norms are always rough guidelines, and particular children may develop more quickly or more slowly than the average.

We noted at the beginning of the chapter that childhood cognition is a mixture of competence and limitations. At no other time during development is this mixture—surprisingly adult-like abilities on the one hand and glaring, hard-to-believe errors on the other—quite so striking or so challenging to explain as it is during the preoperational period. Some of the most fascinating contemporary research in child psychology is directed at exploring the mysteries of the preoperational mind.

MORE ABOUT REPRESENTATION

The defining characteristic of the movement from the sensorimotor to the preoperational period is the onset of representational ability, or what Piaget called **symbolic function**. Piaget defined the symbolic function as the ability to use one thing to represent something else; that is, to use one thing as a symbol to stand for some other thing, which then becomes the symbolized. Symbols can take a variety of forms. They can be mental images, as was likely the case when Piaget's daughter Jacqueline thought through the blades-of-grass problem. They can be physical objects, as when a 3-year-old grabs a broom and rides it as if it were a horse. And, of course, they can be words.

Symbolic function The ability to use one thing (such as a mental image or word) as a symbol to represent something else.

Piaget (1951) cited five kinds of behaviour that become evident at the end of infancy, all of which seem to require representational ability and none of which he had observed earlier in infancy. We have discussed two of these behaviours: the internal problem solving of substage 6, and the ability to handle the invisible displacements version of the object permanence problem. Another is the first appearance of words. Here, Piaget stressed the ability not simply to label present objects, but to talk about objects or events in their absence. The latter is clearly a symbolic achievement. A fourth piece of evidence is the appearance of **deferred imitation**. Although babies imitate from early in life, they can at first imitate only models that are directly in front of them. Only near the end of infancy, according to Piaget, does the baby begin to imitate models from the past—for example, some behaviour that an older sibling performed the week before. The ability to imitate behaviour from the past clearly implies the capacity to store that behaviour in some representational form.

Links to Related Material

In Chapter 11, you will learn how children's increased representational abilities, which are a hallmark of preoperational thought, are tied to the explosion in language development that also occurs around this age.

Deferred imitation Imitation of a model observed some time in the past.

Symbolic play Form of play in which the child uses one thing in deliberate pretence to stand for something else.

The fifth index of the symbolic function is familiar to any parent: the emergence of **symbolic play**. Now is the time that the child's play begins to be enriched by the ability to use one thing in deliberate pretense to stand for something else. Sticks turn into boats, sand piles into cakes, and brooms into horses.

Was Piaget correct about the emergence of representational ability? We have seen consistently from modern research that babies are often more capable than Piaget indicated. The onset of representation is likely no different (Mandler, 2004). Recent research indicates that some forms of representational functioning almost certainly emerge earlier in infancy than Piaget believed. The recent studies of object permanence, for example, seem to demonstrate some capacity to represent unseen objects considerably earlier than Piaget predicted. Furthermore, deferred imitation has been shown in babies as young as 6 months of age (Barr et al., 2005, 2007), and there is suggestive evidence that simple forms may be present as early as 6 weeks (Meltzoff & Moore, 1994). Finally, there is intriguing evidence from studies of infants learning American Sign Language that the first genuinely symbolic signs may emerge as early as 6 or 7 months (Petitto et al., 2004; Thompson et al., 2007) and thus well before both the typical time for the first spoken words and the usual dating for Piaget's substage 6.

One of the clearest signs of the preoperational child's representational skills is the emergence of symbolic play. For example, here a towel and goggles become a superhero's cape and mask. *(Corbis/Media Bakery)*

STRENGTHS OF PREOPERATIONAL THOUGHT

In Piaget's theory, the cognitive structures of later stages are always more powerful and more adaptive than those of earlier stages. Consequently, the onset of representational thought marks a major advance in the child's cognitive abilities.

Representational, in-the-head problem solving is superior to sensorimotor problem solving in a number of ways. Representational intelligence is considerably faster and more efficient. Rather than trying out all possible solutions overtly—a necessarily slow and error-prone process—the representational child can try them out internally, using representations rather than literal actions. When the representational child *does* act, the solution can be immediate and adaptive. Representational intelligence is also more mobile. Sensorimotor intelligence is limited to the here and now—what is actually in front of the child to be acted on. With representational intelligence, however, the child can think about the past and imagine the future. The scope of cognitive activity is thus enormously expanded.

Representational thought is also socially shareable. With the acquisition of language, the child can communicate ideas to others and receive information from them in ways that are not possible without language. Piaget's theory does not place as much stress on either language or cultural transmission as does the sociocultural approach, which we discuss later in the chapter. Nevertheless, he did consistently cite social experience as one of the factors that account for development (Piaget, 1983). And both the extent and the nature of social experience change greatly once the child has entered the preoperational period.

Qualitative identity The knowledge that the qualitative nature of something is not changed by a change in its appearance. In Piaget's theory, this is a preoperational achievement.

The preoperational period is also a time of specific cognitive acquisitions. It is the time during which the child develops a form of knowledge that Piaget labelled **qualitative identity** (Piaget, 1968). Qualitative identity refers to the realization that the nature of something is not changed by a change in its appearance. It is the realization, for example, that a wire remains the same wire even after it has been bent into a different shape. (Note, though, that the child does not yet realize that the length of the wire remains the same—this is a more advanced form of knowledge.) It should be clear that qualitative identity, like object permanence, reflects a central Piagetian theme: the importance of mastering invariants in the environment.

The achievements discussed here hardly exhaust the list of preoperational accomplishments. Indeed, one of Piaget's efforts during the last part of his career was to identify preoperational strengths that had been missed in his earlier studies (Beilin, 1992a, 1992b; Piaget, 1979, 1980). And when we turn to language development in Chapter 11, we will see that the years from 2 to 6 constitute a time of truly remarkable progress with respect to this critical human ability.

LIMITATIONS OF PREOPERATIONAL THOUGHT

Despite the positive features just noted, Piaget focused on weaknesses in preoperational thought, rather than strengths. The weaknesses all stem from the fact that the child is attempting to operate on a new plane of cognitive functioning, that of representational intelligence. The 3-year-old who is quite skilled at the sensorimotor level turns out to be not at all skilled at purely mental reasoning and problem solving. Hence the term *preoperational*, which refers to the fact that the child lacks the "operations" that allow effective problem solving at the representational level.

EGOCENTRISM We saw that infancy begins in a state of profound egocentrism and that a major achievement of infancy is the gradual decentering through which the infant learns what is specific to the self and what exists apart from the self. The preoperational period also begins in a state of egocentrism, but this time at a representational, rather than a sensorimotor, level. In Piaget's view, the young preoperational child has only a very limited ability to represent the psychological experiences of others—to break away from his own perspective to take the point of view of someone whose perspective is different from his own. Instead, the 3- or 4-year-old often acts as though everyone shares his particular point of view—sees what he sees, feels what he feels, knows what he knows, and so on. Note that egocentrism does not mean egotism or selfishness, but rather is simply a difficulty in taking the point of view of another.

TABLE 8.3 CHILDREN RETELL A STORY: SOME PIAGETIAN EXAMPLES OF EGOCENTRIC SPEECH

Story Presented to the Children	Once upon a time, there was a lady who was called Niobe, and who had 12 sons and daughters. She met a fairy who had only one son and no daughter. Then the lady laughed at the fairy because the fairy only had one boy. Then the fairy was very angry and fastened the lady to a rock. The lady cried for 10 years. In the end she turned to a rock, and her tears made a stream, which still runs today.
Examples of Children's Reproductions	Met (6; 4), talking of Niobe: "The lady laughed at this fairy because she [who?] only had one boy. The lady had 12 sons and 12 daughters. One day she [who?] laughed at her [at whom?]. She [who?] was angry and she [who?] fastened her beside a stream. She [?] cried for 50 months, and it made a great big stream." [Impossible to tell who fastened and who was fastened.] Gio (8 years old): "Once upon a time there was a lady who had 12 boys and 12 girls, and then a fairy a boy and a girl. And then Niobe wanted to have some more sons [than the fairy. Gio means by this that Niobe competed with the fairy, as was told in the text. But it will be seen how elliptical his way is in expressing it]. Then she [who?] was angry. She [who?] fastened her [whom?] to a stone. He [who?] turned into a rock, and then his tears [whose?] made a stream which is still running today."

Source: Adapted from *The Language and Thought of the Child* by J. Piaget, 1926, New York: Harcourt Brace, pp. 99, 116, 121.

Preoperational egocentrism is evident in children's speech. Piaget's first book, *The Language and Thought of the Child* (1926), examined both naturally occurring conversations between children and experimentally elicited speech of various sorts. Piaget found that the children's speech was often hopelessly jumbled and hard to decipher, even when they clearly were trying their best to communicate.

Table 8.3 presents some examples from an experiment in which children attempted to retell a story (the phrases in brackets are Piaget's comments on their efforts). Piaget attributed such **egocentric speech** to the young child's basic cognitive egocentrism. Young children often fail to assume the perspective of their listener, acting instead as though the listener already knows everything that they know. Certainly, anyone who has listened to a 3-year-old relate the events of her day has some appreciation of this claim.

FIGURE 8.4

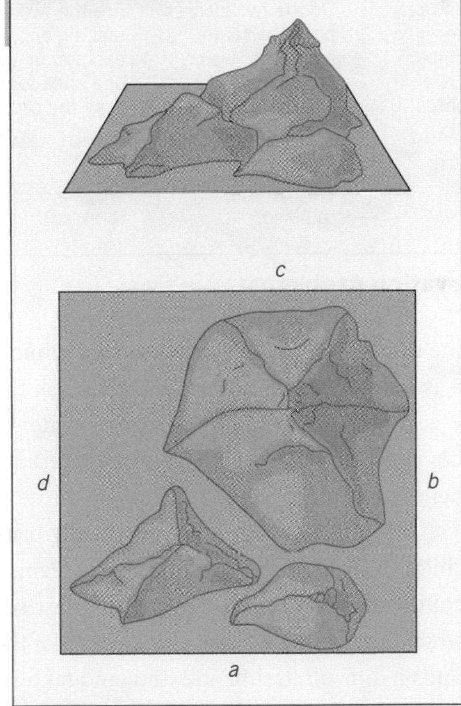

Piaget's three-mountains problem for assessing visual perspective taking. The child's task is to judge how the display looks to someone viewing it from a different perspective. *Adapted from* The Child's Conception of Space *by J. Piaget and B. Inhelder, 1956, London: Routledge and Kegan Paul, 211.*

Piaget also studied the child's ability to assume the visual perspective of another (Piaget & Inhelder, 1956). The best-known task for studying such visual perspective taking is the *three-mountains problem* pictured in Figure 8.4. After walking around the display, the child is seated on one side; the researchers then move a doll to various locations around the board. The child's task is to indicate what the doll would see from the different locations. For many young children, the answer is clear: The doll would see exactly what they see. Again, the young child acts as though his own perspective is the only one possible.

Egocentric speech In Piaget's theory, the tendency for preoperational children to assume that listeners know everything that they know, revealing difficulty with perspective taking.

Centration Piaget's term for the young child's tendency to focus on only one aspect of a problem at a time, a perceptually biased form of responding that often results in incorrect judgments.

Conservation The knowledge that the quantitative properties of an object or collection of objects are not changed by a change in appearance. In Piaget's theory, this is a concrete operational achievement.

CENTRATION The concept of **centration** refers to the young child's tendency to focus on only one aspect of a problem at a time. As an example, consider what is perhaps the most famous Piagetian task: the **conservation** problem. Conservation is the realization that the quantitative properties of objects are not changed by a change in appearance.

The first conservation problem examined in Figure 8.5 relates to number, in which children view two rows of five chips (Piaget & Szeminska, 1952). In this problem, as long as the chips are arranged in one-to-one correspondence, even a 3- or 4-year-old can tell us that the two rows have

FIGURE 8.5

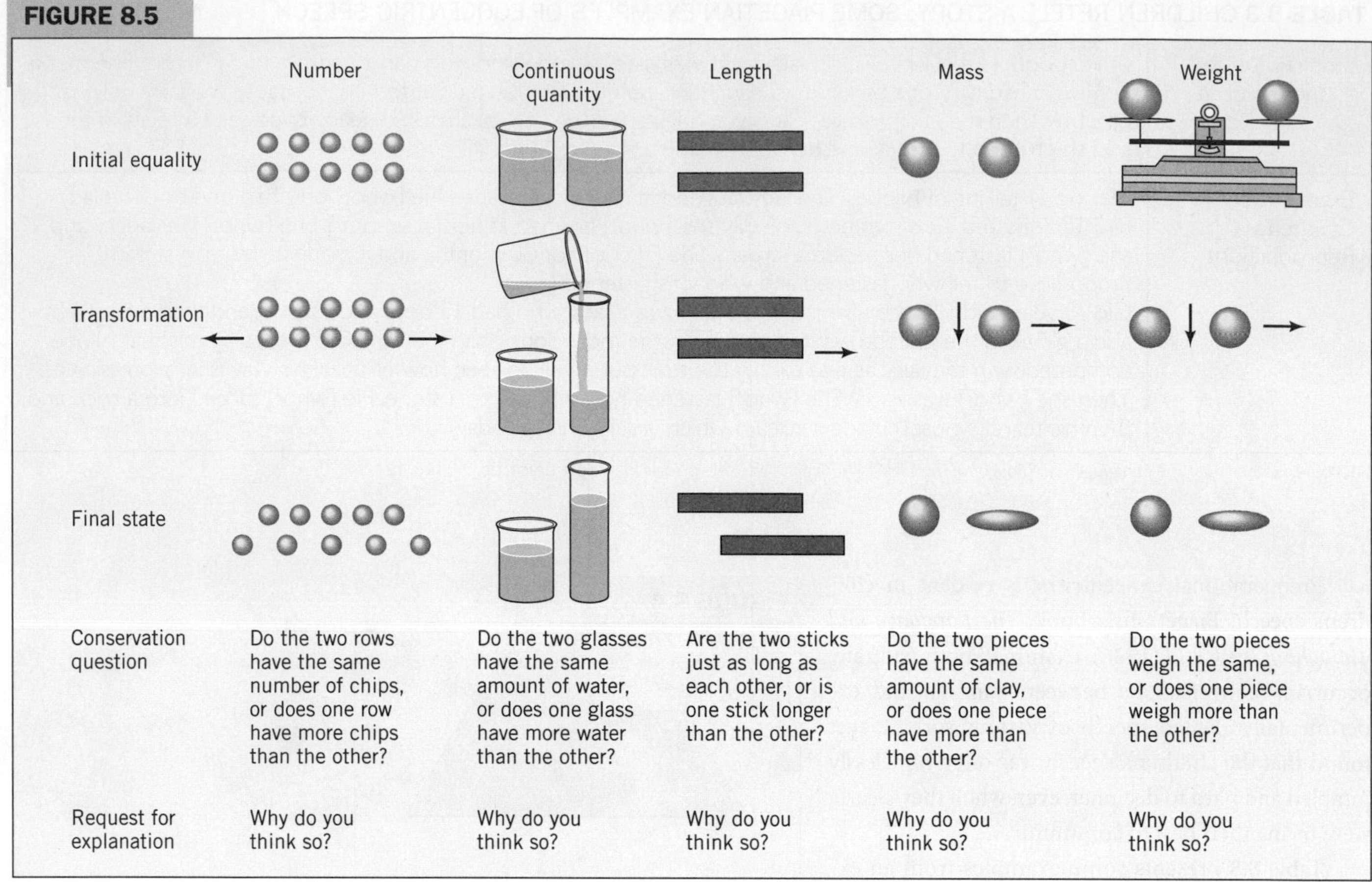

Examples of Piagetian conservation problems.

the same number. But suppose that while the child watches, we spread one of the rows so that it is longer than the other, and then ask the child again about the number. Virtually every 3- or 4-year-old will say that the longer row now has more. If we ask the child why, she finds the answer obvious—because it is longer. In Piaget's terms, the child *centrates* on the length of the row and hence fails to conserve the number.

For Thought and Discussion

Are adults also sometimes egocentric and centred in their thinking? What are some examples from your own experiences and observations?

Centration, then, is a perceptually biased form of responding that is characteristic of young children. For the young child, what seems to be critical is how things look at the moment. The child's attention is captured by the most salient, or noticeable, element of the perceptual display, which in the number task is the length of the rows. Once his attention has been captured, the child finds it difficult to shift attention and take account of other information—for example, the fact that the rows differ not only in length but also in density. Thus the child is easily fooled by appearance and often, as in the conservation task, arrives at the wrong answer.

LEARNING OBJECTIVE 8.3

Identify some strengths and limitations of preoperational thought in children's cognitive development.

1. How is preoperational thinking an advance over sensorimotor cognitive functioning?
2. What cognitive abilities does the child acquire during the preoperational stage?
3. What are two significant limitations of preoperational thinking?
4. What experiments did Piaget use to test the strengths and limitations of young children's thinking?

MIDDLE-CHILDHOOD INTELLIGENCE: THE CONCRETE OPERATIONAL PERIOD

Learning Objective 8.4

Analyze the cognitive task masteries that characterize concrete operational thought.

The concrete operational period is the period of middle childhood, extending from about age 6 to about age 11 or 12.

Discussions of the cognitive differences between preschoolers and school-age children typically note a long list of contrasts (Flavell et al., 2002; Ginsburg & Opper, 1988). If asked to sum up these differences in a single phrase, however, most child psychologists would probably say something like "the older child is just more *logical*." This is not to say that preschoolers are totally illogical; that would be far from the truth. But the preschooler's attempts at logical reasoning are often inconsistent, working impressively in some contexts but going badly astray in others. The young child seems to lack an overall logical system that can be applied with confidence to a wide range of problems, particularly the kinds of scientific and logical problems that Piaget stressed. The older child, in contrast, does possess such a system.

A SAMPLING OF TASKS

For the most part, Piaget used the same tasks to study the preoperational and concrete operational periods. The difference between periods lies in the pattern of response. The preoperational child fails at all the tasks, whereas the concrete operational child begins to succeed at them. The older child's success is not instantaneous—mastery is spread across the entire period of middle childhood.

CONSERVATION The conservation of number problem described earlier is just one example of a conservation task. Conservation can be examined in any quantitative domain, including mass, weight, and volume; length, area, and distance; and time, speed, and movement, as shown in Figure 8.6 (Piaget, 1969, 1970; Piaget & Inhelder, 1974; Piaget, Inhelder, & Szeminska, 1960). As can be seen, the typical starting point is a demonstration that two stimuli are equal on some quantitative dimension. While the child watches, one of the stimuli is then transformed so that they no longer look equal. To conserve the quantity, the child must be able to overcome the misleading perceptual appearance. This is precisely what the preoperational child cannot do.

Different forms of conservation are mastered at different times. Conservation of number is typically one of the first to be acquired, appearing by about age 5 or 6. Conservation of mass and conservation of continuous quantity are also relatively early achievements. Conservation of length and conservation of weight are more difficult, typically coming two or three years after the first conservations. Other forms of conservation emerge still later.

For Thought and Discussion

What are some examples of real-life situations in which young children might make errors in conservation?

FIGURE 8.6

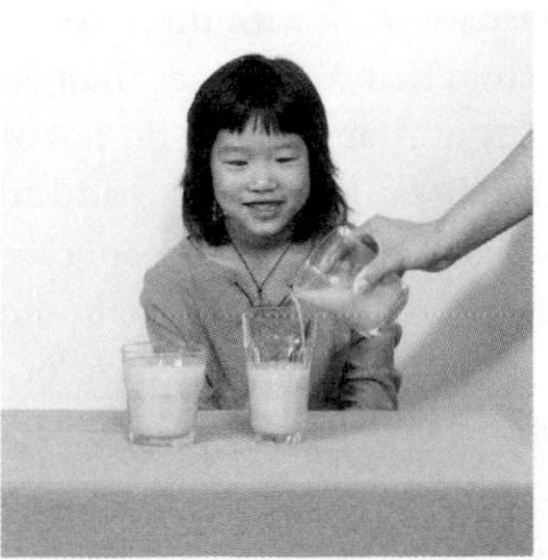

To understand conservation of quantity, the child must overcome misleading perceptual appearances. In the test of conservation of a liquid quantity, the preoperational thinker believes the tall, skinny glass has more juice than the shorter (but wider) glass. (*Ellen B. Senisi/The Image Works*)

CLASSES Investigators, both before and since Piaget, have studied how children form groups or classes when asked to sort an array of objects. Do they sort on the basis of colour or shape, for example, and can they consistently follow whatever criteria they select? Piaget's focus, however, was not simply on the child's ability to group objects sensibly. His interest was in the child's understanding of the structure or logic of any classification system formed.

Class inclusion The knowledge that a subclass cannot be larger than the superordinate class that includes it. In Piaget's theory, a concrete operational achievement.

The best-known task for probing the child's understanding of classes is the **class inclusion** problem. Suppose that we present the child with 20 wooden beads, 17 red and 3 white. The child agrees that some of the beads are red, some are white, and all are wooden. We then ask the child whether there are more red beads or more wooden beads. Or we might ask which would make a longer necklace, all the red beads or all the wooden beads.

Whatever way we word the question, the preoperational response is the same: "There are more red beads than wooden beads." The child is apparently unable to think about a bead as belonging simultaneously to both a subclass (all the red ones) and a superordinate class (all the wooden ones). Instead, once the child has focused on the perceptually salient subclass—the many red beads—the only comparison left is with the other subclass—the few white beads. Note again the role of *centration* in the preoperational child's thinking—the tendency to focus on what is perceptually obvious and to ignore other information. The result is that the child makes a fundamental logical error and judges that a subclass is larger than its superordinate class.

The concrete operational child, in contrast, can solve this and other versions of the class inclusion problem. Furthermore, the concrete operational child, according to Piaget, appreciates the logical necessity of the class inclusion answer. The child does not simply *know* that there are not more roses than flowers or more dogs than animals. The child who truly understands the structure of classes knows that there can *never* be more roses or more dogs—that it is logically impossible for a subclass to be larger than the superordinate class (Miller, 1986).

RELATIONS In addition to understanding classes, the child must come to understand the relations between classes. Thus, another Piagetian task having to do with relational reasoning is the **seriation** task (Piaget & Szeminska, 1952). To study seriation, we might present 10 sticks of different lengths haphazardly arranged. The child's task is to order the sticks in terms of length. We might expect that any child who is persistent enough will eventually arrive at the correct solution through trial and error. Yet most young children fail the task. They may end up with just two or three groups of "big" and "little" sticks, rather than a completely ordered array. Or they may line up the tops of the sticks but completely ignore the bottoms. Even if the child succeeds through trial and error, she is unlikely to be able to solve further variants of the problem—for example, to insert new sticks into the completed array. What seriation requires is a systematic and logical approach in which the child is able to think of each stick as being simultaneously longer than the one that precedes it, and shorter than the one that comes after it. It is this sort of two-dimensional, non-centrated approach to problem solving that the preoperational child lacks.

Seriation The ability to order stimuli along some quantitative dimension, such as length. In Piaget's theory, this is a concrete operational achievement.

Transitivity The ability to combine relations logically to deduce necessary conclusions—for example, if A>B and B>C, then A>C. In Piaget's theory, this is a concrete operational achievement.

The preoperational child also fails to appreciate the **transitivity** of quantitative relations (Piaget et al., 1960). Suppose we work with three sticks—A, B, and C—that differ only slightly in length. We show the child that A is longer than B and that B is longer than C. We then ask about the relative lengths of A and C, but do not allow the child to compare them perceptually. Solving this task requires the ability to add together the two premises (A>B and B>C) to deduce the correct answer (A>C). The concrete operational child has this ability (though not immediately—transitivity emerges at about age 7 or 8). The preoperational child does not, and so is likely to fall back on guessing or some other irrelevant strategy. Note that in both transitivity and class inclusion, the correct answer follows as a logically necessary implication from the information available. That is, it is not simply a fact that A happens to be longer than C; rather, if A is longer than B and B longer than C, then A *has* to be longer than C.

For Thought and Discussion

Children who solve problems quickly are generally viewed as more intelligent, but this value placed on speed is not universal. What other cognitive values may differ from culture to culture?

THE CONCEPT OF OPERATIONS

Interesting though the empirical studies may be, Piaget's primary purpose was never simply to document what children know or do not know. His goal was always to use children's overt performance as a guide to their underlying cognitive structures. During middle childhood, these structures are labelled *concrete operations.* An **operation** always involves some form of action—*operating* on the world in order to understand it. However, operations are a system of *internal* actions. They are the logical, in-the-head form of problem solving, toward which the child has been slowly moving ever since the onset of representational intelligence.

Operations Piaget's term for the various forms of mental action through which older children solve problems and reason logically.

An additional feature of concrete operational thought is **decentration**: the ability to simultaneously keep in mind multiple aspects of a situation. The preoperational child, as we saw earlier, tends to centrate on one aspect of the task and fails to notice other aspects. In contrast, concrete operational children are able to appreciate that while some features of a problem may change, others remain constant.

Decentration The ability to keep in mind multiple aspects of a situation, all at the same time. For Piaget, this is a feature of concrete operational thought.

Let us apply the notion of intelligence-as-internal-action to one of the concepts discussed earlier—working with classes, for example. Piaget argued that what a child knows about classes is a function of various mental actions that the child can perform. Simply to think about an object as belonging to a certain class is a form of action. Classes are not environmental givens; rather, they are cognitive constructions. To add together two subclasses (for example, red beads and white beads) to get the superordinate class (wooden beads) is a form of action. To compare the sizes of two subclasses, or of subclass and superordinate, is a form of action. In general, classification is a matter of mental activity: creating and disbanding classes, comparing different classes, and logically adding, subtracting, or multiplying classes.

What about conservation? Piaget identified various mental actions through which the child might arrive at a correct conservation judgment. In particular, decentration plays a critical role in solving conservation tasks. In the conservation of number task, the child might reason that the change in one dimension—say, the length of the row—is compensated for or cancelled out by the change in the other dimension—the spacing between objects. Such reasoning by means of *compensation* involves a kind of logical multiplication of the two dimensions (increase in length versus decrease in density implies no change in number). Or the child might reason that the spreading transformation can be undone and the starting point of equality re-established, a form of reasoning that Piaget labelled **reversibility**. Reversibility is a property of operational structures that allows the cognitive system to correct, or reverse, potential disturbances and thus to arrive at an adaptive, non-distorted understanding of the world. It is this power that concrete operational thought has and that preoperational thought lacks.

Reversibility Piaget's term for the power of operations to correct for potential disturbances and thus arrive at correct solutions to problems.

MORE ON THE PREOPERATIONAL–CONCRETE OPERATIONAL CONTRAST

Is young children's thinking really as riddled with deficiencies as Piaget claimed? Are the differences between early childhood and later childhood really so great? A number of recent research programs have suggested that the answer to both questions is no. Here, we discuss research about three of the topics reviewed earlier: perspective taking, symbolic ability, and conservation.

PERSPECTIVE TAKING We begin with the concept of visual perspective taking that Piaget's three-mountains task is meant to tap. As an examination of Figure 8.4 makes clear, the three-mountains task requires more than simply avoiding an egocentric response. To come up with the correct answer, the child must engage in a fairly complicated process of spatial calculation. Perhaps the young child's problems with this task tell us more about such spatial computation skills than about egocentrism. When the task is simplified, young children often appear considerably less egocentric. Children as young as 3 years can predict the other's viewpoint when familiar toys, rather than Piagetian mountains, serve as landmarks (Borke, 1975). Even 2-year-olds can demonstrate some awareness of the other's viewpoint in very simple situations. When asked to

Research indicates that children's thinking in early childhood is more advanced than Piaget claimed, as is evident by children's ability to tailor their speech when talking to 2-year-olds versus 4-year-olds or adults. (*Zefa/Media Bakery*)

help an adult find an object, for example, the 2-year-old will hand an object that is hidden from the adult (but not the child) rather than an object in plain view to both of them (Moll & Tomasello, 2006). Similarly, 2-year-olds realize (popular myth notwithstanding) that the fact that *their* eyes are closed does not mean that other people also cannot see (Flavell, Shipstead, & Croft, 1980). Even 12-month-olds will point to objects that they want an adult to notice, a behaviour that suggests some realization that the adult does not necessarily see what they see (Tomasello, Carpenter, & Liszkowski, 2007).

Children's ability to tailor their speech to the needs of others also turns out to be more advanced than one would expect from Piaget's accounts of egocentric speech. Four-year-olds use simpler speech when talking to 2-year-olds than when talking either to other 4-year-olds or to adults (Shatz & Gelman, 1973). Thus, they adjust the level of their communication to the cognitive resources of the listener. Indeed, even 2-year-olds talk somewhat differently to their infant siblings than to adults (Dunn & Kendrick, 1982). Children can also adjust to temporary variations in what the listener knows, as opposed to the general differences that exist between babies and adults. For example, they describe an event differently, depending on whether the adult to whom they are talking was present when the event occurred (Menig-Peterson, 1975). Daniela O'Neill (2005), of the University of Waterloo, reports that children make distinct inferences about what listeners know and structure their communications differently in response to variations in listeners' past experiences.

Links to Related Material

In Chapter 11, you will learn more about how children and adults adjust their speech when talking to young children—a phenomenon known as infant-directed speech.

SYMBOLIC ABILITY The rudimentary forms of symbolic play that emerge by the end of infancy increase in both frequency and complexity across the preschool years (Howes, Unger, & Matheson, 1992; Hughes, 2009). Whereas infants' first play efforts are limited to their own actions (e.g., pretending to go to sleep), eventually props of a variety of sorts can be incorporated. Initially, the props must be physically close to their real-life counterparts; with development, more distant symbols can be used, including imagination in the absence of any prop. Initially, most play episodes consist of isolated actions; eventually, single acts of pretense evolve into sequences of related actions. And, of course, developments do not cease at age 5. Play is a ubiquitous childhood activity, linked to numerous cognitive and social developments, and we therefore return to the topic later in this chapter, as well as in Chapter 15 when we discuss children's relations with their peers.

Children also come to appreciate the representational nature of pictures. Although infants can recognize the correspondence between object and picture, they apparently do not yet realize that a picture is simply a symbolic depiction of the real thing. A 9-month-old presented with a realistic colour photograph of an object pats and rubs the photo as though it were the object itself (Pierroutsakos & DeLoache, 2003). By 19 months, this confusion has disappeared, and pointing and vocalizing replace the manual exploration. Other developments soon follow. Fifteen-month-olds, having experienced a book-reading interaction during which they learned the label "blicket" for a pictured object, can transfer that label to the real item by choosing which of two objects is a blicket (Ganea et al., 2009). Eighteen-month-olds do not care whether the picture they are viewing is right side up or upside down; by 30 months, a preference for the standard upright orientation has emerged (DeLoache et al., 1996). Finally, by age 3 or 4, children, like most adults, begin to take into account the artist's intent when identifying a picture (Bloom & Markson, 1998; Browne & Wooley, 2001). The same emphasis on intent rather than product is also evident when children themselves produce the picture, as anyone who has ever discussed a drawing with a 4-year-old knows.

The preschool child also makes some initial advances in the mastery of conventional symbol systems, such as maps and scale models (Uttal, 2000; Vasilyeva & Huttenlocher, 2004). An especially interesting example in the latter category comes in a program of research by Judy DeLoache and associates (DeLoache, 2000, 2002, 2011; Troseth, Pickard, & DeLoache, 2007). A Snoopy doll (Big Snoopy) is hidden somewhere in the room, and the child's job is to find it. As Figure 8.7 shows, the room offers a number of possible hiding places. As the figure also shows, however, there is a helpful addition to the task: a model of the room that reproduces all of its features in miniature. A miniature Snoopy (Little Snoopy) is hidden in the same place in the model of the room as the Big Snoopy is hiding in the real room, and the question is whether children can use this symbolic equivalence to solve the task. By 3 years of age they can: once they see Little Snoopy disappear into his hiding place, they can run immediately to the matching place in the real room to find Big Snoopy.

FIGURE 8.7

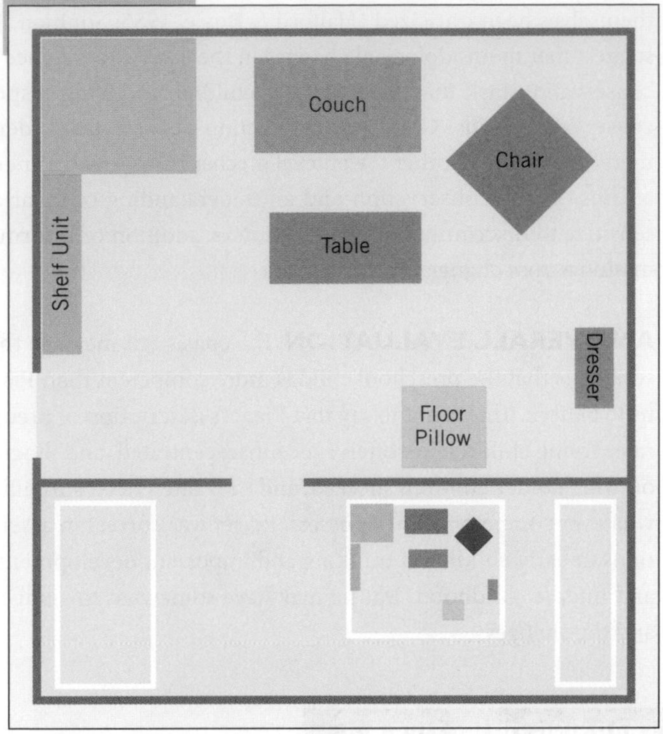

Couch
Chair
Table
Shelf Unit
Dresser
Floor Pillow

Diagram of the experimental arrangement in the DeLoache research on early symbolic ability. The darkened areas in the scale model correspond to labelled items of furniture in the room. *From "Young Children's Understanding of the Correspondence between a Scale Model and a Larger Space" by J. S. DeLoache, 1989,* Cognitive Development, 4, *125. Copyright © 1989 by Elsevier. Reprinted with permission.*

DeLoache argues that the challenge for the young child lies in the need for **dual representation**, which is the realization that an object can be represented in two ways simultaneously. In the find-Snoopy task, the model and miniature dog are not only symbols for their life-size counterparts, they are also real objects in themselves. Two-year-olds are apparently unable to simultaneously think about them as both objects and symbols, but 3-year-olds can.

Dual representation The realization that an object can be represented in two ways simultaneously.

The dual-representation hypothesis suggests an interesting prediction: young children might show greater success if the symbol were less object-like. This proves to be the case. When photographs of the room replace the scale model, children as young as 2.5 years are able to use the symbols to find Snoopy.

CONSERVATION Research suggests that there may be earlier, partial forms of the understanding of conversation that were missed in Piaget's studies. As with perspective taking, investigators have simplified the conservation task in various ways. They have reduced the usual verbal demands, for example, by allowing the child to pick candies to eat or juice to drink rather than answer questions about "same" or "more." Or they have made the context for the question more natural and familiar by embedding the task within an ongoing game. Although such changes do not eliminate the non-conservation error completely, they often result in improved performance by supposedly preoperational 4- and 5-year-olds (Donaldson, 1982; Miller, 1976, 1982). Indeed, in simple situations, even 3-year-olds can demonstrate some knowledge of the invariance of number.

In a study by Rochel Gelman (1972), for example, the 3-year-old participants first played a game in which they learned, over a series of trials, that a plate with three toy mice affixed to it was a "winner" and a plate with two toy mice was a "loser." Then, in a critical test trial, the three-mice plate was surreptitiously transformed while hidden. In some cases, the length of the row was changed; in other cases one of the mice was removed. The 3-year-olds were unfazed by the change in length, continuing to treat the plate as a winner. An actual change in number, however, was responded to quite differently, eliciting search behaviours and various attempts at an explanation. The children thus showed a recognition that number, at least in this situation, should remain invariant.

Note, however, that studies purporting to show earlier competence on conservation tasks have themselves been criticized (Halford & Boyle, 1985; Sophian, 1995b). In particular, these critiques suggest that methodological changes in the early competence studies relative to the more classical conservation task may bias younger children to giving responses that appear to be evidence of conservation skills. Children's completion of these tasks, demonstrating early competence, may therefore be due to other lower level mechanisms—such as perceptual rather than cognitive mechanisms of true conservation and an understanding of invariance. Thus, children may simply be sensitive to discriminating the deletion or addition of information, rather than conserving information across changes in the display.

AN OVERALL EVALUATION The consistent message that emerges from the studies just described is that the preschool child is more competent than Piaget's research and theory would lead us to believe. This is not to say that Piaget's description of preoperational thinking is totally inaccurate. Young children are often egocentric, centrated, and illogical. They fail in a wide range of tasks on which older children succeed, and they often need simplified situations or special help to show whatever competence they possess. Piaget was correct in asserting that there are important limitations in early childhood thinking and important developmental changes between early childhood and middle childhood. But he may have somewhat misjudged the nature of both the limitations and the changes.

LEARNING OBJECTIVE 8.4

Analyze the cognitive task masteries that characterize concrete operational thought.

1. How is operational thinking different from preoperational thinking?
2. How do concrete operational children perform on problems of conservation and classification?
3. How do seriation and transitivity tasks reveal the relational logic used by concrete operational thinkers?
4. What competences have been shown to exist earlier than Piaget proposed?

Learning Objective 8.5

Explain the characteristics and outcomes of formal operations compared with concrete operations.

ADOLESCENT AND ADULT: THE FORMAL OPERATIONAL PERIOD

Formal operations is the final period in Piaget's stage hierarchy. Once acquired, formal operations are assumed to last throughout the lifetime. The onset of the period is usually at about age 12 or 13, around the beginning of adolescence. But formal operations may emerge later than this or not at all. As we will see, the evidence suggests that not everyone reaches the formal operational period.

CHARACTERISTICS OF FORMAL OPERATIONAL THOUGHT

We have already discussed the meaning of the term *operations*. But what about the term *concrete*? The concrete part of the label refers to the basic limitation of concrete operational thought. As we have seen, the concrete operational child operates cognitively by means of representations rather than overt actions. Nevertheless, concrete operational children are still limited to dealing largely with what is directly in front of them—with what is concrete, tangible, and real. What the child at this stage cannot yet do well is deal with the hypothetical—with the whole world of possibility rather than immediate reality.

Formal operational thinkers show no such limitation. The distinguishing characteristic of the formal operational period is the capacity for **hypothetical–deductive reasoning**. The formal operational thinker moves easily and surely through the world of "what-if," "might-be," and "if-then." The adolescent, in fact, seems more at home with the hypothetical—with imagined worlds, counterfactual propositions, and life dreams—than in the world of mundane reality.

Hypothetical–deductive reasoning A form of problem solving characterized by the ability to generate and test hypotheses and draw logical conclusions from the results of the tests. In Piaget's theory, this is a formal operational achievement.

The deductive part of hypothetical–deductive is also important. To qualify as formal operational, thought must do more than simply imagine possibilities. The formal operational thinker possesses a rigorous logical system for evaluating hypotheses and deducing necessary outcomes. As the term operations implies, this system again involves various forms of mental action.

Piaget's favourite way of characterizing the difference between concrete operations and formal operations was to talk about a reversal in the relation between reality and possibility. For the concrete operational child, the starting point is always immediate reality. From this point, the child can make very limited extensions into the hypothetical. For the formal operational thinker, in contrast, the starting point is the world of possibility—whatever it is that might be true. From this starting point in the possible, the thinker works back to what happens to be true in the situation under study.

A RESEARCH EXAMPLE: REASONING ABOUT PENDULUMS

Inhelder and Piaget's (1958) tasks for studying formal operations consist mostly of problems in scientific reasoning. In one task, for example, the participant must determine what factors (length, thickness, shape, and so on) influence the bending of a rod. In another, the task is to experiment with various chemical solutions to determine which combinations produce a specified outcome. Among the other content areas examined are projection of shadows, determinants of floating, conservation of motion, and laws of centrifugal force.

The example that we will describe is drawn from the domain of physics. In this task, the participant is shown a simple pendulum consisting of a weight hanging on a string. Other weights and strings are also available for experimentation. The problem is to figure out what determines the frequency of oscillation of the pendulum, that is, how fast the pendulum swings back and forth. Is it the heaviness of the weight? The length of the string? The height from which the weight is dropped? The force with which it is pushed? Or perhaps some combination of two or more of these factors?

It turns out that the only factor that really has an effect is the length of the string. But the point is not that the formal operational thinker knows this in advance because she probably does not. The point is that the formal operational thinker possesses a set of cognitive structures that will allow systematic solution of the problem. The solution requires first identifying each of the potentially important variables—weight, length, and so on—and then systematically testing them out, varying one factor at a time while holding other factors constant, and drawing logical conclusions. In the case of the pendulum, the performance of all relevant tests leads to the conclusion that if the string is short the pendulum swings fast, and only if the string is short does the pendulum swing fast. As with all Piagetian stages, the achievements of formal operations are clearest when contrasted with the preceding period. The concrete operational child is unlikely to solve the pendulum problem. The 9- or 10-year-old faced with such a task will do some intelligent things, including accurately testing some of the possible variables. But the younger child is not able to generate and examine the full range of possibilities on which a logical conclusion depends. Instead, the child may find that a heavy weight on a short string swings fast and conclude that both the weight and length are important, a conclusion that is not valid in the absence of further tests.

Note that the formal operational approach to the problem embodies the kind of reversal between reality and possibility that Piaget stressed. The formal operational thinker begins by considering all the various possibilities—maybe the weight is important, maybe the length is important, and so on. At first, these are merely hypotheses; none of them have yet been observed, and most of them will turn out to be false. Yet it is only by systematically considering all the possibilities that the subject can determine what happens to be true. Thus, the movement of thought is from the possible to the real.

MORE RECENT WORK ON FORMAL OPERATIONS

For Thought and Discussion

Are you a formal operational thinker? In what contexts or tasks are you most likely to function at this highest level of cognitive development?

Later studies using the Inhelder and Piaget tasks have typically found lower levels of performance than Inhelder and Piaget reported (Shayer, Ginsburg, & Coe, 2007; Shayer & Wylam, 1978). Indeed, some studies have found substantial proportions of adults who fail the usual formal operational tasks (Kuhn & Franklin, 2006; Nigro, 2007).

That Piaget may have *overestimated* this ability runs counter to what we identified earlier as a common conclusion about Piagetian procedures—that they typically lead to some underestimation of children's competence. In fact, some researchers have suggested that underestimation may also occur at the formal operational level. The Inhelder and Piaget tasks are unfamiliar to most people, and the usual method of administering them may not elicit the individual's optimal performance. Studies have shown that the addition of a simple hint or prompt concerning the appropriate procedure can lead to a marked improvement on later trials (Danner & Day, 1977; Stone & Day, 1978). More extended training procedures, as well as other procedural simplifications, have elicited formal operational performance in children as young as 9 or 10 years (Fabricius & Steffe, 1989; Kuhn, Ho, & Adams, 1979).

Another possible approach is to vary the content of the tasks. Perhaps people use formal operations when reasoning about content that is interesting and familiar to them. For some people, the science problems used by Inhelder and Piaget may provide such content; others, however, may require tasks in literary analysis, or auto mechanics, or cooking. Piaget himself, in fact, suggested this possibility (Piaget, 1972). In support of this idea, De Lisi and Staudt (1980) demonstrated that college students' ability to reason at a formal operational level depended on the fit between academic training and specific task: physics majors did best on the pendulum task; English majors excelled on a task involving analysis of literary style; and political science majors earned their highest scores on a problem in political reasoning.

Findings from cross-cultural research also illustrate the importance of specific experience. Although people from non-Western cultures seldom do well on the Inhelder and Piaget problems, they may show impressive levels of performance when operating in more familiar and culturally significant domains. For example, prior to the development of magnetic compasses, Micronesian navigators sailed their canoes for hundreds of miles from one island to another without the aid of instruments, an achievement no Western sailor would attempt to duplicate. The navigators' ability to maintain course depended on a complex—and culturally transmitted—computational system in which star positions, rate of movement, and fixed reference points were systematically combined in ways that seem fully equivalent to the highest levels of performance shown by Inhelder and Piaget's participants (Hutchins, 1983).

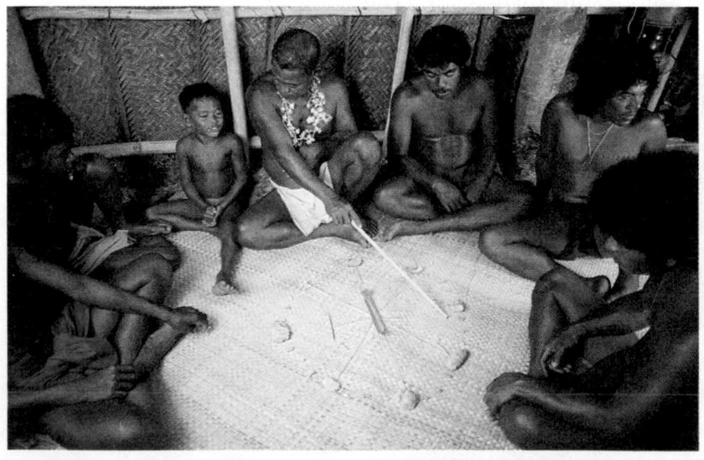

Formal operational reasoning is not limited to the science laboratory. The navigational achievements of Micronesian sailors depend on a complex system of computations and logical deductions. (*Steve Thomas, stevethomashome.com*)

Still one more indication that experience can be important comes from across-time comparisons of performance on formal operational tasks. Flieller (1999) reported that adolescents tested in the 1990s earned higher scores on such measures than did comparable samples from the 1960s and early 1970s. The most plausible explanation for this rise in performance lies in changes in relevant experience across the 25-year span, perhaps especially improvements in education.

Level of performance has not been the only point of contention in follow-up work on formal operations. Piaget's theory of formal operational thought structures has also been subject to criticism, including many of the same criticisms about his claims concerning concrete operations. The degree of within-stage consistency is an issue. Although some studies report fairly strong correlations among formal operational tasks (Eckstein & Shemesh, 1992), low to moderate relations are probably a more common finding (Martorano, 1977). Furthermore, the specific logical structures that Piaget believed underlie formal operational performance have been severely criticized by logicians (Braine & Rumain, 1983; Ennis, 1976). As with earlier Piagetian stages, few dispute that Piaget identified interesting forms of thought or that his theory may partially explain what is happening. But, as Daniel Keating (1988) of the University of Toronto pointed out, the theory does not seem to be completely satisfactory, and debates continue about the best way to characterize this level of thinking (see also Braine & Rumaine, 1983; Byrnes, 1988; Eckstein & Shemesh, 1992; Ennis, 1976; Martorano, 1977; Moshman, 1998).

LEARNING OBJECTIVE 8.5

Explain the characteristics and outcomes of formal operations compared with concrete operations.

1. What is the chief difference between formal operations and concrete operations?
2. How does the pendulum task test for the use of hypothetical–deductive reasoning?
3. Why is there debate about formal operations as a stage of cognitive development?
4. How do interest, experience, and culture influence performance on formal operational tasks?

EVALUATION OF PIAGET'S THEORY

Learning Objective 8.6

Explain the general characteristics of Piaget's theory and evaluate the theory overall.

Piaget's work remains the field's richest source for identifying some of the fundamental developmental questions; however, his theory sets forth some strong claims. In this section, we consider the status of Piaget's claims with respect to three central issues: whether development progresses through distinct stages, whether some aspects of development are universal across cultural settings, and how best to explain cognitive change.

STAGES

What must be true for a stage theory to be valid? Most theorists agree that at least three criteria are important. One is that development includes *qualitative* as well as quantitative changes; that is, changes in *how* the child thinks and not merely in the amount the child knows or the speed at which the child can do things. Piagetian theorists maintain that development does show qualitative change from one period to the next. They argue, for example, that there is a qualitative difference between a sensorimotor child, who must act out all his adaptation to the world, and a preoperational child, who can solve problems mentally through the use of symbols. Similarly, there is a qualitative difference between the preoperational response to a conservation task and the concrete operational response. Younger children treat conservation as a problem in perceptual estimation, always judging in terms of how things look. Older children do not even need to look at the stimuli; for them, conservation is a matter of logical reasoning, not of perceptual judgment.

A second criterion is that the stages follow an *invariant sequence*—each stage builds on the one before, and no stage can be attained until the preceding one has been mastered. The child cannot become preoperational without the sensorimotor developments that make representational thought possible. Similarly, concrete operations build on the achievements of the preoperational period.

The third criterion has created the most problems. Piaget's theory maintains that each stage can be characterized by a set of interrelated cognitive structures—for example, the concrete operations of middle childhood. Once developed, these structures determine performance on a wide range of cognitive tasks. This position implies that there should be important *concurrences* in development. That is, if two or more abilities are determined by the same underlying structures, then they should emerge at the same time. Children's cognitive endeavours should show a good deal of consistency. The problem for Piaget's theory is that children's performance is often far from consistent. They may, for example, succeed on some presumably concrete operational tasks, yet fail totally on others. Piaget did not claim perfect consistency; he was the first, in fact, to demonstrate that various concrete operational concepts may be mastered at different times. He referred to the difference with which such concepts are mastered as reflecting a *horizontal décalage* (*décalage* being a French term for a "gap" or "lag" between events). Most commentators, however, believe that Piaget never satisfactorily explained the inconsistencies that his research uncovered. And research that followed Piaget has revealed even more inconsistencies in development, including instances in which abilities that Piaget explicitly claimed as concurrences are mastered at different times (de Ribaupierre et al., 1991; Jamison, 1977; Kreitler & Kreitler, 1989).

What, then, is the status of the concept of stages? The issue continues to be a source of debate (Feldman, 2004; Fischer & Bidell, 1998; Lourenco & Machado, 1996; Miller, 2011). Some researchers believe that Piaget's stage model is basically accurate, even though specific details may need correcting. Others believe that cognitive development does in fact occur in stages, but that the stages are different from those posited by Piaget. And still others believe that the concept of stage serves no useful purpose and should be abandoned.

UNIVERSALITY

For Thought and Discussion

On the basis of your observations, are children of the same age more similar or more different in their cognitive development? Is any one child more consistent or more inconsistent than another in his or her thinking? Are you and your peers all at the same stage of cognitive development?

In Piaget's view, all children the world around pass through the same stages in the same sequence. And all children develop basic forms of knowledge, such as object permanence and conservation.

The study of development in other cultures provides a natural testing ground for the Piagetian claim of universality. We have long known that children growing up in Canada or the United States show the same basic patterns of development that Piaget first identified in children in Switzerland some 50 or 60 years ago. But would development still follow the Piagetian mould in non-Western societies?

The answer turns out to be yes and no. Cross-cultural research indicates that the specific experiences available to children can affect the development of Piagetian concepts in a variety of ways (Laboratory of Comparative Human Cognition, 1983; Rogoff & Chavajay, 1995). Culture can affect the rate and level of development: in some cultures, development lags several years behind the norms reported in other settings. Culture can also affect the final level of development: in some cultures, especially if children lack formal schooling, few individuals attain formal operations. Indeed, even the order in which certain abilities emerge may vary across cultures. For example, children from pottery-making families show precocious mastery of conservation of substance relative to other abilities (Price-Williams et al., 1969). Similarly, the navigation through the spatial terrain that is part of life in nomadic societies is associated with accelerated development of spatial abilities in children from such groups (Dasen, 1975a).

Inuit children and children of other nomadic cultures have well-developed spatial abilities. (© *Yva Momatiuk and John Eastcott*)

At the same time, cross-cultural research also provides some support for the Piagetian claim of universality. No one has found a culture in which children do not eventually acquire forms of knowledge such as object permanence and conservation, or in which children master conservation without going through an initial phase of non-conservation, or in which the order of the four general periods of development is reversed. Indeed, even some of the reported lags in rate of development disappear when the tests are made appropriate to the cultural setting—for example, when children are interviewed in their native language by a native speaker (Nyiti, 1982) or when the children themselves play an active role in the assessment situation (Greenfield, 1966).

For Thought and Discussion

What aspects of cognitive development would you expect to stay the same across cultures? Why?

COGNITIVE CHANGE

Most of Piaget's research was directed to the question that has been our focus throughout the chapter: What are the most important changes that occur in the course of cognitive development? In his theorizing, however, he also devoted considerable attention to the second general question that a theory of development must address: How can we explain the changes that research has identified?

Piaget's position on the nature–nurture issue is definitely interactionist. In his theory, biology and experience act together to produce changes in the child's cognitive abilities. More specifically, Piaget (1964, 1983) identified four general factors that contribute to cognitive change. Three of the factors are found to some extent in every theory of development. First, biological maturation plays a role. Learning and development occur within constraints set by the child's maturational level, and some kinds of development may be impossible until maturation has progressed sufficiently.

Experience is also important. Piaget divided experience into two categories: physical experience and social experience. The former includes the child's interactions with inanimate objects; the latter, the child's interactions with people. In both cases, Piaget stressed the importance of assimilation and accommodation. Children must fit experiences, physical or social, into what they already understand. And they must actively construct new knowledge, as opposed to having knowledge imposed ready-made upon them.

Every theory talks in some way about maturation, physical experience, and social experience. The fourth factor, however, is uniquely Piagetian. **Equilibration** is another legacy of Piaget's biological training. Piaget used this term to refer to the general biological process of self-regulation. It was for him the most important of the four factors, the one that, in a sense, explained the other three.

Equilibration Piaget's term for the biological process of self-regulation that propels the cognitive system to higher forms of equilibrium.

What did Piaget mean by self-regulation? The notion is easiest to understand in conjunction with a closely related Piagetian construct**, equilibrium**. Equilibrium refers to balance within the cognitive system. It exists when the child's cognitive structures can respond to any environmental challenge without distortion or misunderstanding. Such an adaptive response implies a balance between assimilation and accommodation. The child neither distorts reality to make it fit existing structures (which would be an excess of assimilation), nor distorts current knowledge in an attempt to make sense of something new (which would be an excess of accommodation). It is the self-regulating process of equilibration that guards against such distortions and acts to maintain equilibrium.

Equilibrium A characteristic of a cognitive system in which assimilation and accommodation are in balance, thus permitting adaptive, non-distorted responses to the world.

In Piaget's view, the cognitive system seeks always to reach and maintain states of equilibrium. Suppose, however, that the child encounters some new event that cannot immediately be understood. This new event will evoke disequilibrium, or cognitive conflict—some sort of disturbing imbalance within the cognitive system. The child will feel a need to get rid of the conflict and will continue to think and act until the event is understood and equilibrium restored. Thus, equilibration also accounts for the directionality in development, for the fact that development moves always in an upward, progressive direction. When disequilibrium exists, equilibrium can be restored by evolving a higher, better level of understanding and, consequently, moving from lower stages into higher ones.

Equilibration, however, is a very general notion that does not tell us how specific cognitive changes come about. At various points, Piaget did attempt to specify the equilibration process more exactly (Piaget, 1957, 1977b). Most critics, however, have concluded that none of the versions is very satisfactory, and the theory remains vague and hard to test (Chapman, 1992; Zimmerman & Blom, 1983).

For Thought and Discussion

What might be some real-life examples of events that cause disequilibrium and equilibration in the process of cognitive change?

LEARNING OBJECTIVE 8.6

Explain the general characteristics of Piaget's theory and evaluate the theory overall.

1. On what key issues do evaluations of Piaget's stage theory focus?
2. What are the questions and uncertainties regarding these key issues of Piagetian theory?

Learning Objective 8.7

Discuss and describe more recent research of children's cognitive development that has been influenced by Piaget's cognitive-developmental approach.

NEW DIRECTIONS

The Piagetian legacy of the basic cognitive-developmental approach has in recent years been extended to a number of interesting developments that received little if any attention in Piaget's own research. We briefly consider two such topics: children's understanding of concepts, and various developments that fall under the heading of "theory of mind."

CONCEPTS

Concept A mental grouping of different items into a single category on the basis of some unifying similarity or set of similarities.

Your ability to cut the world up into meaningful units (e.g., grass, trees, dogs, and birds; running, flying, jumping; clouds, wind, and sun; or happiness, excitement, and fear) is a reflection of the many concepts that you have developed. A **concept** is a mental grouping of different items into a single category on the basis of some underlying similarity—some common core that makes them all, in a sense, the same thing (all birds, all instances of happiness). Concepts are a fundamental way in which we organize the world, and thus their development in childhood is of clear interest. What bases do children use when judging things as similar, and how do these bases change with development?

Figure 8.8 shows one approach to this question. The problems are from an influential program of research by Gelman and associates (Gelman & Bloom, 2007; Gelman et al., 2007; Gelman & Markman, 1986; Gelman & Meyer, 2011). The two possible bases for response should be clear. If perceptual similarity is taken to be critical, then the new item should be judged to be like the one that it most resembles. This means, for example, that the blackbird would be expected to have warm legs at night, just like the similar-looking bat. In contrast, if category membership is more important, then the legs would be expected to be cold, just like those of the other bird. The contrast in these tasks between surface similarity and underlying essence as the basis for judging that things are the same is common in studies of children's concepts.

The expectation has been that young children will be perceptually oriented, forming concepts on the basis of surface appearance rather than oriented to more basic commonalities. There is, certainly, support for this expectation (Mandler, 2004). Piaget's studies furnish many instances of preschool children centrating on what is immediately obvious and ignoring what is beneath the surface.

What has been striking and informative in recent research on children's concepts are demonstrations that, in many cases, young children are *not* perceptually bound. Often, in fact, preschool children seem to cut the world up in essentially the same way as do adults. This, for example, was the major conclusion from the research summarized in Figure 8.8. Despite the compelling perceptual cues, most 4-year-olds opted for category membership as the relevant basis for inference, judging that the bird's legs would get cold, that the shark would breathe under water, and so forth. A subsequent study using simplified procedures showed that even 2.5-year-olds had some ability to overlook perceptual appearance in favour of category membership (Gelman & Coley, 1990).

Why is there a more positive picture of preschoolers' competence in recent research? Two factors are probably important. One is the methods used. Many of the older studies based their

FIGURE 8.8

This bird's legs get cold at night. *This bat's legs stay warm at night.* *See this bird. Do its legs get cold at night, like this bird, or do its legs stay warm at night, like this bat?*

This fish stays under water to breathe. (picture of tropical fish)
This dolphin pops above the water to breathe. (picture of dolphin)
See this fish. Does it breathe under water, like this fish, or does it pop above the water to breathe, like this dolphin? (picture of shark, looks like the dolphin)
This puppy hides bones in the ground. (picture of brown dachshund)
This fox hides food in the ground. (picture of red fox)
See this puppy. Does it hide bones in the ground, like this puppy, or does it hide food in the ground, like this fox? (picture of red dog, looks like the fox)

Sample items from Gelman and Markman's studies of children's concepts. *From "Categories and Induction in Young Children" by S.A. Gelman and E. M. Markman, 1986,* Cognition, 23, *183–209. Copyright © 1986 Elsevier. Reprinted with permission.*

conclusions about early concepts on children's responses to explicit instructions to sort items into categories (e.g., "Show me which ones go together"). The Gelman and Markman procedure, in contrast, is tied to a natural, everyday use of concepts—drawing inferences about new instances from what is already known. Our concept of "dog," for example, allows us to form expectations with respect to a number of attributes (likely behaviours, preferred diet, internal organs, etc.) even for dogs we have never met—indeed, even for breeds of dogs we have never seen. The grounding of the response measure in this natural function of concepts may be one explanation for the impressive performance in recent research.

The type of concept at issue is probably important as well. Some studies have used arbitrary concepts created on the spot for the purposes of research—for example, the category of blue circles in a study of sorting behaviour. There is nothing arbitrary, however, about the concepts that children naturally form—such concepts reflect important commonalities among real-life experiences that children extract as they attempt to make sense of the world. The focus on familiar and interesting material may also contribute to the good performance in recent research.

Concepts are far too plentiful and diverse to permit a case-by-case discussion of their development. We will, however, single out one general category that has been the target of much interesting recent research: children's concepts of biology and animacy. Questions of life—of living versus non-living, of origins, of growth—have fascinated children for as long as they have fascinated scientists (including Piaget). As you might expect, the main message to emerge from Piaget's studies was one of confusion and misunderstandings on the part of the child. A basic confusion concerned a failure to distinguish between living and non-living, which Piaget labelled **animism**: the tendency to attribute properties of life to non-living things. The young child who indicates that the sun shines "because it wants to" is engaging in animistic thinking, as is the child who is concerned that a piece of paper will be hurt if cut. According to researchers at the University of Calgary, children even ascribe animistic characteristics to robots (Beran, Ramirez-Serrano, Kuzyk, Fior, & Nugent, 2011). It should be clear that such reasoning represents an error and signals an important gap in biological understanding.

Animism Piaget's term for the young child's tendency to attribute properties of life to non-living things.

The concept of biology—distinguishing living from non-living—can be confusing to children. This is reflected in animism, children's tendency to attribute properties of life to non-living things. (*Design Pics/Media Bakery*)

Studies since Piaget's have confirmed that young children do manifest animism in their thinking, along with confusion with regard to biological phenomena (Carey, 2000). However, other recent studies indicate that animism may be less pervasive than Piaget believed. Three-year-olds, for example, are fairly good at judging which things can move by themselves (e.g., animals) and which things cannot (e.g., statues, plants) (Massey & Gelman, 1988). They also realize that only living things grow, that growth is inevitable (for example, you cannot keep a baby pet small and cute just because you want to), and that growth is directional; that is, people, plants, and animals get bigger, not smaller, as they age (Inagaki & Hatano, 2006; Rosengren et al., 1991). Though this understanding is far from complete, and there are disagreements about what knowledge to attribute to preschoolers (Solomon et al., 1996), there is clearly a stronger starting point than we once believed.

THEORY OF MIND

Theory of mind Thoughts and beliefs concerning the mental world.

We have seen that the preschool period is a time of impressive accomplishments in the domain of conceptual understanding. The preschool child also makes major strides with respect to a variety of forms of knowledge that fall under the heading of **theory of mind**. Theory of mind refers to children's understanding of the mental world—what they think about such phenomena as thoughts, beliefs, desires, and intentions. Do children realize, for example, that there is a distinction between the mental and the non-mental, that thoughts are in our minds and not part of the physical world? Do they realize, despite this distinction, that the mental and the non-mental are connected, that our experiences lead us to have certain thoughts and beliefs, and that these thoughts and beliefs in turn direct our behaviour? Do they appreciate the distinctions among different mental states, that to think something is not necessarily the same as to know something, or that the intention to achieve a goal is no guarantee that the goal will actually be reached?

False belief The realization that people can hold beliefs that are not true. Such understanding, which is typically acquired during the preoperational period, provides evidence of the ability to distinguish the mental from non-mental.

In just the last decade, theory of mind has emerged as one of the most active arenas for research in cognitive development (Laranjo et al., 2010; Legerstee, 2005; Sabbagh et al., 2006; Wellman, 2011). Recent research has even started to attempt to delineate the neural mechanisms underlying children's theory of mind (e.g., Liu et al., 2009). A topic of particular interest has been children's understanding of **false belief**: the realization that it is possible for people to hold beliefs that are not true. Consider the scenario depicted in Figure 8.9. To any adult, the answer to the question of where Sally will search for her marble is obvious—in the basket, where she last saw it. After all, she has no way of knowing that the marble has been moved during her absence. Note, however, that to arrive at this answer we must set aside our own knowledge of the true state of affairs to realize that Sally could believe something that differs from this true state, that she could hold a false belief. We can do this only if we realize that beliefs are mental representations that need not correspond to reality.

Three-year-old children typically have great difficulty understanding false beliefs, and most fail tasks such as the one in Figure 8.9. Four-year-olds are much more likely to understand that they can hold a belief that is false, and that a representation can change even when the reality does not. They are also more likely to realize that others could hold false beliefs in tasks of the hidden-marble sort. This developmental transition in false-belief reasoning is supported by research by Cristina Atance of the University of Ottawa and Daniel Bernstein of Kwantlen University in Surrey, BC (Atance, Bernstein, & Meltzoff, 2010). These researchers

FIGURE 8.9

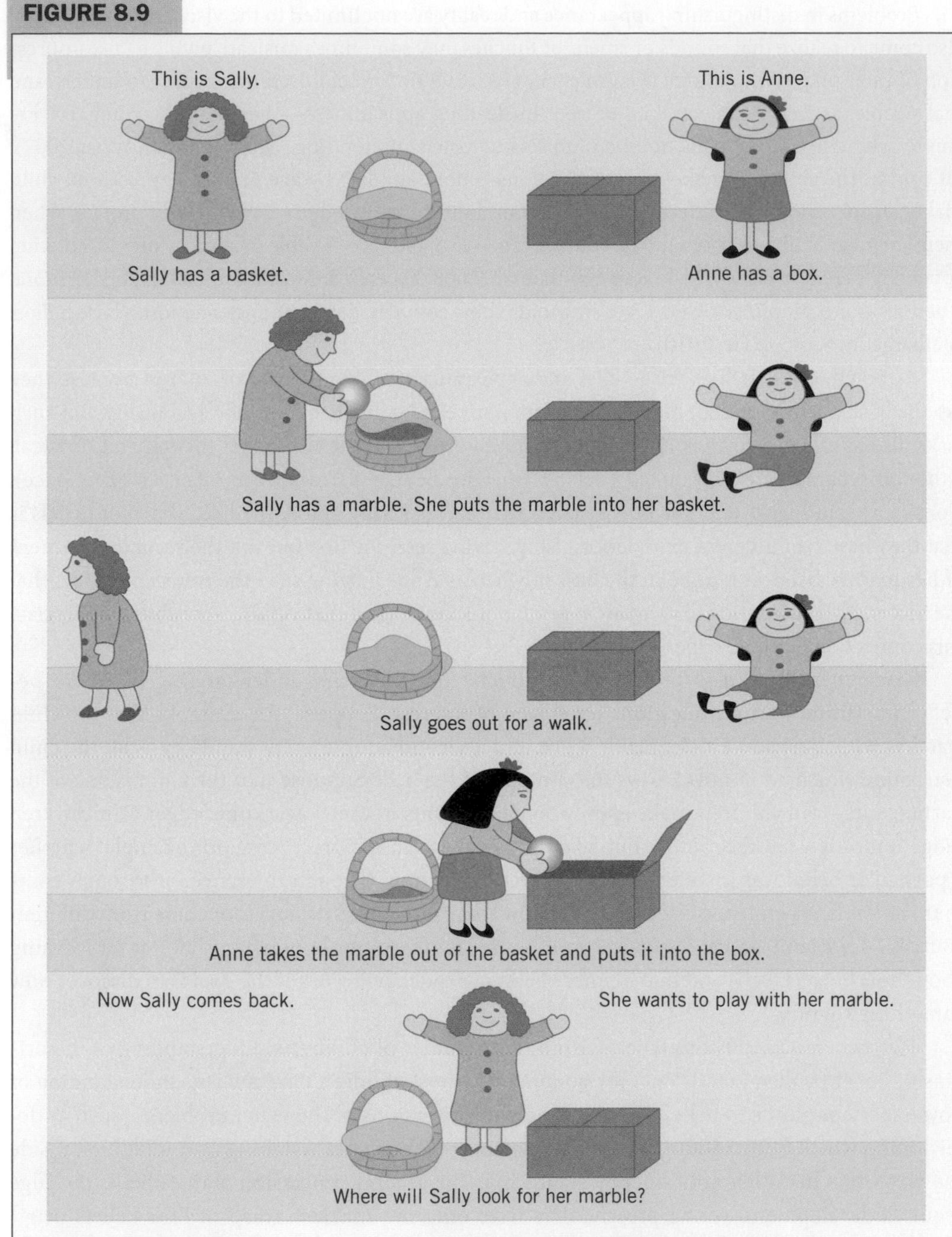

This is Sally.
This is Anne.
Sally has a basket.
Anne has a box.
Sally has a marble. She puts the marble into her basket.
Sally goes out for a walk.
Anne takes the marble out of the basket and puts it into the box.
Now Sally comes back.
She wants to play with her marble.
Where will Sally look for her marble?

Example of a false-belief task. To answer correctly, the child must realize that beliefs are mental representations that may differ from reality. *From* Autism: Explaining the Enigma *by U. Frith, 1989, Oxford: Basil Blackwell, 160. Copyright © 1989 by Basil Blackwell. Reprinted by permission.*

observed that the speed with which children respond to false-belief questions shows a distinct change in pattern around 4 years of age. Interestingly, under certain circumstances even adults sometimes show difficulties in false-belief tasks, as noted by Susan Birch of the University of British Columbia (Birch & Bloom, 2007)

Further evidence of the young child's difficulty in distinguishing representations from reality comes from another popular task in recent theory-of-mind research. As the name suggests, the **appearance–reality distinction** concerns the ability to distinguish between the way things appear and the way they really are. Suppose, for example, that we show a child a red car, cover the car with a filter that makes it look black, and then ask what colour the car "really and truly is." A 3-year-old is likely to reply "black"; a 6-year-old will almost certainly (and perhaps scornfully) say "red."

Appearance–reality distinction Distinction between how objects appear and what they really are. Understanding the distinction implies an ability to judge both appearance and reality correctly when the two diverge.

Problems in distinguishing appearance and reality are not limited to the visual realm. Children also come to realize that sounds or smells or touches may sometimes mislead, giving a false impression of their underlying source (Flavell et al., 1983, 1989). And children must come to understand that people, as well as objects, can present misleading appearances—they may be crying, for example, when they are actually not sad or upset but instead pretending (Mizokawa & Koyasu, 2007). Of course, the ability to make such distinctions is not complete by age 6; but the preschool child makes major strides in mastering this important kind of knowledge (Flavell, 1986). In fact, when their language skills are taken into account, even 3-year-olds are capable of successfully completing appearance–reality tasks (Deák, Ray, Brenneman, 2003; Hansen & Markman, 2005). Furthermore, when tasks are simplified, even 17-month-olds show some evidence of understanding false beliefs (Baillargeon, Scott, & He, 2010).

As noted, tasks such as false-belief and appearance–reality tasks are of interest because they tap the basic realization that mental representations can be distinct from physical reality. But such tasks also speak to a further important realization: the understanding that mental and physical, although separate, are also linked (that is, what we believe follows from what we experience). Consider again Figure 8.9. The only reason, after all, that Sally and Anne hold different beliefs is that they have had different experiences: Sally, having seen the first but not the second placement of her marble, believes it to be in the basket, whereas Anne, having seen the transfer, realizes that the box is the true location. As we saw, it is not until about age 4 that children are able to appreciate this connection between experience and belief.

Researchers have also probed more directly for children's understanding of where beliefs come from. Various questions have been of interest. Suppose, for example, that the child watches while one adult looks inside a box and a second adult merely stands by—can the child determine which adult now knows the contents of the box? Suppose that the child is one of the participants—can children make appropriate judgments of their own knowledge? Can children judge not only what they know, but *how* they know? Can they recapture, for example, whether a particular belief was instilled through direct perception, through inference, or through communication from someone else? Do they know what sorts of knowledge *can* come from different sources—for example, that vision is a good source for learning about colour but not for learning about how objects feel—and that neither vision nor touch will work if the goal is to discover how something sounds?

Two general conclusions emerge from these studies of children's understanding of the origins of belief (Miller, 2000). First, by about age 5, most children have a basic understanding of how experience leads to belief and can handle most versions of the belief problems (such as determining which of two adults knows the contents of a box after watching one adult look inside the box while the other adult merely stands by). The second conclusion is that this knowledge requires development: young preschoolers have only the shakiest grasp of how beliefs originate. Thus, 3-year-olds are unable, seconds after learning the contents of a container, to indicate whether they learned through sight or touch or being told (O'Neill & Chong, 2001). Or, asked to determine the colour of an unseen object, 3-year-olds may be quite content to explore via touch rather than sight (O'Neill, Astington, & Flavell, 1992). Even 4-year-olds may report that they have always known a fact that the experimenter, in fact, taught them just moments earlier (Taylor, Esbensen, & Bennett, 1994).

Links to Related Material

In Chapters 12 and 13, you will learn how infants' and children's social interactions, particularly with their parents, play a key role in the development of their social understanding of others and the self.

One of the most interesting of ongoing research efforts concerns possible relations between theory-of-mind understanding and social behaviour. That is, children's understanding of the mental world can help them interact with other people, and interactions with others can also help teach children about beliefs and other mental states. Sandra Bosacki of Brock University and Janet Astington of the University of Toronto (1999), for instance, have reported a positive relation between number of siblings and false-belief understanding; that is, children from relatively large families, and thus with a higher probability of social experiences through which they can learn about mental states, are generally faster to master false belief (see also

ON THE CUTTING EDGE 8.1
THEORY OF MIND IN INFANCY

A 5-week-old infant imitates mouth openings produced by an adult, but not similar-looking movements produced by an inanimate object (Legerstee, 1991). A 4-month-old reaches to retrieve an object that has just disappeared from view, but vocalizes to bring back a person who has moved out of sight (Legerstee, 1994). A 7-month-old shows increased attention when an inanimate object moves on its own—not, however, when a person moves (Spelke, Phillips, & Woodward, 1995).

Despite the concentration of research on the preschool period, no investigator of theory of mind believes that understanding of mental states begins to emerge only at age 3. As the examples just cited show, infants demonstrate an awareness quite early on in life that people are different from other objects. Indeed, some ability to distinguish the social and non-social worlds is present in simpler form from birth (Wellman, 2011). Recall from Chapter 7 that infants only a day or two old find the human face and human voice especially interesting to look at or listen to.

Of course, theory of mind encompasses more than simply a realization that people are somehow different from other things. The core understanding is how they are differ-ent—namely, that only people have mental states, such as thoughts and desires and beliefs. Furthermore, these mental states, although distinct from the physical world, are also connected to it; that is, beliefs, desires, and so on are about something. How might infants show a dawning awareness of mental states and how they relate to the world? Consider the following two developments that are evident by about 1 year of age.

A mother and baby are playing together on the floor. At one point, the mother turns her head and gazes toward the door of the room. The infant notices the mother's movement, stares for a moment at her face, and then turns and also gazes toward the door. This episode illustrates the phenomenon known as **joint attention**: the ability to follow into and share the attentional focus of someone else. It is an achievement of infancy because it is not something that babies can do from the start. And it seems to imply some understanding, although probably only at an implicit level, of mother as a psychological being: Mommy is having an interesting visual experience, and if I look where she is looking, then I will, too.

Joint attention Using cues (such as direction of gaze) to identify and share the attentional focus of another.

Let us take our illustrative episode one step further. Suppose that what mother and baby see at the door is a stranger—some adult whom the baby has never encountered before. Uncertain how to respond, the baby turns back and looks at the mother's face. If the mother smiles and greets the stranger, the baby will probably respond positively as well; on the other hand, if the mother reacts with fear or distress, there is a good chance that the baby's reaction will also not be a happy one. The baby is engaging in **social referencing**: looking to another for cues about how to interpret and respond to an uncertain situation. Like joint attention, social referencing seems to imply some understanding that mother is experiencing a psychological state—in this case, an emotion that is relevant to the child's own emotional reaction. Like joint attention, social referencing is not present early in infancy, but instead emerges around the end of the first year. And like joint attention, social referencing is specific to the human objects in the baby's environment. Infants do not follow the gaze of a favourite doll, and they do not turn to a teddy bear for guidance when trying to make sense of something new.

Social referencing Using information gained from other people to interpret uncertain situations and to regulate one's own behaviour.

We should add that there are disagreements among researchers with respect to exactly when joint attention and social referencing emerge, and also with respect to how much knowledge about others' mental states such behaviours imply (Moore & Corkum, 1994; Repacholi, 1998; Tomasello, 1999b). Even on the most positive reading, these achievements of infancy constitute a limited step into the mental world of others. Still, they may well be a starting point on which the accomplishments of the preschool period can build.

Perner, Ruffman, & Leekam, 1994; Peterson, 2000; Ruffman et al., 1998). Additionally, Maria Legerstee of York University has examined how early social interactions, particularly social interactions with parents, provide the foundation upon which the understanding of other's mental states develops (Legerstee, 2005; Legerstee, Markova, & Fisher, 2007; Legerstee, Pasic, Barillas, & Fahy, 2004).

Further evidence for links between theory-of-mind understanding and social behaviour is provided by the phenomenon of childhood autism. Autism is a severe disorder that is likely biological in origin. It is characterized by a number of abnormalities in development, including difficulties in social interaction. From early on in life, children with autism show little interest in other people and little ability to form interpersonal relationships. And research demonstrates that these children also show marked deficiencies with regard to theory-of-mind understanding (Baron-Cohen, 2000b; Frith, 1989). Even when other aspects of mental functioning are relatively unimpaired, children with autism typically perform very poorly on theory-of-mind tasks. As Baron-Cohen (1995) observed, these children's insensitivity to the thoughts, wishes, and feelings of others is not surprising; they may literally not know that such psychological states exist. The consequences of such "mind blindness" (Baron-Cohen, 1995) are poignant testimony to the importance of theory of mind to normal social relations.

LEARNING OBJECTIVE 8.7

Discuss and describe more recent research of children's cognitive development that has been influenced by Piaget's cognitive-developmental approach.

1. What is the nature of the child's capacity for understanding concepts?
2. What is meant by "theory of mind"?
3. How do studies of false belief and the appearance–reality distinction inform us about the development of the theory of mind?
4. What factor has been shown to interact with the development of theory of mind?

Learning Objective 8.8

Analyze the three main themes on which sociocultural approaches to development are based.

VYGOTSKY AND THE SOCIOCULTURAL APPROACH

Like the work of Piaget, the ideas of Soviet scholar Lev Vygotsky about cognitive development, referred to as the *sociocultural approach*, have had a profound impact on the study of child development. As with Piaget's theory, the sociocultural approach focuses on the development of intellectual skills and sees the child as an active participant in development. The approaches differ, however, in their views on how change occurs, the factors that influence the process, and the outcomes of development. According to the sociocultural approach, cognitive development is fundamentally a social and cultural process. Numerous studies drawing on Vygotsky's work have been published in recent decades, reflecting growing interest in the cultural context of child development. What different developmental pathways can be observed among children of different cultures and of different ethnic groups within cultures?

The sociocultural approach answers this question in more than one way, as it is not a single theory but a family of theoretical frameworks. The common core that unites these theories is a focus on the social and cultural foundations of developmental processes. According to the sociocultural approach, individuals inherit their environments as much as they inherit their genes. These environments are organized by **culture**—the accumulated body of knowledge of a people encoded in language and embodied in the beliefs, values, norms, rituals, physical artifacts, institutions, and activities that are passed down from one generation to the next (Cole, 1996). Throughout the life course, biological and cultural aspects of development act in concert. Individual growth and development are the products of the coordination of these two organized, dynamic systems. Thus, socioculturalists believe that individual development must be understood in—and cannot be separated from—its social and cultural/historical context (Cole, 2006; Gauvain, Beebe, & Zhao, 2011; Rogoff, 2003).

Culture The accumulated knowledge of a people encoded in their language and embodied in the physical artifacts, beliefs, values, customs, institutions, and activities passed down from one generation to the next.

Three themes in Vygotsky's writings have proven to be especially influential in guiding contemporary sociocultural theory and research (Wertsch, 1985). The first theme is that individual mental development has its origins in social sources. The second is that the study of mental functioning requires the study of change across multiple levels, ranging from momentary learning to species history. The third is that human thought and action are mediated by cultural tools. We discuss each of these themes in more detail below.

For Thought and Discussion

Sociocultural theories emphasize that learning is inherently social. For example, how might a seemingly solitary activity—such as studying for a geography test—be considered a social activity?

THE SOCIAL ORIGINS OF THOUGHT

According to Vygotsky, children acquire knowledge and cognitive skills by participating in cultural activities with more experienced partners. During these interactions, children are introduced to the new ways of thinking of the more knowledgeable members of their society and children then internalize these skills and use them independently.

Vygotsky believed that the most productive interactions occur in what he termed the zone of proximal (or potential) development. The **zone of proximal development** is the distance between what a child can accomplish on his own and what the child can achieve under the guidance of an adult or in collaboration with a more capable peer. The zone of proximal development involves activities that are slightly beyond the child's current capabilities but can be accomplished with help. Interactions within the zone of proximal development promote cognitive growth because the social support allows children to extend current skills to a higher level of competence. The concept of the zone of proximal development has played a role in understanding the success of adult–child interactions in tasks requiring the child to copy what an adult model does (Kleinspehn-Ammerlahn et al., 2011), learning numerical skills (Heine et al., 2010), and learning to plan and use strategies to solve problems (Radziszewska & Rogoff, 1988).

Zone of proximal development The distance between what a child can accomplish independently and what the child can accomplish with the help of an adult or more capable peer.

Scaffolding A method of teaching in which the adult adjusts the level of help provided in relation to the child's level of performance, the goal being to encourage independent performance.

Sociocultural researchers have studied the ways in which other people support and encourage children's development. One way in which experienced partners assist children's learning is through a process known as scaffolding (Pea, 2004). **Scaffolding** refers to learning situations in which more capable partners adjust the level of help they provide in response to the child's level of performance. The process of scaffolding entails moving to more direct, explicit forms of teaching if the child falters, and to less direct, more demanding forms of teaching as the child moves closer to independent mastery. Scaffolding appears to be effective not only in producing immediate success, but also in instilling the skills necessary for independent problem solving in the future.

Scaffolding best captures the processes involved in deliberate instruction. Much of what children come to know is not the result of explicit teaching, however, but rather is a by-product of participating in routine cultural activities. These cultural activities—be they household chores, economic pursuits, or religious practices—may well serve as learning opportunities, but their primary function is social rather than instructional.

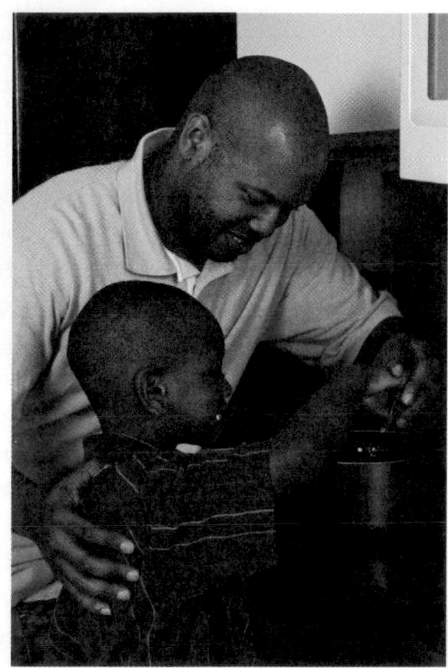

Guided participation in activities with a parent is an important way for young children to become competent in everyday activities. (© *CJMGrafx/iStock*)

Barbara Rogoff (1990) coined the term **guided participation** to describe the process by which young children become competent though participating in everyday, purposeful activities under the guidance of more experienced partners. As in scaffolding, the more expert partner is sensitive to the capabilities of the learners and structures the tasks accordingly by assigning simple chores and adapting tools to the learners' abilities. As children grow more competent, their roles and responsibilities change. In the process, so does their understanding of the task.

Guided participation The process by which young children become competent by participating in everyday, purposeful activities under the guidance of more experienced partners.

THE CULTURAL/HISTORICAL CONTEXT OF DEVELOPMENT

The second theme in Vygotsky's writing is that to understand human cognition, we need to understand its origins and the transitions it has undergone over time (Chaiklin, 2011). Vygotsky proposed the study of development over four interrelated time frames: ontogenetic, microgenetic, phylogenetic, and cultural/historical.

- **Ontogenetic development** occurs across the years of an individual's life, such as infancy, childhood, and adolescence.
- **Microgenetic development** is moment-to-moment learning by individuals as they work on specific problems.
- **Phylogenetic development** refers to the development of the species: existing human capabilities are products of biological evolution. Of particular interest to sociocultural theorists are

Ontogenetic development Development across the years of an individual's life, such as childhood.

Microgenetic development Moment-to-moment learning of individuals as they work on specific problems.

Phylogenetic development Development of the species.

the capabilities that distinguish humans from other animals. These include the use of tools such as language, and social-cognitive abilities that support learning in social contexts.

Cultural/historical development Development that occurs over decades and centuries and leaves a legacy of tools and artifacts, value systems, institutions, and practices.

- **Cultural/historical development** occurs over decades and centuries and leaves a legacy of tools and artifacts, value systems, institutions, and practices.

Individual development unfolds in a particular cultural and historical niche that itself is dynamic and changing. Socioculturalists believe that individual development must be studied in its cultural context. Moreover, socioculturalists study how changes in cultural practices and institutions (e.g., the introduction of formal schooling, moving to a market economy, invention of new technologies) shape the human mind.

TOOLS AND ARTIFACTS

A third theme in Vygotsky's writings is that human thought and action are mediated by material and symbolic tools (Vygotsky, 1981). *Tools and artifacts*, in this context, refer to all the means individuals have at their disposal to achieve desired goals, from simple objects (such as sticks and rope) to complex technological devices (such as smartphones and laptop and tablet computers). Tools and artifacts also include representations (such as maps), sign and symbol systems (such as language), and social practices (such as routines and rituals that organize and structure human activity).

Children learn how to use these cultural tools through interactions with parents, teachers, and more experienced peers. As a result of using these tools—first in cooperation with others and later independently—the child develops **higher mental functions**: complex mental processes that are intentional, self-regulated, and mediated by language and other sign systems. Examples include focused attention, deliberate memory (consciously using strategies for remembering things), and verbal thinking (thought using words that denote abstract concepts).

Higher mental functions Complex mental processes that are intentional, self-regulated, and mediated by language and other sign systems.

Vygotsky believed that the particular structure and content of higher mental functions vary with social experience. Cultural tools for thinking both enhance and transform mental capabilities. Formal tools and systems for measuring time or distance, for example, enhance human thinking by improving accuracy. As children learn how to use these tools, their thinking is transformed, and they come to think about time and distance differently; that is, in units such as minutes, seconds, inches, or metres.

INTERACTIONS WITH TOYS AND OBJECTS Piaget viewed developmental differences in the ways infants use objects in play and problem solving as a reflection of fundamental changes in underlying cognitive abilities. Sociocultural researchers, in contrast, focus on cultural practices that shape those encounters. Cultural practices dictate how much contact children have with objects, which objects young children have access to, and whether they use the objects in work or play, in solitary activity or jointly with others.

The number and types of objects infants and toddlers are allowed to explore vary widely among cultures. Some communities, such as one Mayan village in rural Guatemala, provide infants with few toys and actively restrict exploration of other objects (Gaskins, 1999). Others, such as the !Kung, a hunter–gatherer society of Africa, allow infants access to a variety of objects, including twigs, grass, stones, and household implements (Bakeman et al., 1990). In still other cultures, caregivers encourage infants to manipulate tools used by older children and adults in productive work, or miniature versions of tools fashioned by adults for small hands (Lancy, 1996). The Aka, a hunter–gatherer group in the tropical rainforests of the Central African Republic, for example, begin to teach their infants how to use sharp objects, such as knives, digging sticks, and axes, before the children reach their first birthday (Hewlett et al., 2011).

In wealthy, industrialized societies, caregivers provide infants with an abundant supply of specially manufactured toys and structure their joint play episodes around these toys (Whiting & Edwards, 1988). For example, one study of Canadian infants reported that the babies had an average of 27 toys by the time they were 3 months of age. By 9 months, they averaged nearly 60 toys (Pomerleau, Malcuit, & Sabatier, 1991)!

For Thought and Discussion

Was early exposure to a variety of objects, especially toys, emphasized in your family? Why might object play be given less importance in other families, communities, or societies?

For Thought and Discussion

What are some examples of other cultural tools or artifacts that changed the way you reason or solve problems?

Links to Related Material

Earlier, you learned how Piaget's theory described how interactions with objects change over the course of infancy. Here, we will consider how social and cultural contexts affect the development of these interactions.

Links to Related Material

In Chapters 15 and 16, you will learn about gender differences in play preferences and the role of play in peer relations.

In other cultural communities, object play takes a back seat to social interaction, as illustrated by this depiction of the environment of infants and toddlers in a working-class Black community in the southern United States:

> During their first year, children spend their waking hours in the laps of adults or on the hips of older children; they have no occasions to sit alone and play with baby toys. As children become mobile and move about on their own, they are in demand by older children and adults of the community as toys themselves. They are looked on as entertainers, and all of their waking hours are spent in the company of others. (Heath, 1983, pp. 76–77)

According to the sociocultural approach, these variations in children's early experiences with objects can only be understood within a broad cultural context that includes the physical environment (whether infants spend their time indoors or outdoors), social environment (whether the infants are usually in the company of other children or adults, or are alone), and customs of child care (whether infants are free to move about or physically restrained) (Super & Harkness, 1986). It may seem unwise, for example, to put potentially dangerous objects such as knives and axes in the hands of infants, but the practice is common in cultures where infants are rarely beyond arm's reach of a caregiver and have many opportunities to observe the tools being used by older children and adults (Rogoff, 2003).

IMPLICATIONS OF OBJECT PLAY FOR DEVELOPMENT The differing cultural ideas about the role of object play in development lead to an obvious question: Do different cultural practices have different developmental results? Specifically, does playing with toys during the early years foster cognitive development? Evidence is mixed. Some studies suggest that early experience exploring objects may not be essential for normal cognitive development. Despite wide cultural differences in access to objects, infants the world over follow the same sequence of sensorimotor development and use the same procedures to manipulate and explore objects (e.g., mouthing, squeezing, dropping). Other studies, however, have shown a positive relationship between infants' access to toys and their performance on assessments of cognitive development during infancy and early childhood (Bradley et al., 1994; Franchin et al., 2011). And the amount and quality of infants' object play alone and with caregivers predicts children's current and subsequent performance on various measures of cognitive competence (Bornstein et al., 2008; Tamis-LeMonda et al., 2002; van den Boom, 1994).

Whether or not there is a relation between the availability of toys and performance on measures of cognitive ability may depend on the cultural group or social context in which it is being assessed. For example, although the provision of toys during infancy is highly predictive of the intellectual capabilities of Caucasian North American children, access to toys does not predict the intelligence test performance of Hispanic children (Bradley et al., 1994). These findings highlight again the importance of examining object play in its broader cultural context. Nevertheless, as predicted by sociocultural theory, infants spend more time exploring objects and engage in more focused and complex exploration when interacting with caregivers than when playing alone (Hofsten & Siddiqui, 1993; Lockman & McHale, 1989; Tamis-LeMonda & Bornstein, 1991). Along these lines, Ann Bigelow of St. Francis Xavier University has found that infants exhibit more advanced play when engaged in joint attention with their mothers than when not (Bigelow, MacLean, & Proctor, 2004). Infants and toddlers are also far more likely to use objects as tools to solve problems (e.g., using a stick to retrieve an out-of-reach toy) by observing others use them, rather than by discovering how to do so on their own (Chen & Siegler, 2000; Rakoczy, Tomasello, & Striano, 2005). Joint play with caregivers or older children appears to be particularly important for the development of pretend play, a topic we discuss in more detail below.

THE ROLE OF PRETEND PLAY

Early encounters with objects are important opportunities for infants to learn about cultural tools and artifacts, particularly when those encounters involve other people. In addition to object play, pretend play also seems to develop within the context of joint action with caregivers or older children. Symbolic or pretend play—the "voluntary transformation of the here and now" (Garvey, 1990)—becomes more sophisticated during the preschool years. During this time, children's burgeoning symbolic skills support increasingly complex and abstract pretend or make-believe sequences. The role of symbolic function can be seen in **solitary pretense**, in which children pretend by themselves. Solitary pretense can be quite simple or very complex, as when a preschooler acts out a complicated drama with a collection of dolls and stuffed animals. Because of their interest in the cultural transmission of information, sociocultural theorists focus on **sociodramatic play** in which two or more people enact related roles (e.g., mother and baby, driver and passenger, pet and owner).

Solitary pretense Pretend play engaged in by a child playing alone.

Sociodramatic play Play in which two or more people enact a variety of related roles.

For Vygotsky, make-believe play is a unique activity in which children try out a number of different skills within their zone of proximal development. They exercise their budding representational abilities as they create imaginary situations, substituting objects for other objects within a play-frame (pretending that a block is a telephone, for example). In addition, they create scenes within which they enact certain social rules (pretending to be the daddy, for example, who helps the baby to put on her shoes). The particular themes enacted in such scenes vary, as one would expect, with the particular social activities the children engage in on a daily basis. Worldwide, the most common themes enacted in toddlers' pretense are those centred on domestic life (such as cooking, eating, child care), adult work activities (such as hunting, planting, fishing), and adult rituals (such as marriage, dancing) (Power, 2000).

Pretend play can be found in every society, but there are wide cultural variations in when, where, and how often it occurs (Cote & Bornstein, 2009; Lillard, Pinkham, & Smith, 2011). The extent to which children engage in pretend play depends on the significance caregivers place on play relative to other, competing activities (Lillard et al., 2011). In many societies, caregivers depend on small children to perform important chores, such as tending livestock or the garden and running errands, allowing children little time for pretend play. In other cultures, caregivers dismiss pretend play as mere amusement and do little to encourage it. For example, Farver (1999) found that Korean American children whose parents had recently immigrated to Los Angeles engaged in pretend play less often than did Caucasian American children, both at home and at school. The differences between the two groups were found to be related to adult beliefs about the value of play.

In cultures where adults believe pretend play facilitates development, caregivers view their own participation in play as both appropriate and desirable, and participate actively in children's pretending (Haight, Parke, & Black, 1997). Parent–child pretend play is common among families in Turkey, Argentina, China, and in Caucasian North American communities (Bornstein et al., 1999; Göncü et al., 2000; Haight et al., 1999), where such play is viewed as a type of instruction as well as a form of play. These findings show variation in the themes of pretend play, the importance placed on pretend play, and the particulars of who engages in pretend play with children.

Links to Related Material

In Chapter 10, you will learn more about cultural differences in definitions of intelligence and parental involvement in schooling.

Piaget viewed pretend play as a natural outcome of children's developing symbolic abilities, but Vygotsky claimed that pretend play grows out of the child's collaborations with others. Although early studies of pretend play tended to focus on solitary play, observational studies in everyday settings reveal that most pretend play takes place in a social context with other people acting as either spectators or partners. Studies also reveal that pretend-play partners often scaffold young children's pretense, thereby scaffolding the development of a wide variety of cognitive skills.

According to Vygotsky, the most powerful cultural tool is language. Language is the primary means by which members of a cultural community pass on knowledge and values surrounding cultural practices to succeeding generations. Language also functions as a tool in its own right, shaping children's thinking and problem solving. Vygotsky held a very different view from Piaget of the role of language, the topic we turn to next.

LEARNING OBJECTIVE 8.8

Analyze the three main themes on which sociocultural approaches to development are based.

1. What temporal and cultural contexts did Vygotsky identify, and why are they important to the study of development?
2. What applications based on Vygotsky's theory demonstrate how children learn through social interaction?
3. According to Vygotsky, what are the roles of cultural tools and artifacts in cognitive development?
4. According to the sociocultural view, what is the significance of pretend play in cognitive development?

PIAGET AND VYGOTSKY ON LANGUAGE AND THOUGHT

Learning Objective 8.9

Compare and contrast the theories of Piaget and Vygotsky on the role of language in cognitive development.

Piaget believed that language is a verbal reflection of the individuals' conceptual understanding. Language reflects cognition. As you read earlier, at the end of infancy and the sensorimotor period, children become capable of thinking symbolically. According to Piaget, the acquisition of language symbols speeds up thinking because a sequence of thoughts can usually be carried out more quickly than a sequence of actions. But because language reflects thought, language developments cannot cause cognitive development. Rather, for Piaget, cognition determines language.

Piaget found support for this view in two different forms of speech often used by young children: egocentric speech (defined earlier in this chapter) and collective monologues. If you have had the chance to observe young children, you have seen how they often talk out loud to themselves when playing or trying to solve problems. In Piaget's theory, this kind of egocentric speech or "talk for self" is diagnostic of young children's inability to decenter, or to take the perspective of another.

Another form of speech used by young children is what Piaget termed a **collective monologue**, in which children use egocentric speech in play with other children. You may notice that while preschoolers often appear to be playing and conversing together, their remarks actually focus on what they are doing by themselves, with no real regard for their partner and no apparent intention of communicating with anyone. There may be a turn-taking structure to their "conversations," with each child speaking after the other has finished, but the content of what each child contributes relates only to what he just said. Each child narrates an event to himself without considering what the other child is talking about. Piaget believed that collective monologues give way to genuine dialogues as children develop the ability to adopt others' points of view.

Collective monologue Piaget's term for young children's tendency to use egocentric speech with each other during play, resulting in non-communication.

Vygotsky took a completely different perspective on the relationship between language and thought. He believed that the onset of language is one of the most important events in a child's life, with the power to transform early abilities into a qualitatively new form of thinking. It is with the onset of language that "elementary mental functions" are transformed into "higher mental functions" (Wertsch, 1985). Although Piaget believed that language is a reflection of inner cognitive workings, Vygotsky maintained that language in a sense "precedes" thought. According to Vygotsky, language is social from the outset since it is first used to communicate in interaction with others. Thus, language precedes thought in the sense that it is first experienced on the social plane, and then is later internalized as individual thought.

Vygotsky pointed out that children's development always occurs in a context organized and watched over by adults, and thus that children's experience of language is social from the outset. Children's first words are communicative acts, mediating their interactions with the people

Private speech Speech children produce and direct toward themselves during a problem-solving activity.

around them. To Vygotsky, this sequence suggests a progression from social and communicative speech to internal dialogue, or **private speech**, in which thought and language become intimately interconnected. Thus, language allows thought to be individual and social at the same time. It is the medium through which individual thought is communicated to others, while at the same time it allows social reality to be converted into the idiosyncratic thought of the individual.

Vygotsky's notion of private speech therefore differs from Piaget's notion of egocentric speech (Vygotsky 1934/1962). First, Vygotsky noted that private speech occurs when the child is having difficulty or is doing a difficult task, suggesting that it serves a particular cognitive function rather than simply reflecting a lack of cognitive ability for perspective taking. Thus, far from being non-social, Vygotsky (1934/1962) maintained that young children's private speech grows out of their interactions with parents and more experienced others as they work together on various tasks. For example, much of a parent's speech involves guiding and regulating the child. Over the course of many interactions, children begin to use versions of their parents' instructional comments to direct their own behaviour. Thus, according to Vygotsky, this kind of talk was a child's way of self-guiding or self-directing. Gradually, the controlling speech becomes internalized as thought, as children eventually produce "silent statements" (thoughts) similar to the verbal ones (Winsler, 2009). Self-regulation thus develops out of the child's social interactions—a process Vygotsky called **sociogenesis** (Van der Veer & Valsiner, 1988).

Sociogenesis The process of acquiring knowledge or skills through social interactions.

Vygotsky also challenged Piaget's claim that the language in private speech and collective monologues is not intended to communicate anything. He posited that the same factors that encourage speech directed to others would promote greater amounts of private speech. To test this hypothesis, he created a series of situations that discouraged or prevented social interaction and then measured preschoolers' private speech. Vygotsky placed children in a very noisy classroom with peers who spoke a foreign language, or with peers who were deaf and had no oral language. In both situations self-talk declined significantly. Conversely, private speech increases when children are in the presence of responsive social partners (Goudena, 1987). Thus, private speech is not simply egocentric speech reflecting an inability to consider another's point of view.

Later research has identified other factors that affect the frequency with which children talk to themselves while solving problems. Private speech occurs most often on tasks that are challenging, although not impossibly difficult (Behrend et al., 1989; Berk & Garvin, 1984; Kohlberg et al., 1968; Matuga, 2003). It is also most evident at the beginning of a new task and at times of greatest difficulty, but decreases as children master the task (Berk, 1994; Meichenbaum & Goodman, 1979).

Links to Related Material

Here, you learned about the role of self-regulation and private speech in children's cognitive development. In Chapter 13, you will learn more about the role of private speech in the development of self-control, and how training in self-instruction has been used to help children who are impulsive.

Other evidence supporting the idea that private speech is used for self-guidance comes from research done with children who have learning and behaviour problems. These children have been found to rely on private speech for a longer period of time than do their peers (Berk & Landau, 1993; Winsler et al., 2007), suggesting that such verbalizations may be a way of compensating for impairments in certain cognitive functions. In addition, Robert Duncan of St. Francis Xavier University and Michael Pratt (1997) of Wilfrid Laurier University have also found that in middle and later childhood, a greater proportion of private speech takes the form of whispering, presumably reflecting its gradual internalization (see also Müller, Jacques, Brocki, & Zelazo, 2009; Winsler, 2009).

LEARNING OBJECTIVE 8.9

Compare and contrast the theories of Piaget and Vygotsky on the role of language in cognitive development.

1. How did Piaget and Vygotsky differ in their view of how language and thought are related?
2. How did Vygotsky's notion of private speech differ from Piaget's concept of egocentric speech?
3. What did Vygotsky mean by the notion of sociogenesis?

THE IMPACT OF PIAGET AND VYGOTSKY ON EDUCATION

Learning Objective 8.10

Evaluate the contributions of Piaget and Vygotsky to education.

North American child psychologists began to discover Piaget in the late 1950s and the early 1960s as translations and summaries of his books began to appear (Flavell, 1963). Since that time, Piaget's writings have inspired literally thousands of studies of children's thinking and researchers have extended his work as it applies to the field of education and other areas (Chapman, 1988; Ginsburg & Opper, 1988; Modgil & Modgil, 1976). Piaget wrote two books about education (Piaget, 1971, 1976), and others have written extensively about the educational implications of his work (Cowan, 1978; DeVries & Zan, 1994; Duckworth, 1987; Kamii & DeVries, 1993).

Three main principles underlie Piagetian approaches to education. One is an emphasis on **discovery learning** or active learning. This emphasis relates to Piaget's belief that children learn by acting on the world, not by passively taking in information. Piaget distrusted educational methods that are too passive, rote, or verbal. In his view, education should build on the child's natural curiosity and natural tendency to act on the world to understand it. Knowledge is more meaningful when children construct it themselves rather than when it is imposed on them.

Discovery learning An educational approach based on Piaget's idea that children learn by acting on the world individually, not by passively taking in information.

The Piagetian approach to education emphazises active learning—building on a child's natural curiosity and natural tendency to act on the world in order to understand it. (*Image Source/iStock*)

A second, related principle arises from Piaget's mechanisms of development—assimilation, accommodation, and equilibration—and their timing. Piaget believed that, while all children go through the same sequence of stages, they do so at their own pace. A child's *readiness to learn* depends on the child's current level of thinking. Experience—educational or otherwise—does not simply happen to the child; rather, the child must always integrate it with existing cognitive structures through the processes of assimilation and accommodation. A new experience will be beneficial only if the child can make some sense of it. In addition, a child's *motivation to learn* depends on the timing of educational experiences. For children to move ahead in their cognitive development, they must experience disequilibrium, or a challenge to their thinking. Thus, development takes place when children are ready for an experience, and the experience provokes them to advance their level of thinking.

A third principle, based on the idea that children move through cognitive stages at different rates, is that teachers must be sensitive to *individual differences* among students in a classroom. Piaget's diagnostics about what a child does or does not know at different stages of development helps teachers to understand where the child is in development and what naturally comes next. Because children go through the same cognitive stages at different rates, however, learning must be based on the skill level and developmental pacing of individual children.

Based on these three principles, Piagetian-inspired classrooms are structured so that children have ample opportunities to learn through active exploration of their environment. Unlike traditional teacher-centred classrooms, Piagetian-inspired classrooms have activity centres in which children can engage in hands-on activities of their own choosing. Allowing children to select activities for themselves is also consistent with the idea that skills should not be imposed on children before they are ready. Thus, teachers in Piagetian-inspired classrooms introduce activities that appropriately challenge each child at her level of development. Teachers in Piagetian-inspired classrooms also evaluate children differently. Because children are expected to develop at their own pace according to their own readiness to learn, they are not evaluated against a set standard for the whole classroom. Rather, children are each evaluated in comparison with their own prior developmental achievements.

Vygotsky's work has also had an important influence on educational practices, such as in the use of scaffolding and cooperative learning. Vygotsky, like Piaget, recognized the importance of active learning and of recognizing children's individual differences in cognitive development (Miller, 2001). Where the two theorists diverge is in how they view the relationship between the classroom experience and cognitive development. For Piaget, the classroom exists to provide children with rich opportunities to explore and discover on their own. For Vygotsky, the emphasis is not on individual discovery, but rather on **assisted discovery** through interactions between teacher and student, as well as between students. The role of the teacher is to carefully guide each child, according to his current ability level, to improve skills in using and manipulating the symbolic systems of his culture. The emphasis then, is on the child's interactions with others as he participates in meaningful activities with others in the classroom.

Assisted discovery An educational approach based on Vygotsky's idea that children learn through interactions between teachers and students as well as between students.

Another important difference between Piagetian and Vygotskian approaches to education is in the role played by peers. An important aspect of children's play is that it usually takes place within the context of social interaction with other children. Research has suggested that play with peers may provide a richer context for the development of cognitive skills than play with adults (Farver, 1993; Farver & Wimbarti, 1995).

Sociocultural researchers interested in education have also found that interaction with peers plays a special role in cognitive development in the classroom. The traditional view of a typical classroom is one in which the teacher is the sole authority who provides information to students who passively listen and learn from the teacher, not from their fellow students. As we have seen, Piagetian approaches to schooling challenge this view, suggesting that children play a more active role. Piagetian approaches also emphasize the importance of peers in providing alternative perspectives that motivate students to reevaluate their own views. Vygotskian theory and research also challenge the view of the passive learner and point out the important role that peers play in student learning (Miller, 2001). Beyond these points, however, Piagetian and Vygotskian views of peer learning differ.

Links to Related Material

Here, you learn about the role of peers in children's learning and cognitive development. In Chapter 15, you will learn about the role of peers in children's social and emotional development.

Peer learning has been an active area of study in developmental psychology for many decades (for reviews see Azmitia, 1996; De Lisi & Goldbeck, 1999; Garton, 1992; Hogan & Tudge, 1999; Rogoff, 1998). There is, in fact, much interest in peer learning in today's schools (Webb & Palincsar, 1996), fuelled by a belief that collaborative group work promotes greater understanding and higher levels of achievement than solitary efforts, not just in school settings but perhaps in most settings (Hinds & Kiesler, 2002).

For Thought and Discussion

Some students and their parents resent peer learning, arguing that it holds back the more capable students. What do you think? Under what conditions do you think peer learning works best?

Much of the initial interest in peer learning was based on Piaget's theory (Piaget, 1932). Piaget proposed that during peer interaction, children are exposed to ways of thinking about problems or issues that conflict with their own. Piagetians call this **sociocognitive conflict** (Bearison, 1982; Doise & Mugny, 1984; Piaget, 1932). According to this perspective, cognitive change occurs when children work to reconcile the discrepancy between their views and those held by peers.

Sociocognitive conflict Cognitive conflict that arises during social interaction.

An assumption that underlies Piagetian studies of peer learning is that logical and cogent arguments will most likely persuade individuals to change their thinking because these arguments are more likely to reflect correct understanding than flawed reasoning. Piaget was not suggesting that the social context was responsible for cognitive change. Rather, Piaget believed that cognitive growth is fuelled by the child's recognition that her views are different and perhaps less logical than the views of her peers. Thus, the experience and resolution of sociocognitive conflict pushes development forward.

In one study, for example, grade 2 students worked in pairs on Piagetian conservation tasks (Miller & Brownell, 1975). It was found that conservers and non-conservers asserted their views equally often, but that conservers were able to offer a greater variety of arguments to support their answers. Consequently, non-conservers were more likely to be convinced by their conserving partners than the other way around. This pattern of change—non-conservers advancing through the influence of conservers—has been replicated many times (Murray, 1982).

While the Piagetian approach to peer learning stresses conflict and resolution, the sociocultural approach emphasizes cooperation and coordination. According to the sociocultural view, peer learning is best achieved when students cooperate to achieve a common learning objective. In *peer collaboration*, or cooperative learning, rather than placing one student in an authoritative role of "teacher," as is often done in tutoring or mentoring, the learning partners start out with roughly the same levels of competence and work together to create new knowledge.

Students sharing responsibility for a task are more likely to engage in cooperative dialogues to actively resolve differences of opinion (Forman & McPhail, 1993; Tudge, 1992). In situations with more or less equal distribution of power and knowledge, children may feel more comfortable questioning others' ideas and more motivated to understand those ideas (Bearison & Dorval, 2002; Damon, 1984; Hatano & Iagnaki, 1991). Partners negotiate—or co-construct—new understandings as they clarify, refine, extend, and build on each other's reasoning (Forman & Cazden, 1985; Forman & McPhail, 1993). Success depends on the ability of the learning partners to establish **intersubjectivity**—a commitment to find common ground on which to build shared understanding (Rommetveit, 1979; Vass, 2007).

In simple situations, even young children can collaborate successfully. (*Digital Vision/Media Bakery*)

Studies of collaboration on a variety of tasks, including conservation tasks, mathematical problem solving, scientific reasoning, and even writing, show that students who work on problems with partners of relatively equal ability often produce solutions superior to those of individuals working alone. In addition, collaboration can promote a deeper understanding of the problem or concept that lasts over time (Forman & McPhail, 1993; Levin & Druyan, 1993; Tudge, 1989, 1992).

Intersubjectivity A commitment to find common ground on which to build shared understanding.

PEER LEARNING IN CLASSROOMS

Research on peer interaction in classroom settings has taken on a new look as educators have come to view academic disciplines as cultural communities (Brown, 1997; Brown, Collins, & Duguid, 1989; Lave & Wenger, 1991). According to this perspective, to be competent in a discipline requires that students be socialized to think, talk, and act like a member of that cultural community. Because "real" mathematicians and scientists do their work in social settings, it follows that students should learn to do so as well.

To do math and science with other people, children need to master the discourse styles used in those communities. As we have already noted, however, children often struggle to engage in meaningful discussions with peers, particularly when the content is challenging. Consider, for example, the discussion of photosynthesis among a group of grade 4 and 5 students shown in Table 8.4.

Links to Related Material

Here, you learn about the role of peers in children's learning in the classroom. In Chapter 10, you will learn about the role of peers in the success that children have in school.

Although conversations among actual scientists *sometimes* deteriorate to the level depicted in this excerpt, the situation is far from ideal. Consequently, teachers and researchers have devised a variety of techniques that structure or scaffold students' group problem-solving interactions (Brown & Palincsar, 1989; O'Donnell & King, 1999). For instance, even the poorly coordinated discussion of photosynthesis excerpted in Table 8.4 was salvaged by the use of prescribed prompts printed on cards that the students were instructed to ask themselves or their partners as they worked on each task.

Students who participated in groups supported by the scaffolded explanation-based intervention developed more accurate understanding of photosynthesis than did students in a group whose interactions were not scaffolded. Similar findings have been reported in other studies

TABLE 8.4 DISCUSSION OF PHOTOSYNTHESIS AMONG GRADE 4 AND 5 STUDENTS

Brandon:	How about leaf cells and oxygen—Leaf cells. . .
Steve:	Release
Brandon:	Leaf cells give off
Steve:	Release
Sam:	Give off
Steve:	Release, release, release!
Sam:	Release?—Give off is easier
Brandon:	Give off
Steve:	Okay give off
Sam:	Majority wins!

Source: Adapted from "Using Explanatory Knowledge During Collaborative Problem Solving in Science" by E. B. Coleman, 1998. *Journal of the Learning Sciences*, 7, 406. Copyright © 1998 by Lawrence Erlbaum Associates, Inc. Reprinted by permission.

Whole-class discussions enable teachers to model appropriate discourse and scaffold student discussion. (*Banana Stock/Media Bakery*)

designed to improve the quality of children's discussions of scientific phenomena (Palincsar & Herrenkohl, 1999).

Whole-class discussions offer another opportunity for teachers to model appropriate discourse and scaffold student discussion. Teachers can rephrase student responses, introducing new, more formal terminology or elaborating on the answer in a way that redirects the discussion. Teachers can ask students to clarify or expand on their own reasoning, and they can request students to evaluate other students' answers (Forman & Ansell, 2002; O'Connor, 1996). Unfortunately, teachers in North America often fail to take advantage of the opportunities afforded by whole-class discussion. Japanese classrooms, in comparison, provide an interesting contrast and suggest ways in which discussions can be organized to promote peer learning. For instance, in Japanese classrooms, students do most of the explaining (Stigler et al., 1996). We discuss this issue further in *Application 8.1*.

CONCLUSION: COMPARING SOCIOCULTURAL AND PIAGETIAN APPROACHES

As you have seen, the sociocultural approach is similar in several ways to the Piagetian view. Socioculturalists and Piagetians study many of the same aspects of mental functioning, including attention, memory, conceptual understanding, and academic skills. Both approaches view the child as an active participant in his or her own development (as opposed to a passive recipient of environmental input), and both hold that development involves qualitative as well as quantitative change (Miller, 2001).

The approaches differ, however, in explaining the mechanisms of change. Piagetians focus on processes internal to the individual child, such as the reorganization of cognitive structures,

APPLICATION 8.1
SCAFFOLDING GROUP DISCUSSION: THE HYPOTHESIS–EXPERIMENT– INSTRUCTION METHOD

A common concern voiced by teachers wary of using whole-class discussion to promote student learning in mathematics and science classrooms is that students may not be able to generate plausible solutions (most notably the correct one) worthy of discussion. One way to remedy this problem is through the use of a Japanese educational intervention known as *hypothesis–experiment–instruction.*

In this intervention, the teacher provides three or four plausible alternatives along with a problem. For example:

Taro drinks 1/2 litre of milk at breakfast and 1/5 litre at supper. How many litres of milk does he drink a day?

1/2 + 1/5 = 2/7, answer is 2/7 litre
0.5 + 0.2 = 0.7, answer is 0.7 litre
1/2 + 1/5 = 7/10, answer is 7/10 litre

Students are then asked to choose one of the solutions and to write down the reasons for their choices. Students' choices, counted by a show of hands, are tabulated on the blackboard. Next, one or two students who support each alternative are invited to state the reasons for their choices, after which all students are invited to discuss them. During the discussion, the teacher acts as a neutral moderator, taking care not to endorse some ideas over others. Following the discussion, students are asked to choose an alternative once again.

Implementation of this intervention in Japanese mathematics and science classrooms has yielded positive results (Hatano & Inagaki, 1991; Inagaki, 1981; Inagaki et al., 1998). In class discussion, children as young as grades 4 and 5 have been able to generate arguments for and against each alternative, including the correct answer. Despite the fact that only a small minority of students have an opportunity to speak, most students tend to shift toward the appropriate solution without feedback from the teacher. And, following the discussion, students accurately recall the reasonable explanations offered by their classmates.

These findings reveal that children can develop correct understanding through peer interaction without its being "authorized" by the teacher. This process is aided by the fact that students are more likely to be persuaded by classmates known to be high achievers than by less able students, and by those arguments received favourably by the greatest number of students.

The hypothesis–experiment–instruction method has been used effectively in groups as large as 40 to 45 students. Of particular interest is that even in large groups, "silent" students are as likely to adopt the correct solution as are students who are vocal. Inagaki and colleagues suggest that these students may actively try to find among the speakers an "agent" who "speaks" for them in the discussion. If they can find such an agent, these students are then able to participate vicariously in the discussion. Even if they cannot find an agent, students nonetheless engage with others' arguments in their own minds. In the words of the researchers, "active participation is the prerequisite for the construction of knowledge, but it may take forms other than speaking out" (Inagaki et al., 1998, p. 523).

Might this method work equally well in North American classrooms? Perhaps, but Inagaki and colleagues caution that it depends on two key variables highly associated with Japanese school culture (Hatano & Inagaki, 1998). First, students need to feel comfortable making mistakes and revealing confusion in public. This is possible in Japanese classrooms where all children, regardless of their academic achievements, are genuinely valued by their peers (Lewis, 1995). In this environment, children can expect moral support for their efforts to learn. Additionally, children recognize that they have a responsibility to contribute their ideas—even the wrong ones—to aid the group's success. Inagaki and colleagues argue that unless the teacher can create a climate in which mistakes are viewed positively, discussions that highlight student errors might prove devastating.

A second factor is what the authors call "socialization for listenership" (Inagaki et al., 1998). Japanese children come to school prepared to learn from their peers. They listen to classmates eagerly and carefully. Moreover, as long as they have some sense of participation, they do not grow frustrated or inattentive when not given an opportunity to express their own ideas. As the following comment by one frustrated child illustrates, North American students often begrudge the amount of time devoted to discussion:

> There's so much work and you're always doing conversations and I'm not learning anything. In kindergarten I got all information like a computer would. I can't do that now. I knew all I had to know for first and second grade in kindergarten. It's conversation, conversation, and we hardly get anything accomplished. (Peter, Grade 2, quoted in Nicholls & Hazzard, 1993, p. 172)

Nurturing an appreciation for what others have to say—and the skill to learn from their peers—may prove to be an even more formidable challenge for teachers hoping to encourage class discussion than creating a climate in which students feel free to make mistakes.

increased speed of task completion, and the child's individual attempts to understand the world. From this perspective, cognitive change takes place when children actively explore, manipulate, and experiment on their surroundings.

Sociocultural theorists, in contrast, believe that developmental change is socially mediated and takes place within the context of social interaction. According to this perspective, development is the direct result of interactions with other people and the tools and artifacts that are the products of human culture. The emphasis is on how children's actions are shaped not only by their own active attempts, but by participation in meaningful activities with others. In this view, children, their caregivers, and their peers are active participants in the process of development.

The Piagetian approach views cognitive development as changes in internal mental capabilities. Sociocultural theories, in contrast, situate thinking in practice. That is, development takes place in the way a child participates in socially meaningful activities. Thus, the development of a particular skill cannot be isolated from the social and cultural purposes to which it is put. Children learn not only the skill, but also the values surrounding its use. As Goodnow (1990) notes: "We do not simply learn to solve problems. We learn also what problems are worth solving, and what counts as an elegant rather than simply an acceptable solution" (p. 260). What develops, then, is a culturally constructed system of knowledge that includes goals, values, and motivation (Miller, 2001).

Another difference is in the degree of emphasis on stages and the gradualness and continuity of development from stage to stage. Piaget described a set of stages that a child must pass through in succession. He believed that the stages are consistent for children of every culture. Sociocultural theorists, on the other hand, anticipate variability in both performance content and the sequencing of cognitive abilities of children from different sociocultural communities. Socioculturalists accept the possibility that cognitive development could occur in stage-like fashion if cultures organized children's experiences in that way, but they do not agree that there are universal stages in children's cognitive development (Rogoff, 1998, 2003).

One final difference is in how the two approaches view the outcome or endpoint of development. In Piaget's view the endpoint of development is the ability to think in abstract ways that follow rules of logic. As the individual passes through each successive stage, his thought becomes increasingly detached from material circumstances, until as a young adult the individual is able to mentally manipulate variables to solve a problem. This, for Piaget, is a culmination of an individual human's cognitive capacity.

Sociocultural theorists, on the other hand, question whether there is some ideal endpoint of development (Rogoff, 1998, 2003). They maintain that the kind of abstract thought characterized by Piaget's final stage of development may itself be a product of culturally situated values. Instead, sociocultural theorists argue that cultural groups define the endpoint of development in accordance with the values and practices of their particular communities. Thus, the hypothetical-deductive reasoning that Piaget found characterizes adult thought in Western culture may not characterize the endpoint of development for other cultural groups in which abstract reasoning is not highly valued.

Sociocultural approaches also have challenges to face, however. Critics point out that those working within the sociocultural framework often idealize learning (Anderson, Reder, & Simon, 1996). As Goodnow (1996) observed, "one rarely finds, within Vygotskian-style analyses of learning, accounts of expert-novice interactions that depart from a picture of 'willing teachers/eager learners' " (p. 356). She points out that experts are not always so willing to give away all that they know. And novices are sometimes reluctant to take over responsibility for their own learning when they have the competence to do so. To better understand the social origins of thought (and to have broader application to real-world learning), researchers need to examine learning in these less-than-optimal situations.

Another challenge sociocultural researchers face is how to integrate data across multiple spheres of development. You may recall in Urie Bronfenbrenner's ecological systems model, for example, that social and cultural contexts of development include the microsystem, mesosystem, exosystem, macrosystem, and chronosystem. Without data from these multiple levels of development, although we may accumulate information about lives in different cultures and test the universality of psychological theories, we cannot really gain much insight into the dynamic processes of development in a cultural context. As Bronfenbrenner pointed out, in the past too much research failed to consider development in context, but "we now have a surfeit of studies on 'context without development' " (1986, p. 288).

A final criticism of the sociocultural approach is that it tends to neglect the role of basic cognitive skills such as memory, attention, and the acquisition of expertise in cognitive development. These skills play a major role in children's increasing ability to solve problems and to think efficiently. In fact, the information-processing perspective, to which we turn in the next chapter, is a major contemporary alternative that many researchers believe offers a number of attractive contrasts to Vygotskian and Piagetian approaches to cognitive development.

Links to Related Material

In Chapter 9, you will learn more about cognitive skills such as memory, attention, and the acquisition of expertise, skills that are not addressed by sociocultural approaches to cognitive development.

LEARNING OBJECTIVE 8.10

Evaluate the contributions of Piaget and Vygotsky to education.

1. On what three principles are Piagetian-inspired classrooms based?
2. What kinds of learning activities are you likely to find in a Vygotskian-inspired classroom?
3. How did Piaget's and Vygotsky's views differ on the role of peers in learning and development?
4. What is the role of peers in learning in the classroom?
5. In what key ways are the sociocultural and Piagetian approaches alike?
6. How do the two approaches differ in both the means and the ends of cognitive development?
7. What challenges to their work do socioculturalists continue to face?

SUMMARY

KEY TERMS

A-not-B error, p. 268
animism, p. 289
appearance–reality distinction, p. 291
assisted discovery , p. 302
centration, p. 275
class inclusion, p. 278
cognition, p. 262
collective monologue, p. 299
concept, p. 288
conservation, p. 275
cultural/historical development, p. 296
culture, p. 294
decentration, p. 279
deferred imitation, p. 273
discovery learning, p. 301
dual representation, p. 281
egocentric speech, p. 275
egocentrism, p. 269
equilibration, p. 287
equilibrium, p. 287
false belief, p. 290
guided participation, p. 295
higher mental functions, p. 296
hypothetical–deductive reasoning, p. 283
intentional behaviour, p. 266
intersubjectivity, p. 303
invariants, p. 269
joint attention, p. 293
mental representation, p. 267
microgenetic development, p. 295
object permanence, p. 268
ontogenetic development, p. 295
operations, p. 279
phylogenetic development, p. 295
private speech, p. 300
progressive decentering, p. 269
qualitative identity, p. 274

reversibility, p. 279
scaffolding , p. 295
sensorimotor schemes, p. 265
seriation, p. 278
social referencing, p. 293
sociocognitive conflict , p. 302
sociodramatic play , p. 298
sociogenesis, p. 300
solitary pretense , p. 298
symbolic function, p. 273
symbolic play, p. 273
theory of mind, p. 290
transitivity, p. 278
zone of proximal development , p. 295

LEARNING OBJECTIVES

LEARNING OBJECTIVE 8.1 Define the concepts from biology that Piaget used to explain cognitive development and evaluate his theory of stages.

1. *What is the role of organization in the development of cognitive structures?*
   Organization is a basic biological principle in Piaget's theory. For Piaget, the essence of intelligence lies in the underlying organization. Cognitive structures are ways of organizing information to understand it more effectively.

2. *What processes of adaptation are essential for cognitive change and how do they work?*
   Organization is accomplished through the process of adaptation, which involves the complementary processes of assimilation and accommodation. Assimilation entails interpreting new experiences in terms of what we already understand. Accommodation involves changing our cognitive structures to fit with environmental realities.

3. *What four periods of cognitive development did Piaget propose and how do they differ?*
   Piaget proposed the following periods: sensorimotor, preoperational, concrete operational, and formal operational. In the sensorimotor period (0 to 2 years), infants understand the world through the overt actions they perform on it. In the preoperational period (2 to 6 years), the child can use mental representations rather than overt actions to solve problems, resulting in faster and more efficient thinking. The concrete operational period (6 to 12 years) brings the advent of mental operations, a system of logical problem solving. In the formal operational period (12 years to adult), the acquisition of hypothetical–deductive reasoning enables children to generate and systematically test abstract hypotheses about things that do not currently exist.

LEARNING OBJECTIVE 8.2 Trace the substages and benchmarks of the sensorimotor period in child development.

1. *What distinguishes the first two substages of Piaget's sensorimotor period of cognitive development?*
   In substage 1, simple reflexes become the infant's first sensorimotor schemes used to make sense of the world. During substage 2, schemes become more adaptive and more flexible.

2. *What role do schemes and procedures play in cognitive development?*
   Schemes are fairly limited. Infants do not deliberately vary their schemes, and are only aware of the external environment to the extent that it triggers the infant's action patterns. Procedures reflect the infant's developing knowledge of what she can do to produce desirable outcomes.
3. *When during infancy does intentional behaviour develop?*
   Intentional behaviour involves the ability to separate means from ends. The infant uses a scheme as a means to lead to some other scheme, which becomes the goal or end of the action. Piaget felt the infant is capable of such intentional behaviour at 8 to 12 months of age.

4. *What is object permanence, and how do infants develop this knowledge?*
   Object permanence is the knowledge that objects continue to exist independent of our perception of them. It is only during substage 3 (4 to 8 months) that babies begin to search for

hidden objects. Then, in substage 4 (8 to 12 months), infants can search systematically, even for objects that are hidden entirely from view.

5. *How do contemporary studies inform Piaget's classic work on cognitive development in infancy?*
Some contemporary researchers have found that object permanence may develop earlier than Piaget believed. In addition, recent research reveals that infants' abilities to imitate are more sophisticated than Piaget thought.

LEARNING OBJECTIVE 8.3 Identify some strengths and limitations of preoperational thought in children's cognitive development.

1. *How is preoperational thinking an advance over sensorimotor cognitive functioning?*
The onset of symbolic function (representational thought) marks a major advance in the child's cognitive abilities. Representational thought is faster and more mobile than sensorimotor intelligence, and it is also socially sharable.

2. *What cognitive abilities does the child acquire during the preoperational stage?*
During this stage, the child develops qualitative identity, or the realization that the basic nature of something is not changed by changes in its appearance.

3. *What are two significant limitations of preoperational thinking?*
Egocentrism and centration are two significant limitations. Egocentrism refers to the young child's acting as though everyone shares his point of view. Centration refers to the inability to distinguish appearance from reality, and to focus only on one aspect of a problem at a time.

4. *What experiments did Piaget use to test the strengths and limitations of young children's thinking?*
The best-known task for studying perspective taking is the three-mountains problem. Piaget also used various conservation experiments. One of the best-known is the conservation of liquid experiment, where children view water levels in different-sized containers.

LEARNING OBJECTIVE 8.4 Analyze the cognitive task masteries that characterize concrete operational thought.

1. *How is operational thinking different from preoperational thinking?*
Operations are mental activities such as reversing, combining, or separating information in a logical fashion. Operational thinking involves a system of internal mental activities that support logical thought. The relational abilities acquired during the operational stage are a major advance over earlier preoperational thinking.

2. *How do concrete operational children perform on problems of conservation and classification?*
In conservation problems, concrete operational children can accurately represent and operate on each aspect of the transformation. For example, the child can appreciate that while the height of water in a tall, thin glass has increased, its width has narrowed, and the amount of the water remains constant. In classification problems, the child can solve class inclusion problems. The child appreciates that it is impossible for a subclass to be larger than a superordinate class.
3. *How do seriation and transivity tasks reveal the relational logic used by concrete operational thinkers?*
Seriation requires that the child appreciate multiple relations among items—one item may be simultaneously longer than the one that precedes it, and shorter than the one that comes after it. Transitivity involves appreciating that if item A is longer than item B, and item B is longer than item C, then item A must be longer than item C.

4. *What competencies have been shown to exist earlier than Piaget proposed?*
   Recent research reveals that young children may not be as illogical as Piaget believed. Young children can predict another's viewpoint when using familiar toys rather than Piagetian mountains. They also can adjust their level of communication to take into account the abilities of the listener. They can also adjust to temporary variations in what the listener knows. They describe an event differently depending on whether the listener was present when the event occurred.

   Rudimentary forms of mental representation, such as learning sign language or deferred imitation, have been found in some infants as early as 6 or 7 months of age. In addition, the capacity to appreciate the representational nature of pictures, as well as the symbolic nature of maps and scale models, becomes evident by the end of infancy. Finally, if simpler tasks are used, some knowledge of invariance of number (conservation) can be seen in early childhood.

LEARNING OBJECTIVE 8.5 Explain the characteristics and outcomes of formal operations compared with concrete operations.

1. *What is the chief difference between formal operations and concrete operations?*
   The distinguishing characteristic of the formal operational period is the capacity for hypothetical–deductive reasoning.

2. *How does the pendulum task test for the use of hypothetical–deductive reasoning?*
   The pendulum task challenges individuals to identify each of the potentially important variables—weight, length, and so on—and then to systematically test them out. The participant must be able to generate all possible combinations of variables, keep track of what has been done and what remains to be done, and draw logical conclusions from the pattern of results.

3. *Why is there debate about formal operations as a stage of cognitive development?*
   Researchers have found that extended training and simpler procedures can elicit formal operational performances in children as young as 9 or 10 years. Similarly, people may use formal operations when reasoning about content that is familiar to them. These findings suggest an environmental influence rather than a developmental change.

4. *How do interest, experience, and culture influence performance on formal operational tasks?*
   Across-time comparisons of performance on formal operational tasks indicate that experience can play an important role in formal operational thought. Adolescents tested in the 1990s earned higher scores on these tasks than did those from the 1960s and early 1970s, suggesting that improvements in education may specifically engage students in hypothetical–deductive reasoning. Cross-cultural research also suggests that the specific experiences available to children can affect both the rate and final state of development. In societies without formal schooling, for example, few individuals attain formal operations.

LEARNING OBJECTIVE 8.6 Explain the general characteristics of Piaget's theory and evaluate the theory overall.

1. *On what key issues do evaluations of Piaget's stage theory focus?*
   Three key issues regarding Piaget's stage theory have been evaluated for their validity: the concept of stages, the universality of the stages, and the factors that contribute to cognitive change.

2. *What are the questions and uncertainties regarding these key issues of Piagetian theory?*
   Researchers have found inconsistencies in terms of whether stages best describe cognitive development. Questions have also been raised concerning the universality of the theory:

cross-cultural studies suggest variations in the course of development in different cultural societies. Finally, Piaget's theory has been criticized for a lack of specificity in describing the factors that cause developmental change.

LEARNING OBJECTIVE 8.7 Discuss and describe more recent research of children's cognitive development that has been influenced by Piaget's cognitive-developmental approach.

1. *What is the nature of the child's capacity for understanding concepts?*
   Concepts are cognitive structures used to organize experiences into meaningful categories on the basis of similarity of items or events. Though preschoolers' concepts often are perceptually oriented, in many situations their concepts can reflect other fundamental similarities. Indeed, young children do show the ability to understand the biological distinction between animate and inanimate items.

2. *What is meant by "theory of mind"?*
   Theory of mind refers to children's understanding of the mental world. Research in this area is concerned with children's realization that mental states, thoughts, beliefs, desires, and intentions are part of an individual and not part of the physical world. Researchers have also been interested in children's understanding of how these mental states can affect behaviour. Attainment of a theory of mind has been consistently found by early childhood.

3. *How do studies of false belief and the appearance–reality distinction inform us about the development of theory of mind?*
   False belief is the realization that people can have beliefs that are not true. The appearance–reality distinction involves the ability to distinguish between the way things appear and the way they really are. Tasks assessing children's capacities in these areas have been used to investigate their level of theory of mind. Results have shown distinct limitations in preschoolers' theory of mind. However, children overcome these limitations by early childhood.

4. *What factor has been shown to interact with the development of theory of mind?*
   There is a relation between theory-of-mind understanding and social interactions with others. The connection between theory of mind and social behaviour is supported by studies of children with autism, who have both difficulties in social interactions and in theory-of-mind understanding.

Learning Objective 8.8 Analyze the three main themes on which sociocultural approaches to development are based.

1. *What temporal and cultural contexts did Vygotsky identify, and why are they important to the study of development?*
   Vygotsky proposed the study of development over four interrelated temporal contexts: ontogenetic, microgenetic, phylogenetic, and cultural/historical. Ontogenetic development takes place across the life of an individual. Microgenetic development refers to moment-to-moment learning. Phylogenetic development describes the development of the species. Cultural/historical development occurs over decades and centuries in particular times and places, leaving a legacy of tools, artifacts, value systems, institutions, and practices.

2. *What applications based on Vygotsky's theory demonstrate how children learn through social interaction?*
   By participating in culturally meaningful activities with more knowledgeable members of their society, children internalize the values, customs, beliefs, and skills of their culture, and over time come to use them independently. The zone of proximal development refers to the distance between what a child can accomplish independently and what the child can

accomplish with the help of an adult or more capable peer. Interactions within the zone of proximal development promote cognitive development. Scaffolding refers to the ways more capable partners adjust the level of help in response to the child's level of performance. Guided participation is the process by which young children become competent through participating in everyday, purposeful activities under the guidance of more experienced partners.

3. *According to the Vygotsky, what are the roles of cultural tools and artifacts in cognitive development?*
   Children learn how to use cultural tools through interactions with parents, teachers, and more advanced peers. Children's thinking grows more sophisticated as they master the tools provided by their culture. Children's experiences with objects and tools, and the impact of such experience on their cognitive development, are influenced by the views and expectations of the culture in which they grow up.

4. *According to the sociocultural view, what is the significance of pretend play in cognitive development?*
   For Vygotsky, pretend or make-believe play is a unique activity in which children try out a number of different skills in their zone of proximal development. They exercise their developing representational abilities as they create imaginary situations, substituting objects for other objects within a play-frame. In addition, they create scenes within which they enact certain social rules and activities. Cultures vary in the value they place on pretend play.

LEARNING OBJECTIVE 8.9 Compare and contrast the theories of Piaget and Vygotsky on the role of language in cognitive development.

1. *How did Piaget and Vygotsky differ in their view of how language and thought are related?*
   Piaget believed that language is a verbal reflection of the individual's conceptual understanding. For Piaget, cognition determines language. Vygotsky believed that the onset of language transforms "elementary mental functions" into "higher mental functions." For Vygotsky, language precedes thought.

2. *How did Vygotsky's notion of private speech differ from Piaget's concept of egocentric speech?*
   According to Vygotsky, children's experience of language is social from the start. Their first words are communicative acts, mediating their interaction with the people around them. This sequence suggests a progression from social and communicative speech to internal dialogue or private speech. Piaget believed that children's egocentric speech ("talk for self") was the result of the inability to take the perspective of another.

3. *What did Vygotsky mean by the notion of sociogenesis?*
   According to Vygotsky, young children's private speech grows out of interactions with parents as they work together on tasks. During these tasks, children begin to use versions of their parents' instructional comments to direct their own behaviour, using self-talk in a self-directing manner. Gradually, the controlling speech becomes internalized as thought. Self-regulation thus develops out of the child's social interactions, a process Vygotsky referred to as sociogenesis.

LEARNING OBJECTIVE 8.10 Evaluate the contributions of Piaget and Vygotsky to education.

1. *On what three principles are Piagetian-inspired classrooms based?*
   The first principle is an emphasis on discovery (or active) learning. Children learn by acting on the world, rather than by passively taking in information. The second principle is a child's readiness to learn. The child must integrate experience with existing cognitive structures

through the process of assimilation and accommodation. The third principle is that teachers must be sensitive to individual differences among students in the classroom.

2. *What kinds of learning activities are you likely to find in a Vygotskian-inspired classroom?*
Vygotsky believed that children learn best through assisted discovery, which occurs via interactions between teacher and student as well as between students. The role of teacher is to carefully guide each child according to his ability level. The emphasis is on the children's interactions as they participate in meaningful activities with others in the classroom.

3. *How did Piaget's and Vygotsky's views differ on the role of peers in learning and development?*
For Piaget, cognitive growth is fuelled by the child's recognition that her views are different from those of her peers. The experience and resolution of sociocognitive conflict pushes development forward. Vygotsky's explanation of peer influence focuses on cooperation to achieve a common learning objective, rather than conflict resolution. Students sharing a responsibility for a task are more likely to engage in cooperative dialogues to resolve differences of opinion.

4. *What is the role of peers in learning in the classroom?*
Students who participate in groups supported by teacher-created scaffolding interventions develop better understanding of a problem than those in groups that do not receive scaffolding. Whole-class discussion is another means for teachers to structure discussion among students through rephrasing questions, elaborating answers, encouraging the expansion of students' reasoning, and having students evaluate one another's answers.

5. *In what key ways are the sociocultural and Piagetian approaches alike?*
Both approaches view the child as an active participant in her own development, and both hold that the individual undergoes qualitative as well as quantitative change over the course of development.

6. *How do the two approaches differ in both the means and the ends of cognitive development?*
Piagetians focus on processes internal to the child, such as the reorganization of cognitive structures, as the child attempts to understand the world. Sociocultural theorists believe that development takes place within the context of social interaction: it is the direct result of interactions with other people and the tools and artifacts of human culture. In the Piagetian view, the endpoint of development is the ability to think in abstract ways that follow rules of logic. Sociocultural theorists question whether there is an ideal endpoint of development. They maintain that the kind of abstract thought characterized by Piaget's final stage of development may itself be a product of culturally situated values.

7. *What challenges to their work do socioculturalists continue to face?*
Critics point out that socioculturalists often idealize learning. Another challenge is how to integrate data across multiple spheres of development. Without data from the multiple levels of development (e.g., microsystem, mesosystem, exosystem, macrosystem, and chronosystem), although we may accumulate information about lives in different cultures and test the universality of psychological theories, we cannot really gain much insight into the dynamic processes of development in context.

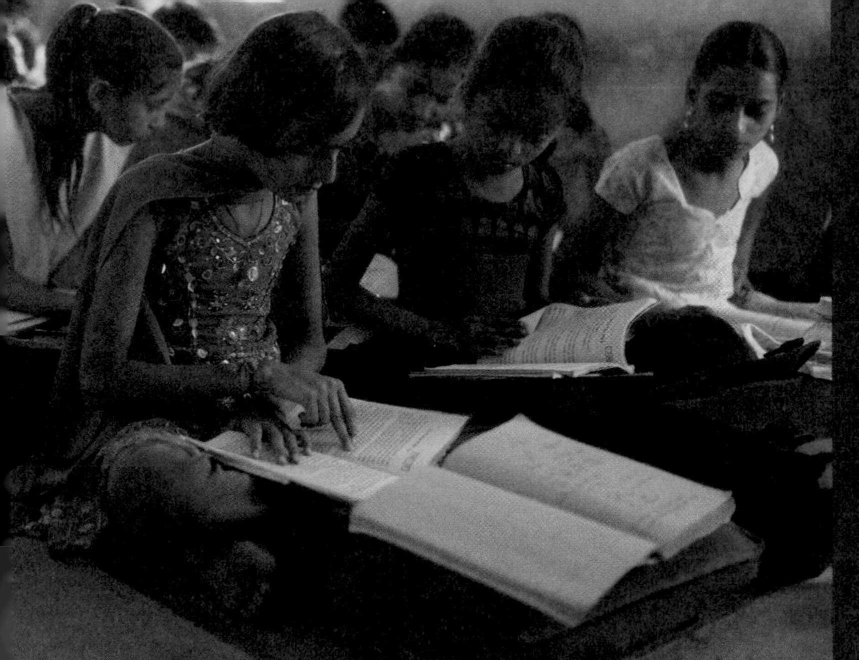

CHAPTER 9

COGNITIVE DEVELOPMENT: THE INFORMATION-PROCESSING APPROACH

Children who have witnessed a crime are just as accurate as adults in identifying the perpetrator in a police lineup. However, if the criminal is not among those in the lineup, children between the ages of 5 and 13 are also more inclined to pick out an innocent person. Those under age 5 have difficulty identifying the right person, even when the criminal is present. These are the research findings of psychologist Joanna Pozzulo, a professor at Carleton University in Ottawa.

Children may identify the wrong person for a number of reasons. "One theory is that the whole lineup task places pressure on the witness, and children feel that pressure more than adults," says Dr. Pozzulo. "Also, children's memory traces may be weaker than adults'; they may have a lower threshold for a match between their memory trace and the lineup member."

Still, children's memories can be accurate. Dr. Pozzulo has also found that when asked to describe situations or unfamiliar people, children report significantly fewer details but are not less accurate than adults—if they are given open-ended questions. When children receive suggestive or leading questions, their descriptions become less reliable.

"When interviewing children who have witnessed criminal activity, you have to be careful in how you ask the questions and what sort of interview protocol you're using," says Dr. Pozzulo. "If you're giving children positive reinforcement for certain types of answers, that's going to produce potentially erroneous reports."

Improper questioning of child witnesses has resulted in a number of court cases in which innocent people have been wrongly accused. The sexual abuse case in Martinsville, Saskatchewan, is one of the more famous Canadian examples. In this case, children's accounts of abuse—provided during what were later found to be inappropriate interviews—contributed to the wrongful prosecution of daycare providers, who were later acquitted.

Although cases like this call into question the reliability of children's testimony, Dr. Pozzulo says it does have a place in court proceedings. "Children have a lot of valuable information to provide," she says. "With proper techniques, both in interviewing and lineup procedure, you can get just as reliable evidence with children as you can with adults." This chapter will examine children's memory and other basic psychological processes of their cognitive development. ■

Exactly how does memory work? How are memories stored and how are they retrieved? Questions like these are central to our understanding of human cognition. Such questions can also have important real-life implications, as you can see in the examples just discussed and will see again when we return to the topic of children as witnesses later in the chapter.

The workings of memory and other basic psychological processes are the focus of scientists seeking to understand children's cognitive development from the information-processing perspective. As we noted in the preceding chapter, information processing has emerged as the major contemporary approach to the study of children's thinking.

In this chapter, we first summarize some of the most important characteristics of information-processing theory and research. We then move on to aspects of child development that have especially intrigued information-processing researchers. We consider several important areas of development, including memory, executive function, problem solving, and academic skills. The chapter concludes with the challenging issue of cognitive change.

Learning Objective 9.1

Define the information-processing approach and describe three methods of studying information processing.

THE NATURE OF THE INFORMATION-PROCESSING APPROACH

As many commentators have noted, information processing is not a single theory, but rather a general framework within which researchers have developed a number of specific theories (Kail & Miller, 2006; Klahr & MacWhinney, 1998; Siegler, 2005). The common core that unites the different theories is the shared assumption implied by the name of the approach: thinking is information processing (Siegler & Alibali, 2005). The information to be processed can take many forms across different contexts and developmental levels; it might, for example, be a hard-to-work toy, a spatial landmark, a numerical symbol, or an instruction from the teacher. The processing can also take many forms, depending on the demands of the task: attention to critical features, insertion into a conceptual category, and comparison with past memory input. Beyond basic cognitive development, the information-processing approach has also become the framework for understanding a whole range of developmental domains such as intelligence, emotional processing and behaviour in children, and adolescent antisocial behaviour. The goal of the information-processing approach, therefore, is to specify such underlying psychological processes—and the developmental changes they undergo.

Children's environments present information and cognitive challenges of many sorts. How children come to understand and respond adaptively to these challenges are the concern of the information-processing approach. (*PhotoDisc, Inc.*)

Two metaphors are instructive in characterizing the information-processing approach. One is the flowchart; the other is the computer.

THE FLOWCHART METAPHOR

Figure 9.1 shows the symbolic representation of a typical information-processing theory. This particular theory, which deals with memory, contains a number of details that do not concern us here. However, its general features are characteristic of the information-processing approach. The starting point is some environmental input, and the end point is some response output. Between stimulus and response, a number of psychological processes intervene to interpret and code the environmental input and transform it into mental information that can be used to initiate response outputs.

In the case of memory, the initial input is assumed to be acted on and transformed in various ways. Imagine, for example, that a 6-year-old in a grade 1 classroom has just heard a word for the first time. This word enters the *sensory register*—in this case, the auditory register—where a literal representation of a stimulus can be held for perhaps a second at most. The word then moves to *short-term*, or *working memory*, which is the centre for active and conscious processing. Although

FIGURE 9.1

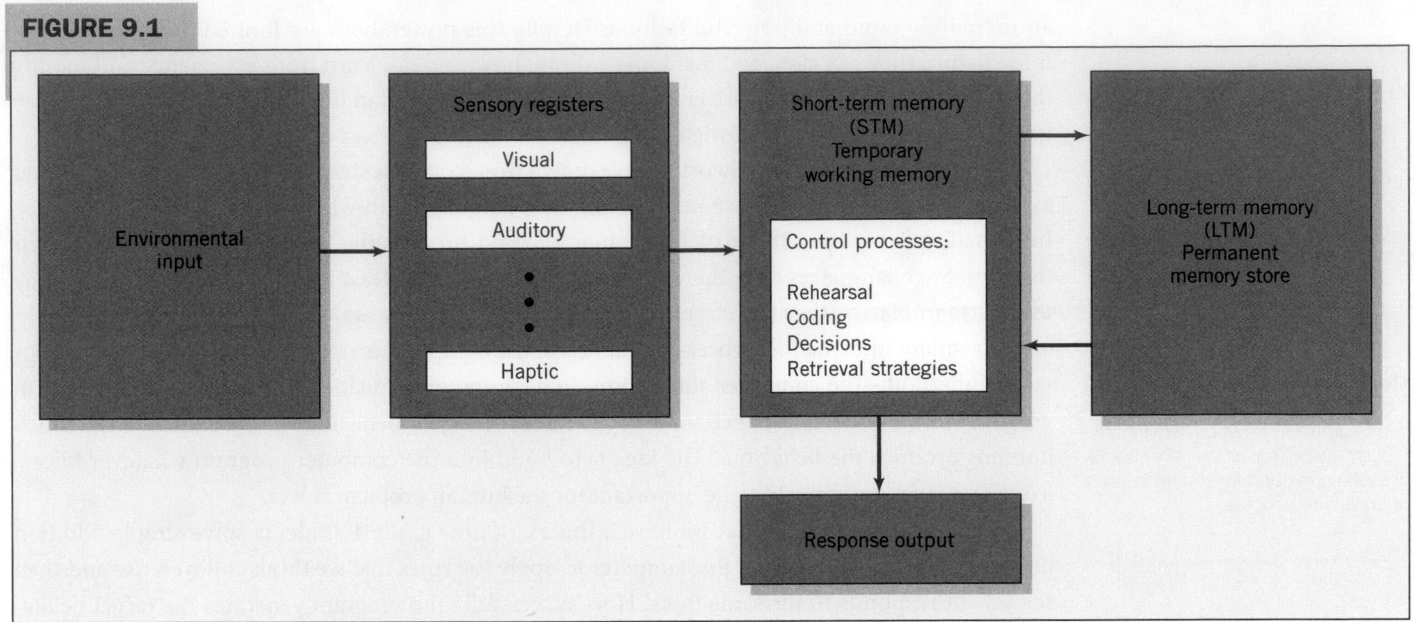

An example of an information-processing model of memory that illustrates the kind of flowchart representation with which information-processing theorists attempt to describe the sequence of information processing. *From "The Control of Short-Term Memory" by R.C. Atkinson and R. M. Shiffrin, 1971, Scientific American, 225, 82. Copyright credit Allen Beechel.*

information typically stays for only a few seconds in short-term memory, various strategies (some of which we will consider shortly) may considerably prolong its lifetime. Finally, the word may be transferred to *long-term memory*, where, as the name suggests, it can exist indefinitely. Getting the word to long-term memory is, of course, the teacher's goal when presenting a new term to be learned. And all of us in fact do have thousands of words stored in permanent memory.

As the figure indicates, more general psychological processes also play a role. *Control processes* affect the maintenance of information and the movement from one store to another. *Response-generating mechanisms* are necessary to explain the eventual overt response—for example, the child's ability to say a recently learned word.

The origin of the term *flowchart* should be evident from this example. Information-processing theorists attempt to capture the orderly flow of information through the cognitive system. The origin of the term *information processing* should also be evident. Information is acted on, or processed, in various ways as it moves through the system. The external stimulus and the external response—the concerns of traditional learning theory—are only the end points. The real goal of the psychologist—or so maintains the information-processing theorist—is to specify as completely and precisely as possible what comes between stimulus and response. Furthermore, the goal of the neuropsychologist and neuroscientist is to specify the brain and neural substrates through which this information processing occurs. And as our example suggests, even in a seemingly simple case, such as hearing a new word, quite a bit may be going on.

THE COMPUTER METAPHOR

The preceding section described a cognitive system that can transform a variety of inputs into a variety of outputs in a systematic and intelligent way. In doing so, it uses stored information and stored rules of various sorts. What sort of intelligent system operates in this way? To anyone immersed in modern technological society, the answer should be obvious—a computer.

Information-processing theorists find the computer to be a useful tool on a variety of levels. At the most general level, the computer serves as a helpful metaphor for thinking about human cognition. Humans and computers are alike in a number of ways. Both store representations or symbols and manipulate these symbols to solve problems. Both perform a variety of such manipulations in an incredibly rapid and powerful fashion. Despite this power, both are limited in the amount of information they can store and manipulate. Both, however, can learn from experience and modify their rule systems in a progressively adaptive direction. Understanding the operations of computer intelligence may thus lead to insights about human intelligence as well.

Information-processing theorists have drawn from computer technology in more specific ways as well. Theorists of intelligence must decide on a language with which to formulate their theory. Information-processing theorists have often adopted pre-existing computer languages for their theories. Such languages have the virtues of precision and (at least to the information-processing theorist) familiarity; they therefore are good vehicles for testing and communicating theories.

Computer simulation Programming a computer to perform a cognitive task in the same way in which humans are thought to perform it. An information-processing method for testing theories of underlying process.

For many information-processing theorists, the computer is not just a metaphor. It also provides a method—the **computer simulation**. In a computer simulation, the researcher attempts to program a computer to produce some segment of intelligent behaviour in the same way in which humans produce the behaviour. The idea is to build into the computer program whatever knowledge and rules are thought to be important for the human problem solver.

Suppose, for example, that we have a theory of how grade 1 students solve simple addition problems. We might program the computer to apply the rules that we think children use and then see how it responds to the same tasks. How successfully the program generates the target behaviour—in this case, the pattern of grade 1 student responses—is a test of the investigator's theory of how children arrive at their answers.

Computer simulations also offer a powerful method for testing theories of underlying process and its development. Nevertheless, many simulations are limited in that they are static; at best, they tell us what the cognitive system is like at one point in development. They do not model the developmental change in cognition. A relatively recent advancement is the creation of programs that can actually change from one level of understanding to another.

Links to Related Material

In Chapter 6, you read how the brain is constructed of millions of interconnected neurons. Here, you learn about computer models of cognitive development that attempt to simulate these neural networks.

Each computer simulation of development includes a set of rules intended to model the starting-point level of understanding of a child who has not yet mastered the knowledge (Shultz, 2003)—for example, a rule system that uses only the length of the row when judging number and hence fails conservation-of-number tasks. Each also includes mechanisms for changing the initial rules in response to experience—for example, the capacity to benefit from experiences of counting and measurement in the case of conservation and thereby to construct more complex rules. Each includes tests in which the program is exposed to the relevant experiences and both its immediate and more long-term responses are recorded. Finally, each reports some success at modelling the acquisition of new knowledge. That is, they create programs that modify their own rule systems with experience and hence change from lower to higher levels of understanding. The forms of knowledge for which change has been successfully modelled include conservation, transitivity, physical reasoning, and arithmetic.

Connectionism Creation of artificial neural networks, embodied in computer programs, that solve cognitive tasks and modify their solutions in response to experience. A methodological and theoretical approach adopted by a subset of information-processing researchers.

Today, many of the ongoing efforts to create self-modifying systems take an approach labelled **connectionism**. The starting point for advocates of connectionism is a basic limitation with regard to the flowchart and computer metaphors: they are simply metaphors. That is, the human brain is not in fact a flowchart with different boxes, nor is it a digital computer, though there are many similarities. Chapter 6 discussed what it in fact is: an extraordinarily complex system of neural connections.

Connectionism attempts to mirror this aspect of the human brain. Rather than strings of symbols, therefore, connectionist computer programs take the form of *artificial neural networks*. Such networks consist of multiple interconnected processing units, just as the brain consists of multiple interconnected neurons. The units are arranged in layers, including an *input layer* that takes in information about the task facing the system and an *output layer* that generates an eventual response. Networks also often contain one or more sets of *hidden layers* representing the information used to execute the task. Connections among units vary in strength (or weights), just as is true for connections among neurons in the brain. Also like neurons in the brain, when the amount of activation received from its connecting units is sufficient, a unit fires. The sum of the activated units determines the response to the task. That is, the pattern of activity that eventually reaches the set of output units determines the network's response to the task (Westermann, Sirois, Shultz, & Mareschal, 2006).

Neural networks are programmed to change or "learn" with experience. The network uses feedback on the accuracy of each output to modify connection strengths among the units. When the response is correct, the connections that produced it are strengthened slightly; when the response is wrong, the connections are weakened. As a result, patterns of activation change throughout the network. This is how learning occurs and how new, more accurate responses gradually replace old, incorrect ones. Researchers can thus ask not only whether the model produces responses like a child at a given time, but also whether the model shows the same pattern of learning over time that real children demonstrate (Mareschal, 2010). When networks perform similarly to human children, researchers conclude that they have created a plausible model of how learning occurs in the task under investigation.

For Thought and Discussion

What might be some limitations of the computer metaphor for understanding cognitive development? What aspects of cognition are not currently captured in a computer program?

Problem-solving tasks are just one of a number of content areas to which the connectionist approach has been applied. Other topics include infant perception (Mareschal & Johnson, 2002), categorization (French, Mareschal, Mermillod, & Quinn, 2004), object permanence (Munakata, 1998), Piagetian concrete operational concepts (Buckingham & Shultz, 2000), and language (MacWhinney & Chang, 1995). We will see an application of this approach to language in Chapter 11.

Information-processing researchers have used a variety of techniques to study the process of change. We next examine a method that has been emphasized in recent information-processing research: microgenetic techniques.

MICROGENETIC STUDIES Computer simulations typically complement studies of human performance, which often employ a microgenetic technique. Recall from Chapter 2 that a microgenetic study begins with the selection of a sample of children who are thought to be in a transitional phase for the knowledge being studied; that is, they are close to moving to a higher level of understanding. The children are observed as they attempt to solve a variety of problems that assess the abilities of interest. Typically, there are many such problems in each experimental session and several such sessions across a period of weeks or months. The goal is to observe processes of change as the change occurs—something that is usually not possible when we assess children only once or twice.

Links to Related Material

In Chapter 2, you learned about the microgenetic method as a way to understand developmental changes. Here, you read about how this methodology has been used to study children's understanding of arithmetic.

An analogy that Siegler (2006) uses in contrasting microgenetic techniques with the standard longitudinal approach is the difference between a snapshot and a movie. With longitudinal research we get snapshots—pictures of the cognitive system at different points in time. With microgenetic research we get a movie—a continuous record of change over time.

A classic example of a microgenetic study is provided by some of the work on arithmetical strategies, discussed later in the chapter. Siegler and Jenkins (1989) selected 10 children who did not yet use the min strategy (that is, counting up from the larger addend) when solving simple arithmetic problems. These children then participated in three experimental sessions per week across a period of 11 weeks. During each session, they attempted to solve seven addition problems; across sessions the complexity of the problems increased. Both videotapes of the children's performance and direct questioning were used to infer the strategies underlying their answers. Through this approach, Siegler and Jenkins were able to document the gradual discovery of the min strategy by seven of the eight children who made it through all 11 weeks. Because of their extensive observational records, they knew when and how the strategy first appeared,

This child has not yet discovered the min strategy for solving addition tasks. The min strategy involves counting up from the larger of two addends to arrive at a sum. For example, the problem 10 + 2 would be solved by thinking "10, 11, 12; the answer is 12." Microgenetic studies can capture the cognitive process of this discovery. What other kinds of things can microgenetic techniques tell us? (*PhotoDisc, Inc.*)

as well as what preceded it and to what it subsequently led. The examples in Table 9.1 include the first appearance of the strategy for one of the children, Brittany.

In discussing the strengths of the microgenetic approach, Siegler (2006) identifies five issues related to cognitive change for which microgenetic techniques can provide valuable data. Such techniques can inform us about the *path* of cognitive change: the sequences and levels through which children move in acquiring new knowledge. They can provide information about the *rate* of change: how quickly or slowly different forms of knowledge are mastered. Microgenetic findings speak to the issue of *breadth* of change: when a new competency (such as a particular arithmetical strategy) is acquired and how narrowly or broadly it is applied. They are relevant to the question of possible *variability* in the pattern of change: Do all children follow the same route in mastering a new concept? As we have seen, a major conclusion from microgenetic research is that often

TABLE 9.1 PROTOCOLS ILLUSTRATING CHILDREN'S USE OF THE MIN STRATEGY TO SOLVE ADDITION PROBLEMS

Experimenter	(E):	How much is 6 + 3?
Lauren	(L):	(Long pause) Nine.
	E:	OK, how did you know that?
	L:	I think I said…I think I said...oops, um…I think he said …8 was 1 and… um…I mean 7 was 1, 8 was 2, 9 was 3.
	E:	OK.
	L:	6 and 3 are 9.
	E:	How did you know to do that? Why didn't you count "1, 2, 3, 4, 5, 6, 7, 8, 9"? How come you did "6, 7, 8, 9"?
	L:	'Cause then you have to count all those numbers.
	E:	OK, well how did you know you didn't have to count all of those numbers?
	L:	Why didn't…well I don't have to if I don't want to.
Experimenter	(E):	OK, Brittany, how much is 2 + 5?
Brittany	(B):	2 + 5-(whispers)-6, 7-it's 7.
	E:	How did you know that?
	B:	(excitedly) Never counted.
	E:	You didn't count?
	B:	Just said it—I just said after 6 something—7—6, 7.
	E:	You did? Why did you say 6, 7?
	B:	'Cause I wanted to see what it really was.
	E:	OK, well—so, did you—what—you didn't have to count at 1, you didn't count, 1, 2, 3, you just said 6, 7?
	B:	Yeah—smart answer.
Experimenter	(E):	OK, Christian, How much is 1 + 24?
Christian	(C):	1 + 24!?
	E:	Yep.
	C:	Umm…25.
	E:	How did you know that?
	C:	I…counted in my head.
	E:	How did you count it in your head?
	C:	What was it again?
	E:	1 + 24.
	C:	I went…1, 2, 3, 4, 5, si…I went, 24 1 1, 1, well. …I'll try to get you to understand, Ok?
	E:	OK.
	C:	I went 24 + 1…(whispers) 24…(whispers) 25…that's what I did.
	E:	OK, that's good, well why didn't you count 1, 2, 3, 4, 5, 6, 7, 8, 9, 10, all the way to 24?
	C:	Aww, that would take too long…silly.

Source: From *How Children Discover New Strategies* by R. S. Siegler and E. Jenkins, 1989, Mahwah, NJ: Erlbaum, 66, 80, 91.

children do not; there can be substantial variability en route to the same end point. This variability in the route that children can take is a substantial component of Siegler's Overlapping Waves Theory, which we will discuss later in this chapter. Finally, microgenetic methods can provide information about the *sources* of change: the experiences and processes through which new knowledge is constructed.

COMPARISONS WITH PIAGET

Because the most complete discussion of intelligence and cognitive change has been the Piagetian approach, comparing the information-processing approach with this view is instructive.

Information-processing approaches to child development share several similarities with Piaget's approach. The first similarity is in the content studied. Information-processing researchers recognize the importance of the concepts identified by Piaget, and much of their research involves attempts to apply information-processing techniques to Piagetian tasks and abilities. Second, similarity exists at a general theoretical level. Information-processing theories, like Piagetian theory, fall within the cognitive-developmental approach to child development. Information-processing theorists agree with Piaget that a complex system of mental rules underlies cognitive performance, and that one job of the theorist is to discover what these rules are. Finally, some information-processing theorists follow Piaget in dividing development into distinct stages. Although the stages are not identical to Piaget's, they typically show some important similarities. For example, Juan Pascual-Leone of York University in Toronto has theorized that the development of mental attention and rules or operations for its deployment in various tasks are responsible for apparent stages (congruent with Piaget's) of cognitive development (Pascual-Leone, 1987; Pascual-Leone & Johnson, 1999).

Because of their grounding in Piaget, this group of information-processing theorists is often referred to as neo-Piagetian (Case & Okamoto, 1996; Fischer & Bidell, 1998; Morra, Gobbo, Marini, & Sheese, 2008; Pascual-Leone, 1987). The issue of stages, however, also illustrates a difference between the information-processing and Piagetian approaches. Most information-processing theorists do not subscribe to a stage model of development. Furthermore, even those who may find stages useful differ in important ways from Piaget. The stages proposed by Piaget are the broadest, most general stages that the field of child psychology has seen. To say that a child is in the stage of concrete operations is to make a strong (and, as we saw, debatable) claim about how the child will perform on a wide range of cognitive tasks. Information-processing stage theories tend to be more limited in scope, focusing on specific skills and particular aspects of the child's development. A model might, for example, concentrate on the acquisition of spatial skills, without making any claims about the child's level of performance on other tasks. One way to summarize this difference is to say that the information-processing theorist's stages are more *domain-specific*; that is, more concerned with distinct aspects, or domains, of development.

Other differences between the information-processing and Piagetian approaches can be inferred from the flowchart and computer metaphors. Piaget's theoretical emphasis was always on the logical rules underlying problem solving, such as the concrete operations of middle childhood and the formal operations of adolescence. Piaget had little to say about many more process-oriented questions that are central to the information-processing researcher. How exactly does the child attend to new information? How is this information taken in and represented in memory? How is it retrieved in the service of problem solving? It would be difficult to construct a full flowchart model of problem solving, let alone a computer simulation, from Piaget's theoretical accounts. Information-processing theorists attempt to develop models that are more specific and more complete than those offered by Piaget.

These goals have both methodological and theoretical implications. Methodologically, the emphasis on precision and testability has led to a number of distinctive methods for studying children's thinking. We have already mentioned one such method—the computer simulation technique—and we describe others later. Theoretically, the emphasis on completeness has meant a concern with many aspects of children's development in addition to the kinds of logical reasoning stressed by Piaget. Much of the work on attention discussed in Chapter 7 was carried out within an information-processing perspective. The same is true for much of the work on memory that we consider next.

LEARNING OBJECTIVE 9.1

Define the information-processing approach and describe three methods of studying information processing.

1. What are the goals of the information-processing approach to cognition?
2. How does the information-processing approach reflect a computer metaphor?
3. What are the strengths and limitations of connectionism in the information-processing approach?
4. What can we learn from microgenetic studies of cognition?
5. What are the similarities and differences between the information-processing approach and Piaget's approach?

Learning Objective 9.2

Explain the information-processing model of memory, and trace developmental changes in the kinds of memory.

MEMORY IN INFANCY

All information-processing models rely on a theory of memory. Children can learn from their experiences only if they can somehow retain information from these experiences over time. To be learned at all, information must first enter the brain through the senses. Once there, the information may be lost and thus forgotten. Alternatively, the information may undergo further mental processing in which it is encoded and stored to be retrieved when needed at a later time. Questions of memory—of how information is taken in, stored, and retrieved—are therefore central to information-processing accounts of development. Because development starts in infancy, the examination of memory must also start with the infant.

We begin our discussion with a very basic question: Can babies remember? We have already encountered a number of findings that tell us the answer is yes. Many of the findings from the study of infant perception discussed in Chapter 7 imply the use of memory—for example, the infant's preference for the mother's voice. Much of the behaviour that we as adults produce would be impossible if we did not remember and were not guided by past experience. The same is true of infants.

How well do babies remember? This question is harder to answer. Even a young infant's memory is in some respects surprisingly good. In other respects, however, infant memory is limited, and many important developmental advances have yet to come.

Event memory Scripts for sequences of familiar actions or routine events in one's daily world.

Script A representation of the typical sequence of events in a familiar context.

Constructive memory The ways that individuals interpret the information they take in in terms of their pre-existing knowledge, which affects what they remember.

Autobiographical memory Specific, personal, and long-lasting memory about the self.

For Thought and Discussion

Autobiographical memory is constructed within the larger contexts of family and community history and biography. How did family photos influence your memories as a child?

In late infancy, children begin to construct their memories through social interaction and social mediation. In **event memory**, for example, children develop scripts for sequences of familiar actions or routine events in their daily world (Hudson & Mayhew, 2009). A **script** is a representation of the typical sequence of events in a familiar context. Children come to regard their scripts—such as the "birthday party" script or the "going to the store" or the "finding my way home" script—as natural and logical, and may even resist attempts to change them. Scripts are both the product and the process of constructive memory and can lead to both improved memory and memory distortions. **Constructive memory** refers to the ways that individuals interpret the information they take in in terms of their pre-existing knowledge, which affects what they remember. Parents and teachers use prompts and cues during social interaction to help children develop event memory and constructive memory. **Autobiographical memory**, on the other hand, refers to specific, personal, and long-lasting memory about the self. Autobiographical memory contains information about unique events such as the first day of school or a vacation to the beach. These memories are part of one's life history and are culturally constructed through verbal and social interaction.

Event memory and autobiographical memory are of particular interest to sociocultural theorists. However, psychologists using the information-processing approach focus on two other basic forms of memory that begin in infancy: recognition and recall. **Recognition memory** refers to the realization that some perceptually present stimulus or event has been encountered before. You would be demonstrating recognition memory, for example, if you realized that you had already seen the flowchart memory model (see Figure 9.1) when you encountered the same figure in some other book.

Recognition memory The realization that some perceptually present stimulus or event has been encountered before.

Recall memory refers to the retrieval of some past stimulus or event when the stimulus or event is *not* perceptually present. You would be demonstrating recall memory if you were able to draw the flowchart model (or at least parts of it!) in the absence of any stimulus input. We begin with recognition, then move on to recall.

Recall memory The retrieval of some past stimulus or event that is not perceptually present.

RECOGNITION MEMORY

METHODS OF STUDY How might we determine whether babies can recognize stimuli that they have previously experienced? The most common method has been the habituation–dishabituation procedure. With this procedure, as you may recall, we examine the infant's response to a repeated stimulus; a decline in response as the stimulus becomes familiar is referred to as *habituation.* Such a decline in interest is possible only if the infant can recognize the repeated stimulus as something that has been experienced previously; if there were no such memory, every appearance of the stimulus would be experienced as a novel event. Similarly, *dishabituation,* or the recovery of response when the stimulus changes, can occur only if the infant is able to compare the new stimulus with some memory of the original.

Links to Related Material

In Chapter 1, you read a description of the habituation–dishabituation procedure. In Chapter 7, you read about studies of infant perception that used the habituation–dishabituation procedure to assess whether the infant perceptually recognizes objects that have been seen before. Here, you learn more about the development of recognition memory in infants.

In order for information encountered during infancy to be developmentally useful, that information needs to be available in memory over long delays. Though the habituation–dishabituation procedure has demonstrated infants' ability to recognize a familiar stimulus and discriminate a novel stimulus after both short and long delays, this procedure has been abandoned because a number of factors were identified that called into question whether it could unequivocally determine whether infants could remember information over long delays (Hayne, 2004). Of particular concern was the tendency of dishabituation to disappear when delays were longer than a few seconds or minutes. As a consequence, classical conditioning and operant conditioning paradigms have also been used to explore infant memory over long delays. As noted in Chapter 1, learning refers to the lasting effects of experience on behaviour, and thus any demonstration of learning necessarily tells us something about memory, and memory over the long term, as well.

One way in which operant conditioning has been employed to study infant memory is pictured in Figure 9.2. As the figure shows, the ribbon linking ankle and mobile confers a potential power on the infant—kicking the leg will make the mobile jump. Infants as young as 2 months can learn this relation; the rate of kicking increases when the kicking pays off in the reinforcement of a dancing mobile (Rovee-Collier, 1999). Once this response has been established, various modifications can be introduced to probe the infant's memory. We can test for memory of the training mobile, for example, by assessing whether the infant exhibits recognition of the familiar training mobile—indicated by a high rate of kicking similar to the end of learning when the memory was first formed. Additionally, memory of the training mobile is assessed by whether the infant discriminates a novel mobile—as indicated by a decrease in kicking relative to the end of learning and similar to before they learned to kick to move the mobile. Or we can test the duration of the memory by seeing how the infant responds a day or a week or a month after the original conditioning.

MEMORY IN NEWBORNS A number of questions about infant memory have been explored with these procedures. A natural first question is how early in life babies can remember. The answer seems clear: from birth (or possibly even earlier—recall the suggestion in Chapter 7 that babies may remember some events that they experienced prenatally). Habituation studies are one basis for this conclusion. Habituation is not easy to demonstrate in newborns, and for years infant

FIGURE 9.2

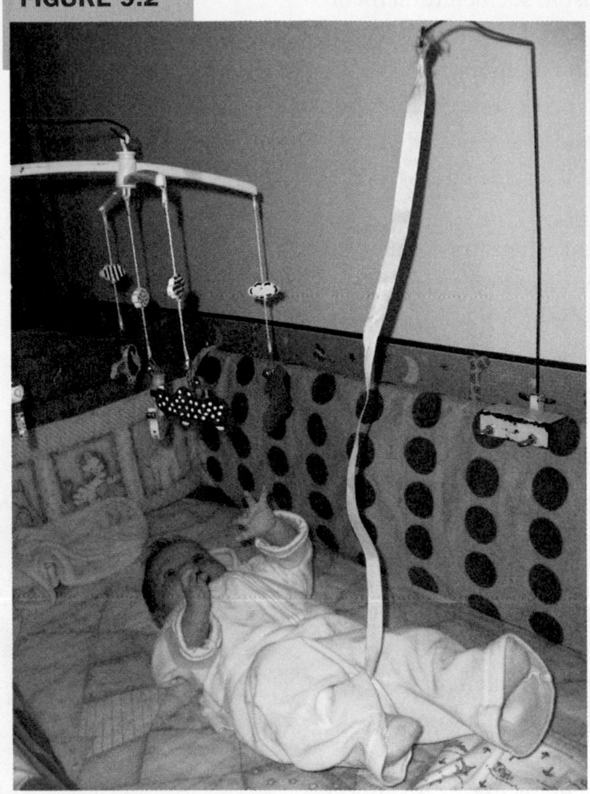

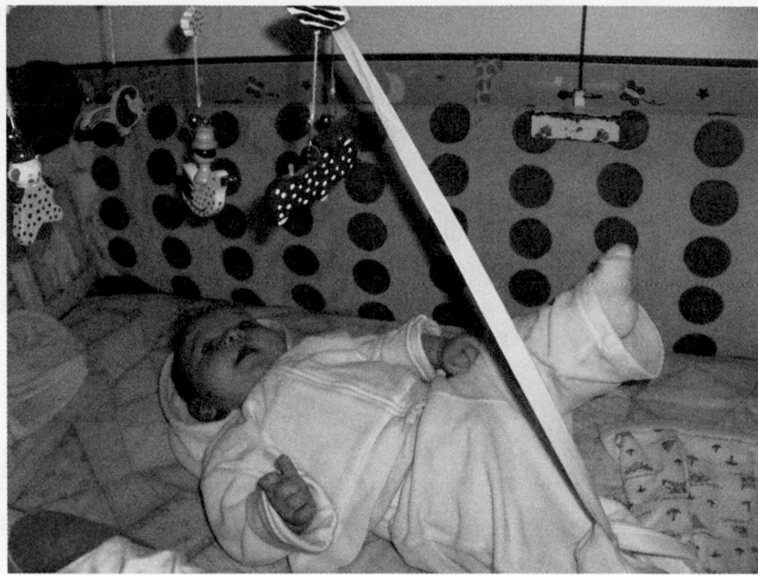

An experimental arrangement for studying infants' ability to learn and remember. When the ribbon is attached to the baby's ankle (as in the right-hand photo), kicking the leg makes the mobile above the crib move. Learning is shown by increased kicking whenever the ribbon is attached and the mobile is present. *Courtesy of Carolyn Rovee-Collier.*

researchers disagreed about whether such early habituation was possible (Slater, 1995). It now seems clear, however, that a newborn infant—given optimal circumstances—can show habituation across a range of modalities: visual (Courage & Howe, 2001; Slater et al., 1991; Turati et al., 2006), auditory (Zelazo, Weiss, & Tarquino, 1991), and tactile (Kisilevsky & Muir, 1984). Thus, newborns do possess some degree of recognition memory.

Conditioning studies are a further source of evidence for neonatal memory. As with habituation, conditioning can be difficult to produce in very young infants, and the question of whether newborns can be conditioned was a topic of debate for many years. Today, however, most researchers agree that both classical conditioning and operant conditioning are possible from birth (Lipsitt, 1990; Taddio et al., 2002). We have already seen some examples of the latter. Recall the finding that newborns prefer a stimulus to which they have been exposed prenatally (DeCasper & Fifer, 1980). The newborns showed this preference by adjusting their sucking to produce the desired stimulus—for example, their own mothers' voices. Adjusting behaviour to obtain reinforcement is a form of operant conditioning.

An example of classical conditioning in newborns is provided by a study in which 1- and 2-day-old infants received a sucrose solution delivered to the lips (Blass, Ganchrow, & Steiner, 1984). The solution functioned as an unconditioned stimulus that elicited the unconditioned response of sucking. The conditioned stimulus consisted of the experimenter's stroking the baby's forehead immediately before delivery of the sucrose. After a few pairings of the stroking with the solution, the babies began to suck in response to the stroking alone—a clear indication that conditioning had occurred.

DEVELOPMENTAL CHANGES Although memory may be present from birth, newborns' and young infants' memories are not as powerful as those of older infants. Developmental improvements of various sorts occur during the first year or so of life. One important change is in how long material can be retained. Most demonstrations of memory in newborns involve only a few seconds between presentation of a stimulus and the test for recognition of that stimulus. What such habituation studies show, then, is very short-term memory. As infants develop, the length of time across which they can remember their experiences steadily increases, soon reaching impressive levels. At 3 months of age, babies may recognize a photo of a face initially viewed for only 2 minutes after a delay of 2 minutes but not of 24 hours (Pascalis, de Haan, Nelson, & de Schonen, 1998). However, by 5 months of age, they exhibit recognition after a delay of 2 weeks (Fagan, 1973). With a more dynamic, moving stimulus, recognition has been demonstrated across a 3-month delay in babies who were only 3 months old at the time of initial exposure (Bahrick & Pickens, 1995). We should add, however, that even newborns are not limited to very brief memories. Newborns can remember speech stimuli across a period of at least 24 hours (Swain, Zelazo, & Clifton, 1993). And the studies of memory for speech sounds experienced prenatally (DeCasper & Spence, 1991; see Chapter 7) have typically involved even longer intervals between the last prenatal exposure and the first postnatal test.

The mobile procedure shown in Figure 9.2 provides another approach to assessing the durability of infant memory. Some suggest this method is better and more systematic at assessing memory function than visual-preference/habituation procedures (Wilk, Klein, & Rovee-Collier, 2001). The question is how long babies can remember the association between kicking and the movement of the mobile. This procedure also reveals both impressive early capacity and developmental improvements in long-term memory with age (Rovee-Collier, 1999). Two-month-olds, for example, can remember the association for 3 days; by 3 months of age, the span has stretched to 8 days; and by 6 months, some retention is still evident 21 days after conditioning (Rovee-Collier & Shyi, 1992). With even older infants, using a variation of this operant conditioning paradigm in which infants had to press a lever to move a toy train on a track, the duration of their retention continues to increase in a linear manner (Figure 9.3). Nine-month-olds remember for 6 weeks; 12-month-olds for 8 weeks; 15-month-olds for 10 weeks; and 18-month-olds for a staggering 13 weeks. More remarkable is that the span over which infants can remember can be prolonged (or shortened) depending on the amount of attention allocated during encoding and retrieval (Adler & Rovee-Collier, 1994; Adler, Gerhardstein, & Rovee-Collier, 1998).

FIGURE 9.3

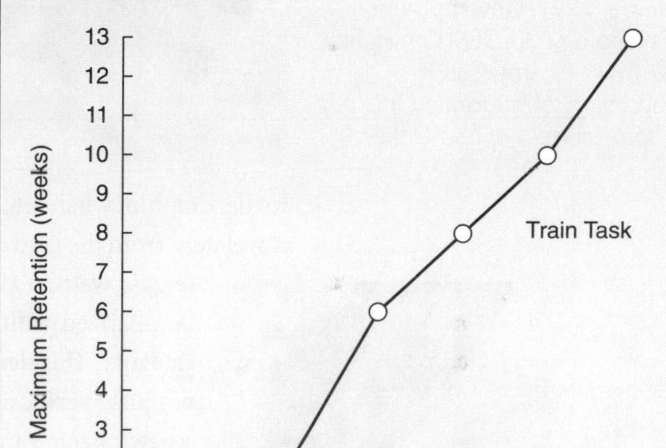

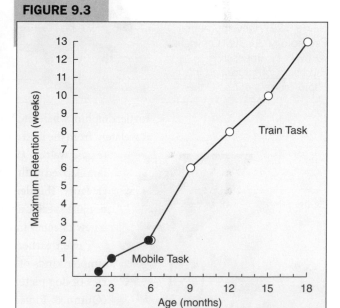

Maximum duration of retention over the first 18 months of life. Filled circles show retention on the mobile task, and open circles show retention on the train task; 6-month-olds were trained and tested in both tasks. *From "The Development of Infant Memory" by C. Rovee-Collier, 1999,* Current Directions in Psychological Science, *8, 83. Copyright © 1999 by Blackwell Publishers, Inc.*

Memory is even better if the infant is given a brief reminder during the delay period. In a number of studies by Rovee-Collier and colleagues (Adler, Wilk, & Rovee-Collier, 2000; Hildreth & Rovee-Collier, 2002; Joh, Sweeney, & Rovee-Collier, 2002), the experimenter jiggled the mobile on the 13th day of the delay period while the infant simply watched. Infants given this reminder showed much more kicking on day 14 than did a control group that received no such help. Such priming of memory through a brief re-encounter with the original experience is referred to as **reactivation**. If the reminders are frequent enough, the original memory may be preserved indefinitely. In one study, for example, 2-month-olds who received periodic reactivation experiences still remembered the kicking response five months after initial exposure to the mobile (Rovee-Collier, Hartshorn, & DiRubbo, 1999). In a further demonstration, 6-month-olds who received periodic reactivations continued to show memory at 2 years of age—1.5 years after the original learning experience (Hartshorn, 2003)! Naturally occurring instances of reactivation may be a major way to prevent forgetting and keep memories alive (Hayne, 2004; Rovee-Collier & Hayne, 1987).

Reactivation The preservation of the memory for an event through re-encounter with at least some portion of the event in the interval between initial experience and memory test.

In addition to duration, another basic question about memory concerns what information is retained. Babies' habituation to a stimulus tells us that they recognize some aspect of the stimulus, but it does not tell us exactly what they are remembering. The mobile paradigm, in contrast to habituation, tells us that young infants' memories do retain specific details of the information that

FIGURE 9.4

Pictures of the land and sea animals used by Oakes and colleagues in the study of infant categorization. *From "By Land or by Sea: The Role of Perceptual Similarity in Infants' Categorization of Animals" by L.M. Oakes, D.J. Coppage, & A. Dingel, 1997,* Developmental Psychology, *33, 398. Copyright © 1999 by American Psychological Association, Inc. Photo courtesy of Lisa Oakes.*

was encountered and what that information might be (Rovee-Collier, 2001). In fact, young infants' memories have been shown to contain details about perceptual features and their relations (Adler & Rovee-Collier, 1994; Bhatt & Rovee-Collier, 1994), the serial order of event components (Gulya, Rovee-Collier, Galluccio, & Wilk, 1998), and even a category of experienced items (Hayne, Rovee-Collier, & Perris, 1987; Merriman, Rovee-Collier, & Wilk, 1997), as well as other details.

What is remembered also shows developmental improvements across infancy. Older infants can remember more information as well as more complex information than younger infants (Olson & Sherman, 1983). Older infants can also abstract and remember general categories of information and not just specific stimuli (Mandler, 2000). In one study, for example, 10- and 13-month-old infants were shown a series of toys from one of two different kinds of animals (land animals: zebra, cow, bear, etc.; or sea animals: turtle, dolphin, whale, etc.). The infants were then given a choice of looking at either of two stimuli: a novel item from the land animal category (e.g., a rabbit), or a novel item from the sea animal category (e.g., a walrus) (Figure 9.4). If the 13-month-old, but not the 10-month-old, infants were familiarized with land animals, they looked longer at the novel item from the sea animal category. This demonstrates that around approximately 13 months of age, infants recognize not just specific animals, but also group those animals into various categories, and they find a new category more interesting than a familiar one (Oakes, Coppage, & Dinger, 1997).

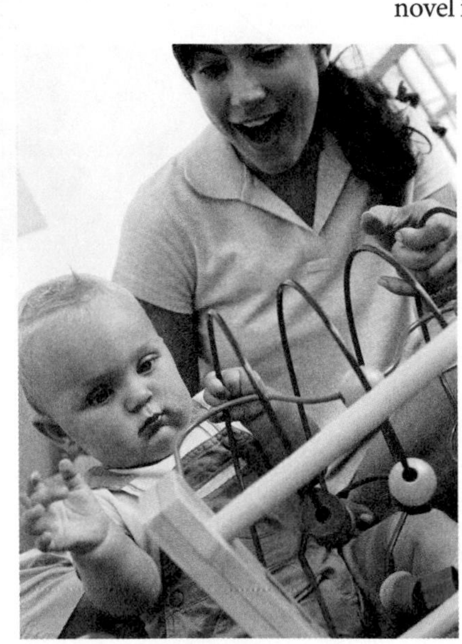

While babies may recognize stimuli, their responses do not tell us exactly what they are remembering. (*Banana Stock*)

Even earlier success has been demonstrated for recognition of other perceptually simpler kinds of categorical distinctions. By 4 months, for example, infants shown a series of dog pictures look more at a picture of a bird than they do at one of another dog (Quinn & Eimas, 1996). Infants as young as 3 months can distinguish animals from furniture, and they can even make some discriminations within each of these categories (Behl-Chadha, 1996; Quinn, 1999). Three-months-olds can also form simple categories based on colour or shape (Hayne, 1996). Even newborns show some basic categorization ability of spatial relations of up versus down and left versus right between objects (Gava, Valenza, & Turati, 2009).

What might explain the apparent developmental trend in categorization from simple perceptual characteristics and features to more complex stimuli and perceptual characteristics? The likely candidate can be found in the specialization of cortical regions in the developing brain with continued experience with examples of various categories. In particular, recent ERP studies have indicated that as the visual cortex receives more input about examples of a particular category, neurons in this area become more finely tuned in their capacity to discriminate individual items within that category (Grossmann, Gliga, Johnson, & Mareschal, 2009). Further, these finely tuned neurons then provide input to the prefrontal cortex—which, as we saw in Chapter 6, does not reach functional maturity until some time in the second half of the first year of life—in which categorical responses occur. The fine tuning of neurons in the visual cortex with age and the maturational time course of the prefrontal cortex likely then provide the basis for making ever sharper distinctions between more complex categories.

Links to Related Material

In Chapter 6, you read of development of the brain, particularly the relatively late maturation of frontal areas. Here, you learn the impact of these trends in brain development on the capacity of infants to form ever more complex categories.

The ability to move beyond specific experiences to abstract, more general categories is an essential component in our attempts to make sense of the world. The studies just reviewed suggest that this ability emerges very early.

RECALL MEMORY

The research that we have described indicates clearly that recognition memory is present from birth. But what about recall? Can infants also actively call to mind previously experienced stimuli or events? Unfortunately, there is no clear agreement on exactly what a young infant might do that would demonstrate recall, and thus no agreement on exactly when recall emerges. It does seem clear, however, that recall is present by the end of infancy, as infants could not show deferred imitation, for example, without the ability to recall a model from the past, nor could they produce words appropriately without some capacity for recall.

As we saw in our discussions of Piagetian research in Chapter 8, evidence suggests that simple forms of recall emerge earlier than previously proposed (Mandler, 1998). The infant's search for vanished objects is one kind of evidence. By the end of the first year, most infants can find objects that are hidden in a single location. Most have also learned the permanent locations for familiar and valued objects, such as the cupboard in which a favourite cereal is kept (Ashmead & Perlmutter, 1980). The ability to find an object that one has not seen for days would certainly seem to imply some capacity for recall.

Studies of deferred imitation provide further evidence for recall memory in infancy. By 6 months of age, infants can imitate a novel action that they viewed a full 24 hours earlier (Barr, Dowden, & Hayne, 1996). By 9 months of age, the delay over which infants can recall novel action increases to five weeks (Carver & Bauer, 2001). Ten- to 11-month-olds can recall actions over delays of three months (Carver & Bauer, 2001). By 14 months, infants can recall unusual actions, like pressing one's forehead against a panel to turn on a light, a full four months after they witnessed an adult doing this (Bauer et al., 2000; Meltzoff, 1995). Even older infants, 20 months of age, can exhibit recall over delays as long as one year (Bauer et al., 2000).

Even after lengthy intervals, infants can remember and imitate not only isolated behaviours, but also simple sequences of action (Bauer, 2002; Bauer & Lukowski, 2010). Thirteen-month-olds, for example, can reproduce three-action sequences for such events as giving a teddy bear a bath (first place in tub, then wash with sponge, then dry with towel), or constructing a simple rattle (place ball in large cup, invert small cup into large, shake) (Bauer & Mandler, 1992). By 24 months, children can remember sequences of five actions (Bauer & Travis, 1993), and by 30 months, children can retain as many as eight separate steps (Bauer & Fivush, 1992). Memory for the order in which events occur is an important form of knowledge to which we will return. These studies indicate that such memory has its origins in infancy (Hayne, Rovee-Collier, & Perris, 1987; Merriman, Rovee-Collier, & Wilk, 1997), but the capacity to store order information in memory requires a couple of years to fully coalesce (Bauer, 2005).

We saw that infants' ability to recognize familiar stimuli may eventually extend across a considerable period of time. The same appears to be true of early recall. Some memory for two-action sequences has been demonstrated after 6 months for infants who were only 10 months old at the time of initial learning (Carver & Bauer, 2001). Infants who are 16 months old at the time of learning show some recall of three-action sequences 8 months later (Bauer, Hertsgaard, & Dow, 1994). Even more impressive is that information originally learned in a non-verbal task is recalled much later with a verbal report once the appropriate language has been acquired (Bauer, Kroupina, Schwade, Dropik, & Wewerka, 1998). In this research, 16- and 20-month-olds learned to imitate simple sequences of actions, similar to the teddy bear and rattle tasks described earlier. When the infants were retested , they showed the ability to verbally recall and report the sequence of actions that they had seen modelled non-verbally a full year earlier!

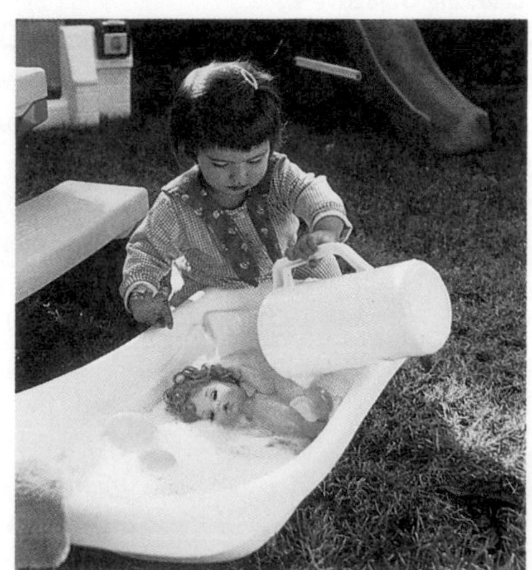

Memory for the order of events emerges early in life. Even 1-year-olds can remember simple sequences, such as the order to follow in giving a doll a bath. (*Michael Newman/Photo Edit*)

What might account for the developmental changes in event memory described here? Changes in the brain structures that are responsible for event memory are likely a major cause (Bauer, Larkina, & Deocampo, 2011). In particular, portions of the hippocampus in the temporal lobe develop early, likely supporting the establishment of event memories in early infancy (Bauer, 2009; Nelson, 2006; Seress & Abraham, 2008). Other areas of the hippocampus receive information from distributed brain regions, including cortical regions. They are therefore responsible for the consolidation of information for storage, and show a more protracted developmental time course. The prefrontal cortex, which has been implicated in working memory and associating and encoding to-be-remembered information, also shows protracted development well into adolescence (Benes, 2001). Together, these prolonged periods of development are likely responsible for the course of development in memory behaviour (Bauer, Larkina, & Deocampo, 2011).

Infantile amnesia The inability to remember experiences from the first two or three years of life.

For Thought and Discussion

What is your first memory? How old were you? How might you explain your infantile amnesia?

The studies just discussed are relevant to one of the classic puzzles in child psychology: the phenomenon of **infantile amnesia**, or the inability to remember experiences from the first two or three years of life. The absence of long-term memories from infancy would be easy to explain if infants did not form long-term memories; as we have just seen, however, this is not the case. Why, then, have all such memories disappeared by later childhood? There is little consensus on what the correct explanation may be, beyond a general agreement that several factors probably contribute (Hayne, 2004; Howe, 2000; Newcombe et al., 2000). Among the contributors that have been proposed are immaturity of parts of the brain; qualitative differences between early and later memory systems (for example, non-verbal versus verbal); quantitative changes in basic memory processes of encoding, retention, and retrieval; the lack of a sense of self in infancy; and the absence of a social system within which to share and rehearse memories.

LEARNING OBJECTIVE 9.2

Explain the information-processing model of memory, and trace developmental changes in the kinds of memory.

1. What is the memory store model in the information-processing approach?
2. What kinds of memory are present in infancy and how are they different?
3. How do researchers study recognition and recall memory in infants and young children?
4. How does memory change as children develop?

Learning Objective 9.3

Describe how memory develops in older children and the tools that contribute to this development of memory.

MEMORY IN OLDER CHILDREN

Beyond infancy, most studies of how children remember have concentrated on various forms of recall. The most general change in this type of memory is an obvious one: older children remember better than younger children. This fact was undoubtedly apparent to parents and teachers long before there was research to verify it. It has also long been apparent to test makers. All the IQ tests described in Chapter 10 include memory as one of their components. On average, the older the child, the better the performance on such memory measures.

Developmental improvements in memory are of considerable practical importance because they influence what parents and teachers expect of children and how they treat children. A 10-year-old can be entrusted with a string of verbal instructions that would overtax the memory of a 4-year-old. Such improvements are also of theoretical interest. How can we explain the fact that older children remember better than younger ones? Several kinds of explanation have been offered, and each seems to capture part of the basis for developmental change. Here, we consider three possible contributors to the developmental improvement in memory: greater use of mnemonic strategies, greater knowledge about memory, and more powerful cognitive structures.

THE ROLE OF STRATEGIES

Imagine you are confronted with the following task. A list of words, such as that in Table 9.2, is presented to you at the rate of one every five seconds. There is a 30-second delay following the last word, and you must then recall as many of the words as possible. How might you proceed?

Adults faced with such a task are likely to do any of a variety of things to help themselves remember. They may say the words over and over again as the list is presented and during the delay period. They may seek to make the list more memorable by grouping the words into categories—noting, for example, that several of the items name foods and several others name animals. Or they may attempt to create associations among the words by imagining a scenario in which several of the words are linked—for example, a mental image of a cow eating a banana while riding a bicycle.

The approaches just sketched are examples of **mnemonic strategies**. A mnemonic strategy is any technique that people use in an attempt to remember something. The examples just given correspond, in fact, to three of the most often studied strategies in research on memory: *rehearsal* of the items to be recalled (the saying-over-and-over technique), *organization* of the items into conceptual categories (grouping into foods, animals, and so on), and *elaboration* of the items by linkage in some more general image or story (the picture of the cow on the bicycle).

Mnemonic strategies Techniques (such as rehearsal or organization) that people use in an attempt to remember something.

For Thought and Discussion

What mnemonic strategies do you find most effective for you in your studies? How do those strategies work?

TABLE 9.2 ITEMS TO BE RECALLED ON A SHORT-TERM MEMORY TEST

Cow	Truck
Tree	Hat
Banana	Bear
Bicycle	Apple
Dog	Flag
Orange	Horse

DEVELOPMENTAL CHANGES IN STRATEGY USE An increase in the tendency to use strategies is one important source of the improvements in memory that come with age. Dozens of studies have demonstrated that older children are more likely than younger children to generate and employ mnemonic strategies (Bjorklund, Dukes, & Brown, 2009; Murphy, McKone, & Slee, 2003). This finding holds for the three strategies just mentioned: rehearsal (Guttentag, Ornstein, & Siemens, 1987), organization (Hasselhorn, 1992), and elaboration (Kee & Guttentag, 1994). It also holds for other mnemonic strategies that develop across childhood—for example, the ability to direct one's attention and effort in optimal ways, such as by attending to central rather than irrelevant information (Miller, 1990) or by concentrating on difficult rather than easy items, as Akira Kobasigawa, of the University of Windsor, and his collaborators point out (Dufresne & Kobasigawa, 1989).

Do strategies work? In general, the answer is yes. Children who use strategies show better recall than children who do not. Children do not always benefit from their initial attempts to employ a strategy, perhaps because executing a new strategy places too great a demand on their limited information-processing resources (Woody-Dorning & Miller, 2001). This failure of a recently developed strategy to facilitate recall is labelled a **utilization deficiency** (Miller, 2000; Schwenck, Bjorklund, & Schneider, 2007). Usually, however, even young children derive some benefit from the use of strategies; their main problem is simply that they do not generate strategies in the first place. Before about age 5 or 6, it apparently simply does not occur to children that it makes sense to do something to help themselves remember. This failure to generate strategies spontaneously, even though the child is capable of executing and benefiting from a strategy, is referred to as a **production deficiency** (Flavell, 1970; Waters, 2000).

Utilization deficiency The failure of a recently developed mnemonic strategy to facilitate recall.

Production deficiency The failure to spontaneously generate a mnemonic strategy.

Strategies increase not only in frequency but also in complexity, as children get older. Rehearsal is a relatively simple strategy and is, in fact, one of the first to emerge, typically appearing at about age 6 or 7. Organization appears somewhat later, and elaboration later still. There are also developmental changes in complexity within a particular strategy. Younger children's rehearsal efforts, for example, tend to be limited to naming each item as it appears. Older children are more likely to repeat larger chunks of the list each time ("cow," "cow-tree," "cow-tree-banana," and so on) (Ornstein, Naus, & Liberty, 1975). In general, older children can generate more complex strategies than younger children, they are better able to match a particular strategy to a particular task, and they are more skilled at executing their strategies—all of which contributes to their superior memory performance.

We noted that on many memory tasks, children younger than 5 or 6 years of age do not display strategies. Does this mean that the young child is totally incapable of generating a mnemonic strategy? Not at all. If the task is sufficiently simplified, even quite young children may use rudimentary strategies. In one study, 3-year-olds played a game in which they had to keep track of a toy dog that had been hidden under one of several cups. During the delay between hiding and retrieval, many of the children sat with their eyes glued to the critical cup and a finger planted firmly on it (Wellman, Ritter, & Flavell, 1975). These are simple strategies, but they *are* strategies, and they work for even young children. Children who produced such strategies showed better recall than children who did not. Other studies using a similar hide-and-seek procedure have demonstrated that children as young as 18 to 24 months can produce and benefit from simple strategies (Wellman, 1988).

FIGURE 9.5

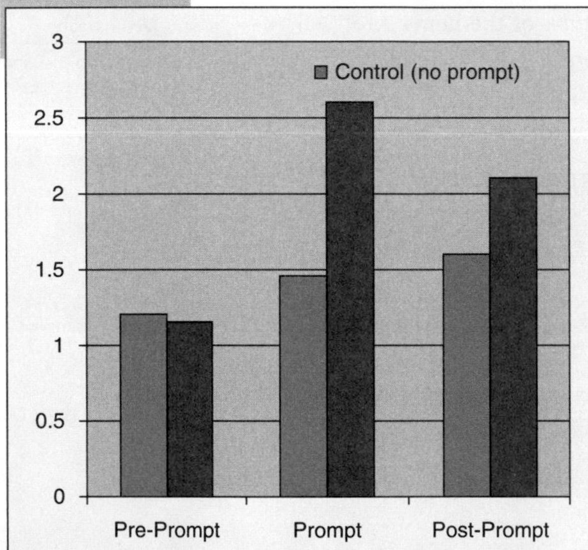

The number of strategies used by children to recall picture items across three phases (Pre-Prompt, during the Prompt, and Post-Prompt) of a sort–recall task, depending on whether or not they received a prompt to sort the pictures. Those who received a prompt to sort used more strategies and exhibited better recall than those who did not receive a prompt. *From "Developmental and individual differences in young children's use and maintenance of a selective memory strategy" by C. Schwenck, D.F. Bjorklund, and W. Schneider, 2009,* Developmental Psychology, *45, 1041. Copyright © 2009 by American Psychological Association.*

Furthermore, younger children can also exhibit strategy use if they are explicitly taught a simple strategy. In a recent study, 4-year-olds played a different type of game in which they were given a set of picture cards, some of which belonged to a particular category such as items for being sick (thermometer, bandage, pills, etc.). The children then needed to sort and/or cluster the items appropriately and subsequently recall the items (Schwenck, Bjorklund, & Schneider, 2009). Children who were explicitly prompted to sort the picture items showed better recall than children who were not, and they were more likely to sort or cluster the items (see Figure 9.5). The general conclusion to be drawn from such research should sound familiar from the discussion of preschoolers' strengths in Chapter 8. Young children are by no means as competent as older children—in memory or in logical reasoning. When tested in simple and familiar contexts or given explicit instruction, however, they can sometimes show surprising abilities.

Just as strategies may begin to develop earlier than experts once thought, so they may continue to develop beyond the grade-school years that have been the focus of most memory research. Complex mnemonic strategies continue to be refined well into adolescence and even adulthood (Pressley, Levin, & Bryant, 1983). Of particular interest to both researchers and teachers have been the various **study strategies** that students develop to cope with school material. Study strategies include specific techniques, such as note-taking and outlining. They also include more general methods, such as allocation of study time to important or not-yet-mastered material, and self-testing to determine what has been learned and what needs to be studied further.

Study strategies Mnemonic strategies (such as outlining and note-taking) that students use in an attempt to remember school material.

As with strategies in general, study strategies improve with age. As children develop, the frequency with which they use such techniques increases, as does the complexity of the strategies they generate. And, again, as with strategies in general, study strategies are beneficial. Research reveals a clear relation between the use of appropriate study techniques and the quality of the child's learning (Paris & Oka, 1986; Pressley, Forrest-Pressley, & Elliot-Faust, 1988).

Clearly, the work on study strategies is not just of scientific interest; it also speaks to important applied questions concerning the bases for children's academic performance. If we can identify and help children who have poor study strategies, then perhaps we can improve their chances of success in school. Such has proven to be the case. A number of intervention programs have verified the value of explicitly teaching study skills to children (Brown & Campione, 1990; Pressley et al., 1988).

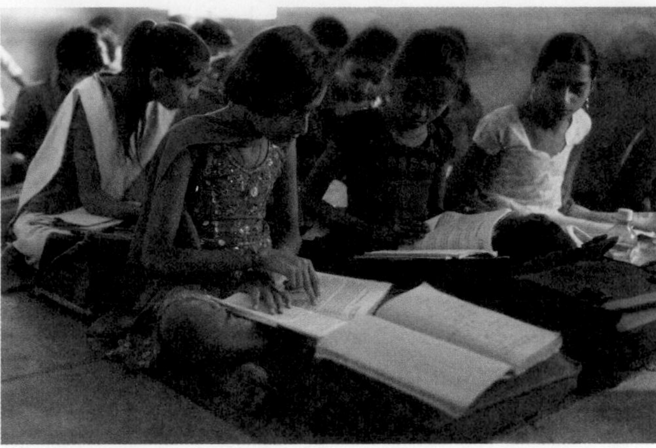

Mnemonic strategies are not limited to laboratory settings. Study strategies can help to ensure that important material is remembered and improve the quality of the student's learning. (© *Tim Graham/Corbis*)

VARIABILITY IN STRATEGY USE Although new and more complex strategies emerge with development, this does not mean that earlier strategies necessarily disappear. One interesting finding from recent memory research concerns the surprising variability in children's strategy use. Rather than employ a single preferred strategy, many children try out and combine several different approaches, sometimes generating as many as three or four strategies within even a single trial (Coyle, 2001; Coyle & Bjorklund, 1997). A particular child, for example, might not only rehearse the items to be remembered, but also name the categories to which they belong, and perhaps sort them into groups as well. In fact, children who use more than one strategy in their recall outperform children who use a single strategy (Schneider et al., 2009).

Why are children so variable in their approach to memory tasks? It has been argued that such variability is adaptive in that it provides experience from which children can eventually determine the optimal strategy for a particular task from the many possible strategies that children initially explore (Siegler & Svetina, 2006). Research on strategies illustrates one important theme of the information-processing approach (Siegler, 1998). The child's—and, for that matter, the adult's—information-processing capacities are always limited. Only a limited amount of information can fit in short-term memory, for example, and this information typically can be held only briefly. If new information can be rehearsed, however, its lifetime can be extended considerably. If the child can think in terms of categories and not merely in terms of individual items, then much more can be retained. Much of development consists of the creation of techniques to overcome information-processing limitations and thereby increase the power of the cognitive system (Siegler & Svetina, 2006). Mnemonic strategies are a prime example of such techniques.

THE ROLE OF METAMEMORY

Although strategies are an important source of developmental improvements in memory, they are not the only contributor. What children know about memory also changes with age, and these changes in knowledge contribute to changes in memory (DeMarie & Ferron, 2003).

Metamemory refers to knowledge about memory. It includes knowledge about memory in general—for example, the fact that recognition tasks are easier than recall tasks, or that a short list of items is easier to memorize than a long list. It also includes knowledge about one's own memory—for example, the ability to judge whether one has studied long enough to do well on an exam.

Metamemory Knowledge about memory.

DEVELOPMENTAL CHANGES IN METAMEMORY Psychologists have been interested in metamemory for two general reasons. First, it is an important outcome of the child's cognitive development. Traditionally, research on cognitive development has concentrated on the child's understanding of external stimuli and events—in some cases physical stimuli (as in Piaget's conservation tasks), and in some cases social ones (as in studies of interpersonal understanding). Children's thinking is not limited to external stimuli, however; it also encompasses the internal, mental world. Flavell (1971) was among the first child psychologists to focus explicitly on "thinking about thinking," and he coined the term metacognition to refer to thoughts that have mental or psychological phenomena as their target. With *metamemory*, the focus is on thoughts about memory. So, metamemory includes "knowledge and beliefs about the capacities, functioning, limitations and development of one's own memory and the human memory system in general" (Pierce & Lange, 2000).

Children's thinking about memory changes in a variety of ways as they develop. Here, we note just a few examples. A basic question is whether the child realizes that there is such a thing as memory. Even young children show some such knowledge. They may behave differently, for example, when told to remember something than when told simply to look, thus demonstrating some awareness that remembering may require special cognitive activities (Baker-Ward, Ornstein, & Holden, 1984). They also have some understanding of the relative difficulty of different memory tasks. By age 5 or 6, most children realize that familiar items are easier to remember than unfamiliar ones (Kreutzer, Leonard, & Flavell, 1975), that short lists are easier to learn than long ones (Wellman, 1977), that recognition is easier than recall (Speer & Flavell, 1979), and that forgetting becomes more likely over time (Lyon & Flavell, 1993).

For Thought and Discussion

What other aspects of cognitive development might help account for changes in children's metacognitive awareness as they age?

In other respects, however, young children's metamemory is limited. They do not always behave differently when faced with an explicit request to remember (Appel et al., 1972). They do not yet understand many phenomena of memory, such as the fact that related items are easier to recall than unrelated ones (Kreutzer et al., 1975), or that remembering the gist of a story is easier than remembering the exact words (Kurtz & Borkowski, 1987). In addition, their assessment of their own mnemonic abilities is far too optimistic. In one study, for example, over half of the preschool and kindergarten participants predicted that they would be able to recall all 10 items from a list, a performance that no child in fact came close to achieving (Flavell, Friedrichs, & Hoyt, 1970). Furthermore, young children do not adjust their expectations readily in response to feedback; even after recalling only two or three items on one trial, they continue to assert that they will get all 10 on the next attempt (Yussen & Levy, 1975). Older children are both more modest and more realistic in assessing their own memories (Schneider & Pressley, 1997).

EFFECTS OF METAMEMORY ON MEMORY PERFORMANCE The second general reason for interest in metamemory concerns its possible contribution to developmental changes in memory performance. Older children know more about memory than do younger children; older children also remember better than do younger children. It is easy to see how these two facts might be related. Knowledge of the demands of different sorts of memory tasks should help the child select the best strategy for remembering. Knowledge of one's own memory should be important in deciding such things as how to allocate attention and what material to study further.

Obvious though the knowledge–behaviour relationship seems, demonstrating it empirically has proven surprisingly difficult. Many early studies that assessed both metamemory and memory performance (usually focusing on the child's use of strategies) reported only modest correlations at best between the two (Cavanaugh & Perlmutter, 1982). Though a more recent analysis of over 60 studies and 7,000 children found a much stronger relation with a correlation of .41 between metamemory and memory performance (Schneider & Pressley, 1997), the strength of this relation was affected by many factors, including the type and difficulty of the task and the age of the children. Thus, the knowledge that children can demonstrate about memory does not always relate clearly to how they perform on memory tasks. The following quotation, taken from one of the first metamemory studies, suggests a possible reason for this discrepancy. Here, a little girl describes a wonderfully complex procedure for memorizing phone numbers (her metaknowledge), but then suggests at the end that her actual behaviour might be quite different.

> Say the number is 633–8854. Then what I'd do is say that my number is 633, so I won't have to remember that, really. And then I would think now I've got to remember 88. Now I'm 8 years

> old, so I can remember, say my age two times. Then I say how old my brother is, and how old he was last year. And that's how I'd usually remember that phone number. [Is that how you would most often remember a phone number?] Well, usually I write it down. (Kreutzer et al., 1975, p. 11)

Despite the difficulty in establishing knowledge–behaviour links, most researchers remain convinced that the growth of metamemory is one source of developmental improvement in memory. It is simply hard to believe that what children know does not exert an important influence on how they behave. Indeed, more recent studies of the issue have been more successful than earlier work at identifying relations between knowledge and behaviour (Schneider, 1999). One promising approach has been to train children in various forms of metamemory and then look for possible effects on subsequent memory performance (Ghatala et al., 1985; Pressley, Borkowski, & O'Sullivan, 1985). Such training does in fact improve memory.

Like the work on mnemonic strategies, research on this topic has applied as well as theoretical implications. For example, it may prove possible to help children with memory problems by teaching them about memory itself. Indeed, some of the most successful of the strategy training programs discussed earlier included instruction in metamemory. Apparently, children are most likely to benefit from memory training if they learn not only what to do, but also why to do it.

The studies of metamemory illustrate a second general theme of the information-processing approach. We have stressed the information-processing theorist's emphasis on the many different processes that go into intelligent behaviour. These processes do not occur in isolation, however, nor do they occur without direction. The child must somehow select and coordinate specific cognitive activities, and a full model of intelligence must explain how this selection and coordination occur. The case of mnemonic strategies provides a good illustration. A strategy, such as rehearsal, does not simply happen. Rather, other cognitive processes must decide that rehearsal is an appropriate strategy, monitor its execution, and evaluate its success. In short, some sort of "executive" must control the more specific forms of information processing. Work on metamemory is directed toward one sort of executive control—children's knowledge of memory as a determinant of the ways in which they go about remembering.

THE ROLE OF KNOWLEDGE

Memory and knowledge are in fact closely related. What we know about a topic is an important determinant of how well we learn and remember information about that topic (Chi, Glaser, & Farr, 1988; Ornstein et al., 2006; Schneider & Bjorklund, 1998). Older children generally know more about all sorts of things than do younger children; thus, older children generally remember better than do younger children.

Studies that have attempted to specify the ways in which knowledge affects memory have taken a variety of directions. Here, we discuss such research under two headings: constructive memory and expertise.

CONSTRUCTIVE MEMORY The notion of constructive memory is most easily introduced through example. Table 9.3 provides an example used in research with grade-school children. The children were first read the story and then asked the eight questions listed beneath it.

Any reader is likely to spot a difference between the first four questions and the last four. The first four tap verbatim memory for information that was given directly in the story. The last four, however, concern information that was never explicitly provided. We are never told, for example, that Linda likes to take care of animals. Yet any adult reader of the story knows that she does. So, it turns out, do most young children.

The ability to answer questions 5 through 8 is a function of constructive memory. Constructive memory refers to the ways in which people's general knowledge system interprets the information they take in and thus affects what they remember. The basic idea is that we do not simply record

TABLE 9.3 STORY USED IN STUDY OF CONSTRUCTIVE MEMORY WITH CHILDREN

Linda was playing with her new doll in front of her big red house. Suddenly, she heard a strange sound coming from under the porch. It was the flapping of wings. Linda wanted to help so much, but she did not know what to do. She ran inside the house and grabbed a shoe box from the closet. Then Linda looked inside her desk until she found eight sheets of yellow paper. She cut the paper into little pieces and put them in the bottom of the box. Linda gently picked up the helpless creature and took it with her. Her teacher knew what to do.

1. Was Linda's doll new?
2. Did Linda grab a match box?
3. Was the strange sound coming from under the porch?
4. Was Linda playing behind her house?
5. Did Linda like to take care of animals?
6. Did Linda take what she found to the police station?
7. Did Linda find a frog?
8. Did Linda use a pair of scissors?

Source: From "Integration and Inference in Children's Comprehension and Memory" by S. G. Paris, 1975. In F. Restle, R. Shiffrin, J. Castellan, H. Lindman, and D. Pisoni (Eds.), *Cognitive Theory,* Vol. 1, Mahwah, NJ: Erlbaum, 233. Copyright © 1975 by Lawrence Erlbaum Associates. Reprinted by permission.

memories as a digital audio recorder or video camera would. Memory always involves acting on and integrating new experiences in light of what we already know—it always involves an attempt to *understand,* not just record. In our attempt to understand, we continually draw inferences and go beyond the information given. The eventual memory is therefore truly a construction, not merely a direct duplication of experience. This is why we, and the 6-year-old, can come away from the story in Table 9.3 knowing that Linda likes to take care of animals.

It seems clear that memory is constructive from early in life. At every age, children filter new experiences through their existing knowledge systems, and what they ultimately remember depends on how they interpret experiences. Constructive memory does change across childhood, however, and the changes are of two general sorts.

First, with increased age, memory becomes even more constructive, as children become increasingly active in processing information and increasingly likely to draw inferences that allow them to go beyond the literal input. The complexity of these inferences that children can draw increases as they get older and their cognitive abilities increase. In the injured-bird story, for example, even most 5-year-olds could answer questions 7 and 8. Questions 5 and 6, however, require a somewhat higher-order inference and hence were solved at a slightly later age. Furthermore, as children get older, there is also an increased likelihood that they will draw inferences when the content of a story or an event fades from memory.

Second, constructive memory can operate in a negative as well as a positive direction. When some new experience is too advanced for the child, the child's memory of the experience is likely to be simplified and perhaps even distorted. Other factors besides cognitive level can sometimes result in such "constructive" distortions. It has been shown, for example, that children's beliefs about gender differences may influence how they process information about males and females. Children who viewed pictures in which gender-stereotypical activities were reversed (e.g., a girl sawing and a boy playing with dolls) showed a tendency on a later memory test to "correct" these images, reporting, for example, that it was the boy who did the sawing (Martin & Halverson, 1983a). Similarly, children's beliefs about different ethnic groups can influence what they remember about members of those groups (Bigler & Liben, 1993), just as their stereotypes about old age can colour their memories of particular elderly individuals (Davidson, Cameron, & Jergovic, 1995).

The constructive nature of memory, then, is, as Ornstein and Haden (2001) put it, "a double-edged sword" (p. 204). In general, constructive memory is a positive force, helping us understand experience more adaptively. But in particular instances, constructive memory can distort and mislead. In *Application 9.1* we discuss one situation in which it may be essential to know how accurate children's memories are and how memories are constructed.

APPLICATION 9.1
CHILDREN'S EYEWITNESS TESTIMONY

According to the Canadian Incidence Study of Reported Child Abuse and Neglect (Trocmé, MacLaurin, Fallon, Daciuk, Billingsley, Tourigny, et al., 2001), 135,573 child maltreatment investigations were carried out in Canada in 1998. Of this number, 10 percent involved sexual abuse as the primary reason for investigation. In most instances of alleged abuse, the child witness is also the target of the abuse. In many, the child is the only witness.

Can the testimony of a young child be trusted? Should such testimony be admissible in court? As the figures just cited indicate, questions like these can be critically important to answer. They can also be very difficult to answer. Researchers who seek to study children's memory for abuse face some obvious challenges: experiences of abuse are typically highly traumatic; they may continue for extended periods of time; and they often involve the child as a participant and not merely as a bystander. Furthermore, what children say about abuse may involve more than simply what they remember. Complex social and emotional factors may be important, such as the child's guilt about being a participant or reluctance to implicate a parent or friend. Questioning by a parent or authority figure may lead the child to particular responses, especially if questioners believe that they already know the truth or if, as advocates within the court system, they have an interest in a particular outcome. All these characteristics make memory of abuse different from the kinds of memory that psychologists usually study—or that they *can* easily study in an ethically acceptable way.

Researchers have tried in various ways to discover or devise memory tests that bear some similarity to the abuse situation. Some have created experimental settings that reproduce some elements of the real-life situations of interest—for example, a Simon Says game in which child and experimenter touch parts of each other's bodies (White, Leichtman, & Ceci, 1997) or children's birthday parties in which the child is hugged and kissed (Bright-Paul & Jarrold, 2009). Others have focused on memory for naturally occurring traumatic experiences—for example, going to the dentist (Peters, 1991), receiving an injection (Goodman et al., 1991), or undergoing urinary catheterization (Quas et al., 1999). Still others have investigated children's long-term recall of highly traumatic, naturally occurring events that affected them directly, such as major hurricanes (Fivush, Sales, Goldberg, Bahrick, & Parker, 2004). Although such experiences can hardly equal the trauma of abuse, they do capture some of its characteristics.

In many studies, researchers have also attempted to simulate the types of questioning that suspected victims of abuse must undergo. A child may be questioned several times across a period of weeks, for example, or the interviewer may include some deliberately leading questions in an attempt to determine how suggestible the child is. Children may be told to "keep a secret" about what happened to them during the experimental session (Bottoms et al., 1990), or a police officer rather than research assistant may do the questioning (Tobey & Goodman, 1992).

Such studies suggest several conclusions about children as witnesses (Bjorklund, 2000b; Bottoms & Goodman, 1996; Ceci & Bruck, 1995, 1998; Eisen, Quas, & Goodman, 2002). First, research verifies that recall memory improves with age and that older children typically report more of their experiences than do younger children (Ornstein et al., 2006). The memories of 3-year-olds (the youngest age group tested in such research) are especially shaky. Second, as the delay between an event and questioning about it increases, the completeness and accuracy of recall decline; this is especially true for young children (Pipe & Salmon, 2009). In many real-life cases, there are delays, often substantial ones, before children are first questioned, and so this finding is a cause for concern. Such effects have been demonstrated by Carole Peterson of Memorial University of Newfoundland, who has shown effects on young children's memory recall by delaying interviews 1 or even 5 years (Peterson et al., 2005; Peterson & Parsons, 2005). Third, in at least some cases, young children are more suggestible than are older children or adults; that is, they are more likely to be influenced by leading questions from an adult authority figure. This finding indicates the need for caution in accepting the reports of young children who have undergone repeated and leading questioning, as is often true in investigations of suspected abuse.

On the other hand, in many studies, memory differences between younger and older children or between children and adults are not very great. Age differences, as well as memory inaccuracies in general, are most likely when specific questions are used; conversely, they are minimized by the use of free recall measures that allow children to say what happened in their own words. Furthermore, the memory problems that children do show are mainly errors of omission, rather than of commission; that is, they are more likely to fail to report certain details than they are to introduce false information. This finding suggests that any clearly spontaneous mentions of abuse by children should be taken very seriously.

Having offered these conclusions, we should add that there remains much controversy about exactly what the research shows and what the implications are for children's legal testimony. Fortunately, one point on which all researchers agree is that more study is necessary, and the topic of eyewitness memory is currently the focus of an extraordinarily active research effort. Among the topics being explored in this research is how best to question children to meet two goals: maximize the accuracy of testimony and minimize stress to the child (Goodman et al., 1992; Lamb & Poole, 1998; Ornstein et al., 2006; Peterson & Parsons, 2005; Poole & Lindsay, 2002). Having to provide testimony can add to the trauma of an already traumatic situation. It is therefore important to devise procedures that protect the child from further harm.

FIGURE 9.6

Meaningful and random configurations of chess pieces. Because they can make use of their knowledge of chess, chess players show better memory of the left-side array than the right-side one. *From "Chess Expertise and Memory for Chess Positions in Children and Adults" by W. Schneider, H. Gruber, A. Gold, and K. Opwis, 1993, Journal of Experimental Child Psychology, 56, 335. Copyright © 1993 by Academic Press. Reprinted by permission.*

EXPERTISE Like constructive memory, expertise is easiest to introduce through examples. Imagine that you viewed each of the arrays pictured in Figure 9.6 for 10 seconds and then attempted to reproduce as much of each configuration as you could remember. If you do not play chess, chances are that you would find the two arrays equally difficult to recall; both, after all, contain the same number and the same variety of stimuli. If you are a chess player, however, the array on the left would almost certainly be easier to remember. It would be easier because the pieces are in positions that might actually occur in a game, whereas those in the array on the right are randomly arranged. You could therefore draw on your knowledge of chess as you took in the information, stored it in memory, and retrieved it during reproduction.

As you may have guessed, the kinds of results just sketched are not purely hypothetical; such outcomes have emerged in a number of research projects. The examples pictured in Figure 9.6 are from a study by Schneider and associates (1993). This study, along with several similar studies, provides support for each of the expectations just discussed: expert chess players show better memory for real chess positions than for random ones; chess experts remember chess configurations better than do chess novices; and the expert–novice differences are especially marked when real positions are the target. Researchers interested in the role of knowledge in developmental change, therefore, often compare experts and novices (e.g., Chase & Simon, 1973; McPherson & Thomas, 1989; Schneider, Gruber, Gold, & Opwis, 1993).

Expertise Organized factual knowledge with respect to some content domain.

The Schneider and colleagues study demonstrates the effects of expertise on memory. The term **expertise** (also sometimes called *content knowledge* or the *knowledge base*) refers to organized factual knowledge about some content domain; that is, what we know about some subject. Someone's expertise may be high with regard to chess or dinosaurs or birds, but low when the topic turns to baseball or cooking or physics. When expertise is high, then memory also tends to be high. Variations in expertise contribute to variations in memory within individuals. Chess experts, for example, show better memory of chess positions and other chess-related information than they do of most other topics. Variations in expertise also contribute to differences in memory across individuals. Thus, chess experts remember more about chess than do chess novices, just as experts in baseball or cooking or physics remember more about their specialty than do most people. Finally, variations in expertise contribute to the aspect of memory that is our main concern here: developmental changes in memory across the span of childhood. Older children possess more expertise for most topics than do younger children, and this greater expertise is one reason they remember more (Murphy, McKone & Slee, 2003).

Expertise can affect memory in several ways. One way is through the form in which the knowledge is represented. In the case of chess, for example, experts store larger and more complex patterns of possible positions (approximately 50,000 board patterns) than do non-experts (only about 1,000 board patterns), and this rich organizational structure helps them quickly make sense of positions that actually arise (Bedard & Chi, 1992). It is likely that the rich organizational structure of experts is due to their representations being focused on those features that differentiate between examples of some content domain, such as chess board patterns, than on those features that make those examples similar (Blair & Sommerville, 2009). Another way is through effects on other contributors to memory, such as mnemonic strategies. Research has shown that children use strategies most effectively in content areas in which they are especially knowledgeable (Bjorklund, Muir-Broaddus, & Schneider 1990). Finally, perhaps the most general effect of expertise is on speed of processing. When knowledge about some domain is high, information relevant to that domain can be taken in and processed more rapidly, thus freeing cognitive resources for other activities, such as generating strategies (Bjorklund & Schneider, 1996).

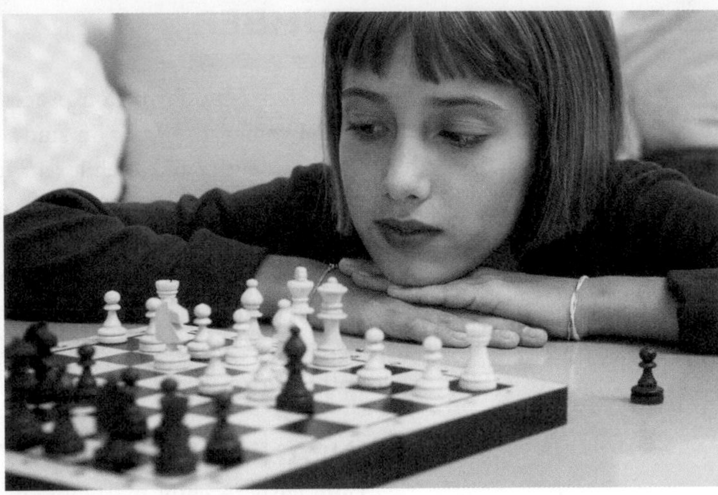

Knowledge about a particular content domain affects the ease with which information is processed and remembered. In some cases, children may possess greater expertise than adults. (© *Franziska Tetzner/Corbis*)

An additional finding from the Schneider and colleagues (1993) study makes one more important point about expertise. In addition to the comparison of experts and novices, the study included an age dimension. Half the chess experts were adults and half were 10- to 13-year-old children; similarly, half the novices were adults and half were children. The design of the study (patterned after an earlier, classic study by Chi, 1978) therefore allowed the researchers to look separately at the effects of age and expertise, two factors that are usually closely linked and thus hard to pull apart. On memory tasks that did not involve chess, the adults, not surprisingly, demonstrated better memory than the children. On the memory-for-chess measure, however, expertise, not age, proved critical. Thus, the 10-year-old experts outshone the adult novices in reproducing chess positions—despite the fact that the adults, in general, had greater memory spans.

The point that this study makes is that, in at least some instances, it is expertise, and not other factors associated with age, that is critical to memory. Other researchers have also found that young participants can equal or even outperform older ones when the content is something they know well. Among the content areas for which child superiority has been demonstrated are dinosaurs (Chi & Koeske, 1983), cartoon figures (Lindberg, 1980), baseball (Recht & Leslie, 1988), and soccer (Schneider, Korkel, & Weinert, 1987).

The work on expertise brings us to another general theme of the information-processing approach. The role of factual knowledge is heavily stressed in contemporary information-processing accounts of not only memory, but also reasoning and problem solving (DeLoache, Miller, & Pierroutsakos, 1998; Hmelo-Silver & Pfeffer, 2004). The more the children already know, the more they will understand any new experience. The more they understand, the more they will remember. And the more they understand and remember, the more likely they are to reason and to solve problems in effective and adaptive ways.

For Thought and Discussion

Are you an expert in something? What makes you an expert, and how did you become one?

LEARNING OBJECTIVE 9.3

Describe how memory develops in older children and the tools that contribute to this development of memory.

1. What are mnemonic strategies, and how do they contribute to memory development in children?
2. What is metacognition, and how does this ability contribute to memory development?
3. What does research on novices and experts tell us about the role of knowledge in cognitive development?

Learning Objective 9.4

Describe the development in the understanding of number from infancy to school age.

NUMBER

We noted that information-processing studies of memory often have applied value as well as theoretical value—the work on study strategies in school is a clear example. The same point applies to research directed to children's understanding of number. Making sense of numbers is a task to which children (and teachers) devote hundreds of hours across many years in school. Research that informs us about the processes of children's mathematical thinking can help make these experiences happier ones for both teacher and child.

One point that relevant research makes is that children's understanding of number starts well before age 5 or 6. We therefore begin with developments that precede the first exposure to formal arithmetic in school, focusing first on infancy and then on the preschool period.

INFANTS' RESPONSE TO NUMBER

Until fairly recently, most child psychologists would have dismissed the idea that infants are at all sensitive to number. This is no longer the case. Although there are, as we will see, disputes with regard to the extent of infant numerical competence, it now seems clear that some ability to respond to number is present from early in life.

What sorts of sensitivity to number might infants show? One basic question concerns the ability to discriminate between sets of different numerical size. A number of investigators have used the habituation–dishabituation methodology to probe for early ability to discriminate set sizes (Brannon, Abbott, & Lutz, 2004; Starkey & Cooper, 1980; Trehub, Thorpe, & Cohen, 1991; Xu & Arriaga, 2007). In these studies, the infant is first repeatedly shown collections of a particular size (say, three objects) until attention drops off. A new set size (say, four objects) is then presented. Do infants notice the change? As long as the set sizes are small, as in the example, babies as young as 3 months apparently do. In fact, Daniel Keating, of the University of Toronto, and his collaborator (Antell & Keating, 1983), report successful discrimination of two versus three by newborns!

That infants can discriminate differences in set size is certainly impressive. Even more impressive is the suggestion that babies may be capable of very simple forms of arithmetic. Evidence derives from an extension of the Baillargeon possible event–impossible event procedure. In this case, however, the impossible event involves a violation of the laws of arithmetic. Figure 9.7 shows some examples—the top part shows a violation of the principles of addition; the bottom part shows a violation of subtraction.

Wynn (1992, 1995, 1998) reported that 5-month-old infants who witness such events react as we would expect them to react if they understood the arithmetical operations involved; that is, they show little dishabituation to the possible events, but a marked recovery of interest when the rules of addition or subtraction are apparently violated. This outcome is certainly compatible with the hypothesis of early arithmetical competence; unfortunately, it does not definitively establish it. As some thought about Figure 9.7 should reveal, the impossible events in these studies encompass not only arithmetical impossibilities, but also physical impossibilities—an object either magically disappears (in the addition condition) or magically appears (in the subtraction condition). It is possible, therefore, that the infants' increase in attention reflects their knowledge about objects, rather than anything specific about numbers (Haith & Benson, 1998).

Other researchers have suggested that Wynn's findings, as well as additional demonstrations of infant numerical discriminations, might be due to simple perceptual discriminations of other factors that correlate with quantity or number, such as surface area and object perimeter length (Clearfield & Mix, 2001; Feigenson, Carey, & Spelke, 2002; Newcombe, 2002). Clearfield (2004), for example, even found that in a task that required habituation to the number of times that a puppet jumped, infants were more likely to base their discriminations on the amount of jump time than the number of jumps. In her study, after being habituated to either two or three 1-sec jumps,

FIGURE 9.7

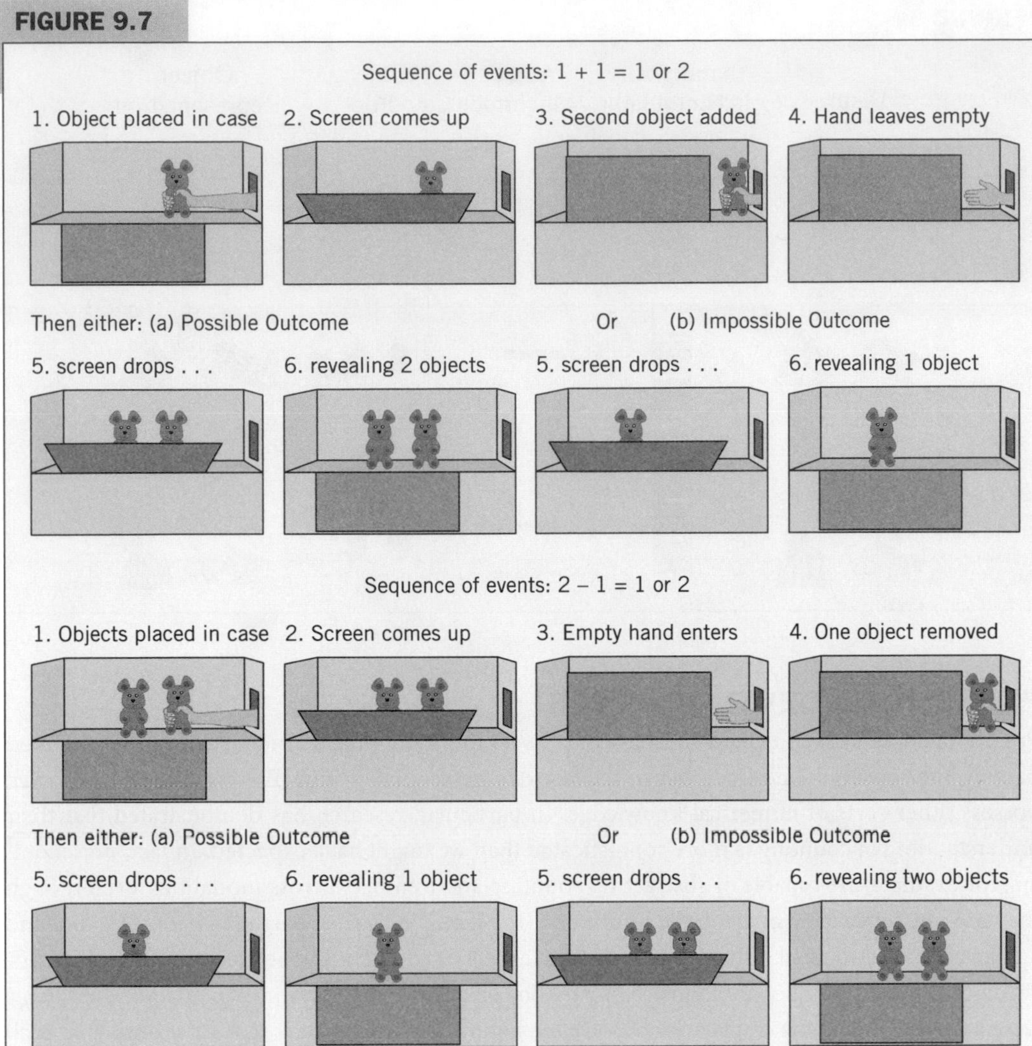

Possible and impossible outcomes in Wynn's study of infants' arithmetical competence. *From "Addition and Subtraction by Human Infants" in* Nature *(1992) Figure 1, 749. Reprinted by permission from* Nature*. Copyright © 1992 Nature Publishing Group/Macmillan Publishing Ltd.*

infants looked longer at a display with the familiar number of jumps but a novel jump time (e.g., two 1-1/2-sec jumps if habituated to two 1-sec jumps) than at a display with a novel number of jumps but with a familiar jump time (e.g., three 2/3 sec jumps if habituated to two 1 sec jumps). Pulling apart whether infants are discriminating on the basis of number or some other perceptual characteristic is a challenging task, and efforts therefore continue to specify exactly what, if anything, babies know about arithmetic (Cohen & Marks, 2002; Mix, Huttenlocher, & Levine, 2002; Cordes & Brannon, 2008).

Gallistel and Gelman (1992) have proposed that the apparent quantitative or number skills in infants are due to the existence of a preverbal counting mechanism that represents quantities. This counting mechanism could function in one of two ways (see Figure 9.8). First, there might be a numerosity accumulator that accumulates the representations of three or four items (whatever they are). The second way is a mechanism that represents and marks objects; the markers can then be counted and thereby give number incidentally. Support for such a counting of object markers comes from research by Lana Trick of the University of Guelph, who has demonstrated development in the capacity to track and enumerate multiple items. She notes increases in the number of items that can be marked and tracked with increases in age (Trick, Audet, & Dales, 2003; Trick, Jaspers-Fayer, & Sethi, 2005). Interestingly, Trick's research has identified that short-term memory can mark around three to four items in early development, consistent with the preverbal counting mechanism of Gallistel and Gelman.

FIGURE 9.8

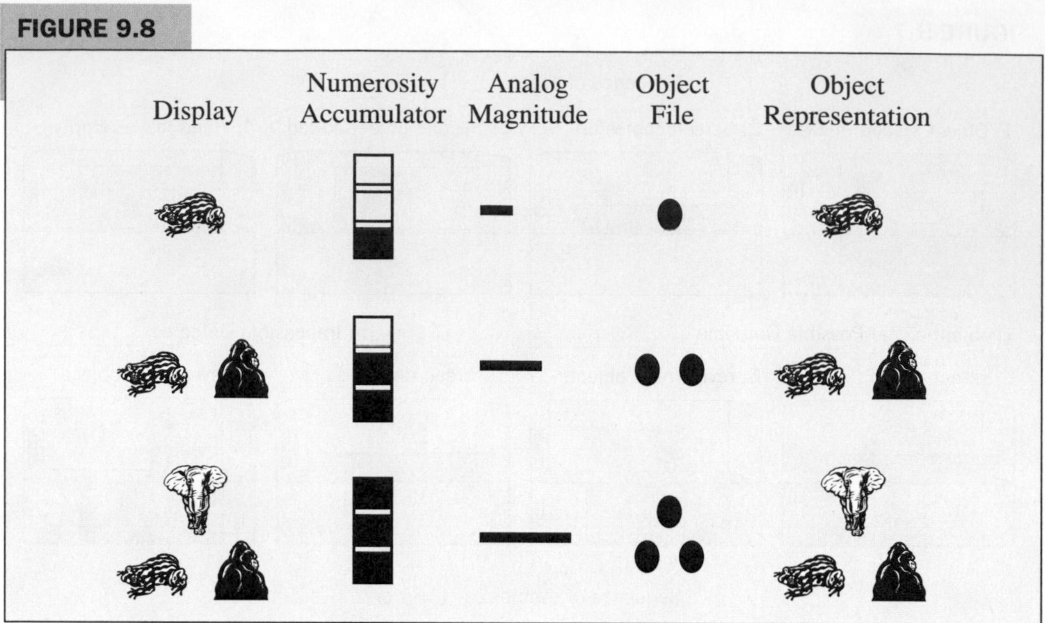

Representations of the ways that a counting mechanism might function. The numerosity accumulator exactly represents the number of objects. The object file marks each object in short-term memory and these markers can then be counted. *From D. C. Geary, "Development of mathematical understanding," 2006. In D. Kuhn and R. S. Siegler (Eds.),* Handbook of Child Psychology, *6th edition, Volume 2: Cognition perception, and language (p. 783). Hoboken, NJ: John Wiley & Sons.*

PRESCHOOL DEVELOPMENTS

Preschoolers, as we saw in Chapter 8, have only a very limited appreciation for the aspect of number: namely, the conservation of number in the face of a perceptual change. Preschoolers do, however, possess other sorts of numerical knowledge. In particular, research has demonstrated that their understanding of counting is more sophisticated than we might have expected. In fact, preschoolers, for example, are capable of abstracting counting and numbers across modalities, even though they are not yet capable of symbolic arithmetic (for example, 3 + 5). Barth, La Mont, Lipton, and Spelke (2005) conducted a study in which preschoolers had to choose between displays that consisted of different numbers of items (comparison) or between displays in which additional items were added to one of the displays (addition); see Figure 9.9. The displays to be discriminated each consisted of items from the same modality (i.e., visual dots) or different modalities (i.e., visual dots versus beeps) to test their ability to abstract their numerical representations. Preschoolers were as accurate with their numerical discriminations in addition tasks as they were in comparison tasks, regardless of the modalities in which the numerical information was conveyed. Thus, even preschoolers, who are not yet able to master symbolic arithmetic, are capable of abstracting counting across differences between the items being counted.

Although counting is an automatic activity for most adults, accurate counting in fact depends on an appreciation of a number of underlying rules or principles. In addition to the abstraction of counting illustrated in our discussion above, Rochel Gelman and associates (Gelman, 1982, 1991; Gelman & Gallistel, 1978) have identified four other principles that a counting system must honour (see Table 9.4). As you can see, the first three principles deal with how to count, the fourth deals with what can be counted, and the fifth is a combination of the features of the first four.

Research by Gelman and colleagues indicates that children as young as 3 or 4 years have some understanding of these principles. Of course, preschoolers are unlikely to be able to verbalize the principles explicitly. But when asked to carry out counting tasks, they generally act in ways that accord with the principles (for example, applying just one number name to each item), and they also are able to spot violations of the principles when they watch others count. Young children, it is true, do not always follow the principles perfectly, and their specific ways of applying them may differ from those of adults (e.g., the 3-year-old who demonstrates the stable-order principle by always counting, "1, 2, 6"). Nevertheless, both Gelman's work and that of other researchers (e.g., Barth, La Mont, Lipton, & Spelke, 2006; Sophian, 1995b, 1998) indicate that counting is a systematic, rule-governed behaviour from early in life. It is also a frequent activity—something that children the world around seem to do naturally, often for the pure pleasure of counting.

FIGURE 9.9

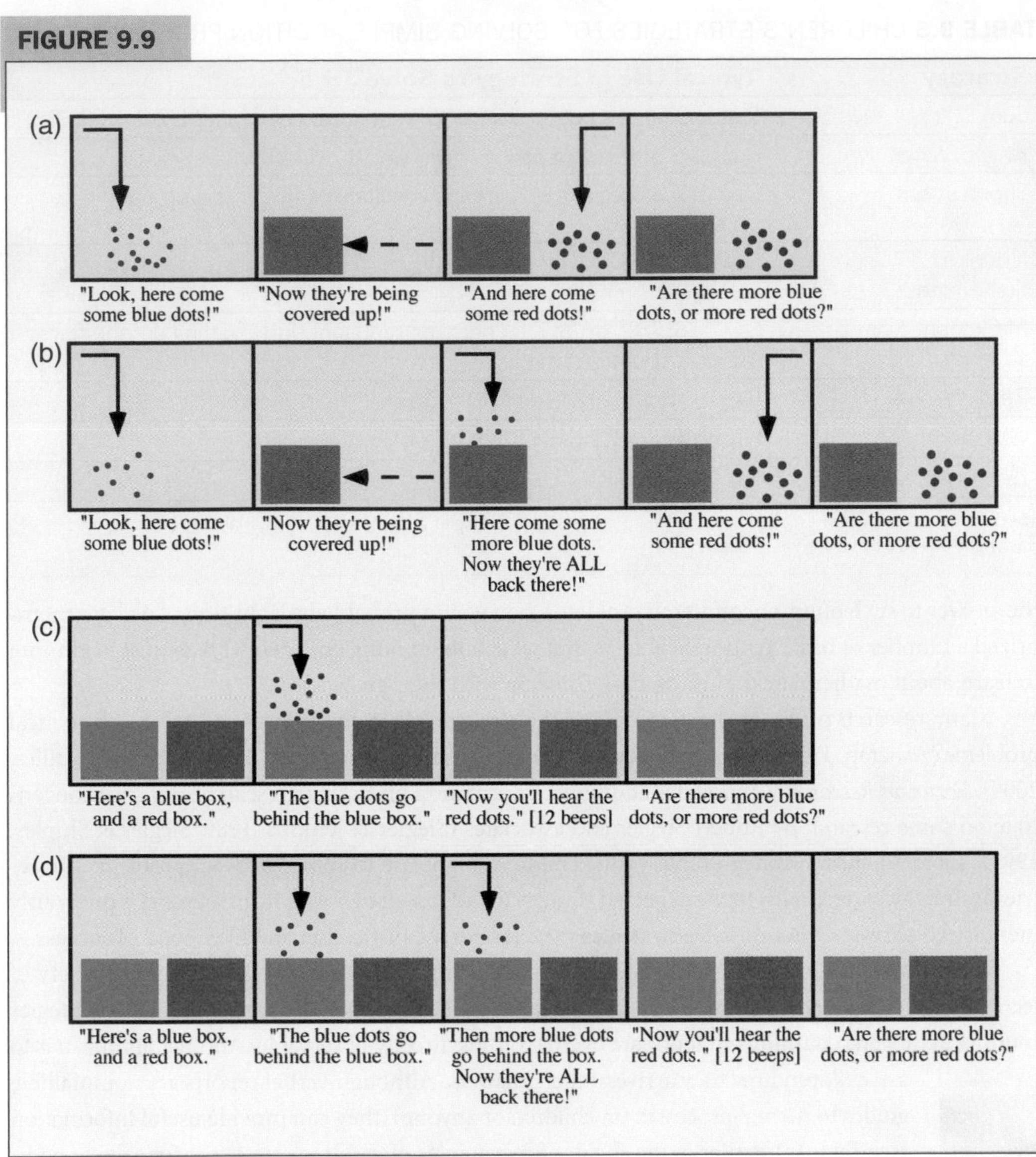
(a)
"Look, here come some blue dots!"
"Now they're being covered up!"
"And here come some red dots!"
"Are there more blue dots, or more red dots?"
(b)
"Look, here come some blue dots!"
"Now they're being covered up!"
"Here come some more blue dots. Now they're ALL back there!"
"And here come some red dots!"
"Are there more blue dots, or more red dots?"
(c)
"Here's a blue box, and a red box."
"The blue dots go behind the blue box."
"Now you'll hear the red dots." [12 beeps]
"Are there more blue dots, or more red dots?"
(d)
"Here's a blue box, and a red box."
"The blue dots go behind the blue box."
"Then more blue dots go behind the box. Now they're ALL back there!"
"Now you'll hear the red dots." [12 beeps]
"Are there more blue dots, or more red dots?"

Sequence of displays shown to preschoolers to test their ability to discriminate number from the same and different modalities in comparison and addition tasks. (a) Comparison of visual arrays; (b) Addition and comparison of visual arrays; (c) Comparison of visual arrays and auditory sequences; and (d) Addition and comparison of visual arrays and auditory sequences. *From H. Barth, K. La Mont, J. Lipton, and E. S. Spelke, "Abstract Number and Arithmetic in Preschool Children," 2005.* Proceedings of the National Academy of Sciences of the United States of America, 102, *14117, Figure 1. Copyright © 2005 by National Academy of Sciences, U.S.A.*

TABLE 9.4 WHAT YOUNG CHILDREN KNOW ABOUT NUMBER: THE GELMAN AND GALLISTEL COUNTING PRINCIPLES

Principle	Description
One–one	Assign one and only one distinctive number name to each item to be counted.
Stable-order	Always recite the number names in the same order.
Cardinal	The final number name at the end of a counting sequence represents the number of items in the set.
Abstraction	The preceding counting principles can be applied to any set of entities, no matter how heterogeneous.
Order-irrelevance	The items in a set can be counted in any order.

Source: Based on information from *The Child's Understanding of Number* by R. Gelman and C. R. Gallistel, 1978, Cambridge, MA: Harvard University Press.

ARITHMETIC

We turn now to older children and the sorts of arithmetical problems that are the subject of instruction in school.

Suppose you were asked how you come up with answers to simple addition problems, such as 4 + 2 and 3 + 5. Your response would probably be that you simply know—that you have memorized

TABLE 9.5 CHILDREN'S STRATEGIES FOR SOLVING SIMPLE ADDITION PROBLEMS

Strategy	Typical Use of Strategy to Solve 3 + 5
Sum	Put up 3 fingers, put up 5 fingers, count fingers by saying "1, 2, 3, 4, 5, 6, 7, 8."
Finger recognition	Put up 3 fingers, put up 5 fingers, say "8" without counting.
Shortcut sum	Say "1, 2, 3, 4, 5, 6, 7, 8," perhaps simultaneously putting up one finger on each count.
Count-from-first-addend	Say "3, 4, 5, 6, 7, 8" or "4, 5, 6, 7, 8," perhaps simultaneously putting up one finger on each count.
Min (count-from-larger-addend)	Say "5, 6, 7, 8," or "6, 7, 8," perhaps simultaneously putting up one finger on each count beyond 5.
Retrieval	Say an answer and explain it by saying "I just knew it."
Guessing	Say an answer and explain it by saying "I guessed."
Decomposition	Say "3 + 5 is like 4 + 4, so it's 8."

Source: Adapted from *How Children Discover New Strategies* by R. S. Siegler and E. Jenkins, 1989, Mahwah, NJ: Erlbaum, 59. Copyright © 1989 by Lawrence Erlbaum Associates. Adapted by permission.

the answer to such often-encountered problems. You would probably be right—all of us *have* memorized a number of basic arithmetical facts. But what about young children who are just beginning to learn about mathematics? How do they come up with their answers?

Many research programs have examined the strategies that children use to solve arithmetical problems (Ashcraft, 1990; Bisanz & LeFevre, 1990; Bjorklund & Rosenblum, 2002; Lemaire & Callies, 2009). *Focus on Research 9.1* provides additional information on Bisanz's research. Here, we concentrate on some research by Robert Siegler and associates (Siegler & Jenkins, 1989; Siegler & Shipley, 1995). Table 9.5 shows strategies that young children might use to solve the 3 + 5 problem. The retrieval strategy corresponds to the expected strategy for adults—retrieving from memory a previously memorized answer. Other possible strategies vary in both sophistication and likelihood of success.

How can we determine which strategy a child is using? Siegler and colleagues use a variety of techniques. One approach is simply to watch children as they work on the problems. Some strategies (putting up fingers, counting out loud) are overt and thus directly observable. Another approach is to ask children how they arrive at their answers. Although verbal reports are not infallible guides to mental processes (in children or anyone), they can provide useful information (see Table 9.1 earlier in the chapter for examples of children's strategies for solving addition problems).

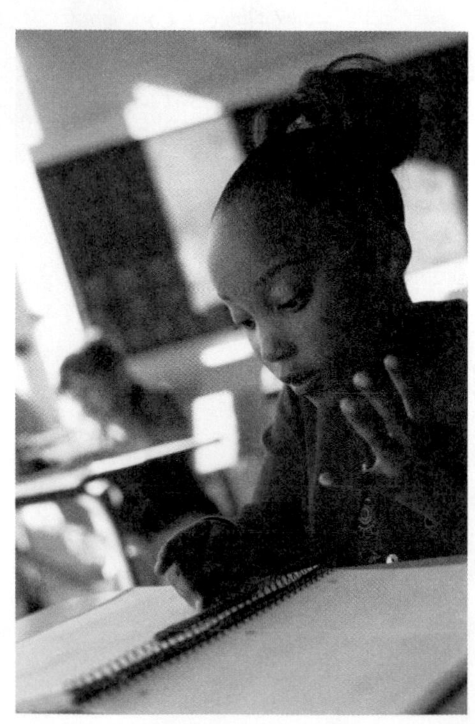
Counting on the fingers is one of the first arithmetical strategies that children develop. (© *JDC/LWA/Corbis*)

A third approach makes use of a central information-processing methodology: the measurement of response time as a guide to processes of solution. A child using the count-from-first-addend strategy, for example, should take longer to solve 3 + 7 than to solve 3 + 5; a child using the min strategy, however, should be equally quick on both problems. Examination of response times across a range of problems can help specify the strategies being used.

One of the most interesting findings from the Siegler research concerns the diversity of strategies that children use. We might have expected that a child at any point in development would have a single method of solving addition problems. In fact, children typically employ a number of different strategies, sometimes going with one approach, sometimes trying something different.

Children's selection from among strategies is not random, but often adaptively geared to the problem at hand. They may, for example, use the retrieval strategy for simple and familiar problems, but fall back on one of the more certain counting strategies when faced with a more complex task. In general, children seem to strive for a balance of speed and accuracy, selecting the fastest strategy that is likely to yield a correct response. With development, there is a predictable progression from less efficient to more efficient strategies, culminating in the ability to retrieve answers from memory rather than continually having to calculate them anew. With development, speed and accuracy increase as well. These increases come in part from the emergence of more efficient strategies and in part from increased skill in executing any particular strategy (Berg, 2008).

These conclusions about strategies are not limited to the domain of addition. Both subtraction and division, for example, are also characterized by the use of multiple strategies rather than a single, consistent approach (Siegler, 2006), as is reading (Siegler, 1988). So, too, as we saw earlier in this chapter, are many memory tasks.

Siegler (2000) captures these points about strategies in his "overlapping waves" model, depicted in Figure 9.10. The contrast drawn is with a strong version of a stage theory (what Siegler refers to as a staircase model) in which, at any point, children have a single way of solving a problem and in which lower-level approaches are abruptly replaced by higher ones. In fact, children often have multiple ways of solving problems, and the transitions across development are often gradual rather than abrupt. Accordingly, what changes with development is the frequencies with which any of the multiple problem-solving strategies are used.

FIGURE 9.10

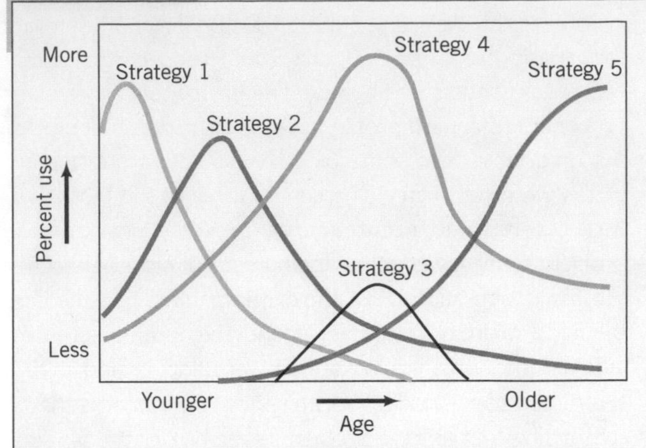

Siegler's overlapping waves model. *From* Emerging Minds: The Process of Change in Children's Thinking *by R. S. Siegler, 1996, New York: Oxford University Press, 89. Copyright © 1996 by Oxford University Press. By permission of Oxford University Press, Inc.*

The research discussed in this section has implications for teaching arithmetic. One is that teachers should be sensitive to the beliefs and strategies that children bring to the classroom setting. We have seen that learning about numbers begins very early in life; thus, it is not surprising that even grade 1 students have their own strategies for solving arithmetic problems.

Teachers should realize, furthermore, that not all grade 1 students will have the same strategies and that they should adjust instruction, as much as possible, to the individual child's level of development. Lower-level strategies, such as counting on one's fingers, should not necessarily be discouraged; children may need experience with the simpler strategies to arrive at answers that they can eventually retrieve from memory. Educators must be sensitive to the natural sequence of development and to the need for advanced knowledge to build on lower-level understanding.

For Thought and Discussion

Think about the possible application of the approach to another academic subject, such as reading, writing, or science. How would information-processing researchers study the topic, and what sorts of conclusions might they offer?

FOCUS ON RESEARCH 9.1
THE INVERSION PRINCIPLE AS A STRATEGY FOR SOLVING MATHEMATICS PROBLEMS

Jeffrey Bisanz is a professor of developmental psychology and director of the Centre for Research in Child Development at the University of Alberta. An important part of his research is devoted to the study of the mathematical abilities of children. His work provides an excellent illustration of the way in which information-processing theory researchers investigate cognitive development.

One of the topics recently investigated by Dr. Bisanz concerns the understanding that children have about the notion of inversion to solve simple arithmetic problems. Although it is usually necessary to be able to count in order to solve problems involving addition and subtraction, there are some cases in which it is possible to solve such problems just on the basis of logic. For example, if you are asked to find the result of 4 + 2 − 2, you realize that adding and subtracting the same quantity to an initial quantity does not change this quantity. You can solve this problem without having to count. Put another way, you can solve the problem by using a shortcut that allows you to provide the right answer faster than if you had decided to perform the two arithmetic operations.

Several studies indicate that children already have some grasp of the inversion principle at the beginning of the school-age period, and they use this principle more systematically as they get older (Bisanz & Lefevre, 1990; Bryant, Christie, & Rendu, 1999; Klein & Bisanz, 2000). To investigate this issue, researchers ask children to solve problems of the $a + b - b$ type (inversion problems) and others of the $a + b - c$ type (standard problems). If children have some grasp of the inversion principle, they are expected to solve inversion problems faster and more accurately than standard problems, and this is exactly what has been consistently found.

The fact that children in grade 1 already have some grasp of the inversion principle raises an interesting question. Is their understanding of this principle a product of their formal instruction in arithmetic, or did they already have some grasp of this principle prior to the beginning of their formal education? To

(continued)

The Inversion Principle as a Strategy for Solving Mathematics Problems *continued*

investigate this intriguing question, Dr. Bisanz and his collaborators (Rasmussen, Ho, & Bisanz, 2003) used blocks instead of numerical symbols when presenting preschool children with inversion and standard problems. An initial quantity of blocks was put on a table, then some blocks were added, and then some blocks were subtracted. The central array of the blocks was always covered with a cloth, so that children could not solve the problem simply by counting the number of blocks after the two successive operations. First, the experimenters told the children the initial quantity of blocks; second, they added some blocks, indicating how many blocks they were adding; and third, they subtracted some blocks, indicating how many blocks they were subtracting. To make the problems even harder, the blocks were the same size in one condition and were different sizes in another condition. In the latter condition, children could not simply remember the length of the initial array of blocks and compare it with that of the final array of blocks.

Consistent with the hypothesis that children use shortcuts to solve inversion problems, accuracy was higher (three times higher) for inversion problems than for standard problems. Around 70 percent of the preschool children demonstrated the expected pattern of results. Furthermore, the children were as successful with the tasks when the blocks were of different sizes as when the blocks were of the same size. This result is very interesting because it means that children have a quantitative grasp of the inversion principle prior to the beginning of their formal instruction in arithmetic.

LEARNING OBJECTIVE 9.4

Describe the development in the understanding of number from infancy to school age.

1. What is infants' understanding of number?
2. What is the understanding of number in preschoolers?
3. How do school-age children solve arithmetical problems?

Learning Objective 9.5

Analyze the abilities and skills children use to solve problems, and give examples of how research on problem solving can be applied.

PROBLEM SOLVING

No one has to read a textbook to know that children's problem-solving abilities improve dramatically across childhood. The tasks that the school system sets for its students, the ways in which parents attempt to reason with and control their children, the opportunities and the expectations that society in general holds—all are quite different for 15-year-olds than for 5-year-olds. As with the study of memory, the challenge for the researcher is to describe exactly how children's abilities change—and then to explain why these changes come about.

Children's problem-solving abilities, in fact, change in many ways as they develop (DeLoache, Miller, & Pierroutsaksos, 1998; Ellis & Siegler, 1994). Here, we consider development under three headings. We begin with the idea that some kinds of problem solving may be explained by the formation of rules for combining information and making judgments. We then discuss situations in which reasoning by analogy is an effective problem-solving strategy. We conclude with a central theme in information-processing theory—the contribution of memory to children's problem solving.

THE DEVELOPMENT OF RULES

Rules Procedures for acting on the environment and solving problems.

Deanna Kuhn and Sam Franklin (2006) have proposed that a strong factor in the development of children's cognition thinking is the shift to rule-based thinking. **Rules** are procedures for acting on the environment and solving problems. They take the form of "if…then" statements. *If* A is the case, *then* do X; *if* B is the case, *then* do Y; and so forth. A simple and familiar example concerns the rules for behaviour at traffic lights: if the light is green, then proceed; if the light is red, then stop (unfortunately, rules for yellow lights seem to be more variable!).

The rules for traffic lights are relatively simple ones, and children must deal primarily with simple rules in early childhood. We begin with research on preschoolers' ability to follow simple rules of the if…then sort. We then move on to some of the more complex forms of rule-based reasoning that emerge later in development.

For Thought and Discussion

How might children's ability to solve conservation tasks reflect the development of rule-based problem solving?

PRESCHOOLERS' RULE-BASED REASONING Although young children—as we hope is clear by now—have many cognitive strengths, there are times when they surprise us with what they cannot yet do or do not yet understand. Some recent studies by Philip Zelazo, formerly of the University of Toronto, and collaborators (Zelazo & Frye, 1998) provide another striking example (see also Zelazo 1999; Zelazo, Carlson, & Kesek, 2008).

The basic task in this research—labelled *the dimensional-change card sort*—is illustrated in Figure 9.11. The child is given a series of cards that vary in both shape and colour and is instructed to sort them by one of the two dimensions. If the task is the "colour game," for example, then the instructions will be to put the red ones in the box with the red picture and the blue ones in the box with the blue picture. Most 3-year-olds readily learn this task. After several such trials the rule changes: now the task becomes the "shape game," and the instructions are to put the cars in one box and the flowers in the other. Most 4-year-olds easily make the switch. Most 3-year-olds do not. Even when they receive the new instructions at the start of every trial, and even when they themselves succeed in verbalizing the new rule, 3-year-olds continue to sort according to the original rule.

FIGURE 9.11

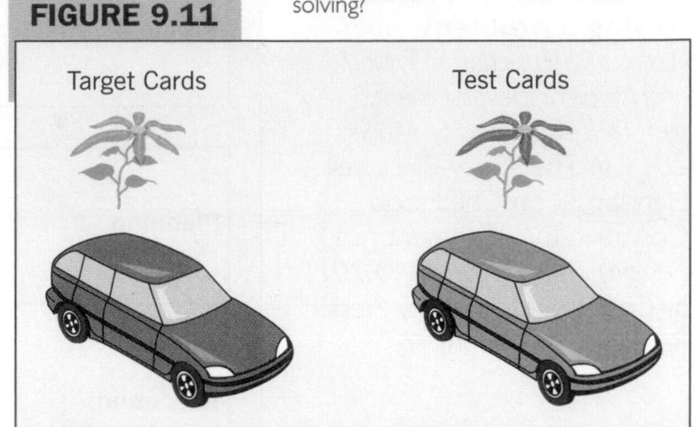

Dimensional card sort task used in Zelazo and Frye's study of early rule following. *From "Cognitive Complexity and Control: II. The Development of Executive Function in Childhood," by P. D. Zelazo and D. Frye, 1998,* Current Directions in Psychological Science, 7, *122. Copyright © 1998 by Cambridge University Press. Reprinted by permission.*

What the dimensional-change task shows is that 3-year-olds are capable of rule-based problem solving, but with some definite limitations. Three-year-olds can handle two simple rules at a time—for example, if red, do this; if blue, do this. Even this, it is worth noting, is an accomplishment; 2-year-olds are able to learn and follow only one rule at a time. What the 3-year-old cannot yet do is embed these simple rules within a more complex rule system, in which selection of one of the simple rules is contingent on a prior, higher-order rule. Successful performance on the change trials requires this sort of embedded rule structure. The child must be able to reason in the following way: if this is the colour game (higher-order rule), then it is "if red do this and if blue do this"; if this is the shape game, then it is "if car do this and if flower do this."

In addition to illustrating the sorts of rules that young children can follow, the dimensional-change task suggests some general conclusions about contributors to children's problem solving. Success on the task requires a number of component processes. The child must have sufficient short-term memory capacity to keep in mind several rules at the same time. The child must be capable of inhibiting the original response once a new response is called for. Finally—and in Zelazo and Frye's (1998) analysis, most critically—the child must have sufficient metacognitive ability to reflect on the rules that he or she has learned and to note the relations among them. The term **executive function** refers to general problem-solving components of this sort, and to process components that enable control over thoughts and actions. These components include processes such as memory and planning and inhibition and self-awareness that play a role in virtually every form of reasoning and problem solving. Recent research has shown that developmental improvements in executive function contribute to developmental advances on a wide range of cognitive tasks (Hughes, 2002; Keenan, 2000). Further, Zelazo has demonstrated that problem-solving tasks, such as the dimensional-change task, are associated with areas of the prefrontal cortex, which are also implicated in executive function (Kerr & Zelazo, 2004; Zelazo & Müller, 2011).

Executive function General components of problem solving, such as short-term memory, metacognitive awareness, and inhibition.

Links to Related Material

In Chapter 6, the development of the cortical regions responsible for executive functions was discussed. Here, the development in executive function behaviour is discussed.

According to Zelazo and Müller (2011) there are four processes or phases for solving a problem, the passage through which is related to executive function and its development (see Figure 9.12). The initial phase is *problem representation* in which the nature of the problem, including its relevant dimensions, and the goal are identified. Studies of problem representation, for example, have indicated that there is significant development between 3 and 5 years of age in the ability to understand and follow task instructions and identify the key dimensions stipulated in the instructions (e.g., Jacques & Zelazo, 2001). The next phase is *planning* in which a plan for solving the problem is chosen. To assess planning, the Tower of London is used, in which coloured balls on three pegs must be

FIGURE 9.12

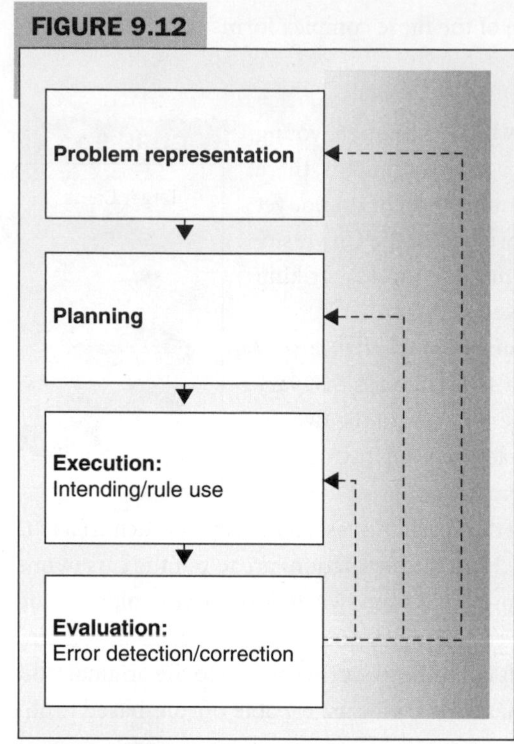

Zelazo and Müller's problem-solving framework for how mechanisms of executive function control relate to solving a problem. *From "Executive Function in Typical and Atypical Development," by P. D. Zelazo and U. Müller, 2011, in* The Wiley-Blackwell Handbook on Childhood Cognitive Development *(2nd Edition), 578. Copyright © 2011 by Cambridge University Press. Reprinted by permission.*

FIGURE 9.13

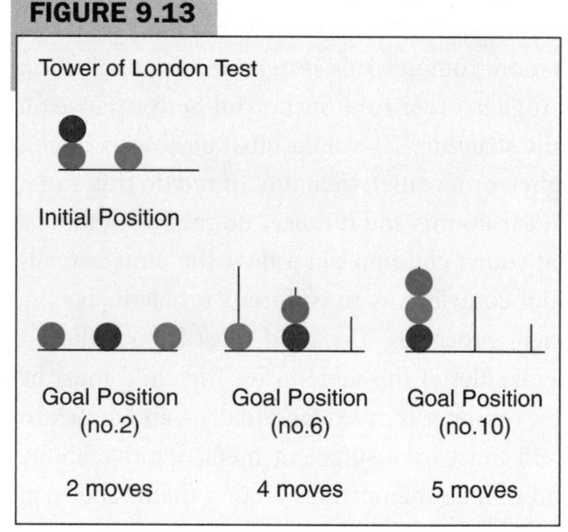

Tower of London used in tests of problem solving and executive function. Children are initially given coloured balls in a particular arrangement on three pegs and are then required to move the balls, one at a time, to match a final goal position. The goal positions can be set to require any number of moves, such as 2, 4, or 5 moves shown here, for successful completion of the goal.

moved from an original arrangement to match a target arrangement and children are required to describe how they would move the balls to match the target arrangement (see Figure 9.13). Using the Tower of London, findings indicate that there is an increase with age in the number of moves that can be planned to match the target arrangement, though even 8-year-olds still cannot plan as many moves as adults (Luciana & Nelson, 1998).

REASONING BY ANALOGY

Analogical reasoning A form of problem solving in which the solution is achieved through recognition of the similarity between the new problem and some already understood problem.

To many students, the term *analogical reasoning* doubtless conjures up images of tests and complex verbal problems of the "A is to B as C is to ___?" sort. In fact, the scope of the concept is a good deal broader than this. **Analogical reasoning** refers to a form of problem solving in which the solution is achieved through recognition of a similarity between the new problem (such as figuring out the relation between C and D) and an already understood problem (such as the relation between A and B). Some forms of such reasoning, including many verbal analogies, are complex and late to develop, which is why analogies are a common item on standardized tests. Some forms, however, are evident very early in development. Here, we consider two examples, one with infants and one with preschoolers.

Chen, Sanchez, and Campbell (1997) used the following task with 10- to 13-month-olds (see Figure 9.14). Infants were presented with an attractive toy, such as the toy car pictured on the right side of the figure. Two factors, however, prevented them from immediately grasping and playing with the toy: a barrier intervened between infant and toy, and the toy was too far away to reach. To solve the problem, therefore, the infant needed to push aside the barrier, grasp the string connected to the toy (while ignoring the other, non-helpful string), and pull the toy within range. The infants were first given a chance to solve the problem on their own, and few could do so. When a parent then modelled the solution, however, many more infants succeeded.

The test for analogical problem solving followed. The infants received a series of further problems that retained the same general solution structure as the original problem, but varied a number of specific perceptual features—for example (as the figure shows), a different goal object, a different-coloured barrier, a different string arrangement. The question was whether they could recognize the relation between the original problem and the new one and transfer the original solution appropriately. Not all could, especially at the younger end of the 10- to 13-month span. By the third problem, however, the average success rate had risen to better than 60 percent, a figure much higher than performance on the initial trial. Although they obviously could not put the process in words, the infants seemed to be engaging in reasoning of the following sort: "This barrier is like the one I pushed aside before, and this string is like the one I pulled before, and so if I want to get this new toy..."

Not only does language come to contribute to children's reasoning as they get older, but they also show reasoning by relational similarity rather than perceptual similarity. That is, they are able to solve a problem on the basis of recognizing the relation between items (for example, 'bird' goes with 'nest'). A study by Goswami and Brown (1990) best illustrates reasoning on the basis of relational similarity. Four-, 5-, and 9-year-old children were shown a pair of pictures (for example, bird and nest) about which they must ascertain the relation. They were also shown another picture (for example, dog). The children were then given a set of four pictures, one of which would fit the same type of relation with dog as existed between bird and nest (that is, doghouse; see Figure 9.15). On this reasoning task, children of all ages chose the correct picture above chance levels (25 percent), with a clear developmental trend appearing. Four-year-olds chose correctly 59 percent of the time, 5-year-olds chose correctly 66 percent of the time, and 9-year-olds chose correctly an incredible 94 percent of the time. Since the bird and dog are not perceptually similar, children had to use the similarity of the relation between bird and nest to correctly choose doghouse for dog. This shows a clear advance in the sophistication of children's reasoning ability as it continues to develop through much of early childhood.

FIGURE 9.14

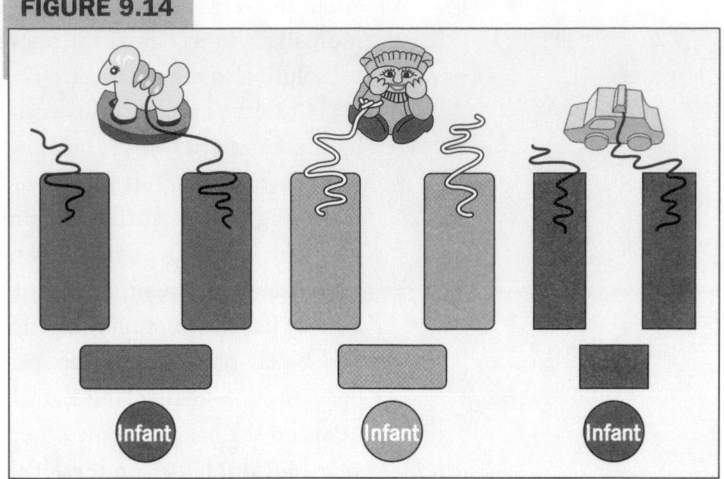

Configuration of problems in Chen et al.'s study of analogical problem solving in infants. *From "From Beyond to Within Their Grasp: The Rudiments of Analogical Problem Solving in 10- and 13-Month-Olds" by Z. Chen, R. P. Sanchez, & T. Campbell, 1997,* Developmental Psychology, 33, 792. *Copyright © 1997 by the American Psychological Association. Reprinted by permission.*

As children develop, the sorts of relations they can recognize across problems become progressively less dependent on perceptual similarity; they also are more likely to be embedded in language. Consider an example of analogical problem solving in preschoolers (Brown, Kane, & Echols, 1986). Children first heard a story in which a genie needed to transport some jewels over a wall and into a bottle. The genie solved her problem by rolling up a piece of poster board so that it formed a tube, placing one end of the tube in the mouth of the bottle, and rolling the jewels through the tube and into the bottle. The children were then asked to demonstrate a solution to the following problem: the Easter Bunny needs to transport his eggs across a river and into a basket on the other side. Despite the presence of a piece of posterboard, few 3-year-olds spontaneously recognized the analogy to the genie task, although with help (for example, questioning

FIGURE 9.15

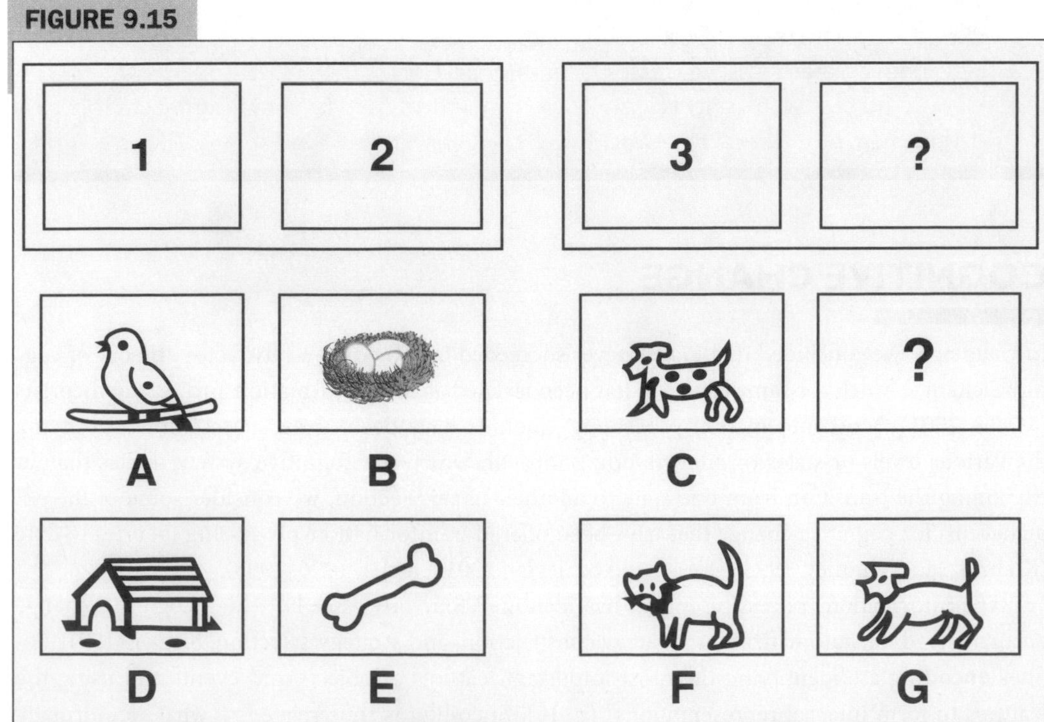

One set of stimuli used in the Goswami and Brown (1990) study of children's ability to use relational similarity in their analogical reasoning. Children had to select one of the pictures from D through G that would correctly fit the missing box on the top row to complete the analogy. *From Figure 1, "Higher-order structure and relational reasoning: Contrasting analogical and thematic relations" by U. Goswami, & A.L. Brown, 1990,* Cognition, 36, 211. *Copyright © 1990 by the Elsevier Science Publishers. Reproduced by permission.*

about the central elements in each story) some eventually succeeded. Five-year-olds were much more likely to recognize the relevance of the original story and to hit immediately on an analogical solution to the new task.

Children's ability to use relational similarity for analogical reasoning can also be affected by the familiarity or prior knowledge of the material that is being related, as well as the relations themselves. This should not be surprising considering that we already defined analogical reasoning as recognizing the similarity between a new problem and some already understood problem. Thus, analogical reasoning works precisely because the child is already familiar in some way with the original problem. Goswami (1995) demonstrates the effect of familiarity in a study using a relation that exists in the Goldilocks and the Three Bears story. In this study, 3- and 4-year-old children were presented with the relation that Daddy bear's stuff is big, Mommy bear's stuff is smaller, and Baby bear's stuff is smallest. They used this relation to relate or order items on the basis of some other dimension such as quantity, loudness, temperature, etc. Four-year-olds did better on these tasks than did the 3-year-olds, though even they exhibited better than chance performance. As a result of being familiar with the underlying relation, very young children are capable of analogical reasoning on the basis of relational similarity, even with no perceptual similarity.

These examples of early analogical reasoning are obviously very simple, and they do not negate the fact that important developmental advances occur in this form of problem solving. To a good extent, however, what seems to develop is not the basic capacity to reason by analogy, which appears to be present from early in life, but rather knowledge about the particular items and particular relations that enter into particular analogies (Goswami, 1992, 1996). The point here is a simple one: if children do not yet know what A or B is, then they cannot use the relation between A and B to reason analogically about C and D. We saw that what is known about a topic can be important for memory. The same point applies to problem solving.

LEARNING OBJECTIVE 9.5

Analyze the abilities and skills children use to solve problems, and give examples of how research on problem solving can be applied.

1. What are children's problem-solving skills?
2. How does children's use of rule-based reasoning develop?
3. How does children's ability to reason by analogy develop?
4. How do perceptual similarity, language, relational similarity, and familiarity contribute to the development of analogical reasoning?

Learning Objective 9.6

Describe the mechanisms that have been proposed to account for cognitive change.

COGNITIVE CHANGE

In Chapter 8, we concluded that Piaget never succeeded in providing a satisfactory theory of cognitive change. Much the same criticism has been levelled against information-processing theorists (Miller, 2001). Most information-processing accounts have been more successful at specifying the various levels or states of understanding through which the cognitive system moves than at explaining the transition from one state to another. In this section, we consider some of the explanations for cognitive change that have been offered in information-processing theories to date (Klahr & MacWhinney, 1998; McClelland & Siegler, 2001; Siegler, 1996, 1998).

Encoding Attending to and forming internal representations of certain features of the environment. A mechanism of change in information-processing theories.

The information-processing model has identified four processes by which cognitive change occurs: encoding, automatization, strategy construction, and strategy selection. Siegler (1991) defines **encoding** as "identifying the most important features of objects and events and using the features to form internal representations" (p. 10). Encoding is thus related to what we normally mean by *attention*, but it carries some further implications as well. One is the idea that information processing is always active, rather than passive, because the child attends to only some features of the environment and uses only some features to arrive at judgments. The other is the emphasis on how the child interprets or represents the encoded information. Encoding involves not simply attending to, but also forming some sort of representation of what has been attended to, and it is this representation that guides subsequent problem solving.

Let us consider how the concept of encoding can be applied to the example of the first phase of *problem representation* in Zelazo and Müller's (2011) framework for problem solving. In this example, the task in which pictures had to be paired on the basis of matching on a particular dimension (e.g., size or colour) was first demonstrated to children as a form of instruction (Jacques & Zelazo, 2001). Children were then presented with three pictures and were required to match two of them on one dimension. Then they were given a second set of three cards and were required to match two of those on a different dimension. Children 2 years of age were unable to encode and understand the task requirements and identify the key dimensions as instructed by the demonstration. Three-year-olds were able to do the task, but did more poorly than 4- and 5-year-olds. These findings indicate that encoding the relevant requirements of the task is critical to forming a representation of the problem, which in turn supports successful completion of the problem-solving task.

A second mechanism is **automatization**. As noted, there is a characteristic progression in the development of any cognitive skill. At first, the skill—precisely because it is new—requires considerable attention and effort, and few resources may be left for any other sort of cognitive processing. With practice, however, execution of the skill becomes more automatic, cognitive resources are freed, and more advanced forms of problem solving become possible. Automatization is a primary mechanism by which the cognitive system overcomes inherent limitations on the amount of information that can be processed.

Automatization An increase in the efficiency with which cognitive operations are executed as a result of practice. A mechanism of change in information-processing theories.

The same can be said for a third mechanism, **strategy construction**. Like automatization, strategies serve to overcome processing limitations by increasing the efficiency with which information is handled. The child who realizes the organization inherent in a set of items, for example, may need to remember only the general categories and not every individual item. Similarly, a child who has developed the min strategy for adding numbers will need to count just twice, rather than eight times, when adding 2 plus 8.

Strategy construction The creation of strategies for processing and remembering information. A mechanism of change in information-processing theories.

A final, closely related mechanism is **strategy selection**. As we have seen, children often try out a variety of strategies when they are in the process of developing a new form of competence. We discussed examples with respect to both memory and arithmetic, and the same finding has emerged for other kinds of problem solving as well (Ellis, 1997; Rosengren & Braswell, 2001). Given this multiplicity of approaches, a main task for development is selecting the strategy or combination of strategies that provides the optimal approach to problem solving. Over time, these relatively effective approaches come to be used more and more, whereas less effective strategies are gradually discarded (Siegler & Svetina, 2006).

Strategy selection Progressively greater use of relatively effective strategies rather than with relatively ineffective ones.

Siegler (1996) argues that cognitive development across the course of childhood is in many respects parallel to biological evolution in the history of a species. In both evolution and development, change builds on initial diversity and variation. In the case of evolution, the diversity is in the distribution of genes within a species; in development, it lies in the variation in problem-solving approaches (multiple strategies, different encodings, etc.) that characterize the initial response to a task. In both evolution and development, the initial variation is followed by selection based on differential success: reproductive success in the case of evolution, and problem-solving success in the case of development. And in both evolution and development, successful variants are preserved and passed on—to the next generation in the evolution of species, to future problem-solving efforts in the development of the child. In Siegler's analysis, the parallels between biology and psychology are not surprising because they follow from the similar tasks of evolution and development: to produce adaptive change over time.

LEARNING OBJECTIVE 9.6

Describe the mechanisms that have been proposed to account for cognitive change.

1. What are the four mechanisms of cognitive change?
2. What is the relation between change mechanisms and biological evolution?

CONCLUSION

The information-processing approach has been a major position in the study of cognitive development for several decades now. During that time, it has achieved some noteworthy successes, as our discussions throughout this chapter should make clear. Nevertheless, even its strongest advocates clearly regard their efforts as work in progress—already fruitful, to be sure, but with much still to be done. In that spirit, we focus here on some of the challenges that remain for workers in this tradition.

One challenge concerns scope. Information-processing research has addressed many different aspects of child development. Information-processing theories have been more limited. To date, information-processing theorists have been most successful at constructing precise models of specific, but also somewhat limited, aspects of child development—what Klahr and MacWhinney (1998) refer to as "toy versions" of the larger domains of interest. There is as yet no information-processing theory that rivals Piaget's theory in the scope of phenomena it encompasses.

A second challenge relates to the computer metaphor that has guided so much work in this tradition. One obvious difference between humans and computers concerns the social context for intelligent behaviour. Humans, unlike computers, interact constantly with other humans, and these interactions are both an important context for exercising cognitive skills and one of the sources of those skills. Information-processing conceptions, it is true, have begun to influence the study of social behaviour; we will see a number of examples in the later chapters of the book. Information-processing researchers have also begun to explore the social contributors to information-processing skills. Nevertheless, the social world has been a relatively neglected topic for most information-processing researchers.

A final challenge relates to the issue with which we concluded our discussion: cognitive change. Despite much recent attention to the question, information-processing theorists are still far from producing a completely satisfactory explanation of how cognitive change comes about. On the other hand, they have generated both specific models of the change process and the methods for testing the models. Thus, they seem clearly to be moving in the right direction.

SUMMARY

KEY TERMS

analogical reasoning, p. 346
autobiographical memory, p. 322
automatization, p. 349
computer simulation, p. 318
connectionism, p. 318
constructive memory, p. 322
encoding, p. 348
event memory, p. 322
executive function, p. 345
expertise, p. 336
infantile amnesia, p. 328
metamemory, p. 331
mnemonic strategies, p. 329
production deficiency, p. 329
reactivation, p. 325
recall memory, p. 323
recognition memory, p. 323
rules, p. 344
script, p. 322
strategy construction, p. 349
strategy selection, p. 349
study strategies, p. 330
utilization deficiency, p. 329

LEARNING OBJECTIVES

LEARNING OBJECTIVE 9.1 Define the information-processing approach and describe three methods of studying information processing.

1. *What are the goals of the information-processing approach to cognition?*
   The goal of the information-processing approach is to specify the steps by which the mind transforms sensory inputs into cognitive or behavioural outputs.

2. *How does the information-processing approach reflect a computer metaphor?*
   Psychologists have observed that computers can systematically transform a variety of inputs into a variety of outputs. To do so, computers require precise programs that specify each step of the transformation. Information-processing theorists see in the digital computer a useful metaphor for the human mind.

3. *What are the strengths and limitations of connectionism in the information-processing approach?*
   The connectionist approach has provided insight into a host of aspects of cognitive development, including infant perception, object permanence, Piagetian concrete operational concepts, category learning, and language. However, the use of connectionism as a tool for understanding cognition has also been criticized. Similarities between such networks and human brains often are exaggerated, and connectionist systems always require hundreds or even thousands of trials to learn simple tasks. These models never experience the "aha moments" of insight that humans often report, in which an answer simply becomes clear.

4. *What can we learn from microgenetic studies of cognition?*
   There are five issues related to cognitive change for which microgenetic techniques can provide valuable data: the path of cognitive change (the sequences and levels through which children move in acquiring new knowledge); the rate of change (how quickly or slowly different forms of knowledge are mastered); the breadth of change (when a new competency is acquired, how narrowly or broadly is it applied; variability in the pattern of change (children often do not all follow the same route in mastering a new concept); and the sources of change (the experiences and processes through which new knowledge is constructed).

5. *What are the similarities and differences between the information-processing approach and Piaget's approach?*
   Both information processing and Piaget emphasize concepts or cognitive structures. Further, some information-processing researchers have proposed stage theories that are related to Piaget's stages. However, information-processing theorists do not subscribe to the broad, general stages advocated by Piaget. Information-processing models are more domain-specific, precise, and more testable.

LEARNING OBJECTIVE 9.2 Explain the information-processing model of memory, and trace developmental changes in the kinds of memory.

1. *What is the memory store model in the information-processing approach?*
   In the memory store model, the information first enters the sensory register, where a literal image of a stimulus can be held, but only for a matter of milliseconds. The information then moves to short-term, or working memory, the centre for active and conscious processing. Although information typically remains in short-term memory only for a few seconds, various strategies may prolong it. Finally, the information may be transferred to long-term memory, where it can exist indefinitely. Getting the information to long-term memory is the goal when new information is to be learned.

2. *What kinds of memory are present in infancy and how are they different?*
   Event memory is when children develop scripts for sequences of familiar actions or routine events in their daily world. A script is a representation of the typical sequence of

events in a familiar context, such as "birthday party," or "going to the store." Constructive memory refers to the ways that individuals interpret the information they acquire in terms of their pre-existing knowledge, which affects what they remember. Autobiographical memory refers to specific, personal, and long-lasting memory about the self. Infants are also capable of recognition memory, which is the realization that some perceptually present stimulus or event has been encountered before, and recall memory, which refers to the retrieval of some past stimulus or event when the stimulus or event is not perceptually present.

3. *How do researchers study recognition and recall memory in infants and young children?*
   Researchers study recognition memory in infancy through the habituation–dishabituation procedure. Even newborn infants show habituation across a range of modalities, including visual, auditory, and tactile modalities. Recall memory is difficult to study in infancy because infants cannot produce verbal reports or drawings to show what they recall. However, studies of deferred imitation provide compelling evidence of recall memory in infancy.

4. *How does memory change as children develop?*
   Older children remember better than do younger children. On average, the older the child, the better the performance on memory measures. Research verifies that recall memory improves with age, and that older children typically report more of their experiences than do younger children.

LEARNING OBJECTIVE 9.3 Describe how memory develops in older children and the tools that contribute to this development of memory.

1. *What are mnemonic strategies, and how do they contribute to memory development in children?*
   A mnemonic strategy is any technique that people use to help them remember something. There are three well-studied mnemonic strategies: rehearsal, organization, and elaboration. Rehearsal is the saying over and over technique. Organization is grouping into conceptual categories. Elaboration is linking items with a general image or story.

2. *What is metacognition, and how does this ability contribute to memory development?*
   Metacognition is knowledge about thinking. Children's thinking about memory (metamemory) changes as they develop. Even young children realize that there is such a thing as memory. By age 5 or 6, most children realize that familiar items are more easily remembered than unfamiliar ones. Research suggests that the knowledge–behaviour relationship is difficult to demonstrate empirically. However, training programs in memory strategies have been found to improve performance.

3. *What does research on novices and experts tell us about the role of knowledge in cognitive development?*
   Where expertise is high, so is memory, and variations in expertise contribute to variations in memory. In addition, variations in expertise contribute to developmental changes in memory across the span of childhood. Older children posses more expertise for most topics than do younger children, and this greater expertise is one reason they remember more. Experts have a greater quantity of knowledge, and are able to represent more than just individual bits of information in memory. They are also capable of representing relationships among individual items. Expertise is also influential in reasoning and problem solving. Expertise affects the speed of processing. When knowledge about some domain is great, information relevant to that domain can be taken in and processed more rapidly, thus freeing cognitive resources for other activities.

LEARNING OBJECTIVE 9.4 Describe the development in the understanding of number from infancy to school age.

1. *What is infants' understanding of number?*
   An understanding of number begins to emerge in infancy. Infants can detect differences in the number of items in a set. Some research suggests that the rudimentary form of simple arithmetical operations is functioning in infancy. However, this finding is controversial and may be due to simpler mechanisms, such as perceptual discrimination.

2. *What is the understanding of number in preschoolers?*
   Preschool children demonstrate knowledge of the basic principles that underlie counting, though they are unable to explicitly verbalize these principles. Their ability to count, however, is often inaccurate.

3. *How do school-age children solve arithmetical problems?*
   Studies of arithmetic in school-age children indicate that children develop a variety of strategies to solve arithmetical problems. Some of the strategies they use include using their fingers, counting out loud, and retrieving from memory. As captured by Siegler's overlapping waves model, children typically use several strategies rather than just one. With increased age, there is a gradual shift to more efficient strategies from less effective ones.

LEARNING OBJECTIVE 9.5 Analyze the abilities and skills children use to solve problems, and give examples of how research on problem solving can be applied.

1. *What are children's problem-solving skills?*
   Children use two kinds of problem-solving skills: 1) forming rules for combining information and making judgments and 2) reasoning by analogy. Developmental changes in basic cognitive abilities affecting memory and knowledge also contribute to problem-solving ability.

2. *How does children's use of rule-based reasoning develop?*
   Preschoolers are capable of rule-based problem solving, but with some definite limitations. At first, children can follow only one rule at a time. However, eventually higher-order rule-following capabilities emerge. Finally, enough metacognitive ability develops to allow children to reflect on the rules they have learned and note the relation among them. The term executive function refers to these problem-solving capabilities.

3. *How does children's ability to reason by analogy develop?*
   Some forms of analogical reasoning, including verbal analogies, are complex and late to develop; other forms are evident early in development. Infants are able to problem solve in situations where the problem solving is modelled by a parent. As children develop, they recognize relationships across problems and gradually depend less on perceptual similarity. Domain-specific knowledge about particular items and their relationships eventually develops.

4. *How do perceptual similarity, language, relational similarity, and familiarity contribute to the development of analogical reasoning?*
   Early in development, analogical reason seems to be controlled by the perceptual similarity between problems. That is, the problems being related share some similar perceptual features, such as colour or shape. As children develop during the preschool years, their analogical reasoning becomes more likely to be embedded in language. Older children, with more language skills, are capable of recognizing the relation in a story that they hear and are able to benefit from verbal questioning about central elements of the story. With continued development, children's analogical reasoning no longer relies on perceptual similarity but they use relational similarity—solving a problem on the basis of recognizing the relation between items

(for example, that bird goes with nest). However, with the support of knowledge or having familiarity with the underlying relation (for example, relations in the Goldilocks and the Three Bears story), very young children are capable of analogical reasoning on the basis of relational similarity, even with no perceptual similarity.

LEARNING OBJECTIVE 9.6 Describe the mechanisms that have been proposed to account for cognitive change.

1. *What are the four mechanisms of cognitive change?*
   Siegler identifies encoding, automatization, strategy construction, and strategy selection as the four mechanisms of cognitive change. Encoding is the identifying of the most important features of objects and events and using them to form internal representations. Young children are sometimes incapable of encoding critical information. Automatization is the process by which practice makes the skill automatic. Cognitive resources are then freed, and more advanced forms of problem solving become possible. Strategy construction refers to the idea that children realize the organization inherent in a set of items, thus increasing the efficiency with which information is handled. In strategy selection, the child selects the strategy that supplies the optimal solution.

2. *What is the relation between change mechanisms and biological evolution?*
   In both evolution and cognitive development, change builds on initial diversity and variation. In the case of evolution, the diversity is in the distribution of genes within a species; in development, it lies in the variation in problem-solving approaches (for example, the multiple strategies proposed by Siegler) that characterize the initial response to a task. In both evolution and development, the initial variation is followed by selection based on differential success of the initial response. Consequently, in both evolution and cognitive change, successful variants are preserved and passed on to the next generation in the evolution of species or to future problem-solving efforts in the development of the child.

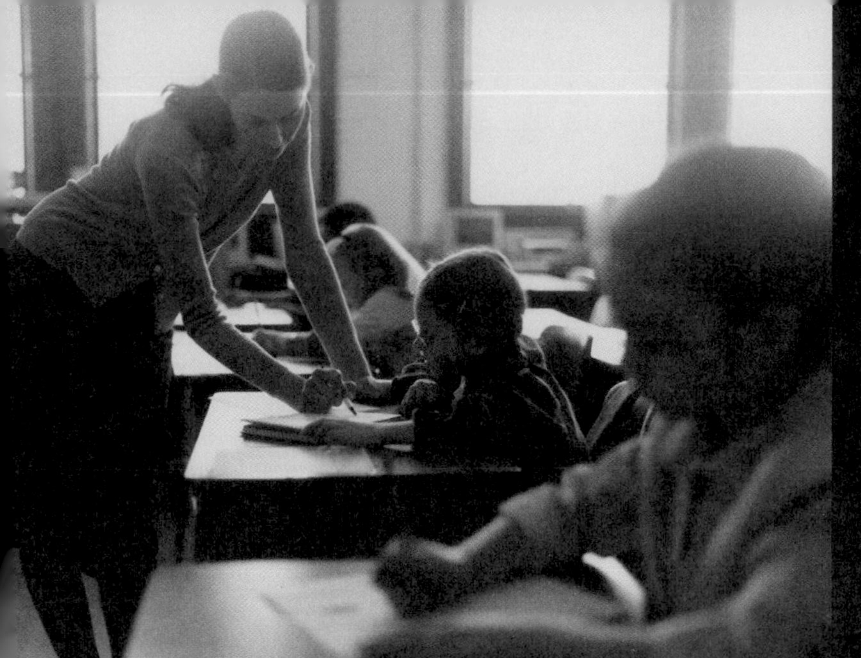

CHAPTER 10

INTELLIGENCE AND SCHOOLING

When children are hungry or malnourished, have a disability that's not accommodated, have emotional and behavioural problems, or feel disconnected from their culture, learning in school can be a challenge.

A national program, Aboriginal Head Start, has worked for over 15 years to improve the learning environment for Aboriginal children across Canada who often have poorer outcomes at school than the general Canadian population. The program, funded by the federal government, provides a half-day of learning to preschool children as young as 3. Parents and elders help teachers show the children proper nutrition and provide healthy meals in the classroom, teach them their Aboriginal language and culture, and provide a supportive learning environment.

"Unfortunately some of the kids come through with some very traumatic times ... and for them to have an opportunity for people to give unconditional love and that kind of care is a big transition," says Alan Knockwood, a participating parent on the Indian Brook First Nation in Nova Scotia.

"I think the Head Start program is a good thing for children, especially when they aren't able to speak," says Bonnie Nickel, a parent on Seabird Island, British Columbia. The local program provides a speech therapist and helps students with physical disabilities as well as emotional and behavioural problems.

Aboriginal Head Start also helps the whole family, participants say. "The program has a direct impact on the future development of these children, and also on the development of what's going on in the families...because the children are bringing home what they've learned," says Chief Gilbert Whiteduck of Kitigan Zibi Anishinabeg, Quebec. Mary Brown, a former consultant for the program in Winnipeg, agrees. "We're trying to instill in the children a lifelong desire to learn and for the parents to get involved at an earlier stage in their children's life and realize how important education is for their children."

This chapter explores additional early intervention programs and other environmental factors that can influence intelligence and learning. The chapter also discusses how intelligence is defined and measured and how schooling can affect intellectual development.

Source: "Aboriginal Head Start on Reserve," Health Canada, 2011, www.hc-sc.gc.ca/fniah-spnia/famil/develop/ahsor-papa_intro-eng.php; "Aboriginal Head Start on Reserve Program Sharing Circle Stories," Health Canada, 2009, www.hc-sc.gc.ca/fniah-spnia/famil/ahsor-papa_video-eng.php.

Psychometric An approach to the study of intelligence that emphasizes the use of standardized tests to identify individual differences among people.

In this chapter, we consider the issues of intelligence and schooling. Our focus is on a particular approach to defining and measuring intelligence: the **psychometric**, or intelligence-test, approach. Consideration of this approach will both broaden our picture of children's intellectual development and immerse us in some of the most controversial issues in the field.

Why has the intelligence-test approach been so controversial? At least part of the answer lies in some important differences between this approach and the Piagetian and information-processing perspectives. Some of the differences relate to the distinction between normative and idiographic approaches to development, one of the general issues identified in Chapter 1. Piaget's approach falls clearly under the normative heading in that his emphasis was always on similarities in children's development; that is, forms of knowledge that all children develop and stages through which all children move. Information-processing researchers have paid more attention to individual differences than did Piaget; however, they too have tended to concentrate on basic processes that are common to all children.

In contrast, the main objective of the intelligence-test approach is to identify differences in children's cognitive abilities. Furthermore, an IQ test identifies not only differences, but *ordered* differences—it indicates that one child is more or less intelligent than another, or that a particular child is above or below average in intelligence. IQ tests thus involve an evaluative component that is impossible to escape, which is one reason why they have always been controversial. The evaluative nature of IQ provides a point of contrast not only with Piaget and information processing, but also with the sociocultural perspective. As we have seen, sociocultural researchers often identify differences in what children know or how they think; their emphasis, however, is on the cognitive strengths that children develop within a particular cultural setting, not on the deficiencies of one group relative to another.

Another difference between the intelligence-test approach and the other perspectives concerns purpose and uses. The research discussed in the two preceding chapters was very much theoretically oriented, its goal being to identify basic cognitive processes. Although such research has practical applications (e.g., effects on school curriculum), to date, such applications have been limited and secondary to the basic theoretical aims. In contrast, the psychometric approach has been pragmatically oriented from the start. As we will see, IQ tests were designed for practical purposes, and they have always had practical uses—most notably, to determine what kind of schooling a child is to receive. This factor, too, contributes to the controversy. In contrast to many measures used by psychologists, IQ tests can make a real difference in a child's life.

We begin this chapter by reviewing what IQ tests for children look like, along with some of their strengths and weaknesses. We then move on to some of the theoretical issues that have been the focus of research in the psychometric tradition. Because of the importance of the question, we pay special attention to the role of experience in the development of intelligence, with a focus on schooling as it both contributes to and is affected by individual differences in intelligence. Although our emphasis is on IQ, we occasionally broaden the scope to include other ways to assess differences in intellectual ability. And in the final part of the chapter, we break away from the traditional IQ approach to consider some recent and exciting alternative approaches to studying intelligence.

Learning Objective 10.1

Explain how intelligence traditionally is defined and measured.

THE NATURE OF IQ TESTS

Before we discuss results from the use of IQ tests, it is important to have some idea of how such tests are put together and what kinds of abilities they measure. We begin, therefore, with an overview of the history and construction of IQ tests. We take a brief look at several specific tests, and then turn to the important question of how to evaluate such measures.

THE BINET APPROACH TO MEASURING INTELLIGENCE

IQ tests were originally devised for purposes of school placement in Paris school systems in the early 1900s. Such educational applications remain important for contemporary IQ tests. (*Culver Pictures Inc.*)

The first successful intelligence test was developed in Paris in 1905 by Alfred Binet and Theodore Simon. From its very start, the IQ approach was tied to success in school. Binet and Simon had been hired by the school authorities in Paris to develop a test that could be given to children who were having difficulty in school. The goal was to distinguish between children who were capable, perhaps with extra help, of succeeding in school and children who were simply not intelligent enough to cope with the regular curriculum. Once the latter group had been identified, they could be placed in special classes from which they might benefit.

Binet and Simon took a pragmatic approach to their task. They tried out a large number of possible items for their test, looking at performance across both a range of ages and a range of ability levels (i.e., children who were known to do well in school and children who were known to do poorly in school). All the items kept for the test were items on which older children, on average, did better than younger children. Such improvement with age was one of Binet and Simon's criteria for a measure of childhood intelligence. These items also tended to differentiate between academically successful children and those who were less successful, which, of course, was the immediate purpose for which the test was designed (Saklofske, Weiss, Beal, & Colson, 2003). The test items, some of which appear in modified form in contemporary IQ tests, included identification of parts of the body, naming of familiar objects, and distinguishing between abstract words—for example, indicating the difference between liking and respecting.

The Stanford-Binet Intelligence Scale (Roid, 2003; Roid & Pomplun, 2005) is the direct descendant of the original Binet-Simon test. It was developed in 1916 by Lewis Terman at Stanford University and has been revised several times since (it is now in its fifth edition). The Stanford-Binet Scale shares several features with Binet's original instrument. Although it can be used with adults, it is primarily a test of childhood intelligence, applicable to every age group within the span of childhood except infancy, and stresses the kinds of verbal and academic skills that are important in school. Specifically, the current edition of the Stanford-Binet test assesses fluid reasoning, knowledge, quantitative processing, visual-spatial processing, and working memory, providing an overall IQ score as well as verbal and non-verbal IQ scores.

The Stanford-Binet test—and, indeed, every other standardized test of intelligence—shares one other important feature with Binet's original test. Binet's approach to measuring intelligence was based on comparing the performances of different groups of children. All contemporary tests of intelligence are comparative, or relative, measures. There is no absolute metric for measuring intelligence, as there is for measuring height or weight. Instead, a child's intelligence is reported as a function of how that child's performance compares with that of other children the same age. Binet used the concept of *mental age* to indicate level of performance relative to other children. Take a child of 8 years old, for example. If that child were able to answer questions at a level equivalent to the average 9-year-old, that child would be said to have a mental age of 9, even though his or her chronological age is actually 8. Similarly, if the child answered at a level equivalent to the average 7-year-old, that child's mental age would be considered to be 7.

Terman took Binet's concept of mental age a step further. Terman used both mental age and chronological age to report children's performance on the Stanford-Binet test. The *Intelligence Quotient* (or *IQ* for short) was a ratio of mental age divided by chronological age, times 100 (i.e., MA/CA × 100). Thus, an 8-year-old child answering questions at the mental age level of an

FIGURE 10.1

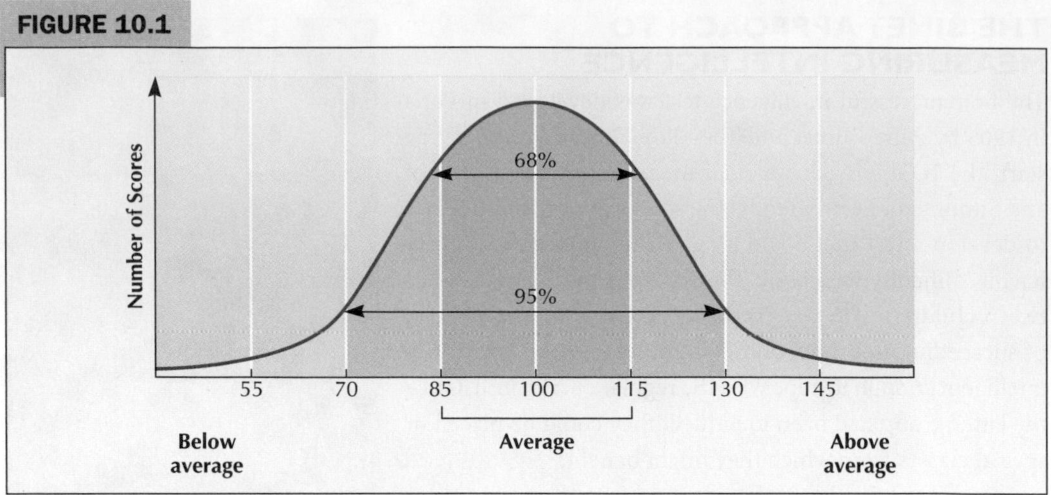

Frequency distribution of IQ scores. IQ scores are distributed in a bell-shaped curve with a mean of 100 and a standard deviation (the variability of scores with respect to the mean) of 15. Approximately 68 percent of the population scores between 85 and 115, while 95 percent scores between 70 and 130.

8-year-old would have an intelligence quotient of 100 (i.e., 8/8 × 100). Likewise, an 8-year-old answering at the level of a 9-year-old would have an intelligence quotient of 112.5 (i.e., 9/8 × 100), and an 8-year-old performing at a mental age of 7 years would have an intelligence quotient of 87.5 (i.e., 7/8 × 100).

Modern intelligence tests no longer make use of the concept of mental age. Nevertheless, modern tests have retained IQ as their measure of analysis, as well as the notion of 100 as representing the average IQ. Children who outperform their peers have above-average IQs; children who lag behind their age group have below-average IQs. The greater the discrepancy from average, the higher or lower the IQ will be. Figure 10.1 shows the distribution of IQ scores.

OTHER TESTS OF CHILDHOOD INTELLIGENCE

The leading alternative to the Stanford-Binet is a series of tests developed by David Wechsler. There are two Wechsler tests designed for childhood: the Wechsler Intelligence Scale for Children (WISC-IV), which is intended for ages 6 to 16, and the Wechsler Preschool and Primary Scale of Intelligence (WPPSI-III), which is intended for ages 2½ to 7 years (Wechsler, 2002, 2003). The Wechsler test bears many similarities to the Stanford-Binet test, including a focus on academically relevant skills.

The WISC-IV test is divided into four scales assessing different aspects of intellectual performance. The scales include: Verbal Comprehension (e.g., tests such as vocabulary and general information), Perceptual Reasoning (e.g., non-verbal tests such as reproducing a geometric design using coloured blocks), Working Memory (e.g., tests of short-term memory, mental arithmetic, etc.), and Processing Speed (e.g., tests such as copying symbols paired with numbers, scanning for target symbols in a list, etc.). The test therefore yields both an overall IQ and separate scores on each of these four scales (Prifitera, Weiss, Saklofske, & Rolphus, 2005). Some examples of the kinds of items included on the Wechsler test are shown in Table 10.1. These examples are similar, although not identical, to those used on the actual test.

A relatively recent entry to the field of childhood assessment is a test developed by Alan and Nadeen Kaufman (1983, 2004). The Kaufman Assessment Battery for Children, second edition, or KABC-II, marks an explicit effort to minimize cultural content in the construction and administration of a test (Kaufman et al., 2005). The KABC-II thus attempts to respond to a long-standing criticism of traditional IQ tests—namely, that such measures may discriminate against children from poor or minority families. Motivated by another criticism levelled at traditional measures, that they are empirically derived instruments lacking a clear theoretical rationale, the KABC-II is also grounded in information-processing conceptions of intelligence. The KABC-II examines

TABLE 10.1 TYPES OF ITEMS INCLUDED ON THE WECHSLER INTELLIGENCE SCALE FOR CHILDREN–FOURTH EDITION

Verbal Comprehension

Information
How many wings does a bird have?
How many nickels make a dime?
What is pepper?

Vocabulary
What is a______? What does______ mean?
Hammer
Protect
Epidemic

Perceptual Reasoning

Block Design
Copy this design with blocks.

Picture Completion
What is missing from this ambulance?

Working Memory

Arithmetic
Sam had three pieces of candy, and Joe gave him four more. How many pieces of candy did Sam have altogether? If two apples cost $0.15, what will be the cost of a dozen apples?

Digit Span
Repeat the following numbers:
4 1 7
7 1 9 5 4 8 2

Processing Speed

Coding
Write the appropriate number above each symbol.

1	2	3	4	5							
⊛	✱	❄	❉	❋	❄	⊛	❋	✱	❉	⊛	❋

Source: Adapted from sample items from the *Wechsler Intelligence Scale for Children, Fourth Edition (WISC-IV)*. Copyright © 2003 NCS Pearson, Inc. Block design, picture completion, and coding illustrations adapted from Huffman, K., (2004). *Living Psychology.* Hoboken, NJ: John Wiley & Sons, Inc. Adapted by permission. All rights reserved.

broad cognitive abilities, including visual processing, fluid reasoning, short-term memory, and long-term storage and retrieval.

Other tests of childhood IQ focus on infancy, the one age period not encompassed by the Stanford-Binet and Wechsler tests. The best-known measure of infant development is the Bayley Scales of Infant and Toddler Development (Bayley, 2005). Not surprisingly, measures of infant intelligence tend to stress sensorimotor skills, as opposed to the academic and verbal emphasis found in tests for older children. Perhaps because of this different focus, tests of infant intelligence do not accurately predict IQ measures taken later in childhood (we discuss this under "Stability of IQ" later in the chapter). The Bayley test, for example, is divided into a motor scale (with items assessing control of the body, muscular coordination, manipulatory skill, and so on) and a mental scale (including items assessing sensory–perceptual acuity, vocalization, and memory). Table 10.2 presents some items from the mental scale.

TABLE 10.2 EXAMPLES OF ITEMS FROM THE BAYLEY SCALES OF INFANT AND TODDLER DEVELOPMENT

Age Placement (in months)	Ability Measured	Procedure	Credit
1	Habituates to rattle	Shake rattle at regular intervals behind child's head	If child shows an initial altering response that decreases over trials
6	Smiles at mirror image	Place mirror in front of child	If child smiles at image in mirror
12	Pushes car	Push toy car while child watches, then say to child, "Push the car, push the car like I did"	If child intentionally pushes car so that all four wheels stay on table
17–19	Uses two different words appropriately	Record the child's spontaneous word usage throughout the exam	If child uses two (non-imitative) words appropriately
23–35	Points to five pictures	Show pictures of 10 common objects (e.g., dog, book, car), say "Show me the ________."	If child either correctly points to or names at least five pictures

Source: Sample items from the *Bayley Scales of Infant Development*, Second Edition (BSID-II).

EVALUATING INTELLIGENCE TESTS

How can we decide whether a test that claims to measure intelligence really does? A standardized test of intelligence—or, indeed, of any attribute—must meet two criteria: reliability and validity.

Reliability The consistency or repeatability of a measuring instrument. A necessary property of a standardized test.

RELIABILITY The consistency or repeatability of measurement is referred to as **reliability**. Does the test give us a consistent picture of what the child can do? Or do scores on the test fluctuate from one testing occasion to the next, perhaps sometimes coming out very high and sometimes very low? Clearly, a test that lacks reliability can hardly provide an accurate measure of the child's ability.

The notion of reliability does not mean that children's IQ scores can never change. Scores often do go up or down as children develop and may also reflect changes within the child, such as fatigue, spurts and lags in development, and so on. Reliability refers to short-term consistency; that is, the constancy of the measuring instrument, not of the child. The major tests of childhood IQ, such as the Stanford-Binet and Wechsler tests, possess good reliability.

Validity The accuracy with which a measuring instrument assesses the attribute it is designed to measure. A necessary property of a standardized test.

VALIDITY The second criterion that a test must meet is validity. The **validity** of a test can be summarized as follows: does the test actually measure what it claims to measure? Do scores on the Stanford-Binet test, for example, really reflect individual differences in children's intelligence? Or do the scores have some other basis—perhaps differences in motivation, in general test-taking ability, or in familiarity with the specific test content?

The validity of a test can be determined in various ways. The approach most commonly used for IQ tests is labelled *criterion validity.* To determine criterion validity, we first specify some external measure, or criterion, of the attribute that we are attempting to assess. We then see whether scores on the test relate to performance on this external criterion. For tests of childhood IQ, the most common external criterion has been performance in school or on standardized tests of academic ability. Tests such as the Stanford-Binet do, in fact, relate to academic performance, with typical correlations of about .5 to .6 (Brody, 1997; Sternberg, Grigorenko, & Bundy, 2001). Thus, on average, the higher the child's IQ, the better the child does in school.

Academic performance is not the only correlate of IQ. IQ also correlates with most standard laboratory measures of learning and cognitive performance—not perfectly, to be sure, but with typical values of around .5 (Jensen, 1981). In adulthood, IQ correlates, again at a mid-range level, with indices of occupational status and with measures of job performance (Hunter & Hunter, 1984). It is this ability to predict important aspects of everyday intelligent behaviour that constitutes the argument for IQ tests as valid measures of intelligence.

For Thought and Discussion

IQ is moderately related to a child's school performance. What other factors, in addition to IQ, do you think may be related to how well a child does at school?

It is important to note some qualifications to the points just made. Consider the relation between IQ and performance in school. A correlation of .5 to .6 indicates a moderate relation between IQ and academic performance. But, if the correlation is .5 to .6 (rather than a higher value such as .8 or .9), there must also be a number of exceptions to this on-the-average relation. There must be, therefore, some children with high IQs who do poorly in school, and some with average or below-average IQs who do well in school. Knowing a child's IQ does not allow us to predict that child's school performance (or, indeed, anything else) with certainty. Furthermore, as we saw in Chapter 2, a correlation in itself does not allow us to determine the cause and effect. Thus, simply knowing that IQ correlates with school performance does not allow us to conclude that children do well or poorly in school because of their IQs. This is one possible explanation for the correlation, but it is not the only one. All we know for certain is that there is a relation between the two variables.

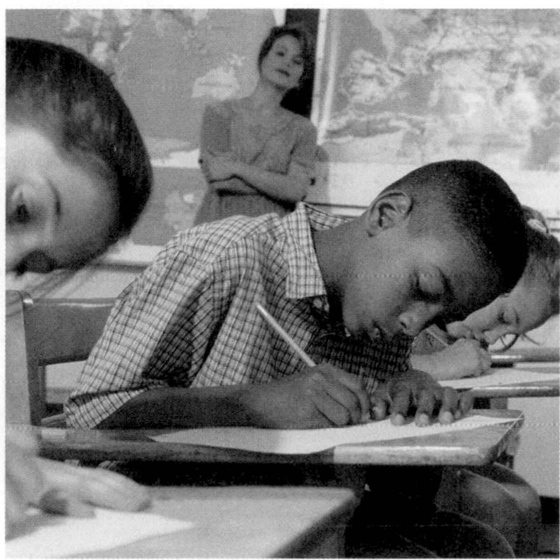

IQ tests are most successful at measuring skills necessary for success in school. Such tests may not capture forms of intelligence that are important in other contexts. *(Media Bakery)*

Finally, we can note that there is a kind of "inbred" relation between IQ tests and school performance. IQ tests for children were originally devised to predict school performance, and this is what they do (although not perfectly). Performance in school is important in our culture; so, too, is performance in the occupational contexts to which school success often leads (Sternberg, 2004). It is reasonable to argue, therefore, that IQ tests do measure something of what we mean by intelligence in our culture. But the qualifications implied by this wording are important. IQ tests may not tap cognitive skills that are important in other cultures (Sternberg, 2009c), such as the ability to navigate in a society in which sailing is important, or the ability to track and hunt food in a hunter-gatherer society. These tests may not even tap skills that are important for some subgroups within our own Western culture, such as the ability to do chores on the family farm or to cope with the challenges of life in an inner-city ghetto. And for any individual, at best they measure something of intelligence, not everything that we would want this term to mean. The two preceding chapters considered numerous aspects of intelligence that are not well captured by IQ tests. Later in this chapter, we will see that even within the psychometric tradition, there are a number of interesting alternatives to IQ.

LEARNING OBJECTIVE 10.1

Explain how intelligence traditionally is defined and measured.

1. What is the purpose of intelligence testing?
2. What is the Stanford-Binet, and how does it define and measure IQ?
3. Identify three IQ or developmental tests in addition to the Stanford-Binet that are commonly used with children.
4. How can we tell whether an IQ test accurately measures intelligence?

Learning Objective 10.2

Understand the organization and stability of intelligence, and the origins of individual differences.

ISSUES IN THE STUDY OF INTELLIGENCE

We have emphasized the pragmatic origins and uses of IQ tests. But the early pioneers of intelligence testing, including Binet, were also interested in theoretical questions about the nature of intelligence. In addition to cognitive-developmental and sociocultural approaches, IQ tests have long served as another context for addressing basic questions about cognitive development. In this section, we consider some of the theoretical issues that have most intrigued researchers in the intelligence-test tradition.

ORGANIZATION OF INTELLIGENCE

The question of the organization or structure of intelligence is a basic issue that any approach to intelligence must confront. We have seen how Piagetian and information-processing researchers have examined this question. Psychometric researchers also study the organization of intelligence, but the methods they use are different from those we have encountered thus far.

In the psychometric approach, conclusions about the organization of intelligence are based on the individual differences that IQ tests elicit. The issue is whether these differences show consistent and interpretable patterns, patterns that can tell us something about how intelligence is organized.

Let us consider two opposed possibilities. Suppose that intelligence is a unitary trait; that is, that there is a single "general intelligence" that people possess in varying degrees. If so, then the particular task that we use to measure intelligence should not really matter. Some people—those who are high in general intelligence—will do well whatever the task, and some will do poorly whatever the task. This outcome would be reflected in uniformly high correlations among different measures of intelligence.

Consider now a very different hypothesis. Perhaps there is no such thing as general intelligence. Perhaps, instead, there are various specific intelligences—verbal intelligence, mathematical intelligence, spatial intelligence, and so on. People may be high in one form of intelligence, but low in some other form. What happens, then, if we administer a test battery that assesses these different forms of intelligence? We no longer expect uniformly high correlations among our measures. Instead, a particular task should correlate most strongly with other tasks that are measuring the same kind of intelligence. Verbal tasks, for example, should correlate strongly with other verbal tasks, but weakly or not at all with measures of spatial ability.

The preceding example summarizes the psychometric approach to the organization of intelligence: that is, determine how intelligence is organized by examining the pattern of correlations across different measures of intelligence. In practice, the approach is more complicated than this brief description suggests. Psychometric researchers use a complex statistical procedure called *factor analysis* to make sense of the large number of correlations that their research yields. There are disagreements about exactly how to carry out and interpret factor analyses, and results may vary depending on the method used. Results may also vary across different batteries of tasks or different samples of participants. Thus, psychometric researchers provide no single, agreed-on answer to the structure question (Sternberg, 2009a), but they have offered some interesting theories and related findings.

GENERAL VERSUS SPECIFIC We have already previewed the question that has generated the most interest and debate among researchers of the organization of intelligence: Is intelligence a single general ability, or does intelligence consist, instead, of a number of specific abilities?

The earliest proponent of the general-intelligence view was the inventor of factor analysis, Charles Spearman. Spearman proposed what has come to be called a *two-factor theory of intelligence* (Spearman, 1927). One factor is general intelligence, or ***g***. In Spearman's view, *g* permeates every form of intellectual functioning and is the most important determinant of individual differences on any test of intelligence. The second factor is *s*, Spearman's label for specific abilities that contribute to performance on particular tasks. Spearman used his newly developed technique of

g General intelligence; g is assumed to determine performance on a wide range of intellectual measures.

factor analysis to analyze correlations among different measures of intelligence. His conclusion was that the consistently positive correlations across measures were evidence for the existence and importance of *g*.

Other theorists have argued for a more differentiated model. Louis Thurstone, for example, developed an intelligence test designed to assess seven primary mental abilities: verbal comprehension, verbal fluency, number, spatial visualization, memory, reasoning, and perceptual speed (Thurstone, 1938; Thurstone & Thurstone, 1962). Thurstone regarded these seven abilities as largely independent and equal in importance.

Seven is by no means the maximum number of abilities that have been proposed. In J. P. Guilford's (1988) structure of the intellect model, there are at least 180 somewhat distinct mental abilities!

For Thought and Discussion

Do you think there is one basic type of intelligence that cuts across all tasks, or are there different kinds of intelligence? How much of your intelligence do you think is due to experience and how much to inheritance?

CONCLUSIONS What is the solution to the general-versus-specific dispute? As is often the case, the answer probably lies somewhere between extreme positions (Sternberg & Grigorenko, 2002b). The consistent finding of positive correlations among different measures of intelligence is evidence that something like general intelligence does exist. The fact that the correlations are far from perfect is evidence that more specific subskills also exist. This sort of solution is sometimes referred to as a **hierarchical model of intelligence**—intelligence is organized in a hierarchical fashion, with broad, general abilities at the top of the hierarchy and more limited, specific skills nested underneath (Sternberg, 2009a). This model probably corresponds to the intuitions that most of us hold about intelligence. We have some ability to rank-order people, including ourselves, along some general dimension of intelligence. But we also realize that different people have different strengths and weaknesses, and that we may outshine a particular peer in some respects and yet lag behind in others.

Hierarchical model of intelligence A model of the structure of intelligence in which intellectual abilities are seen as being organized hierarchically, with broad, general abilities at the top of the hierarchy and more specific skills nested underneath.

STABILITY OF IQ

Do children's IQs remain stable as they develop, so that we can assume that a child who scores 100 at age 4 will also score 100 at ages 8 or 12 or 20? Or can a child's IQ change? This is a question of both theoretical and practical importance.

Answering the question requires a longitudinal approach, in which the same children are tested repeatedly across some span of time. Researchers have conducted many longitudinal studies of IQ, including some lifespan efforts that began in the 1920s (Bayley, 1970). We therefore have quite a bit of data on this issue. Several conclusions emerge.

PREDICTION FROM INFANCY A first conclusion is that traditional tests of infant intelligence do not predict well to tests of later intelligence. The correlation between performance on the Bayley Scales, for example, and performance on later tests is typically close to 0 (Lipsitt, 1992; McCall, 1981). There are some exceptions to this statement: as Linda Siegel (1989, 1992) of the University of British Columbia points out, very low scores on infant tests may sometimes indicate a problem in development, and scores on particular subparts of an infant test (such as items dealing with fine motor skills) may relate to measures of similar skills on childhood tests. For the most part, however, individual differences in infant scores do not tell us much about how children will differ later in development.

Why is there this gap between infant intelligence and later intelligence? The usual explanation stresses the differences in the content of infant tests and childhood tests (Brownell & Strauss, 1984). Tests such as the Stanford-Binet and WISC emphasize symbolic abilities (such as language), as well as abstract, higher-order reasoning and problem solving. Infant tests necessarily stress quite different things—manual dexterity, visual and auditory alertness, and so on. This explanation is related to the continuity–discontinuity issue introduced in Chapter 1. The argument is that there is a discontinuity in the nature of intelligence between infancy and later childhood. Intelligence in infancy requires different skills from those required by later intelligence, and thus it is not surprising that variations in infant development do not relate to variations in later development.

There is almost certainly some truth to the discontinuity argument. But to many psychologists, there is something unsatisfactory about any extreme version of the hypothesis. Surely there must be *some* continuity from infancy to childhood, *some* aspect of intelligence that is common across all age periods. But what might this common thread be?

Research suggests that the common thread may be response to novelty. This conclusion comes from longitudinal studies in which children who were first tested as infants are later assessed for childhood IQ. Investigators have reported positive correlations between various measures of response to novelty in infancy and later measures of intelligence (Colombo & Mitchell, 2009; Kavsek, 2004). For example, babies who show an especially strong preference for new, as opposed to familiar, stimuli tend to do well on later IQ tests (Colombo et al., 2004; Kavsek, 2004). Similarly, babies who are quick to habituate to familiar stimuli tend to perform well on later tests (Bornstein et al., 2006; Domsch et al., 2009). The relations that have been demonstrated are modest in size, with typical correlations in the range of .35 to .40 (Fagan el al., 2007; Kavsek, 2004). Nevertheless, these findings provide a first piece of evidence for some continuity in intelligence from infancy to later childhood.

As might be expected, the studies of response to novelty have led to the creation of a new approach to assessing infant intelligence. In the Fagan Test of Infant Intelligence developed by Joseph F. Fagan (Fagan, 2005; Fagan & Detterman, 1992), babies are shown a picture to look at for a brief period, after which the original picture is paired with a slightly different, novel picture (see Figure 10.2). The measure of interest is how long the baby looks at the novel compared with the familiar. The greater the interest in novelty, the higher is the score on the test. And the higher the Fagan score, the higher, on the average, is the later IQ.

FIGURE 10.2

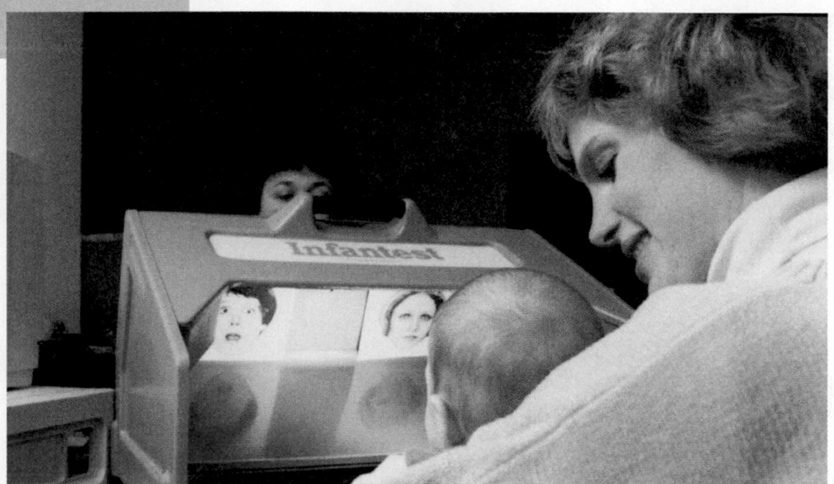

The Fagan Test of Infant Intelligence. Infants are first exposed to one of the two members of each stimulus pair, and then given a chance to look at either the familiar stimulus or the novel alternative. A relatively strong preference for novelty correlates positively with later IQ. *From "Predictive Validity of the Fagan Test of Infant Intelligence" by J. F. Fagan III, P. Shepherd, and C. Knevel, 1991, Meeting of the Society for Research in Child Development, Seattle. Copyright © 1993 by J. F. Fagan III. Reprinted by permission.*

PREDICTION ACROSS CHILDHOOD After infancy, scores from traditional IQ tests begin to correlate significantly from one age period to another. The correlation is not perfect, however. A typical set of findings is shown in Table 10.3

TABLE 10.3 CORRELATIONS IN IQ ACROSS DIFFERENT AGES

Age	3	6	9	12	18
3		.57	.53	.36	.35
6			.80	.74	.61
9				.90	.76
12					.78

Source: Based on information from "The Stability of Mental Test Performance between Two and Eighteen Years" by M. P. Honzik, J.W. MacFarlan, and L. Allen, *Journal of Experimental Education, 17*, 323, 1948. Published by Heldref Publications, 1319 Eighteenth St., N.W., Washington, D.C. 20036-1802. Copyright © 1948.

Two rules for predicting stability in IQ can be abstracted from the data in the table. The first rule is that the degree of stability decreases as the time period between tests increases. Thus, we typically find more similarity in IQ between ages 3 and 6 than between ages 3 and 12. This pattern fits what we would expect from common sense: the longer we wait between tests, the more chance there is for some change to occur. Indeed, this pattern is not limited to IQ, but applies generally whenever we measure stability or change across varying time periods (Nunnally, 1982).

For Thought and Discussion

Do you know your IQ? How is it possible for someone's IQ score to be different today than it was in childhood?

The second rule involves the age at which the child's IQ is assessed. Consider the comparison between the 3-to-6 correlation and the 9-to-12 correlation in Table 10.3. Both reflect a 3-year interval; hence, by our first rule, we would expect them to be equivalent. But the correlation is greater between ages 9 and 12 than it is between ages 3 and 6. In general, the older the child, the higher the correlation in IQ for any given span of time. This pattern, too, fits common sense. As children get older, major changes in their abilities relative to those of other children become less and less likely.

Another way to examine the stability question is to ask about the magnitude of changes in IQ. If children's IQs do change (and the less-than-perfect correlations between ages tell us that they do), how large can the changes be? One study found that 79 percent of a sample of children shifted at least 21 points in IQ between the ages of 2.5 and 17. For 14 percent of the children, the change was 40 points or more (McCall, Applebaum, & Hogarty, 1973).

In summary, probably the most reasonable position on the stability issue is one that avoids extreme statements in either direction. It is not correct to suggest that IQ varies wildly as children develop and that childhood IQ therefore has no predictive value. IQ shows moderately good stability, and the stability increases as the child gets older. On the other hand, it is also not correct to suggest that a child's IQ is fixed and unchangeable. IQs do change, and, in some cases, they change dramatically. We consider some of the reasons for change shortly.

ORIGINS OF INDIVIDUAL DIFFERENCES

Our discussion of IQ has already touched on two of the issues introduced in Chapter 1—normative versus idiographic emphasis and continuity versus discontinuity. We turn next to the third and most general issue—nature versus nurture. The question of the origin of differences in intelligence has been perhaps the most common—and certainly the most heated—context for debates about the relative contributions of biology and experience to human development.

Links to Related Material

In Chapter 3, you read how family or kinship studies have been used to examine the role of nature versus nurture in human development. Here, you learn more about how kinship studies help us understand genetic versus environmental influences on IQ scores.

We first considered this question in Chapter 3 in the discussion of hereditary transmission. As we noted, researchers use three main approaches to study this question: family studies, adoption studies, and twin studies.

FAMILY STUDIES Family studies (also labelled kinship studies) capitalize on our knowledge of the degree of genetic relation among different sorts of relatives. Parent and child, for example, have 50 percent of their genes in common. Two siblings also share an average of 50 percent of their genes. For grandparent and grandchild, the average amount of genetic overlap is 25 percent. For first cousins, the overlap is 12.5 percent. In general, if we know the type of relation between two people, we know their degree of genetic similarity. Knowing this, we can then see whether similarity in IQ relates to similarity in genes.

Similarity in IQ *does* relate to similarity in genes. Table 10.4 shows typical correlations in IQ across different degrees of relation. These findings fit nicely with what would be expected from a genetic model of intelligence.

ADOPTION STUDIES The problem in interpreting the family studies, of course, is that genetic similarity is not the only possible explanation for similarity in IQ. The pattern shown in Table 10.4 might also be accounted for by environmental factors. Siblings, after all, usually share similar experiences. Parents are typically an important part of their children's environments. We would expect some relation between the parent's IQ and the child's IQ solely for environmental reasons.

TABLE 10.4 CORRELATIONS IN IQ AS A FUNCTION OF DEGREE OF GENETIC RELATION

Relation	Median Correlation
Siblings	.55
Parent–child	.50
Grandparents–grandchild	.27
First cousins	.26
Second cousins	.16

Source: Adapted from "Genetics and the Development of Intelligence" by S. Scarr-Salapatek, 1975. In F. D. Horowitz (Ed.), *Review of Child Development Research*, 4, 33, Chicago: University of Chicago Press. Copyright © Society for Research in Child Development. Adapted by permission.

You may recall that studies of adopted children offer a way to disentangle the genetic and environmental explanations for parent–child similarity. Two sets of correlations are relevant. One is the correlation between the adopted child's IQ and the biological parents' IQs. In this case, the usual genetic basis for a correlation remains, but the environmental basis is ruled out. The other correlation of interest is that between the adopted child's IQ and the adoptive parents' IQs. In this case, the environmental basis remains, but the genetic contribution is ruled out.

Before discussing findings, we should note that adoption studies are not really as easy to interpret as this description suggests. In some cases, for example, when the separation of mother and infant does not occur at birth, the biological mother provides part of the post-birth environment. Moreover, in all cases, the biological mother provides the prenatal environment, which—as we saw in Chapter 4—can be important. There is also the possibility of selective placement, through which adoption agencies attempt to match characteristics of the adoptive parents with characteristics of the biological parents. To the extent that selective placement occurs, parent–child correlations cannot be clearly interpreted as either genetic or environmental (Gregory et al., 2011).

Two main findings emerge from adoption studies (Petrill et al., 2004; Plomin & Spinath, 2004). One concerns the pattern of correlations. Typically, the adopted child's IQ correlates more strongly with the IQs of the biological parents than with the IQs of the adoptive parents. This finding provides evidence for the importance of genetic factors. The biological parents make relatively little contribution to an adopted child's environment, but they do provide the child's genes. Recall from our discussion in Chapter 3 that studies of siblings paint a similar picture: stronger correlations for biological siblings than for children adopted into the same home.

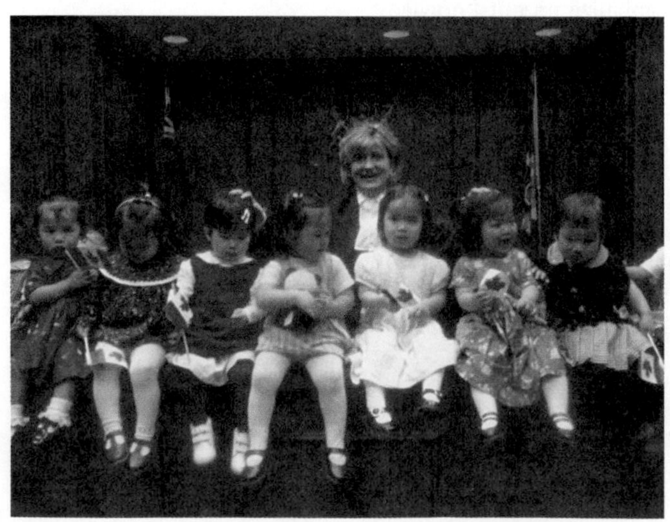

These Chinese babies have been adopted and sworn in as Canadian citizens. Do you think their new environments will boost their IQs? (*Paul Irish/The Canadian Press*)

The second finding concerns average level of IQ. In most studies, adopted children tend to have above-average IQs (van Ijzendoorn, Juffer, & Poelhius, 2005). Why should this be? The most plausible explanation is environmental: parents who adopt children are not a random subset of the population of parents, nor are adoptive homes a random subset of the population of homes. Adoptive parents tend to be highly motivated parents, and adoptive homes tend to be privileged in various ways (such as having a large number of books available and access to good-quality schools for the children). These factors apparently boost the IQs of children who grow up in such settings. Thus, adoption studies provide evidence for *both* genetic and environmental effects.

TWIN STUDIES The logic of the twin-study approach was explained in Chapter 3. As discussed in that chapter, there are two types of twins: monozygotic (or identical) twins, who are genetically identical; and dizygotic (or fraternal) twins, who have approximately 50 percent genetic overlap and thus are no more related than are ordinary siblings. Researchers have compared correlations in IQ for members of identical twin pairs with correlations in IQ for members of fraternal twin pairs. If genes are important, the correlations for identical twins should be higher than those for fraternal twins.

Identical twins not only look alike but may also be treated alike. Could similarities in their environment account in part for their similar IQs? (© *Ace Stock Limited/Alamy*)

The results from many such studies were summarized in Table 3.3. The consistent finding is that identical twins *are* more similar (Bishop et al., 2003; Bouchard & McGue, 2003; Plomin & Spinath, 2004). The same pattern emerges for tests of more specific abilities—for example, verbal and mathematical skills or spatial reasoning ability (Plomin, 1990).

Like family studies, twin studies are compatible with a genetic model, but they do not prove it correct. Environmental factors again provide an alternative explanation. Perhaps identical twins are treated more similarly than are fraternal twins. If so, the greater similarity in IQ may have both an environmental and a genetic basis (Gregory et al., 2011).

Researchers have tried in various ways to control for this environmental alternative. Some have attempted to measure aspects of the twins' environments to see whether identical twins are, in fact, treated more similarly than are fraternal twins. Investigators have concluded that such differential treatment is less marked than is often claimed; furthermore, to the extent that it does occur, it appears to be elicited by pre-existing characteristics of the twins, such as the greater physical similarity or more similar temperaments of identical twins. In this view, then, the similarity between identical twins leads to their being treated similarly, not the reverse (Lytton, 1977, 1980, 2000).

The most widely cited attempt to control for environmental factors comes from the study of twins reared apart. If identical twins are separated early in life and reared in unrelated environments, then there is no environmental basis (other than prenatal experiences) for their developing similarly. The twins still share 100 percent of their genes, however. Should their IQs still be correlated, powerful evidence for the importance of genes would be gained. Table 10.5 summarizes results from studies of twins reared apart. The values in the table indicate that separated twins correlate quite substantially in IQ. Indeed, the reported correlations for identical twins, even when reared apart, are higher than those for fraternal twins reared in the same home (Plomin & Spinath, 2004)!

THE CONCEPT OF HERITABILITY The three kinds of evidence that we have considered all point to the same conclusion: differences in genes and differences in environments can both lead to differences in IQ. This conclusion is important, but very general. Can we go beyond a general statement that both factors are important, and say something about their relative importance?

TABLE 10.5 CORRELATIONS IN IQ OF RELATED AND UNRELATED CHILDREN REARED TOGETHER OR APART

Relationship and Rearing Condition	Average Correlation	Number of Pairs
Identical twins reared together	.86	4,672
Fraternal twins reared together	.60	5,533
Siblings reared together	.47	26,473
Unrelated children reared together	.32	714
Identical twins reared apart	.72	6

Source: Adapted from "Familial Studies of Intelligence: A Review" by T. J. Bouchard, Jr. and M. McGue, 1981, *Science, 212*, 1056. Copyright © 1981 by the American Association for the Advancement of Science. Adapted by permission.

Jerry Levey and Mark Newman, identical twins separated at birth and reared apart, met at a firefighters' convention. Do you think their IQs would be similar? Why? (*T. K. Wanstal/The Image Works*)

We must emphasize that the question of relative importance makes sense only when we are talking about differences among people. Any individual's intelligence clearly depends on both genes and environment. There is no way, when talking about an individual's development, to disentangle the two factors or to label one as more important than the other. We simply would not exist without both genes and environment, let alone have a height or weight or an IQ to explain.

Suppose, however, that we are studying a sample of people who differ in IQ and we wish to determine the origin of these differences. In this case, the question of relative importance makes sense. The differences among the members of our sample may be totally or predominantly genetic in origin, totally or predominantly environmental in origin, or may reflect a mixture of genetic and environmental contributions.

Researchers who attempt to determine relative importance make use of exactly the sorts of data that we have been discussing—data from kinship studies, adoption studies, and twin studies. What they add to these data is a set of statistical procedures for calculating the heritability of IQ. The term **heritability** refers to the proportion of variance in a trait that can be attributed to genetic variance in the sample being studied. It is, in other words, an estimate of the extent to which differences among people come from differences in their genes as opposed to differences in their environments. The *heritability index* provides a measure of that estimate. It is a statistic that ranges from 0 (all of the differences are environmental in origin) to 1 (all of the differences are genetic in origin).

Heritability The proportion of variance in a trait (such as IQ) that can be attributed to genetic variance in the sample being studied.

A heritability index can be computed in various ways, depending on the degree to which people are related, whether they share the same or different environments, and so on (Plomin, 1990). One method is to use data from identical and fraternal twins, where both groups of twins have been reared together, using the following formula:

$$\text{Heritability} = (\text{correlation between identical twins} - \text{correlation between fraternal twins}) \times 2$$

Entering the average correlations from Table 10.5 into this formula provides the following estimate of heritability:

$$\text{Heritability} = (.86 - .60) \times 2 = .52$$

Thus, on the basis of these data, we would estimate the heritability of IQ to be .52. This is indeed consistent with the most widely accepted contemporary estimates of the heritability of IQ that place the value at about .40 to .70, with figures toward the lower end of the range more typical in childhood and somewhat higher values for adult samples (Grigorenko, 2000; Plomin & Spinath, 2004). By these estimates, then, approximately half the variation in people's IQs results from differences in their genes. The conclusion that genes are important should come as no surprise in light of the evidence that we have reviewed. The heritability estimates follow directly from the findings just discussed—the similarity in IQ between identical twins, the correlations in IQ between adopted children and their biological parents, and so on.

It is important to note some limitations of the heritability index. First, heritability can be calculated in different ways, and the value obtained may vary depending on the method used and on the particular data that the researcher decides to emphasize. Second, whatever the heritability may be, the value is specific to the sample studied and cannot be generalized to other samples. The value is specific to the sample studied because it depends on two factors: the range of environmental differences in the sample, and the range of genetic differences in the sample. If we increase either range, we give that factor more chance to have an effect; conversely, if we decrease either range, we give that factor less chance to have an effect. In either case, we change the heritability.

Let us consider an example of this point, using not intelligence but height as the outcome we wish to explain. Imagine an island on which every person receives exactly 100 percent of his or her nutritional needs (Bjorklund, 2000a). In this case, the heritability for height has to be close to 1 because there is no variability in the main environmental contributor to differences in height (i.e., nutrition). If a factor does not vary in some sample of people, it cannot produce differences among those people. Suppose, however, that famine strikes part of the island. Some people still receive 100 percent of their nutritional needs; others, however, fall well short of this ideal. Over time, people in the better-nourished group grow taller than people in the poorly nourished group. In this case, the heritability for height becomes less than 1 because environmental as well as genetic differences are now contributing to variations in height. Because the range of environmental differences has grown, the relative importance of genes and environment has changed.

In a parallel fashion, the heritability of IQ has also been found to vary depending on the environment. In impoverished, low socioeconomic status environments, most of the variability in IQ scores is due to environment, while the contribution of genes is minimal. In high socioeconomic environments, the effects are reversed: most of the variability in IQ scores is due to heredity (Turkheimer, Haley, Waldron, D'Onofrio, & Gottesman, 2003). How could it be that the IQs of children from disadvantaged backgrounds are less affected by their genes than are the IQs of children from more enriched backgrounds? As Alison Gopnik (2009) explains, for children living in disadvantaged circumstances, environmental variations can make a big difference. The effects of going to a better school, for example, may greatly overshadow differences due to heredity. On the other hand, in high socioeconomic groups, there is less variability in the environment—all the children, for example, are already going to good schools—and so differences between them more likely reflect the effects of heredity (Gopnik, 2009).

FIGURE 10.3

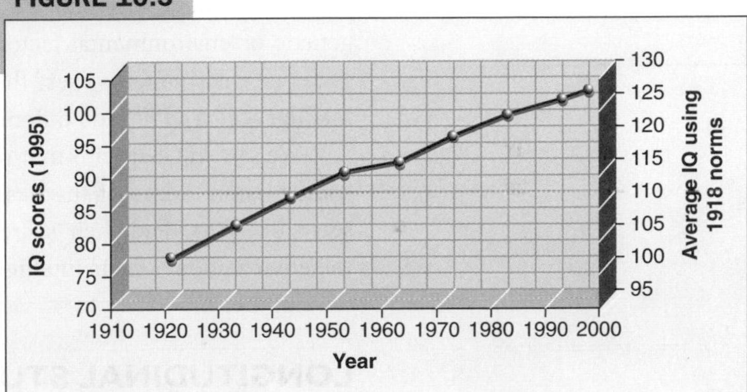

The Flynn Effect. Flynn demonstrated that intelligence scores have increased from 1918 to 1995. The right axis of the graph shows that if the 1918 scales were used today, the average IQ score in the United States would be 125. The left axis shows that if the 1995 scales were used, the average IQ score in 1918 would equate to a score of 76 today. *Adapted from Comer, R., & Gould, E. (2011).* Psychology Around Us *(p. 329). Hoboken, NJ: Wiley. Based on Flynn, J. R. (1998). IQ gains over time: Toward finding the causes. In U. Neisser (Ed.),* The rising curve: Long-term gains in IQ and related measures *(p. 37). Washington, DC: American Psychological Association.* Adapted with permission of the illustrator.

The sample-specific nature of heritability has two further important implications. First, a particular heritability value—based as it is on the current range of genes and environments—tells us nothing for certain about what might happen in the future. In particular, heritability does not tell us about the possible effects of improvements in the environment. Height, for example, typically shows high heritability, yet average height has increased over the last 100 years, presumably because of improvements in nutrition (Angoff, 1988). Likewise, performance on IQ tests has improved steadily ever since the tests were first introduced, with an average gain of about 3 points per decade. Indeed, this is one major reason why IQ tests must be periodically revised and re-normed. This phenomenon of increasing IQ performance over time is known as the **Flynn Effect**, named after James Flynn, the New Zealand researcher who most fully documented these changes (Flynn, 2006, 2007). (Figure 10.3 illustrates how intelligence scores increased between 1918 and 1995.) Thus, however high heritability may be, improvements in the environment could still lead to gains in children's intelligence.

Flynn Effect Increase over time in the average level of performance on IQ tests.

Second, heritability tells us nothing for certain about comparisons between samples that were not included in the heritability estimate. Going back to our example of the heights of the inhabitants of an island, knowing what the heritability for height is on Island A, for example, does not tell us why its residents are taller or shorter than residents of Island B. Whatever the heritability may be within one group, differences between groups could result solely from differences in their genes, solely from differences in their environments, or from some combination of genes and environment.

LEARNING OBJECTIVE 10.2

Understand the organization and stability of intelligence, and the origins of individual differences.

1. Is intelligence a unitary trait?
2. Do children's IQs remain stable as they develop?
3. What do we know about the heritability of IQ?

Learning Objective 10.3

Understand the ways in which the environment affects IQ.

CONTRIBUTIONS OF THE ENVIRONMENT

In the preceding section, we discussed some of the limitations of the heritability index. However, we have yet to note what is perhaps the most important limitation. At best, heritability estimates answer the question of *how much*: How much of the variation among people can be attributed to genetic or environmental factors? Such estimates tell us nothing about the processes by which genes or environments exert their effects. *How* is a genotype translated into a particular level of intelligence? And *how* do different environments shape different kinds of cognitive development?

We saw in Chapter 3 that researchers are just beginning to unravel the mysteries of genetic transmission. Some of the basic principles and mechanisms have been discovered, and more seem likely to yield their secrets in the near future. Our focus now is on the ways in which the environment affects intelligence. We begin with the contribution of home life to intellectual development.

LONGITUDINAL STUDIES

Several kinds of research provide evidence about the contribution of family experience to children's intelligence. The longitudinal studies mentioned earlier are one source of evidence. Such studies have shown that IQ is not perfectly stable as children develop, and that a particular child's IQ may go up or down by 30 or 40 points across childhood. Researchers have sought to discover whether these changes in IQ can be linked to characteristics of the children's environments.

Sameroff and associates, for example (Sameroff et al., 1993), followed a sample of children and their parents from the time the children were 4 until they reached the age of 14. Included at both time periods was an assessment of the extent to which the child's family life was characterized by each of the risk factors listed in Table 10.6. At both age periods, the children's IQs were negatively related to the number of risk factors; that is, the more risk factors present, the lower, on average, were the IQs. No single category of risk emerged as critical; rather, what seemed important was the accumulation of different forms of risk. Furthermore, risk at age 4 proved predictive of IQ at age 13. Children with difficult early environments were most likely to experience continued problems in intellectual adaptation. The negative impact of early risk, it is important to note, is not limited to IQ scores, but extends as well to measures of language development and performance in school (Burchinal et al., 2000; Caughy, 1996).

McCall and colleagues (1973) focused more directly on parents' contributions to stability or change in IQ. They analyzed patterns of IQ change for 80 children participating in a long-term longitudinal study. They found that two aspects of parental behaviour showed the strongest relation to IQ change. Children who declined in IQ tended to have parents who made relatively little effort to stimulate them or to accelerate their development, and who also fell at the extremes in their use of punishment (either very high or very low). In contrast, children who increased in IQ tended to have parents who emphasized intellectual acceleration and who were intermediate in the severity of their discipline. Thus, the most adaptive parental pattern appeared to be one that stressed stimulation and intellectual encouragement within a general context of structure and control. Similar conclusions have emerged from other studies of the child-rearing antecedents of intellectual competence (Wachs, 1992; Williams, 1998).

TABLE 10.6 RISK FACTORS IN THE SAMEROFF ET AL. STUDY OF FAMILY ENVIRONMENT AND IQ

Risk Factor	Description
Occupation	Head of household is unemployed or holds low-skilled occupation.
Mother's education	Mother did not complete high school.
Family size	Family has four or more children.
Father's absence	Father is not present in the home.
Stressful life events	Family experienced at least 20 stressful events during the child's first 4 years.
Parenting perspectives	Parents hold relatively rigid and absolutist conceptions of children and child rearing.
Maternal anxiety	Mother has unusually high anxiety.
Maternal mental health	Mother has relatively poor mental health.
Mother–child interaction	Mother shows little positive affect toward child.

Source: Adapted from "Stability of Intelligence from Preschool to Adolescence: The Influence of Social and Family Risk Factors" by A. J. Sameroff, R. Seifer, A. Baldwin, and C. Baldwin, 1993, *Child Development, 64*, p. 85. Copyright © 1993 by the Society for Research in Child Development. Adapted by permission.

RESEARCH WITH THE HOME

To identify the environmental contributors to intellectual development, we must have a way to assess the quality of the child's environment. Undoubtedly the most popular contemporary approach to measuring the home environment is an instrument called the **HOME (Home Observation for Measurement of the Environment)**. In this section, we review findings from research with the HOME.

HOME (Home Observation for Measurement of the Environment) An instrument for assessing the quality of the early home environment. Includes dimensions such as maternal involvement and variety of play materials.

The infant version of the HOME, developed by Caldwell and Bradley (1984; Linver, Martin, & Brooks-Gunn, 2004), consists of 45 items intended to tap the quality of the child's environment during the first three years. Each item is scored either yes (this feature is characteristic of the child's environment) or no (this feature is not characteristic). The 45 items are, in turn, grouped into six general subscales. The subscales and examples of the corresponding items are shown in Table 10.7. Scoring on the HOME is conducted during a one-hour home visit and is based on a combination of interviews with the parent and observation of parent–child interaction.

Of course, the infant environment, important though it may be, is not our only concern. There has long been a preschool version of the HOME as well. The preschool HOME is similar in structure to the infant scale, but includes 55 items and eight subscales. More recently, HOME scales have been developed for the periods of middle childhood and adolescence (Bradley et al., 2000).

Do scores on the HOME relate to children's IQs? Many studies indicate that they do (Bradley, 1994, 1999). In general, the higher the score on the HOME (that is, the greater the number of "yes" answers), the better is the child's development. There is some evidence that each of the subscales correlates with IQ, although which scales predict most strongly varies to some extent across studies and across age periods. Perhaps the most consistently important dimensions are parental involvement, play materials, and variety of stimulation.

Measures on the HOME relate to contemporaneous measures of the child's intelligence. That is, scores on the infant version of the HOME correlate with infant intelligence (Barnard, Bee, & Hammond, 1984), scores on the preschool version correlate with preschool intelligence (Espy, Molfese, & DiLalla, 2001; Siegel, 1984), and scores on the middle childhood version correlate with childhood intelligence (Luster & Denbow, 1992). Measures on the HOME also relate to future intelligence. In one study, for example, the correlation between the HOME score at 6 months and IQ at 4.5 years was .50; the correlation between the HOME at 24 months and IQ at 4.5 years was .63

TABLE 10.7 SUBSCALES AND EXAMPLES OF ITEMS ON THE HOME (INFANT VERSION)

Subscale 1. Emotional and Verbal Responsivity of Parent
• Parent responds to child's vocalizations with a verbal response. • Parent spontaneously praises child's qualities or behaviour twice during visit. • Parent tells child the name of some object during visit or says name of person or object in a "teaching" style. • Parent caresses or kisses child at least once during visit.
Subscale 2. Avoidance of Restriction and Punishment
• Parent does not express overt annoyance with or hostility toward child. • Parent neither slaps nor spanks child during visit. • Parent does not scold or derogate child during visit.
Subscale 3. Organization of Physical and Temporal Environment
• Child gets out of house at least four times a week. • Child has a special place in which to keep his or her toys and "treasures." • Child's play environment appears safe and free of hazards.
Subscale 4. Provision of Appropriate Play Materials
• Parent provides learning equipment appropriate to age—cuddly toy or role-playing toys. • Parent provides eye–hand coordination toys that permit combinations—stacking or nesting toys, blocks or building toys. • Parent provides toys for literature or music.
Subscale 5. Parental Involvement with Child
• Parent "talks" to child while doing housework. • Parent structures child's play periods. • Parent provides toys that challenge child to develop new skills.
Subscale 6. Opportunities for Variety in Daily Stimulation
• Parent reads stories at least three times weekly. • Family visits or receives visits from relatives. • Child has three or more books of his or her own.

Source: Adapted from "174 Children: A Study of the Relationship between Home Environment and Cognitive Development during the First 5 Years" by R. H. Bradley and B. M. Caldwell, 1982. In A.W. Gottfried (Ed.), *Home Environment and Early Cognitive Development*, New York: Academic Press, 7–8.

(Bradley & Caldwell, 1984a). Other studies have demonstrated relations between HOME scores in infancy and both IQ and school performance during the grade-school years (Bradley & Caldwell, 1984b; Olson, Bates, & Kaskie, 1992). Thus, the quality of the child's early environment is predictive of various aspects of the child's later intelligence.

Although the HOME is a valuable source of evidence with respect to experience and intelligence, one caution should be noted. Research suggests that genetic factors may also contribute to findings with the HOME (Braungart, Fulker, & Plomin, 1992; Cherny, 1994; Cleveland et al., 2000). Genetically based characteristics of children may influence the HOME score itself because such characteristics will affect the treatment that children receive from their parents (recall Bronfenbrenner's notion of developmentally generative characteristics, discussed in Chapter 1). And genetic characteristics of the parents may affect both the home environment and the child's intelligence, thus contributing to the correlation between HOME measures and children's IQs (Lytton, 2000). The conclusion that both genes and environment are important for intelligence—and that the two factors are often very difficult to separate—should be familiar by now.

FAMILIES AND ACHIEVEMENT: CROSS-CULTURAL RESEARCH

As we discussed in Chapter 2, comparison of different cultures allows us to explore variations in experience and development that might not be evident within a single cultural setting. Some of the most interesting results from such comparisons concern performance on the kinds of academic measures that are often linked to IQ. Differences in mathematical and science achievement between cultures are especially striking.

American children, on average, do not perform well in mathematics and science. This conclusion has emerged from several surveys of cross-national differences in recent years. The contrast with children from Asian countries is especially marked. For example, in a couple of recent international surveys, American students scored in the bottom third of 15-year-old students from 41 countries in mathematical ability (Bussière, Cartwright, & Knighton, 2004) and at the 50th percentile of 57 participating countries in terms of science ability (Bussière, Knighton, & Pennock, 2007). Over the past two decades, a similarly disappointing picture has been painted for American children, while children from China and Japan, in contrast, have consistently been found to be near the top of the range (Geary, 1996; U.S. Department of Education, 2001).

Canadian students from every province, by way of comparison, perform significantly better on standardized tests of both mathematics and science than their American counterparts (Bussière et al., 2001, 2004, 2007), with their performance rivalling that of Chinese and Japanese students. Figure 10.4 illustrates the mathematical performance of 15-year-olds from 41 countries.

FIGURE 10.4

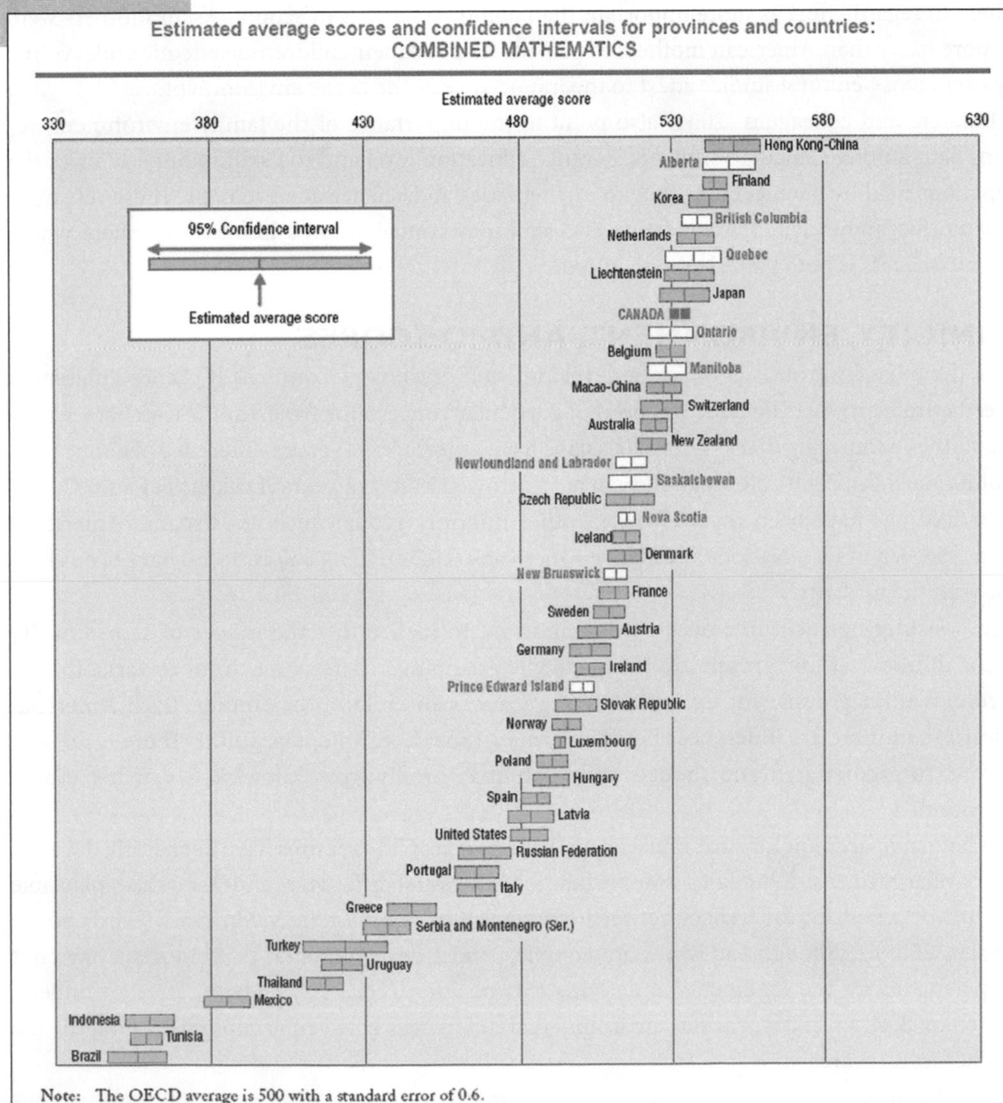

Estimated Average Scores and Confidence Intervals for Provinces and Countries: Combined Mathematics. Source: *Adapted from Statistics Canada publication* The Performance of Canada's Youth in Mathematics, Reading, Science and Problem Solving: 2003 First Findings for Canadians Aged 15, *Catalogue 81-590-X, no. 2.*

Why do American children do so poorly in mathematics and science? It is tempting to indict the school system, and schools, as we discuss more fully in the next section, can be quite important. Some differences between Asians and Americans, however, are evident by age 5, before most children have even started school (Stevenson, Lee, & Stigler, 1986). Furthermore, Asian American students in the United States often outperform Caucasian students, even though both groups are moving through the same school systems (Sue & Ozaki, 1990). These findings suggest that schools are not the sole explanation; the family environment also contributes.

The most ambitious attempt to identify family bases for academic achievement is a program of research by Stevenson and associates (Chen & Stevenson, 1995; Stevenson, Chen, & Lee, 1993; Stevenson et al., 1990). The child participants in the project were grade 1 and 5 students from the United States, China, and Japan. The children took a variety of achievement tests, and the results fit those of previous research—poorer performance in mathematics by American children than by children from China or Japan. Many of the grade 1 students were retested in grades 5 and 11, and the original results were confirmed; if anything, the cross-national gap in achievement had widened.

The children's mothers also participated in the study, and it was their beliefs and practices that constituted the main focus of the research. Mothers in all three cultures were interested in and supportive of their children's academic development. At the same time, the maternal interviews revealed cross-cultural differences in beliefs and practices that might well contribute to the superior performance of Asian children. Asian mothers, for example, were more likely than American mothers to regard effort as more important than ability in success in school. Asian mothers were also more likely than American mothers to provide help for their children's academic endeavours. Thus, such cross-cultural studies attest to the importance of the home environment.

Bussière and colleagues (2004) also point to the importance of the family environment, reporting that among Canadian students, parents' education level and the skill requirements of the occupations held by parents contribute to mathematics and science achievement. These researchers argue that higher parental education and skill may contribute to a home atmosphere where academic success is both valued and nurtured.

ETHNICITY, ENVIRONMENT, AND IQ SCORES

One of the most controversial topics in developmental psychology concerns IQ-score differences between ethnic groups. The issue has been of particular concern for American researchers, where many studies comparing Blacks and Caucasians have reported an average difference of about 10 to 15 points (Loehlin, 2000), although the gap has narrowed in recent years (Dickens & Flynn, 2006). Similar findings have been reported when other minority groups such as Hispanic Americans (Sattler, 1988), and First Nations and Native Americans (Dolan, 1999; Salois, 1999) have been compared with the majority.

In considering such differences, it is important to realize that the ranges of scores on IQ tests for different ethnic groups are completely overlapping. There is much more variability in IQ scores within groups (for example, among Caucasian children or among Black American children) than there are differences between groups (Suzuki & Valencia, 1997). There is no way, therefore, to predict anything about a child's abilities simply from knowing his or her ethnic background.

What could account for such inter-group discrepancies? The reasons have been hotly debated. Some have argued that if heredity is important for individual differences in IQ, it is also plausible that it is important for differences between ethnic groups (Herrnstein & Murray, 1994; Rushton & Jensen, 2005). Although the issues are complex, most developmental psychologists have not been persuaded by the arguments underlying this position (Dickens & Flynn, 2001; Sternberg, Grigorenko, & Kidd, 2005). Various environmental differences between groups could underlie the difference in IQ scores.

Social and economic disadvantage is one major environmental difference that must be considered. Minority children are disproportionately more likely to be living in poverty (Duncan &

Magnuson, 2005). And the consequences of living in poverty—poor nutrition, poor medical care, lack of educational resources, psychological and emotional stress—have well-documented negative effects on children's intellectual development (Sattler & Hoge, 2006; Duncan & Brooks-Gunn, 1997, 2000).

Cultural and experiential differences are other environmental factors that may be important. It has been argued that IQ tests and the testing situation may be culturally biased in favour of the middle-class majority. Questions have been raised as to whether they are fair tests of intellectual ability for all children. The argument is that both the communication style of testing and the types of knowledge required for successful performance on the test may be culturally bound, and that lack of exposure to these required skills can undermine performance (Ceci, 1996; Sternberg, 2004; Sternberg et al., 2005). Administration of the tests is another primary issue. A component of many IQ tests involves a series of factual questions asked by an adult examiner. This type of adult–child interchange, although common in middle-income Caucasian families from a very early age, may be less common as an interactional style in other cultural settings (Brooks-Gunn & Markman, 2005; Heath, 1989). As a result, the traditional testing setting may be uncomfortable or unpractised for children not familiar with this form of interaction, placing them at a disadvantage.

It has also been argued that many test items, especially those assessing vocabulary and general knowledge, may be conceptualized in favour of the majority culture's perspective. Furthermore, even performance on items believed to assess more general and inborn abilities rather than those one might acquire through learning, such as quickly assembling geometric shapes with coloured blocks, may be influenced by environmental factors. Experience with games involving similar visual-spatial abilities, such as video games that require rapid mental rotation and manipulation of visual images, may produce practice effects that can contribute positively to children's performance on such tests (Quaiser-Pohl et al., 2006; Terlecki & Newcombe, 2005). Not all groups have equal access to such resources.

Finally, even the notion of "trying one's best" on a test, or of trying to solve problems or to perform tasks "as quickly as possible," may represent middle-class values not necessarily shared by other groups. Children from some groups may see little value in trying hard on the test. Others may be reluctant to respond quickly on timed tasks, viewing it as a sign of competitiveness, which is frowned upon in some cultures (Sattler, 1988). Even expectations that children hold about their likely performance on tests may lead to self-fulfilling prophecies that can affect performance. (We discuss one such self-fulfilling prophecy, *stereotype threat*, in *Application 10.1* later in the chapter.) Moreover, aspects of the interaction between tester and child may carry different meaning in different cultures: pauses, prompts, and interruptions, along with non-verbal communication such as nodding, eye contact, and so on, can convey different meanings to those from different cultural backgrounds, which could affect test performance (Sattler & Hoge, 2006).

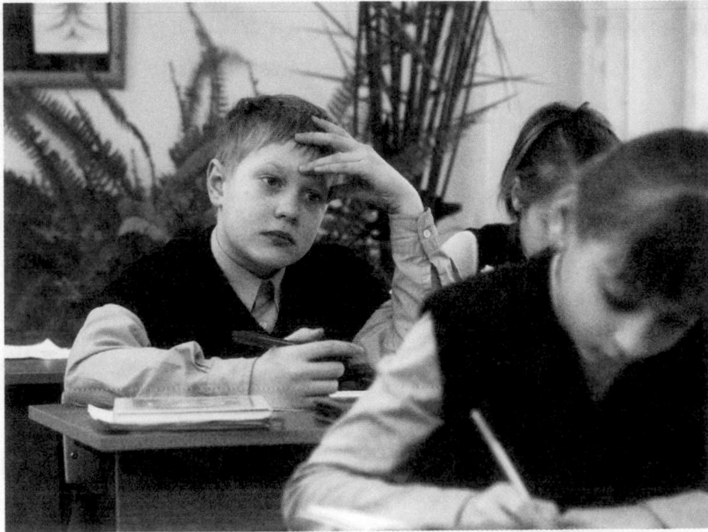

Various factors such as environment, experiences, and motivation should be considered when interpreting IQ scores of a particular child. (© *Nikolay Titov/iStock*)

Awareness of such potential differences is important both during the administration of the test and in the interpretation of a child's performance on the test. Such differences do not necessarily render the test invalid—IQ tests have been found to predict academic achievement in minority groups as well as in middle-class Caucasian groups (Sattler, 2001). However, as we have seen throughout this chapter, a child's score on an IQ test involves a complex interplay among heredity, environment, range of experiences, and motivation. As a consequence, caution must be exercised when comparing IQ scores between groups, and especially when interpreting the IQ score of a particular child.

EARLY INTERVENTION PROGRAMS

Given the importance of environmental factors, especially for children living in impoverished circumstances (Gopnik, 2009; Turkheimer et al., 2003), a number of programs have sought to improve children's environments, thereby enhancing children's intellectual development. The largest category of such intervention efforts has been directed toward a specific population: young children (usually from families of low-income or minority status) who are perceived as being at risk for school failure. The interventions involve provision of enriched environmental opportunities, and the goal is to enhance the children's prospects for success in school and in later life.

THE ABECEDARIAN PROJECT The Abecedarian Project in North Carolina (Ramey et al., 2000; Ramey, Ramey, & Lanzi, 2001) is one of the most successful of the many intervention efforts that were launched in the 1960s and 1970s. It focused on low-income children and their families. Children were enrolled as infants, with an average age of 4 months at the start of the project. Half the infants were randomly assigned to the treatment group, and half were assigned to an untreated control group. The infants in the treatment group attended a special childcare centre for eight hours a day, 50 weeks a year. The centre was of very high quality, with a low child-to-teacher ratio and a curriculum designed to promote cognitive development. Children remained in the centre until age 5, with appropriate changes in the curriculum as they grew older. They were also given nutritional supplements and health benefits, and their mothers received instruction in principles of child development. Finally, for half the sample, aspects of the intervention remained in effect through the first three years of elementary school.

The intervention had an immediate effect on IQ, with some differences between the treatment and control participants emerging at as early as 6 months of age. The differences increased throughout the duration of the program; by preschool, the average IQ difference between treatment and control was 17 points. Although the superiority of the treatment participants decreased across the school years, it did not disappear. Furthermore, the treatment participants consistently outperformed their counterparts on various measures of academic achievement. In follow-up studies, some effects of the intervention were still evident on cognitive and academic measures when participants reached 21 years of age (Campbell et al., 2001).

In addition to demonstrating the possibility for long-term success of the intervention, the Abecedarian Project provides evidence with regard to the effects of variations in the timing and intensity of intervention. Some children in the project received intervention only during the preschool years, and some only during the early school years. Although there were some benefits in both cases, the greatest gains by far were shown by the children for whom intervention began early and extended late.

PROJECT HEAD START Project Head Start is an American intervention that is significantly larger in scope than the Abecadarian Project. It is directed primarily toward low-income preschool children and their families. There are approximately 2,500 Head Start centres spread across the United States.

Head Start emphasizes family and community involvement. Parents are encouraged to volunteer in their children's classrooms and are also given a voice in decisions about the direction of the program. Rather than seeking only to correct deficiencies in the child's background, Head Start is designed to build on existing interests and strengths. Although academic readiness is always part of a Head Start curriculum, other aspects of the child's development are stressed as well. Social skills are important, as is the development of self-confidence and motivation. So, too, is the child's physical development—an emphasis on nutrition and dental and medical care has been part of Head Start since its inception.

Does Head Start work? Initial evaluations of Head Start focused on IQ gain, and many commentators were dismayed when Head Start failed to produce lasting improvements in children's IQs. In the years since the initial assessment, however, it has become clear that Head Start, like intervention programs in general, can have a number of beneficial effects that are not captured by IQ scores (Lee et al., 1990; Zigler & Finn-Stevenson, 1999; Zigler & Styfco, 1993). These effects include greater success in school, better health status, gains in social competence, and increased involvement of the family in the child's education.

BETTER BEGINNINGS, BETTER FUTURES In 1990, the Ontario government initiated a 25-year longitudinal early intervention project known as Better Beginnings, Better Futures. The program is offered to children in economically disadvantaged neighbourhoods in a number of Ontario cities. As described by Ray Peters and Kelly Petrunka of Queen's University in Kingston, Ontario, and Robert Arnold of the University of Windsor, the project has the following five goals:

a. "To reduce or prevent emotional and behavioural problems and promote healthy development of young children
b. To support and strengthen parents and families in responding to the needs of children
c. To develop a local organization to provide programs for young children
d. To encourage neighbourhood parents to participate with service providers in developing and carrying out programs
e. To establish and coordinate partnerships with existing service providers, such as schools" (Peters et al., 2003, p. 217).

The program was initiated in eight Ontario communities, including one First Nations community. As is the case with the Head Start programs just discussed, the procedures employed by individual Better Beginnings, Better Futures projects vary from community to community; the program is tailored to the needs of the residents. Several programs are school-based, whereas others take place outside the school. Programs intervene on a variety of levels, including nutrition and meals, classroom enrichment, homework help and tutoring, programs for parents, after-school activities, and so on.

Follow-up studies of participants in the Better Beginnings, Better Futures program suggest it is effective. Improvements associated with the program have been reported in children's emotional and behavioural problems, as well as in their social skills. Although no consistent overall change has been found in scholastic achievement across the eight different sites, the program appears to have had the effect of reducing participants' need for special education services. In addition, results indicate positive consequences of the program not just for the child participants, but also for their parents. Improvements have been reported in children's and parents' health, and some settings have reported improvements in parenting skills. Moreover, parents in more than half the sites involved reported improvements in neighbourhood quality of life (Peters, 2005; Peters et al., 2003).

ABORIGINAL HEAD START Aboriginal Head Start is an early intervention program for First Nations, Inuit, and Métis children. It was initiated in 1995 by the Canadian federal government to facilitate the development of Aboriginal children by meeting their psychological, emotional, social, health, and nutritional needs. It consists of a half-day preschool program for children 3 to 5 years of age, and is designed to prepare children for elementary school. The program is funded by the Public Health Agency of Canada and is offered at no cost to participants. Aboriginal Head Start programs are designed, controlled, and administered by local communities in 126 urban and northern communities in all ten provinces and three territories. Parents are directly involved in the programs. Approximately 3,900 Aboriginal children are involved in AHS programs. According to the Public Health Agency of Canada (2004), the program emphasizes the following six areas:

1. to foster a positive identity as Aboriginal children and develop children's knowledge of their language and culture

2. to support and encourage children to develop an enthusiasm for learning that will remain with them throughout school
3. to empower parents and caregivers in the area of health, to improve self-care, and to develop social support networks
4. to provide children with good nutrition, and to provide educational resources to parents and caregivers concerning nutrition
5. to assist families in taking advantage of community resources available to them
6. to help parents become more confident as caregivers and more aware of their children's development, and to improve family relationships

For Thought and Discussion

If you were developing an intervention program for an at-risk population, what would your program emphasize, and how would you measure its effectiveness?

Project evaluations of Aboriginal Head Start done at the community level suggest that this project is effective. Gains have been reported in many areas of children's development, and similar gains have been reported in parenting skills for adult participants (Public Health Agency of Canada, 2004). A National Impact Evaluation is underway to assess the impact of the Aboriginal Head Start program as a whole.

CONCLUSIONS FROM EARLY INTERVENTION PROGRAMS

What do the results from early intervention programs tell us? Reviews of the intervention literature support several general conclusions (Brooks-Gunn, 2003; Peters, 2005; Ramey et al., 2001).

First, although not all projects have examined effects on children's IQ, those that have done so find an immediate positive effect on children's IQ, which typically persists for at least a year or two after the program has ended. The IQ effects, however, do show a definite tendency to diminish with time. The main effect of intervention seems to be to minimize the declines in IQ that the children would otherwise experience.

Second, positive effects of intervention are often more marked on measures other than IQ. Even in the absence of IQ gain, participation in early intervention is often associated with higher scores on standardized achievement tests, lower probability of being assigned to special education classes, and lower probability of being retained in a grade. In some projects, there is also evidence for positive effects on self-concept, achievement motivation, and maternal attitudes toward schooling. Such findings have reinforced long-standing criticisms of the practice of using IQ scores as the main index of the success of intervention. Not only is IQ an incomplete measure of intellectual ability (Sternberg, 2009c), but other kinds of effects (such as the effect on school performance) may be more important for the child's development. Furthermore, IQ tests cannot measure the non-intellectual benefits that some programs may have (improved nutritional status, better social competence, and so on).

What is the rationale for offering early intervention programs? What factors contribute to the success of these programs? (*Yellow Dog Productions/Getty Images*)

A third set of conclusions concerns the specific features of intervention that produce positive effects. Ramey and Ramey (1998) identified six principles that capture much of what is known about the contributors to successful intervention. Table 10.8 summarizes these principles. Note the mixed message that emerges from this summary. On the positive side, it is clear that intervention programs *can* produce genuine and lasting benefits for children and their families, and that psychologists and educators have learned much about the factors that determine success. On the negative side, it is clear that success does not come easily; rather, a continued societal commitment will be required to ensure that the necessary resources are devoted to the task.

TABLE 10.8 PRINCIPLES OF SUCCESSFUL INTERVENTION (RAMEY & RAMEY)

Principle	Description
Principle of developmental timing	Programs that begin early and extend later in development are more successful than those of briefer duration.
Principle of program intensity	Programs that are more intensive (with regard, for example, to number of hours and range of activities) are more effective than less intense programs.
Principle of direct provision of learning experiences	Programs that provide direct learning experiences to children are more effective than those that rely on indirect methods (e.g., parent training).
Principle of program breadth and flexibility	Programs that provide more comprehensive services and use multiple routes are more effective than programs that are narrower in focus.
Principle of individual differences	Some children show greater benefits from participation than do others.
Principle of environmental maintenance of development	Maintenance of positive effects over time depends on adequate environmental supports.

Source: Adapted from "Early Intervention and Early Experience" by C.T. Ramey and S.L. Ramey, 1998, *American Psychologist, 53,* 109–120. Copyright © 1998 by the American Psychological Association. Adapted by permission.

APPLICATION 10.1
REDUCING STEREOTYPE THREAT IN MINORITY POPULATIONS

We have been discussing how environmental factors can affect children's academic and test performance. Researchers have also found that attitudes that children hold about their own abilities can influence performance. One such attitude is **stereotype threat**—the extra pressure that people feel in situations in which their performance may confirm a negative stereotype about their group (Steele & Aronson, 1995). Importantly, students can suffer stereotype threat even if they do not believe the stereotype, but it is more damaging to performance when the stereotype is endorsed (Schmader, Johns, & Barquissau, 2004). Researchers have demonstrated stereotype threat under controlled laboratory conditions, as well as in real-world classrooms (Good, Aronson, & Inzlicht, 2003). For instance, females tend to perform more poorly on assessments of mathematical ability when researchers invoke the stereotype that females are less capable in math (Cadinu, Maass, Rosabianca, & Kiesner, 2005). Invoking the stereotype may involve comments made by or expectations of parents or teachers (Bhanot & Jovanovic, 2005), or may even involve something as simple as providing math problems with pictures of only males in the examples. (We discuss such gender-based stereotypes in Chapter 16.)

Stereotype threat Extra pressure people feel in situations in which their performance may confirm a negative stereotype held about their group.

Stereotype threat is not limited to mathematics and females. For example, in a classic study, Steele and Aronson (1995) found that Black American students performed significantly worse on a standardized test when the test was presented as a diagnostic measure of their intellectual abilities in contrast to its being presented as simply a problem-solving task. This effect was not seen in a group of Caucasian American students, whose performance on the test was the same under both conditions. Simply asking students to indicate their race on a test form can be sufficient to induce stereotype threat (Steele & Aronson, 1998). Even Caucasian American males, who normally do not show evidence of stereotype threat, have been found to show impaired performance on difficult mathematics assessments when told that Caucasian Americans may be inferior to Asian Americans in mathematics (Aronson et al., 1999).

As illustrated in Figure 10.5, theorists believe that stereotype threat undermines performance in two ways. First, in the short run, it raises anxiety and impairs test performance. For example, under conditions of stereotype threat, Black-American college students report feeling more anxious. Higher levels of anxiety have been confirmed through blood pressure measures (Blascovich. Spencer, Quinn, & Steele, 2001). Second, stereotype threat can hamper academic performance through the ways students cope with the threat it poses to their self-esteem. To protect themselves, students may "disidentify," or disengage, from the threatened domain. Students tend to base their self-esteem on domains in which they can excel and devalue domains in which success is less likely (Marsh, Trautwein, Lüdtke, Koeller, & Baumert, 2005). Disengagement can be short-lived, as when a student discounts the importance of a poor exam score. It can also contribute to a general disidentifying with academics over time. For example, females asked to complete a difficult math task under stereotype threat conditions reported more negative thoughts specifically related to the test and to math than those who completed the task under no-threat conditions (Cadinu et al., 2005). Other research has indicated that stereotype threat actually interferes with the working memory capacity available to individuals in the

(continued)

Application 10.1 Reducing Stereotype Threat in Minority Populations *continued*

stereotype conditions (Schmader, 2010; Schmader & Johns, 2003).

Negative stereotypes (e.g., girls are bad at math) can create situational pressure that causes a decrease in performance. How do we help students demonstrate their actual ability and knowledge? Researchers have explored several means of alleviating stereotype threat. One approach is to redefine the testing situation to make it less threatening (Alter et al., 2010; Steele & Aronson, 1995). Although this manipulation has proven to be effective in laboratory settings, it would be difficult to readily apply it in real-world situations. For instance, it would not be realistic to tell students that a test is not important.

In real-world settings, directly countering the stereotype appears to help. For instance, when women are told that females perform just as well as males on specific kinds of math problems, their performance improves (Johns, Schmader, & Martens, 2005). This result suggests that teaching students about stereotype threat might offer a practical way to reduce its negative effects. Drawing students' attention to the accomplishments of members of their group also appears to inoculate vulnerable students against the threat (McIntyre, Paulson, & Lord, 2003). For example, shortly after the election of Barack Obama as the first Black president in the United States, some researchers noticed a positive effect on Black Americans' academic performance, a phenomenon aptly labelled the "Obama Effect" (Marx, Ko, & Friedman, 2009).

We know from decades of research that cultural stereotypes are very difficult to change, even among young children. We also know that children gain knowledge of stereotypes at a very young age. Nevertheless, current research suggests that it may be possible to create contexts—in classrooms and even entire schools—in which negative stereotypes do not apply.

FIGURE 10.5

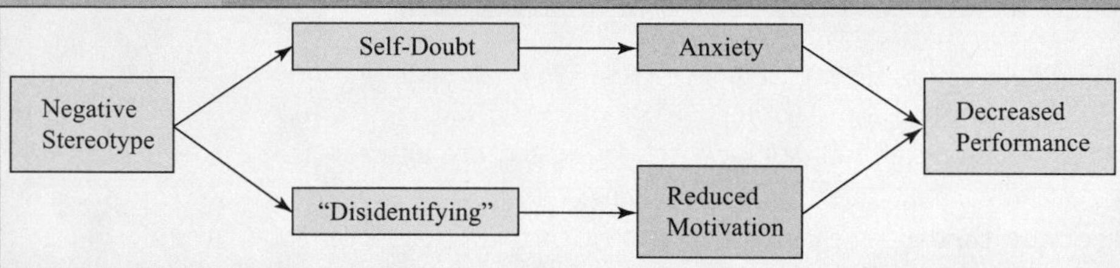

Stereotype threat. The two ways in which stereotype threat can undermine performance: (1) anxiety that results from self-doubt can decrease test performance and (2) reduced motivation associated with disidentifying as a way to protect self-esteem can negatively affect performance. *Adapted from Huffman, K., Younger, A., and Vanston, C. (2010).* Visualizing Psychology, *Canadian Edition, (p. 231). Toronto: John Wiley & Sons Canada, Ltd.*

For Thought and Discussion

Have you experienced stereotype threat? In what areas other than academic performance could group stereotypes have a negative effect on performance?

LEARNING OBJECTIVE 10.3

Understand the ways in which the environment affects IQ.

1. How does the family environment influence IQ?
2. What might account for minority group differences in IQ scores?
3. What are some examples of early intervention programs?
4. Are early intervention programs effective?
5. What is stereotype threat and how does it influence test performance?

Learning Objective 10.4

Evaluate different aspects of the schooling experience and how these affect cognitive development.

SCHOOLING: VARIATIONS AND EFFECTS

The average North American child spends approximately 15,000 hours in school between the ages of 5 and 18. Clearly, school is a major setting within which children in our society exercise—and develop—their intellectual abilities. What do we know about the impact of schooling on cognitive development? In addressing this question, we draw from the same two general kinds of evidence that were the focus of our discussions of the family. In this case, we begin with comparisons of different cultures, after which we turn to variations within Western culture.

CROSS-CULTURAL STUDIES

A difficulty in determining the effects of schooling in Western culture is its pervasiveness: virtually every child goes to school. When we broaden our scope to encompass other cultures, this uniformity no longer holds. Of course, if we simply compare cultures with and without schooling, it will be difficult to interpret our results because the cultures may differ in a number of ways apart from the presence or absence of school. Most informative, therefore, are cases in which only some children within a culture go to school or in which schooling has been recently introduced, allowing us to make a before-and-after comparison. Psychologists have been able to find and to study a number of such cases (Barber, 2005; Ceci, 1996; Cole, 1999). Several conclusions emerge.

A first conclusion is that some aspects of children's cognitive development seem to be more strongly and consistently affected by schooling than others. Many of the kinds of knowledge studied by Piaget fall into the relatively unaffected category. Schooling does sometimes influence the development of Piagetian concepts—most obviously, effects on the rate at which knowledge is acquired. Most studies, however, report no clear qualitative differences between schooled and unschooled children in their mastery of concepts such as conservation, nor is there any lasting advantage for children who have been to school.

Other aspects of cognitive development appear to be affected more by schooling. Skill at various kinds of perceptual analysis can be facilitated by schooling; for example, the ability to match stimuli or to construct models of familiar patterns. Schooling can also affect memory: schooled children not only perform better on a variety of memory tasks, they are also more likely to use mnemonic strategies to help themselves remember. Schooling also affects how children classify objects. Children who have been to school are more likely to group objects in terms of general categories (e.g., all of the foods together), rather than functional or thematic relations (e.g., ice cream and spoon together). Similarly, schooling affects how children think about words and use language, with schooled children more likely to think in terms of general categories and abstract relations. Finally, and perhaps most generally, schooling improves children's ability to reflect on their own cognitive processes—to think about thinking (de Jager, Jansen, & Reezigt, 2005). As we saw in Chapter 9, such metacognition has emerged as an active area of current research interest.

Why does schooling produce these effects? Rogoff (1981) discusses four factors that may play roles. Perhaps the most obvious explanation is that schooling directly teaches many of the specific skills in which schooled children excel. Classification, for example, is a common activity in school, and committing material to memory is even more common. A more general proposal is that schooling exerts its effects through its emphasis on the search for general rules—for universal systems of knowledge (such as mathematics) within which specific instances can be understood. A third possibility stresses the differences between teaching in school and teaching outside school. Teaching in school often involves the verbal transmission of information that is far removed from its everyday context, a style of instruction that may promote verbally based, abstract modes of thought. Finally, perhaps the most general explanation concerns a primary goal of most forms of schooling: the development of literacy. It has been argued that literacy, like verbally based teaching, promotes abstract, reflective styles of thinking. And, of course, as Keith Stanovich (1993) of the University of Toronto points out, reading can also be the door to a vast world of experiences and knowledge that could never be acquired first-hand.

AMOUNT OF SCHOOLING

We touched on some evidence about schooling in Canada and the United States in the points just made about cross-national differences. Here, we take up the topic more fully. We begin with research on the amount of schooling, after which we turn to the more difficult question of the nature or quality of schooling.

It has long been known that there is a positive relation between number of years of education completed and IQ; that is, the more years of schooling people complete, the higher (on the average) are their IQs (Barber, 2005; Jencks, 1972). The usual explanation has been that people who are

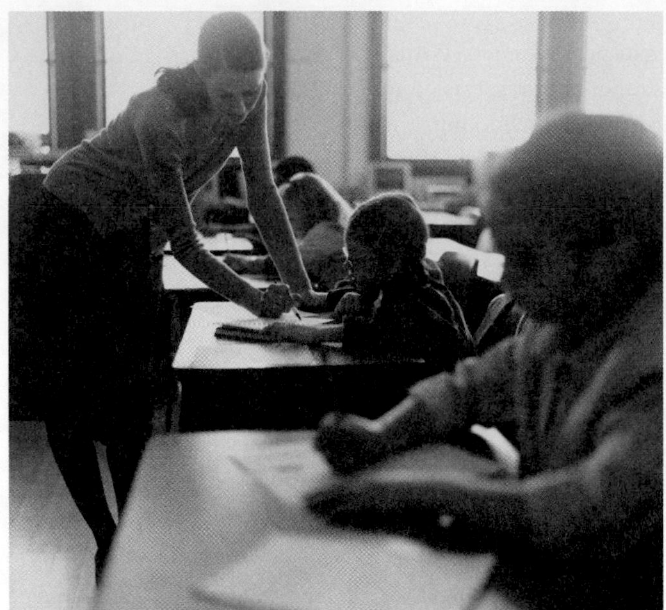

Not only do IQ tests predict success in school; recent evidence suggests that schooling can increase IQ. (*PhotoDisc, Inc./Getty Images*)

more intelligent tend to stay in school longer. This factor is almost certainly part of the basis for the correlation. It can also be argued, however, that the cause and effect may also flow in the opposite direction; that is, that schooling may actually increase IQ (Barber, 2005; Ceci & Williams, 1997, 2007). A variety of evidence supports this argument. First, children who drop out of school decline in IQ relative to children who stay in school, even when the two groups were initially equal in IQ. Second, children's IQs have been shown to decline slightly across the months of summer vacation and then to rise again during the school year. Third, children whose birthdays fall in late December, making them just barely old enough to qualify for school entry, obtain higher IQ scores by age 8 than children whose birthdays fall in early January of the next year, making them fall just short. The point is that the two groups are virtually the same age, but one group has had a year more of schooling. Using this approach, Morrison and colleagues (Christian, Bachnan, & Morrison 2001; Morrison, Griffith, & Alberts, 1997; Morrison, Smith, & Dow-Ehrensberger, 1995) have demonstrated that starting school relatively early can nurture a number of specific cognitive abilities.

For Thought and Discussion

Why does IQ predict success in school? Why does schooling then increase IQ? Do you think that intelligence tests should be used to track students' schooling?

In speculating about why schooling boosts IQ, Ceci draws on the cross-cultural evidence just discussed. We saw that schooling affects perceptual analysis, memory, language use, and classification. These skills, Ceci notes, are precisely the kinds of abilities that are stressed on IQ tests. This overlap is, of course, no accident: IQ tests were designed, in part, to predict school performance. It is not surprising, therefore, that being good at IQ-type skills is helpful in school. But it is also not surprising that experiences in school can nurture IQ.

QUALITY OF SCHOOLING

As might be expected, quality of schooling is more difficult to define and study than quantity (Eccles & Roeser, 1999; Good & Brophy, 2000). Despite the difficulties, however, few doubt that there can be important differences in the quality of the education that different children receive. Some schools consistently produce more successful outcomes than others—even when the children being served are initially equivalent. And some teachers within a school consistently have happier and more productive classrooms than others.

Michael Rutter (1983) has provided one of the most helpful surveys of the research about quality of schooling. One of the interesting messages from his review concerns factors that do *not* make much of a difference. Rutter found little evidence, for example, that variations in school success (such as performance on standardized tests, attendance rates, and graduation rates) are associated with the financial or physical resources available to the school, with the overall size of the school, or with the size of the class within the school. This conclusion does not mean that such factors are never important—no one would advocate a class size of 50 for kindergarteners. Indeed, more recent research indicates that small class size can sometimes be beneficial, especially in the early grades and perhaps especially for low-income students (Finn et al., 2001, 2005; Nye, Hedges, & Konstantopoulos, 2001). Nevertheless, the variations that are normally found along dimensions such as school and class size do not seem to be major contributors to school success.

What factors *do* influence school success? The dimensions that emerge as important in Rutter's review have to do mainly with emphasis and organization. Successful schools have a clear emphasis on academic goals, accompanied by clearly defined procedures for achieving those goals. Teachers plan the curriculum together, actively teach important content, assign and grade homework regularly, and, in general, hold high but realistic expectations for their students. Discipline within successful schools tends to be firm but fair—sufficient to maintain focus on the task at hand, but not so punitive as to arouse anxiety or resentment. Students in successful schools are helped to feel part of the school through opportunities to participate in school-related activities, as well as by the chance to have a voice in decisions concerning the school. Finally, teachers in successful schools manage their classrooms in an organized and efficient manner, maximizing the time spent on the lesson of the moment, rather than on peripheral concerns (e.g., distributing papers, setting up equipment). This same variable of classroom management has also proven important in the comparison of Asian and North American schools.

That organization and efficiency are desirable qualities in the school environment is not really in dispute; the challenge is how to achieve these characteristics. Other dimensions along which classrooms and schools vary are the subject of considerably more debate. One is the practice of **ability grouping**; that is, the separation of students who differ in ability (often as determined by standardized tests) into distinct groups for instruction. In the early school years, grouping is most likely to be at the within-class level; for example, the "red robins" and the "bluebirds" reading groups. By intermediate school and high school, grouping is more often at the between-class level; for example, separate curricula for college- or university-bound students and vocational-track students.

Ability grouping Separation of students into groups of similar ability for purposes of instruction.

For Thought and Discussion

What have been your experiences with between-class and within-class ability groupings? What were some benefits and drawbacks of these approaches?

Is ability grouping a desirable educational practice? There is no simple answer to this question. The basic rationale behind the procedure—that instruction should fit the developmental level and interests of the student—is one with which no educator would disagree, and achieving such a fit is generally easier in a small and similar-ability group than in a diverse class of 30. Furthermore, some forms of ability grouping have been shown to work well for some students. In particular, placement in challenging educational tracks with peers of similar ability is generally beneficial for students of relatively high academic ability (Fuligni, Eccles, & Barber, 1995; Pallas et al., 1994).

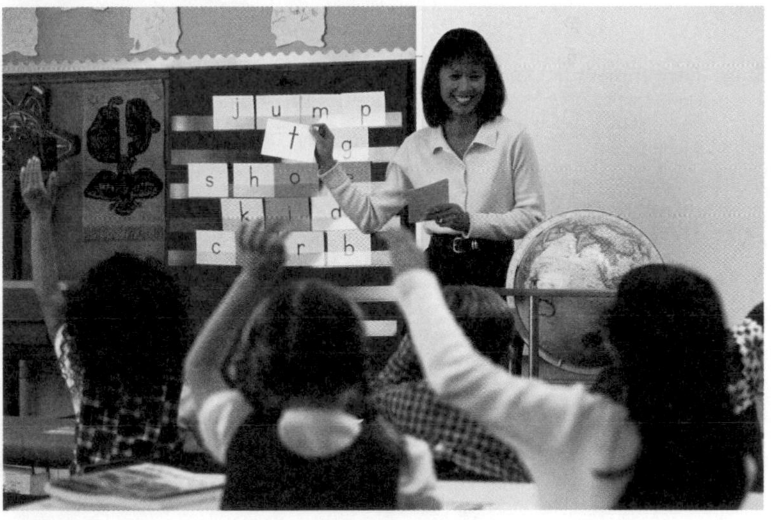

It is not uncommon for a first-grade teacher to have some students who are still struggling to learn the alphabet and others who read fluently and independently. As a teacher, how would you work with students who have yet to demonstrate proficiency in basic skills while at the same time not holding back the educational development of the other children in the class? (©*Jim Cummins/Corbis*)

Ability grouping is also sometimes beneficial for children whose academic performance or test scores consign them to lower-level tracks. In balance, however, the practice may carry more drawbacks than advantages for such children (Hallinan & Kubitschek, 1999; Oakes, Gamoran, & Page, 1992). One problem is that the assignment to a particular group may not always be an accurate reflection of the child's true ability or potential; even when objective measures are equated, low-income and minority children tend to be disproportionately represented in lower-level tracks (Ansalone, 2005; Dornbusch, 1994). Even when the placement is appropriate, children in lower-level tracks may not receive content that is sufficiently challenging to elicit their full potential, and the instruction they receive may not be of the same quality as that given their higher-track peers (Achinstein et al., 2004; Dornbusch et al., 1996; Dreeban & Barr, 1988). They also lack the opportunity to interact with high-ability students, missing out on opportunities for spontaneous peer tutoring (Saleh et al., 2007). In addition, the negative labels that can accompany placement in the "slower" groups could adversely affect the child's self-image, which in turn may affect subsequent academic expectations and motivation (Eccles, 2007; Saleh et al., 2005; Stipek, 2002). As we will see in Chapter 13, beliefs about one's competence can be a powerful contributor to how one actually performs.

Whether or not ability grouping is used, every school system necessarily makes decisions with regard to one basis for grouping students: namely, age of child. These decisions include the age at which formal schooling should begin (typically 5 years of age in Canadian and American school systems) and the points at which movement will occur from one level or grade to the next (typically one-year increments in Canadian and American schools). In most communities, children do not remain in the same school throughout their educational careers, and thus decisions must also be made about how many transitions from one school to another there will be and when the transitions

Links to Related Material

In Chapter 13, you will read more children's academic self-concept and how it can affect school achievement.

For Thought and Discussion

Which school transition had the greatest impact on you? How were you affected and why?

will occur. Many Canadian and American students experience two transitions: one from elementary school to either middle or intermediate school (grades 6, 7, and 8) or junior high (grades 7, 8, and sometimes 9), and again from intermediate/middle school or junior high to high school.

The first of these transitions, in particular, can pose some special challenges. In part, these challenges stem from changes in the nature of schooling between elementary school and middle school or junior high. Most children now attend a school that is considerably larger than what they had been accustomed to. Rather than stay with a single teacher throughout the day, they now move from teacher to teacher for different subjects; as a result, there is less opportunity to form a close relationship with a supportive adult. Grading standards are typically more stringent than was formerly the case, and there is increased emphasis on competition and comparison with peers. Teachers are more likely to provide instruction to entire classes rather than to individual groups, and there is more emphasis on teacher control and discipline.

Jacquelynne Eccles and colleagues have argued that the inherent challenges posed by such changes in schooling are magnified by the developmental changes that occur during early adolescence (Eccles et al., 1996; Gutman & Eccles, 2007). Early adolescence is a time of heightened self-consciousness, a heightened desire and a heightened capacity for decision-making and autonomy, an increased concern with close peer relations, and an increased need for supportive adults outside the home. It is, in short, a time when young people need exactly the sorts of things that the new structure of schooling tends to discourage. The relevant theoretical notion is labelled **stage–environment fit**: development proceeds most smoothly when the environmental opportunities and challenges during a particular time period match the capacities and needs of the developing child. Eccles maintains that the typical middle school or junior high provides a poor fit for young adolescents.

Stage–environment fit Degree to which environmental circumstances match the capabilities and the needs of the child at particular points during development.

Two general kinds of evidence provide support for this argument. First, early adolescence—and thus the middle school or junior high years—is a period of heightened risk for a number of psychological problems, including declines in self-esteem, lowered academic motivation, poorer academic performance, and increases in truancy and delinquency (Anderman & Midgley, 1997; Eccles & Roeser, 1999; Harter, 2006b). Furthermore, these effects are not necessarily short-lived; declines in self-esteem during junior high are predictive of continued problems throughout high school (Eccles et al., 1997). Second, such negative outcomes are considerably less likely when students do not experience the typical post-grade school transition, either because they remain in the same school or because their new school incorporates positive features (e.g., the opportunity to form supportive relationships with teachers) that were typical of the earlier school experience (Roeser, Eccles, & Sameroff, 2000; Rudolph et al., 2001).

Links to Related Material

In Chapter 13, you will read more about the decline in children's self-esteem in early adolescence.

CONTEXTUAL CONTRIBUTORS TO SCHOOLING

In Chapter 1, we introduced Bronfenbrenner's ecological systems theory (Bronfenbrenner, 1979). As we saw, schools fall within the environmental layer labelled the *microsystem*, as do families and peers. The *mesosystem* refers to interrelations among the child's microsystems. A consideration of schooling provides a clear illustration of the importance of the mesosystem because the success of schooling depends very much on other important social contexts in the child's life.

Peers are important at the time of the first school transition: the entry into school at age 5 or 6. Children who have several good friends when they start kindergarten are happier in school than are children who lack such friendships; they develop more positive attitudes toward school; and they show greater gains in performance across the school year. Conversely, being rejected by peers is associated with unfavourable attitudes and poorer school performance (Ladd, Kochenderfer-Ladd, & Rydell, 2011).

Peer relations remain important as children progress through school. Association with academically oriented peers promotes academic motivation and achievement; conversely, association with antisocial peers is linked to poor grades and dropping out of school (Gest et al., 2005, 2006; Ryan, 2001). Throughout grade school and high school, children who lack friends are less well-adjusted in the classroom, show higher rates of absenteeism, and are more at risk for being retained at a grade (Ladd et al., 2011). They are also less likely to complete school: in a classic analysis of the research, Jeff Parker and Steve Asher (1987) reported that children who are

Links to Related Material

In Chapter 15, you will read more about children's relationships with peers and the consequences of peer rejection.

rejected by their peers are two to eight times more likely to drop out of school than are children in general.

The family is also important to success in school. We saw earlier that the quality of the home environment is one contributor to the child's intellectual abilities, which, of course, contribute to performance in school. The importance of the family, however, extends beyond stimulation of intellectual development alone. From the start of school, children's adjustment to school and their academic performance are linked to the quality of family relations and family support (Cowan & Cowan, 2002; Eccles, 2007; Entwisle & Alexander, 2000). A variety of aspects of family life are important, including the number of parents or other adults in the home, the stability of the family structure, the quality of relations with the parents, and the degree of parental support for academic achievement. Researchers at the University of Victoria have found that frequent family moves may also have negative consequences, especially for shy/withdrawn children (Hoglund & Leadbeater, 2004). These factors, in turn, affect a variety of outcomes in the school setting, ranging from adjustment to kindergarten, to coping with the transition to middle school or junior high, to the probability of dropping out of high school. It is worth noting that one of the ways in which parents affect their children's school success is by influencing the peers with whom they associate, which, as we have seen, can be one contributor to academic attitudes and performance (Dishion & Bullock, 2002).

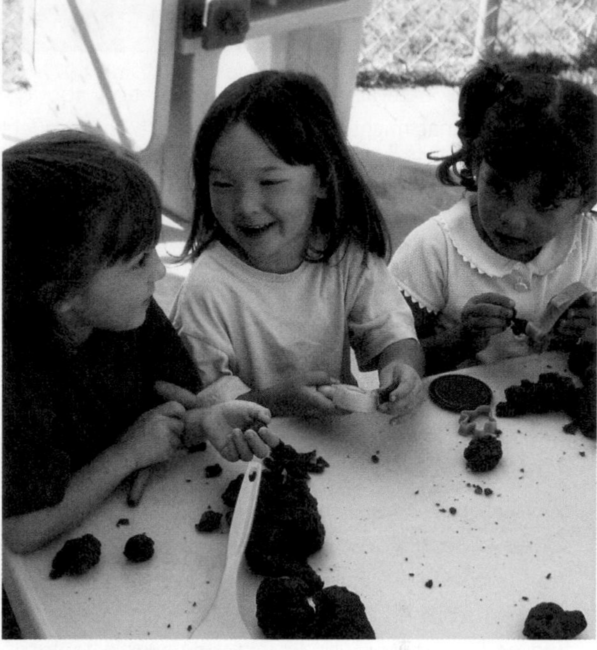

Children who have several good friends when they start kindergarten are happier in school, develop more positive attitudes toward school, and show greater gains in performance at school. Why is friendship so important, and why is rejection by peers associated with poorer school performance? (©*Tom Prettyman/PhotoEdit*)

Parents' direct involvement with school is also important. Parents can take an active role in their children's schooling in a number of ways, including parent–teacher conferences, monitoring and helping with homework, and selection of curricular and eventual career-track options (Christenson & Sheridan, 2001; Epstein, 2002). The dimension of parental involvement, however, is itself an example of a contextual effect. On average, low-income and minority parents are less likely to be involved in their children's schooling than are middle-income parents. In many instances, this lack of involvement is less a matter of interest and concern than of possibility. For parents who are coping with the challenges of poverty, dangerous neighbourhoods, and uncertain employment, finding time and energy for their child's schooling may be an insurmountable task (Elias et al., 2005; Lee & Burkham, 2002; Brooks-Gunn et al., 1997). And, as researchers in Montreal report, living in a consistently poor family greatly increases the risk of children's academic and behaviour problems at school (De Civita, Pagani, Vitaro, & Tremblay, 2004, 2007).

For Thought and Discussion

In what ways were your parents involved in your schooling? How did this affect your academic achievement?

Links to Related Material

In Chapter 12, you will read more about how children's early social and emotional development, including the quality of their relationship with their parents, influences their adjustment to school.

Finally, in addition to peers and parents, an important contextual contributor is the child's general cultural background. Because of the diversity of North American society, different children often bring different experiences, beliefs, and values to the school setting. The potential importance of this dimension is expressed in the **cultural compatibility hypothesis**: classroom instruction will be most effective when it matches patterns of learning that are familiar in the child's culture (Slaughter-DeFoe et al., 1990; Tharp, 1989).

Cultural compatibility hypothesis The hypothesis that schooling will be most effective when methods of instruction are compatible with the child's cultural background.

A good example of this principle can be found in the comparison of wait-times—the length of time one participant in a dialogue waits before responding to the other. Many First Nations children tend to pause when giving answers, creating the impression (at least for non-Native teachers) that they have finished responding (Spielmann, 2002). The result is that they may be interrupted before they have completed their answers. In this case, the teacher's wait-time is too short. In contrast, native Hawaiian children prefer a short wait-time because in their culture, prompt response and overlapping speech patterns are signs of interest and involvement. Teachers, however, often interpret the Hawaiian child's quick responses as rude interruptions, and their attempts to curtail such behaviour may lead to general uncertainty and inhibition (White & Tharp, 1988). Thus, in both cases, although in different ways, the teacher's unfamiliarity with the child's cultural background can create problems for the child in school. (*Research Classic 10.1* discusses a famous study of the effects of teacher expectations about their pupils.)

RESEARCH CLASSIC 10.1
PYGMALION IN THE CLASSROOM

Teachers naturally welcome information about their students that might help them to teach more effectively. For many, results from standardized assessment tests—such as IQ and academic achievement measures—are useful sources of information. Normally, of course, such tests are designed to be as accurate as possible. One of the most famous experiments in child psychology, however, was built around the provision of deliberately inaccurate test information to teachers.

Robert Rosenthal and Lenore Jacobson (1968) informed a group of elementary-school teachers that a new test of intellectual potential had been developed to measure children's readiness to "bloom." The test, the teachers were told, could identify those children who were most likely to show spurts or leaps forward in their academic performance during the coming year. Each teacher was also given a list of the children from his or her classroom that the test had identified as likely bloomers. In fact, however, a table of random numbers had been used to select the supposed bloomers. These children were no different from any other children in the class.

What would be the point of deliberately misleading teachers in this way? Rosenthal and Jacobson's study grew out of previous research by Rosenthal on a phenomenon known as the researcher expectancy effect. Across a series of experiments, Rosenthal (1976) had demonstrated that researchers' expectations can affect the results they obtain. For example, testers who believe that their subjects will perform well on some cognitive measure typically elicit better performance than do testers who believe that their subjects will perform poorly. The effect extends even to animal research. Testers who are told that they are working with "maze-bright" rats obtain better performance than testers who believe that their rats are "maze-dull."

The work on researcher expectancy effects is of considerable methodological significance, for it identifies a source of bias that may seriously affect the outcomes of research. The point of the Rosenthal and Jacobson study was to see whether expectancy effects extend beyond the laboratory to the real-life settings within which children develop. Do the expectations that teachers hold about their students affect the way the students perform? In particular, can the creation of positive expectancies—as was done with respect to the bloomers—lead to positive outcomes for the children?

The answer to this question turned out to be a qualified yes. Rosenthal and Jacobson did not find any effects of expectancies for the older children in the study. In grades 1 and 2, however, the effects were dramatic. Children who had been identified as bloomers easily outperformed their classmates on an IQ test given at the end of the year. By the end of the year, the bloomers were also earning better grades in reading and arithmetic. Apparently the teachers' expectancies acted as *self-fulfilling prophecies*: children who were expected to perform well did perform well.

The Rosenthal and Jacobson study is not only one of the most famous, but also one of the most controversial experiments in child psychology. The original study has been subjected to a number of criticisms, and its results have not always been replicated in follow-up research (Good, 1993; Wineberg, 1987). Clearly, children's intellectual performance has many determinants, and teachers' expectations are at best one of many contributors. Nevertheless, the weight of the evidence has convinced most critics that expectancies can make a difference—not always, certainly, but in some classrooms and for some children. What teachers expect of their students has been shown to affect how they behave toward those students, and the teachers' behaviour has in turn been shown to affect, for better or for worse, how the children perform (Weinstein, 2002). In some cases, such as when the student adopts the teacher's positive views, this can work to the student's advantage. However, if a student perceives a negative view from a teacher, he or she may adopt that view and start to live up to it. Unfortunately, the potential negative effects appear to be even stronger for students from at-risk groups, such as minorities (McKown & Weinstein, 2002).

Expectancies themselves can have many bases. Among the sources that have been identified are standardized test scores (the basis explored in the Rosenthal and Jacobson study), gender, social class, race, physical attractiveness, and presence of an older sibling in the school system (Dusek & Joseph, 1983; Jones & Myhill, 2004). Anyone who has ever followed an older sibling through school should be able to appreciate this last factor.

Rosenthal and Jacobson entitled their book *Pygmalion in the Classroom*. In the Pygmalion legend, a sculptor's skill and devotion transform a mass of stone into a perfect, living woman. Teachers' effects on students are neither this powerful nor (unfortunately) this positive. But teachers can have effects, and the expectancies that they form are one determinant of what these effects may be. A challenge for teachers, then, is to monitor their expectancies and the subsequent treatment of their students. It is important to have positive, yet realistic, expectations for students of all kinds. Researchers have found that teachers can modify and increase their expectations for students with lower abilities (Weinstein, Madison, & Kuklinski, 1995). Awareness of the problem is one of the first steps toward modifying these expectancies.

LEARNING OBJECTIVE 10.4

Evaluate different aspects of the schooling experience and how these affect cognitive development.

1. Identify cognitive effects of schooling that have been found by researchers.
2. Discuss how teacher expectations, class and school size, school transition, and school effectiveness affect cognitive outcomes for children.
3. Define and describe the evidence for and against the effectiveness of ability grouping.
4. Explain how family and peers can contribute to school success.

ALTERNATIVE CONCEPTIONS OF INTELLIGENCE

Learning Objective 10.5

Identify alternative conceptions of intelligence.

In our discussion of intelligence and how it is measured, we touched on some ways other than IQ measurement to assess children's competence. To finish this chapter, we return to this topic. In this section, we broaden the scope to consider some recent theories and programs of research that represent significant departures from the traditional IQ perspective.

EVOLUTIONARY APPROACHES

As we have seen, traditional approaches to intelligence focus primarily on abilities associated with success in school. School—and the disciplines taught in school—are, however, very recent developments. The human capacity to read and write can be traced back fewer than 10,000 years. To this day, there are societies in which the majority of citizens cannot read and where formal education is unknown. Consequently, many theorists are dissatisfied with current formulations that define intelligence primarily in terms of school-related skills.

In recent years, there has been growing interest in understanding human intelligence in light of evolution. According to this perspective, intelligence is the ability to adapt to the environment. The issue is, *which* environment? Natural selection occurs over thousands of years. The changes that have occurred in modern times have occurred far too rapidly for humans to have had the opportunity to evolve cognitive capabilities specifically in response to them.

According to evolutionary theory, modern cognitive abilities reflect adaptations to the recurring pressures faced by our human ancestors during primeval times. Evolutionary psychologists label the environment that produced a species' evolved tendencies its **environment of evolutionary adaptedness**, or **EEA** (Simpson & Belsky, 2008). For humans, the EEA is presumed to have occurred two to three million years ago during the Pleistocene era, at which time humans and their protohuman ancestors lived as hunter–gatherers.

Environment of evolutionary adaptedness (EEA) The environment that produced a species' evolved tendencies.

Based on studies of modern hunter–gatherer groups and observations of our closest genetic relatives—chimpanzees—evolutionary psychologists have painted a portrait of the lives of these early humans. They contend that early humans probably lived in small bands of 30 to 60 people and survived by gathering fruits, nuts, vegetables, and tubers; scavenging food left over from animal kills; and hunting. The social organization of the hunter–gatherer groups included a gender division of labour, with females primarily responsible for food gathering and the care and nurturing of children, and males primarily responsible for hunting. It is likely that some males had more than one mate, whereas others had no access to females. To survive, early humans had to cooperate and compete, both within groups and with people from the outside (Bjorklund & Pellegrini, 2002b).

Of course, life has changed much over the past 100,000 years. But, as already noted, natural selection works too slowly for civilization and the associated changes in social roles, tools, and technology to have substantially affected the structure and organization of the human mind. What this means is that many of the problems our minds are designed to solve are not the ones common to modern life—such as learning to read, solving algebra equations, and operating complex machines—but are, rather, the problems our hunter–gatherer ancestors faced generation after generation.

What might those problems have been? Surely finding food would be one (along with knowing which foods to eat and which to avoid). And our ancestors likely faced numerous problems centred around the complexities of social life, such as attracting and choosing mates, recognizing kin, and inferring other's motives, intentions, and knowledge (Simpson & Belsky, 2008).

Evolutionary psychologists believe that over many generations, humans evolved a neuropsychological system specially adapted to solving these "ancient" problems. Moreover, this system is organized into specialized modules or cognitive systems dedicated to solving certain kinds of problems—specifically, problems related to human survival and reproduction. These modules are not "preformed"; rather, they emerge with species-typical experience over the course of development.

One example of this approach is a model developed by David Geary (1998). As shown in Figure 10.6, Geary's model includes two overarching domains—social and ecological. These domains reflect the types of information that must be processed for humans to survive and reproduce in the natural habitat. Each of the domains consists of two more specific domains, each of which comprises even more specific domains. Thus, there are modules for language and for processing faces, a module for processing information about kin and a separate one for strangers, modules for plants and for moving through the physical world. Geary acknowledges that the list of domains is not complete. For instance, there is no domain for numerical information, even though Geary himself believes such a domain exists. Indeed, some evolutionary psychologists believe the number of modules dedicated to solving specific types of adaptive problems to be quite large (Cosmides & Tooby, 2001).

Biologically primary abilities Evolved abilities shaped by natural selection to solve recurring problems faced by ancestral humans.

Geary refers to the abilities shown in Figure 10.6 as biologically primary abilities. **Biologically primary abilities** have been shaped by natural selection and have evolved to deal with problems faced by our ancestors (Geary, 2005, 1995b). These abilities (e.g., language, face recognition) are universal. They are found in all cultures and are acquired easily by all normally developing children in all but the most deprived environments. Indeed, children are highly motivated to master these abilities and actively pursue opportunities to do so through play, social interaction, and the exploration of objects and the environment (Geary, 2002).

Biologically secondary abilities Non-evolved abilities that co-opt primary abilities for purposes other than the original evolution-based function and appear only in specific cultural contexts.

Skills such as reading and higher mathematics are called biologically secondary abilities. **Biologically secondary abilities** are highly specialized neurocognitive systems that build on the biologically primary abilities. Reading, for example, builds on the cognitive and brain systems involved in language acquisition and production. Biologically secondary abilities are the product of

FIGURE 10.6

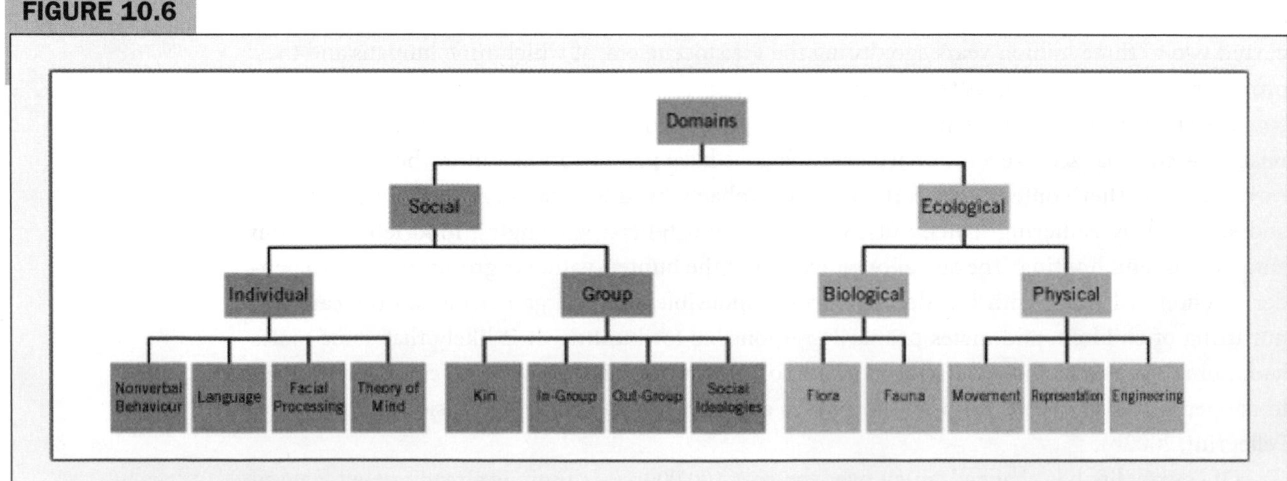

Proposed domains of the human mind. *From* Male, Female: The Evolution of Human Sex Differences *by D. C. Geary, 1998, Washington, DC: American Psychological Association, 180. Copyright © 1998 by the American Psychological Association.*

culture, not biological evolution. Acquisition of these abilities depends on growing up in a culture that deliberately teaches the skills. For instance, children in illiterate cultures do not spontaneously learn to read. In contrast to biologically primary abilities, which most children readily (and happily) acquire without formal instruction, acquisition of biologically secondary abilities is much more variable. It also often depends on tedious practice and external inducements (Geary, 2002).

From the perspective of evolutionary theory, reading and the other skills taught in school are "unnatural." Consequently, it is understandable that some children have a good deal of difficulty mastering such skills as reading and higher mathematics. Indeed, different cultures approach teaching mathematics somewhat differently. There are also a variety of ways that cultures use to foster literacy.

The idea that many human cognitive abilities are domain-specific or modularized is widely accepted by evolutionary psychologists. Most evolutionary psychologists do not endorse the idea of domain-general cognitive abilities or the notion of general intelligence. Moreover, because evolutionary psychology is primarily concerned with species-wide cognitive adaptations, they have devoted little attention to the topic that is at the heart of the psychometric approach: the study of individual differences in intelligence. Evolutionary psychologists have, however, devoted considerable attention to the study of gender differences in cognitive abilities, a topic that we will discuss in Chapter 16.

DYNAMIC TESTING

As we have seen, a central theme in the sociocultural approach to children's development is the cultural determination of individual development. In this view, much of what children learn is acquired from the culture around them, and much of the child's problem solving is mediated through adult help. This emphasis is captured in Vygotsky's notion of the *zone of proximal development*, or what children can do with appropriate help from others, which we discussed in Chapter 8.

From the sociocultural perspective, assessments of ability that focus on the child in isolation, as do IQ tests, are misleading. Such a focus, at best, captures the products of learning; it does not reveal the processes by which children acquire new skills. Furthermore, such a focus may miss important differences among children. Vygotsky used the following example to make this point. Imagine two children who each achieve a mental age of 7 on a standard intelligence test, and who therefore are equally intelligent from this perspective. With hints and prompts from an adult, however, one might be able to solve problems that are two years beyond his mental age, whereas the other can go only six months beyond. The two children have different zones of proximal development.

In recent years, a number of researchers have attempted to develop **dynamic assessments**—methods of assessing intelligence that build on the concept of the zone of proximal development and the child's ability to profit from instruction (Feuerstein et al., 1995; Lidz & Elliott, 2000; Sternberg & Grigorenko, 2002a; Tzuriel, 2001). Different investigators have taken somewhat different approaches. One common strategy, however, has been a *test-train-test procedure*. With this approach, the child first attempts to solve a set of problems on his or her own, much as on a standard IQ test. Following this determination of independent performance, the tester provides a standardized set of prompts designed to help the child arrive at an answer. The prompts are arranged in a graduated series, starting out as fairly subtle and indirect and becoming progressively more explicit until the solution is reached. The child's zone for that kind of problem solving can be determined from the number of hints needed—the fewer the hints, the wider the zone. In the final phase, the child is presented with problems that vary in their similarity to those on which help was given. This final phase provides a measure of the child's ability to transfer the skills learned with adult help.

Dynamic assessment Method of assessing children's abilities derived from Vygotsky's concept of the zone of proximal development. Measures the child's ability to benefit from adult-provided assistance, typically in a test-train-retest design.

Links to Related Material

We discussed Vygotsky's notion of the zone of proximal development in Chapter 8. Here you see how it can be applied to the assessment of intelligence.

Studies using the approach have confirmed Vygotsky's claim that IQ tests provide an incomplete picture of children's intelligence. IQ scores do relate to both speed of initial learning and breadth of transfer. The relation is not perfect, however, and many children's ability to profit from help is not predicted by their IQs. Children, in short, are a good deal more variable than IQ tests indicate. In a sense, of course, this fact has always been known; we saw that IQ scores are a far-from-perfect predictor of school performance or any other important outcome. What dynamic assessments do is specify one of the important dimensions not captured by IQ—the ability to profit from help provided by other people (Sternberg, 2004).

Assessing children's ability with standard IQ tests is relatively easy; there are many such instruments to choose from, and most can be administered in approximately one hour. Dynamic testing is more challenging on a number of dimensions: in the degree of training necessary to carry out such assessments; in the amount of time required to complete an assessment (up to 10 hours per child in some approaches); and in the interpretation of the results. Although several individual research programs have demonstrated the potential value of dynamic assessment, the approach has yet to result in a generally accepted, widely applied method of testing intelligence. Nevertheless, the approach remains, in the words of one recent evaluation, "a wonderful idea... with enormous promise" (Sternberg & Grigorenko, 2002a, p. viii).

GARDNER'S MULTIPLE INTELLIGENCES

Howard Gardner (1983, 1993b, 1999) has proposed a theory of intelligence that is, in some respects, similar to those of factor-analytic theorists, such as Thurstone and Guilford. Like these theorists, Gardner believes that intelligence is considerably more diversified and multifaceted than the notion of general intelligence admits. Unlike most psychometric researchers, however, Gardner does not rely solely on factor analyses of standardized tests to draw conclusions about different forms of intelligence. And the kinds of intelligence that he proposes go well beyond the ones that psychometric theorists usually consider.

Gardner's general thesis is that humans possess at least eight relatively distinct *intelligences*, defined as the "ability to solve problems or fashion products that are of consequence in a particular cultural setting or community" (Gardner, 1993, p. 15). We consider what some of these intelligences are shortly. First, however, we must ask about evidence. How can the existence of a distinct intelligence be demonstrated? Gardner suggests a number of kinds of evidence, or signs, that can help point the way. First, there must be experimental evidence in support of the intelligence. The factor-analytic studies discussed earlier are one possible experimental approach to distinguishing different sorts of intelligence; information-processing demonstrations of the distinctiveness of different cognitive domains (see Chapter 9) are another. Next, the intelligence should be specifiable in terms of a set of distinct core operations; that is, it should be possible to say what it "is." Third, the intelligence should show a distinct developmental history, progressing predictably from rudimentary to advanced. In addition, it should show a distinct evolutionary history, growing in complexity as the species grows more complex in the course of its evolution.

Two final signs discussed by Gardner concern deviations from the normal developmental path. Gardner argues that isolation by brain damage can be informative. For example, the fact that linguistic abilities can be either selectively impaired or selectively spared in cases of brain injury is evidence for a separate linguistic intelligence. Similarly, the existence of individuals with exceptional talents in one particular domain is a possible sign. In the so-called savants, for example, remarkable mathematical ability may be coupled with subnormal general intelligence, suggesting that a distinct mathematical intelligence exists. And children who compose symphonies at age 10, as did Mozart and Mendelssohn, are evidence for a musical intelligence.

For Thought and Discussion

How well does Gardner's theory of multiple intelligences apply to you and people you know?

As noted, Gardner uses such evidence to propose the existence of at least eight distinct human intelligences. Table 10.9 summarizes the intelligences. Some are familiar. Gardner marshals evidence in support of a linguistic intelligence, a spatial intelligence, and a logical-mathematical intelligence.

Although the evidence that he uses is sometimes unusual (for example, an analysis of the drawings of a child with autism in the discussion of spatial intelligence; see Figure 10.7), these are forms of intelligence that are talked about in some way by every theorist.

TABLE 10.9 GARDNER'S MULTIPLE INTELLIGENCES

Type of Intelligence	Description	Possible Vocations
Linguistic	Sensitivity to spoken and written language, ability to use language to achieve goals	Writer, lawyer, poet
Logical-mathematical	Ability to analyze problems logically, carry out mathematical operations, investigate issues scientifically	Mathematician, scientist
Musical	Appreciation of musical patterns, skill in the composition and performance of music	Musician, composer
Bodily kinesthetic	Ability to use one's body or parts of the body (e.g., hands, feet) to solve problems or fashion products	Dancer, athlete, craftsperson
Spatial	Ability to perceive spatial relationships and manipulate patterns of space	Navigator, pilot, architect
Naturalist	Ability to recognize and classify flora and fauna	Biologist, naturalist
Interpersonal	Ability to understand the desires and intentions of other people and to work effectively with others	Clinician, salesperson, politician
Intrapersonal	Capacity to understand oneself and to use this understanding to direct one's life effectively	Relevant to almost any profession

Source: Adapted from *Intelligence Reframed* by H. Gardner, 1999, New York: Basic Books.

Other intelligences are less familiar. We have already mentioned, for instance, the idea of a musical intelligence. In Gardner's view, musical ability meets all the signs for consideration as a distinct form of intelligence. Musical ability has both an evolutionary and a developmental history, it can appear in isolated form in cases of brain injury or musical prodigy, and it can be analyzed in terms of a set of core elements (pitch, rhythm, timbre, and so on). Similar arguments are offered in support of a bodily kinesthetic intelligence, a naturalist's intelligence, and two forms of personal intelligence—one concerned with the understanding of self (intrapersonal intelligence) and one concerned with understanding others (interpersonal intelligence).

We noted that the Vygotskian approach is beginning to have an impact on both psychological assessment and educational practice. The same is true of the theory of multiple intelligences. Recent years have seen the formation of a number of schools inspired by Gardner's framework, as well as the creation of methods of assessing children's abilities that encompass a wider range of skills and contexts than do IQ tests (Chen & Gardner, 1997; Kornhaber, 1994). As with the dynamic assessments inspired by Vygotsky, such efforts face formidable practical obstacles, and applications to

FIGURE 10.7

Drawing made by a 5-year-old girl with autism. This drawing illustrates one kind of evidence offered by Gardner in support of his theory of a distinct form of spatial intelligence. *From* Frames of Mind: The Theory of Multiple Intelligence *by H. Gardner, 1983, New York: Basic Books, 189. Copyright © 1983 by Basic Books. Reprinted by permission.*

date have been limited. Both approaches, however, have the potential to enrich our understanding of how children differ in intelligence, as well as to reveal and nurture intellectual strengths that might not otherwise be apparent.

GIFTEDNESS AND CREATIVITY

By one definition of *giftedness*, gifted children are simply those who score at the top of the IQ range—perhaps IQs of 130 or 140 or above. This is the most common definition in Canadian and American school systems.

However, not all psychologists agree that the standard IQ approach captures everything that the concept of giftedness should embody (Moran & Gardner, 2006). One of the most forceful advocates of an alternative approach to the study of gifted children is Ellen Winner (1996, 2000). In Winner's view, high-IQ children represent only one form of giftedness—they are gifted with respect to the kinds of abilities (verbal skills, mathematical understanding, logical reasoning) that are stressed on IQ tests and in school. Even within the domain of IQ-type skills, however, such children are not necessarily exceptional across the board; a child, for example, might be gifted in math but only average on other dimensions. More generally, Winner argues that "global giftedness" is the exception rather than the rule; more typical is exceptional performance in just one domain of development. Furthermore, these domains, she maintains, include more than just the verbal and mathematical abilities valued in school. Primarily through analyses of dozens of case studies, Winner provides examples of giftedness not only in mathematics and language, but also in art and in music. Figure 10.8 shows some of the drawings produced by a child identified as gifted in art.

Clearly, exceptional performance in some domain is the starting point for any conception of giftedness. Winner argues that gifted children display three further characteristics. One is *precocity*—gifted children not only possess exceptional abilities, but also demonstrate their abilities very early in development. The drawing of the cat in Figure 10.8 may not seem remarkable in itself (even though it is probably better than most of us could do!); what is remarkable is that it was produced by a 3-year-old. A second characteristic is what Winner labels *marching to their own drummer.* Gifted children learn not only faster, but in qualitatively different ways from children in general, and much of what they learn they discover for themselves, rather than acquiring from others. Finally, gifted children possess *a rage to master*—they are strongly motivated, perhaps even driven, to conquer their domain of interest. For example, the little girl who was the source for the drawings in Figure 10.8 produced 4,000 paintings in a span of three years!

FIGURE 10.8

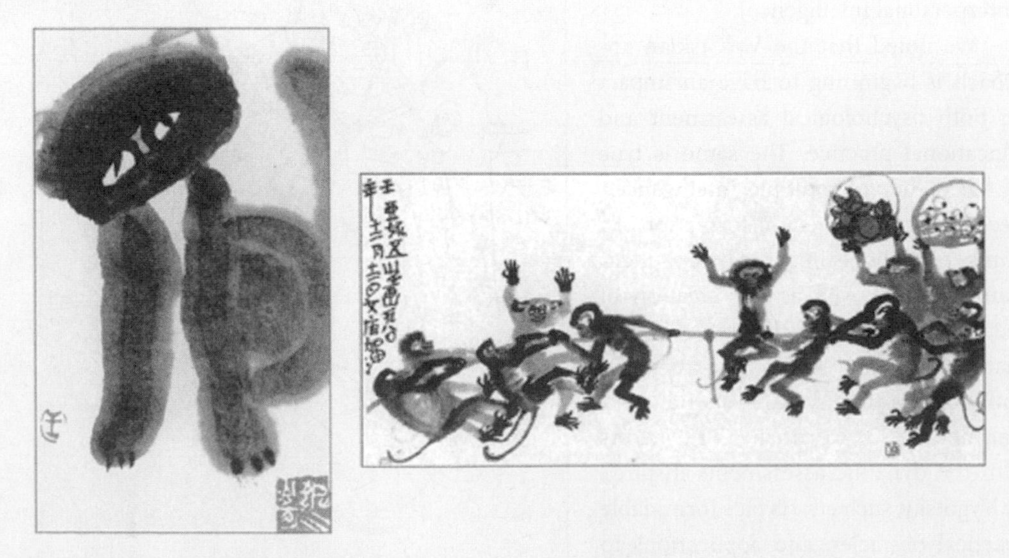

Drawings made by a young girl identified as gifted in art. *The cat was drawn at age 3 and the monkeys at age 5. From* Gifted Children *by E. Winner, 1996, New York: Basic Books, 84–85. Copyright © 1996 by Basic Books. Reprinted by permission.*

Where does giftedness come from? Winner's answer is definitely of the nature *and* nurture sort—as is that of most psychologists and educators who have considered the question (e.g., Feldman, 1986; Gottfried et al., 1994). She dismisses as a myth the idea that parents or other environmental forces can turn any child into a gifted child. There must be a biological starting point, and only some children are born with the capacity to achieve exceptional levels in math or music or art. Biology is not sufficient, however; there must also be a supportive environment. It is true, as we have seen, that gifted children in part create their own environment. For their full potential to emerge, however, they cannot do it alone; they must receive help from parents, teachers, or other supportive adults.

If the definition of giftedness has been problematic for psychologists, that for *creativity* has proven to be even more so. At the adult level, the meaning—if not the production—of creativity is fairly straightforward: creativity involves the ability to generate novel outcomes that are valued in some context. But what can children do that merits the label *creative* or that might be predictive of eventual adult creativity?

One approach emphasizes the distinction between convergent thinking and divergent thinking (Guilford, 1985; Wallach & Kogan, 1966). **Convergent thinking** is right-answer-oriented thinking—the form of thinking we engage in when faced with a task (e.g., a mathematical problem, a logical deduction) for which there is a single, definite solution. Convergent thinking is what IQ tests measure. In contrast, **divergent thinking** involves the ability to generate multiple and original possible solutions for tasks that do not have a single right answer. For example, thinking of unusual uses for a newspaper or coat hanger would be forms of divergent thinking, as would be coming up with different possible interpretations for a squiggle drawing.

Convergent thinking A form of thinking in which the goal is to discover the correct answer to problems with a definite solution—the form of thought emphasized on IQ tests.

Divergent thinking A form of thinking in which the goal is to generate multiple possible solutions for problems that do not have a single correct answer—the form of thought hypothesized to be important for creativity.

The unusual uses and squiggles tasks are, in fact, among the tasks used to measure for problems that do not have a single correct answer—the form of divergent thinking in childhood (Wallach & Kogan, 1966). Tasks like these do succeed in identifying individual differences in the capacity for divergent thinking, differences that are evident from early on in childhood. Furthermore, these differences are only weakly, if at all, related to IQ. Thus, tests of divergent thinking meet one of the criteria for a measure of creativity: they appear to be tapping something other than simply intelligence in the IQ sense.

A capacity for divergent thinking is almost certainly necessary for creativity, but most investigators believe that it is not sufficient. There is, after all, a gap between generating lots of ideas for some topic and actually producing a genuinely creative product. Furthermore, measures of divergent thinking are at best weak predictors of real-world creative performance.

Most contemporary accounts of creativity are what Robert Sternberg (2009b) labels *confluence theories*, in that they stress the coming together or confluence of multiple contributors that must work together to make creativity possible. One example is the *investment theory* of creativity proposed by Sternberg (2009b; Sternberg, & Lubart, 1996). The basic idea of investment theory is implied by the name: creativity requires a willingness to invest or commit a number of resources to the task at hand—to buy low, in the sense of pursuing novel or out-of-favour topics, and sell high, in the sense of persisting until a valued outcome is produced. The necessary cognitive resources include, but are not limited to, an aptitude for divergent thinking. Also important are knowledge with regard to the specific problem domain and an ability to evaluate the adequacy of the ideas that one has generated. Cognitive factors, in turn, must be joined by the right sort of personality attributes—in particular, an ability to tolerate ambiguity and a willingness to take risks. There must be strong motivation to persist in the face of obstacles. And there must be a supportive environmental context.

The importance of this last contributor is worth reiterating. However strong the cognitive and personality resources may be, creative potential can flourish only if the environment provides the opportunity. We saw the same point with respect to giftedness, and, of course, it applies as well to other cognitive achievements, including intelligence in the IQ sense and performance in school. Cognitive abilities always develop and are expressed within an environmental context, and some children experience more supportive contexts than do others.

For Thought and Discussion

To what extent and in what ways are you creative? Did adults in your life nurture your creativity?

LEARNING OBJECTIVE 10.5

Identify alternative conceptions of intelligence.

1. Describe the evolutionary approach to intelligence.
2. Explain the notion of dynamic assessments.
3. Describe the multiple intelligences identified in Gardner's model.
4. Explain what is meant by giftedness.

CONCLUSION

We have discussed a number of issues related to intelligence, IQ testing, and academic achievement throughout this chapter. What is intelligence, where does it come from, why are there differences among individuals and among groups, and what effects does intelligence have? An interesting commentary on these very issues was published by psychologist Ulrich Neisser and colleagues in 1996, and we highly recommend it for those with a continuing interest in the issues addressed in this chapter. We will not attempt to summarize all of the points made in the commentary, but we will note three of the general conclusions that the authors emphasize because they mirror conclusions that we have attempted to convey in our own discussion of the issues.

A first conclusion is that we have learned much about intelligence in the almost 100 years since intelligence tests first appeared. Much of Neisser and colleagues' article, like much of the current chapter, is devoted to documenting these gains in knowledge. As we noted at the outset of the chapter, intelligence testing has had both applied as well as theoretical effects on school curricula, for example, or on the design and evaluation of intervention programs. Whether intelligence tests can really be considered, as one of their proponents has claimed, as "psychology's most telling accomplishment to date" (Herrnstein, 1971, p. 45) is debatable. But they certainly are among the most influential.

A second conclusion is that these undeniable achievements are accompanied by large areas of uncertainty and debate. The greatest uncertainty, not surprisingly, is associated with the hardest-to-study topics. Thus, we know, for example, that both genes and environment contribute to differences in IQ, and we know something about their typical relative contribution. But we still have much to learn about how genes or environments produce their effects. Nor do we know why there are on-average group differences on some measures of intellectual performance.

A final conclusion concerns limitations of another sort. IQ tests provide a sampling of intellectual abilities, but they do not exhaust the domain of human intelligence. As Neisser and colleagues (1996) note, "We know much less about the forms of intelligence that tests do not easily assess: wisdom, creativity, practical knowledge, social skill, and the like" (p. 95). Furthermore, the psychometric focus on individual differences may cause us to lose track of the important ways in which all children are similar in their intellectual development. Similarly, the frequent focus on problems in development may cause us to miss the strengths that particular children possess. It is in this respect that the approaches to cognitive development that we considered in the preceding two chapters provide a valuable complement to the intelligence-test perspective. These approaches concentrate on basic developments common to all children, and they remind us that all children show impressive intellectual achievements.

These points emerge even more clearly in the next chapter, when we turn to the topic of language development. We will see that the focus of most research on language has been on similarities rather than on differences among children. We will also see that mastery of language is a remarkable cognitive achievement—perhaps the most impressive achievement that the human species shows.

SUMMARY

KEY TERMS

ability grouping, p. 383
biologically primary abilities, p. 388
biologically secondary abilities, p. 388
convergent thinking, p. 393
cultural compatibility hypothesis, p. 385
divergent thinking, p. 393
dynamic assessment, p. 389
environment of evolutionary adaptedness (EEA), p. 387
flynn effect, p. 369
g, p. 362
heritability, p. 368
hierarchical model of intelligence, p. 363
HOME (home observation for measurement of the environment), p. 371
psychometric, p. 356
reliability, p. 360
stage–environment fit, p. 384
stereotype threat, p. 379
validity, p. 360

LEARNING OBJECTIVES

LEARNING OBJECTIVE 10.1 Explain how intelligence traditionally is defined and measured.

1. *What is the purpose of intelligence testing?*
   The purpose of IQ tests is to measure individual differences in intellectual ability. Such tests were originally devised for practical purposes, and they have always had practical applications—school placement, for example. Such real-world applications contribute to the controversy that has always surrounded IQ tests.

2. *What is the Stanford-Binet, and how does it define and measure IQ?*
   The Stanford-Binet intelligence scale is primarily a test of childhood intelligence applicable to every age group except infancy. It yields an IQ score that summarizes the child's ability. It stresses the kinds of verbal and academic skills that are important in school—quantitative reasoning, fluid reasoning, visual-spatial processing, knowledge, and working memory.

3. *Identify three IQ or developmental tests in addition to the Stanford-Binet that are commonly used with children.*
   The most commonly used alternative tests for children are two tests designed by David Wechsler: the Wechsler Preschool and Primary Scale of Intelligence (WPPSI-III), intended for children aged 2½ to 7 years, and the Wechsler Intelligence Scale for Children (WISC-IV), intended for children aged 6 to 16. The WISC-IV is divided into four scales assessing different aspects of intellectual performance. The Kaufman Assessment Battery for Children (KABC-II) marks an explicit effort to include cultural diversity and cultural fairness in the construction and administration of a test. The best-known measure of infant development is the Bayley Scales of Infant and Toddler Development.

4. *How can we tell whether an IQ test accurately measures intelligence?*
   Two criteria are applied to determine if a test that claims to measure intelligence really does so. Any test of a stable attribute must demonstrate reliability; that is, it must give a consistent, repeatable picture of what the child can do. The major IQ tests do possess satisfactory reliability. The test must also demonstrate validity; that is, it should relate to other external measures of ability. Tests of childhood IQ do relate to measures of academic performance, an important external criterion of childhood intelligence. The correlation is not perfect, however. Furthermore, the academic focus of most IQ tests means that they may not be good measures of other kinds of intelligence.

LEARNING OBJECTIVE 10.2 Understand the organization and stability of intelligence, and the origins of individual differences.

1. *Is intelligence a unitary trait?*
   Organization is one major issue in the study of intelligence. Psychometric researchers draw inferences about how intelligence is organized from patterns of correlations across different measures of intelligence. Factor analyses of such correlations provide evidence both for the existence of general intelligence, which affects performance on many tasks, and for more specific abilities, which contribute to performance on specific tasks.

2. *Do children's IQs remain stable as they develop?*
   The question of the stability of IQ is another central issue in the psychometric approach to intelligence. Longitudinal studies indicate that traditional measures of infant IQ have little relation to later IQ. Recent evidence suggests, however, that response to novelty may provide a link between infancy and later childhood. After infancy, IQ begins to correlate from one age to another, and the stability increases as the child gets older. The correlations are not perfect, however, and substantial changes in IQ do sometimes occur.

3. *What do we know about the heritability of IQ?*
   The question of heritability concerns the origins of individual differences in IQ. Three methods of study have been prominent: family studies, adoption studies, and twin studies. All three methods suggest a substantial genetic contribution to individual differences in intelligence, and yet all three also indicate the importance of the environment. Estimates of the heritability of IQ suggest that 40 to 70 percent of the variation among people is genetic in origin. Performance on IQ tests has increased steadily over time (the Flynn Effect), with an average gain of 3 points per decade. This increase is evidence of the role of the environment.

LEARNING OBJECTIVE 10.3 Understand the ways in which the environment affects IQ.

1. *How does the family environment influence IQ?*
   The home environment is one context within which intellectual abilities develop. Longitudinal studies indicate that risk factors in the child's environment, such as family stresses, are predictive of declines in IQ over time. Studies that measure variations in the home environment (often using the HOME instrument) suggest that the quality of the experience within the home influences both current and future intellectual competence. Examinations of the bases for cross-national differences in mathematical achievement provide further evidence for the importance of parental values and practices.

2. *What might account for minority group differences in IQ scores?*
   A number of minority groups score lower on average than Caucasian children on IQ tests. Several factors may contribute to these differences. Social and economic disadvantage is one major environmental difference that must be considered. Cultural and experiential differences may also contribute to children's test performance. Motivational factors may influence test performance as well.

3. *What are some examples of early intervention programs?*
   The Abecedarian Project is a successful intervention program focused on low-income children and families in North Carolina. Project Head Start is a nationwide American intervention directed at low-income preschool children and their families. Better Beginnings, Better Futures is a 25-year longitudinal intervention project offered to children in economically disadvantaged neighbourhoods in a number of Ontario cities. Aboriginal Head Start is an early intervention program for First Nations, Inuit, and Métis children.

4. *Are early intervention programs effective?*
   Early intervention programs have been found to have positive effects on children's development. Immediate effects are generally greater than are long-term effects. School performance is generally more affected than is IQ. Programs that introduce the greatest changes in the child's environment have generally had the greatest impact.

5. *What is stereotype threat and how does it influence test performance?*
   Stereotype threat is the extra pressure that people, especially those who are members of minority groups, feel in situations in which their performance may confirm a negative stereotype. This stereotype and its related anxiety then interfere with performance. The stereotype threat effect has been well-documented with students of varying ages, from young children to adults. Experimental interventions suggest some possible means for countering its effects.

LEARNING OBJECTIVE 10.4 Evaluate different aspects of the schooling experience and how these affect cognitive development.

1. *Identify cognitive effects of schooling that have been found by researchers.*
   Schools can affect children's intellectual development. Cross-cultural studies indicate that schooling promotes a number of cognitive skills, including memory, classification, and metacognition. Some aspects of children's cognitive development, such as the Piagetian concept of conservation, are less strongly and consistently affected. Schooling also affects how children think about words and use language, as schooled children are more likely to think in terms of general categories and abstract relations. The development of literacy promotes abstract, reflective styles of thinking, and reading exposure is strongly linked to cognitive development. Amount of schooling also appears to be important in the development of IQ.

2. *Discuss how teacher expectations, class and school size, school transition, and school effectiveness affect cognitive outcomes for children.*
   One of the greatest challenges teachers face is treating everyone equally and fairly. Teachers often have more positive expectations for students they perceive to be of higher ability. Students who perceive their teachers as supportive and caring are more motivated to engage in academic work than students who see their teachers as unsupportive and uncaring.

   School transitions can be stressful times for children. Adjustments to new adult authority figures, physical environments, schedules, peers, and academic expectations add to the stress. Development proceeds most smoothly when the environmental opportunities and challenges during a particular time period match the capacities and needs of the developing child (stage–environment fit).

   School effectiveness is difficult to define and study. In general, effective schools are comfortable places to learn where education is actively pursued. Teachers in successful schools manage their classrooms in an organized and fair manner. Students in effective schools are helped to feel part of the school through opportunities to participate in school-related activities, as well as chances to have a voice in decisions concerning the school. It is important for the school and teacher to find an appropriate match between the students they have and the teaching methods they use.

3. *Define and describe the evidence for and against the effectiveness of ability grouping.*
   Ability grouping is designed to decrease the heterogeneity that teachers must work with in the classroom. Students are assigned to particular classrooms based on some measure of ability. Supporters of ability grouping argue that the practice permits teachers to devise and deliver a curriculum that more closely meets the needs of all the students in the group. Some forms of ability grouping have been shown to work well for some students. Critics argue that students

who are tracked receive a poorer educational environment, can be stigmatized, and demonstrate lower levels of academic performance.

4. *Explain how family and peers can contribute to school success.*
Children's adjustment to school and their academic performance are related to the quality of family relations and family support. The parents' direct involvement with the school is also important. Good relationships with peers are related to positive attitudes toward school. Children rejected by their peers do more poorly in school and are more likely to drop out.

LEARNING OBJECTIVE 10.5 Identify alternative conceptions of intelligence.

1. *Describe the evolutionary approach to intelligence.*
Evolutionary accounts contrast cognitive abilities that likely proved adaptive in the ancestral past with those necessary to survive in the modern world. Cognitive abilities that have been shaped by natural selection are called biologically primary abilities. These abilities are supported by dedicated neurocognitive systems and are readily acquired by children the world over. Biologically secondary abilities are culture-specific. Acquisition of these skills, which include reading and higher mathematics, requires deliberate instruction.

2. *Explain the notion of dynamic assessments.*
Dynamic testing has its origins in the sociocultural approach. Sociocultural theorists emphasize what children can do with appropriate help from others. Theoretically, this emphasis is reflected in the concept of the zone of proximal development, and pragmatically, it forms the basis for dynamic assessments; that is, assessments that add a social dimension to the evaluation of intellectual ability. Dynamic assessments measure the child's ability to benefit from adult-provided assistance, typically in a test-train-retest design. Such assessments reveal individual differences among children that are not identified by standard IQ measures.

3. *Describe the multiple intelligences identified in Gardner's model.*
Gardner posits eight distinctive intelligences, collectively defined as the ability to solve problems or fashion products that are important in a particular cultural setting or community. The eight intelligences are (1) linguistic: ability to use language to achieve goals; (2) logical-mathematical: ability to analyze problems logically; (3) musical: appreciation and skill in the composition and performance of music; (4) bodily kinesthetic: ability to use one's body to solve problems or fashion products; (5) spatial: ability to perceive spatial relationships; (6) naturalist: ability to recognize and classify flora and fauna; (7) interpersonal: ability to understand the desires and intentions of other people and work effectively with others; and (8) intrapersonal: capacity to understand oneself and use this understanding to direct one's life effectively.

4. *Explain what is meant by giftedness.*
Studies of giftedness and creativity attempt to identify forms of exceptional intellectual accomplishment that are not captured by IQ. Many psychologists believe that giftedness involves more than simply high IQ; children may be gifted in specific domains of development rather than in general, and these domains include abilities (e.g., in art or music) that are not part of standard conceptions of intelligence. It has been argued that creativity also requires more than intelligence in the psychometric sense. Confluence models of creativity stress the convergence of multiple contributors to creativity, including divergent thinking, personality attributes, and motivation.

CHAPTER 11

LANGUAGE DEVELOPMENT

In the fifth century B.C.E., Greek historian Herodotus reported what may have been the first scientific experiment. According to Herodotus, Egyptian pharaoh Psammentichus had sought to determine which was the earliest (and therefore the most natural) human language. To answer this question, the pharaoh ordered that two infants be reared in an isolated mountain hut without any exposure to language. If the infants nevertheless learned to speak, as the pharaoh believed they would, then the language that emerged must be the original human tongue. The infants did in fact eventually speak, and the first word uttered was bekos, which, it turned out, was the word for bread in the ancient language of Phrygia (now part of Turkey). The honour of the original language was therefore ceded to the Phrygians (Fromkin & Rodman, 1988).

The report by Herodotus is just one of many accounts of attempts, spread across many centuries, to identify the first human language. The reported results have varied. One experiment, carried out by King James IV of Scotland, led to the conclusion that the original language was Hebrew (Fromkin & Rodman, 1988). Another study was inconclusive because the isolated babies, deprived of social contact, died before they could produce any words (Ross & McLaughlin, 1949).

We will not attempt to solve the mystery of the first human language in this chapter. Our focus will be on how children today master the particular language to which they are exposed. We will see, however, that this problem is perhaps no less difficult than the one that confronted Psammentichus. The question of how children learn language is one of the most challenging and fascinating topics in the modern science of child psychology. ■

Productivity The property of language that permits humans to produce and comprehend an infinite number of statements.

ANY STUDENT WHO HAS SPENT four years in high school or college attempting to learn a second language can appreciate the struggle of trying to memorize how each verb is conjugated or what endings signify past, future, and subjunctive forms. Yet, that very same student, during the first four years of life, very likely acquired the rudiments of his or her native language rather easily, with no textbooks, classroom instruction, or studying. How is such an impressive feat accomplished?

We can immediately rule out simple explanations of either the nature or nurture sort. The remarkable feat of language development would be easy to understand if language were simply an inherited ability that is passed along in the genes, emerging according to a biological timetable. As we saw in Chapter 1, even animals with very limited cognitive capabilities can display extremely complex behaviour if it is the product of millions of years of evolution. Various properties of language rule out such an explanation, however. One is **productivity**. Whereas communication in other species involves a small set of inborn messages that the animal can send and also recognize, humans can produce—and comprehend—an infinite number of sentences. Many of the statements we speak and hear every day are ones we have never used or encountered in exactly the same form, yet they give us little trouble. Such statements are obviously not the sorts of messages that are passed along genetically from generation to generation.

A second property of language that argues against a purely genetic explanation is its variety. Language consists not of one tongue used by all members of the species, but of thousands of languages. Furthermore, different languages do not simply substitute one word for another; they use different grammatical structures. The word order used to ask a question in Japanese, for example, is different from the corresponding order in French. Yet, children readily learn the particular language to which they are exposed. And a child of Japanese parents growing up in a French-speaking home will learn French, not Japanese. We are reminded of the story of the little American girl whose parents had just adopted a baby from Korea. "I can't wait until he gets older," she remarked, "so that he can teach me to speak Korean."* Whatever language abilities children inherit from their parents, the ability to speak and comprehend their native tongue is not one of them.

We can begin, then, by ruling out a simple nature solution to the fascinating puzzle of human language. Clearly, language must be, at least in part, learned. But some of the same properties of language that argue against a direct genetic explanation also pose problems for any simple learning account. Language, as we said, is infinitely productive, and children continually produce and understand sentences that they have not encountered before. The rules that underlie such sentences are quite complex, yet children master them very quickly. And they do so even though their parents do not explicitly teach them most of the rules, nor (as we will see) do they necessarily provide clear models or reinforcements from which children might learn the rules. These arguments suggest that there may, indeed, be a strong biological basis on which experience operates.

Our coverage of the active field of language development focuses on two traditional developmental issues. One is a description of the typical course of language development, beginning with the infant's earliest recognition abilities and continuing through to the child's first words, sentences, and more complex utterances. The second involves proposed explanations of language acquisition and the research findings that support them.

This chapter is divided into five parts. We begin by considering modern theories of language development. Next, we examine what is known about the period before the child begins to speak—a period that many researchers feel is important in laying the groundwork for language development. Within this section, one of the major topics discussed is how young children learn the sounds of their language (phonology). In the remaining sections, we discuss the development of the three principal areas of language: its meaning (semantics), its structure (grammar), and its function (pragmatics).

*We thank Harriet Rheingold for this story.

THEORIES OF LANGUAGE DEVELOPMENT

Learning Objective 11.1

Compare and contrast four major theories of language development.

The theoretical debate over language development is not new. Today, the theoretical approaches to language follow roughly the four traditions we described in Chapter 1, including a biologically oriented model, cognitive approaches, sociocultural approaches, and environmental/learning analyses. Here, we outline the fundamental ideas of these theories, and in later sections we examine what the data from research with children have to say about them.

NATIVIST THEORY

The modern debate over language development began around 1960. Before then, most North American psychologists viewed language learning in terms of conditioning and learning principles. In his book *Verbal Behavior* (1957), B.F. Skinner argued that the same operant principles used to explain other forms of human behaviour could be used to explain the acquisition of language.

The first important challenge to Skinner's views came from Noam Chomsky, a linguist at the Massachusetts Institute of Technology (MIT). The **nativist theory** of language development proposed by Chomsky put a heavy emphasis on inborn processes and biological mechanisms, in contrast to the environmentalist emphasis of Skinner's theory. Chomsky and other nativist theorists contend that language acquisition must have a strong biological basis because young children acquire language so rapidly and so easily during a period of development when their cognitive abilities are still rather unsophisticated (Chomsky, 1959, 1965; Lenneberg, 1967; Pinker, 1994).

Noam Chomsky's nativist theory dominated research on language acquisition throughout the 1960s. *(Getty Images)*

For several reasons, these theorists rule out the possibility that language is acquired by means of rewards, punishments, and imitation. First, adults do not appear to reinforce or punish children for the accuracy of their speech (a point we will discuss again shortly), as an environmental analysis would seem to suggest. In addition, learning by imitation would require that children be exposed to consistently good models of speech and language. However, much of the everyday adult speech that children hear is not well formed and accurate; it includes short pieces of sentences, hesitating stops and starts, slang words, and errors of many types. The productivity property of language also argues against learning by imitation because children produce many statements they have never heard spoken precisely in that way. Similarly, they cannot be imitating adult speech when they produce forms such as "Mommy goed here" or "me up."

Nativist theory A theory of language development, originated by Chomsky, that stresses innate mechanisms separate from cognitive processes.

A final argument comes from linguistic analyses of human language. Such analyses reveal that the rules we use in speaking or comprehending language are extremely complex. But adults do not specifically teach children these rules. None of us, in fact, could accurately describe the intricate system of language regulations we use so effortlessly to produce and understand good speech and to recognize when speech is not good. These problems and others have led theorists in this tradition to conclude that environmental/learning accounts of language development are inadequate. The only alternative, they suggest, is that children are born with special brain mechanisms—separate from other cognitive processes—that allow them to acquire language quickly and easily.

For Thought and Discussion

What are some other examples of errors that reveal children's application of language rules?

According to Chomsky's original model, language can be described in terms of two types of structures. A language's **surface structure** consists of the rules governing the way that words and phrases can be arranged, which may vary considerably from one language to another. The **deep structure** of language, in contrast, refers to the inborn rules humans possess that underlie any language system.

Language acquisition, therefore, requires a speech-analyzing mechanism, which Chomsky called the **language acquisition device (LAD)**. Whenever a child hears speech—good, bad, or

Surface structure Chomsky's term for the way words and phrases are arranged in spoken languages.

Deep structure Chomsky's term for the inborn knowledge humans possess about the properties of language.

Language acquisition device (LAD) Chomsky's proposed brain mechanism for analyzing speech input; the mechanism that allows young children to quickly acquire the language to which they are exposed.

Transformational grammar A set of rules developed by the LAD to translate a language's surface structure to a deep structure that the child can innately understand.

whatever—this hypothetical brain mechanism begins to develop a **transformational grammar** that translates the surface structure of the language into the deep structure that the child can comprehend. The development of these transformational rules is assumed to take place over several years, explaining why the child's initial language skills are rather limited, but also why they progress so rapidly.

Evidence for such a deep structure to language can be found in a series of very interesting studies conducted by Susan Goldin-Meadow (2003). These studies looked at how American and Chinese deaf children, not exposed to either spoken language or sign language, spontaneously develop their own "home signs" and begin to communicate with their parents using gestures. Despite clear differences in the languages spoken by the parents (English versus Mandarin), and different cultural and parent–infant interactional styles, there were some striking similarities in the sentence structure of the home signs used by these two groups of children. The children broke scenes they wanted to describe into components of subjects, actions, and objects (i.e., who does what to whom), and tended to order these components in sequences that were similar for all the deaf children, regardless of the language spoken by their parents. Interestingly, the sequencing of components did not necessarily parallel the syntax of the spoken language of their parents. The syntax of the spoken language of their parents, which differed in English and Mandarin, might be considered the surface structure of each particular language, whereas the syntax expressed by the children in their home signs, which was remarkably similar in American and Chinese children, might be considered to represent a deeper structure of language, which apparently does not require much learning.

We should note that more recent models in this tradition have diverged in various ways from Chomsky's original formulation. Chomsky's own theory has undergone many specific changes over the years, the largest change occurring in a paper he wrote with Marc Hauser and Tecumseh Fitch in 2002. In this paper, they proposed that most language abilities involve cognitive and perceptual mechanisms (e.g., memory, hearing) that are shared with other psychological abilities and that are found in other species. This position changed Chomsky's theory in two ways. The first is that language was no longer seen as extraordinarily complex. The second is that language was no longer seen as extremely "special," since many of its mechanisms are shared with other cognitive processes. Nevertheless, it is still a nativist argument: children start the task of language learning with innate abilities, albeit abilities shared with other cognitive processes. Other theorists, however, such as Stephen Pinker (2004; Pinker & Jackendoff, 2005), a Canadian cognitive scientist at Harvard University, argue strongly for Chomsky's original position, that language is innate and special. This emphasis on the natural, biologically prepared nature of language development is well captured in the title of Pinker's (2004) book devoted to this position, *The Language Instinct*.

One major feature of language development that is used by nativists as proof for the biological bases of language development is the existence of a sensitive period for language acquisition (see Chapter 1 for a discussion of sensitive periods). This is the idea, first proposed by the famous neuroscientist Wilder Penfield of McGill University in 1959, that language can only be learned before a certain age and cannot be acquired after that point—essentially a biological deadline for learning language. The most famous illustration of this sensitive period is the case of "Genie," a young girl who was not exposed to language until 13 years of age because of abuse and neglect (Curtiss, 1977). Although regularly exposed to language after her rescue, Genie never fully acquired language, especially grammar skills.

Links to Related Material

In Chapter 1, you read about sensitive periods—times in development when certain behaviours are more easily learned—which ethologists believe reflect the biological programming of a species. Here, you learn about the sensitive period for language learning, which nativists view as evidence for the biological basis of language development.

One problem with using Genie as evidence for a sensitive period is that, as with all single case studies, we cannot necessarily generalize this finding, especially considering the early trauma Genie experienced. However, there is a group of individuals with normal early childhood experiences who do not have regular exposure to language: deaf children of hearing parents. The children cannot hear the spoken language of their parents, and the parents, for the most part, do not have knowledge of a sign language. Therefore, many of these children learn sign language when they enter the educational system. Newport (1990) found that adult signers who acquired sign after early childhood performed less well in sign language measures than adult signers who learned the language during early childhood. This finding provides further proof for a sensitive period. Finally, the most common example of the sensitive period, one that you may have experienced yourself, is the fact that people cannot fully learn a second language after early childhood. People who acquire a second language as a teenager or adult, even if regularly used, perform less well on language tests than native speakers (Johnson & Newport, 1989). This is an argument for starting second language training, like immersion programs, as early as possible. (We discuss immersion schooling later in the chapter.)

The nativist model solves several of the problems of an environmental approach. The rewards and punishments that would be necessary to operantly condition children's speech are not important to this model. Rather, children need only a few critical bits of speech input to develop a grammar and thus to trigger a great deal of language development. Once children grasp the structural rules, or grammar, of the language, they can understand and produce an infinite number of sentences. In addition, according to this model, the analyzing and processing mechanisms needed have evolved specifically for language acquisition and are concerned only with the abstract structure of speech (e.g., subject-verb-object), not with its meaning or content. These two points mean that language acquisition should put few demands on children's cognitive abilities, making highly sophisticated language learning possible in a cognitively immature organism.

Nativists believe that children's learning of language is due to innate abilities. (*© Nina Vaclavova/iStock*)

Chomsky's approach dominated language research and theory throughout the 1960s, and it remains a major position today. Beginning around 1970, however, alternative views of language development began to emerge. These views have a number of points in common. In particular, each places more emphasis on the environmental contributors to language acquisition than does the nativist approach; in addition, the various models overlap in the assumptions they make and the kinds of evidence they cite. Nevertheless, there are also differences among them in emphases and specific claims, differences that correspond to general themes of the remaining three theoretical approaches.

ENVIRONMENTAL/LEARNING APPROACHES

We saw that Skinner's analysis of language behaviour fell out of favour when Chomsky convincingly argued that the environment alone cannot explain the facts of normal language development. Nevertheless, learning-based approaches to this topic did not stop. Contemporary work in this tradition differs in two main ways from its predecessors.

First, most work is now directed by more cognitively oriented theories of learning than the operant conditioning model of Skinner. In particular, more recent work has been grounded in Bandura's social-cognitive model (see Chapter 1), with its emphasis on observational learning and related cognitive processes (Zimmerman, 1983). Chomsky argued that children cannot learn language simply by imitating what they hear, because they can produce and understand an unlimited number of new sentences. But as we saw in Chapter 1, social-learning theorists have shown that learning by imitation need not involve exact copying. They argue, therefore, that modelling and observational learning may account for the kind of rule-based system that children come to use (Bandura, 1986; Whitehurst & DeBaryshe, 1989).

The second difference concerns evidence for the role of environmental factors. As we saw, one of Chomsky's most important criticisms of Skinner's approach was that the environment does not present the child with a good model of language from which to learn. But research has shown that people do not talk to infants or young children in the same way that they talk to proficient speakers. Instead, mothers (and fathers, and even older children) use a distinct style of speech termed **infant-directed speech**. This style of speech was formerly called "motherese," however that is now considered a flawed term as it is not just mothers who can produce this type of speech, but also other adults and even older children. Infant-directed speech is characterized by slow, careful pronunciation and exaggerated intonation. It consists primarily of familiar words, there is much

Infant-directed speech (formerly known as "motherese") Simplified speech directed at very young children by adults and older children.

repetition, and sentences tend to be short, simple, and grammatically accurate (Fernald, et al., 1989; Hampson & Nelson, 1993). These findings indicate that the input children receive may well be clearer and more helpful than Chomsky claimed. Further, children with more one-on-one language input from adults have more advanced language development, suggesting that experience with language does affect rates of learning (Hoff, 2006).

Finally, nativist theorists have argued that parents do not specifically train children in the rules of language. Yet, recent analyses of parent–child interactions indicate that parents do sometimes respond to the grammatical accuracy of their children's speech, providing them with a variety of forms of feedback and instruction (Moerk, 2000; Saxton, 1997). Taken together, these findings suggest that social and environmental factors may play a significant role in children's language acquisition.

For Thought and Discussion

If language has a strong biological basis, how did there come to be so many different languages? Do you think there will be more or fewer languages in the future? Why?

COGNITIVE-DEVELOPMENTAL MODELS

The major emphasis of the cognitive-developmental approach to language is, not surprisingly, on cognitive contributors to language acquisition. Whereas nativist theorists believe that language does not depend on children's general cognitive abilities and is more or less separate from them, cognitive theorists assume that even very young children have a good deal of knowledge about the world and that they use this knowledge to help them learn language. These researchers contend that children do not simply acquire a set of abstract linguistic rules. Rather, they acquire language forms that they can "map onto" cognitive concepts they already possess.

Some cognitive language research has been based on Piaget's theory (Bates & Snyder, 1985). Most interest has centred on the transition from the later sensorimotor abilities of the toddler to the early preoperational abilities of the preschooler—a time when children are just beginning to combine words into two- and three-word phrases. This research has examined the relations between certain mental operations and corresponding language forms (Gopnik & Meltzoff, 1996; Tamis-Lemonda & Bornstein, 1994). For example, it appears that infants need a concept of object permanence before they begin using disappearance words, such as *all gone* (Gopnik & Meltzoff, 1987). Similarly, the kinds of meanings that children convey in their earliest sentences (e.g., agents acting on objects) correspond closely to the kinds of understanding that they developed during the sensorimotor period. Words can also influence concepts (Gopnik, 2001). Infants as young as 3 months learn a new object category (e.g., dinosaurs) if trained on a set of examples from the object category (e.g., a stegosaurus, a brontosaurus) paired with a consistent word, rather than if the examples are paired with a consistent musical tone (Ferry, Hespos, & Waxman, 2010).

For Thought and Discussion

What are some other examples of the two-way interaction between language and thought?

A second cognitive approach is based on a belief that children use their early cognitive concepts as a means of extracting the rules of language from the speech they hear. Recall that the nativist view is that children analyze speech into its abstract, grammatical structure. This cognitive model, in contrast, holds that children first analyze speech into meaning-based, or *semantic*, concepts that involve relations among objects, actions, and events. According to this view, children have a very early understanding of concepts such as *agent* (the person who performs an action), *action* (something that is done to a person or object), and *patient* (the person who is acted on). When young children hear speech, they presumably analyze it into these cognitive concepts, focusing, for example, on who did what to whom. They then develop simple rules regarding these concepts—such as "agents are usually named at the beginning of a statement"—that they use to guide their own speech (Bowerman, 1976).

A third cognitive approach stems from recent connectionist work within the information-processing perspective. As we saw in Chapter 9, connectionism involves the creation of self-modifying computer simulations in the form of artificial neural networks, the goal being to model forms of learning that humans show. A related approach to connectionism is called statistical, or distributional, learning. Theorists in this area propose that children can track regularities in language input, such as syllables co-occurring to form words or subject words preceding action words in English word order (Saffran, Aslin, & Newport, 1996). They use these high probability co-occurrences to rapidly learn about words and grammar (Soderstrom, Conwell, Feldman, & Morgan, 2009). Like the nativist approach, these theorists argue that the child's ability to track probabilities and distributions is innate. However, unlike most nativist approaches, they do not necessarily believe that language is special, as these abilities are applied across many domains, like tracking visual input (Saffran, 2003).

Links to Related Material

In Chapter 9, you read about connectionism as a model for cognitive development. Here, you learn how connectionist models may help us understand language acquisition.

SOCIOCULTURAL APPROACHES

The sociocultural approach to language stresses the cognitive abilities children bring to the task of language acquisition, in conjunction with a supportive and helpful social environment. It thus shares emphases with the two approaches just discussed. Nevertheless, it also adds some distinctive themes of its own.

One emphasis is on the functional basis for language acquisition and language use (MacWhinney & Bates, 1993; Ninio & Snow, 1999). Sociocultural theorists maintain that the child's primary motivation for acquiring language is social interaction—to communicate ideas and to be understood. The emphasis is thus on *pragmatics,* or the uses to which language is put. Children are seen as inherently social beings, and language is a primary way by which they enter into and affect their social world.

A further, related emphasis is on the preverbal origins of language acquisition. Social interaction begins at birth, and children therefore have many opportunities to learn about the nature of language well before the first words appear. Jerome Bruner (1983, 1999) has proposed that the typical social environment of infants (in most cases their parents), in fact, provides many structured opportunities for language learning to take place. These opportunities make up what Bruner (in deliberate contrast to Chomsky's LAD) refers to as **LASS**, or the **language acquisition support system**.

Language acquisition support system (LASS) Bruner's proposed process by which parents provide children with assistance in learning language.

The central component of the LASS is the *format.* Formats are similar to the scripts we discussed in Chapter 9. They consist of structured social interactions, or routines, that commonly take place between infants and their mothers. Familiar formats include looking at books together, playing naming games ("Where's your nose?" "Where's your mouth?") and action games (peekaboo, hide-and-seek), and singing songs with gestures ("The Itsy Bitsy Spider"). Such activities appear to be common across a range of cultures. Variations of the peekaboo game, for example, were found in all 17 cultural settings examined by Fernald and O'Neill (1993).

For Thought and Discussion

What formats or structured interactions did you enjoy as a child? What formats might you present to a child in your care?

The format allows a child to learn specific language elements within a very restricted context—usually simply by memorizing words and their corresponding actions. Gradually, the parent may change the formats so that they include more elements or require a greater contribution from the child. In this way, additional language can be learned and previously acquired responses can be applied in new ways. Within these formatted interactions, the parent also provides other sorts of scaffolding for language acquisition, such as simplifying speech, using repetition, and correcting the child's inaccurate or incomplete statements (Snow, Perlmann, & Nathan, 1987).

A final emphasis of the sociocultural approach is on the rich set of social-cognitive abilities that both children and adults bring to the interactions that underlie language learning (Snow, 1999; Tomasello, 2003). Children's ability to learn from others is a central theme of the approach, not just with respect to language, but in general. It is no surprise, therefore, that children are seen as possessing special sensitivity to the messages they receive from other people. In particular, as we will see, work that comes under the heading "theory of mind" (see Chapter 7) documents a number of social-cognitive skills that can help explain the accomplishments of language acquisition.

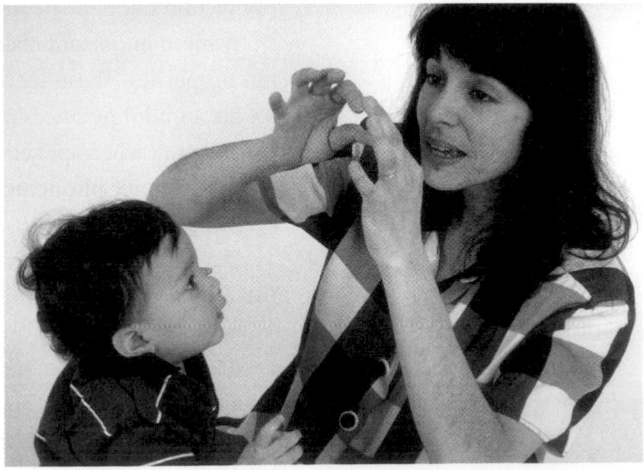

Jerome Bruner believes that young children learn language through structured play experiences called formats. *(Laura Dwight/Corbis Images)*

LEARNING OBJECTIVE 11.1

Compare and contrast four major theories of language development.

1. What are the four major theories of language development?
2. In the behavioural view, through what processes do children learn language?
3. In the nativist view, how does biology take precedence over the environment in language learning?
4. How do the cognitive-developmental approach and the sociocultural approach differ in their explanations of language acquisition?

Learning Objective 11.2

Trace the developments in the first year of life that establish the preverbal basis for language learning.

THE PREVERBAL PERIOD

From the abstract world of theories, we turn to the real world of children learning language. Development in many areas begins at birth or even before. But children typically do not produce their first identifiable word until about 1 year of age, and they do not begin to combine words until about 18 months. Just how important is the preverbal period in language development?

Some theorists have argued that the process of language development is discontinuous, with the events of the preverbal period having little connection to later language learning (Bickerton, 1984; Shatz, 1983). Most, however, believe that language acquisition represents a continuous process, and that abilities developed during infancy form the building blocks of the language skills that appear later on (Bloom, 1998; Golinkoff & Hirsh-Pasek, 1999). As we will see, much recent evidence supports the continuity point of view.

SPEECH PERCEPTION

Before babies can learn language, they must be able to perceive the sounds through which language works. How early is the perception of speech sounds apparent? The answer to this question takes us into the area of **phonology**, the study of speech sounds.

Phonology The study of speech sounds.

Human speech actually consists of a continuous stream of sound. To comprehend language, the listener therefore must divide this stream into segments of various sorts, including syllables, words, and statements. The listener must also attend to other characteristics of speech, such as rising and falling intonations, pauses between words and phrases, and stress placed at different points.

Phonologists characterize speech in several ways. Speech therapists, for example, are most concerned with *phonetic* properties, which refer to the different kinds of sounds that can be articulated by our vocal apparatus—lips, tongue, larynx, and so on. Articulation skills develop in a predictable order, with some sounds, such as *r*, appearing later than others (which explains why a young child might be heard to say, "The wabbit is wunning").

A more important characteristic of speech for infants learning language, however, is its *phonemic* properties. These are the contrasts in speech sounds that change the meaning of what is heard. Not all sound differences produce different meanings. The *a* in the word *car,* for example, sounds very different when spoken by someone from Alabama and by someone from Nova Scotia. But they represent a single **phoneme** because they fall within a class of sounds that all convey the same meaning. As a result, an English-speaking listener would recognize both words as meaning "automobile."

Phoneme A sound contrast that changes meaning.

If a sound variation crosses the boundary from one phoneme category to another, however, a different meaning is produced, as when *car* becomes *core*. The sound difference between these two words may actually be smaller than that between the two regional pronunciations of *car* we just described. But *car* and *core* are perceived as different words—that is, words with different meanings—because in English they represent different phoneme categories. The English language, in fact, uses about 45 phonemes. Other languages use more or fewer. According to Pinker (1994), the range extends from as few as 11 (in Polynesian) to as many as 141 (in the Khoisan or "Bushman" language).

This topic is important for our understanding of language development because research has shown that babies are surprisingly skilled in this area. From an early age, they show evidence of **categorical perception**—the ability to discriminate when two sounds represent two different phonemes and when, instead, they lie within the same phonemic category. This ability has been investigated extensively in infants and has been demonstrated across a wide range of speech sounds in babies as young as 1 month (Aslin, Jusczyk, & Pisoni, 1998; Eimas, Siqueland, Einar, Jusczyck, & Vigorito, 1971; Jusczyk, 1997). Indeed, as Sandra Trehub (1976) of the University of Toronto points out, infants have been shown to display categorical perception of some speech contrasts found only in languages they have never heard. These findings suggest that categorical perception is an innate ability and thus universal among children. But biology is only part of the story.

Categorical perception The ability to detect differences in speech sounds that correspond to differences in meaning; the ability to discriminate phonemic boundaries.

Experience also plays a role in early speech perception. Studies indicate that the more babies are exposed to a language, the sharper their phonemic discriminations in that language become (Kuhl et al., 2006). Linda Polka of McGill University has demonstrated that this is especially true for phonemic discriminations that are more difficult to perceive, such as the difference between the words "doze" and "those" (Polka, Colontonio, & Sundara, 2001; Sundara, Polka, & Genesee, 2006). Conversely, lack of exposure dulls these abilities. For example, the distinction between the sounds *r* and *l*, which is not a phonemic contrast in the Japanese language, is a well-known problem for Japanese speakers of English. Studies show that adult Japanese not only have difficulty pronouncing these sounds, but also struggle to discriminate them (Miyawaki et al., 1975). Young Japanese infants, however, have no difficulty discriminating this contrast, suggesting that this ability gradually decreases in children learning Japanese as a result of their having little need to use it (Eimas, 1975). In fact, more recent research specifies exactly when the loss occurs: 7-month-old Japanese infants can make the *r* versus *l* discrimination; 11-month-olds cannot (Kuhl, 2001).

This pattern turns out to be a general one, now demonstrated across a variety of speech contrasts and a variety of languages. By the end of the first year, as reported by Janet Werker and Richard Tees (1999) of the University of British Columbia, babies lose a good deal of their ability to discriminate sound contrasts that are not present in the language to which they have been exposed, but they maintain those contrasts present in their language (see also Best, 1995). Interestingly, bilingual infants appear to keep the sounds of both of their languages active. In a study conducted at both the University of British Columbia and the University of Ottawa, researchers demonstrated that French–English bilingual infants maintained consonant contrasts in both English and French (Burns, Yoshida, Hill & Werker, 2007).

Experience with language also helps babies conquer the formidable task, mentioned earlier, of segmenting the continuous stream of speech they hear into individual words. Recent research indicates that babies bring some impressive skills to this task. One cue to word boundaries is frequency of co-occurrence: The syllables that make up a word (for example, *ba* and *by* in *baby)* occur together more often in speech than do syllables that span adjacent words (for example, *ty* and *ba* in *pretty baby).* By 8 months of age, infants can abstract and use such frequency information to distinguish common from less common patterns of speech sounds (Aslin, Saffran, & Newport, 1999). Recognizing which sounds occur together is a critical step in isolating individual words from the ongoing speech stream.

Any language provides additional cues about word boundaries beyond simple frequencies of occurrence. A further cue that babies learning English use is the location of a word's stress. In English, most words are stressed on the first syllable. By 9 months of age, American babies prefer listening to words stressed on the first syllable, presumably because this is the pattern they are used to hearing (Jusczyk, Cutler, & Redanz, 1993). In addition, they are more successful at segmenting words from the speech stream when the emphasis is on the first syllable (e.g., kingdom, hamlet) than when it comes later (e.g., device, guitar) (Jusczyk, Houston, & Newsome, 1999).

Since infants narrow their phoneme categories around the same time they begin learning words, many researchers assumed that infants would apply their phoneme perception skills to early word learning and would not confuse similar sounding words, like *boat* and *goat.* However, researchers have demonstrated that infants initially have difficulty *applying* their perceptual skills to word learning, confusing similar-sounding new words (Nazzi, 2005; Stager & Werker, 1997; Werker, Fennell, Corcoran, & Stager, 2002). Linking a word to an object requires many cognitive skills: infants must perceive and attend to the details of both the word and object; encode the relevant information; and then retrieve and maintain access to that information. This strain limits the cognitive resources of novice word learners, and they lose some information in the process. If this is the case, decreasing the difficulty of the task should help the infants to apply phonemes to words. Christopher Fennell of the University of Ottawa has shown that 14-month-olds succeed in distinguishing between similar sounding words that they are already familiar with, such as *ball* and *doll* (Fennell & Werker, 2003; Swingley & Aslin, 2002). Infants this age also succeed when they are trained on words they already know prior to learning similar sounding new words in a laboratory task (Fennell & Waxman, 2010). These findings demonstrate that infants have the underlying ability to apply their speech perception skills to early words, but task difficulty masks this ability.

Research on infant speech perception, then, suggests the influence of both nature and nurture. Perhaps from birth, babies possess an ability to discriminate a wide range of speech contrasts. They are, in the words of one leading researcher, "universal linguists" (Kuhl, 1991). But the environment very quickly begins to fine-tune these discriminations, eliminating those that are not needed, and improving the child's ability to use those that remain.

LISTENING PREFERENCES

Babies not only discriminate various types and properties of speech, they also prefer some speech sounds to others. As might be expected, infants prefer normal speech to either jumbled words or music (Colombo & Bundy, 1981; Glenn, Cunningham, & Joyce, 1981). Newborn infants even prefer natural speech over non-speech audio stimuli that maintains the duration, loudness, and modulations of speech (Vouloumanos & Werker, 2007). They also prefer listening to their mothers' voices over virtually any other type of sound (DeCasper & Fifer, 1980; Mehler et al., 1978). Newborns also prefer listening to their own language over a rhythmically distinct foreign language (see Chapter 6), demonstrating the role of prenatal listening experience (Nazzi & Ramus, 2003). In a fascinating study conducted at the University of British Columbia, Krista Byers-Heinlein and her colleagues demonstrated that infants who heard two languages prenatally, in other words newborns of bilingual mothers, preferred *both* maternal languages at birth (Byers-Heinlein, Burns, & Werker, 2010).

Perhaps even more theoretically important is the *type* of speech that infants prefer. We noted earlier that adults talk to babies differently than they talk to other adults, using the style of speech that has been labelled *infant-directed speech.* Several research teams, including Judith Pegg and Janet Werker of the University of British Columbia and Peter McLeod of Acadia University (Pegg, Werker, & McLeod, 1992), have presented babies with recordings of mothers speaking to their infants and mothers speaking to other adults. These investigators report that infants consistently prefer the mother-to-baby talk (see also Cooper & Aslin, 1990; Fernald, 1993). This preference is evident in the first days of life, although young infants are not yet sensitive to all the tone-of-voice cues to which older babies respond (Cooper & Aslin, 1994). Interestingly, the phenomenon is not limited to the auditory medium. Deaf mothers of deaf infants use a form of infant-directed speech in the sign language they direct to their babies, slowing down and exaggerating their gestures, and their babies are more attentive to such input than they are to adult-directed signs (Masataka, 1996). Indeed, even hearing infants who have never been exposed to signs find the infant-directed speech form of sign language especially interesting (Masataka, 1998).

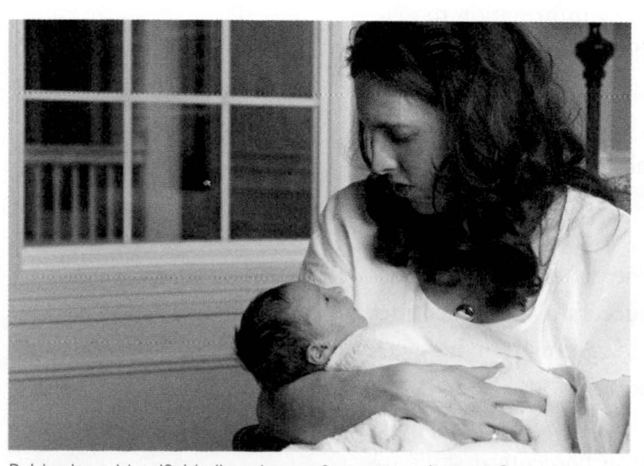

Babies have identifiable listening preferences, such as preferring the mother's voice to that of other adults. (© *jclegg/iStock*)

The findings from studies of infant-directed speech are important because they suggest that the adjustments speakers make when talking to an infant may actually increase the likelihood that the baby will be listening.

But the benefits of infant-directed speech extend beyond simply heightening interest in the speech signal. For example, the early preference we noted for the mother's voice is most evident when the speech is infant-directed speech (Mehler et al., 1978). Similarly, infants are better at detecting boundaries between clauses (Kemler Nelson et al., 1989).

Infants also discriminate phonemic categories more easily when listening to infant-directed speech than when listening to adult-directed speech (Karzon, 1985; Liu, Kuhl & Tsao, 2003). Janet Werker of the University of British Columbia and colleagues in Japan demonstrated how infant-directed speech may aid phoneme discrimination by showing that mothers highlight phoneme categories in infant-directed speech in both English and Japanese (Werker et al., 2007). Infants at 7 months of age are also better at using frequency of syllable co-occurrence to detect word boundaries, as discussed in the previous section, when the stimuli is infant-directed speech (Thiessen, Hill, & Saffran, 2005). Infants also remember words presented in infant-directed speech better than words presented in regular adult-styled speech (Singh et al., 2009). Thus, adults' natural way of talking to babies may help babies take the initial steps toward making sense of speech.

EARLY SOUNDS

Before babies speak words, they produce other sounds. As Joanna Blake (2000) of York University notes, this process is not random; rather, children's preverbal sounds follow a reasonably predictable course (see also Oller, 2000). The very earliest sounds consist of non-speech utterances that include whimpers and cries, burps, grunts, and other physiological noises. At about 2 months of age, babies begin to produce one-syllable vowel sounds known as **cooing**—*ah*, *oo*—and occasionally a consonant-vowel combination, such as *goo*. Whereas the earlier sounds usually signalled some form of discomfort, these new sounds frequently are accompanied by smiling or laughing and seem to convey more positive emotions (Blount, 1982).

Cooing A stage in the preverbal period, beginning at about 2 months, when babies primarily produce one-syllable vowel sounds.

At about 6 months of age, **reduplicated babbling** appears (Ferguson, 1983). Here, the infant strings together several identical sounds, as in *babababa*. In the months that follow, the baby adds more and more sounds, including some that occur only in other languages. Research indicates, in fact, that the babbling of children from different language backgrounds is very similar (Locke, 1989).

Reduplicated babbling A stage in the preverbal period, beginning at about 6 months, when infants produce strings of identical sounds, such as *dadada*.

As infants approach the end of the first year, their babbling loses its duplicated quality, and they begin to combine different sounds, as in *da-doo* or *boo-nee*. This later phase of babbling is characterized by "speechiness"; that is, it begins to include certain fundamental qualities of speech. For example, babies add changing intonation to their sounds so that their babbling includes the same patterns of rising and falling pitch that we might hear in adult speech (Clumeck, 1980). In addition, many of the sounds that infants produce late in the babbling period are sounds that they will display when they first begin to produce words (Oller, 2000).

Babbling is so similar among infants of different language groups that biological mechanisms undoubtedly play a major role. But when infants finally begin to speak, they say only words from the language they have been hearing. Does this mean that speech emerges separately from babbling? Or, instead, does the form of babbling steadily gravitate toward the language the child hears—a theoretical notion called **babbling drift** (Brown, 1958b)? Evidence has been reported on both sides of this issue, but it seems to be accumulating in favour of the drift hypothesis (Blake, 2000; Boysson-Bardies, 1999; Locke, 1993). For example, at the end of the first year of life, French-learning infants produce consonants that include sound cues specific to French much more than do English-learning infants of the same age (Whalen, Levitt, & Goldstein, 2007). In a study conducted at McGill University, researchers demonstrated that English-learning infants produced different vowels than French-learning infants (Rvachew et al., 2008). In either case, this issue nicely illustrates the difference between the continuity and discontinuity views of children's preverbal abilities.

Babbling drift A hypothesis that infants' babbling gradually gravitates toward the language they are hearing and soon will speak.

The possible role of environmental factors in babbling has also led researchers to examine the *vocalizations* of deaf infants. If babies do not hear speech, will they still display babbling? The answer is yes, but the nature and course of babbling are not identical to the typical pattern for hearing children. Differences are most marked near the end of the babbling stage, and include a delay in the onset of reduplicated babbling and a reduced number of well-formed syllables (Oller & Eilers, 1988). Such findings suggest that although early vocal babbling is probably guided by innate mechanisms, hearing speech may be a necessary experience for the emergence of the more complex aspects of later babbling. However, as we will discuss shortly, deaf infants babble manually (i.e., with their hands).

What about infants who are prevented from babbling? This unusual situation can occur, for example, in children who have severe respiratory problems and must breathe through a surgically implanted tube in the trachea. Clinical studies of such cases show that when the tube is eventually removed and normal breathing is resumed, the child's ability to articulate words lags behind that of age-mates for some time. This finding suggests that the opportunity to babble may provide important practice in the development of articulation. Also, the sounds produced by these children resemble those of deaf children, suggesting further that hearing one's own speech (that is, babbling), along with the speech of others, may be necessary for articulatory skills to develop properly (Locke & Pearson, 1990).

At least one type of babbling, however, does not require vocal skills. In studies done at McGill University, Laura Ann Petitto has shown that deaf children learning sign language display a sort of gestural babbling, producing partial forms of appropriate hand and finger gestures (Petitto & Marentette, 1991). Interestingly, hearing babies of deaf parents also babble gesturally, demonstrating that exposure to sign language is key to gestural babbling (Petitto, Holowka, Sergio, Levy, & Ostry, 2004). These findings support the belief that early babbling has a strong biological basis, as infants appear to be born with the ability to babble either auditorally or visually.

GESTURES AND NON-VERBAL RESPONSES

Gestures are an important component of human communication (McNeill, 1992). As early as the preverbal period, hearing infants use gestures, combined with other non-verbal responses, to perform many of the functions of vocal language (Acredolo & Goodwyn, 1990; Adamson, 1995; Goldin-Meadow, 2007).

One basic function of language is to make *requests*. Infants first use gestural responses for communicating requests at around 8 to 10 months of age, usually with their mothers (Bruner, Roy, & Ratner, 1982). Babies who want their mother to bring a toy, join in a game, or open a box learn to signal these desires with various non-verbal behaviours. For example, a baby who wants a toy may reach toward it while looking back and forth between the toy and his mother. Sometimes the reaching includes fussing or crying, which stops when the mother complies with the request (Bates, Camaioni, & Volterra, 1975).

A second function of early gestures is *referential communication*; that is, talking about something in the environment (Bates, O'Connell, & Shore, 1987). This form of behaviour usually appears at about 11 or 12 months and may initially involve only *showing*, in which the baby holds up objects for the adult's acknowledgment. From showing, it may evolve into *giving*, in which the baby offers objects to the adult, again apparently for approval or comment. Eventually, infants develop *pointing* and *labelling*—the baby uses a gesture to draw attention to an object, such as a cat that has just walked into the room, while producing a vocalization and alternating glances between the adult and the object (Leung & Rheingold, 1981).

Referential communication may involve showing and giving. *(Image Source/Getty Images)*

Infants also appear to be able to accept gestures as labels for objects, indicating that gestures can serve as "words" (Namy & Waxman, 1998). However, as they grow older, infants learning spoken languages become less willing to accept gestures as names for objects, preferring spoken words.

Not all infant gestures are used for communicating; some are used for *symbolizing* objects or events (Acredelo et al., 1999).

For example, a child may put her fist to her ear and speak into it as if it were a telephone, or hold her arms out to signify an airplane. Children also use gestures to label events (clapping hands to mean "game show") or to label attributes of objects (raising arms to mean "big"). These gestures frequently are not directed at anyone else—in fact, they often occur when the child is alone—and serve primarily to name things, not to communicate the names to others.

Is this early system of gestures related to the emergence of language? The answer seems to be yes: earlier use of gesture predicts earlier language development (Özçaliskan & Goldin-Meadow, 2010). The names for objects that infants gesture toward tend to become infants' first words (Iverson & Goldin-Meadow, 2005). When words first appear, gesture labelling and word labelling are positively correlated; that is, children who do more gesturing also tend to use more words (Blake, 2000). Also, infants' use of word–gesture combinations (e.g., point at bottle and say "Mommy") predicts their later use of two-word combinations, their first sentences (Özçaliskan & Goldin-Meadow, 2005).

BABY SIGN LANGUAGE Teaching infants and toddlers a simple system of symbolic gestures, known as "baby sign," has been shown in some studies to facilitate the mastery of spoken language (Goodwyn, Acredolo, & Brown, 2000). This method has become quite popular in North America, with many different businesses and programs promoting it as a language learning aid. Advocates of this technique argue that infants seek to communicate through whatever means they have available, and initially they have more control over the movements of their hands than over the products of their vocal apparatus (Bonvillian, 1999). Gestures are thus a natural early step on the road of communication. When spoken language does emerge, it can build on this gestural starting point. Goodwyn, Acredolo, and Brown (2000) contend that the use of these signs allows young children to communicate more easily with parents, reduces their frustration about communication, and gives them practice with symbols, thus preparing them for word learning.

Proponents of baby sign contend that it allows infants to communicate more easily with their parents, although there are few controlled studies of its effectiveness. (*David Young-Wolff, PhotoEdit*)

However, a review of the literature performed by researchers at the University of Ottawa and the University of Waterloo found that very few studies on baby sign have actually been conducted. Further, many of those studies lacked adequate experimental controls, obscuring the findings (Johnston, Durieux-Smith, & Bloom, 2005). It is also important to stress that "baby sign" is not the same as a sign language, like American Sign Language (ASL). Sign languages, like spoken languages, have expansive vocabularies and possess grammar. Baby sign consists of isolated signs, that may or may not be based on words from sign languages, and these signs are never combined into sentences. Despite the debate over whether baby sign accelerates language development or not, its use provides for increased parent–child interactions, which can never be a bad thing for development.

DEAF INFANTS Studies of deaf children provide an interesting addendum to work on the development of gestures. Deaf children who learn a sign language do, of course, eventually master a gestural system that far surpasses that of hearing children. The acquisition of sign languages in children who learn these languages from birth proceeds in very much the same manner as learning spoken languages in terms of the stages children progress through and the milestones that they achieve (Petitto, 2000). One striking finding concerns deaf children who, at least for a while, are not exposed to a conventional sign system. Despite the absence of the usual supports for language, many such children spontaneously develop a complex gestural system, the home signs discussed earlier in the chapter (Coppola & Newport, 2005). Even more fascinating is the case of Nicaraguan Sign Language, a sign language that emerged over the past few decades. This language was created when deaf children who had created home signs in their individual homes began attending the same school. Out of a desire to communicate with one another, the children adapted their home signs into a common system, thus creating a new language with an expansive vocabulary and grammatical rules (Senghas, Kita, & Özyürek, 2004). We can see again a conclusion that emerged from studies of babbling in deaf children: humans seem to be born with a strong tendency to develop language, if at all possible.

TRANSITION TO WORDS

Around 12 months of age, most children utter what their parents consider to be their first word. Students unfamiliar with infants might assume that one morning a baby looks up from his cereal and says "granola." But in fact, the production of words appears to involve a more gradual and continuous process, and the timing of the first word is highly variable across infants (Fenson et al., 1994).

Late in their first year, infants begin to utter specific sounds (or sound combinations) with increasing frequency—for example, *dee-dee*. Parents often notice that these sounds have become favourites for the child. Soon, the baby begins to attach these utterances to particular objects, situations, or people, such as calling the television *deedee* (Kent & Bauer, 1985). At this point, such sounds would seem to be functioning as words for the child. But parents may not attribute much significance to this phase because none of the infant's words correspond to any of their own. Finally, though, the child begins to produce an utterance, even if it is a bit distorted, that the parents recognize, calling the television *dee-vee*. The parents jubilantly record this event as a milestone in the baby's development.

The continuity view of language development finds support during this period as well. For example, children more quickly learn words that involve sounds and syllables they are already using, suggesting that early speech builds on babbling skills (Schwartz et al., 1987). Additional evidence is that other preverbal communication forms do not immediately stop when words appear. For some time after the baby's first words, babbling continues, along with communicative and symbolic gesturing (Vihman & Miller, 1988). Together, these findings suggest that the transition between the preverbal period and the emergence of speech is relatively smooth and continuous, rather than abrupt and discontinuous.

LEARNING OBJECTIVE 11.2

Trace the developments in the first year of life that establish the preverbal basis for language learning.

1. How does speech perception develop?
2. What preverbal speech sounds do infants use?
3. What is the role of non-verbal communication in language acquisition?

Learning Objective 11.3

Describe the processes by which children first use words and develop vocabulary.

Semantics The study of meaning in language.

SEMANTICS

Once children have begun speaking, their use of language expands at a breathtaking rate. We begin our look at this period of language development with the concept of **semantics**, the study of the meanings conveyed in language. Semantics encompasses both the meanings of individual words and the meanings expressed by words in combination.

A well-known investigator of children's language recounts how her 18-month-old daughter began to use the word "hi" to mean that some sort of cloth was covering her hands or feet (for example, her hands were inside a shirt or a blanket was laid across her feet). The child apparently had come to make this unlikely association as a result of her mother's showing her a finger puppet that nodded its head and said "hi." Rather than interpreting the word as a greeting, the child had instead assumed that it meant the mother's fingers were covered by a cloth (Bowerman, 1976).

This anecdote illustrates two points about semantic development. The first is that learning the meaning of words is not as simple a task as it might appear, especially around the age of 2. Not only do children hear adults speaking thousands of different words (one estimate is that 2-year-olds hear 20,000 to 40,000 words per day! [Chapman et al., 1992]), but they also must learn that words are of different types, such as those that stand for objects ("hat" and "Mommy"), actions ("eat" and "talk"), and states ("happy" and "red").

Second, the more psychologists study word learning, the more they come to realize how closely this process is tied to children's concept development. Names of things (such as "cat") usually label an entire class of things (the family's pet kitten, a stuffed toy, Garfield), as do names of actions, states, and so on. Furthermore, the same thing can be called by many different names (for example, animal, horse, stallion, and Champ). How the young child knows what class of things to attach a new word to and how this learning develops are issues of considerable importance to understanding language acquisition (Bloom, 1993; Waxman, 2004).

Related to both of the above points is the idea that a child must understand that a word is a symbol for something. The word "cat" stands for the group of animals that purr, have tails, and live in our homes. However, "cat" is not a part of the animal, like their tails or purring abilities. There is nothing about the word that directly relates to cats, except for the fact that English speakers have agreed that this is their name. If it were tied directly to the animal, these creatures would not be called "gato" in Spanish or "kedi" in Turkish. This illustrates the concept that words have completely arbitrary relationships to the concepts they label. Imagine the challenges for young children to discover the connections between these completely arbitrary symbols and the objects, actions, properties, and concepts they experience in their everyday world. Yet, as we will see, they succeed with this challenge.

EARLY LEXICAL DEVELOPMENT

The acquisition of words and their meanings typically begins in the baby's second year. Infants' first words usually name things that are familiar or important to them, such as food, toys, and family members. These words, we will see, also serve a variety of pragmatic functions, including requesting things, asking questions, and complaining. In this section, we examine the emergence of children's first words and the importance of the errors children make when attempting to relate words to objects and events in their world.

FIRST WORDS AND THE NAMING EXPLOSION By the age of 18 months, children possess an average **lexicon**, or vocabulary, of about 100 spoken words and about 200 words that they understand (Fenson et al., 1994). There are, however, substantial individual differences, a point to which we return shortly.

Lexicon A vocabulary or repertoire of words.

Around this time, many children display what has been termed the **naming explosion**, in which they begin to label everything in sight. Some psychologists, such as Diane Poulin-Dubois of Concordia University, Susan Graham of the University of Calgary, and Lorrie Sippola of the University of Saskatchewan (Poulin-Dubois, Graham, & Sippola, 1995), believe that this burst of vocabulary is related to the child's emerging ability to categorize objects. Word learning continues rapidly for the next few years, and, as Jeremy Anglin (1993) of the University of Waterloo points out, by the age of 6, children have a lexicon of about 10,000 words, which means that they have learned, on average, six new words a day between the ages of 18 months and 6 years.

Naming explosion A period of language development, beginning around 18 months, when children suddenly begin to acquire words (especially labels) at a high rate.

Semantic development proceeds faster for comprehension than for production. Children typically comprehend words before they begin to produce them. Children comprehend high-frequency words, like "mommy," as early as 6 months of age (Tincoff & Jusczyk, 1999). Children also comprehend more words than they normally speak (Fenson et al., 1994). This pattern is evident from the very beginning and continues into adulthood.

For Thought and Discussion

What were your first words or those of a child you know?

TABLE 11.1 TYPICAL EARLY WORDS: THE FIRST WORDS IN FIVE CHILDREN'S LEXICONS

Child	Words
Jane	Daddy, Mommy, Daniel, girl, ball, cracker, cookie, that, school, bye
Leslie	Daddy, ball, duck, doggie, kitty, donkey, bottle, apple, thank you, bowwow
Lisa	Daddy, Mommy, Daisy, puppy, ball, see, hi, yes, where
Paul	Daddy, Mommy, Papa, boat, truck, map, this, sit, umm
Mark	Ma, dog, milk, water, car, here, bye-bye, no

Source: Adapted from "Structure and Strategy in Learning to Talk" by K. Nelson, 1973, Monographs of the Society for Research in Child Development, 38 (Serial No. 149). Copyright © 1973 by the Society for Research in Child Development, Inc., University of Michigan, Center for Human Growth & Development.

Children's first words usually label common objects. *(© Petro Feketa/iStock)*

What sorts of words are present in children's early lexicons? Table 11.1 provides some typical examples. For most children, nouns (especially object words) predominate, and nouns remain more common than verbs and action words throughout language development. In most languages, in fact, nouns are understood earlier, spoken earlier and more frequently, and even pronounced better (Camarata & Leonard, 1986; Gentner, 1982; Nelson, Hampson, & Shaw, 1993; Waxman & Lidz, 2006).

INDIVIDUAL AND CULTURAL DIFFERENCES Despite the commonalities just noted, children do not all follow the same pattern of lexical development. Indeed, one of the major changes in the study of language development in recent years has been the realization that there are important individual differences in how children go about the task of learning language (Goldfield & Snow, 2001; Pine, Lieven, & Rowland, 1997; Shore, 1995).

One obvious difference is in the size of children's early vocabularies. We would expect, of course, that young children will vary in how quickly they learn words; the extent of the variation, however, may be surprising. In the most thorough examination of the issue (Fenson et al., 1994), the number of words produced at 16 months ranged from 0 to 347. At 25 months, the range was from 7 to 668. Comparable differences were found for children's comprehension of words. Some individual factors lead to larger vocabulary sizes in early childhood: being the oldest child in a family (probably due to more time spent with mom and dad); hearing more adult speech; faster word recognition skills; and being female (Fenson et al., 1994; Fernald, Perfors, & Marchman, 2006; Jones & Adamson, 1987).

Referential style Vocabulary acquired during the naming explosion that involves a large proportion of nouns and object labels.

Expressive style Vocabulary acquired during the naming explosion that emphasizes the pragmatic functions of language.

There are differences not only in the number, but also in the types of words that are found in children's early lexicons. The nouns-first pattern described earlier is not universal. Two kinds of early development have been identified (McCabe, 1989; Nelson, 1973). Some children, who display what is called a **referential style**, follow the nouns-first mode. These children produce a large proportion of nouns, especially object names, and use language primarily to label things. Other children display an **expressive style**. This style includes a larger mix of word types, more "frozen phrases" (e.g., "What's that?" "Lemmee see"), and a greater emphasis on language as a pragmatic tool for expressing needs and for social interaction. The two groups seem to have somewhat different ideas about the purpose of language, with referential children focusing on its informational function, and expressive children more concerned with interpersonal uses. On average (and, of course, with many exceptions), referential children are more likely to be girls, firstborns, and from middle- or upper-income homes.

What could produce these two different patterns of early language acquisition? One influential model stresses the contexts within which language learning takes place and the interplay of biological and environmental factors (Nelson, 1985; Shore, 1995). This contextual explanation stresses the transactional nature of development discussed in Chapter 1. Certain characteristics that differentiate children with the two styles—such as gender and birth order—affect the type of language environment to which the children are exposed. For example, in some samples, parents have been found to speak to their infant daughters more than to their infant sons, using more complex language and more supportive forms of speech (Gleason & Ely, 2002; Leaper, Anderson, & Sanders, 1998). These different environments, in turn, lead children to develop either a referential or an expressive pattern of vocabulary acquisition.

Just as there are differences among children within a culture, so are there differences across cultures and languages. The nouns-first pattern, for example, is more marked in children learning English than is the case in several other languages whose early acquisition has been studied. Children learning Korean, for instance, are slower on average to acquire object names than are children learning English, and the same is true of children learning Mandarin Chinese (Choi, 1997, 2000; Kim, McGregor, & Thompson, 2000; Lavin, Hall, & Waxman, 2006; Tardif, 2006; Tardif, Gelman, & Xu, 1999). On the other hand, children in both cultures are faster to acquire verbs than are children in English-speaking homes. These differences, in turn, relate to differences in the kinds of speech input that parents in the different cultures provide. North American parents tend to include a high proportion of object labels in speech to their children; they are also more likely to elicit nouns than verbs when prompting the child to produce words (Goldfield, 2000). In contrast, parents in Korea and China include a higher proportion of verbs in their speech than do English-speaking parents, and they also provide more cues to the meanings of verbs. The general conclusion is the same as that for individual differences within a culture: children best learn the words for which their parents provide helpful input.

THE NATURE OF CHILDREN'S EARLY WORDS Psychologists have learned a great deal about children's semantic development by examining the kinds of errors they make. Word learning typically begins with a child attaching a specific label to a specific object, such as learning that the pet poodle is a "doggie." Next, the child begins to extend that label to other examples of the same object, using "doggie" to label the dogs he or she sees in books or on TV. These extensions demonstrate that the child is forming an object category that is defined by certain features.

Most children, however, make errors when attempting to extend these early labels, and may also use "doggie" to describe a cat, a fox, a rabbit, and so on. Such **overextensions** are very common in the early stages of semantic development in many languages (Rescorla, 1980). Why they occur is not certain. One obvious possibility is that children's initial categories are simply too broad; they do not yet understand the specific features that define the concept (Mandler, 2004). However, this explanation does not fit very well with the fact that overextensions are more common in production than in comprehension. For example, a child who calls an apple a ball might, if shown an apple, a ball, and a pear, be able to *point to* the apple (Naigles & Gelman, 1995). Further, in neuro-imaging work, young word learners display a brain response that indicates semantic violations when they see a picture labelled with the wrong category name (e.g., hearing the word "cat" and seeing a picture of a dog; Torkildsen et al., 2006). This indicates that their initial categories are well-formed, and that overextensions are the result of production difficulties.

Overextensions An early language error in which children use labels they already know for things whose names they do not yet know.

If overextensions do not always reflect a lack of understanding, then maybe they reflect a lack of vocabulary. If she does not know the word "apple," a child may use the name of a similar object, such as "ball," simply to achieve the communication function of talking about the object. Such errors may also result from momentary memory problems: a failure to retrieve the correct label under the time pressure of generating a word. In fact, the evidence suggests that all of these factors contribute to overextension errors (Behrend, 1988; Gershkoff-Stowe, 2001; Hoek, Ingram, & Gibson, 1986).

Another type of semantic error involves applying labels too narrowly, rather than too broadly. A child who has learned to apply the label "bird" to robins and wrens, for example, may not apply it to ostriches. Such **underextensions** are less common in production than are overextensions. Underextensions are frequent, however, in comprehension. For example, when shown a group of

Underextensions An early language error in which children fail to apply labels they know to things for which the labels are appropriate.

different animals, young children often do not point to the ostrich in response to the instruction "show me a bird," but instead select a non-member of the category, such as a butterfly (Kay & Anglin, 1982).

Both overextensions and underextensions are indications that children, for a while, use words differently than do adults. **Coining** occurs when children create new words that are not part of the adult language. We saw earlier that children sometimes name an unfamiliar object by overextending the label of a similar object. Thus, a child who sees a lawn rake for the first time may call it a fork, even though the child understands that the label is not correct. But another device that children use to deal with gaps in their vocabulary is simply to coin a new name for the object. Our first-time viewer of a rake might instead call it a grass-comb. Here are some more examples, taken from reports by Clark (1995) and Becker (1994): "fix-man" for mechanic, "many talls" for height, "nose beard" for moustache. Word coining is common in young children, gradually decreasing as their lexicon grows (Windsor, 1993). Such inventiveness provides a nice example of a point that we will re-encounter frequently: the creativity that children bring to the task of language learning.

Coining Children's creation of new words to label objects or events for which the correct label is not known.

A final characteristic of children's utterances during the one-word phase concerns their communicative function. We might expect that when children produce one-word utterances they are simply labelling objects in their environment—thus "ball" means "that's a ball," "Daddy" means "that's Daddy," and so forth. Although this is sometimes true, it is not always the case, especially near the end of the one-word phase. Instead, sometimes young children use one word to express an entire sentence or idea—thus "ball" might mean "I want the ball," or "the ball hit me," or perhaps any of several other meanings. We call such words **holophrases**, meaning single-word sentences (Dore, 1985). Making sense of them—for either parent or psychologist—must clearly depend on context.

Holophrases A single word used to express a larger idea; common during the second year of life.

FIRST WORD COMBINATIONS Children begin to combine words as they approach age 2. As with holophrases, they may sometimes use the same phrase to express different meanings, depending on its function. For example, "Daddy hat" may represent a name for an article of clothing, a demand for the father to take off his hat, or perhaps a simple description of the father putting on his hat (Bloom, 1973). Again, contextual cues are important in interpreting what the child is trying to communicate.

Table 11.2 gives some functions of early word combinations. Studies in various cultures reveal that the same dozen or so functions appear first in a variety of languages (Bowerman, 1975; Brown, 1973). This cross-language commonality suggests that the kinds of things children attempt to communicate during this period are influenced by their level of cognitive development. Because cognitive development is similar across different cultures, so, too, are aspects of early language.

MECHANISMS OF SEMANTIC DEVELOPMENT

Since the early 1970s, a variety of explanations for semantic development have been proposed. We will discuss several potential contributors to early word learning. We begin with the proposal that children use grammatical cues to help determine the meanings of certain words. We then consider the claim that children are predisposed, perhaps by biology, to interpret words in certain ways. Finally, we consider the environmental contributors to word learning, focusing both on what parents do to help their children learn words and on the social-cognitive skills that children bring to the task of word learning.

GRAMMATICAL CUES In our discussion of theories, we saw that cognitive-developmental theorists argue that children use their knowledge of the meaning or semantics of utterances to help figure out the grammatical structure. In such cases, learning of grammar builds on a prior knowledge of semantics. But the reverse direction is also possible. Perhaps once children have mastered some aspects of grammar, they can use this knowledge to make sense of new words.

TABLE 11.2 SOME FUNCTIONS OF FIRST WORD COMBINATIONS

Function	Purpose	Examples
Nomination	Naming, labelling, or identifying	Bunny Ernie.
Negation	Rejecting or denying	No nap. No wet.
Non-existence	Describing something that is gone or finished	No milk. All-gone story.
Recurrence	Describing or demanding the repetition of something	More pat-a-cake. More milk.
Entity-attribute	Describing a characteristic of an object	Ball big.
Possessor-possession	Naming two nouns, the first possessing the second	Mommy sock.
Agent-action	Describing a person performing an action	Daddy jump.
Action-object	Describing an action being performed on an object	Hit ball.
Agent-patient	Describing a person doing something to another person	Oscar Bert.
Action-patient	Describing an action being performed on a person	Feed baby
Entity-location	Naming a noun and its place	Ball up. Baby chair.

How might this process work? Imagine that a child who does not yet know the word "spatula" hears the sentence, "Give me the spatula." From its placement following "the," the child can use her knowledge of grammar to infer that "spatula" is a noun and probably the name of an object. If the spatula is the only nearby object whose name she does not know, then the child is in position to make a correct name-object pairing and thus learn a new word. Suppose, instead, that the child already knows the word "spatula" and hears the sentence "Give me the grey spatula." From the fact that it follows an article and precedes a noun, the child can determine that "grey" must be an adjective. If further cues indicate what type of adjective is at issue (e.g., "Give me the grey spatula, not the white one"), then the child may learn a new colour term.

There are, in fact, numerous grammatical cues to word meaning, in English and in other languages (Bloom, 1996, 2000). Table 11.3 summarizes some of the most important examples in English.

Can children use such information? The usual approach to this question has been to do experimental studies in which children have a chance to learn a new word based on the grammatical cues available in a sentence. Studies of this sort demonstrate that children can exploit a variety of

TABLE 11.3 SYNTACTIC CUES TO WORD MEANING

Syntactic Cues	Usual Type of Meaning	Examples
"This is a fep/the fep."	Individual members of a category	cat, forest
"These are feps."	Multiple members of a category	cats, forests
"This is fep."	Specific individual	Fido, John
"This is some fep."	Non-indivuated stuff	water, sand
"John feps."	Action with one participant	sleeps, stands
"John feps Bill."	Action with two participants	hits, kisses
"This thing is feppy."	Property	big, good
"The dog is fep the table."	Spatial relationship	on, near

Source: From *How Children Learn the Meanings of Words* by P. Bloom, 2000, p. 205, Cambridge, MA: MIT Press. Copyright © 2000 by the MIT Press. Reprinted by permission.

grammatical cues—including all those listed in the table—to narrow down the possible meanings of new words (Bloom, 1996; Gleitman & Gillette, 1999; Hall, Lee, & Belanger, 2001). This process is called **syntactic bootstrapping** because the child's prior knowledge of grammar underlies, or "bootstraps," learning of semantics. Young children, with their more limited grasp of grammar, use such cues less successfully than do older children, and grammar alone is seldom a sufficient basis for determining meaning (Waxman & Booth, 2001, 2003; Waxman & Markow, 1995). But it can be helpful. Further, young word learners can recognize familiar words quicker when the words are presented in sentences than when they are presented alone, indicating that the syntax cues in sentences facilitate word processing (Fernald & Hurtado, 2006). Infants can also learn new words in more detail (e.g., all the sounds of the word) when they are presented in sentences than when presented alone (Fennell & Waxman, 2010).

Syntactic bootstrapping A proposed mechanism of semantic development in which children use syntactic cues to infer the meanings of words.

Children can sometimes acquire the meaning of a new word from only a brief exposure, a process called fast-mapping. (*Courtesy of CJW*)

CONSTRAINTS We saw that most children have learned thousands of words by the time they start school. Most of these are words that no one has explicitly taught them. And in some cases, the learning is quite rapid. Children as young as 3 years can sometimes acquire at least a partial meaning of a word after only one exposure to it, a process called **fast-mapping** (Carey, 1977; Gershkoff-Stowe & Hahn, 2007). Preschoolers can even use this process when watching TV programs, demonstrating in some studies a very rapid acquisition of new words used by the story characters (Rice & Woodsmall, 1988).

Fast-mapping A process in which children acquire the meaning of a word after a brief exposure.

But note how difficult this task really is. When a child sees a cat and hears Mommy say, "There's kitty," how does the child know that "kitty" refers to the cat rather than, say, its ears, its colour, or its behaviour? In any situation in which a child hears a new word, there are many logically possible meanings for that word. How does the child avoid the many false directions and zero in on the one correct meaning?

Some psychologists contend that children can accomplish this task only if they are predisposed to relate labels to objects in particular ways. That is, when children hear a new word, they automatically make certain assumptions (usually accurate) regarding what it probably means. The assumptions, or **constraints**, rule out the many false possibilities, and thus permit children to quickly acquire the meanings of new words (Markman, 1991; Waxman, 1990). Several such constraints have been proposed to govern early word learning (Hollich, Hirsh-Pasek, & Golinkoff, 2000; Woodward, 2000; Woodward & Markman, 1998). For example, children assume that a new word refers to a whole object, not parts or aspects of an object. If they hear the word "truck" for the first time and see a truck, they assume it labels the whole vehicle, not its wheel or door. This is known as the **whole-object assumption** (Markman & Wachtel, 1988). Another constraint related to the physical nature of the object being labelled is the **shape bias**. Children tend to extend labels to new items based on similarities in shape, not texture or colour. For example, if a child hears a new word like "blicket" and simultaneously sees a novel object that is star-shaped, red, and fuzzy, the child will select another star-shaped object when asked for another "blicket" and will ignore red or fuzzy objects as possibilities (Diesendruck & Bloom, 2003). Two other important constraints are lexical contrast and mutual exclusivity, discussed below.

Constraints Implicit assumptions about word meanings; hypothesized to narrow down the possibilities that children must consider, thereby facilitating the task of word learning.

Whole-object assumption The child's hypothesis that a new noun refers to an entire object, not its constituent parts.

Shape bias The child's assumption that a new word is extended to things of a similar shape.

Lexical contrast theory A theory of semantic development holding that (1) children automatically assume a new word has a meaning different from that of any other word they know, and (2) children always choose word meanings that are generally accepted over more individualized meanings.

According to **lexical contrast theory** (Clark, 1987, 1993), when children hear an unfamiliar word, they automatically assume the new word has a meaning different from that of any word they already know. This assumption motivates them to learn exactly what the new word means. A second part of this theory holds that when a choice must be made, children always replace their current meanings or categories with those they decide are more conventional or accepted. For example, a child who has been assuming that foxes are called "dogs" should, on learning that "fox" has its own separate meaning, replace the incorrect label, "dog," with the correct label, "fox." This mechanism helps bring the child's categories in line with those of adults. There is evidence from both naturalistic and experimental studies that children often do honour the principle of contrast.

Principle of mutual exclusivity A proposed principle of semantic development stating that children assume that an object can have only one name.

The **principle of mutual exclusivity** (Markman, 1989, 1991) states simply that children believe that objects can have only one name. So, when a youngster hears a new word, she is more likely to attach it to an unknown object than to an object for which she already has a label. This strategy has the advantage of limiting the possible choices when a child is trying to attach meaning to a new word. Suppose, for example, that a toddler knows "kitty" but not "doggie." If her mother points in the direction of a cat and dog and says, "See the doggie," the child should assume, based on mutual exclusivity, that "doggie" cannot refer to the cat because she already knows a name for cats. She is therefore more likely to attach the label to the correct referent. This constraint appears to be very powerful in early word learning. Toddlers will assume that a new label refers to a new object, even where an adult gives a strong social-pragmatic cue that a new label refers to a familiar object. Three-year-olds who see two objects, one familiar (e.g., a toy car) and one novel (e.g., a fish tackle), will select the novel object when they hear a novel label, even when an adult points directly to the familiar object when saying the new label (Jaswal & Hansen, 2006).

Is mutual exclusivity present from the beginning of word learning? Researchers at the University of British Columbia tested to see if 12-month-old infants have an implicit assumption that hearing two different labels means that there should be two different objects present. Infants watched an adult look into a box and say two novel labels three times each, or one novel label six times. The infants were then allowed to reach into the box, without being able to look directly into the box. After pulling out one object, infants who heard two novel labels spent more time searching inside the box than infants who heard one label, indicating that they assumed two objects should be in the box based on hearing two novel labels (Xu, Cote, & Baker, 2005).

The principle of mutual exclusivity poses an interesting challenge to one specific group of word learners: bilingual children. These children need to overcome the constraint of mutual exclusivity because every object necessarily has two labels; the family pet is "dog" in English and "chien" in French. It appears that bilingual children do not apply mutual exclusivity between their languages, accepting two labels for the same object when it is clear that the labels come from different languages (Au & Glusman, 1990). However, they do apply mutual exclusivity within each of their languages, assuming a new label refers to a new object when it is clear that both labels are in the same language, albeit at slightly lower rates than their monolingual peers (Davidson, Jergovic, Imami, & Theodos, 1997; Davidson & Tell, 2005). Research conducted in Vancouver, a multilingual city, demonstrates that children learning three languages apply mutual exclusivity even less than do bilingual children (Byers-Heinlein & Werker, 2009). In *Application 11.1* we discuss bilingual children.

As with lexical contrast, research indicates that young children often do adhere to the principle of mutual exclusivity, and that doing so can be helpful in learning new words (Merriman, 1997; Woodward & Markman, 1998). Interestingly, some of the support for the principle comes not from the successes, but from the difficulties that young children sometimes have in learning words. For example, the strategy causes temporary problems as children encounter the hierarchical nature of word categories. A dog, for instance, can also be called an animal, a mammal, a beagle, and so forth. Two-year-olds sometimes balk at referring to their pet pooches by more than one name, which is what we would expect if they believe that objects can have only a single label (Gelman, Wilcox, & Clark, 1989; Mervis, 1987).

Although mutual exclusivity and other proposed constraints seem to account well for some aspects of early word learning, we should note that not all psychologists are convinced that the notion of constraints is really helpful (Bloom, 1998; Déak, 2000; Diesendruck & Bloom, 2003). Disagreements revolve around several points: whether children's word learning biases really are as consistent and strong as the label "constraint" implies; whether, assuming that constraints exist, they are present from the start of word learning or emerge only later; and whether, again assuming their existence, constraints are innate or derived from experience. There are also concerns about the scope of such explanations; that is, how much of early word learning they can account for. Constraints positions have focused on how children learn nouns, yet children clearly must learn other types of words as well (Tomasello & Merriman, 1995). Finally, even if constraints provide a helpful start toward word learning, we still need to know how children use the speech around them to figure out exactly what words mean. We turn to this question next.

THE CONTRIBUTION OF PARENTS Whatever innate predispositions children may bring to the task of semantic development, experience is clearly necessary to complete the process. Children are not born knowing the meanings of any specific words; rather, they can learn words only if their social environment provides them with sufficient information about what different words mean. What do parents do that might help their children in this task?

Undoubtedly one important process is *modelling.* Although children sometimes make up their own words, much of what they say reflects what they have heard. We have already seen that children's early words tend to be those that are used most frequently by their parents. Furthermore, the more speech parents address to young children, the faster their early vocabularies grow (Hoff & Naigles, 2002; Snow, 1999).

The specific labels that children attach to objects can also be affected by parental modelling. Not surprisingly, children tend to learn such words as "dog" before they learn either "animal" (the superordinate category under which dogs fall) or "poodle" (a subordinate category within the category of dogs). At least part of the basis for this ordering lies in parents' labelling practices—parents are more likely to say "Look at the dog" than either "Look at the animal" or "Look at the poodle" (Callanan, 1985). Furthermore, when parents do use subordinate labels for objects, they usually do so for non-typical examples—such as identifying a robin as a bird but an ostrich as an ostrich (White, 1982). This suggests one explanation for children's underextensions: they may fail to extend a label to non-typical examples of a category because they seldom hear anyone use the label for such examples.

Parents' modelling of words can occur either incidentally, in the normal course of conversation, or explicitly, in an attempt to teach the child a new word. In what has been called the Original Word Game (Brown, 1958a), parents sometimes do, in fact, specifically show a child an object, tell the child its name, encourage the child to say the name, and then provide feedback as to the accuracy of the child's responses. This kind of modelling is given most often to infants and occurs less as children grow older. With older children, most labels occur in a less structured fashion, simply in everyday conversations between parent and child (Chouinard & Clark, 2003). Whether intended as teaching or not, however, such conversations can be a rich source of information about word meaning.

Finally, parents' use of infant-directed speech may aid young infants' ability to learn words. Young word learners are better able to segment words out of running speech when listening to infant-directed speech (Thiessen, Hill, & Saffran, 2005). After being exposed to words presented in infant-directed speech and in adult-directed speech, 8-month-old infants only remembered the word presented in infant-directed speech when tested 24 hours later (Singh, Nestor, Parikh, & Yull, 2009). The enhanced word processing abilities arising from this style of speech may directly aid vocabulary development.

SOCIAL-COGNITIVE CONTRIBUTORS Whatever the source or intent of a label, children can learn its meaning only if they can figure out what the speaker is referring to. This is the problem we considered earlier in our discussion of constraints: how does the child know that "kitty" refers to the cat, rather than to any number of other logically possible alternatives? It is here that the social-cognitive abilities stressed by the sociocultural approach come in.

Part of the answer to this puzzle seems to lie in parents' sensitivity to their child's interest and attention. Studies of parent–child interaction indicate that parents talk most about objects or events to which their children are already attending (Harris, Jones, & Grant, 1983), and that children are most successful at learning new words when parents have accurately judged their focus of attention (Mundy et al., 2007; Tomasello & Farrar, 1986). In the "kitty" example, the argument is that the mother would not have said "kitty" if the child's attention had been focused on the cat's ears, the nearby dog, or any of the other features of the situation. Because the parent labels what the child is attending to, the child is in a good position to link label and referent. However, some sociocultural theorists point out that joint attention is not necessary for word learning. Some cultures do not encourage one-on-one joint attention learning episodes, and children in these cultures do not appear to have major vocabulary delays (Akhtar, 2005). It has been shown that infants can learn words via "overhearing," or listening to third-party conversations (Floor & Akhtar, 2006).

Furthermore, children themselves play an active role in this process. The child's role is important because even the most sensitive parent is not always going to be successful in judging his or her child's attentional focus. Recall, however, the early theory-of-mind developments discussed in *On the Cutting Edge 8.1*. This work reveals that the process goes in both directions: from late in the first year, infants are surprisingly good at discerning the *parent's* focus and thereby linking what the parent says with the correct object or event (Baldwin, 1995; Baldwin & Moses, 2001); and from early in life, it is children, not parents, who initiate and direct many of the conversations from which words and other aspects of language are learned (Bloom et al., 1996; Tomasello, Carpenter, & Liszkowski, 2007).

APPLICATION 11.1
LANGUAGE DIFFERENCES AT HOME AND IN SCHOOL: TEACHING (AND LEARNING) ONE LANGUAGE OR TWO?

Over 6 million Canadians reported that their mother tongue was a language other than English or French in the 2006 census (Statistics Canada, 2007b). When children from these households enter the school system, they present an obvious challenge for educators. What is the best way to educate children who may have limited abilities in the majority language?

Approaches to this issue take a variety of forms, but they divide into two general categories (Brisk, 1998; Hakuta, 1999). Programs that follow a bilingual model use both the minority and the majority language for instruction. There are many variants of such programs, depending on the specific emphases and time course (structured immersion, transitional bilingual education, two-way bilingual education, etc.); the common element, however, is the use of two languages. The second category, in contrast, consists of majority-only programs. Here, as the name suggests, instruction occurs in the majority language only, and use of the minority language is minimized and may even be explicitly discouraged.

Although the types of programs employed often reflect political, rather than educational, factors, policy makers typically attempt to support their decisions with scientific data regarding bilingual learning. One of the most important questions has been whether children learning two languages have more difficulty learning the majority language. For many scientists, answering this question requires a basic understanding of how the bilingual process works (Genesee, Paradis, & Crago, 2004).

One theory has been that bilingual children initially approach the task of learning two languages as if they were learning only one. That is, they do not separate the two forms of speech input, but develop a single language system that includes elements of each. Only with increasing age do these children presumably learn to differentiate the two tongues, gradually treating them as independent languages (Volterra & Taeschner, 1978).

This theory has principally grown out of the observation that younger bilingual children display a good deal of code-mixing, or combining forms from the two languages within the same utterance (Redlinger & Park, 1980). Mixing occurs at all levels of speech, including articulation, vocabulary, inflections,

(continued)

Application 11.1 Language Differences at Home and in School: Teaching (and Learning) One Language or Two? *continued*

and syntax. The assumption has been that mixing reflects confusion on the part of the bilingual child, who cannot separate the two languages. A related finding is that children in bilingual homes acquire both languages more slowly than do peers who are learning only one language, although this lag gradually disappears and the children's proficiency in both languages eventually reaches that of monolingual children (Oller & Pearson, 2002).

More recent research strongly challenges the single-system hypothesis (Bialystok, 2001; Genesee, Nicoladis, & Paradis, 1995; Paradis, Nicoladis, & Genesee, 2000). Studies of infant speech perception, for example, indicate clearly that babies can differentiate sounds and phonemes found in different languages (Eilers & Oller, 1988;). By 4 months of age, infants growing up in bilingual homes can differentiate sounds from the two languages, even when the languages are rhythmically similar (Bosch & Sebastian-Galles, 2001). Hence, perceptual confusion does not appear to be a problem.

Even when there appears to be perceptual confusion in bilingual children, it may not indicate a bilingual "delay." Christopher Fennell of the University of Ottawa demonstrated that bilingual infants begin using phonemes to distinguish similar-sounding nonsense words at a slightly later age (20 months) than do monolingual infants (17 months). However, he proposed that this was adaptive. By reducing the amount of information they are processing in words for a longer developmental period than monolingual children, young bilingual children can keep up with their monolingual peers, as evidenced by the fact that bilingual and monolingual children learn words at similar rates. Further, there would be little cost to the approach of not using speech sounds in detail, as there are few similar-sounding words in the early vocabularies of infants (Fennell, Byers-Heinlein, & Werker, 2007).

It has also been suggested that children's substitution of a word in one language for the same word in the second language may simply reflect the overextension principle. Thus, the child may substitute in this way if she does not know the appropriate word in the second language or if it is simply easier to do so (Vihman, 1985). Furthermore, modelling by parents has been implicated in children's language mixing. Studies of bilingual children's home environments indicate that their parents often speak to them using parts of both languages simultaneously, and that parents generally respond positively to the child's code-mixing (Goodz, 1989; Lanza, 1997). It is not surprising, then, that bilingual children often mix parts of their two languages.

Another claim made in the older research literature was that bilingualism results in cognitive deficits. Theoretically, the bases for this claim were the slower growth of language skills in bilingual children, and the suggestion that hearing and learning two languages confuses children. Empirically, the claim found support in studies that reported on the average cognitive deficits in samples of bilingual children. It has now become clear, however, that various methodological weaknesses (concentration on low-income samples, use of inappropriate measures) render the results of the earlier research suspect. As Ellen Bialystok (2007) of York University points out, bilingual children, in fact, have been shown to be more advanced in some areas of cognition than are monolingual children.

It appears, then, that exposure to two languages does not present an unusually difficult challenge to young children, who can apparently separate and acquire both systems. This would suggest that majority-only educational policies, in which non-native children are required from the start of school to use and learn only the majority language, may be misguided. Indeed, as Fred Genesee (1994) of McGill University notes, research that compares different approaches to educating bilingual children generally favours some form of transitional approach in which both languages are used at the early grades and children gradually develop competence in the majority language (see also Greene, 1998). Note that in addition to its purely academic benefits, this approach has the virtue of acknowledging the value of the child's family and cultural background.

A different approach to bilingual education, French immersion, has developed in Canada over the last 30 years. French immersion programs are offered across the country to English-speaking children, with the goal of fostering their abilities in Canada's other official language. Such programs take various forms and have largely proven to be successful. We discuss French immersion programs in *Focus on Research 11.1*.

Research indicates that teaching non-native children in their own language does not interfere with their learning of the majority language. (*Creatas / Fotosearch*)

FOCUS ON RESEARCH 11.1
FRENCH IMMERSION IN CANADIAN SCHOOLS

In the 1960s, faced with a feeling of isolation from the French community surrounding them and a lack of competence in their ability to converse in French, a group of English speaking parents in the Montreal suburb of St. Lambert, Quebec, began meeting to discuss how best to improve French language instruction in English-speaking schools (Genesee & Gandara, 1999). They sought not simply to improve children's second language learning, but also to improve relations between English- and French-speaking Quebecers (Genesee & Gandara, 1999). With the advice of Dr. Wallace Lambert of the Psychology Department at McGill University and Dr. Wilder Penfield of the Montreal Neurological Institute, these parents proposed an experimental kindergarten immersion class (Genesee, 1987). Their program formed the basis for the first French immersion program in Canada, initiated in 1965.

To try to create a system that paralleled the processes that occur during first language acquisition, it was decided to offer instruction in all subjects in French, rather than offering instruction solely in French language skills (Genesee, 1987). Dr. Fred Genesee of McGill University in Montreal, who has extensively researched bilingual education programs, describes the goals of the program as not simply to develop competency in French, but also to promote and maintain competence in English, to ensure academic achievement, and to develop an appreciation of francophones and their language and culture.

Since that first program was developed, other immersion programs were implemented in English schools in Quebec and subsequently have become popular all across Canada. Indeed, in the 2006–2007 academic year, there were 314,680 students enrolled in French immersion programs across the country (Canadian Parents for French, 2008). Figure 11.1 shows the percentage of students enrolled in French immersion programs in each province and territory (there is no French immersion in Nunavut).

French immersion has taken various forms. The initial program in St. Lambert was what has come to be referred to as an "early immersion" program. Early immersion programs begin in the lower elementary school grades, and may involve either total immersion or partial immersion. Not all immersion programs begin at such a low grade, however. "Delayed immersion" or "middle immersion" programs do not begin to use French as the language of instruction until grade 4 or 5, although students typically receive core French instruction of 20 to 45 minutes a day for several years prior to beginning immersion. "Late immersion" programs delay instruction in French until the end of elementary school or the beginning of high school (Canadian Council on Learning, 2007; Genesee, 1987).

Does immersion work? Results indicate that it does. As Dr. Genesee (1987) points out, students who have participated in French immersion show excellent French comprehension skills and high levels of skill in speaking and writing French. In general, the more exposure to French, the better the students' proficiency. Thus, as might be expected, exposure that begins early and is either concentrated or extended appears to be associated with very high levels of proficiency. However, even immersion that begins late appears to be beneficial. Indeed, Dr. Genesee suggests that older children, perhaps because of their more advanced cognitive abilities, may actually be quite efficient at second language learning. Opportunities to converse in French outside of the classroom foster second language learning even further.

FIGURE 11.1

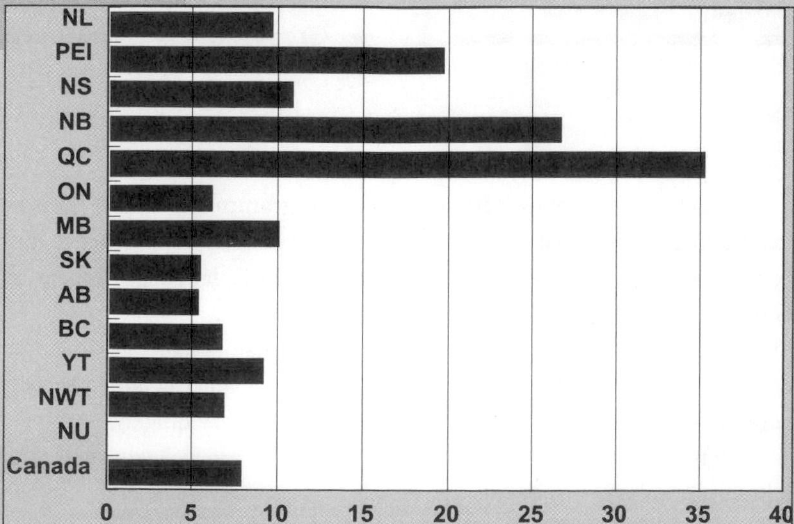

Percentage of children enrolled in French immersion in 2007 by province and territory. *Source: Canadian Parents for French (2008).*

Does French immersion have a negative effect on children's competence in English? A common concern of parents contemplating French immersion for their children is that early immersion might have deleterious effects on their children's English abilities. Indeed, a goal of most French immersion programs has been to promote and maintain competence in English concurrently with developing competence in French. Consequently, students in French immersion typically also receive formal instruction in English language arts. In general, results indicate that students in early total immersion programs may show some initial lag in English reading and spelling skills; however, such lags tend to disappear after English language arts instruction is introduced. Students in partial immersion or delayed or late immersion show no lags in English language abilities (Genesee,

(*continued*)

Focus on Research 11.1 French Immersion in Canadian Schools *continued*

1987). In fact, recent results reported by Statistics Canada (Allen, 2004) found that children from French immersion programs actually outperformed their peers from non-immersion programs on tests of English reading achievement when tested at age 15. There are differences, however, between the groups of immersion and non-immersion students in the Statistics Canada study. Socioeconomic status differences, differences in educational background of their parents, and a higher proportion of girls in French immersion programs may have contributed to the findings of superior reading achievement of the immersion students (Allen, 2004). Nevertheless, even when these factors were taken into account, immersion children still outperformed their non-immersion counterparts. Thus, it does appear that for most children, French immersion does not negatively influence their later English language skills. Moreover, evidence suggests that there are no negative effects of immersion on children's performance in other academic subjects (Genesee, 1987).

Does French immersion instill in children an appreciation of French Canadians and their language and culture? A goal of French immersion programs was to instill in children an appreciation of the language and culture of francophones. Has this goal been achieved? According to Genesee and Gandara (1999), immersion students in lower grades report more favourable views of French Canadian language and culture than do their non-immersion counterparts. These differences appear to fade with time, however. A similar pattern has been found in the attitudes of late immersion students, whose attitudes were more favourable in the beginning of immersion in grade 7, but became similar to those of non-immersion children in grade 11.

Genesee and Gandara (1999) suggest that what may underlie this fading in positive attitudes may be a lack of contact between anglophone and francophone children. Indeed, these researchers point out that anglophone students who are educated in French language schools continue, as they get older, to display a more positive view of francophones and their culture. Such findings point again to the value of extracurricular French language activities, and perhaps student exchange programs, in maintaining the gains of French immersion programs.

LEARNING OBJECTIVE 11.3

Describe the processes by which children first use words and develop vocabulary.

1. What are the characteristics of children's first words, and at what rate do children acquire vocabulary?
2. What are some individual and cultural differences in children's language learning?
3. What can we learn about language learning from the semantic errors that children make?
4. By what processes do children learn the meaning of words?
5. What roles do parents and children themselves play in semantic development?

Learning Objective 11.4

Describe the processes by which children learn to communicate grammatically.

Grammar The study of the structural properties of language, including syntax, inflection, and intonation.

Syntax The aspect of grammar that involves word order.

GRAMMAR

All human languages are structured and follow certain rules called **grammar**. Many of these rules seem arbitrary, such as the English rule that adding *-ed* to a verb puts it in the past tense. But as nativist theorists suggest, some rules may have a biological basis; that is, languages appear to be structured in such a way that humans learn them very easily.

Understanding the acquisition of grammar has posed one of the major challenges to language researchers. As noted at the beginning of the chapter, children are not explicitly taught the structure of their language (at least not before school age), yet they learn it very quickly. Making this feat all the more impressive is the fact that most adults, even those who are well educated, cannot describe our complex linguistic rules in any detail.

The grammar of most languages involves three principal devices: word order, inflections, and intonation. Word order, called **syntax**, is most important for the English language and is thus the aspect of grammar on which we focus here. The sentences "John hit the car" versus "The car hit John," or "I did pay" versus "Did I pay?" illustrate how necessary it is to take into account the order of words. **Inflections** are certain endings added to words to modify their meanings. Common examples include plural endings (cat*s*), possessive endings (Mary'*s*), and past-tense endings (work*ed*). Some languages rely much more heavily than does English on inflections to communicate meaning. (For example, in Turkish, a verb can have up to 3,000 different inflections!) Finally, *intonation* can alter grammar. A rising tone at the end of a sentence, for example, can transform a statement into a question.

Inflections The aspect of grammar that involves adding endings to words to modify their meaning.

DEVELOPMENT OF GRAMMAR

Most children do not begin to combine words into the first simple sentences until about 18 months. However, various precursors to sentence formation may be evident prior to this point. As we saw, the meanings and pragmatic functions that children convey with their one-word utterances expand across the one-word phase, moving from simple labels to more sentence-like communications. Also, near the end of this period, many children begin to produce many single-word utterances in a row; the child may use one word to call the mother's attention to an object, and then a second word to comment on the object (e.g., "milk hot"). These multiple one-word utterances can be distinguished from the two-word sentences that will soon appear by the longer pause that occurs between the words (Branigan, 1979). The child seems to be on the brink of producing sentences—just not quite ready to put the parts together.

EARLY WORD COMBINATIONS By age 2, most children have overcome this limitation and are producing two- and three-word sentences, such as "Mommy chair" and "all gone cookie." Investigators have discovered that children's first word combinations are not random, but rather follow certain patterns or orders. As a result, much research has been devoted to trying to understand these earliest indications of grammatical knowledge.

The principal method of investigation used has been to collect samples of a child's speech—usually in the natural environment—and to analyze its structure. Many such studies are longitudinal, with samples gathered over a period of months or years to examine how grammar evolves (Bates & Carnevale, 1993).

Researchers have also devised a number of ingenious experimental techniques to probe for knowledge that may not be evident in children's spontaneous speech (McDaniel, McKee, & Cairns, 1997; Menn & Ratner, 2000). Such techniques can be used to assess children's comprehension of different linguistic forms, as well as their ability to produce forms that may not occur in a spontaneous speech sample.

The first syntactic rules that many children develop seem to be built around individual words. For example, a child may say "all-gone doggie," "all-gone milk," and "all-gone Mommy," using "all-gone +_____" as a basic rule (Maratsos, 1983). Children display a degree of individuality in these rules, however. Another child might develop rules around other words, for example "_____+ on" or "I +_____" (Bloom, Lightbrown, & Hood, 1975; Braine, 1976). Furthermore, not all children begin with the "familiar word +_____" formula; some show a greater variety of items and combinations in their initial sentences. We can see again that there are individual differences in how children go about learning language.

The next phase of grammatical development is the emergence of **telegraphic speech**. As the child's sentences grow from two to three or four words and beyond, they begin to resemble telegram messages. That is, they leave out non-essential function words, such as *a, the,* and *of,* and also certain parts of words, such as endings and unstressed syllables. Thus, a child who hears "Billy, we're going to the parade" may repeat "Billy go 'rade." Over time, however, the telegraphic nature of children's speech greatly diminishes, as children expand their utterances and add more and more elements of the adult language (Bowerman, 1982).

Telegraphic speech Speech from which non-essential function words (e.g., in, the, with) are omitted; common during early language learning.

We noted that children take somewhat different approaches to early sentence construction. One consistent characteristic, however, is an emphasis on word order. No child ever generates sentences by randomly combining all the words in her lexicon in all possible ways; rather, only certain orders and certain combinations appear in children's early utterances. Indeed, even children who are not yet producing sentences are responsive to word order in the sentences they hear (Gertner, Fisher, & Eisengart, 2006; Hirsh-Pasek & Golinkoff, 1996; Mandel, Kemler Nelson, & Jusczyk, 1996). From the start, therefore, children seem to be sensitive to one of the basic properties of grammar.

OVERREGULARIZATION As mentioned, the rule-learning at the core of children's acquisition of grammar also is evident in certain types of mistakes they make. A good example involves inflections. The English language uses inflectional rules to change a verb to the past tense (*-ed* is added, as in "talk*ed*" and "play*ed*") and a noun from singular to plural (*-s* or *-es* is added, as in cup*s* and dish*es*). But unfortunately for English-speaking children, English also contains a large number of irregular forms that are exceptions to these rules—the verb forms *go/went*, *eat/ate*, and *see/saw*, for example, and the noun forms *mouse/mice*, *foot/feet*, and *sheep/sheep.*

At first, children may produce a correct irregular form if it is part of a chunk of adult speech that they are copying. Thus, even 2-year-olds may be heard to say "ate" or "feet." But as they begin to learn the inflectional rules of the language, children tend toward **overregularization**, sometimes applying the rules to nouns and verbs that have irregular forms. Now the child will be heard to say "I knowed her," or "Look at the mans." Interestingly, the correct forms do not altogether disappear, so that a child may at one time say "I ate" and at another time say "I eated." Eventually, the correct and incorrect forms may merge, and the child may begin to produce words such as "wented" and "mices." The final disappearance of the overregularized forms seems to take place word by word, with some errors persisting longer than others (Marcus, 1996).

Overregularization An early structural language error in which children apply inflectional rules to irregular forms (e.g., adding *ed* to say).

Although such forms as "mans" or "eated" may be quite noticeable to the adults around the child, overregularizations, in fact, occur in only a minority of the cases in which children cope with irregular words. One extensive survey, based on more than 11,000 past-tense utterances, reported overregularizations in only about 4 percent of the possible instances (Marcus et al., 1992). Nevertheless, overregularizations are informative because a word such as "eated" could not be an imitation of anything the child has heard. Instead, the errors children make suggest that they are not merely imitating, but are developing a system of rules. Overregularizations are not limited to children who are learning English; indeed, such errors may be more striking in more highly inflected languages that offer more opportunity for children to make mistakes (Slobin, 1985b). (An early study of children's understanding of inflections is described in *Research Classic 11.1.*)

CHARACTERIZING CHILDREN'S LANGUAGE All researchers of child language agree that some sort of structured rule system underlies even the earliest sentences that children produce. What they do not agree on is how best to characterize the system. Two opposing positions exist.

One possibility, favoured by cognitively-oriented researchers, is that children's early sentences are organized in terms of meaning-based, or semantic, categories (Schlesinger, 1988). These categories, in turn, reflect the kinds of cognitive concepts that the 2- or 3-year-old child has come to understand. The small set of basic meanings that appear consistently in children's first sentences are compatible with this cognitive model (see Table 11.2).

The other possibility, favoured by nativist researchers, is that even the earliest sentences reflect knowledge of abstract grammatical categories, such as subject, verb, and object (Lidz, 2007, 2010). In this view, syntax, not semantics, underlies sentence formation.

As an example of how these models differ, consider the sentences in Table 11.4. The sentences in the left column all lend themselves to a similar semantic description. Each includes at least two components of a basic three-part structure: an *agent* (e.g., Jamie) who *acts* (e.g., hits) on an *object*

RESEARCH CLASSIC 11.1
ADDING ENDINGS TO "WUGS" AND THINGS

Even before the appearance of Chomsky's critique of learning theories of language acquisition, other researchers had questioned the early view that language is learned piecemeal through reinforcement of early babbling or imitation of adult speech. One alternative possibility was that children develop general rules that regulate their early speech productions

To explore this possibility, Jean Berko, a doctoral student at MIT conducted a simple but ingenious experiment (Berko, 1958). Children ages 4 through 7 were shown a series of pictures of nonsense objects and activities that had been given nonsense names—the most famous, perhaps, was a small, bird-like creature that Berko called a "wug," shown in Figure 11.2.

The aspect of grammar that Berko examined was inflectional endings—such as adding the *s* or *z* sound to create the plural (cats, dogs) and the *d* or *t* sound to create the past tense (played, walked). To investigate a child's use of inflectional endings, Berko presented the child with a sequence similar to the following: "This is a cup. Now there is another one. There are two of them. There are two_____."

But what if the child added the correct ending sound to the word? Would that demonstrate that the child knew the rule for plurals? Perhaps. But it could simply mean that the child had previously been reinforced for saying "cups" when more than one was present, or that the child was imitating her parents' use of this plural form.

To eliminate these alternative explanations, Berko used nonsense terms. For example, on one trial examining possessive endings, the children were told: "This is a bik who owns a hat. Whose hat is it? It is the_____." As predicted on this and many of the other trials, children supplied the correct inflectional ending. Because these terms were new, the children could not have learned them either through reinforcement or through imitation of what they had heard. Rather, this classic study showed that the children had acquired a set of inflectional rules that they could systematically apply even to unfamiliar words.

FIGURE 11.2

This is a wug.

Now there is another one.

There are two of them.

There are two __________.

An example of a stimulus used to demonstrate that children's early use of inflectional endings involves rules. *From "The Child's Learning of English Morphology" by J. Berko, 1958, Word, 14, 155. Reprinted by permission of Jean Berko Gleason.*

or recipient of the action (e.g., ball). Each sentence can also be analyzed as consisting of certain syntactic categories (nouns and verbs) and syntactic relations (subject-verb, verb-object). But—or at least as many researchers argue—there is no reason to credit the child with such abstract grammatical knowledge as long as a simpler, semantically based system can account for all the sentences that we hear.

TABLE 11.4 SAMPLE SENTENCES

Jamie hits ball.	Jamie is hit.
Baby drinks juice.	Jamie has freckles.
Mommy play.	Baby liked juice.
Throw ball.	Thunder scary.

But consider the sentences in the right column. Now there is no longer a one-to-one relation between a semantic description and a syntactic one. In the first sentence, for example, *Jamie* is the semantic object (because she is the one receiving the action), but she is also the grammatical subject. In the second sentence, *Jamie* is again the subject, but now is the possessor of an attribute rather than an agent who performs an action. In both the second and third sentences, the verb is no longer an action word, and in the fourth, the subject is no longer an object name.

The debate about how to characterize early language centres on whether children's initial knowledge about language is limited to consistent meanings or extends to the abstract categories represented in the second group of sentences. As you might expect, semantic analyses find their strongest support with regard to children's initial sentences, which are much more likely to consist of combinations of the "Mommy play" sort than they are to include such constructions as "is hit" or "baby liked" (de Villiers, 1980; Maratsos, 1988). In addition, children's earliest sentences, although occasionally creative constructions, keep fairly close to the adult models around them; they do not yet show the full productivity that will eventually characterize the child's language (Tomasello, 2006). It is possible therefore—or at least some researchers maintain—to account for them with a fairly limited set of rules.

Even in the case of the earliest sentences, however, there are disputes about whether a semantic analysis is sufficient to capture all of the child's knowledge (Radford, 1990). And most researchers agree that soon thereafter, some grammatical competence must be assumed, not only to account for utterances like those in the right column of Table 11.4, but also to explain the emergence of more complex sentence forms, such as passives and negations. Exactly when and how knowledge of grammar emerges remains one of the most actively debated topics in the study of child language (de Villiers & de Villiers, 1999; Maratsos, 1998; Mintz, 2003; Soderstrom, Conwell White, & Morgan, 2007; Tomasello, 2009).

MECHANISMS OF GRAMMAR ACQUISITION

As we have just suggested, no area of language development is more complex than that of grammar. As with semantics, many explanations for the mastery of grammar have been proposed. Some researchers even argue that grammar has its roots in the preverbal infants. For example, grammar words, such as articles and prepositions, tend to be acoustically different from the majority of words in a language. They tend to be short, with clipped vowels and reduced volume: "the" and "on" sound different than "pretty" and "baby." Rushen Shi of the University of Quebec at Montreal has demonstrated that even newborn infants can discriminate lists of grammar words from lists of non-grammar words, and that this ability is present across infants being raised in languages other than English, such as Turkish, Chinese, and French (Shi & Gauthier, 2005; Shi, Morgan, & Allopenna, 1999; Shi, Werker, & Morgan, 1999). Shi argues that this acoustic distinction allows infants to eventually concentrate on grammar words as an important class of word, and can be thought of as an acoustic bootstrapping into grammar.

Rather than attempting to examine all theories of grammar acquisition, we focus on those that are currently of greatest interest to language researchers.

SEMANTIC BOOTSTRAPPING One proposed model of the acquisition of grammar grows out of the semantics-versus-syntax debate discussed in the preceding section. Even the most cognitively oriented researchers agree that children eventually master a system of grammatical rules. What they maintain, however, is that this acquisition builds on prior semantic understanding. According to this view, children first learn semantic categories, such as agent and action, which follow naturally from early achievements in cognitive development. Once these categories are established, young language learners begin to note that other words can perform the same roles in sentences as the words that make up their own utterances. For example, nouns in general, not just object labels, can serve as the subject of a sentence or can follow the word *the.* Similarly, verbs in general, not just action words, can be the predicate of a sentence or can precede the object or patient. In this way, abstract grammatical categories slowly grow out of what was at first a purely semantic system.

For Thought and Discussion

What is an example of language learning in which a child might use both semantic bootstrapping and syntactic bootstrapping at the same time?

Earlier, we discussed the notion of syntactic bootstrapping: the idea that children use their knowledge of grammar to learn about semantics. The form of learning just discussed is known as **semantic bootstrapping**: use of knowledge of semantics to learn about grammar (Bowerman, 1988; Pinker, 1987). The two kinds of learning are not, of course, incompatible; as language develops, the various components might well build on each other in a back-and-forth, reciprocal fashion. Given the complexity of language acquisition, it certainly makes sense that children would make use of any source of information available to them.

Semantic bootstrapping A proposed mechanism of grammatical development in which children use semantic cues to infer aspects of grammar.

Semantic bootstrapping has a role even in many nativist accounts of language acquisition (Pinker, 1987). Theorists in this tradition, however, do not believe that children's initial categories are purely semantic, or that meaning alone is sufficient to teach children about syntax. Their view, rather, is that much of the basic structure of language—in particular, those aspects that are universal across languages—is innate. The reasons for this claim are the arguments given earlier: the apparent unlearnability of many language rules, given the complex, non-obvious nature of the rules and the very limited evidence available to children. Experience remains necessary in this view—not to teach the child the rules, however, but simply to indicate how the rules are expressed in his or her language.

STRATEGIES The position just discussed assumes that children possess innate knowledge about the rules of language. An alternative possibility is that children's innate endowment consists not of rules, but of cognitive strategies that allow them to acquire the rules rapidly.

One proposal of this type is based on the notion of **operating principles** (Slobin, 1982, 1985a). After studying more than 40 languages, Slobin extracted a number of strategies, which he called operating principles, that describe how to learn the rules of any language. Among the most important strategies are (1) "Pay attention to the order of words," (2) "Avoid exceptions," and (3) "Pay attention to the ends of words."

Operating principles A hypothetical innate strategy for analyzing language input and discovering grammatical structure.

We have already seen that children increasingly focus on word order, or syntax, in speech. And children's overregularizations may result, in part, from their avoiding exceptions and applying inflectional rules across the board. Evidence supporting children's use of the third operating principle was reported in an interesting study. The method used to address this issue involved teaching English-speaking children several artificial language rules and examining which were acquired most easily. First, the children were taught the names of two new animals—"wugs" and "fips" (Figure 11.3). Next, they learned two new verbs—"pum" (meaning to toss an animal vertically into the air) and "bem" (meaning to toss an animal horizontally across the table surface). Finally, the children were taught two variations of these verbs. If the animal's actions were observed by one other animal, the verbs describing them were "pumabo" or "bemabo"; if the animal's actions were observed by several other animals, the verbs became "akipum" or "akibem." The researchers hypothesized that if children use a strategy of paying attention to the ends of words, the verbs with a suffix (*-abo*) should be acquired more quickly than the verbs with a prefix (*aki-*). In support of Slobin's model, children learned the suffixed verbs more easily (Daneman & Case, 1981).

Slobin's full model includes more than 40 operating principles. These principles consist of what Slobin (1985a) refers to as the child's **language-making capacity**, or **LMC**. In contrast to Chomsky's LAD, the LMC does not include innate knowledge about the rules of language. Instead, it consists of learning strategies for rapidly acquiring such knowledge.

Language-making capacity (LMC) Slobin's proposed set of strategies or learning principles that underlie the acquisition of language.

A more recent proposal that involves strategies for acquiring grammar is the **competition model** (Bates & MacWhinney, 1987; MacWhinney, 1987; MacWhinney & Chang, 1995). The competition model is a blend of sociocultural and information-processing approaches. According to

Competition model A proposed strategy children use for learning grammar in which they weight possible cues in terms of availability and reliability.

FIGURE 11.3

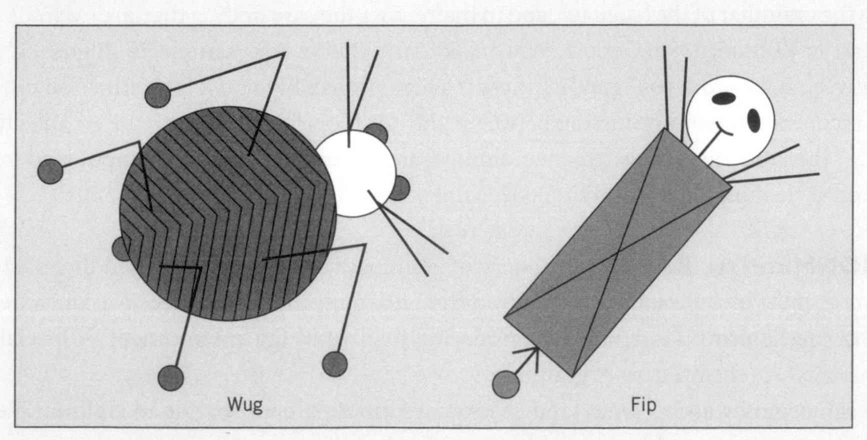

Artificial language concepts, along with these two imaginary animals, were used to compare children's acquisition of suffixed and prefixed verbs. *From "Syntactic Form, Semantic Complexity, and Short-Term Memory: Influences on Children's Acquisition of New Linguistic Structures" by M. Daneman and R. Case, 1981,* Developmental Psychology, *17, 369. Copyright © 1981 by the American Psychological Association.* Reprinted by permission.

this account, young children hearing speech examine the various grammatical cues of their language, such as word order, endings, and intonation, and then focus on the one they believe is most useful for learning the structure of the language. The cue they select can vary from one language to another and, significantly, is thought to change as the child matures.

Initially, children focus on the cue that is most *available.* In English and French, for example, children's first attempts to learn grammar involve word order. Because word order is important in these languages, it is a cue that is frequently available to provide information useful for learning language rules. In Turkish, in contrast, word order is less important, and language-learning children typically focus first on the inflections in the speech they hear. In the second stage, children select the cues that are most *reliable,* meaning those that most consistently provide clues to grammatical structure. In the final stage, children note cues that are in *conflict with* one another, and then focus on the one that most often "wins out" and best reveals the language's structure.

The sociocultural origins of the competition model are evident in two emphases. One emphasis is on the helpful input provided by the adults in the speech environment around the child, input that helps the child make adaptive choices among the cues. The other emphasis is on the pragmatic bases for language acquisition and use. Children's mastery of language is motivated by the various uses to which language can be put.

The information-processing aspect of the competition model is seen in the use of computer simulations to embody and test the model's propositions. These simulations are in the form of artificial neural networks; they thus provide another example of the connectionist approach introduced in Chapter 9. As we saw, in connectionist simulations, learning involves the adjustment of activation strengths with experience, as shifting patterns of connections among the underlying units gradually make some responses more likely and some less so. An example in the domain of language is mastery of the English past tense. Proponents of the competition model have demonstrated that a computer programmed with the strategies identified in the model and given appropriate linguistic input shows patterns of acquisition of the past tense that are similar to those shown by children, including a phase of overregularization prior to full mastery (MacWhinney & Leinbach, 1991).

Note that in this approach, neither the computer program nor children are seen as acquiring discrete rules for language (such as add *-ed* to make a verb past tense); what they acquire, rather, are patterns of response that fit the cues available to them. This approach therefore stands in marked contrast to more traditional rule-based accounts of language acquisition. Whether connectionist models can account for all of the phenomena for which rule-based accounts were developed is currently a subject of dispute (Klahr & MacWhinney, 1998; Marcus, 2001; Pinker, 1999). But they clearly provide an ongoing challenge to the traditional view.

A new approach to grammar acquisition is related to connectionism and to the frequency tracking strategy discussed earlier in the section on word learning. Essentially, researchers are asking if the distributional patterns in children's input could be a reliable source of information for learning the grammar of the language, and in many cases they are finding they are (Marcus, Vijayan, Bandi Rao, & Vishton, 1999; Gerken, Wilson, & Lewis, 2005). For example, in English, if there is a word between the words "you" and "it," there is a high probability that it is a verb: "You put it"; "You see it." In contrast, a word occurring between "the" and "one" will probably be an adjective: "The red one"; "The little one." These "frequent frames" are present in the parental input, and infants are quite good at tracking them (Gomez, 2002; Mintz, 2003; Weisleder & Waxman, 2010).

ENVIRONMENTAL BASES Any theory of grammatical development, even the most strongly nativist one, must include some contribution from learning and experience. We conclude our discussion of mechanisms, therefore, by considering the role of the environment—especially of the child's parents—in the mastery of grammar.

We can begin by asking what kind of language input parents provide to children. Recall that Chomsky claimed that children should have difficulty extracting structural rules from everyday speech because such speech typically provides poor models of good language. But research has now demonstrated that both adults and children change aspects of their speech when talking to babies and toddlers (Fernald et al., 1989). This is the infant-directed speaking style, already discussed at various points. Infant-directed speech, you may recall, includes helpful-looking adjustments of a variety of sorts. Mothers tend to speak slowly and use short utterances, often three words or fewer. Usually mothers pronounce the words very clearly, and the speech rarely contains grammatical errors. When talking about an object or situation, mothers label it frequently and use a good deal of repetition in their descriptions and comments. And the focus of their speech usually is on the here and now, rather than on more distant or abstract events.

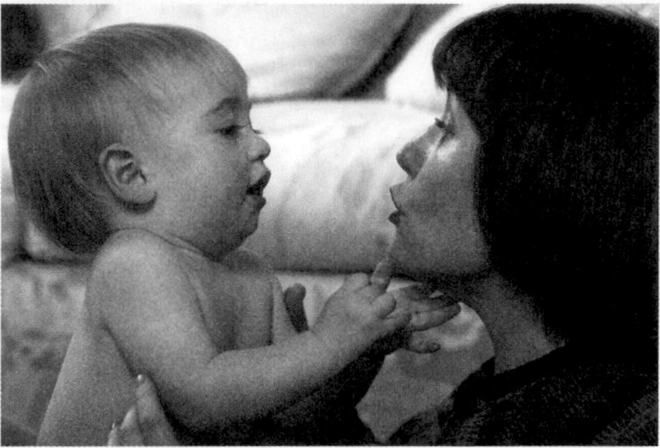

Infant-directed speech is one of many ways in which parents help their children master language. (*Jonathan Nourok/PhotoEdit*)

Fathers display many of the same speech adjustments, although they generally are less sensitive to the infant's level of linguistic development (McLaughlin et al., 1983; Ratner, 1988). In fact, some researchers have suggested that the father's speech serves as a bridge between the fine-tuned adjustments of the mother and the complex and erratic speech of the outside world (Gleason & Weintraub, 1978; Mannle & Tomasello, 1987; Tomasello, Conti-Ramsden, & Ewert, 1990).

But do all these infant-directed speech adjustments have any effect on the child's language development? We noted earlier that some aspects of phonological development, such as the ability to discriminate phonemes, are facilitated by infant-directed speech. However, attempts to find a convincing connection between the overall degree of maternal speech adjustment and the child's level of grammar development have failed to discover a strong relation (Murray, Johnson, & Peters, 1990; Valian, 1999). And attempts to uncover positive effects of more specific speech changes (length of utterance, amount of repetition, and so on) have offered only scattered support (Furrow, Nelson, & Benedict, 1979; Hoff-Ginsberg, 1990; Hoff-Ginsberg & Shatz, 1982; Kemler-Nelson, Hirsh-Pasek, Jusczyk, & Cassidy, 1989).

For Thought and Discussion

Are you aware of having used infant-directed speech with a child? If you had not used this type of speech, how would your communication with the child have been altered?

Do these results mean that simplifications in the speech directed toward language-learning children are of little value for grammar? Not necessarily. One possibility is that some *minimum* amount of simplification is important, but the additional degree of infant-directed speech provided to some children is of no extra benefit (Scarborough & Wyckoff, 1986). Another possibility is that the methods and measures used by researchers have simply not been appropriate or sensitive enough to detect all the relations that exist between the adults' input and the children's output (Schwartz & Camarata, 1985; Snow et al., 1987). At present, therefore, the role of infant-directed speech in grammatical development remains to be established.

We turn now to one of the contributors discussed with respect to semantic development: parental modelling. We know, of course, that imitation of parental models cannot be the whole story. As Chomsky pointed out, our ability to produce entirely novel statements means that language must be based on more than merely copying what we hear. In addition, young children produce word combinations that they have probably not heard ("all-gone Daddy"), along with overregularizations not found in adult speech ("I hurted my foots"). These forms clearly do not arise from imitation in any simple sense.

But perhaps those imitations that occur are *progressive*. That is, perhaps when youngsters do repeat their parents' comments, they tend to imitate language structures more complex than those they use themselves. These structures may then begin to find their way into the children's own spontaneous speech. Whether this is the case or not seems to depend on how *imitation* is defined.

When imitation is defined as immediate and exact copying of an utterance, several findings emerge. The first is that most children display very little imitation, although a few imitate a great deal (Bloom, Hood, & Lightbrown, 1974). Furthermore, such imitations are rarely progressive. In fact, they often are even shorter and less complex than the syntax the child usually uses (Ervin, 1964; Tager-Flusberg & Calkins, 1990). Finally, the proportion of immediate and exact imitations declines over the first few years of language learning (Kuczaj, 1982).

A different picture emerges when imitation is defined more broadly. For example, we might look for *expanded imitations*, in which the child adds something to the utterance that was just heard; or *deferred imitations*, in which the copying occurs at some later time; or *selective imitations,* in which the child imitates the general form of a language structure—such as a prepositional phrase—but uses different words (Snow, 1983; Whitehurst & Novak, 1973). The research evidence suggests that these forms of imitation sometimes *are* progressive. Thus, at least in some cases, a more advanced language structure does first appear in a child's imitation of adult speech, and then gradually finds its way into the child's spontaneous, non-imitative speech (Bloom 1973; Snow & Goldfield, 1983).

The final mechanism we consider that might help children master grammar is feedback, or correction in response to utterances that are grammatically incorrect. Such feedback is called *negative evidence* because it provides information about what is *not* correct in language (in contrast, parental modelling of correct language provides what is called *positive evidence*). The question of negative evidence is important because it relates to a central claim in the Chomskian approach to language acquisition. Nativist theorists maintain that some grammatical rules could be learned only if negative evidence is available; otherwise, children could never avoid all the false starts and wrong directions that are compatible with the speech input they hear. They also claim that children do not receive such feedback—and thus that knowledge of the rules must be innate.

Do children receive negative evidence? The answer to this question is not a simple yes or no. Indeed, the issue of negative evidence is one of the most controversial topics in the study of language development (Bohannon et al., 1996; MacWhinney, 2004; Morgan, Bonamo, & Travis, 1995; Valian, 1996).

Parents rarely respond to their children's ungrammatical statements with simple disapproval, such as "No, you didn't say that right." Instead, feedback regarding the accuracy of a child's remark usually involves its content, or truth value, such as "No, the block isn't red, it's blue" (Brown & Hanlon, 1970; Demetras, Post, & Snow, 1986). Thus, most children apparently do not receive the kind of negative evidence that nativist theorists have stressed. But parents do provide helpful feedback in more subtle ways (Bohannon & Stanowicz, 1988; Chouinard & Clark, 2003; Moerk, 2000; Strapp, 1999).

Expansion A repetition of speech in which errors are corrected and statements are elaborated.

Recasts A response to speech that restates it using a different structure.

Clarification question A response that indicates that a listener did not understand a statement.

Research has shown, for example, that mothers frequently respond to their children's ill-formed statements (such as "Mouses runned in hole, Mommy!") in one of three ways. An **Expansion** involves repeating the child's incorrect statement in a corrected or more complete form ("Yes, the mice ran into the hole!"). A **Recast** involves restating the child's remark using a different structure ("Didn't those mice run into that hole!"). A **Clarification question** signals that the listener did not understand the comment and that the child should attempt the communication again ("What happened? What did those mice do?") (Demetras et al., 1986; Hirsh-Pasek, Treiman, & Schneiderman, 1984; Penner, 1987).

Are these forms of feedback helpful? Research suggests that they are. Children appear to be sensitive to such parental responses; it has been shown, for example, that they are much more likely to imitate a correct grammatical form following a parental recast than following ordinary speech (Saxton, 2000). And there is evidence, from both experimental and correlational studies, that providing children with such feedback can accelerate the development of correct grammar (Farrar, 1990, 1992; Moerk, 1996).

LEARNING OBJECTIVE 11.4

Describe the processes by which children learn to communicate grammatically.

1. What are children's first sentences, and how do they change?
2. What kinds of errors can signal progress in grammatical development?
3. How do children acquire grammar through semantic bootstrapping?
4. How do we know that children use innate cognitive strategies to acquire grammar?
5. How do infant-directed speech, imitation, and modelling help children learn language?
6. What kinds of feedback best help children acquire correct grammar?

PRAGMATICS

Learning Objective 11.5

Describe the means by which children learn the pragmatics of language use.

We have seen that language has both structure (grammar) and meaning (semantics). But it also performs a function in that it gets people to do things we would like them to do. When a toddler points to the refrigerator and says "cup," for example, she is not as likely to be labelling the refrigerator as she is to be asking her mother to fetch her a cup of juice. The study of the social uses of language is called **pragmatics** (Ninio & Snow, 1996).

Pragmatics The study of the social uses of language.

As we saw, the sociocultural approach has placed the greatest stress on the pragmatic aspect of language development. From this perspective, children do not learn language simply because of an innate quest to understand linguistic structure. Instead, they are motivated to acquire language because it provides them with a very powerful tool—the ability to communicate easily with others and to effectively achieve their goals (Lohmann, Tomasello, & Meyer, 2005; Ninio & Snow, 1999).

To be effective communicators, children first must learn to express their needs or desires in ways that can be understood by others. In the beginning, babies cannot always accomplish this, and sometimes their attempts to convey their wants are frustrated by their parents' failure to understand exactly what is being requested. This frustration is an important motivator for the child to acquire skills that will make communication easier. But the process operates in the other direction as well. Effective communication also involves understanding what parents and others are saying in order to follow their directions, answer their questions, or comply with their requests. Communication, of course, is a two-way street.

We begin our discussion of pragmatics with a look at how children use speech to control others and to get their own way. Then, we examine the development of conversation skills and the ability to communicate effectively with others.

SPEECH ACTS

Before acquiring speech, infants use other tools for communication, such as crying, facial expressions, and gestures (Reddy, 1999; Sachs, 2001). In one study, mothers engaged in a turn-taking game (for example, taking turns squeezing a squeak toy) with their 1-year-old babies. Once the game was going smoothly, they were instructed not to take a turn and simply to sit silently and motionlessly. The babies reacted by performing a variety of behaviours clearly designed to communicate to the mother that it was her turn. These included vocalizing at her, pointing to the toy, and picking up the toy and giving it to her (Ross & Lollis, 1987).

With the acquisition of language, children add verbal responses to this repertoire of communication devices. Now children achieve various goals by directing words and phrases at other people. Such pragmatic use of language is referred to as a **speech act** (Astington, 1988; Dore, 1976). Researchers have found that even the earliest words that infants utter usually serve several pragmatic functions (Bretherton, 1988). "Mama," for example, is generally first used both to call the mother and to request things from her (as when the baby says "mama" while pointing to a toy on a shelf). In time, this word also begins to serve the more common purpose of naming the parent (Ninio & Snow, 1988). Later in the one-word period, babies begin to use relational words—those connecting several objects or events—in a number of pragmatic ways. For example, they may use "more" to request that an activity be continued, as well as to describe a block being added to a pile (McCune-Nicolich, 1981).

Speech act An instance of speech used to perform pragmatic functions such as requesting or complaining.

As children's cognitive and linguistic abilities grow, so too do the range and effectiveness of their speech acts. In one longitudinal study, the number of communicative attempts per minute more than doubled between the ages of 14 and 32 months, and the number of different types of speech acts more than tripled. In addition, the proportion of attempts that were judged as interpretable—and therefore more likely to be successful—rose from 47 to 94 percent (Snow et al., 1996). Children also move from using speech acts for the here and now to using them to refer to future or past events or other places (Adamson & Bakeman, 2007).

Adults also produce speech acts that must be comprehended by the language-learning infant if adult and child are to communicate effectively. The comprehension side of communication also improves greatly with development. The child's task is complicated, however, by the fact that the function of some speech he or she hears may not be obvious. When a mother says, "May I open it for you?" she is not really asking the child a question as much as she is offering help. And when she says, "I didn't mean to break it," she is doing more than describing her intentions; she is actually apologizing to the baby. We will return to this aspect of pragmatics shortly.

DISCOURSE

Discourse Language used in social interactions; conversation.

Links to Related Material

In Chapter 8, you read about the cognitive developmental phenomenon called egocentric speech. Here, you learn how children develop an understanding of socially appropriate discourse.

Regardless of what theory of language acquisition they favour, all researchers agree that language is most often used in social contexts. Speech during social interaction is called **discourse** or, more commonly, conversation (Hicks, 1996).

When people have conversations, they must, of course, adhere to the grammatical rules of the language if they are to understand one another. But they also must follow certain social rules of discourse. The most obvious of these is turn taking, with each participant alternating between the role of speaker and of listener. This basic rule of conversation is one of the first acquired by children. As we have seen, it may actually be learned during the preverbal period (Collis, 1985).

Some other rules of discourse are more difficult, however, and are learned later. One of these is the answer-obviousness rule. Some statements that are phrased as questions may actually be intended as directives, such as, "Could you hand me that pencil?" How do listeners know in these situations which function the speaker intends? Most often, we solve the problem by considering the context in which the remark is made (Shatz & McCloskey, 1984). For example, we would very likely treat the remark as a directive if the speaker were about to write a note, if a pencil were visible but out of the speaker's reach, and if the pencil were within our reach. Another kind of cue we often use in such situations, however, is the obviousness of the answer. Because we realize that the speaker in our example knows that we could pass the pencil, we do not treat the remark as a request for information. Instead, we view it as a directive. Discourse rules of this sort are clearly more difficult to learn than is turn taking, and the answer-obviousness rule is not apparent in children until about age 5 (Abbeduto, Davies, & Furman, 1988).

Other discourse rules appear even later. For example, understanding that in a conversation one should (1) say something that relates to what the speaker has just said, (2) say something that is relevant to the topic under discussion, and (3) say something that has not already been said involves discourse rules that most children do not use consistently until 6 or 7 years of age (Conti & Camras, 1984).

SOCIAL REFERENTIAL COMMUNICATION

Social referential communication A form of communication in which a speaker sends a message that is comprehended by a listener.

An even more advanced conversational skill involves the ability to effectively communicate information about something that is not known to the other participant in the conversation, as when one child describes his or her new computer game to a classmate in such a way that the other child understands how it is played. This form of communication is called **social referential communication**. In formal terms, such communication occurs when a speaker sends a message that is comprehended by a listener. The communication is social because it occurs between two people; it is referential because the message is in a symbolic form (the child is using language to convey the information and not simply showing the classmate what to do); and it is communication because it is understood by the listener (Resches & Perez Pereira, 2007; Whitehurst & Sonnenschein, 1985).

Research on social referential communication has been conducted primarily in laboratory settings. To study this process, researchers have generally used a task of the following sort (see Figure 11.4). Two children sit across from one another at a table, separated by a screen or partition. One child is designated the speaker, the other the listener. Both children are given identical sets of stimuli, such as blocks of different sizes, patterns, or colours. The speaker's task is to send messages that describe a block. The listener's task is to use the messages to select the correct block from the available array. In some experiments, the listener can ask questions or comment on the usefulness of the speaker's descriptions. The success of the communication is measured by how often the listener selects the correct item. Using this procedure, psychologists have been able to identify many of the factors that influence children's communication abilities.

FIGURE 11.4

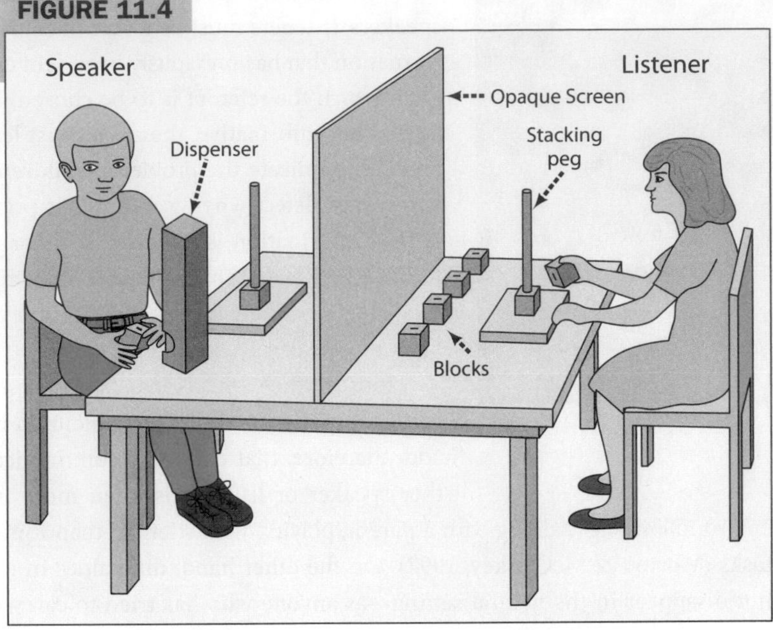

Example of an arrangement used to study social referential communication in children. The speaker's task is to describe the target object in his set clearly enough so that the listener can pick the same object in her set. *From "The Development of Communication: Competence as a Function of Age" by R. M. Krauss and S. Glucksberg, 1969,* Child Development, *40, 259. Copyright © 1969 by the Society for Research in Child Development. Reprinted by permission.*

For children to effectively engage in social referential communication—as speakers or as listeners—they must learn a number of important skills. In the role of speaker, children must become aware of listener cues, meaning simply that they must adjust messages to meet the needs of the listener. For example, if the listener is far away, the message should be loud; if the listener is running out the door, the message should be brief; and if the listener is someone of higher status (for example, a teacher or a preacher), the message should be polite.

A good example of a young child's failure to take listener cues into account is the little boy who talks with his grandmother on the phone and answers her questions by nodding his head. The same phenomenon is evident in experimental tasks of the sort pictured in Figure 11.4 when young children in the speaker role say, "It's this one," or perhaps simply point to the intended target.

Although children are often insensitive to the characteristics of the listener, they do sometimes adjust their speech in response to one important listener characteristic—namely, age. We have seen that adults tend to use the simplified infant-directed style of speech when talking to young children. So, it turns out, do children; children as young as 4 simplify their speech when addressing toddlers or infants (Sachs & Devin, 1976; Shatz & Gelman, 1973). They also alter their speech depending on the social status of the peer to whom they are talking (Kyratzis, Marx, & Wade, 2001). As we would expect, this ability improves as children grow older. Grade 5 students, for example, make more effective speech modifications when talking to younger children than do grade 1 students (Sonnenschein, 1988). Even grade-school students, however, still show a tendency to overestimate the comprehension abilities of young listeners (Miller, Hardin, & Montgomery, 2003; Montgomery, 1993).

Another useful listener cue involves *common ground,* the information shared by the speaker and listener. If the listener, for example, knows the speaker's birthday, then the message "Come over on my birthday" will be sufficient; if the listener does not possess the information, the message will be inadequate. Kindergarteners have some understanding of the common-ground principle, but this ability, too, improves with age (Ackerman & Silver, 1990; Ackerman, Szymanski, & Silver, 1990).

Perhaps the most important listener cues involve feedback. If the listener does not appear to comprehend, the speaker should change the message and try again. In simple situations with very clear cues, even 2-year-olds show some ability to adjust their messages when a listener has misunderstood (Ferrier, Dunham, & Dunham, 2000; Shwe & Markman, 1997). In general, however, sensitivity to listener feedback is limited in young children, who often persist with the same types of messages even when the listener clearly does not understand (Robinson, 1981).

To become effective communicators, children must acquire both speaker and listener skills. (*PhotoDisc, Inc.*)

As listeners, children need to learn certain rules as well. Like speakers, listeners must be aware of context cues, including the information that has previously been sent and the nature of the array from which the referent is to be chosen. In addition, when a message is not informative, the child must learn to recognize this fact and communicate the problem. Children as young as 5 years can sometimes detect when a message is poorly constructed or when critical information is missing. At this age, however, they will often proceed with the inadequate information, whereas by age 7, they are more likely to seek clarification or additional information from the speaker (Ackerman, 1993).

Most of the conclusions just discussed were derived from the sorts of experimental measures pictured in Figure 11.4. We should add, therefore, that children's communicative performance, as either speaker or listener, is often more impressive in the natural environment (e.g., talking with a parent, playing with friends) than it is on unfamiliar laboratory tasks (Warren & McCloskey, 1997). On the other hand, difficulties in communicating clearly do not disappear in the natural setting—as anyone who has tried to carry on a conversation with a 4-year-old can attest.

How referential communication skills develop is an important question. Environmental factors certainly play a role. One study, for example, found that children whose mothers provided them with specific feedback regarding how their messages were inadequate developed their communication skills most rapidly (Robinson, 1981). But such skills must also depend on the emergence of certain cognitive abilities. For example, as children's egocentric view of the world decreases, they develop a better appreciation for how another person might view a situation. And as their theory of mind understanding improves (see Chapter 8), they come to realize that listeners with different cognitive capabilities (such as children versus adults) may interpret the same information differently (Chandler & Lalonde, 1996; Taylor, Cartwright, & Bowden, 1991).

Links to Related Material

In Chapter 8 you read about children's developing theory of mind. Here you learn more about how theory of mind can influence how children use language with others.

ON THE CUTTING EDGE 11.1
IS LANGUAGE SEPARATE FROM GENERAL COGNITIVE ABILITY? THE MESSAGE FROM WILLIAMS SYNDROME

Carl is an extremely friendly 8-year-old who approaches strangers as though they were long-time friends. He likes to talk, his vocabulary is varied, and he speaks in complete sentences. He also demonstrates impressive sensitivity to the feelings of others. Despite these accomplishments, however, Carl's abilities in most respects fall well below those of a typical 8-year-old. He cannot yet tie his shoelaces or fasten small buttons, he cannot reproduce simple spatial patterns, and he struggles to produce a recognizable drawing. His IQ is 54, which places him in the moderate to severe mental retardation range (Mervis et al., 1999).

Carl has Williams syndrome, a genetically based disorder that occurs in 1 per 20,000 births. As the description of Carl suggests, individuals with Williams syndrome show a very uneven profile of cognitive abilities. Their IQs are well below average, they have difficulty maintaining attention, and they experience special difficulty with spatial and numerical problem solving. Yet, they demonstrate both interest and skill when social stimuli are the target; they are especially good, for example, at face processing. And their proficiency with language far surpasses what would be expected given their level of general intelligence. It also surpasses that found in other syndromes that produce similar levels of intelligence. Individuals with Down syndrome, for example, seldom achieve the level of language mastery that is typical in Williams syndrome (Harris et al., 1997).

Williams syndrome has been of interest to students of language because of its relevance to one of the central claims in Chomsky's nativist theory. Recall that Chomsky argued that language is made possible by specially selected mental faculties that are largely independent of other cognitive abilities. This position implies that it should be possible to find instances in which language and general intelligence are dissociated—either impairments in language exist despite generally good intelligence, or intact language abilities exist in the face of serious intellectual

(*continued*)

On the Cutting Edge 11.1 Is Language Separate from General Cognitive Ability? The Message from Williams Syndrome *continued*

deficits. A disorder labelled Specific Language Impairment provides an example in the first category. Children with Specific Language Impairment have normal intelligence by most measures, but are seriously delayed in the mastery of language (Fletcher, 1999). Williams syndrome has been cited by nativist theorists as evidence for the second sort of dissociation (Pinker, 1999).

That Williams syndrome results in a strikingly uneven pattern of abilities is not in dispute. Indeed, the general conclusion that emerges from study of the syndrome is compatible with arguments that we have seen at various points throughout the book. We saw in Chapter 8 that Piaget's general stage model has been challenged by demonstrations that children's cognitive performance is often uneven across different tasks. We saw in Chapter 9 that an emphasis on the domain-specific nature of cognitive development is a characteristic of many information-processing theories of development. Recall also the discussion of Gardner's theory of separate intelligences in Chapter 10.

Whether Williams syndrome really provides evidence for the kind of separate language faculty proposed by nativist theorists is more controversial. Although their eventual linguistic achievements are impressive, individuals with Williams syndrome are slower than most children to move through the initial phases of language mastery (Paterson et al., 1999). In addition, there is evidence that the path they take to mastery may be in some ways different from the typical path. For example, toddlers with Williams syndrome produce far fewer gestures than do normally developing toddlers, and they are less likely to engage in joint attention with their caregivers (Laing et al., 2002). They are also less likely to abide by the constraints (e.g., lexical contrast) that seem to govern much early word learning in normal development (Karmiloff & Karmiloff-Smith, 2001). Finally, they appear to have impaired pragmatic skills, such as having disconnected stories and not asking for clarification when a message is misunderstood (Asada, Tomiwa, Okada, & Itakura, 2010; John, Rowe, & Mervis, 2009). Many researchers believe that mastery of language in this population is dependent—more than is true in normal development—on the attributes that people with Williams syndrome do possess: namely good auditory memory coupled with intense social interest.

Whatever their ultimate implication for theories of language development, the achievements of individuals with Williams syndrome do mirror a central theme of this chapter: children strive to master language, and they are flexible and resourceful learners who use whatever means may be available to them in this effort.

LEARNING OBJECTIVE 11.5

Describe the means by which children learn the pragmatics of language use.

1. What is involved in the knowledge of pragmatics?
2. How do children use speech acts to communicate?
3. What strategies do children learn to apply in discourse?
4. What skills do children need for social referential communication?

CONCLUSION

Developmental psychologists, like researchers in the other natural sciences, attempt to identify processes that are general and fundamental. Rather than considering each event or behaviour unique, scientists search for principles and laws that can explain and interrelate them across the many domains of human development.

During the 1960s, the study of language became an exception to this approach. Language was believed to be different, requiring special mechanisms and processes independent of other behaviours. The basic cognitive and learning processes that psychologists used to explain other aspects of development were thought to be inadequate, and even irrelevant, in explaining language acquisition. Perhaps this separation occurred because the nativist model was developed outside traditional psychology by theorists who were trained primarily in linguistic structure, rather than in human behaviour. As we have seen throughout this chapter, however, the situation has changed considerably.

With the development of new theoretical models and better research techniques, language study has come back into the mainstream of child psychology. The view that language is either independent of cognitive abilities or insensitive to social and environmental factors no longer finds much support among developmental researchers. This is not to say that language does not possess its own unique characteristics, as nativist theorists continue to emphasize. But there can be little doubt that language development is very much interrelated with other developmental processes that both affect it and are affected by it.

SUMMARY

KEY TERMS

babbling drift, p. 409
categorical perception, p. 407
clarification question, p. 432
coining, p. 416
competition model, p. 429
constraints, p. 418
cooing, p. 409
deep structure, p. 401
discourse, p. 434
expansion, p. 432
expressive style, p. 414
fast-mapping, p. 418
grammar, p. 424
holophrases, p. 416
infant-directed speech, p. 403
inflections, p. 425
language acquisition device (LAD), p. 401
language acquisition support system (LASS), p. 405
language-making capacity (LMC), p. 429
lexical contrast theory, p. 418
lexicon, p. 413
naming explosion, p. 413
nativist theory, p. 401
operating principles, p. 429
overextensions, p. 415
overregularization, p. 426
phoneme, p. 406
phonology, p. 406
pragmatics, p. 433
principle of mutual exclusivity, p. 419
productivity, p. 400
recasts, p. 432
reduplicated babbling, p. 409
referential style, p. 414
semantic bootstrapping, p. 428
semantics, p. 412
shape bias, p. 418
social referential communication, p. 434
speech act, p. 433
surface structure, p. 401
syntactic bootstrapping, p. 418
syntax, p. 424
telegraphic speech, p. 425
transformational grammar, p. 402
underextensions, p. 415
whole-object assumption, p. 418

LEARNING OBJECTIVES

LEARNING OBJECTIVE 11.1 Compare and contrast four major theories of language development.

1. *What are the four major theories of language development?*
   The dominant theoretical approach prior to the 1960s was the learning approach (Skinner), which contends that language learning is based on experience. The nativist approach proposed by Chomsky emphasizes the interaction of inborn processes and biological mechanisms with environmental influences. The cognitive-developmental approach to language focuses on the cognitive contributions to language acquisition. The sociocultural approach, influenced by Vygotsky, stresses the cognitive abilities children bring to the task of language learning in conjunction with the cultural context, which affects early social interactions, and therefore may differentially promote cognitive mastery.

2. *In the behavioural view, through what processes do children learn language?*
   According to Skinner, children learn language just as they learn any other skill or behaviour, through operant conditioning. Skinner maintained that there is nothing unique or special

about language. Children utter sounds at random and are more likely to repeat the sounds that caregivers reinforce.

3. *In the nativist view, how does biology take precedence over the environment in language learning?*
   Chomsky and his followers believe that language acquisition must have a strong biological basis because young children acquire language early and rapidly. Evidence for the inborn tendency to acquire language is found in the universality of human language abilities; in the regularity of the production of sounds, even among deaf children; and in the invariant sequences of language development, regardless of the specific language.

4. *How do the cognitive-developmental approach and the sociocultural approach differ in their theory of language acquisition?*
   Cognitive theories emphasize the active role of the learner in language acquisition. This approach focuses on the link between language learning and the child's developing understanding of concepts and relationships. As children mature cognitively, they are able to advance in language development. Evidence for this view comes from the progressive, stage-like, development of speech. The sociocultural approach emphasizes that the basis for language acquisition and use is social interaction. The child's primary motivation for acquiring language is social interaction—to communicate ideas and to be understood.

LEARNING OBJECTIVE 11.2 Trace the developments in the first year of life that establish the preverbal basis for language learning.

1. *How does speech perception develop?*
   Speech perception—the ability to discriminate and attend to speech sounds—enables listeners to divide speech, a continuous series of sound, into segments. As listeners divide the stream of sounds into syllables, words, and sentences, they also attend to other characteristics of speech, such as intonations, pauses, and the placement of stress. Infants perceive and distinguish phonemes—the smallest sound unit that signals a change in meaning. From an early age, infants show evidence of categorical speech perception. Experience also plays an important role in early speech perception. Two-day-old infants already show a preference for hearing their own language. And the more babies are exposed to a language, the more language-specific their phonemic discriminations become. Some phonemic distinctions become sharper with experience and, conversely, lack of exposure dulls other distinctions. Interestingly, when infants begin learning words, they appear to be unable to use all the information present in the speech signal, confusing similar-sounding words. However, infants can distinguish similar-sounding words when the task is made easier, indicating that it is not a problem perceiving the phonemic information, but in applying it to the difficult task of word learning.

2. *What preverbal speech sounds do infants use?*
   Children develop language in stages tied to maturation. Before they develop language, infants use prelinguistic vocalizations. During the first month, the primary sound that infants make is crying. During the second month, infants begin cooing, using their tongues and extended vowel sounds to articulate. Coos express feelings of pleasure or positive excitement. Between 6 and 9 months of age, infants begin babbling, the first vocalizing that sounds like human speech. The babbling of infants begins to take on the properties of the language they are hearing, a concept called babbling drift.

3. *What is the role of non-verbal communication in language acquisition?*
   Non-verbal aspects of communication, such as gestures, are important preverbal skills used by all infants to perform many of the functions of vocal language. Infants first use gestures to

communicate requests at about 8 to10 months of age. Children also use gestures to symbolize objects or events. Babies learning spoken languages will even accept gestures as labels for objects in early word learning, but this tendency decreases with age.

LEARNING OBJECTIVE 11.3 Describe the processes by which children first use words and develop vocabulary.

1. *What are the characteristics of children's first words, and at what rate do children acquire vocabulary?*
   Children first understand words before they produce words. For most children, nouns (especially object words) predominate and remain more common than verbs and action words throughout language development. After 18 months, rapid growth, termed the naming explosion, takes place in the number of new words learned. Children often maintain this rapid rate of vocabulary acquisition throughout the preschool period, when they can effortlessly acquire an average of nine new words per day. However, there are generally great individual differences in the size and range of vocabulary development.

2. *What are some individual and cultural differences in children's language learning?*
   One difference is in the size of children's early vocabularies. Another is in the rate at which children learn words. There is wide variability in the number of words in children's vocabularies, with word production ranging from several to hundreds. Comparable differences are found for children's comprehension of words. There also are differences in the types of words found in children's early lexicons. Some children display a referential style, producing a large proportion of nouns. Other children display an expressive style, which includes a larger mix of word types, more "stock phrases," and a greater emphasis on language as a pragmatic tool for expressing needs and for interacting socially. The two styles reflect different culturally defined ideas about the purpose of language. Also, some cultures have languages that have more verbs than do other cultures.

3. *What can we learn about language learning from the semantic errors that children make?*
   Psychologists have learned a great deal about children's semantic development by examining the kinds of errors they make. In early word learning, children attach a specific label to a specific object. Next, the child begins to extend that label to other examples of the same object. These extensions demonstrate that the child is forming an object category that is defined by certain features. Most children, however, make errors when attempting to extend these early labels and may also use a specific label to describe something else. These overextensions are common in the early stages of semantic development and may reflect either a lack of understanding or a lack of vocabulary. Young children may also apply labels too narrowly (underextensions), but these are less common in production than overextensions. Word coining occurs when children create new words that are not a part of adult language.

4. *By what processes do children learn the meaning of words?*
   Various explanations have been proposed for semantic development—the processes by which children come to learn the meaning of words. In one process, children use grammatical cues to help them determine the meaning of certain words. The reverse is also possible. Once children have mastered some aspects of grammar, they can use grammatical cues to narrow down the possible meaning of new words to process words faster. This process is called syntactic bootstrapping, because the child's prior knowledge of grammar underlies, or "bootstraps," the learning of semantics. Most children have learned thousands of words by the time they start school, and most of these words are those they learned on their own through exposure. Children's word learning can occur rapidly, sometimes after only a brief exposure, through a

process called fast-mapping. Children use assumptions, or constraints, to govern early word learning. Lexical contrast theory suggests that when children hear an unfamiliar word, they automatically assume the new word has a different meaning from any word they already know, motivating them to learn exactly what the new word means. In addition, children always replace their current meanings with those they think are more conventional or correct. The principle of mutual exclusivity states that children believe that objects can have only one name, which limits the possible choices when a child is trying to attach meaning to a new word. Interestingly, bilingual children, who need two labels for every object, only apply mutual exclusivity within each of the languages, but not between their languages.

5. *What roles do parents and children themselves play in semantic development?*
   Children can learn words only if their social environment provides them with sufficient information about what different words mean. Parents and other caregivers help children in this task through modelling. Parents' modelling of words can occur either incidentally in the normal course of conversation, or explicitly in an attempt to teach the child a new word.

LEARNING OBJECTIVE 11.4 Describe the processes by which children learn to communicate grammatically.

1. *What are children's first sentences, and how do they change?*
   Most children begin to combine words into the first simple sentences at around 18 months. Children begin to produce strings of single-word utterances, using one word to call attention to an object and then a second word to comment on the object. Multiple one-word utterances can be distinguished from the two-word sentences that will soon appear by the longer pause that occurs between words. Children show great variety of items and combinations in their initial sentences. The next phase of grammatical development is telegraphic speech. As the child's sentences grow, they become truncated, resembling telegram messages. Sentences focus on high-content words and omit unnecessary function words.

2. *What kinds of errors can signal progress in grammatical development?*
   As children learn the inflectional rules of language, they tend toward overregularization, or applying the regular rules to nouns and verbs that have irregular forms. Usage is inconsistent, but eventually the correct and incorrect forms may merge. Thus, the application of rules, even when overregularized, represents progress in language development.

3. *How do children acquire grammar through semantic bootstrapping?*
   Semantic bootstrapping is using word meanings to help learn about grammar. An example of semantic bootstrapping is using prior knowledge of noun and pronoun categories to determine the grammatical forms surrounding them in a sentence. In the sentence, "These pencils belong in this box," the child may know that "this" means one of something, while "these" means more than one. This knowledge may then help the child form the plural and singular forms of the nouns in the sentence correctly.

4. *How do we know that children use innate cognitive strategies to acquire grammar?*
   Researchers have found that children's use of innate cognitive strategies allows them to acquire grammatical rules rapidly. An example is children's development of rules for inflections of words, such as forming plurals.

5. *How do infant-directed speech, imitation, and modelling help children learn language?*
   In infant-directed speech, adults modify their language when speaking to young children. Mothers tend to speak slowly, use short utterances, and focus on the here and now rather than

on more distant or abstract events. Imitation is not exact copying of parental models of grammar. Rather, the child adds something to the utterance that was just heard, or copies it at some later time, or copies a particular grammatical form using different words.

6. *What kinds of feedback best help children acquire correct grammar?*
   Feedback provides information about what is not correct in language. Adults frequently respond to children's ill-formed statement in one of three ways. Expansions involve repeating the child's statement and adding something to make it more complex. Recasts involve restating what the child said in a different, more correct way. Clarification questions signal that the listener did not understand the comment and that the child should attempt the communication again. Research suggests that these forms of feedback are helpful to children and that children appear to be receptive to such responses.

LEARNING OBJECTIVE 11.5 Describe the means by which children learn the pragmatics of language use.

1. *What is involved in the knowledge of pragmatics?*
   Pragmatics is the practical knowledge of how to use language to communicate. It involves knowing how to begin and continue a conversation, how to ask for things, how to tell a story or joke, and how to adjust comments to the listener's perspective.

2. *How do children use speech acts to communicate?*
   With the acquisition of language, children add verbal responses to their repertoire of communication devices and achieve goals by directing words and phrases to other people. Such pragmatic uses of language are referred to as speech acts. Even the first words that infants utter serve pragmatic functions. In the one-word period, babies begin to use relational words, those connecting several objects or events, in pragmatic ways toward multiple goals. As their cognitive and linguistic abilities grow, children's speech acts increase in range and effectiveness.

3. *What strategies do children learn to apply in discourse?*
   Speech during social interaction is called discourse. When people have conversations, in addition to adhering to the grammatical rules of the language, they also must follow the social rules of discourse, such as turn taking, with each participant alternating between the roles of speaker and listener. Some other rules of discourse are more difficult, however, and are learned later. Another example is the answer-obviousness rule. Statements phrased as questions are actually intended as directives. For example, the answer to "Could you hand me that pencil?" is obvious in that the listener knows to hand the speaker the pencil rather than answer the question.

4. *What skills do children need for social referential communication?*
   Social referential communication involves sending a message that a listener comprehends; the communication is social because it occurs between two people; it is referential because the message is in a symbolic form; and it is communication because it is understood by the listener. To be effective, children must learn a subset of important skills. In the role of speaker, the child must become aware of listener cues, adjusting his or her messages to meet the listener's needs. Young children often fail to take into account listener cues and situational factors. Children also sometimes adjust their speech in response to the listener's age. Another useful listener cue involves common ground—information that is shared by both speaker and listener. Feedback is perhaps the most important listener cue. If the listener does not appear to understand what is being communicated, the speaker should change the message and try again. Listeners must also be aware of context cues, including information that has been given previously and the subject to which the information refers.

CHAPTER 12

EARLY SOCIAL AND EMOTIONAL DEVELOPMENT

It's estimated that around 10 to 20 percent of mothers suffer from postpartum depression (PPD) after their babies are born. Apart from the obvious effects on the mother, PPD can have a lasting negative impact on her child, even after the mother has recovered. Children of mothers with PPD can have growth and developmental problems, including behavioural problems.

Intervention programs have long focused on improving the mood of depressed mothers, but with limited success. A new approach realizes that since recovering from depression can take a long time, if mothers can't easily change how they feel, they can at least try changing how they interact with their babies.

The Keys to Caregiving program, developed by NCAST Programs (Nursing Child Assessment Satellite Training) at the University of Washington, is used internationally to model nurturing behaviour by parents, including during feeding time. Mothers are shown how best to respond to the cues their infants give them as part of their nonverbal communication.

Researchers at the University of Alberta and University of New Brunswick studied the program's effects on mothers with PPD. Mothers of three-month-olds attended five weekly sessions of Keys to Caregiving. After the intervention, although the mothers' depression ratings did not change, the babies showed a marked increase in their levels of interest and joy. "This study suggests that intervention that focuses on what mothers do with their infants instead of how they feel can be effective in increasing infants' positive responsiveness and improving infant outcomes," the authors write.

In this chapter we will study infants' temperament and their emotional development. We will also examine the development of their early attachments to their caregivers, and how this may be influenced by the ways their caregivers interact with them.

Source: Jung, V., Short, R., Letourneau, N., & Andrews, D., "Interventions with depressed mothers and their infants: Modifying interactive behaviours," *Journal of Affective Disorders, 98*(3), 2007, 199–205.

"Keys to Caregiving program information page," NCAST, available at www.ncast.org/index.cfm?fuseaction=category.display&category_id=28

Desjardins, Sylvain-Jacques, "Post-partum depression has an impact on children: Effects continue long after treatment," *Concordia Journal*, May 24, 2007.

HUMANS ARE A VERY SOCIAL SPECIES. We organize into groups, ranging in size from families to communities to nations, and we spend a good deal of time interacting with one another. From early on, children form many social relationships. Some of these relationships, such as those with occasional babysitters, are very brief and of little consequence. But others, such as those with family members and certain friends, will last for many years and may affect children's later development and personality in important ways (Caspi & Shiner, 2006; Thompson, 2006).

Understanding social development has not been easy, however, because the complexity of social interaction poses certain obstacles to its scientific study. Consider the following mother–infant interaction, which represents the relatively simple dyadic, or two-person, situation. A mother talks to her baby, and he begins to smile; when she moves a toy in front of him, the baby follows it with his eyes; and when she makes a strange face at him, he becomes still and stares attentively.

A baby's social interactions are transactional. Babies not only respond to their environment, but also influence it. *(Purestock)*

What causes these changes in the baby's behaviour? Clearly, the changes are being determined, or caused, by what the mother is doing. But there is more to the interaction than that because the influence here is undoubtedly bidirectional. That is, the baby's responses also influence the mother's behaviour. For example, if the baby gazes at her with apparent interest, the mother is likely to continue what she is doing. If the baby begins to act bored, she may step up her actions, perhaps tickling him or adding attention-getting vocalizations. If the baby begins to fret, the mother may tone down her responses or even end the interaction altogether.

This relatively simple example illustrates the challenge that faces psychologists in their attempts to identify the determinants of social interactions. In the case of the baby's behaviour, certainly one determinant is the mother's behaviour. But the baby's behaviour and personal characteristics also affect the kinds of things the mother does. In that sense, then, the baby is a *producer* of his own environment (Lerner, 1982).

We have already encountered this general idea in earlier chapters—first, in Chapter 1, when we discussed Bandura's model of reciprocal determinism and Bronfenbrenner's notion of developmentally generative and disruptive behaviours, and then in Chapter 3, in the behaviour-genetic models of Scarr and Plomin. The essential point here is that psychologists have come to understand that human social behaviour is *transactional*—each person's actions both affect and are affected by the actions of others. We will see many examples of this in the remainder of the book.

This chapter is the first of five that deal with children's social and personality development. We focus here on social interactions during the first years of life. To begin, we survey the approaches of the four major theoretical traditions to infant social development. Next, we consider how the infant and the caregiver develop an early communication system as they learn to regulate one another's behaviour. Then, we look at the baby's temperament, or individual style of responding. Finally, we examine the topic that traditionally has been of greatest interest to researchers—the nature of the attachment process that produces the unique emotional bond between caregiver and child.

Learning Objective 12.1

Understand the major theoretical approaches to early social development.

THEORIES OF EARLY SOCIAL DEVELOPMENT

Social development during the first years of life is distinctive in several important ways. First, although children eventually come to have many social contacts—family, friends, teachers, and so on—the social world of infants in most Western cultures has traditionally consisted of relatively few individuals, such as the mother, father, and siblings. Second, these initial relationships appear to be more influential and to have longer-term effects on the child's social, personality, and even cognitive development than do many of the relationships that develop later on. Finally, children appear to develop strong emotional relationships—especially with the mother but also with the father and others—more easily and intensely during the infant years, suggesting that early social development may involve psychological processes that are different from those that operate later on in life.

Researchers from each of the four major theoretical approaches have taken an interest in early social development. And, as you might expect, their different views have led them to pursue different questions and aspects of this area. Much of the focus has been on the attachment process, which we discuss in detail later in the chapter.

EVOLUTIONARY AND BIOLOGICAL APPROACHES

According to evolutionary approaches, the social behaviours we observe in today's infants and caregivers represent millions of years of gradual adaptation to the environment. Much of this work has involved other species, with theorizing regarding human development based largely on the views of John Bowlby, discussed in Chapter 1.

In contrast to the young of many other species, human infants are relatively helpless at birth and remain unable to survive on their own for years. If babies are not fed, sheltered, and protected, they will certainly die. And because humans produce comparatively few offspring (whereas fish, for example, lay thousands of eggs), our species would quickly become extinct if a high percentage of babies did not survive long enough to reproduce.

Evolutionary theorists believe that the process of natural selection has provided infants and mothers with an innate system of behaviours designed to ensure the infant's survival (Simpson & Belsky, 2008). Perhaps the most important of these built-in behaviours is for the infant to develop a relationship with the **primary caregiver**—usually the mother—that accomplishes two goals: it keeps her nearby, and it motivates her to provide adequate caregiving. For the first six or seven months, the baby can remain close to the mother only by drawing her near. Crying is by far the most effective behaviour for doing this. Later, as locomotor abilities develop, the child can stay near the mother by crawling or running after her.

Primary caregiver The person, usually the mother, with whom the infant develops the major attachment relationship.

The infant promotes caregiving behaviours in several ways. One is by making interactions very pleasant for the mother, such as by smiling, vocalizing, and making eye contact with her. Proper caregiving is also encouraged when babies reduce signs of distress in response to the mother's attention, such as when they stop fussing when picked up. Finally, some ethologists believe that the physical appearance of babies—large heads, round faces, and large eyes—may also serve to maintain the mother's interactions because she innately finds these features "cute" (George & Solomon, 2008). Interestingly, researchers have found that the preference for baby-like features is found in both adult men and women, but is most prominent in women. Moreover, development is characterized by a shift from a preference for adult features in middle childhood to favouring infant features beginning in early adolescence, corresponding with the onset of the ability to reproduce (Fullard & Reiling, 1976).

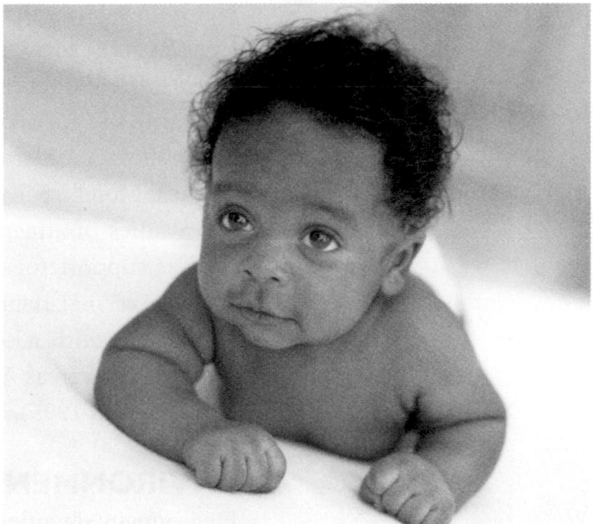

According to ethologists, aspects of babies' physical appearance may be innately "cute" and so elicit caregiving. (*Caren Alpert/The Image Bank/Getty Images*)

The caregiver, too, presumably has built-in mechanisms for doing what is necessary for the infant's survival. This individual's job is to "read" the infant's signals and decide what is wrong, what to do in response, and when it has been effective. Innate caregiving patterns are obvious with other mammals, where mothers of even first litters appear to know exactly how to care for their young. As we saw in Chapter 1, ethologists characterize these more complex sequences of innate behaviours as modal action patterns, and assume that they are triggered by certain stimuli (such as the sound or smell of the newborn pups). It is not easy to determine what portion of the caregiving provided by human mothers is innate, however, because new mothers in most cultures typically acquire much of this information through social sources (e.g., by observing or conversing with other mothers).

The behaviours that serve to keep mother and baby together during the early weeks and months of life emerge as part of an *attachment process* that also includes a strong emotional bond. At first, the baby emits care-seeking behaviours to virtually anyone. But if the mother responds to these bids in a sensitive and consistent way, the baby gradually comes to use the mother as a source of comfort and reassurance when upset and a secure base from which to explore the world. As we will discuss in more detail, this behaviour characterizes what is known as a *secure* attachment. Bowlby and others of this tradition believe further that the attachment process in humans occurs during a sensitive period in the baby's development, as is the case for the imprinting process that produces attachment in some other species (Marvin & Britner, 2008).

According to Bowlby and most adherents of attachment theory, sensitive, responsive mothers and securely attached infants are nature's prototype, shaped by forces in our evolutionary past (Beaulieu & Bugental, 2007; Chisolm, 1996). Less responsive mothers—or infants who do not seek out their mothers for comfort and reassurance—are viewed as abnormal and maladaptive. More recently, however, a number of evolutionary theorists have questioned the premise that there is a single, species-appropriate type of mother–infant relationship (Simpson & Belsky, 2008). To understand their objections, it is helpful to recall some of the work that shaped Bowlby's thinking.

Bowlby's model of the mother–infant relationship was heavily influenced by observations of modern hunter–gatherer groups, such as the !Kung. Many evolutionary theorists believe these groups live much as our ancestors did. Therefore, the way these groups deal with environmental constraints should reflect the pressures faced by our ancestors in the evolutionary past. !Kung infants, it should be noted, were found to be in physical contact with their mothers 70 to 80 percent of the time during their first year of life (Konner, 1972).

Of course, it is impossible to know very much about the features of the environments in which humans evolved. However, contemporary evolutionary psychologists increasingly suspect that the environment was not quite as ideal as Bowlby imagined (Simpson & Belsky, 2008). It was probably highly unstable, with unpredictable changes in climate and habitat (Bjorklund & Pellegrini, 2002a). Consequently, many evolutionary psychologists contend that humans are equipped with a flexible behavioural repertoire that allows persons to form social bonds that are adaptive, given local ecological and social conditions. Indeed, studies of modern hunter–gatherer groups other than the !Kung show considerable variability in the nature of early social relationships (Hewlett et al., 2000; Tronick, Morelli, & Ivey, 1992).

Studies of attachment in high-risk samples in modern industrialized societies provide further support for the idea that whether a particular form of attachment relationship is adaptive or maladaptive depends on the situation. For instance, children who form a secure attachment with a severely depressed caregiver place themselves at risk for psychological problems, whereas children who do not form a close attachment are less at risk (Radke-Yarrow et al., 1995).

ENVIRONMENTAL/LEARNING APPROACHES

Environmentally oriented theorists do not deny that infants and mothers possess many built-in responses that may contribute to early caregiving and the attachment process. But the main concern of these theorists is with the infant's **socialization**—the process by which a child's behaviour is moulded to fit with the society's roles, beliefs, and expectations (Bugental & Grusec, 2006; Maccoby, 2007). Socialization is assumed to continue throughout childhood and is thought to affect many of the child's more complex social behaviours, such as moral development and interactions with peers. The process, however, begins in infancy and can be observed in the way the baby's first social interactions are influenced by others.

Socialization The process through which society moulds the child's beliefs, expectations, and behaviour.

According to the environmental/learning view, caregiver–infant social behaviours result from interaction between the two individuals, with each influencing the behaviour of the other. Rather than appealing to special evolutionary mechanisms unique to this area, however, psychologists of this tradition assume that these interactions can be explained by social-learning processes, including reinforcement, punishment, and observational learning (Gewirtz & Pelaez-Nogueras, 1992a; Hay et al., 1985).

For example, this approach contends that infants produce behaviours that encourage the mother to approach and remain close (crying, smiling, vocalizing, and so on) because these behaviours result in either positive reinforcement (milk, a rattle, or being rocked) or negative reinforcement (the removal of a wet diaper). Similarly, the mother learns to respond to these behaviours because they also result in either negative reinforcement (the baby stops crying) or positive reinforcement (the baby smiles, coos, and clings).

Much of the evidence supporting the social-learning model derives from studies showing that infant social behaviours can be influenced by reinforcement processes. Infant vocalizations, for example, will increase if reinforced and decrease if subjected to an extinction procedure (Poulson & Nunes, 1988). The same is true for infant smiling (Etzel & Gewirtz, 1967; Zelazo, 1971). Likewise, certain behaviours common in infants, such as separation protest and social referencing (both of which we will discuss later in the chapter), can be produced through conditioning processes (Gewirtz & Pelaez-Nogueras, 1991a, 1992b). And similar experiments have demonstrated that infant behaviours can serve to increase (reinforce) or decrease (punish) the social behaviour of the caregiver (Gewirtz & Boyd, 1976, 1977). Together, these studies show that it is theoretically possible to explain changes in caregiver–infant interaction by applying social-learning principles. But exactly how important such principles are in the development of the typical infant–caregiver relationship remains unresolved (Hay, 1986; Schaffer, 1986).

For Thought and Discussion

Have you ever engaged in mutual smiling with an infant? Have you noticed how reinforcing an infant smile can be?

COGNITIVE-DEVELOPMENTAL APPROACHES

The cognitive-developmental tradition contends that to understand children's early social development, we should search for the cognitive processes that underlie social behaviours. This approach is based on the concept of **social cognition** (Lewis & Carpendale, 2011), which refers to children's and adults' understanding of human behaviour and social interactions. For example, it explores how children learn to predict another person's behaviour by appreciating what the other person is thinking, what he or she believes to be true, or what he or she wants to achieve. Social cognition is thought to begin in infancy, such as with a baby's ability to follow and make use of another person's eye gaze, or to reference his or her facial expression or vocal intonation for clues about how to react to novel stimuli. Ways in which these behaviours may demonstrate a budding theory of mind are discussed in Chapter 8.

Social cognition Knowledge of the social world and interpersonal relationships.

Internal working models An infant's and a caregiver's cognitive conception of each other, which they use to form expectations and predictions.

As applied to attachment, the cognitive tradition overlaps somewhat with the evolutionary approach in that both are concerned with how infants and mothers cognitively represent their relationships with each other (Main, Kaplan, & Cassidy, 1985). Bowlby adopted the notion of mental representations from cognitive psychology, and proposed that infants and caregivers develop **internal working models** of each other and use these models to interpret events and predict what will happen (Bowlby, 1973; Bretherton & Munholland, 2008). For example, an infant may develop expectations regarding the mother's behaviour as a result of the type of treatment she provides. If she responds quickly and reliably to the infant's signals of distress or care-seeking, the baby may develop the expectation that the mother will be available if needed and so will be less likely to cry when left alone (Weinfield, Sroufe, Egeland, & Carlson, 2008). Likewise, the caregiver may develop an internal working model of the infant that leads her to expect the baby will be eager to interact with her. As a result, she may become more likely to play with the infant (Crowell & Feldman, 1991; George & Solomon, 1989). Internal working models are also important for the infant's development of a sense of self, a topic we consider in the next chapter.

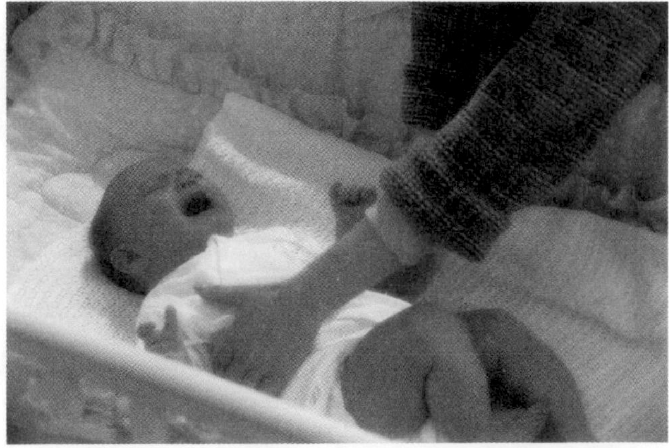

When the caregiver responds reliably to the infant's signals of distress, such as picking up the infant when she cries, the infant is likely to develop the expectation that the caregiver will be there when needed. (*Comstock Images/Getty Images*)

SOCIOCULTURAL APPROACHES

Sociocultural approaches to early social and emotional development focus on the solutions cultures devise to deal with one basic universal reality—that the survival of infants depends on bonds with caregivers who will protect and nurture them (Rogoff, 2003). Sociocultural theorists acknowledge that infants and mothers possess many built-in responses that shape early caregiving and the attachment process. At the same time, however, these theorists point to variations in caregiving arrangements that have been observed across cultures and history. Such variations, they argue, indicate that early development is due not to biology alone, but also to the interaction of biology with culture.

As is true of environmental/learning approaches, sociocultural perspectives on early social and emotional development focus on socialization practices. However, sociocultural approaches diverge from the traditional environmental/learning view in their scope. Environmental/learning theorists primarily focus on the interactions between infants and their caregivers. Sociocultural theorists contend that to understand these interactions, it is essential to place them in a cultural context. Consequently, sociocultural studies of early development focus on levels or contexts of development beyond the infant or the infant–caregiver dyad.

Theorists have proposed several frameworks to help organize research on early development in its cultural context. One of these frameworks, described in Chapter 1, is Bronfenbrenner's bioecological model (Bronfenbrenner & Ceci, 1994; Bronfenbrenner & Morris, 2006). This model stresses the interactions of a changing organism in a changing environment composed of immediate settings and the larger social and cultural contexts in which the settings are embedded. Of particular interest are the ways in which various spheres—the home, the school, the parents' workplace, the local community, national policies—interact and shape development.

Indeed, studies show that conditions outside of the caregiver–infant dyad can influence the quality of the relationship. For example, family stress, family support, employment, and changes in supplemental childcare have all been shown to affect the mother–infant relationship, either directly or indirectly through the marital relationship (Corwyn & Bradley, 1999; Fish, 2001; Thompson, Lamb, & Estes, 1982; van Bakel & Riksen-Walraven, 2002; Vondra, Hommerding, & Shaw; 1999).

Another model, known as the *developmental niche*, was devised by Charles Super and Sara Harkness to provide a framework for thinking about parenting as a culturally constructed interface between the larger environment and the development of children. The developmental niche is composed of three subsystems: the physical and social settings in which the child lives, cultural customs of child care and child rearing, and the psychology of the caregivers. The psychology of the caregivers includes their beliefs regarding the nature and needs of children, their child-rearing goals, and their understanding of effective rearing techniques (Harkness & Super, 2002; Super & Harkness, 1997, 2002).

As we see throughout this and subsequent chapters, socialization practices are largely compatible with parental child-rearing goals and beliefs. For instance, in cultures with high infant mortality rates, the parental goal is to maximize survival. Parents in these cultures tend to have more children than in communities with low child mortality rates. They also tend to provide very attentive physical care during the first two or three years, when the children are at greatest risk (LeVine, 1988; LeVine et al., 1994).

LEARNING OBJECTIVE 12.1

Understand the major theoretical approaches to early social development.

1. How does the ethological approach explain infant–mother attachment?
2. Explain how the environmental/learning approaches view early infant social behaviour.
3. How is cognitive development related to early social development?
4. How do sociocultural approaches conceptualize early social development?

MUTUAL REGULATION BETWEEN INFANTS AND CAREGIVERS

Learning Objective 12.2

Understand the development of early communication between the infant and caregiver.

The attachment process that becomes so evident by the end of the baby's first year has roots in early infancy (Marvin & Britner, 2008). Right from birth, mothers and newborns begin to interact in ways that will draw them into a close emotional relationship. A most important feature of these early interactions is that each individual both influences the other's behaviour and adjusts to it, producing a smooth-running system of mutual regulation (Bornstein & Tamis-LaMonda, 1990; Tronick, 1989).

The key to the development of this two-way system is effective communication between the infant and the caregiver. Chapter 11 described how babies use gestures and babbling to send messages even before they can speak. But the baby's ability to convey wants and needs and to mobilize the caregiver into action begins even earlier.

CRYING

By far the most important form of communication for the newborn is crying. Not only is crying one of the baby's strongest and clearest responses, but it is one to which caregivers appear to be especially responsive (Nader, Job, Badali, & Craig, 2004). Crying is part of the infant's larger affective communication system, which we discuss next. But because it has generated so much research on its own, we consider crying here separately.

Darwin believed that crying in newborns evolved as a means of providing the mother with information about the baby's state or condition (Darwin, 1872). Ethologists today continue to assume that crying serves as a stimulus to trigger innate caregiving behaviours by the mother (Simpson & Belsky, 2008; Zeifman, 2001). Learning theorists point out that crying (like sucking and some other early, reflex-like behaviours) also soon comes under the baby's voluntary control. When this occurs, crying becomes modifiable by its consequences; that is, it can be conditioned. If a baby's crying results in his caregiver's presence (as it often does), he or she may learn to use this response purposefully as a way of summoning care (Gewirtz, 1991; Lotem & Winkler, 2004).

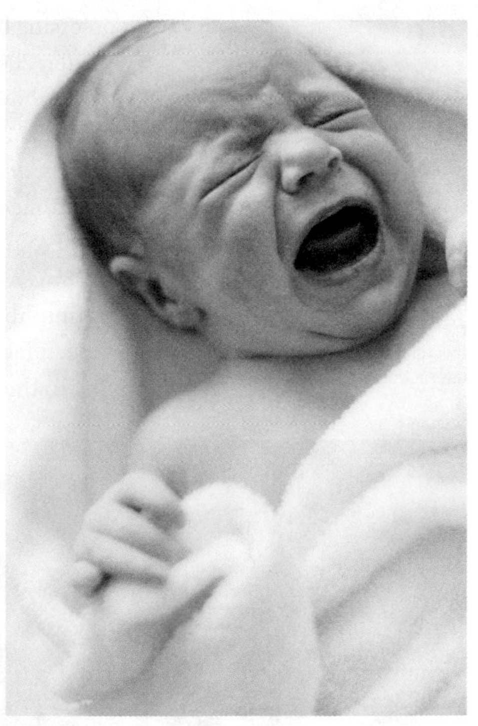

Crying is one of the baby's strongest and clearest responses. (© *Amanda Rohde/iStock*)

For crying to serve as a form of communication, two conditions are necessary. First, different types of cries should communicate different messages. And they do; infants' pain cries differ in pitch and intensity from hunger cries (Soltis, 2004). In addition, variations in cries can convey other information. For example, as the pitch of crying increases, adult listeners tend to perceive the baby's problem as becoming more serious and urgent (Leger et al., 1996; Zeskind & Marshall, 1988).

The other condition necessary for crying to be communicative is that listeners must be able to discriminate one type from another. Caregivers must understand whether the baby is saying, for example, "I'm hungry," "I'm wet," or "I'm frightened." As we saw in Chapter 5, there is debate about exactly which dimensions adults can distinguish. Nevertheless, a number of studies have reported that adult listeners can be quite good at interpreting babies' cries (Soltis, 2004). This ability is based, in part, on experience. In general, parents and other adults who have spent time around infants are better at decoding infant crying than are adults with little experience (Gustafson, Wood, & Green, 2000). Such experience can help parents learn to read contextual cues—such as the infant's facial expressions—that are important for decoding infant cries (Craig, Grunau, & Aquan-Assee, 1988; Gustafson et al., 2000).

The communication role of crying thus has elements of both nature and nurture. At first, crying is innately elicited by various internal stimuli (such as hunger) and external stimuli (such as a diaper pin). Such crying serves primarily to draw the mother near. With experience, however, the caregiver becomes more accurate at reading the information in these signals, and babies learn to use the crying response as a means of controlling the mother's attention and care.

EMOTIONS AND THE AFFECTIVE SYSTEM

Research on crying indicates that many of the early messages sent by babies involve "dislikes." Newborns also can communicate "likes," using behaviours such as smiling, vocalizing, and gazing at an object they find interesting (Brazelton, 1982). These aversions and preferences are the internal reactions, or feelings, we call **emotions**. On seeing his mother, for example, an infant might experience joy, which might be followed by anger as she prepares to leave, sadness when she is gone, and fear when he hears an unfamiliar sound. Some researchers believe that emotions also carry with them a readiness for action—the child experiences a particular feeling in preparation for doing something (Campos, Frankel, & Camras, 2004; Saarni, Campos, Camras, & Witherington, 2008).

Emotions An internal reaction or feeling which may be either positive (such as joy) or negative (such as anger), and may reflect a readiness for action.

The outward expression of emotions is called **affect**. Many theorists believe that initially a close correspondence exists between what babies feel and what they express. That is, early on, affect accurately reveals emotion (Malatesta et al., 1989). It is widely believed that the infant's ability to display different affective states is an important component in the mutual regulation between babies and their mothers (Adamson & Bakeman, 1991; Fogel & Thelen, 1987).

Affect The outward expression of emotions through facial expressions, gestures, intonation, and the like.

DEVELOPMENT AND EXPRESSION OF EMOTIONS Although affective responses can take a number of forms, such as gestures and vocalizations, much of our understanding of babies' early emotional development has come about through the study of facial expressions (Camras & Fatani, 2008). Even newborns possess all the facial muscle movements necessary to produce virtually any adult emotional expression. Researchers have developed detailed coding procedures for assessing babies' facial expressions, involving separate ratings for the brow, eye, and mouth regions (Oster, 2005).

Babies' facial expressions of the basic emotions appear at different points in development (Camras & Fatani, 2008; Ekman, 1993). There is some disagreement about exactly what these basic or *primary emotions* are (Oster, 2005; Sroufe, 1996), but we will consider several that have been mentioned frequently.

From birth, babies can indicate *distress* by crying and *interest by* staring attentively (Lewis, 2008b). As we saw in Chapter 7, one stimulus that reliably elicits interest is the human face, illustrating how evolution encourages infant–mother interaction right from the beginning. Another inborn facial expression is *disgust,* which is elicited by unpleasant tastes or odours, usually signalling to the caregiver that feeding is not going the way it should (Oster, 2005).

Links to Related Material

In Chapter 7, you read how newborns enjoy looking at the human face. Here, you learn more about how this tendency sets the stage for social interaction.

By 3 months of age, smiling (reflecting *pleasure)* appears in response to familiar events, such as the voice or face of a person the infant knows (Lewis, 2008b). Researchers have identified different types of smiles in babies, varying according to the components of lip retraction, cheek raising, and jaw dropping. Recent research suggests that 6- and 12-month-old infants display different smiles in response to different types of pleasure, such as the enjoyment of different components of a face-to-face caregiver–child interaction, including anticipation of the caregiver's behaviour and satisfaction after its completion (Fogel et al., 2000). This further suggests that the positive emotional experience of children is rather complex, even midway through the first year of life.

Research suggests infants display different smiles in response to different types of pleasure, such as enjoyment of different aspects of the interaction with a caregiver. (© *Quavondo/iStock*)

Sadness and *anger*—demonstrated experimentally by inducing frustration (e.g., by removing a teething toy or by restraining the baby's arm)—are first evident in facial expressions at around 4 months of age (Lemerise & Dodge, 2008; Lewis, 2008b). Facial expressions indicating fear do not appear until about 7 or 8 months (Lewis, 2008b).

Because they are assumed to reflect the infant's emotions, an infant's expressions can be used to infer how the baby is feeling about a situation. For example, researchers taught babies to pull a string tied to one arm to produce a pleasant visual and auditory stimulus. The babies displayed expressions of joy during the learning process, but displayed expressions of anger when the pulling no longer produced a reward (Lewis et al., 1990; Sullivan, Lewis, & Alessandri, 1992). Thus, the infants appeared to experience the two situations in much the same way adults would. Nevertheless, researchers cannot be certain that babies' affective responses are identical to those of adults, and we clearly have more to learn in this area (Saarni et al., 2008).

In the middle of the second year, infants become increasingly aware of themselves. We can see such self-awareness in their ability to recognize pictures of themselves or their reflection in a mirror (Lewis & Ramsay, 2004). (We discuss the development of a sense of self in Chapter 13.) As their sense of self emerges, a set of *secondary emotions* develops (Lewis, 2008b). These "self-conscious" emotions initially include *embarrassment*, *empathy*, and *jealousy*. Embarrassment is related to a feeling of exposure and is reflected in repeatedly looking away, often accompanied by a shy smile (Lewis, 2008a). Empathy is the ability to vicariously experience another's emotional state or reaction, particularly distress. Rudimentary signs of empathy can be seen early in infancy when some infants cry in response to the crying of another (Hoffman, 2008). However, it is not until infants acquire a sense of self that they are able to realize that the distress of others is not their own. (We discuss the development of empathy in children in Chapter 14.) Jealousy also emerges in the second year of life. One situation in which jealousy can often be seen in young children is when a parent directs more attention to a sibling. For example, many firstborn children show jealousy upon the arrival of a newborn younger sibling with whom they must now share the attention of their parents (Howe, Ross, & Recchia, 2011). (We discuss children's relations with their siblings in Chapter 15.)

Links to Related Material

Here, you learn about the emergence of self-conscious emotions. In Chapter 13, you will learn about the child's developing sense of self.

Links to Related Material

In this chapter, you learn about early signs of empathy in children. In Chapter 14, you will learn about the stages children pass through as empathy develops.

Links to Related Material

In this section, you learn about the emergence of jealously in children. In Chapter 15, you will learn more about both the negative as well as the positive aspects of sibling relationships.

Later, as children develop the ability to compare themselves to a standard, some time between 2 and 3 years of age, another set of secondary emotions—"self-conscious evaluative" emotions—emerges. These include *shame*, *guilt*, and *pride*. As Lewis (2008b) points out, these emotions require the ability to compare one's behaviour to a standard. These standards can be external rules and expectations, such as those imposed by parents, or they can be children's own internal expectations of themselves. Failure to meet the standard results in feelings of shame and guilt, whereas successfully meeting the standard results in feelings of pride.

SOCIALIZATION OF EMOTIONS The emergence of emotions in infancy is guided primarily by biological processes and is universal across cultures (Izard, 1995). However, even in early infancy, this development is shaped by cultural practices (Saarni et al., 2008). In cultures where infants are in nearly constant physical contact with caregivers, they have little need to express their emotions. For example, among the Inuit of Arctic Quebec, infants are almost always found in a pouch inside their mother's parka. Under these circumstances, the infant's small postural changes or movements are sufficient to elicit a response from caregivers. Indeed, observers often remark on how little infants cry in communities where they are constantly held (Crago, 1988).

Modelling is another way in which emotions are socialized. Most mothers, for example, display only a few facial expressions to their babies, most of which are positive (Malatesta, 1985). The babies, in turn, tend to match these expressions (Haviland & Lelwica, 1987). This is particularly true in Japan, where the expression of negative emotion is discouraged. Japanese parents model restraint of emotion, and actively avoid confrontations and contests of will in which negative emotions are likely to be expressed. When Japanese parents do oppose their children, they tend to express it indirectly via silence, indifference, or shunning (Azuma, 1996; Lebra, 1994; Miyake et al., 1986).

Inuit mothers are in nearly constant physical contact with their babies, and as a result the babies rarely need to cry. *(Jeff McIntoch/ The Canadian Press)*

Socialization of emotions also occurs through reinforcement processes. In face-to-face interactions with their babies, mothers more often respond positively to their babies' expressions of positive emotions than to displays of negative emotions (Thompson & Meyer, 2007). This process—perhaps in combination with the modelling just described—may be one reason that infants' positive emotional signals typically increase while their negative responses decrease over the course of the first year (Malatesta et al., 1989).

Older infants and preschoolers generally learn to identify and label their emotions through conversations with parents about feelings and through everyday experiences (Thompson & Meyer, 2007). Many parents talk frequently with their children about emotions, pointing out how a child is feeling (e.g., "You seem to be angry with Mommy" or "That baby must be feeling upset about dropping her ice cream cone") or the implications of the child's actions on the feelings of others (e.g., "You made your little brother sad") (Harris, 2008).

At first, children's affective expressions closely mirror their emotions. But over time, they increasingly learn to control their affective displays so that what they express may not necessarily reflect what they are actually feeling. Why would children attempt to mask their feelings? Saarni and colleagues (2008) describe four broad categories of reasons reported by children: to avoid negative outcomes; to protect self-esteem; out of a concern for others' feelings and their well-being; and to fit with norms and conventions. Many of these reasons reflect children's increasing awareness of the emotional **display rules** of their culture—the expectations or attitudes regarding the expression of affect. Children begin to show an understanding of such display rules as early as age 2 (Lewis & Michaelson, 1985). For example, boys may learn that displaying fear or pain is not seen as appropriate, so they often try to inhibit such expressions of emotion.

Display rules The expectations and attitudes a society holds toward the expression of affect.

For Thought and Discussion

What emotional display rules were part of your socialization as a child in your family? How do you think your experiences with display rules affected your social and emotional development?

How parents respond to young children's emotional reactions can influence children's ability to control or *regulate* their emotional reactions. Negative parental responses, such as reactions that are punitive or dismissing, can interfere with children's ability to regulate emotional arousal and can actually increase their arousal and emotional dysregulation (Denham, Bassett, & Wyatt, 2007; Moore, 2011). By contrast, warm parental responses help reduce emotional arousal. Responses that are supportive and comforting give the message that parents are sensitive to and accepting of the child's feelings and open to discussing them (Eisenberg et al., 1996; Moore, 2011).

Supportive and comforting parental responses help children manage negative emotional reactions. (© *Karen Struthers/iStock*)

Thompson and Meyer (2007) describe a number of ways in which parents help their children manage negative emotional arousal. Parents may distract children's attention from frightening or frustrating situations or alter their interpretation of the situation (e.g., saying something like "It's just a story!"). In addition, parents may problem-solve with their child, suggesting alternative, more adaptive ways to react (e.g., asking for an adult's intervention rather than hitting a child who is annoying them). Such positive and sensitive parental responses can help children find ways to cope with negative emotional arousal, foster positive feelings about themselves, and increase their skill at understanding emotions (Moore, 2011; Thompson, 2008; Thompson & Meyer, 2007).

RECOGNIZING EMOTIONS Just as the baby influences the mother through the display of affective responses, the mother can influence the baby. But before this form of regulation can occur, the baby must be able to recognize and interpret the mother's responses, a task that is more difficult than simply producing one's own expressions of emotion (Denham, 1998).

An infant's ability to recognize facial expressions of emotion seems to develop in stages (Baldwin & Moses, 1996; Nelson, 1987; Walker-Andrews, 1997). Babies younger than 6 weeks are not very good at scanning faces for detail. As a result, they do not recognize different emotional expressions (Field & Walden, 1982). Soon after, however, infants begin to show evidence of discriminating facial expressions of emotions. For example, babies who have been habituated to a photo of a smiling face show renewed attention when the photo is changed to one depicting a frowning face (Barrera & Maurer, 1981a). Babies of this age discriminate even better when they view talking faces displaying various emotions—although under these circumstances the voice may also provide important cues (Caron, Caron, & MacLean, 1988).

But do babies in this second stage have any real understanding of the emotions that are being expressed? Probably not. It is more likely that they simply can tell that the faces look different, without appreciating that a sad look represents unhappiness or a smiling face joy (Widen & Russell, 2008). Once infants reach 5 to 6 months of age, however, they appear to develop a clearer understanding of the meanings of emotional expressions. This is shown, for example, by the fact that at this age, babies begin to display the same emotion as displayed on the face they are viewing (smiling at a happy face) and prefer some emotional expressions to others (Balaban, 1995; Haviland & Lelwica, 1987; Ludemann, 1991; Widen & Russell, 2008).

Near the end of the first year, infants begin to use information about other people's emotional expressions to regulate their own behaviour—the social referencing process described in Chapter 7 (Feinman et al., 1992; Laible & Thompson, 2007; Thompson, 2006). Babies are especially likely to look to their mothers or fathers for this type of guidance when they are uncertain about what to do next, such as when they encounter an unfamiliar object or person. They then use the parent's expression as a guide to how to react in the situation.

In a study that illustrates this process very clearly, 1-year-old infants and their mothers were studied as they interacted on the visual-cliff apparatus described in Chapter 7. (Recall that in the visual-cliff procedure, infants are placed on a glass-covered table, near an apparent drop off. By 9 months of age, most babies show fear and are unwilling to cross over the deep side of the cliff.) The baby was placed on the shallow side, and the mother and an attractive toy were positioned at the deep end. This situation produced uncertainty in the infants, who generally responded cautiously and frequently looked up at their mothers as if attempting to gain information as to how to respond. The mothers were trained to produce a number of affective facial expressions, including fear, happiness, anger, interest, and sadness.

Links to Related Material

In Chapter 7, you read about how the visual-cliff procedure is used to study perception in infants. Here, you learn more about how social information from the parents can influence an infant's behaviour during this procedure.

The question of interest to the researchers was whether the mother's expression would regulate the infant's behaviour on the visual cliff. The results indicate that it did. When the mother expressed joy or interest, most babies crossed over to the deeper side to reach her. If she expressed fear or anger, however, very few of them ventured onto the deep portion of the apparatus (Sorce et al., 1985). Similar results have been found when mothers were instructed to express different emotions toward an unfamiliar person or a new toy—babies' willingness to approach and interact with the person or toy depended on the nature of the mother's reaction—both her facial expression and her vocal intonation (Baldwin & Moses, 1994; Boccia & Campos, 1989; Mumme, Fernald, & Herrera, 1996). Thus, babies as young as 1 year old appear to be able to use another person's emotional reactions as a gauge for understanding the environment and adjusting to it.

Research has found that infants may bring some awareness of the social context into play in social-referencing situations, and this ability develops across the first year of life. For example, when presented with the ambiguous novel stimulus of a barking toy dog, 10-month-olds were likely to look at their mothers' faces only if the mother was attending to them, whereas 7-month-olds did not make this distinction (Striano & Rochat, 2000).

Finally, mothers have been shown to use the infant's tendency for social referencing to their advantage. In a study examining the emergence of emotions, mothers were asked how they usually responded when an event—such as abruptly encountering an unfamiliar animal or hearing a loud sound—caused their baby to display surprise. Many mothers reported that immediately after exhibiting surprise, the baby appeared for a moment to be uncertain as to how to respond and then entered a state of either joy or distress. If during that brief moment the mother communicated a positive reaction to the infant, perhaps by smiling or speaking in a pleasant voice, the baby's response was more likely to be a pleasant one and distress was avoided (Klinnert

FOCUS ON RESEARCH 12.1
CHILDREN'S ABILITY TO RECOGNIZE EMOTIONS FROM FACES

The research described so far in this chapter has reviewed the very beginning of emotion recognition. With increasing age, children become able to impute much more specific meaning to facial expressions. Two-year-old children can categorize the facial expressions of basic emotions at a better-than-chance level when they are asked to choose which of two alternative facial expressions depicts a particular emotion (Russell & Bullock, 1985). The ability to categorize facial expressions improves substantially during childhood. By around the age of 10, children can recognize most basic emotions at a level of accuracy comparable to that found in adults (Gross & Ballif, 1991).

Happiness, sadness, and anger are generally recognized earlier than disgust, surprise, and fear, while some distinctions between emotions seem to be particularly hard to make, even for school-age children. Pierre Gosselin, of the University of Ottawa, found that the poor performance of children in recognizing fear, surprise, and disgust results from some specific confusions (Gosselin, 2005; Gosselin & Pélissier, 1996; Gosselin & Larocque, 2000). Children often confuse surprise expressions with those of fear, and disgust expressions with those of anger (Gagnon, Gosselin, der Buhs, Larocque, & Milliard, 2010). According to Gosselin, these confusions result, at least in part, from limitations of the perceptual system in discriminating facial patterns. For example, fear and surprise share several facial features in the eye and forehead regions, making them more difficult to distinguish.

To test this hypothesis, Gosselin and Simard (1999) presented school-age children with pairs of photographs of fear and surprise, such as those shown in Figure 12.1. The pairs differed in the number of facial features distinguishing the two emotions. The researchers found that recognition accuracy was positively related to the number of differences between the various facial patterns. Specifically, performances were better when judgments were based on photographs from the first row of Figure 12.1, rather than on those of the two other rows.

However, perceptual limitation is not the only explanation that accounts for the confusion between emotions. James Russell investigated children's use of verbal labels when instructed to categorize facial expressions. His research suggests that confusion between emotions might also arise from conceptual limitations in children's cognitive development. In a series of studies, Widen and Russell (2003) identified a systematic order in the emergence of verbal labels, and found that the words "scared" and "surprised" are not completely differentiated before the age of 5, while the word "disgusted" is not conceptually differentiated from the other terms describing negative emotions before the age of 6.

FIGURE 12.1

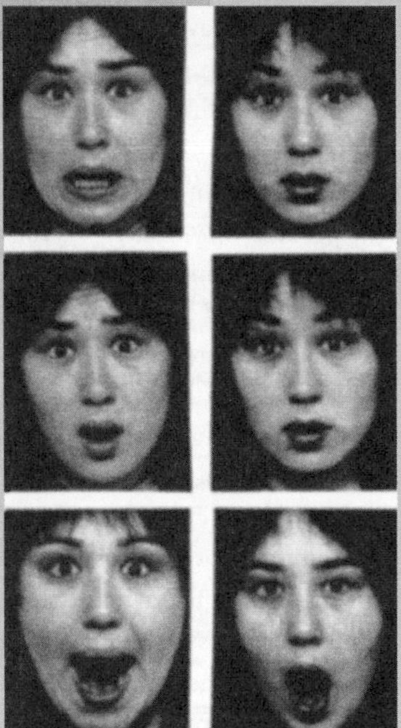

Photographs of one model showing the three contrasts shown to participants. Fear patterns appear at left and surprise patterns at right. In the first contrast (first row), both patterns include the raising of the brows, the raising of the upper eyelid, and the opening of the mouth. However the fear pattern includes two additional action units: the lowering of the brows and the stretching of the lip. In the second contrast (second row), both patterns include the raising of the brows, the raising of the upper eyelid, and the opening of the mouth. The fear pattern includes one additional action unit: the lowering of the brows. In the third contrast (third row), both patterns include the raising of the upper eyelid and the opening of the mouth. The fear patterns include one additional action unit: the stretching of the lip. *Photographs from Glles Kirouac. Copyright from the* Journal of Genetic Psychology, *1999, 160(2), 186 (Figure 1), published by Heldref Publications, 1319 Eighteenth Street, NW, Washington, DC. Fax (202) 296-5149.*

et al., 1984). This study and others suggest that mothers intuitively understand (or perhaps have learned through experience) that their babies look to them when feeling uncertain and that they have some ability to influence the infants' responses to the situation (Hornik & Gunnar, 1988). See *Focus on Research 12.1* for a discussion of children's ability to recognize emotions from faces.

FACE-TO-FACE INTERACTIONS

During the first three or four months of life, much of the infant's contact with the caregiver involves face-to-face interactions, such as those that occur during feeding, diapering, and, in some cultures, play. Psychologists have come to attach considerable significance to these early interactions, believing that they are fundamental to the development of an effective communication system between mother and baby, and ultimately to the development of a strong attachment relationship (Brazelton & Yogman, 1986; Isabella, 1993, 1994).

Researchers can closely investigate these early dyadic interactions in laboratory settings. The baby and mother sit facing each other, with the mother typically instructed to play with the infant in her normal fashion. As they interact, one camera records the caregiver's face, and another records the baby's. By replaying the two recordings side by side—often comparing only one frame at a time—investigators can examine the interactions in great detail. This technique, known as **microanalysis**, has helped reveal the subtle ways in which infant and caregiver influence one another (Beebe et al., 2010; Kaye, 1982; Lamb, Thompson, & Frodi, 1982). Study of these early interactions has revealed two principal features characteristic of both newborn behaviour in general and caregiver–infant dyadic exchanges in particular: cycles and patterns.

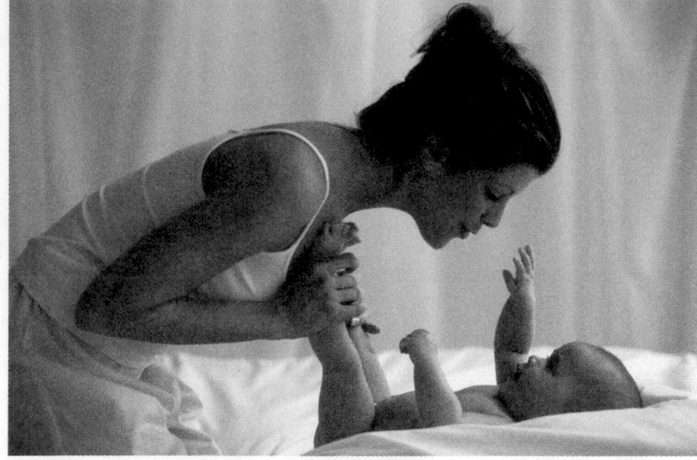

Face-to-face interactions during the early months appear to play an important role in the development of infant–caregiver attachment. (*Purestock*)

Microanalysis A research technique for studying dyadic interactions, in which two individuals are simultaneously video recorded with different cameras and then the tapes are examined side-by-side.

CAREGIVER–INFANT INTERACTION CYCLES Newborns appear to cycle from states of attention and interest to states of inattention and avoidance. During the attention phase, they make eye contact with the caregiver and often display positive affect, such as by smiling and vocalizing, whereas during the inattention phase they avoid eye contact and are more likely to show distress. Some psychologists believe that periods of attention can become too arousing and stressful for infants, and that infants keep this stimulation under control by turning away and perhaps by self-comforting, for instance, by putting the thumb in the mouth (Field, 1987; Gianino & Tronick, 1988). Early face-to-face interactions are important because they reveal the baby's capability for emotion regulation, whereby the infant increases positive feelings and decreases negative feelings by adjusting his or her behaviour (Thompson, Flood, & Lundquist, 1995; Thompson & Meyer, 2007).

CAREGIVER–INFANT INTERACTION PATTERNS Early interactions produce patterns of behaviour between the caregiver and the infant. As the caregiver comes to recognize the baby's cycles of attention and inattention, she adjusts her behaviour to them. Microanalytic studies of caregiver–infant interaction during the first four months have shown that caregivers gradually learn to concentrate their affective displays (talking, tickling, and smiling) during those times when the baby is attending to them. When the baby looks away, the caregiver's responses decline. Soon, the infant and caregiver develop an **interactional synchrony** in behaviour so that they are both "on" or both "off" at about the same time (Jaffe, 2001; Saarni et al., 2008). In this way, the caregiver maximizes her opportunities to "teach" the baby, and the baby can regulate the amount of interaction that takes place.

Interactional synchrony The smooth intermeshing of behaviours between caregiver and baby.

Once a synchronous pattern has developed between caregiver and baby, a second pattern begins to emerge. The caregiver waits for the baby to respond, and then she responds back. Sometimes these responses are imitative (the caregiver produces the same sound that the baby has just made), sometimes they are repetitive (she wiggles the baby's toes after each response), and sometimes they take other forms. But all of them serve to "answer" the infant's responses. This *turn-taking* pattern between caregivers and babies may represent the first conversational "dialogues," which later become more obvious as speech and language develop (Beebe et al., 1988, 2010; Masataka, 1993; Mayer & Tronick, 1985). Babies appear to enjoy turn-taking episodes, often displaying a good deal of smiling and positive vocalizations (Tronick, 2005).

Investigators have explored how individual differences among infants produce variation in mother–infant interactive behaviours. In one study, mothers were observed interacting with their

Links to Related Material

In Chapter 5, you read about infants' arousal states. Here, you learn more about how parents use these states to time their interactions with infants during periods of alertness.

Affect mirroring The degree to which caregivers gauge their communicative behaviours to respond to input from their infants.

For Thought and Discussion

Based on your observations or experience, in what ways is the process of parent–child interaction both bidirectional and transactional?

2- and 3-month-old babies, and researchers noted their levels of **affect mirroring**, or the degree to which they gauged their communicative behaviours to respond to input from their infants (Legerstee & Varghese, 2001). Infant behaviour patterns corresponded to the level of maternal affect mirroring, with the infants of mothers high in this measure displaying more positive affect, attention toward their mothers, and social expectancy (preference for responsive input, smiles, and the like) than infants of mothers low in affect mirroring.

WHEN INTERACTION IS DISRUPTED What happens when face-to-face interactions are disrupted? A revealing experimental technique (Figure 12.2) involves having the mother present the baby with no expression at all. The results of this *still-face paradigm* have been fairly consistent across a number of studies (Adamson & Frick, 2003; Bertin & Striano, 2006; Mesman et al., 2009). Generally, babies initially attempt to engage the mother's attention, sometimes by pointing, vocalizing, or looking at her inquisitively. When the mother fails to respond, the infants usually begin to show signs of distress and protest, they reduce their overall level of positive affect, and often gaze in a different direction. These findings are consistent with the belief that the infant and mother develop an interaction pattern within the first few months that becomes comfortable for both of them. When one member of the pair (in this case, the mother) violates that pattern, however, the system is disrupted, and the other member (here, the baby) has difficulty coping with the new interactional style.

The importance of a smooth-running pattern of infant–caregiver interactions can also be seen in studies with mothers who are clinically depressed. These mothers have been found to be much less positive or responsive to their babies, and they do not synchronize well with the infants' behaviours. The babies, in turn, are less active and attentive and spend much of their time crying or displaying other forms of distress (Jung et al., 2007; Tronick, 2008). Importantly, however, such infants do not display this sort of behaviour with their nursery teachers (Pelaez-Nogueras et al.,

FIGURE 12.2

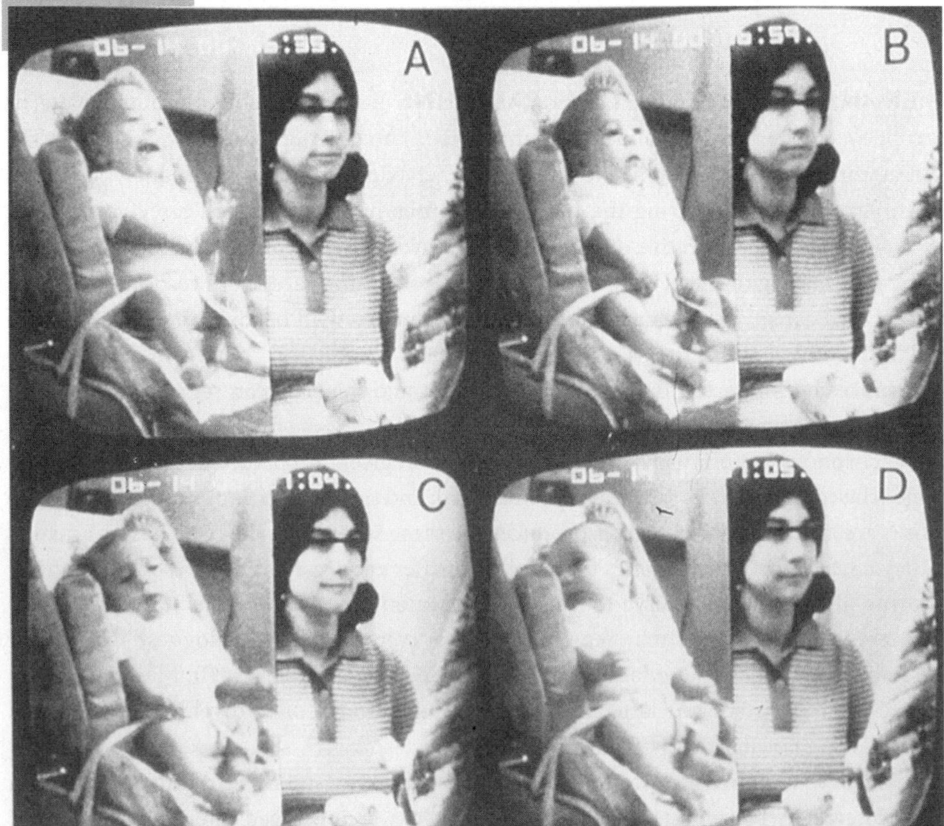

Still-face paradigm. In (a) the infant actively greets the mother, but the mother maintains a blank facial expression. In (b) the infant notices the mother's failure to respond and attempts to gain her attention. When the attempt doesn't work, in (c) the infant shows signs of distress and protest, and turns away. Finally, in (d) the infant turns fully away from the mother. Usually, the infant will repeat the cycle several times in an attempt to engage the mother. *Source: Tronick, E. (2009). Social interaction. In J. B. Benson & M. M. Haith (Eds.)* Social and emotional development in infancy and early childhood *(pp. 429-436). New York: Academic Press.*

1994), suggesting that it is, indeed, the absence of a synchronous relationship with the caregiver that causes the infants to respond in this way. Moreover, researchers at the University of Alberta and the University of New Brunswick (Jung, Short, Letourneau, & Andrews, 2007) have found that teaching depressed mothers to better respond to their infants can alleviate some of these effects.

Disruptions in face-to-face interactions can also occur if the baby is premature. Studies have shown that preterm babies spend more time asleep, are less alert and responsive when awake, smile less and are more irritable (Goldberg & DiVitto, 2002), are more quickly overaroused by social stimulation, and spend more time averting their gaze from the caregiver. In turn, their mothers spend less time in face-to-face interaction with them, smile at and touch them less, are less skilled at reading their emotional signals, and engage in fewer episodes of turn-taking with them (Goldberg & DiVitto, 2002; Kropp & Haynes, 1987; Lester, Hoffman, & Brazelton, 1985; Malatesta et al., 1986). Recent studies indicate, however, that encouraging mothers to hold their preterm infants can stimulate face-to-face interactions (Goldberg & DiVitto, 2002). With time, preterm babies appear to catch up, and by 8 months of age engage in as much face-to-face contact as did full-term infants at 4 months of age (Goldberg & DiVitto, 2002). Moreover, it is important to point out that prematurity does not necessarily prevent the development of a secure attachment relationship (Goldberg & DiVitto, 2002; van IJzendoorn et al., 1992).

LEARNING OBJECTIVE 12.2

Understand the development of early communication between the infant and caregiver.

1. Is crying a form of communication?
2. Trace the development of the expression and understanding of emotions in children.
3. What effect do face-to-face interactions have on infants' emotional development?

TEMPERAMENT

Learning Objective 12.3

Define temperament and describe its role in child development.

The child's role in infant–caregiver interactions is greatly influenced by his or her personality. For example, mothers often respond differently to happy, friendly babies who like to cuddle than to fussy, irritable babies who squirm when held. For infants, personality does not yet include many components that are evident later on, such as beliefs, attitudes, and values. For this reason, the study of infant personality is generally restricted to emotional expressiveness and responsiveness to environmental stimulation. These components of personality are called **temperament** (Rothbart & Bates, 2006).

Temperament The aspect of personality studied in infants, which includes their emotional expressiveness and responsiveness to stimulation.

Temperament is meant to describe the baby's behavioural style, reflecting not so much *what* babies do as *how* they do it. For example, two babies may both enjoy riding in a mechanical swing, but one may react exuberantly, shrieking with delight, whereas the other may remain calm and even fall asleep. Most researchers view temperament as simply one of the many individual differences, or traits, that make each child unique (Bates & Wachs, 1994).

DEFINING TEMPERAMENT

Psychologists' definitions of temperament vary considerably (Goldsmith et al., 1987). We begin, therefore, simply by considering three questions that have guided their attempts to define this concept.

IS TEMPERAMENT INHERITED? A fundamental question is whether babies inherit their response styles, just as they inherit the shapes of their noses or the colour of their hair. There is considerable support for this idea.

We saw in Chapter 3 that studies comparing identical twins with fraternal twins provide strong evidence that at least some portion of temperament is transferred through the genes. Research shows that identical twins are more similar to each other than fraternal twins on a variety of behavioural measures, ranging from descriptions by parents of the baby's irritability, to ratings by trained observers of the child's reactions to strangers, to laboratory tests of the infant's fear responses on the visual-cliff apparatus. Twin studies have also found genetic effects in temperament traits among toddlers and preschoolers (Emde et al., 1992; Goldsmith, Buss, & Lemery, 1997; Plomin et al., 1993; Robinson et al., 1992).

IS TEMPERAMENT STABLE? Regardless of the origins of temperament, another theoretical question is whether it remains constant over the years. Does the fearful baby who cries at an unfamiliar face at 6 months of age also shy away from new people at 20 months and avoid playmates at 42 months? This kind of stability over time and across situations has traditionally been viewed as an important defining component of responses that reflect temperament.

Research suggests that certain aspects of infants' behavioural style do indeed remain reasonably stable over time. A longitudinal study over seven years found that observational assessment of infant temperament was related to parent reports of the children's temperaments at age 7 on several dimensions: fear, frustration-anger, and approach tendencies (Rothbart, Derryberry, & Hershey, 2000). Other research suggests a link between early and later negative emotionality (such as fear or fussiness), reactions to new situations or people, and attention span (Guerin & Gottfried, 1994; Pedlow et al., 1993; Ruddy, 1993). Not all measures of temperament, however, display this sort of stability.

The question of stability—or lack thereof—has been of interest to both nature and nurture theorists (Hooker et al., 1987). Those who favour a genetic model of temperament argue that when some aspect of a child's response style is found to be stable across years, this stability is most easily explained by assuming that the trait is simply part of the child's genetic structure. Environmentalists, however, contend that such stability could just as easily result from the child's remaining in a fairly constant environment (Bates, 1987; Rothbart & Bates, 2006; Wachs, 1988).

Lack of stability in temperament likewise can be handled by both nature and nurture models. Changes in behavioural style obviously could result from changes in the child's environment. But studies by Warren Eaton (1994), of the University of Manitoba, have also shown that genetically related children tend to show similar *patterns of change* in some temperamental behaviours, which could mean that temperament develops according to some genetic plan (see also Matheny, 1989). More research on this issue is needed.

IS TEMPERAMENT EVIDENT EARLY IN LIFE? A third important question in defining temperament is whether the child's response style is apparent from very early on. Again, the evidence is mixed. Research has found that certain characteristics of the fetus—such as heart rate and activity level—are reasonably stable during the last months of pregnancy, and are also fairly good predictors of how the mother later rates her infant's temperament (DiPietro et al., 1996b, 2002; Eaton & Saudino, 1992). These data seem to suggest that temperament begins in the womb. However, only some of the temperamental differences among newborns—usually those involving irritability and other forms of negative responding—are still observable after several years (Plomin et al., 1993; Riese, 1987; Stifter & Fox, 1990; Worobey & Blajda, 1989); many early differences disappear.

In sum, although many psychologists believe that temperamental behaviours are genetic, stable, and apparent early, not all agree. And the research evidence at this point does not settle the issue.

CONCEPTUALIZING TEMPERAMENT

Since systematic studies of infant temperament began in the middle of the 20th century, researchers have focused on different answers to the question of how best to conceptualize temperament. In this section, we examine three models of temperament and then describe some research concerning the physiological processes involved.

AN EARLY APPROACH: GOODNESS OF FIT The most widely used classification of temperament was developed in the 1950s by two pediatricians, Alexander Thomas and Stella Chess. An important overarching dimension identified by this pair concerns the **goodness of fit** between the baby's response style and his or her physical and social surroundings (Chess & Thomas, 1996; Thomas & Chess, 1977). The degree of goodness of fit determines the degree of influence of infant temperament on later development. This notion meshes well with the transactional view of early social development, and has become an important concept in temperament research (Sanson, Hemphill, & Smart, 2002; Seifer, 2000; Wachs, 1994; Windle & Lerner, 1986).

Goodness of fit A concept describing the relation between a baby's temperament and his or her social and environmental surroundings.

Thomas and Chess' research project, named the **New York Longitudinal Study (NYLS)**, continued for more than 40 years (Chess, 2005) and represents one of the most important longitudinal efforts in modern child psychology (Chess & Thomas, 1996; Thomas & Chess, 1986; Thomas, Chess, & Birch, 1968). The research began as an effort to predict children's psychological adjustment by identifying potential problems early. The strategy was to develop categories of infant temperament and then to examine whether these categories related to the child's social and emotional development at later ages. After extensive interviews with parents of infants, Thomas and Chess identified three clusters of characteristics that occurred frequently, leading them to conclude that they had identified three early behavioural styles. They labelled these styles "easy," "difficult," and "slow to warm up."

New York Longitudinal Study (NYLS) A well-known longitudinal project conducted in the United States by Thomas and Chess to study infant temperament and its implications for later psychological adjustment.

The *easy baby* is rhythmic and usually has regular patterns of eating, sleeping, and toileting. He or she adapts well to changing situations and generally has a positive, happy mood. Easy babies are willing to approach new objects or people, and their reactions (of all types) are typically of low to moderate intensity. Thomas and Chess found that about 40 percent of the babies they studied could be classified as this type.

The *difficult baby* is just the opposite. His or her schedules are less predictable, he or she is uncomfortable when situations change, and often cries or displays a negative mood. These babies also withdraw from new experiences and react intensely to most environmental stimulation. This pattern was evident in about 10 percent of the infants.

The *slow-to-warm-up baby,* too, adapts poorly to changing situations and tends to withdraw from unfamiliar people or objects. He or she is typically less active, however, and responds at a relatively low intensity. About 15 percent of the babies were classified as this type. (The remaining 35 percent of the infants in the project did not fit into any of these three categories.)

For Thought and Discussion

How would you characterize your temperament? Has it remained stable since you were a child? Which aspects, if any, have changed?

Although the NYLS approach remains a widely used method of categorizing infant temperament, it does have its critics. One problem is its heavy reliance on parental report as a means of obtaining information. Parents' descriptions of their babies' behaviour have the advantage of reflecting a wide range of behaviours and situations, but this method is also open to biases of several sorts (Kagan & Fox, 2006; Rothbart & Bates, 2008). Some parents are undoubtedly more objective than others, and some are better than others at observing and describing what their children do. Parents also may tend to report what they assume the researchers would like to hear, presenting, for example, a consistent description of the infant from one interview to the next, or portraying the child in a more positive than realistic light. And parents' descriptions sometimes reflect their own reactions to the infant's behaviour. Some parents, for example, might describe a response style as stubborn, while other parents would describe it as self-assured (Bates & Bayles, 1984; Kagan, 1994).

Links to Related Material

In Chapter 2, you read about some of the advantages and disadvantages of interview methods. Here, you learn more about how this method has been used to study infant temperament.

An alternative to the interview is the questionnaire, which asks parents to respond to a series of objective questions about the child's typical behaviour and reactions to situations. The best-known questionnaires have been designed according to the NYLS classification scheme (Carey & McDevitt, 1978; Fullard, McDevitt, & Carey, 1984; Medoff-Cooper, Carey, & McDevitt, 1993). Questionnaires offer the advantage of producing quantitative information that can be easily summarized and compared. But they suffer from some of the same potential biases as parent interviews, and they involve additional issues, including how well the parents understand the questions, how well they can compare their child with others (as some of the items require), and how they are feeling about the child when they fill out the instrument (Kagan & Fox, 2006; Mebert, 1991).

EAS MODEL Another popular method of classifying infant temperament was developed by a research team headed by Robert Plomin (Buss & Plomin, 1984, 1986). This model is strongly biological in its approach, viewing temperament as inherited personality traits that show an early onset.

According to these researchers, a baby's temperament can be measured along a few main dimensions. Because these theorists originally identified emotionality, activity, and sociability as the key components, this classification scheme has been commonly referred to as the **EAS model**. A fourth component, shyness, has often been included as well.

EAS model Plomin and Buss' theory of temperament, which holds that temperament can be measured along the dimensions of emotionality, activity, and sociability.

Emotionality in this model refers to how quickly a baby becomes aroused and responds negatively to stimulation from the environment. A baby rating high on this dimension, for example, would be awakened easily by a sudden noise and would cry intensely in reaction. Plomin believes that differences on this dimension represent inherited differences in infants' nervous systems, with some infants having a quicker "trigger" and automatically experiencing greater arousal than others. During the first few months of life, emotionality is revealed through general distress reactions (such as crying) in unpleasant situations. Later in the first year, emotionality begins to evolve toward either fear or anger responses. Which behavioural style develops, Plomin contends, depends on the infant's experiences.

Activity describes the baby's tempo and energy use. Babies rating high on this dimension are moving all the time, exploring new places, and frequently seeking out vigorous activities. Like most definitions of temperamental traits, this one describes only how the baby behaves and not precisely what the baby likes to do. The researchers use the analogy of the controls of an automobile: the activity level presumably determines how fast the infant can go, but the environment determines the direction that the infant will take.

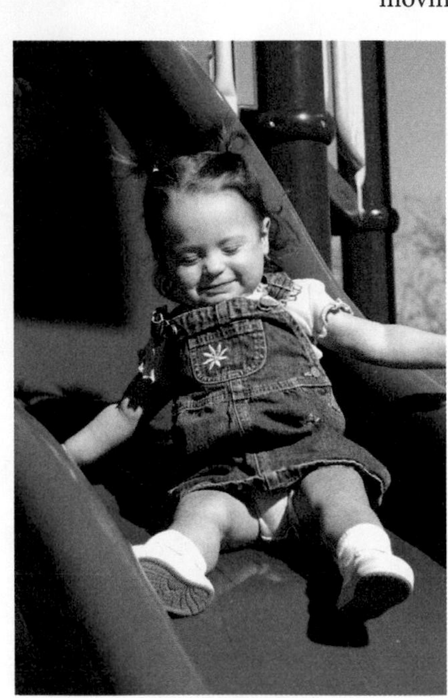

Babies rating high in the *activity* dimension are constantly seeking out vigorous activities and exploring new places. (© *Thomas Polen/iStock*)

Sociability refers to an infant's preference for being with other people. Babies rating high on this dimension do not like to spend time alone and often initiate contact and interaction with others. This trait is not meant to describe the closeness of a baby's relationship with the caregiver or other significant people, which is assumed to be influenced by the child's experiences. It is simply a measure of how much a given child innately prefers the stimulation derived from people rather than from things, and it is perhaps most clearly assessed in the baby's reactions to unfamiliar people when the strength of a prior relationship does not come into play.

Finally, *shyness* refers to the child's response to unfamiliar persons, both at home and elsewhere. It is more a measure of wariness than of social activity, which is what the sociability scale measures. Researchers have supported the inclusion of separate subscales for shyness and sociability (Boer & Westenberg, 1994) and have found evidence for the stability of the EAS-based temperament measures from ages 18 months through 50 months (Mathiesen & Tambs, 1999).

Although the EAS model views temperament as a biological concept, the researchers are interactionist in their conception of social development. In their view, although the baby's levels of key temperamental characteristics may be determined by genes, the baby's overall social development will depend on how these characteristics interact with characteristics of the social and physical environment.

The EAS Temperament Survey is used to measure temperament according to this model. This is typically a written questionnaire, completed by a child's parents, that asks about the child's behavioural patterns.

ROTHBART'S MODEL A third model of temperament has been proposed by Mary Rothbart. This model also has a strong biological flavour, viewing temperament as reflecting inborn differences in infants' physiological functioning. It, too, employs a parent questionnaire to assess an infant's temperament, although this information is supplemented by laboratory measures and by data collected in the home by professional observers (Goldsmith & Rothbart, 1991). Rothbart views temperament as consisting of individual differences in two areas—reactivity and self-regulation (Rothbart & Bates, 2008).

Reactivity is similar to Plomin's dimension of emotionality in that it refers to how easily and intensely a baby responds to stimulation. The major difference is that Rothbart also includes positive arousal, as illustrated by a baby's smiling and laughing at a new toy.

The other component of temperament according to this model is the baby's ability to increase or reduce this reactivity. This ability, termed *self-regulation*, is assumed to be inborn and to vary from child to child. Control of arousal by infants can take a number of forms, such as how long a baby looks at a stimulating object before turning away, or how he or she approaches and explores it. The specific behaviours used for self-regulation change as the baby gets older, but the underlying temperamental trait presumably determines the infant's success in achieving it (Rothbart & Posner, 1985).

Like the schemes previously described, Rothbart's model is interactionist. Even though the reactivity and self-regulation abilities of babies differ from birth, the child's caregivers and physical surroundings are assumed to play major roles in determining the path that development will take.

AN EMPHASIS ON PHYSIOLOGICAL PROCESSES

Some investigators have focused on physiological contributions to temperament and have de-emphasized the role of environmental factors. Of particular interest have been individual differences in *stress reactivity*, which is often evidenced by increased levels of the hormone cortisol (Gunnar & Quevedo, 2007). For example, high cortisol response has been found to be associated with being prone to distress at various points during the first 12 months of life (Gunnar et al., 1989, 1992, 1996). Similarly, high cortisol response to stressors may be associated with high emotionality (Ramsay & Lewis, 2001).

Extremely shy and inhibited children show indications of greater stress reactivity even in infancy, as can be seen in the distress of this infant as her mother leaves her at the daycare. (*Banana Stock*)

Overall, researchers interested in the physiological aspects of temperament have focused on negative emotionality. Researchers tend to agree that extremely shy and inhibited children show greater stress reactivity, indications of which are present early in infancy (Kagan & Snidman, 2004; Rosenbaum et al., 1993; Schmidt & Fox, 1998; Schmidt et al., 1997, 1999). We return to the topic of inhibition later in this section. Evidence is also mounting that stress reactivity may be related to aggression; to extroverted, sensation-seeking behaviours; and to low self-control (Dettling, Gunnar, & Donzella, 1999; Gunnar et al., 1997; Tout et al., 1998).

Of course, an important issue relevant to any research on physiology and temperament concerns the direction of causation. Are rises in cortisol, for example, a cause of the behaviours that constitute temperament, or are they simply markers of a child's temperamental tendencies?

TEMPERAMENT AND SOCIAL INTERACTIONS

Although, as noted, physiological responses have been the focus of some researchers, most researchers who study temperament have at least some appreciation for the interactional role of temperament and early social development. An infant's social interactions are influenced not only by personality, but also by the degree to which these characteristics match the demands or expectations of the environment (Putnam, Sanson, & Rothbart, 2002; Sanson & Rothbart, 1995). For example, if a mother's personality is very methodical, she may have considerable difficulty with a baby whose behavioural style is irregular and unpatterned. As a result, she may frequently attempt to do certain things, such as feed or put the baby down for a nap, when the child is not interested, perhaps producing repeated conflict and tension for both of them. That same baby, however, may develop a smoother relationship with a mother whose own behaviour is not very structured. A mismatch can similarly occur with the physical environment. A baby who has a high activity level, for example, may have trouble living in a small apartment, and a baby who has a low threshold for distraction may not do well in a noisy neighbourhood.

The quality of children's social interactions, as we have seen, can also affect their cognitive development. Thus, the temperamental characteristics of the child come into play in this area of development as well. One research team found that when mothers viewed their infants as having a more difficult temperament, they tended to provide them with fewer learning and discovery opportunities during their daily interactions (Gauvain & Fagot, 1995). Importantly, follow-up observations at age 5 revealed that these children did not perform as well on tasks involving cognitive problem solving (Fagot & Gauvain, 1997).

The interactional model of temperament and social relationships has implications for the role that infant personality may play in the attachment process, too. We consider this issue later in the chapter.

TEMPERAMENT AND BEHAVIOUR PROBLEMS

We mentioned earlier that the NYLS project was motivated by the search for early predictors of children's psychological adjustment. Other investigators have taken a similar clinical approach to investigations of temperament. Most of this work has focused on two categories of infant personality: the level of difficulty and the level of inhibition (Bates, Wachs, & Emde, 1994; Newman et al., 1997).

DIFFICULT INFANTS Thomas and Chess reported early in their longitudinal study that babies classified as difficult displayed more behavioural problems during early childhood than did infants in the other categories (Thomas, Chess, & Birch, 1968). This finding spurred a number of investigations aimed at determining whether this classification scheme might serve as an early screening device for identifying children at risk for later problems (Rothbart, Posner, & Hershey, 1995).

Interestingly, in a follow-up of their original longitudinal subjects, Thomas and Chess (1984) indicated that the majority of those who displayed temperamental difficulties during early childhood showed no evidence of these difficulties by early adulthood. Others have reported similar findings (Korn, 1984; Lee & Bates, 1985). Nevertheless, it is useful to ask whether assessments of a difficult temperament during infancy and early childhood correlate positively with reports of behaviour and adjustment problems in later childhood, adolescence, or even adulthood. Some studies have indeed reported such correlations (e.g., Bates et al., 1991; Caspi et al., 1995, 1996; Goldsmith et al., 2001; Halverson & Deal, 2001; Rothbart, Ahadi, & Hershey, 1994; Tubman et al., 1992). But exactly why difficult infants tend to develop these sorts of problems later on remains unresolved.

One possibility is that those aspects of the baby's temperament that produce the classification of difficult infants, such as frequent crying and irritability, increase the chances that parents will respond to the infant in a less than optimal manner, leading to problems in the child–caregiver relationship and ultimately to behaviour problems in the child. This explanation is related to the goodness-of-fit concept described earlier (Bates, 1990; Chess & Thomas, 1987).

A very different explanation is that the positive correlation lies primarily in the eyes of the beholders (that is, the parents). According to this analysis, the fact that some parents rate their babies as difficult and later report them as having behaviour problems results from the parents' attitudes, expectations, or approaches to child rearing, not from the child's characteristics (Garrison & Earls, 1987; Sanson, Prior, & Kyrios, 1990). Several studies, for example, have found that a baby's temperament during the first year—as measured by parent questionnaires—could be accurately predicted by assessment of the mother's personality characteristics and expectations when the child was still in the uterus (e.g., Diener, Goldstein, & Mangelsdorf, 1995; Mebert, 1989,1991; Vaughn et al., 1987).

Finally, having a "difficult" temperament—although perhaps posing certain long-term risks—nevertheless may afford children some ethological advantages. For example, a cross-cultural study of babies during a drought in East Africa found that those classified as difficult were most likely to survive, presumably because they were most demanding of attention and care from their mothers (DeVries & Sameroff, 1984).

Inhibition The tendency to quickly respond in a negative manner to an unfamiliar situation.

INHIBITED INFANTS Inhibition has been a focus of investigation by researchers for several years (Kagan & Fox, 2006; Kagan & Snidman, 2004). **Inhibition** can be defined as a tendency to quickly respond in a negative manner to an unfamiliar situation. For example, an inhibited baby would be cautious when presented with a toy very different from any previously encountered. As inhibited children approach 1 year of age, they become more timid, shy, and fearful, especially when encountering new situations or people (Schmidt & Fox, 1997). Like difficult babies, inhibited infants also are at risk for a variety of behaviour problems in later childhood and beyond (Kagan, 1997; Rubin & Asendorpf, 1993).

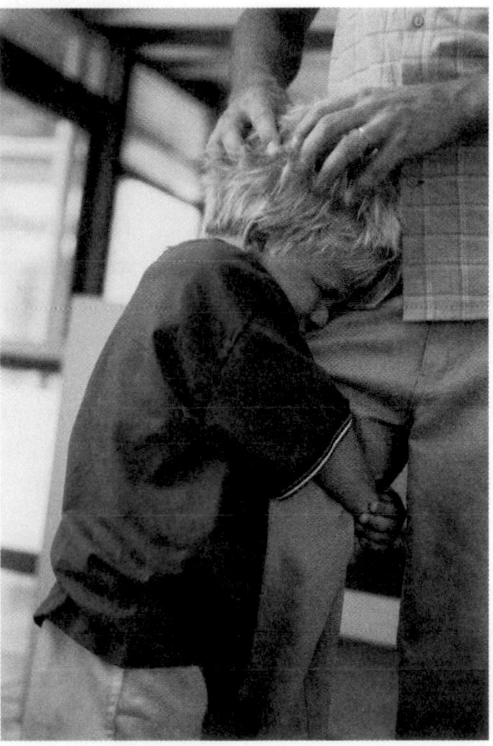

Inhibition is a fear of unfamiliarity that appears to have a biological basis, but it is likely also affected by socialization influences. (*Media Bakery*)

The best-known research on inhibited children has been conducted by Jerome Kagan and his colleagues (Kagan & Snidman, 2004; Kagan, 1994, 1998). Kagan's research has involved an impressive longitudinal study designed to determine whether certain behaviours and physiological responses of inhibited children display an early onset and are stable over childhood (Kagan, Snidman, & Arcus, 1992).

Kagan's approach was to first identify groups of 2-year-olds who were either very inhibited or very uninhibited. He did this by observing how a large group of children reacted in a laboratory setting with unfamiliar people or objects. About 15 percent of the children responded to the new situations in a very timid manner and were thus selected for study. The 15 percent who responded in the most outgoing and fearless manner comprised the uninhibited comparison group. The children were studied again at 5.5 years and at 7.5 years of age to see whether their early response styles were still apparent, as we would expect if inhibition is a stable trait (Reznick et al., 1986).

Two sorts of measurement were used. The first was a set of behavioural measures, including children's performance on a series of problem-solving tasks with an unfamiliar adult, their interactions with unfamiliar peers, and their social behaviour in school. On these measures, about 75 percent of the children who had been identified as inhibited or uninhibited displayed behaviours consistent with their classification even six years later. In addition, most of the inhibited children were found to have developed other fears or anxieties, such as fear of the dark or fear of going away to camp (Kagan, Reznick, Snidman, Gibbons, & Johnson, 1988). Moreover, in a follow-up study, Schwartz, Snidman, and Kagan (1999) found that those who had been inhibited as children were more likely at 12 to 14 years of age to display characteristics of social anxiety when interacting with a stranger.

Suspecting that inhibition might have a biological basis, the researchers also looked at a number of physiological responses (such as heart rate and pupil dilation) that are commonly associated with human stress reactions (Kagan, Reznick, & Snidman, 1987; Schmidt & Fox, 1997; Schwartz et al., 2003). The physiological data were reasonably consistent with the behavioural findings. Children identified at age 2 as being inhibited continued to show evidence of greater physiological arousal in new situations as second graders (Kagan, Reznick, & Snidman, 1988). These studies suggest that some timid children may be displaying a temperamental trait that is apparent from infancy, remains reasonably stable over the years, and has a biological basis (Kagan & Snidman, 2004). Findings in Sweden by other researchers support these conclusions (Broberg, Lamb, & Hwang, 1990; Kerr, Lambert, & Bem, 1996; Kerr et al., 1994).

Links to Related Material

In Chapter 15, you will read more about shy/withdrawn children, and the help that teachers and parents can provide to shy children.

Even if true, however, these results tell only part of the story. For example, only those children at the extremes of inhibition displayed the sort of stability that is presumed characteristic of a temperamental trait; the rest of the children's levels of inhibition varied considerably over time (Kagan, Reznick, & Gibbons, 1989; Reznick et al., 1989). And even within the extreme groups, some children's inhibition did not remain constant.

Shyness and timidity, like a difficult temperament, also can be influenced by factors related to experience and socialization. For instance, babies who display the negative emotionality characteristic of this trait during the early months are more likely to reduce their crying and fussing if their mothers are sensitive, responsive, and highly involved with them (Belsky, Fish, & Isabella, 1991; Matheny, 1986). We discuss shyness further in Chapter 15 in *Focus on Research 15.1*.

LEARNING OBJECTIVE 12.3

Define temperament and describe its role in child development.

1. What is temperament?
2. Outline three models of temperament.
3. Discuss how temperament may be related to children's social interactions.

Learning Objective 12.4

Explain the role of attachment in child development.

ATTACHMENT

We now come to the topic that is central to this chapter: How do parents and babies develop the intense emotional relationship that characterizes infancy and early childhood? We have seen that this process appears to be continuous, beginning with the earliest interactions between infants and their parents. In particular, the development of the affective system—which is at the heart of infant–caregiver mutual regulation—is important in setting the stage for the social relationship that is about to form. The baby's temperament undoubtedly plays a role in this process as well.

DEVELOPMENTAL COURSE OF ATTACHMENT

The infant's attachment to the caregiver can first be clearly observed at 6 to 8 months of age. However, the actual process begins shortly after birth and continues well beyond this time. Here, we describe the phases of attachment development that roughly correspond to those proposed in several theoretical models of this process (Bowlby, 1982; Schaffer & Emerson, 1964).

PHASE I (BIRTH TO 8–12 WEEKS): INDISCRIMINATE SOCIAL RESPONSIVENESS

At first, babies do not focus their attention exclusively on their parents and will at times respond positively to anyone. Nevertheless, they do behave in ways that are important for the development of an attachment relationship with the caregiver. Infants come into the world with a number of built-in responses that appear designed to draw the parents near (such as crying), and keep them close at hand (quieting and smiling, for example). And although babies in this stage may not reserve their sociability solely for the caregiver, they can recognize her in a number of ways. As we saw in Chapter 7, newborns prefer to look at their mother rather than at a stranger within only a few days of birth, even though their attention is directed to peripheral information like her hairline and the shape of her head (Bushnell, 2001). Moreover, they recognize and prefer the sound of her voice, a preference that can even be seen in full-term fetuses (Kisilevsky et al., 2003, 2009).

Caregivers, too, very quickly learn to recognize their babies. Within a day or two after giving birth, for example, mothers can identify their own children solely on the basis of smell (Bornstein, 2002; Kaitz et al., 1987) or by touching a hand or cheek (Kaitz et al., 1992, 1993).

An important difference, however, is that although the baby displays attachment only after several months have passed, the mother's emotional bond to the baby develops very quickly. Some believe that **maternal bonding** occurs during a sensitive period immediately following birth and is facilitated by skin-to-skin contact with the baby (Kennell, 2002; Klaus & Kennell, 1976; Klaus, Kennell, & Klaus, 1995). Based on this view, many hospitals and neonatal intensive care units have made it easier for mothers to spend more time with their newborns during the presumably crucial first hours and days of life.

Maternal bonding The mother's emotional attachment to the child, which appears shortly after birth and which some theorists believe develops through early contact during a sensitive period.

Research indicates that although such early contact may be important for some mothers under some circumstances, it certainly does not appear necessary for a strong maternal bond (George & Solomon, 2008). Mothers and babies separated during the first days after birth by illness are no less likely than pairs not separated to develop strong attachment relationships (Rode et al., 1981). This can also hold true for adoptive mothers and their babies, especially if the adoption takes place early in infancy (Dozier & Rutter, 2008).

PHASE 2 (2 TO 7 MONTHS): DISCRIMINATE SOCIAL RESPONSIVENESS During the second stage, infants become more interested in the caregiver and other familiar people, and direct their social responses to them. Although strangers continue to be accepted, they now assume a second-class status.

Across this period, the infant and caregiver develop interactional patterns that permit them to communicate and that establish a unique relationship between them. The child develops a cognitive representation, or internal working model, of the caregiver based on how reliable and trustworthy she is seen to be (Bretherton & Munholland, 2008). The baby also looks to the caregiver when anxious or uncertain for information regarding how he or she should feel—the social-referencing process described earlier—and the caregiver uses this communication system to exert some control over the child (Ainsworth, 1992).

Also important to the attachment process, babies now begin to develop a sense of self, and to understand that they are separate from the rest of the world and that they can do things to affect it. We discuss these processes in detail in the chapter that follows.

PHASE 3 (8 MONTHS TO 2½ YEARS): FOCUSED ATTACHMENT The attachment bond becomes clearest in the third quarter of the first year and remains very strong until about age 2½ . The appearance of attachment behaviours is very much tied to development in two other areas. One of these is emotional. Around this time, fear begins to emerge as a dominant emotion. With improvements in memory and other cognitive functions, babies begin to recognize what is strange or unfamiliar, and they generally react to such experiences negatively (Marvin & Britner, 2008). **Wariness of strangers** becomes common, often causing the baby to cry and retreat to the mother. Being apart from the caregiver produces **separation protest**, which also involves crying and sometimes searching after the mother. Both forms of distress are typically reduced once the baby is back in contact with the caregiver.

Wariness of strangers A general fear of unfamiliar people that appears in many infants at around 8 months of age and indicates the formation of the attachment bond.

Separation protest Crying and searching by infants separated from their mothers; an indication of the formation of the attachment bond.

Links to Related Material

In Chapter 5, you read about motor development in the first two years of life. How do you think the infant's increasing motor skills might affect the infant's ability to display attachment behaviours toward the parent?

The other related development is physical. Around 6 to 8 months of age, most babies begin to crawl. This ability gives infants their first opportunity to have considerable control over where they are, and it is crucial in the attachment process—the baby no longer needs to rely on crying or related behaviours to gain proximity to his or her mother (or father), but can crawl to her and follow her around.

The full-blown attachment process becomes evident when the infant puts these two developments together and begins to treat the caregiver as a secure base. Now the infant's increased mobility allows her to regulate feelings of fear and insecurity by controlling the distance between her and the caregiver. When she is feeling secure, she ventures boldly from the mother or the father to explore her environment, but when an unfamiliar person or situation appears, she returns to the mother or the father for comfort and security (Bowlby, 1988; Marvin & Britner, 2008).

Most infants form attachments to more than one individual involved in their care (Berlin, Cassidy, & Appleyard, 2008). As might be expected, the mother is usually a significant attachment figure (Cassidy, 2008). Many fathers are also involved in the care of their infants and can be

Links to Related Material

Here we discuss how not only mothers, but often fathers, grandparents, and even siblings can serve as attachment figures. In Chapter 15, you will read more about the other roles played by these family members.

just as nurturing and competent as mothers (Lamb & Lewis, 2010). Not surprisingly, therefore, infants usually also develop attachment relationships with their fathers (Grossmann et al., 2008). Other attachment figures may include older siblings, aunts, grandparents, or perhaps a daycare worker (Cassidy, 2008). The number of people with whom the infant develops attachment relationships is not limitless, however, being restricted to perhaps three or four. Moreover, these multiple attachments are not all equal in importance to the infant. Usually, a particular caregiver (often the mother) serves as the infant's primary attachment figure, while the infant's other attachment figures are less important in the hierarchy (Cassidy, 2008; Zeifman & Hazan, 2008).

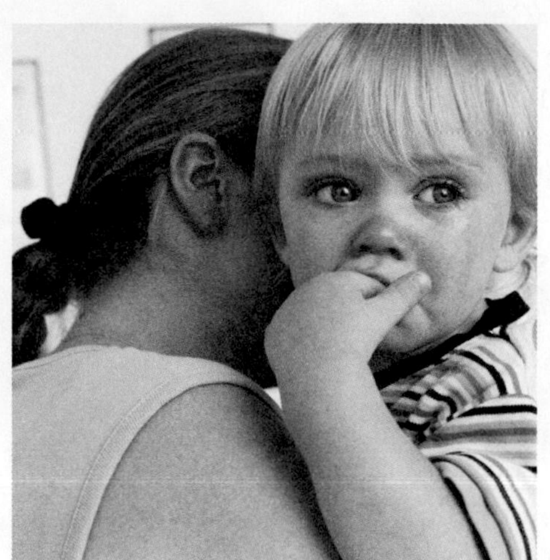

One clear sign that attachment has developed is that the infant clings to, and is reluctant to separate from, the caregiver. (*Banana Stock*)

PHASE 4 (3 YEARS AND ON): GOAL-CORRECTED PARTNERSHIPS As children enter the preschool years, they become better able to modulate their own reactions and responses and, as a consequence, have decreasing need to seek proximity with their attachment figures. Furthermore, their developing cognitive abilities foster an increasing understanding of their caregivers as separate individuals with goals of their own. As they gain greater insight into their caregivers' behaviours and motivations, children engage in relationships with them that are more reciprocal than in the earlier phases of attachment—more of a partnership, where they are able to negotiate plans and activities with their caregiver (Marvin & Britner, 2008; Simpson & Belsky, 2008). Through this, children become capable of complex relationships. This final phase marks the beginning of lifelong mature attachment behaviours. As they enter adolescence, children display less attachment to parents and transfer their needs for emotional security to peers and eventually to romantic partners and other intimate relationships (Zeifman & Hazan, 2008).

ASSESSING ATTACHMENT

To study the attachment process, researchers must have reliable and valid methods for assessing the nature and quality of the infant–caregiver relationship. Two major methods have been developed for this purpose: the Strange Situation procedure and the Attachment Q-Set.

Strange Situation procedure Mary Ainsworth's laboratory procedure for assessing the strength of the attachment relationship by observing the infant's reactions to a series of structured episodes involving the mother and a stranger.

STRANGE SITUATION PROCEDURE The older and more popular way of assessing the strength and quality of the attachment relationship is the **Strange Situation procedure.** This method was developed in the 1960s by Mary Ainsworth as part of a longitudinal study of the attachment process (Solomon & George, 2008). (See *Canadian Contributions 12.1* for a review of Ainsworth's career.)

The Strange Situation is a laboratory procedure that involves studying the child interacting with the mother (or the father) and with an adult stranger in an unfamiliar setting. This approach ensures that the situation will be at least mildly stressful for the child, and so will elicit secure-base attachment behaviours toward the caregiver. The procedure is typically conducted when the infant is between 12 and 20 months of age, a point at which the attachment relationship should be clearly established. Of particular interest are the baby's reactions when separated from the caregiver and when reunited with her or him.

The method consists of eight episodes, summarized in Table 12.1. Episode 1 simply involves introducing the caregiver and baby to the laboratory room, which contains several chairs and an array of toys, and is designed to encourage exploration by the infant. Observers are positioned behind one-way windows where they can observe and video record the behaviours of the infant for later scoring. The next two episodes provide pre-separation experiences for the baby. In episode 2, the caregiver and infant are alone, and the observers note the baby's willingness to explore the new toys and situation. In episode 3, a stranger joins them; after one minute of silence, the stranger begins a conversation with the caregiver and also attempts to engage the baby in play.

Episode 4 represents the first separation, in which the caregiver leaves the child alone with the stranger. This episode may last for three minutes, but is cut short if the baby shows too much

CANADIAN CONTRIBUTIONS 12.1
MARY AINSWORTH (1913–1999)

Although born in Glendale, Ohio, Mary Ainsworth received her education entirely in Canada. She arrived in Toronto with her family when she was 5 years old, and started her training in psychology in 1929 at the University of Toronto. There she completed her B.A., M.A., and Ph.D. degrees. Her interest in developmental psychology began when she undertook her doctoral research within the framework of the security theory under the supervision of Professor William Blatz. Her dissertation (Ainsworth, 1940) was devoted to the construction of self-report pencil-and-paper scales to assess young adults' relations with their parents and peers.

Between 1939 and 1950, she held various clinical and academic positions in Toronto. In 1950, she joined the Tavistock Clinic in London (UK), directed by John Bowlby, where she studied the effect of mother–infant separation in early childhood on personality development. In 1954, she moved to Africa for a research position at the East African Institute of Social Research in Kampala, Uganda. There she undertook her famous work on Ganda mother–infant interactions and maternal practices. After a two-year appointment in Kampala, which had a profound effect upon her thinking, she continued her work on attachment in the United States, first at The Johns Hopkins University and later at the University of Virginia.

TABLE 12.1 STRANGE SITUATION PROCEDURE

Episode Number	Person/People Present	Duration	Brief Description of Action
1	Mother, baby, and observer	30 sec.	Observer introduces mother and baby to experimental room, then leaves.
2	Mother and baby	3 min.	Mother is non-participant while baby explores. If necessary, play is stimulated after 2 min.
3	Stranger, mother, and baby	3 min.	Stranger enters. Min. 1: stranger silent. Min. 2: stranger converses with mother. Min. 3: stranger approaches baby. After 3 min., mother leaves unobtrusively.
4	Stranger and baby	3 min. or less[a]	First separation episode. Stranger's behaviour is geared to that of baby.
5	Mother and baby	3 min. or less[b]	First reunion episode. Mother greets and comforts baby, then tries to settle baby again in play. Mother then leaves, saying bye-bye.
6	Baby alone	3 min. or less[a]	Second separation episode.
7	Stranger and baby	3 min. or less[a]	Continuation of second separation. Stranger enters and gears behaviour to that of baby.
8	Mother and baby	3 min.	Second reunion episode. Mother enters, greets baby, then picks baby up. Meanwhile, stranger leaves unobtrusively.

[a] Episode is curtailed if the baby is overly distressed.

[b] Episode is prolonged if more time is required for the baby to become re-involved in play.

distress. Episode 5 involves the return of the caregiver and the departure of the stranger. How the infant reacts to the reunion with the caregiver is carefully noted. The caregiver remains with the infant for at least three minutes, offering comfort and reassurance, and attempts to get the baby re-involved with the toys.

In episode 6, the second separation takes place. Now, the caregiver leaves the baby alone in the room, again for a maximum of three minutes, depending on the child's level of distress. The stranger returns in episode 7 and attempts to interact with the baby. Episode 8 is the second reunion, during which the caregiver greets and picks up the baby, while the stranger leaves.

Links to Related Material

In Chapter 8, you read how Piaget emphasized the importance of active exploration during the sensorimotor period. To what extent do you think that a secure attachment relationship might promote active exploration in an infant?

Three patterns of responses were originally found to describe most infants who have undergone this procedure (Solomon & George, 2008; Weinfield et al., 2008). Infants exhibiting pattern B are considered to be *securely attached* to the caregiver. They feel secure enough to explore freely during the pre-separation episodes, but they display distress when the caregiver leaves and respond enthusiastically when she returns. About 65 percent of North American babies tested react in this manner. Pattern A babies are described as *insecure-avoidant.* They generally show little distress at separation, and when the caregiver returns they tend to avoid her. This pattern represents about 20 percent of North American infants. Pattern C babies are termed *insecure-resistant.* They give evidence of distress throughout the procedure, particularly during separation. Reunions with the caregiver produce a mixture of relief at seeing her and anger directed toward her. Only about 15 percent of North American infants respond in this way.

Most infants have been found to fit into Ainsworth's three original categories of attachment. However, these three categories proved insufficient to account for all types of mother–infant interaction patterns (Lyons-Ruth & Jacobvitz, 2008). More recently, researchers have described a fourth type of attachment, dubbed *insecure-disorganized/disoriented* (pattern D) (Main & Hesse, 1990; Solomon & George, 2011). The infant with this attachment pattern displays an unpredictable, distressed response to separation from and reunion with the mother. The pattern is thought to emerge as a by-product of unusual, disrupted maternal behaviours that are frightening to the infant and result in the infant's feeling unprotected and abandoned (George & Solomon, 2008; Moss, Bureau, St-Laurent, & Tarabulsy, 2011). For example, mothers of children classified as disorganized are more likely to show both withdrawing behaviours (Lyons-Ruth et al., 1999) and frightened behaviours (Abrams et al., 2006; Schuengel et al., 1999) in the Strange Situation procedure. As will be discussed later in the chapter, maltreatment in infancy is associated with a higher incidence of disorganized attachment patterns (Barnett et al., 1999; Belsky & Fearon, 2008). Furthermore, the fear and disorganization evident in infants showing this pattern endure over time: children who receive a disorganized classification as infants have been found to display continued maladjusted behaviours as 6-year-olds, and even as young adults (Hesse & Main, 2000; Main, Hess, & Kaplan, 2005; Moss et al., 2011).

It is important to understand that although the Strange Situation procedure focuses on the infant's behaviour, it is designed to assess the quality of the relationship between caregiver and baby. Pattern B infants are assumed to have developed a secure, healthy attachment to the caregiver, whereas the relationships developed by pattern A, C, and D infants are assumed to be less than optimal.

An important advantage of this procedure is that it is a structured observation method (as discussed in Chapter 2) and can thus be applied in the same way at different times and by different researchers. Because it is video recorded, it also can be re-observed by other researchers or for other reasons. The major disadvantages are that it involves only a very brief sampling of the child's interactions, it occurs in an unfamiliar setting and environment, and the mother's behaviour is strictly directed.

Attachment Q-Set (AQS) A method of assessing attachment in which cards bearing descriptions of the child's interactions with the caregiver are sorted into categories to create a profile of the child.

ATTACHMENT Q-SET An alternative approach to assessing attachment that avoids the problems just mentioned is the **Attachment Q-Set** (AQS) (Solomon & George, 2008; Waters, 1995).

TABLE 12.2 SAMPLE ITEMS FROM THE ATTACHMENT Q-SET ILLUSTRATING THE BEHAVIOUR AT HOME OF A CHILD WHO IS SECURELY ATTACHED OR INSECURELY ATTACHED TO THE MOTHER

Secure Attachment	Insecure Attachment
Child readily shares with mother or lets her hold things if she asks to.	Child refuses to share with mother.
Child is happy or affectionate when returning to mother between or after play times.	When child returns to mother after playing, he is sometimes fussy for no clear reason.
When child is upset or injured, mother is the only one he allows to comfort him.	When he is upset or injured, child will accept comforting from adults other than mother.
Child often hugs or cuddles against mother, without her asking or inviting him to do so.	Child doesn't hug or cuddle much unless mother hugs him first or asks him to give her a hug.
When child finds something new to play with, he carries it to mother or show it to her from across the room.	Child plays with new object quietly or goes where he won't be interrupted.
Child keeps track of mother's location when he plays around the house.	Child doesn't keep track of mother's location.
Child enjoys relaxing in mother's lap.	Child prefers to relax on the floor or on furniture.
Child actively goes after mother if he is upset or crying.	When child is upset about mother leaving him, he sits right where he is and cries. Doesn't go after her.
Child clearly shows a pattern of using mother as a base from which to explore. Moves out to play; returns or plays near her; moves out to play again, etc.	Child is always away from mother or always stays near her.

Source: From Parke, R. & Clarke-Stewart, A. (2011). *Social Development*, Table 4.4, p. 121. Hoboken, NJ: John Wiley & Sons, Inc. Derived from Waters, E. (1987). Attachment Q-set (Version 3), http://www.psychology.sunysb.edu/attachment/measures/content/aqs_items.pdf.

Rather than studying attachment in the laboratory, this evaluation is conducted in the home and over a much longer period of time.

The procedure usually involves trained observers who visit the infant and mother in their own home, sometimes more than once, and observe their interactions in a variety of typical activities. After completing several hours of observation, each observer evaluates the nature and quality of the mother–baby relationship using the Q-sort method—a rating technique used in social science research, in which prepared statements are sorted into categories. Sometimes, the mothers themselves serve as the observers and evaluators.

The AQS consists of 90 items, each describing the behaviour of an infant or young child (ages 1–5) interacting with the mother. (See Table 12.2 for sample items.) Each item is printed on a card, and the observer is instructed to sort the 90 cards into nine piles ranging from "least like the child" (piles 1–3) to "most like the child" (piles 7–9).

When the cards have all been sorted, the researcher compares the observer's profile of the child with a profile of a "securely attached child" prepared by experts in the field. The higher the correlation with the expert description, the more securely attached the child is assumed to be.

The AQS offers some advantages over the Strange Situation procedure. It involves a much wider array of behaviours on the part of both the mother and the baby, and is also applicable to a broader age-range of children (Solomon & George, 2008; van IJzendoorn et al., 2004). However, it focuses on attachment security–insecurity and does not distinguish between different types of insecure attachment (Moss, Bureau, Cyr, & Dubois-Comtois, 2006; Thompson, 2006). Nevertheless, studies that have included both methods have generally found that they classify children as secure or insecure in about the same way (Pederson & Moran, 1996; Vaughn & Waters, 1990; van IJzendoorn et al., 2004).

CULTURAL DIFFERENCES IN ATTACHMENT Most of the early work on attachment was done in the United States. But as this research spread to other countries and cultures, it became obvious that attachment to some degree varies with the cultural context in which it develops (Thompson, 2006; van IJzendoorn & Sagi-Schwartz, 2008). This conclusion was initially based on studies using the Strange Situation procedure and has since been confirmed by research involving the Q-Set approach, demonstrating that the differences may not be merely methodological (Sagi et al., 1995).

What cross-cultural contrasts have researchers found? A notable example is work undertaken in Germany. Because Germany's Western industrialized culture is not widely different from the North American culture, we might expect patterns of attachment in these two cultures to be very similar. Researchers have found, however, that in the German samples, fewer infant–caregiver pairs display the secure (pattern B) attachment and more are classified as pattern A, or insecure–avoidant. This difference does not appear to result from less maternal sensitivity among German mothers. Rather, the investigators speculated that German mothers' emphasis on building independence in their children resulted in the infants' appearing less interested in their mothers during reunions (Grossmann & Grossmann, 1990; Grossmann et al., 1985).

Very different results have been reported in studies of Japanese children, which have found a higher percentage of pattern C, or insecure–resistant, attachments. In the Japanese culture, mothers rarely leave their babies with others, and so the Strange Situation procedure may prove more stressful for the infants (Rothbaum, Kakinuma, Kagaoka, & Azuma, 2007; Saarni et al., 2008; Takahashi, 1986, 1990).

Whatever the pattern of attachment displayed in a particular culture, it is clear that cultural differences do exist. Such differences appear compatible with the view of evolutionary psychologists, mentioned earlier, that the social bonds infants form with caregivers are flexible, depending partly on the particular environment in which they live.

DETERMINANTS OF ATTACHMENT

The measures of attachment we have been discussing raise two important questions: What factors produce different patterns of attachment between infant and caregiver? What significance do they have for the child's development? The first issue involves the origin of patterns of attachment. Several factors have been suggested as determining what kind of attachment relationship develops (Belsky & Fearon, 2008; Cummings & Cummings, 2002).

PARENTAL RESPONSIVENESS Many theorists contend that the major influence on the quality of attachment is the parents' responsiveness to the baby. When parents respond to their infants' bids for attention in a reliable and consistent way, and when their interactions with their infants are warm and responsive, infants are likely to develop a sense of confidence in the parent as a source of comfort and protection, leading to a secure attachment relationship (Weinfield et al., 2008). Such parents are more sensitive to their infants' needs, are able to "read" their infants' mental states (Meins et al., 2001, 2003), and adjust their behaviour to that of their babies (Ainsworth, 1983; Belsky, 2006; Sroufe, 2005). By contrast, infants who have not experienced such reliable care, whose parents respond in a manner that is inconsistent, indifferent, or even rejecting, are less likely to develop such confidence in the parent. As a result, they are also less likely to develop a secure attachment relationship with that parent (Belsky & Fearon, 2008; Weinfield et al., 2008).

Examples of the sensitive care associated with secure attachment can be seen in everyday situations, such as feeding, responding to crying, and interacting with the infant. Securely attached infants have mothers who are more responsive to their signals—feeding them at a comfortable pace, recognizing when they are done or ready for more, and recognizing their taste or texture preferences (Ainsworth et al., 1978; Egeland & Farber, 1984; Sroufe et al., 2005). Another revealing situation involves responsiveness to crying. Mothers of securely attached babies are less likely to ignore their crying, are quicker to respond, and are more effective in comforting the baby (Belsky, Rovine, & Taylor, 1984; Del Carmen et al., 1993). Another everyday situation involves the mother's bodily contact with her infant. When mothers of secure babies are holding them, they tend to be more affectionate, playful, and tender toward the children (Sroufe, 2005; Tracy & Ainsworth, 1981).

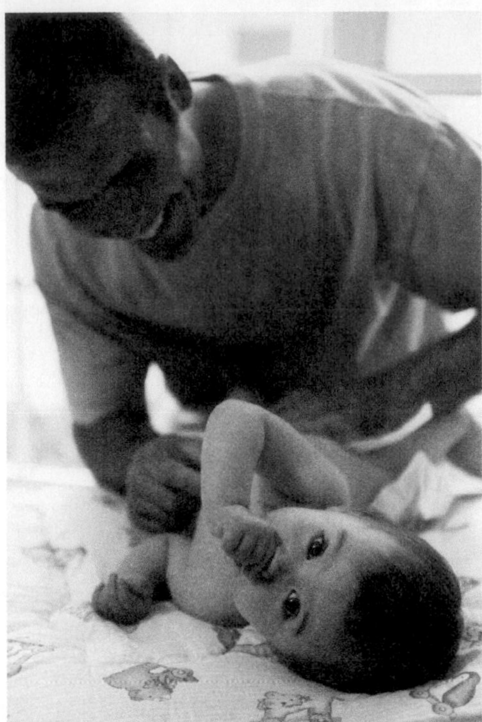

Secure attachments are most likely to develop when the caregiver is sensitive and responsive to the infant's needs. *(Purestock)*

In face-to-face interactions, securely attached infants have caregivers who more easily synchronize their actions to mesh with those of the baby (interactional synchrony and turn taking), which also serves to lengthen their time together (Belsky, 2006; Isabella & Belsky, 1991). Indeed, overall levels of acceptance, rejection, and sensitivity by mothers across a variety of everyday activities have been shown to predict which of the three major attachment classifications their babies will exhibit in the Strange Situation (Belsky, 2006; De Wolff & van IJzendoorn, 1997; Pederson & Moran, 1996; Sroufe et al., 2005).

Still other kinds of evidence link the caregiver's behaviour to the quality of the attachment relationship. For example, babies can develop different attachment relationships with different caregivers (e.g., the mother, the father, professional caregivers), which should not be surprising if caregivers respond differently to the child (Howes & Spieker, 2008).

Moreoever, as mentioned, the proportion of infants in different attachment classifications varies from culture to culture, again presumably as a result of different caregiving practices (Sagi et al., 1995; Thompson, 2006; van IJzendoorn & Sagi, 1999). Finally, interventions designed to increase mothers' sensitivity to their infants have also produced more secure attachment relationships between them (Bakermans-Kranenburg, van IJzendoorn, & Juffer, 2003, 2005; van IJzendoorn, Juffer, & Duyvesteyn, 1995). Thus, quality of care seems to be central to the development of the attachment relationship. In fact, recent physiological research underscores its importance further, indicating that quality of care may even play a role in the actual shaping of the physiological systems that underlie a child's reactivity to stressful situations (Fox & Hane, 2008). (In *Research Classic 12.1*, we discuss early research looking at one aspect of quality of care—"contact comfort.")

For Thought and Discussion

Caregiver sensitivity and responsiveness are so important that interventions have been designed for parents of infants with attachment problems. Do you think society should mandate such interventions to improve parenting?

It seems clear, then, that the security of the relationship between the infant and the caregiver depends heavily on the kinds of care the child receives. Yet, it should also be clear by this point that infants have more than a little to do with how their mothers treat them.

ATTACHMENT ACROSS GENERATIONS It is reasonable to ask why some mothers respond more sensitively to their babies than do others. One answer seems to involve the mother's recollections of her own childhood experiences. The idea is that individuals form a working model of close relationships as young children, a prototype that endures with time and affects various close relationships in the future, both with romantic partners and with their own children (Bretherton & Munholland, 2008; Roisman et al., 2001; Zeifman & Hazan, 2008). One approach to studying this phenomenon has been to have mothers describe their childhood attachment relationships using an instrument called the **Adult Attachment Interview**. Data collected are then used to classify mothers as displaying one of four adult attachment styles (Hesse, 2008; Main & Goldwyn, 1998).

Adult Attachment Interview
An instrument used to assess an adult's childhood recollections of the attachment relationship with the primary caregiver.

Autonomous parents present an objective and balanced picture of their childhood, noting both the positive and negative experiences; *dismissing* parents claim to have difficulty recalling their childhoods and appear to assign little significance to them; *preoccupied* parents tend to dwell on their early experiences, often describing them in a confused and highly emotional manner; and *unresolved* parents have experienced attachment-related trauma that they have not yet resolved, such as the loss of or abuse from a mother or father (Crowell, Fraley, & Shaver, 2008).

For Thought and Discussion

What pattern of attachment did you experience as a child? How do you think your experience might affect your attachment style with a child you care for?

The assumption underlying this research is that mothers' memories and feelings regarding their own attachment security will be expressed in their caregiving toward their child, and so affect

RESEARCH CLASSIC 12.1
MOTHER LOVE: HARLOW'S STUDIES OF ATTACHMENT

Much of the early work on attachment involved other species, in part because this research often was conducted by ethologists—scientists who traditionally study behaviour in a wide range of animal species. But the focus on other species also reflects the fact that some questions cannot easily be addressed by research with humans. A classic study conducted in the 1950s by Harry Harlow at the University of Wisconsin illustrates this point.

Harlow was interested in determining the role of feeding in the attachment process. Many psychologists at that time accepted the learning-theory view that a baby's emotional attachment to the mother is based on her role as a powerful reinforcer. Not only does she provide the infant with social stimulation, remove wet diapers, and comfort him when he is upset, she is, perhaps most importantly, the source of the baby's nourishment. Because food is so fundamental to sustaining life, many researchers assumed that the baby becomes emotionally drawn to the mother as a result of her being associated with food.

To test this hypothesis, a psychologist would need to manipulate when, how, and by whom a baby is fed. For ethical reasons, we cannot conduct such research with human babies. Harlow approached the issue using what he felt was the best available alternative—baby rhesus monkeys. In addition to feeding, Harlow suspected that the opportunity to cuddle with the mother would also influence the attachment process. So, he conducted the following study.

A group of rhesus monkeys was removed from their mothers immediately after birth and raised in a laboratory with two surrogate "mothers" constructed of wood and wire (Figure 12.3). One of the surrogates was covered with terry cloth to which the baby monkey could cling; the other surrogate was made only of wire mesh. For half the infants, food was made available in a bottle on the cloth mother; for the other monkeys, food was attached to the wire mother. To assess the infant's "love" for the mothers, Harlow used two measures: the amount of time spent with each surrogate, and the degree to which the mother provided the baby monkey with security in fear-producing situations.

The results were dramatic and surprising. The baby monkeys spent an average of 17 to 18 hours a day on the cloth mother and less than one hour a day on the wire mother, regardless of which mother provided the food.

Likewise, when frightened, the monkeys consistently sought out the cloth mother for security; when only the wire mother was available to them, the infants seemed to find little comfort in its presence (Harlow & Harlow, 1966). Harlow's research thus demonstrated that the most important factor in the development of attachment in rhesus monkeys is not feeding, but rather the opportunity to cling and snuggle, which he called "contact comfort."

The relevance of these findings to our species remains unclear, partly because we cannot replicate Harlow's procedures by depriving human babies of contact with their caregivers. But this classic research did prompt investigators to begin examining factors other than conditioning and learning principles in their search for the determinants of human attachment. It also served as a reminder that even widely held ideas regarding the causes of behaviour should not be accepted without scientific verification.

FIGURE 12.3

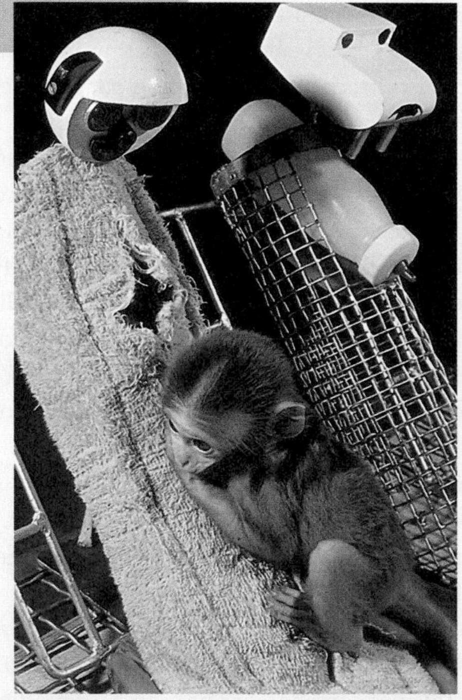

Harry Harlow found that contact comfort, rather than feeding, was the most important determinant of a rhesus monkey's attachment to its caregiver. (*Nina Leen/Time Life Pictures/Getty Images*)

the infant–caregiver relationship (Hesse, 2008; Mikulincer & Shaver, 2007). Several studies have shown that adult attachment classifications are, indeed, reasonably good predictors of the patterns of attachment these mothers form with their own babies (Arnott & Meins, 2007; Posada et al., 1995; van IJzendoorn, 1992, 1995). Even more impressive, they can predict both forward and backward; that is, mothers' interviews during pregnancy predict their later attachment to their infants (Steele, Steele, & Fonagy, 1996; Ward & Carlson, 1995), and mothers' interviews when their children are age 6 correlate positively with their attachments when the children were only 12 months old (Main et al., 1985).

Other research has suggested that the impact of adults' memories of their childhood attachment patterns is importantly mediated by the nature of the current family environment (Cowan et al., 1996). A dysfunctional working model of close relationships may make one more likely to become involved in a marriage characterized by conflict, a reality that may, in turn, make adults poor communicators and less effective parents.

TEMPERAMENT AND ATTACHMENT We have seen that an infant's temperament can affect how the child interacts with the caregiver, as well as in other social situations. Some researchers believe that temperament may therefore play a role in the attachment process. This could happen in two different ways (Seifer & Schiller, 1995).

First, the infant's temperament may interfere with a valid assessment of his or her attachment classification. For example, some researchers suspect that infants who are fearful and inhibited tend frequently to be classified as pattern C in the Strange Situation procedure—not because they actually have this sort of relationship with the caregiver, but because their overreaction to the unfamiliar situation gives the appearance of insecure attachment (Calkins & Fox, 1992; Kagan & Fox, 2006; Thompson, Connell, & Bridges, 1988). Temperamental characteristics involving activity level, distractibility, or soothability likewise are suspected to affect ratings in the Strange Situation (Goldsmith & Harman, 1994). This issue does not appear to present a serious problem (Sroufe et al., 2005), however, and use of the Q-Set methodology has helped address it (Vaughn, Bost, & van IJzendoorn, 2008).

The second (and more important) role for temperament is that it may directly affect the type of attachment relationship the child develops with the caregiver. This idea relates to the goodness-of-fit concept discussed earlier in the chapter. For example, babies who are irritable or have other characteristics of a difficult temperamental style might be a challenge to respond to in a prompt and sensitive manner. Another possibility is that a baby's temperament may influence how sensitive the child is to the parent's caregiving—the same type of caregiving could be received differently by different infants. Either of these situations could result in a child being less likely to develop a secure attachment with the caregiver (Belsky & Fearon, 2008).

There is some evidence that temperament may affect the attachment relationship in this second, more direct way (Seifer et al., 1996; van den Boom, 1994). For example, babies who tend to be more irritable or who less readily orient themselves to people or objects may be more likely to develop insecure attachments (Spangler & Grossmann, 1993; Susman-Stillman et al., 1996).

However, other researchers continue to find no clear temperament–attachment link (Vaughn et al., 2008). Thus, the precise relationship at work here remains uncertain and is the subject of continuing research.

CONSEQUENCES OF ATTACHMENT

Another major issue in attachment research concerns a simple question: Does it matter? One answer to this important question is that securely attached infants display a variety of other positive characteristics not found in infants whose caregiver relationships are of lower quality. These include features of both cognitive and social development, as will be discussed. It is likely that as a result of being secure in the caregiver's presence, the infant feels comfortable in exploring the surrounding social and physical environment and thus develops important cognitive and social skills.

Ross Thompson (2000) cautions, however, that when we consider the mechanisms by which early attachment may produce long-term consequences, we must remember that early influence develops in context. In other words, attachment relationships do not exist in isolation. They are importantly shaped by the child's changing levels of cognitive understanding, as well as by other features of the parent–child relationship, such as how conflict is handled. Especially important is the continuity of care the child receives (Belsky, 2006; Sroufe, 2005). A child who has been securely attached and who continues to receive sensitive care is likely to remain secure. If the quality of care deteriorates, however, attachment status may also change in a negative direction (Weinfield, Sroufe, & Egeland, 2000; Sroufe et al., 2005). The converse is also true: improvements in quality of care can result in positive changes in attachment security (Sroufe et al., 2005; Thompson, 2008). The influence of attachment over time, therefore, may depend on several influential variables.

COGNITIVE COMPETENCE Several studies have shown that securely attached infants later become better problem solvers and show less negative affect in response to challenges than do insecure children (Sroufe et al., 2005; Weinfield et al., 2008). Securely attached children have also have been found to be more curious and to explore more (Slade, 1987a). In addition, competence in cognitive and language development is associated with the sensitivity mothers express toward their infants in play situations (Laible & Thompson, 2007; Lewis, 1993a).

Other research has found cognitive benefits associated with secure attachment in older children. Seven-year-olds in Iceland, who were classified as securely attached based on their responses to a story about separation, were more likely than their peers to display multiple positive characteristics at ages 9, 12, and 15 years (Jacobsen & Hofmann, 1997). These included possession of a strong sense of self, attentiveness in school, and higher grades. Likewise, securely attached 6-year-olds in Montreal were found to score higher at age 8 than their peers on measures of academic competency, including communication, cognitive engagement, and mastery motivation (Moss & St-Laurent, 2001).

SOCIAL AND EMOTIONAL COMPETENCE Children who were securely attached as infants also seem to be more socially competent than insecure children. They tend to be more cooperative, participate more actively in the peer group, and have better relations with their peers (Booth-Laforce & Kerns, 2009; Kerns, 2008). In addition, they are less likely to develop emotional or behaviour problems than those who are insecurely attached (Sroufe et al., 2005; Weinfield et al., 2008). Indeed, likely as a result of their parents' sensitivity to their feelings, securely attached children are more skilled at understanding emotions (Laible & Thompson, 1998; Thompson, 2008) and develop better ability to regulate their own emotions (Sroufe et al., 2005; Thompson & Meyer, 2007). The advantages continue into adolescence, where those who were securely attached as infants not only participate well in group situations, but are more independent and more likely to show leadership qualities (Sroufe et al., 2005; Weinfield et al., 2008). Finally, preliminary longitudinal evidence suggests that attachment security in infancy may even shape young adults' views of ideal romantic partners (Grossman et al., 2008) and their relations with romantic partners in terms of conflict and collaboration (Roisman, Collins, Sroufe, & Egeland, 2005).

In contrast, insecurely attached children are more likely to have difficulty with social interactions than are their securely attached counterparts. Children classified as insecure–avoidant (pattern A) have a greater tendency to isolate themselves and avoid contact (Sroufe, 2005). Those classified as insecure–resistant (pattern C), although interested in interaction, often have ineffectual interactional skills and tend to hover at the periphery of group activities (Sroufe, 2005). Finally, those classified as insecure–disorganized/disoriented (pattern D) tend to be more aggressive (Main et al., 2005) and display more adjustment problems than do their securely attached peers (Bernier & Meins, 2008; Moss et al., 2004, 2006; Tarabulsy et al., 2008).

There is evidence that the social benefit conferred on securely attached children may have its roots in the more sensitive and responsive caregiving provided by their parents. Mothers of securely attached children have been found to be more adept in modulating the style and degree of the feedback they provide to their children during a cognitive task, favouring positive over negative comments and intervening only when asked. Mothers of insecurely attached children tended to be less skilled at recognizing their children's level of competence and responding appropriately (Meins, 1997).

It is important to note that this body of evidence does not mean that insecurely attached babies are doomed to problems. Change can occur (Sroufe et al., 2005). It has been shown, for example, that some insecure babies can benefit from daycare experiences, suggesting that environmental influences play an important role in the development of their later social competence (Egeland & Heister, 1995).

LEARNING OBJECTIVE 12.4

Explain the role of attachment in child development.

1. Trace the development of attachment in infants.
2. How is attachment assessed?
3. What individual differences in attachment have researchers identified?
4. What are the causes and consequences of individual differences in attachment?

EFFECTS OF EARLY EXPERIENCE

Learning Objective 12.5

Explain how early experience can affect later social, emotional, and cognitive development.

An important issue in the discussion of early social development concerns the magnitude of its impact over time. In earlier sections of this chapter, we discussed how social elements like early temperament and relationships may influence various aspects of a child's future. Next, we focus on special circumstances to further explain how early experience helps lay the groundwork for later social, emotional, and cognitive development.

EFFECTS OF EARLY DAYCARE

One of the most obvious societal changes in Canada and the United States in the latter part of the 20th century involved the increased number of women working outside the home. Currently, there are almost as many women as men in the workforce in Canada, a participation rate that is among the highest in the world (Marshall, 2006). The incidence of Canadian mothers with children aged 3 to 5 years who worked outside the home grew from 68 percent in 1992 to 75.8 percent in 2005 (Friendly & Beach, 2005; Friendly, Beach, Ferns, & Turiano, 2007). Similar trends have occurred in the United States. As a result, some of the job of child care must be assigned to others, such as those who provide care in daycare centres (Scarr, 1998). Two topics that have generated a great deal of interest and debate concern what happens to the mother–infant attachment process when babies are cared for out of the home (Howes & Spieker, 2008), and whether particular features of child care are associated with negative outcomes (Brooks-Gunn, Han, & Waldfogel, 2002).

Time in daycare is becoming a more common experience for children. For many, this experience begins early in life. (*Banana Stock*)

Early studies reported that infants whose mothers were employed were less likely to be classified as securely attached in the Ainsworth Strange Situation procedure than those whose mothers stayed at home (Barglow, Vaughn, & Molitor, 1987; Belsky, 1988; Belsky & Rovine, 1988; Lamb, Sternberg, & Prodromidis, 1992). And infants whose mothers worked full-time were less likely to be securely attached than those whose mothers worked part-time (Clarke-Stewart, 1989). Such evidence suggested that leaving infants with daycare providers might be inadvisable, although there was considerable disagreement concerning the issue among child development experts.

One objection to these findings had to do with the use of the Strange Situation to assess the effects of daycare on attachment. An important requirement of the Strange Situation procedure is that the infant must experience it as somewhat stressful. This experience of stress is what causes the baby to show anxiety when the mother leaves and to greet her enthusiastically when she returns—reactions that lead to the baby's being classified as securely attached.

The problem with using this method to assess the impact of daycare is that infants left frequently in daycare may not find the Strange Situation particularly stress-inducing. After all, their mothers routinely leave them with others and then later return to pick them up. Perhaps after babies have gained enough experience with this routine, the Strange Situation does not evoke the level of anxiety necessary for them to display the secure-base behaviours normally indicating secure attachment.

The debate over daycare was further fuelled by later findings that failed to replicate the results of earlier investigations (Burchinal et al., 1992; Roggman, et al., 1994; Stifter, Coulehan, & Fish, 1993). Why the negative effects of daycare seemed to disappear was unclear. One possible reason was that the number of mothers of infants in the workforce had increased over time; therefore, the working-mother group may have become more similar to the mothers who stayed at home than in previous years. Other possibilities were that publicizing the potential negative effects of early daycare had led parents to be more selective in choosing daycare arrangements or to consider more carefully their own role in their children's development, leading to improvement in the quality of the home environment. The later studies of infant daycare were also stronger methodologically than the early studies, which often involved small numbers of children and lacked adequate controls.

To help resolve the debate, the American federal government funded a large-scale longitudinal study to explore a variety of outcomes associated with the onset, duration, and quality of daycare. The study enrolled over 1,000 children shortly after birth in 10 localities across the United States. The NICHD Early Childcare Research Network has issued regular reports of its findings since the study began in 1994. Regarding the impact of daycare on attachment status, no evidence was found that placing a child in daycare in and of itself affects the security of the child's attachment to the caregiver one way or the other at 15 months of age (Friedman & Boyle, 2008).

Evidence does indicate, however, that a child whose mother is low in sensitivity is more likely to be classified as insecurely attached when (1) the daycare centre also does not provide a high level of care, (2) the child spends a great deal of time in daycare, or (3) the child has had many different childcare arrangements (Howes & Spieker, 2008). A related finding is that boys are more likely to be classified as insecurely attached when they spend a great deal of time in daycare, whereas girls are more likely to receive such a classification when they spend little time in daycare (Howes & Spieker, 2008).

The NICHD research team also made direct observations of mother–child interaction when the children were 6, 15, 24, and 36 months of age (NICHD Early Childcare Research Network, 1999). This study found that infants and toddlers who spent more hours in daycare experienced somewhat less sensitive mothering and were less positively engaged with their mothers than children not in child care. However, the lesser amount of maternal sensitivity was not of sufficient magnitude to disrupt the formation of a secure infant attachment. Moreover, children in higher-quality programs experienced greater maternal sensitivity, regardless of the number of hours in care. It may be that using higher-quality daycare provides mothers with role models for involved caregiving or emotional support. This, in turn, allows mothers to be more emotionally available to their children.

Investigators involved with the NICHD study have also focused on the cognitive characteristics of children in early daycare. One recent study examined school readiness skills (e.g., children's knowledge of colour, letters, and numbers) among 3-year-old children (Brooks-Gunn, Han, & Waldfogel, 2002). Children placed in daycare before 9 months of age were found to have lower school readiness scores on average around the time of their third birthdays, and the effect was greater for infants who spent more than 30 hours per week in daycare. As with the effects of daycare on attachment, the negative effects of early and full-time child care were larger for children with mothers who were less sensitive, and for boys (compared with girls).

Recent analyses, however, have found that the quality of care is again important (NICHD Early Childcare Research Network, 2002). Compared with children in lower-quality care, those in higher-quality care, in care that improved in quality over time, and in centre-based arrangements had better language, cognitive, and pre-academic skills at age 4½. However, children who spent more hours in out-of-home care were reported to have more behaviour problems at ages 4, 5, and during the kindergarten year, regardless of program quality (NICHD Early Childcare Research Network, 2003).

Results from the NICHD study and other investigations indicate that early child care is associated with both risks and benefits, even when such factors as ethnicity, family income and education, and parenting quality are controlled for. Consequently, many researchers and policy makers have shifted their attention to ways to improve the quality of the care children receive (Friendly et al., 2007; National Research Council & Institute of Medicine, 2000; National Research Council, 2001). We describe one such effort in *Application 12.1*.

For Thought and Discussion

What factors do you think are most important in ensuring positive outcomes for children who spend time in daycare? Who do you think should pay for quality child care?

APPLICATION 12.1
FOSTERING POSITIVE TEACHER–CHILD RELATIONSHIPS DURING EARLY CHILDHOOD

Most research on attachment has concentrated on children's relationships with their parents. And, as we have seen, secure attachments with parents have been linked to later social and cognitive competence. Many young children, however, spend a good deal of time with daycare providers or preschool teachers. Does the quality of their relationships with these caregivers have similar long-term effects?

Research suggests that it does. Compared with peers who have negative relationships with teachers, children who are emotionally close to their teachers during early childhood begin school with better school readiness skills, achieve more academically, and have better relations with peers (Burchinal et al., 2002; Howes, Hamilton, & Philipsen, 1998; Peisner-Feinberg et al., 2001). One longitudinal study even documented effects lasting through the end of elementary school (Hamre & Pianta, 2000).

Attachment theory offers some insight into why the effects of these early relationships are so long lasting. According to attachment theory, young children are better able to attend to and learn from adults with whom they have close relationships than from adults with whom they have detached or conflicted relationships (Pianta, 1999). Thus, children who have positive relations with caregivers are more likely to engage in the kinds of interactions that foster the language skills and other competencies required to succeed during the first years of school.

Moreover, the relationships children form with nonparental caregivers and teachers during early childhood support the development of an internal working model of teacher–child relationships that will help organize children's interactions with teachers and other adults during later school years. Children whose early experiences suggest that adults cannot be trusted to care for them or to help them are prone to distrust the teachers they encounter later.

Unfortunately estimates suggest that fewer than half the children in typical community child care have emotionally secure relationships with caregivers, and the numbers are even lower for children who come from difficult life circumstances—involving maltreatment, parental psychopathology, substance abuse, and poverty (Howes, Galinsky & Kontos, 1998; Howes & Ritchie, 1999). Research also suggests that daycare providers and teachers vary widely in their ability to foster positive relationships with the children in their care (Howes & Hamilton, 1992a).

As with parent–child attachment, children are more likely to form secure bonds with caregivers who are sensitive and responsive to their needs (Howes, 2011). Teachers, like parents, naturally vary in their sensitivity. We have seen that short-term attachment intervention programs with mothers can be quite effective in changing maternal sensitivity and children's attachment (van IJzendoorn, Juffer, & Duyvesteyn, 1995). Might similar targeted interventions increase the sensitivity of childcare providers as well?

To examine this question, researchers (Howes, Galinsky & Kontos, 1998) implemented an intervention in a daycare centre located on-site at a large corporation. All of the caregivers at the centre participated in an intensive 20-hour training program designed to encourage positive interactions with the children. Thirty-six children participated in the study, randomly selected from a larger number of children whose families were willing to have them participate.

(continued)

Application 12.1 Fostering Positive Teacher–Child Relationships During Early Childhood *continued*

Observers rated caregiver sensitivity and children's attachment security before and six months following the intervention. At the first observation, 25 of the 36 children were deemed to have insecure attachments with the classroom teacher. Following the intervention, 21 of these children had secure relations with the caregiver. Analysis of the ratings of teacher sensitivity showed that the caregivers of children who became secure or stayed secure increased in sensitivity and decreased in detachment during their interactions with the children.

These findings suggest that modest interventions can increase caregivers' sensitivity to children and thereby foster the kinds of close relationships that are linked to positive developmental outcomes years later. These relationships may be especially valuable for children who lack opportunities to form secure emotional bonds with other adults in their lives (Howes & Ritchie, 2002; Pianta, 1999).

EFFECTS OF MALTREATMENT ON ATTACHMENT

Although the family is typically a source of security and protection for the young child, sometimes it can be just the opposite. Child maltreatment is a tragic reality of some households, and it is a problem that may be growing (Emery & Laumann-Billings, 1998).

Abuse and neglect have major developmental consequences for growing children. By 1 year of age, maltreated infants tend to lag in both social and cognitive development, and these problems typically continue into childhood and adolescence (Trickett & McBride-Chang, 1995). Many developmental researchers believe that these deficits result from the lack of a secure attachment relationship with the mother. A great deal of research has focused on the attachment process in infants who have been abused or who are at risk for abuse (Cicchetti, 2010; Cicchetti & Valentino, 2010).

Sensitive and responsive caregiving growing out of mutual infant–caregiver regulation is thought to provide the basis for secure attachment. However, many abusive parents fail to develop a smooth and effective communication system with their infants. Although babies will become attached even to parents whose caregiving is of poor quality, the attachment relationship suffers. Perhaps for this reason, the insecure attachment patterns occur more frequently among maltreated infants (Carlson et al., 1989; Rogosch et al., 1995).

Some parents maltreat their infants in ways that involve physical punishment, active hostility, and intrusiveness into the baby's world. Rather than synchronizing their behaviour with that of the child, they often insensitively forge ahead with whatever they are doing (such as feeding a baby before he or she is hungry), focusing more on their own needs than on those of the infant. This caregiving style has been referred to as *overstimulating* and has been linked to physical abuse, such as beating and battering, and to the insecure–avoidant pattern of attachment (pattern A). In contrast, the insensitive care of some mothers takes the form of withdrawal and underinvolvement. This style, termed *understimulating*, has been associated with physical and emotional neglect and appears to be a cause of the insecure–resistant pattern of attachment (pattern C) (Belsky, 2006; Belsky & Fearon, 2008). (In *On the Cutting Edge 12.1*, we discuss one infant behaviour that sometimes triggers maltreatment: persistent crying during the first few months of life.)

Maltreated infants cannot always be classified according to Ainsworth's three original patterns because they often fail to display any coherent pattern of reactions to the Strange Situation. These infants frequently exhibit elements of each category, sometimes accompanied by bizarre responses, such as freezing, assuming unusual postures or expressions, and making interrupted or mistimed movements. Such behaviours, which are sometimes also seen in non-abused children, led to the development of the fourth classification, insecure–disorganized/disoriented (pattern D), described earlier (Lyons-Ruth & Jacobvitz, 2008). Parenting behaviour that is frightening to the infant (Abrams et al., 2006; Beksky & Fearon, 2008; Madigan et al., 2006) and that results in the infant's feeling abandoned or unprotected (George & Solomon, 2008; Moss et al., 2011) is associated with disorganized/disoriented attachment. These children are especially at risk for developing socio-emotional and adjustment problems (Bernier & Meins, 2008; Moss et al., 2004, 2006; Tarabulsy et al., 2008).

The conclusions that can be drawn from research on abused infants support a transactional model of attachment (Crittenden & Ainsworth, 1989). Evolution has provided that babies will become attached even to caregivers who provide minimal or deviant care, but the interactions between these mothers and babies clearly affect the quality of the relationship that develops. This, in turn, affects the child's later social, emotional, and cognitive development (van IJzendoorn et al., 1992).

ON THE CUTTING EDGE 12.1
PERSISTENT INFANT CRYING AND THE RISK OF SHAKEN BABY SYNDROME

Many parents face the stress of trying to cope with a baby who just won't stop crying. The crying always seems to happen in the evening or late afternoon, and no matter what parents do, it often doesn't seem to help. They pick the baby up, they try cuddling and soothing her, but the crying often goes on and on, sometimes for hours. They search through parenting magazines and baby books, but all seem to offer different advice (Catherine et al., 2008), and none of it seems to work. Parents frequently feel exhausted, isolated, and conclude they must be doing something wrong (Barr, 2006; Long, 2004).

In fact, such crying is quite common. Many infants go through a phase of heavy and persistent crying in the first few months of life. Ronald Barr (2006) of the Faculty of Medicine of the University of British Columbia notes that such persistent crying seems particularly unique to the early months of infancy; at no other point in their development will infants display such prolonged, inconsolable crying. Barr (2006) describes six properties that characterize early, persistent infant crying:

- The amount of crying increases over the first few weeks of life, peaks in the middle of the second month, then declines by the fourth or fifth month.
- The crying is unexpected, unpredictable, and seems unrelated to anything aversive in infant's environment.
- The infant is inconsolable; soothing has little effect.
- The infant grimaces and appears to be in pain, but in fact is not.
- The crying episodes are long, averaging 35 to 40 minutes, and sometimes lasting as long as several hours.
- The bouts of crying tend to occur in the evening or late afternoon.

According to Barr, such persistent crying is usually not an attempt to communicate distress, despite the apparent pain expression on the infant's face. Rather, it seems to be simply a part of the infant's normal behavioural development. Moreover, the vast majority of infants—around 95 percent—who engage in such crying are perfectly healthy and not in distress (of course it is important to check with the infant's doctor to ensure that nothing physical is indeed wrong). Such prolonged infant crying in the early months is frequently seen not only in babies in Canada, but also in most Western societies, and it has even been documented in a number of non-Western, hunter–gatherer societies, such as the !Kung, who maintain consistent close physical contact with their young infants (Barr, 2006). In fact, similar prolonged crying in the early months has even been reported in other species, such as chimpanzees (Bard, 2000).

FIGURE 12.4

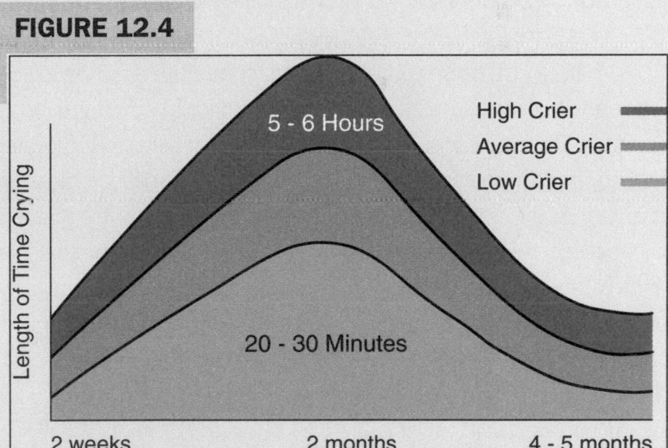

Early infant crying peaks at about 2 months, on average, and then declines by the fourth or fifth month. The length of the crying episodes varies from infant to infant. The average episode is 35 to 40 minutes; however, some infants cry for shorter periods, and some cry for much longer periods. *Source: Barr, R. (2011). Why does my baby cry so much? Retrieved May 30, 2011 from http://www.purplecrying.info/sections/index.php?sct=2&sctpg=10&.*

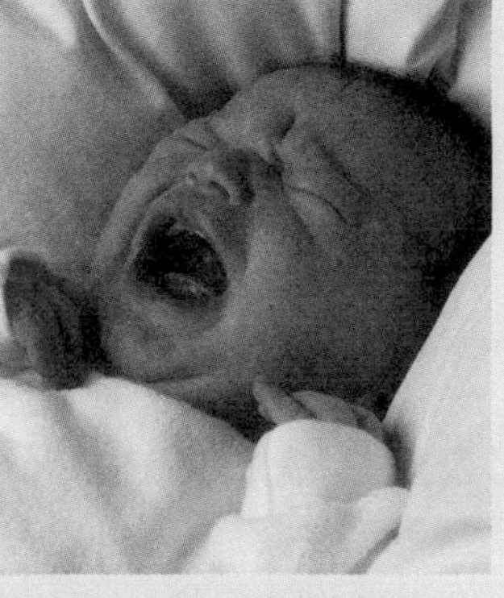

Persistent crying early in infancy is often accompanied by a facial expression that gives the impression of pain. (© *Kemter/iStock*)

In general, there are no negative outcomes associated with such early crying, and most infants simply grow out of it. Nevertheless, prolonged crying can have serious negative effects on parents. The persistence of the crying, coupled with its occurrence in the late afternoon or evening when parents are often tired after the workday, can be a source of great frustration to many parents. Their lack of ability to console and

(*continued*)

On The Cutting Edge 12.1 Persistent Infant Crying and The Risk of Shaken Baby Syndrome *continued*

soothe their baby, no matter what they do, can lead parents to view themselves as ineffectual. Indeed, it can be easy to view the crying as a sign that the baby is an obstinate and ungrateful little creature. As one mother said to her baby in frustration: "Why can't you just be happy for a while?" Another said: "Well, if I'm holding you, walking around with you, and can't stop you from crying, why am I bothering with you at all?" (Long, 2004, p. 62).

Out of frustration, some parents react physically, picking up their crying baby and shaking him or her (Barr, Barr, Fujiwara, et al, 2009). Such shaking can have serious consequences and can result in severe brain injury. Shaken Baby Syndrome (SBS) is a clinical disorder that occurs in about 25 to 31 out of 100,000 children who are less than 1 year of age (Barr, Barr, Fujiwara, et al., 2009). The majority of infants with SBS have lifelong neurological damage, and for about a quarter of babies, the brain injury is fatal (Barr, Rivara, Barr, et al., 2009). It seems that a major trigger for SBS is persistent crying in infancy (Barr, Trent, & Cross, 2006; Lee, Barr, Catherine, & Wicks, 2007).

What can be done to help parents cope with a crying infant? There are no easy cures for crying, and in fact promising parents a method that will console their infant often only leads to greater frustration. Barr stresses that it is important to make it clear to parents that this is a normal part of infant development—that it is not because the parents are doing something wrong or that the infant is being obstinate. Barr and his colleagues have recently developed an intervention program designed to work with parents. Called "The Period of PURPLE Crying," the program consists of an 11-page booklet and 12-minute video on crying and a method for helping parents deal with the stresses associated with infant crying.

The term "PURPLE" is designed to help parents recognize and remember the six characteristics of early crying, helping to reinforce the understanding that such crying is a normal part of infant development. PURPLE stands for the following: "P for Peak pattern, in which crying increases, peaks during the second month, and then declines; U for Unexpected timing of prolonged crying bouts; R for Resistance to soothing; P for Pain-like look on the child's face; L for Long crying bouts; and E for late afternoon and Evening clustering" (Barr, Barr, Fujiwara, et al., 2009, p. 728). The PURPLE program stresses to parents that persistent early crying is normal, suggests ways that parents can soothe their infants, prepares them for the fact that soothing won't always work, and explains to them why it is so frustrating when babies cannot be soothed. The program provides three "action steps" for parents to use to deal with a crying baby: (1) use typical comfort responses—"carry, comfort, walk, and talk"; (2) if becoming too frustrated by the crying, put the baby back in the crib, walk away, and calm yourself for 5 or 10 minutes; and (3) never hurt or shake the infant (Barr, Rivara, Barr, et al., 2009).

Does the intervention work? Preliminary evidence suggests that it does. Two recent studies using the PURPLE method with mothers in Vancouver and Seattle indicate that use of the program results in greater knowledge of infant crying and the dangers of infant shaking (Barr, Barr, Fujiwara, et al, 2009; Barr, Rivara, Barr, et al., 2009). Moreover, parents who participated in the program were likely to share information about coping with crying and preventing shaking with other parents. The PURPLE method is advocated by the National Center on Shaken Baby Syndrome and has been adopted by a number of Canadian hospitals, including the BC Children's Hospital in Vancouver and the Children's Hospital in London, Ontario. More information about the intervention can be found at the following website: www.purplecrying.info.

LEARNING OBJECTIVE 12.5

Explain how early experience can affect later social, emotional, and cognitive development.

1. Discuss what is known about early daycare and attachment.
2. Discuss the effects of early abuse on attachment.
3. Discuss what is known about persistent crying in early infancy and the PURPLE intervention program.

CONCLUSION

We said at the beginning of this chapter that social development is a complex topic. By now, that should be very clear. But it is important to understand that this complexity is of two different types.

The first concerns social interactions themselves. Because these behaviours are transactional—with people continually affecting one another—it becomes difficult to separate the causes of social behaviours from their effects. Even in the infant–mother relationship, as we have seen, social influences can be subtle and highly interrelated. Identifying the determinants of the baby's and the mother's behaviours thus can be a very challenging task.

The second reason this topic is so complex is that social development is affected by more than social influences. How the child interacts with other people is the result of biological processes, cognitive abilities, and non-social environmental factors—in addition to the influences of others in the child's world. Only recently have psychologists begun to appreciate the extent to which these non-social factors are involved in the development of social relationships, as we shall continue to see in later chapters.

In this chapter, we have focused on the attachment process and the developmental events that lead up to it. Other social relationships and processes also occur during infancy, and we consider those in the chapters that follow. In addition, we examine social development beyond the early years as the child grows away from the caregiver and the home to become a member of the larger society.

SUMMARY

KEY TERMS

Adult Attachment Interview, p. 471
affect, p. 450
affect mirroring, p. 456
Attachment Q-Set (AQS), p. 468
display rules, p. 452
EAS model, p. 460
emotions, p. 450
goodness of fit, p. 459
inhibition, p. 463
interactional synchrony, p. 455
internal working models, p. 447
maternal bonding, p. 465
microanalysis, p. 455
New York Longitudinal Study (NYLS), p. 459
primary caregiver, p. 445
separation protest, p. 465
social cognition, p. 447
socialization, p. 446
Strange Situation procedure, p. 466
temperament, p. 457
wariness of strangers, p. 465

LEARNING OBJECTIVES

LEARNING OBJECTIVE 12.1 Understand the major theoretical approaches to early social development.

1. *How does the ethological approach explain infant–mother attachment?*
   Ethologists contend that evolution has provided many of the responses necessary for the infant's survival. Babies are programmed by nature to produce behaviours that keep the primary caregiver close at hand and encourage her to provide appropriate caregiving. The caregiver, in turn, is biologically predisposed to read and respond to the infant's signals. Infant–mother attachment results from these innate behaviours. Most adherents of attachment theory consider sensitive, responsive mothers and securely attached infants to be nature's prototype. Recent evolutionary theory also holds that attachment need not follow one pattern and may develop differently, depending on environmental variables.

2. *Explain how the environmental/learning approaches view early infant social behaviour.*
   Social-learning theorists have been concerned mainly with the infant's socialization. According to this view, mother–infant attachment responses result from social-learning processes, with the infant and caregiver each providing consequences for the other's behaviour. Infant behaviours such as crying, smiling, and vocalizing can both influence and be influenced by the caregiver's response through a conditioning process.

3. *What individual differences in attachment have researchers identified?*
   Mary Ainsworth identified three common patterns of infant response: pattern A, insecure–avoidant; pattern B, securely attached; and pattern C, insecure–resistant. Most babies display pattern B, but the proportion of infants in each classification varies across cultures, apparently reflecting different attitudes toward child rearing. Because Ainsworth's three original categories proved insufficient to account for all types of parent–infant interaction, researchers have described a fourth type of attachment: pattern D, insecure–disorganized/disoriented.

4. *What are the causes and consequences of individual differences in attachment?*
   The quality of the infant–caregiver attachment relationship appears to result primarily from the caregiver's responsiveness. Caregivers who are more sensitive to their babies' signals and who adjust their behaviour to mesh with that of their children are more likely to develop secure attachment relationships. The mother's recollections of her childhood and the infant's temperament also play a role. Secure attachment to the caregiver has several positive effects on the child's development. Children who were securely attached as infants display greater cognitive and social competence than their insecurely attached counterparts. Securely attached children are also less likely to develop emotional and behaviour problems.

LEARNING OBJECTIVE 12.5 Explain how early experience can affect later social, emotional, and cognitive development.

1. *Discuss what is known about early daycare and attachment.*
   An increasing number of mothers work outside the home and leave some of the job of childrearing to others. Early studies on the results of this practice reported that infants whose mothers were employed were less likely than those whose mothers stayed at home to be classified as securely attached. Later studies failed to replicate these findings, however, and a large-scale governmental study found no evidence that placing a child in daycare in itself affects the security of the child's attachment to the caregiver. Evidence does indicate, however, that a child whose mother is low in sensitivity is more likely to be classified as insecurely attached when (1) the daycare centre also does not provide a high level of care, (2) the child spends a great deal of time in daycare, or (3) the child has had many different childcare arrangements.

2. *Discuss the effects of early abuse on attachment.*
   Abuse and neglect have major negative effects on both social and cognitive development. Many researchers believe that these effects result from the lack of a secure attachment relationship with the parents. Parental care that is overstimulating and abusive is more frequently associated with insecure–avoidant attachment. Parental care that is understimulating and characterized by neglect tends to be associated with insecure–resistant attachment. Parental care that is frightening to the infants and results in feelings of abandonment is associated with insecure–disorganized/disoriented attachment.

3. *Discuss what is known about persistent crying in early infancy and the PURPLE intervention program.*
   It is quite common during the first few months for infants to engage in bouts of prolonged, inconsolable crying in the evening. Such crying can be quite frustrating for parents, and some react by violently shaking the baby. Shaken Baby Syndrome results in serious brain damage and even death. The PURPLE intervention program seeks to help parents cope with the potential frustration that can result from such excessive crying. The program helps parents realize that bouts of prolonged crying are normal in early infancy, as are the feelings of frustration that often result.

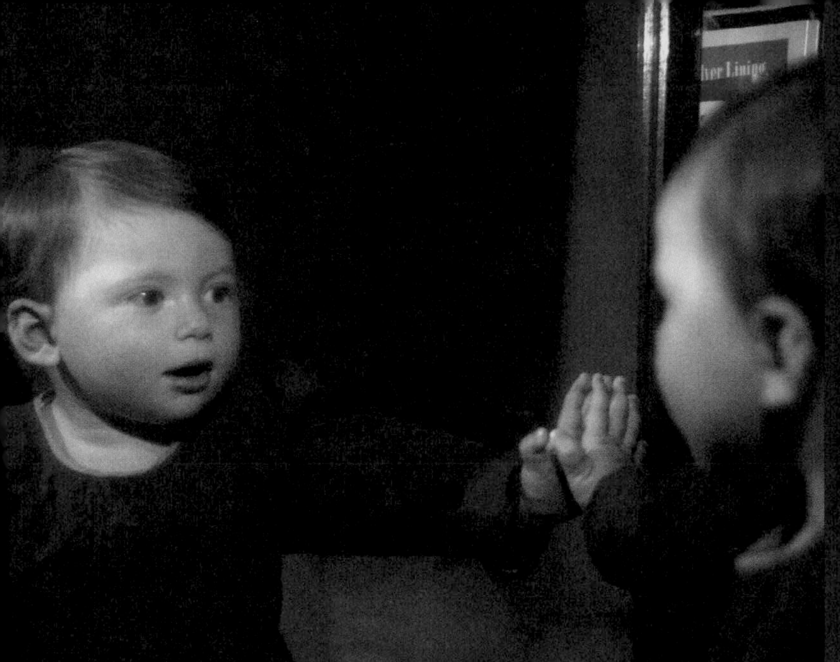

CHAPTER 13

DEVELOPMENT OF THE SELF

One day, when Joanne Klauke-LaBelle was teaching music to a group of children in her home in Sarnia, Ontario, a teenage boy came over to talk with her. She told him she was busy but would call him later. He went home and committed suicide.

Klauke-LaBelle was so distraught, she researched suicide and vowed to help prevent it. In 1995 she started Harmony for Youth, a non-profit program aimed at boosting self-esteem for at-risk youth through the arts. "The arts offer a unique avenue for youth to vent, release emotion, and find an alternative, constructive way of self-expression, thus reducing self-mutilation, use of drugs and alcohol, and suicide," says the Harmony for Youth website.

There are no waiting lists or prerequisites. Students take music and other arts lessons for free, as long as they "pay it forward:" For each hour of instruction, they must do an hour of community service. "They find out their value in the community through volunteering," says Klauke-LaBelle.

Part of the youths' volunteer and esteem-building hours are spent giving over 200 concerts a year in places such as nursing homes and on Parliament Hill. The program's volunteers and participants also help out in the broader community. When Hurricane Katrina devastated the southern United States, Klauke-LaBelle and a team of Harmony volunteers went to Houston to donate 500 pairs of drumsticks and other items.

Harmony for Youth opened a branch in Houston, and many more in Canada, including on First Nations reserves, have followed.

It also launched a suicide resource centre in Sarnia. "Mental health is something we need to talk about, and we need to talk about it daily," Klauke-LaBelle said at the centre's opening.

In this chapter we examine the development of the self, beginning in infancy. We discuss the development of the self-concept, self-esteem, and self-control, as these aspects of the self develop through childhood.

Source: "Harmony bio," Harmony for Youth, no date, available at http://www.harmonyforyouth.org/images/newsletters/Harmony%20Bio%2008-09.pdf

Punch, Daniel, "Harmony volunteers help 'pay it forward,'" *Sarnia Observer*, July 13, 2009.

Young, Heather Linda, "Resource centre music to Harmony's ears," *Sarnia This Week*, October 5, 2011. ■

Existential self The "I" component of the self, which is concerned with the subjective experience of existing.

Categorical self The "Me" component of the self, which involves one's objective personal characteristics.

Self-system The set of interrelated processes—self-knowledge, self-evaluation, and self-regulation—that make up the self.

Self-knowledge (self-awareness) The part of the self-system concerned with children's knowledge about themselves.

Self-evaluation The part of the self-system concerned with children's opinions of themselves and their abilities.

Self-regulation The part of the self-system concerned with self-control.

OVER THE YEARS, psychologists have conceptualized the self using several schemes. One early and influential view, first proposed over 100 years ago by William James (1890, 1892), divides the self into two major components: the subjective "I" and the objective "Me." The I, or **existential self**, is the subjective experiencer of the world, whereas the Me, or **categorical self**, is an objective entity seen and evaluated in the world. The I includes a sense of personal identity, a sense of being able to do things (personal agency), and an awareness of one's continuing existence across time (Harter, 2003, 2008; Moore & Lemmon, 2001). The Me includes such traits as physical appearance, personality traits, and cognitive abilities (Harter, 2003, 2008).

A more recent conceptualization posits that the self is a broad concept that can be divided into three distinct but interrelated elements: self-knowledge, self-evaluation, and self-regulation (Harter, 2006b). Together, these compose the **self-system**.

- **Self-knowledge (self-awareness)** is concerned with the questions: What do children know about themselves as distinct, enduring individuals? When do they acquire this knowledge? How is this knowledge related to their understanding of other aspects of their social and physical environments?
- **Self-evaluation** concerns the questions: Does the child have high or low self-esteem? What factors influence children's opinions of themselves? How do these opinions affect their behaviour?
- Finally, **self-regulation** is concerned with the questions: How and when do children acquire self-control? What variables influence this process?

Our coverage of the self in this chapter focuses on these three major elements. Throughout the chapter, we also maintain our interest in the themes that have guided our discussions in other areas: what the four principal theoretical traditions have to say about this topic, how it looks from the nature and the nurture perspectives, and how researchers have investigated it.

Learning Objective 13.1

Compare and contrast five theoretical perspectives on the development of the self-system.

THEORIES OF THE SELF

The three components of the self-system cover a very broad range of topics and issues. Perhaps for that reason, no theoretical perspective explains all aspects of this complex area. In this section, we begin by considering what each of the major theories has to say about the self—approaches that will be revisited in later sections of the chapter as well.

COGNITIVE-DEVELOPMENTAL APPROACHES

The concept of the self and its relation to other aspects of development has been of considerable interest to cognitive-developmental psychologists. Those working from the framework of information-processing theory focus on how children's cognitive abilities to process information limit and shape the development of the self. Other theorists have proposed normative models of self-development based largely on Piaget's theory (Harter, 2006b, 2008; Selman, 1980).

Self-schema An internal cognitive portrait of the self used to organize information about the self.

INFORMATION-PROCESSING MODEL Children's information-processing abilities—how they encode, interpret, and remember information—contribute to the creation of self-relevant cognitive structures that, in turn, influence how further information is processed. Specifically, researchers believe that, over time, each child develops a **self-schema**, an internal notion of "who I am," composed of various features and characteristics. As a child encounters new information, the self-schema works to filter, interpret, and organize that information. Whenever we encounter new events or information, we attempt to understand them in terms of these cognitive structures (Kihlstrom et al., 2003). Support for the existence of such structures is found in studies showing that people are better able to recall words and events that they can apply to themselves than to recall descriptors that do not seem to relate to them (Pullybank et al., 1985; Skowronski et al., 1995).

For example, developmental psychologists have wondered whether being asked to process information in a self-relevant way would influence children's memory for that information. Specifically, researchers presented children with lists of words spoken one at a time. Half the words were followed by the question, "Is this word like you?" and the other half were followed by, "Is this a long word?" As predicted, answering the first question regarding the word's relatedness to oneself made children more likely to recall the word later than did the second question, which was neutral in regard to the self.

A second variable focused on how children's levels of self-esteem and depression influence their memories. Half the words presented to the children described positive personal traits (brave, helpful, and so on); the other half described negative personal traits (such as lonely and ugly). Again, as predicted, children who were high in self-esteem and were not depressed showed better recall of the positive traits, whereas depressed children with low self-esteem showed better recall of the negative traits (Hammen & Zupan, 1984; Zupan, Hammen, & Jaenicke, 1987). Similar research has found that children of depressed mothers also are more likely to remember negative rather than positive self-information (Taylor & Ingram, 1999).

This type of research illustrates how powerfully children's self-schemas can influence how they relate to the world around them. For example, children whose self-esteem is high are apparently more attuned to information that is consistent with a positive view of themselves. They may be likely to notice compliments, which, in turn, should further enhance their self-image. Children low in self-esteem, in contrast, are more aware of information that confirms their negative feelings and thus likely serves to decrease self-esteem even more.

A DEVELOPMENTAL MODEL: SELMAN'S WORK ON SELF-AWARENESS A detailed account of children's self-awareness has been presented by Robert Selman (1980). In the tradition of other cognitive-developmental theories, the model was developed from extensive clinical interviews with children and emphasizes development through stages.

Selman presented children of various ages with brief stories in which the main character faces a conflict or dilemma. The children were then asked a series of questions regarding what the character was thinking and feeling and how the dilemma would be resolved. The focus was not so much on the children's solutions as on the type of reasoning they used to arrive at the solutions.

Using these responses, Selman identified a five-stage progression in self-awareness. The model includes some assumptions that are common to most stage theories. That is, the stages (1) follow a fixed sequence through which all children pass with no regression to earlier stages, (2) are consistent across different problems and situations, (3) are universal across cultures, and (4) develop as a result of changes in the child's cognitive abilities (Gurucharri & Selman, 1982).

The five stages are summarized briefly below. Note that Selman's stages begin with the infant's awareness of only the physical self and progress gradually to greater appreciation for other features of the self, such as an understanding of the potential for a private or "hidden" self, which appears in middle childhood, and the recognition in adolescence that the self may include unconscious components.

Level 0 (Infancy): Children understand their physical existence but do not display an awareness of a separate psychological existence. The child does not, for example, distinguish between physical behaviour (such as crying) and simultaneous emotional feelings (such as being sad).

Level 1 (Early Childhood): The child now separates psychological states from behaviour and believes that thoughts can control actions. But the child also believes that inner thoughts and feelings are directly represented in outward appearance and behaviour, so that someone's self can be known simply by observing the person's actions and statements (for example, that a person who is whistling and smiling must be happy).

Level 2 (Middle Childhood): The child appreciates that feelings and motives can be different from behaviour, and thus that the self can, to some degree, be hidden from others; it cannot, however, be hidden from oneself.

Level 3 (Preadolescence): Children in later childhood show a growing belief that the self represents a stable component of personality. They believe that people can observe and evaluate their inner selves, suggesting that the mind (which does the observing) is somehow separate from the self (which is observed).

Level 4 (Adolescence): Ultimately, the adolescent comes to believe that the self cannot ever be completely known because some aspects of personality remain at an unconscious level.

ENVIRONMENTAL/LEARNING APPROACHES

Social-learning theorists have proposed a number of psychological processes that are relevant to the self. Two theoretical models have been developed by Albert Bandura: one involves self-evaluation, while the other involves self-regulation.

Self-efficacy Bandura's term for people's ability to succeed at various tasks, as judged by the people themselves.

Bandura's self-evaluation model is built around the concept of **self-efficacy**, a person's ability, as judged by that person, to carry out various behaviours and acts (Bandura, 1997, 2001, 2006). Bandura observes that just as infants and young children do not understand the operations of the physical and social world very well, they also do not know much about their own skills and abilities. Studies have shown, for example, that parents (and teachers) can predict how well children will perform on academic tasks much better than can children themselves (Miller & Davis, 1992; Stipek & MacIver, 1989). Similarly, in everyday situations, parents must frequently warn children, for example, that they are swimming out too far, that a particular library book will be too difficult for them to understand, or that they can never finish the largest ice cream sundae on the menu. Such verbal instructions from parents, along with many trial-and-error experiences, help young children gradually learn the limits of their talents and capabilities; that is, accurately judge their self-efficacy (Maddux & Gosselin, 2003).

As children grow, two other mechanisms promote the development of self-efficacy judgments. One is modelling, which children come to use as a way of estimating the likelihood of success at a task (Maddux & Gosselin, 2003). For example, a child might reason, "If that little girl [who is my size and age] can jump over that fence, I can probably do it, too." Using vicarious experiences in this way obviously involves somewhat sophisticated cognitive abilities in that the child must determine the appropriate models and situations for making comparisons.

Another way in which children learn to estimate their potential for success is through awareness of internal bodily reactions. For example, feelings of emotional arousal (e.g., tension, a nervous stomach, or a fast heart rate) frequently become associated with failures. As a result, children begin to interpret these feelings as indications of fear, anxiety, or lack of confidence, and they learn to use them to decide that failure is close at hand (Maddux & Gosselin, 2003).

For Thought and Discussion

How have your beliefs about self-efficacy directly affected decisions you made recently? Do you think that following your self-efficacy judgments is always wise?

Self-efficacy judgments are important because they are believed to significantly affect children's behaviour. Bandura contends, for example, that greater feelings of self-efficacy produce increased effort and persistence on a task and thus, ultimately, a higher level of performance. This concept is especially relevant in the area of children's academic achievement and how it relates to their self-evaluations—a topic we discuss later in the chapter.

Bandura also proposed a theoretical mechanism to explain the development of self-regulation (Bandura, 1991a). Early on, children's behaviour is only externally controlled through such processes as modelling, consequences (reinforcement and punishment), and direct instruction. With experience, however, children learn to anticipate the reactions of others, and they use this knowledge to self-regulate their behaviour. For example, as a child learns (through external processes) how the teacher expects her to behave in the classroom, she begins to monitor her behaviour to conform to these expectations. Gradually, the child internalizes the rules, and they become her own personal standards. Now the child's behaviour comes under the control of her **evaluative self-reactions**; that is, the child notes whether her behaviour has met her personal standards and then applies self-sanctions in the form of self-approval ("I did well today") or self-disapproval ("I shouldn't have done that"). According to Bandura, self-regulation occurs as children become motivated to behave in ways that match their internal standards and that lead to feelings of self-satisfaction.

Evaluative self-reactions Bandura's term for consequences people apply to themselves as a result of meeting or failing to meet their personal standards.

EVOLUTIONARY AND BIOLOGICAL APPROACHES

Two approaches to the self fall under the framework of evolutionary and biological approaches—Bowlby's attachment theory and evolutionary psychology. Historically, Bowlby's theory has proven to be the more influential.

BOWLBY'S ATTACHMENT THEORY In his landmark writings on attachment, John Bowlby discussed his belief that the sense of self begins to develop within the context of infant–caregiver interactions and is promoted by responsive caregiving. These ideas have been elaborated by other developmental theorists. For example, responsive caregiving leads to a more secure attachment between baby and mother, which, in turn, should affect the infant's development of an internal working model of the self (as well as of the mother) (Bretherton & Munholland, 2008). Babies whose caregivers are sensitive and responsive should construct an internal model of the self as lovable and worthy of attention; babies whose caregivers are neglectful and insensitive should form models of the self as unworthy (Weinfield et al., 2008). We will see shortly that evidence from both normal and clinical populations of children provides support for these ideas.

EVOLUTIONARY PSYCHOLOGY In recent years, evolutionary psychologists have taken up the issue of the self. Researchers working within this framework are interested in three questions: (1) At what point in human evolution did the modern self emerge? (2) What is the adaptive function of having a self? (3) What is the neuropsychological basis of the self?

To address the first question, evolutionary psychologists explore the existence of self-consciousness among non-human species. Although evolutionary theorists have long suspected that species other than humans may possess a self-concept (Darwin, 1871/1896), documenting self-consciousness among species that cannot talk about the self challenged researchers for decades (Lewis, 2011; Mitchell, 2003).

Great strides in the study of animal self-awareness occurred in 1970 with the publication of a paper on primate mirror self-recognition by Gordon Gallup, Jr. As described in *Research Classic 13.1*, Gallup described an experimental procedure that provided compelling evidence that chimpanzees are able to recognize their images in mirrors. Since Gallup's pioneering study, scientists have tested many other species for mirror self-recognition. These include a wide variety of primates, fish, birds, dolphins, and even elephants (presumably using a very large mirror!). Among primates, only hominids (orangutan, bonobo, chimpanzee) show clear evidence of self-recognition (the evidence regarding gorillas is mixed) (Barth et al., 2004; De Veer et al., 2003; Heschel & Burkart, 2006). Studies using variations on the mark test suggest bottle-nosed dolphins may also have the capacity for self-recognition (Barth et al., 2004; Herman, 2002).

Although some skeptics remain, most scientists agree that chimpanzees and several other great apes and perhaps dolphins have some kind of rudimentary self-concept. The exact nature of this self-concept is, however, hotly debated (Barth et al., 2004; Gallup, Anderson, & Shillito, 2002; Povinelli & Bering, 2002).

For Thought and Discussion

From an evolutionary perspective, what would be the selective value of self-awareness for primates such as humans?

The second question of interest to evolutionary psychologists concerns how (or why) the self evolved. Many evolutionary psychologists believe that human intellectual capabilities were shaped by selection pressures associated with living in a group with a complex social organization (Bjorklund & Pellegrini, 2002a, 2002b). According to this perspective, self-awareness is important because it lays the foundation for other capabilities required for group living, most notably the ability to understand the mental states of others. Indeed, the species that show self-recognition do live in complex social groups. However, other species (e.g., spotted hyenas) live in social groups and do not exhibit self-awareness (Holekamp & Engh, 2002).

The third question of interest to evolutionary psychologists is the neurological basis of the self. As described in earlier chapters, evolutionary psychologists generally believe that evolved human capabilities are encapsulated in modules in the brain. Studies of children with autism—who exhibit impairment in both self-recognition and the ability to draw inferences about others' mental states—provide some support for the modularized view of self-knowledge (Baron-Cohen, 2000).

Further evidence can be found in studies of clinical patients with damage to specific regions in the frontal cortex. These individuals show impairments in the ability to recognize their own faces and to engage in self-evaluation as well as in autobiographical memory (Gallup et al., 2002; Keenan, Wheeler, & Ewers, 2003). There is also some evidence that gorillas, which may not show self-recognition, have a smaller, less well-developed frontal cortex than the other great apes that have the capacity for self-recognition (Semendeferi, 1999). The same is true of monkeys, which do not show self-recognition (Semendeferi et al., 2002). However, recent studies using brain-imaging techniques suggest that in average human adults, a neural network involving both right and left hemisphere brain structures is involved in self-recognition (Kircher et al., 2001). These findings caution against taking an overly simplistic view of the way the brain is involved in various kinds of self-understanding.

RESEARCH CLASSIC 13.1
THE MONKEY IN THE MIRROR: PRIMATE SELF-RECOGNITION

The concept of the self was at one time held to be a uniquely human capacity. In the late 1960s, Gordon Gallup, Jr. decided to test this claim by assessing whether chimpanzees have the capacity for self-recognition—a very basic aspect of the self. One way to measure self-recognition is to observe reactions to one's image in a mirror.

There had been reports of home-reared apes using mirrors to explore their teeth (Mitchell, 2003). However, these observations and those of babies playing with mirrors were open to interpretation. Both apes and babies might enjoy interacting with mirror images without recognizing the images as themselves. Researchers needed a technique that would allow them to make the distinction.

Gallup (1970) first gave several preadolescent chimpanzees 10 days of individualized exposure to mirrors. In each case, the chimp initially reacted to its reflection as if the reflection were another chimp (e.g., bobbing, vocalizing, threatening). After about three days, however, the chimpanzees began to behave in ways similar to the reports of home-reared apes and suggestive of self-recognition. For instance, they would pick food from between their teeth, make bubbles, and manipulate wads of food with their lips while watching their images in the mirror.

To test whether the chimpanzees had truly learned to recognize their own images, Gallup devised what has come to be known as the mark test. Gallup anaesthetized each animal and applied red dye to an eyebrow ridge and to the opposite ear. On waking, the chimpanzees at first almost never touched the marks. When the mirror was reintroduced, however, the chimps began to frequently touch the marks. Clearly they related the marks they saw in the mirror to their own bodies.

Gallup's study has had an enduring effect on developmental psychology. Though researchers had long been interested in babies' reactions to their mirror images (e.g., Gesell, 1925; Shirley 1933), they were reluctant to conclude that an infant recognized the image until he or she could label it (e.g., "It's me!"). As we have seen, reliance on verbal measures of understanding often underestimates what infants really know. The mark test pioneered by Gallup provided researchers with a tool to assess self-recognition among preverbal infants. (Interestingly, unbeknownst to Gallup, Beulah Amsterdam [1972] was using a similar technique with human infants around the same time.) Although researchers now employ a variety of techniques to assess children's self-recognition, the mark test is still in use today.

SOCIOCULTURAL APPROACHES

The sociocultural approach focuses on the socialization of the self and self-understanding through participation in cultural practices, customs, and institutions. Socialization practices reflect each culture's model of the self. These models, in turn, derive from societal ideals and values and vary from culture to culture.

CULTURAL MODELS OF THE SELF Cultural models of the self vary across a number of dimensions (Cross & Gore, 2003). Of these, the most extensively documented is the relation of the self to others. As we saw in Chapter 8, cultural communities with roots in Western European traditions tend to draw a clear distinction between the self and others. In this view, the self is independent, self-contained, and autonomous. In many other cultures, the boundary between the self and others is less clearly drawn. In this model, which is common in many East Asian, Central and South American, and Native American groups, the self and others are seen as interdependent or interconnected.

Although the self–other dimension has been most widely studied cross-culturally, conceptions of the self vary in other ways as well. Cultures differ in the age at which they assign "selfhood" or person-status to an individual. For instance, in some cultures, children are not considered "persons" until they are several months or even years old (Riesman, 1992).

Even more dramatic variations are found in how cultures perceive the self through space and time. Some Native American societies believe that the self may leave the body and metamorphose into other forms, such as an eagle or bear. Cultures that endorse the idea of reincarnation believe that a self may have previously inhabited other bodies (Barth, 1997). And, of course, there is considerable cultural variation in beliefs about the existence of the self after biological death.

Cultures also vary in terms of the ideal self. In Caucasian North American communities, for example, the ideal person is independent. In these communities, individuals strive to distinguish themselves from the crowd. Personal economic and psychological needs take precedence over those of the group. In contrast, in many East Asian societies, the ideal person is closely connected with others. In these communities, individuals strive to conform, maintain harmonious interpersonal relations, and bring favour to the family (Ho, 1995; Markus & Kitayama, 1991; Tu, 1994).

Although every culture provides a broad outline of the ideal self, cultures also provide some options. The range of possible selves varies widely across cultures. In diverse, heterogeneous cultures, there is a veritable supermarket of identities from which to choose (Mathews, 1996). In others, there are relatively few options (e.g., in some cultures, women are seen mainly as wives and mothers) (Cross & Gore, 2003).

In contrast to the autonomous view of the self stressed in Western thought, many cultures view self and others as interdependent. (*Kevin Frayer/The Canadian Press*)

CULTURAL SHAPING OF THE SELF From the first days of an infant's life, caregivers adopt practices that are largely compatible with their own cultural views of the self. Consider, for example, sleeping arrangements. From the first weeks of life, most infants in North American Caucasian families sleep in their own beds, often in their own rooms (Goldberg & Keller, 2007). Although parents offer a variety of reasons for this practice (including safety concerns), a significant number believe that sleeping apart trains children to be independent (Germo et al., 2007; Goldberg & Keller, 2007; McKenna & Volpe, 2007).

Autonomy training pervades other aspects of child rearing as well. For instance, most Caucasian North American parents begin to teach children that they have the right to an opinion by offering choices (e.g., "Do you want the red cup or the blue cup?") long before children can articulate a reply (Markus & Kitayama, 1994). Once a child is old enough to engage in conversation, middle-income parents try not to infringe on the child's right to voice his or her point of view, even if the child is mistaken or fabricating events (Wiley et al., 1998).

For Thought and Discussion

How did social and cultural contexts shape your self-concept?

Adult reactions to disputes among children provide further evidence for the socialization of an autonomous self in Caucasian North American communities. When siblings tussle over video game controls or the favoured seat in the car, for example, middle-income parents often respond by establishing rules for equal, separate turn-taking. In the process, children learn to defend their individual rights and to respect the rights of others (Rogoff, 2003).

In contrast, in cultures that hold a model of the self that emphasizes the interconnectedness of the self with others, caregivers adopt socialization practices compatible with this view (Harkness & Super, 2002). In Japan, for example, infants and toddlers sleep next to their mothers and later with siblings or other family members. In contrast to Caucasian American parents, who believe children should be socialized for independence, for Japanese parents, co-sleeping is one means by which to foster healthy dependence and close bonds with others (Caudill & Weinstein, 1969).

Whereas Caucasian American children are encouraged to speak up and defend their individual rights, children in Japan are taught to rely on others to sense and meet their needs and, in turn, to empathize and be sensitive to the needs of others (Markus & Kitayama, 1994; Roland, 1988). These values are also reflected in adult reactions to children's disputes. Japanese children are taught to sacrifice their personal interests for the sake of interpersonal harmony and that "to lose is to win" (Lebra, 1976; Zahn-Waxler et al., 1996). (See *Focus on Research 13.1* later in this chapter for further discussion of the impact of culture on the self.)

LEARNING OBJECTIVE 13.1

Compare and contrast five theoretical perspectives on the development of the self-system.

1. According to contemporary views, what are the three components of the self-system?
2. How do cognitive-developmental approaches view the development of the self?
3. How do environmental/learning approaches contribute to our understanding of the development of the self?
4. What are examples of biological and evolutionary approaches to questions about the self?
5. What important information do sociocultural approaches provide in understanding the self?

SELF-KNOWLEDGE

Learning Objective 13.2

Trace the development of self-knowledge from infancy, identifying the processes by which changes in the self-system occur.

Our look at the research evidence on the self-system begins with perhaps the most basic questions: what do children know about the self, and when do they know it? It is not uncommon to hear a toddler proudly announce that he is a big boy or that his name is Jeremy. But he may, as yet, have very little understanding of his physical characteristics (heavy or slight), his personality (shy or bold), or his living conditions (middle-income or poor). As we will see, children's self-knowledge develops steadily across the childhood years and is interwoven with the development of other cognitive and socialization processes.

DISCOVERY OF THE SELF IN INFANCY

When do babies first understand that they exist separately from the surrounding world? This question has long been of interest in developmental psychology. Some researchers believe that babies have an inborn awareness of their existence, or at least that awareness develops within the first weeks of life (Butterworth, 1995; Gibson, 1993; Samuels, 1986). Others argue that nothing of what babies do requires us to assume they have self-awareness prior to their first birthday (Kagan, 1991). Unfortunately, like many issues involving non-verbal infants, this one is not easily settled.

THE ROLE OF PERCEPTION Perceptual processes are thought to play an important role in infants' first coming to recognize their separateness (Rochat, 2001, 2003, 2011). For example, we have seen that within only weeks after birth, infants can imitate certain adult facial expressions. This finding has been interpreted to mean that newborns can connect sensory (visual) input with the corresponding motor responses—a capability that lays the groundwork for their realizing that they can interact with and affect the world around them (Meltzoff, 2011; Rochat, 2003).

Links to Related Material

In chapters 8 and 12, you read about infants' early capacities to imitate adult facial expressions. Here, you learn more about how this and other early perceptual capacities may be linked to the infant's developing sense of agency.

By 3 months of age, infants seem to perceive that they control their own body movements. One study had babies seated in an apparatus in which they could see live images of their legs transmitted on two television monitors in front of them. Different images—sometimes reversed or upside down—were presented on each screen, and it was clear from the babies' looking responses that they could easily detect when the timing or direction of the leg movements they viewed did not correspond to what they were doing (Rochat & Morgan, 1995). Mark Schmuckler (1995) of the University of Toronto has reported the same findings with infants' arm movements.

Studies of perception also have shown that in the months that follow, the self becomes much more clearly defined. As we saw in Chapter 7, when 6-month-olds are taught to look for an object located in one position relative to themselves (say, to the left) and then are rotated to the opposite orientation (so that the object is to their right), they continue to search for the object by looking left. The addition of visual cues or landmarks to encourage more appropriate searching has little effect on babies of this age (Acredolo, 1985). This approach, of course, results in unsuccessful searching and gradually gives way to more effective, environmentally guided perceptual strategies as the baby approaches 1 year. But in using themselves as anchor points when searching, young infants demonstrate at least a crude awareness of their own separate existence.

PERSONAL AGENCY Along with infants' knowledge that they exist apart from the things around them comes an understanding of **personal agency**; that is, an understanding that they can be the agents or causes of events that occur in their worlds. Now babies move toys and put things in their mouths and bang blocks, all suggesting an awareness both that they are separate from these things and that they can do something with them (Morin, 2004; Rochat, 2011). Personal agency also appears to develop through babies' early interactions with caregivers (Emde et al., 1991; Morin, 2004; Sroufe, 1990). Theorists concur that when parents are more sensitive and responsive to their infants' signals, babies more quickly develop an understanding of the impact they can have on their environments (e.g., "I can make Mommy come by crying").

Personal agency The understanding that one can be the cause of events.

A related question is whether babies first acquire an understanding of the self or of the mother. In one study, babies aged 6 months and older watched an adult model eat a Cheerio. They were then given one and instructed either to feed it to themselves or to feed it to their mothers. Significantly more babies at each age level were able to follow the first instruction than were able to follow the second (Pipp, Fischer, & Jennings, 1987). These findings are consistent with others in showing that infants learn to direct actions or speech toward themselves before they direct those same responses toward their mothers or others (Bretherton & Beeghly, 1982; Huttenlocher, Smiley, & Charney, 1983), suggesting that with respect to agency, self-knowledge ("I can do it to me") precedes mother-knowledge ("I can do it to her"). This difference reverses by age 2, when toddlers are better able to direct actions toward their mothers and other objects than toward themselves. This change may result from older infants' becoming more self-conscious (Lewis, 2008a, 2011) and therefore less comfortable with directing actions toward themselves. Or it may reflect the child's increasing focus on interpersonal relations and newly emerging capacity for play (Pipp-Siegel & Foltz, 1997).

SELF-RECOGNITION

As babies approach age 2, they display an increasing awareness of the self. Perhaps the form of self-knowledge that has attracted the most research is infants' ability to recognize what they look like.

Visual self-recognition The ability to recognize oneself often studied in babies by having them look into mirrors.

VISUAL SELF-RECOGNITION IN INFANCY A number of researchers have investigated the development of **visual self-recognition** by examining babies' reactions to mirror reflections. The major issue in this research concerns whether babies actually recognize the reflected images as themselves.

During their first year, babies will smile and vocalize at their mirror reflections (Rochat, 2003). There is some evidence that babies can distinguish between their own image and that of another child. When infants as young as 3 months of age are shown still images of themselves and another baby, they exhibit a clear preference for looking at the other child. This finding indicates not only that they can discriminate between the two images, but that their own is familiar to them (Bahrick, 1995; Bahrick et al., 1996).

Visual self-recognition has been the most commonly used method of assessing infants' and toddlers' self-awareness. (*Vanessa Berberian/Image Bank/Getty Images*)

By about 5 months of age, this procedure reveals another interesting finding. When the still images are altered (such as by placing coloured marks on the cheeks of both babies), the looking preference changes, and infants spend more time looking at their own images (Bahrick, 1995; Neilsen et al., 2003). Whether babies this young realize that what they are seeing is themselves, however, is not known.

One sure way to know if a toddler recognizes herself in a mirror is if she labels the image ("It's me!" or "Amy!"). Pronouns, such as *me* and *mine*, as well as the child's name, enter the child's vocabulary during the second year of life (Rochat, 2011). By their second birthday, most children can apply these labels to their reflections in mirrors. But researchers have long been curious as to whether children recognize mirror images as themselves even before they can apply the appropriate labels (Lewis & Ramsay, 2004).

To investigate whether an infant understands that the image in the mirror is himself or herself, psychologists use the mark test described earlier (*Research Classic 13.1*). A coloured mark is surreptitiously placed on the infant's face in a location where she cannot normally see it, such as on her forehead. The baby is then placed before a mirror, and the investigators note whether she attempts to touch the mark. If she does, they conclude that she understands that the marked face in the mirror is her own. Using this measure, researchers have not found self-recognition in infants younger than 15 months of age; self-recognition does not occur reliably until about 24 months (Courage et al., 2004; Lewis & Ramsay, 2004).

Visual self-recognition has also been investigated with a variety of other techniques. For instance, researchers at St. Francis Xavier University (Bigelow, 1981) compared infants' reactions to videotapes or photographs of themselves with their reactions to tapes or photos of similar peers (see also Suddendorf, Simcock, & Nielsen, 2007). Researchers at Memorial University of Newfoundland and Lakehead University (Courage, Edison, & Howe, 2004) had infants point to pictures of themselves in a group of photos after hearing their names. Evidence from these measures places self-recognition several months later than do the mirror-technique findings.

When the marked-face type of procedure includes a delay, the age of self-recognition rises even further. One study had 2-, 3-, and 4-year-old children play a simple game, during which the experimenter frequently patted the child on the head and at some point surreptitiously placed a large sticker on the child's head. Shortly thereafter, the child was invited to watch a videotape of the game, which clearly showed the experimenter placing the sticker on the child's head. None of the 2-year-olds searched for the stickers on their own bodies, and only 25 percent of the 3-year-olds did so—even though they typically could label their video image with a confident "That's me!" Only the 4-year-olds searched consistently for the sticker (Povinelli, 1995, 2001).

These marked-face procedures may, however, underestimate the dawning of self-recognition because these actions require several accompanying cognitive achievements. As Mary Courage of Memorial University and Mark Howe of Lakehead University point out, mark-directed behaviour may reflect more than self-recognition; it may signify a broad shift in cognitive development as the child approaches 2 years of age (Courage & Howe, 2002).

INDIVIDUAL DIFFERENCES IN SELF-RECOGNITION Regardless of the method used, self-recognition appears at different ages for different infants. What could be the source of these differences? One hypothesis is that self-recognition relates to temperament. Specifically, babies who react strongly in stress situations (and so are usually classified as difficult) are thought to develop a sense of self earlier than do other babies in order to deal better with the intensity of the stimulation they experience. Consistent with this idea, infants who react most strongly to vaccinations at 6 months of age also are most likely to show mirror self-recognition at 18 months of age (Lewis & Ramsay, 1997).

Another source of individual differences in self-recognition is attachment. Researchers have confirmed that children who are securely attached have a better understanding of both personal agency and physical characteristics than do children in other attachment classifications (Pipp, Easterbrooks, & Harmon, 1992; Verschueren, Marcoen, & Schoefs, 1996). Moreover, infants whose relationships with their mothers are characterized by emotional responsiveness show better self-recognition than do other children (Harel et al., 2002). Thus, a secure attachment relationship appears to promote the development of the self.

Why might this be? As we indicated earlier, some psychologists believe that mother–child interaction provides an infant with the opportunity to first develop a concept of a separate self. And as mentioned in Chapter 12, a secure attachment to the caregiver promotes exploration and cognitive development in the baby—all factors that may contribute to the development of self-recognition.

One research team has sought to investigate the relationship between attachment and self-recognition in cases where children have been abused and neglected. The maltreated infants were found to be less securely attached and displayed less evidence of self-recognition (Cicchetti, 2010). Moreover, the maltreated infants responded more negatively to their mirror reflections, which the researchers speculate may indicate the beginnings of a low sense of self-worth (Cicchetti, 2010). Research with abused children has also found that their language is less likely to involve descriptions of themselves or of their internal states and feelings (Cicchetti & Rogosch, 2001; Coster et al., 1989).

SELF-AWARENESS AND AWARENESS OF OTHERS One consequence of infants' increasing awareness of their own identities may be a greater awareness of the separateness and distinctiveness of others. That is, as we become more self-aware, we should simultaneously become more other-aware. There is some evidence that infants draw distinctions between themselves and others at a very young age. In one study, for example, infants 4 months of age responded differently to a live video of an adult mimicking their behaviour than to their own live video image. In this study, infants' behaviours toward the mimicker were more social than were their reactions to their own image, with more smiling and longer gazes. In addition, when the video images of both the infants and their adult mimickers were frozen for one minute, infants made more attempts to re-engage the adult image, suggesting recognition that another person—but not one's own image—is a potential social partner. This difference was present in both 4- and 9-month-old children, with a large increase in re-engagement behaviours across the two ages (Rochat & Striano, 2002).

Links to Related Material

Here, you learn about the child's developing sense of self and other. In Chapter 15, you will read more about children's early peer interactions.

Further evidence for children's developing appreciation of the existence and individuality of others can be found in an early type of play termed *synchronic imitation*. In synchronic imitation, preverbal children play with similar toys in a similar fashion (Asendorpf, 2002; Neilsen & Dissanayake, 2004). For example, one toddler might bang a spoon. This is followed by another toddler banging her spoon, which is followed by the first toddler banging his spoon, and on and on to the great glee of all (except perhaps the daycare provider). To synchronize his play with that of a peer, a child must have some understanding of the other child's intentions and behaviour. This type

Links to Related Material

In Chapter 12, you read about the self-conscious emotions that emerge as children acquire a sense of self. Here, you learn how such self-awareness develops in infants.

Links to Related Material

Here, you learn about children's developing sense of self and its relation to the emergence of empathy. In Chapter 14, you will read more about the development of both empathy and prosocial behaviour in children.

of play would thus seem to require some degree of self- and other-awareness. Consistent with this view, 18-month-olds who give evidence of mirror self-recognition display more synchronic imitation with same-age peers (and also with adults) than do infants who do not recognize themselves in the mirror (Asendorpf & Baudonniere, 1993; Asendorpf et al., 1996).

Self-recognition has also been linked to the emergence of the self-conscious emotions of embarrassment, empathy, and jealousy, which emerge in the second half of the first year (Lewis, 2008a, 2008b; Lewis & Sullivan, 2005). As we discussed in Chapter 12, the experience of these secondary emotions requires a sense of self-awareness. A little later, between the ages of 2 and 3 years, self-conscious evaluative emotions such as pride, shame, and guilt emerge, as children become able to evaluate the self relative to some social standard (Lewis, 2008a, 2008b). A number of researchers have linked these affective experiences with the development of prosocial behaviour and a moral sense (Eisenberg, 2010; Gibbs, 2010). We return to this topic in Chapter 14.

DEVELOPMENTAL CHANGES IN SELF-DESCRIPTIONS

Psychologists have typically assessed older children's self-knowledge by examining their descriptions of themselves. This method has taken various forms, ranging from very unstructured interviews (which might include such general questions as "Who are you?") to very structured questionnaires (which might require answers to such written items as "How old are you?" and "What is your favourite outdoor game?"). Regardless of the method used, researchers have found a relatively predictable pattern of development (Harter, 2006b, 2008).

By the age of 2, many children display knowledge of some of their most basic characteristics. For example, they know whether they are girls or boys, and that they are children rather than adults (Campbell et al., 2002; Ruble, et al., 2006). These category labels are undoubtedly learned through modelling and other learning processes (Leaper & Friedman, 2007), as children repeatedly hear themselves referred to with phrases such as "my little boy," or as they receive approval when they correctly state their age or other personal characteristic. But, as we will see, cognitive development also plays a role in the self-discovery process.

In the preschool years, as shown in Table 13.1, self-descriptions usually involve physical features, possessions, and preferences (Harter, 2003, 2006b). Thus, a 4-year-old might say that she lives in a big house, has a dog, and likes ice cream. This information, however, is not always completely accurate, and children's descriptions are often unrealistically positive. During this period, there is a focus on objective, here-and-now attributes—a finding that corresponds well with Piaget's description of preoperational children's view of the world.

But it is incorrect to assume, as some psychologists have done, that children of this age can comprehend only specific characteristics of themselves and do not understand more general traits, such as being messy or having a big appetite. The self-description a young child offers seems to depend heavily on how the information is sought. Children give more general responses when questions are structured to encourage generality ("Tell me how you are at school with your friends") than when questions seek more specific information ("Tell me what you did at school with friends today") (Eder, 1989, 1990).

TABLE 13.1 CHILDREN'S SELF-DESCRIPTIONS THROUGH THREE AGE PERIODS

Age Period	Piagetian Stage	Focus of Self-Descriptions	Examples
Early childhood	Preoperational	Physical characteristics, possessions, preferences	"I have freckles." "My cat is white."
Middle and later childhood	Concrete operations	Behavioural traits and abilities, emotions, category membership	"I'm a good singer." "I'm a happy kid."
Adolescence	Formal operations	Attitudes, personality attributes (sometimes opposing or associated with different roles), beliefs	"I'm patriotic." "I can be persuasive." "I'm not a quitter."

In middle childhood, self-descriptions change in several ways, reflecting the shift to concrete operational abilities. Rather than limiting their statements to the here-and-now and the physical, 6- to 10-year-olds begin to talk about less tangible characteristics, such as emotions ("Sometimes I feel sad"), and to combine separate attributes (good at climbing, jumping, and running) into an overall category ("I'm a good athlete") (Harter, 2003,2006b). The accuracy of children's information also improves during this period, although they generally continue to stress their positive, rather than negative, characteristics (Phillips & Zimmerman, 1990; Ruble & Dweck, 1995).

In later childhood, descriptions may be based on social comparisons with others, as children evaluate their skills or talents relative to those of friends or classmates ("I'm the best skater on the street") (Harter, 2003, 2006b). Children also can include opposing attributes, such as "I'm good at spelling, but bad at math," in their descriptions. But the earlier tendency to stress positive attributes now sometimes gives way to more intense negative self-evaluations and more general feelings of low self-worth (Harter, 2006b).

As children enter adolescence, their self-descriptions continue to change. The formal operational child thinks and self-describes in more abstract and hypothetical terms. Rather than focusing on physical characteristics and possessions (as in early childhood) or on behavioural traits and abilities (as in middle and later childhood), the adolescent is concerned with attitudes ("I hate chemistry"), personality attributes ("I'm a curious person"), and beliefs involving hypothetical situations ("If I meet someone who has a different idea about something, I try to be tolerant of it") (Harter, 2003, 2006b; Rosenberg, 1986b).

By middle adolescence, the self typically differentiates into more roles. For example, adolescents give different responses when asked to describe themselves in the classroom, at home, and with friends. Sometimes, these differences involve opposing or conflicting attributes, such as being shy in the classroom but outgoing with friends. For the first time, such conflicts produce feelings of confusion and distress (Harter, 2006b).

For Thought and Discussion

Are you aware of displaying false self behaviour? In what contexts? What are the main contrasts between your ideal and real self?

Later in adolescence, these opposing characteristics are often combined into single personality styles ("cheerful" and "sad" are combined into "moody"), and this more complex view of the self comes to be viewed as legitimate and normal (Harter, 2003, 2006b). Adolescents now can display **false self behaviour**, meaning that when necessary, they can purposely behave ("act") in ways that do not reflect their true selves (Harter et al, 1996). The limits of self-development are not yet known, but the self apparently continues to differentiate throughout adolescence and adulthood (Block & Robins, 1993; Hart & Yates, 1996; Harter, 1999).

False self behaviour Behaving in a way that is knowingly different from how one's true self would behave.

ADOLESCENCE AND CULTURAL IDENTITY Adolescence is also the time when many youth begin to explore their cultural heritage and its relevance for their identity. Most of what is known about the development of cultural identity is based on studies of ethnic-minority youth. According to one model (Phinney & Kohatsu, 1997), there are three phases in ethnic identity development. During the initial phase, young people give little consideration to their cultural or ethnic identities. One reason may be that race and ethnicity are simply not sufficiently salient to warrant their attention. Alternatively, they may refuse to consider what it means to belong to an ethnic minority and may simply adopt the views of others without question. In the words of one Mexican American male, "I don't go looking for my culture. I just go by what my parents say and do, and what they tell me to do, the way they are" (Phinney, 1993, p. 68).

During the second phase, however, adolescents grow increasingly interested in learning about their ethnic and cultural heritage and the role it may play in their lives. Transition to this phase may be triggered by personal experiences with prejudice, stereotyping, or racism. Growing awareness of the discrepancies between the values of the dominant culture and the minority culture or exposure to role models or to the history or culture of one's group may also inspire exploration of cultural identity. This process of exploration may lead to the third phase, in which the adolescent commits to his or her ethnic identity (Spencer & Markstrom-Adams, 1990).

Not all ethnic-minority adolescents develop a strong ethnic identity; for some, the process of exploration leads to a lessening of ethnic ties. Others, however, develop a bicultural identity that includes identification with both the majority culture and their ethnic culture (Berry, 2007; Cross & Gore, 2003). For example, Sophie Gaudet and Richard Clément (2005) of the University of Ottawa investigated the process by which the effects of cultural loss and maintenance might occur concomitantly among the Fransaskois, a small and dispersed francophone group living in Saskatchewan. The Fransaskois have been severely affected by acculturation over the past 50 years, with a 50 percent decrease in their population. Gaudet and Clément found that it can be important for adolescents to balance their minority cultural identity with adopting some characteristics of the majority out-group. Thus, greater confidence in speaking English, as well as the maintenance of a francophone identity, were both positively related to the adjustment and self-esteem of the Fransaskois adolescent participants.

Similarly, Catherine Costigan and colleagues at the University of Victoria (Costigan & Dokis, 2006; Costigan, Su, & Hua, 2009), in their study of the children of Chinese immigrants to Canada, also found that many youths maintain a bicultural orientation. These researchers reported that children of Chinese immigrants were often able to participate in the majority Canadian culture, while still maintaining a strong sense of ethnic identity. How children adjust under such circumstances depends in part on how committed their parents are to their ethnic identity. Overall, these results suggest that operating in the host culture does not necessarily interfere with ethnic identity and values. Indeed, John Berry (2007) of Queen's University argues that *integration*—which includes maintaining a positive ethnic and Canadian identity, being able to converse in both one's ethnic language and that of the majority culture, and developing friends from both cultures—is often associated with the best adaptation outcome for immigrant youth. Berry points out that such positive adaptation best takes place in societies that promote multiculturalism, as is our policy in Canada.

To date, as suggested earlier, researchers have paid little attention to the development of cultural identity among children and adolescents of the majority culture. However, a number of theorists have recently proposed that nearly everyone—not just members of racial or ethnic minority groups—participates in more than one cultural community (Arnett, 2002; Rogoff, 2003). For example, many people regard themselves as members of a national—or even global—community, and of more local or specific communities defined by regional values and traditions (e.g., western, rural), religion, as well as ethnic heritage (such as Scottish descent).

FOCUS ON RESEARCH 13.1
SELF-CONTINUITY, CULTURAL IDENTITY, AND SUICIDE AMONG FIRST NATIONS YOUTH

Most young people succeed in giving a satisfactory meaning to their lives. This search for meaning often takes the form of questions such as: What do I want to become? What do I want to accomplish in my life? Unfortunately, too many young people cannot find answers to these questions, and instead decide to take their own lives. Adolescents and young adults commit suicide almost twice as often as other members of the overall population. An even more troubling fact is the prevalence of suicide among First Nations youth. These young people commit suicide five times more often than do Canadian young people overall.

What can explain the higher prevalence of suicide among First Nations youth? Could it be that the challenge of finding their own identity is especially difficult for them as a result of the past governmental policies aimed at undermining First Nations cultures? The report of the Royal Commission on Aboriginal Peoples (Indian and Northern Affairs Canada, 1996) strongly suggests that this could be the case. Over the last century, several First Nations communities were forced to leave their home regions, children were removed from their parents and educated in residential schools, and traditional ways of life were ridiculed, if not criminalized.

Recently, researchers at the University of British Columbia, Simon Fraser University, and the University of Victoria examined the factors contributing to suicide among the First Nations youth of British Columbia (Chandler, Lalonde, Sokol, & Hallett, 2003; Chandler & Proulx, 2006). The researchers were especially interested in the protective effects that cultural continuity may have against suicide. They reasoned that communities that have successfully worked to protect and promote their culture would have a lower suicide rate among their youth than communities that have not done this. What they called *cultural continuity* was indexed by six variables that were representative of the various ways in which First Nations communities had fared in their struggles to resist the sustained history of acculturative practices. These variables included efforts made to challenge federal and provincial governments for

(continued)

Focus on Research 13.1 Self-Continuity, Cultural Identity, and Suicide among First Nations Youth *continued*

title to traditional lands; efforts to obtain self-governance; efforts to regain responsibility for education, health care, police, and fire services; and success in erecting permanent structures specially designed for the preservation and promotion of culture.

The results obtained were very informative. First, as shown in Figure 13.1, there were great differences in the youth suicide rate among the 29 tribal councils the researchers examined. Six of them experienced no suicides during the six-year period of the study, while 11 had rates below 100 per 100,000, and two had rates above 400 per 100,000.

Figure 13.2 shows the rate of suicide as a function of the number of cultural factors present in a given community. The suicide rate in First Nations youth was almost 140 per 100,000 in communities with no cultural factor; it was around 80 for those with three or four factors; and it was just above zero for those with six factors. In a recent continuation of this research, Hallett, Chandler, and Lalonde (2007) found that one important cultural factor that plays an important protective role is knowledge of a First Nations language. Suicide rates were low to absent in communities where the majority of members reported a conversational knowledge of a First Nations language, but were six times higher when fewer than half of the members were able to converse in the language.

These data provide strong support for the protective effect that cultural continuity may have against suicide among young First Nations people.

FIGURE 13.1

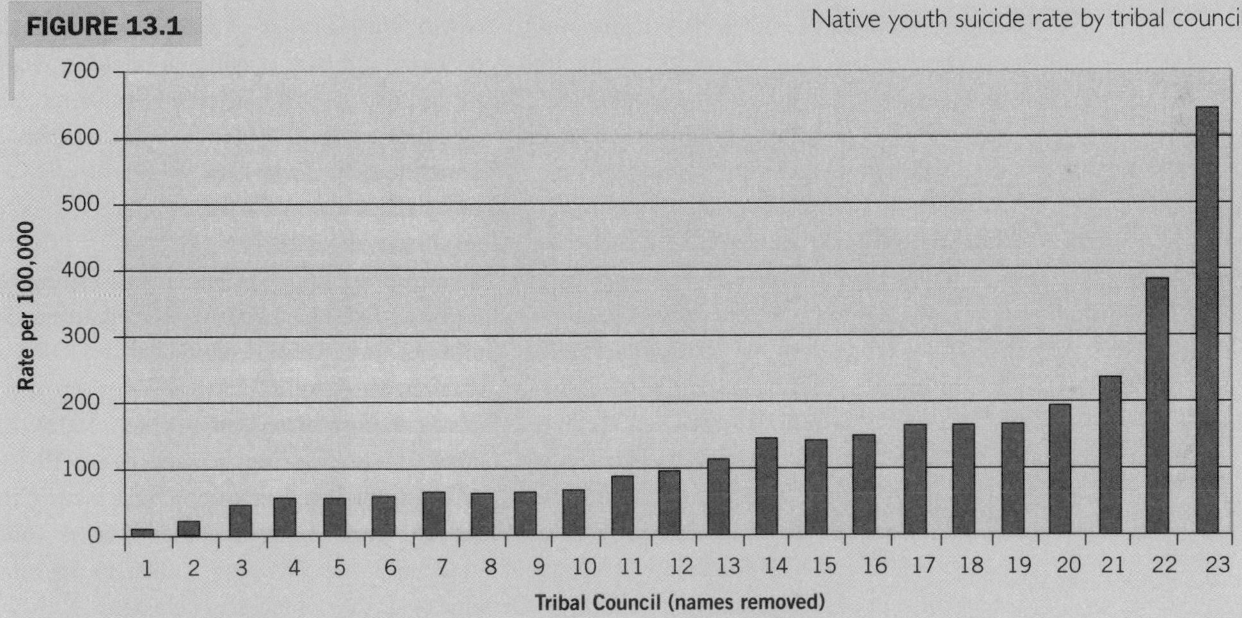

Native youth suicide rate by tribal council.

FIGURE 13.2

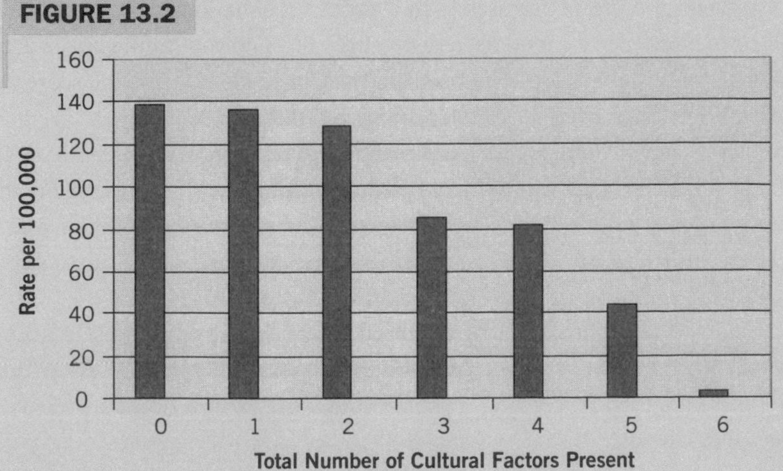

Native youth suicide rate by the number of cultural factors present in the community.

From "Personal persistence, identity development, and suicide: A study of Native and non-Native North American adolescents," by M. J. Chandler, C. E. Lalonde, B. W. Sokol, D. Hallett. In *Monographs of the Society for Research in Child Development, Vol 68*(2), June 2003, vii–130, Boston: Blackwell Publishing.

LEARNING OBJECTIVE 13.2

Trace the development of self-knowledge from infancy, identifying the processes by which changes in the self-system occur.

1. How can you tell when an infant discovers the self as a separate entity with personal agency?
2. How does self-recognition in infants change over time, and what factors are related to this ability?
3. How do children's self-descriptions change from early childhood to adolescence?

Learning Objective 13.3

Describe the development of self-esteem, ways to measure it, and the contexts that shape the way children evaluate themselves.

SELF-EVALUATION

As children grow, they not only come to understand more about themselves; they also begin to evaluate this information. Participation in school or on athletic teams encourages children to compare themselves with other children and also with their images of who they would like to be. Such self-evaluations usually bring both good news and bad, as children come to recognize their strengths and weaknesses and their positive and negative attributes. Self-evaluation, like self-knowledge, develops as children grow and is influenced by both cognitive and socialization variables (Harter, 2008).

MEASURING SELF-ESTEEM

Self-esteem (self-worth) A person's evaluation of the self and the affective reactions to that evaluation.

Looking-glass self The conception of the self based on how we think others see us.

Competence Self-evaluation that includes both what one would like to achieve and one's confidence in being able to achieve it.

The opinions children develop about themselves have been referred to as their **self-esteem**, or **self-worth** (Harter, 2003, 2006b). Self-esteem is assumed to include not only children's cognitive judgments of their abilities, but also their affective reactions (pride, shame, etc.) to these self-evaluations.

This concept is not new. Two traditional views of self-esteem have long been part of the developmental literature. According to the idea of the **looking-glass self** (Cooley, 1902), the psychological portraits we paint of ourselves are based on how we think others see us. That is, we view other people's reactions to us as "reflections" of who we are. The **competence** view of the self (James, 1892) holds that our level of self-esteem results from a combination of what we would like to achieve and how confident we feel about achieving it—an idea very similar to the more recent concept of self-efficacy (Bandura, 2006; Cervone et al., 2004; Maddux & Gosselin, 2003).

Links to Related Material

In Chapter 12, you read about how quality of attachment may influence later social and emotional development, including self-esteem. Here, you learn more about the development and measurement of self-esteem during childhood.

METHODS OF MEASUREMENT The most common method of assessing children's self-esteem has been through questionnaires. Typically, such instruments present children with a list of questions designed to tap their opinions of themselves in a variety of situations or contexts (such as, "Are you usually willing to help when a friend needs a favour?" and "Do you think you are artistic?"). The responses to these questions are combined and analyzed to produce an overall score that represents the child's level of self-esteem (Ghaderi, 2006; Keith & Bracken, 1996).

Attempts to capture self-esteem in a single score, however, have met with the same problems as attempts to describe children's intelligence with a single IQ score. Intuitively, it seems unlikely that children would evaluate themselves similarly in all areas—academics, appearance, athletics, and so on. And research has demonstrated that evaluations across different areas are often not consistent (Harter, 2006b; Marsh, Craven, & Martin, 2006).

An alternative to the single-score method is to conceptually divide children's lives into a number of domains (social skills, physical skills, and so on), and then assess children's self-evaluations separately in each. The results are then reported as a profile across the various domains. We consider an example of this approach next.

HARTER'S SELF-PERCEPTION PROFILE FOR CHILDREN Susan Harter has developed a set of popular instruments for measuring self-esteem at various stages of development. Each instrument assesses self-evaluations in specific domains as well as overall self-worth. For instance, the Self-Perception Profile for Children (Harter, 1985b, 2003), designed for children ages 8 and older, assesses children's opinions of their overall worth as well as their self-evaluations in five separate domains: scholastic competence, athletic competence, social acceptance, behavioural conduct, and physical appearance. Three additional domains—close friendship, romantic appeal, and job competence—are included on the adolescent version of the scale (Harter, 1988b, 2003). There are also versions for use with college students and adults, which include an even greater number of domains (Harter, 1999, 2003). Each item on the questionnaire presents two related statements, one describing a competent child and the other a less competent child. A child completing the instrument selects the statement that best describes him or her and then marks the box indicating whether the statement is "really true for me" or "sort of true for me." Figure 13.3 shows sample items from the scholastic competence area and the domain of behavioural conduct.

Children respond to six items in each of the six areas, and their scores are used to construct a profile of their self-esteem. Results allow the researcher to note both global self-worth and differences from one domain to the next. It should be noted that the tester cannot simply sum an individual's scores across the separate domains to obtain a score of global self-worth. Instead, the global score reflects responses to its own separate scale. In addition, the global score is imperfectly predicted by responses to the other scales.

FIGURE 13.3

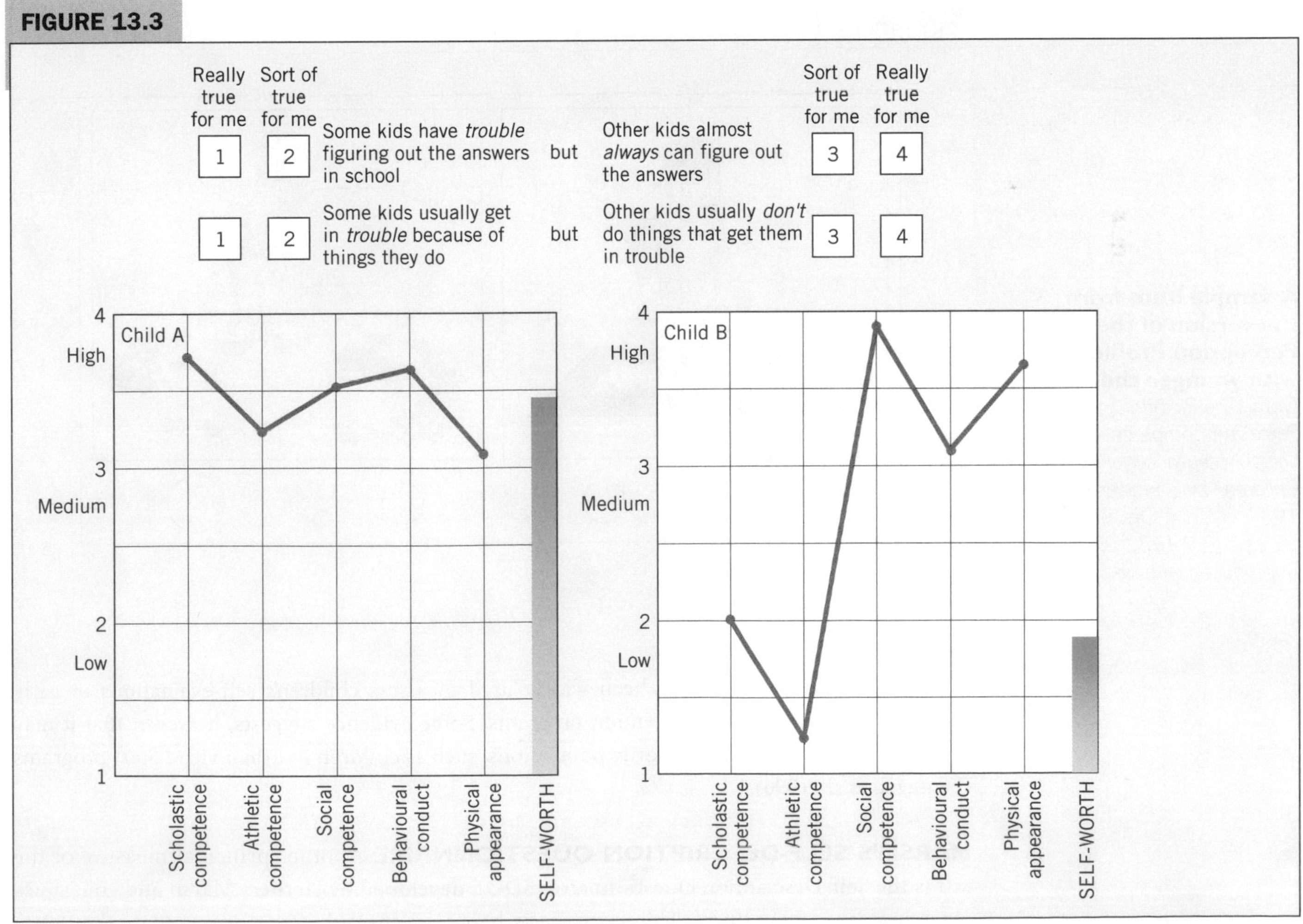

Two sample items from the Self-Perception Profile and examples of the scoring profiles from two children.
From "The Pictorial Scale of Perceived Competence and Social Acceptance for Young Children," by S. Harter & R. Pike, 1984, in Child Development, 55, pp.1969-1982, Blackwell. Reproduced with permission.

To assess the looking-glass self, Harter constructed additional items that ask children to rate how they believe other people feel about them. Consistent with that model, youngsters who felt others had high regard for them also rated themselves high on the self-worth items. To examine the competence view of the self, she asked children to rate how important each of the five areas was to them. In support of this model, children who rated themselves as very competent in areas they felt were important also had high self-worth scores (Harter, 1986). Harter concluded from her research that older children's feelings of self-esteem are based on both how they believe others evaluate them and how they evaluate themselves (Harter, 2006b; Harter & Whitesell, 2003).

Preschoolers differ from older children in their levels of self-understanding, their self-descriptions, and their general cognitive development. Measuring their self-concepts thus presents a unique challenge. For younger children between the ages of 4 and 7, Harter modified the Self-Perception Profile to create the Pictorial Scale of Perceived Competence and Social Acceptance (Harter & Pike, 1984). As shown in Figure 13.4, the items consist of pictures—for example, a girl who is good at puzzles (left) and a girl who is not good at puzzles (right). The child points to the circle indicating whether a picture is a little like her (small circle) or a lot like her (large circle). Because children younger than age 8 may not be able to form an overall judgment of their self-worth, only four individual content areas are assessed.

FIGURE 13.4

A sample item from the version of the Self-Perception Profile used with younger children. *From "The Pictorial Scale of Perceived Competence and Social Acceptance for Young Children," by S. Harter & R. Pike, 1984, in* Child Development *55, pp. 1969-1982, Blackwell. Reproduced with permission.*

Harter's pictorial scale has been widely used to assess children's self-evaluations in early childhood education and intervention programs. Some evidence suggests, however, that it may not be well-suited for some minority populations, such as children in urban Head Start programs (Fantuzzo et al., 1996).

MARSH'S SELF-DESCRIPTION QUESTIONNAIRE Another principal measure of the self is the Self-Description Questionnaire (SDQ), developed by Herbert Marsh and colleagues (Marsh et al., 1984, 2005). This measure is based on the belief that individuals develop a multidimensional and hierarchical self-concept. Different versions have been devised for preschoolers, preadolescents, adolescents, and young adults (Byrne, 1996; Marsh et al., 2002, 2005, 2006).

The new version for 4- to 5-year-olds uses an interview procedure in which the child is first asked a "yes" or "no" question, such as the following:

"Can you run fast?"
"Do you like the way you look?"
"Do you have lots of friends?"
"Do your parents smile at you a lot?"
"Are you good at counting?"

After answering "yes" or "no," the child is asked to clarify whether he or she means "yes/no always" or "yes/no sometimes." Using this procedure, preschoolers are able to distinguish among different aspects of self-concept (physical ability, appearance, relationships with peers, relationships with parents, verbal skills, and math skills).

THE DEVELOPMENTAL PROGRESSION OF SELF-ESTEEM

The developmental course of self-esteem is relatively clear. Although very young children may not have a well-developed sense of overall self-worth, the self-esteem scores of preschool and kindergarten children are generally high, likely reflecting an inflated view of themselves. Self-esteem drops slightly during the first years of elementary school as children begin to encounter external feedback and social comparisons (Harter, 2006b; Robins & Trzesniewski, 2005). During middle and later childhood, self-esteem scores are more stable. But the transition to adolescence often poses problems. Many investigators have found that at about age 11 or 12, self-esteem scores dip, only to increase again over the subsequent years (Harter, 2006b; Twenge & Campbell, 2001). Several explanations have been offered for the drop in self-esteem in early adolescence. We discuss some of these below.

Self-consciousness A concern about the opinions others hold about oneself.

Links to Related Material

In Chapter 8, you read about Piaget's formal operational stage of cognitive development. Here, you learn how this may affect self-consciousness and self-esteem in early adolescence.

INCREASED SELF-CONSCIOUSNESS One factor that may play a role in the temporary deterioration of self-esteem is the child's level of **self-consciousness**, or concern about the opinions of others (Tangney, Stuewig, & Mashek, 2007). Cognitive-developmental theorists suggest that this tendency increases with the emergence of formal operational abilities. At this stage, children become so much better at taking the perspective of others that they develop a preoccupation with how other people regard their appearance, behaviour, and so forth (Bell & Bromnick, 2003; Rankin et al., 2004; Schwartz et al., 2008). Psychologist David Elkind (2007) coined the term *imaginary audience* to aptly describe adolescents' preoccupation with the opinions of others. This increased self-consciousness leads to more critical self-evaluations, which, in turn, can lower self-esteem.

Early adolescence is a time of increased self-consciousness and often lower self-esteem. How is Elkind's term *imaginary audience* descriptive of the thinking of children at this age? (© *Michael Newman/PhotoEdit*)

CHANGES ASSOCIATED WITH PUBERTY The dip in self-worth among early adolescents may also be caused, in part, by the biological changes associated with puberty. Some researchers have suggested that pubertal changes produce physical and psychological stress in children that leads to depression and other negative emotional states (Harter, 2006b; Michael & Eccles, 2003). Other evidence has shown that the relationship between puberty and depression is connected with the young person's body image, self-esteem, and experience of stressful life events (Marcotte et al., 2002). Thus, the physical changes associated with puberty likely represent one element of a complex array of factors that dampen self-esteem in early adolescence.

CHANGING SCHOOLS An environmental variable that contributes to a drop in self-esteem involves whether children remain in their own school or move to a new one following grade 5 or 6. Researchers at Laval University (Cantin & Boivin, 2004) report that moving to a new school produces a noticeable decline in self-esteem scores, a decline that is greater for girls than for boys. Similar findings have been reported in other studies, especially if the new school is large and ethnically diverse (Eccles et al., 1997; Gutman & Eccles, 2007; Simmons et al., 1987). Children who remain in the same school show no such change (Rosenberg, 1986b). This phenomenon appears to affect a wide range of young people: a study of youth in poor urban settings, for example, found that the drop in self-esteem associated with the transition to middle or junior high school was present, regardless of ethnicity or gender (Seidman et al., 1994). We consider the role that changing schools plays in academic problems in a later section.

GENDER DIFFERENCES IN SELF-ESTEEM

We have seen that psychologists have identified broad trends in self-esteem in children and in the way self-esteem typically changes with age. We should note, however, that girls and boys exhibit some differences in self-esteem measures.

Links to Related Material

In this chapter, you learn about gender differences in self-esteem. In Chapter 16, you will read more about the impact of gender on child development.

In self-evaluative judgments across different domains, boys show much less variability than girls from one domain to the next (Harter, 2008). Although girls typically evaluate their conduct in a more positive light than do boys, they provide much more negative assessments of their physical appearance and athletic competence. These gender differences are consistent among cultures and across development, holding from elementary school through college. Females' perceptions of their athletic abilities are thought to arise from the traditionally greater emphasis on males' athletic prowess and participation, whereas their low ratings of their own physical appearance are believed to stem from the greater emphasis on female appearance and the more limited yet unrealistic expectations of what constitutes female beauty.

The developmental course of self-esteem also differs for boys and girls. Beginning in middle to late childhood, boys report higher global self-esteem than do girls, with the greatest differences occurring in adolescence (Harter, 2006b; Robins & Trzesniewski, 2005). Here again, self-ratings of perceived physical appearance are a source of male–female contrast. As Figure 13.5 shows, beginning in grade 4, girls' perceptions of their physical attractiveness decline markedly. By the last half

FIGURE 13.5

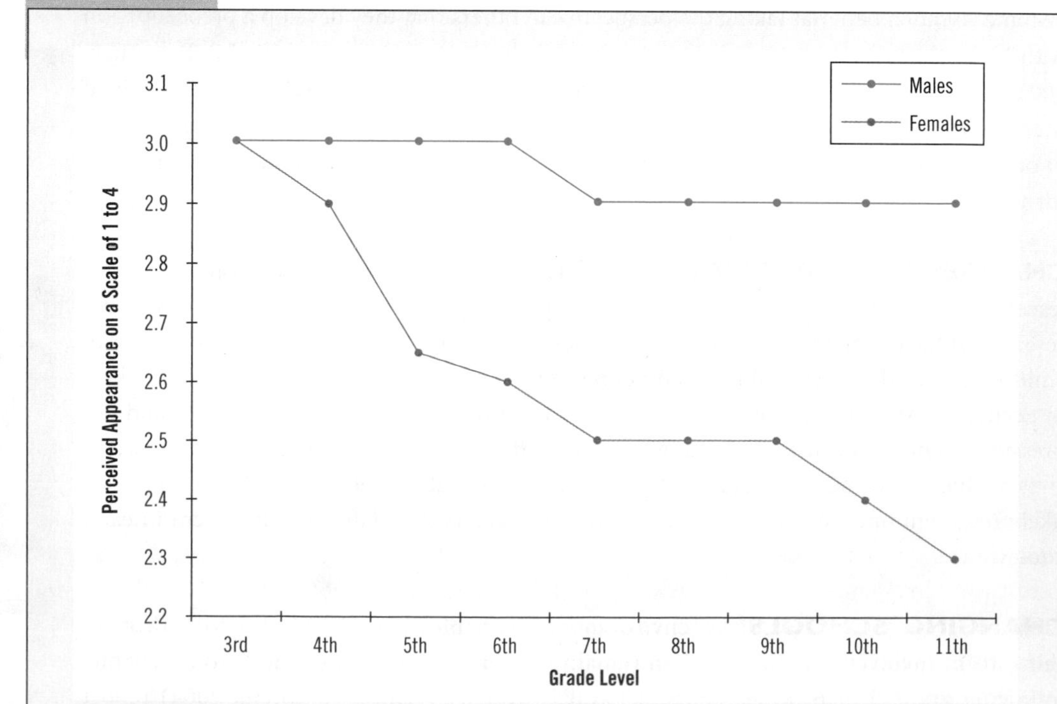

Perceived physical appearance on the Self-Perception Profile for males and females as a function of grade level. *From "The development of self-esteem," by S. Harter, in M. Kernis (Ed.),* Self-esteem issues and answers: A sourcebook of current perspectives, 2006, *pp. 144-150, New York: Psychology Press. Original source:* The construction of the self: A developmental perspective, *by S. Harter, 1999, New York: Guilford.*

of high school, girls have dramatically lower self-ratings than do boys, whose scores decline only a little with age. This trend may be particularly troubling, given that perceived physical appearance has been shown to be an effective predictor of global self-worth (Harter, 2003, 2006a). We will discuss further the issue of gender differences in the section of Chapter 16 dealing with the development of gender identity.

For Thought and Discussion

What are some examples of the effects of gender roles and experiences on your self-esteem?

ACADEMIC SELF-CONCEPT

The factors affecting self-esteem have also been investigated in the classroom, especially with regard to children's perceptions of their academic competence, or **academic self-concept**. We review some of these findings next.

Academic self-concept The part of self-esteem that involves children's perceptions of their academic abilities.

AGE AND GENDER DIFFERENCES Prior to entering school, children have no basis for an academic self-concept. Some research has examined the reactions of infants and preschoolers to other sorts of achievement tasks, however, and has found that a developmental progression does exist (Stipek, Recchia, & McClintic, 1992). Infants, for example, have little understanding of success and failure and so do not behave in ways that give any evidence of self-evaluation. However, even before the age of 2, children begin to show that they anticipate how adults will react to their achievements, such as when they look up for approval after making a stack of blocks. They also express delight at their successes and display negative reactions to their failures. By age 3, most children prefer to engage in activities at which they win rather than lose.

Children's academic self-concept generally is highest in kindergarten and steadily declines through at least grade 4. This trend has been noted in children's spontaneous classroom comments to other students, in their statements during interviews, and in their responses to questionnaires (Benenson & Dweck, 1986; Butler, 1990; Dweck, 2002; Rhodes & Brickman, 2008). One cause of this decline may be as simple as the fact that older children realize that bragging is not socially appropriate, and so they increasingly avoid giving glowing descriptions of their abilities (Ruble & Frey, 1987).

DWECK'S MOTIVATIONAL MODEL OF ACHIEVEMENT Children's academic self-concept, of course, derives mainly from their academic performance. Those who do well in school are likely to develop high opinions of their competence, whereas poor performers are likely to develop low opinions. How well a child performs in school depends partly on his or her academic abilities and partly on the amount of effort and motivation the child puts forth.

Links to Related Material

In Chapter 10, you read about the influence of teacher expectations on children's academic performance. Here, you learn more about the role of achievement motivation in children's school performance.

Based on over 20 years of research, Carol Dweck and her colleagues have developed a theoretical model that attempts to explain the complex role that motivation plays in children's academic success (Dweck, 1999, 2002). The model focuses on two patterns of motivation that have been observed in both younger and older children, and that are reflected in their affect, cognitions, and behaviour.

MOTIVATION PATTERNS Children in achievement situations generally react to failure experiences in one of two ways (Dweck, 2002; Grant & Dweck, 2003). Some children display a *mastery-oriented* pattern. Despite having just failed at a task or problem, these children retain a positive mood and express high expectations for success on future attempts. As a result, they tend to persist at the task and seek out similar challenging problems. This motivational pattern usually leads to improved academic performance over time.

Performance in school is one important contributor to academic self-concept. Academic self-concept can, in turn, affect how well children do in school. (© *Christopher Futcher/iStock*)

Other children, however, display a *helpless* pattern. When they encounter failure, their affect conveys sadness or disappointment, and they express doubt that they can ever succeed at the task. These children show little persistence in the activity and tend to avoid similar challenges in the future. Academic performance in these children often remains considerably below what it could be. What could produce these very different responses to failure? Dweck's model proposes that at the heart of the problem are children's feelings of self-worth. Children who develop the helpless pattern typically believe that their self-worth depends on the approval and positive judgments of others. As a way of validating their self-worth, they seek out situations in which success involves receiving such approval. If the situation produces failure instead, these children view the absence of approval as a blow to their "goodness" as a person (self-worth), which then leads to the helpless pattern of negative affect, low expectations for future success, low persistence, and avoidance of similar situations.

For Thought and Discussion

What attributions do you tend to use for your academic successes and failures? What does this tendency tell you about your motivation?

In contrast, children who develop the mastery-oriented pattern do not believe that their self-worth depends on the opinions of others. They tend to seek out situations in which, whether successful or not, they will learn from their experiences. When these children fail, therefore, they view it simply as an opportunity to improve their ability on the task and so display the opposite pattern of affect, expectations, and persistence.

THE DEVELOPMENT OF MOTIVATION: WORK WITH PRESCHOOL CHILDREN Dweck and colleagues have examined the achievement motivation of preschool-age children and have found that even at these young ages, children display patterns of persistence or helplessness. In these studies, 4- and 5-year-olds were asked to solve several puzzles, but only one could actually be solved; the others had been modified. For example, in a jigsaw puzzle, pieces might have been removed and pieces from a different puzzle added. After spending time with the puzzles, children were given the opportunity to indicate which one they would like to play with again. More than a third of the children said they would like to work again on the single solved puzzle, despite having just completed it.

Interestingly, when asked to explain their choice, these "non-persisters" did not say that the solved puzzle was challenging or that repeating it would provide them with good practice. Instead, these young children said such things as "Because it was the easiest" or "Because I already know how to do it." These children also displayed negative affect toward the task and expressed lower expectations for success on another task. Children who chose to persist on one of the unsolved puzzles showed the more positive pattern of reactions (Smiley & Dweck, 1994).

CHILDREN'S IMPLICIT THEORIES OF INTELLIGENCE In older children, the model becomes more complex. Beyond 10 years of age or so, children's cognitive abilities permit them to develop certain self-conceptions. One of these is a "theory of intelligence." Some children come to believe in an **entity model**, in which the amount of a person's intelligence is fixed and unchangeable. Others subscribe to an **incremental model**, in which a person's intelligence can grow with experience and learning. A second self-conception involves children's "attributions for success or failure." Some children believe that success or failure results primarily from the amount of ability a person has; other children believe it depends on the amount of effort a person applies to a task (Blackwell, Trzesniewski, & Dweck, 2007; Dweck & Molden, 2005).

Entity model The belief that a person's intelligence is fixed and unchangeable.

Incremental model The belief that a person's intelligence can grow through experience and learning.

Children who develop the helpless pattern, as we might expect, generally believe that the amount of their intelligence is fixed (entity model) and that their lack of success derives from a lack of ability. These two beliefs combine to give the child little reason for optimism in the face of failure—after all, ability is unchangeable and the child simply has too little of it. Predictably, then, these children feel helpless and hopeless.

A very different outlook, however, results from the two opposite beliefs, which are generally held by mastery-oriented children. If intelligence can grow (incremental model) and success depends largely on one's effort, then failure experiences need not lead to feelings of despair or pessimism. These children believe they can do better next time simply by trying harder.

Research has likewise supported this portion of the model. For example, one study found that grade 5 children who displayed elements of the helpless pattern (non-persistence and low expectations for future success) following failure on a task were more likely to hold the entity view of intelligence, whereas children displaying the mastery-oriented pattern tended to believe in the incremental view (Cain & Dweck, 1995).

Studies also revealed that girls—especially bright girls—are particularly vulnerable to the helpless pattern. Girls are also more likely to hold an entity theory of intelligence. Compared with boys, girls more often pick tasks at which they can perform well and show impairment when tasks grow difficult. When the going gets tough, girls are also more likely to blame their abilities (Dweck, 1999, 2007). We speculate about a possible cause of this gender difference in the following section.

THE EFFECTS OF PRAISE AND CRITICISM Another important component of Dweck's model of achievement motivation concerns caregivers' responses to children's performance. How are failures and successes handled? What aspects of the child's performance are the targets of praise or criticism? The answers to such questions have been found to be of substantial consequence. In fact, Dweck (1999; Dweck & London, 2004) asserts that the feedback children receive from adults is the source of patterns of motivation, having more impact than the child's temperament.

As you might expect, Dweck's team hypothesized that criticism could have a negative impact on children. Specifically, the researchers targeted criticism that judged the children themselves—their stable traits—rather than their situation-specific effort. In contrast, criticism that focused on the children's effort or strategies was thought to promote the desirable mastery-oriented motivational pattern. What about praise? Here, too, the researchers hypothesized that praise directed toward the child's efforts or problem-solving processes would be beneficial, just as with criticism. Praise could end up having a negative impact, they argued, when focused on children's enduring traits.

To test these hypotheses, kindergarteners participated in a role-playing exercise in which they imagined they had done some well-intentioned act for their teacher that ended up being a disappointment. For example, in one scenario, the children imagined creating a picture of a family and then realizing that a child in the painting had no feet:

> You spend a lot of time painting a picture of a family to give to your teacher. You pick out colors you think are nice and carefully draw each person. As you are about to give it to your teacher you say to yourself, "Uh oh, one of the kids has no feet." But you worked really hard on the picture and want to give it to her. You say, "Teacher, here's a picture for you." (Heyman, Cain, & Dweck, 1992, p. 404)

Interestingly, noting a flaw like this did not produce particular concern for kindergarteners on their own. Reactions changed, however, when the scenario included criticism from the teacher, who the children were told had said, "What, no feet? I don't call this drawing the right way. I'm disappointed."

About a third of the young children responded to this input by lowering their own evaluation of the painting: what they thought was fine before was now judged to be inadequate. Children with this downward reaction also reported more negative emotion than did the other children and were less willing to persist on the task, evidence of a helpless reaction (Dweck, 1999, 2002). These helpless children also imagined that their painting's shortcoming would elicit negative reactions from their parents and teachers, suggesting that their parents would respond with statements such as "You are very bad" or "That's bad work." Finally, this negativity extended to these children's self-evaluations: nearly two-thirds of the helpless children said that their performance indicated they were not being good kids—a sentiment shared by fewer than 10 percent of the mastery-oriented children. Thus, it appears that a strong relationship exists between the child's motivation pattern and his or her reactions to criticism.

Dweck and colleagues have also demonstrated effects of differing kinds of criticism and praise using hypothetical scenarios as described above (Dweck, 2002; Kamins & Dweck, 1999). Feedback was provided in response to children's errors. Some children received criticism that offered information about their strategy use (e.g., "Maybe you should think of another way to do it"). Other criticism focused on the child's behaviour ("That's not what I call doing it the right way") or on the child as a whole ("I'm disappointed in you"). Children who received strategy-specific feedback fared the best, giving their work the highest self-rating, reporting the most positive overall feelings, and providing the best solutions for future improvement.

Analogous results were found for children's responses to praise. Receiving person-oriented praise was actually associated with increased vulnerability to failure, whereas praise directed at effort or strategy use produced the most mastery-oriented responses. In explaining these findings, Dweck proposes that believing that one is good when one does something correctly leaves one open to the alternative conclusion that one is bad when failure results. Thus, despite the common intuition that praise is bound to be beneficial for children, research suggests that certain forms of praise can, in fact, have later negative consequences.

For Thought and Discussion

Why is praise directed toward effort, skills, and knowledge better than praise directed at personal qualities? What might be some ways to foster a mastery-orientation to achievement without abandoning person-oriented praise?

Dweck also contends that performance-based praise may underlie girls' greater vulnerability to helplessness. Girls are usually the stars of elementary school. According to Dweck, young girls—especially bright ones—are likely fed a steady diet of praise during the early years of school. They are, after all, generally better behaved than boys and comply more readily with adult requests. Moreover, very capable girls are unlikely to struggle very much with the academic demands of the first years of school. The lesson girls may learn is that they can measure their traits from the outcomes and praise they receive.

Because the requirements of the classroom are less compatible with the needs of the average boy, they are more likely to experience both failure and criticism. These early difficulties may, however, prove advantageous over time because through them boys learn that persistence can lead to success.

THE ROLE OF SOCIAL COMPARISONS We have seen that academic self-image is affected by children's academic performance and by the types of attributions they make regarding failure. But the general decline over the elementary grades in children's self-evaluations of competence may involve yet another factor.

Social comparison Comparing one's abilities to those of others.

Children, like adults, contrast their abilities with those of others and draw conclusions about themselves from those assessments—a process called **social comparison**. This process begins as early as kindergarten, but its function changes with age (Pomerantz et al., 1995; Stipek, 1992; Wheeler & Suls, 2005).

Kindergarteners use what their classmates are doing or saying primarily as a way of making friends or learning how things are done. For example, a child may comment to a classmate that he is colouring on the same page of his book. Social comparisons, at this point, do not appear to have much impact on the child's self-image (Aboud, 1985; Stipek & Tannatt, 1984). As children proceed through the early grades, however, their social comparisons increasingly involve academic performance, and they begin to use the comparisons to evaluate their own competence relative to others (Butler, 1992; Pomerantz et al., 1995).

By grade 2, children's spontaneous self-evaluative remarks become positively correlated with the number of social comparisons they make; that is, children with lower opinions of their competence make fewer social comparisons (Ruble & Frey, 1991). Why? One interpretation of this finding is that in continually comparing their performance with that of peers, many children unhappily discover that their work is not as good as they had believed. A child who once found great pleasure in drawing may discover that his artwork is not as attractive as that of his classmates. As a result, he may lower his opinion of his drawings, but also begin to avoid comparing his work with that of other children. If this interpretation is correct, we would expect academically successful children to seek out more information about their performance than would children who are lower achievers. And research has found just that: high-achieving students show more interest in comparing their performance with that of classmates and also in discovering the correct answers to problems (Ruble & Flett, 1988).

This developmental change in the use of social comparisons is not inevitable, however, and can be influenced by the atmosphere of the educational environment. For example, in Israel, the communal kibbutz environment places more emphasis on cooperative than on competitive learning, and fosters concern with mastering skills rather than with surpassing others. As a result, even older children in the kibbutz environment have been found to use social comparison primarily as a means of acquiring new abilities and much less for self-evaluation (Butler & Ruzany, 1993). Social comparisons are more likely to be interpreted in a positive way when the individuals perceive the social environment as cooperative rather than competitive (Buunk, Zurriaga, Piero, Nauta, & Gasalvez, 2005).

The relation between social comparison and academic self-concept, then, is bidirectional. Social comparisons can affect children's self-image by giving them information about how they are performing relative to other children. But children's self-image may affect their willingness to engage in social comparisons, depending on how pleasant or unpleasant they expect the resulting information to be (Buunk, Kuyper, & van der Zee, 2005; Pomerantz et al., 1995).

PARENTAL INFLUENCES Children's academic self-concept is also affected by the attitudes, expectations, and behaviours of their parents. Studies have shown that parents' perceptions of their children's academic abilities are good predictors of children's self-perceptions of ability (Eccles, 2007; Fredricks & Eccles, 2005; Midgett et al., 2002; Spinath & Spinath, 2005).

How do such expectations produce their effects on children's self-perceptions? There are three main venues through which parents positively influence their children's academic self-concept (Grolnick & Beiswenger, 2006; Pomerantz, Grolnick, & Price 2005). The first is by being involved in their children's school lives through participating in school activities, helping with homework, and getting involved in learning activities. One example is parents' reading with their children, which researchers at Carleton University have found fosters the development of language and reading skills (Sénéchal, 2006; Sénéchal & LeFevre, 2002). The second venue entails providing structure and assistance, in accordance with children's levels of ability. Such ability-related structure tends to foster children's cognitive and academic competence (Pratt et al., 1988). The third venue involves providing *autonomy support*; that is, allowing children to play an active role in their own activities, solve their own problems, and so on, which can lead to a sense of competence.

Links to Related Material

Here, you learn about the role that parenting plays in the development of children's positive academic self-concept. In Chapter 15, you will learn more about different parenting styles and their effects on child development.

The child's perception of parental involvement and of any educational barriers parents might impose is also important (Wettersten et al., 2005). Moreover, fathers have been found to play an important role in fostering children's academic self-concept: The fathers of children with high academic self-concept are warmer and more supportive than those of children with lower academic self-concept (Wagner & Phillips, 1992). Indeed, in several studies, college students recalled that continuing support from their fathers was instrumental in their success in school (Kim & Chung, 2003; Schaffer & Blatt, 1990).

Research suggests that fathers may be especially important contributors to children's academic self-concept. (*Purestock*)

EFFECTS OF ACADEMIC SELF-CONCEPT Children's perception of their academic competence has perhaps been of such interest to psychologists because of its applied value—academic self-concept influences academic achievement (Byrne, 1996; Marsh et al., 2005; Spinath et al., 2006). Studies examining feelings of competence and perceived self-efficacy report that children who view themselves as academically skilled are more motivated to succeed, more persistent in their work, and more willing to seek out challenging tasks or problems (Eccles et al., 2006). A high academic self-concept, even when it is an overestimate of the child's abilities, also correlates positively with (and probably contributes to) a high level of self-esteem (Connell & Ilardi, 1987; Harter, 1985a).

Children with low opinions of their academic abilities are less motivated to work. One study found that even among children whose academic skills were high, those who held an incorrectly low opinion of their competence approached new tasks with less effort and optimism than did their classmates (Phillips, 1984, 1987). Thus, for some children, academic success may hinge as much on academic self-concept as it does on academic ability.

The value of academic success to the child may seem obvious, but its effects can reach beyond the classroom. For example, research indicates that when children have academic (and social) failure experiences at school, their relations with their parents often suffer—the children tend to become more demanding and unreasonable, while the parents become more disapproving and punitive (Repetti, 1996). These home experiences, in turn, may further erode the child's attitude toward school, in effect producing a vicious circle.

LEARNING OBJECTIVE 13.3

Describe the development of self-esteem, ways to measure it, and the contexts that shape the way children evaluate themselves.

1. What is self-esteem and how is it measured?
2. How does self-esteem change across childhood and adolescence, and how does it differ for boys and girls?
3. What factors are believed to contribute to the formation of academic self-concept?
4. What roles do children's theories of intelligence and attributions play in achievement motivation?
5. What roles do criticism, praise, and social comparison play in the development of academic self-concept?
6. What is the impact of academic self-concept on children's development and future prospects?

Learning Objective 13.4

Analyze the mechanisms and processes by which children develop self-control.

SELF-REGULATION

We have examined how growing children gain knowledge of the self and how their continual evaluation of this knowledge produces a positive or negative view of the self. In this section, we consider a third process—how the self comes to regulate, or control, children's behaviour.

Self-regulation is a crucial aspect of human development. If children did not learn to control their own behaviour—to avoid the things they must avoid, to wait for the things they cannot have right away, to alter strategies that are not working—they would be constantly at the mercy of the moment-to-moment pushes and pulls of their environments. They would simply be "weathervanes," as Bandura puts it (1986, p. 335). The development of self-control is one of the child's most impressive accomplishments. Self-control indicates, at the very least, that the child knows what demands are made by the surrounding world, realizes what behaviours relate to those demands, and understands how to adjust behaviours to meet the demands (Vaughn, Kopp, & Krakow, 1984). How does such self-control develop, and what are its effects?

For Thought and Discussion

How would we be "weathervanes" in the absence of self-control? How do other species exhibit self-control in their behaviour?

THE EMERGENCE OF SELF-CONTROL

During early infancy, self-regulation mostly involves involuntary biological processes (Rothbart & Posner, 1985; Stifter & Braungart, 1995). For instance, babies reflexively squint in response to bright light. And even young infants control sensory input by turning away or even falling asleep when stimulation from caregivers or surroundings becomes overwhelming. Such responses serve important regulatory functions, but there is no evidence that the infants who engage in them are cognitively aware of what is happening.

By the beginning of the second year, babies have developed many voluntary behaviours and can act on their environments in purposeful ways (Rochat, 2011). Children act to accomplish things or to produce outcomes, such as when a baby grabs for a toy he or she would like to play with or pushes over a tower of blocks to watch it crash to the floor. But at this point, the child's ability to monitor behaviours and to adjust them as necessary is still limited (Bullock & Lutkenhaus, 1988).

Self-control becomes more effective and obvious during the third year, as children begin to resist having everything done for them and to assert their desire to do things for themselves (Bullock & Lutkenhaus, 1990; Grolnick, Bridges, & Connell, 1996). Much of the external control children have experienced thus far has involved verbal instruction from their parents. In asserting their independence, children sometimes attempt to take on this role themselves, and they adopt some of the same regulating commands. A 2-year-old might, for example, say "No, no, no," as she reaches for a forbidden object. Or she may direct her own behaviour much as her mother has directed it previously (e.g., "Put the spoon in the bowl"). At this point, some verbal control over children's behaviour has begun to move from external sources to children themselves. But the progression is not yet complete. The final step comes when children internalize the control, directing their behaviour silently through thought rather than speech. This form of self-regulation is generally not apparent before 3 years of age.

During the third year as well, most children begin to pay attention to simple standards set by others or by themselves, and monitor their activities with respect to those standards. For instance, a child making a birthday cake out of sand may try several combinations of mud, water, sticks, and grass to get it just right. As children come to recognize standards, they also begin to react emotionally when they meet or fail to meet them. Thus, as discussed in Chapter 12, we begin to see the expression of the self-conscious evaluative emotions of pride, shame, and guilt at this time (Lewis, 2008a; Lewis & Sullivan, 2005).

The changes in self-regulation observed during the early years reflect two important developments. First, regulation shifts from external to internal control. Initially, caregivers largely regulate children's behaviour directly or do so indirectly by supporting children's own efforts at self-regulation. Gradually, however, regulation shifts to the child. Second, self-control grows more elaborate and sophisticated (McClelland et al., 2010). We discuss the shift from external to internal control and the use self-instruction as a means of helping impulsive children gain internal control in *Application 13.1*.

APPLICATION 13.1
SELF-DIRECTED SPEECH AS A MEANS OF DEVELOPING SELF-CONTROL

Many psychologists believe the transition from external control to self-control is guided in part by the child's language. This proposition was clearly articulated in the writings of Russian psychologist Lev Vygotsky (1934/1962), whose work is described in chapters 1 and 8. Vygotsky was intrigued by the observation that preschoolers often talk to themselves while working on a task—a behaviour now generally referred to as **private speech**. He argued that young children's private speech grows out of their interactions with parents and other adults as they work together on tasks. Much of a parent's speech in such situations involves guiding and regulating the child, and young children's actions, thus, tend to be initially controlled externally. With time, children begin to use their parents' instructional comments (although not always in versions as complete or well formed) as self-directed speech guiding their own behaviour. As they grow older, children's private speech becomes internalized, directing their behaviour in terms of inaudible inner speech. Thus, private speech is important in children's movement from "other-regulation" to self-regulation (Winsler, 2009).

Private speech Speech children produce and direct toward themselves during a problem-solving activity.

Observations of children's private speech indicate that it does indeed follow the development progression described by Vygotsky. By preschool age, many children can be heard talking to themselves as they plan and solve problems (Müller, Jacques, Brocki, & Zelazo, 2009; Winsler, 2009). Gradually, as they move into middle childhood, a greater proportion of their private speech takes the form of whispering and inaudible mutterings, presumably reflecting its gradual transformation into inner speech (Müller et al., 2009; Winsler, 2009), although it may become more audible at times, such as when they tackle a difficult problem.

Application 13.1 Self-Directed Speech as a Means of Developing Self-Control *continued*

Given the apparent self-regulatory function of private speech, Canadian psychologist Donald Meichenbaum of the University of Waterloo hypothesized that it might be used to help children who are highly impulsive gain better self-control. Meichenbaum (1977) noted that the private speech of impulsive preschool children included very little self-guiding speech; consisting instead of mostly self-stimulating verbalizations such as animal noises, repeated words, and singing. This contrasted with the private speech of non-impulsive preschoolers, which was more inward-directed and consisted more often of self-guiding verbalizations. In a classic study, Meichenbaum (1977) developed a program to teach self-guiding private speech to impulsive children, to help them deal with their self-regulatory deficits.

The training required impulsive children to solve a set of difficult problems. Initially, they watched an adult solve a problem while guiding his or her behaviour by talking aloud. Next, they solved the problem while the adult provided verbal instructions to guide the child's behaviour. In the next step, the children solved the problem while guiding their behaviour using their own spoken self-instructions. Following this, they then whispered the self-directed instructions while completing the task. In the final step, they performed the task using internal private speech to guide their performance. Through these steps, Meichenbaum attempted to parallel the process by which children's behaviour gradually comes under the control of their private speech.

The following is an example of the self-instructions provided by the adult models as they undertook the task in the initial step. The task consisted of copying a complicated line pattern: "Okay, what is it I have to do? You want me to copy the picture with different lines. I have to go slowly and carefully. Okay, draw the line down, down, good; then to the right, that's it; now down some more and to the left. Good, I'm doing fine so far. Remember, go slowly. Now back up again. No, I was supposed to go down. That's okay. Just erase the line carefully... good. Even if I make an error I can go on slowly and carefully. I have to go down now. Finished. I did it" (Meichenbaum & Goodman, 1971, p. 117).

Several sessions were necessary to increase the self-control abilities of impulsive children, with more demanding problems introduced as the training proceeded. In a follow-up, the benefits of the training were still evident one month after the intervention, with 60 percent of the impulsive children spontaneously talking to themselves while working on problems (Meichenbaum & Goodman, 1971).

In the years that have followed Meichenbaum's original investigations, researchers have further examined the utility of self-instructional training for impulsive children. Findings have not always been as promising as those initially reported by Meichenbaum. Research has supported the notion that self-instructional training can help focus impulsive children's attention on the task on which they are working. However, its usefulness is limited, especially if used as the sole intervention for severe cases of impulsivity (Hinshaw, 2000; Kendall & Choudhury, 2003; Winsler, 2009). Rather, self-instructional training is most effective when used in combination with other behavioural and cognitive interventions.

Since Meichenbaum's classic studies, self-instructional training has been further refined and applied to the treatment of a number of problem behaviours. Indeed, training in self-instructions has become one of the best-known components of cognitive-behavioural therapy. Used in combination with a variety of other cognitive-behavioural procedures, training in self-instructions is a valuable ingredient of interventions for problems of impulse control (Finch et al., 1993), anger (Nelson & Finch, 2000; Gibbs, 2010), disruptiveness and aggression (Friedberg & McLure, 2002; Goldstein, 2004a), and anxiety (Eisen & Kearney, 1995; Friedberg & McLure, 2002). Self-instructional training has also been incorporated into many cognitive-behavioural interventions used with adults. It is remarkable how Vygotsky's observations of little children talking to themselves inspired an idea that has become a core component of many current interventions for behaviour disorders.

COMPLIANCE

Compliance The child's ability to go along with requests or adopt the standards of behaviour espoused by caregivers.

One of the earliest indices of self-control is compliance. **Compliance** refers to children's ability to go along with requests or adopt the standards of behaviour espoused by caregivers (Kopp, 1982). Children begin to understand caregiver wishes and expectations around the end of the first year (Kaler & Kopp, 1990). However, during the months that follow, children are more likely to refuse, ignore, or subvert parents' behavioural requests than comply with them.

The kinds of situations in which parents expect compliance vary widely. For instance, sometimes caregivers direct children to stop or refrain from doing something—for example, playing with the electric socket, interrupting when mom is on the phone, or going on the street. To comply with these requests, children must be able to inhibit a behaviour (Lagattuta, 2005). In other situations, parents want their children to perform desired behaviour, such as brushing teeth, saying "thank you," and helping with chores (Gralinski & Kopp, 1993; Kochanska & Aksan, 1995).

To study the development of compliance, researchers look at children's behaviour in both kinds of situations—"Don't" and "Do." For example, in one study, Grazyna Kochanska and colleagues (2001) followed a group of children longitudinally from shortly after their first birthdays until age 4. Compliance in "Don't" situations increased dramatically during the second year of life. By the time they were 4 years old, children complied with parental prohibitions nearly 80 percent of the time. In contrast, compliance in "Do" situations was far more difficult to achieve.

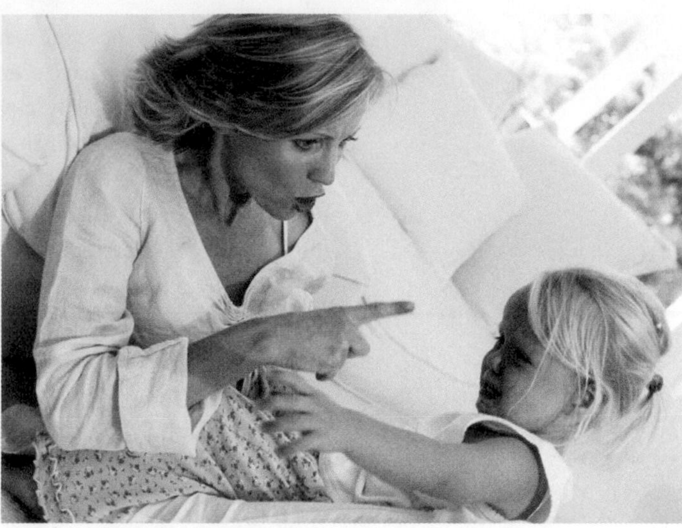

By the age of 4, children comply with parental prohibitions most of the time. *(Banana Stock/Media Bakery)*

Moreover, the quality of children's compliance differed between the two contexts. In "Don't" situations, children usually complied wholeheartedly. Kochanska termed this **committed compliance**. Committed compliance describes children's behaviour when they embrace the caregiver's agenda, adopt it as their own, and follow caregiver directives in a self-regulated way (e.g., saying "No, no, don't touch").

Compliance in "Do" situations was less likely and usually achieved grudgingly. In this type of compliance, termed **situational compliance**, children essentially cooperate with parental directives, but with little enthusiasm. Situational compliance also requires a good deal of sustained caregiver support, such as reminding the child to continue or framing the activity (e.g., toy clean-up) as some kind of game. Situational compliance is often fleeting and disappears if caregivers grow distracted, leave the room, or otherwise withdraw control.

Committed compliance Compliant behaviour that results from a child's internalizing the instruction of an adult; results in positive emotion.

Situational compliance Obedience that results from a child's awareness of an adult's will in a particular situation; does not reflect enduring behavioural change.

"Do" requests appear to be more challenging for young children than "Don't" requests. There may be several reasons for this difference. One possibility is that the neuropsychological correlates that underlie the ability to inhibit a behaviour mature before those required to sustain a prolonged flow of behaviour (Rothbart, 1989). Another possibility is that parents impose "Don't" commands earlier and expect children to comply with them at a younger age than with "Do" commands. It is noteworthy that many "Don't" commands involve safety issues (e.g., "*Don't* jump on the bed." "*Don't* poke the dog." "*Don't* touch the stove.").

Links to Related Material

Here, you learn about the development of compliance in childhood. In Chapter 15, you will read more about how different parenting styles may produce different types of compliance in children.

There are also striking individual differences in the ease with which parents and children achieve compliance. Some children are eager to comply with caregivers, whereas others readily comply with one parent but not the other. For other children, achieving compliance is a struggle, regardless of who else is involved in the interaction. What might underlie these differences?

One contributing factor may be children's temperaments. As discussed in Chapter 12, children vary along a number of temperament dimensions, including fearfulness and the ability to regulate their behaviour (inhibitory control). Children who are more cautious or who are able to inhibit a dominant response have been found to be more compliant (Kochanska, Aksan & Joy, 2007; Rothbart & Hwang, 2005; Rothbart, Ahadi, & Evans, 2000). Another factor that matters a great deal is the quality of the relationship between the parent and the child: parental warmth is associated with higher levels of self-control in young children and teens (Eisenberg et al., 2005).

Children are most likely to comply in dyads marked by a happy mood and in which partners are mutually responsive to one another's needs and desires (Aksan, Kochanska, & Ortmann, 2006; Kochanska, 2002). Longitudinal studies show that mothers in dyads with a mutually responsive orientation have a history of being responsive to their children's signals of need, signs of distress, bids for attention, and social overtures (Kochanska, 1997b). During the second year, children whose mothers were responsive to their needs tend to adopt a similar attitude—or what Kochanska terms a *responsive stance*—toward maternal wishes. Children with a responsive stance happily embrace the mother's agenda and eagerly comply with her requests. Kochanska believes that a responsive stance is an intermediate step between simple cooperation and genuine internalization of parental values and standards.

Studies of Japanese mother–child relations provide additional support for Kochanska's model of compliance. As we have seen in this chapter and also in Chapter 12, the mother–child relationship in Japan is especially close. Mothers are highly responsive (even indulgent in the view of many Westerners) to their infants' needs. Japanese parents try to avoid direct confrontations and contests of will with their children, rarely scold them directly, and often back down when children resist their requests (Lebra, 1994; Vogel, 1963/1991). Although giving children such a free reign might seem destined to create demanding tyrants, Japanese children, in fact, make fewer demands on parents, give fewer commands, and are less likely to assert that they will not obey (Caudill & Schooler, 1973). Indeed, the "terrible twos," a phenomenon North American parents are led to believe is unavoidable and normative, is virtually unheard of in Japan.

To understand why Japanese children tend to be more compliant than their North American counterparts and at a younger age, we can return to Kochanska's model. The goal of Japanese parenting techniques is to encourage children to *want* to adhere to parental and societal values and standards (Fogel, Stevenson, & Messigner, 1992; Rothbaum et al., 2000). In other words, by virtue of creating a warm, close, and responsive parent–child relationship, Japanese parents are, in effect, fostering a receptive stance.

Many Canadian and American parents, in contrast, try to *convince* children to go along with parental requests (Fogel et al., 1992). To convince them, North American parents are often forced to resort to power assertion or appeals to the parents' authority. Power assertion encompasses a range of behaviours, including taking toys from children, spanking, and verbal threats. As we discuss in greater depth in Chapter 14, although power assertion is often effective in the short run (e.g., a child who is slapped upon touching an attractive toy will likely stop immediately), it is less likely to promote the internalization of values and standards than other techniques.

There are undoubtedly many reasons why Japanese and North American parents adopt such different approaches to the socialization of self-control. Nonetheless, a number of theorists contend that the North American approach is a natural outgrowth of the joint emphasis on autonomy and independence (Fogel et al., 1992; Rogoff, 2003; Rothbaum et al., 2000). As we have seen, parents begin to encourage children to assert their own wishes and desires from a very early age. It should not be surprising, then, to discover that toddlers and preschoolers have their own opinions about a variety of issues, including the reasonableness of parental requests and directives!

RESISTANCE TO TEMPTATION

As children grow older and spend more time outside of the immediate supervision of adults, they learn to inhibit forbidden behaviours, even when no one is watching them. How does this kind of self-control come about?

Forbidden-toy paradigm An experimental procedure for studying children's resistance to temptation in which the child is left alone with an attractive toy and instructed not to play with it.

A well-known method for studying resistance to temptation uses the **forbidden-toy paradigm**. Typically, an experimenter puts a child in a room where there is an attractive toy and tells the child not to touch or play with the toy (analagous to the "Don't" situation already described). Outside the room, observers monitor the child's behaviour through a one-way mirror. The investigators are interested in how long the child waits before breaking the rule or how much time the child spends playing with the forbidden toy.

Researchers have explored whether having children produce self-instructional statements during their waiting time affects their ability to resist temptation. In one study, 3- to 7-year-old children were placed in a room with several attractive toys on a table behind them. They were instructed not to turn around and look at the toys while the experimenter was out of the room. Some of the children were also told that to help them keep from looking, they should repeat out loud a relevant statement, such as "I must not turn around." Children in a second group were told to use an irrelevant self-instruction, such as "hickory, dickory, dock." Those in a third group were given no self-instructional advice and waited silently. For younger children, producing a verbal self-instruction led to greater resistance than remaining silent. Interestingly, the actual content of the instruction did not matter—the relevant and irrelevant instructions worked equally well. For older children, the content of the self-instruction did make a difference, with the relevant statement proving most effective (Hartig & Kanfer, 1973).

Several other factors have also been shown to influence children's behaviour in forbidden-toy settings. For example, Joan Grusec (1979), of the University of Toronto, and her collaborators note that seeing an adult model break the rule and play with the toy makes children more likely to do so. On the other hand, providing children with a good rationale for following the prohibition ("Don't touch the toy; it's fragile and might break") increases the likelihood that they will resist (Parke, 1977), as does teaching children to develop their own plans or strategies for dealing with the temptation (Patterson, 1982).

DELAY OF GRATIFICATION

Another popular approach to studying children's self-control has been the **delay-of-gratification technique**. Typically, the child is presented with two choices: a small reward that is available immediately or a larger reward that can only be obtained later. This situation is analogous to many choices children (and even adults) encounter every day: Should I use this week's allowance to buy a small toy or combine it with next week's and buy a larger toy? Should I eat this snack now or save my appetite for a better meal later? Perhaps because this experimental task is a bit more complex than that involving resistance to temptation, more factors have been shown to influence children's ability to delay gratification (Eigsti et al., 2006; Mischel & Ayduk, 2004; Mischel, Shoda, & Rodriguez, 1989).

Delay-of-gratification technique
An experimental procedure for studying children's ability to postpone a smaller, immediate reward in order to obtain a larger, delayed one.

In one study, while waiting for the better reward, children were directed to produce either a relevant statement ("I am waiting for the marshmallow"), an irrelevant statement ("one, two, three"), or nothing. Once again, either of the self-statements increased waiting time for younger children, but only the relevant verbalizations were of assistance to the older children (Karniol & Miller, 1981).

Another method for helping children delay gratification is to reduce or alter the attention they pay to the tempting object (the smaller but immediately available reward) (Mischel et al., 1989; Peake, Hebl, & Mischel, 2002). When the object is out of sight, for example, children will wait much longer. The same is true when they spend the waiting time playing with a toy or engaging in some other distracting activity. Even when they are thinking about the tempting object, children will wait longer if they are instructed to think only about certain objective properties of the object (say, the shape or colour of a candy bar), rather than about its appealing properties (the candy bar's smell or taste).

As children grow older, their understanding of these delay strategies increases. For example, when presented with various waiting techniques and asked to select the ones that would work best, preschoolers display little knowledge of what strategies would be more effective. Grade 3 students, however, show an impressive understanding. And by grade 6, the large majority of children clearly seem to know that redirecting one's attention from the reward and various other forms of distraction are the methods most useful in delaying gratification (Mischel & Ayduk, 2004; Mischel et al., 1989; Yates, Yates, & Beasley, 1987).

Children's use of distraction strategies in other contexts may be related to their ability to delay gratification. Toddlers who were able to use self-distraction to cope with a period of separation from their mothers were found to be able to delay gratification at age 5 for longer periods than were children who did not show that early coping ability (Sethi et al., 2000). These researchers also explored how delay of gratification is related to children's reactions to their mothers' behaviours in a play setting. The key predictor of preschool delay of gratification was toddlers' response to their mothers: the greatest success in delay of gratification at age 5 was observed in the children who as toddlers had distanced themselves from controlling mothers or those who had engaged themselves with non-controlling mothers. Thus, the ability to delay gratification may be an indication of a child who is generally well-equipped to navigate social experiences and adjust his or her responses to best fit a situation.

Not surprisingly, then, the ability to delay gratification has been linked to children's social competence as well. Children who respond impulsively often experience problems in their social interactions with other children, in part because they fail to acquire all the necessary information about a situation before making a decision (Eisenberg, Pidada, & Liew, 2001; Frankel & Feinberg, 2002; Hughes et al., 2000). One study investigated the relation between a child's ability to delay gratification (in the standard tasks described here) and how many witness statements the child chose to hear before deciding whether another child was guilty of having caused a problem. As predicted, those children who were good at delaying gratification also waited to hear more testimony before making their decisions (Gronau & Waas, 1997).

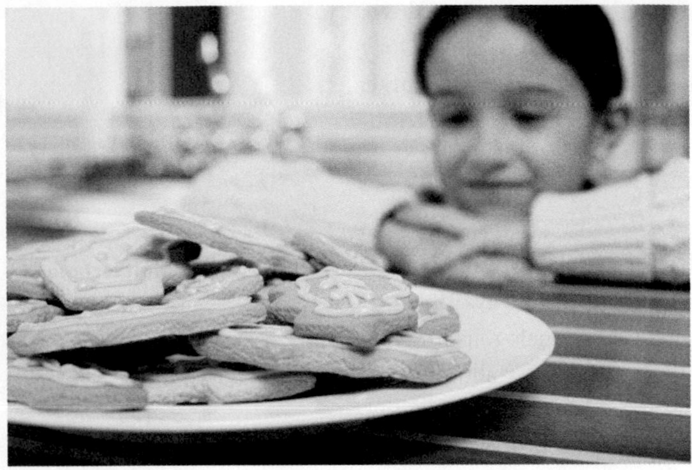

A child's ability to delay gratification appears to remain stable over time, and may predict future happiness and social competence. (*Digital Vision*)

Finally, children's ability to cope with temptation in this type of experimental situation appears to reflect a surprisingly stable personality characteristic. In one study, adolescents who had participated as preschoolers in delay-of-gratification research of the type described earlier were studied again 10 years later. Parents were asked to complete several questionnaires concerned with aspects of their children's present cognitive skills, social competence, and ability to cope with stress. The results indicated that children who had been better at delaying gratification in their early years were much more likely to be rated by parents as stronger in each of these three areas. For example, the children who had waited the longest during the experimental procedures (especially those who had spontaneously developed good coping strategies) were now reported to be the most academically successful, the best at getting along with peers, the best at coping with problems, and the most confident and self-reliant (Mischel & Ayduk, 2004; Mischel, Shoda, & Peake, 1988; Shoda, Mischel, & Peake, 1990). These rather remarkable findings indicate that a child's early ability to delay gratification may be one long-term predictor of that child's eventual success and happiness.

For Thought and Discussion

Why do you think the ability to delay gratification is so important in child development?

LEARNING OBJECTIVE 13.4

Analyze the mechanisms and processes by which children develop self-control.

1. What trends do we see in the development of self-regulation?
2. How do children learn different types of compliance?
3. What can we learn about self-control from experiments using the forbidden-toy paradigm and the delay-of-gratification technique?

CONCLUSION

This chapter has covered a variety of topics that may seem only loosely connected to one another. Why a baby watches herself in a mirror may seem unrelated to why she does or does not give up a smaller reward to wait for a larger one in kindergarten, or why she lowers her opinion of herself in junior high school. The lack of an immediately obvious connection between these aspects of child development reflects the fact that the self has only recently become a topic of major research interest.

Our examination of the self has, however, nicely illustrated an important theme of this book and of modern child psychology: social and cognitive development are so interdependent that it is difficult to study either one alone. Although, for clarity, we have often discussed these two domains separately, it should be apparent that one cannot be completely understood without the other. We have seen, for example, that children's growing knowledge about themselves and their increasingly accurate evaluations of their abilities have major influences on their interactions with other people. On the other hand, social interactions play an important role in the development of children's thinking and problem-solving skills. This theme emerged in earlier chapters and will continue to find its way into our discussions as we look further at children's social development.

SUMMARY

KEY TERMS

academic self-concept, p. 505
categorical self, p. 486
committed compliance, p. 513
competence, p. 500
compliance, p. 512
delay-of-gratification technique, p. 515
entity model, p. 506
evaluative self-reactions, p. 489
existential self, p. 486
false self behaviour, p. 497
forbidden-toy paradigm, p. 514
incremental model, p. 506
looking-glass self, p. 500
personal agency, p. 493
private speech, p. 511
self-consciousness, p. 503
self-efficacy, p. 488
self-esteem (self-worth), p. 500
self-evaluation, p. 486
self-knowledge (self-awareness), p. 486
self-regulation, p. 486
self-schema, p. 486
self-system, p. 486
situational compliance, p. 513
social comparison, p. 508
visual self-recognition, p. 494

LEARNING OBJECTIVES

LEARNING OBJECTIVE 13.1 Compare and contrast five theoretical perspectives on the development of the self-system.

1. *According to contemporary views, what are the three components of the self-system?*
   Three distinct but interrelated components—self-knowledge, self-evaluation, and self-regulation—comprise the self-system. Self-knowledge (or self-awareness) is concerned with what children know about themselves and when this knowledge is acquired. Self-evaluation refers to children's opinions of themselves. Self-regulation refers to children's self-control and its development.

2. *How do cognitive-developmental approaches view the development of the self?*
   Cognitive-developmental theorists have offered several models concerning the development of the self. Information-processing theorists view the self as part of the larger memory system. Children are believed to construct self-schemas, which they use to organize information related to the self and which influence how they perceive and interact with the world. Based on interviews with children, Selman proposed a five-stage model of self-awareness that begins with the infant's inability to differentiate the physical and psychological selves and ends with the adolescent's belief that aspects of the self remain unconscious and unknowable.

3. *How do environmental/learning approaches contribute to our understanding of the development of the self?*
   Social-learning theory has contributed two models of the self, both proposed by Bandura. Self-efficacy judgments—judgments concerning one's own ability to succeed at various tasks—are assumed to be inaccurate in early childhood but to improve gradually with the help of four processes: verbal instruction from parents and other adults, success and failure experiences, observation of relevant models, and monitoring of internal bodily reactions. Self-efficacy judgments appear to have important effects on children's behaviour. Self-regulation is assumed to occur when children internalize the standards they have acquired through external processes and then use evaluative self-reactions to keep their behaviour consistent with these standards.

4. *What are examples of biological and evolutionary approaches to questions about the self?*
   Evolutionary and biological perspectives on the self include Bowlby's attachment theory and evolutionary psychology. According to Bowlby, infants construct an internal working model of the self through their interactions with caregivers. Children whose caregivers are responsive to their needs develop a working model of the self as worthy and lovable. Evolutionary psychologists are interested in the evolutionary roots of the self. Research from this perspective focuses on the nature of self-understanding and self-related behaviours among non-human species.

5. *What important information do sociocultural approaches provide in understanding the self?*
   According to the sociocultural approach, the self is shaped through participation in cultural practices that reflect cultural models of the self. Cross-cultural studies show striking variability in cultural models of the self. The dimension of the self that has been most widely studied is the relation of the self to others.

LEARNING OBJECTIVE 13.2 Trace the development of self-knowledge from infancy, identifying the processes by which changes in the self-system occur.

1. *How can you tell when an infant discovers the self as a separate entity with personal agency?*
   Perceptual processes play an important role in infants' recognizing their separateness. By 3 months of age, infants perceive that they control their own body movements. Along with infants' knowledge that they exist apart from the things around them comes an understanding of personal agency—that they can be the agents or causes of events that occur in their worlds. Babies manipulate objects, suggesting an awareness both that they are separate from things, and that they can do something with them. Personal agency also develops through babies' interactions with caregivers. When parents are more sensitive and responsive to their infants' signals, babies more quickly develop an understanding of their impact on their environments and the self as separate from the mother.

2. *How does self-recognition in infants change over time, and what factors are related to this ability?*
   As infants approach the end of their second year, they begin to show recognition of themselves. Research with mirrors and videotapes indicates reliable self-recognition by about 2 years of age. However, not until about 4 years of age do children display recognition of self-images videotaped earlier. It may be that experimental procedures that require children to use mirror or video information underestimate the dawning of self-recognition because these actions require several accompanying cognitive achievements.

   Individual differences are found in the development of self-recognition. Self-recognition may occur earlier in babies with difficult temperaments. Research of maltreated infants suggests that self-recognition is influenced by the security of the infant–caregiver attachment.

   Increases in self-awareness are accompanied by increases in other-awareness. Infants who display self-recognition are also more likely to engage in synchronic imitation and to help someone in distress.

3. *How do children's self-descriptions change from early childhood to adolescence?*
Self-knowledge in children beyond the infant years has been assessed principally through examination of their self-descriptions. Self-descriptions by preschoolers reflect preoperational thinking and typically include references only to objective, here-and-now characteristics. In middle childhood, the concrete operational child focuses to a greater degree on non-tangible characteristics, such as emotions, and on membership in various categories. Adolescents' formal operational abilities lead to more abstract and hypothetical self-descriptions, concerned often with attitudes, personality characteristics, and personal beliefs, sometimes involving conflicting attributes. During adolescence, many youth grow increasingly interested in and committed to their ethnic and cultural identities.

LEARNING OBJECTIVE 13.3 Describe the development of self-esteem, ways to measure it, and the contexts that shape the way children evaluate themselves.

1. *What is self-esteem and how is it measured?*
The evaluative opinions children develop about themselves are referred to as their self-esteem, or self-worth. Children's self-esteem is assumed to include both cognitive judgments and affective reactions to those judgments. Questionnaires are the most common methods used to assess children's self-esteem. Instruments such as Harter's Self-Perception Profile for Children and Marsh's Self-Description Questionnaire present children with questions designed to tap their opinions of themselves in a variety of contexts. The responses to these questions can be combined to produce an overall score representing the child's level of self-esteem. By age 7 or 8, children in Western cultures have usually formed at least four broad areas of self-esteem: academic competence, social competence, physical/athletic competence, and physical appearance. These categories become more refined and distinct with age. As children mature, they also gain the ability to combine their separate self-evaluations into a general psychological image of themselves—an overall sense of self-esteem.

2. *How does self-esteem change across childhood and adolescence, and how does it differ for boys and girls?*
Kindergarteners tend to have a relatively high level of self-esteem, which remains stable until early adolescence. At about age 11 or 12, children report a dip in self-esteem. This drop in self-esteem has been attributed to several changes that typify adolescence, including the stress of school transitions, increased self-consciousness, and the biological changes associated with puberty. Beginning in middle to late childhood, boys report higher global self-esteem than girls, with the greatest differences occurring in adolescence. This difference may be due in part to gender differences in perceptions of physical attractiveness.

3. *What factors are believed to contribute to the formation of academic self-concept?*
Children's perception of their academic competence, or academic self-concept, is one factor that affects self-esteem. Academic self-concept generally is highest in kindergarten and steadily declines through at least grade 4. Older children learn that bragging is not socially appropriate, and so increasingly avoid giving glowing descriptions of their abilities.

4. *What roles do children's theories of intelligence and attributions play in achievement motivation?*
Some children believe in an entity model of intelligence, in which intelligence is fixed and unchangeable. Others develop an incremental model, in which intelligence can grow with experience and learning. These models relate to children's attributions for success or failure. Some children believe that success or failure depends on how much ability one has, while others believe it depends on how much effort one applies. Children who attribute their lack of success to lack of ability tend to learn helplessness and fail to persist. Children who focus on effort and skill-building, on the other hand, have reason for optimism in the face

of failure. They become mastery-oriented, believing they can do better in the future by trying harder.

5. *What roles do criticism, praise, and social comparison play in the development of academic self-concept?*
The feedback children receive from adults is one source of academic motivation. However, not all praise is beneficial. Person-oriented praise is associated with increased vulnerability to failure, whereas praise directed at effort produces the most mastery-oriented responses. As children move through the early grades, they increasingly use social comparisons in developing their academic self-concept. This process may explain the general decline in academic self-image: many children must lower their assessments of their abilities as they compare themselves with other children. Parents' interaction styles also influence children's academic self-concepts.

6. *What is the impact of academic self-concept on children's development and future prospects?*
Academic self-concept influences children's academic achievement. High self-image improves motivation and success, and low self-image reduces them, even among children whose low self-image inaccurately reflects their high academic ability. Subjective perception of ability (rather than actual ability) determines whether children will attempt or avoid challenges.

LEARNING OBJECTIVE 13.4 Analyze the mechanisms and processes by which children develop self-control.

1. *What trends do we see in the development of self-regulation?*
The development of self-regulation is a major achievement. Little meaningful self-regulation is evident during the first year of life, but by the third year children consistently regulate their activities with respect to producing outcomes. Self-directed private speech appears to play a role in self-regulation. The changes in self-regulation observed during the early years reflect two important developments: a shift from external to internal control, and an increase in the sophistication of self-control.

2. *How do children learn different types of compliance?*
Children begin to understand caregiver wishes and expectations around the end of the first year. Compliance is an early index of self-control. Research has indicated that children display two contrasting types of compliance to authority: committed compliance and situational compliance. Only committed compliance, wherein the child adopts the caregiver's viewpoint as his or her own, can be considered a demonstration of self-regulation. Factors influencing compliance include the child's temperament, parental warmth and responsivity, and type of request ("Do" vs. "Don't").

3. *What can we learn about self-control from experiments using the forbidden-toy paradigm and the delay-of-gratification technique?*
Resistance-to-temptation studies examine the common situation in which children must withhold a prohibited behaviour. Using the forbidden-toy paradigm, investigators have found that the ability to resist temptation is influenced by a number of factors, including appropriate self-statements, modelling, and a good rationale or plan for resisting the prohibited act. Delay-of-gratification studies examine children's ability to forgo smaller, immediate rewards in order to receive larger, delayed ones. Factors that affect waiting time include self-statements and various methods of reducing attention to the tempting, immediately available reward. Children's understanding of effective delay strategies increases as they get older. The ability to delay gratification during the preschool years has been linked with parents' ratings of their adolescents' cognitive, social, and coping abilities.

CHAPTER 14

MORAL DEVELOPMENT

In the popular children's book, *The Cat in the Hat*, it is a cold and rainy day and Sally and her brother are bored; their mother has gone out. A mischievous cat appears on the doorstep with promises of "good games" and amusing "tricks" that would undoubtedly annoy their mother. Despite the warnings of the fish (the parental voice), the children let the cat into the house and all kinds of chaos ensues. The children grow concerned, but the cat shows up with an amazing machine that restores order and all is well, except, perhaps, the children's state of mind. They wonder—should we tell mother, or not? (And, the author asks, would you?)

Generations of children have felt the rush of adrenaline as the cat breaks rule after rule in this story and in its sequel, *The Cat in the Hat Comes Back*. The stories appeal strongly to children who are old enough to know about family and societal rules and to spend increasing amounts of time unsupervised and outside of direct adult control. They delight in imagining what they might do—if they could be certain they would not be caught. Would they eat cake in the bathtub? Fly kites in the house? Juggle mother's china? Try on father's shoes?

The violations depicted by Dr. Seuss are relatively minor, and that is part of their appeal to young listeners. As we discuss shortly, by the time children are old enough to appreciate Dr. Seuss, they can already distinguish between the fanciful infractions of the Cat in the Hat and more serious transgressions, and most children would not find these latter sorts of violations so amusing. Why this is so, and how children come to understand various kinds of rules and follow them, even when parents or other authority figures are not around, is the focus of this chapter. ■

MORALITY INVOLVES ISSUES of right and wrong, good and evil. If any society is going to survive, it must have rules that make clear to its citizens what is permitted and what is prohibited. Children's moral development involves the ways in which they come to understand and follow (or not follow) the rules of their social world. Until fairly recently, the study of moral development was left primarily to philosophers and religious scholars. Today, developmental psychologists also have a great deal of interest in this topic.

Contemporary research focuses on three facets of morality: affect, cognition, and behaviour. Research on affect focuses on the emotions associated with moral behaviour, such as empathy and guilt. Research into the cognitive underpinnings of moral development investigates how children think about what they and others do. Studies of this type focus on children's ability to examine a situation and decide whether a person's behaviour was appropriate, and whether the person should be punished. Ultimately, of course, researchers aim to explain children's behaviour—for example, why children steal, which children are more likely to start fights, and what factors promote sharing and cooperation among youngsters.

Increasingly, models of moral development incorporate all three facets. Historically, however, each of these facets has been studied in isolation. This is due, in part, to the ways in which the four major approaches to development have conceptualized moral development.

Learning Objective 14.1

Understand four theoretical approaches to the study of moral development.

THEORIES OF MORAL DEVELOPMENT

Two theoretical issues have dominated the study of moral development. One is whether children's moral beliefs and behaviours reside in the child and simply emerge over time, or whether they reside in the culture and are transmitted to the child. The second issue involves the generality of moral rules. If they emerge from the child, they must have a large biological component, making them universal for all members of our species. On the other hand, if they develop within the social group, they are more arbitrary and thus can vary from one culture to the next. These two questions lie at the heart of much of the research on this topic.

COGNITIVE-DEVELOPMENTAL APPROACHES

The cognitive tradition has been most concerned with the development of children's *moral reasoning* as they struggle with issues involving moral rules and social conventions. Some of these issues, such as physician-assisted suicide or the death penalty, are complex, with compelling arguments on both sides. Older children and adults will often examine the various arguments and weigh the evidence on all sides. As we have seen, however, young children often have difficulty taking multiple perspectives into account. They tend to consider only some of the information at hand and arrive at fairly simplistic solutions. Based on these observations, cognitive developmentalists have concluded that advances in moral reasoning abilities depend heavily on children's improving cognitive abilities. Their advancing moral understanding, in turn, is thought to produce more mature moral behaviours.

Three models have guided much of the cognitive research on moral development. Like so much in developmental psychology, this line of inquiry began with the pioneering work of Jean Piaget.

PIAGET'S THEORY Piaget made a brief foray into the realm of children's reasoning about moral issues, and his groundbreaking studies have proven to be very influential. Piaget's model of moral development grew out of his early work with children in Geneva, Switzerland, during the 1920s and 1930s. To investigate how children's conceptions of morality develop, Piaget used two very different methods.

One was a naturalistic approach in which he observed children playing common street games, such as marbles. Piaget closely examined how youngsters created and enforced the rules of their games, and he questioned them about circumstances under which the rules could be modified or even ignored. Piaget's second approach was more experimental and involved presenting individual children with **moral dilemmas** to solve. These took the form of short stories in which the child had to determine which of two characters was "naughtier." For example, in one story a little boy named Augustine accidentally makes a large ink stain on the tablecloth while trying to be helpful and fill his father's ink pot, whereas a little boy named Julian makes a small ink spot on the tablecloth while engaging in the forbidden act of playing with his father's pen.

Moral dilemmas Stories used by Piaget and others to assess children's levels of moral reasoning.

From this research, Piaget developed a four-stage model of moral development that focused on the way children follow rules (Piaget, 1932). In the first stage (2 to 4 years), children have no real conception of morality. Much of their behaviour involves play and imaginative games that have no formal rules, although at times they may invent certain restrictions as part of the play (e.g., all green blocks must be put in the same pail). The idea of following someone else's rules does not appear consistently until the second stage (5 to 7 years). When rule-following emerges, children approach the concept in an absolute manner. Social rules are viewed as *heteronomous* (or externally dictated) commands presented by people in authority (usually parents), and they cannot be changed. Children in this second stage, called the stage of **moral realism**, do not think to question the purpose or correctness of a rule, even though they may not like to follow it. Thus, Piaget observed that younger children playing marble games were usually very inflexible about changing any rules, even if it would have made the game more convenient or more fun.

Moral realism Piaget's second stage of moral development, in which children view rules as absolute, externally dictated, and unchangeable.

Piaget noted two interesting characteristics that grow out of this absolutist orientation. Most children in the second stage evaluate moral situations largely in terms of their physical and objective consequences. They view actions that cause greater damage as more wrong morally than actions causing less damage, regardless of the character's motives or intentions. Hence, the helpful Augustine was usually seen as naughtier than the disobedient Julian because he made the larger ink stain.

Another characteristic of this stage is **immanent justice**. Because these children believe so firmly in the authority of a rule, they feel that punishment must always occur when the rule is broken. Thus, if a child steals a cookie when no one is looking and then loses his baseball the following day, he may assume that he has been punished for the theft.

Immanent justice Literally inherent justice; refers to the expectation of children in Piaget's stage of moral realism that punishment must follow any rule violation, including those that appear to go undetected.

In Piaget's third stage (8 to 11 years), the child gradually realizes that rules are agreements created by people to help or protect one another. Obeying these rules is no longer viewed as simply following someone else's orders, but as an autonomous or personal decision to cooperate with others. Piaget observed, for example, that at this stage children could adapt marble-game rules, if necessary, to fit the circumstances of the moment (too many players, too few marbles, and so on).

Piaget studied common children's games as a way of examining children's conceptions of rules. (© *Tim Gainey/Alamy*)

Furthermore, at this stage, children's more advanced cognitive abilities allow new factors to enter into their moral evaluations. What a person was trying or meaning to do—that is, the person's motives or intentions—may become as important as the outcome of the behaviour. Accordingly, with increasing age, children were more likely to judge Julian's forbidden behaviour as naughtier, even though it caused less damage. Because the morality of following a rule is now evaluated in relation to other factors in the situation, Piaget referred to this third level as the stage of **moral relativism**.

Moral relativism Piaget's third stage of moral development, in which children view rules as agreements that can be altered and consider people's motives or intentions when evaluating their moral conduct.

In the final stage, which Piaget discussed only briefly, children become capable of developing new rules when the circumstances require it. They also begin to extend their moral reasoning beyond the personal level to larger societal and political concerns.

Piaget believed that both cognitive factors and social experience underlie the development of moral reasoning (Horn, Daddis, & Killen, 2008). As children move away from the egocentrism of early childhood, they become better able to evaluate the morality of a situation from multiple perspectives. Thus, the narrow focusing on unchangeable rules and objective consequences gives way to a broader, more flexible view of the world as the child gets older.

Piaget also emphasized the importance of social experiences in children's moral development. Of particular importance are children's interactions with peers. During their early years, children learn that parents usually dictate and enforce the rules of behaviour. In their desire to please their parents, children adopt the belief that they live in a world where rules must be followed. But the one-way nature of this rule system keeps children from expressing their own points of view or appreciating that there can be different opinions on moral questions. Piaget believed that through their interactions with peers, children learn that there can be several perspectives on an issue and that rules are the result of negotiating, compromising, and respecting the points of view of other people.

KOHLBERG'S MODEL A second influential cognitive theory of moral development was proposed by Lawrence Kohlberg, who drew much of his inspiration and methodology from Piaget's earlier work (Colby & Kohlberg, 1987; Kohlberg, 1969, 1981). Like Piaget, Kohlberg rejected the idea that moral development is a simple transmission of moral rules from parents and other adults to children.

Kohlberg's method, like Piaget's, involved presenting research participants with moral dilemmas to assess their level of moral reasoning. But Kohlberg's stories did not require a simple choice as to who was naughtier. Instead, they presented the child with a dilemma in which a story character must choose, for example, between obeying a law (or rule) and breaking the law for the benefit of an individual person. For each dilemma, the child is asked what the character should do and why. In Kohlberg's model, the second question is especially important because it reveals the child's level of reasoning. The Heinz dilemma, which follows, is one of the best known of Kohlberg's moral dilemmas:

For Thought and Discussion

How would you respond to the Heinz dilemma? Do you think Heinz should have stolen the drug? Why or why not? Can you see why this story is referred to as a moral dilemma?

> In Europe, a woman was near death from a special kind of cancer. There was one drug that doctors thought might save her. It was a form of radium that a druggist in the same town had recently discovered. The drug was expensive to make, but the druggist was charging 10 times what the drug cost him to make. He paid $200 for the radium and charged $2,000 for a small dose of the drug. The sick woman's husband, Heinz, went to everyone he knew to borrow the money, but he could gather together only about $1,000, half of what it cost. He told the druggist that his wife was dying and asked him to sell it cheaper or let him pay later. But the druggist said, "No, I discovered the drug, and I'm going to make money from it." So Heinz got desperate and broke into the man's store to steal the drug for his wife (Kohlberg, 1964, pp. 18–19).

The questions asked are "Should Heinz have done that?" and then "Why?" (or "Why not?").

From his research, Kohlberg concluded that moral reasoning develops in three predictable levels, termed **preconventional**, **conventional**, and **postconventional**. Within each level are two stages, each of which can be divided into a social perspective component and a moral content component. The model is described in Table 14.1. In his later writings, Kohlberg suggested that the sixth stage is actually more theoretical than real. Few individuals attain this level, and none of the individuals that Kohlberg studied ever displayed it. Nevertheless, Kohlberg speculated that a seventh stage of moral development might also exist that goes beyond these levels of moral reasoning and enters the realm of religious faith (Kohlberg, Levine, & Hewer, 1983).

Preconventional level Kohlberg's first two stages of moral development. Moral reasoning is based on the assumption that individuals must serve their own needs.

Conventional level Kohlberg's third and fourth stages of moral development. Moral reasoning is based on the view that a social system must be based on laws and regulations.

Postconventional level Kohlberg's final stages of moral development. Moral reasoning is based on the assumption that the value, dignity, and rights of each individual person must be maintained.

An important aspect of Kohlberg's model is how the two components of each stage interact. The social perspective component indicates the point of view from which the moral decision is made. For example, the child in the first stage is egocentric and sees all situations from a personal point of view. With development, the child becomes better able to appreciate the dilemma from the perspective of others or in terms of what is best for society as a whole. Advances in this area are thought to be related to cognitive development. But advances in perspective-taking are not sufficient for moral reasoning to advance. They must be accompanied by development of

TABLE 14.1 KOHLBERG'S STAGE MODEL OF MORAL REASONING

	Social Perspective	Moral Content
LEVEL I PRECONVENTIONAL Stage 1: Heteronomous morality ("Morality derives from power and authority.")	Children cannot consider more than one person's perspective. They tend to be egocentric, assuming that their feelings are shared by everyone.	This stage is equivalent to Piaget's moral realism. Evaluations of morality are absolute and focus on physical and objective characteristics of a situation. Morality is defined only by authority figures, whose rules must be obeyed.
Stage 2: Individualism and instrumental purpose ("Morality means looking out for yourself.")	Children understand that people have different needs and points of view, although they cannot yet put themselves in the other's place. Other people are assumed to serve their own self-interests.	Moral behaviour is seen as valuable if it serves one's own interests. Children obey rules or cooperate with peers with an eye toward what they will get in return. Social interactions are viewed as deals and arrangements that involve concrete gains.
LEVEL II CONVENTIONAL Stage 3: Interpersonal conformity ("Morality means doing what makes others like you.")	People can view situations from another's perspective. They understand that an agreement between two people can be more important than each individual's self-interest.	The focus is on conformity to what most people believe is right behaviour. Rules should be obeyed so that people you care about will approve of you. Interpersonal relations are based on the Golden Rule ("Do unto others ...").
Stage 4: Law and order ("What's right is what's legal.")	People view morality from the perspective of the social system and what is necessary to keep it working. Individual needs are not considered more important than maintaining the social order.	Morality is based on strict adherence to laws and on performing one's duty. Rules are seen as applying to everyone equally and as being the correct means of resolving interpersonal conflicts.
LEVEL III POSTCONVENTIONAL Stage 5: Social contract ("Human rights take precedence over laws.")	People take the perspective of all individuals living in a social system. They understand that not everyone shares their own values and ideas, but that all have an equal right to exist.	Morality is based on protecting each individual's human rights. The emphasis is on maintaining a social system that will do so. Laws are created to protect (rather than restrict) individual freedoms, and they should be changed, as necessary. Behaviour that harms society is wrong, even if it is not illegal.
Stage 6: Universal ethical principles ("Morality is a matter of personal conscience.")	People view moral decisions from the perspective of personal principles of fairness and justice. They believe each person has personal worth and should be respected, regardless of ideas or characteristics. The progression from Stage 5 to Stage 6 can be thought of as a move from a social-directed to an inner-directed perspective.	It is assumed that there are universal principles of morality that are above the law, such as justice and respect for human dignity. Human life is valued above all else.

Source: Based on information from L. Kohlberg, "Moral Stages and Moralization: The Cognitive-Development Approach," 1976, in T. Likona (Ed.), *Moral Development and Behavior: Theory, Research, and Social Issues* (New York Holt, Rinehart and Winston).

the moral content component, which is assumed to be more strongly influenced by the child's experiences with moral situations. Kohlberg's theory thus resembles Piaget's in assuming that moral development results from a combination of improving cognitive skills and repeated encounters with moral issues.

Movement from stage to stage in Kohlberg's model closely follows the Piagetian process of accommodation. Movement occurs when the child can no longer handle new information within his or her current view of the world—or, in Piagetian terms, when the child can no longer assimilate new information within his or her existing structure of schemes. Kohlberg's model

For Thought and Discussion

What is an example of a moral dilemma or conflict that you have recently faced in your own life? Do you approach all issues within the same level of moral reasoning, or is your reasoning for some issues higher (or lower) than for others?

places particular importance on *role-taking* opportunities, which occur when children participate in decision-making situations with others and exchange differing points of view on moral questions. The contrasting viewpoints produce cognitive conflict, which the children eventually resolve by reorganizing their thinking into a more advanced stage of reasoning. This process occurs gradually. Thus, although a person's general level of moral reasoning can be generally classified into one of Kohlberg's stages, the individual may approach certain specific issues at a higher or lower stage of reasoning.

Several other characteristics of Kohlberg's stage model are similar to Piaget's theory. For instance, each stage forms a *structured whole*, with children in that stage generally responding consistently to different dilemmas and situations. Also, the stages follow an *invariant sequence*, so all children experience them in the same order and with no regression to earlier stages. Finally, the progression of stages is *universal* for all people and all cultures.

For Thought and Discussion

What are examples of issues that some Canadians regard as matters of personal choice, but that others classify as rule violations in the moral domain?

Social conventions Rules used by a society to govern everyday behaviour and maintain order.

TURIEL'S MODEL Elliot Turiel has developed a model that has much in common with those of Piaget and Kohlberg, including the methods used to assess children's reasoning. Like Piaget and Kohlberg, Turiel and colleagues interviewed children about hypothetical situations. Some of these stories involved themes highly reminiscent of those in the stories of Piaget and Kohlberg (e.g., stealing, breaking a promise). Other stories involved other rule violations, such as undressing on the playground, not saying grace before eating, a boy's wanting to become a nurse and care for infants when he grows up, and the like (Turiel, Killen, & Helwig, 1987). The stories were designed to depict rule violations in three distinct domains.

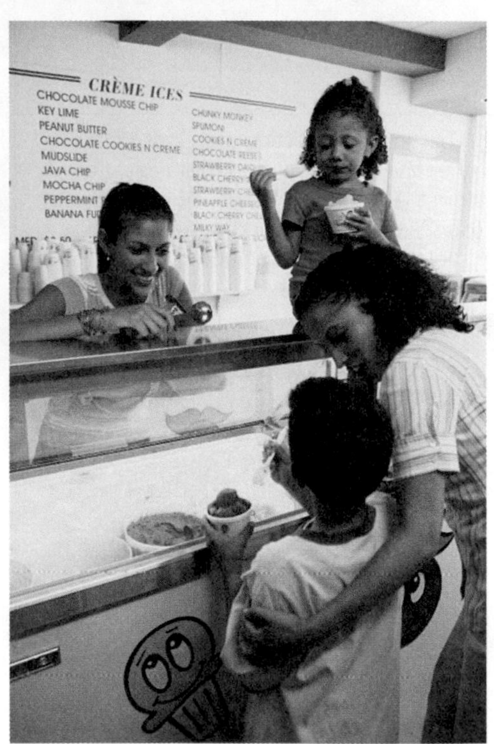

According to Turiel's model, children can distinguish between moral rules and social conventions, such as saying "please" and "thank you," at a very early age—a result of their social interactions. (*Blend Images/Media Bakery*)

The *moral domain* is concerned with people's rights and welfare. Issues concerning fairness and justice, such as lying, stealing, and killing, fall into this category. The *social domain* involves **social conventions**, the rules that guide social relations among people. Being polite, wearing appropriate clothing, and addressing people using the proper titles (Professor Jones, Dr. Brown, Ms. Smith, etc.) are behaviours that fall within this domain. There are also matters of personal choice, the *personal domain*, in which individual preferences take priority. These issues do not violate the rights of others or harm others, and they are not socially regulated (or only weakly so). In many Canadian families, these issues include one's hairstyle, choice of friends, and leisure activities.

A central premise of Turiel's *domain theory* is that children can distinguish among these domains from a very early age (Turiel, 2006). Of particular interest is the distinction between moral rules and social conventions. In the models of Piaget and Kohlberg, rules and conventions initially fall within a single domain for children and do not divide into separate cognitive categories until later on. In fact, by age 3, children in many societies understand that moral violations (e.g., hitting another child) are more wrong than violations of social conventions (e.g., eating ice cream with fingers) (Smetana, 2006). And by age 4, children assert that a moral transgression would be wrong, even if an adult did not see it and there was no rule to prohibit it (Smetana & Braeges, 1990).

How do children come to make these distinctions? Children's understanding of issues within the moral domain is thought to result from their social interactions—especially with peers—through both being victims of immoral acts and witnessing the consequences of such acts for others (Nucci, 2008). Children's understanding of social conventions is assumed to result from their experiences in a variety of social settings, where the conventions often differ from one setting to another. One very important context involves culture. Domain theory predicts that children in all cultures will distinguish between the moral and conventional domains at an early age, but that particular social conventions may vary from one culture to the next (Miller, 2006; Turiel, 2002, 2006).

EVOLUTIONARY AND BIOLOGICAL APPROACHES

As we have seen, cognitive-developmental theorists view reasoning as the primary determinant of moral behaviour. Theorists working within the evolutionary approach have a markedly different perspective. Much of their work has involved relating human behaviour to that observed in other species, whose intellectual capabilities are very different from those of humans. Scientists working within this tradition contend that there must be some biological basis for human morality because every known human culture has developed some kind of moral system to structure interactions among members. Moreover, they argue, it is implausible that the capacity for moral behaviour suddenly appeared among humans in the absence of any semblance of moral behaviour in other species. Thus, evolutionary theorists believe the rudiments of human morality must exist in the behaviour of non-human primates. The behaviours that have attracted most of their attention include altruism (or prosocial behaviour) and aggression (Bjorklund & Pellegrini, 2011; Brosnan, 2006; de Waal, 1996).

ALTRUISM Altruistic behaviours are those that benefit someone else but offer no obvious benefit—and perhaps even some cost—to the individual performing them. Giving money to a charity, sharing a candy bar, and risking one's life to save someone else's are examples. As mentioned in Chapter 1, this prosocial behaviour has been a particular challenge to classical evolutionary models because self-sacrifice would not seem to fit with Darwin's proposed mechanisms. How can a behaviour that does not increase a person's own chances of survival and reproduction be passed on in the species? It would seem, instead, that people who act selfishly and think first about themselves would be more likely to survive to pass along their genes. This dilemma, called the **paradox of altruism**, was discussed by Darwin and has been studied and debated ever since (Hastings, Zahn-Waxler, & McShane, 2006; Simpson & Beckes, 2010).

For Thought and Discussion

Do you believe that altruism ever occurs in the absence of any reward whatsoever? If so, what would be an example?

Paradox of altruism The logical dilemma faced by ethological theorists who try to reconcile self-sacrificial behaviour with the concepts of natural selection and survival of the fittest.

Sociobiologists have attempted to resolve this problem by adding two concepts to Darwin's notion of survival of the fittest (Dawkins, 1976; Maynard Smith, 1976; Simpson & Beckes, 2010). **Kin selection** proposes that humans (and some other animals) behave in ways that increase the chances for the survival and reproduction of their genes, rather than of themselves. A person can pass on genes either by reproducing or by increasing the reproductive chances of someone who has the same or similar genes. The more genes the second individual shares with the first, the more reasonable it becomes to try to save that individual's life (and reproductive capability). Therefore, we would predict that a mother should be more likely to risk her life for her child than for her husband because her child shares many of her genes. Similarly, any family member, or kin, should be favoured over any unrelated individual.

Kin selection A proposed mechanism by which an individual's altruistic behaviour toward kin increases the likelihood of the survival of genes similar to those of the individual.

But people perform acts of altruism directed toward non-family members every day. How does evolutionary theory explain such behaviour? Here, theorists propose a process called **reciprocal altruism**. According to this idea, people are genetically programmed to be helpful because (1) it increases the likelihood that they will someday in turn receive aid from the person they helped or from some other altruistic member of their group, or (2) by helping someone else in their social group, they help ensure that genes similar to their own will be passed on in the species (Simpson & Beckes, 2010; Trivers, 1971, 1983).

Reciprocal altruism A proposed mechanism by which an individual's altruistic behaviour toward members of the social group may promote the survival of the individual's genes through reciprocation by others or may ensure the survival of similar genes.

AGGRESSION Aggression and mechanisms for controlling aggression have been another favourite area of study for those espousing an evolutionary approach. Viewed from this perspective, one function of aggression is to increase the likelihood of survival of an individual's genes—believed by some to be the most important evolutionary function of any behaviour. Aggression serves this purpose in many ways, such as by helping the individual obtain food, protect the young, or preserve valuable hunting territory. In such cases, evolutionary processes clearly favour the stronger, smarter, or more skilled members of the species.

Aggression in many species can lead to physical combat. Some conflicts, however, do not progress to this point, but are resolved when one animal displays threatening gestures (such as certain facial expressions and body postures) and the other animal backs down, perhaps making submissive gestures. Such behaviours have adaptive value for both individuals—the attacker gains possession of the desired property and the retreating animal avoids injury or death. In some species that form social groups, such as monkeys, a **dominance hierarchy** develops, in which each member of the group fits somewhere on a dominance ladder. Each monkey controls those lower in the hierarchy (often simply by threats), but submits to those higher on the ladder. Even though initially created through aggression, such a structure ultimately reduces the overall physical conflict that might otherwise occur in the group (Bjorklund & Pellegrini, 2011; Pellegrini et al., 2007). The structure and function of dominance hierarchies in children's social interactions has been a favourite focus of ethologists, as we will see in Chapter 15.

Dominance hierarchy A structured social group in which members higher on the dominance ladder control those who are lower, initially through aggression and conflict but eventually simply through threats.

For Thought and Discussion

Do you think that humans are aggressive by nature, making warfare inevitable? If not, why is there persistent conflict?

Dominance hierarchies are one way of managing conflicts of interest among group members. In recent years, ethologists have expanded their focus to include non-aggressive methods of managing conflict (Aureli & de Waal, 2000; de Waal, 2005). For example, high-ranking male chimpanzees intervene in fights among juveniles and come to the aid of low-ranking females under attack. Researchers have also observed that chimpanzees massively bark in protest when an adult male punishes a juvenile too roughly. And many primates have a repertoire of "peacemaking" behaviours, including special calls, facial expressions, and rituals such as kissing and embracing that serve to restore damaged relationships following conflicts. These more advanced methods of conflict management require the ability to keep track of past social exchanges and, some ethologists believe, at least a rudimentary capacity for empathy and sympathy (Flack & de Waal, 2000; Verbeek, 2006). As we will see, these emotions play a key role in linking moral reasoning to moral action among humans.

ENVIRONMENTAL/LEARNING APPROACHES

The environmental/learning approach also has much to say about moral development. The essence of the social-learning view is that the social behaviours we traditionally label in terms of moral development are acquired and maintained through the same principles that govern most other behaviours. Although social-learning theorists agree that these processes are affected by developmental advances in cognitive abilities (Perry & Perry, 1983), they emphasize environmental mechanisms, such as reinforcement, punishment, and observational learning (modelling and imitation). This emphasis argues against a stage model of development in which moral behaviours emerge according to an internal timetable that is universal for all children. Instead, it predicts that behaviours should develop more individually, depending primarily on each child's social environment and personal experiences.

Most of the research within the social-learning tradition has involved *moral conduct*—both prosocial and antisocial behaviours—rather than moral reasoning (Grusec, 2006). This difference has resulted principally because social-learning theorists, unlike cognitive developmentalists, believe that moral reasoning and moral conduct are somewhat independent processes that can be influenced by different factors. As a result, social-learning theorists are less inclined to expect a child's moral behaviour to show consistency across situations or between knowledge and conduct (Gewirtz & Pelaez-Nogueras, 1991b).

The principal spokesperson for the social-learning account of moral development has been Albert Bandura, and most of the research conducted within this tradition is based on his views (Bandura, 1986, 1989b, 1991b). Bandura's theory, described in Chapter 1, holds that reinforcement and punishment are major processes by which children acquire moral behaviours. In simplest terms, children are more likely to produce behaviours (prosocial or antisocial) that are approved or rewarded, and tend to inhibit behaviours that are ignored or punished (Dishion & Piehler, 2009; Snyder, 2005). In addition, children come to discriminate the reinforcement possibilities that exist in different settings, such as the praise parents provide for good grades versus the pressure peers may exert for skipping school.

Another process that Bandura considers crucial for understanding moral development is observational learning. Children learn many of the rules and practices of their social world by watching others, such as parents and peers. Moreover, their behaviour can be affected by what they observe on television, in movies, and on the Internet, by the video games they play, or even by what they read in books and magazines (Bushman & Huesmann, 2010; Huesmann & Kirwil, 2007).

With development, reinforcement and observational processes become internalized, and children learn to use them to regulate their own behaviour. As we saw in Chapter 13, Bandura proposes that through the use of evaluative self-reactions and self-sanctions, children come to regulate their behaviour to match the moral standards they set for themselves. We will have much to say about the contributions of social-learning researchers when we discuss children's prosocial development and aggression later in the chapter.

SOCIOCULTURAL APPROACHES

The sociocultural approach to moral development focuses on how children come to understand moral and social rules and abide by them in the context of everyday activities. Like those working within the framework of social-learning theory, sociocultural researchers view moral development as a process of socialization. Sociocultural theorists believe children develop moral understanding during their interactions with parents and other more mature members of their communities. During these interactions, adults and other partners "scaffold" children's moral development by making salient the features of moral situations that are important for children to understand (we discussed the sociocultural notion of scaffolding in Chapter 8). Sometimes caregivers and others make explicit reference to rules (e.g., "Never hit small children"). Other times, the message is tacit, and children must draw inferences based on others' reactions to their transgressions. And, in some situations, caregivers engage in lengthy discussions with children that highlight why some act is right or wrong. In these ways, the moral concepts of a culture are communicated to children (Miller, 2006; Grusec, 2006; Shweder et al., 1987; Tappan, 1997, 2006).

The sociocultural approach views moral concepts as part of a child's cultural heritage—much like conceptions of the self, norms for emotional expression, and language—that have been passed on from generation to generation. This does not mean that socioculturalists endorse the idea that cultures "stamp" their moral codes onto the young. Rather, like cognitive developmentalists, those working within this framework acknowledge that children actively construct their understanding of morality (Miller, 2006; Tappan, 2006). But, whereas cognitive developmentalists see this as a largely individual process fuelled by children's social experiences, socioculturalists regard the process itself as a social one in which other people assist children's moral development by structuring and interpreting situations through the lens of a particular—not necessarily universal—moral system.

Sociocultural theorists believe children develop moral understanding through interactions with parents and other members of their community. These interactions can include explicit references to rules or tacit inferences. *(Comstock/Media Bakery)*

Much sociocultural research on moral development focuses on children's involvement in moral situations that naturally arise during everyday life. For example, researchers have devoted considerable attention to the ways caregivers foster children's moral development in the context of sibling interactions (Dunn, 2006, 2007). Of growing interest is how participation in cultural institutions (such as schools, religious institutions, organized sports, and community service organizations) contributes to children's moral development (Hart et al., 2006, 2008; Kerestes et al., 2004; Reinders & Youniss, 2006; Shields & Bredemeier, 2008). And, in keeping with Bronfenbrenner's ecological model, researchers working within this tradition are also concerned with how aspects of parents' lives, such as the nature of their employment, directly and indirectly affect children's involvement in prosocial and antisocial activities (Elder & Conger, 2000; Fletcher, Elder, & Mekos, 2000). We consider these contexts of children's moral development in greater detail later.

LEARNING OBJECTIVE 14.1

Understand four theoretical approaches to the study of moral development.

1. What is Piaget's model of moral development?
2. How did Kohlberg conceptualize moral development?
3. What are the main features of Turiel's view of moral development?
4. How does the evolutionary approach explain moral development?
5. What is the focus of the sociocultural approach to moral development?

Learning Objective 14.2

Understand what research has found concerning children's moral reasoning.

MORAL REASONING

How well has research evidence supported the theories we have just examined? We investigate this question, along with other issues, with reference to three important topic areas: moral reasoning, prosocial behaviour, and aggression. We begin with a discussion of research on children's moral reasoning.

FIGURE 14.1

An example of drawings used to convey motive, action, and outcome in stories. When pictures such as these accompany stories involving moral dilemmas, even 4- to 6-year-olds sometimes use story characters' motives as a basis for evaluating their behaviour. *From "Factors Influencing Young Children's Use of Motives and Outcomes as Moral Criteria," by S.A. Nelson, 1980,* Child Development, *51, 823–829. Copyright © 1980 by the Society for Research in Child Development. Reprinted by permission.*

EVALUATING PIAGET'S MODEL

Piaget's account of children's moral development has generally fared well empirically. Numerous studies show that with age, children increasingly consider motives and intentions when evaluating the morality of actions (Lapsley, 2006). In addition, various cognitive measures, including perspective-taking and mental state understanding, have been associated with children's level of moral judgment (Dunn & Herrera, 1997; Kurdek, 1980).

Piaget's idea that peer relations are an important context for moral development is also supported by research (Lapsley, 2006). As we discuss in detail later, children's peer relations provide many opportunities to tackle moral issues, such as kindness and unkindness, exclusion from play, failure to share, and so forth. Moreover, research by Lawrence Walker of the University of British Columbia and Karl Hennig of the University of Guelph (Walker, Hennig, & Krettenauer, 2000) supports Piaget's contention that children can achieve advances in moral reasoning via discussions with peers. And, consistent with Piaget's prediction, children with punitive parents who reinforce strict adherence to rules tend to display less mature moral reasoning and behaviour (Hoffman, 2000; Walker & Hennig, 1999; Walker & Taylor, 1991).

That said, some aspects of Piaget's theory have not held up as well to scrutiny. As will become clear, parents play a far more important role—and a different one—in the development of children's morality than Piaget envisioned. Piaget also appears to have underestimated the moral reasoning abilities of young children. When Piaget's dilemmas are presented in ways that make intentions more *salient*, for example, by stating the intention at the end of the story or adding pictures like that shown in Figure 14.1, even young children can take motives into account (Chandler, Greenspan, & Barenboim, 1973; Helwig, Zelazo, & Wilson, 2001; Jones & Thomson, 2001).

Other research shows that even young children consider a variety of factors in addition to motives and damage when assessing a character's morality. For example, young children believe that taking a toy from a friend is more wrong than taking a toy from a non-friend (Slomkowski & Killen, 1992). Most important, children in many societies judge the breaking of moral rules more harshly than the violation of social conventions.

For Thought and Discussion

What advice might a Piagetian psychologist give to those wishing to reduce aggressive behaviour and promote prosocial behaviour?

EVALUATING KOHLBERG'S MODEL

Like Piaget's model of moral development, Kohlberg's theory is supported by a good deal of empirical research. Studies that use Kohlberg's methods and criteria for scoring responses generally show that individuals progress through the sequence proposed by Kohlberg in the predicted order (Armon & Dawson, 1997; Rest et al., 1999; Walker, 1989). One of the most convincing studies is an investigation that followed a group of boys from age 10 through to adulthood (Colby et al., 1983). As shown in Figure 14.2, at age 10, the boys primarily used preconventional reasoning—emphasizing obeying authority or acting in one's own self-interest.

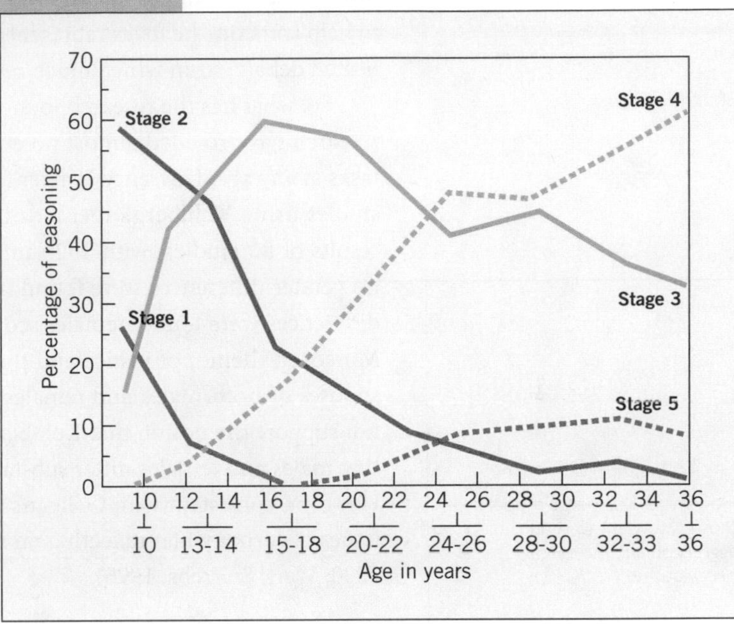

Mean percentage of moral reasoning by age group.
From A. Colby L. Kohlberg, J. C. Gibbs, and M. Lieberman, "A Longitudinal Study of Moral Judgment," 1983, Monographs of the Society for Research in Child Development, *48, 1–2. Reprinted by permission.*

From the ages of 14 to 24, Stage 3 reasoning predominated. During these years, the subjects were concerned with conforming to expectations to win others' approval. Even by age 36, only a small number were reasoning at the postconventional (Stage 5) level.

There is also support for the idea that individuals will consistently apply the same level of moral reasoning across a range of problems (Walker & Taylor, 1991). A typical study, for example, found that 60 percent of the time, the reasoning of research participants across a series of moral dilemmas involved only one stage, and 90 percent of the time it involved two adjacent stages (Walker, DeVries, & Trevarthen, 1987). Nevertheless, an individual's level of reasoning is not always consistent. It can even be influenced by characteristics of the dilemma itself, such as whether the dilemma involves general moral issues or personally experienced problems (Carpendale & Krebs, 1995; Teo et al., 1995).

A larger question raised by Kohlberg's theory is whether the model is universal, applying equally well to people of all cultures. Studies in non-technological societies, for example, show that individuals rarely progress to the fifth stage, while many people in more technologically advanced cultures do make this progression (Snarey, 1985). This finding is not a major problem for Kohlberg's theory, which incorporates the idea that culture and experiences help determine what stage a person ultimately reaches (Kohlberg, 1984). A more serious concern is that Kohlberg's moral dilemmas do not adequately address certain moral issues and concepts found in other cultures (Miller, 2006).

In some Chinese cultures, for example, the conflict between what is right for the individual and what is right for society is not ideally resolved by choosing one over the other (as is required in Kohlberg's hypothetical dilemmas). Instead, the most appropriate solution is thought to be reconciling the two interests by arriving at a compromise solution (Dien, 1982). And according to Hindu beliefs in India, the very fact that Heinz finds himself in a dilemma is an indication of his prior sins or negligence, from which he will not escape by committing further sinful actions, such as stealing (Shweder & Much, 1987). Kohlberg's model, then, is not applicable to everyone in these cultures.

Applicability should be universal not only across cultures, but between sexes as well. Recall that Kohlberg's theory focuses on justice reasoning as the best indicator of moral development. In one early study, Kohlberg reported that the moral reasoning of females generally was not as advanced as that of males (Kohlberg & Kramer, 1969). Not surprisingly, the notion that females engage in less sophisticated moral reasoning than do males was not well received, particularly by women. In response, Carol Gilligan asserted that women's moral reasoning is not lower than that of males, just different from it. Gilligan stressed that females are socialized to an "ethic of care" that is devalued in Kohlberg's system. In a book entitled *In a Different Voice*, Gilligan (1982) argued that Kohlberg's model underestimates the moral reasoning of females because their moral reasoning is less concerned with justice—whether someone has the right to do something based on laws or rules—and more concerned with issues of responsibility and care—whether someone has an *obligation* to do something based on the value of a personal relationship. For example, arguing that Heinz should steal the drug because saving a life is more important than obeying laws reflects a justice orientation, whereas arguing that Heinz should steal the drug because he has an obligation to help someone he loves represents a care orientation. Not surprisingly, Gilligan's book sparked a heated debate, from which much research ensued.

So, what has the research found? Contrary to Kohlberg's early findings and Gilligan's premise, research has provided almost no evidence that males and females score differently on Kohlberg's tasks at any age. Lawrence Walker (1991, 2006) of the University of British Columbia surveyed all studies using Kohlberg's methods in which gender differences could be reported. Analyzing the results of 80 studies, with 152 samples, and a total of 10,637 participants, Walker reported that no gender differences were found in 86 percent of these studies! Of the remaining studies where differences were found, females scored higher in 6 percent, and males scored higher in 9 percent. Moreover, themes of justice and themes of care were found to appear virtually equally in the responses of both males and females (Jaffee & Hyde, 2000; Walker, 2006). In short, research does not support the notion that Kohlberg's approach is biased in favour of one sex over the other, nor that males and females differ substantially in their approaches to moral dilemmas (Walker, 2006). However, consistent with Gilligan's views, there is some evidence that females may focus more on issues of caring when reflecting on moral issues they have faced in their own lives (Jaffee & Hyde, 2000; Wark & Krebs, 1996).

For Thought and Discussion

How might Kohlberg's model help those who want to reduce childhood aggression and increase prosocial behaviour?

EVALUATING TURIEL'S MODEL

Turiel's domain theory, too, is supported by a considerable body of evidence. The claim that moral reasoning involves several independent domains of social cognition and that children distinguish among these from an early age has found support in many studies (Smetana, 2006; Wainryb, 2006). For example, even preschool children generally believe that breaking a moral rule (such as stealing) is always wrong, whereas breaking a social convention (such as eating with your hands) depends on the setting and situation. Likewise, they believe that it is wrong to do something immoral, whether or not an explicit rule about it exists. Ignoring a social convention, however, is acceptable if there is no specific rule prohibiting it. Similarly, in situations involving harm and justice (moral rules), children judge that peers, parents, and other adults all have the authority to intervene to protect another person. And they believe it is not legitimate for a teacher or other authority figure to compel a child to violate moral rules. In contrast, children believe teachers and other authority figures have the right to make their own rules in their own arenas of influence. So, teachers can make rules in the classroom, but not in children's homes (Smetana, 2006). Finally, when asked which is more wrong, a minor moral misdeed (stealing an eraser) or a major social-conventional transgression (wearing pyjamas to school), most children choose the former (Catron & Masters, 1993; Laupta & Turiel, 1993; Smetana & Braeges, 1990; Smetana et al., 1993; Tisak & Turiel, 1988).

Turiel's belief that children's moral reasoning will be influenced by the context in which it takes place similarly has much support (Turiel, 2006). For example, when the violation is presented as part of a story, children view the breaking of a moral rule as always wrong. However, when the same rule is broken within their real-life experience, children are more willing to consider other factors (such as motives or intentions) in determining the wrongness of the act (Smetana, 2006). Likewise, physical harm (pushing someone down) is viewed by children as always wrong, whereas psychological harm (calling someone stupid) is viewed as wrong when it occurs in real life, but as much more acceptable when it occurs as part of a game (Helwig et al., 1995).

Children in Western societies appear to reason in ways consistent with Turiel's model. But do children in other cultures draw similar distinctions among moral rules, social conventions, and matters of personal choice? And do they make these distinctions at similar ages? The evidence here is intriguing and is the focus of considerable debate. Although researchers using culturally appropriate versions of Turiel's stories have replicated his findings in a diverse array of societies (Smetana, 2006; Turiel, 2006), research also shows considerable cultural variability in how children classify various kinds of rule violations. For example, compared with children from middle-income families, those in lower-income families are less likely to draw clear distinctions between moral rules and social conventions, and they view fewer issues as matters of personal choice (Nucci, 1997). These findings suggest there are some acts involving harm and justice that are universally regarded as wrong (e.g., breaking promises, destroying property), but the category of moral transgressions may be wider in some cultures than others.

For Thought and Discussion

How might you use Turiel's model to teach children moral reasoning skills?

DISTRIBUTIVE JUSTICE AND RETRIBUTIVE JUSTICE

We have been focusing on the ideas of Piaget, Kohlberg, and Turiel, but the moral concepts assessed by their methods are not the only areas of moral reasoning of interest to psychologists. Here, we briefly consider research on two other aspects of children's moral reasoning: distributive justice and retributive justice.

DISTRIBUTIVE JUSTICE The question of how to distribute a limited amount of resources among a group of deserving people—called *distributive justice* (Damon, 1983)—is usually assessed using a reward-allocation task. In the typical study, a group of children perform a task together for which they are to receive some sort of payment. One child is then asked to divide the pay among the participants. Usually the situation is designed so that the children perform different amounts of work.

Children's reasoning regarding distributive justice appears to develop in several stages (Lapsley, 2006). Up to about 4 years of age, children's reward distribution is characterized by self-interest; they tend to take a large portion of the earnings for themselves, regardless of the amount of work they contributed. At 5 or 6 years of age, children begin to divide rewards according to an equality principle, with all children receiving the same share, whatever their input. By about 7 years of age, children start to use equity as the basis for reward allocation; children who do more work are given more of the reward, although not always in the correct proportions.

Children's allocation of rewards appears to be influenced not only by their cognitive development—such as their understanding of proportions—but also by situational variables. For example, children distribute more reward to those whom they consider to be in greater need or whom they see as kind and helpful (Kienbaum & Wilkening, 2009; McGillicuddy-De Lisi et al., 1994). Culture may also play a role: children from more collectivistic cultures tend to be more egalitarian in their distribution of rewards than are those from more individualistic cultures (Nisan, 1984; Rochat et al., 2009). Also, if children believe they will interact again with someone who has done relatively little work, they tend to reward that person using the equality rule, rather than the more advanced equity rule (Graziano, 1987).

RETRIBUTIVE JUSTICE Children's concepts of justice have also been examined with a view toward determining what factors children use in assigning blame or responsibility; that is, their concept of *retributive justice*. Even young children appear to approach such problems in essentially the same way as adults.

As noted in a series of studies by Thomas Schultz of McGill University (Schultz & Darley, 1991; Schultz & Wright, 1985; Schultz, Wright, & Schleifer, 1986), when presented with a story about a character who broke a rule, both children and adults first examine whether any harm or damage was done. If none occurred, they typically do not pursue the issue of responsibility and justice. When damage is perceived to have occurred, people in both age groups then attempt to determine whether the story character was responsible. If no blame can be assigned to the character, punishment typically is not considered necessary. If, however, the character is deemed responsible for the harm, both children and adults proceed to the questions of whether punishment is warranted and, if so, how much. At both ages, then, they appear to follow a three-step line of reasoning: Harm? Responsibility? Punishment?

Although their approach to punishment situations may be similar to that of adults, children predict that the approach followed by adults will be different from their own. For example, when children were presented with several stories in which a character had bad intentions and produced a bad outcome, they rated the character's behaviour negatively. When asked to predict how adults would evaluate the behaviour, the children predicted that the adults would also view the behaviour negatively, but they would focus more on the outcome of the bad behaviours than on the character's motives and would evaluate the character's behaviour more harshly than the children had. These predictions proved to be inaccurate when the children's parents were then also asked to rate the story characters (Saltzstein et al., 1987).

These findings indicate that children's moral reasoning in situations involving responsibility for damage does not represent a simple imitation of what they expect from adults. Furthermore, children's predictions about the harshness of adults' judgments may reflect their view of adults as the creators and enforcers of social rules.

SOCIAL AND FAMILY INFLUENCES ON MORAL REASONING

Researchers working within each of the four theoretical traditions agree that social factors play a role in moral development, although they disagree as to the nature and importance of that role. In this section, we consider several of the most important functions of the social world in the development of morality.

PEERS Both Piaget and Kohlberg argued that children's interactions with peers are an important impetus for moral growth (Bukowski et al., 2009). Researchers have examined this issue using a variety of approaches. One indirect test of the role of peers in children's moral development is whether children who have greater peer experience engage in more advanced moral reasoning. And, indeed, correlational studies generally have demonstrated a positive relation between aspects of a child's peer interactions (such as popularity) and the child's level of moral maturity (Dunn, Cutting, & Demetriou, 2000; Enright & Satterfield, 1980; Peterson & Siegal, 2002; Schonert-Reichl, 1999). It is likely, however, that the direction of influence between peer relations and moral development goes both ways: children who reason competently about moral issues are likely to be attractive companions and friends.

Other researchers have followed in Piaget's footsteps and have observed children's social interactions in situations where moral issues are involved. There have been numerous studies of this type in homes, in schools, and on playgrounds, involving children as young as age 2 through junior high (Much & Shweder, 1978; Nucci & Nucci, 1982a, 1982b; Nucci & Turiel, 1978; Turiel, 2002). These studies show that situations involving issues of fairness and harm arise frequently in children's interactions with peers. Moreover, from a very early age, children respond to moral transgressions, usually by talking about the injury or loss experienced by the victim and asking the perpetrator to consider how it would feel to be the victim of the transgression. We discuss children's moral reasoning about peer relations in *On the Cutting Edge 14.1*.

Both Piaget and Kohlberg believed that children's moral reasoning is strongly influenced by their interactions with peers. Interactions with peers may cause children and adolescents to discover or doubt some points of view on moral questions, which may lead to a higher level of moral reasoning. (© *Tom Grill/Corbis*)

Other researchers have used experimental approaches to examine the impact of peer interaction on moral reasoning (Berkowitz et al., 1980; Kruger 1992; Kruger & Tomasello, 1986; Walker et al., 2000). In these studies—which typically involve older elementary school children or adolescents—researchers begin by interviewing children individually about some type of moral dilemma. Various materials are used, including Kohlberg's dilemmas and situations personally experienced by the interviewees. The children are then paired with peer partners and asked to discuss and reach consensus about the dilemmas. Following the discussion, each partner is interviewed again, sometimes after considerable time has elapsed.

Studies using this approach show that discussing moral issues with peers can foster advances in children's moral reasoning. Findings also suggest that interactions among peers with somewhat different perspectives on the problems are most beneficial (Berkowitz et al., 1980). And, there is some evidence that peer interactions that promote moral growth differ in important ways from parent–child interactions associated with higher levels of moral reasoning (Walker et al., 2000).

ON THE CUTTING EDGE 14.1
CHILDREN'S REASONING ABOUT THE MORALITY OF PEER EXCLUSION

Exclusion by peers is a normal experience for many children. As early as the preschool years, children prefer some playmates to others (Hay, Caplan, & Nash, 2009; Howes, 2009). During middle childhood and adolescence, children sort into social groups or cliques that—by definition—include some peers and exclude others (Killen et al., 2009). Moreover, many groups organized for children by adults also practise exclusion. Boys are excluded from Girl Guides, for example, and less-skilled soccer players are excluded from the travelling team.

Viewed from the perspective of Turiel's domain theory, peer exclusion has some elements of a moral situation (Killen & Rutland, 2011). After all, as anyone who has ever felt its sting knows, exclusion can hurt (i.e., it can cause psychological harm). Moreover, as we will discuss in Chapter 15, exclusion can also restrict children's opportunities to acquire valuable social skills and can negatively impact their social and academic performance (Ladd et al., 2011). Considered from this perspective, exclusion can be unfair—an issue in the moral domain. Acts of exclusion that occur in the absence of harmful intent, however, may not appropriately be classified as moral events, fitting better into the social or the personal domains (Killen & Rutland, 2011).

Are children aware of the moral complexities of exclusion? Most people generally view the choice of friends as a personal—not a moral—issue (Nucci, 2008). But what if a child refuses to consider someone as a friend, not on the basis of shared interests or likeability, but because of gender or race? Do children view this as a personal decision because it concerns friendship? Or do they view it as a moral issue because it may hurt feelings or be unfair? To study this issue, Melanie Killen and colleagues (2002) interviewed grades 4, 7, and 10 students from ethnically diverse schools in a suburban area in Maryland. The researchers presented the students with six scenarios depicting exclusion in three contexts—friendship, the peer group, and the school. In half of the scenarios, the exclusion was based on gender, and in the other half it was based on race.

The friendship scenario involved a Caucasian boy who did not want to be friends with a new neighbour because the neighbour was either a girl or was Black. The peer group scenario involved a music club, either all boys or all Caucasians, whose members did not want to let a girl or a Black child join the club. The school scenario involved a town that did not allow girls or Black children to go to school. After each scenario was described, students were asked whether it was "Okay" to exclude the child and also to explain their answers.

At all ages, the children judged exclusion differently depending on whether it occurred in the context of a friendship, the peer group, or the school. They almost universally regarded exclusion in school on the basis of either gender or race as unacceptable. In the friendship and peer group contexts, they judged exclusion on the basis of gender as less negative than exclusion on the basis of race (see Figure 14.3).

The justifications children offered for their judgments also varied across the three contexts, although it should be noted that most justified their judgments in terms of moral rules. They were especially likely to refer to fairness in response to exclusion in school. As one grade 4 boy responded, "It's not all right because it's not like girls have this certain disease. There is no difference between anybody and everybody should be able to go to school" (p. 52). Justifications based on personal choice appeared only in the friendship context, and most often when exclusion was based on gender: "I think it's up to him, even though I don't think it's very nice for him to not hang out with Sally just because she's a girl. But I do think it's his choice" (grade 10 male) (p. 52).

References to social convention, or group functioning, occurred most often in the context of the peer group, especially with respect to exclusion on the basis of gender: "I think that Mike and his friends are right for not letting her in the club because it's their club.... If she wanted to make her own group, then she can do it and make it so no boys are allowed" (grade 7 boy) (p. 56).

A particularly interesting finding was that although children of all ages viewed exclusion negatively, older children were less likely to do so. Compared with younger students, grade 10 students were less likely to negatively evaluate exclusion in the context of friendships and the peer group. This was especially true for exclusion based on gender.

(continued)

On the Cutting Edge 14.1 Children's Reasoning about the Morality of Peer Exclusion *continued*

This study raises a number of intriguing questions. One question has to do with a long-standing issue in the study of moral development—the relation between moral reasoning and moral behaviour. The children in this study were remarkably uniform in their opposition to exclusion, and they explained their opposition in terms of moral rules. In real life, however, most children do practise exclusion. More research is needed to understand how children reconcile their moral beliefs about exclusion with their actual practices.

Another question is whether the same findings would emerge in a different sample. The students in this study lived among families of varied cultural backgrounds and attended ethnically diverse schools. As one Black adolescent put it, "I live with Cambodians, Ethiopians, and Asians, all kinds of people, and everyone has a heart" (p. 99). Perhaps these experiences fostered a greater appreciation for moral issues related to race.

Finally, what are we to make of the finding that negative ratings of exclusion in the context of friendship and peer relations decline with age? The answers to all these questions await further study. In the meantime, one thing is clear—friendships and peer groups are important contexts for the development of children's moral reasoning.

FIGURE 14.3

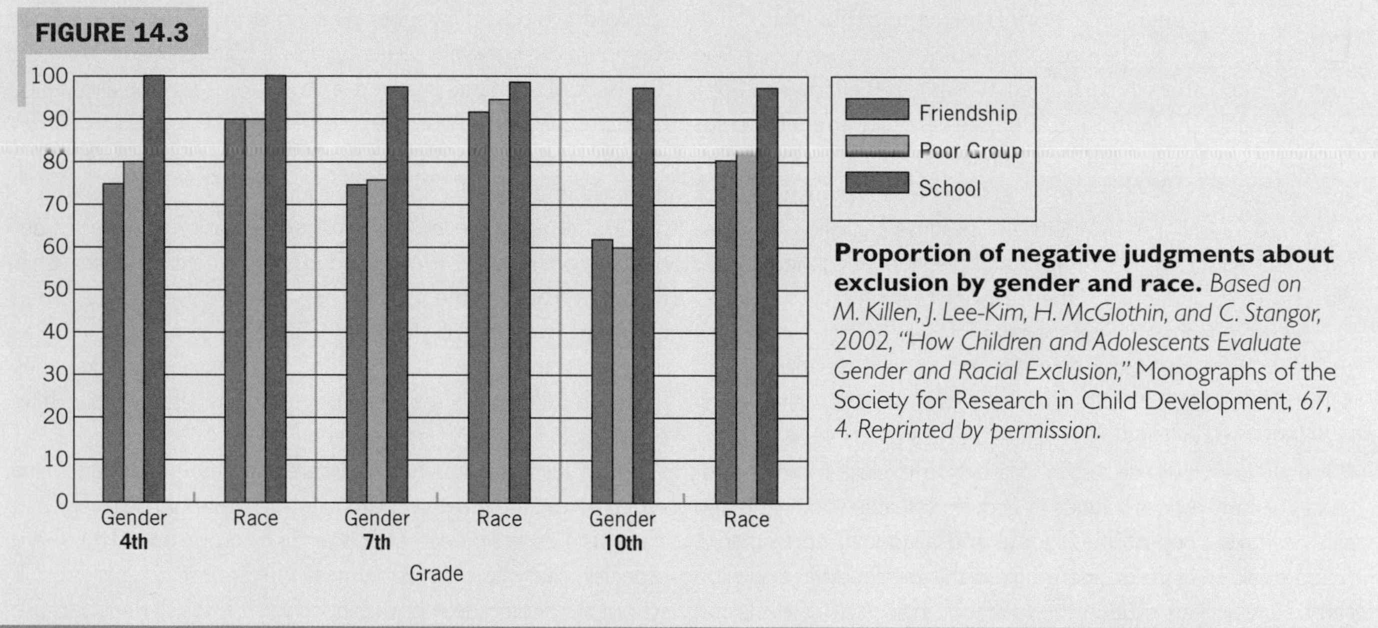

Proportion of negative judgments about exclusion by gender and race. *Based on M. Killen, J. Lee-Kim, H. McGlothin, and C. Stangor, 2002, "How Children and Adolescents Evaluate Gender and Racial Exclusion,"* Monographs of the Society for Research in Child Development, 67, *4. Reprinted by permission.*

PARENTS As we have seen, discussions of moral issues with peers can foster moral growth. Research shows that dialogues with parents can also foster this growth (Grusec, 2006). For example, in one impressive investigation, Lawrence Walker and John Taylor of the University of British Columbia recruited children ranging in age from 6 to 16, along with their parents, to participate in two laboratory sessions two years apart. In the first session, both parents and children responded individually to a set of Kohlberg's moral dilemmas and then to a real-life dilemma they had recently experienced in their own lives.

Following the individual interviews, the children and their parents were asked to discuss one of the Kohlberg dilemmas on which they had displayed some disagreement during the individual interviews, as well as a real-life dilemma that had been volunteered by the child. The same procedure was repeated two years later.

Links to Related Material

In Chapter 8, you read about the zone of proximal development and the related notion of scaffolding. Here you read how these concepts have been applied to the development of children's moral reasoning.

The study resulted in a number of interesting findings. One was that parents lowered their level of reasoning during the family conversations, whereas children raised theirs. These findings are consistent with Vygotsky's notion of a zone of proximal development (discussed in Chapter 8). By aiming their reasoning at—but not beyond—the upper bounds of the child's capabilities, parents provided a scaffold for the child's acquisition of a more advanced moral understanding.

Walker and Taylor also found that the nature of the interactions differed across the two kinds of dilemmas. When discussing the hypothetical dilemma, parents tended to challenge children's reasoning and adopt a rather opinionated lecturing-type style. When discussing the child's real-life dilemma, in contrast, parents tended to be more supportive, focusing on drawing out the child's opinion and trying to understand it. Interestingly, the quality of the interactions on the real-life dilemmas—but not the hypothetical ones—predicted children's moral reasoning two years later (Walker & Taylor, 1991).

Another way parents influence children's moral understanding is through discipline for misconduct. When parents punish children, they generally hope that children will not only avoid engaging in the inappropriate behaviours again, but also will gradually assume responsibility for enforcing the rules (Grusec, 2006). Children seem to accomplish this by *internalizing* the rules and prohibitions presented by their parents (Hoffman, 1994; Tappan, 1997, 2006).

Links to Related Material

Here you read about how parents' responses to misbehaviour are related to children's moral understanding. In Chapter 15, you will read about styles of parenting and their outcomes.

The effectiveness of discipline in promoting internalization of the parents' values and morals depends on a number of factors (Grusec, 2006; Grusec & Davidov, 2007). One involves the style of punishment parents employ. Three general classes of parental discipline have been identified (Hoffman, 1970, 1984). *Power assertion* involves the use of commands, threats, and physical force. *Love withdrawal* refers to the use of verbal disapproval or ridicule, or the withholding of affection from the child. *Induction* involves reasoning with the child to explain why certain behaviours are prohibited, and often encourages feelings of guilt in the child by pointing out how the misbehaviour may have caused harm or distress to someone else.

A number of studies have found that an inductive approach to discipline is associated with the most advanced levels of moral reasoning; love-withdrawal techniques result in somewhat lower levels, and power assertion produces the least mature forms of reasoning (Hart, 1988b; Weiss et al., 1992). Adolescents reared in an environment where parents tend to use an inductive approach show higher levels of moral reasoning than those whose parents use other approaches (Boyes & Allen, 1993; Gibbs, 2010). Similarly, discussions with children about moral issues lead to similar moral perspectives between parent and child (Pratt, Arnold, Pratt, & Diessner, 1999).

Another factor that affects how well discipline promotes internalization involves the child's temperament. Recent studies have identified *fearfulness* as an inborn trait that influences whether children will internalize their parents' rules (Kochanska et al., 2007; Rothbart & Hwang, 2005). For fearful children who are prone to being timid and anxious, gentle discipline and the avoidance of power tactics seem best to promote the development of conscience (internalization) in the child. For fearless children, the best disciplinary approach capitalizes on the child's positive motivation to accept the parents' values, and so involves a cooperative and responsive approach by the adult. The goodness-of-fit concept discussed in Chapter 12 thus applies here as well. The type of discipline that is most effective with a particular child is the one that best "fits" with the child's personality and temperament (Laible & Thompson, 2007).

Links to Related Material

In Chapter 12, you read about the concept of goodness of fit. Here, you learn more about how goodness of fit relates to parental discipline strategies and children's moral development.

MORAL REASONING AND MORAL CONDUCT

A central issue in the study of moral development is the relationship between moral reasoning and moral behaviour. When this issue is raised, the scenario that typically comes to mind is one in which an individual presumed to possess sophisticated powers of moral reasoning—a politician, a religious figure, or a business leader, for example—engages in immoral activity. But when we study moral development among children, we often see that the opposite can also be true—children often behave in moral ways without being able to explain very clearly why.

The different theoretical perspectives address this issue somewhat differently. Piaget believed that thought follows from action, and so he anticipated that children's behaviour should, initially at least, be more advanced than their reasoning. Kohlberg, in contrast, believed that moral thought and moral action should be consistent (although not perfectly so), and he claimed that the evidence shows that they are (Kohlberg, 1987; Kohlberg & Candee, 1984). Social-learning theorists make a different prediction. They argue that moral reasoning and conduct may show some correspondence, but that the correspondence need not be very strong because what children say and what they do involve somewhat independent processes (Bandura, 1991b; Liebert, 1984).

The evidence on this question does not strongly support Kohlberg's position. Studies based on Kohlberg's method have found only a modest relation between a child's level of moral reasoning and the child's moral behaviour (Blasi, 1980, 1983; Rholes & Lane, 1985; Straughan, 1986). In most children, this relation simply does not hold.

Children's moral behaviour is undoubtedly influenced by many factors. One of the most important is one we have largely neglected so far—moral affect or emotions. We consider the role of affect in the discussions of the development of prosocial and aggressive behaviour that follow.

LEARNING OBJECTIVE 14.2

Understand what research has found concerning children's moral reasoning.

1. Does research support Piaget's model?
2. Has Kohlberg's model been supported by research?
3. Has Turiel's model stood up under the scrutiny of research?
4. Discuss how children allocate rewards and punishments.
5. How do peers and parents influence children's moral reasoning?

Learning Objective 14.3

Understand the development of prosocial behaviour and identify its determinants.

Prosocial behaviour The aspect of moral conduct that includes socially desirable behaviours, such as sharing, helping, and cooperating; often used interchangeably with altruism by modern researchers.

Empathy The ability to vicariously experience or share another's emotional state or condition.

Sympathy Feeling of concern for another in reaction to the other's situation or emotional state without necessarily sharing the same emotional state.

PROSOCIAL BEHAVIOUR

We turn now to moral conduct—how children act as opposed to how they think. Specifically, we examine **prosocial behaviour**—those acts that society considers desirable and attempts to encourage in children. Three forms of prosocial behaviour that have been studied extensively are *helping* (which includes comforting and caregiving), *sharing*, and *conflict resolution* (Eisenberg, Fabes, & Spinrad, 2006). It is widely believed that the roots of prosocial behaviour lie in the capacity to feel empathy and sympathy, and so we begin our discussion of prosocial development with these topics.

EMPATHY AND SYMPATHY

Most theorists acknowledge that moral action requires more than moral thoughts; it also requires what have come to be known as moral emotions. Two of the moral emotions are empathy and sympathy. **Empathy** is the ability to vicariously experience (or share) another's emotional state or condition. **Sympathy**, in contrast, involves feeling sorrow and concern for another in reaction to his or her situation or emotional state, without necessarily sharing the same emotion (Eisenberg, 2010). As we saw earlier, evolutionary theorists believe that the capacity to feel these emotions is also present in some non-human primate species (de Waal, 2008; Verbeek, 2006).

How does empathy develop in children? According to Martin Hoffman (2000, 2008), true empathy requires a sense of the self and others as separate individuals who have independent thoughts, feelings, and perceptions. Hoffman suggests that empathy gradually develops in a sequence of six stages as children mature cognitively.

Empathy involves the ability not only to understand someone else's feelings, but also to share them. (*PhotoDisc, Inc./Media Bakery*)

STAGE 1: GLOBAL EMPATHIC DISTRESS. The first precursor signs of empathy are apparent during the early months of life when infants reactively cry upon hearing the cries of other infants. Hoffman (2008) points out that this is not simply imitation, nor is it a pain response to aversive stimulation; newborns do not cry when they hear their own tape-recorded crying, nor do they react as strongly to equally noxious non-social stimuli (Martin & Clark, 1982; Sagi & Hoffman, 1976). Rather, such crying is a reaction of distress in response to the distress of another person.

STAGE 2: EGOCENTRIC EMPATHIC DISTRESS. At around 11 or 12 months, infants respond to the distress of others as though they themselves were in distress. At this point in their development, they feel empathic distress, but lack clear boundaries between the self and others. Consequently, they respond to distress in others by comforting themselves (e.g., sucking their thumbs) or seeking comfort from caregivers.

In neither of these first two stages can infants yet *feel* true empathy; at this point in development, they are unable to differentiate the distress of another from their own feelings of distress (Gibbs, 2010). Nevertheless, the fact that their responding is contingent on the distress reaction of another is what justifies calling these reactions *precursors* to empathy (Hoffman, 2008).

STAGE 3: QUASI-EGOCENTRIC EMPATHIC DISTRESS. As children develop a sense of themselves as distinct individuals, their reactions to the distress of others change. As we saw in Chapter 13, midway through their second year, infants' sense of self becomes clearer, as can be seen in their ability to recognize their own image in a mirror. Around this time, when confronted with someone who is distressed, they realize the distress belongs to the other rather than to themselves. Consequently, they respond by kissing, hugging, or otherwise trying to help (Hoffman, 2008). However, they have difficulty distinguishing between their own thoughts and feelings and those of others. As a result, the help they offer often reflects what they would like, and not necessarily what would be most helpful to the other person. For example, Hoffman (2008) describes one toddler who responded to a crying friend "with a sad look, and then gently took the friend's hand and brought him to his own mother, although the friend's mother was present" (p. 444). Nevertheless, during this stage, children respond out of a sense of sympathy for the victim, rather than just to alleviate their own empathy-induced distress.

STAGE 4: VERIDICAL EMPATHY. As children move into their third year, they come closer to feeling what others are actually feeling. They now understand that other people have inner states (thoughts, feelings, and perceptions) that are different from their own and can now offer more appropriate help and comfort. We should note, however, that the understanding that emerges during this stage is not *always* put to its best use. For example, a child may understand very well why a sibling is distressed and how best to comfort her, and yet choose to do the exact opposite (Dunn, 1988)!

STAGE 5: EMPATHIC DISTRESS BEYOND THE SITUATION. During middle childhood, children are able to consider the broader features of other people's lives. Thus, they are able to empathize not only with those currently experiencing a distressing situation, but also with individuals whom they imagine to have generally sad or unpleasant lives because of illness, poverty, and the like. To Hoffman, this reflects mature empathy, which he describes as a response to multiple cues, including the emotional expression of others, as well as their behaviour, their immediate situation, and their life condition.

STAGE 6: EMPATHY FOR DISTRESSED GROUPS. The highest level of empathy emerges in adolescence. At this level, owing to their developing abstract reasoning abilities (Gibbs, 2010), youth are able to empathize with not only the plight of individuals, but also of entire classes of people, such as the homeless, social outcasts, and victims of war or disaster. This form of empathy motivates some to intervene to try to aid those in distressed groups, through policy-making, outreach work, or social activism (Hoffman, 2008).

DEVELOPMENT OF PROSOCIAL BEHAVIOUR

We look next at the development of prosocial behaviour in the three major areas mentioned earlier: helping, sharing, and conflict resolution.

When faced with someone who is distressed, young children often attempt to comfort or to help. (*Stockbyte/Media Bakery*)

HELPING The results of empirical studies on the development of early helping behaviour are largely consistent with Hoffman's six-stage theory of the development of empathy. Of particular note are a series of longitudinal studies conducted by Carolyn Zahn-Waxler and colleagues, who tracked changes in children's reactions to others' distress during the second and third years of life (Hastings, Zahn-Waxler, & McShane, 2006; Zahn-Waxler & Radke-Yarrow, 1982; Zahn-Waxler et al., 1992, 2001).

Each of the studies involved maternal reports of children's reactions when confronted with the distress of another in the context of everyday activities. In some of the studies, these reports were supplemented by home and laboratory visits, during which mothers and experimenters staged events designed to elicit concern. For example, the mother might pretend to cry, cough, or choke, or feign an injury to her knee. Coders recorded the children's reactions to the incidents. Typical behaviours included hugs or kisses, words of comfort (e.g., "You be okay"), putting on a bandage, asking if the mother was all right, facial expressions of concern, and expressions of personal distress.

As Hoffman's theory predicts, when confronted with someone distressed, the younger toddlers primarily became distressed themselves. But many of the older toddlers actually attempted to help the victim, although the help was not always appropriate, as when one youngster tried to feed his cereal to his ailing father (Zahn-Waxler et al., 1992). As the children grew older, both the frequency and sophistication of the helping increased. With age, children were increasingly likely to express their concern verbally, fetch a bandage or a blanket, or ask an adult to intervene.

Similar age-related increases in helping have been reported in studies of siblings and peers. Young children show an increased tendency to comfort a sibling in distress between the ages of 15 and 36 months—but only if the child was not the cause of the sibling's distress (Dunn, 1988). Observations in preschools reveal that young children will also comfort peers in distress, especially if the pair have an ongoing friendly relationship (Farver & Branstetter, 1994). Moreover, initiating such prosocial behaviour leads peers to reciprocate with similar behaviour (Persson, 2005). Thus, as Paul Hastings and William Utendale of Concordia University and Caroline Sullivan of the University of Ottawa (2007) point out, preschoolers who show unselfish concern for others tend to receive similar concern from their peers.

Further evidence for the early development of prosocial behaviour comes from observations of children as they follow parents and older siblings about during their daily activities (Rogoff, 1990, 2003). Toddlers are often eager to help others perform household chores (Rheingold, 1982). There are, however, cultural variations in how often young children have the opportunity to "pitch in" and how others respond to their offers of help. In communities where children are integrated into the lives of adults, toddlers' imitation of adult activities is expected and encouraged, and even small children are assigned simple chores (Rogoff, 2003). Also, studies in a variety of cultures show that participation in chores is associated with prosocial behaviour (Elder & Conger, 2000; Whiting & Whiting, 1975).

Together, these findings paint a positive picture of the prosocial tendencies of young children. But are older children and adolescents also enthusiastic helpers? Research suggests that generally they are: helping actually increases with age. Moreover, compared with younger children, older children and adolescents are more likely to help even at some cost to themselves, perhaps because older children are better able to recognize possible physical, psychological, or moral gains from assisting others (Eisenberg, Spinrad, & Sadovsky, 2006).

Of course, individuals—whatever their age—do not always offer to help even when they can. Obstacles to helping include not knowing how to help, lack of confidence in one's ability to help, and fear that helping will make the situation worse or will otherwise be unappreciated. Additionally, children and adolescents sometimes fail to help because they feel that someone else is responsible or it is not appropriate for them to help (Eisenberg & Fabes, 1998). Studies show that children are more likely to help when they have been shown how to assist and when they have been assigned responsibility to help (Peterson, 1983a, 1983b; Staub, 1971). We return to this topic later in our discussion of intervention programs aimed at peer bullying and victimization.

SHARING Another prosocial behaviour of considerable interest to researchers and caregivers alike is sharing. As we all know, young children do not always readily share. Still, like helping, sharing emerges remarkably early. Toward the end of the first year, babies will often hand a toy or some of their food to their mother or to another child (Hay et al., 2009). Sharing can serve a variety of interpersonal functions. For young children who have as yet only limited verbal capabilities, sharing is one way in which to initiate or maintain social interactions with adults or peers (Hay et al., 1995, 2009). It also may be a means by which children resolve conflicts among themselves (Butovskaya et al., 2000; Caplan et al., 1991). Children are especially likely to share when they are involved in a give-and-take relationship with the other person and have experienced some "receiving" as well as "giving" (Hay & Murray, 1982; Levitt et al., 1985). Interestingly, similar "rules" appear to guide food sharing and grooming among chimpanzees (de Waal, 1997, 2000). Finally, as with helping, older children are more likely to share than are younger ones (e.g., Benenson et al., 2003; Eisenberg, Fabes, & Spinrad, 2006).

CONFLICT RESOLUTION A third type of prosocial behaviour is conflict resolution. Although estimates vary, conflict among peers and siblings appears to be a fairly regular occurrence during childhood and adolescence (Howe, Ross, & Recchia, 2011; Laursen & Pursell, 2009). Because many of these conflicts occur away from adult eyes, there must be some mechanism in place to keep children's conflicts from escalating out of control.

Conflict is, in fact, resolved in a variety of ways. The methods can be placed in three broad categories. *Negotiation* and compromise are attempts to reduce conflict, and they often result in positive, constructive outcomes. *Disengagement*, which tends to occur when there is no resolution to the conflict, includes withdrawal (walking away from the dispute) or shifting the focus or topic. *Coercion* occurs when one party gives in to the demands of another, often in response to threats, power assertion, or other negative ploys (Laursen, Hartup, & Koplas, 1996; Laursen & Pursell, 2009).

The relative use of these resolution strategies changes with age (Laursen, Finkelstein, & Betts, 2001; Laursen & Pursell, 2009). Children resolve most disputes with coercion, making less use of negotiation or disengagement. Adolescents, in contrast, tend to favour disengagement, followed by coercion, then negotiation. Young adults strongly favour negotiation and use coercion and disengagement less frequently. Children tend to display higher conflict resolution skills when reasoning about hypothetical dilemmas than when dealing with actual disputes. Moreover, the particular methods used also vary depending on the relationship. Negotiation and compromise are more common in conflicts among children who are friends—where there is a desire to maintain the relationship—than among children who are simply acquaintances (Laursen & Pursell, 2009). We discuss this issue further in Chapter 15.

Links to Related Material

In Chapter 15, you will read about differences in conflict resolution between friends and non-friends, and how skill at resolving conflict is related to popularity.

In addition to studying how children resolve conflicts, researchers have also investigated the ways children "make peace" with one another following conflict (Fujisawa, Kutsukake, & Hasegawa, 2006; Verbeek, Hartup, & Collins, 2000). **Peacemaking** refers to a friendly post-conflict reunion between former opponents, and has been studied not only in children but in non-human primates as well. Peacemaking can immediately follow the conflict or can occur after a delay or cooling-off period. In some species, peacemaking involves conspicuous behaviours that are rarely observed in other social contexts, whereas in other species the behaviours are more implicit (de Waal, 1993, 2005; Verbeek, 2006). Studies show that children use both explicit and implicit behaviours to reconcile with peers. We have already mentioned one—sharing toys. Others include invitations to

Peacemaking A friendly post-conflict reunion between former opponents often characterized by invitations to play, hugs, apologies, object sharing, and silliness.

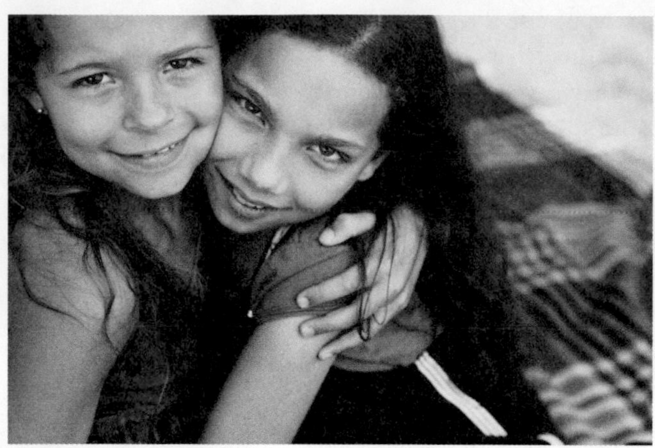
Peacemaking behaviours include hugs, apologies, and sharing of toys. (© *Roy McMahon/Corbis*)

play, apologies, and hugs. Although girls and boys tend not to differ in their peacemaking tendencies, they sometimes differ in the methods they use to make peace. One approach used often by boys but rarely by girls is acting silly to make others laugh (Butovskaya et al., 2000). Next, we briefly consider the general issue of sex differences in prosocial behaviour.

GENDER DIFFERENCES IN PROSOCIAL BEHAVIOUR

One of the most widely held gender stereotypes is that females are kinder, more generous, and more caring than males (Eagly, Wood, & Diekman, 2000; Shigetomi, Hartmann, & Gelfand, 1981). In fact, empirical evidence suggests only a modest sex difference favouring girls (Eagly & Crowley, 1986; Eisenberg, Fabes, & Spinrad, 2006). As infants and toddlers, girls tend to display more personal distress, empathy, and other expressions of concern than boys, though the difference is not great (Zahn-Waxler et al., 2001). Sex differences in empathy grow larger with age and are greatest when measured by self-report. Girls are also more likely to be kind and considerate, but are not more inclined to share, comfort, or help (Eisenberg, Fabes, & Spinrad, 2006).

BIOLOGICAL DETERMINANTS OF PROSOCIAL BEHAVIOUR

We earlier discussed evolutionary explanations of a species-wide capacity for prosocial behaviour, but individual differences in prosocial behaviour also exist. Some children seem inordinately caring and compassionate, whereas others appear to care little about the welfare of other beings. Are these differences solely due to socialization, or might biological factors also play a role?

There is some evidence that genetic factors contribute to individual differences in prosocial behaviour (Knafo & Israel, 2010). Studies involving adult twins have found greater similarity in self-reported empathy and altruism among pairs of identical twins than among fraternal twin pairs (Knafo & Plomin, 2006). Similar findings have been reported in twin studies with children (Knafo, Zahn-Waxler, Davidov, et al., 2009: Knafo & Plomin, 2006; Volbrecht et al., 2007; Zahn-Waxler et al., 2001): identical twins are more similar on measures of empathic concern and prosocial behaviour than are fraternal twins.

Is there a gene for kindness? Probably not. So, how might genetic factors produce differences in prosocial behaviour? A likely possibility is that individual differences in prosocial responding are related to differences in temperament. Studies have linked children's tendencies to feel negative emotions, such as anxiety, sadness, and guilt, as well as their responses to these emotions, with their tendency to feel empathy and sympathy. Children who experience negative emotions, but are not overcome by them, are especially likely to feel sympathy for the plight of others. In contrast, children who are overcome by high levels of negative emotions tend to focus on themselves and their own feelings of distress (Eisenberg, 2010; Eisenberg, Fabes, & Spinrad, 2006). Of course, feeling bad is not always sufficient to prompt action. Inhibited or cautious children may not always be able to bring themselves to help someone even if they want to (Barrett & Yarrow, 1977; Denham & Couchoud, 1991; Young, Fox, & Zahn-Waxler, 1999).

COGNITIVE AND AFFECTIVE DETERMINANTS OF PROSOCIAL BEHAVIOUR

Although the capacity for prosocial behaviour is grounded to some extent in biology, there exists extensive evidence that other factors also play a role. In this section, we consider cognitive and emotional factors that may affect prosocial development.

EMPATHY Early studies that relied on self-report found little relation between empathy and prosocial behaviour (Eisenberg, Spinrad, & Sadovsky, 2006). In recent years, however, the assessment of empathy has focused on physiological responses. Researchers have, for example, measured children's emotional arousal and facial expressions as they view videotapes designed to induce feelings of sympathy for a story character. Children whose responses were strongest were most likely to share or display other prosocial behaviours when given the opportunity (Eisenberg, 2010; Eisenberg, Fabes, & Spinrad, 2006; Fabes et al., 1994). Moreover, looking at parent reports of children's empathy, Janet Strayer of Simon Fraser University and William Roberts of Thompson Rivers University (1989) found significant correlations between empathy and children's prosocial behaviour at home.

PROSOCIAL REASONING We have seen that cognitive-developmental psychologists believe that moral reasoning processes lie at the heart of moral development. Their models would then predict a positive relation between a child's moral reasoning and his or her altruistic behaviour (Krebs & Van Hesteren, 1994).

Investigations of this issue have typically evaluated the child's level of moral reasoning through the use of *prosocial dilemmas*. These stories differ from those of Piaget and Kohlberg in that they place less emphasis on breaking rules or laws. Instead, the story character usually must decide whether to help someone, often at some personal expense. For example, one story requires a little girl to choose between helping a hurt child and being on time for a birthday party (Eisenberg, 1982).

Investigations comparing children's prosocial reasoning with their prosocial behaviour have generally found a modest positive relation (Eisenberg, 2010; Eisenberg, Fabes, & Spinrad, 2006). This finding is similar to studies pertaining to Kohlberg's justice reasoning dilemmas, which reveal a small relation between how children think about moral issues and how they act.

MENTAL STATE UNDERSTANDING The ability to understand a situation from someone else's point of view is also basic to cognitive-developmental explanations of prosocial behaviour. For example, in several studies, children who were better at telling a story from another person's point of view were more prosocial with peers (Eisenberg, 1986, 1987; Eisenberg et al., 1995). Understanding (but not necessarily experiencing) the feelings and emotions of another person is also correlated with prosocial behaviour (Garner, Jones, & Miner, 1994; Moore & Eisenberg, 1984). Exposure to children's storybooks can contribute to such understanding. Raymond Mar of York University, Jennifer Tackett of the University of Toronto, and Chris Moore of Dalhousie University (2010) point out that children's literature contains frequent reference to the inner states of the characters in the story. These researchers report that parents can foster the development of young children's understanding of others' thoughts and feelings by reading stories to them. In addition, children who do well as preschoolers on various types of "mind-reading" tasks (for example, the false-belief tasks described in Chapter 8) are better able to resolve conflicts with friends during elementary school (Dunn, 1999).

Links to Related Material

In Chapter 8, you read about false belief tasks and children's developing theory of mind. Here, you learn that performance on false belief tasks relates to conflict resolution skills in elementary school.

SOCIOCULTURAL AND FAMILY DETERMINANTS OF PROSOCIAL BEHAVIOUR

Over the course of childhood and adolescence, prosocial behaviours increase in frequency. Clearly, developmental changes in children's affective and cognitive capabilities contribute to this increase. But increases in prosocial responding also coincide with changes in children's social experiences. Among these are changes in the settings children inhabit, the roles they play, the kinds of activities they engage in, and the expectations of others. In this section, we describe some ways that children's social experiences contribute to prosocial development. We begin the discussion with opportunities for prosocial behaviour.

OPPORTUNITIES FOR PROSOCIAL BEHAVIOUR One context in which children can practise prosocial behaviour is the home. Do children who routinely perform chores and contribute to the functioning of the household develop a stronger prosocial orientation than peers not assigned chores? The answer appears to be a qualified yes, if their work involves benefits to other family members (Grusec & Davidov, 2007; Grusec et al., 1996). One source of supporting evidence comes from research reported by Whiting and colleagues (Whiting & Whiting, 1975; Whiting & Edwards, 1988). These investigators observed children between the ages of 3 and 11 in six different countries, and reported that the factors that were predictive of prosocial/nurturant behaviour in these children (i.e., offering help and support to others) were participation in chores, and especially participation in the care of infants.

A more recent study of Iowa farm youth also examined the effects of contributing to the functioning of the household. Elder and Conger (2000) followed more than 400 grade 7 students over a period of six years during a time when many Iowa farmers were struggling economically. As is true in many farm families, the youth in this study made a significant economic contribution to the household through their labour on the farm and the money they earned by raising livestock or in part-time jobs. Even as grade 7 students, the adolescents took their responsibilities quite seriously. Most rated their chores as very important, a higher rating than that provided by youth from non-farm families. When asked as grade 12 students about what made their work important, many focused on the importance of being counted on and the experience of being interconnected with others. As one boy noted, "If I help the family, it saves the family money as whole. So we can take the money we save . . . and apply it to maybe . . . a new truck" (Elder & Conger, 2000, p. 90).

The opportunity to fulfill productive roles also fostered a sense of adult status among the farm youth. For many other adolescents, voluntary community service may serve a similar function, providing opportunities to practise helping others and perhaps increasing feelings of prosocial commitment (Hart et al., 2008; Zaff et al., 2010).

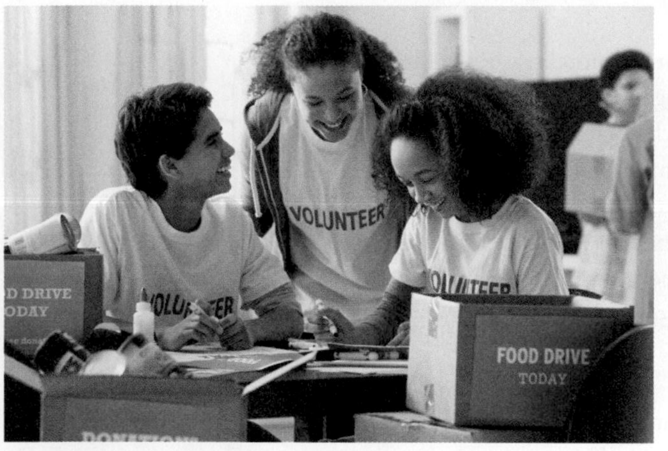

For many adolescents, voluntary community service provides opportunities to practise proscocial behaviour. (© *JLP/Jose L. Pelaez/Corbis*)

COMMUNICATION OF VALUES Another way parents may foster a prosocial orientation is through the values they communicate to children (Grusec & Davidov, 2007). As we have already seen, children whose parents employ inductive techniques and talk with them about the impact of their actions on others display more mature moral reasoning than do those whose parents use other disciplinary techniques (Gibbs, 2010; Grusec, 2006; Hoffman, 1975).

Compelling support for the power of parental communication of values comes from studies of people who show unusual levels of altruism. For example, during interviews after World War II, individuals who risked their own lives to rescue Jews from the Nazis in Europe often reported having learned values of caring, generosity, and respect for all human life from their parents and other influential adults. Neighbours who were not involved in rescue activities did not often mention learning these values (Oliner & Oliner, 1988).

MODELLING Of course, children learn not only from what parents say, but also from what they do. Laboratory studies have shown that children share more or are more helpful after observing a model performing similar behaviours (e.g., Eron & Huesmann, 1986; Lipscomb, McAllister, & Bregman, 1985; Radke-Yarrow & Zahn-Waxler, 1986). Children are especially likely to imitate adults with whom they have a positive relationship. Thus, parents who are sympathetic tend to have children who behave in a sympathetic manner (Eisenberg, Fabes, & Spinrad, 2006). Indeed, parents who respond sensitively to their children's distress model caring behaviour, which their children, in turn, are more likely to display in their own interactions with others (Grusec & Davidov, 2007).

Some psychologists have attempted to use modelling in applied settings to increase prosocial behaviour. Children's educational television, for example, often includes moral themes and prosocial messages (Hogan & Strasburger, 2008; Jordan, Schmitt, & Woodard, 2001). A review of 34 studies (with a total sample of over 5,000 children) found that viewing prosocial TV programming has a modest effect on prosocial behaviour. The effects were greater when supplemental materials were added, such as guided lessons, games, and general discussion designed to enhance program content (Mares & Woodard, 2005).

SECURE ATTACHMENT One important consequence of sensitive parental care is secure attachment. As we discussed in Chapter 12, being securely attached leads to greater skill in children's ability to understand feelings (Thompson, 2008), and may motivate altruistic behaviour through conferring on the child a sense of being valued and cared for (Mikulincer & Shaver, 2010).

REINFORCEMENT Will children be more altruistic if their altruism is reinforced? This straightforward question has been answered positively many times in laboratory studies, demonstrating clear effects of reward and praise on children's prosocial behaviours (Eisenberg, Fabes, & Spinrad, 2006; Eisenberg & Murphy, 1995). As noted by Rosemary Mills of the University of Manitoba, and Joan Grusec of the University of Toronto (1989), praise is especially effective in promoting altruism if it emphasizes that the child is a generous or helpful person (e.g., "You were a very kind girl for sharing your candy"). Applied psychologists have used reward programs as a way of increasing prosocial behaviours in the classroom and other naturalistic settings (CPPRG, 1999; Walker, Colvin, & Ramsey, 1995).

Do reinforcement processes play a role in maintaining altruism under everyday circumstances, when no psychologist is involved? They may indeed. One study investigating preschool children's naturally occurring altruistic behaviour found that peers often respond positively to this type of behaviour, such as by smiling, thanking the child, or doing something nice in return (Eisenberg et al., 1981). Similar research conducted in home settings by Mills and Grusec (1988) indicated that mothers, like peers, often respond to altruistic behaviour with some form of praise or verbal approval (see also Eisenberg et al., 1992). Research also shows that parental reinforcement is key to adolescents' involvement in community activities, particularly when the parents themselves do not participate (Fletcher, Elder, & Mekos, 2000). And older siblings who are cooperative and helpful tend to promote prosocial interactions among younger family members (Dunn, 2006; Dunn & Munn, 1986).

Finally, even in the absence of external rewards or approval, reinforcement processes can still be in operation. Witnessing the joy experienced by someone we have just helped, for example, or sharing that person's relief from distress can reinforce our helping behaviour (Batson, 2010). Whether pure altruism ever occurs remains a matter of debate, but there can be no doubt that much of children's prosocial behaviour occurs because it rewards the giver as well as the receiver.

LEARNING OBJECTIVE 14.3

Understand the development of prosocial behaviour and identify its determinants.

1. What are Hoffman's six stages in the development of empathy?
2. Identify three major categories of prosocial behaviour and describe how these develop.
3. What are some gender differences in prosocial behaviour?
4. What factors contribute to the development of prosocial behaviour?

AGGRESSION

Learning Objective 14.4

Describe the factors that contribute to aggressive behaviour and discuss ways of reducing aggression in children.

At the opposite end of the spectrum from prosocial behaviour is the antisocial behaviour of aggression. Whether it takes the form of destroying a preschool playmate's block tower, teasing and taunting by a grade 4 student, or fighting between teenage gangs, aggression is a common and important aspect of child development that has been studied extensively (Bushman & Huesmann, 2010; Dodge, Coie, & Lynam, 2006).

DEFINING AGGRESSION

Aggression Behaviour that is intended to cause harm to persons or property and that is not socially justifiable.

Psychologists define **aggression** as behaviour that is intended to cause harm to persons or property and that is not socially justifiable. Note that by this definition, aggression is always based on a social judgment that takes into account both the individual's motives and the context in which the behaviour occurs (Bushman & Huesmann, 2010).

Proactive aggression Aggression intended to obtain something or achieve a goal. Sometimes also referred to as instrumental aggression.

Aggression can be divided into types based on its function and form. In terms of function, psychologists distinguish between proactive aggression and reactive aggression. **Proactive aggression** (also referred to as *instrumental* aggression) is behaviour intended to obtain something or achieve a goal (Coyne, Nelson, & Underwood, 2011). Although the goal is frequently an object (e.g., a desired toy) or an activity (e.g., a turn on the swing), it may also be social status in the peer group. Bullying, which we discuss later in the chapter, is an example of proactive aggression aimed at increasing the bully's status in the eyes of others (Salmivalli, Peets, & Hodges, 2011).

Reactive aggression Aggression in response to provocation by another individual and frequently accompanied by anger. Sometimes referred to as hostile aggression.

Reactive aggression (also sometimes referred to as *hostile* aggression), on the other hand, is behaviour that occurs in reaction to provocation by someone else. It is usually motivated by anger, resulting from a perceived threat, insult, or frustration attributable to another individual, and is often an impulsive reaction (Coyne et al., 2011; Parke & Clarke-Stewart, 2011).

Aggression can also take various forms. Perhaps the most noticeable form of aggression is *physical* aggression. Hitting, shoving, and even biting are obvious examples of this form of aggression. But aggression can also be *verbal*. Yelling at someone or calling someone names would fit this category. In addition, both physical and verbal aggression can be direct or indirect (Coyne et al., 2011).

Relational aggression Aggression designed to damage or disrupt social relationships.

A form of aggression that has been studied extensively in recent years is **relational aggression.** Relational aggression is aimed at damaging or manipulating social relationships. Like physical and verbal aggression, relational aggression can also be direct or indirect (Crick, Ostrov, & Yawabata, 2007; Ostrov & Crick, 2007). Table 14.2 shows some examples of direct and indirect physical, verbal, and relational aggression.

TABLE 14.2 EXAMPLES OF DIRECT AND INDIRECT PHYSICAL, VERBAL, AND RELATIONAL AGGRESSION

Physical aggression	**Direct**	Pushing, hitting, kicking, punching, or shoving a person
	Indirect	Destroying a person's property, getting someone else to physically hurt the person
Verbal aggression	**Direct**	Insulting, putting down, name-calling, or teasing a person
	Indirect	Gossiping, saying mean things behind a person's back, urging someone else to verbally abuse the person
Relational aggression	**Direct**	Excluding, threatening to stop liking a person
	Indirect	Spreading rumours or lies, exposing secrets about a person, ignoring or betraying the person, building an alliance that excludes the person

Source: From Table 12.1 in Parke, R. & Clarke-Stewart, A. (2011). *Social Development*. Hoboken, NJ: John Wiley & Sons, Inc., p. 395.

AGE AND GENDER DIFFERENCES IN AGGRESSION

The forms of aggression we have been discussing occur in different proportions among children of different ages and sexes. Children begin to use physical aggression, such as hitting and pushing, to resolve conflicts by the end of their second year of life. Longitudinal studies conducted by

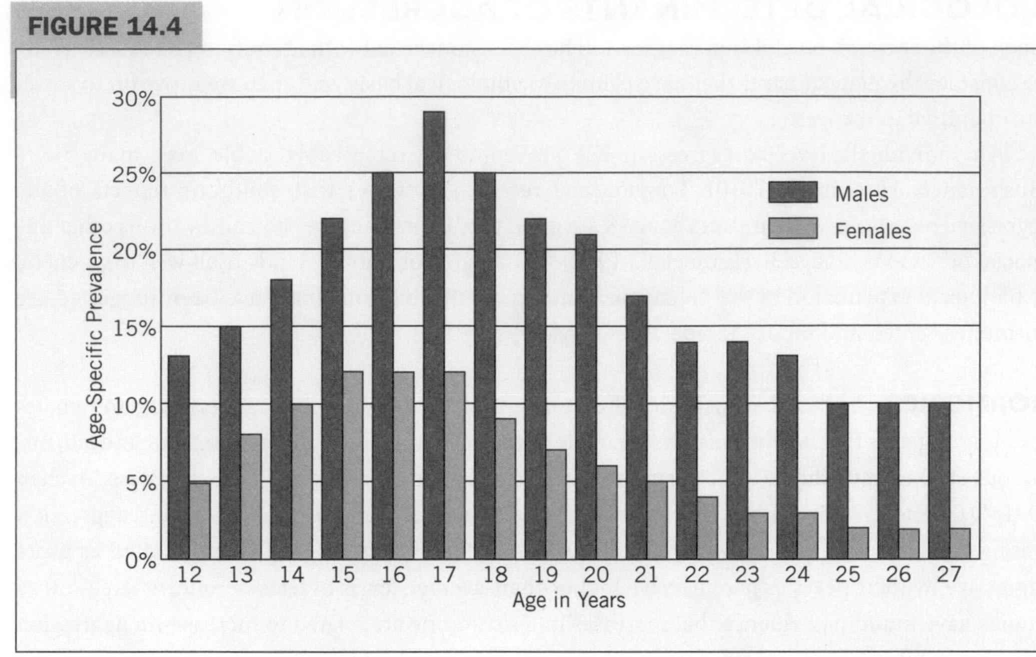

FIGURE 14.4

Prevalence of self-reported violence for males and females of different ages. *From J. D. Coie and K.A. Dodge, "Aggression and Antisocial Behavior," 1998, in W. Damon (Series Ed.) & N. Eisenberg (Vol. Ed.),* Handbook of Child Psychology: Volume 3. Social, Emotional, and Personality Development *(5th ed.), New York: Wiley. Reprinted by permission.*

Canadian researchers reveal that for the majority of children, the use of physical aggression declines over the preschool and early elementary school years, while verbal aggression becomes more common (Côté, Vaillancourt, Barker, Nagin, & Tremblay, 2007; Côté, Vaillancourt, LeBlanc, Nagin, & Tremblay, 2006; Tremblay & Nagin, 2005).

The decline in physical aggression in the preschool years coincides with an improved ability to resolve conflicts verbally and to control emotions and actions (Dionne, 2005; Dionne, Boivin, Tremblay, Laplante, & Perusse, 2003). Most children continue to show a decline in overt physical aggression during elementary school, a decline that continues throughout adolescence (Dodge et al., 2006). However, during middle childhood, some children manifest serious problems with aggression and other forms of antisocial behaviour (Côté et al., 2006; Dodge et al., 2006). Then, during adolescence, a second group of aggressive children emerges who engage in acts of serious violence (Dodge et al., 2006; Moffitt, 2007). Adolescent violent crime peaks at age 17, when 29 percent of males and 12 percent of females report engaging in at least one serious violent act. As can be seen in Figure 14.4, there is a large difference in the number of males and females who engage in violent behaviour during adolescence and early adulthood.

Links to Related Material

In Chapter 16, you will read more about gender differences in aggression, as well as in other aspects of children's social interactions.

This sex difference in rates of aggression begins long before adolescence and is observed in all cultures of the world. Boys begin to display more physical and verbal aggression as preschoolers and continue to do so throughout the elementary-school years (Murray-Close, Ostrov, & Crick, 2007; Ostrov & Crick, 2007).

Also, beginning with the preschool years and extending into adolescence, girls display more relational aggression than do boys (Crick et al., 2007; Murray-Close et al., 2007; Ostrov & Crick, 2007). In the later elementary grades, another gender difference begins to become apparent. Aggression by boys toward other boys becomes increasingly physical in nature, but aggression by boys toward girls drops markedly. Aggression by girls remains primarily relational and is directed predominantly toward other girls (Cairns et al., 1989; Galen & Underwood, 1997; Underwood, 2003).

Aggression in girls is often relational and directed toward other girls. *(Banana Stock/Media Bakery)*

BIOLOGICAL DETERMINANTS OF AGGRESSION

Much of the research on children's aggression has been concerned with identifying its causes. Here, we consider the determinants that have primarily a biological basis, and then we move on to social and cognitive influences.

An individual's level of aggression has proven to be remarkably stable over many years (Bushman & Huesmann, 2010). Longitudinal research indicates that children's reports of the aggressive behaviour of their peers at age 8 are good predictors of aggression and various other antisocial behaviours at age 30 (Eron et al., 1987). This degree of stability lends itself well to a genetic or biological explanation of the behaviour. Among the mechanisms that have been suggested are hormones, genes, and inborn temperament styles.

HORMONES The fact that males in all cultures of the world are more aggressive than females certainly suggests that hormones play some role in the development of aggression. And, indeed, numerous studies have shown a link between levels of testosterone and *adult* aggressiveness (Archer, 1991; O'Connor, Archer, & Wu, 2004). Evidence for a link between hormone levels and aggression among *adolescent* samples, however, is mixed. Some studies have found that boys rated as more aggressive by their peers or parents have higher-than-average levels of testosterone, whereas other studies have found no evidence that increases in testosterone are related to increases in aggression (Booth, Granger, Mazur, & Kivlighan, 2006). To further complicate matters, there is some evidence that testosterone levels are more closely linked to social dominance than aggression per se, and that hormone levels can change in response to particular kinds of competitive experiences (Dodge et al., 2006; Rowe et al., 2004). If hormone levels do contribute to individual differences in aggression, the process is likely to be indirect and to vary with the individual's experience and developmental status (Booth et al., 2006).

GENES The strongest evidence that aggression is genetically mediated comes from work with animals in which scientists (or animal breeders) breed animals specifically to be high or low in aggressiveness (Maxson & Canastar, 2007). The situation appears to be far more complicated in humans, for whom environmental factors play a key role in the development of aggression and for whom the behaviours regarded as aggressive vary widely in form and function.

Nonetheless, there is evidence that genes do play a role in human aggression. Numerous studies of adult twins have reported more similar levels of aggression among identical (monozygotic) twins than among fraternal (dizygotic) twins or other siblings (Rhee & Waldman, 2011). Twin studies involving children have also demonstrated significant genetic influences on aggression and antisocial behaviour (Moffitt, 2005; Rhee & Waldman, 2011). Moreover, twin studies have found that environmental risk factors interact with genetic effects. The negative effects of environmental risk, such as physical maltreatment, are much greater for a child who has a twin high in aggression than for a child whose twin is non-aggressive (Jaffee et al., 2005).

Links to Related Material

In Chapter 12, you read about dimensions of temperament. Here, you learn more about how early temperament may relate to the development of aggressive behaviour.

TEMPERAMENT One manifestation of genetic effects is temperament. We saw in Chapter 12 that some babies are born with "difficult" response styles. They fuss, cry, and are more demanding than other infants of the same age. This personality dimension is quite stable across childhood, prompting researchers to investigate whether it bears some relation to the development of aggressive behaviour.

One team of researchers tested this hypothesis by asking a group of mothers to rate their 6-month-old infants on a temperament questionnaire that allowed the researchers to identify difficult babies. Over the course of the next five years, the same mothers periodically evaluated their children's aggressive behaviour. As predicted, the early temperament ratings were quite good predictors of which children would display greater amounts of aggression (Bates et al., 1991). Longitudinal studies have reported similar results extending into adolescence (Caspi et al., 1995; Olson et al., 2000).

As children move into the preschool years, other temperament dimensions, such as impulsivity and poor regulatory control, become predictive of later aggressiveness. Children who are highly impulsive during early childhood are more likely to engage in fighting and delinquency during early adolescence, aggression and criminal activity during late adolescence, and violence in adulthood (Caspi et al., 1995; Tremblay et al., 1994).

Why might these early temperament dimensions be predictive of later antisocial behaviour? One possibility is that a difficult early temperament reflects an underlying problem that is stable and manifests itself in different ways at different ages. Another possibility is that children with difficult temperaments elicit or evoke harsh and punitive parenting, which contributes to the development of aggressive behaviour. Evidence for such a phenomenon has been reported (Ge et al., 1996; O'Connor et al., 1998; Rubin et al., 2003). Next, we discuss the impact of parenting on the development of aggression.

SOCIOCULTURAL AND FAMILY DETERMINANTS OF AGGRESSION

Social and situational factors are very important determinants of aggressive behaviour. Social-learning theorists believe that aggression is controlled largely by learning principles (Bandura, 1986, 1989b, 1994). Their research indicates, for example, that gender differences in physical aggression may result because boys—by their own report—expect less disapproval for this sort of behaviour and are less bothered by the disapproval when it occurs (Boldizar et al., 1989; Perry et al., 1989). Environmental influences can also be illustrated by a consideration of three familiar contexts in which aggressive behaviour develops: family interactions, relationships with peers, and exposure to violence on television and in video games.

FAMILY PROCESSES Children's aggression often stems from their interactions with parents and siblings. Parents of aggressive children are more likely to deal with misbehaviour by using power-assertion methods of discipline, such as physical punishment, than by using verbal explanation or reasoning (Chamberlain & Patterson, 1995; Rubin, Stewart, & Chen, 1995; Schwartz et al., 1997). Canadian researchers Janet Strayer and William Roberts (2004) suggest that lack of warmth, low empathy, and greater demandingness on the part of parents may be associated with higher levels of anger in their children. Elisa Romano of the University of Ottawa reports a similar connection between maternal hostility and aggression in children (Romano, Tremblay, Boulerice, & Swisher, 2005). Furthermore, recent research finds that aggressive behaviour and harsh discipline affect one another reciprocally: aggressive children elicit harsh discipline from their parents, which in turn leads to higher levels of aggressiveness in the children (Sheehan & Waston, 2008). For social-learning theorists, these findings suggest two processes that may be at work here. First, parents who use harsh discipline may be modelling aggressive behaviour to their children, who go on to imitate what they see. Second, these parents may be reacting to their children's misbehaviour in ways that actually promote aggression. Indeed, there is evidence from the Concordia Risk Study in Montreal (see Chapter 2) that these processes may even continue from one generation to the next: children who are highly aggressive and isolated are more likely than those who are not aggressive to have aggressive children themselves when they grow up (Serbin et al., 2002).

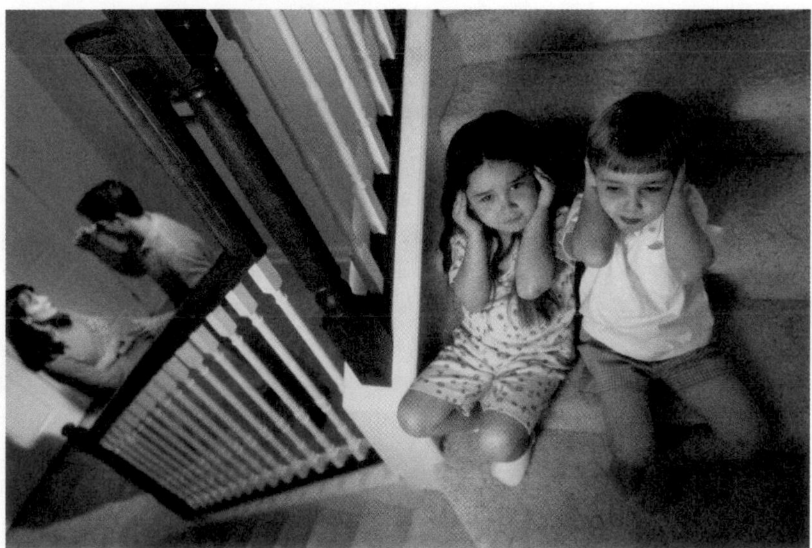

Parents' aggressive behaviour may become a model to their children, who may go on to imitate the aggressive behaviour. (*Purestock*)

Links to Related Material

Here you learn how harsh methods of discipline by parents are associated with aggressive behaviour in children. In Chapter 15, you will learn more about the different styles of discipline employed by parents and their effect on children's behaviour.

Coercive family process Gerald Patterson's term for the method by which some families control one another through aggression and other coercive means.

These family processes associated with aggression are well-illustrated by a series of studies conducted by Gerald Patterson and his colleagues (Patterson, 1982; Patterson, Reid, & Dishion, 1992; Snyder & Patterson, 1995). Patterson found that families of aggressive children commonly display a troublesome pattern of interactions, which he termed **coercive family process** (Dishion & Patterson, 2006; Reid, Patterson, & Snyder, 2002; Snyder, Reid, & Patterson, 2003). These households are characterized by very few friendly, cooperative comments or behaviours, and by a high number of hostile and negative responses. Commonly, the parents spend a good deal of time scolding, berating, or threatening the children, and the children nag or disobey the parents and tease or frustrate one another.

In such environments, aggression is used as a means of stopping or escaping from these sorts of aversive experiences. For example, a little girl may tease and taunt her brother, who punches her to make her stop, which leads his mother to spank him for punching his sister. Thus, both the children and parents use aggression to control one another and to get what they want.

Patterson refers to this pattern as *coercion* because the family members achieve their goals through threats, commands, and other coercive behaviours, rather than through cooperative, prosocial means. Children who learn this style of interaction at home—and who fail to learn more positive interpersonal skills—also display aggression in other settings, and many go on to delinquency and other serious forms of antisocial behaviour (Dishion & Patterson, 2006).

PEER RELATIONS Aggression is considered a social problem primarily because it causes harm to others. But psychologists also warn that aggressive children, by failing to acquire appropriate social skills, run the risk of being rejected by their peer group and becoming outcasts (Asher & McDonald, 2009; Dodge et al., 2003).

We will see in Chapter 15 that these concerns have some foundation. Aggressive children often have poor interpersonal skills, and aggression runs high among unpopular, rejected children (although the cause-and-effect relation probably operates in both directions). But does this mean that highly aggressive children never have friends? Or that they are never members of stable social groups?

Links to Related Material

Here you learn about the peer relationships of aggressive children. In Chapter 15, you will learn more about children's peer relationships, including how popular and rejected children differ from each other.

These questions were addressed in a large-scale study of the social patterns of aggressive children (Cairns et al., 1988). The researchers identified a group of boys and girls in grade 4 and grade 7 who were very aggressive, based on reports from their teachers, principals, and counsellors. They selected as well a comparison group of non-aggressive children who were similar in age, gender, race, and other related characteristics. The social patterns of the two groups were measured using interviews with classmates, ratings by teachers, and self-ratings. The data from these measures were analyzed to answer several questions. First, did the children group themselves into social clusters in which certain children spent a great deal of time together? If so, which children were members of these groups? Were any of the clusters made up predominantly of aggressive children? Finally, how often were aggressive children nominated as "best friends" by their classmates?

The results proved somewhat surprising. In the social clusters that were identified, aggressive children were just as likely to be members as those who were non-aggressive. Children high in aggression often tended to hang around together, forming their own clusters. And aggressive children had just as many peer nominations as best friend as did non-aggressive children. The best-friend relationships, however, involved aggressive children nominating one another and non-aggressive children nominating one another. Subsequent research has confirmed these findings. It appears that although many children dislike aggressive peers (perhaps as a result of being the recipients of their aggressive behaviour), a portion of the peer group likes these aggressive children, likely because of their shared aggressiveness (Crick et al., 2009). We discuss children who are both liked and also disliked by their peers in Chapter 15.

These findings, once again, demonstrate how studies of children in their natural environments often turn up unexpected results. The widely held belief that aggressive behaviour automatically sentences a child to a life of social isolation is overstated. Many aggressive children have networks of friends who are similar to themselves. Although these clusters may encourage and thus perpetuate antisocial behaviour, they also appear to provide friendships and social support. Thus, although many aggressive children may fail to develop good interpersonal skills and may be rejected by their peers, some are socially competent enough to make and maintain friends (Crick et al., 2009).

TELEVISION AND VIDEO GAME VIOLENCE The prevalence of violence on television is well documented. Surveys of television programming reveal that over 70 percent of children's prime time programs and over 90 percent of Saturday morning dramatic programming depict violent acts. An average of 5.3 violent acts per hour occur during prime time shows, and 23 violent acts per hour occur in Saturday morning shows (Huston & Wright, 1998). The amount of aggression and violence shown on television is particularly striking in light of the amount of television children watch—about 22 hours per week for the typical school-age child (Comstock & Scharrer, 2006). The number of violent acts viewed during these hours adds up—by age 21, the average child has witnessed about 8,000 television murders (Huston & Wright, 1998).

Beginning with Bandura in the 1960s, researchers have repeatedly demonstrated that children can learn new forms of aggression and can be stimulated to perform them by viewing a violent film model (Bandura, 1973, 1983, 1994). But, could simply watching television at home have a similar effect? The findings of a classic study that investigated the impact of the introduction of television into a Canadian community in the 1970s suggest that it can. In the days prior to Internet access and widespread cablevision and satellite television, there was little in this community by way of media models. This "natural experiment" revealed that the introduction of a single television channel (where there had previously been no television service) was associated with increases in both aggressive behaviour and sex-typed attitudes in the child residents of the community (Joy, Kimball, & Zabrack, 1986; Kimball, 1986).

So does the average child really become more aggressive simply as a result of watching a typical diet of current network programming? The answer, based on dozens of studies, appears to be yes (Bushman & Huesmann, 2010; Comstock & Scharrer, 2006). Moreover, the effects of violence can take several forms.

The most obvious effect is that children imitate the violent acts they see. They are especially likely to do so when the violence is performed by the "good guys," and also when the aggression successfully achieves its purpose. A somewhat less obvious effect is that television violence increases the likelihood of all other forms of aggression in children, even those that do not resemble the behaviour of the television models. And the effects are long term—one study, for example, found that the amount of violence boys view at age 8 is a predictor of their level of crime at age 30 (Huesmann & Miller, 1994). Similarly, researchers have reported that viewing television violence from ages 6 to 10 is associated with elevated aggressive behaviour in both males and females 15 years later in young adulthood (Huesmann et al., 2003). Not all individuals are equally likely to be affected, however. Children are more readily affected than adults, as are those who are already aggressive, lower in IQ, and from lower socioeconomic backgrounds (Huesmann & Kirwil, 2007). Moreover, the relation between violence and aggression appears to be circular: television violence stimulates aggression, and more aggressive children also tend to watch more violent television (Huesmann, Lagerspetz, & Eron, 1984). Nevertheless, even when these factors are controlled for statistically, the relationship between viewing violence on television and later aggressive behaviour holds true (Huesmann & Kirwil, 2007).

Violence in video games is a current concern. Could playing video games affect children's behaviour? Indeed, it could. Bushman and Huesmann (2010) point out three characteristics of violent video games that may cause children to be even more likely to imitate the violence they are exposed to through this medium than through television or film. First, video games allow children to participate actively in the violence, rather than simply watching it passively. Second, video games are unique in that they allow players to take the perspective of the character performing the violence. Third, video

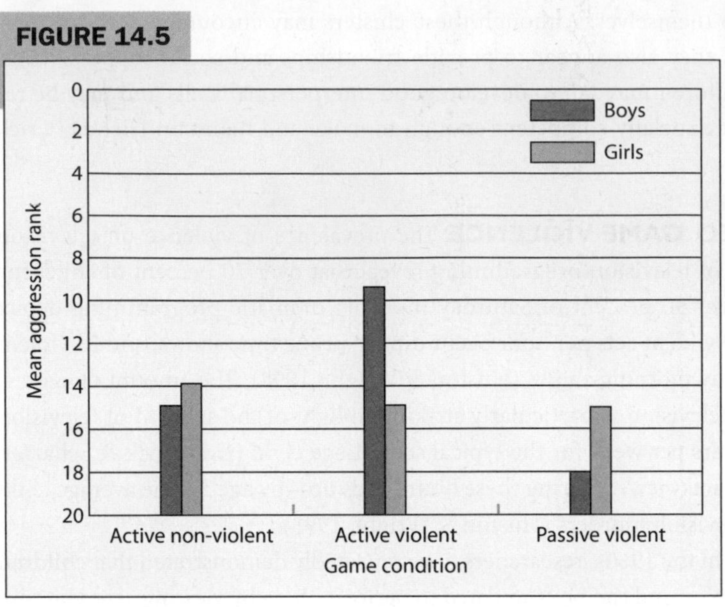

Mean levels of aggression displayed by children after actively participating in a violent video game, passively watching a violent video game, or actively participating in a non-violent video game. Boys who actively played the violent video game were reported by peers to be more aggressive following the game than were those who passively watched the game or who played a non-violent game. No differences were found across the three conditions in aggressive behaviour displayed by girls. *From H. Polman, B. Orobio de Castro, & M. van Aken, 2008, "Experimental study of the differential effects of playing versus watching violent video games on children's aggressive behavior,"* Aggressive Behavior, *34 (3), p. 261.*

games reward participants for destroying their opponents, awarding points for successful kills, often accompanied by encouraging comments, such as "Great shot!" and "What a kill!". As we know from the discussion of social learning theory in Chapter 1, such reinforcement can increase the likelihood that a child will display a modelled behaviour. Thus, video games would appear to offer a particularly effective medium for the learning of aggressive behaviour.

What has research shown about the effects of violent video games? Exposure to violent video games has been linked to increases in aggressive thoughts and behaviour. In addition, active exposure to video game violence may result in a numbing of participants' sensitivity to the distress of others in "real life," perhaps reducing their likelihood of intervening to help others (Anderson, 2004; Anderson et al., 2007, 2010; Bushman & Anderson, 2009; Gentile et al., 2004).

Are the effects of simply watching media violence different from actually participating in it? A recent study suggests that this may be the case. Polman, Orobio de Castro, and van Aken (2008) assigned preadolescent students to one of three experimental conditions. One group played a violent video game. A second group watched the game being played on a screen in an adjacent room, without actually participating in the game. A third group played a video game that was low in violence. Following this, the children interacted as usual with their peers in the classroom and playground, and the researchers collected ratings of their levels of aggressiveness from their classmates (who knew nothing of the conditions of the study). As shown in Figure 14.5, boys who actively played the violent video game showed more aggressive behaviour than did those who simply watched the game or who played a non-violent game. No differences were found between the three conditions for girls. These results clearly suggest an effect of participation, especially for boys, that extends beyond simple exposure to media violence.

For Thought and Discussion

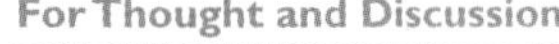

Earlier in the chapter we discussed how not just aggressive behaviour, but also prosocial behaviour, can be learned through exposure to models in television programming. Could the same be applied to video games? Could video games be developed that model prosocial behaviour to children?

Finally, violence on TV and in video games can also make children more tolerant of aggression and less bothered by it (Carnagey, Anderson, & Bushman, 2007; Funk et al., 2004). How long these consequences last is unclear. The immediate effects of media violence are typically short-lived (Huesmann & Kirwil, 2007). It is likely, therefore, that the effects of playing violent video games also dissipate when the game is over. Nevertheless, we know there are long-term consequences of a steady diet of violent media exposure (Huesmann & Kirwil, 2007). Whether there are similar long-term consequences of regularly playing violent video games, although likely, remains to be examined (Carnagey et al., 2007).

EXPOSURE TO REAL-LIFE VIOLENCE Not all the violence that children witness comes in the form of movies or television programs. Many children experience repeated violence first-hand in their everyday lives. Sometimes it occurs in the home among family members, perhaps in the form of spouse or child abuse. And increasingly, children around the world are exposed to political, ethnic, or community violence (Flannery et al., 2007; Garbarino & deLara, 2004; Klingman, 2006).

What happens to children whose development takes place in the context of such violence? Psychologists have typically approached this issue by identifying children who have been exposed to real-life violence and comparing their development with that of children who have not had such experiences. Of greatest interest have been subsequent psychological or behavioural problems, such as aggression, anxiety and phobias, depression, and the like. Typically, this information is gathered by interviewing parents or teachers, or by having them complete questionnaires concerning children's behaviour problems. The children themselves may also be interviewed about their personal experiences and their feelings about the events taking place around them. Sometimes, they are asked to draw pictures depicting where they live and what it is like to live there. These drawings, like the one shown in Figure 14.6, frequently reveal children's perceptions of, and ideas about, the world in which they live.

FIGURE 14.6

Drawing by a 9-year-old Palestinian child. Note the soldiers with guns standing over the small children near their house. *From "Coping with the Consequences of Living in Danger: The Case of Palestinian Children and Youth,"* by K. Kostelny & J. Garbarino, 1994, International Journal of Behavioral Development, *17*, 595–611.

The overriding conclusion is that even when children are not physically injured by real-life violence, they are often invisible or silent victims of the traumatic events (Flannery et al., 2007; Klingman, 2006; Osofsky, 2004; Phares, 2008). Younger children, in particular, seem to be more greatly affected in these situations. Common problems include evidence of fear and anxiety—such as withdrawal, constant crying and clinging, sleep disturbances, and bedwetting—with boys being somewhat more vulnerable to these problems than girls. Such children also tend to display increased use of aggressive words, aggressive play, and a general preoccupation with aggressive themes.

BULLYING AND VICTIMIZATION A survey of grade 6 to 10 Canadian children found that almost 35 percent of boys and 30 percent of girls reported being victimized by peers at school during the previous six weeks (Craig & Harel, 2004). Similar findings have been reported in studies conducted in many other countries (Rigby, 2008). For most students, these negative experiences are relatively infrequent and have no serious impact on long-term adjustment. For others, however, bullying is a frequent and long-standing problem in their lives.

According to Wendy Craig of Queen's University and Debra Pepler of York University (2003), approximately 10 percent of Canadian boys and 7 percent of Canadian girls report having bullied others, and 17 percent of boys and 18 percent of girls report having been the targets of bullying at least twice in the previous week. A sizeable number of children are bullied several times per week, and many of these victims are tormented for years by their peers (Sohlberg & Olweus, 2003). Not surprisingly, these children are at heightened risk for a variety of problems, including loneliness, depression, anxiety, low self-esteem, peer rejection, and academic difficulties (Ladd & Ladd, 2001).

In recent years, investigators have devoted considerable effort to understanding bullying and victimization. One thing we have learned is that bullying is largely a group phenomenon. Peers are present during the vast majority of bullying episodes (Atlas & Pepler, 1998; Hawkins, Pepler, & Craig, 2001), and most bullies seem to thrive on the reactions of their audience (Salmivalli et al., 2011). Surprisingly, although peers frequently witness the victimization, they seldom intervene and put a halt to attacks on peers.

Why do children so often stand by and watch as others are teased, assaulted, and humiliated by bullies? Research suggests that most children do not support the practice of bullying (Charach, Pepler, & Ziegler, 1995; Rigby & Slee, 1993). Indeed, in a survey of 211 Toronto students aged 4 to 14 years (Charach et al., 1995), 90 percent of children reported that it is disturbing to watch

Onlookers are often present during episodes of bullying. Although most report they find it uncomfortable to watch such events, they seldom intervene. (*Media Bakery © Ocean/Corbis*)

bullying, and 43 percent reported that they almost always tried to help a victim. Nonetheless, observational studies show that peers actually intervene only 10 to 20 percent of the time (Atlas & Pepler, 1998; Craig & Pepler, 1995; Hawkins et al., 2001; Salmivalli et al., 2011).

One reason children choose not to intervene is that they may believe that victims bring harassment on themselves. Some children do, indeed, elicit attacks by showing off, tattling, spreading rumours, or otherwise behaving obnoxiously (Graham & Juvonen, 1998a; Olweus, 2001). In such cases, children may feel that—to some degree—the victim "deserves" the harassment.

Such provocative victims, however, constitute only a minority of children who are picked on. Most victims do not provoke others, but are perceived instead as weak and vulnerable (Bosacki, Marini, & Dane, 2006; Olweus, 2001). But, that perception too may have negative implications. Children may fail to intervene on behalf of such peers because they appear cowardly and fail to defend themselves (Graham & Juvonen, 1998a). Boys in particular are unlikely to come to the aid of peers who express fear (Terwogt, 2002). This view of the victim as weak and cowardly contrasts with the view many children hold of the bully. Although they may not "like" the bully, they frequently view him or her as powerful and high in social status (Vaillancourt, Hymel, & McDougall, 2003). Some peers may not intervene, therefore, because of a desire to increase their own status through association with the bully (Junoven & Galván, 2008). Finally, some may also fail to stop bullying because they fear the bully will turn on them if they intervene (Junoven & Galván, 2008).

As our understanding of bullying has grown, it has become increasingly clear that it is unreasonable to expect students to work out such peer problems on their own (Craig, Pepler, & Blais, 2007). Researchers have developed a number of school-based programs designed to reduce school bullying (Rigby, 2008).

A promising Canadian intervention to prevent victimization has been developed over the past 10 years at the University of Victoria. Named the WITS Program, this comprehensive school-based initiative is aimed at children in kindergarten to grade 6 and involves the participation of teachers, police volunteers, and student athletes from universities and high schools (Leadbeater, 2008, 2010; Leadbeater & Hoglund, 2006; Woods, Coyle, Hoglund, & Leadbeater, 2007). The WITS acronym stands for Walk away, Ignore the bully, Talk it out, and Seek help. The WITS program is also available as a series of French lessons for use in francophone schools, as well as a series of Aboriginal-themed lessons. A five-year longitudinal study of 409 children from 17 schools shows that participation in the program is associated with decreases in classroom physical and relational victimization. The manual for the program and many additional related resources are available online at www.witsprogram.ca.

Another well-known anti-bullying program was developed and implemented by Dan Olweus and colleagues in Norwegian schools. The Olweus intervention program has four major goals (Olweus, 1997). The first is to increase awareness of the bullying problem. Second, the program aims to actively involve teachers and parents. Implicit in this goal is the recognition that adults have some responsibility to control what goes on among students at school. A third goal is to develop clear rules against bullying. These rules include explicit statements that bullying is not allowed, that students are to help those who are bullied, and that students should attempt to include peers who are easily left out in their activities. A final goal is to provide support and protection for victims. The Olweus program has been found to reduce bullying by 50 to 70 percent in Norwegian schools (Olweus, 1997, 2001, 2004). The program has also become popular in schools across North America.

Bullying is a major concern in many countries around the world (Rigby, 2008). In Canada, an anti-bullying network has recently been established, consisting of researchers from universities across the country together with a large number of national organizations that work with children and youth. This network, named PREVNet (Promoting Relationships and Eliminating Violence Network), has the goal of designing a national strategy to deal with bullying in Canada (Craig & Pepler, 2007). PREVNet seeks to enhance bullying awareness, to provide assessment and intervention tools, and to promote policy related to bullying (PREVNet, 2010). Further information on this network can be found at www.prevnet.ca. In *Focus on Research 14.1*, we discuss bullying that occurs not on the playground, but electronically in cyberspace.

FOCUS ON RESEARCH 14.1
CYBER BULLYING: WHEN BULLYING MOVES FROM THE PLAYGROUND TO CYBERSPACE

In 2005, CBC news reported on an Ontario high-school student who had been the victim of a website devoted to humiliating him. A friend informed him of a website that had his name on it. When he checked out the site, he found it was full of degrading comments about him and his family. His family contacted the police, but they were told there was little that could be done unless the site contained actual threats of harm. They then contacted the website host to get the site removed, but only after seven frustrating months of repeated emails, letters, and ultimately threats of legal action were they eventually able to get the site taken down (CBC News, 2005).

Was this student's humiliating ordeal an isolated phenomenon? Apparently not. In fact, it is an example of a growing problem. With the explosion of electronic communication in recent years, bullying has moved into cyberspace. Online bullying, referred to as *cyber bullying*, has become widespread (Kiriakidis & Kavoura, 2010). Cyber bullying refers to the intentional and repeated use of communication technology to inflict harm on another (Kiriakidis & Kavoura, 2010; Kowalski, Limber, & Agatson, 2008).

Between 11 and 29 percent of North American children and youth report having been the targets of cyber bullying, and as many as 50 percent report having observed an instance of cyber bullying (Kowalski & Limber, 2007; Patchin & Hinduja, 2006). Similar figures are reported in Canadian surveys (Mishna & MacFadden, 2008). Clearly, cyber bullying is a problem, and it is on the rise. Almost every young person in North America has access to a computer, at home or at school (Kowalski & Limber, 2007; Mishna et al., 2009). Indeed, 94 percent of Canadian youth have Internet access in their homes (Media Awareness Network, 2005), and many also have their own cell phones (Cassidy, Jackson, & Brown, 2009). Thus, this form of harassment is readily available to many youth. Chat rooms, instant messaging, social networks, and websites are the favoured venues for cyber bullying (Kowalski et al., 2008).

Cyber bullying can take various forms. Among the more commonly reported types are the following (Calvete et al., 2010, Kowalski et al., 2008; Willard, 2007):

- *Flaming* (online fights that use antagonistic and vulgar language)
- *Harassment* (sending repeated offensive messages to a victim)
- *Slandering/denigration* (spreading/posting derogatory and untrue information in an attempt to harm a person's reputation)
- *Impersonation/hacking* (harming people's reputation by impersonating them and using their account to spread negative information about others)
- *Defamation/outing (trickery)* (sharing secrets or spreading embarrassing confidential information about someone)
- *Ostracism/exclusion* (intentionally excluding or blocking an individual from online activities such as chat rooms or social networking groups)
- *Cyberstalking* (sending repeated threats or attempts to intimidate)
- *Happy slapping* (recording and sharing a video of someone being attacked)

Cyber bullies don't restrict their aggressive behaviour to electronic media. Some studies find that the perpetrators of cyber bullying are also bullies in the schoolyard (Kowalski et al., 2008). Likewise, the victims of cyber bullying may also be victims of bullying at school (Juvonen & Gross, 2008; Kowalski et al., 2008). Indeed, bullying in the schoolyard may precede instances of cyber bullying away from the schoolard for many victims (Cassidy et al., 2009).

As is often the case with schoolyard bullying, youth who are socially isolated or who have poor social relationships may be at a higher risk for victimization by cyber bullies (Calvete et al., 2010). The consequences of repeated cyber bullying can be serious. Anxiety, stress, depression, and embarrassment are often reported by victims (Kiriakidis & Kavoura, 2010; Raskauskas & Stoltz, 2007), and some researchers have found a higher incidence of suicidal thoughts among victims (Hinduja & Patchin, 2010).

(continued)

Focus on Research 14.1 Cyber Bullying: When Bullying Moves from the Playground to the Computer *continued*

Like schoolyard bullies, cyber bullies thrive on an audience. A major difference between the two forms of bullying, however, is that in most cases the identities of the cyber bully and the bystanders are concealed (Kowalksi et al., 2008). Such anonymity reduces the risk of negative consequences for the bully (Calvete et al., 2010), and may even encourage some bystanders to join in the attack (Kowalski et al., 2008). Indeed, in some cases the cyber bully may have been a recent victim of bullying, and finds it less threatening to retaliate anonymously via cyber bullying than would be the case in the schoolyard (Kowalski et al., 2008; Willard, 2007).

As with traditional forms of bullying, onlookers appear reluctant to intervene or inform authorities when they witness cyber bulling (Juvonen & Gross, 2008; Li, 2007). Some reasons for their reluctance include fear of retaliation by the bully, worry that parents will curtail their Internet privileges, a feeling that the problem belongs to the victim and not anyone else, and a concern that authorities would be ineffective in stopping the bullying anyway (Cassidy et al., 2009; Kowalski et al., 2008).

How can we combat cyber bullying? Some individuals believe the government should not be involved in censoring or otherwise controlling the content of material posted on the Internet, as this constitutes a violation of freedom of expression (CBC News, 2005). Others feel, however, that freedom of expression should have limits, especially when it is harmful to others (CBC News, 2005). In fact, many provinces have begun developing policies to combat bullying and cyber bullying, as have school boards across the country. It is difficult, however, for schools to monitor online harassment, as it frequently does not take place on school property.

Nevertheless, in recent years, schools have begun to take action. For example, 11 students from the Toronto area were given suspensions from school for posting disparaging comments about their principal online (CBC News, 2007). The Canadian government, too, is considering means for dealing with Internet harassment. Finally, an Alberta father and educator, Bill Belsey, has developed an acclaimed website—www.cyberbullying.ca—which provides a wealth of information for parents, educators, and victims of cyber bullying. Informing people about the prevalence of cyber bullying, its consequences, and the risk factors associated with it is a vital first step in reducing its harmful effects on youth.

For Thought and Discussion

Do you think Internet service providers should report people who harass and bully others online? If so, how should they deal with issues of privacy for their clients?

COGNITIVE AND AFFECTIVE INFLUENCES ON AGGRESSION

Any complete understanding of children's aggression must include the cognitive processes that control it. Much research in this area has involved studying how children process and react to information pertaining to the social world in which they live.

Consider the following scenario. Dave has spent the afternoon building a sandcastle at the beach. Ted comes running over, trips, and falls on Dave's sandcastle, smashing it. Ted tells Dave he's sorry and offers to help Dave rebuild the damaged sandcastle. How does Dave respond? Does he laugh it off and let Ted off the hook, or does he blow up and retaliate against Ted? Similar situations happen frequently in children's social worlds. Two things are important here: first, something negative happened to Dave, and second, the intentions of the culprit, Ted, were not overtly malicious (at worst, they were ambiguous).

Although non-aggressive children would likely not be pleased with the situation, most would accept Ted's apology and maybe even take him up on his offer of restitution. By contrast, aggressive children are much more likely to react with hostile retaliation. What underlies these different reactions to the same situation?

Social-cognitive theorists argue that aggressive children, likely because of their life experiences, expectations, and even their temperament, tend to view and respond differently than non-aggressive children to situations where they experience negative consequences (Pettit & Mize, 2007). Kenneth Dodge and colleagues (Crick & Dodge, 1994; Dodge et al., 2006; Dodge & Pettit, 2003) have developed a social information-processing model that explains aggressive children's reactions to such situations in terms of a sequence of emotional and mental steps that ultimately culminates in an aggressive response (Pettit & Mize, 2007).

First, the child must attend to and encode the social cues relevant to the situation. What were the cues in this situation? The most important is that the sandcastle Dave was working on was damaged. But were there other important cues? Did Ted have a look of surprise on his face, or was it one of hostility? Did Dave notice that Ted tripped before landing on the sandcastle? Aggressive children are not good at considering the cues in such situations. When asked to recall the details, they recall fewer relevant social cues than do non-aggressive children and focus especially on those that are negative (Dodge et al., 2003). As a result, they tend to jump to conclusions about the situation without taking into account all the relevant factors (Dodge, 2006; Dodge et al., 2006).

Next, the child must interpret the cues he or she has noticed. Here, an important consideration is determining the intent of the perpetrator. Did Ted intend to do harm to Dave, or was his act accidental? Studies have repeatedly found that aggressive children are more likely to conclude the former than the latter (Dodge et al., 2006). They are not good at considering the feelings and perspectives of others (Cohen & Strayer, 1996; Eisenberg, 2010), and when they are at the receiving end of a negative act, aggressive children assume that the intent of the perpetrator must have been malicious (Dodge et al., 2006; Dodge & Crick, 1990). Such an assumption of negative intent has been referred to as a *hostile attribution bias* (Dodge, 2006), because it occurs even when there is little or no evidence to support it. Having concluded that someone has acted toward them with negative intent, there is a good likelihood that aggressive children will then retaliate with an aggressive response (Dodge, 2006; Pettit & Mize, 2007).

In the next step in the sequence, the child must consider possible ways to respond. Here, again, aggressive children show deficits. They may not be able to come up with many solutions as to how to respond (Shure & Spivack, 1980), or the responses they can think of are frequently negative or aggressive (Dodge et al., 2003, 2006). Thus, while Dave could laugh, tell Ted he's a clumsy oaf, and maybe even accept his offer to help rebuild the sandcastle, if he is aggressive he is more likely to think of retaliating—perhaps yelling at Ted or hitting him.

Next, the child must decide whether to act on the selected response. Here the question is, what will be the outcome of the selected behaviour? Aggressive children have more difficulty thinking through the consequences of their behaviour than do non-aggressive children. They often justify their aggressive responses as legitimate and acceptable reactions to the perpetrator's behaviour (Crick & Werner, 1998; Erdley & Asher, 1998; Gibbs, 2010). And they may even expect their retaliation to have positive effects (Dodge et al., 2006; Fontaine et al., 2010; Pettit & Mize, 2007). In fact, many aggressive children mistakenly think their behaviours are more positively regarded by the peer group than they really are (David & Kistner, 2000). Thus, although Dave may be upset and feel like hitting Ted, most non-aggressive children would consider the possible negative outcomes of such action (e.g., punishment by an adult who sees the retaliation, negative response by peers) and usually decide against this. Aggressive children, in contrast, are more likely to follow through on their aggressive choice of action, thinking that the perpetrator deserves it, or even considering retaliation a matter of honour (Dodge, 2006).

This sequence of steps then leads to the final step—enactment of the response. For aggressive children, the response is usually one of retaliation. Figure 14.7 illustrates the sequence of steps.

Although the social information-processing model breaks things down into a series of sequential steps, the whole process actually takes place in a split second, with little awareness on the part of the aggressive child. At each step along the way, we can see deficits that increase the likelihood that an aggressive child will respond with aggressive behaviour. Moreover, these steps provide points where psychologists can intervene in an attempt to derail this automatic process. We discuss social-cognitive intervention methods later.

FIGURE 14.7

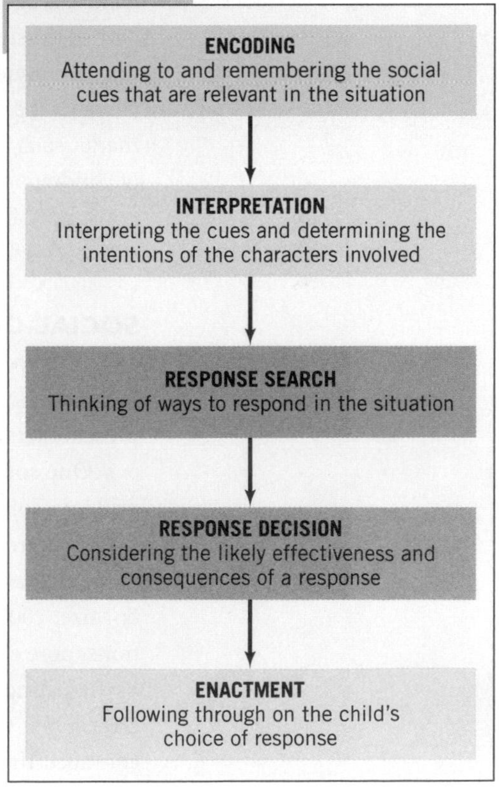

ENCODING
Attending to and remembering the social cues that are relevant in the situation

↓

INTERPRETATION
Interpreting the cues and determining the intentions of the characters involved

↓

RESPONSE SEARCH
Thinking of ways to respond in the situation

↓

RESPONSE DECISION
Considering the likely effectiveness and consequences of a response

↓

ENACTMENT
Following through on the child's choice of response

The sequence of steps in the processing of social information. Many aggressive children show deficits at each step in the process.

CONTROLLING AGGRESSION

Our discussion of the causes of aggression indicates that it is a complex social behaviour with biological, social, and cognitive elements. This complexity has made the task of preventing or reducing aggression a major challenge. Researchers have learned that aggressive youth may follow one of a number of routes, or "developmental trajectories" (Moffitt, 2007). Consequently, "one-size-fits-all" interventions are unlikely to work equally well with all children. Psychologists have also learned that preventing the development of antisocial behaviour in the first place is generally more effective than treating youth after they have begun to engage in problem behaviour (Fields & McNamara, 2003). And researchers have learned much about which kinds of interventions do work—and which do not. We discuss some approaches next.

Catharsis The psychoanalytic belief that the likelihood of aggression can be reduced by viewing aggression or by engaging in high-energy behaviour.

CATHARSIS It was once believed that aggression is a means of venting steam and that it can thus be prevented by having the aggressive child channel energy into other behaviours or experience aggression vicariously. Hitting a punching bag or watching a wrestling match, then, could take the place of engaging in aggressive behaviours. Psychoanalytic theory refers to these substitute behaviours as forms of **catharsis**. The cathartic process has even been used to defend the existence of violent television programs and aggression-related toys (Feshbach & Singer, 1971).

Research evidence, however, does not support this theory. As we have seen, viewing violence on television and in video games increases, rather than decreases, the probability of aggression. And studies with both children and adults indicate that engaging in high-energy behaviours does not make aggression any less likely (Bushman & Huesmann, 2010). Not surprisingly, methods aimed at curbing aggression through catharsis have generally proven to be ineffective.

PARENT TRAINING It is well established that parents' child-rearing methods are related to children's aggression (Dishion & Patterson, 2006; Dodge et al., 2006). One of the most straightforward and successful approaches to handling this source of aggression has been the use of parent training techniques, in which parents are taught more effective ways of interacting with their children (Forehand & Kotchick, 2002; Lochman & Wells, 2004). Parents learn to reduce the use of negative remarks, such as threats and commands, and replace them with positive statements and verbal approval of children's prosocial behaviours (Farrell & Vulin-Reynolds, 2007). They are also trained in applying non-physical punishment in a consistent and reasonable manner when discipline is required. The results of this form of intervention are often dramatic in changing both parents' and children's behaviour.

SOCIAL-COGNITIVE METHODS Another way to reduce aggression is to focus on cognitive and affective processes, which, as the social information-processing model shows, tend to be different for aggressive children. These approaches have been used with children ranging in age from preschoolers to adolescents.

One social-cognitive approach involves preventing aggressive responses through training in problem-solving techniques (Gibbs, 2010; Goldstein, 2004a; Kazdin, 2003, 2005). As discussed earlier, aggressive children show deficits in the ability to generate non-aggressive solutions to social problems, as well as in thinking through the consequences of the solutions they choose (Pettit & Mize, 2007). The social problem-solving method teaches children to deal with problem situations more effectively by generating and examining various strategies for confronting the problem. Participating children listen to stories in which a character faces potential conflict, and then they are trained to analyze the problem and develop constructive solutions. Gradually, they are encouraged to apply these new skills in real-life situations. Similar programs have been used with aggressive adolescents (Goldstein, 2004a, 2004c; Lochman et al., 2007).

Another approach aims at increasing children's empathy, teaching them to take the perspective of the other child and try to understand that child's emotional reactions. Such approaches have found some success in reducing conflict and aggression (Barriga et al., 2009; Gibbs, 2010; Glick & Gibbs, 2011). In addition, many psychologists have found it beneficial to incorporate training in anger management into interventions focusing on social problem-solving (Goldstein, 2004c; Lochman et al., 2006; Nelson et al., 2006).

A third approach is to focus on the attributions children make about the intentions of others (Graham & Hoehn, 1995; Graham et al., 1992; Graham & Juvonen, 1998b). The premise of this

FIGURE 14.8

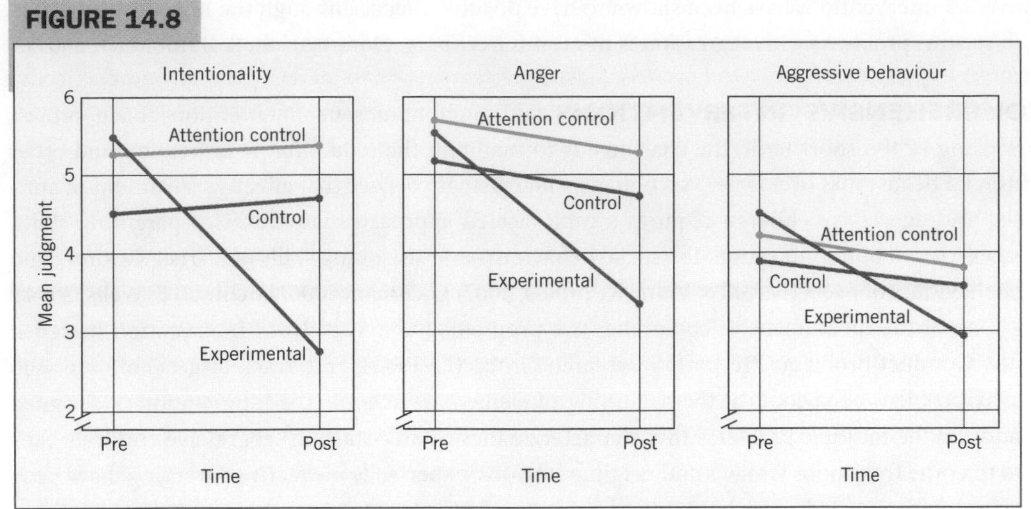

Results of an intervention study with aggressive children. The experimental group received attributional training and decreased the most on the three measures of interest. *Adapted from "An Attributional Intervention to Reduce Peer-Directed Aggression among African-American Boys," by C. Hudley & S. Graham, 1993,* Child Development, *64, 124–138. Copyright © 1993 by the Society for Research in Child Development. Reprinted by permission.*

approach, as discussed earlier, is that aggressive children are likely to interpret negative actions by their peers (such as bumping into them in the school hallway) as intentional and hostile. This attribution produces anger, which then gives rise to aggressive, retaliatory behaviour (Dodge, 2006).

Using this model as a basis, psychologists developed an intervention program designed to interrupt the social information-processing sequence leading to aggression (Hudley & Graham, 1993). The intervention involved children in grades 4 to 6 who had been selected on the basis of teacher and peer ratings of their aggression. Each child was assigned to one of three groups: an experimental group that received attribution training, an attention control group that received training only in academic skills, and a second control group that received no training.

The attribution training involved teaching the children to recognize cues to another person's intentions (such as facial expressions), to encourage non-hostile attributions when the peer's actions were ambiguous (e.g., "he probably did it by accident"), and to generate non-aggressive responses to the peer's behaviour. The training lasted six weeks and included a variety of methods, such as storytelling, role playing, videos, and group brainstorming.

Before and after the training, all participants were given a series of assessments designed to determine how likely they were to (a) attribute hostile intentions in an ambiguous situation, (b) become angry in response to such attributions, and (c) respond with aggressive behaviour. The results of the intervention are shown in Figure 14.8. We can see that the attributional training worked very well. On each of the three measures, children in the experimental group scored the lowest on the post-test that followed the training and showed by far the greatest change. These data provide good evidence that intervening in aggressive children's social information processing by changing their hostile attributions can reduce their aggression.

SCHOOL-BASED UNIVERSAL PROGRAMS An alternative approach to controlling aggression is to shift the focus away from the individual child and instead toward the school—one of the primary socialization contexts of children's lives. Several intervention programs share a common goal of reducing aggressive behaviour and increasing prosocial behaviour by altering the social environment of the school (Battistich, 2008; Flannery et al., 2003; Nucci, 2008). Although the specifics of the programs differ, they all aim to create caring school communities. In contrast to the other intervention efforts we have described, most of these "universal interventions" involve all children in a classroom or school and not just those deemed to have behaviour problems (Farrell & Vulin-Reynolds, 2007). The University of Victoria WITS anti-bullying program (Leadbeater, 2008, 2010), described earlier in the chapter, is an example of a school-based universal program (although not all such programs focus on bullying). Key to the success of the programs is helping teachers foster a prosocial orientation among students toward classmates and their community.

Universal interventions have been shown to have positive effects, although the impact on children with serious problems with aggression is modest (Greenberg, Domitrovich, & Bumbarger, 2001).

COMPREHENSIVE INTERVENTIONS Although numerous interventions have proven promising in the short term, the challenge is to maintain the reduction in aggression and other antisocial behaviours over time. Psychologists increasingly believe that effective treatment of antisocial and aggressive children requires a multifaceted approach that addresses parenting skills, teacher–parent communication, the social behaviours and reasoning skills of at-risk children, and the behaviours of peers (Farrell & Vulin-Reynolds, 2007; Lochman, 2006; Lochman & Wells, 2004).

One of the most intensive comprehensive programs is the Fast Track intervention designed by the Conduct Problems Prevention Research Group (CPPRG). Fast Track targets children who display problem behaviours at the beginning of elementary school. The intervention is designed to address the multiple problems that characterize these "early-starting" aggressive children: they tend to come from poor families and neighbourhoods, experience ineffective parenting, have poor relations with peers, do poorly in school, and attend schools that cannot control disruptive and violent behaviour. The program seeks to improve these various areas of children's lives.

Fast Track begins in grade 1 and continues through grade 10. It includes both a universal curriculum for all children, and a specialized program that targets high-risk children and their families. The universal curriculum fosters emotion regulation and prosocial skills in the regular education classroom. The specialized program includes weekly enrichment sessions during school hours. High-risk children and their parents participate in these sessions, which are designed to further advance children's social skills and peer relations, and to improve parenting skills, parent–child relations, and the parent–school partnership. The children also receive academic tutoring. In addition, the program includes home visits designed to develop trusting relationships with the parents and children and to promote general problem-solving skills for the entire family (CPPRG, 1992, 1999, 2004).

Does Fast Track work? A longitudinal study designed to assess the effectiveness of this comprehensive program was initiated in 1990. Nearly 900 grade 1 students with behaviour problems were randomly assigned to intervention (Fast Track) or control classrooms. Results of ongoing evaluations are promising. By grade 4, 48 percent of children in the control group had been placed in special education compared with 36 percent of children in the intervention group. The intervention also lowered arrest rates. By grade 8, 42 percent of the control group had been arrested, contrasting with 38 percent of Fast Track children. And among children in grade 9, the intervention reduced serious conduct disorders by more than a third, from 21 to 13 percent (CPPRG, 2002, 2007; Crawford, 2002).

Fast Track is an expensive program. Is the reduction in rates of serious antisocial behaviour obtained so far worth the cost? Kenneth Dodge, one of the program directors, thinks so. He observes, "If each career criminal costs society $1.3 million and the Fast Track program costs $40,000 per child, the program will prove to be a wise economic investment if just 3 percent of children are saved from careers of violent crime" (Crawford, 2002, p. 38).

LEARNING OBJECTIVE 14.4

Describe the factors that contribute to aggressive behaviour and discuss ways of reducing aggression in children.

1. What kinds of aggressive behaviour do children exhibit?
2. How does aggressive behaviour vary by age and sex?
3. What evidence is there for a biological explanation of aggression?
4. What role do sociocultural and family factors play in the development of aggressive behaviour?
5. What are some cognitive factors that contribute to aggression in children?
6. What techniques have been used to control children's aggression?

CONCLUSION

At the beginning of this chapter, we noted that two issues have dominated the study of moral development. One issue is whether morality lies within the child and simply emerges over time or is transmitted from adults and society to the child. The second is whether moral rules are universal—shared by all cultures.

Developmental psychology has made significant progress in understanding these two issues since Piaget initiated the study of children's moral reasoning in the 1930s. With respect to the first issue, the most accurate answer is probably neither. Scientists now believe that humans are born with the capacity to experience emotions that underlie moral behaviour. However, the development of a moral sense, and ultimately moral behaviour, depends on a complex interplay between cognitive abilities and experience with other people who themselves adhere to a moral code and enforce compliance among others.

We have also learned much about the second issue, although it also is far more complex than envisioned by early researchers. Moral rules are universal in the sense that every known culture has a legacy of agreed-upon rules that structure the interactions among members. At the same time, there exists considerable cultural variation in these rules. Moreover, this variation is not as insignificant as was once believed (e.g., variations in levels of moral reasoning achieved in different cultures). Widely divergent beliefs permeate cultural ideologies around the world and are the basis on which people justify such acts as slavery, ethnic cleansing, widow burning, and infanticide.

Researchers have looked at how children and adults reason about moral beliefs that differ from their own. These studies show that, beginning in childhood, people wrestle with the issue of what makes beliefs with which they disagree more or less legitimate. One consistent finding is that beginning as young as age 3, people do not judge moral beliefs that differ from their own as legitimate grounds on which to base actions that they would consider immoral (Wainryb, 2000).

SUMMARY

KEY TERMS

aggression, p. 546
catharsis, p. 558
coercive family process, p. 550
conventional level, p. 524
dominance hierarchy, p. 528
empathy, p. 538
immanent justice, p. 523
kin selection, p. 527
moral dilemmas, p. 523
moral realism, p. 523
moral relativism, p. 523
paradox of altruism, p. 527
peacemaking, p. 541
postconventional level, p. 524
preconventional level, p. 524
proactive (instrumental) aggression, p. 546
prosocial behaviour, p. 538
reactive (hostile) aggression, p. 546
reciprocal altruism, p. 527
relational aggression, p. 546
social conventions, p. 526
sympathy, p. 538

LEARNING OBJECTIVES

LEARNING OBJECTIVE 14.1 Understand four theoretical approaches to the study of moral development.

1. *What is Piaget's model of moral development?*

   Piaget proposed a four-stage model. Children in the first stage show very little understanding of rule following. In the stage of moral realism, children view rules as absolute and base their moral evaluations largely on the physical and objective aspects of a situation. Increased interaction with peers combines with a movement away from egocentric thinking in the stage of moral relativism, during which children approach rules more flexibly and are able to take subjective factors into account. In the final stage, moral reasoning can extend to hypothetical situations and to issues in the larger society.

2. *How did Kohlberg conceptualize moral development?*
   Kohlberg's model consists of three levels of moral reasoning—preconventional, conventional, and postconventional—each composed of two stages. The two components of each stage, social perspective and moral content, represent cognitive and environmental influences, respectively. According to Kohlberg, movement from stage to stage occurs when the child experiences cognitive conflict; each stage represents a structured whole; the stages follow an invariant sequence; and the model is universal across cultures and sexes.

3. *What are the main features of Turiel's view of moral development?*
   Turiel believes that children's moral reasoning involves several domains of social cognition. Even very young children can distinguish issues in the moral domain, which is concerned with people's rights and welfare, and the social domain, which is concerned with social conventions. Turiel also argues that understanding of such issues is influenced by their context and by situational factors.

4. *How does the evolutionary approach explain moral development?*
   The evolutionary approach explains moral development in terms of evolutionary principles. For the so-called paradox of altruism, sociobiologists have argued that self-sacrificial behaviour can be explained by a focus on the survival of the genes, rather than of the individual, through the processes of kin selection and reciprocal altruism. In the area of aggression, ethologists have been especially interested in how primate social groups—including humans—regulate conflict through dominance hierarchies and non-aggressive means of resolving disputes.

5. *What is the focus of the sociocultural approach to moral development?*
   The sociocultural approach focuses on both moral reasoning and moral behaviour. This approach emphasizes children's moral development in the context of everyday activities, such as family interactions and participation in cultural institutions. Sociocultural theorists view moral development as a social process in which other people assist children's moral development by structuring and interpreting situations for them.

LEARNING OBJECTIVE 14.2 Understand what research has found concerning children's moral reasoning.

1. *Does research support Piaget's model?*
   Research generally supports Piaget's model, but suggests that he somewhat underestimated younger children's moral reasoning. When the story characters' motives are made salient in the classic moral dilemmas, even preschoolers can use this information as a basis for moral evaluations.

2. *Has Kohlberg's model been supported by research?*
   Research has generally supported Kohlberg's contention that moral reasoning displays consistency across situations and that children proceed through the stages in an invariant order. The universality of the model is less well documented, and in some cultures Kohlberg's theory clearly does not apply. Questions have also been raised as to whether Kohlberg's model applies equally to males and females.

3. *Has Turiel's model stood up under the scrutiny of research?*
   Turiel's domain theory has found support in research. Studies suggest that children do distinguish between moral and societal rules from an early age. Their moral reasoning also appears to be influenced by contextual factors, including culture. Although there are some acts that are

universally regarded as wrong, in some cultures moral transgressions may constitute a wider category than in others.

4. *Discuss how children allocate rewards and punishments.*
   Children's allocation of rewards seems to follow a predictable sequence, moving from self-interest to equality and then to equity, but it is also influenced by situational variables. Children's reasoning about application of punishment uses much the same pattern found in adults: Was harm done? If so, was the person in question responsible? If so, is punishment warranted?

5. *How do peers and parents influence children's moral reasoning?*
   Interactions with peers, especially in situations of moral conflict, stimulate the development of moral reasoning. Dialogue with parents, particularly about real-life dilemmas, also fosters moral growth. Parental disciplinary techniques affect moral reasoning and the degree to which children internalize parents' standards. Induction is most effective in stimulating moral development and internalization among children in Canada and the United States. The temperamental trait of fearfulness in the child helps determine the type of discipline that will promote the development of conscience.

LEARNING OBJECTIVE 14.3 Understand the development of prosocial behaviour and identify its determinants.

1. *What are Hoffman's six stages in the development of empathy?*
   Hoffman has proposed a six-stage theory of empathy development. During the first stage, infants cry reflexively on hearing another infant cry. During the second stage, the distress of others produces personal distress, and infants respond by seeking comfort themselves. In the third stage, toddlers interpret the distress of another correctly but often respond inappropriately because of limited ability to understand mental states of others. In the fourth stage, children recognize the distress of others and now respond in appropriate ways. In the fifth stage, children empathize with the general conditions of people's lives. In the sixth stage, children empathize with entire classes of largely unknown people.

2. *Identify three major categories of prosocial behaviour and describe how these develop.*
   Major categories of prosocial behaviour are helping, sharing, and conflict resolution. Clear evidence for helping behaviour emerges during the second year of life, when toddlers try to comfort others who are distressed. Generally, helping increases over the course of childhood and adolescence. Sharing also emerges early—by the end of the first year of life. Sharing serves a number of interpersonal functions. Children are most likely to share with friends and those who have given them help in the past. Like helping, sharing increases with age. Another prosocial skill is conflict resolution. During childhood, children tend to use coercion to resolve conflicts. This gradually gives way to the more prosocial approach of negotiation. Studies of children's peacemaking show that children are able to resolve past conflicts and repair damaged relationships. Children use both verbal and non-verbal behaviours to reconcile with peers, including sharing of toys or food, invitations to play, apologies, and touching or hugs.

3. *What are some gender differences in prosocial behaviour?*
   There is little empirical support for a gender difference in prosocial behaviour, although girls tend to display more empathy and concern for others. This sex difference grows larger with age and is largest on self-report measures.

4. *What factors contribute to the development of prosocial behaviour?*
   Biology, affect, cognition, and socialization all contribute to the development of prosocial behaviour. It is believed that genes influence prosocial development through temperament.

Studies have shown that children's prosocial behaviour is modestly related to empathy, prosocial reasoning, and their mental state understanding. Parents contribute to children's prosocial development by providing opportunities to practise prosocial behaviours and by modelling and reinforcing prosocial behaviour.

LEARNING OBJECTIVE 14.4 Describe the factors that contribute to aggressive behaviour and discuss ways of reducing aggression in children.

1. *What kinds of aggressive behaviour do children exhibit?*
   Proactive (instrumental) aggression is aimed at obtaining something desirable or to achieve a goal. Reactive (hostile) aggression occurs in reaction to provocation by someone else and is usually motivated by anger. Aggression can be physical (hitting, kicking, biting) or verbal (name-calling teasing, threats), and may be direct or indirect. Relational aggression, which can also be direct or indirect, is aimed at damaging or manipulating social relationships.

2. *How does aggressive behaviour vary by age and sex?*
   In preschoolers, physical aggression gradually gives way to verbal aggression. In school-age children, the overall level of aggression tends to decrease with age. Boys are more physically aggressive than girls, especially toward one another; girls display more relational aggression.

3. *What evidence is there for a biological explanation of aggression?*
   The fact that aggression is a very stable characteristic over the life span lends itself to a biological explanation of aggressive behaviour. One such explanation of aggression has linked it to blood levels of the hormone testosterone. There is also evidence for a genetic basis for aggression, which may, in part, be manifested through a "difficult" temperament.

4. *What role do sociocultural and family factors play in the development of aggressive behaviour?*
   Situational factors are assumed to influence aggression by way of the social-learning principles of reinforcement, punishment, and observational learning. The families of aggressive children engage in an ongoing pattern of coercive interactions in which members control one another through aggressive behaviour. Violence on television and in video games also increases the likelihood of aggression in child viewers. The effects may include direct imitation of the violent behaviour, an increase in overall aggression, and an increase in children's tolerance of aggression in others. Long-term exposure to real-life violence can have negative consequences for many children. Bullying, either in the schoolyard or in cyberspace, can have serious negative consequences for its victims.

5. *What are some cognitive factors that contribute to aggression in children?*
   Aggressive children appear to be deficient in a number of cognitive areas, including moral reasoning and empathy. Dodge's social information-processing model describes a sequence of emotional and mental steps that are involved in aggressive responding. These steps include attending to and encoding social cues, interpreting these cues, considering ways to respond, and selecting an appropriate response and acting on it. At each step in the sequence, aggressive children show deficits that ultimately lead to an aggressive response.

6. *What techniques have been used to control children's aggression?*
   Parent training has been effective in reducing children's aggression. Social-cognitive interventions, including training in problem solving, perspective taking, anger management, and attribution, have also been used to help children control their aggression. School-based programs, as well as comprehensive interventions such as Fast Track, have also proven effective.

CHAPTER 15

FAMILIES AND PEERS

If a child were somehow able to find sustenance and protection from the elements, would she develop in much the same way as a child subject to the socializing influences of parents, peers, and human culture? Or would she emerge a wild animal? Remarkably, over the course of human history, several children have found themselves in circumstances much like these. Such cases, referred to as feral (or wild) children, provide unique insights into the importance of human socialization.

One of the best-documented cases occurred in the early 1900s in India. The Reverend A.J. L Singh, a Christian missionary working in Calcutta, discovered two young girls living among wolves in the jungle outside a small village. Singh estimated the larger one to be about 8 years of age. He named her Kamala. The smaller one, whom Singh guessed to be about a year and a half, he named Amala.

Singh took the girls to an orphanage he operated with his wife. At the time of their rescue, the girls were half-savage, more like beasts than humans. They ate, drank, and walked like dogs and seemed not to feel heat or cold. The girls showed no fear of the dark, preferring to explore the compound at night and stay indoors, sheltered from the sun, during the day. The girls also remained aloof and shy. Initially, they refused to interact with anyone. They were particularly uncomfortable around the other children, and the mere presence of another child in the room was enough to prevent them from even moving. When they were approached, they often made faces and bared their teeth.

Within about a year of their capture, both girls grew quite ill with dysentery, and the younger one, Amala, died. Over time, her remaining sister, Kamala developed affection for Mrs. Singh and gradually acquired the rudiments of human behaviour. She learned to walk upright, wear human clothing, use the toilet, and relate to the other children, and she even acquired a small vocabulary. But at the time of her death eight years later, Kamala—although grown—functioned at the level of a child of a year and a half.

Although the outcomes vary somewhat depending on the extent of isolation, one thing is clear: human children raised outside of human culture, without peers or family, never develop normal human capacities. Why this is so, and how family and peers influence development, is the focus of this chapter. ■

A CENTRAL ASPECT of being human is being socialized by other humans—as the sad cases of Kamala and Victor make clear. Normal development requires a social world and social experiences of many forms and from very early in life. Children encounter many people who influence them as they develop. For most, however, the family and peer group are the principal agents of socialization. It is with family and peers that this chapter is concerned.

Learning Objective 15.1

Discuss four theoretical approaches to socialization.

THEORIES OF SOCIALIZATION

Socialization is one of the central issues in the field of child psychology, and each of the major theoretical traditions has therefore had much to say about the topic. To a good extent, the pictures they provide complement, rather than contradict, one another.

EVOLUTIONARY APPROACHES

We have already seen some of the emphases that evolutionary approaches bring to the study of socialization. The overriding theme is that of a biological basis for adaptive behaviour, a basis set by the evolutionary history of the species. This biological pretuning is evident very early. As we saw in Chapter 12, ethologists believe that evolution has provided infants with a number of characteristics, both physical and behavioural, that elicit appropriate caregiving responses from the adults around them and hence promote survival. Evolution has also provided adults with natural responses to these infant characteristics—for example, relieving the distress of a crying baby.

In most cultures throughout human history, mothers have assumed a much greater role in child care. (*Corbis/Media Bakery*)

Although any adult is presumably set by evolution to respond to children in appropriate ways, theorists from the sociobiology and evolutionary psychology perspectives add two further ideas (Bjorklund, Younger, & Pellegrini, 2002). One is that parents are especially likely to engage in caregiving practices that promote the development of their children, because doing so serves to perpetuate their genes. (Of course, there is no claim that this is a conscious motivation on the parents' part.) The second, which we will discuss in Chapter 16, is the idea that evolution has provided males and females with somewhat different priorities with regard to mating and subsequent child care. According to *parental investment theory* (Trivers, 1972), females have considerably more investment in the survival and well-being of their offspring than do males. And, indeed, in most cultures at most points in human history, mothers have assumed a much greater role in child care than have fathers.

Ethologists also contend there is an innate underpinning to many of the behaviours that children direct toward their peers. We have already seen this argument applied to two important classes of social behaviour: altruism and aggression. Ethologists do not claim that such behaviours are totally under genetic control, because experience is clearly necessary for their emergence. But they do claim there is an important biological basis, set by evolution, on which experience operates. Recall that in the case of aggression, evolution is also assumed to have built in various controls, the function of which is to prevent intraspecies aggression from becoming too severe. We discussed one such control in Chapter 14: the formation of a dominance hierarchy, or a kind of social pecking order, that determines who wins out over whom in social disputes. Once the hierarchy is established, disputes can be resolved simply through members' knowledge of their relative status and thus without use of force. A range of different species form dominance hierarchies, and so, as we saw, do human children (Bjorklund & Pellegrini, 2002a, 2011). Such hierarchies are evident on the school playground (Pellegrini et al., 2007), and they are also evident in the summer camp encounters of adolescents (Savin-Williams, 1987). We can see two emphases of the ethological approach in the work on dominance hierarchies: the value of comparative study and the importance of studying behaviour in the natural setting.

ENVIRONMENTAL/LEARNING APPROACHES

The goal of the environmental/learning approach has always been to identify basic learning principles that apply across a range of situations, age groups, and types of behaviour. From this perspective, socialization does not require the discovery of new processes of learning; the task, rather, is to explain how the basic processes apply in the socialization context. Indeed, John Watson, whom we discussed as one of the pioneers of the approach in Chapter 1, wrote advice pamphlets in which he instructed parents in the application of the basic learning techniques that had been identified in laboratory study.

What has changed over the years in environmental/learning approaches to socialization is not the guiding philosophy, but rather the particular forms of learning that are stressed. Early versions emphasized direct learning via reinforcement and punishment. Such processes remain important in contemporary accounts; clearly, one way in which parents influence their children is by reinforcing and thereby strengthening some behaviours and punishing and thereby weakening others. Often, of course, parents' delivery of reinforcing or punishing consequences is intentional, but this is not always the case. Parents may sometimes unintentionally strengthen behaviour that they do not wish to promote. Patterson's (1982) work on coercive processes in the home setting as antecedents of aggression (Chapter 14) provides one example.

In modern versions of social-learning theory—most notably, Bandura's work (Bandura, 1986, 1989a, 2001)—reinforcement and punishment are joined by a third important socialization process: observational learning that results from exposure to a model. Thus, another basic way that parents influence their children is by providing models of behaviour that may then affect the child's behaviour. Again, parents may do this either intentionally or unintentionally, and the result may be either desirable or undesirable behaviour on the child's part. The topic of aggression again provides an example of the latter; recall that large amounts of physical punishment by parents is associated with heightened aggression in children, an outcome that may result from the aggressive model provided by a punitive parent.

Like parents, peers can also affect a child's behaviour and development in several ways. One way again is through reinforcement and punishment, and peers provide many reinforcing or punishing consequences as a child develops—attention, praise, acquiescence to the child's wishes, sharing or refusing to share, criticism, disapproval. Many of these consequences are, to be sure, unintended, but they may function as reinforcements or punishments nonetheless. Peers are also important as models of behaviour; indeed, for some behaviours (e.g., forms of play) peers may be even more important models than are parents. Finally, peers contribute to the development of self-efficacy—children's conceptions of which behaviours they are capable of performing. One source of self-efficacy judgments is the child's observation of the behaviour of others, and peers are clearly a natural comparison group.

Of course, none of the roles just cited is unique to peers. But peers may be especially important sources of such effects, especially as children grow older. The sheer amount of time spent with peers guarantees that any child will be exposed frequently to the behaviour of other children and will experience frequent consequences from other children in response to his or her behaviour. Furthermore, for most children, the importance of being accepted by other children guarantees that peers will be effective agents of reinforcement and punishment, as well as potent models for a wide range of behaviours. And, of course, the behaviours that peers model and reinforce may differ from the behaviours that adults try to promote.

COGNITIVE-DEVELOPMENTAL APPROACHES

Bandura's version of social-learning theory places considerably more emphasis on cognition than did its predecessors in the environmental/learning tradition. Nevertheless, it is within the cognitive-developmental approach, not surprisingly, that cognitive factors are accorded their most prominent role.

A cognitive emphasis in the study of parenting is a relatively recent emergence. The first wave of child-rearing studies were inspired primarily by either Freudian theory or learning theory, neither of which put much emphasis on how parents think about their children or the tasks of child rearing. Such is no longer the case. In recent years, a substantial research literature has grown up devoted to the study of parents' beliefs about children (Bugental & Happaney, 2002; Goodnow, 2002; Russell, 2011). In retrospect, the general conclusions that emerge from this literature are perhaps not surprising. Parents do hold beliefs of various sorts, both about children in general and about their own children in particular. Some of these beliefs are unconscious and implicit, such as the internal working models (Bretherton & Munholland, 2008) discussed in Chapter 12. Other beliefs may be the result of deliberately thinking about children and child rearing (Hawk & Holding, 2006). There are marked individual differences among parents in the ways that they think about children, as well as differences in belief systems across different cultures or subcultures (Harkness, Raeff, & Super, 2000; Sigel & McGillicuddy-De Lisi, 2002). Although the relation is far from perfect, beliefs do relate to parental behaviour—for example, a belief that children learn best through self-discovery is associated with non-directive, child-oriented methods of teaching (Sigel, 1986). Finally, parental beliefs also relate to children's development (Murphey, 1992). Again, the relation is far from perfect, but in general more accurate or sophisticated beliefs are associated with more positive developmental outcomes.

Contemporary approaches to child rearing also emphasize the child's cognitive contribution. Rather than simply adhering (or failing to adhere) to parental directives, children are seen as striving to make sense of both their parents' positions and their own eventual behaviour (Why should I clean my room? Why should I not hit other children?). The ways in which they do so change as their cognitive capacities change, which is one reason that a 12-year-old and a 3-year-old require somewhat different socialization practices. In general, from this perspective, socialization involves not only the teaching of specific behaviours, but also the transmission of general attitudes or belief systems.

Cognitive-developmental theorists also address the role of peers in the socialization process. One well-cited example is Piaget's (1932) description of how peers contribute to changes in moral reasoning (Rubin et al., 2009), which was discussed in Chapter 14. In Piaget's view, because children lack the power and authority of the adult, they conform to what they perceive to be the adult's views. The result is moral realism, characterized by a rigid view of right and wrong. When children interact with peers, however, the relation is much more one of equals, and there is a continual need for cooperating, negotiating, and taking the point of view of the other. Interaction with peers, therefore, leads to the ability to consider different perspectives, an ability central to the more advanced form of reasoning known as moral relativism. More generally, interaction with peers is important in breaking down the child's egocentrism and encouraging more mature forms of thought.

Peers are also important in Kohlberg's (1987) theory of moral development. As in Piaget's theory, movement through Kohlberg's stages results partly from biological maturation. Achieving a new stage, however, requires not only a sufficient level of maturation, but also experience with moral issues. Kohlberg especially stressed experiences in which the child encounters different points of view and thus is forced to consider and integrate different perspectives. Such experiences of cognitive conflict may be especially likely in the give-and-take of the peer group.

In addition to their role in promoting cognitive change, peers are important as objects of the child's thought. Thinking about other children falls under the heading of *social cognition*—the child's understanding of the social and interpersonal world (Harris, 2006; Lewis & Carpendale, 2011). Social cognition is of interest both in itself and because of its possible effects on the child's social behaviour. A basic principle of the cognitive-developmental approach is that the child's cognitive level is an important determinant of the child's behaviour, including behaviour toward other people. Thus, the cognitive theorist would expect older children to show more complex and mature forms of social behaviour because of their greater cognitive maturity. And within an age group, the theorist would expect children who are advanced in their level of social reasoning to be advanced in their social behaviour as well. Later in the chapter, we will see how well these expectations are borne out by research.

SOCIOCULTURAL APPROACHES

As we have seen in previous discussions of theories, sociocultural approaches share a number of assumptions with the other general theoretical traditions. Theorists who subscribe to this approach certainly agree, for example, that parental models can be important contributors to children's behaviour, and that children's cognitive capacities affect both what they bring to and what they take away from socialization encounters. In the other approaches, however, development is seen as residing primarily within the child; it is affected by and often expressed within social contexts, but the child and the social world are separate entities. For sociocultural theorists, in contrast, development is always embedded within and is inseparable from a sociocultural context. To a good extent, therefore, development *is* socialization.

Because of this inherently social emphasis, it is no accident that our earlier discussions of this approach have already said quite a bit about the roles of family and peers in children's development. Recall that a key notion in both cases is Vygotsky's concept of the zone of proximal development. Parents can direct their child's development most successfully when they work within the child's zone for a particular domain, either through scaffolding in the case of explicit instructional encounters, or through guided participation as they socialize the child in the ways of the home or the community more generally. Although our earlier discussion stressed effects on the child's cognitive development, the same principle applies to other developmental outcomes that parents attempt to instill—for example, assuming responsibilities around the household or behaving in prosocial ways toward a younger sibling.

Peers are also important in sociocultural approaches to development. In contrast to cognitive-developmental theories, however, the emphasis is not on the clash of differing perspectives but on the transmission of knowledge or skills from a more expert peer to a less expert peer (Tudge & Rogoff, 1989). Thus, just as children benefit from interactions with a parent or teacher, they may also be helped to achieve new levels of understanding when they interact with a more competent peer.

Bronfenbrenner's (1992; Bronfenbrenner & Morris, 2006) ecological systems theory adds a further important point. Not only are children affected by the various microsystems (family, peers, school) within which they develop; also important are the ways in which these systems relate to one another—the layer referred to in Bronfenbrenner's model as the mesosystem. We will see several examples of this point later in the chapter. Bronfenbrenner's model also captures an emphasis that is central to theory and research in the sociocultural perspective: the importance of the macrosystem, or the general culture within which development occurs. Socialization practices often vary in important ways across cultures or subcultures; furthermore, the impact of a particular practice may differ across different cultural settings. We will see examples of these points as well.

LEARNING OBJECTIVE 15.1

Discuss four theoretical approaches to socialization.

1. How do evolutionary approaches view socialization?
2. What is the major focus of environmental/learning approaches to socialization?
3. What does the cognitive-developmental approach to socialization emphasize?
4. How does the sociocultural perspective view socialization?

SOCIALIZATION WITHIN THE FAMILY

Learning Objective 15.2

Analyze the influence of parents and other family members on childhood socialization.

For most children, the most important socialization context, especially in the early years, is the family. Our discussion of socialization begins, therefore, with life in the home. We focus first on the role of the parents. In the next section, we will consider the contribution of other family members, such as siblings, grandparents, and so on. We will also later look at the effects of different kinds of family arrangements, examining the effects of divorce, remarriage, blended families, and so on.

PARENTING STYLES

Parental warmth A dimension of parenting that reflects the amount of support, affection, and encouragement the parent provides to the child.

Parental control A dimension of parenting that reflects the degree to which the child is monitored disciplined and regulated.

Parenting style The overall pattern of child rearing provided by a parent, typically defined by the combination of warmth and control that the parent demonstrates.

Authoritative parenting A style of parenting characterized by firm control in the context of a warm and supportive relationship.

Authoritarian parenting A style of parenting characterized by firm control in the context of a cold and demanding relationship.

Permissive parenting A style of parenting characterized by low levels of control in the context of a warm and supportive relationship.

Uninvolved (disengaged) parenting A style of parenting characterized by low levels of both control and warmth.

Research on child rearing has always had a strong idiographic focus. Parents differ in how they socialize their children—indeed, the same parent may even treat two children in the same family differently. The goal in most studies of childrearing is twofold: to identify the important differences among parents and to determine what effects, if any, these variations have on children's development.

What are the significant dimensions along which parenting might vary? Although many distinctions have been proposed, two dimensions have consistently emerged as important (Maccoby & Martin, 1983). One is **parental warmth** (sometimes labelled *acceptance/responsiveness*): the amount of support, affection, and encouragement the parent provides, as opposed to hostility, shame, or rejection. You will not be surprised to learn that a high standing on the dimension of parental warmth is generally associated with positive child outcomes. The second dimension is **parental control** (sometimes labelled *demandingness*): the degree to which the child is monitored, disciplined, and regulated, as opposed to being left largely unsupervised. Control also appears in general to be beneficial, although the results are more variable and complex than those for warmth.

One reason that conclusions regarding control (and to some extent even those for warmth) vary is that the effects of any one aspect of parenting depend on other aspects of parenting; that is, the overall context within which it is expressed. This realization, in fact, reflects one of the major changes in the study of child rearing over the years. Initially, studies of parenting tended to focus on specific parental behaviours in isolation—for example, method of feeding in infancy or amount of physical punishment in later childhood. Contemporary research is more likely to encompass multiple parental practices and dimensions in an attempt to capture the overall pattern of child rearing, what is referred to as **parenting style**.

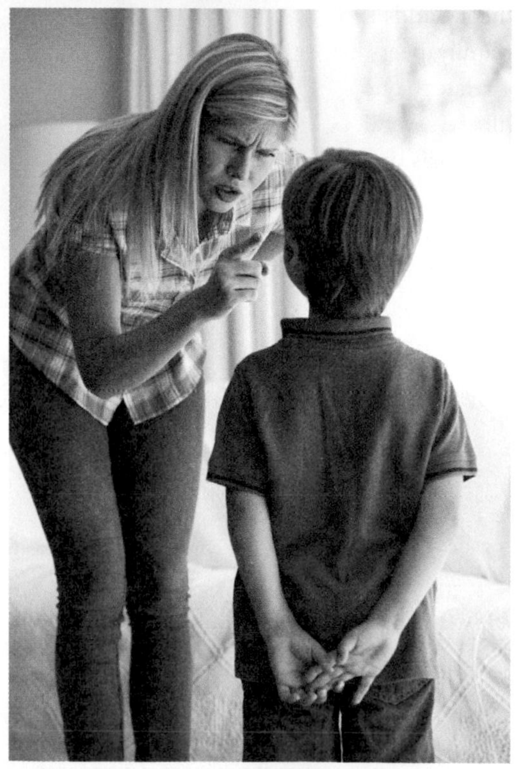

The authoritative style of child rearing is characterized by firm control in the context of a warm and supportive relationship. Why do you think the authoritative child-rearing style is effective? (© *Mark Bowden/iStock*)

The most influential conceptualization of parenting style was developed by Diana Baumrind (1971, 1989, 1991). (*Research Classic 15.1* describes the original Baumrind research.) Baumrind's approach combines the dimensions of warmth and control to yield four parenting styles, which are summarized in Table 15.1. As can be seen, the **authoritative parenting** style is characterized by a high degree of both warmth and control. Authoritative parents tend to be caring and sensitive, while at the same time setting clear limits and maintaining a predictable environment. They also provide rationales for why they expect certain behaviour from the child. In contrast, the **authoritarian parenting** style combines high control with low warmth. Authoritarian parents are very demanding, they exercise strong control over their children's behaviour, and they enforce their demands with threats and punishments, rather than reasons.

The **permissive parenting** style represents a third possible combination of the two dimensions. Permissive parents are high in warmth but low in control. These parents are loving and emotionally sensitive, but set few limits on behaviour and provide little in the way of structure or predictability. Finally, the **uninvolved parenting** style (also termed the *disengaged parenting* style) is the label for parents who are low on both dimensions. These parents set few limits, but they also provide little in the way of attention, interest, or emotional support.

Baumrind's approach has proven to be successful at identifying individual differences among parents across a range of different populations and child ages. As noted, however, the measurement of parental characteristics is usually just the first step in studies of parenting. A further step is to determine how the variations in parenting affect children's development. Here, too, the approach has proven to be very influential.

TABLE 15.1 PARENTING STYLES

		Parental Control	
		High	**Low**
Parental Warmth	**High**	Authoritative	Permissive
	Low	Authoritarian	Uninvolved

CHARACTERISTICS OF DIFFERENT PARENTING STYLES

Authoritative Parenting
Is accepting of child; displays frequent expressions of affection
Sets high standards for behaviour
Maintains consistent discipline and limit setting
Employs reason rather than force
Listens to child's point of view

Authoritarian Parenting
Shows little warmth; may be actively rejecting
Sets high standards for behaviour
Expects strict obedience
Uses harsh, punitive discipline
Does not listen to child's point of view

Permissive Parenting
Is highly accepting; displays frequent expressions of affection
Is undemanding with regard to child's behaviour
Has lax rules; is inconsistent about discipline
Employs reason rather than force
Encourages child to express his or her point of view

Uninvolved Parenting
Is emotionally detached; withdrawn
Is undemanding with regard to child's behaviour

Baumrind reported, and later studies have largely confirmed, that the authoritative style is associated with the most positive child outcomes (Baumrind, 1971; Parke & Buriel, 2006; Steinberg, 2001). Children of authoritative parents tend to be curious, self-confident, and well-behaved. They perform well in school, they are popular with peers, and they are responsive to parental messages. Their self-esteem is high, and their probability of engaging in deviant activities (e.g., drug use in adolescence) is low.

For Thought and Discussion

Which of Baumrind's parenting styles would you say best describes how your parents disciplined you?

The other parenting styles are linked to more negative outcomes, although in somewhat different ways. Children of authoritarian parents tend to be anxious, easily upset, and low in self-confidence. They often react with anger and aggression when frustrated, a tendency that negatively affects their relations with peers. They are at risk for conduct problems, and their performance in school is typically not equal to that of children from authoritative families. Indeed, Canadian data from the National Longitudinal Study of Children and Youth (Thomas, 2004) confirm the association between punitive parenting and aggression in children. A sample of 1,967 Canadian children was examined at age 2 to 3 years and again at age 8 to 9 years. At both ages, parenting that involved high levels of physical punishment, yelling, and scolding was associated with higher levels of defiance, anger, and physical aggression than was disciplining based more on verbal correction, explanation, and teaching alternative behaviour.

For Thought and Discussion

Why do you think punitive parenting is associated with negative outcomes?

Such correlational findings, of course, do not imply that punitive parenting causes aggressive behaviour in children (see Chapter 2 for a discussion of correlational studies and cause-and-effect conclusions). It may well be that aggressive children tend to elicit such disciplinary responses from their parents. However, the relation between punitive parenting and aggression is further underscored in this Canadian survey by the finding that if parents changed their practices over the 6-year interval of this study, children's aggression changed accordingly. Thus, if parents became more punitive, aggression increased, whereas if they became less punitive, aggression decreased (Thomas, 2004). Similar connections between punitive, hostile parenting and children's aggression have been reported by researchers in Ottawa, Montreal, and Quebec City (Romano et al., 2005; Zoccolillo et al., 2005).

Just as the pattern for authoritarian rearing (anxious, aggressive, etc.) might be predicted from knowledge of the style, so the outcomes for children of permissive parents are what we might expect. These children tend to be impulsive, immature, and disobedient. They are overly dependent on adults, they do not persist well in the face of difficulty, and they often do not do well in school. In adolescence, they show a heightened probability of various forms of rebellious, antisocial behaviour.

Finally, the uninvolved style seems to be associated with the most negative outcomes, which is not surprising given that uninvolved parents are low in both warmth and control. Children of

RESEARCH CLASSIC 15.1
PARENTING STYLES: THE WORK OF DIANA BAUMRIND

The field of child psychology has seen literally thousands of studies of parental child-rearing practices, dating back more than 100 years. Probably no entry in this long list has been more influential than a series of studies carried out by Diana Baumrind more than 40 years ago (Baumrind, 1967, 1971; Baumrind & Black, 1967).

Any researcher of child rearing must surmount at least two major challenges. One is getting accurate measures of parents' behaviour. Child rearing, after all, is something that occurs primarily in the privacy of the home, with parent and child as not only the only participants, but also often as the only witnesses. How can we learn what parents do with their children? Most researchers have solved this problem by asking parents what they do; that is, collecting self-reports of typical behaviour via either questionnaires or interviews.

Baumrind made use of parental reports in her research as well. The core of the measurement, however, came from direct observation of parent–child interactions. Trained observers visited the homes of the participants (4-year-old children and their parents) on two occasions for several hours at a time, during which they made extensive observations of the interactions between the parents and the child. The visits extended from about an hour before dinner until the child's bedtime, a time deliberately selected because, in the researchers' words, it is a "period commonly known to produce instances of parent–child divergence." Certainly anyone who has been a parent of a preschooler can relate to this assertion.

Several hours of detailed observation of family interactions yield a wealth of information about both parent and child behaviours. A second challenge in child-rearing research is to make sense of all this information—to abstract general principles and processes from the hundreds of specific interchanges between parent and child. Drawing partly from theory and partly from past research, Baumrind identified 15 "clusters" of parental behaviour, that is, sets of interrelated behaviours that appeared to capture important dimensions of child rearing and important differences among parents. Examples of the clusters include Directive versus Non-directive, Firm versus Lax Enforcement Policy, Encourages versus Discourages Independence, and Expresses Punitive versus Nurturant Behaviour.

The next step was to determine whether the clusters—which themselves were composites of numerous specific behaviours—could be organized into larger, more general categories. Baumrind's answer was yes, and this aspect of the work yielded two conclusions that have affected the study of child rearing ever since. One was the identification of the three general styles of child rearing that we described previously: authoritative, authoritarian, and permissive (the uninvolved category was a later addition). The second—made possible by the inclusion of a battery of child outcome measures—was a demonstration of the effects of the different styles. Baumrind reported that the authoritative style was consistently associated with the most positive child outcomes.

Since the original studies, Baumrind's approach to conceptualizing child rearing has proven informative across a range of ages, measurement techniques, and cultural groups. As the text indicates, however, the extension of the approach to different groups has sometimes resulted in conclusions different from those that held for the Caucasian middle-income families that made up Baumrind's sample. It is worth noting that Baumrind herself anticipated such variation. Indeed, she was the first to demonstrate that a particular parental style could have a different meaning in different cultural groups.

uninvolved parents often form insecure attachments in infancy, they show low social and academic competence as they develop, and they are at heightened risk for substance abuse and delinquency in adolescence. At the extreme, the uninvolved style becomes neglect, a form of child abuse associated with a range of negative outcomes.

We should qualify these conclusions in two ways. First, these are on-the-average findings, and as such, they do not apply to every child. Not all instances of authoritative rearing lead to positive outcomes, and children whose parents exhibit one of the other styles are certainly not doomed to failure. Many such children turn out fine.

The second qualification is that effects of the different styles may vary across groups. We consider this issue next.

ETHNIC AND CULTURAL DIFFERENCES

Most of the research just summarized was with Caucasian, predominantly middle-income families. Extension of the approach to other populations reveals both some similarities and some important differences.

Perhaps the clearest findings involve the authoritative and authoritarian styles. The authoritative style has been shown to be beneficial across a range of different populations. These include Canadian children (Thomas, 2004) and subgroups within the United States, such as African American, Hispanic American, and Asian American samples (Brody & Flor, 1998; Glasgow et al., 1997; Steinberg et al., 1991). They also include samples from other countries such as China (Chen et al., 2011) and India (Pinto, Folkers, & Sines, 1991). On the other hand, the benefits of authoritative rearing—and the superiority of this style to other methods of child rearing—are often smaller or less consistent in populations other than middle-income Western Caucasians. In some instances, they vary for different members of the same ethnic group. For example, authoritative rearing appears to be generally beneficial for adolescents from second-generation Chinese American families. For first-generation families, however, few benefits are evident (Chao, 2001).

In many cultures, great emphasis is placed on family unity and respect for elders. What implications might this have for research on the effects of different parenting styles? (© *Alex Mares-Manton/Asia Images/Corbis*)

Conclusions regarding authoritarian rearing change in two ways when a wider range of settings and populations are taken into account. One concerns frequency: in many groups, the authoritarian pattern is more common than in Caucasian samples. This is true for African American and Asian American samples in the United States, as well as for samples of Chinese parents and children (Greenberger & Chen, 1996; Parke & Buriel, 2006). Two factors—either alone or in combination—appear to account for this finding. One is cultural beliefs and values. In China, for example, family unity and respect for elders are central goals of socialization, and parental concern for children is expressed more through close supervision and frequent teaching than through displays of overt affection (Chao & Tseng, 2002). Many Black families within the United States share a similar emphasis on communal values, respect for parents and other adults, and close control of children's activities (Parke & Buriel, 2006).

The other factor is economic and personal necessity. For families living in dangerous neighbourhoods and under conditions of poverty, reasoning with the child and encouraging independence may be risky luxuries. Firm and immediate control may be a higher priority for parents in such circumstances—and may, in fact, make more sense for the overall well-being of the child (Furstenberg, 1993).

This last point suggests that in some contexts, the authoritarian style might actually be beneficial for children's development. And this leads to the second way in which conclusions about authoritarian rearing have been found to vary across groups. Although an extreme standing on this dimension is probably not optimal in any context, authoritarian rearing does, indeed, have beneficial—or at least not clearly detrimental—effects in some contexts. This is the case, for example, for many African American samples within the United States (Dodge et al., 2006; Lamborn, Dornbusch, & Steinberg, 1996), as well as for Chinese families in China and Chinese American families in the United States (Chao & Tseng, 2002). It is also at least sometimes the case for families living in poverty (Baldwin, Baldwin, & Cole, 1990).

What these differences suggest is that the meaning of a particular parental style cannot be defined solely in terms of objective attributes, such as amount of physical discipline or expressions of overt affection. The meaning, rather, lies in how the parents' practices are interpreted by the child, which in turn depends on the overall cultural context within which they occur. One Asian American student makes this point when talking about the firm and at times even punitive control that characterizes his culture's parenting: "That's how we know our parents love us" (Bronfenbrenner, 1993, p. 39).

THE ROLE OF FATHERS

Our discussions to this point have been of "parents," but in fact, most of the research has concentrated on mothers. There are theoretical reasons for this emphasis in that the theories that have guided socialization research have stressed the mother. There are also pragmatic reasons—mothers, in fact, have typically been more involved in early child care than fathers.

But this is not to say, of course, that fathers are unimportant to children's lives. In recent years, fathers have assumed an increased role in children's care, in part because of social changes in Canada and the United States that have resulted in more mothers entering the workforce. There are now almost as many Canadian women in the workforce as men, and over the past 30 years, married Canadian men have taken on a greater share of household and childcare duties (Marshall, 2006). In a parallel fashion, research interest in the role of fathers in children's development has also increased over this period (Lamb, 2010).

Fathers' interactions with their children, especially with boys, tend to centre on physical play. *(PhotoDisc, Inc.)*

How do mothers and fathers typically compare in their caregiving activities? Any summary must be prefaced by the acknowledgment that there are wide variations across families and no single pattern is going to characterize all fathers. In general, however, fathers—despite their increased involvement in recent years—devote less time to child care than do mothers (Marshall, 2006). Furthermore, the time that they do spend tends to be distributed differently. Although research suggests that most fathers are as skilled and sensitive in performing basic caregiving activities (e.g., feeding, diapering, putting to bed) as are mothers (Lamb & Lewis, 2010), most fathers do not, in fact, engage in such activities as often as women. Instead, fathers' interactions with their children more often centre on physical stimulation and play, especially with boys (Lamb & Lewis, 2010; Parke & Buriel, 2006). This emphasis emerges early in infancy and continues through childhood (Russell & Russell, 1987).

Links to Related Material

In Chapter 12 you read about young children's attachment to their fathers. In Chapter 16 you will read about fathers' attitudes about gender. Here, you learn more about the role of fathers in children's lives.

We should add, however, that the pattern is not universal. Although father as play partner is a common role across many cultures (Lamb & Lewis, 2010), there are exceptions. In Sweden, for example, there are few mother–father differences in the tendency to engage children in play (Lamb et al., 1982), and the same is true for Israeli kibbutz families (Sagi et al., 1985). In both instances, the society's egalitarian political views may account for the similarity in parental roles (although with definite limitations—mothers still perform most of the basic caregiving activities).

What fathers do with their children is one of the questions of interest in research on the fathers' role in their children's lives. The other question is what effects these paternal behaviours have. What do we know about fathers' contribution to children's development?

Some of the things we know are discussed in other chapters. In Chapter 16, we will see that fathers, on average, seem to hold stronger views about gender-appropriate behaviour than do mothers, and are more likely to treat boys and girls in ways that might promote sex differences in development. In Chapter 12, we saw that fathers as well as mothers can serve as attachment figures for infants. Most babies with a father in the home become attached to their fathers, and the probability of a secure attachment is as great with the father as with the mother (Grossmann et al., 2008). Furthermore, as we discuss more fully later in the chapter, secure attachment to the father is predictive of later positive outcomes in much the same way as is secure attachment to the mother.

As children develop, many fathers (as well as mothers) also play important roles in promoting and managing their relations with peers, arranging and supervising contacts, offering support and advice concerning conflict, and so on (Ladd & Pettit, 2002; Pleck 2010). (We discuss how parents manage their children's peer interactions later in the chapter.) Fathers have also been found to make an important contribution to their toddlers' and preschoolers' intellectual growth and language development through reading to them and engaging them in conversations (Pancsofar et al., 2010). Moreover, recent longitudinal Canadian research shows that fathers' use of positive forms of parental control with their preschool-age children is predictive of the children's better cognitive and behavioural functioning more than six years later (Pougnet, Serbin, Stack, & Schwartzman, 2011). And we saw in Chapter 13 that fathers also contribute to children's school performance: warmth and support from fathers play a positive role in children's academic self-concept and contribute to their school success (Kim & Chung, 2003; Schaffer & Blatt, 1990).

How do children's relationships with their father compare to their relationships with their mother? Some children have closer, more satisfactory, or more intense relations with one parent than with the other (Collins & Russell, 1991; Russell, Mize, & Bissaker, 2002). In the majority of cases, however, relations with the two parents—for both sons and daughters—are more alike than different (Lamb, 2010).

Research on parenting styles finds similar effects for both mothers and fathers. In general, the attributes that characterize successful parenting for fathers turn out to be the same as those that are important for mothers—namely, a warm and involved relationship with the child, firm but not punitive control, and frequent use of verbal reasoning. Thus, just as for mothers, the authoritative style of parenting appears most adaptive for fathers' socialization of their children (Marsiglio et al., 2000; Pleck, 2010).

For Thought and Discussion

Do you think that children raised by their fathers develop differently from those raised by their mothers?

THE CHILD'S CONTRIBUTION

Parenting style may lead to particular outcomes in children. But the reverse is also possible: characteristics of the child can influence parenting style. Beginning with a classic paper by Richard Bell (1968), researchers have been increasingly interested in how characteristics of the child can influence parents' behaviour. Perhaps the clearest example comes from the work on temperament discussed in Chapter 12. As we saw, infants enter the world with somewhat different temperaments, including variations along dimensions (e.g., irritability, emotionality, sociability) that could clearly affect the ways parents interact with them. Although the relationship between temperament and parent behaviour is often complex (Bates & Pettit, 2007), temperamental characteristics do appear to affect parental behaviour (Parke & Buriel, 2006; Putnam, Sanson, & Rothbart, 2002). Infants with difficult temperaments, for example, receive more total caregiving time in the early months of life than do other infants, presumably because their characteristics force attention in a way that those of easier-to-handle babies do not (Crockenberg, 1986). This changes, however, and by the second half of the first year, difficult infants receive less soothing and less maternal involvement, likely because their mothers have too often found their efforts to be frustrating and unrewarding (van den Boom & Hoeksma, 1994). Other temperamental dimensions have also been shown to have predictable effects on parental behaviour—activity level, for example, or inhibition/timidity (Kochanska et al., 2007).

Some parents adapt more successfully than others to the child's characteristics, described in Chapter 12 as the idea of goodness of fit. Development proceeds most successfully when parents are able to match their caregiving practices to the nature and needs of the child (Laible & Thompson, 2007). For example, early difficult temperament is moderately predictive both of continued difficult temperament and of various behavioural problems in later childhood (Gallagher, 2002). However, parental response to the difficult temperament plays a role in later outcomes. Some parents are successful at gradually moderating their child's problematic attributes, whereas others respond to

Links to Related Material

In Chapter 12, you read about infant temperament. Here, you learn more about how different dimensions of child temperament affect the parenting that children receive.

the child in ways that perpetuate or even aggravate the difficulties. Note the transactional nature of the developmental process: characteristics of the child elicit particular behaviours from the parent; these parental behaviours, in turn, alter characteristics of the child; the child then brings a somewhat different set of characteristics to future socialization encounters with the parent; and so on throughout development.

As the point just made suggests, effects of children's characteristics on parental behaviour are not limited to the early years or to inborn temperamental qualities. Child effects are a pervasive finding across a range of ages and socialization contexts. For example, children who display committed compliance (see Chapter 13) are likely to receive milder and more verbal forms of discipline than are children whose compliance is more of the forced, situational sort (Kochanska, 1997a). As Leon Kuczynski of the University of Guelph and Grazyna Kochanska (1995) point out, children who resist maternal requests elicit stronger demands and more restrictions from the mother than do children who are easier to control. Adolescents who engage in antisocial behaviour receive harsher forms of parental discipline than do adolescents who are better behaved (Neiderhiser et al., 1999).

Having stressed effects of the child on the parent, we should add that the fact that children can affect their parents does not mean that parent and child play equal roles or have equal impact in most socialization exchanges (Maccoby, 2002). Nor, of course, does it mean that parent–child correlations are due solely to the effects of the child. But it does indicate the need for caution in interpreting any simple correlation between parental practices and children's development.

LEARNING OBJECTIVE 15.2

Analyze the influence of parents and other family members on childhood socialization.

1. What are four major parenting styles that have been identified?
2. What are the different outcomes associated with these styles of parenting?
3. To what extent do fathers play a role in parenting?
4. What is the child's contribution to the socialization process?

Learning Objective 15.3

Analyze the ways that families function as a social system.

THE FAMILY AS A SYSTEM

Determining what mothers or fathers do is important, but a sole focus on one or even both parents provides an incomplete picture of life in the family, for several reasons. Most obviously, most families contain more members than a child and two parents, such as siblings, perhaps grandparents, and other family members as well. Furthermore, the impact of the characteristics and behaviours of any one family member can depend on the family system as a whole. For example, parenting practices take a somewhat different form and have different effects when conflict between parents is high than when parental relations are more harmonious. Similarly, a parent's behaviour toward a firstborn child typically changes in predictable (and, from the child's point of view, not desirable) ways when a second child arrives on the scene. Finally, not all families fit the two-parent, two-child nuclear family mould. Families come in many forms, and the different forms can have definite effects on how children develop.

In this section of the chapter, we consider aspects of family life that are not captured when the focus is on parenting practices alone. We begin with a consideration of the role of siblings in children's development.

SIBLINGS

In Canada, the United States, and Europe, approximately 80 percent of children have siblings; most spend more time with their siblings than with their parents; and for many, relationships with siblings will be the longest-lasting relationships they will ever have (Dunn, 2007; Howe, Ross, & Recchia, 2011). What do we know about sibling relations and their possible effects on other aspects of development?

RELATIONS AMONG SIBLINGS One thing we know is that sibling relations come in many forms. Some of the variations are obvious and objective. Any child is either the older or the younger member of a sibling dyad. Siblings can be the same gender or different genders. They can be close in age or widely separated. And they can number only two or perhaps a dozen. The former, however, is a good deal more likely in Canada than the latter (Statistics Canada, 2006). Indeed, only 6 percent of North American families have four or more children (Fields & Casper, 2001). Growing up with lots of siblings is a less common experience than it once was.

More important, however, are variations in *quality* of the sibling relationship—variations that are only weakly predicted by such characteristics as age spacing or gender composition. Siblings spend more time in one another's company than with parents or even peers, and come to know one another well (Dunn, 2007). Such proximity can have both positive and negative ramifications: it can result in mutual support, but also in conflict (Howe et al., 2011). There is considerable variability in the closeness of sibling relationships from family to family. Judy Dunn, a leading researcher of sibling relations, summarizes the differences as follows:

> Some siblings describe their affections and interest in their siblings vividly in interviews and show cooperation, insight, and empathy in most of their interactions. Others describe their feelings of irritation, hostility, and dislike and show this hostility and aggression in their interactions with their siblings. Others show and describe their *ambivalent* feelings" (Dunn, 2007, p. 310).

What causes such striking variations? As is true for many aspects of development, temperament plays a role. Siblings typically get along best when they have similar temperaments—for example, both are active and outgoing (Brody, 1996). Because temperament is only moderately heritable, however, many siblings will, in fact, not have similar temperaments. Furthermore, a difficult temperament for either member of a sibling pair is predictive of eventual difficulties in their relationship (Brody, Stoneman, & McCoy, 1994).

Parents are also important. The same qualities that make up successful parenting in general—warmth, reasoning, firm but non-punitive control—also enhance the probability of positive relations among siblings (Brody, 1998; Furman & Lanthier, 2002). The parents' own relationship can contribute as well. Positive relations among siblings are most likely when the parents' relationship is positive (although siblings may also provide important support for one another when there is conflict between parents) (Dunn, 2007). General parenting practices are not the only way parents can affect sibling relations. Also important is the *equality* of parenting (Howe et al., 2011). One predictor of difficulty in sibling relationships is differential treatment by parents; that is, one sibling's receiving overall more attention, more affection, weaker discipline, and so forth than the other (Dunn, 2002; Furman & Lanthier, 2002). This may happen (or at least children may feel that it happens) fairly frequently, with as many as one in two children reporting that their parents don't treat them the same as their siblings (Howe & Recchia, 2008). What seems to be especially important, however, is not so much the *existence* of differential treatment, but the child's *interpretation* of the treatment (Kowal & Kramer, 1997; Kowal et al., 2002). Difficulties in the sibling relation are most likely when children both perceive that they are being treated unequally and regard the differential treatment as unfair (Howe & Recchia, 2008).

For Thought and Discussion

Can you think of situations where children might not perceive differential treatment by their parents as unfair? Why do you think the child's interpretation of the treatment is so important?

CHANGES WITH DEVELOPMENT For the first child in a family, sibling relations begin with the birth of a second child. As Canadian researchers Nina Howe, Hildy Ross, and Holly Recchia (2011) point out, the arrival of a new sibling is often greeted both positively and negatively by the firstborn. Many firstborns display interest and affection toward the new family member; however, this interest may be mixed with negative feelings, especially if the firstborn is very young. The addition of a new sibling is usually accompanied by a decline in both the amount and the positiveness of mother–child interaction for the firstborn (Baydar, Greek, & Brooks-Gunn, 1997). This loss of attention often precipitates an increase in behaviour problems for the older child. We can see here

Sibling rivalry Feelings of competition resentment and jealousy that can arise between siblings.

the beginnings of what is sometimes regarded as the most worrisome aspect of sibling relations: the existence of **sibling rivalry**, or negative, competitive feelings between two or more siblings.

Links to Related Material

In Chapter 12 you read about the emergence of self-conscious emotions, including jealousy, in the second year of life. Here you read about one manifestation of jealousy in children—sibling rivalry.

Usually, the strong negative reaction lasts only a few months, however, and, as Howe and Recchia (2008) note, there are a number of actions parents take to help reduce its severity. Many parents attempt to prepare the older child for the new sibling's arrival through such activities as reading the older child stories about babies, involving the older sibling in the preparation of the nursery, making contact with families who already have a younger sibling, and so on. Some parents also find it helpful to allow the older sibling to help out with some of the care for the new infant. Ensuring that the older child continues to receive attention, perhaps special attention from the father, can also be valuable (Howe & Recchia, 2008). Finally, close friendships can sometimes help mitigate the intensity of negative feelings, presumably because they provide an opportunity to discuss the older sibling's feelings about the situation with a friend (Dunn, 2004). Nevertheless, in some cases the rivalry continues beyond this initial period of adjustment (Howe & Recchia, 2008).

Initially, a new sibling has little to offer to an older child in the family. By about 1 year of age, however, the younger sibling begins to present possibilities as a play partner, and by the time a baby brother or sister reaches age 2 or 3, most siblings are spending considerable amounts of time together. These interactions tend to be marked by strong expressions of emotion on both sides of the sibling pair, with the balance of positive and negative emotions varying markedly across dyads. As a result, conflict is common, with an average of eight (albeit often minor) skirmishes per hour in young siblings (Howe et al., 2011). In fact, Dunn (1993) reports one case in which a sibling pair produced 56 conflicts in an hour! In most cases, however, such conflict is a normal part of sibling relationships, and may even be useful in teaching children conflict-resolution skills (Howe & Recchia, 2008).

Both cooperation and conflict are frequent components of sibling interaction. (© *Judy Barranco/iStock;* © *Tatiana Gladskikh/iStock)*

As they develop, interactions between siblings change in various ways (Brody, 1996). Interactions become less physical and more verbal, and they also become more wide-ranging in their topics and concerns. In addition to serving as play partners, siblings begin to perform various other roles for each other. They can be sources of support in times of stress, as well as sources of advice or information when some problem arises. They provide help with school work, and they consult each other on family issues and other personal matters (Tucker, McHale, & Crouter, 2001). Typically, the provision of information or support flows from older to younger, but this is not always the case, especially as children grow older (Howe et al., 2011).

For Thought and Discussion

Was there sibling rivalry in your family? What impact do you think birth order had on your development?

As children develop, there are changes in the balance or symmetry of their interactions. Initially, older siblings take the lead in most dealings with their younger siblings, initiating both more positive and more negative actions, and generally directing the course of the interaction. Younger siblings, in turn, are more likely to give in to and to imitate their older partner (Teti, 1992).

Such asymmetry lessens with age, and by adolescence the relations between siblings are typically more egalitarian. Now the younger sibling may sometimes be the dominant member, and can even be the one who provides nurturance or help (Buhrmester & Furman, 1990).

Another change that is evident by adolescence is a decline in the relative importance of siblings as sources of intimacy or help. As we will see, by adolescence, friends are more likely to play these roles, and children thus have less need to turn to their siblings for support (Buhrmester & Furman, 1990).

EFFECTS OF SIBLINGS Siblings spend thousands of hours together as they grow up, they imitate each other frequently from early in life (Abramovitch, Corter, & Pepler, 1980), and they eventually exchange information and opinions (often conflicting ones!) on dozens of different issues. There are probably few aspects of development that are not potentially affected by growing up with siblings.

The presence of siblings in a family can have important cognitive benefits. Sibling interactions are a frequent context for teasing, tricks, and sharing of emotions. It is no surprise, therefore, that such interactions can help children learn about other minds and how they can differ from their own. Indeed, growing up with siblings—perhaps especially older siblings—is associated with accelerated development of various theory-of-mind skills, which are a natural by-product of the kinds of interactions in which siblings engage (Dunn 2007; Kavanaugh, 2006).

Links to Related Material

In Chapter 8, you read about the development of theory of mind. Here, you learn more about how sibling interactions can improve a child's theory-of-mind skills.

Siblings can also be effective teachers of each other. Indeed, research suggests that siblings may be both more likely to teach and more skillful in teaching a younger child in need than are peers, even peers who are older (Howe & Recchia, 2008). Many parents capitalize on this fact by entrusting an older child to convey a household chore or a social expectation (e.g., how to behave in church, what to say when Grandma gives you a gift) to a younger brother or sister.

Siblings can also affect aspects of one another's social development. The topic of gender-role development provides one obvious example. Siblings, especially those who are older, are both models of gender-role behaviour and potential agents of reinforcement or punishment for behaviours they see in their siblings. As we will see in Chapter 16, siblings do have an effect; in general (with some exceptions and complications), same-sex older siblings promote gender-typical behaviour and opposite-sex siblings make counter-stereotypical behaviour more likely (McHale et al., 2001, 2003; Rust et al., 2000). Likewise, as we will discuss later in the chapter, interactions with siblings have implications for the development of social skills important in relationships with peers (Howe et al., 2011).

One more point is worth noting: millions of children in a large number of cultures around the world receive much of their early care and socialization from older siblings (Zukow-Goldring, 2002). And of course, the older siblings are themselves socialized by the adults of the community for the role of caregiver—a prime example of the guided participation model of cultural transmission stressed in the sociocultural approach to development.

GRANDPARENTS AND OTHER FAMILY MEMBERS

In Canada, almost half a million children live in a home with one or more grandparents—in most instances, with one or more parents as well (Statistics Canada, 2003). In more than 12 percent of these families, however, the grandparent is the only caregiver (Statistics Canada, 2007a). Millions of other children, of course, make visits to and receive visits from grandparents, and surveys indicate that such contacts are moderately frequent in a majority of cases (Smith & Drew, 2002). The majority of older Canadians have grandchildren, and for some, being a grandparent is central in their lives (Rosenthal & Gladstone, 2000).

Grandparents can play many roles in their grandchildren's lives. They can be a source of emotional or financial support for the parents, and they can be mentors, playmates, babysitters, or substitute parents for grandchildren (Rosenthal & Gladstone, 2000). How involved grandparents are in their grandchildren's lives depends on a number of factors. One such factor is family structure. In families with two parents, grandparents tend to stay more in the background and have less direct involvement with the grandchildren. When one parent is absent, however, the role of grandparents generally increases, and children similarly report an increased closeness to them. When there is no parent present, as is the case for more than 65,000 Canadian children (Statistics Canada, 2007a), the role of the grandparent is obviously maximal.

Another factor is gender. On average, grandmothers are more involved in and derive more satisfaction from the grandparent role than do grandfathers (Creasey & Koblewski, 1991; Somary & Stricker, 1998). Research on whether, and how, grandparenting varies as a function of gender of child or age of child has yet to yield consistent results (Smith & Drew, 2002). Such research, however, does reveal expected changes with age in how children perceive their grandparents, from a view of the grandparent as a dispenser of gifts or treats in early childhood to an emphasis on companionship and support by late childhood and adolescence.

One situation in which the presence of a grandmother can be very important is that of teenage motherhood. Co-residence of daughter and mother becomes more likely when a new baby arrives, and a grandmother in the home can be a source of both expertise and welcome hands-on help (Stevens, 1984). Having a grandmother present is not always a benefit, however. In some cases the presence of her own mother can interfere with the new mother's becoming comfortable and effective in the parenting role, with detrimental effects on both her parenting skills and the child's development (Moore & Brooks-Gunn, 2002).

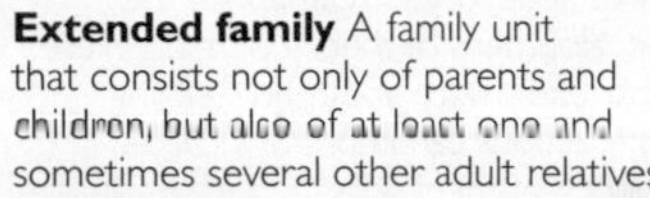
Extended family A family unit that consists not only of parents and children, but also of at least one and sometimes several other adult relatives.

There are some cultures in which the presence of grandparents in the home is a good deal more typical than is the case for Caucasian Canadian and Caucasian American families. In China, for example, three-generation households are common (Shu, 1999), and the same is true for Black families in the United States (Parke & Buriel, 2006). More generally, in many cultures, the modal family pattern is not the nuclear family but the **extended family**; that is, a family unit that consists not only of children and parents, but also of at least one and often several other adult relatives. The extended family is a legacy of family patterns in Asia and Africa, where newly married couples often join one of the parents' households rather than starting a household of their own.

In many cultures, the extended family is a common—and often beneficial—arrangement. (*Blend Images/Media Bakery*)

As we would expect of any long-established cultural tradition, the extended family is associated with beneficial effects in cultures in which it is the norm. The extended family structure has been shown to provide social and financial support to members of the younger generation, to facilitate the transmission of cultural history and values, and to reduce the probability of negative developmental outcomes (Taylor, Casten, & Flickinger, 1993; Wilson, 1995).

DIVORCE

Divorce is an increasing reality in the lives of many children. The number of divorces in Canada began rising in the early 1970s, and peaked in 1987 following changes to the Divorce Act that allowed for divorce after only one year of separation. Divorce rates have remained high in Canada, and, at present, more than 38 percent of Canadian marriages end in divorce (Statistics Canada, 2005). (Figure 15.1 shows the number of divorces in Canada from 1969 to 2003.) Although this figure may appear discouraging, it is substantially less than the 50 percent divorce rate frequently reported for American marriages (Hetherington & Stanley-Hagan, 2002). Furthermore, this same figure viewed from the other direction also indicates that more than 60 percent of Canadian marriages do *not* end in divorce. Nevertheless, about 30 percent of children in Canada experience the effects of divorce (Wu & Schimmele, 2009).

Because much of what is known about the effects of divorce is negative, we should begin with two qualifications. First, the findings to be discussed are on-the-average outcomes that do not apply to every child. Not all children are negatively affected by divorce, and the effects that do occur vary in severity across different children. Indeed, following an initial period of difficulty, most children do adapt to their new circumstances (Emery, 2004; Wu & Schimmele, 2009).

FIGURE 15.1

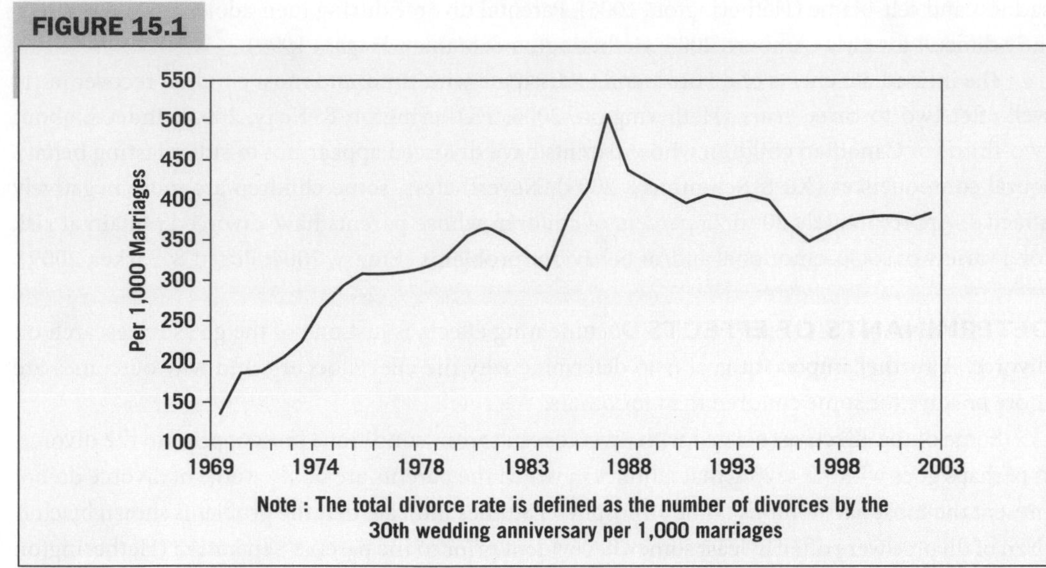

Number of divorces in Canada from 1969 to 2003. The divorce rate increased through the 1970s, reaching its peak in 1987 following changes to the Divorce Act. It has levelled off at around 38 percent, where it has remained for a number of years. *From Wu, Z. & Schimmele, C. (2009). Divorce and repartnering. In M. Baker (Ed.),* Families: Changing trends in Canada. *Toronto, ON: McGraw-Hill Ryerson, Figure 8.1, p. 159.*

Second, evaluations of the negative consequences of divorce must be placed in the context of the alternative, which, in many cases, is for parents to stay together in an unhappy marriage with daily conflict in the home. Experts disagree with regard to the extent to which an unhappy marriage should be preserved for the sake of the children (Hetherington & Kelly, 2002; Wallerstein, Lewis, & Blakeslee, 2000). In fact, negative effects have also been found for marriages that, although intact, are high in conflict (Amato, 2006). Thus, in some instances, divorce may be the better of two unfortunate alternatives.

EFFECTS OF DIVORCE On average, children whose parents have divorced do not fare as well as those who come from intact families. Negative outcomes have been found across many aspects of development (Amato, 2006; Pruett & Barker, 2009).

Effects are generally most evident in the time period immediately following the divorce. The first year or so following a divorce is especially a time of heightened anxiety, depression, and parent–child conflict. The life changes that typically follow divorce, including increased loneliness, task overload, and financial stress, pose significant challenges for competent parenting (Weinraub, Horvath, & Gringlas, 2002). Often, both child and parent struggle to adjust to new and stressful circumstances, and the negative reactions of each can affect the other in a cyclical, escalating fashion. Moreover, the conflict between parents often spills over into the parent–child relationship, impacting negatively on the quality of parents' relations with their children (Amato, 2006; Hetherington, 2006).

The immediate effects of divorce vary to some extent as a function of both the age and the gender of the child. Preschool-age children are in some ways especially vulnerable because they lack the cognitive resources necessary to understand the reasons for the divorce, and may assume that they themselves were somehow to blame (Amato, 2006). Fears of abandonment and worry about the safety of the absent parent are among the more common effects seen in preschoolers (Wallerstein, 2008). In elementary-school-age children, declines in academic performance and increases in aggressive behaviour, especially among boys, are frequently reported (Amato, 2006). In adolescence, negative effects may include a heightened probability of premature sexual activity, substance abuse, and school dropout or delinquent behaviours (Hetherington & Clingempeel, 1992; Pruett & Barker, 2009).

Thus, each segment of the developmental span presents its own vulnerabilities. Furthermore, boys and girls may react in different ways. Boys are typically more impacted by divorce than are girls, at least in terms of overt effects such as increased aggression and defiant behaviour (Pruett & Barker 2009). Girls, however, may be more vulnerable to effects of an internalizing sort, such as sadness and self-blame (Hetherington, 2006). Parental divorce during their adolescence is particularly difficult for girls (Ambert, 2005; Hetherington & Stanley-Hagan, 1999).

The immediate effects of divorce tend to dissipate with time, and most children recover fairly well after two to three years (Hetherington, 2006; Hetherington & Kelly, 2002). Indeed, about two-thirds of Canadian children whose parents have divorced appear not to suffer lasting behavioural consequences (Xu & Schimmele, 2009). Nevertheless, some children are more negatively affected. Approximately 20 to 25 percent of children whose parents have divorced remain at risk for a variety of socio-emotional and/or behaviour problems (Emery, 2004; Pruett & Barker, 2009).

DETERMINANTS OF EFFECTS Documenting effects is just one of the goals in research on divorce. A further important goal is to determine why the effects occur—and why outcomes are more positive for some children than for others.

Some of the effects associated with divorce result from conditions present prior to the divorce. It perhaps goes without saying that families in which the parents are on the verge of divorce do not present the most harmonious home atmosphere. Studies indicate that the problems shown by children of divorce were often at least somewhat evident prior to the parents' separation (Hetherington & Stanley-Hagan, 2002).

Changes in the child's experiences following the divorce are also important. Most obviously, one of the parents with whom the child has lived his or her entire life (typically the father) is no longer in the home, and thus a source of affection and support is no longer so readily available. In many cases, the family's economic situation worsens appreciably, and the financial circumstances put additional stress on a mother who is now trying to cope with the role of single parent. Often, the mother's parenting practices become harsher and less consistent, with predictable negative effects on the children's behaviour (Hetherington & Kelly, 2002). More positively, when mothers are able to maintain an authoritative style of parenting, their children are more likely to adapt successfully following divorce (Wolchik et al., 2000).

The father's behaviour is also important. Sheer amount of time with the father does not appear to be critical, but the quality of the time is (Pruett & Barker, 2009). As we would expect, children generally adjust most successfully when the relationship with the father is warm and supportive (Amato & Gilbreth, 1999; Whiteside & Becker, 2000).

Thirty years ago, mother-only custody was the outcome for almost 80 percent of divorces in Canada. Since then, the number has dropped to around 50 percent, while shared parenting (also known as joint custody) has become increasingly common (Kruk, 2008; Statistics Canada, 2007a). Shared parenting arrangements typically entail equally shared rights and responsibilities by the two parents, although the children do not necessarily reside for equal periods of time in each parent's home. In fact, arrangements where children live half of the time with each parent are not frequent in Canada, occurring in about 6 to 12 percent of divorces (Wu & Schimmele, 2009). At least for younger children, primary residence with the mother and frequent time spent with the father is the most common arrangement, occurring in slightly more than 80 percent of Canadian divorces (Wu & Schimmele, 2009). Such arrangements often change, however, as the child grows older and as more time has passed since the separation (Wu & Schimmele, 2009).

For Thought and Discussion

Why do you think completely shared living arrangements following divorce, where a child spends half of the time with each parent, are not that common in Canada? What might be some advantages and disadvantages of such an arrangement? Why might the child's age be important to consider?

Shared parenting arrangements allow children to experience continued contact with their father, which, in all but a very few cases, has been found to be beneficial to children's adjustment (Bauserman, 2002; Juby, Billette, Laplante, & Le Bourdais, 2007). As with any post-divorce arrangement, the success of shared parenting depends on how committed and effective each parent is in the parenting role, as well as how successfully the parents are able to work together. Although not all fathers maintain contact with their children following divorce, the percentage of fathers who do so has increased considerably over the past 30 years (Amato & Dorius, 2010). Almost half of divorced Canadian dads maintain regular contact with their children, seeing them on a weekly or biweekly basis. Another 32 percent maintain some contact, albeit on a less regular basis, while 19 percent have no direct contact at all (although they may maintain some telephone or mail contact) (Juby et al., 2007). Factors that are positively related to the father's continued contact with his children include his income, education, religiosity, and a cooperative relationship with the children's mother (Amato & Dorius, 2010). Factors associated with reduced father contact include remarriage by either parent, especially if the remarriage occurs shortly after the divorce and if the father is in a new marriage that produces children (Amato & Dorius, 2010). Fathers who establish close connections with their children in the period immediately following separation are likely to remain closely involved, both emotionally and financially, with their children as they grow up (Juby et al, 2007).

REMARRIAGE Approximately 75 percent of divorced parents eventually remarry (although, unfortunately, the incidence of divorce in these marriages is even higher than in first marriages) (Browning & Bray, 2009; Hetherington & Stanley-Hagan, 2002). As a consequence, more than one-third of Canadian children whose parents have divorced experience the introduction of a new step-parent into their lives within two years of their parents' separation; within seven years of the separation, three-quarters of Canadian children have been introduced to one or more new step-parents (Juby, Le Bourdais, & Marcil-Gratton, 2005). The addition of a step-parent to the child's life brings both challenges and opportunities. When both parents bring children to the new marriage, then there are step-siblings as well, and still more new challenges. The conjunction of two families to form a new one is referred to as a **blended family**.

Blended family A new family unit resulting from remarriage that consists of parents and children from previously separate families.

Initially, adjustment to the new family situation following remarriage is often shaky for both child and step-parent. This is especially true during early adolescence (a shaky time in general for parenting!) and for girls' adjustment to a stepfather (Hetherington & Stanley-Hagan, 2002). Boys are more likely to adjust favourably to a stepfather, presumably because they perceive less threat to their relationship with the mother than do girls.

Because the majority of children reside principally with their mother, less is known about the effects of a new stepmother in the home (Juby et al., 2005). Studies indicate, however, that this situation can also be difficult. As with stepfathers, however, initial difficulties are often, although not always, smoothed out with time (Hetherington & Stanley-Hagan, 2002). Important in both cases is the relationship between the newly married parents.

Despite the difficulties just noted, step-parents can be a wonderful addition to the lives of children who have experienced a divorce. Especially when step-parents are involved with the children and skillful in their parenting efforts, positive effects on family life and children's development are evident (Hetherington, 2006; Hetherington & Stanley-Hagan, 2002). Unfortunately, step-parents, on average, are less involved and less skillful than parents in general; thus, not all children reap these potential benefits.

ALTERNATIVE FAMILY COMPOSITIONS

We have already touched on some of the many forms that families can take. Children can grow up with two parents, just one, or none. In the case of divorce and blended families, they may eventually have more than two parents, with step-parents joining their lives in addition to the biological parents. The number of siblings in the home can vary from zero to many, and this, too, may change if the child becomes part of a blended family. Finally, the child may grow up as part of an extended family, with anywhere from one to perhaps half a dozen or so grandparents, aunts, and uncles as part of the family unit.

In this section, we consider three further variations in family composition: single parents who have never married, families created through adoption, and families with gay or lesbian parents.

SINGLE PARENTS WHO HAVE NEVER MARRIED Single-parent families have become more common over the past few decades, accounting for 15.9 percent of all Canadian families in the 2006 census (Statistics Canada, 2007a). Forty years ago, divorce and separation accounted for almost all children in single-parent homes. Over the years, this number has declined considerably, while the number of children living in single-parent families headed by a never-married parent has increased (Weinraub et al., 2002).

Adolescent parents (usually mothers) are among the most disadvantaged of single parents. Births to teenagers in both Canada and the United States have declined significantly over the last 25 years (Dryburgh, 2000; Martin et al., 2002). Nevertheless, recent data reveal over 14,000 births per year to Canadian teenager mothers (Statistics Canada, 2007). Most teens who give birth keep their babies (Leadbeater & Way, 2001), and as many as 79 percent of all teenage mothers are not married. Teenage mothers are more likely than other parents to come from poor families, to have low educational backgrounds, and to live in impoverished neighbourhoods (Leadbeater & Way, 2001). They have frequently attended poor-quality schools and suffered from school failure. They are more likely to drop out of school than other teens, and their life circumstances often limit their ability to become self-sufficient. Attaining a higher level of education and controlling future births are important factors in improving the life course of a teen mother (Weinraub et al., 2002).

The relatively disadvantaged life circumstances of many teenage mothers, combined with their young age, create a context that affects the development of their children in unique ways. Adolescents who become parents, like all parents, must develop an identity as a parent and negotiate new family dynamics that arise following a baby's birth. In addition, teenage parents are at the same time confronted with their own developmental needs related to being an adolescent: finding an identity of their own and negotiating autonomy from their family of origin. Combining these two major life transitions (becoming a parent and being an adolescent) into the same time period can place considerable stress on the teen mother (Moore & Brooks-Gunn, 2002). Furthermore, the financial and educational limitations typically experienced by adolescent mothers contribute to making teen parenthood an exceptionally difficult life circumstance to traverse successfully (Leadbeater & Way, 2001). The high rates of problem behaviour among children of teen parents attest to this difficulty (Patterson & Hastings, 2007).

Despite the gloominess of this scenario, some teenage mothers manage to cope well with their circumstances. University of Victoria psychologist Bonnie Leadbeater, in collaboration with Niobe Way of New York University, studied a sample of 126 inner-city teenage mothers in New York City. Although all faced the struggles described above, 15 of the mothers and their children were found to be holding their own at a six-year follow-up. Leadbeater and Way (2001) describe a number of factors that contributed to the success of these "resilient" mothers. Having supportive relationships with family members was important, as was the positive attitude of their families toward education. The presence of positive role models, combined with an optimistic/confident attitude and a desire to succeed, fostered resiliency, as did having access to an affordable post-secondary education.

In the 1990s, the birth of a child to sitcom character Murphy Brown (played by Candace Bergen), a single professional woman, stirred a national controversy in the United States regarding the importance of fathers in children's lives. Murphy Brown's choice to have a child on her own became a rallying point for those on both sides of the political spectrum. If aired today, do you think this sitcom situation would cause the same furor that it did 20 years ago? (*CBS/Landov LLC*)

While single mothers who are adolescents are frequently disadvantaged, a very different group of single parents is older, professional women who have never married, but who choose to raise a child on their own (Jadva, Badger, Morrissette, & Golombok, 2009; Patterson & Hastings, 2007). Called *single mothers by choice* or SMC, these women first came to national attention in the 1990s, when the television sitcom character, Murphy Brown, chose to bring a child into the world knowing that she would not have the help or support of a partner. Typically, single mothers by choice are in their 30s and early 40s, and of upper-middle class socio-economic status. Like Murphy Brown, they are usually financially secure, well educated, and employed in well-paying professional jobs (Jadva et al., 2009). Some of these mothers choose single parenthood through adoption, while many choose to have children through anonymous donor insemination (Single Mothers by Choice, 2009).

An international support and informational group for these women, called Single Mothers by Choice, was founded in 1981 with just eight members. It currently has over 2,000 members (Single Mothers by Choice, 2009). Research on outcomes for children reared by women who are single mothers by choice is limited, reflecting the relatively recent growth of this phenomenon in our society (Golombok, 2006). Although single parenthood is certainly fraught with challenges, research available thus far indicates that children reared by single mothers by choice may not face the same developmental risks as children in single-parent homes created through divorce or teen parenthood. Longitudinal studies are currently following a set of SMC families as the children grow up (Murray & Golobok, 2005). Such research is necessary to better understand the effects of growing up in this unique context.

ADOPTION Adoption in Canada is a provincial responsibility, and, except for data on international adoptions, the Canadian government does not maintain statistics on overall adoption rates (Adoption Council of Canada, 2005). In the United States, approximately 2 to 4 percent of children are adopted (Brodzinsky & Pinderhughes, 2002); a slight majority of these are kinship adoptions, while the rest of these children go to families with whom they have no biological ties. In addition, adoptions from other countries have become increasingly common.

Adoptions from other countries have become increasingly common in Canada, numbering 2,122 in 2009 (Hilborn, 2010). On average, girls outnumber boys by about two to one, with the largest number of either sex being less than 4 years old. Data source: Adoption Council of Canada, 2007. (© *China Photos/X01183/Corbis*)

Adoptions occur for many reasons, under many circumstances, and at many points in adopted children's lives—all of which complicate the task of determining what effects, if any, adoption has on children's development. It is clear that the majority of adopted children develop in ways that are indistinguishable from those of children being reared by their biological parents. However, certain groups of children appear to be at greater risk for the later development of problems. In particular, those who are older at the time of adoption; those who have had more adverse experiences, such as health problems, multiple changes in caregiving environment, or a history of neglect or abuse; and boys all show a higher risk for adjustment and behavioural problems than do other children (Brodzinsky & Pinderhughes, 2002; Peters, Atkins, & McKay, 1999). Nevertheless, adopted children, even those from adverse backgrounds, often do better than similar children who were not adopted (Brodzinsky & Pinderhughes, 2002; Hocksbergen, 1999; van IJzendoorn et al., 2005). Thus, adoption can actually serve as a protective factor against the damaging effects of adverse environmental circumstances. Recall that we discussed one such effect in Chapter 10: adopted children on average have higher IQs than would be expected based on the background of their biological parents (van IJzendoorn et al., 2005).

GAY AND LESBIAN PARENTHOOD Adoption is one method through which individuals or couples who are lesbian or gay add children to their family. In other cases, the children of gay or lesbian parents are the result of a previous heterosexual relationship by a parent who has now committed to a gay or lesbian sexual orientation. Still other parents make use of alternative methods of conception, such as donor insemination, as discussed in Chapter 4 (Patterson & Hastings, 2007).

Children raised in gay or lesbian homes may grow up in single-parent or in two-parent families (Patterson & Hastings, 2007), and the total number of such families is not known. However, Statistics Canada included information on the number of same-sex couples (both common-law and married) in the 2006 census. In their responses, 45,345 Canadian couples indicated that they were same-sex; 54 percent of these were males and 46 percent were females. Of these couples, 16.3 percent of females and 2.9 percent of males reported having children (Statistics Canada, 2007a).

Research on the possible effects of this family structure is a fairly recent endeavour; such research faces a number of methodological challenges, and all who evaluate the research agree that more study is needed (Golombok, 2006; Golombok & Tasker, 2010; Herek, 2006). Thus far, however, findings suggest that children growing up with lesbian or gay parents develop much as do children in other family structures (Patterson & Hastings, 2007). Most of the research has involved children raised by lesbian parents (Golombok & Tasker, 2010; Herek, 2006), and has failed to find consistent effects of any sort that differentiate these children from those in other family arrangements. This conclusion holds across a range of outcomes, including self-esteem, intelligence, family relations, and peer relations (although some children report occasional homophobic teasing from peers) (Gartrell et al., 2005; Patterson & Hastings, 2007). There are fewer studies of children raised in families with gay men as parents, and thus less is known about their development (Golombok & Tasker, 2010). Available evidence, however, does not suggest that gay men differ as parents from heterosexual men (Herek, 2006). Indeed, as Patterson and Hastings (2007) point out, desire and ability to parent effectively may be more important contributors to parenting than is sexual orientation.

Links to Related Material

In Chapter 16, you will read about the development of sexual orientation. Here, you learn more about the development of children growing up in families headed by gay and lesbian parents.

One of the most frequently examined outcomes of gay and lesbian parenting is gender-role development and sexual identity. Once again, there is little information currently available on the development of children raised by gay men (Herek, 2006); more information is available on children raised in lesbian families. Some studies suggest that these children may be less strongly sex-typed than those raised in heterosexual families (Stacey & Biblarz, 2001), although many other studies have not found reliable differences in this area (Herek, 2006). Moreover, as adolescents and young adults, these children appear no more likely to adopt a same-sex sexual orientation than are young adults in general (Herek, 2006; Patterson & Hastings, 2007). (We discuss socialization accounts of sexual orientation further in Chapter 16.)

LEARNING OBJECTIVE 15.3

Analyze the ways that families function as a social system.

1. How do sibling relationships influence child development?
2. What role do grandparents play in child development?
3. How does divorce affect child development?
4. What do we know about children raised by single parents who have never married?
5. How does adoption affect child development?
6. How does gay and lesbian family structure work as a context for child development?

Learning Objective 15.4

Trace the development of peer relations and discuss how peers influence each other's development.

SOCIALIZATION BY PEERS

How do children interact with one another? What factors affect these interactions, and how do interactions with peers, in turn, affect other aspects of the child's development? To address these questions, we first consider how peer relations change as children grow older; that is, the developmental aspect of peer relations. We then discuss the various processes and contexts through which peers influence each other's development. In the next section, we take up the important question of individual differences in the quality of peer relations.

TYPICAL PEER RELATIONS

For Thought and Discussion

Is experience with peers necessary for development? Could a child reared solely in the company of adults develop normally? Why or why not?

The most obvious developmental change in peer relations is an increase in amount. As children grow older, they spend more and more time with peers and relatively less time with adults, including their parents (Ellis, Rogoff, & Cromer, 1981). The change in amount of time spent with peers is a backdrop to the issue we now address—changes in the nature or quality of children's relations with their peers. Here, too, changes with age are dramatic.

INFANCY Unlike older children, infants cannot spontaneously seek out their peers for companionship or pleasure. If infants find themselves together, it is because adults have placed them together.

Adults often do place babies together, however, and the likelihood of such contact is increasing as more and more mothers enter the labour force (Marshall, 2006). Three or four infants may be cared for in the home of one mother, or half a dozen or so may occupy the infant room of a daycare centre.

Interest in other children emerges quite early. Infants as young as 6 months look at, vocalize to, smile at, and touch other infants (Hay, Caplan, & Nash, 2009). Such behaviours are, to be sure, limited in both frequency and complexity. They also have been characterized as *object-centred* because infants' early interactions often centre on some toy of mutual interest. Indeed, toys remain an important context for interaction throughout infancy.

Relations with peers change in various ways as babies develop (Hay et al., 2009; Rubin et al., 2006). Initially, simple and discrete behaviours, such as a touch, begin to be coordinated into more complex combinations, such as a touch in conjunction with a smile, perhaps followed by a vocalization. Reciprocity becomes more and more likely as one-way social acts evolve into more truly social interchanges. Bouts of mutual imitation develop, in which toddlers both imitate their partner and take pleasure in being imitated themselves (Asendorpf, 2002; Neilsen & Dissanayake, 2004). Positive emotional responses become more marked as infants begin to derive obvious enjoyment from the company and the behaviour of their peers. Unfortunately, negative responses also become more evident, especially in disputes over toys. Nevertheless, most social interchanges among infants are positive (Hay et al., 2009). And the cognitive level of a child's play is generally higher when peers are present than when they are not (Rubenstein & Howes, 1976).

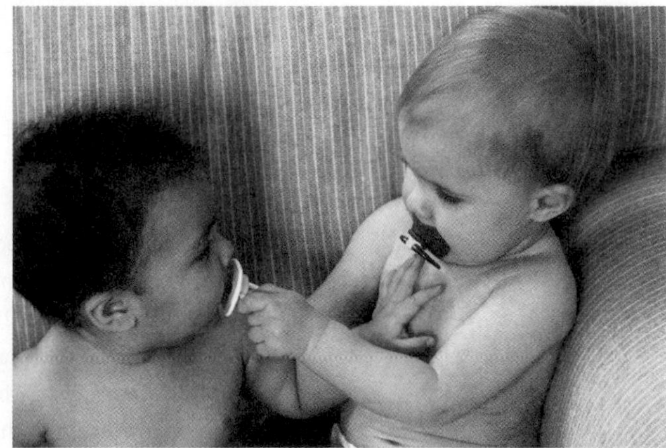

For many children, interaction with peers begins very early in life. (*Brand X Pictures*)

THE PRESCHOOL PERIOD We have already seen numerous differences between what infants can do and what preschoolers can do. It should be no surprise to learn that peer relations also differ between the two periods. The preschooler occupies a larger social world than the infant, with a greater number and variety of playmates (Howes, 2009). The preschooler's social world is also more differentiated. The preschool-aged child can direct different behaviours to different social objects and form somewhat different relations with different peers (Coplan & Arbeau, 2009). The complexity of social interactions increases as symbolic forms of behaviour begin to predominate over physical ones. The same goal that was once accomplished with a pull or a shove can now be achieved (at least sometimes) with a verbal request (Hay et al., 2009). Children also become more skilled at adjusting such communications to the different needs of different listeners (Garvey, 1986; Shatz & Gelman, 1973), and the first truly collaborative problem solving emerges (Brownell & Carriger, 1990; Holmes-Lonergan, 2003).

Of course, none of these developments is instantaneous—skill in interacting with peers increases gradually between the ages of 2 and 5, and indeed for some time afterward. The preschooler's social competence is impressive compared with that of the infant, but there is still a long way to go. Nevertheless, the skills acquired during this period lay the groundwork for the interactions and relationships that will be developed at later periods (Fabes, Martin, & Hanish, 2009).

Much of the research concerned with peer relations during the preschool years has focused on children's play. One common approach to categorizing play is shown in Table 15.2. As you can see, the categories vary in the cognitive complexity of the play, ranging from the simple motor exercise of functional play to the give-and-take intricacies of games with rules. As would be expected, children of different ages are likely to engage in different types of play. Functional play emerges early and predominates during the infant and toddler years, whereas games with rules are infrequent among children younger than grade-school age (Rubin, Fein, & Vandenberg, 1983).

The category of **pretend play** has been of special interest to investigators of preschool development. Studies have demonstrated that both the frequency and the complexity of pretend play

Pretend play A form of play in which children use an object or person as a symbol to stand for something else.

TABLE 15.2 TYPES OF PLAY CLASSIFIED ACCORDING TO COGNITIVE LEVEL

Type	Description	Examples
Functional	Simple, repetitive muscular movements performed with or without objects	Shaking a rattle; jumping up and down
Constructive	Manipulation of objects with intention of creating something	Building a tower of blocks; cutting and pasting pictures
Pretend	Use of an object or person to symbolize something that it is not	Pretending that a log is a boat; playing Batman and Robin with a friend
Games with rules	Playing games in accordance with prearranged rules and limits	Playing hopscotch; playing checkers

Source: Based on information from *The Effects of Sociodramatic Play on Disadvantaged Preschool Children* by S. Smilansky 1968, New York: Wiley.

increase across the preschool years (Howes & Lee, 2006). Research also suggests that pretend play can have beneficial effects on both the child's cognitive development and the child's relations with peers (Coplan & Arbeau, 2009). Both parents and siblings can be important contributors to the earliest forms of pretend play.

Another popular approach to categorizing play is shown in Table 15.3. Here, the focus is on the social organization, rather than the cognitive level of the child's play. The usual assumption has been that the various types of play develop in the order shown in the table. Thus, 2-year-olds are most likely to be found in solitary or onlooker behaviour; in 5- and 6-year-olds, cooperative and associative play are common. A particularly interesting category is that of **parallel play**, in which two or more children play next to each other, using the same sorts of materials and perhaps even talking, yet without any genuine interaction. Anyone who has watched groups of 3- and 4-year-olds can verify that such "semi-social" play is common.

Parallel play A form of play in which children play next to each other and with similar materials but with no real interaction or cooperation.

Links to Related Material

In Chapter 8, you read about some of the cognitive developments that underlie changes in pretend play across the preschool years. Here, you learn more about the development of different types of pretend play.

The categories listed in Table 15.3 were developed decades ago (Parten, 1932). Although recent research verifies that children today show the same general patterns of play, such research also suggests some qualifications and complexities in the developmental picture (Howes & Lee, 2006; Rubin et al., 2006). Not all children progress in the order shown in the table, nor do the early categories of play necessarily disappear as children grow older; solitary and parallel play are still common among 4- and 5-year-olds (Tieszen, 1979). What does change with age is the cognitive maturity of the play. The non-social play of 2- and 3-year-olds consists mainly of various kinds

TABLE 15.3 TYPES OF PLAY CLASSIFIED ACCORDING TO SOCIAL LEVEL

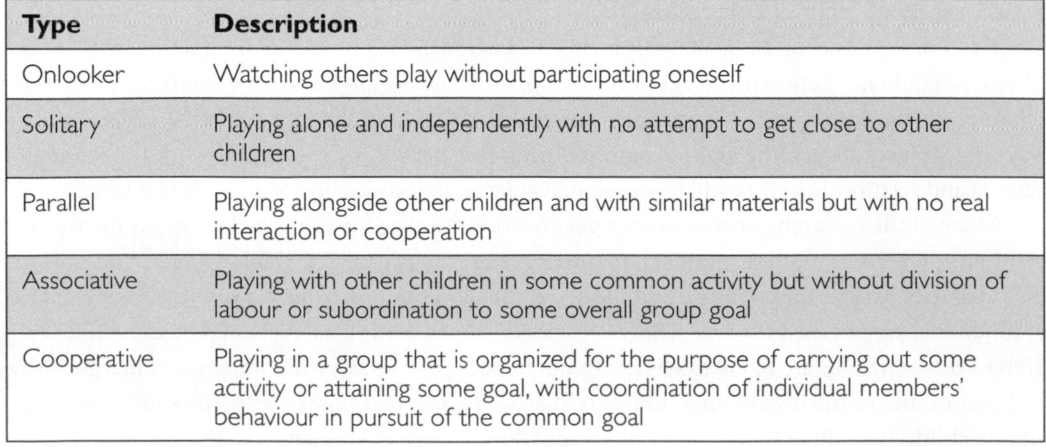

Type	Description
Onlooker	Watching others play without participating oneself
Solitary	Playing alone and independently with no attempt to get close to other children
Parallel	Playing alongside other children and with similar materials but with no real interaction or cooperation
Associative	Playing with other children in some common activity but without division of labour or subordination to some overall group goal
Cooperative	Playing in a group that is organized for the purpose of carrying out some activity or attaining some goal, with coordination of individual members' behaviour in pursuit of the common goal

Source: Based on information from "Social Participation among Preschool Children" by M. B. Parten, 1932, *Journal of Abnormal and Social Psychology, 27*, 243–269.

A child may still engage in solitary play at the age of 4 or 5. (*Banana Stock*)

of functional play (see Table 15.2). Older children are more likely to embed even their non-social play in a constructive or dramatic context (Rubin, Watson, & Jambor, 1978). Because of this interplay of cognitive and social factors, modern scales to assess play typically include both cognitive and social dimensions (Howes, Unger, & Seidner, 1989; Rubin, 1989).

Parallel play is a familiar sight among preschoolers. *(Banana Stock)*

LATER CHILDHOOD AND ADOLESCENCE As children develop, their play continues to evolve through the hierarchies shown in Tables 15.2 and 15.3. By age 8 or 9, children have become enthusiastic participants in games with rules, as any visit to a school playground or toy store will readily verify. By middle childhood, children's play is also more likely to fall within the most advanced of the categories in Table 15.3—cooperative play.

These changes in both the cognitive level and the social organization of play, in turn, relate to more general factors in the child's development. Increased experience with peers clearly plays a role as children spend more and more time with a wider variety of children. Indeed, effects of experience are evident well before this point; from infancy on, children with more extensive peer experience are more positive and skilled in peer play (Howes & James, 2002; NICHD Early Childcare Research Network, 2001). Advances in cognitive level also contribute. In particular, gains in perspective-taking skills during middle childhood may underlie both the new-found facility at games with rules and the general ability to interact cooperatively.

One of the most striking developmental changes in peer relations is the increased importance of groups as a context for peer interaction. For psychologists, the term **group** describes something more than just a collection of individuals. Hartup (1983) suggests the following criteria for determining that a group exists: "social interaction occurs regularly, values are shared over and above those maintained in society at large, individual members have a sense of belonging, and a structure exists to support the attitudes that members should have toward one another" (p. 144).

Preschool children occasionally interact in ways that seem to fit this definition. The same four boys, for example, may play together in similar ways every day, demonstrating clear leader-and-follower roles in their play, as well as a clear sense of "we" versus "they" in their relations with those outside their group. Nevertheless, during the grade-school years, membership in groups assumes a clear significance in the lives of most children. Some such groups are formal ones with a substantial degree of adult input, such as Girl Guides and Boy Scouts, 4-H clubs, and hockey leagues. Other groups are more informal, child-created, and child-directed, reflecting mutual interests of the group members.

For Thought and Discussion

What are some examples of your play as a child that reflect the social and the cognitive levels of play?

Group A collection of individuals who interact regularly in a consistent structured fashion and who share values and a sense of belonging to the group.

Clique A kind of group typical in adolescence consisting usually of 5 to 10 members whose shared interests and behaviour patterns set them apart from their peers.

Crowds Large loosely organized groups that serve to structure social identity in high school.

In the early teen years, the more loosely structured groups of middle childhood coalesce into *cliques* (Killen et al., 2009). **Cliques** are small groups of 5 to 10 friends who interact frequently and whose shared interests and behaviour patterns set them apart from both their peers and the adult world. Typically, clique members are similar in family background, values, and attitudes. In early adolescence, cliques are usually same-sex, but by the mid-teens mixed-sex cliques are more common. Cliques offer members a place to find emotional support and companionship, as well as a place to begin to explore one's social (and sexual) identity during the teen years.

How do cliques and crowds serve to structure social life and identity in high school? *(Rubberball/Mike Kemp/Getty Images)*

During high school, groups of cliques often come together to form *crowds*. **Crowds** are large, loosely organized groups that serve to structure social identity in high school (Horn, 2003, 2006; Kindermann & Gest, 2009). Most adults will remember a variety of high school crowds by their general label and reputation: the "jocks," who typically are popular and

For Thought and Discussion

What labels and reputations identified crowds in your high school? How did membership in a crowd affect your development during adolescence?

involved in athletics; the "geeks" or "nerds," who often are considered technologically sophisticated but socially awkward; the "goths," who distinguish themselves with their dark clothing, chains, and body piercings; the "druggies" who use drugs and are known for skipping school and getting into fights; and others (you may have different terms for these, and other, crowds).

Crowds such as these provide adolescents with a forum for exploring social identity. After high school, the power of crowds declines in the lives of individuals. However, even in adulthood, people seek like-minded groups of others with whom they socialize and often identify with in terms of personal interests and lifestyle choices.

How does membership in a group affect peer relations? A classic study of this question is the Robbers Cave experiment (Sherif et al., 1961). For this study, 22 grade 5 boys, initially unacquainted, were recruited to attend one of two summer camps. In each camp, the boys engaged in typical activities—hiking, sports, crafts, and the like. Thanks to the manipulation of the experimenters, they also coped with various unexpected challenges—for example, preparing a meal when the staff had failed to do so. In both camps, divisions of labour and cooperative problem solving ensued, both in response to immediate crises and with respect to longer-term group organization and group goals. Leaders and followers emerged. And both camps adopted names—Rattlers in one case, Eagles in the other.

Initially, neither group was aware of the other. After five days, however, the experimenters arranged for the two groups to meet "accidentally." A series of competitions (baseball, tug of war, and so on) followed, engineered so that neither group enjoyed more success than the other. The immediate effects of the competitions on group cohesiveness were detrimental; bickering followed any defeat, and the leader of one group was actually overthrown. Over time, however, the between-group competitions led to a heightened sense of within-group—"us" versus "them"—solidarity. At the same time, the rivalry between groups escalated, eventually reaching the point of physical violence. Only through cooperative efforts to solve further experimentally engineered crises (for example, a non-functioning water supply on a hot day) did the two groups begin to resolve their conflict and develop between-group friendships.

The Robbers Cave experiment is a classic study of group formation. From "The Robbers Cave Experiment" by M. Sherif, O. J. Harvey, B. J. White, W. R. Hood, and C. W. Sherif, Wesleyan University Press, 1988, p. 103. © 1988 Muzaref Sherif and reprinted by permission of Wesleyan University Press.

The Robbers Cave experiment suggests several conclusions about children's groups that are verified by more recent research (Bigler, Brown, & Markell, 2001; Fine, 1987; Nesdale & Flesser, 2001). Most generally, it is clear that children tend to form groups based on common interests and goals, and that groups serve as a source of self-identity and gratification. Groups are organized, with rules and norms that must be adhered to and divisions of the members into leaders and followers. Work in support of common goals is one source of group cohesiveness; competition with other groups is another source. Between-group rivalry is clearly the most worrisome aspect of group functioning, since attitudes and behaviours toward outsiders may become quite negative. More positively, the same factors that promote within-group cohesion—in particular, working toward a common goal—can also serve to reduce between-group hostility.

COGNITIVE CONTRIBUTIONS

We turn now to the role that cognitive development plays in peer relations. As the name suggests, cognitive factors are stressed most heavily in the cognitive-developmental approach. But any theoretical perspective must allow some role for cognitive factors. It seems obvious that how children think about peers must affect their behaviour toward peers. The question is exactly how these factors contribute.

A reasonable first step is to ask which cognitive factors might be important. The most popular candidate has been perspective taking. The ability to adopt the perspective of another—to figure out what someone else feels, thinks, wishes, or the like—seems clearly relevant to the ability to interact

TABLE 15.4 EXAMPLES OF ITEMS USED TO ASSESS CHILDREN'S SOCIAL PROBLEM-SOLVING SKILLS

Stimulus	Narration	Questions
Picture of one girl swinging and another girl standing nearby	This girl's name is Laurie, and this is Kathy. Laurie is 5 years old. Kathy is 7 years old. Kathy is older than Laurie. Kathy has been on the swing for a long, long time. Laurie would really like to play on the swing.	What could Laurie say or do so that she could play on the swing? If that didn't work, what else could Laurie do or say? What would you do or say if you wanted to play on the swing?
Picture of a boy riding a tricycle and a girl standing nearby	This boy's name is Bert, and this girl's name is Erika. They are both 5 years old. Bert, the boy, has been on the tricycle for a long, long time. Erika, the girl, would like to ride the tricycle.	What could Erika say or do so that she could ride the tricycle? If that didn't work, what else could Erika do or say so that she could have the tricycle? What would you do or say if you wanted to ride on the tricycle?
Picture of a school setting with two girls sitting near each other	This girl's name is Kim, and this is Jenny. Kim and Jenny are both 5 years old. They are both the same age. Kim and Jenny are in the same class at school, but this is Jenny's first day at the school. Jenny is a new girl in the class. Kim would like to get to know Jenny better.	What could Kim say or do to get to know Jenny? If that didn't work, what else could Kim do or say to get to know Jenny? What would you do or say to get to know Jenny?

Source: Adapted from *The Social Problem-Solving Test—Revised* (pp. 3, 4) by K. H. Rubin, 1988, Waterloo, Ontario: University of Waterloo Press. Copyright © 1988 by K. H. Rubin. Reprinted by permission.

with others. More broadly, researchers have stressed various aspects of social cognition—the child's thoughts and level of reasoning with respect to other people. How, for example, do children reason about the causes of other people's behaviour, or about the morality of various behaviours, or about the nature of friendship (Harris, 2006)? Finally, Canadian researchers Kenneth Rubin and Linda Rose-Krasnor (1986; 1992) have moved closer to actual social interaction by focusing on **social problem-solving skills**, the skills needed to resolve social dilemmas. An example of an approach to assessing social problem-solving skills is shown in Table 15.4. Models of the skills needed to solve such problems have often been grounded in information-processing conceptions of the components—such as attention, representation, and memory—of problem solving in general (Crick & Dodge, 1994; Gifford-Smith & Rabiner, 2004; Rose-Krasnor & Denham, 2009).

Social problem-solving skills Skills needed to resolve social dilemmas.

Skills, such as those assessed by the tasks in Table 15.4, improve with age, as do perspective-taking and information-processing abilities more generally. The parallel changes with age in cognitive skills and peer relations are compatible with the idea that cognitive advances lead to social advances—as children can do more cognitively, they also can do more socially. This kind of evidence, however, is very indirect. Stronger support for the role of cognitive factors in peer relations comes from two further sorts of data. If the cognitive-developmental position is correct, we would expect to find cognitive-social links within an age group—children who are advanced in the relevant cognitive abilities should also be advanced in their peer relations. We would also expect that teaching children relevant cognitive skills would lead to advances in their social behaviour as well.

Both kinds of evidence have, in fact, been obtained. Research has shown that there is a positive relation between level of cognitive development and level of peer relations. Perspective taking has been the most frequently examined cognitive variable, and a variety of forms of perspective taking have been shown to relate to how children interact. Measures of communication skill, both in speaking and listening, also relate positively to peer interaction (Gottman, Gonso, & Rasmussen, 1975). So do various measures of social cognition—for example, level of moral judgment (Gibbs, 2010) and attributions concerning the intentions underlying behaviour (Dodge, 2006). And so do measures of the kind of social problem-solving skills described in Table 15.4 (Goldstein, 2004c). The aspects of peer relations that have been found to relate to cognitive development include play (Rubin & Maioni, 1975), prosocial behaviour (Wentzel & Erdley, 1993), and aggression (Rubin, Bream, & Rose-Krasnor, 1991).

In general, the results from studies that attempt to train relevant cognitive skills are compatible with those from correlational research. Not all training studies produce positive results, and the effects that do occur are generally modest in magnitude. Nevertheless, most of the evidence suggests that training in cognitive skills does have some effect on how children behave with peers. Training in perspective taking, for example, has been shown to lead to decreased aggression (Gibbs, 2010; Goldstein, 2004b) and increased helpfulness and cooperation (Iannotti, 1978). Teaching children social problem-solving skills has been shown to result in improvements in prosocial behaviour and general social adjustment (Weissberg, 1985). Note that work of this sort has applied as well as scientific value, a point to which we return later.

PROCESSES OF PEER INFLUENCE

As they develop, children spend increasingly more time with peers, and they interact in increasingly varied and complex ways. How do experiences with peers affect children's development? We begin by considering some of the processes stressed in social-learning accounts of peer relations.

One important process is modelling. Children clearly imitate other children; one study conducted in a preschool setting by Canadian researchers Rona Abramovitch and Joan Grusec (1978) reported an average of 13 imitative acts per child per hour. A variety of behaviours have been shown to be susceptible to the effects of peer models, including compliance with adult instructions (Ross, 1971), sharing (Elliott & Vasta, 1970), social participation (O'Connor, 1972), and problem solving (Butler, 1996). Indeed, as we noted in our discussion of infancy, some capacity for imitative learning emerges even before the usual age for preschool attendance. Research has shown simple forms of peer imitation in children as young as 15 to 20 months (Asendorpf, 2002; Neilsen & Dissanayake, 2004).

Reinforcement and punishment occur frequently when children interact with each other (Charlesworth & Hartup, 1967; Furman & Gavin, 1989). Among the reinforcements children deliver are help-giving, praise, smiling or laughing, affection, and compliance. Among the punishments they deliver are non-compliance, blaming, disapproval, physical attack, and ignoring. Children are most likely to repeat a response that results in reinforcement and least likely to repeat one that results in punishment (Hartup, 1983). Children are also most likely to continue to play with peers from whom they generally receive positive consequences (Snyder et al, 1996; 2005). Among the aspects of development that have been shown to be responsive to peer consequences are gender-typed behaviours (Leaper & Friedman, 2007), aggression (Bukowski et al., 2007; Dishion & Piehler, 2009), modes of initiating interaction (Leiter, 1977), and on-task behaviour in the classroom (Sage & Kindermann, 1999).

We noted earlier that children's reinforcement of their peers is often unintentional. The same is true, of course, for many instances of modelling. These processes are not necessarily inadvertent, however, even in children as young as preschool age. Preschool children often use imitation of peers as a technique to win friends or to enter ongoing groups—a successful technique, in that imitation is generally responded to positively (Grusec & Ambramovitch, 1982). And anyone who has spent much time around young children is familiar with their deliberate manipulation of reinforcement through such promises as "I'll be your friend if..." and the corresponding threat "I won't be your friend unless..." (Howes, 2009).

CONFORMITY TO PEERS We have seen that groups play an increasing role in most children's lives as they move through the late childhood and early adolescent years. To many adults, the importance of peer-group membership for the grade-schooler or adolescent raises the disturbing possibility that peers may come to outweigh parents as a source of behaviours and values. What do we know about the influence of peers in general, and about the relative influence of peers and parents in particular?

The issue of peer influence turns out to be one of those "it depends" issues (Berndt, 1989a; Urberg, 1999). Peers can clearly be an important source of values. But how important they are depends on a number of factors. Peer influence varies with age, reaching a peak, at least by some measures, in early adolescence and declining thereafter (Berndt, 1979; Constanzo, 1970). Peer influence varies from child to child; some children are a good deal more susceptible to pressures from the peer group than are others (Allen, Porter, & McFarland, 2006). And peer influence, as well as the relative importance of peers and parents, varies from one area of life to another. In areas such as clothing, music, and choice of friends, peers are often more important than parents, especially by adolescence. In areas such as academic planning and occupational aspirations, however, parents usually have the dominant voice (Berndt, Miller, & Park, 1989; Sebald, 1989; Steinberg, 2001).

This discussion is not meant to imply that peers are never a negative influence. In particular cases, they clearly can be (Dishion & Piehler, 2009)—in problem areas as serious as smoking (Urberg, Degirmencioglu, & Pilgrim, 1997), drinking (Cleveland & Wiebe, 2003), drug use (Dinges & Oetting, 1993; Mounts & Steinberg, 1995), bullying (Espelage, Holt, & Henkel, 2003), delinquency (Snyder et al., 2005, 2008), and gang violence (Lahey et al., 1999). Despite these cautionary points, it is important to remember that membership in groups, in addition to simply being enjoyable for children, often nurtures positive behaviours and values, as well as promotes a number of social skills that will remain valuable throughout life. Furthermore, surveys reveal that the common perception of a clash in values between peers and parents is overstated; on most questions, peers and parents are more similar than different in their views (Brown, 1990; Newman, 1982). In part, this similarity results from the fact that parents help determine the peers with whom the child associates (Collins et al., 2000)—a point to which we return shortly.

LEARNING OBJECTIVE 15.4

Trace the development of peer relations and discuss how peers influence each other's development.

1. How do infants interact with their peers?
2. Describe how peer interactions develop in the preschool period.
3. Describe the characteristics of peer interaction in the elementary-school and adolescent years.
4. What role does cognitive development play in children's peer relations?
5. In what ways can peers be considered as socializing agents for one another?

VARIATIONS IN PEER RELATIONS

Learning Objective 15.5

Discuss the contributors to and benefits of friendship.

Our emphasis thus far has been on general processes in peer relations and general changes that accompany development. But peer relations do not follow a single general pattern. For some children, life in the peer group is a good deal more enjoyable and fulfilling than it is for others. In this section, our focus shifts to individual differences in the quality of peer relations. We begin with the most important peer relationship: friendship. We then consider status in the peer group more generally.

FRIENDSHIP

According to the dictionary, the word peer means "equal." Clearly, however, some peers (to borrow from George Orwell's *Animal Farm)* are more equal than others. Relations among peers, like peers themselves, differ. In this section, we focus on the closest and most significant peer

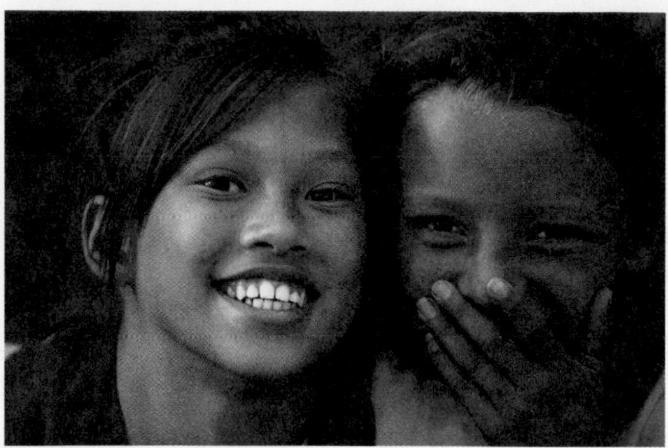

The most important peer relationship is that of friendship. (*PhotoDisc, Inc.*)

relationship—friendship. We begin by considering what children themselves mean by the word *friend.* We then examine how friendships are formed and how friendship influences children's behaviour and development.

CONCEPTIONS OF FRIENDSHIP Consider the following answers in response to the question "What is a friend?"

"A friend is a person you like. You play around with them."

"Friends don't snatch or act snobby, and they don't argue or disagree. If you're nice to them, they'll be nice to you."

"A person who helps you do things. When you need something, they get it. You do the same for them."

"Someone you can share things with and who shares things with you. Not material things; feelings. When you feel sad, she feels sad. They understand you."

"A stable, affective, dyadic relationship marked by preference, reciprocity, and shared positive affect."

It does not take much psychological insight to guess that these answers were given by respondents of different ages—or to figure out which is the definition offered by professional researchers. The first four answers (drawn from studies by Rubin, 1980, and Youniss and Volpe, 1978) came from children ranging in age from 6 to 13. The last (from Howes, 1987, p. 253) is typical of how psychologists define **friendship**.

Friendship An enduring relationship between two individuals characterized by loyalty, intimacy, and mutual affection.

Despite their diversity, the different definitions do share some common elements. All agree that there is something special about a friend that does not apply to peers in general. All state or imply that friendship is not just any sort of relationship, but a relationship of affection—friends like each other. And all acknowledge that friendship is a two-way, reciprocal process. One child may like another child, but liking alone does not make one a friend. For friendship to exist, the affection must be returned.

As the examples indicate, the presence of these common elements does not rule out the possibility that children's reasoning about friendship might change with age. At a general level, a description of the changes that occur should sound familiar because such changes parallel more general advances in the way children think about the world (Hartup & Abecassis, 2002; Rawlins, 1992). Young children's thinking about friendship tends to focus on concrete, external attributes—a friend is someone who is fun to play with and who shares things. Older children are more capable of penetrating beneath the surface to take into account more abstract aspects of friendship, such as caring for another person. For young children, friendship is often a momentary state dependent on specific acts just performed or about to be performed. Older children are more likely to see friendship as an enduring relationship that persists across time, and even in the face of occasional conflicts. Finally, although even young children realize the importance of mutual liking between friends, qualities such as loyalty and intimacy do not become central in children's thinking about friendship until late childhood or adolescence.

For Thought and Discussion

How do you define friendship? What factors have determined who your friends are? How are you and your friends similar?

DETERMINANTS OF FRIENDSHIP Friends are not selected randomly. As children develop, they are exposed to many different people, but only a few of these potential friends ever become actual friends. On what basis are these selections made?

Studies of friendship formation show a rare unanimity in agreeing that one general factor is central to most friendship choices. This factor is similarity (Aboud & Mendelson, 1996, Bukowski, Motzoi, & Meyer, 2009)—children tend to pick friends who are similar to themselves. Similarity is not the only criterion used; children may sometimes seek out friends who are more popular than they are (Hirsch & Renders, 1986) or who have a higher socio-economic status (Epstein, 1983). Nevertheless, similarity seems to be a major contributor to most friendship selections.

Various kinds of similarity are important. One is similarity in age. Friendships are most common among children who are close in age. Mixed-age friendships are found, of course, especially when children move outside the same-age groupings imposed by school (Epstein, 1989). Even when not constrained by adults, however, most children tend to pick friends who are about the same age (Berndt, 1988).

Similarity in gender is also important. As we will see in Chapter 16, a preference for same-sex friends emerges in the preschool years and becomes quite strong by middle childhood (Rose & Smith, 2009). Indeed, throughout much of childhood, gender is a better predictor of friendship choices than age (Epstein, 1986; Maccoby, 2000b). By adolescence, of course, cross-sex romantic relationships have begun to emerge (Shulman & Collins, 1997); even here, however, same-sex friendships continue to predominate (Hartup, 1993).

Links to Related Material

In Chapter 16, you will read about the preference for same-sex friendships that is often evident in childhood. Here, you learn more about factors that influence the development of friendships.

Finally, still another contributor to friendship choices is similarity in ethnicity and race (Graham, Taylor, & Ho, 2009). This preference, although less evident in preschoolers (Howes, 2009), increases with age and, in elementary school, some studies find that children are at least twice as twice as likely to choose as friends those who are of a similar racial/ethnic background to themselves (Graham et al., 2009). It should be noted, however, that the strength of this tendency depends on a number of factors, including the degree of integration in both the school system and the neighbourhood (Epstein, 1986).

Although the variables of age, gender, and race are important, they do not completely explain friendship selection. Most children encounter many peers who are similar to them in age, gender, and ethnicity or race, yet only some of these peers are selected as friends. What seems to be important in addition to general similarity to a peer is specific similarity in behaviours and interests—what psychologists call **behavioural homophily**. The word homophily means "love of the same" (Retica, 2006), and one reason that children become friends is that they like to do the same sorts of things (Rubin et al., 2006; Ryan, 2001).

Behavioural homophily Similarity between peers in behaviours and interests. Such similarity is one determinant of friendship selection.

This pattern is evident as early as the preschool period (Rubin et al., 2006), and it eventually extends to various settings in which children find themselves. Among older children, friends tend to be similar in their orientation toward school; they show correlations, for example, in educational aspirations and achievement test scores (Ide et al., 1981). They also tend to be similar in what Berndt (1988) labels their "orientation toward children's culture," or what they like to do outside of school (music, sports, games, and so on). They tend to be similar in general behaviour patterns and personality—for example, in the tendency to be shy or aggressive (Bukowski et al., 2009).

Although the relation between similarity and friendship is well established, the causal basis for the relation is less clear. There are two possibilities. Do children become friends because they have similar interests and preferences, or do children develop similar interests and preferences because they are friends (Kindermann & Gest, 2009; Ryan, 2001)? Answering this question requires longitudinal study in which patterns of similarity can be traced over time. Such studies suggest that the cause and effect flow in both directions (Bukowski et al., 2009). Children who later become friends are more similar initially than are children who do not become friends, indicating that similarity is, indeed, a determinant of friendship selection. But children who are friends become more similar over time, indicating that friendship also promotes further similarity.

Children derive much pleasure from interacting with friends. What aspects of friendship and friendship choices are evident in this photo? (© *Bartosz Hadyniak/ iStock*)

What are the processes through which friendships are initially formed? A classic study by John Gottman (1983) provides an exceptionally detailed account.

The participants in Gottman's research were children between the ages of 3 and 9, none of whom knew one another at the start of the study. Pairs of same-aged children were randomly formed, and each pair then met in the home of one of the children for three play sessions across a period of four weeks. The questions were whether the children would become friends and, if so, what processes led to friendship formation.

Gottman found that some of the children did, indeed, become friends, whereas others did not. What aspects of the interaction differentiated the two groups? Several processes proved important. Children who became friends were more successful at establishing a *common-ground activity*—that is, agreeing on what to do—than were children who did not become friends. Eventual friends showed greater *communication clarity* and were more successful at exchanging information than were non-friends. Eventual friends were more skilful at *resolving conflict*—an important skill, for conflict is frequent in young children's interactions. And eventual friends were more likely to engage in *self-disclosure,* or sharing of personal information about oneself.

Other studies of friendship formation support Gottman's conclusion that processes such as exchange of information and resolution of conflict play central roles (Grusec & Lytton, 1988). As we will see, processes of this sort do not disappear once a friendship has been formed. The same kinds of skills that help build a friendship are also central to the ways friends interact with each other.

BEHAVIOUR WITH FRIENDS That behaviour is different with friends than with non-friends seems almost part of the definition of friendship. But exactly how does behaviour differ as a function of friendship? Some differences are obvious. Children spend more time with friends than with non-friends, and they typically derive more pleasure from interacting with friends (Newcomb & Bagwell, 1995). Friends, clearly, are fun to be with. In this section we focus on several further areas of possible differences between friends and non-friends.

Links to Related Material

In Chapter 14, you read about the development of prosocial behaviour. Here, you learn how prosocial behaviour relates to the development of children's friendships.

PROSOCIAL BEHAVIOUR As we saw in Chapter 14, the term prosocial behaviour refers to forms of conduct that society considers desirable and whose development is thus encouraged in children. Examples of prosocial behaviour include helping someone in need, comforting someone in distress, and sharing with others. It seems reasonable to expect that such clearly positive behaviours will be more likely with friends than with peers in general.

For the most part, this prediction is borne out by research (Underwood, Mayeux, & Galperin, 2006). Children share more with friends than with classmates who are merely acquaintances (Jones, 1985). Cooperation in carrying out some common task is generally greater among friends than non-friends, as is equity in dividing any rewards that are obtained (Berndt, 1981). As Canadian researchers Bukowski, Motzoi, and Meyer (2009) point out, even as early as the preschool years, children may cooperate and share more with friends than with non-friends. They are more likely to offer help to a friend in distress than to a mere acquaintance (Costin & Jones, 1992). Preschoolers also deliver reinforcements more often to friends than to peers in general (Masters & Furman, 1981). In fact, participating in cooperative activities can even have positive benefits for children who are not well liked by their peers, resulting in decreases in the negative behaviours such children tend to display (Schneider et al., 2011).

CONFLICT We turn next to a less positive side of peer interaction. The definition psychologists give to conflict is a broad one: conflict refers to "a state of disagreement that may be manifest in terms of incompatible or opposing behaviors and views" (Laursen & Purcell, 2009, p. 267). The core notion is thus one of opposition between individuals, a notion conveyed by words such as *refusing, denying, objecting,* and *disagreeing* (Hartup, 1992).

Defined this broadly, conflict is clearly a frequent component of peer interaction (Rubin et al., 2006; Shantz & Hartup, 1995). It is also a frequent component of interaction between friends; indeed, conflicts probably occur most often among friends (Laursen & Purcell, 2009). This situation results, in part, simply because friends spend so much time together. But it also reflects the freedom and security that friends feel with one another and thus their ability to criticize and to disagree without threatening the relationship (Hartup et al., 1993).

The important difference between friends and non-friends, therefore, is not the probability of conflict, but the ways conflict is handled (Laursen & Purcell, 2009). Although exceptions certainly occur, conflicts are generally less heated among friends than among non-friends. Friends use what Hartup (1992) refers to as "softer" modes of managing conflicts than do non-friends: they are more likely to attempt to reason with the other person and less likely to get into extended chains of disagreement. They are also more likely to resolve the conflict in an equitable, mutually satisfactory way. And they are more likely to let bygones be bygones and to continue playing together following the conflict (Laursen & Purcell, 2009). We saw that the ability to resolve conflicts satisfactorily plays a role in forming a friendship. The findings just mentioned indicate that such skills are also important for maintaining a friendship. Indeed, the ability to overcome conflicts and remain close can be seen as one definition of the term friendship.

INTIMACY "A friend is someone with whom to share one's innermost thoughts and feelings." This quotation came from a 13-year-old, and it is usually not until late childhood or adolescence that the emphasis on intimacy in children's talk about friendship emerges.

Do friends, in fact, interact in more intimate ways than do non-friends? Children's own statements about friendship provide one source of evidence. If a girl says she shares things with her best friend that she can share with no one else, there seems little reason to doubt the accuracy of her statement. In one series of studies, statements of this sort were absent among kindergarteners, but were offered by approximately 40 percent of the grade 6 participants (Berndt, 1986).

Intimacy—sharing one's innermost thoughts and feelings—is an important characteristic of children's friendships in middle childhood and adolescence. (© *Avril O'Reilly/Alamy*)

Observations of children's interactions also provide evidence about the role of intimacy in friendship. Children who are friends or who are in the process of becoming friends are more likely than non-friends to talk about feelings and to engage in various forms of self-disclosure (Gottman, 1983). Because this difference emerges as early as the preschool years, these data suggest that intimacy may be a characteristic of friendship long before children begin to talk about intimacy as being important. On the other hand, the frequency of such intimate disclosures does increase as children grow older (Berndt & Perry, 1990; Buhrmester & Prager, 1995). And the importance of intimacy as a determinant of the quality of friendship is greater for adolescents than for younger children (Buhrmester, 1990; Hartup, 1993). It is worth noting that in addition to age differences, there are gender differences in this aspect of friendship. Many studies find that girls' friendships are characterized by a higher degree of intimacy than are those of boys. This difference begins to emerge by middle childhood and increases into adolescence (Rubin, Dwyer, Booth-LaForce, Kim, Burgess, & Rose-Krasnor, 2004; Underwood, 2004; Underwood & Buhrmester, 2007; Zarbatany, McDougall, & Hymel, 2000).

Contextual differences in boys' and girls' interactions may, at least in part, play a role in these gender differences. Girls prefer to interact in smaller groups than do boys, which may provide greater opportunity for more intimate interactions (Rose & Smith, 2009). In addition, ethnic/cultural differences may also be important. Although Caucasian boys' friendships tend to be lower in intimacy than those of girls, this may not hold true for all groups. Interviews with a sample of inner-city Black and Hispanic teenage boys (Way, 2004) suggest that intimacy—expressed in terms of self-disclosure, sharing money, and mutual protection—may be an important component of friendship in this group. How these boys' reports of intimacy would compare to those of a similar group of girls, however, was not reported. Clearly, further research on factors related to gender differences in intimacy is needed.

EFFECTS OF FRIENDSHIP Friendship, as we have seen, can have a number of positive effects on the ways in which children interact. The effects that we have discussed, however, have all been fairly immediate and short-term. In this section, we turn to the more long-term impact of childhood friendship. Do children with many friends develop differently from children with few or no friends? Do children with high-quality friendships differ in their development from children whose friendships are less satisfactory?

Both common sense and the studies already discussed suggest that the answer to these questions should be positive. And research on the long-term consequences of friendship, in fact, confirms the expectation. We have already discussed one benefit of friendship: children with satisfactory friendships adjust more successfully to school than do children who lack such support (see Chapter 10). Here, we consider two others.

Links to Related Material

In Chapters 10 and 13, you read about relationships that researchers have found between friendship and school adjustment, and friendship and self-esteem. Here, you learn more about the positive effects of friendship in children's lives.

SELF-ESTEEM One effect of friendship is on the child's self-esteem. We saw in Chapter 13 that children vary in how positively they feel about different aspects of their lives (academic abilities, physical prowess, etc.). We saw also that the successes or failures a child experiences in a particular domain are one determinant of these feelings of self-worth. The specific example discussed was academic self-concept; as we would expect, children who do well in school tend to feel better about their academic competence than children who do less well.

Children's success in the peer group also affects self-esteem. The primary measure used in this research is the Self-Perception Profile for Children, which we described in Chapter 13. Not all examinations of the issue have found relations between friendship quality and self-esteem (Berndt, 2002). In most studies, however, children with relatively satisfactory friendships have been reported to have more positive scores on the Self-Perception Profile than do children who lack such friendships (Berndt & Keefe, 1995; Keefe & Berndt, 1996). As we might expect, the greatest differences tend to be on the social acceptance subscale, but the effects are not limited to perceptions of peer relations. Global self-worth—the most general index of self-evaluation—also tends to be higher in children who have satisfactory friendships.

Social support Resources (both tangible and intangible) provided by other people in times of uncertainty or stress.

SOCIAL SUPPORT Perhaps the most general benefit of friendship is that it provides social support. The term **social support** refers to resources provided by other people in times of uncertainty or stress. We all need such support on occasion, even if the help is simply in the form of someone "being there" during a difficult time. Research with adults has shown that success in obtaining support is an important determinant of people's ability to cope with stress (Sarafino, 2008).

Social support is also important in the lives of children (Vitaro, Boivin, & Bukowski, 2009). The supports that children need can take a variety of forms, depending on the particular situation. One important category is *emotional support*—behaviours of others that offer needed comfort or reassurance and in general enhance the self-esteem of the recipient. Providing reassurance after a potentially embarrassing failure is a form of emotional support, as is lending a sympathetic ear when a friend has frustrations to vent. Other forms of support include *instrumental support* (provision of tangible resources to help solve practical tasks), *informational support* (provision of information or advice about how to cope with problems), and *companionship support* (sharing of activities and experiences).

Just as it can take many forms, support can come from many sources. As we would expect, parents tend to be the most important sources of support for most children. A variety of other sources can also be important, however, including peers, siblings, grandparents, teachers, and even pets. Among peers, friends—not surprisingly—typically rank highest. In one study, friends were judged second only to parents as sources of emotional support, and friends headed the list when children were in need of companionship (Reid et al., 1989). Furthermore, as Canadian researchers Cathy Denton and Lynne Zarbatany (1996), point out, the value of friends as sources of support increases as children grow older. Older children, as we have seen, emphasize such qualities as intimacy, and trust in their thinking about friendship and in their behaviour with friends. It is not surprising, then, that development brings an increased tendency to turn to friends in times of need. Indeed, the presence of just one close friend can shield children from the negative consequences of victimization by peers (Vitaro et al., 2009).

POPULARITY AND PROBLEMS

Friendships do not exhaust the category of peer relations—for children or for any of us. In addition to the peers who become friends, children interact with a wide range of other children as they develop. They also form opinions—sometimes positive, sometimes negative—about many of these peers, and, of course, any child is him- or herself the subject of evaluation by other children in the peer group. In this section, we consider a question that is of considerable importance in the lives of many children: What are the factors that determine whether a child is generally liked or disliked by other children?

MEASURING SOCIAL STATUS The first question concerns measurement. How can we determine which children are doing well in the peer group and which are not? The most common approach has been to ask children themselves, the assumption being that a child's peers should be the best judges of that child's standing among peers. Such peer-based evaluations of social standing are referred to as **sociometric techniques** (Asher & McDonald, 2009; Hymel, Closson, Caravita, & Vaillancourt, 2011).

Sociometric techniques
Procedures for assessing children's social status based on evaluations by the peer group. Sociometric techniques may involve ratings of degree of liking or nominations of liked or disliked peers.

Researchers have used a variety of sociometric approaches. In the *nomination technique*, the child is asked to name some specific number of well-liked peers—for example, "Tell me the names of the kids in the class you really like." The technique can also be directed to negative relations—"Tell me the names of the kids in the class you don't like very much." In the *rating-scale technique,* the child is asked to rate each of her classmates along the dimension of interest. The child might be asked, for example, to rate each classmate on a five-point scale ranging from "really like to play with" to "really don't like to play with."

What is the evidence that sociometric measures yield a valid picture of a child's social standing? Sociometric scores correlate with teacher ratings of popularity or social competence; that is, the children who are identified by their peers as well liked also tend to be the ones whom teachers identify as popular (Green et al., 1980). Sociometric scores also correlate with direct observations of children's social interactions (Bukowski & Hoza, 1989; Newcombe, Bukowski, & Pattee, 1993). Even sociometric assessments by children as young as preschool age show correlations with such external measures and thus some evidence of validity (Denham & McKinley, 1993; Wu et al., 2001).

For Thought and Discussion
What might a sociometric study of your peer relations show? How did peer acceptance influence your feelings of self-worth as a child?

POPULARITY However it is measured, *popularity* seems easy to define. A popular child is one who is well liked by his or her peers. In terms of sociometric techniques, such children receive high ratings and are the objects of many positive and few, if any, negative choices. What underlies such positive status?

Some examinations of this question have focused on relatively indirect predictors of popularity. Two factors, in particular, emerge as important. One is intellectual ability. Both IQ scores (Czeschlik & Rost, 1995) and measures of academic performance (Green et al., 1980) have been found to correlate with sociometric ratings. The second is physical attractiveness. On average, relatively attractive children (as rated either by adults or by children themselves) are more popular than are relatively unattractive children (Blachman, 2005; Langlois et al., 2000).

It is perhaps not surprising that intellectual ability correlates with popularity, given the importance of the school as a context for observation of peers. But why should physical attractiveness relate to popularity? Although no one knows for sure, an intriguing suggestion is that attractive and unattractive children may actually behave differently. In one study, 5-year-olds rated as unattractive showed more aggression and were more boisterous in their play than were their more attractive counterparts (Langlois & Downs, 1979). Thus, part of the reason for the unattractive child's social problems may lie in the child's behaviour. On the other hand, there is also ample evidence that both adults and children in North American society tend to hold a "beauty is good" stereotype, evaluating attractive individuals positively even in the absence of objective evidence (Ramsey & Langlois, 2002; Ritts, Patterson, & Tubbs, 1992). Such stereotypes, moreover, may begin to operate very early: infants as young as 6 months of age have been found able to discriminate between attractive and unattractive faces (Ramsey et al., 2004). Moreover, mothers of relatively attractive newborns respond more positively to their babies than do mothers whose infants are less attractive (Langlois et al., 1995). Thus, part of the basis for the unattractive child's difficulties may stem from stereotyped expectations about what attractive and unattractive people are like.

As noted, the research we have considered thus far has concerned relatively indirect predictors of popularity. We turn next to direct measures of behaviour. Presumably, popular children become popular because they behave in ways that other children find attractive. What do we know about behavioural contributors to popularity?

In general, the behavioural correlates of popularity are not at all surprising. Popular children tend to be friendly, socially visible, outgoing in their behaviour, and reinforcing in their interactions with others (Asher & McDonald, 2009; Cillessen & Mayeux, 2004). At a more specific level, three sets of social skills seem to be especially important (Asher, Renshaw, & Hymel, 1982). Popular children are skilled at *initiating interaction* with other children. They enter ongoing groups smoothly and set about making friends in a carefully paced but confident manner, not forcing themselves on other children but also not giving up at the slightest rebuff. Popular children are also skilled at *maintaining interaction*. They reinforce other children, show sensitivity to the needs and wishes of others, and communicate effectively in the role of both speaker and listener. Finally, popular children are skilled at *resolving conflict*. The popular child knows how to defuse touchy situations in ways agreeable to all parties, using reasoning, rather than force, and drawing on general principles of fairness and general rules for how people should interact.

This list of contributors to popularity should sound familiar. The kinds of social skills that help make a child popular are the same sorts of skills that we saw are important for forming and maintaining friendships. The concurrence is what we would expect—popular children are children who have the qualities desirable in a friend.

SUBTYPES OF POPULARITY? Sometimes children use the term "popular" to refer to peers whose behaviour is far from friendly, kind, and prosocial. Are there popular peers who behave in unfriendly ways? Researchers in this area have recently distinguished between *sociometric popularity* and *perceived popularity* (Asher & McDonald, 2009; Cillessen & Mayeux, 2004; Hymel et al., 2011). Sociometric popularity, which we have been discussing, refers to children who are well-liked in the peer group, and is assessed by asking children, "Who do you like?" Perceived popularity, by contrast, refers to children of high social standing, who are viewed as cool, arrogant, dominant, and often athletic (Cillessen & Mayeux, 2004). Perceived popularity is assessed by asking children, "Who is popular?" (Asher & McDonald, 2009). Peers high in perceived popularity often form high-status cliques and may be manipulative and aggressive (both physically and relationally) in their interactions with non-clique members. Cillessen and Mayeux (2004) argue that the status of children high in perceived popularity should perhaps be referred to as "dominant" rather than popular, given that children's attitudes toward such peers are often not favourable—children frequently describe such peers as "stuck up" and often assume that their actions are motivated by negative intentions. Although children may describe such peers as popular, how they feel about them depends on age. In intermediate grades, such peers are not necessarily viewed negatively, and some may even be viewed positively (Asher & McDonald, 2009; Vaillancourt & Hymel, 2006). However, as grade level increases, peers high in perceived popularity (especially girls) are viewed increasingly negatively by their schoolmates (Asher & McDonald, 2009).

PROBLEMS IN PEER RELATIONS Popularity is the bright side of the sociometric picture. But not everyone is popular, and not everyone develops satisfactory friendships. Problems in peer relations are a topic not only of scientific interest, but also of great practical importance in the lives of many children. As explained by Canadian researchers Shelley Hymel, Tracy Vaillancourt, and Patricia McDougall (Hymel et al., 2002), problems in peer relations can take many forms, and different investigators have proposed different classification systems (Cillessin, 2009; Cillesin & Bellmore, 2011).

Rejected child A child who receives few positive and many negative nominations in sociometric assessments by peers. Such children seem to be disliked by the peer group.

Neglected child A child who receives few nominations of any sort, positive or negative, in sociometric assessments by peers. Such children seem to be ignored by the peer group.

Controversial child A child who receives both many positive and many negative nominations in sociometric assessments by peers.

One often-used system distinguishes between rejected children, neglected children, and controversial children. The **rejected child** receives few positive but many negative nominations from his or her peers.

The rejected child seems to be actively disliked. The **neglected child**, in contrast, receives few nominations of any sort, positive or negative, from peers. The neglected child seems to be less disliked than ignored. Finally, the **controversial child**, as the name suggests, receives a mixed evaluation from the peer group, earning both positive and negative nominations. The rejected-neglected-controversial distinction has been the focus of much research, and so we begin by reviewing findings concerning these three groups. As we go, however, we also note some qualifications to the general conclusions because not all children with problems fall clearly into one of these categories.

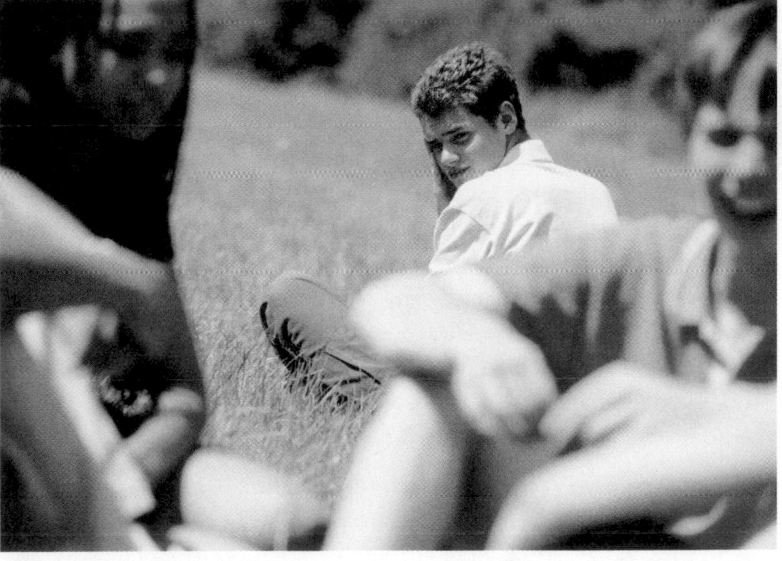

Neglected children make fewer and more hesitant attempts to make new friends, and are often perceived by their peers as being shy and socially withdrawn. (© *Corbis*)

Studies of rejected children suggest several ways in which their behaviour may contribute to their social difficulties (Cillesin & Bellmore, 2011; Rubin et al., 2006). Probably the most consistent correlate of peer rejection is aggression. Peers report, and behavioural observations confirm, that many rejected children are well above average in levels of aggression. Longitudinal studies indicate that the cause and effect actually flow in both directions: aggression leads to being rejected by the peer group, but being rejected also increases later aggression (Bukowski, Brendgen, & Vitaro, 2007; Dodge et al., 2003). More generally, rejected children often show behaviour that is antisocial, inappropriate to the situation at hand, and disruptive to ongoing group activities. Their attempts to enter new groups or to make new friends tend to be especially maladroit, consisting of overly intrusive and even bizarre overtures whose outcome, predictably, is exactly the opposite of their intent (Cillesin & Bellmore, 2011; Putallaz & Wasserman, 1990). Aggressive behaviour, as well as bullying and victimization, were discussed in more detail in Chapter 14.

The picture for neglected children is different. Neglected children are often perceived by their peers as being shy and socially withdrawn (Coie & Kupersmidt, 1983; DeRosier & Thomas, 2003). This perception is not surprising, given that many neglected children are less talkative and less socially active than are other children. Compared with most children, neglected children make fewer and more hesitant attempts to enter groups and make new friends. They also tend to give up quickly when their tentative and not very skilled efforts do not meet with success.

As befits their in-between sociometric status, controversial children typically show a mixture of positive and negative social behaviours (Newcomb et al., 1993; Rubin et al., 2006). Like rejected children, controversial children tend to rank high on measures of aggression (DeRosier & Thomas, 2003). But, like popular children, they also tend to score high on measures of sociability. This category also overlaps to some degree with perceived popularity, discussed earlier (Asher & McDonald, 2009).

Links to Related Material

In Chapter 14, you read about aggressive behaviour and bullying. Here, you learn more about how such behaviour is related to rejection by peers.

The patterns just described reflect typical, average differences among groups of children. As such, they do not apply to all rejected or neglected children. For example, only some neglected children show the shy behavioural style described; others are indistinguishable in their behaviours from sociometrically average children (Rubin et al., 2006). Similarly, although about 40 to 50 percent of rejected children seem to earn their status through high aggression and lack of control, for another 10 to 20 percent, social withdrawal appears to be a more important contributor (Bukowski et al., 2007; Rubin et al., 2006). In fact, Kenneth Rubin (1993) has argued that **social withdrawal**—that is, self-imposed isolation from the peer group—can be an important problem in itself, even in the absence of rejection or neglect. We discuss such shy/withdrawn children further in *Focus on Research 15.1*.

Social withdrawal Self-imposed isolation from the peer group.

For Thought and Discussion

Were you or a member of your family shy or withdrawn as a child? How did this characteristic affect development? What kinds of responses were most helpful?

Finally, not all unpopular children are totally lacking in friends. As we saw in Chapter 14, aggressive, rejected children, in particular, may have a small set of close friends. These children are not generally liked by the peer group, however, and the friends they do have are often other aggressive children who are more likely to maintain rather than moderate their antisocial behaviour (Vitaro et al., 2009).

FOCUS ON RESEARCH 15.1
CHILDREN WHO ARE PAINFULLY SHY AND WITHDRAWN

Some children interact infrequently with others, choosing instead to withdraw from the peer group. Some of these socially withdrawn children may simply be uninterested in social interaction. However, as Robert Coplan and colleagues at Carleton University note, many children withdraw because of shyness and social anxiety (Coplan, Girardi, Findlay & Frohlick, 2007; Coplan, Prakash, O'Neil, & Armer, 2004). Such shy/withdrawn children have received less research attention than their aggressive peers; however, there has been a recent increase in focus on shyness in children (Rubin, Coplan, Bowker, & Menza, 2011).

What Are Shy/Withdrawn Children Like?

Shy/withdrawn children interact infrequently with their peers, tend to withdraw from social encounters, are likely to be timid and reserved, and talk less than their non-shy peers (Evans, 2010; Younger, Schneider, Wadeson, Guirguis, & Bergeron, 2000). Shy children display such inhibition in unfamiliar social situations, in the presence of peers, and in the classroom.

What Are Shy/Withdrawn Children Like in School?

One of the most noticeable characteristics of shy/withdrawn children is their tendency to talk considerably less than others. Mary Ann Evans (2010) of the University of Guelph reports that children who are very shy talk infrequently in class, take longer to make their first remarks, and their statements are usually significantly shorter than those of their classmates. Shy children frequently prefer not to answer questions in class, and, when called on by the teacher, often fail to respond.

According to Evans, this lack of verbal participation in class may actually lead to a perception on the part of teachers of poorer academic competence in the shy child. Shy children's "communication reticence" is evident not only to their teachers, but also to their peers. Alastair Younger of the University of Ottawa asked 227 children from grades 1, 3, 5, and 7 how they could tell that a peer was shy. The overwhelming majority of children from all grade levels responded that shy children "do not talk much" (Younger, Schneider, & Guirguis-Younger, 2008).

What Do Shy/Withdrawn Children Think of Themselves?

Shy/withdrawn children are aware of their shyness and view themselves negatively in some areas. Shelley Hymel of the University of British Columbia, Erik Woody of the University of Waterloo, and Anne Bowker of Carleton University (1993) report that shy/withdrawn elementary school-aged children view themselves more negatively in social and athletic areas and, to some extent, in terms of physical appearance. Not surprisingly, shy/withdrawn children also report being lonely (Gazelle & Ladd, 2003).

According to Hymel and colleagues, however, shy children are not completely lacking in positive social skills. Although poorer in such social skills as leadership and sense of humour than their more outgoing peers, they are equal in other skills such as cooperativeness, behavioural conduct, and relations with adults. Nevertheless, shy/withdrawn children tend to perceive themselves as less socially competent than others. As Hymel points out, such negative self-perceptions can lead to a vicious cycle whereby negative self-perceptions can lead a child to develop negative expectations of social interactions, and thus to behave in ways that may actually evoke negative experiences from their peers.

(*continued*)

Focus on Research 15.1 Children Who are Painfully Shy and Withdrawn *continued*

What Do Shy/Withdrawn Children's Peers Think of Them?

Shy/withdrawn children tend to undervalue their social skills and view themselves as disliked by the peer group. But, are they really viewed negatively by the peer group? As discussed in this chapter, some researchers have argued that shy/withdrawn children are not disliked by their peers, but rather occupy the sociometric position of "Neglected"—neither liked nor disliked. Others have argued that such children tend to be among those in the "Rejected" category, although perhaps for different reasons than for aggressive children. Which of these is true?

Alastair Younger suggests that how children view their shy peers may depend on age. He has reported that in early elementary school grades, children do not pay much attention to the behaviour of shy/withdrawn peers (Younger, Gentile, & Burgess, 1993). Although many children are aware of their shy classmates, even in grade 1 (Coplan et al., 2007; Younger et al., 2008), their behaviour is not necessarily viewed negatively. With increasing age, however, children pay more attention to the behaviour of shy peers, and view it more negatively. Thus, although some shy/withdrawn children may be excluded from the peer group even in early grades (Gazelle & Ladd, 2003; Hart et al., 2000), such exclusion appears to increase with age (Rubin & Coplan, 2007; Younger et al., 1993). Consequently, the same behaviours that led to being "Neglected" at an earlier age may lead some (although by no means all) shy children to be "Rejected" in later elementary school.

As Lynn Alden (2005) of the University of British Columbia suggests, shyness can interfere with the development of children's peer relationships, and negative experiences with peers can serve to exacerbate the shy child's already-existing self-doubt and social anxiety. Indeed, Michel Boivin of Laval University and Shelley Hymel of the University of British Columbia have observed that some shy/withdrawn children may come to be victimized by peers and made fun of and called names (Boivin & Hymel, 1997; Boivin, Hymel, & Hodges, 2001). Canadian researchers Kenneth Rubin, Kim Burgess, and Robert Coplan (2002) suggest that partly as a consequence of this negative peer response and the loneliness and poor self-regard that ensue, some shy children may be more likely to experience anxiety and depression at later ages. Indeed, Kim Burgess and Alastair Younger (2006), in research conducted at the University of Ottawa, found that highly withdrawn children in grades 6 and 7 reported more depression and anxiety and, in some cases, experienced more somatic symptoms such as headaches, stomach aches, fatigue, and nausea, than did their non-withdrawn peers. Thus, shyness/withdrawal, particularly when accompanied by peer rejection, may have the potential to lead to unhappiness and emotional distress as children develop.

Help for Shy/Withdrawn Children

Shy/withdrawn children can be helped in various ways. In the classroom setting, there are a number of steps that teachers can take to gently encourage the participation of shy children. Interviews with several teachers conducted by Mary Ann Evans (2010) suggest the value of maintaining a quiet, orderly class. Teachers also report that it is helpful to spend time alone with the shy child after school, engaging him or her in discussion about family and interests, leading to the development of trust and a relationship. Teachers can also gently reinforce children's participation in class discussion, without drawing attention to the child, with patient attention and encouragement.

From the peer side of things, children who are shy and withdrawn can often benefit from social skills training interventions, of the sort described in *Application 15.1*. Such interventions can be most successful when conducted in a group of children with similar problems. Helen Bienert and Barry Schneider (1995) of the University of Ottawa report that modelling social skills such as how to approach others, how to initiate activities, and how to initiate and respond to conversation, followed by practice in the group, can be an effective intervention (see also Sweeney & Rapee, 2001). Interventions that include pairing the shy/withdrawn child with a non-shy peer, perhaps a peer who is a couple of years younger than the shy child, have also been found to be helpful (Furman, Rahe & Hartup, 1979; Zimbardo & Radl, 1999).

Parents can help as well. Many shy/withdrawn children are more comfortable in the familiar setting of their home. It can be beneficial to encourage the shy child to invite a friend over to spend time in this less threatening setting (Zimbardo & Radl, 1999). Although parents of shy children may often want to shield their child from stressful situations, such overcontrol and overprotection can actually serve to maintain or exacerbate the child's anxiety (Rubin et al., 2009, 2011). Lynn Alden (2005) suggests that by gently encouraging engagement with life, parents can help the shy child learn to cope with social anxiety. In their book *The Shy Child,* Zimbardo and Radl (1999) offer valuable examples of encouragement that can help children build confidence in social interactions, including practising making eye contact, developing a sense of humour, and developing listening skills. It is also valuable to help shy children to focus on their areas of competence and interest—be they academics, hobbies, or other activities—to help them view themselves as persons with strengths in various areas, rather than just as persons with perceived weaknesses in the areas of social interaction (Zimbardo & Radl, 1999).

These are some ways in which shy children can be helped and encouraged. Other suggestions for shy children, as well as for their parents and teachers, can be found at the following website: www.shykids.com.

The message from this discussion is that problems in peer relations can take many forms and can have many sources. Is it possible, despite this diversity, that the various problems have a common underlying core? The common element that has been most often proposed is a cognitive one. Earlier we reviewed evidence indicating that social-cognitive skills are important for successful peer relations. Perhaps children with social problems acquire their status because they lack such skills. Simply put, such children do not know how to make or maintain friends.

Research to investigate the hypothesis that cognitive deficits underlie social problems is similar to the research discussed earlier in the chapter. Again, the findings are mixed. Not all studies find relations between cognitive and social skills, and when relations do emerge, they are seldom large (Crick & Dodge, 1994; Dodge & Feldman, 1990). Clearly, cognitive deficits are at best only one contributor to problems in peer relations. A variety of studies suggest, however, that cognitive problems do indeed contribute. Unpopular children are often lower in perspective-taking skills than are their more popular peers (Jennings, 1975). Rejected children have difficulty judging the intentions behind the behaviour of others, a deficiency that may contribute to their high levels of aggression (Dodge, 1986; Dodge et al., 2006). And, both rejected and neglected children show deficits in the kind of social problem-solving skills illustrated in Table 15.4 (Rubin & Rose-Krasnor, 1986, 1992). This finding makes sense because the kinds of solutions such dilemmas call for are precisely the behaviours that rejected and neglected children fail to show.

STABILITY OF SOCIOMETRIC STATUS An important question in the study of peer relations concerns the stability of sociometric status over time. Do popular children remain popular and unpopular children remain unpopular as they grow up? This question is of pragmatic as well as theoretical importance. Clearly, there is less reason for concern if children with problems are simply going to outgrow them as they develop.

Findings of longitudinal studies discussed by Bill Bukowski of Concordia University and colleagues (Cillessen, Bukowski, & Haselager, 2000) and by Patricia McDougall of the University of Saskatchewan and colleagues (2001) indicate that children with problems do *not* automatically outgrow them. Some, of course, do; early peer status is no more perfectly predictive of later development than is any other early childhood measure. For many children, however, early rejection or neglect or withdrawal does predict continuing rejection or neglect or withdrawal. The category of rejection is especially stable over time. And rejected children are the ones who are at greatest risk for a number of problems later in life, including juvenile delinquency, dropping out of school, academic and job problems, and mental illness (Coie, 2004; Gest et al., 2006; Ladd et al., 2011; McDougall, Hymel, Vaillancourt, & Mercer, 2001). Although less is known about the long-term consequences of early social withdrawal, the evidence suggests that withdrawn children are also at risk for later problems, such as anxiety and depression (Rubin et al., 2011), as well as poorer social and romantic competence (Gest el al., 2006). *Application 15.1* explores intervention programs designed to help children who are having difficulty in the peer group.

Across a range of cultures, aggression is found to be one of the strongest and most consistent predictors of peer rejection. (© *1MoreCreative/iStock*)

CULTURAL VARIATIONS Recent years have seen the extension of sociometric research to a number of new settings beyond Canada and the United States. The picture that emerges from these studies is, in some respects, similar to what is found with North American samples, and in some respects it is different.

APPLICATION 15.1
INTERVENTIONS TO HELP CHILDREN WITH PROBLEMS

Problems in peer relations are not just a source of anxiety and unhappiness in childhood; such problems place children at greater than average risk for a variety of negative outcomes later in life. Can children who are having difficulty in the peer group be helped by intervention programs designed to improve their success?

As discussed by Canadian researchers Barry Schneider, Jane Ledingham, and Kenneth Rubin (1985) in their book *Children's Peer Relations,* a variety of intervention approaches have been tried (see also Bierman & Powers, 2009; Ladd, Buhs, & Troop, 2002). Some are grounded in social-learning theory. Modelling, for example, has been used in an attempt to increase social skills and social acceptance (Goldstein, 2004a). Shaping of desirable social behaviours through reinforcement has also been explored (O'Connor, 1972). Other approaches have their origins in cognitive-developmental theory. Included in this category are attempts to improve peer relations through teaching perspective-taking skills (Goldstein, 2004a) and through training in social problem-solving abilities (Kazdin, 2003, 2005). Still other programs are more eclectic, encompassing a number of different training techniques in an effort to promote the needed social skills (Erdlen & Rickrode, 2007; Simmerman & Christnor, 2007).

A particularly interesting form of intervention is labelled **peer-mediated intervention** (Odom & Strain, 1984). This approach focuses not only on the target child, but also on the group of peers with whom the child interacts. The attempt is to use responses from these other children (for example, offers to play, praise for desirable behaviour) to promote more effective social behaviours in the target child.

Peer-mediated intervention Form of intervention for children with sociometric problems in which responses of the peer group are used to elicit more effective social behaviours from the target children.

Intervention efforts do have beneficial effects (Asher, Parker, & Walker, 1996; Goldstein, 2004b; Schneider & Byrne, 1985). All of the approaches we mentioned have yielded positive results in terms of both the social skills being taught and subsequent sociometric status. These effects are, to be sure, limited in various ways. Not all children benefit from intervention, and we have limited information about the long-term impact of such programs. Nevertheless, the picture is encouraging. Especially heartening is the fact that rejected children, who may be most at risk for later problems, can be helped through intervention to improve their social status (Asher, 1985).

It is interesting to note that one technique that has proven effective with some rejected children is training in academic skills (Coie & Krehbiel, 1984; Wanzek, Vaugh, Kim, & Cavanaugh, 2006). Apparently, for those doing poorly at school, the improvement in the rejected child's academic performance has a beneficial impact on the child's self-concept and general classroom behaviour—changes that, in turn, affect how the peer group evaluates the child.

Let us first consider a major similarity. In North American samples, one of the strongest and most consistent predictors of peer rejection is aggression. This finding has proven to be general across a range of cultures. Similar aggression–rejection links have been demonstrated in China (Chen & French, 2008; Chen, Rubin, & Li, 1995), in Italy (Attili, Vermigli, & Schneider, 1997), in the Netherlands (Cillessen et al., 1992), and in Costa Rica (Kupersmidt & Trejos, 1987). These findings confirm what most of us would predict: hitting other children is not an effective way to win friends or earn group approval, whatever the specific cultural setting in which the child is developing.

On the other hand, not all findings from North American samples have proven to be generalizable to other cultures. Recall that Canadian and American children who are shy and reserved in their interactions with peers are at risk of being neglected by the peer group. In China, however, there is no association between a reserved pattern of behaviour and neglect. To the contrary, Chinese children who are quiet and non-assertive tend to be above average in popularity (Chen et al., 2011). They also are rated by their teachers as especially competent, and they hold a disproportionate number of leadership positions within the school (Chen, 2002; Chen, Rubin, & Sun, 1992).

Why might a similar behaviour pattern lead to such different outcomes in different cultures? The most likely answer concerns cultural values and expectations. In China, a cautious, self-restrained style of interpersonal interaction is regarded as a sign of competence and maturity (Chen et al., 2011; Chen & French, 2008). Adults therefore encourage such a behaviour pattern in children, and children themselves come to value it and to reward it in their peers.

In a sense, then, the comparison of Chinese and North American children reveals similarities as well as differences. In any culture, there are expectations about appropriate forms of behaviour—expectations held by children as well as adults. Children whose behaviour is in accord with cultural values and expectations are the ones who are most likely to find acceptance in the peer group.

LEARNING OBJECTIVE 15.5

Discuss the contributors to and benefits of friendship.

1. How does children's understanding of friendship develop?
2. What factors are related to friendship formation?
3. Outline the characteristics and benefits of friendship.
4. Describe the correlates of popularity in children.
5. How do rejected, neglected, and controversial children differ?

Learning Objective 15.6

Understand how experiences within the family contribute to children's behaviour with friends.

FAMILY AND PEERS

For most children, the family and the peer group are the two most important microsystems within which development occurs. In this final section, we consider how these two major social worlds relate. We begin by examining how children's relations with their siblings compare with their peer relations. We then explore the contribution of parents to children's peer relations.

SIBLINGS AND PEERS

There are both obvious similarities and obvious differences in children's relations with their siblings and their relations with their peers, especially with their friends. On the one hand, both "sibships" and friendships are intimate, long-lasting relationships that are the context for frequent and varied interactions—usually positive in tone, but including moments of conflict and rivalry as well. Both relationships involve partners who are close in age, and hence interactions are likely to be more egalitarian and symmetrical than are interactions with adults, such as parents or teachers.

On the other hand, siblings (unless they are twins) are not identical in age, and the younger–older contrast introduces a basic asymmetry not necessarily found with friends. Furthermore, siblings, unlike friends, are not together by choice and do not have the option of terminating the relationship if negative aspects begin to outweigh positive ones (Howe et al., 2011). As one researcher put it, "Siblings do not choose each other, very often do not trust or even like each other, and may be competing strongly for parental affection and interest; the sources of conflict and hostility in this relationship are likely to be very different from those leading to tension in a friendship" (Dunn, 1992, p. 7).

This analysis suggests that we should expect some similarity, but hardly perfect similarity, between sibling relations and peer relations. And this, in fact, is what research shows. Let us first consider some similarities. As we have seen, siblings clearly can perform the same roles and fulfill the same needs that are important among friends—as objects of pleasure or companionship, for instance, or as sources of affection, or as confidants for intimate interchanges (Dunn, 2007; Howe et al., 2011). Less positively, siblings, like friends, may also sometimes be targets for hostility and conflict. Especially among younger children, conflicts among siblings are a depressingly familiar experience for many parents (Howe & Recchia, 2008). Some conflict is inevitable in any long-term, intimate relationship, and siblings, like friends, are no exception to this rule.

Along with these general similarities in sibling and peer relations come differences. Some differences follow from the differences in age between siblings and the contrasting roles played by the younger child and older child. Sibling interchanges, especially early in development, tend to be less symmetrical and egalitarian than those among friends, both because of the younger–older contrast and because of the forced, not chosen, nature of the sibling relationship. This factor also contributes to differences in the domain of conflict. Although conflicts occur in both relationships, they tend to be more frequent between siblings than between friends (Buhrmester, 1992), and they also take somewhat different forms in the two contexts. Children are less likely to reason with siblings than with friends, less likely to attempt to take the sibling's point of view, and more likely to judge perceived transgressions negatively when the perpetrator is a sibling (Slomkowski & Dunn, 1993). Again, the forced nature of the sibling relationship may account for the siblings–friends differences.

Our discussion so far has concerned general similarities or differences between sibling relations and peer relations. But it is also important to ask about within-child links between the two social worlds. Does a particular child tend to show the same sorts of behaviours with peers as with siblings? Does the overall quality of a child's peer relations mirror the quality of relations with siblings?

The answer turns out to be "sometimes but not always" (Dunn & McGuire, 1992). Research makes clear that there is no simple, direct carry-over of relations forged with siblings to relations with peers (Ross & Howe, 2009). Indeed, some examinations of the issue report little if any association between how children behave with siblings and how they behave with peers (Cutting & Dunn, 2006; McElwain & Volling, 2005). Such findings demonstrate once again the importance of context for children's behaviour—what we see in one social context does not necessarily hold true when we move to a different context.

For Thought and Discussion

How would you compare and contrast your sibships and your friendships while you were growing up?

In other studies, sibling–peer connections do emerge, but they are seldom strong. As we might expect, links tend to be greater with friendship (another intense, dyadic relationship) than with peer relations in general (Stocker & Dunn, 1990). In some cases, the direction of the relation is positive. For example, studies have shown positive correlations between cooperation with siblings and cooperation with friends (Stocker & Mantz-Simmons, 1993), between aggression with siblings and aggression toward peers (Vandell et al., 1990), and between the overall quality of sibling relations and the quality of peer relations (Seginer, 1998). In other cases, the direction is negative. For example, children with relatively hostile sibling relations sometimes form especially close friendships (Stocker & Dunn, 1990); similarly, children who are unpopular with peers may rank high on affection and companionship with their siblings (East & Rook, 1992). What seems to be happening in these cases is a kind of compensation: when one component of children's social world is unsatisfactory, they may try especially hard to obtain pleasure and support from other components.

PARENTS AND PEERS

In Chapter 10, we saw one example of Bronfenbrenner's (1992) concept of the mesosystem, or the interrelationships among the various microsystems in the child's life. There our focus was on the ways in which relations with parents and peers contribute to children's success in school. Here, we take up another aspect of the mesosystem: relations between life with parents and life in the peer group. The specific question on which we focus is one of interest to any parent: what do parents do that helps or hinders their children's success with peers? The answer, we will see, is that parents do a variety of things that can be important (Reich & Vandell, 2011; Ross & Howe, 2009).

EARLY CONTRIBUTORS Parents' contribution to peer relations can begin very early in life, before most children have even begun to interact with peers. As we saw in Chapter 12, infants differ in the security of the attachments they form with the caregiver, and these differences in turn relate to the sensitivity and responsiveness of caregiving practices. As we also saw, secure attachment in infancy is associated with a number of positive outcomes in later childhood, including various aspects of peer relations. Children who were securely attached as infants tend to do well on measures of social competence and popularity later in childhood (Booth-Laforce & Kerns, 2009; Kerns, 2008). They also tend to form more harmonious and well-balanced friendships than do children with a history of less secure attachments (Booth-LaForce, Oh, Kim, Rubin, Rose-Krasnor, & Burgess, 2006; Booth-LaForce, Rubin, Rose-Krasnor, & Burgess, 2004; Schneider, Atkinson, & Tardif, 2001).

Links to Related Material

In Chapter 12, you read about the relation of quality of attachment to later peer relations. Here, you learn more about the impact of early attachment relationships on the quality of children's friendships.

Parents may also contribute to the development of the forms of play that occupy a central position in children's early interactions with their peers. Before they embark on pretend or dramatic play with peers, many children have spent dozens of hours engaged in such play with their mothers and fathers at home. Observational studies verify that joint pretend play is a frequent activity in many households, and that parents (mothers, in particular, in these studies) often assume a directive role in such play (Tamis-LeMonda, Uzgiris, & Bornstein, 2002). Research suggests, moreover, that children can acquire social skills in play with parents that carry over to later interactions with peers (Ross & Howe, 2009). It has been shown, for example, that parents' expression of positive emotions during play is linked to children's subsequent expression of positive emotions with peers, which, in turn, is related to acceptance by the peer group (Isley et al., 1999). Similarly, mothers' use of other-oriented reasoning in resolving conflicts with their children is related to the children's subsequent success in resolving conflicts with friends (Herrera & Dunn, 1997).

PARENTS AS MANAGERS Parents' involvement in early play represents a relatively indirect contribution to eventual peer relations. Parents may also take a more direct role in promoting and managing their children's encounters with peers. Ladd and Pettit (2002) discuss four ways parents may influence the frequency and nature of peer interactions:

a. *As designers* of the child's environment, parents make choices that affect the availability of peers and the settings (such as a safe versus a hazardous neighbourhood) within which peer interactions take place.
b. *As mediators,* parents arrange peer contacts for their children and regulate their choice of play partners.
c. *As supervisors,* parents monitor their children's peer interactions and offer guidance and support; and finally.
d. *As consultants,* parents provide more general advice and emotional support with respect to peer relations, especially in response to questions and concerns from the child.

One way parents influence peer interactions is through initiating and arranging peer contact, such as with a birthday party. (*Blend Images*)

Research indicates that parents vary in the frequency and the skill with which they perform these various roles, and that these variations in parental behaviour, in turn, relate to variations in children's peer relations (Ladd & Pettit, 2002). It has been found, for example, that peer acceptance in preschool is related to the extent to which parents initiate play opportunities for their children (Ladd & Hart, 1992). Play among children, especially toddlers or preschoolers, proceeds more smoothly and happily when a parent is present to facilitate and direct (Bhavnagri & Parke, 1991). And play opportunities are more frequent and friendship networks larger when children grow up in safe neighbourhoods with closely spaced houses than when conditions are less conducive to peer interaction (Medrich et al., 1982).

PARENTS' CHILD-REARING STRATEGIES Although these kinds of direct management can undoubtedly be important, most attempts to identify the parental contribution to peer relations have focused on general child-rearing strategies that either nurture or fail to nurture the social skills necessary for success with peers. Several dimensions emerge as important. One correlate of sociometric status and social skills is parental warmth (Ross & Howe, 2009). Children who come from homes that are characterized by high levels of warmth, nurturance, and emotional expressiveness tend to do well in the peer group (Eisenberg, Fabes, & Spinrad, 2006); conversely, children whose home lives are less harmonious are at risk for peer problems as well. The extreme of the latter situation arises in cases of physical abuse or neglect. Children who have been abused show special difficulty in responding appropriately when peers exhibit signs of distress (Klimes-Dougan & Kistner, 1990). Children who have been maltreated also show heightened levels of aggressiveness and social withdrawal (Ladd & Pettit, 2002). Not surprisingly, abused children tend to fare poorly on sociometric measures, and their unskilled behaviour with peers often perpetuates their difficulties (Bolger & Patterson, 2001; Cicchetti, 2010).

The parent's methods of controlling and disciplining the child can also be important. Parents of popular children tend to use an authoritative approach (Ross & Howe, 2009). They neither rigidly direct the child's every action nor allow too much leeway because of lack of time or interest. These parents are involved in the lives of their children, but the goal of their socialization seems to be to promote autonomy and not merely immediate compliance. When discipline becomes necessary, parents of popular children tend to prefer verbal rather than physical methods, reasoning with the child and negotiating rather than imposing solutions. As Ross and Howe (2009) suggest, such an approach models to children a caring, positive approach to relationships, which may then influence their relationships with their peers. In contrast, techniques of power assertion (threats and physical punishment) are likely to characterize the home lives of children with peer problems (Ladd & Pettit, 2002; Rubin & Burgess, 2002).

These conclusions about the contribution of parents to peer relations should not sound new or surprising. They fit with the general conclusions about the effects of parental practices discussed earlier in the chapter. They also fit with what we would expect from theory. Support for cognitive-developmental positions is evident in the value of rational, cognitively-oriented techniques of control and discipline. Support for social-learning theory can be seen in the clear role of parental reinforcements and parental models in fostering social skills. Indeed, the importance of parents as models is perhaps the clearest conclusion to be drawn from studies of the family's contribution to peer relations: parents who are warm and friendly and effective with others have children who are warm and friendly and effective with others.

For Thought and Discussion

How did parenting styles and child-rearing strategies in your family affect your peer relations during childhood and adolescence?

In discussing links between family and peer experience, we have emphasized the contribution of parents to the child's success with peers. We should add, however, that effects can clearly flow in the other direction as well. In *On the Cutting Edge 15.1* we discuss some recent research that explores how satisfactory relations with peers can buttress children against the effects of family adversity.

ON THE CUTTING EDGE 15.1
PEER RELATIONS AS A SOURCE OF RESILIENCE

It is well established that children exposed to aversive family environments during early childhood are at elevated risk for the development of behaviour problems. Of course, exposure to difficult family experiences does not foreordain adjustment problems. Many children reared in difficult circumstances nonetheless show good adjustment later in life. Psychologists refer to children who adapt positively in the face of significant adversity as **resilient children** (Luthar, Cicchetti, & Becker, 2000; Masten et al., 1999).

Studies of resilient children have revealed that a variety of factors contribute to children's ability to overcome negative experiences. These include personal characteristics of the child (e.g., socially responsive temperament, high self-esteem), aspects of the family (e.g., the availability of alternative caregivers), and characteristics of the child's wider social network (e.g., supportive neighbours or social agencies) (Cochran & Niego, 2002; Werner & Smith, 1982).

Resilient children Children who adapt positively and develop well despite early environmental adversity.

In one study, researchers explored whether peers might buffer children from the effects of exposure to a family environment characterized by high levels of marital conflict and physical aggression (Criss et al., 2002). The investigation was part of a larger, longitudinal study of children's socialization known as the Child Development Project (Pettit et al., 2001). More than 550 children and their families in Tennessee and Indiana were recruited for the study when they registered for kindergarten. The families were primarily of middle-income and Caucasian backgrounds. During the summer before the children entered kindergarten, the parents were interviewed and they completed questionnaires about a variety of issues. Based on the parents' responses, each family was rated on three dimensions of family adversity: ecological disadvantage, violent marital conflict, and harsh discipline.

(continued)

On the Cutting Edge 15.1 Peer Relations as a Source of Resilience *continued*

Data on children's peer relations were collected during kindergarten and grade 1. To assess children's peer relations, the researchers used two of the sociometric techniques described earlier. During individual interviews, children were shown a class roster and asked to nominate up to three peers they liked and three peers they disliked. They were also asked to rate how much they liked each peer. The measures provided an index of how much each child was generally liked by peers, as well as his or her number of friends.

Children's adjustment was based on teacher ratings. During the spring of grade 2, teachers completed the Child Behavior Checklist, a widely used checklist of behaviour problems that includes such items as "gets in many fights" and "disobedient at school."

As expected, the researchers found that children exposed to higher levels of family adversity in early childhood exhibited greater numbers of problem behaviours in grade 2. However, children reared in adverse circumstances but who had positive peer relations displayed far fewer behaviour problems than other children raised in comparable family situations. Moreover, the positive impact of peers was found for all three kinds of family adversity.

The results of this study suggest that positive peer relations can serve as a protective factor against family adversity. The findings also raise a number of intriguing questions. One question is how peer relations might moderate the effects of negative family environments. Theorists have proposed a number of explanations. One possibility is that positive peer relationships provide a "remedial" context in which children can practise certain skills not picked up at home (Price, 1996). For instance, a child whose parents are too stressed to help the child learn how to manage his or her emotions may learn how to do so in the context of peer interaction.

Another possibility is that relationships with peers may foster the child's engagement in school and foster positive relations with teachers. A positive orientation toward school may, in turn, decrease the child's tendency toward social deviance. A third possibility is that peers may serve as a form of "behavioural intervention." The negative reactions of peers, and possibly the peers' parents, to inappropriate behaviour (e.g., aggression) may teach the at-risk child that behaviours that are normative in his or her own home are unacceptable outside of it.

Finally, children's relationships with peers may also indirectly modify parents' behaviours. By interacting with the parents of their children's friends, mothers may learn more effective means of discipline and of resolving marital conflicts (Fletcher et al., 1995). Establishing a network of relations with other parents may also reduce family stress by providing social support. Thus, peer relations may lead to improvements in the behaviour of children at risk via their positive influence on parenting.

LEARNING OBJECTIVE 15.6

Understand how experiences within the family contribute to children's behaviour with friends.

1. How do relationships with siblings compare with peer relationships?
2. In what ways do parents contribute to children's peer relationships?

CONCLUSION

In 1998, Judith Harris published a book titled *The Nurture Assumption,* a book that quickly became one of the most talked about and controversial publications in the field. The book was an extension of an earlier article by Harris (1995), the opening lines of which set forth her basic thesis: "Do parents have any important long-term effects on the development of their child's personality? This article examines the relevant evidence and concludes that the answer is no" (p. 458). Rather than parents' practices being of any importance, Harris argued that children's development was shaped by two main forces: the genes with which they were born and experiences in the peer group as they grew up.

Most child psychologists have not been persuaded by Harris' arguments, and many, in fact, have offered explicit counterarguments to her position (e.g., Collins et al., 2000; Maccoby, 2000a, 2002; Vandell, 2000). As our discussions throughout this chapter suggest, we are not persuaded either. We believe that a substantial body of evidence indicates that parents can be important from birth, both in shaping eventual individual differences among children (the idiographic side of development) and in aiding the development of species-wide competencies and attributes (the normative side of development).

Whatever its ultimate fate, however, *The Nurture Assumption* does serve to provide a valuable reminder of several important points. One is that although parents may be important for their children's development, they are very far from being all-important. Many factors contribute to making all of us what we ultimately become. These factors clearly include the two determinants emphasized by Harris: peers and genes. Psychology's growing appreciation of the importance of genetic factors was a theme of earlier chapters, and the potential contributions of peers should be clear from the discussions in this chapter. Nor do genes and peers exhaust the non-parental sources of children's development. If you need to be reminded of this point, simply look back at all the forces in the Bronfenbrenner ecological systems model (Figure 1.1).

A second point concerns the challenges in doing research on some of the most basic and important issues in the field, including socialization. If fundamental uncertainties still exist after a century of child-rearing research, it is not because of either lack of effort or lack of competence on psychologists' part. Rather, it is because child rearing is considerably more difficult to study than are most topics that science addresses—indeed, more difficult than most topics within psychology.

A final point is that despite the challenges, the scientific method has brought genuine advances in our understanding of child rearing specifically, and of childhood more generally. There was a time when the expert scientific advice to parents about how to treat children was John Watson's (1928) "Never hug or kiss them, never let them sit in your lap" (p. 81). We have come a long way since then. The same story could be told for dozens of other topics considered in this book. At the same time, there is still much to be learned about almost every topic we have considered. The power of the scientific approach is verified daily in the study of child psychology. But the mysteries of human development yield their secrets slowly.

SUMMARY

KEY TERMS

authoritarian parenting, p. 570
authoritative parenting, p. 570
behavioural homophily, p. 595
blended family, p. 583
clique, p. 589
controversial child, p. 601
crowds, p. 589
extended family, p. 580
friendship, p. 594
group, p. 589
neglected child, p. 601
parallel play, p. 588
parental control, p. 570
parental warmth, p. 570
parenting style, p. 570
peer-mediated intervention, p. 605
permissive parenting, p. 570
pretend play, p. 587
rejected child, p. 601
resilient children, p. 609
sibling rivalry, p. 578
social problem-solving skills, p. 591
social support, p. 598
social withdrawal, p. 602
sociometric techniques, p. 598
uninvolved (disengaged) parenting, p. 570

LEARNING OBJECTIVE 15.1 Discuss four theoretical approaches to socialization.

1. *How do evolutionary approaches view socialization?*
   Evolutionary approaches reflect the assumption that evolution has provided an important innate basis for many social behaviours. Infants enter the world with characteristics that elicit appropriate caregiving, and adults, in turn, are equipped with natural responses to these

characteristics. Many behaviours toward peers (such as altruism and aggression) are also assumed to have an innate underpinning that reflects the evolutionary history of the species.

2. *What is the major focus of environmental/learning approaches to socialization?*
The environmental/learning approach to socialization stresses the application of general learning principles. Both parents and peers can affect children's development in several ways. Both may reinforce or punish certain behaviours and thereby increase or decrease their likelihood. Both may serve as models who influence the child's subsequent behaviour. Finally, peers, in particular, can be an important source for self-efficacy judgments.

3. *What does the cognitive-developmental approach to socialization emphasize?*
The cognitive-developmental approach emphasizes the cognitive resources that both parents and children bring to the task of socialization. Parents hold beliefs of various sorts about children, beliefs that contribute to both their socialization practices and the child's development. Children, in turn, are active cognitive processors in socialization interchanges. Children also form beliefs about other children, and such beliefs are one determinant of how they behave toward peers. Interaction with peers can also serve as an important impetus for cognitive change. Both Piaget and Kohlberg stressed conflict with peers as one source of the ability to consider different points of view.

4. *How does the sociocultural perspective view socialization?*
For theorists in the sociocultural perspective, development is always embedded within a social context, and thus questions of socialization are central to the approach. Both parents and peers can nurture development most effectively when they provide experiences that are within the child's zone of proximal development for the task in question. In addition to the various microsystems (such as family and peers) within which development occurs, the sociocultural approach stresses the relations among systems and the effects of the general culture on socialization and development.

LEARNING OBJECTIVE 15.2 Analyze the influence of parents and other family members on childhood socialization.

1. *What are four major parenting styles that have been identified?*
The goals of most child-rearing studies are to identify important differences among parents and to determine the effects of these variations on children's development. One influential approach, proposed by Diana Baumrind, identifies four general parenting styles that vary along the dimensions of warmth and control. The authoritative style is characterized by firm control in the context of a warm, supportive relationship. In contrast, the authoritarian style is high in control but low in warmth. The permissive style shows the opposite pattern to the authoritarian style, and is high in warmth and low in control. Finally, the uninvolved style is low on both warmth and control.

2. *What are the different outcomes associated with these styles of parenting?*
In general, the authoritative style is associated with the most positive outcomes in both social and cognitive domains. The other parenting styles are linked to more negative outcomes, although in somewhat different ways. Children of authoritarian parents tend to be anxious, easily upset, and low in self-confidence. They often react with anger and aggression when frustrated. Children of permissive parents tend to be impulsive, immature, disobedient, and dependent. Children of uninvolved parents show poor social and academic competence, and may be at risk for later delinquency. These effects are not inevitable, however, and they may vary across different populations. In particular, authoritarian parenting appears to have beneficial effects in some cultural contexts and in some environmental conditions.

3. *To what extent do fathers play a role in parenting?*
Studies of socialization are increasingly taking into account the father's contribution to parenting, as well as that of the mother. Although paternal involvement has increased in recent years, fathers typically devote less time to child care than do mothers. In many cultures, fathers' interactions with the child centre on play, rather than more general caregiving. Fathers can be effective caregivers, however. The same attributes that characterize successful parenting for mothers (warmth and control) are equally important for fathers.

4. *What is the child's contribution to the socialization process?*
Most child-rearing studies are correlational, which means that the direction of cause and effect is uncertain. In some instances, however, the causal direction is from child to parent, as characteristics of children influence the ways that parents treat them. Work on temperament provides the clearest example of this point. Variations in irritability, activity level, emotionality, timidity, and sociability can affect the ways that parents interact with children. Characteristics of the child can elicit particular behaviours from the parent. Parental behaviours, in turn, can alter characteristics of the child.

LEARNING OBJECTIVE 15.3 Analyze the ways that families function as a social system.

1. *How do sibling relationships influence child development?*
Relations among siblings vary markedly in quality, from close and supportive to distant and at times hostile. The children's temperaments are one contributor to these variations; parental practices are another. With development, relations among siblings typically become broader in scope and more symmetrical. Growing up with siblings can affect a number of aspects of development, including theory-of-mind skills in the cognitive realm and gender-role development in the social realm.

2. *What role do grandparents play in child development?*
Grandparents can play a variety of roles in their grandchildren's lives, from occasional play partner to principal caregiver. Grandmothers are typically more involved than are grandfathers, and in some cultures grandparents have greater involvement than in others. More generally, the extended family is the norm in a number of cultural settings, and in such settings the extended family is associated with positive developmental outcomes.

3. *How does divorce affect child development?*
Divorce has become more prevalent in recent years and is associated with a number of negative outcomes, both immediate and long-term. Effects are not inevitable, however, and both their occurrence and their magnitude depend on a number of factors. Among these factors are the age and sex of the child, the parenting styles experienced by the child following divorce, and the post-divorce living circumstances, including whether one or both parents remarry.

4. *What do we know about children raised by single parents who have never married?*
The number of single-parent families is increasing in Canada. Adolescent parents are the most disadvantaged of single parents. High rates of problem behaviour are found among children of teen parents. A very different group of single parents is older, professional women who choose to raise a child on their own. Research available thus far indicates that children reared by such single mothers by choice may not face the same developmental risks as children in single-parent homes created through divorce or teen parenthood.

5. *How does adoption affect child development?*
Adopted children are at greater than average risk for a number of negative outcomes. Nevertheless, most adopted children turn out fine, and outcomes for many are more positive than would have been the case had they stayed in their family of origin.

6. *How does gay and lesbian family structure work as a context for child development?*
   Studies of children growing up with lesbian or gay parents do not indicate negative effects of such family arrangements. Most current research has examined children of lesbian parents, and there has been much less study of gay men as parents. Research has found few consistent effects differentiating these children from those in other family arrangements. This conclusion holds across a range of outcomes, including self-esteem, intelligence, family relations, and peer relations, as well as gender-role development and sexual identity.

LEARNING OBJECTIVE 15.4 Trace the development of peer relations and discuss how peers influence each other's development.

1. *How do infants interact with their peers?*
   Children's peer relations undergo dramatic changes with development. Infants as young as 6 months show interest in and positive behaviours toward other babies. As infants develop, their interactions with peers become more frequent, more complex, and more reciprocal. Negative peer interactions are also evident, particularly disputes over toys.

2. *Describe how peer interactions develop in the preschool period.*
   During the preschool years, peer interactions continue to grow in frequency and complexity. Relations with peers become more differentiated, and symbolic forms of interaction begin to predominate over physical ones. Play increases in both cognitive level and social organization as cooperative play becomes increasingly likely.

3. *Describe the characteristics of peer interaction in the elementary-school and adolescent years.*
   Development during the elementary-school years is partly a continuation of trends present earlier. In addition, groups, both formal and informal, begin to assume a prominent role. Studies of children's groups reveal the importance of common interests and goals for group formation, as well as the importance of organization and agreed-on norms for effective group functioning. During high school, groups of cliques often come together to form crowds—large, loosely organized groups that serve to structure social identity in high school.

4. *What role does cognitive development play in children's peer relations?*
   A factor stressed especially in the cognitive-developmental approach to peer relations is the cognitive level of the child. Cognitive level is by no means a perfect predictor of peer interaction. Nevertheless, evidence from both correlational research and experimental training studies suggests that cognitive factors such as social problem-solving skills, perspective taking, and information-processing abilities do contribute to peer relations.

5. *In what ways can peers be considered as socializing agents for one another?*
   As they interact more, children become important socializing agents for one another, especially by delivering reinforcements and punishments for particular behaviours and by serving as models. The peer group is an influential source of values and behaviour, both positive and negative. Parents remain influential as well, and, on many issues, the views of peers and of parents are more similar than different.

LEARNING OBJECTIVE 15.5 Discuss the contributors to and benefits of friendship.

1. *How does children's understanding of friendship develop?*
   A particularly important peer relation is friendship. Children themselves agree with this assessment—from the preschool years on, children talk about friends as being different from peers in general. Children reason about friendship in increasingly sophisticated ways as they develop. Young children tend to think of friends in concrete terms as sources of immediate

pleasure; older children are more likely to see friendship as an enduring relationship characterized by such attributes as intimacy and loyalty.

2. *What factors are related to friendship formation?*
Children tend to pick friends who are similar to themselves. Similarities in age, gender, and race have all been shown to influence selection. Similarities of a more behavioural sort also play a role. Friends tend to be similar in academic orientation, and they often share the same outside-of-school interests. Studies suggest that a variety of processes contribute to friendship formation, including exchange of information, self-disclosure, and successful resolution of conflict.

3. *Outline the characteristics and benefits of friendship.*
Behaviour with friends differs from that with non-friends in a number of ways. Prosocial behaviours, such as sharing and helping, are generally more common with friends. Although conflict does not disappear once a friendship has been formed, resolution of conflict is usually more successful among friends than among non-friends. Finally, sharing of intimate information is more likely among friends, and the importance of intimacy for friendship increases as children get older. Friendship can have long-term as well as immediate benefits. Among the aspects of development that are influenced by the quality of friendships are self-esteem and availability of social support in times of need.

4. *Describe the correlates of popularity in children.*
Children show important individual differences in the quality of their peer relations. Typically, such differences have been assessed through sociometric techniques—judgments offered by the child's peers. Children are defined as popular if they are the objects of many positive and few negative judgments. Studies of the determinants of popularity have explored both relatively indirect predictors and more direct behavioural correlates. Variables in the first category that correlate with popularity include intellectual ability and physical attractiveness. The behavioural skills that seem to distinguish popular from less popular children are of three sorts: skill in initiating interaction, skill in maintaining interaction, and skill in resolving conflict.

5. *How do rejected, neglected, and controversial children differ?*
Sociometric assessments also identify children with problems in peer relations. The rejected child receives few positive but many negative nominations from the peer group, whereas the controversial child receives many choices in both categories, and the neglected child receives few nominations of any sort. Both rejected and neglected children show deficits in social skills, although their behavioural problems take different forms. Many (although not all) rejected children are characterized by aggressive, antisocial, and inappropriate behaviour. Many (although again, not all) neglected children are characterized by shy and withdrawn behaviour. Some shy, withdrawn children, however, become rejected and may be victimized by other peers. Controversial children are liked by many peers, but disliked by many others. They are often sociable, but tend to also be high on aggression. Training in social skills can be helpful for many children with peer relationship problems.

LEARNING OBJECTIVE 15.6 Understand how experiences within the family contribute to children's behaviour with friends.

1. *How do relationships with siblings compare with peer relationships?*
Siblings are in many respects similar to peers as social objects, and sibling relations show many of the characteristics important in relations with peers, especially friends. Both relationships involve partners who are close in age, and hence interactions are likely to be more egalitarian and symmetrical than are interactions with adults, such as parents or teachers. Sibling

relationships and friendships are different in some respects, however, and specific qualities of sibling relations are only sometimes reflected in relations with peers.

2. *In what ways do parents contribute to children's peer relationships?*
Parents can contribute to their children's behaviour with peers in a number of ways. Secure attachment to the parent during infancy is associated with positive peer relations in later childhood. Parents' participation in early pretend play may facilitate the emergence of play with peers. Both the frequency and the nature of peer interactions may be affected by various parental actions, ranging from choice of neighbourhood to direct initiation and management of peer encounters. Finally, parents' child-rearing practices can help instill the social skills necessary for success in the peer group. Among the parental practices that can be beneficial are creation of a warm and supportive family atmosphere, use of cognitively oriented techniques of discipline, and provision of models of socially appropriate actions in the parents' own behaviour.

CHAPTER 16

GENDER-ROLE DEVELOPMENT AND SEX DIFFERENCES

Large toy manufacturers and retailers have been accused of driving stereotypes by allowing on-line shoppers to "shop by gender" and by dividing their stores into very obvious pink versus blue toy sections. But are they creating the stereotype, or merely responding to it?

Extensive studies have been conducted to determine the source of sex-role stereotyping. While some parents (and commercial forces) consciously reinforce "girl" behaviour in girls and "boy" behaviour in boys, most stereotype perpetuation appears to be unintentional.

Research has shown that parents who would be appalled by suggestions that they treat their sons and daughters differently, in fact do, and in stereotypical ways. One early North American study showed that parents provided more explanations to their sons than daughters at a science exhibit, a traditionally male domain. Girls also tend to be praised and encouraged more for "feminine" behaviours, such as caring for younger siblings.

The cycle then self-perpetuates through observational learning, as sex-stereotyped mothers and fathers become models for daughters and sons, respectively.

Then of course, there is biology. Boys and girls *are* biologically different, and even young babies are aware of these differences. At Concordia University in Montreal, researchers found that babies as young as 9 months old correctly paired (as measured by length of gaze) female voices with female faces and male with male.

The forces of socialization, observational learning, and innate biological differences interact in very complex—and often subtle—ways to support society's gender stereotypes. In this chapter, in addition to looking at stereotypes, we also introduce the prominent theories of gender-role development, discuss perceived and real sex differences, and explore the development of sexual relationships and behaviour. ■

IN THIS CHAPTER, we consider various aspects of gender-role development and sex differences, including the origin of sex differences, how gender roles develop and what they mean, and why this area has attracted so much attention. First, however, we should clarify the terminology we will be using throughout the chapter.

When to use the label *gender* rather than *sex* has been a matter of some debate among researchers (Halpern, 2012). Some authors have argued that the term sex should be reserved for differences between males and females that are biological in origin, whereas gender should be used to describe differences that result from experience and socialization. However, in actual fact, it is very difficult to separate these two influences in the individual's development as female or male (Best, 2010; Halpern, 2012). Consequently, in this chapter, we use the terms interchangeably to refer to an individual's maleness or femaleness. The biological process through which these physical differences emerge is called **sexual differentiation**. When we refer to a sex difference, however, we are saying simply that males and females differ on the particular personality trait or psychological characteristic under discussion; we are not assuming anything about the biological or environmental origins of that difference.

Sexual differentiation The biological process through which physical differences between sexes emerge.

The term **gender role** (or *sex-role stereotype)* refers to a pattern or set of behaviours considered appropriate for males or females within a particular culture (Wood & Eagly, 2010). In most cultures, for example, the male gender role is characterized by such traits as leadership, independence, and aggressiveness, whereas females are expected to be nurturing, dependent, and sensitive (Best, 2001, 2010; Seem & Clark, 2006). **Sex typing** is the process by which children develop the behaviours and attitudes considered appropriate for their gender. This process is assumed to involve a combination of biological, cognitive, and social mechanisms (Best, 2010; Powlishta et al., 2001).

Gender role A pattern or set of behaviours considered appropriate for males or females within a particular culture.

Sex typing The process by which children develop the behaviours and attitudes considered appropriate for their gender.

Learning Objective 16.1

Understand four theoretical approaches to gender development.

THEORIES OF GENDER-ROLE DEVELOPMENT AND SEX DIFFERENCES

The past three decades have seen dramatic changes in the roles of men and women. In Canada, we are not surprised to learn that the next governor general or prime minister will be a woman, that the next NASA space mission will include a female Canadian astronaut, that the young mother next door is an army reservist, or that the best doctor in town is a woman. The roles of men have also changed. Increasing numbers of Canadian men share child care and household responsibilities with mothers (Marshall, 2006), and although still relatively uncommon, some fathers opt to be stay-at-home dads. The study of gender roles covers many different questions and issues. And as usual, theorists from the four major traditions have different things to say about the nature and causes of this aspect of development.

EVOLUTIONARY AND BIOLOGICAL APPROACHES

The evolutionary and biological family of theories focuses on the contributions of innate biological factors to the development of sex differences, gender roles, and sexual orientation. Evolutionary theory provides a broad framework for studying sex differences, whereas research on more immediate biological processes provides insight into the mechanisms by which sex differences are expressed in each succeeding generation.

EVOLUTIONARY APPROACHES As we have seen, evolutionary approaches to development focus on the adaptive function of behaviours and traits. Most of these adaptations are species-wide and occur in both males and females. For instance, according to the evolutionary approach, a capacity to form attachments with caregivers has evolved in both male and female infants (Simpson & Belsky, 2008). To understand sex differences, however, evolutionary theorists must address why behaviours adaptive for one sex may not be adaptive for the other. To answer this question, evolutionary theorists point to the different roles males and females play in reproduction.

One way in which the reproductive roles of males and females differ is in the relative investment each makes to parenting and to mating (Trivers, 1972). For females, each copulation brings with it the possibility of conception and nine months of pregnancy. In traditional societies and in our ancestral past, it also means several years of nursing and caring for offspring. Thus, females have a large potential investment in each copulation. In theory, males need to invest little more than sperm and the energy required for copulation. As a result of these differences in parental investment, natural selection favoured somewhat different reproductive strategies for females and males. According to the evolutionary position, females evolved to be choosier about their mates and to invest more in parenting, whereas males, who invest much less in individual offspring, evolved to focus their reproductive efforts largely on mating (Buss & Kenrick, 1998; Kenrick & Luce, 2000).

Support for the evolutionary origins of human sex differences can be found in ethological studies that show similar behaviour patterns among the females and males of many non-human species. Evolutionary theorists contend that sex differences that emerge during childhood reflect and help the young prepare for later reproductive roles (Geary & Bjorklund, 2000). Thus, higher rates of aggression and dominance displayed by boys are seen as preparation for adult male competition over mates. And girls' greater inhibitory control reflects the challenges they will face in choosing mates and caring for young, demanding infants (Bjorklund & Pellegrini, 2011).

PSYCHOBIOLOGICAL APPROACH Clearly, modern sex differences can be interpreted as reflecting the evolutionary past. But to understand how this past is expressed in each succeeding generation, we must look to more immediate causes, such as genes, hormones, and brain structure and organization.

Researchers interested in the biological underpinnings of sex differences have concentrated much of their attention on hormones. During the prenatal period, fetal hormones guide the development of male or female reproductive organs and external genitals (Hines, 2009). There is growing evidence that prenatal sex hormones also affect the organization of the central nervous system (e.g., the size of brain structures, connections between nerve cells). Sex hormones after puberty are believed to activate the neural systems and behavioural patterns laid down earlier.

Hormones contribute not only to behavioural differences between males and females, but also to differences within each sex. Individual differences in masculinity and femininity are sometimes due to hormonal disorders (Hines, 2009). Other differences may be due to naturally occurring variations in hormone levels (Auyeung et al., 2009). In addition, hormone levels can be influenced by innumerable environmental factors, such as outside temperature, immunological reactions, and maternal stress.

The idea that biology and experience interact in development is not unique to evolutionary accounts. It characterizes the sociocultural approach as well. We turn to this approach next.

SOCIOCULTURAL APPROACHES

According to the sociocultural approach, gender roles develop as children participate in and prepare for the adult roles they are expected to play in their communities (Rogoff, 2003). Gender differences arise because, in most cultures, males and females occupy very different social roles (Eagly et al., 2000; Wood & Eagly, 2002, 2010). Historically, these social roles have been closely tied to biological differences between males and females—in particular, differences in child bearing and child rearing and differences in size and strength. The gender roles of girls and boys parallel those of the adults around them and exert a powerful influence on how, with whom, and where children spend their time (Wood & Eagly, 2002). Like their mothers, girls around the world devote more time to child care and household chores than do boys. Boys, in contrast, spend more time in unsupervised activities and play (Larson & Verma, 1999). Compared with boys, girls are also more likely to be found at home or close to home (Weisner, 1996; Whiting & Edwards, 1988).

Sociocultural theorists contend that sex differences observed among children and adults *follow* from the roles commonly held by females versus males. This view contrasts with that held by evolutionary psychologists, who believe that intrinsic, inborn differences between the sexes give rise to and maintain gender roles. To be sure, sociocultural theorists acknowledge that females and males have biological differences that may affect what activities they pursue. They point out, however, that male and female roles vary among cultures, which indicates that the roles cannot be fixed aspects of male and female inheritance (Best, 2010).

Sociocultural theorists also recognize that gender roles affect behaviour through cognitive and social processes. Exactly how these processes operate is the focus of the remaining two perspectives: the cognitive-developmental and environmental/learning approaches.

COGNITIVE-DEVELOPMENTAL APPROACHES

The cognitive-developmental approach to gender-role development focuses on the child's understanding of the concepts of male and female and his or her ability to identify with one of them. These models emphasize the child's growing knowledge regarding gender and gender roles, and how this knowledge translates into the sex-typed behaviours that we commonly observe (Liben & Bigler, 2002; Martin, Ruble, & Szkrybalo, 2002).

KOHLBERG'S STAGE MODEL The earliest cognitive-developmental model of gender role development was proposed by Lawrence Kohlberg (1966). Kohlberg believed that children construct their gender identity from what they see and hear around them. Once established, this gender identity serves to organize and regulate children's gender learning and behaviour.

Gender constancy The belief that one's own gender is fixed and irreversible.

A key component of Kohlberg's model is the development of **gender constancy**—the belief that one's own gender is fixed and irreversible (Martin et al., 2002; Ruble et al., 2007). This understanding is similar to the Piagetian concept of conservation of physical properties discussed in Chapter 8. Children who have achieved gender constancy understand that their sex is a permanent attribute tied to biological properties, and that changes in superficial characteristics, such as hair length, clothing, or activities, will not turn them into a member of the opposite sex.

Gender identity The ability to categorize oneself as male or female.

Gender stability The awareness that all boys grow up to be men and all girls become women.

Gender consistency The recognition that an individual's gender remains the same despite changes in dress, hairstyle, activities, or personality.

Kohlberg proposed that gender constancy develops in three stages: **gender identity** ("I am a boy/girl"), **gender stability** ("I will grow up to be a man/woman"), and **gender consistency** ("I cannot change my sex"). Furthermore, according to Kohlberg's theory, children reliably behave in gender-typed ways only after they have developed gender constancy—not until about 6 years of age (Halim & Ruble, 2010).

Studies of the development of gender constancy in societies as diverse as Egypt, Kenya, and Nepal, as well as North America, have confirmed that children do, indeed, progress through Kohlberg's stages in the proposed order (see Gibbons, 2000, for a review). The idea that gender constancy precedes children's adherence to gender norms is not, however, supported by empirical research. Children show gender-typed toy preferences, emulate same-sex models, and reward peers for gender-appropriate behaviour years before they understand that gender is a permanent, unchanging attribute.

Moreover, although numerous studies have shown significant relationships between levels of gender constancy and gender-appropriate preferences and behaviours, other studies have failed to demonstrate a link or have found stronger relationships at lower—rather than higher—levels of gender constancy, quite the opposite of what Kohlberg originally proposed (Ruble et al., 2006, 2007).

GENDER SCHEMA THEORY Theorists working within the framework of information processing have proposed an alternative theory of gender-role development, based on the concept of schemas. Proponents of this approach explain developmental changes in children's gender-role behaviour in terms of mental models that organize children's experiences concerning gender. Specifically, children form **gender schemas**—cognitive representations of the

Gender schemas Cognitive representations of the characteristics associated with being either male or female.

characteristics associated with being either male or female (Bem, 1981; Martin et al., 2002, Ruble et al., 2006).

According to this theory, children categorize gender-relevant stimuli (people, toys, activities) as "for girls" or "for boys." These schemas result principally from two factors: the child's inborn tendency to organize and classify information from the environment, and the preponderance of gender-distinguishing cues (such as clothing, names, and occupations) that make these concepts easily identifiable.

The child then adopts one of the schemas: girl or boy. This self-schema, in turn, affects the child in two ways. First, it prompts the child to pay greater attention to information relevant to his or her own gender. A girl may notice television ads for a new Barbie doll, for example, whereas a boy may be more attuned to commercials announcing the release of a new action hero movie. Second, it influences the child's choice of activities. For instance, a girl may decide to play with Barbie dolls and a boy to take karate lessons (Leaper & Friedman, 2007; Martin et al., 2002).

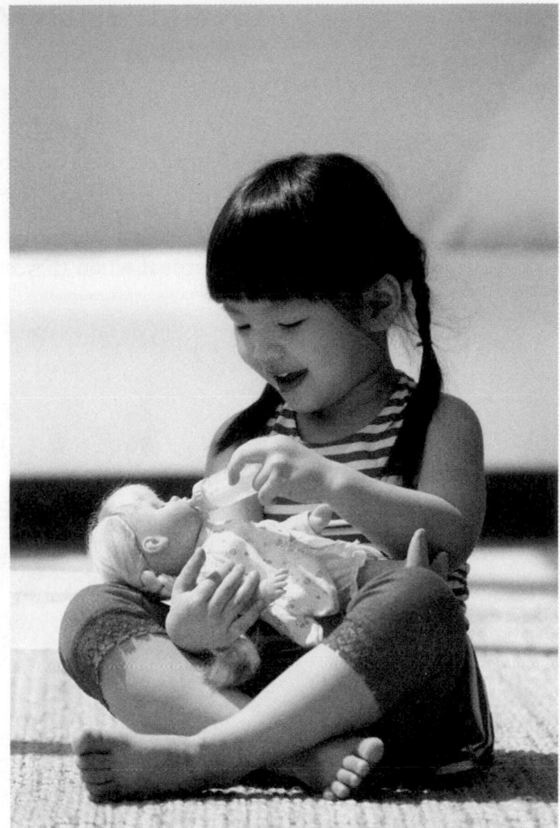

According to gender schema theory, children categorize gender-relevant stimuli, such as toys, as "for girls" or "for boys," and adopt one of those schemas, which influences their self-regulated behaviour. (© *Cedric Lim/AsiaPix/Corbis*)

Gender schema theory has much in common with Kohlberg's theory. In both approaches, for example, children are motivated to behave in ways that are consistent with what they know or believe about gender. An important difference between the two theories, however, is the level of knowledge or understanding required for the child to begin to act in accordance with gender norms. Kohlberg believed that children do not behave in sex-typed ways until they achieve gender constancy, a milestone not typically attained until 6 years of age or later. According to gender schema theory, children begin to organize their experience and behave in ways compatible with gender norms once they can identify themselves as male or female—an achievement typically reached between the ages of 2 and 3.

What does research have to say about gender schema theory? As we discuss in more detail later, there is considerable evidence that young children do use gender as a means to categorize their world and that knowledge of gender categories influences children's processing of information. The link between gender-role knowledge and gender-typed behaviour is less straightforward. For example, children often show gender-typed toy preferences or identify specific toys as being more appropriate or typical for one gender or the other even before they can label themselves as girls or boys (Serbin et al., 2001). Gender schema theorists argue, however, that these children may know more about gender roles than they are given credit for; that is, the standard ways of assessing gender knowledge may underestimate what children understand about gender (Liben & Bigler, 2002; Martin et al., 2002).

Another potential problem with the theory is that greater amounts of gender role knowledge do not always translate into more gender-typed behaviour. That is, some children show impressive knowledge of gender-role stereotypes, but nonetheless choose to behave in non-gender-typed ways. Gender schema theorists do not view this finding as a serious threat to the theory, noting that a variety of situational factors influence whether children will match their behaviour to their gender knowledge structures (Martin et al., 2002).

It is also the case that some children develop *idiosyncratic gender schemas,* or gender schemas that include dimensions more typically associated with the opposite sex. For instance, a "tomboy" may have a schema that is different from the schemas of more typical girls. This schema would likely allow the child greater flexibility than a more traditional gender schema. Nonetheless, it would influence her to behave in certain ways rather than others (Liben & Bigler, 2002).

For Thought and Discussion

What are some examples of things in your everyday life that you probably pay attention to or ignore because they relate to your gender schema?

ENVIRONMENTAL/LEARNING APPROACHES

Within the environmental/learning family of theories, social-learning theorists view gender roles as primarily learned patterns of behaviour that are acquired through experience (Lott & Maluso, 2001). According to this approach, many sex-typed behaviours are products of the same learning principles that govern other social behaviours, including reinforcement processes, observational learning, and self-regulation (Bussey & Bandura, 1999, 2004). Little boys, for example, are more likely to behave in traditionally masculine ways because they receive social approval for this type of behaviour and disapproval when they exhibit traditionally feminine behaviour or preferences. They also observe and imitate models in their environments—ranging from parents to classmates to TV characters—who display gender-related behaviours (Leaper & Friedman, 2007). And, by learning to anticipate how others will respond to their behaviour, they gradually internalize standards regarding what are appropriate and inappropriate gender behaviours, and then self-regulate their behaviour to conform to these standards.

Children observe and imitate models in their environments who display gender-related behaviours. (*Design Pics/Media Bakery*)

Social-learning theorists do not deny that biological distinctions separate males and females, but they argue that many of the sex differences in children's social behaviour and cognitive abilities are not inevitable results of their genetic makeup. Nor do they deny that children develop a cognitive understanding of different gender roles. But this understanding, they believe, is not necessarily the cause of the sex differences we observe in behaviour, especially during early childhood (Bussey & Bandura, 1999, 2004).

LEARNING OBJECTIVE 16.1

Understand four theoretical approaches to gender development.

1. How do evolutionary and biological approaches view gender development?
2. How do sociocultural theorists account for the development of gender roles?
3. Describe two cognitive-developmental approaches to gender-role development.
4. How does social-learning theory view gender roles?

Learning Objective 16.2

Describe the physical, cognitive, and social/personality sex differences that researchers have found.

SOME PERCEIVED AND REAL SEX DIFFERENCES

In this section, we discuss sex differences that are commonly observed during childhood or adolescence. We begin with some guidance on how to interpret research on sex differences. As you may have noticed, studies sometimes yield conflicting results. This is certainly true of research on sex differences. To give just one example, some studies find that parents talk more to girls, others report that parents talk more to boys, and yet others find no differences in the amount of speech parents direct to sons and daughters. How do we know which results to believe?

Meta-analysis A method of reviewing the research literature on a given topic that uses statistical procedures to establish the existence and the size of effects.

To help make sense of discrepant results, researchers employ **meta-analysis**. In meta-analysis, researchers apply statistical rules to a group of studies that all investigate the same issue. Because meta-analysis is based on large amounts of data collected by numerous researchers under widely varying conditions, researchers are better able to draw firm conclusions about the phenomena under study (Borenstein et al., 2009). Meta-analyses are not available for every behaviour and attribute that has attracted the attention of researchers interested in sex differences. However, as you read our discussion of sex differences, pay special attention to those differences supported by studies that have used meta-analysis.

FIGURE 16.1

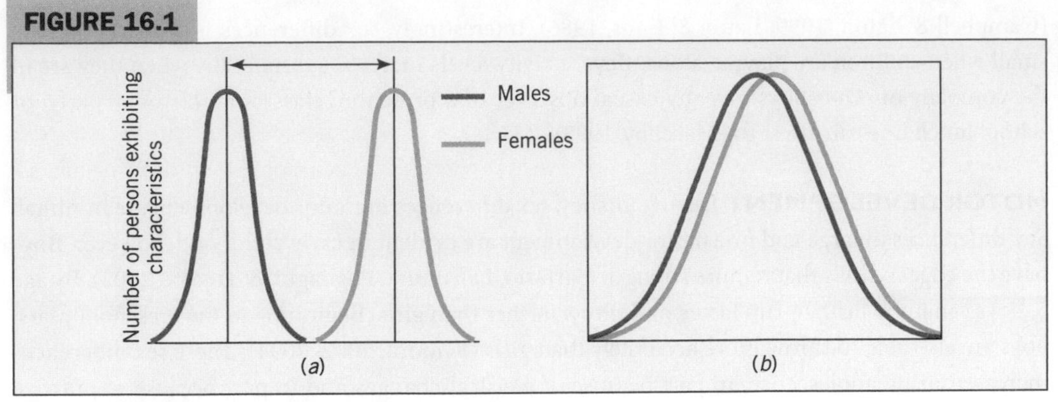

Possible patterns of sex differences. The discussion of sex differences focuses on the differences, on average, between males and females. Generally, the difference within each sex is larger than the difference between males and females, as shown in (*b*).

Another thought to keep in mind is that sex differences represent only the average difference across all males and females. To illustrate the point, consider Figure 16.1, which shows two possible patterns of sex differences. In (*a*), males and females differ so markedly that there is no overlap in their scores. When the topic of sex differences is raised, many people think in terms of the picture represented by graph (*a*). In fact, such a pattern virtually *never* arises in real life.

In graph (*b*), females, on average, outperform males, but there is considerable overlap between males and females. In this situation, many females are actually more different from other females than they are from the average male. Likewise, many males are actually more different from other males than they are from the average female. The general pattern depicted in (*b*) is the most common—although, of course, which sex outperforms the other may differ with the task or ability being assessed. In general, the average difference between males and females is actually smaller than the variability within each sex.

Finally, we caution you not to assume that any differences discussed here primarily reflect innate biological differences. All sex differences are best conceived of as the product of biological and environmental processes acting in combination.

PHYSICAL DIFFERENCES

Physical differences include differences in physical maturity and vulnerability, in activity level, and in motor development.

PHYSICAL MATURITY AND VULNERABILITY At birth, the female newborn is generally healthier and more developmentally advanced than the male, despite being somewhat smaller and lighter. Although she is less muscular and somewhat more sensitive to pain, she is better coordinated neurologically and physically (Garai & Scheinfeld, 1968; Lundqvist & Sabel, 2000; Reinisch & Sanders, 1992; Tanner, 1990). On average, females also reach developmental milestones earlier than males. For instance, girls lose their first tooth at a younger age and begin (and end) puberty sooner.

Males are physically more vulnerable than females from conception on. They are more likely to be miscarried, to suffer from physical and mental illnesses and various kinds of hereditary abnormalities, and to die in infancy (Hartung & Widiger, 1998; Jacklin, 1989). Males are also more likely to suffer physical injuries. This probably reflects a constellation of factors, including boys' higher activity level and greater risk-taking tendencies (Byrnes, Miller, & Schafer, 1999; Laing & Logan, 1999).

ACTIVITY LEVEL On average, boys have higher activity levels than girls. This sex difference first emerges during the prenatal period; male fetuses are more active in the womb (Almli, Ball, & Wheeler, 2001; DiPietro et al., 1996a). Meta-analytic studies reported by Warren Eaton of the University of Manitoba show that this difference is maintained through infancy and childhood

(Campbell & Eaton, 1999; Eaton & Enns, 1986). Interestingly, sex differences in activity level are small when children are playing alone. Boys' activity levels increase substantially when they are in the company of other boys—as any casual observer of a preschool classroom, birthday party, or school lunch line can attest to (Maccoby, 1998).

MOTOR DEVELOPMENT During infancy, sex differences in motor development are minimal. Sex differences in large and fine motor development are evident in early childhood, however. Boys have the edge in skills that require strength (Sartario, Lafrotuna, Pogliaghi, & Trecate, 2002). By age 5, boys can jump farther, run faster, and throw farther than girls. Beginning in the preschool years, boys are also able to throw more accurately than girls (Kimura, 2002, 2004). These sex differences increase during adolescence, in part because of physical changes and in part because of practice (Ruble et al., 2006).

Girls, in turn, have an advantage in motor skills that require a combination of balance and precise movement, such as hopping and skipping. Girls also have better fine motor skills (Ruble et al., 2006), and so initially have an easier time tying shoes and performing tasks required in school, such as writing, cutting paper, and the like.

COGNITIVE DIFFERENCES

According to popular stereotypes, girls are better at verbal tasks, whereas boys are better at mathematics (Halpern, Straight, & Stephenson, 2011). In fact, studies reveal that the differences between males and females in these two cognitive domains are not large (Priess & Hyde, 2010). Furthermore, the differences that do exist are often restricted to specific age groups, to specific kinds of tasks, or to very high-achieving groups. Nevertheless, some differences are observed.

LANGUAGE AND VERBAL ABILITIES There is little doubt that young females, on average, outperform young males in some kinds of verbal skills (Priess & Hyde, 2010; Ullman, Miranda, & Travers, 2008). Female infants tend to produce more sounds at an earlier age than do males, they tend to use words sooner, and the size of their early vocabularies tends to be larger (Bauer, Goldfield, & Reznick, 2002; Galsworthy et al., 2000; Huttenlocher et al., 1991). Girls also tend, on average, to be superior to boys on a variety of measures of grammar and language complexity, such as sentence length, use of pronouns, use of conjunctions, and so on (Kolb & Whishaw, 2009). Girls begin to show marked superiority at about 2 years of age, and the differences continue through adolescence (Koenigsknecht & Friedman, 1976; Schacter et al., 1978).

Throughout the school years, females achieve higher scores in reading and writing (Halpern et al., 2007). Early differences in learning to read may originate in sex differences in the ability to detect the sounds of language (phonology), as females outperform males across a range of phonological tasks (Majeres, 1999). Recent Canadian data show that females continue to outperform males on standardized tests of reading and writing during high school (Bussière et al., 2007). Doreen Kimura of Simon Fraser University also reports that females are superior to males on tests of verbal memory, a superiority that cannot be attributed simply to differences in verbal IQ (Kimura, 2002, 2004; Kimura & Clarke, 2002).

Links to Related Material

We discussed male-female differences in cerebral lateralization in Chapter 6.

In addition to gender differences in reading and writing ability, males are also more likely than females to have serious problems with speech and written language. Compared with girls, boys are more likely to suffer from language difficulties, such as stuttering (McKinnon, McLeod, & Reilly, 2007). They are also more likely to have dyslexia and other types of learning disorders that make learning to read and write difficult (Liederman, Kantrowitz, & Flannery, 2005; Phares, 2008).

Lateralization The specialization of functions in the right and left hemispheres of the brain.

There is evidence that sex differences in verbal and language abilities are biologically based. Of particular importance is brain **lateralization**—the specialization of functions in the right and left hemispheres. Some scientists believe that prenatal exposure to high levels of testosterone—which occurs normally during the development of male fetuses—slows the development of the left hemisphere and enhances the development of the right hemisphere (Rosen, Galaburda, & Sherman, 1990). This process may produce two results significant for sex differences in cognitive abilities.

One is that the right hemisphere is relatively more established in males. You may recall from Chapter 6 that the right hemisphere is specialized for spatial abilities. This may help account for the male advantage in spatial tasks. Second, the brains of females are less lateralized. Female superiority on verbal and language tasks may derive from the fact that they use both hemispheres to process language, whereas males' language processing tends to be localized in the left hemisphere. We return to the topic of lateralization in a later section.

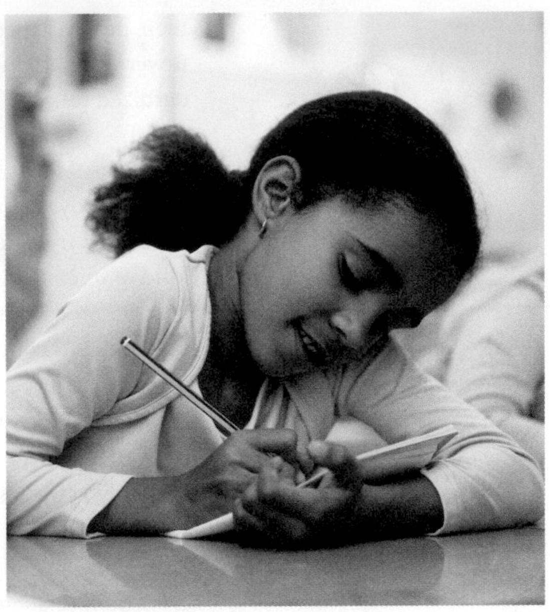

Girls, on average, outperform boys in language skills and in reading and writing. Evidence suggests that this is both biologically and environmentally based. *(PhotoDisc, Inc.)*

Although language skills appear to have biological underpinnings, environment plays a significant role as well. Girls usually experience a richer language environment than boys. Indeed, a meta-analysis of mother–child talk showed that mothers vocalize more to daughters, imitate their vocalizations more, and generally maintain a higher level of mother–infant vocal exchange (Leaper, Anderson, & Sanders, 1998). Moreover, parents tend to believe that their daughters have greater reading ability than their sons—which can affect how they interact with their children—even if their children's actual abilities do not support this belief (Eccles, Arbreton, et al., 1993; Wigfield et al., 2002).

QUANTITATIVE ABILITIES During elementary school, girls and boys are equally interested in mathematics (Andre et al., 1999; Eccles, Jacobs, et al., 1993; Folling-Albers & Hartinger, 1998; Wigfield et al., 1997). Even at this young age, however, females and males appear to differ in the kinds of mathematics in which they do well. Throughout elementary and intermediate school, girls tend to be better at computation (perhaps reflecting their better verbal abilities), whereas boys are better at problem solving and geometry (perhaps reflecting their better visuospatial abilities) (Kimura, 2002; Priess & Hyde, 2010). Notwithstanding these differences, there do not appear to be gender differences in understanding of mathematical concepts (Priess & Hyde, 2010).

By adolescence, males begin to perform significantly better than females on standardized tests of mathematics. For example, in the United States, males, on average, achieve higher scores on Scholastic Aptitude Test (SAT) mathematics tests than do females. Recent Canadian standardized test results show similar differences. On average, 15-year-old Canadian boys achieve higher mathematics test scores than do girls (Bussière et al., 2007), with the most pronounced difference on tests of shape and scale, and the least pronounced difference on measures of quantity (Bussière et al., 2004). The sex difference in scores on standardized exams is especially marked among students of very high ability (Priess & Hyde, 2010). Interestingly, despite these differences on standardized tests of mathematics, girls tend to receive higher grades than boys in mathematics classes in school (Halpern et al., 2007; Priess & Hyde, 2010).

Several studies have shed some light on male–female differences. These studies looked at *how* girls and boys solve mathematical problems—not just whether they solve them correctly or not. Compared with boys, grade 1 girls are more likely to use simpler strategies (e.g., counting on their fingers) that are almost certain to produce correct solutions. Boys, in contrast, tend to use more complex strategies, such as retrieval; but, as a result, they are at greater risk for making mistakes (Carr & Jessup, 1997; Carr, Jessup, & Fuller, 1999).

Some researchers believe that these early differences in the types of strategies preferred by girls and boys contribute to differences in mathematical achievement that persist over time. Despite their earlier "failures," by grade 3, boys are better able to rapidly and automatically retrieve correct answers to arithmetic problems. This ability may lay the foundation for later-developing mathematical competencies. How quickly students retrieve mathematical facts is predictive of their performance on both computational and mathematical reasoning tasks (Geary et al., 2000; Royer et al., 1999). Speedy retrieval may especially advantage males on timed tests, such as standardized tests.

There is also a sex difference in the kinds of strategies used to solve mathematical reasoning problems. Starting in grade 1, girls are more likely to use concrete strategies, such as counting, whereas boys use more abstract approaches (Fennema et al., 1998). By grade 3, girls prefer the conventional strategies taught in school, whereas boys are more likely to use logic, estimation, or some kind of unconventional strategy (Hopkins, McGillicuddy-De Lisi, & De Lisi, 1997).

Differences in strategy preferences can help explain why females tend to perform better in mathematics courses, yet obtain lower scores than males on standardized tests. Although the more orthodox approaches used by girls tend to produce correct solutions on conventional problems, they are less likely to yield results on problems that are unconventional (see Table 16.1 for an illustration). Consequently, girls may perform well on school exams designed to test whether they can correctly apply a strategy taught in class, but may do less well on trickier problems that require a novel approach. Conversely, although mathematics teachers may not always appreciate the creative solutions offered by boys, those approaches may confer an advantage on boys outside of the classroom (Gallagher & De Lisi, 1994; Gallagher et al., 2000).

Why boys and girls approach mathematical problems differently is not well understood. One possibility is that girls rely on safe strategies because they fear making mistakes. Indeed, some

TABLE 16.1 TWO TYPES OF SAT MATH PROBLEMS

Whereas Problem 1 is easily solved using a formula, Problem 2 is more easily solved using non-conventional procedures. Females tend to have better success with the first type of problem.

Problem 1	**Problem 2**
P Q R → 4/n 5/n 1/4 If PQ = QR on the number line above, what is the length of PR?	A blend of coffee is made by mixing Colombian coffee at $8 a kilogram with espresso coffee at $3 a kilogram. If the blend is worth $5 a kilogram, how many kilograms of the Colombian coffee are needed to make 50 kilograms of the blend?
(A) 1/12	(A) 20
(B) 1/9	(B) 25
(C) 1/8	(C) 30
(D) 1/6	(D) 35
(E) 3/16	(E) 40
Answer: (A) 1/12	Answer: (A) 20

Source: Adapted from A. M. Gallagher and R. De Lisi, "Gender Differences in Scholastic Aptitude Test Mathematics Problem Solving among High-Ability Students," *Journal of Educational Psychology, 86,* 1994, 204-211. Adapted by permission.

studies have suggested that females have less confidence in their mathematical abilities than do males, which can have detrimental effects on test performance (Cadinu et al., 2005; Nguyen & Ryan, 2008; Steffens & Jelenek, 2011). (Recall the effects of *stereotype threat,* discussed in Chapter 10.) The gender gap in beliefs involving mathematical competence, however, appears to be decreasing, and girls currently take as many math classes in high school as do boys (Priess & Hyde, 2010; Ruble et al., 2006). Another possibility is that females are more concerned with following rules and meeting teacher expectations (Dweck, 1999). Still another possibility is that sex differences in mathematics performance are related to underlying differences in spatial abilities (Halpern et al., 2007; Nuttall & Pezaris, 2001). We turn to this topic next.

SPATIAL ABILITIES As we have already noted, males do better than females, on average, on tasks involving spatial abilities (Kimura, 2002, 2004; Liben, 2006). Some sex differences in spatial abilities may be observed as early as infancy (Moore & Johnson, 2008; Quinn & Liben, 2008). Later, in the preschool years, boys outperform girls on spatial tasks such as the Mazes Subtest of the Wechsler Preschool and Primary Scale of Intelligence (Levine et al., 1999). Four-year-old boys also outperform girls on spatial transformation tasks, like that shown in Figure 16.2, and show superior performance on three-dimensional spatial tasks such as copying Lego models (Levine et al., 1999; McGuiness & Morley, 1991). In addition, Doreen Kimura (2002, 2004) of Simon Fraser University reports that boys are more accurate than girls on throwing tasks (e.g., throwing darts at a dartboard). Sex differences in spatial abilities increase in adolescence, although the extent of the difference varies with the task, according to a meta-analytic study conducted by Daniel and Susan Voyer of the University of New Brunswick (Voyer, Voyer, & Bryden, 1995).

FIGURE 16.2

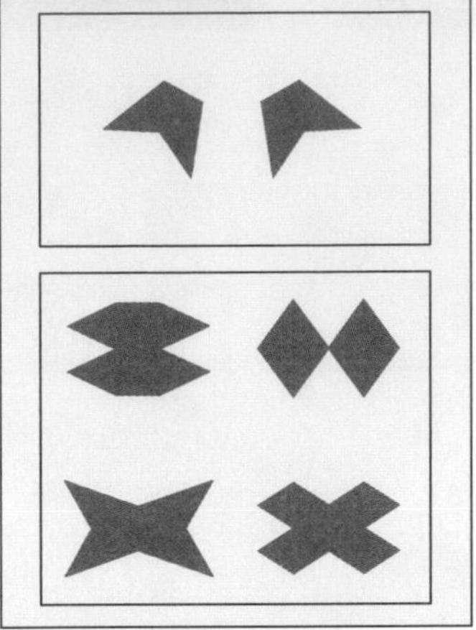

Spatial transformation task. In this spatial transformation task, children select which of the four cards shows what the two pieces in the top card would look like if placed together. *Source: S. C. Levine, J. Huttenlocher, A. Taylor, and A. Langrock, "Early Sex Differences in Spatial Skill,"* Developmental Psychology, *35, 1999, 940-949.* © 1999 American Psychological Association. Adapted with permission.

One type of task on which males do better, on average, than females involves mental rotation—mentally visualizing an object from different perspectives (Hampton, 2008; Kimura 2002, 2004). An example of a mental rotation task appears in Figure 16.3. Early signs of sex differences in mental rotation ability may even be seen in infancy. In two recent studies, researchers habituated 3- to 5-month-old infants to a simple visual stimulus, which was then rotated so that it appeared from a different perspective. Male infants were more likely than female infants to recognize the stimulus as the same object when viewed from this different spatial perspective (Moore & Johnson, 2008; Quinn & Liben, 2008). Another task on which males generally do better is the water level task, shown in Figure 16.4 (Vasta & Liben, 1996) in *Application 16.1*.

What might account for these sex differences in spatial abilities? One explanation, as we have already noted, emphasizes brain lateralization. The right hemisphere is specialized for spatial tasks, and the development of the right hemisphere is promoted by male hormones. However, experiential factors likely play a significant role as well. From early childhood, boys are more likely to participate in activities that promote spatial skills. They spend more time building with blocks, constructing models, and playing videogames and sports (Baenninger & Newcombe, 1995; Subrahmanyam et al., 2001; Quaiser-Pohl et al., 2006; Terlecki & Newcombe, 2005).

Nora Newcombe, an expert on the development of spatial cognition, has argued that the debate over the origins of sex differences in spatial abilities, although interesting, has diverted attention from the fact that spatial skills can be modified through training (Newcombe, Mathason, & Terlecki, 2002). It is widely accepted that spatial skills are important in many daily activities, including navigation, recalling locations, recognizing and manipulating objects, and so on (Tzuriel & Egozi, 2010). Spatial skills are valuable as well in various professions, such as engineering, architecture, and medicine (Liben, 2006; Shea, Lubinski, & Benbow, 2001). Consequently, Newcombe believes society would benefit if more people developed better spatial skills. This raises an interesting question: Should spatial reasoning be taught in school? That is the topic of *Application 16.1*.

FIGURE 16.3

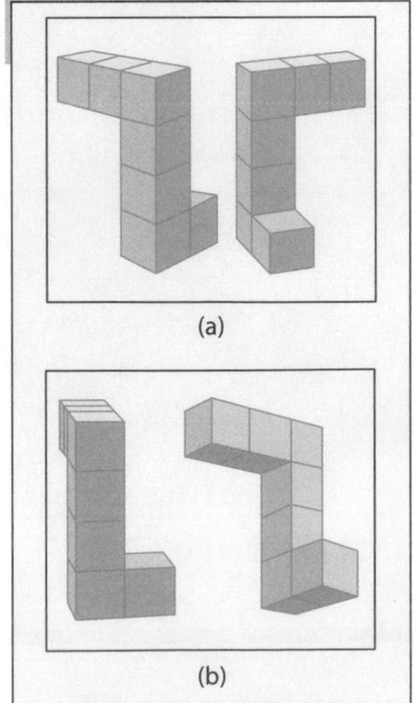

A mental rotation task in which one must decide whether the two objects are the same as in (a), or different, as in (b).

SOCIAL AND PERSONALITY DIFFERENCES

We turn next to social and personality differences between boys and girls, including differences in temperament, emotional development, self-control, aggression, prosocial behaviour, activities and interests, and friends and companions.

TEMPERAMENT As we saw in Chapter 12, infants are born with basic temperamental characteristics. Some babies are easygoing, whereas others are often fussy and irritable. It is clear that temperament varies from infant to infant. But are some dimensions of infant temperament more typical of females, while others more typical of males?

APPLICATION 16.1
SHOULD SCHOOLS TEACH VISUAL-SPATIAL SKILLS?

One of the most robust and reliable findings in research on sex differences is a male advantage on tasks that involve spatial reasoning, such as mental rotation and spatial visualization. At the same time, there is ample evidence that certain experiences promote the development of spatial skills (Baenninger & Newcombe, 1995; Gerson et al., 2001; Feng, Spence, & Pratt, 2007).

Cross-cultural research shows superior spatial abilities among children and adults in cultures that depend heavily on hunting and other activities that require extensive travel (Dasen, 1975b). Moreover, when females travel and hunt as frequently as males, they exhibit comparable spatial skills (Berry, 1966).

Everyday, practical experience performing tasks that entail spatial demands also enhances spatial competence in modern societies. For instance, Ross Vasta and colleagues (1997) found that individuals in occupations that provide extensive experience with liquids in containers—namely bartenders and servers—perform better than adults of equal age, gender, and education on the water level task depicted in Figure 16.4.

Experience playing video games has also been linked to spatial competence (Quaiser-Pohl et al., 2006; Terlecki & Newcombe, 2005). Under naturalistic conditions, it is difficult to know whether time spent playing these games promotes the development of spatial skills, or whether children (and adults) with better spatial skills enjoy playing those games more and so devote more time to them. Although the latter is likely true to some extent, experimental research also supports the idea that playing some kinds of video games does indeed enhance spatial competence (De Lisi & Wolford, 2002; Feng et al., 2007).

Can spatial skills be taught? There is evidence from a variety of sources that suggests that they can. For example, researchers at the University of Toronto recently reported that 10 hours of training in an active, three-dimensional video game produced substantial improvements in spatial attention and mental rotation in undergraduate university students, with female participants showing the greatest gains (Feng, Spence, & Pratt, 2007).

A recent intervention program with grade 1 students adds further support. Tzuriel and Egozi (2010) provided training in representing and transforming spatial information to grade 1 children. The children were given eight weekly 45-minute training sessions where they were provided with geometric shapes and asked to reproduce them by drawing them from memory. They were coached to manipulate the shapes and to consider them from various different perspectives. The children completed a mental rotation task before beginning the training program and again after completing the program. Before beginning the training, boys outperformed girls on the mental rotation task. After completing the program, both boys and girls showed improvements in mental rotation ability. Moreover, girls improved even more so than boys, such that there were no longer gender differences in mental rotation ability.

Other training studies provide further evidence for the effect of experience on spatial abilities. In one study, female college students were taught how to solve the water level problem (Vasta et al., 1996). This task has proven to be notoriously difficult for college-age women; estimates suggest that up to 40 percent of them do not recognize that the water level will remain horizontal when the container is tilted (Halpern, 2012). Simply by receiving practice on a series of problems of increasing complexity (and no feedback), females were able to solve problems as accurately as males.

The fact that spatial skills can be taught has led some theorists to argue that spatial thinking should be included in the school curriculum (Liben, 2006). Schools offer remedial programs for reading—an area in which boys are at increased risk for educational failure. Significant numbers of girls—and a number of boys as well—exhibit serious deficiencies in spatial competence. Yet, schools generally make little effort to address these limitations (Halpern, 2012). Given the importance of spatial abilities for success in our increasingly technological world, should not schools promote these skills as well?

FIGURE 16.4

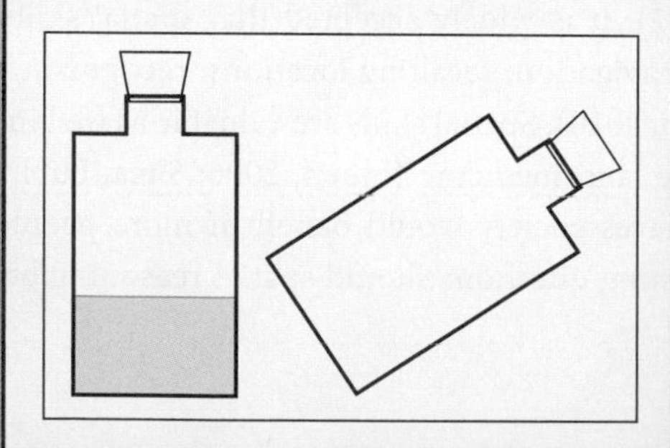

The water level problem. Individuals are asked to predict how the water will look when the bottle is tilted.

From the first days of life, female newborns seem better equipped for social interaction than their male counterparts. Female infants maintain greater eye contact with caregivers (Connellan et al., 2000; Hittelman & Dickes, 1979) and look at faces longer and more often than do males

(Schroeder, 2010). By 3 months of age, they engage in more face-to-face communication (Lavelli & Fogel, 2002). Female babies also smile more during social interactions (Cossette et al., 1996). And these differences persist into adulthood. Adult women maintain eye contact and smile more during social exchanges than do adult males (Brody & Hall, 2010; LaFrance, Hecht, & Paluck, 2003).

Although these differences may seem compelling, there is no evidence to suggest that females are inherently more sociable than males (Maccoby, 1998; Mathiesen & Tambs, 1999; McCrae et al., 2002). What appears to be a female propensity for social interaction during the first months of infancy may instead be related to male infants' greater fussiness and irritability and their less-developed ability to regulate their emotional states (Calkins et al., 2002; Weinberg et al., 1999).

EMOTIONAL DEVELOPMENT As they grow older, both boys and girls become better able to manage their emotions. This improvement is due to both biological maturation and the development of emotion regulation strategies (Compas et al., 2001). Sex differences in the strategies used to regulate emotional states have been observed among children as young as age 2. In one study, for example, toddlers were promised an attractive toy but were made to wait before being allowed to play with it. The girls coped with the stress of the situation by seeking comfort from their mothers, whereas the boys were more likely to distract themselves by playing with the other objects in the room (Raver, 1996).

This gender difference in coping style grows larger over the course of childhood (Rose & Rudolph, 2006). By adolescence, these behavioural styles are incorporated into gender scripts. Adolescents expect females to turn to other people when upset, and expect males to find something else to do when upset (Broderick & Korteland, 2002). A meta-analysis of the adult coping literature confirms the same pattern in adulthood: females are more likely to seek social support and talk about upsetting events and males, in contrast, are more likely to employ distraction or to engage in some kind of physical activity (Tamres, Janicki, & Helgeson, 2002).

One possible reason why girls talk about their feelings with other people more than do boys is that girls are socialized to do so (Fivush & Buckner, 2000). Studies find that parents talk more about the emotional aspects of events with daughters than with sons. Most intriguing is that parents seem to highlight sadness when talking with daughters (Brody & Hall, 2010; Fivush, 2007). This focus on sadness does not appear to be elicited by the girls themselves, as young girls and boys mention sadness equally often. Later in childhood, however, girls are more likely to report feeling sad than are boys (Hughes & Dunn, 2002). Moreover, Mélanie Perron of Laurentian University reports that girls even do better than boys when asked to produce a sad facial expression (Perron & Gosselin, 2004).

There are gender differences in the expression of other negative emotions as well. Parent–child conversations about anger are more common with sons than with daughters (Brody & Hall, 2010). Boys are more likely to express anger in face-to-face interactions (Hubbard, 2001) and, as Carole Peterson and Marlene Biggs (2001) of Memorial University of Newfoundland report, when describing past events. And, boys are better than girls at producing a facial expression of anger (Perron & Gosselin, 2004). Boys are also more likely to deny feeling afraid. For example, one male space camper, when asked if he would like to go into space following the destruction of the *Columbia* shuttle in 2003, replied: "Nooooooo, I'm just not a space person. Not that I'm scared or anything" (Halbfinger, 2003, p. 23).

Boys are also less likely to follow cultural display rules regarding the expression of disappointment. For instance, upon receiving a disappointing gift, girls are better able to mask their disappointment and look pleased. In fact, girls are also better than boys at producing facial expressions of happiness (Perron & Gosselin, 2004). Boys not only are more likely to show disappointment in such situations, but are also less capable of hiding it, even when given incentives to do so (Cole, 1986; Davis, 1995; McDowell, O'Neil, & Parke, 2000).

Links to Related Material

In Chapter 13, you read about the development of self-control in children. Here, you learn more about gender differences in self-control.

SELF-CONTROL As we saw in Chapter 13, the emergence of self-control is one of the hallmark achievements of the preschool period. Children with self-control are able to inhibit impulsive and aggressive behaviour, delay immediate gratification, and comply with caregiver requests and prohibitions.

There is some evidence that girls develop self-regulatory capabilities more rapidly than boys (Basow, 2010). During early childhood, boys have considerably more difficulty than girls with tasks that demand impulse control—for example, whispering on command, walking slowly in a line, and playing games such as Simon Says (Kochanska et al., 1996). Girls also have been found to comply more readily and at a younger age than boys with parental requests to perform unpleasant tasks—such as picking up toys—and prohibitions against touching attractive or dangerous objects (Kochanska & Askan, 1995; Kochanska, Coy, & Murray, 2001; Kuczynski & Kochanska, 1990).

Children with limited self-control are at risk for problem behaviours, such as angry outbursts and other kinds of disruptive actions. Prior to age 4 or 5, girls and boys engage in disruptive and impulsive behaviour equally often (Achenbach, Edelbrock, & Howell, 1987). After this age, however, striking sex differences are found. Whereas most girls show a steady decline in problem behaviours, boys show a lesser decline and, in some cases, even an increase (Prior et al., 1993).

AGGRESSION Perhaps the clearest and largest sex difference in behaviour is that males generally display more aggression than do females—especially the more violent varieties (Bjorklund & Pellegrini, 2011). In the United States, for example, recent statistics indicate that in 2006, males committed about 89 percent of the murders and 79 percent of the aggravated assaults (U.S. Department of Justice, 2007). Many other countries and cultures report similar statistics.

There are gender differences, however, in the type of aggression displayed by children. As discussed in Chapter 14, boys are more likely to display physical aggression such as kicking, hitting, and pushing than are girls of the same age. Indeed, a comparison of 4,640 preschoolers in Austria, Brazil, Canada, China, Italy, Japan, Russia, and the United States found that boys were universally reported to be markedly more physically aggressive than girls (LaFreniere et al., 2002). Boys are also more likely to engage in oppositional behaviour and to damage property. Girls, in contrast, are more likely to engage in relational aggression. As we discussed in Chapter 14, relational aggression involves attempting to harm other children, particularly other girls, by damaging or manipulating social relationships. This is done through activities such as gossip, rumour spreading, threats to withdraw friendship, or social exclusion (Crick et al., 2007; Ostrov, & Crick, 2007). Research shows that girls tend to perceive such forms of aggression as more hurtful than do boys (Rose & Smith, 2009). Gender differences in the types of aggression that children use have been noted in children as young as preschool-aged (Ostrov & Crick, 2007; Ostrov & Keating, 2004) and to persist through high school (Crick et al., 2007; Murray-Close et al., 2007), where the differences appear to peak (Rose & Smith, 2009).

Links to Related Material

In Chapters 14 and 15 you read about the development of aggression and prosocial behaviour and how these relate to children's friendships.

PROSOCIAL BEHAVIOUR We saw in Chapter 14 that girls are generally rated as more generous, helpful, and cooperative than boys by their teachers and peers (Rose & Rudolph, 2006). Some evidence does suggest that girls have better emotional perspective-taking abilities and experience more empathy (Zahn-Waxler et al., 1992, 2001). But when researchers examine children's actual prosocial behaviour, they find few sex differences (Eisenberg, Fabes, & Spinrad, 2006); so, if a difference exists in this area, it appears to be very small.

ACTIVITIES AND INTERESTS Gender differences in activity preferences emerge between the first and second birthdays. Boys show more interest in blocks, transportation toys (such as trucks and airplanes), and objects that can be manipulated (Berenbaum, Martin, Hanish, Briggs, & Fabes, 2008). They also engage in more large-motor activities, including rough-and-tumble play (Blatchford et al., 2003; Fabes et al., 2003; Hines, 2009; Rose & Smith, 2009).

Girls prefer doll play, dress-up, artwork, and domestic activities, such as sewing and cooking (Berenbaum, Martin, Hanish, et al., 2008). They also prefer activities that are less physically active, such as reading and drawing, over those that are more vigorous. This sex difference in participation in vigorous physical activity is maintained throughout childhood and adolescence (Bradley et al., 2000). Nevertheless, whereas boys are inclined to stick to male toys and games, girls are more likely to engage in some activities preferred by the opposite sex (Berenbaum, Martin, Hanish, et al., 2008).

Because sex differences in play preferences emerge so early, it is tempting to believe that somehow boys are born to prefer mechanical toys and girls to prefer dolls. There may, in fact, be some basis for this notion, as similar preferences have also been found in non-human species. Examining the toy preferences of young rhesus monkeys, researchers have found that males show a greater preference than do females for toys with wheels over plush toys, such as stuffed dolls or teddy bears, a sex difference paralleling that found in children (Hassett, Siebert, & Wallen, 2008). However, as we shall see, there are also strong socialization influences on children's toy preferences: parents encourage sex-typed play from the first months of life (Leaper, 2002). This is especially true for boys, who experience considerable pressure from both parents and peers to play with toys deemed appropriate for their sex.

In addition to differing in play preferences, boys and girls exhibit sex-stereotyped television preferences. Boys prefer non-educational cartoons, action programs, and sports. Girls lose interest in non-educational cartoons before boys, and prefer comedy programs and shows with relationship themes (Roberts & Foehr, 2004; Wright et al., 2001).

Studies have also examined boys' and girls' use of computers, and especially the Internet. A recent cross-Canada survey, *Young Canadians in a Wired World*, asked over 5,000 children from grades 4 to 11 about their Internet use (Media Awareness Network, 2005). Boys reported spending slightly more time on-line and considerably more time playing games than did girls. In many other ways, however, boys and girls were found to use computers similarly, reporting little difference in time spent chatting, visiting websites, using email, doing schoolwork, and so on. Further, research also suggests that adolescent boys and girls are equally confident about their computer abilities and are equally skilled (North & Noyes, 2002; Media Awareness Network, 2005). Figure 16.5 shows Canadian boys' and girls' on-line activities on an average school day.

FIGURE 16.5

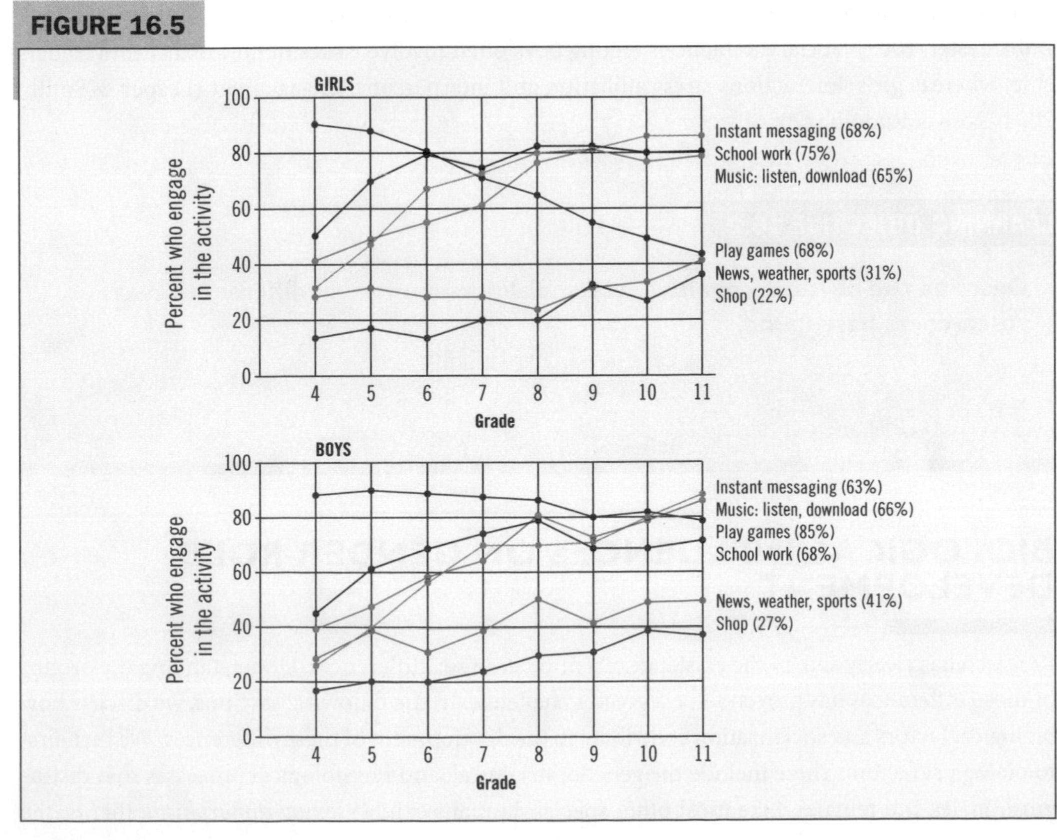

Proportion of children who engage in on-line activities "on an average school day." *From Media Awareness Network,* Young Canadians in a Wired World-Phase II, *2005, Figure 4, p. 19: www.media-awareness.ca/english/research/YCWW/phaseII/.* © 2010 Media Awareness Network, www.media-awareness.ca. Reproduced with permission.

Gender differences also have been found in children's academic interests. Beginning in elementary school, girls are more interested in reading and music, whereas boys express greater interest in sports. At this age, however, girls and boys are equally interested in mathematics and science (Andre et al., 1999; Eccles, Jacobs, et al., 1993; Folling-Albers & Hartinger, 1998; Wigfield et al., 1997). By adolescence, however, boys have traditionally tended to express greater interest in mathematics and science than have girls (Evans, Schweingruber, & Stevenson, 2002; Miller, Blessing, & Schwartz, 2006; Wigfield et al., 2002). Nevertheless, more recent findings suggest that these differences may be on the decline: current research indicates that girls may be as likely as boys to both enrol in and do well in high-school mathematics and science courses (Priess & Hyde, 2010).

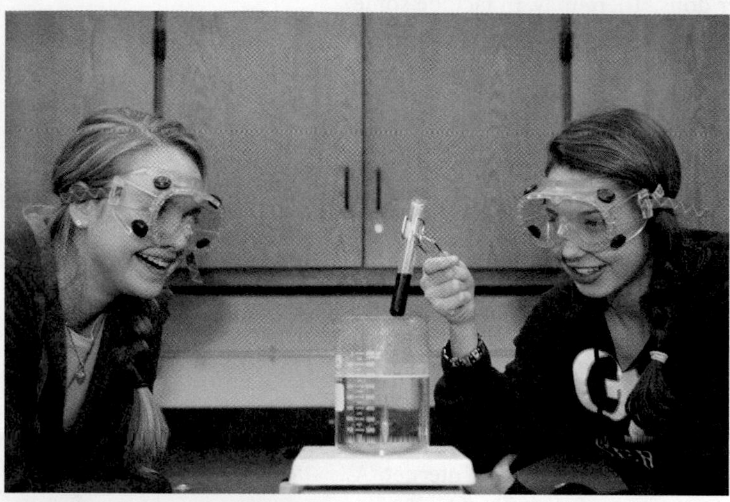

Studies indicate that the gender differences in interest in science is decreasing in North America. (© *Martin Shields/Alamy*)

Although gender differences in *preference* for science may be declining, specific interests of males and females *within* the domain of science tend to differ. Male students tend to be more interested in the physical sciences, engineering, and computer science. Female students, by contrast, are more likely to express interest in people-oriented sciences, such as the biosciences and health fields (Adamuti-Trache, 2006; Halpern et al., 2007; Priess & Hyde, 2010).

FRIENDS AND COMPANIONS Children's social relationships also show sex differences. Although there appear to be no differences between boys and girls in total number of friends (Rose & Smith, 2009), there are differences in the size of the groups in which they play. Beginning in early childhood, boys prefer to interact in large groups, whereas girls generally limit their group size to two or three (Rose & Rudolph, 2006). Boys' and girls' groups are also characterized by different interactional processes. As discussed in Chapter 15, interactions among girls tend to involve more self-disclosure and intimacy than do interactions among boys (Ladd, 2005; Underwood & Buhrmester, 2007). Social interactions among boys often involve issues of dominance and leadership, whereas girls' interactions stress affiliation and interpersonal engagement (Leaper & Smith, 2004; Rose & Rudolph, 2006).

Links to Related Material

Here you learn about gender differences in children's interactions with friends and companions. In Chapter 15, we discussed a variety of other factors related to children's friendships and peer relations.

LEARNING OBJECTIVE 16.2

Describe the physical, cognitive, and social/personality sex differences that researchers have found.

1. What physical sex differences have researchers found?
2. What cognitive sex differences have researchers found?
3. What social and personality sex differences have researchers found?

Learning Objective 16.3

Understand the role of biological influences in the development of sex differences.

BIOLOGICAL INFLUENCES ON GENDER-ROLE DEVELOPMENT

Research has clearly shown the existence of a number of sex differences. Understanding the origins of those differences has proven to be a greater challenge. In the following sections, we discuss how biological factors and socialization contribute to the development of these differences. We turn first to biological factors. These include the genetic, structural, and physiological processes that distinguish males and females. Like most other species, humans exhibit *sexual dimorphism*; that is, the male and female are biologically different for the purpose of reproduction (Rhen & Crews, 2008). As noted earlier, the process through which these biological differences emerge is called *sexual differentiation.* Many of the biological influences on gender-role development appear to result from nature's preparing the individual in this way to participate in the reproduction process.

GENETIC INFLUENCES

As we explained in Chapter 3, the sex chromosomes—referred to as the X and the Y chromosomes—determine whether we develop as males or females. The X chromosome is of about average size as chromosomes go, and carries a good deal of genetic material; the Y chromosome is much smaller and has fewer genes. When the pair of sex chromosomes inherited from the parents consists of two X chromosomes (XX), the individual is female; when it is made up of one of each type (XY), the individual is male.

Links to Related Material

In Chapter 3, you read about the role that the sex chromosomes play in determining gender. Here, you learn more about prenatal sexual differentiation and the influence of prenatal exposure to sex hormones.

The sex chromosomes have no influence on the fertilized zygote for about six weeks. At that point, if the embryo is genetically male (XY), the Y chromosome causes a portion of the embryo to become the male gonadal structure—the testes. Once this is accomplished, the Y chromosome does not appear to play any further role in the process of sexual differentiation. If the embryo is genetically female (XX), the sex chromosomes produce no change at 6 weeks. At 10 to 12 weeks, however, one X chromosome causes a portion of the embryo to become female gonads—the ovaries. From this point on, sexual differentiation is guided primarily by the hormones produced by the testes and the ovaries.

HORMONAL INFLUENCES

A major step in sexual differentiation begins when the newly formed embryonic gonads begin to secrete hormones of different types. Up until about the third month of gestation, the internal sex organs of the fetus can become either male or female. When a Y chromosome causes testes to develop in the embryo, these glands secrete hormones called *androgens*, which cause the male internal reproductive organs to grow (they also secrete a chemical that causes the female organs to shrink). At 5 months, if androgens are present, the external sex organs also develop as male, producing a penis and scrotal sac. If androgens are not present at 3 months, the internal sex organs, and later the external sex organs, develop as female. The hormones produced mainly by the ovaries, estrogen and progesterone, do not play their principal role in sexual differentiation until puberty.

Somewhere between 3 and 8 months after conception, sex hormones are believed to affect the development and organization of the fetal brain. The two major types of organizing effects involve hormonal regulation (how often the body releases various hormones) and brain lateralization.

HORMONAL REGULATION AND ABNORMALITIES In adult humans, the pituitary gland controls the production of hormones by the gonads. One effect of these hormones is to activate certain social behaviours, including dominance, aggression, maternal behaviours, and sexual activity. Some theorists believe that sex differences in these and other social behaviours may be largely controlled by such hormones (Booth et al., 2006; Campbell, 2008).

In support of this idea, researchers have given pregnant monkeys extra doses of testosterone (a type of androgen), for example, and found that the female offspring tended to engage more in rough-and-tumble play and in sexual mounting behaviours—characteristics more common in males of the species (Wallen, 2005).

Recent advances in ways to measure hormone levels in humans have made it possible to examine whether naturally occurring variations in testosterone during the prenatal period are related to the gender-role behaviour of offspring. Researchers measured testosterone levels in maternal blood samples obtained during routine prenatal care. When the children were 8 years old, their parents completed a questionnaire concerning the children's involvement with sex-typed toys, games, and activities. Among both girls and boys, higher levels of testosterone during the prenatal period were associated with higher levels of male-typical play and activities (Auyeung et al., 2009).

Links to Related Material

In Chapter 6, you read how prenatal exposure to testosterone may influence cerebral lateralization. Here you learn about how such prenatal exposure influences later behaviour.

Congenital adrenal hyperplasia (CAH) A recessive genetic disorder in which the adrenal glands produce unusually high levels of male hormones known as androgens.

Another way to study the effects of hormones on development is to study cases where hormonal processes go awry. One such hormonal abnormality, **congenital adrenal hyperplasia (CAH)**, occurs when too much androgen is produced during pregnancy. CAH usually results from an inherited enzyme deficiency that causes the adrenal glands to produce androgens, regardless of the presence or absence of testes (Saucier & Ehresman, 2010). This problem typically begins after the internal sex organs have been formed, but before the external sex organs appear. The incidence of CAH is estimated to be 1 in 15,000 births, distributed approximately equally among males and females (Eckel et al., 2008). The effects of the extra dose of androgens on males are fairly mild (Hines, 2010). These boys are somewhat more inclined toward intense physical activity than are normal boys, but they do not appear to be more aggressive or antisocial (Berenbaum & Snyder, 1995; Hines & Kaufman, 1994).

If, however, the fetus is genetically female (XX), she will have ovaries and normal internal sex organs, but the excessive androgen will cause the external organs to develop in a masculine direction. Often, the clitoris will be very large, resembling a penis, and sometimes a scrotal sac will develop (although it will be empty, because there are no testes) (Chen, 2006).

In a number of rare cases, such females have been mistaken at birth for males and raised as boys (Hines, 2010). In most cases, however, the problem is discovered at birth and corrected by surgically changing the external sex organs and by administering drugs to reduce the high levels of androgens. Although these procedures return the girls to biological normality, the early androgen exposure appears to have some long-term effects. CAH females often have better spatial abilities than normal females (Cohen-Bendahan et al., 2005; Saucier & Ehresman, 2010). Many of these girls also become "tomboys," preferring active play and traditional male-stereotyped toys, while having less interest in activities typical of young females (Cohen-Bendahan et al., 2005; Saucier & Ehresman, 2010).

Androgen insensitivity syndrome (AIS) An X-linked genetic defect in males that prevents the body cells from responding to androgens, the masculinizing hormones.

Another type of hormonal disorder involves androgen insensitivity. **Androgen insensitivity syndrome (AIS)** is an X-linked genetic disorder in males, in which the body cells are prevented from responding to androgens, the masculinizing hormones (Chen, 2006; Hines, 2010). The testes produce hormones, but neither internal nor external male sex organs develop. The substance that usually shrinks the potential female internal sex organs is effective, however, leaving the fetus with neither a uterus nor an internal male system. The external sex organs develop as female. This disorder has been less studied than CAH, partly because it is rare (occurring in about 1 in 50,000 males), and partly because it is generally not diagnosed until adolescence (Cohen-Bendahan et al., 2005; Eckel et al., 2008). The available data suggest that androgen-insensitive males tend to be feminine in appearance, gender identity, preferences, and abilities (Cohen-Bendahan et al., 2005; Hines, 2010; Ruble et al., 2006).

For Thought and Discussion

The media reported about a Canadian family who chose to raise their new baby as "genderless." From what you've read about biological influences on gender, including the effects of prenatal hormones, do you think this is possible?

For Thought and Discussion

How are sexual identity and sex-typed behaviour a product of biology? To what extent are they a product of environment? How would you describe the relationship between these factors?

Taken together, evidence from animals and humans suggests that fetal sex hormones play an important part in producing differences between males and females. But hormonal processes are complex, and scientists still do not understand exactly how they interact with socialization processes (Kimura, 2004; Saucier & Ehresman, 2010). In *Research Classic 16.1*, we present the case of a Canadian boy who was brought up as a girl, and the complications that ensued.

RESEARCH CLASSIC 16.1
WHEN NATURE AND NURTURE CONFLICT

From time to time, researchers come across situations where heredity and environment conflict in their contribution to gender-typed behaviour. One such case concerns a pair of identical twin boys born in Winnipeg, Manitoba, in the 1960s. As an infant, one of the boys suffered severe injury to his penis during circumcision. Learning that it would not be possible to reconstruct the penis, the anguished parents sought advice from a leading sex researcher at The Johns Hopkins University in Baltimore, Maryland. The parents asked if it would be better for their son to live as a physically deformed male or as a female.

(*continued*)

Research Classic 16.1 When Nature and Nurture Conflict *continued*

It was recommended that the child be transformed into a female through surgical construction of female genitalia, followed in later years by further surgery and hormone treatments. In the hope of giving their baby the best chance for a normal life, the parents agreed and proceeded to raise their son—renamed Brenda—as a girl, assured by the doctors that she would remain unaware of her original biology

The details of this extraordinary case were first made public in 1972 (Money & Ehrhardt, 1972). In the report, the authors mentioned Brenda's tomboyishness, but focused primarily on the ways in which her behaviour and interests conformed to female stereotypes, especially in contrast to those of her identical twin brother. In this and subsequent updates on the twins' development, the intervention was portrayed as an unqualified success (Money, 1975).

The case received a great deal of attention in both the scientific literature and the popular press. *Time* magazine opined, "This dramatic case provides strong support for a major contention of women's liberationists: that conventional patterns of masculine and feminine behaviour can be altered. It also casts doubt on the theory that major sexual differences, psychological as well as anatomical, are immutably set by the genes at conception" (*Time*, 1973, cited in Colapinto, 2000, p. 69).

In reality, the case turned out to offer strong support for the biological determinants of psychological gender. From early on, Brenda displayed more interest in toys and activities commonly preferred by boys, despite her parents' best efforts to encourage stereotypically female interests and behaviour. Everyone, including her twin brother, Brian, noticed Brenda's masculinity.

Brenda's tomboyish looks and mannerisms elicited daily teasing and ridicule from peers as early as kindergarten. During early adolescence, Brenda made a brief but concerted effort to look and act more feminine, but the result was an appearance so unusual that even strangers would stop and stare. Moreover, Brenda did not *feel* like a girl—she felt like an oddity.

Finally, Brenda rebelled. She abandoned her efforts to dress and behave like a girl, resisted the annual visits to The Johns Hopkins University, and refused to undergo the vaginal surgery needed to complete her transformation. When Brenda was 14, the physicians assigned to her case declared the sex reassignment a total failure and advised Brenda's parents to tell her the truth. Brenda decided immediately to take steps to return to her original gender as a male and took the name David. He eventually married and became a father to three stepchildren.

The story, unfortunately, had a tragic ending. In 2004, dealing with a number of depressing events in his life (including the loss of his job, the death of his twin brother two years earlier, and personal problems), David took his own life. Whether the nightmare of his earlier childhood experiences also contributed to his suicide is difficult to say.

It would be many years before the rest of the world learned the truth about the twins. Milton Diamond, a biologist who specialized in the effects of prenatal sex hormones on development and who had for years expressed scepticism about the case, and Keith Sigmundson, a psychiatrist who had been involved in the twins' treatment, convinced David to go public with his story (Diamond & Sigmundson, 1997).

In retrospect, one of the most remarkable aspects of this case is that so many people readily accepted the premise that it would be easy to change a normal, healthy baby boy into a girl. Why weren't there more sceptics like Diamond? One explanation is the prevailing view in North America in the 1960s and early 1970s. At the time, the idea that sexual orientation and sex-typed behaviour were primarily the products of socialization resonated with Canadians and Americans, whose gender-role expectations were changing dramatically. Today, the view is far different. Indeed, now many scholars argue that experiential factors, rather than biological ones, are at risk of being overlooked (Lewontin, 2000; Oyama, 2000).

David's difficult childhood as Brenda was captured in this book by John Colapinto, *As Nature Made Him: The Boy Who Was Raised as a Girl*. Copyright © 1999 by John Colapinto. Reproduced by permission of HarperCollins Publishers.

BRAIN LATERALIZATION

As we discussed earlier, the human brain is divided into left and right hemispheres that perform different functions. The left half both controls and receives information from the right side of the body, including the right ear, hand, and foot, and the right visual field of each eye. The right hemisphere controls and receives information from the left side of the body. Among other things, the left hemisphere is primarily responsible for language and speech processes, whereas the right side appears to be more involved with spatial abilities (Kolb & Whishaw, 2009).

Links to Related Material

In Chapter 6, you read about lateralization of the hemispheres of the brain. In this chapter, you learn more about how lateralization relates to gender differences in certain cognitive abilities.

Because the division of these functions corresponds to the cognitive sex differences discussed earlier, some psychologists believe that differences in brain laterality may be important for understanding certain differences in male and female behaviours. As noted earlier, some data suggest that males are more lateralized—that is, their left and right hemispheres function more independently—than are females (Halpern et al., 2007).

Studies of language and verbal abilities provide some support for the idea that brain lateralization plays a role in gender differences. For example, sex differences in hemisphere specialization have been found in both 3- and 6-month-old infants. When they responded to recordings of a voice speaking, female infants showed stronger brainwave reactions to right-ear (left hemisphere) presentations, whereas male infants showed stronger reactions to left-ear (right-hemisphere) presentations (Shucard & Shucard, 1990; Shucard et al., 1981). At 2 and 3 years of age, both sexes begin to process verbal stimuli (such as spoken words) through the right ear, and non-verbal stimuli (such as music) through the left ear (Harper & Kraft, 1986; Kamptner, Kraft, & Harper, 1984). But at this point, males begin to show evidence of greater lateralization than females—for example, performing much better in response to verbal stimuli presented in the right ear than in the left ear, but showing the opposite tendency for non-verbal stimuli (Kraft, 1984).

Other research has reported that verbal abilities in males whose left hemispheres have been damaged (such as through strokes or tumours) are much more impaired than are those in females with a similar degree of damage in that area (Pedersen et al., 1995). More recently, a number of studies using functional magnetic resonance imaging (fMRI) have shown that when males perform phonological tasks, activation is more localized to regions of the left hemisphere, whereas females show more bilateral activation (Ullman et al., 2008). These results suggest that language functioning in females may be more equally spread between the two hemispheres.

The role of brain lateralization in spatial abilities has also been examined in a study of children's haptic (touch) performance. Children in the study first felt a pair of hidden shapes, one with each hand, for 10 seconds. They were then asked to pick out the two shapes from a visual display. For boys, left-hand (right-hemisphere) performance was better than right-hand performance. For girls, left- and right-hand performances were equal (Witelson, 1976).

The evidence that males seem to be more lateralized than females does not in itself provide a simple explanation of verbal and spatial sex differences. It does, however, suggest that some sex differences may literally exist in our brains.

LEARNING OBJECTIVE 16.3

Understand the role of biological influences in the development of sex differences.

1. What role do genetic influences play in the development of gender differences?
2. Explain how fetal hormones affect sexual differentiation.
3. How may brain lateralization be related to sex differences?

SOCIALIZATION AND GENDER-ROLE DEVELOPMENT

Learning Objective 16.4

Understand how society, parents, peers, and the self contribute to gender-role socialization.

Clearly, biological factors make important contributions to gender-role development. They do not, however, operate in isolation. Rather, biological processes interact with environmental forces in shaping gender development. We now turn to these environmental forces.

Environmental influences on the development of gender are usually viewed in terms of socialization. The socialization of gender occurs on multiple levels, ranging from the societal to the self. In the following sections, we highlight two means of socialization: modelling and differential treatment of boys and girls.

SOCIALIZATION BY SOCIETY

In all cultures, children are socialized to gender roles, although the specifics of the roles may differ across time and place. One way children learn about gender roles is through modelling, by observing those around them. In addition, girls and boys may experience differential treatment.

For Thought and Discussion

In what settings and social roles do children learn the behaviours and attributes regarded as appropriate for their gender? How important is it that males and females have equal access to various social roles?

MODELLING As we have seen in earlier chapters, modelling is a powerful means of transmitting values, attitudes, beliefs, and behavioural practices from generation to generation (Bussey & Bandura, 2004). Gender knowledge is no exception.

In many societies, the media have greatly expanded the variety of models available to children. Television, especially, communicates a great deal about social practices and behaviour. Analyses of the contents of both network programs and commercials—in North America and around the world—indicate that TV has generally portrayed characters in very traditional gender roles (Collins, 2011; Leaper & Friedman, 2007). This is especially the case for children's non-educational cartoons (England et al., 2011; Leaper et al., 2002). In addition, music videos, video games, and teen magazines all tend to portray highly stereotyped views of the sexes (Ruble et al., 2006; Wallis, 2011).

For Thought and Discussion

What models do the media offer for what it means to be male and female? How important were these models in shaping your gender role development? How do children decide which messages to pay attention to and which to ignore?

DIFFERENTIAL TREATMENT A second mechanism for the socialization of gender roles is differential treatment of males and females. Differential treatment can take various forms (Bussey & Bandura, 1999; Leaper & Friedman, 2007). One is direct instruction, or the guided participation of the child in cultural practices (Rogoff, 1990). In some cultures, access to formal education and apprenticeships differs for males and females. Cultures also have a sexual division of labour, although the specific tasks assigned to each gender and the extent to which tasks are shared across genders vary widely.

In most cultures boys can venture farther from home without adult supervision than girls can. This provides greater opportunity to explore the environment and pursue risky adventures. (© *Sami Sarkis Lifestyles/ Alamy*)

A second type of differential treatment involves the opportunities and experiences available to males and females. For instance, worldwide, boys are generally granted greater autonomy than girls. They have greater freedom of movement and can be found farther from home without adult supervision (Whiting & Edwards, 1988). As a consequence, males have greater opportunities to explore the environment, pursue risky adventures, and work out interpersonal conflicts without adult intervention.

A third type of differential treatment concerns the expectations societies have for boys and for girls. Different expectations translate into different opportunities and different socialization pressures. In Japan, for example, the expectations for self-control are greater for girls than for boys. Consequently, girls exhibit greater self-regulatory capabilities at a younger age than do boys (Olson & Kashiwagi, 2000).

In recent years, there has been considerable interest in whether males and females experience differential treatment in one of the primary socialization settings for children—the school. Some

For Thought and Discussion

Have you observed or experienced gender bias from teachers? Why do you think this occurs? How important do you think it is to counter this tendency and why?

evidence indicates that teachers do, indeed, treat male and female students differently. Of particular interest has been teacher attention. Studies frequently show that teachers give more attention to boys than to girls (Basow, 2010). However, much of the contact is negative: boys receive more criticism, disapproval, and scolding for misbehaviour than do girls (Watt, 2010).

There is less consensus regarding positive attention. Some studies have found that teachers tend to be more attentive to boys, call on them more often, and allow them more time to speak (Basow, 2010). However, not all studies find such differences (Kleinfeld, 1996). Interestingly, girls view themselves as participating in class as much as boys. Moreover, when asked about whom teachers call on most often and pay the most attention to, many intermediate and high school students, both male and female, report a gender bias, but a bias favouring girls (AAUW/Greenberg-Lake, 1990; Harris, 1997).

If boys do receive more attention from teachers than girls, it may be partly because they actively elicit it. In a survey of over 1,000 grade 6 through 12 teachers, a majority reported that boys demand more attention in the classroom than do girls (Harris, 1997). And an observational study of intermediate-school science classrooms found that half the teachers did call on boys more often than girls. However, in these classrooms, the boys also volunteered to answer questions more frequently than did their female classmates (Altermatt, Jovanovic, & Perry, 1998).

Like the parents described in the following section, teachers sometimes hold gender-stereotyped beliefs about the abilities of males and females. Some studies suggest that teachers attribute greater ability in math and science to males (Li, 1999; Tiedemann, 2000), although not all studies find such beliefs (Helwig, Anderson, & Tindal, 2001). When teachers believe that male and female students are different in terms of ability or interest, it is reflected in the number and kinds of questions they ask of boys and girls, as well as the amount of encouragement they provide (She, 2000).

Evidence that males and females have different experiences in school has fostered concern that schools may short-change students of both sexes. Some have argued that schools undermine girls' self-confidence and career aspirations, and discourage interest in traditionally male domains, such as math and science (Watt, 2010). Partly in response to these assertions, schools and other organizations have done much to transform the educational experiences of many females, with some success. With the exception of physics, female high school students now enrol in as many mathematics and science courses as males (Priess & Hyde, 2010).

Concern is now growing that schools are failing to meet the needs of males (AAUW, 2001; Gally, 2002; Lesko, 2000; Noble & Bradford, 2000; Skelton, 2001). Indeed, the gender gap favouring females in reading achievement is considerably larger than that seen in math and science favouring males (Bussière et al., 2004; National Center for Education Statistics, 1997).

SOCIALIZATION BY PARENTS

Parents, too, can influence children's learning about gender roles through modelling and through differential treatment.

MODELLING Because parents are typically important figures in children's lives, they are especially salient models for what it means to be male or female (Bussey & Bandura, 1999, 2004). As we have seen, however, there is no shortage of gender role models in children's lives. Thus, it can be difficult to isolate the effects of modelling by parents from other models, such as television characters, classmates, and other adults.

One way to address this issue is to examine gender-role development in families in which parents' roles are different from traditional cultural norms. In such situations, parents model behaviour that is different from what children typically observe in other settings. Researchers have examined gender-role development of children in single-parent households and alternative living arrangements (e.g., communes), as well as among children with lesbian parents and in families where fathers are primary caregivers, and so on. Surprisingly, although we might expect differences in gender-role development among children from these different types of families, few such differences have been found (e.g., Golombok & Tasker, 2010; Patterson & Hastings, 2007; Ruble et al., 2006; Stevens et al., 2002).

Another way to examine the effects of parental modelling in gender-role development is to look at homes where parents perform non-traditional jobs and chores. In such homes, children have, indeed, been found to hold less stereotyped ideas about the roles of men and women (Deutsch, Servis, & Payne, 2001; Hoffman & Youngblade, 1999; Serbin et al., 1993; Weisner et al., 1994). The effects, however, are less pronounced for boys than for girls. For example, even in homes where the father is the primary caregiver, boys tend to maintain gender-stereotyped ideas, despite the non-traditional role played by their fathers (Leaper, 2002).

DIFFERENTIAL TREATMENT Another way parents may socialize gender differences is by treating sons and daughters differently. As with influences at the societal level, differential treatment by parents includes instruction, opportunities, and attitudes. For instance, parents are sometimes quite explicit in teaching sons or daughters skills traditionally associated with one or the other gender—as when fathers recruit sons, but not daughters, to help with home repairs. Differential treatment can also be largely unconscious. We have seen, for example, that parents talk about emotions differently with sons and daughters (Brody & Hall, 2010). Most parents are probably unaware of this difference. Nonetheless, a consequence of this differential treatment is that boys and girls learn different ways of expressing and coping with emotions.

Studies show that parents also offer sons and daughters different opportunities. The most notable example is children's play (Leaper, 2002). Parents tend to play differently with sons and daughters. During infancy, parents are more likely to physically stimulate boys than girls (Frisch, 1977; MacDonald & Parke, 1986). This emphasis on physical play with boys is maintained during early childhood. Both mothers and fathers tend to engage in more physical play with sons and pretend play with daughters; however, rough physical play is especially likely among fathers and sons (Lamb & Lewis, 2010; Leaper, 2002; Lindsey & Mize, 2001).

Differential treatment is also apparent in parents' selection of toys. Parents tend to give boys more sports equipment, vehicles, and tools, and girls more dolls and toy kitchen sets. Indeed, in many families, infants are given sex-typed toys within the first few months of life—long before they can express any kind of toy preferences themselves (Leaper, 2002; Leaper & Friedman, 2007; Pomerleau et al., 1990).

Children begin to demonstrate preferences for same-sex toys between their first and second birthdays. Parents encourage gender-appropriate play in their young children, especially boys, by more often offering gender-appropriate or neutral toys than those traditionally viewed as appropriate for the other sex (Wood, Desmarais, & Gugula, 2002). Parents are likely to express approval (smile, act excited, comment approvingly) for gender-appropriate play and activities and to respond negatively to behaviours considered characteristic of the other sex (Leaper, 2002; Leaper & Friedman, 2007).

Parents' gender typing of play tends to be stronger with sons than daughters. This is especially true of fathers. Fathers appear more concerned both that their sons be masculine and that their daughters be feminine, whereas mothers are more inclined to treat their sons and daughters alike (Leaper, 2002; Leaper & Friedman, 2007). These more rigid attitudes are expressed in fathers' descriptions of what constitutes appropriate gender-role behaviours, as well as in their actual interactions with their sons and daughters (Kane, 2006; Lindsey et al., 1997).

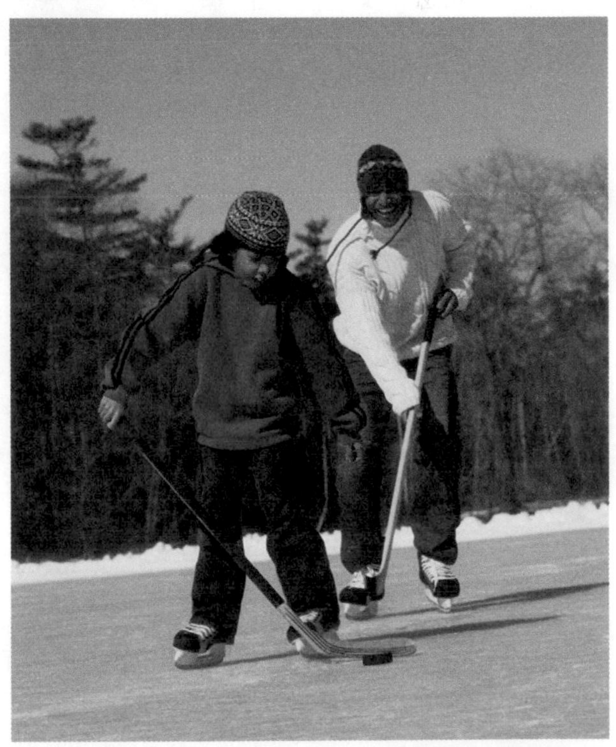

Parents' gender typing of play leads to the development of different sets of knowledge and abilities. For example, a father's physical play with his son fosters visuospatial skills, physical strength, and endurance. *(Blend Images/Media Bakery)*

Sex typing of play is important because different kinds of play provide opportunities to acquire and practise different skills. Female-stereotyped play, such as pretend play involving domestic themes, encourages nurturance and certain types of social understanding. Pretend play also depends more heavily on language than the kinds of activities parents more often enjoy with sons—such as physical play and construction activities. In turn, these male-stereotyped activities foster a different set of knowledge and abilities, including visuospatial skills, physical strength, endurance, and coordination.

As children move into the elementary school years, parents begin to provide them with other kinds of experiences, such as dance classes, music lessons, and sports activities. One study of a group of approximately 600 children found that parents provide different experiences for sons and daughters (Eccles et al., 2000). As shown in Table 16.2, these experiences tend to reflect gender stereotypes and to parallel gender differences in interests and achievement that emerge in later childhood and adolescence. For example, parents are far more likely to encourage sons to either view or participate in sports. Conversely, they more often encourage daughters to read and take music and dance lessons.

Parents also often hold different expectations for sons and daughters. Even before newborns leave the hospital, parents use very different terms to describe their little boys (e.g., "firmer," "better coordinated," "stronger") (Rubin, Provenzano, & Luria, 1974). As infants become mobile, mothers tend to perceive their infant sons as having better-developed crawling abilities—and daughters as having less-well-developed crawling skills—than they really do (Mondschein, Adolph, & Tamis-LeMonda, 2000). During middle childhood, parents rate sons as more capable in sports than daughters (Eccles et al., 2000). And when boys and girls achieve success in sports, parents attribute the success to different factors. Boys' sports achievements are attributed to "natural talent," whereas girls' achievements are attributed to hard work (Eccles, Jacobs, et al., 1993).

TABLE 16.2 PARENTS' PROVISION OF EXPERIENCES FOR DAUGHTERS AND SONS (GRADES 2, 3, AND 5)

Activity	Girls	Boys
Have child read to you	3.10	2.90
Play sports with child	2.63	3.36
Do active, outdoor activities with child	3.20	3.56
Take child to paid sporting event	1.71	1.91
Encourage child to do math- or science-related activities at home	4.01	4.35
Encourage child to work on or play with a computer outside of school	3.70	4.04
Encourage child to read	6.04	5.69
Encourage child to play competitive sports	3.58	4.43
Encourage child to play non-competitive sports	4.54	4.94
Encourage child to take dance lessons	3.56	2.15
Encourage child to take dancing for fun	3.85	2.53
Encourage child to watch sports on TV	2.60	3.07
Encourage child to take music lessons	4.26	3.52
Encourage child to play a musical instrument	4.32	3.67
Encourage child to build, make, or fix things	3.83	4.67
Encourage child to learn cooking and other homemaking skills	4.00	3.59
Ratings were made on 7-point scales: 1 = never/strongly discourage; 7 = almost every day/strongly encourage. All differences between girls' and boys' means are significant at $p < .05$		

Source: Adapted from J. S. Eccles, C. Freedman-Doan, P. Frome, J. Jacobs, & K. S. Yoon (2000). "Gender-Role Socialization in the Family: A Longitudinal Approach," in T. Eckes & H. M. Trautner (Eds.), *The Developmental Social Psychology of Gender*, Mahwah, NJ: Erlbaum. Adapted by permission.

Parents hold different expectations for males and females in the academic realm as well. As noted earlier, parents believe their daughters' reading ability to be better than that of their sons (Eccles, Arbreton, et al., 1993; Wigfield et al., 2002). They also believe that mathematics is more natural for boys than for girls, and tend to underestimate girls' mathematics abilities and overestimate those of boys (Eccles et al., 2000). Similar findings have emerged in parents' beliefs about science abilities: parents generally endorse the cultural stereotype that boys are better in science than are girls (Tenenbaum & Leaper, 2003).

Parents' gender-stereotyped expectations contribute to children's gender-role development in two ways. First, as we have seen, these expectations lead parents to provide boys and girls with different opportunities to develop specific skills and competencies. Second, parents' views of their children's abilities influence children's own developing sense of competence and interest in different domains (Eccles et al., 2000; Tiedemann, 2000; Wigfield et al., 2002). Children whose parents rate their ability as low in a domain tend to also rate their own ability lower than it really is. Furthermore, in North American society, where effort is generally viewed less positively than in many other cultures, children whose parents believe they will have to work hard to be successful at something are likely to lose interest and channel their efforts to domains where they believe they can excel more easily.

SOCIALIZATION BY PEERS

The peer group is another powerful socialization force in children's lives. Studies consistently show that peers reinforce one another for engaging in gender-typed play and punish those who deviate from established norms (Leaper & Friedman, 2007; Rose & Rudolph, 2006). Although boys and girls are both criticized by peers for cross sex play and behaviours, the consequences are especially severe for boys (Basow, 2010).

In one early study, Beverly Fagot (1977) observed children's reactions to cross-gender play in a number of preschool classrooms. Girls who enjoyed boys' activities were allowed to join boys' groups and went back and forth between girl and boy groups with relative ease. The story for boys was quite different. Boys had especially strong reactions to male classmates who violated gender norms. They taunted and teased those who played with the girls, using derogatory terms, such as "sissy boy." When the "offending" boys tried to rejoin the boy groups, they were rejected, criticized, and physically threatened. The negative reactions continued throughout preschool, even though most of the boys learned quite quickly to avoid playing with girls or in girls' activities.

Children actively maintain strictures against cross-sex interaction throughout middle childhood. One particularly revealing study of preadolescents at a summer camp described a set of "rules" that dictate children's interactions with members of the opposite sex (see Table 16.3). These guidelines have come to be known as "the cootie rules" because children observing them often behave as though they have been contaminated by just being near a member of the opposite sex (Sroufe et al., 1993). Basically, the rules state that one cannot freely choose to interact with a peer of the opposite sex, but they acknowledge that contact is sometimes inevitable or unavoidable. Under those circumstances, it is acceptable. Interestingly, children who adhere most closely to the rules and maintain them most actively are liked the most by peers and judged to be most socially competent by adults.

Given their proclivity to avoid contact with the other sex, it is not surprising that children spend much of their time in the company of same-sex peers. In simpler societies, gender segregation is imposed by adults, who manage children's lives in ways that separate boys and girls. For instance, in some societies, boys are assigned chores (such as herding) that take them away from home, whereas girls take on domestic duties that keep them near adult women and other girls (Whiting & Edwards, 1988). In other societies, children attend single-sex schools or are kept largely separate in other ways. However, gender segregation also prevails in societies where children are free to associate—indeed, are encouraged to associate—with opposite-sex peers. Gender segregation emerges

TABLE 16.3 THE "COOTIE" RULES: UNDER WHAT CIRCUMSTANCES IS IT PERMISSIBLE TO HAVE CONTACT WITH THE OTHER GENDER IN MIDDLE CHILDHOOD?

Rule:	The contact is accidental.
Example:	You're not looking where you are going and you bump into someone.
Rule:	The contact is incidental.
Example:	You go to get some lemonade and wait while two children of the other gender get some. (There should be no conversation.)
Rule:	The contact is in the guise of some clear and necessary purpose.
Example:	You may say "Pass the lemonade," to persons of the other gender at the next table. No interest in them is expressed.
Rule:	An adult compels you to have contact.
Example:	"Go get that map from X and Y and bring it to me."
Rule:	You are accompanied by some of your own gender.
Example:	Two girls may talk to two boys, though physical closeness with your own partner must be maintained and physical intimacy with the others is disallowed.
Rule:	The interaction or contact is accompanied by disavowal.
Example:	You say someone is ugly or hurl some other insult or (more commonly for boys) push or throw something at them as you pass by.

Source: L. A. Sroufe, C. Bennett, M. Englund, J. Urban, & S. Shulman. (1993). "The Significance of Gender Boundaries in Preadolescence: Contemporary Correlates and Antecedents of Boundary Relations and Maintenance," *Child Development, 64*, 455-466. Reprinted by permission.

around age 3 to 4 and is routinely observed in mixed-sex settings, such as daycare and preschool. The tendency for children to seek out companions of the same sex and to avoid children of the opposite sex increases dramatically in the elementary school years (Rose & Smith, 2009). Indeed, in a study looking at the friendship patterns of over 700 children in grades 3 and 4, Kovacs, Parker, and Hoffman (1996) found that only 14 percent of the children had friends of the opposite sex.

For Thought and Discussion

What do you think about single-sex schools? Would single-sex schooling be more effective at certain ages? What criteria would you use to determine whether single-sex education "works" and benefits both sexes?

The causes of gender segregation are not well understood (Fagot, Rodgers, & Leinbach, 2000; Maccoby, 2000b; Powlishta et al., 2001). One explanation is that children are naturally attracted to others with play styles that are compatible with their own. And, as we have seen, boys and girls exhibit rather distinct play styles beginning at an early age. Although there is some evidence to support this theory of gender segregation (Moller & Serbin, 1996), it cannot be the whole story. Children often react more positively to others of the same gender before they have had time to learn much about their play styles (Martin, 1989; Serbin & Sprafkin, 1986). Children also exhibit a preference for same-sex adults, for whom play styles are not as important (Serbin & Sprafkin, 1986). In addition, children's preference for same-sex companions extends beyond a willingness to play with them. Children exhibit an own-sex favouritism that colours their perception of a wide variety of sex-typed traits (Powlishta, 1995).

Whatever the causes of gender segregation may be, the consequences of same-sex gender groupings are very important for children's gender-role development. As we saw earlier, boys' and girls' groups differ in size, in the nature of activities, and in the norms for social interaction. According to Eleanor Maccoby (1998), a prominent gender theorist, the dynamics of interaction in boys and girls groups are so different that the groups constitute two separate "cultures of childhood." These two cultures, in turn, foster the development of distinct sets of social-emotional skills and propensities (Underwood, 2003; Underwood et al., 2006).

SOCIALIZATION BY SELF

So far, our discussion of socialization portrays children as largely responding passively to pressures from outside. However, a central premise of socialization accounts of gender-role development is that children participate actively in the process of socialization. Here, we discuss two ways that children can be said to "self-socialize" their gender roles.

One way is through their selection of models. Although children of both genders can learn male and female gender stereotypes by viewing models, they tend to focus on models of their own gender (Halim & Ruble, 2010). Children are better able to recall and imitate the behaviour of same-sex models (Bussey & Bandura, 1984, 1992; Perry & Bussey, 1979). In addition, children are sensitive to the gender appropriateness of the model's activity. If a boy, for example, believes that a behaviour is "girlish," he is unlikely to imitate it, even if it is modelled by a male (Masters, 1979; Raskin & Israel, 1981). The tendency to attend more to same-sex models is especially strong for boys, who often resist imitating behaviours modelled by females. In contrast, although girls prefer to imitate adult women, they will also imitate adult men (Bussey & Perry, 1982; Slaby & Frey, 1975).

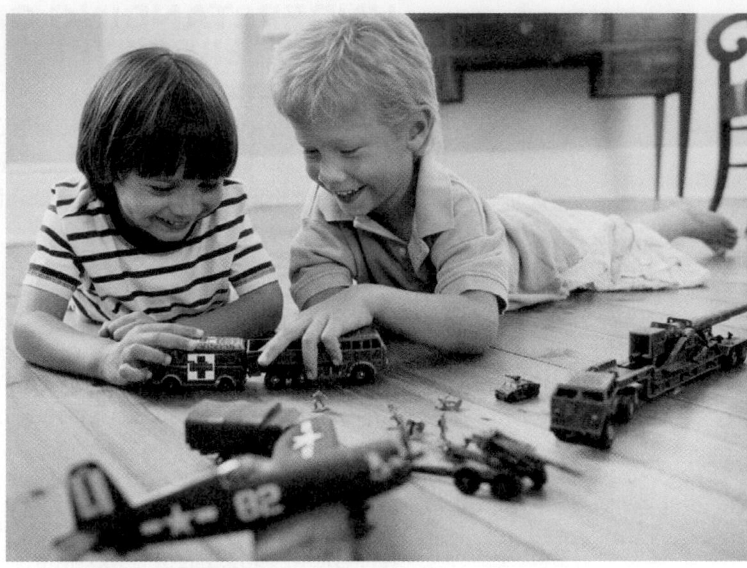

Some studies have shown that young children adapt their toy preferences to win approval from peers. (*Banana Stock/Media Bakery*)

Second, external sanctions (such as negative reactions from parents and peers) are gradually internalized as self-sanctions. As children acquire knowledge about the likely consequences of gender-linked conduct, they come to regulate their actions accordingly (Bussey & Bandura, 1999, 2004). Children's regulation of their own sex-typed play was graphically illustrated in a study that examined preschoolers' reactions to opportunities to play with a variety of gender-typed toys or toys linked to the other gender (Bussey & Bandura, 1992). When only other-sex toys were available, some boys attempted to have the stereotypically feminine toys removed. When that failed, the boys did all they could to avoid playing with the toys. One boy reportedly flung the baby doll across the room and turned his back on it. Others transformed the toys into more masculine props, such as using the eggbeater in the kitchen set as a drill or gun. Children's self-ratings correspond to these behavioural observations. At age 4, both boys and girls rated themselves more positively when they played with own-sex toys and more negatively when they played with toys usually associated with the other sex.

Other studies show that young children adapt their toy preferences to win approval from peers. In one study (Banerjee & Lintern, 2000), boys and girls between the ages of 4 and 9 were instructed to describe their activity and toy preferences twice—once when alone and once when facing a group of same-sex peers. Whereas the older children did not change their self-descriptions when in front of peers, younger boys presented themselves as more sex-typed in front of peers than they did when alone.

The process of self-socialization requires a good deal of knowledge about gender and related attributes. What children know about gender and when they know it is the focus of the next section.

LEARNING OBJECTIVE 16.4

Understand how society, parents, peers, and the self contribute to gender-role socialization.

1. How can gender-role development be viewed as a process of socialization?
2. What roles do parents play in the socialization of gender?
3. How do peers and self contribute to gender-role development?

Learning Objective 16.5

Trace the development of gender-role knowledge and behaviour.

UNDERSTANDING GENDER ROLES AND STEREOTYPES

We have reviewed considerable evidence that socialization processes are involved in sex typing. In this section, we turn to the cognitive processes that influence gender-role development. Of particular interest is the developing child's increasing understanding of gender roles and stereotypes.

THE DEVELOPMENT OF GENDER IDENTITY

We have already mentioned Kohlberg's (1966) stage model of gender constancy, which includes gender identity ("I am a boy/girl"), gender stability ("I will grow up to be a man/woman"), and gender consistency ("I cannot change my sex") (Martin et al., 2002; Ruble et al., 2007). Data from a number of studies have confirmed this theoretical progression. By 3 years of age, almost all children display gender identity. Gender stability follows around 4 years of age, and gender consistency around age 5. Children have a full understanding of gender constancy at around 6 years of age (Halim & Ruble, 2010). Males and females progress through these stages at approximately the same rate (Bem, 1989; Fagot, 1985; Martin & Little, 1990). This progression has been demonstrated in a variety of cultures, although children in many non-Western cultures may proceed through the stages more slowly (Gibbons, 2000; Munroe, Shimmin, & Munroe, 1984).

THE DEVELOPMENT OF GENDER KNOWLEDGE

Recent research shows that children develop some knowledge about gender categories during the first 2 years of life. By just 2 months of age, infants can discriminate male and female voices (Jusczyk, Pisoni, & Mullennix, 1992). By the end of the first year, children are able to categorize people by gender on the basis of features such as voice pitch and hair length (Patterson & Werker, 2002; Poulin-Dubois & Serbin, 2006).

Once the categories of male and female are established, children begin to associate other attributes with gender. By about age 2, children can reliably sort pictures of males and females and their accessories (clothes, tools, and appliances) into separate piles and accurately point to pictures of things for males and things for females (Fagot et al., 1986; O'Brien & Huston, 1985). Diane Poulin-Dubois and Lisa Serbin report that toddlers around age 2 also have some awareness of the typical activities of men and women (Poulin-Dubois & Serbin, 2006; Poulin-Dubois et al., 2002). Within about the first year, they are able to verbally label toys as being for boys or for girls (Weinraub et al., 1984). In *Focus on Research 16.1*, we look at how researchers have investigated awareness of gender-stereotyped activities in infants.

Over the course of early childhood, children begin to incorporate more abstract or metaphorical concepts into their gender stereotypes. For example, perhaps as early as age 2 and certainly by age 4, children come to associate hardness and items such as bears and eagles with boys, and softness, flowers, butterflies, and the colour pink with girls (Eichstedt et al., 2002; Poulin-Dubois & Serbin, 2006; Leinbach et al., 1997). During middle childhood, children gradually add information about occupations, behavioural traits, and personality differences to their stereotypes (Berenbaum, Martin, & Ruble, 2008).

Children's gender stereotypes mirror those of the adults in their cultural communities (Best, 2010). Cross-cultural studies show that male stereotypes are generally learned earlier than female stereotypes, although there are exceptions. Female stereotypes are learned earlier in Germany and in Latin/Catholic cultures (Brazil, Chile, Portugal, Venezuela), where the adult-defined female stereotype is more positive than that of the male (Best, 2001).

FLEXIBILITY OF GENDER STEREOTYPES

The rigidity or flexibility of children's gender stereotypes changes over the course of childhood. During the preschool years, most children view gender roles in inflexible, absolutist terms

FOCUS ON RESEARCH 16.1
PREFERENTIAL LOOKING AS A MEASURE OF INFANTS' AWARENESS OF GENDER-STEREOTYPED ACTIVITIES

Researchers have been intrigued by the question of when children's awareness of gender stereotypes begins to be evident. Using sorting and pointing tasks, investigators have determined that sometime between their second and third birthdays, children display awareness of the stereotyping of traditionally feminine and masculine activities (Fagot et al., 1986; O'Brien & Huston, 1985). Such procedures, however, require a certain degree of verbal ability; that is, children need a sufficient level of language fluency to respond to the investigator's questions or to understand and comply with test instructions (Poulin-Dubois et al., 2002; Serbin, Poulin-Dubois, Colburne, Sen, & Eichstedt, 2001). Such verbally based tasks could underestimate young children's knowledge of gender stereotyping (Serbin et al., 2001; Serbin, Poulin-Dubois, & Eichstedt, 2002). It is possible that awareness of gender stereotypes develops at an even earlier age, perhaps even during infancy before children are able to verbalize such knowledge.

But, how could researchers investigate the existence of such awareness in preverbal infants? A team of innovative researchers from the Centre for Research in Human Development at Concordia University in Montreal employed the *preference method*, pioneered by Robert Fantz (1961), to assess awareness of gender stereotypes in preverbal infants. As discussed in Chapter 7, the preference method involves presenting infants with pairs of visual stimuli and assessing the amount of time spent looking at each member of the pair. Preference is indicated by longer looking times at one item in the pair. Infants' preferences may be related to various characteristics of the stimuli presented to them. One such characteristic may be unexpectedness. Research in the physical domain (e.g., Baillargeon, 1995) has indicated that infants tend to look longer at unexpected or "impossible" events (see Chapter 8).

Using the preference method, Lisa Serbin, Diane Poulin-Dubois, and Julie Eichstedt (2002) presented 24-month-old toddlers with photos of a male and a female engaging in the same activity, and assessed the length of time the infants spent looking at each photo (see Figure 16.6). The activities presented were either stereotypically masculine (e.g., fixing a large toy car, taking out the garbage, or hammering), stereotypically feminine (e.g., feeding a baby, ironing clothes, putting on makeup), or neutral (e.g., putting on shoes, reading, turning on a light). The researchers hypothesized that the infants in their study would stare longer at the mismatched, gender-inconsistent event.

As predicted, the infants stared longer at photos of males engaging in female-stereotyped activities than at photos of females engaging in the same activities, suggesting some awareness of gender stereotypes in infants as young as 24 months of age. No similar differences were found, however, for pictures of males and females engaged in stereotypically male activities. As suggested by Serbin and colleagues, the infants in this study appear to have been more surprised to see males engaging in feminine activities than females engaging in masculine activities, perhaps reflecting more stereotyping of feminine activities in the infants' homes.

In another study, Lisa Serbin, Diane Poulin-Dubois, Karen Colburne, Maya Sen, and Julie Eichstedt (2001) used the preference method with an even younger group of infants. Infants

FIGURE 16.6

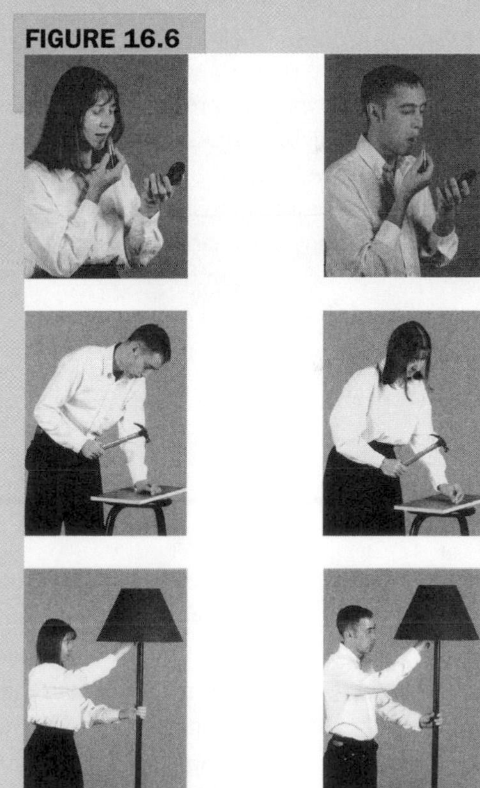

Examples of the pairs of stimuli used by Serbin and colleagues in a study of infants' awareness of gender-stereotyped activities. *Source: Serbin, L.A., Poulin-Dubois, D., & Eichstedt, J. (2002). Infants' responses to gender-inconsistent events.* Infancy, *3, 531–542. Lawrence Erlbaum Associates, Inc. Reprinted by permission.*

Links to Related Material

In Chapter 7 you read how the preference method is used to determine if the infant can discriminate between stimuli. Here you see how the preference method is used to assess awareness of gender stereotypes in preverbal infants.

(continued)

Focus on Research 16.1 Preferential Looking as a Measure of Infants' Awareness of Gender-Stereotyped Activities *continued*

aged 12, 18, and 23 months were shown paired photos of a male-stereotyped and female-stereotyped toy (see Figure 16.7). Male-stereotyped toys included vehicles such as tractors, cars, and trains, whereas female-stereotyped toys included a variety of dolls. Which toy would they look at longer?

At 12 months of age, children of both sexes preferred to look at pictures of dolls over vehicles. The researchers suggested that this preference for dolls might reflect the similarity of dolls to faces, which attract the attention of young infants. At 18 and at 23 months of age, however, girls looked longer at dolls and boys looked longer at vehicles, indicating sex-typed toy preferences in children as young as 18 months. When these pictures were paired with photos of male and female children, the researchers found that 18- and 23-month-old girls, but not boys, matched the gender appropriate faces to the toy presented.

What do these preference method studies tell us? They suggest that gender-stereotyped toy preferences emerge sometime between ages 12 and 18 months, and that awareness of gender stereotypes follows shortly thereafter. Awareness of gender stereotypes may be seen in girls as early as 18 to 23 months of age. Such awareness appears to emerge a little later in boys, somewhere between 24 months and 31 months of age (Poulin-Dubois & Serbin, 2006; Poulin-Dubois et al., 2002; Serbin et al., 2002).

FIGURE 16.7

Examples of paired toys shown to young infants in the study by Serbin and colleagues. *Adapted from Serbin, L. A., Poulin-Dubois, D., Colburne, K. A., Sen, M. G., & Eichstedt, J. A. (2001). Gender stereotyping in infancy: Visual preferences for and knowledge of gender-stereotyped toys in the second year.* International Journal of Behavioral Development, *25, 71-15. International Society for the Study of Behavioural Development.* Adapted by permission.

(consistent with preoperational thinking), and consider cross-sex behaviours to be serious violations of social standards.

By middle childhood, children generally have begun to view gender roles as socially determined rules and conventions that can be approached somewhat flexibly and broken without major consequences (Miller, Trautner, & Ruble, 2006; Trautner et al., 2005). This flexibility reflects several developmental achievements, including more advanced classification skills, a growing awareness of the cultural relativity of gender norms, and an increasingly sophisticated understanding of biology (Halim & Ruble, 2010). For instance, one study presented children with a story of a baby who had been raised on an island with only members of the opposite sex. When asked which gender characteristics the baby would eventually display, children younger than age 9 or 10 predicted that the baby's biological sex would determine its later characteristics. Children above that age, in contrast, believed that the baby would be more influenced by the social environment, and so would adopt the characteristics of the opposite sex (Taylor, 1996).

The transition to junior high school appears to increase adolescents' flexibility toward the roles of males and females. This may occur because the fairly dramatic change in setting and routine forces young adolescents to rethink many of their previous ideas (Katz & Ksansnak, 1994). Nevertheless, across the junior high and high school years, gender stereotypes become increasingly rigid again (Alfieri, Ruble, & Higgins, 1996).

GENDER KNOWLEDGE AND BEHAVIOUR

We have seen that some forms of gender knowledge are present very early in childhood. But does this knowledge affect children's behaviour? Evidence suggests that it does.

TOY AND ACTIVITY PREFERENCES As suggested earlier, sex differences in children's play emerge between the first and second birthdays, before children of both sexes can reliably identify toys as being more appropriate or typical for girls or boys (Campbell, Shirley, & Caygill, 2002; Poulin-Dubois & Serbin, 2006; Serbin et al., 2001). Consequently, gender knowledge is probably not critical for the emergence of sex-typed play. It does, however, exert considerable influence on children's preferences for toys and activities as they grow older (Halim & Ruble, 2010), an effect that seems especially pronounced for boys (Miller et al., 2006). Indeed, by the preschool years, children spend more time exploring own-sex toys and rate such toys as more attractive. They are also more motivated to perform well on own-sex games or tasks (Berenbaum, Martin, Hanish, et al., 2008).

MEMORY Gender stereotypes influence what children remember. Children pay more attention to and remember more about same-sex peers and activities than about other-sex peers and activities (Halim & Ruble, 2010; Martin et al., 2002). Gender information also influences children's memory for scripted sequences of behaviours (see Chapter 8). Boys, but not girls, show better memory for own-gender than for other-gender scripts (Bauer, 1993; Boston & Levy, 1991; Levy & Fivush, 1993).

Children's recall is better when information is consistent with the gender schemas they have formed. For example, in several studies, children were shown a series of pictures, each depicting either a male or female performing a gender-stereotyped activity. The children were later shown two pictures and asked which one they had seen earlier. Children had a more accurate memory for gender-consistent pictures (such as a woman ironing clothes) than for gender-inconsistent pictures (such as a man ironing clothes) (Bigler & Liben, 1990; Boston & Levy, 1991; Liben & Signorella, 1993). Children sometimes even misremember information to make it consistent with their stereotypes (Frawley, 2008; Martin et al., 2002).

SOCIAL JUDGMENTS Children—like adults—use gender knowledge to make inferences and judgments about other people. As in cases of gender-related recall, young children are better able to make stereotypical inferences when given own-sex cues than other-sex cues. For example, a girl told about a child who likes to play with kitchen sets would likely infer that the same child would also like to play with dolls. She would be less likely, however, to draw appropriate inferences if told about a boy who likes to play with trucks.

By around age 8, children are able to use other-gender cues to draw inferences about the opposite sex. Developmental differences also emerge when children are presented with conflicting information about another person, such as a boy who enjoys playing with dolls. Young children tend to reason simply on the basis of the child's gender, and infer that because the unfamiliar child is a boy, he will probably like to play with trucks. Older children rely more on individuating information (e.g., the target child's individual interests, traits, appearance) and infer that this particular boy may not behave in sex-stereotyped ways (Berndt & Heller, 1986; Biernat, 1991; Martin, 1989).

The range of possible inferences increases as children gain additional stereotypical information about the sexes. For example, when told of a boy who admired another child's bicycle, school-age boys and girls were likely to suggest that the boy was the kind of person who likes to steal things. In contrast, when the character was a girl, children were more likely to claim that she was simply trying to be friendly (Heyman, 2001).

LEARNING OBJECTIVE 16.5

Trace the development of gender-role knowledge and behaviour.

1. What is the developmental progression of gender knowledge?
2. What is the developmental course for children's flexibility regarding gender stereotypes?
3. How does gender knowledge influence behaviour?

Learning Objective 16.6

Discuss the development of sexual relationships and behaviour.

DEVELOPMENT OF SEXUAL RELATIONSHIPS AND BEHAVIOUR

Sexual orientation A person's sexual preference. Heterosexuals are attracted to members of the opposite sex and homosexuals are attracted to members of the same sex.

Throughout childhood, the dominant theme in children's relations with the opposite sex is segregation (Rose & Smith, 2009). As children move into adolescence, heterosexual attraction becomes increasingly powerful, opposing the forces of cross-sex avoidance. There is, of course, marked individual variation in sexuality and **sexual orientation**. Nonetheless, most adolescents develop a sexual attraction to those of the opposite sex, and the peer culture of adolescence is dominated by a heterosexual script for appropriate behaviour. In this section, we describe how adolescents manage the transition to adult sexual relationships.

EMERGENCE OF ROMANTIC AND SEXUAL INTEREST

Children are aware of each other as potential romantic and sexual partners from early on. Romantic themes involving dating, courtship, and marriage dominate much of girls' play. In the meantime, boys engage in sexy "locker room" talk about girls' bodies (Maccoby, 1998). "Kiss-and-chase" games that are the mainstay of elementary school playgrounds in industrialized societies are observed in cultures around the world as well (Sutton-Smith & Roberts, 1973). During middle childhood, when children are at the peak of opposite-gender avoidance, children tease each other for "liking" or "loving" a child of the opposite sex (Maccoby, 1998; Thorne, 1993).

How do children move from these kinds of immature relationships to the sexually mature relationships of adulthood? Until recently, sexual maturation was highly regulated by cultural practices and prescribed social expectations. In some cultures, this remains true even today. But in many communities, young people must negotiate their entry into dating and sexuality with little direct support from parents or other adults. In these communities, the peer group serves as an important context for the development of heterosexual relationships.

Adolescents spend much of their time in mixed-sex groups just "hanging out," eventually moving on to more romantic interests and sexual relationships. (© *Adrian Sherratt/Alamy*)

Some theorists have found it helpful to consider the transition as a series of stages or phases (Brown, 1999; O'Sullivan, Graber, & Brooks-Gunn, 2001). Boys and girls typically report experiencing their first romantic interests, or "crushes," between the ages of 7 and 10. Often, these crushes are directed at unavailable targets, such as teachers and celebrities. The age of 10 is typically considered the "magical" age at which sexual attraction develops (Herdt & McClintock, 2001) and interest in romantic and sexual partners begins.

Between the ages of 10 and 14 years, young people spend increasing amounts of time in mixed-sex groups just "hanging out" and going places together. There is initially little intimacy in these encounters. Gradually, activities such as dances and parties that require more intimacy increase in frequency. Games with some sexual content (e.g., Spin the Bottle, Man Hunt, and Seven Minutes of Heaven) and kissing and touching breasts or genitals through clothes become more common (O'Sullivan et al., 2001). Nonetheless, having numerous peers around remains important to ensure that behaviour remains within culturally acceptable boundaries.

By middle adolescence (15 to 16 years), many adolescents are involved in a romantic relationship (Feiring, 1996). Approximately 28 percent of Canadian grade 9 students and 38 percent of grade 11 students report at least one steady relationship in the past year (Boyce et al., 2006). Nonetheless, couples continue to spend much of their time in mixed-sex groups that include peers who are "dating" and other adolescents who are just friends.

During later adolescence, romantic relationships involve greater levels of emotional and sexual intimacy. The relationships are also longer in duration and involve more couple activities than those observed in younger adolescents, when dating activities often occur in a group context (O'Sullivan et al., 2001).

Researchers often focus on age of first intercourse as an important moment in a person's sexual development. However, many adolescents start to experiment with a variety of sexual behaviours before they engage in intercourse. Experimenting with sexual activities typically follows a general sexual script. Adolescents may try various behaviours progressively until they engage in sexual intercourse (Flicker et al., 2009). About 29 percent of Canadian teens aged 15 to 17, and 65 percent of those aged 18 to 19, report having had sexual intercourse at least once (Statistics Canada, 2008).

Researchers at the University of Ottawa examined university students' retrospective evaluations of their first sexual intercourse experience (Reissing, Andruff, & Wentland, 2012). The average age of first intercourse in this study was approximately 17 years for both males and females, which is in line with other Canadian data (Maticka-Tyndale, 2001; Tsui & Nicoladis, 2004). Although males were slightly more likely to report a positive first sexual intercourse experience, in general, both males and females reported a positive first experience if they were not under the influence of drugs and/or alcohol and were in a romantic relationship with their partner.

Relationship status with one's partner seems important for a positive first sexual intercourse experience. Indeed, a study on first sexual intercourse experience conducted at the University of Alberta found that 84 percent of the 384 participants reported having been in a romantic relationship with their first intercourse partner, whom they had dated on average for a total of 7 months (Tsui & Nicoladis, 2004). Sixty-three percent of females and 43 percent of males reported that they believed they were in love with their first intercourse partner at the time of first sexual intercourse.

Most researchers acknowledge that large numbers of adolescents do not conform to the normative ages described above. Studies suggest that there may be cultural differences in the age at which sexual behaviours emerge (Smith & Udry, 1985) and in how various cultures view sexual behaviour during adolescence. Researchers from the University of Windsor, for example, studied adult Iranian immigrants' perceptions of Canadian attitudes toward sexuality (Shirpak, Maticka-Tyndale, & Chinichian, 2007). Many of the participants identified concerns regarding liberal attitudes and adolescent sexuality, especially in terms of the importance of virginity and subsequent expectations of purity for young girls. Given the cultural diversity of Canada, it is important for researchers to continue to examine sexual behaviour in light of cultural differences.

Additionally, some adolescents explore their sexuality in different ways. For example, gay, lesbian, and bisexual young people typically do not have their first same-sex sexual experience within a romantic relationship, in part because of the difficulty of dating someone of the same sex given the heterosexual orientation that dominates adolescent peer culture (Diamond et al., 1999; Herdt & Boxer, 1993). Researchers are beginning to examine the specific sexual scripts that non-heterosexual adolescents use in their dating and sexual relationships, as they may not follow the same patterns as those of heterosexual adolescents (Saewyc, 2011). And some adolescents may skip stages altogether or recycle through the various stages several times (Brown, 1999). For example, some adolescents in the British Columbia Adolescent Health Survey stopped engaging in sexual intercourse and returned to previous sexual activities because they felt they were not prepared to have sexual intercourse (Smith, Stewart, Peled, Poon, & Saewyc, 2009).

ORIGINS OF SEXUAL ORIENTATION

The majority of adolescents develop a heterosexual orientation; however, homosexuality is also found in most cultures (Crompton, 2003). Calculating the actual number of gay people in a society has proven to be very difficult. Estimates of homosexuality depend in large part on how it is defined. For example, asking people if they have ever had any kind of same-sex experience yields different results than does asking people if they have had a same-sex partner in the past five years. Also, many more people report being attracted to someone of the same sex than report having a sexual experience with someone of the same sex.

These and other factors make it difficult to obtain accurate information regarding the actual number of gay people living in different societies. Surveys in North America and Europe estimate the percentage of men who identify themselves as gay to be around 3 to 5 percent of the population, and the percentage of women who identify themselves as lesbian to be around 2 to 3 percent (Diamond, 1993). The percentage is higher if the criteria include romantic attraction, without self-identification as gay or lesbian. In a recent survey of American adolescents, 7.1 percent of males and 5.3 percent of females reported same-sex or both-sex romantic attraction (Russell, 2006). Percentages also vary if questions ask about attraction to individuals of both sexes, rather than just to one sex or the other (e.g., Herbenick et al., 2010).

How does an erotic attraction to one or the other sex or both sexes develop? Most research on the development of sexual orientation has focused on how some individuals develop an attraction to members of their own sex. Researchers have looked to both biological and socialization influences.

BIOLOGICAL INFLUENCES Research on twins and families suggests that sexual orientation may be, in part, hereditary. Although concordance rates vary widely from study to study, the chances that both members of a pair of twins will have a homosexual orientation are significantly greater for identical (monozygotic) twins than for fraternal (dizygotic) twins (Dawood, Bailey, & Martin, 2009; Hershberger, 2001; Zucker, 2001). Studies also find gay men and lesbian women to have more gay and lesbian siblings than heterosexuals. Moreover, gay males are more likely to have gay male siblings than lesbian siblings, whereas lesbian siblings are—to a lesser degree—more likely to have lesbian siblings than gay male siblings (Dawood et al., 2009).

How might genes influence the development of sexual orientation? Some researchers believe certain genes influence the production or impact of prenatal hormones. As we saw earlier, hormones produced by the newly formed testes masculinize the fetus, which includes both the development of the reproductive organs and the organization of the fetal brain. Some researchers argue that sexual orientation may be established during this process (Meyer-Bahlburg et al., 2008; Reinisch, Ziemba-Davis, & Sanders, 1991).

As we have seen, however, hormone levels are influenced by both genetic and environmental factors. Whether a person is chromosomally male (XY) or female (XX), hormonal imbalances— such as those caused by CAH and androgen insensitivity—can affect the individual's gender-related behaviour, personality traits, and sexual preferences (Berenbaum & Snyder, 1995; Meyer-Bahlburg et al., 2008; Zucker et al., 1996). And girls exposed to unusually high levels of masculinizing androgens because of medications prescribed to their mothers to prevent miscarriage may be more likely to develop a lesbian or bisexual orientation than are girls whose mothers did not take such medication (Meyer-Bahlburg et al., 1995). It is not known, however, whether similar processes underlie the development of individuals not affected by these hormonal disorders or exposed prenatally to these medications.

Further evidence to support the role of hormones in sexual orientation is the existence of a birth order difference between gay and heterosexual men (Hershberger, 2001). Specifically, homosexual boys tend to be later in birth order than heterosexual boys. Moreover, the later birth order of gay men depends only on the number of older brothers and not on the number of older sisters (Blanchard & Lippa, 2007; Blanchard et al., 2002: Schwartz et al., 2010). The birth order effect is believed to be due to a maternal immune reaction that lessens the impact of male androgens during the prenatal period (Blanchard, 2004).

SOCIALIZATION An alternative explanation of sexual orientation involves socialization processes. In general, traditional socialization accounts of sexual orientation have not fared well empirically. There is little evidence, for example, that having a non-heterosexual parent predisposes a child to become gay or lesbian (Golombok & Tasker, 2010; Herek, 2006; Patterson & Hastings, 2007). In one study of the sons of gay fathers, researchers found that the sons' identification as either gay or heterosexual was unrelated to the amount of time they had lived with their fathers, how accepting they were of their fathers' homosexuality, and the quality of their relationships with their fathers (Bailey, Nothnagel, & Wolfe, 1995). In general, the proportion of children reared by gay, lesbian, or bisexual parents who adopt a non-heterosexual identity is comparable with that among children raised by heterosexual parents. The fact that child rearing alone is not enough to determine sexual orientation does not mean that socialization is irrelevant, however. Indeed, most scholars believe that sexual orientation is the product of interaction between biology and environment.

AN INTERACTIONIST MODEL Daryl Bem (2000, 2001) has offered one model of how biological factors and experience might interact in the development of sexual orientation. In Bem's model—termed the *Exotic-Becomes-Erotic (EBE) theory*—sexual orientation is the culmination of a complex chain of events that begins with children's temperament. According to Bem, children's inborn temperament shapes their preferences for activities and play partners. As we have seen, some behavioural styles tend to be more characteristic of boys than girls. Specifically, boys tend to have, on average, higher activity levels. They are also more aggressive. Consequently, children higher in activity level and aggression are drawn to male-typical activities, whereas children who prefer quieter play are attracted to female-typical activities.

According to EBE theory, children not only prefer others like themselves, but also perceive children in the other group as different, unfamiliar, even "exotic." These feelings—which gender-conforming children have toward members of the opposite sex, but which gender-non-conforming children have toward members of the same sex—are associated with heightened physiological arousal in the presence of the other-group children.

Initially, of course, children do not interpret this arousal in sexual or erotic terms. Rather, a male-typical child may experience arousal in the presence of girls as antipathy ("girls are yucky"). A female-typical child may experience arousal in the presence of boys as apprehension. Eventually, through a complex process involving maturational, cognitive, and situational factors, this physiological state comes to be experienced as erotic desire.

The idea that individuals come to be attracted to a class of people from whom they felt different in childhood is supported by retrospective interviews of gay men and lesbians and heterosexual adults. When asked about their childhoods, a majority of gay men and lesbians report feeling different from same-sex peers on gender-related characteristics, such as activity preferences. Heterosexual adults rarely report feeling different from same-sex peers because of gender-related characteristics (Bell, Weinberg, & Hammersmith, 1981; Savin-Williams, 1998).

Of course, the reliability of retrospective reports is subject to scrutiny. However, the significance of gender non-conformity for later sexual preference is also supported by prospective studies that follow children to adolescence or adulthood, and by retrospective examination of the content of childhood home videos. Boys who grow up to be gay men are more likely to display gender non-conforming behaviours as children. They avoid rough-and-tumble activities, physical aggression, and competitive sports, and enjoy playing with girls. Girls who grow up to be lesbian are also more likely to display gender non-conforming behaviours as children (Bailey, Dunne, & Martin, 2000; Bailey, Miller, & Willerman, 1993; Bailey & Zucker, 1995; Rieger, Linsenmeier, Gigax, & Bailey, 2008).

Bem's model seems particularly well suited for explaining the sexual orientation of gay men and lesbian women who fit cultural stereotypes—that is, effeminate males and masculine females. But not everyone who is gay or lesbian fits these stereotypes. Can EBE theory explain individual differences in sexual orientation?

Bem contends that it can. The central tenet of EBE theory is that individuals feel different from a class of peers during childhood. What makes a child feel that way may differ across peer subcultures. To illustrate, Bem points to males who are highly interested in computers. In some peer cultures, these males would be regarded as highly masculine, whereas in others they would be regarded as gender-deviant. Bem also points out that an individual child may be gender-non-conforming in some ways, but not feel different from peers if he or she conforms to other gender expectations that are more gender-defining in the culture. In addition, widespread cultural changes can produce cohort effects, and behaviours that are gender-non-conforming in one cohort can become more or less so in a later cohort.

Bem acknowledges that there may be multiple routes to adult sexual orientation, and that EBE theory describes just one of them. He also admits that EBE theory may be completely wrong and that biological factors, such as genes, prenatal hormones, and brain structure may indeed play a more direct and powerful role in the development of sexual orientation than accounted for in his theory (Bem, 2001). It is important to remember, however, that existing evidence for the biological origins of human sexual orientation remains correlational. Bem has made a valuable contribution to the study of the development of both heterosexual and non-heterosexual orientations by cautioning against the overly deterministic view of sexual orientation that is gaining popularity.

LEARNING OBJECTIVE 16.6

Discuss the development of sexual relationships and behaviour.

1. How do romantic and sexual interests emerge?
2. What do we know about the origins of sexual orientation?

CONCLUSION

There have been dramatic changes in the roles of men and women worldwide. In many nations, the roles open to both women and men have expanded considerably. Science has made significant contributions to these societal changes. Early research revealed numerous ways in which child rearing and educational practices blunted the aspirations of young girls. Changes in policies followed, accompanied by a wide range of intervention programs designed to foster gender equity in schools, sports, and the workplace. Studies showed that fathers—not just mothers or mother figures—can serve as primary caregivers. These findings have helped shape decision-making about child care among families and in the courts. And research on the origins of sexual orientation, including longitudinal investigations of children reared in gay and lesbian households, has proven influential in shaping both attitudes and laws regarding the rights of sexual minorities.

We have learned much about gender development during recent years, but numerous questions continue to intrigue the public and scientists alike. Why, for example, do females seem to enjoy caring for children more than males? Why are most of the students who commit violence in schools male? And why, despite the fact that males and females are more alike than different, do we often find it so hard to understand each other?

Although scientists have not yet found firm answers to these questions, one thing has become clear: the process of gender development is far from simple. As in other areas of development, biological, cognitive, and sociocultural factors all play important parts in guiding the child's progress toward a sexual identity.

SUMMARY

KEY TERMS

androgen insensitivity syndrome (AIS), p. 634
congenital adrenal hyperplasia (CAH), p. 634
gender consistency, p. 620
gender constancy, p. 620
gender identity, p. 620
gender role, p. 618
gender schemas, p. 620
gender stability, p. 620
lateralization, p. 624
meta-analysis, p. 622
sex typing, p. 618
sexual differentiation, p. 618
sexual orientation, p. 648

LEARNING OBJECTIVES

LEARNING OBJECTIVE 16.1 Understand four theoretical approaches to gender development.

1. *How do evolutionary and biological approaches view gender development?*
   The biological approach to gender development includes the general framework of evolutionary theory, as well as a focus on specific biological mechanisms, such as genes, hormones, and brain functioning. According to the evolutionary approach, modern sex differences in aggression and dominance, as well as in inhibitory control, reflect the different reproductive challenges faced by males and females in our ancestral past. The psychobiological approach stresses how prenatal exposure to sex hormones contributes both to differences between sexes, and also to individual differences within each sex.

2. *How do sociocultural theorists account for the development of gender roles?*
   Sociocultural theorists contend that sex differences observed among children and adults *follow* from the roles commonly held by females versus males. Proponents of the sociocultural approach place less emphasis on biological factors than do proponents of the evolutionary approach. They emphasize, however, that gender-role behaviour is readily acquired by children who have inherited evolved tendencies to categorize the world and acquire culture.

3. *Describe two cognitive-developmental approaches to gender-role development.*
   The cognitive-developmental tradition has generated two theoretical approaches to gender-role development. One is Kohlberg's stage model of the development of gender constancy, in which children's understanding of gender-role issues proceeds through three stages: gender identity, gender stability, and gender consistency. The second approach is based on the information-processing concept of gender schemas, cognitive representations of the characteristics associated with being male or female. Gender schemas help children organize gender-related information, regulate their gender-role behaviour, and make inferences regarding gender-role issues.

4. *How does social-learning theory view gender roles?*
   Social-learning theory views gender roles primarily as a class of social behaviour acquired and maintained by learning principles, including reinforcement, modelling, and self-regulation. In this view, sex differences are not inevitable and may change with environmental conditions.

LEARNING OBJECTIVE 16.2 Describe the physical, cognitive, and social/personality sex differences that researchers have found.

1. *What physical sex differences have researchers found?*
   Females are generally healthier and more developmentally advanced than males at birth, and reach developmental milestones earlier. Males are more physically active—especially when in the company of other males—and more vulnerable to illness and injury. Sex

differences in infancy are minimal in motor development. However, they are evident in early childhood. By age 5, boys can jump farther, run faster, and throw farther than girls. Girls have the advantage in activities that require a combination of balance and precise movement, such as hopping and skipping, and also with fine motor skills like tying shoes, writing, and cutting paper.

2. *What cognitive sex differences have researchers found?*
Girls outperform boys in their rate of language acquisition. Generally, girls also learn to read more easily. Recent studies show girls outperform boys on language and reading assessment throughout the high school years. Parental expectations and child-rearing practices combine with biological factors to produce this difference.

Boys and girls are initially equally interested in mathematics, but they excel in different aspects of mathematics from an early age. Girls outperform boys in mathematical computation, on average, whereas boys outperform girls in mathematical reasoning. On average, boys also outperform girls on spatial tasks from early childhood on. During adolescence, boys tend to exhibit both greater interest and performance in mathematics, at least when assessed on standardized exams. Both socialization and biological factors have been implicated in sex differences in quantitative and spatial abilities.

3. *What social and personality sex differences have researchers found?*
Male infants are initially fussier and less able to regulate their arousal than are female infants. Perhaps in part as a result, female infants appear better equipped for social interaction. There is no evidence for sex differences in temperament over the long term, however.

Beginning in childhood, males and females use different strategies to regulate their emotions. Females tend to talk about their feelings with others, whereas males tend to use distraction or physical activity. Females are generally more emotionally expressive than males, and talk more often about feeling sad. Males more readily express anger. These differences reflect differences in the kinds of conversations parents have with their children.

Females exhibit greater self-control than males. During early childhood, girls appear better able to control their impulses and comply more readily with parental requests. Girls also have a reputation for being more altruistic, helpful, and cooperative; however, few sex differences in these behaviours have actually been observed. Males display more physical aggression, while females display more social and relational aggression.

To some extent, males and females prefer different activities. Boys tend to enjoy more active play, as well as television and computer games with violent or aggressive themes. Girls enjoy play that is less active and tend to role-play more domestic themes. Males and females also have different academic interests. These differences appear to be influenced by cultural attitudes and opportunities to pursue different roles.

There are no differences between boys and girls in total number of friends. Girls, however, prefer to interact in smaller groups, characterized by higher levels of intimacy and self-disclosure, while boys prefer activities that involve larger groups. Interaction styles also differ: girls tend to be somewhat more concerned with equal participation, and boys are concerned with issues of dominance.

LEARNING OBJECTIVE 16.3 Understand the role of biological influences in the development of sex differences.

1. *What role do genetic influences play in the development of gender differences?*
In humans, the male and female are different for the purpose of reproduction, a characteristic called sexual dimorphism. The process through which these differences emerge is called sexual

differentiation. The sex chromosomes—the X and Y chromosomes—determine whether an embryo develops as male or female. An individual who inherits an X chromosome from each parent is biologically female, while someone who receives an X chromosome from his mother and a Y chromosome from his father is biologically male.

2. *Explain how fetal hormones affect sexual differentiation.*
The principal fetal hormones are androgens in males and progesterone and estrogens in females. The production of androgens by the testes is necessary for the embryo to develop as male. Androgens also affect the organization of the fetal brain.

Hormonal abnormalities in humans illustrate the role of hormones in gender-related behaviours. Congenital adrenal hyperplasia (CAH) results from the overproduction of androgens during gestation. Even with treatment, the personalities of CAH females remain masculinized. CAH males are much less affected. Androgen insensitivity syndrome (AIS) involves a failure of the body cells to respond to androgens. The personalities of androgen-insensitive males tend to be feminized.

3. *How may brain lateralization be related to sex differences?*
Brain lateralization refers to specialization in function of the brain hemispheres. The right hemisphere is more involved with spatial abilities, while the left hemisphere is more involved with verbal abilities. Males appear to be more lateralized than females. This sex difference may be related to behavioural sex differences on verbal and spatial tasks.

LEARNING OBJECTIVE 16.4 Understand how society, parents, peers, and the self contribute to gender-role socialization.

1. *How can gender-role development be viewed as a process of socialization?*
Gender-role socialization occurs at many levels: society, family, peer, and the self. Two mechanisms of socialization are modelling and differential treatment. Children readily learn gender-appropriate conduct by observing those around them. In modern societies, children have an abundance of models to choose from, ranging from family members to characters depicted on television and other media sources. In all societies, males and females are treated somewhat differently. Differential treatment includes direct instruction and guided participation, provision of opportunities and experiences, and expectations. Although the specifics vary from culture to culture, differential treatment fosters the development of different skills, abilities, and attitudes.

2. *What roles do parents play in the socialization of gender?*
Parents model gender roles to their children, although research is not conclusive on how strong the modelling effect is. Parents hold different expectations for sons and daughters and treat them differently from infancy. Parents' gender typing of play tends to be stronger with sons than daughters. This is especially true of fathers.

3. *How do peers and self contribute to gender-role development?*
Peers are also a powerful socialization force. Of particular importance is the same-sex peer group. From an early age, children in all cultures spend much of their time with same-sex peers. Although the causes of gender segregation are not well understood, theorists believe it has important consequences for the development of gender-role behaviour. Children reinforce one another for gender-typed play and punish those, especially boys, who deviate from established norms. Children themselves contribute importantly to the socialization process through their selection of appropriate models and the application of self-sanctions to gender-linked behaviour.

LEARNING OBJECTIVE 16.5 Trace the development of gender-role knowledge and behaviour.

1. *What is the developmental progression of gender knowledge?*

   The key notion in Kohlberg's theory is gender constancy, the realization that one's gender is fixed and irreversible. Gender constancy develops in three stages and is completed by about 6 years of age. Almost all children display the first stage, gender identity, by about age 3. The second stage, gender stability, is acquired by about age 4, and the third stage, gender consistency, is displayed by about age 5. Males and females progress through these stages at about the same rate, and the progression has been demonstrated in a variety of cultures, although children in some non-Western cultures may proceed through the stages more slowly.

   Gender-role knowledge involves awareness of the concepts of male and female and their culturally defined stereotypes. Even young infants can learn to discriminate the categories of male and female. Children generally understand the basic male–female concept by age 2. Gender labelling of toys appears at age 3, and an awareness of sex-typed personality traits at about age 5.

2. *What is the developmental course for children's flexibility regarding gender stereotypes?*

   Gender stereotypes become more flexible over the course of childhood. During the preschool years, most children view gender roles as inflexible and absolute. Cross-gender behaviours are seen as serious violations of social standards. By middle childhood, children begin to realize that gender roles are socially determined and can be broken without any major consequences. The transition to junior high school appears to increase adolescents' flexibility toward the roles of males and females.

3. *How does gender knowledge influence behaviour?*

   Gender knowledge, present very early in childhood, profoundly influences children's behaviour. Gender labelling is the basis for their toy and activity preferences, influencing their motivation, accuracy, and expectancies for success. Sex differences in children's play emerge between the first and second birthdays. By the preschool years, children spend more time exploring own-sex toys and rate own-sex toys as more attractive. Children are more motivated by own-sex games and activities, are more likely to remember more about same-sex peers, and use gender knowledge to make inferences about judgments about other people.

LEARNING OBJECTIVE 16.6 Discuss the development of sexual relationships and behaviour.

1. *How do romantic and sexual interests emerge?*

   Children begin to exhibit interest in others as future sexual partners during middle childhood. Children's sexual relationships gradually evolve from "kiss and chase" games to crushes on unattainable figures (such as celebrities) to increasingly intimate involvements with people they know well. In many communities, adolescents negotiate this transition to intimate relations in the context of the mixed-sex peer group.

2. *What do we know about the origins of sexual orientation?*

   Although most children eventually develop a heterosexual orientation, a minority of children adopt a gay, lesbian, or bisexual orientation. Biological accounts of sexual orientation link sexual behaviour and interest to genes and prenatal hormones.

   There is little evidence that socialization alone shapes the development of sexual orientation or identity. The proportion of children reared by gay, lesbian, or bisexual parents who adopt a non-heterosexual identity is comparable to that among children raised by heterosexual parents. Most contemporary researchers believe that sexual orientation is influenced by both biology and environment, although the processes by which each contributes are far from understood.

GLOSSARY

A

Ability grouping Separation of students into groups of similar ability for purposes of instruction.

Academic self-concept The part of self-esteem that involves children's perceptions of their academic abilities.

Accommodation Changing existing cognitive structures to fit with new experiences. One of the two components of adaptation in Piaget's theory.

Active gene-environment correlation Situation in which genes and environment affect development similarly because children seek out experiences that are compatible with their genetic predispositions.

Adaptation The tendency to fit with the environment in ways that promote survival. One of the two biologically based functions stressed in Piaget's theory.

Adult Attachment Interview An instrument used to assess an adult's childhood recollections of the attachment relationship with the primary caregiver.

Affect The outward expression of emotions through facial expressions, gestures, intonation, and the like.

Affect mirroring The degree to which caregivers gauge their communicative behaviours to respond to input from their infants.

Age of viability The age (presently around 23 or 24 weeks) at which the infant has a chance to survive if born prematurely.

Aggression Behaviour that is intended to cause harm to persons or property and that is not socially justifiable.

Alleles Genes for the same trait located in the same place on a pair of chromosomes.

Amniocentesis A procedure for collecting cells that lie in the amniotic fluid surrounding the fetus. A needle is passed through the mother's abdominal wall into the amniotic sac to gather discarded fetal cells. These cells can be examined for chromosomal and genetic defects.

Amniotic sac A fluid-containing watertight membrane that surrounds and protects the embryo and fetus.

Analogical reasoning A form of problem solving in which the solution is achieved through recognition of the similarity between the new problem and some already understood problem.

Animism Piaget's term for the young child's tendency to attribute properties of life to non-living things.

Anorexia nervosa A severe eating disorder, usually involving excessive weight loss through self-starvation.

A-not-B error Infants' tendency to search in the original location in which an object was found rather than in its most recent hiding place. A characteristic of stage 4 of object permanence.

Anoxia A deficit of oxygen to the cells that can produce brain or other tissue damage.

Apgar Exam An exam administered immediately after birth that assesses vital functions such as heart rate and respiration.

Appearance-reality distinction Distinction between how objects appear and what they really are. Understanding the distinction implies an ability to correctly judge both appearance and reality when the two diverge.

Assimilation Interpreting new experiences in terms of existing cognitive structures. One of the two components of adaptation in Piaget's theory.

At risk Describes babies who have a higher likelihood than other babies of experiencing developmental problems.

Attachment Q-Set (AQS) A method of assessing attachment in which cards bearing descriptions of the child's interactions with the caregiver are sorted into categories to create a profile of the child.

Attention The selection of particular sensory input for perceptual and cognitive processing and the exclusion of competing input.

Attention-deficit hyperactivity disorder (ADHD) A developmental disorder characterized by difficulty in sustaining attention, hyperactivity, and impulsive and uncontrolled behaviour.

Authoritarian parenting A style of parenting characterized by firm control in the context of a cold and demanding relationship.

Autobiographical memory Specific, personal, and long-lasting memory regarding the self.

Automatization An increase in the efficiency with which cognitive operations are executed as a result of practice. A mechanism of change in information-processing theories.

Autosomes The 22 pairs of human chromosomes, other than the sex chromosomes.

Axon A long fibre extending from the cell body in a neuron; conducts activity from the cell.

B

Babbling drift A hypothesis that infants' babbling gradually gravitates toward the language they are hearing and soon will speak.

Baby biography Method of study in which a parent studies the development of his or her own child.

Behavioural homophyly Similarity between peers in behaviours and interests. Such similarity is one determinant of friendship selection.

Behaviour genetics The field of study that explores the role of genes in producing individual differences in behaviour and development.

Behaviourism A theory of psychology, first advanced by John B. Watson, that human development results primarily from conditioning and learning processes.

Biologically primary abilities Evolved abilities shaped by natural selection to solve recurring problems faced by ancestral humans.

Biologically secondary abilities Non-evolved abilities that co-opt primary abilities for purposes other than the original evolution-based function and appear only in specific cultural contexts.

Blended family A new family unit, resulting from remarriage, that consists of parents and children from previously separate families.

Bone age The degree of maturation of an individual as indicated by the extent of hardening of the bones. Also called skeletal maturity.

Brainstem The lower part of the brain, closest to the spinal cord; includes the cerebellum, which is important for maintaining balance and coordination.

Brazelton Neonatal Behavioral Assessment The most comprehensive of newborn assessment instruments; assesses attention and social responsiveness, muscle tone and physical movement, control of alertness, and physiological response to stress.

Brightness constancy The experience that the brightness of an object remains the same even though the amount of light it reflects back to the eye changes (because of shadows or changes in the illuminating light).

Bulimia A disorder of food binging and sometimes purging by self-induced vomiting.

C

Case study A research method that involves only a single individual, often with a focus on a clinical issue.

Catch-up growth Accelerated growth that follows a period of delayed or stunted growth resulting from disease or malnutrition.

Categorical perception The ability to detect differences in speech sounds that correspond to differences in meaning; the ability to discriminate phonemic boundaries.

Categorical self The "Me" component of the self, which involves one's objective personal characteristics.

Catharsis The psychoanalytic belief that the likelihood of aggression can be reduced by viewing aggression or by engaging in high-energy behaviour.

Centration Piaget's term for the young child's tendency to focus on only one aspect of a problem at a time, a perceptually-biased form of responding that often results in incorrect judgments.

Cephalocaudal Literally, head to tail. This principle of development refers to the tendency of body parts to mature in a head-to-foot progression.

Cerebellum Situated behind the brainstem and under the cerebral hemispheres, this distinct and unique looking structure is involved in motor control and learning, attention, language, and regulating emotional responses.

Cerebral cortex The thin sheet of grey matter that covers the brain.

Cerebrum The highest brain centre; includes both hemispheres of the brain and the interconnections between them.

Cesarean section Surgical delivery of the fetus directly from the uterus; performed when normal delivery is prohibited.

CHILDES (Child Language Data Support System) A computerized data-sharing system that makes available the transcribed records from dozens of studies of children's spontaneous speech.

Chorionic villus sampling (CVS) A procedure for gathering fetal cells earlier in pregnancy than is possible through amniocentesis. A tube is passed through the vagina and cervix so that fetal cells can be gathered at the site of the developing placenta.

Chromosomes Chemical strands in the cell nucleus that contain the genes. The nucleus of each human cell has 46 chromosomes, with the exception of the gametes, which have 23.

Chronosystem Bronfenbrenner's term for the passage of time as a context for studying human development.

Clarification question A response that indicates that a listener did not understand a statement.

Classical (respondent) conditioning A form of learning, involving reflexes, in which a neutral stimulus acquires the power to elicit a reflexive response (UCR) as a result of being associated (paired) with the naturally eliciting stimulus (UCS). The neutral stimulus then becomes a conditioned stimulus (CS).

Class inclusion The knowledge that a subclass cannot be larger than the superordinate class that includes it. In Piaget's theory, a concrete operational achievement.

Clique A kind of group typical in adolescence, consisting usually of 5 to 10 members whose shared interests and behaviour patterns set them apart from their peers.

Codominance The case in which both alleles are dominant and each is completely expressed in the phenotype.

Coercive family process Gerald Patterson's term for the method by which some families control one another through aggression and other coercive means.

Cognition Higher-order mental processes, such as reasoning and problem solving, through which humans attempt to understand the world.

Cohort effect A problem sometimes found in cross-sectional research in which people of a given age are affected by factors unique to their generation.

Coining Children's creation of new words to label objects or events for which the correct label is not known.

Colour constancy The experience that the colour of an object remains the same even though the wavelengths it reflects back to the eye change (because of changes in the colour of the illuminating light).

Committed compliance Compliant behaviour that results from a child's internalizing the instruction of an adult; results in positive emotion.

Comparative research Research conducted with non-human species to provide information relevant to human development.

Competence Self-evaluation that includes both what one would like to achieve and one's confidence in being able to achieve it.

Competition model A proposed strategy children use for learning grammar in which they weight possible cues in terms of availability and reliability.

Compliance The child's ability to go along with requests or adopt the standards of behaviour espoused by caregivers.

Computer simulation Programming a computer to perform a cognitive task in the same way in which humans are thought to perform it. An information-processing method for testing theories of underlying process.

Concept A mental grouping of different items into a single category on the basis of some unifying similarity or set of similarities.

Conception The combining of the genetic material from a male gamete (sperm) and a female gamete (ovum); fertilization.

Concrete operations Form of intelligence in which mental operations make logical problem solving with concrete objects possible. The third of Piaget's periods, extending from about 6 to 11 years of age.

Conditioned stimulus (CS) A neutral stimulus that comes to elicit a response through a conditioning process in which it is consistently paired with another stimulus (UCS) that naturally evokes the response.

Congenital adrenal hyperplasia (CAH) A recessive genetic disorder in which the adrenal glands produce unusually high levels of male hormones known as androgens.

Congenitally organized behaviour Early behaviours of newborns that do not require specific external stimulation and that show more adaptability than simple reflexes.

Connectionism Creation of artificial neural networks, embodied in computer programs, that solve cognitive tasks and that modify their solutions in response to experience. A methodological and theoretical approach adopted by a subset of information-processing researchers.

Conservation The knowledge that the quantitative properties of an object or collection of objects are not changed by a change in appearance. In Piaget's theory, a concrete operational achievement.

Constraints Implicit assumptions about word meanings; hypothesized to narrow down the possibilities that children must consider, thereby facilitating the task of word learning.

Constructive memory The ways that individuals interpret the information they take in in terms of their pre-existing knowledge, which affects what they remember.

Constructivism Piaget's belief that children actively create knowledge rather than passively receive it from the environment.

Continuity versus discontinuity debate The scientific controversy regarding whether development is constant and connected (continuous) or uneven and disconnected (discontinuous).

Controversial child A child who receives both many positive and many negative nominations in sociometric assessments by peers.

Conventional level Kohlberg's third and fourth stages of moral development. Moral reasoning is based on the view that a social system must be based on laws and regulations.

Convergent thinking Form of thinking whose goal is to discover the correct answer to problems with a definite solution; the form of thought emphasized on IQ tests.

Cooing A stage in the preverbal period, beginning at about 2 months, when babies primarily produce one-syllable vowel sounds.

Corpus collosum The bundle of nerves that connect the left and right hemispheres of the brain.

Correlation The relation between two variables, described in terms of direction and strength.

Correlation coefficient (*r*) A number between +1.00 and −1.00 that indicates the direction and strength of a correlation between two variables.

Cross-cultural studies Research designed to determine the influence of culture on some aspect of development and in which culture typically serves as an independent variable.

Crossing over The exchange of genetic material between pairs of chromosomes during meiosis.

Cross-sectional design A research method in which people of different ages are studied simultaneously to examine age-related differences in some aspect of behaviour.

Cross-sequential design A research method combining longitudinal and cross-sectional designs.

Crowds Large, loosely organized groups that serve to structure social identity in high school.

Cultural compatibility hypothesis The hypothesis that schooling will be most effective when methods of instruction are compatible with the child's cultural background.

Cultural/historical development Development that occurs over decades and centuries and leaves a legacy of tools and artifacts, value systems, institutions, and practices.

Cultural psychology Study of a single culture from the perspective of members of that culture, the goal being to identify the values and practices important to the culture.

Cultural relativism The belief that each culture should be examined and evaluated on its own terms.

Culture The accumulated knowledge of a people encoded in their language and embodied in the physical artifacts, beliefs, values, customs, institutions, and activities passed down from one generation to the next.

D

Decentration The ability to keep in mind multiple aspects of a situation, all at the same time. For Piaget, this is a feature of concrete operational thought.

Deep structure Chomsky's term for the inborn knowledge humans possess about the properties of language.

Defensive reflex A natural reaction to novel stimuli that tends to protect the organism from further stimulation and that may include orientation of the stimulus receptors away from the stimulus source and a variety of physiological changes.

Deferred imitation Imitation of a model observed some time in the past.

Delay-of-gratification technique An experimental procedure for studying children's ability to postpone a smaller, immediate reward in order to obtain a larger, delayed one.

Dendrite One of a net of short fibres extending out from the cell body in a neuron; receives activity from nearby cells and conducts that activity to the cell body.

Deoxyribonucleic acid (DNA) A stairlike, double-helix molecule that carries genetic information on chromosomes.

Dependent variable The variable that is predicted to be affected by an experimental manipulation. In psychology, usually some aspect of behaviour.

Descriptive research Research based solely on observations, with no attempt to determine systematic relations among the variables.

Developmental pacing The rate at which spurts and plateaus occur in an individual's physical and mental development.

Developmental psychology The branch of psychology devoted to the study of changes in behaviour and abilities over the course of development.

Dialectical process The process in Vygotsky's theory whereby children learn through problem-solving experiences shared with others.

Diffusion tensor imaging (DTI) An imaging technique that measures the diffusion or movement of water molecules through neural tracts that connect brain structures.

Discourse Language used in social interactions; conversation.

Dishabituation The recovery of a habituated response that results from a change in the eliciting stimulus.

Displaced aggression Retaliatory aggression directed at a person or object other than the one against whom retaliation is desired.

Display rules The expectations and attitudes a society holds toward the expression of affect.

Divergent thinking Form of thinking whose goal is to generate multiple possible solutions for problems that do not have a single correct answer; the form of thought hypothesized to be important for creativity.

Dizygotic (DZ) twins Twins who develop from separately fertilized ova and who thus are no more genetically similar than are other siblings. Also called *fraternal twins*.

Dominance hierarchy A structured social group in which members higher on the dominance ladder control those who are lower, initially through aggression and conflict, but eventually simply through threats.

Dominant gene A relatively powerful allele whose characteristics are expressed in the phenotype regardless of the allele with which it is paired.

Dual representation The realization that an object can be represented in two ways simultaneously.

Dynamic assessment Method of assessing children's abilities derived from Vygotsky's concept of the zone of proximal development. Measures the child's ability to benefit from adult-provided assistance, typically in a test-train-retest design.

Dynamic systems Thelen's model of the development of motor skills, in which infants who are motivated to accomplish a task create a new motor behaviour from their available physical abilities.

E

EAS model Plomin and Buss's theory of temperament, which holds that temperament can be measured along the dimensions of emotionality, activity, and sociability.

Ecological perspective An approach to studying development that focuses on individuals within their environmental contexts.

Egocentric speech In Piaget's theory, the tendency for preoperational children to assume that listeners know everything that they know, revealing difficulty with perspective taking.

Egocentrism In infancy, an inability to distinguish the self (e.g., one's actions or perceptions) from the outer world. In later childhood, an inability to distinguish one's own perspective (e.g., visual experience, thoughts, feelings) from that of others.

Electroencephalograph (EEG) An instrument that measures brain activity by sensing minute electrical changes at the top of the skull.

Embryo The developing organism from the third week, when implantation is complete, through the eighth week after conception.

Emotion An internal reaction or feeling, which may be either positive (such as joy) or negative (such as anger), and may reflect a readiness for action.

Empathy The ability to vicariously experience another's emotional state or condition.

Encoding Attending to and forming internal representations of certain features of the environment. A mechanism of change in information-processing theories.

Entity model The belief that a person's intelligence is fixed and unchangeable.

Environment of evolutionary adaptedness (EEA) The environment that produced a species' evolved tendencies.

Equilibration Piaget's term for the biological process of self-regulation that propels the cognitive system to higher and higher forms of equilibrium.

Equilibrium A characteristic of a cognitive system in which assimilation and accommodation are in balance, thus permitting adaptive, non-distorted responses to the world.

Ethnographic methods Methods of study employed in cultural psychology in which the researcher lives as a member of a culture and gathers information about the culture through various techniques (e.g., observations, interviews) over an extended period of time.

Ethology The study of development from an evolutionary perspective.

Evaluative self-reactions Bandura's term for consequences people apply to themselves as a result of meeting or failing to meet their personal standards.

Event memory Recall of things that have happened.

Event-related potentials (ERPs) A technique for measuring the electrical activity of specific brain areas in response to the presentation of a particular stimulus or action.

Evocative gene-environment correlation Situation in which genes and environment affect development similarly because genetically set predispositions of the child elicit compatible experiences from the environment.

Evolutionary developmental psychology A branch of evolutionary psychology that encompasses the evolutionary origins of contemporary cognitive abilities, as well as those that underlie social relations and social interactions.

Executive function General components of problem solving, such as short-term memory, metacognitive awareness, and inhibition.

Existential self The "I" component of the self, which is concerned with the subjective experience of existing.

Exosystem Social systems that can affect children but in which they do not participate directly. Bronfenbrenner's third layer of context.

Expansion A repetition of speech in which errors are corrected and statements are elaborated.

Experience-dependent synaptogenesis Changes in brain structure and function as a result of experience.

Experience-expectant synaptogenesis The mechanism by which synapses are formed, maintained, and pruned based on experiences that are typical for that species. Given the same species-expected environment, all members' brains will develop the same capabilities.

Expertise Organized factual knowledge with respect to some content domain.

Expressive style Vocabulary acquired during the naming explosion that emphasizes the pragmatic functions of language.

Extended family A family unit that consists not only of parents and children, but also of at least one and sometimes several other adult relatives.

Extinction A process related to classical conditioning in which the conditioned stimulus (CS) gradually loses its power to elicit the response as a result of no longer being paired with the unconditioned stimulus (UCS).

F

False belief The realization that people can hold beliefs that are not true. Such understanding, which is typically acquired during the preoperational period, provides evidence of the ability to distinguish the mental from the non-mental.

False self behaviour Behaving in a way that is knowingly different from how one's true self would behave.

Fast-mapping A process in which children acquire the meaning of a word after a brief exposure.

Fetal alcohol syndrome (FAS) A set of problems in the infant and child caused by the mother's use of alcohol during pregnancy; typically includes facial malformations and other physical and mental disabilities.

Fetal distress A condition of abnormal stress on the fetus, reflected during the birth process in an abnormal fetal heart rate.

Fetus The developing organism from the ninth week to the 38th week after conception.

Flynn effect Increase over time in the average level of performance on IQ tests.

Forbidden-toy paradigm An experimental procedure for studying children's resistance to temptation in which the child is left alone with an attractive toy and instructed not to play with it.

Formal operations Form of intelligence in which higher-level mental operations make possible logical reasoning with respect to abstract and hypothetical events and not merely concrete objects. The fourth of Piaget's periods, beginning at about 11 years of age.

Fraternal twins Twins who develop from separately fertilized ova and who thus are no more genetically similar than are other siblings. Also called *dizygotic (DZ) twins.*

Friendship An enduring relationship between two individuals, characterized by loyalty, intimacy, and mutual affection.

Frontal lobe Located at the very front of the brain; functions include working memory, planning, and decision making; involved in executive functions that monitor and choose appropriate behaviours in a given situation or task; also plays a role in associating information in long-term memory.

Functional magnetic resonance imaging (fMRI) The imaging technique that measures the level of oxygenated blood taken up by active brain areas. Oxygenated blood is more magnetized than non-oxygenated blood, leading to higher measurement of the blood oxygen level dependent (BOLD signal) in areas that are active.

G

g General intelligence; *g* is assumed to determine performance on a wide range of intellectual measures.

Gender consistency The recognition that an individual's gender remains the same despite changes in dress, hairstyle, activities, or personality.

Gender constancy The belief that one's own gender is fixed and irreversible.

Gender identity The ability to categorize oneself as male or female.

Gender role A pattern or set of behaviours considered appropriate for males or females within a particular culture.

Gender schemas Cognitive representations of the characteristics associated with being either male or female.

Gender stability The awareness that all boys grow up to be men and all girls become women.

Gene A segment of DNA on the chromosome that codes for the production of proteins. The basic unit of inheritance.

Genetic counselling The practice of advising prospective parents about genetic diseases and the likelihood that they might pass on defective genetic traits to their offspring.

Genomic imprinting The case in which the allele from one parent is biochemically silenced and only the allele from the other parent affects the phenotype.

Genotype The arrangement of genes underlying a trait.

Gesture-speech mismatch Instance in which the meaning conveyed by speech and the meaning conveyed by an accompanying gesture are in conflict. Thought to be an indicator of readiness for change.

Glial cell A cell that wraps itself around the axon.

Goodness of fit A concept describing the relation between a baby's temperament and his or her social and environmental surroundings.

Grammar The study of the structural properties of language, including syntax, inflection, and intonation.

Group A collection of individuals who interact regularly in a consistent, structured fashion and who share values and a sense of belonging to the group.

Guided participation The process by which young children become competent by participating in everyday, purposeful activities under the guidance of more experienced partners.

H

Habituation The decline or disappearance of a response as a result of repeated presentation of the eliciting stimulus. The simplest type of learning.

Haptic perception The perceptual experience that results from active exploration of objects by touch.

Heritability The proportion of variance in a trait (such as IQ) that can be attributed to genetic variance in the sample being studied.

Hierarchical model of intelligence A model of the structure of intelligence in which intellectual abilities are seen as being organized hierarchically, with broad, general abilities at the top of the hierarchy and more specific skills nested underneath.

Higher mental functions Complex mental processes that are intentional, self-regulated, and mediated by language and other sign systems.

Holophrase A single word used to express a larger idea; common during the second year of life.

HOME (Home Observation for Measurement of the Environment) An instrument for assessing the quality of the early home environment. Includes dimensions such as maternal involvement and variety of play materials.

Hostile (retaliatory) aggression Aggression whose purpose is to cause pain or injury.

Hypothesis A predicted relation between a phenomenon and a factor assumed to affect it that is not yet supported by a great deal of evidence. Hypotheses are tested in experimental investigations.

Hypothetical-deductive reasoning A form of problem solving characterized by the ability to generate and test hypotheses and draw logical conclusions from the results of the tests. In Piaget's theory, a formal operational achievement.

I

Identical twins Twins who develop from a single fertilized ovum and thus inherit identical genetic material. Also called *monozygotic (MZ) twins.*

Identification The Freudian process through which the child adopts the characteristics of the same-sex parent during the phallic stage.

Identity In Erikson's theory, the component of personality that develops across the eight stages of life and that motivates progress through the stages.

Imaginary companions Fantasy friends with names and stable personalities that remain a part of children's lives for months or even years.

Imitation Behaviour of an observer that results from and is similar to the behaviour of a model.

Immanent justice Literally, inherent justice; refers to the expectation of children in Piaget's stage of moral realism that punishment must follow any rule violation, including those that appear to go undetected.

Imprinting A biological process of some species in which the young acquire an emotional attachment to the mother through following.

Incomplete dominance The case in which a dominant gene does not completely suppress the effect of a recessive gene, which is then somewhat expressed in the phenotype.

Incremental model The belief that a person's intelligence can grow through experience and learning.

Independent orientation A focus on the self's individuality, self-expression, and personal achievement.

Independent variable The variable in an experiment that is systematically manipulated.

Infantile amnesia The inability to remember experiences from the first 2 or 3 years of life.

Inflections The aspect of grammar that involves adding endings to words to modify their meaning.

Inhibition The tendency to quickly respond in a negative manner to an unfamiliar situation.

Innate releasing mechanism A stimulus that triggers an innate sequence or pattern of behaviours.

Instrumental aggression Aggression whose purpose is to obtain something desired.

Intellectual disability A disorder characterized by limited intellectual and adaptive functioning (formerly known as mental retardation).

Intentional behaviour In Piaget's theory, behaviour in which the goal exists prior to the action selected to achieve it; made possible by the ability to separate means and end.

Interactional synchrony The smooth intermeshing of behaviours between mother and baby.

Interactionist perspective The theory that human development results from the combination of inborn processes and environmental factors.

Interdependent orientation A focus on the self's role within a broader social network, marked by an emphasis on interpersonal connectedness, social obligation, and conformity.

Internalization Vygotsky's term for the child's incorporation, primarily through language, of bodies of knowledge and tools of thought from the culture.

Internal working model An infant's and a caregiver's cognitive conception of each other, which they use to form expectations and predictions.

Intersubjectivity A commitment to find common ground on which to build shared understanding.

Invariants Aspects of the world that remain the same even though other aspects have changed. In Piaget's theory, different forms of invariants are understood at different stages of development.

Interview method Collecting information through verbal reports, such as interviews or questionnaires.

J

Joint attention Using cues (such as direction of gaze) to identify and share the attentional focus of another.

K

Kinetic cues Visual cues that indicate the relative distances of objects through movement either of the objects or of the observer.

Kin selection A proposed mechanism by which an individual's altruistic behaviour toward kin increases the likelihood of the survival of genes similar to those of the individual.

L

Landscape The fourth theme of geography; the overall appearance of an area. Most landscapes comprised a combination of natural and human-induced influences.

Language acquisition device (LAD) Chomsky's proposed brain mechanism for analyzing speech input; the mechanism that allows young children to quickly acquire the language to which they are exposed.

Language acquisition support system (LASS) Bruner's proposed process by which parents provide children with assistance in learning language.

Language-Making Capacity (LMC) Slobin's proposed set of strategies or learning principles that underlie the acquisition of language.

Lateralization The specialization of functions in the right and left hemispheres of the brain.

Law (principle) A predicted relation between a phenomenon and a factor assumed to affect it that is supported by a good deal of scientific evidence.

Learning A relatively permanent change in behaviour that results from practice or experience.

Lexical contrast theory A theory of semantic development holding that (1) children automatically assume a new word has a meaning different from that of any other word they know, and (2) children always choose word meanings that are generally accepted over more individualized meanings.

Lexicon A vocabulary, or repertoire of words.

Locomotion The movement of a person through space, such as walking and crawling.

Longitudinal design A research method in which the same individuals are studied repeatedly over time.

Looking-glass self The conception of the self based on how one thinks others see him or her.

M

Macrosystem The culture or subculture in which the child lives. Bronfenbrenner's fourth layer of context.

Magnetoencephalography (MEG) A technique in which the magnetic field generated by the electrical activity of the brain is measured by sensors placed on the scalp.

Maternal bonding The mother's emotional attachment to the child, which appears shortly after birth and which some theorists believe develops through early contact during a sensitive period.

Maturation The biological processes assumed by some theorists to be primarily responsible for human development.

Mediated memory Remembering that relies on cultural tools and artifacts.

Meiosis The process by which germ cells produce four gametes (sperm or ova), each with half the number of chromosomes of the parent cell.

Mesosystem The interrelationships among the child's microsystems. The second of Bronfenbrenner's layers of context.

Meta-analysis A method of reviewing the research literature on a given topic that uses statistical procedures to establish the existence and the size of effects.

Metamemory Knowledge about memory.

Microanalysis A research technique for studying dyadic interactions in which two individuals are simultaneously video recorded with different cameras, and then the recordings are examined side by side.

Microgenetic development Moment-to-moment learning of individuals as they work on specific problems.

Microgenetic method A research method in which a small number of individuals are observed repeatedly in order to study an expected change in a developmental process.

Microsystem The environmental system closest to the child, such as the family or school. The first of Bronfenbrenner's layers of context.

Midbrain A part of the brain that lies above the brain stem; serves as a relay station and as a control area for breathing and swallowing, and houses part of the auditory and visual systems.

Mitosis The process by which body cells reproduce, resulting in two identical cells.

Mnemonic strategies Techniques (such as rehearsal or organization) that people use in an attempt to remember something.

Modal action pattern A sequence of behaviours elicited by a specific stimulus.

Monozygotic (MZ) twins Twins who develop from a single fertilized ovum and thus inherit identical genetic material. Also called *identical twins.*

Moral conduct The aspect of children's moral development concerned with behaviour.

Moral dilemmas Stories used by Piaget and others to assess children's levels of moral reasoning.

Moral realism Piaget's second stage of moral development in which children's reasoning is based on objective and physical aspects of a situation and is often inflexible.

Moral reasoning The aspect of children's moral development concerned with knowledge and understanding of moral issues and principles.

Moral relativism Piaget's third stage of moral development in which children view rules as agreements that can be altered and consider people's motives or intentions when evaluating their moral conduct.

Moral rules Rules used by a society to protect individuals and to guarantee their rights.

Motherese Simplified speech directed at very young children by adults and older children.

Motion parallax An observer's experience that a closer object moves across the field of view faster than a more distant object when both objects are moving at the same speed or when the objects are stationary and the observer moves.

Myelin A sheath of fatty material that surrounds and insulates the axon, resulting in speedier transmission of neural activity.

N

Naming explosion A period of language development, beginning at about 18 months, when children suddenly begin to acquire words (especially labels) at a high rate.

Nativism The theory that human development results principally from inborn processes that guide the emergence of behaviours in a predictable manner.

Nativistic theory A theory of language development, originated by Chomsky, that stresses innate mechanisms separate from cognitive processes.

Natural selection An evolutionary process proposed by Charles Darwin in which characteristics of an individual that increase its chances of survival are more likely to be passed along to future generations.

Naturalistic observation Systematic observation of behaviour in a natural setting.

Nature versus nurture debate The scientific controversy regarding whether the primary source of developmental change rests in biological (nature) factors or in environmental and experiential (nurture) factors.

Near infra-red spectroscopy (NIRS) An imaging technique in which infrared light is beamed through the skull and brain, and its absorption and scatter by blood oxygen in the brain is measured.

Negative correlation A correlation in which two variables change in opposite directions.

Negative reinforcer A consequence that makes the behaviour it follows more likely through the removal of something unpleasant.

Neglected child A child who receives few nominations of any sort, positive or negative, in sociometric assessments by peers. Such children seem to be ignored by the peer group.

Neuroimaging techniques The technologies and methodologies that enable scientists to generate "structural" and "functional" maps of brain activity through measurements of changes in the brain's metabolism, blood flow, or electrical activity.

Neuron A nerve cell, consisting of a cell body, axon, and dendrites. Neurons transmit activity from one part of the nervous system to another.

Neurotransmitter A chemical that transmits electrical activity from one neuron across the synapse to another neuron.

New York Longitudinal Study (NYLS) A well-known longitudinal project conducted by Thomas and Chess to study infant temperament and its implications for later psychological adjustment.

Non-shared environment A concept used in behaviour genetics to refer to presumed aspects of the environment that children experience differently.

Normative versus idiographic development The question of whether research should focus on identifying commonalities in human development (normative development) or on the causes of individual differences (idiographic development).

Norms A timetable of age ranges indicating when normal growth and developmental milestones are typically reached.

O

Obesity A condition of excess fat storage; often defined as weight more than 20 percent over a standardized, ideal weight.

Object permanence The knowledge that objects have a permanent existence that is independent of our perceptual contact with them. In Piaget's theory, a major achievement of the sensorimotor period.

Objectivity A characteristic of scientific research; it requires that the procedures and subject matter of investigations should be formulated so that they could, in principle, be agreed on by everyone.

Observational learning A form of learning in which an observer's behaviour changes as a result of observing a model.

Observer influences The effects of knowing that you are being observed.

Occipital lobe Located in the rearmost location of the brain, its main function is the processing of visual information; can be subdivided into a number of functional sections, differentiated by the type and complexity of the visual information being processed.

Ontogenetic development Development across years of an individual's life, such as childhood.

Operant behaviours Voluntary behaviour controlled by its consequences. The larger category of human behaviours.

Operant learning A form of learning in which the likelihood of an operant behaviour changes as a result of its reinforcing or punishing consequences.

Operating principle A hypothetical innate strategy for analyzing language input and discovering grammatical structure.

Operating space In Case's theory, the resources necessary to carry out cognitive operations.

Operations Piaget's term for the various forms of mental action through which older children solve problems and reason logically.

Optic flow The sensation that objects are apparently moving as a result of self-produced movement.

Organization The tendency to integrate knowledge into interrelated cognitive structures. One of the two biologically based functions stressed in Piaget's theory.

Orienting reflex A natural reaction to novel stimuli that enhances stimulus processing and includes orientation of the eyes and ears to optimize stimulus reception, inhibition of ongoing activity, and a variety of physiological changes.

Overextension An early language error in which children use labels they already know for things whose names they do not yet know.

Overregularization An early structural language error in which children apply inflectional rules to irregular forms (e.g., adding 'ed' to say).

P

Paradox of altruism The logical dilemma faced by ethological theorists who try to reconcile self-sacrificial behaviour with the concepts of natural selection and survival of the fittest.

Parallel play A form of play in which children play next to each other and with similar materials but with no real interaction or cooperation.

Parental control A dimension of parenting that reflects the degree to which the child is monitored, disciplined, and regulated.

Parental investment The time, energy, and resources required to produce and rear offspring that survive to reproductive age.

Parental warmth A dimension of parenting that reflects the amount of support, affection, and encouragement the parent provides to the child.

Parenting style The overall pattern of child rearing provided by a parent, typically defined by the combination of warmth and control that the parent demonstrates.

Parietal lobe Located above and forward from the occipital lobe; receives information from different senses, particularly touch; integrates multisensory information from different parts of the body; maps perceived objects relative to one's body; is involved in number processing.

Passive gene-environment correlation Situation in which genes and environment affect development similarly because the genes the child receives from the parents are compatible with the environment the parents provide.

Peacemaking A friendly post-conflict reunion between former opponents, often characterized by invitations to play, hugs, apologies, object sharing, and silliness.

Peer-mediated intervention Form of intervention for children with sociometric problems in which responses of the peer group are used to elicit more effective social behaviours from the target children.

Perception The interpretation of sensory stimulation based on experience.

Perinatal period The events and environment surrounding the birth process.

Periods Piaget's term for the four general stages into which his theory divides development. Each period is a qualitatively distinct form of functioning that characterizes a wide range of cognitive activities.

Peripheral vision The perception of visual input outside the area on which the individual is fixating.

Permissive parenting A style of parenting characterized by low levels of control in the context of a warm and supportive relationship.

Personal agency The understanding that one can be the cause of events.

Phenotype The characteristic of a trait that is expressed or observable. The phenotype results from an interaction of genotype and environment.

Phoneme A sound contrast that changes meaning.

Phonology The study of speech sounds.

Phylogenetic development Development of the species.

Pictorial cues Visual cues that indicate the relative distances of objects through static, picturelike information—for example, interposition of one object in front of another.

Placenta An organ that forms where the embryo attaches to the uterus. This organ exchanges nutrients, oxygen, and wastes between the embryo or fetus and the mother through a very thin membrane that does not allow the passage of blood.

Plasticity Changes in brain structure and function as a result of experience.

Polygenic inheritance The case in which a trait is determined by a number of genes.

Positive correlation A correlation in which two variables change in the same direction.

Positive reinforcer A consequence that makes the behaviour it follows more likely through the presentation of something pleasant.

Positron emission tomography (PET) An imaging technique that measures the activity of brain areas by detecting the radiation emitted by an injected glucose-like isotope that has been taken up by cells in the brain as they are doing work.

Post-conventional level Kohlberg's final stages of moral development. Moral reasoning is based on the assumption that the value, dignity, and rights of each individual person must be maintained.

Postural development The increasing ability of babies to control parts of their body, especially the head and the trunk.

Pragmatics The study of the social uses of language.

Preconventional level Kohlberg's first two stages of moral development. Moral reasoning is based on the assumption that individuals must serve their own needs.

Preference method A research method for the study of visual ability in infancy. Two visual stimuli are presented simultaneously, and the amount of time the infant looks at each is measured.

Prehension The ability to grasp and manipulate objects with the hands.

Preoperational Form of intelligence in which symbols and mental actions begin to replace objects and overt behaviours. The second of Piaget's periods, extending from about 2 to about 6 years old.

Pretend play A form of play in which children use an object or person as a symbol to stand for something else.

Preterm Describes babies born before the end of the normal gestation period.

Primary caregiver The person, usually the mother, with whom the infant develops the major attachment relationship.

Principle of mutual exclusivity A proposed principle of semantic development stating that children assume that an object can have only one name.

Private speech Speech children produce and direct toward themselves during a problem-solving activity.

Production deficiency The failure to generate a mnemonic strategy spontaneously.

Productivity The property of language that permits humans to produce and comprehend an infinite number of statements.

Progressive decentering Piaget's term for the gradual decline in egocentrism that occurs across development.

Prosocial behaviour The aspect of moral conduct that includes socially desirable behaviours such as sharing, helping, and co-operating; often used interchangeably with altruism by modern researchers.

Proximal processes Bronfenbrenner and Ceci's term for interactions between the child and aspects of the microsystem that have positive effects on psychological functioning and that help maximize expression of the child's genetic potential.

Proximodistal Literally, near to far. This principle of development refers to the tendency of body parts to develop in a trunk-to-extremities direction.

Psychometric An approach to the study of intelligence that emphasizes the use of standardized tests to identify individual differences among people.

Puberty The period in which chemical and physical changes in the body occur that enable sexual reproduction.

Punisher A consequence that makes the behaviour it follows less likely, either through the presentation of something unpleasant or the removal of something desirable.

Q

Qualitative identity The knowledge that the qualitative nature of something is not changed by a change in its appearance. In Piaget's theory, a preoperational achievement.

Quasi-experimental studies Comparison of groups differing on some important characteristic.

R

Rapid eye movement (REM) sleep A stage of light sleep in which the eyes move rapidly while the eyelids are closed.

Reaction range In Gottesman's model, the term for the range of ability or skill that is set by the genes. The value achieved within this range is determined by the environment.

Reactivation The preservation of the memory for an event through reencounter with at least some portion of the event in the interval between initial experience and memory test.

Recall memory The retrieval of some past stimulus or event that is not perceptually present.

Recapitulation theory An early biological notion, later adopted by psychologist G. Stanley Hall, that the development of the individual repeats the development of the species.

Recast A response to speech that restates it using a different structure.

Recessive gene A relatively weak allele whose characteristics are expressed in the phenotype only when it is paired with another recessive gene.

Reciprocal altruism A proposed mechanism by which an individual's altruistic behaviour toward members of the social group may promote the survival of the individual's genes through reciprocation by others or may ensure the survival of similar genes.

Reciprocal determinism Albert Bandura's proposed process describing the interaction of a person's characteristics and abilities (P), behaviour (B), and environment (E).

Recognition memory The realization that some perceptually present stimulus or event has been encountered before.

Reduplicated babbling A stage in the preverbal period, beginning at about 6 months, when infants produce strings of identical sounds, such as *dadada*.

Referential style Vocabulary acquired during the naming explosion that involves a large proportion of nouns and object labels.

Reflex A biological reaction in which a specific stimulus reliably elicits a specific response; an automatic and stereotyped response to a specific stimulus.

Rejected child A child who receives few positive and many negative nominations in sociometric assessments by peers. Such children seem to be disliked by the peer group.

Relational aggression Aggression designed to damage or disrupt social relationships.

Reliability The consistency or repeatability of a measuring instrument. A necessary property of a standardized test.

Replica toys Toys that resemble real objects, such as dishes, dolls, and vehicles.

Representation The use of symbols to picture and act on the world internally.

Repression Freud's term for the process through which desires or motivations are driven into the unconscious, as typically occurs during the phallic stage.

Resilient children Children who adapt positively and develop well despite early environmental adversity.

Respondent behaviours Responses based on reflexes, which are controlled by specific eliciting stimuli. The smaller category of human behaviours.

Response inhibition The absence of a particular response that has just been modelled; often the result of vicarious punishment.

Reversal-replication (ABAB) design An experimental design in which the independent variable is systematically presented and removed several times. Can be used in studies involving very few research participants.

Reversibility Piaget's term for the power of operations to correct for potential disturbances and thus arrive at correct solutions to problems.

Rules Procedures for acting on the environment and solving problems.

S

Scaffolding A method of teaching in which the adult adjusts the level of help provided in relation to the child's level of performance, the goal being to encourage independent performance.

Scatter diagram A graphic illustration of a correlation between two variables.

Schemes Piaget's term for the cognitive structures of infancy. Consists of a set of skilled, flexible action patterns through which the child understands the world.

School cut-off design Research technique that compares children who are close in age but differ in school experience by one year.

Scientific method The system of rules used by scientists to conduct and evaluate their research.

Script A representation of the typical sequence of actions and events in some familiar context.

Selective attention Concentration on a stimulus or event with attendant disregard for other simultaneously available stimuli or events.

Self-consciousness A concern about the opinions others hold about one.

Self-efficacy Bandura's term for people's ability to succeed at various tasks, as judged by the people themselves.

Self-esteem (self-worth) A person's evaluation of the self and the affective reactions to that evaluation.

Self-evaluation The part of the self-system concerned with children's opinions of themselves and their abilities.

Self-knowledge (self-awareness) The part of the self-system concerned with children's knowledge about themselves.

Self-regulation The part of the self-system concerned with self-control.

Self-schema An internal cognitive portrait of the self used to organize information about the self.

Self-system The set of interrelated processes—self-knowledge, self-evaluation, and self-regulation—that make up the self.

Semantic bootstrapping A proposed mechanism of grammatical development in which children use semantic cues to infer aspects of grammar.

Semantics The study of meaning in language.

Sensation The experience resulting from the stimulation of a sense organ.

Sensitive period A period of development during which certain behaviours are more easily learned.

Sensorimotor Form of intelligence in which knowledge is based on physical interactions with people and objects. The first of Piaget's periods, extending from birth to about 2 years.

Sensorimotor schemes Skilled and generalizable action patterns by which infants act on and understand the world. In Piaget's theory, the cognitive structures of infancy.

Separation protest Crying and searching by infants separated from their mothers; an indication of the formation of the attachment bond.

Seriation The ability to order stimuli along some quantitative dimension, such as length. In Piaget's theory, a concrete operational achievement.

Sex chromosomes The pair of human chromosomes that determines one's sex. Females have two X chromosomes; males have an X and a Y.

Sex differentiation The biological process through which physical differences between sexes emerge.

Sex typing The process by which children develop the behaviours and attitudes considered appropriate for their gender.

Shape bias The child's assumption that a new word is extended to things of a similar shape.

Shape constancy The experience that the physical shape of an object remains the same even though the shape of its projected image on the eye varies.

Short-term storage space In Case's theory, the resources necessary to store results from previous cognitive operations while carrying out new ones.

Sibling rivalry Feelings of competition, resentment, and jealousy that can arise between siblings.

Situational compliance Obedience that results from a child's awareness of an adult's will in a particular situation and does not reflect enduring behavioural change.

Size constancy The experience that the physical size of an object remains the same even though the size of its projected image on the eye varies.

Skeletal maturity The degree of maturation of an individual as indicated by the extent of hardening of the bones. Also called bone age.

Small for gestational age (SGA) Describes babies born at a weight in the bottom 10 percent of babies of a particular gestational age.

Social cognition Knowledge of the social world and interpersonal relationships.

Social comparison Comparing one's abilities to those of others.

Social conventions Rules used by a society to govern everyday behaviour and to maintain order.

Socialization The process through which society moulds the child's beliefs, expectations, and behaviour.

Social-learning theory A form of environmental/learning theory that adds observational learning to classical and operant learning as a process through which children's behaviour changes.

Social problem-solving skills Skills needed to resolve social dilemmas.

Social referencing Using information gained from other people to interpret uncertain situations and to regulate one's own behaviour.

Social referential communication A form of communication in which a speaker sends a message that is comprehended by a listener.

Social support Resources (both tangible and intangible) provided by other people in times of uncertainty or stress.

Social withdrawal Self-imposed isolation from the peer group.

Sociobiology A branch of biology that attempts to discover the evolutionary origins of social behaviour.

Socio-cognitive conflict Cognitive conflict that arises during social interaction.

Sociodramatic play Play in which two or more people enact a variety of related roles.

Sociogenesis The process of acquiring knowledge or skills through social interactions.

Sociometric techniques Procedures for assessing children's social status based on evaluations by the peer group. Sociometric techniques may involve ratings of degree of liking or nominations of liked or disliked peers.

Solitary pretense Pretend play engaged in by a child playing alone.

Speech act An instance of speech used to perform pragmatic functions, such as requesting or complaining.

Spontaneous electroencephalography (EEG) A technique for measuring the spontaneous electrical activity of groups of neurons across the brain to different stimulation conditions using electrodes placed on the scalp.

Stage-environment fit Degree to which environmental circumstances match the capabilities and the needs of the child at particular points during development.

Stereotype threat Extra pressure people feel in situations in which their performance may confirm a negative stereotype held about their group.

Stimulus generalization A process related to classical conditioning in which stimuli that are similar to the conditioned stimulus (CS) also acquire the power to elicit the response.

Strange Situation procedure Mary Ainsworth's laboratory procedure for assessing the strength of the attachment relationship by observing the infant's reactions to a series of structured episodes involving the mother and a stranger.

Strategy construction The creation of strategies for processing and remembering information. A mechanism of change in information-processing theories.

Strategy selection Progressively greater use of relatively effective strategies rather than with relatively ineffective ones. A mechanism of change in information-processing theories.

Structural magnetic resonance imaging (MRI) A technique that images the anatomical structure of the brain by creating a magnetic field that interacts with molecules in the body. When the magnetic field is removed, the molecules emit energy that is detected and from which images of the structures being scanned are produced.

Structured observation Observation of behaviour in settings that are controlled by the investigator.

Study strategies Mnemonic strategies (such as outlining and note taking) that students use in an attempt to remember school material.

Sudden infant death syndrome (SIDS) The sudden and unexpected death of an otherwise healthy infant under the age of 1.

Surface structure Chomsky's term for the way words and phrases are arranged in spoken languages.

Symbolic function The ability to use one thing (such as a mental image or word) as a symbol to represent something else.

Symbolic play Form of play in which the child uses one thing in deliberate pretense to stand for something else.

Sympathy Feeling of concern for another in reaction to the other's situation or emotional state, not necessarily involving an experience of the other's emotional state.

Synapse The small space between neurons across which neural activity is communicated from one cell to another.

Synaptic vesicles Structures near the end of the axon in which neurotransmitters are stored. When encountering an electrical signal coming down the axon, the vesicle moves to the end of the axon and releases its neurotransmitter molecules into the synapse.

Syntactic bootstrapping A proposed mechanism of semantic development in which children use syntactic cues to infer the meanings of words.

Syntax The aspect of grammar that involves word order.

T

Tabula rasa Latin phrase, meaning "blank slate," used to describe the newborn's mind as entirely empty of inborn abilities, interests, or ideas.

Telegraphic speech Speech from which unnecessary function words (e.g., in, the, with) are omitted; common during early language learning.

Temperament The aspect of personality studied in infants, which includes their emotional expressiveness and responsiveness to stimulation.

Temporal lobe Located below the parietal lobe and forward of the occipital lobe; has as its main function the processing of auditory information; functions to process speech and language; involved in object perception and recognition; transfers information from short-term memory, encoding it in long-term memory.

Teratogen An agent that can cause abnormal development in the fetus.

Teratology The study of the effects of teratogens upon development.

Theory A broad set of statements describing the relation between a phenomenon and the factors assumed to affect it.

Theory of mind Thoughts and beliefs concerning the mental world.

Tools of intellectual adaptation Vygotsky's term for the techniques of thinking and problem solving that children internalize from their culture.

Transactional influence A bidirectional, or reciprocal, relationship in which individuals influence one another's behaviours.

Transformational grammar A set of rules developed by the language acquisition device to translate a language's surface structure to a deep structure that the child can innately understand.

Transitivity The ability to combine relations logically to deduce necessary conclusions—for example, if A=B and B=C, then A=C. In Piaget's theory, a concrete operational achievement.

U

Ultrasound imaging A non-invasive procedure for detecting physical defects in the fetus. A device that produces soundlike waves of energy is moved over the pregnant woman's abdomen, and reflections of these waves form an image of the fetus.

Umbilical cord A soft cable of tissue and blood vessels that connects the fetus to the placenta.

Unconditioned response (UCR) The response portion of a reflex, which is reliably elicited by a stimulus (UCS).

Unconditioned stimulus (UCS) The stimulus portion of a reflex, which reliably elicits a respondent behaviour (UCR).

Underextension An early language error in which children fail to apply labels they know to things for which the labels are appropriate.

Uninvolved (disengaged) parenting A style of parenting characterized by low levels of both control and warmth.

Universals of development Aspects of development or behaviour that are common to children everywhere.

Utilization deficiency The failure of a recently developed mnemonic strategy to facilitate recall.

V

Validity The accuracy with which a measuring instrument assesses the attribute that it is designed to measure. A necessary property of a standardized test.

Variable Any factor that can take on different values along a dimension.

Vestibular sensitivity The perceptual experience that results from motion of the body and the pull of gravity.

Vicarious punishment Punishing consequences experienced when viewing a model that affect an observer similarly.

Vicarious reinforcement Reinforcing consequences experienced when viewing a model that affect an observer similarly.

Visual accommodation The automatic adjustment of the lens of the eye to produce a focused image of an object on the light-sensitive tissue at the back of the eye.

Visual acuity The clarity with which visual images can be perceived.

Visual cliff A research method for the study of depth perception in infancy. The infant is placed on a glass-covered table near an apparent drop-off and perception of depth is inferred if the infant avoids the drop.

Visual self-recognition The ability to recognize oneself; often studied in babies by having them look into mirrors.

W

Wariness of strangers A general fear of unfamiliar people that appears in many infants at around 8 months of age and indicates the formation of the attachment bond.

Whole-object assumption The child's hypothesis that a new word refers to a whole object.

X

X-linked disorders Disorders that result from recessive genes located on the X chromosome, leaving males more vulnerable to them.

Z

Zeitgeist The spirit of the times, or the ideas shared by most scientists during a given period.

Zone of proximal development The distance between what a child can accomplish independently and what the child can accomplish with the help of an adult or more capable peer.

Zygote A fertilized ovum.

REFERENCES

A

Abbeduto, L., Davies, B., & Furman, L. (1988). The development of speech act comprehension in mentally retarded individuals and nonretarded children. *Child Development, 59,* 1460–1472.

Abdala, C. & Folsom, R. C. (1995). Frequency contribution to the click-evoked auditory brain stem response in human adults and infants. *Journal of the Acoustical Society of America, 97,* 2394–2404.

Abdulaziz, Y. & Ahmad, S. M. S. (2010). Infant cry recognition system: A comparison of system performance based on mel frequency and linear prediction cepstral coefficients. Paper presented at the conference of Information and Knowledge Management, Shah Alam, Selangor.

Aber, J. L., Bishop-Josef, S. J., Jones, S. M., McLearn, K. T., & Phillips, D. A. (2006). *Child Development and Social Policy: Knowledge for Action.* Washington, DC: American Psychological Association.

Aboud, F. E. (1985). Children's application of attribution principles to social comparisons. *Child Development, 56,* 682–688.

Aboud, F. E. & Mendelson, M. J. (1996). Determinants of friendship selection and quality: Links to child-mother attachment. In W. M. Bukowski, A. F. Newcomb, & W. W. Hartup (Eds.), *The company they keep: Friendship in childhood and adolescence.* New York: Cambridge University Press.

Abramovitch, R., Corter, C., & Pepler, D. J. (1980). Observation of mixed-sex sibling dyads. *Child Development, 51,* 217–229.

Abramovitch, R., Freedman, J. L., Thoden, K., & Nikolich, C. (1991). Children's capacity to consent to participation in psychological research: Empirical findings. *Child Development, 62,* 1100–1109.

Abrams, K. Y., Rifkin, A., & Hesse, E. (2006). Examining the role of parental frightened/frightening subtypes in predicting disorganized attachment within a brief observational procedure. *Development and Psychopathology, 18,* 345–361.

Achenbach, T. M., Edelbrock, C., & Howell, C. T. (1987). Empirically based assessment of the behavioral/emotional problems of 2- and 3-year-old children. *Journal of Abnormal Child Psychology, 15,* 629–650.

Achinstein, B., Ogawa, R. T., & Speiglman, A. (2004). Are we creating separate and unequal tracks of teachers? The effects of state policy, local conditions, and teacher characteristics on new teacher socialization. *American Educational Research Journal, 41,* 557–603.

Ackerman, B. P. (1993). Children's understanding of the speaker's meaning in referential communication. *Journal of Experimental Child Psychology, 55,* 56–86.

Ackerman, B. P., & Silver, S. (1990). Children's understanding of private keys in referential communication. *Journal of Experimental Child Psychology, 50,* 217–242.

Ackerman, B. P., Szymanski, J., & Silver, D. (1990). Children's use of common ground in interpreting ambiguous referential utterances. *Developmental Psychology, 26,* 234–245.

Acredolo, L. P. (1978). Development of spatial orientation in infancy. *Developmental Psychology, 14,* 224–234.

Acredolo, L. P. & Goodwyn, S. W. (1990). Development of communicative gesturing. In R. Vasta (Ed.), *Annals of child development* (Vol. 7). Greenwich, CT: JAI Press.

Acredolo, L. P. (1985). Coordinating perspectives on infant spatial orientation. In R. Cohen (Ed.), *The development of spatial cognition.* Hillsdale, NJ: Erlbaum.

Adams, R. J. (1989). Newborns' discrimination among mid- and long-wavelength stimuli. *Journal of Experimental Child Psychology, 47,* 130–141.

Adams, R. J. (1995). Further exploration of human neonatal chromatic-achromatic discrimination. *Journal of Experimental Child Psychology, 60,* 344–360.

Adams, R. J. & Courage, M. L. (1998). Human newborn color vision: Measurement with chromatic stimuli varying in excitation purity. *Journal of Experimental Child Psychology, 67,* 22–34.

Adams, R. J. & Courage, M. L. (2002). A psychophysical test of the early maturation of infants' mid- and long-wavelength retinal cones. *Infant Behavior and Development, 25,* 247–254.

Adamson, L. B. (1995). *Communication development during infancy.* Madison, WI: Brown & Benchmark.

Adamson, L. B. & Bakeman, R. (1991). The development of shared attention during infancy. In R. Vasta (Ed.), *Annals of child development* (Vol. 8). London: Kingsley.

Adamson, L. B. & Bakeman, R. (2006). Development of displaced speech in early mother-child interactions. *Child Development, 77,* 186–200.

Adamson, L. B. & Frick, J. E. (2003). The still face: A history of a shared experimental paradigm. *Infancy 4,* 451–473.

Adamuti-Trache, M. (2006). Who likes science and why? Individual, family, and teacher effects. Canadian Council on Learning. Available at: 9458A577-2A56-486F-9F80-49DCCD8E05F3/0/WhoLikesScienceJan2007.pdf

Adler, S. A., Gerhardstein, P., & Rovee-Collier, C. (1998). Levels-of-processing effects on infant memory. *Child Development, 69,* 280–294.

Adler, S. A. & Haith, M. M. (2003). The nature of infants' visual expectations for event content. *Infancy 4,* 389–421.

Adler, S. A., Haith, M. M., Arehart, D. M., & Lanthier, E. C. (2008). Infants' visual expectations and the processing of time. *Journal of Cognition and Development, 9,* 1–25.

Adler, S. A. & Orprecio, J. (2006). The eyes have it: Visual pop-out in infants and adults. *Developmental Science, 9,* 189–206.

Adler, S. A. & Rovee-Collier, C. (1994). The memorability and discriminability of primitive perceptual units in infancy. *Vision Research, 34,* 449–459.

Adler, S. A., Wilk, A., & Rovee-Collier, C. (2000). Reinstatement versus reactivation effects on active memory in infants. *Journal of Experimental Child Psychology, 75,* 93–115.

Adolph, K. E. (2000). Specificity of learning: Why infants fall over a veritable cliff. *Psychological Science, 11,* 290–295.

Adolph, K. E. & Berger, S. E. (2006). Motor development. In D. Kuhn and R. S. Siegler (Eds.), *Handbook of child psychology* (Vol. 2, Cognition, perception, and language). Hoboken, NJ: Wiley.

Adoption Council of Canada. (2005). Personal communication, January 20, 2005.

Adoption Council of Canada. (2007). Downward trend continues: Citizenship and Immigration Canada releases statistics for 2006. Available at: www.adoption.ca/ACCArticle_2006Stats.htm

Agrell, S. (November 6, 2007). "Daycare may help at-risk toddlers soothe their aggression." *The Globe and Mail.*

Ainsworth, M. D. S. (1940). *An evaluation of adjustment based upon the concept of security.* University of Toronto Studies, Child Development Series, no. 9. Toronto: University of Toronto Press.

Ainsworth, M. D. S. (1983). Patterns of infant-mother attachment as related to maternal care: Their early history and their contribution to continuity. In D. Magnusson & V. Allen (Eds.), *Human development: An interactional perspective.* New York: Academic Press.

Ainsworth, M. D. S. (1992). A consideration of social referencing in the context of attachment theory and research. In S. Feinman (Ed.), *Social referencing and the social construction of reality in infancy.* New York: Plenum.

Ainsworth, M. D. S., Blehar, M. C., Waters, E., & Wall, S. (1978). *Patterns of attachment: A psychological study of the Strange Situation.* Hillsdale, NJ: Erlbaum.

Akhtar, N. (2005). Is joint attention necessary for early language learning? In B. Homer & C. Tamis-LeMonda (Eds.), *The development of social cognition and communication.* Mahwah, NJ: Erlbaum.

Aksan, N., Kochanska, G., & Ortmann, M. R. (2006). Mutually responsive orientation between parents and their young children: Toward methodological advances in the science of relationships. *Developmental Psychology, 42,* 833–848.

Alarcon, M., Plomin, R., Fulker, D. W., Corley, R., & DeFries, J. C. (1999). Molarity not modularity: Multivariate genetic analysis of specific cognitive abilities in parents and their 16-year-old children in the Colorado Adoption Project. *Cognitive Development, 14,* 175–193.

Alden, L. E. (2005). Interpersonal perspectives on social phobia. In W. R. Crozier & L. E. Alden (Eds.), *The essential handbook of social anxiety for clinicians* (pp. 168–192). Hoboken, NJ: John Wiley & Sons, Inc.

Aldridge, M. A., Braga, E. S., Walton, G. E., & Bower, T. G. R. (1999). The intermodal representation of speech in newborns. *Developmental Science, 2,* 42–46.

Alfieri, T., Ruble, D. N., & Higgins, E. T. (1996). Gender stereotypes during adolescence: Developmental changes and the transition to junior high school. *Developmental Psychology, 32,* 1129–1137.

Allen, J. P., Porter, M. R., & McFarland, F. C. (2006). Leaders and followers in adolescent close friendships: Susceptibility to peer influence as a predictor of risky behavior, friendship instability, and depression. *Development and Psychopathology, 18,* 155–172.

Allen, M. (2004). Reading achievement of students in French immersion programs, Statistics Canada, *Educational Quarterly Review,* Volume 9, number 4, pp. 25–30. Catalogue 81-003-XIE.

Almeida, J., Mahon, B. Z., & Caramazza, A. (2010). The role of the dorsal visual processing stream in tool identification. *Psychological Science, 21,* 772–778.

Almli, C. R., Ball, R. H., & Wheeler, M. E. (2001). Human fetal and neonatal movement patterns: Gender differences and fetal-to-neonatal continuity. *Developmental Psychobiology, 38,* 252–273.

Alter, A. L., Aronson, J., Darley, J. M., Rodriguez, C., & Ruble, D. N. (2010). Rising to the threat: Reducing stereotype threat by reframing the threat as a challenge. *Journal of Experimental Social Psychology, 46,* 166–171.

Altermatt, E. R., Jovanovic, J., & Perry, M. (1998). Bias or responsivity? Sex and achievement-level effects on teachers' classroom questioning practices. *Journal of Educational Psychology, 90,* 516–527.

Amato, P. R. (2006). Marital discord, divorce, and children's well-being: Results from a 20-year longitudinal study of two generations. In A. Clarke-Stewart & J. Dunn (Eds.), *Families count: Effects on child and adolescent development* (pp. 179–202). New York: Cambridge University Press.

Amato, P. R. & Dorius, C. (2010). Fathers, children, and divorce. In M. E. Lamb (Ed.) *The role of the father in child development* (5th edition, pp. 177–200). Hoboken, NJ: Wiley.

Amato, P. R. & Gilbreth, J. G. (1999). Nonresident fathers and children's well-being: A meta-analysis. *Journal of Marriage and the Family, 61,* 557–573.

Ambert, A.-M. (2005). *Divorce: Facts, causes, and consequences.* Ottawa, ON: Vanier Institute of the Family.

American Academy of Pediatrics. (2000). Changing concepts of sudden infant death syndrome: Implications for infant sleeping environment and sleep position. *Pediatrics, 105,* 650–656.

American Academy of Pediatrics. (2008). Maternal phenylketonuria. *Pediatrics, 122,* 445–449.

American Association of University Women. (2001). *Beyond the gender wars: A conversation about girls, boys, and education.* Washington, DC: AAUW.

American Association of University Women/ Greenberg Lake. (1990). *Expectations and aspirations: Gender roles and self-esteem.* (Data Report and Banners). Washington, DC: Greenberg-Lake.

American Psychiatric Association. (2000). *Diagnostic and statistical manual of mental disorders* (4th ed., text rev.). Washington, DC: Author.

American Psychological Association. (2002). Ethical principles of psychologists and code of conduct. *American Psychologist, 57,* 1060–1073.

American Psychological Association. (2005). *Guidelines for ethical conduct in the care and use of animals:* Available at: www.apa.org/science/anguide.html

Amso, D. & Johnson, S. P. (2005). Selection and inhibition in infancy: Evidence from the spatial negative priming paradigm. *Cognition, 95,* B27–B36.

Amsterdam, B. (1972). Mirror self-image reactions before the age of two. *Developmental Psychobiology, 5,* 297–305.

Anagnostou, E. & Taylor, M. J. (2011). Review of neuroimaging in autism spectrum disorders: What have we learned and where we go from here. *Molecular Autism, 2,* 4.

Anand, K. J. S. & Scalzo, F. M. (2000). Can adverse neonatal experiences alter brain development and subsequent behavior? *Biology of the Neonate, 77,* 69–82.

Ancora, G., Maranella, E., Locatelli, C., Pieratoni, L., & Faldella, G. (2009). Changes in cerebral hemodynamics and amplitude integrated EEG in an asphyxiated newborn during and after cool cap treatment. *Brain Development, 31,* 442–444.

Anderman, E. M. & Midgley, C. (1997). Changes in achievement goal orientations, perceived academic competence, and grades across the transition to middle-level schools. *Contemporary Educational Psychology, 22,* 269–298.

Anderson, C. A. (2004). An update on the effects of playing violent video games. *Journal of Adolescence, 27,* 113–122.

Anderson, C. A., Gentile, D. A., & Buckley, K. E. (2007). *Violent video game effects on children and adolescents: Theory, research, and public policy.* New York: Oxford University Press.

Anderson, C. A., Shibuya, A., Ihori, N., Swing, E. L., Bushman, B. J., Sakamoto, A., Rothstein, H. R., & Saleem, M. (2010). Violent videogame effects on aggression, empathy, and prosocial behavior in Eastern and Western countries: A meta-analytic review. *Psychological Bulletin. 136,* 151–173.

Anderson, D. R., Lorch, E. P., Field, D. E., Collins, P. A., & Nathan, J. G. (1986). Television viewing at home: Age trends in visual attention and time with TV. *Child Development, 57,* 1024–1033.

Anderson, J. R., Reder, L. M., & Simon, H. A. (1996). Situated learning and education. *Educational Researcher, 25,* 5–11.

Anderson, P. & Doyle, L. W. (2003). Neurobehavioral outcomes of school-age children born extremely low birth weight or very preterm in the 1990s. *JAMA-Journal of the American Medical Association, 28,* 3264–3272.

Andre, T., Whigham, M., Hendrickson, A., & Chambers, S. (1999). Competency beliefs, positive affect, and gender stereotypes of elementary students and their parents about science versus other school subjects. *Journal of Research in Science Teaching, 36,* 719–747.

Anglin, J. M. (1993). Vocabulary development: A morphological analysis. *Monographs of the Society for Research in Child Development, 58* (10, Serial No. 238).

Angoff, W. H. (1988). The nature-nurture debate, aptitudes, and group differences. *American Psychologist, 43,* 713–720.

Anisfeld, M. (1996). Only tongue protrusion modeling is matched by neonates. *Developmental Review, 16,* 149–161.

Anisfeld, M., Turkewitz, G., Rose, S. A., Rosenberg, F. R., Sheiber, F. J., Couturier-Fagan, D. A., et al. (2001). No compelling evidence that newborns imitate oral gestures. *Infancy, 2,* 111–122.

Ansalone, G. (2005). Getting our schools on track: Is detracking really the answer? *Radical Pedagogy, 6,* no pagination specified.

Antell, S. E. & Keating, D. P. (1983). Perception of numerical invariance in neonates. *Child Development, 54,* 695–701.

Anzures, G., Quinn, P., Pascalis, O., Slater, A., & Lee, K. (2009). Categorization, categorical perception, and asymmetry in infants' representation of face race. *Developmental Science, 13*(4), 553–564.

Apgar, V. (1953). A proposal for a new method of evaluation of the newborn infant. *Current Researches in Anesthesia and Analgesia, 32,* 260–267.

Appel, L. F., Cooper, R. G., McCarrell, N., Sims-Knight, J., Yussen, S. R., & Flavell, J. H. (1972). The development of the distinction between perceiving and memorizing. *Child Development, 43,* 1365–1381.

Appley, M. (1986). G. Stanley Hall: Vow on Mount Owen. In S. H. Hulse & B. F. Green (Eds.), *One hundred years of psychological research in America.* Baltimore: Johns Hopkins University Press.

Archer, J. (1991). The influence of testosterone on human aggression. *British Journal of Psychology, 82,* 1–28.

Ark, W. S. (2002). Neuroimaging studies give new insight to mental rotation. Proceedings of the 35th Annual Hawaii International Conference on System Sciences, 1822–1828.

Armon, C. & Dawson, R. L. (1997). Developmental trajectories in moral reasoning across the lifespan. *Journal of Moral Education, 26,* 433–453.

Arnett, J. (2002). The psychology of globalization. *American Psychologist, 57,* 774–783.

Arnott, B. & Meins, E. (2007). Links among antenatal attachment representations, postnatal mind-mind-edness, and infant attachment security: A preliminary study of mothers and fathers. *Bulletin of the Menninger Clinic, 71,* 132–149.

Arseneault, L., Moffitt, T. E., Caspi, A., Taylor, A., Rijsdijk, F. V., Jaffee, S. R., et al. (2003). Strong genetic effects on cross-situational antisocial behaviour among 5-year-old children according to mothers, teachers, examiner-observers, and twins' self-reports. *Journal of Child Psychology and Psychiatry, 44,* 832–848.

Arsenio, W. (2010). Social information processing, emotions, and aggression: Conceptual and methodological contributions of the special section articles. *Journal of Abnormal Child Psychology: An official publication of the International Society for Research in Child and Adolescent Psychopathology, 38*(5), 627–632. doi:10.1007/s10802-010-9408-z.

Asada, K., Tomiwa, K., Okada, M., & Itakura, S. (2010). Fluent language with impaired pragmatics in children with Williams syndrome. *Journal of Neurolinguistics, 23*(6), 540–552.

Asato, M. R., Terwilliger, R., Woo, J., & Luna, B. (2010). White matter development in adolescence: A DTI study. *Cerebral Cortex, 20,* 2122–2131.

Asendorpf, J. B. (2002). Self-awareness, other-awareness, and secondary representation. In A. Meltzoff & W. Prinz (Eds.), *The imitative mind: Development, evolution, and brain bases* (pp. 63–73). New York: Cambridge University Press.

Asendorpf, J. B. & Baudonniere, P. (1993). Self-awareness and other-awareness: Mirror self-recognition and synchronic imitation among unfamiliar peers. *Developmental Psychology, 29,* 88–95.

Asendorpf, J. B., Warkentin, V., & Baudonniere, P. (1996). Self-awareness and other-awareness II: Mirror-self recognition, social contingency awareness, and synchronic imitation. *Developmental Psychology, 32,* 313–321.

Ashcraft, M. H. (1990). Strategic processing in children's mental arithmetic: A review and proposal. In D. F. Bjorklund (Ed.), *Children's strategies: Contemporary views of cognitive development.* Hillsdale, NJ: Erlbaum.

Asher, S. R. (1985). An evolving paradigm in social skill training research with children. In B. H. Schneider, K. H. Rubin, & J. E. Ledingham (Eds.), *Children's peer relations: Issues in assessment and intervention.* New York: Springer-Verlag.

Asher, S. R. & McDonald, K. L. (2009). The behavioral basis of acceptance, rejection, and perceived popularity. In K.H. Rubin, W. M. Bukowski, & B. Laursen (Eds.) *Handbook of peer interactions, relationships, and groups* (pp. 232–248). New York: Guilford.

Asher, S. R., Parker, J. G., & Walker, D. L. (1996). Distinguishing friendship from acceptance: Implications for intervention and assessment. In W. D. Bukowski, A. F. Newcomb, & W. W. Hartup (Eds.), *The company they keep: Friendship in childhood and adolescence.* New York: Cambridge University Press.

Asher, S. R., Renshaw, P. D., & Hymel, S. (1982). Peer relations and the development of social skills. In S. G. Moore (Ed.), *The young child: Reviews of research* (Vol. 3). Washington, DC: National Association for the Education of Young Children.

Ashmead, D. H., Davis, D. L., Whalen, T., & Odom, R. D. (1991). Sound localization and sensitivity to inter-aural time differences in human infants. *Child Development, 62,* 1211–1226.

Ashmead, D. H. & Perlmutter, M. (1980). Infant memory in everyday life. In M. Perlmutter (Ed.),

New directions for child development: No. 10. Children's memory. San Francisco: Jossey-Bass.

Aslin, R. N. & Hunt, R. H. (2001). Development, plasticity, and learning in the auditory system. In C. A. Nelson & M. Luciana (Eds.), *Handbook of developmental cognitive neuroscience.* Cambridge, MA: MIT Press.

Aslin, R. N., Jusczyk, P. W., & Pisoni, D. B. (1998). Speech and auditory processing during infancy: Constraints on and precursors to language. In W. Damon (Series Ed.) & D. Kuhn & R. S. Siegler (Vol. Eds.), *Handbook of child psychology: Vol. 2. Cognition, perception, and language* (5th ed.). New York: Wiley.

Aslin, R. N., Pisoni, D. B., & Jusczyk, P. W. (1983). Auditory development and speech perception in infancy. In P. H. Mussen (Series Ed.) & M. M. Haith & J. J. Campos (Vol. Eds.), *Handbook of child psychology: Vol. 2. Infancy and developmental psychology* (4th ed.). New York: Wiley.

Aslin, R. N., Saffran, J. R., & Newport, E. L. (1999). Statistical learning in linguistic and nonlinguistic domains. In B. MacWhinney (Ed.), *The emergence of language.* Mahwah, NJ: Erlbaum.

Aslin, R. N. & Shea, S. L. (1990). Velocity thresholds in human infants: Implications for the perception of motion. *Developmental Psychology, 26,* 589–598.

Astington, J. W. (1988). Children's production of commissive speech acts. *Journal of Child Language, 15,* 411–423.

Atance, C. M., Bernstein, D. M., & Meltzoff, A. N. (2010). Thinking about false belief: It's not just what children say, but how long it takes them to say it. *Cognition, 116,* 297–301.

Atkinson, J. (1998). The "where and what" or "who and how" of visual development. In F. Simion & G. Butterworth (Eds.), *The development of sensory, motor, and cognitive capacities in early infancy: From perception to cognition* (pp. 3–20). Hove: Psychology Press.

Atkinson, J. (2000). *The developing visual brain.* Oxford Psychology Series. Oxford: Oxford University Press.

Atkinson, J. & Braddick, O. (2003). Neurobiological models of normal and abnormal visual development. In M. de Haan & M. H. Johnson (Eds.), *The cognitive neuroscience of development* (pp. 43–71). Hove, UK: Psychology Press.

Atkinson, J., Wattam-Bell, J., & Braddick, O. (2002). Development of directional and orientational-selective VEP responses: Relative functional onset of dorsal and ventral stream processing in human infants. *Association for research in vision and ophthalmology: Abstract,* 3992.

Atkinson, R. C. & Shiffrin, R. M. (1971). The control of short-term memory. *Scientific American, 225,* 82.

Atlas, R. S. & Pepler, D. J. (1998). Observations of bullying in the classroom. *Journal of Educational Research, 92,* 86–99.

Attili, G., Vermigli, P., & Schneider, B. H. (1997). Peer acceptance and friendship patterns within a cross-cultural perspective. *International Journal of Behavioral Development, 21,* 277–288.

Au, T. K. & Glusman, M. (1990). The principle of mutual exclusivity in word learning: To honor or not to honor? *Child Development, 61,* 1474–1490.

Audibert, F. (2009). Preimplantation genetic testing. *Journal of Obstetrics and Gynaecology in Canada,* 31, 761–767.

Aureli, F. & de Waal, F. B. M. (2000). *Natural conflict resolution.* Berkeley: University of California Press.

Auyeung, B., Baron-Cohen, S., Ashwin, E., Knickmeyer, R., Taylor, K., Hackett, G., & Hines, M. (2009). Fetal testosterone predicts sexually differentiated childhood behavior in girls and in boys. *Psychological Science, 20,* 144–148.

Aylward, G. P. (1997). *Infant and early childhood neuropsychology.* New York, NY: Plenum Press.

Azevedo, F. A. C., Carvalho, L. R. B., Grinberg, L. T., Farfel, J. M., Ferretti, R. E. L., Leite, R. E. P., Filho, W. J., Lent, R., & Herculano-Houzel, S. (2009). Equal numbers of neuronal and nonneuronal cells make the human brain an isometrically scaled-up primate brain. *The Journal of Comparative Neurology, 513,* 532–541.

Azmitia, M. (1996). Peer interactive minds: Developmental, theoretical, and methodological issues. In P. B. Baltes & V. M. Staudinger (Eds.), *Interactive minds: Life-span perspectives on the social foundations of cognition.* New York: Cambridge University Press.

Azuma, H. (1996). Cross-national research on child development: The Hess-Azuma collaboration in retrospect. In D. Schwalb & B. Schwalb (Eds.), *Japanese childrearing: Two generations of scholarship.* New York: Guilford.

B

Baenninger, M. & Newcombe, N. (1995). Environmental input to the development of sex-related differences in spatial and mathematical ability. *Learning and Individual Differences, 7,* 363–382.

Bahrick, L. E. (1983). Infants' perception of substance and temporal synchrony in multimodal events. *Infant Behavior and Development, 6,* 429–451.

Bahrick, L. E. (1992). Infants' perceptual differentiation of amodal and modality-specific audio-visual relations. *Journal of Experimental Child Psychology 53,* 180–199.

Bahrick, L. E. (1995). Intermodal origins of self-perception. In P. Rochat (Ed.), *The self in infancy: Theory and research.* Amsterdam: Elsevier.

Bahrick, L. E., Hernandez-Reif, M., & Flom, R. (2005). The development of infant learning about specific face-voice relations. *Developmental Psychology, 41,* 541–552.

Bahrick, L. E. & Lickliter, R. (2000). Intersensory redundancy guides attentional selectivity and perceptual learning in infancy. *Developmental Psychology 36,* 190–201.

Bahrick, L. E. & Lickliter, R. (2002). Intersensory redundancy guides early perceptual and cognitive development. In R.V. Kail (Ed.), *Advances in child development and behavior* (Vol. 30). Orlando, FL: Academic Press.

Bahrick, L. E., Netto, D., & Hernandez-Reif, M. (1998). Intermodal perception of adult and child faces and voices by infants. *Child Development, 69,* 1263–1275.

Bahrick, L. E. & Pickens, J. N. (1994). Amodal relations: The basis for intermodal perception and learning in infancy. In D. J. Lewkowicz & R. Lickliter (Eds.), *The development of intersensory perception: Comparative perspectives.* Hillsdale, NJ: Erlbaum.

Bahrick, L. E. & Pickens, J. N. (1995). Infant memory for object motion across a period of three months: Implications for a four-phase attention function. *Journal of Experimental Child Psychology, 59,* 343–371.

Bahrick, L. E., Walker, A. S., & Neisser, U. (1981). Selective looking by infants. *Cognitive Development, 13,* 377–390.

Bailey, J. M., Dunne, M. P., & Martin, N. G. (2000). Genetic and environmental influences on sexual orientation and its correlates in an Australian twin sample. *Journal of Personality and Social Psychology, 78,* 524–536.

Bailey, J. M., Miller, J. S., & Willerman, L. (1993). Maternally rated childhood gender nonconformity in homosexuals and heterosexuals. *Archives of Sexual Behavior, 22,* 461–469.

Bailey, J. M., Nothnagel, J., & Wolfe, M. (1995). Retrospectively-measured individual differences in childhood sex-typed behavior among gay men: Correspondences between self and maternal reports. *Archives of Sexual Behavior, 24,* 613–622.

Bailey, J. M. & Zucker, K. J. (1995). Childhood sex-typed behavior and sexual orientation: A conceptual analysis and quantitative review. *Developmental Psychology, 31,* 43–55.

Bailey, S. M. & Garn, S. M. (1986). The genetics of maturation. In F. Falkner & J. M. Tanner (Eds.), *Human growth: A comprehensive treatise.* New York: Plenum.

Baillargeon, R. (1994). How do infants learn about the physical world? *Current Directions in Psychological Science, 3,* 133–140.

Baillargeon, R. (1995). A model of physical reasoning in infancy. In C. Rovee-Collier & L. P. Lipsitt (Eds.), *Advances in infancy research* (Vol. 9, pp. 305–371). Norwood, NJ: Ablex.

Baillargeon, R., Lee, J., Gertner, Y, & Wu, D. (2011). How do infants reason about physical events? In U. Goswami (Ed.). *The Wiley-Blackwell handbook of childhood cognitive development, second edition* (pp. 11–48). Chichester, UK: Blackwell Publishing Ltd.

Baillargeon, R., Scott, R. M., & He, Z. (2010). False-belief understanding in infants. *Trends in Cognitive Sciences, 14,* 110–118.

Baird, A. A., Kagan, J., Gaudette, T., Walz, K. A., Hershlag, N., & Boas, D. A. (2002). Frontal lobe activation during object permanence: data from near-infrared spectroscopy. *Neuroimage, 16,* 1120–1125.

Bakeman, R., Adamson, L. B., Konner, M., & Barr, R. G. (1990). !Kung infancy: The social context of object exploration. *Child Development, 61,* 794–809.

Baker, B. L., Birch, L. L., Trost, S. G., & Davison, K. K. (2007). Advanced pubertal status at age 11 and lower physical activity in adolescent girls. *The Journal of Pediatrics, 151,* 488–493.

Baker, T. J., Norcia, A. M., & Candy, T. R. (2011). Orientation tuning in the visual cortex of 3-month-old human infants. *Vision Research, 51,* 470–478.

Baker, T., Tse, J., Gerhardstein, P. C., & Adler, S. A. (2008). Contour integration by 6-month-olds: Discrimination of distinct contour shapes. *Vision Research, 48,* 136–148.

Bakermans-Kranenburg, M. J., van IJzendoorn, M. H., & Juffer, F. (2003). Less is more: Meta-analysis of sensitivity and attachment interventions in early childhood. *Psychological Bulletin, 129,* 195–215.

Bakermans-Kranenburg, M. J., van IJzendoorn, M. H., & Juffer, F. (2005). Disorganized infant attachment and preventive interventions: A review and meta analysis. *Infant Mental Health Journal, 26,* 191–216.

Baker-Ward, L., Ornstein, P. A., & Holden, D. J. (1984). The expression of memorization in early childhood. *Journal of Experimental Child Psychology, 37,* 555–575.

Balaban, M. T. (1995). Affective influences on startle in five-month-old infants: Reactions to facial expressions of emotion. *Child Development, 66,* 28–36.

Baldwin, A., Baldwin, C., & Cole, R. E. (1990). Stress-resistant families and stress-resistant children. In J. E. Rolf, A. S. Masten, D. Cicchetti, K. N. Wechterlein, & S. Weintraub (Eds.), *Risk and protective factors in the development of psychopathology.* New York: Cambridge University Press.

Baldwin, D. A. (1995). Understanding the link between joint attention and language. In C. Moore & P. J. Dunham (Eds.), *Joint attention: Its origins and role in development.* Hillsdale, NJ: Erlbaum.

Baldwin, D. A. & Moses, L. J. (1994). Early understanding of referential intent and attentional focus: Evidence from language and emotion. In C. Lewis & P. Mitchell (Eds.), *Children's early understanding of mind.* Hillsdale, NJ: Erlbaum.

Baldwin, D. A. & Moses, L. J. (1996). The ontogeny of social information gathering. *Child Development, 67,* 1915–1939.

Baldwin, D. A. & Moses, L. J. (2001). Links between social understanding and early word learning: Challenges to current accounts. *Social Development, 10,* 309–329.

Baltimore, D. (2001). Our genome unveiled. *Nature, 409,* 814–816.

Bandura, A. (1965). Influence of models' reinforcement contingencies on the acquisition of imitative responses. *Journal of Personality and Social Psychology, 1,* 589–595.

Bandura, A. (1973). *Aggression: A social learning analysis.* Englewood Cliffs, NJ: Prentice Hall.

Bandura, A. (1977). *Social learning theory.* Englewood Cliffs, NJ: Prentice Hall.

Bandura, A. (1978). The self system in reciprocal determinism. *American Psychologist, 33,* 344–358.

Bandura, A. (1983). Psychological mechanisms of aggression. In R. G. Geen & E. I. Donnerstein (Eds.), *Aggression: Theoretical and empirical reviews* (Vol. 1). New York: Academic Press.

Bandura, A. (1986). *Social foundations of thought and action: A social cognitive theory.* Englewood Cliffs, NJ: Prentice Hall.

Bandura, A. (1989a). Regulation of cognitive processes through perceived self-efficacy. *Developmental Psychology, 25,* 729–735.

Bandura, A. (1989b). Social cognitive theory. In R. Vasta (Ed.), *Annals of child development* (Vol. 6). Greenwich, CT: JAI Press.

Bandura, A. (1991a). Self-regulation of motivation through anticipatory and self-regulatory mechanisms. In R. A. Dienstbier (Ed.), *Nebraska symposium on motivation: Vol. 38. Perspectives on motivation:* Lincoln: University of Nebraska Press.

Bandura, A. (1991b). Social cognitive theory of moral thought and action. In W. M. Kurtines & J. L. Gewirtz (Eds.), *Handbook of moral behavior and development: Vol. 1. Theory.* Hillsdale, NJ: Erlbaum.

Bandura, A. (1994). Social cognitive theory of mass communication. In J. Bryant & D. Zillman (Eds.), *Media effects: Advances in theory and research.* Hillsdale, NJ: Erlbaum.

Bandura, A. (1997). *Self-efficacy: The exercise of control.* New York: W. H. Freeman.

Bandura, A. (2001). Social cognitive theory: An agentic perspective. *Annual Review of Psychology, 52,* 1–26.

Bandura, A. (2006a). Adolescent development from an agentic perspective. In F. Pajares & T.C. Urdan (Eds.) *Self-efficacy beliefs of adolescents. (pp. 1-44).* Greenwich, CT: Information Age Publishing.

Bandura, A. (2006b). Social cognitive theory. In S. Rogelberg (Ed.). *Encyclopedia of Industrial/Organizational Psychology.* Beverly Hills: Sage Publications.

Bandura, A. (2007). Albert Bandura. In G. Lindzey & W.M. Runyan (Eds.) *A history of psychology in autobiography*, Vol. IX. (pp. 43–75). Washington, DC: American Psychological Association.

Bandura, A. & Walters, R. (1963). *Social learning and personality development.* New York: Holt, Rinehart, & Winston.

Banerjee, R. & Lintern, V. (2000). Boys will be boys: The effect of social evaluation concerns on gender-typing. *Social Development, 9,* 397–408.

Banks, M. S. & Ginsburg, A. P. (1985). Infant visual preferences: A review and new theoretical treatment. In H. W. Reese (Ed.), *Advances in child development and behavior* (Vol. 19). Orlando, FL: Academic Press.

Barber, N. (2005). Educational and ecological correlates of IQ: A cross-national investigation. *Intelligence, 33,* 273–284.

Bard, C., Hay, L., & Fleury, M. (1990). Timing and accuracy of visually directed movements in children: Control of direction and amplitude components. *Journal of Experimental Child Psychology, 50,* 102–118.

Bard, K. A. (2000). Crying in infant primates: Insights into the development of crying in chimpanzees. In R. G. Barr, B. Hopkins, & J. A. Green (Eds.) *Crying as a sign, a symptom, and a signal* (pp. 157–175). London, UK: MacKeith Press.

Barglow, P., Vaughn, B. E., & Molitor, N. (1987). Effects of maternal absence due to employment on the quality of infant-mother attachment. *Child Development, 58,* 945–954.

Barkley, R. A. (2006). *Attention-deficit hyperactivity disorder: A handbook for diagnosis and treatment* (3rd ed.). New York: Guilford.

Barnard, K. E., Bee, H. L., & Hammond, M. A. (1984). Home environment and cognitive development in a healthy, low-risk sample: The Seattle study. In A. W. Gottfried (Ed.), *Home environment and early cognitive development.* New York: Academic Press.

Barnard-Brak, L., Sulak, T., & Ivey, J.K. (2011). Macrocephaly in children with autism spectrum disorders. *Pediatric Neurology, 44,* 97–100.

Barnea-Goraly, N., Menon, V., Eckert, M., Tamm, L., Bammer, R., Karchemskiy, A., Dant, C., & Reiss, A.L. (2005). White matter development during childhood and adolescence: A cross-sectional diffusion tensor imaging study. *Cerebral Cortex, 15,* 1848–1854.

Barnett, C. R., Leiderman, P. H., Grobstein, R., & Klaus, M. H. (1970). Neonatal separation: The maternal side of interactional deprivation. *Pediatrics, 45,* 197–205.

Barnett, D., Hunt, K. H., Butler, C. M., McCaskill, J. W. IV, Kaplan-Estrin, M., & Pipp-Siegel, S. (1999). Indices of attachment disorganization among toddlers with neurological and non-neurological problems. In J. Solomon & C. George (Eds.), *Attachment disorganization.* New York: Guilford.

Baron-Cohen, S. (1995). *Mindblindness: An essay on autism and theory of mind.* Cambridge, MA: MIT Press.

Baron-Cohen, S. (2000a). The cognitive neuroscience of autism: Evolutionary approaches. In M. Gassaniga (Ed.), *The new cognitive neurosciences* (2nd ed.). Cambridge, MA: MIT Press.

Baron-Cohen, S. (2000b). Theory of mind and autism: A fifteen year review. In S. Baron-Cohen, H. Tager-Flusberg, & D.J. Cohen (Eds.), *Understanding other minds: Perspectives from developmental cognitive neuroscience.* Oxford: Oxford University Press.

Barr, R. G. (2004). Early infant crying as a behavioral state rather than a signal. *Behavioral and Brain Sciences, 24,* 460.

Barr, R. G. (2006). Crying behavior and its importance for psychosocial development in children. In R. E. Tremblay, R. G. Barr, & R. DeV. Peters (Eds.) *Encyclopedia on early child development* (pp. 1–10). Montreal, Quebec: Center of Excellence for Early Childhood Development.

Barr, R. G, Barr, M., Fujiwara, T., Conway, J., Catherine, N., & Brant, R. (2009). Do educational materials change knowledge and behaviour about crying and shaken baby syndrome? A randomized controlled trial. *Canadian Medical Association Journal, 180,* 727–733.

Barr, R. G., Dowden, A., & Hayne, H. (1996). Developmental changes in deferred imitation by 6- to 24-month-old infants. *Infant Behavior and Development, 19,* 159–170.

Barr, R. G., Muentener, P., & Garcia, A. (2007). Age-related changes in deferred imitation from television by 6- to 18-month-olds. *Developmental Science, 10,* 910–921.

Barr, R. G., Paterson, J. A., MacMartin, L. M., Lehtonen, L., & Young, S. N. (2005). Prolonged and unsoothable crying bouts in infants with and without Colic. *Journal of Developmental and Behavioral Pediatrics, 26,* 14–23.

Barr, R. G., Rivara, F. P., Barr, M., Cummings, P., Taylor, J., Lengua, L. J., & Meredith-Benitz, E. (2009). Effectiveness of educational materials designed to change knowledge and behaviors regarding crying and shaken-baby syndrome in mothers of newborns: a randomized, controlled trial. *Pediatrics, 123,* 972–80.

Barr, R. G., Rovee-Collier, C., & Campanella, J. (2005). Retrieval protracts deferred imitation by 6-month-olds. *Infancy, 7,* 263–283.

Barr, R. G., Trent, R. B., & Cross, J. (2006). Age-related incidence curve of hospitalized shaken baby syndrome cases: convergent evidence for crying as a trigger to shaking. *Child Abuse and Neglect, 30,* 7–16.

Barrera, M. & Maurer, D. (1981a). The perception of facial expressions by the three-month-old. *Child Development, 52,* 203–206.

Barrera, M. & Maurer, D. (1981b). Recognition of mother's photographed face by the three-month-old infant. *Child Development, 52,* 714–716.

Barrett, D. E. & Yarrow, M. R. (1977). Prosocial behavior, social inferential ability, and assertiveness in children. *Child Development, 48,* 475–481.

Barriga, A. Q., Sullivan-Cosetti, M., Gibbs, J. C. (2009). Moral cognitive correlates of empathy in juvenile deliquents. *Criminal Behaviour and Mental Health, 19,* 253–264.

Barrington, K. J. & Finer, N. (2010). Cochrane review: Inhaled nitric oxide for respiratory failure in preterm infants. *Evidence-Based Child Health: A Cochrane Review Journal, 5*(1), 301–336.

Barth, F. (1997). How is the self conceptualized? Variations among cultures. In U. Neisser & D. A. Jopling (Eds.), *The conceptual self in context: Culture, experience, self-understanding.* Cambridge: Cambridge University Press.

Barth, H., La Mont, K., Lipton, J., & Spelke, E. S. (2005). Abstract number and arithmetic in preschool children. *Proceedings of the National Academy of Sciences, 102,* 14116–14121.

Barth, J., Povinelli, D. J., & Cant, J. G. H. (2004). Bodily origins of self. In D. Beike, J. Lampinen, & D. Behrend (Eds.), *The self and memory* (pp. 11–43). New York: Psychology Press.

Bartrip, J., Morton, J., & de Schonen, S. (2001). Response to mother's face in 3-week to 5-month-old infants. *British Journal of Developmental Psychology, 19,* 219–232.

Basow, A. A. (2010). Gender in the classroom. *Handbook of gender research in psychology: Vol. 1: Gender research in general and experimental psychology* (pp. 277–295). New York, NY: Springer.

Basso, D., Ferrari, M., & Palladino, P. (2010). Prospective memory and working memory: Asymmetrical effects during frontal lobe TMS stimulation. *Neuropsychologia, 48,* 3282–3290.

Bates, E., Camaioni, L., & Volterra, V. (1975). The acquisition of performatives prior to speech. *Merrill-Palmer Quarterly, 21,* 205–226.

Bates, E. & Carnevale, G. F. (1993). New directions in research on language development. *Developmental Review, 13,* 436–470.

Bates, E. & MacWhinney, B. (1987). Competition, variation, language learning. In B. MacWhinney (Ed.), *Mechanisms of language acquisition.* Hillsdale, NJ: Erlbaum.

Bates, E., O'Connell, B., & Shore, C. (1987). Language and communication in infancy. In J. D. Osofsky (Ed.), *Handbook of infant development (2nd ed.).* New York: Wiley.

Bates, E. & Roe, K. (2001). Language development in children with unilateral brain injury. In C. A. Nelson & M. Luciana (Eds.), *Handbook of developmental cognitive neuroscience* (pp. 281–307). Cambridge, MA: MIT Press.

Bates, E. & Snyder, L. (1985). The cognitive hypothesis in language development. In I. Uzgiris & J. M. Hunt (Eds.), *Research with scales of psychological development in infancy.* Champaign-Urbana, IL: University of Illinois Press.

Bates, J. E. (1987). Temperament in infancy. In J. D. Osofsky (Ed.), *Handbook of infant development* (2nd ed.). New York: Wiley.

Bates, J. E. & Bayles, K. (1984). Objective and subjective components in mothers' perceptions of their children from age 6 months to 3 years. *Merrill-Palmer Quarterly, 30,* 111–130.

Bates, J. E., Bayles, K., Bennett, D. S., Ridge, B., & Brown, M. M. (1991). Origins of externalizing behavior problems at eight years of age. In D. Pepler & K. H. Rubin (Eds.), *Development and treatment of childhood aggression.* Hillsdale, NJ: Erlbaum.

Bates, J. E. & Pettit, G. S. (2007). Temperament, parenting, and socialization. In J. E. Grusec & P. D. Hastings (Eds.), *Handbook of socialization: Theory and research* (pp. 153–177). New York: Guilford.

Bates, J. E., Schermerhorn, A. C., & Goodnight, J. A. (2010). Temperament and personality through the life span. In M. E. Lamb & A. M. Freund (Eds.), *The handbook of life-span development, Vol. 2, Social and emotional development* (pp. 208–253). Hoboken, NJ: Wiley.

Bates, J. E. & Wachs, T. D. (Eds.) (1994). *Temperament: Individual differences at the interface of biology and behavior.* Washington, DC: American Psychological Association.

Bates, J. E., Wachs, T. D., & Emde, R. N. (1994). Toward practical uses for biological concepts of temperament. In J. E. Bates & T. D. Wachs (Eds.), *Temperament: Individual differences at the interface of biology and behavior.* Washington, DC: American Psychological Association.

Batson, C. D. (2010). Empathy-induced altruistic motivation. In M. Mikulincer & P. R. Shaver (Eds.), *Prosocial motives, emotions, and behavior: The better angels of our nature* (pp. 15–34). Washington, DC: American Psychological Association.

Batstra, L., Hadders-Algra, M., & Neeleman, J. (2003). Effect of antenatal exposure to maternal smoking on behavioural problems and academic achievement in childhood: Prospective evidence from a Dutch birth cohort. *Early Human Development, 75,* 21–33.

Battistich, V. A. (2008). The Child Development Project: Creating caring school communities. In L. P. Nucci & D. Narvaez (Eds.), *Handbook of moral and character education* (pp. 328–351). New York, NY: Routledge.

Batty, M. & Taylor, M. J. (2006). The development of emotional face processing during childhood. *Developmental Science, 9,* 207–220.

Bauer, D. J., Goldfield, B. A., & Reznick, J. S. (2002). Alternative approaches to analyzing individual differences in the rate of early vocabulary development. *Applied Psycholinguistics, 23,* 313–326.

Bauer, P. J. (1993). Memory for gender-consistent and gender-inconsistent event sequences by twenty-five month-old children. *Child Development, 64,* 285–297.

Bauer, P. J. (2002). Early memory development. In U. Goswami (Ed.), *Blackwell handbook of childhood cognitive development.* Madden, MA: Blackwell Publishers.

Bauer, P. J. (2005). Developments in declarative memory: Decreasing susceptibility to storage failure over the second year of life. *Psychological Science, 16,* 41–47.

Bauer, P. J. (2007). *Remembering the times of our lives: Memory in infancy and beyond.* Mahwah, NJ: Lawrence Erlbaum Associates Publishers.

Bauer, P. J. (2009). The cognitive neuroscience of the development of memory. In M. Courage & N. Cowan (Eds.), *The Development of Memory in Infancy and Childhood, Second Edition* (pp. 155–144). New York, NY: Psychology Press.

Bauer, P. J. & Fivush, R. (1992). Constructing event representations: Building on a foundation of variation and enabling relations. *Cognitive Development, 2,* 381–401.

Bauer, P. J., Kroupina, M. G., Schwade, J. A., Dropik, P. L., & Wewerka, S. S. (1998). If memory serves, will language? Later verbal accessibility of early memories. *Development and Psychopathology, 10,* 655–679.

Bauer, P. J., Larkina, M., & Deocampo, J. (2011). Early memory development. In U. Goswani (Ed.), *The Wiley-Blackwell handbook on childhood cognitive development* (2nd Edition, pp. 153–179). West Sussex, UK: Wiley-Blackwell Publishing.

Bauer, P. J. & Lukowski, A. F. (2010). The memory is in the details: Relations between memory for the specific features of events and long-term recall in infancy. *Journal of Experimental Child Psychology, 107(1),* 1–14.

Bauer, P. J. & Mandler, J. M. (1992). Putting the horse before the cart: The use of temporal order in recall of events by one-year-old children. *Developmental Psychology, 28,* 441–452.

Bauer, P. J. & Travis, L. L. (1993). The fabric of an event: Different sources of temporal invariance differentially affect 24-month-olds' recall. *Cognitive Development, 8,* 319–341.

Bauer, P. J., Wenner, J. A., Dropik, P. L., & Wewerka, S. S. (2000). Parameters of remembering and forgetting in the transition from infancy to early childhood. *Monographs of the Society for Research in Child Development, 65* (4, Serial No. 263).

Bauer, P. J., Wiebe, S. A., Carver, L. J., Lukowski, A. F., Haight, J. C., Waters, J. M., & Nelson, C. A. (2006). Electrophysiological indexes of encoding and behavioral indexes of recall: Examining relations and developmental change late in the first year of life. *Developmental Neuropsychology, 29,* 293–320.

Bauerfeld, S. L. & Lachenmeyer, J. R. (1992). Prenatal nutritional status and intellectual development: Critical review and evaluation. In B. B. Lahey & A. E. Kazdin (Eds.), *Advances in clinical child psychology* (Vol. 14). New York: Plenum.

Baumrind, D. (1967). Child care practices anteceding three patterns of preschool behavior. *Genetic Psychology Monographs, 75,* 43–88.

Baumrind, D. (1971). Current patterns of parental authority. *Developmental Psychology Monograph, 4,* 1–103.

Baumrind, D. (1989). Rearing competent children. In W. Damon (Ed.), *Child development today and tomorrow.* San Francisco: Jossey-Bass.

Baumrind, D. (1991). The influence of parenting style on adolescent competence and substance abuse. *Journal of Early Adolescence, 11,* 56–95.

Baumrind, D. & Black, A. E. (1967). Socialization practices associated with dimensions of competence in preschool boys and girls. *Child Development, 38,* 291–327.

Bauserman, M. (2002). Child adjustment in joint-custody versus sole-custody arrangements: A meta-analytic review. *Journal of Family Psychology, 16,* 91–102.

Baydar, N., Greek, A., & Brooks-Gunn, J. (1997). A longitudinal study of the effects of the birth of a sibling during the first 6 years of life. *Journal of Marriage and the Family, 59,* 939–956.

Bayley, N. (1956). Individual patterns of development. *Child Development, 27,* 45–74.

Bayley, N. (1969). *Manual for the Bayley Scales of Infant Development.* New York: Psychological Corporation.

Bayley, N. (1970). Development of mental abilities. In P. H. Mussen (Ed.), *Carmichael's manual of child psychology* (3rd ed., Vol. 1). New York: Wiley.

Bayley, N. (2005). *Bayley Scales of Infant Development, Third Edition.* San Antonio, TX: Psychological Corporation.

Bearison, D. (1982). New directions in studies of social interactions and cognitive growth. In F. C. Serafica (Ed.), *Social-cognitive development in context.* New York: Guilford.

Bearison, D. & Dorval, B. (2002). *Collaborative cognition: Children negotiating ways of knowing.* Westport, CT: Ablex.

Beauchamp, G. K., Cowart, B. J., Mennella, J. A., & Marsh, R. R. (1994). Infant salt taste: Developmental, methodological, and contextual factors. *Developmental Psychobiology 27,* 353–365.

Beauchamp, G. K. & Menella, J.A. (2009). Early flavor learning and its impact on later feeding behavior. *Journal of Pediatric Gastroenterology and Nutrition, 48,* S25–S30.

Beaulieu, D. A. & Bugental, D. B. (2007). An evolutionary approach to socialization. In J. E. Grusec & P. D. Hastings (Eds.), *Handbook of socialization: Theory and research* (pp. 71–95). New York: Guilford.

Bebbington, M. W., Johnson, M. P., Wilson, D., & Adzick, N. S. (2006). Open fetal surgery. In J. M. Vugt & L. P. Schulman (Eds.), *Prenatal medicine* (pp. 493–507). New York, NY: Taylor and Francis.

Bech, B. H., Nohr, E. A., Vaeth, M., Henriksen, T. B., & Olsen, J. (2005). Coffee and fetal death: A cohort study with prospective data. *American Journal of Epidemiology, 162,* 983–990.

Bechara, A., Damasio, H., Tranel, D., & Damasio, A. R. (1997). Deciding advantageously before knowing the advantage strategy. *Science, 275,* 1293–1295.

Becker, J. (1994). "Sneak-shoes, " "sworders," and "nose-beards": A case study of lexical innovation. *First Language, 14,* 195–211.

Beckwith, L. & Parmelee, A. (1986). EEG patterns of preterm infants, home environment, and later IQ. *Child Development, 57,* 777–789.

Bedard, J. & Chi, M. T. H. (1992). Expertise. *Current Directions in Psychological Science, 1,* 135–139.

Beebe, B., Alson, D., Jaffe, J., Feldstein, S., & Crown, C. (1988). Vocal congruence in mother-infant play. *Journal of Psycholinguistic Research, 17,* 245–259.

Beebe, B., Jaffe, J., Markese, S., Buck, K., Chen, H., Cohen, P., Bahrick, L., Andrews, H., Feldstein, S. (2010). The origins of 12-month attachment: A microanalysis of 4-month mother-infant interaction. *Attachment & Human Development, 12,* 6–141.

Behl-Chadha, G. (1996). Basic-level and superordinate-like categorical representations in early infancy. *Cognition, 60*, 105–141.

Behrend, D. A. (1988). Overextensions in early language comprehension: Evidence from a signal detection approach. *Journal of Child Language, 15*, 63–75.

Behrend, D. A., Rosengren, K. A., & Perlmutter, M. (1989). A new look at children's private speech: The effects of age, task difficulty, and parental presence. *International Journal of Behavioral Development, 12*, 305–320.

Behrman, R. E., Kliegman, R. M., & Jenson, H. B. (Eds.). (2000). *Nelson textbook of pediatrics* (16th ed.). Philadelphia: W. B. Saunders.

Beier, E. G. (1991). Freud: Three contributions. In G. A. Kimble, M. Wertheimer, & C. L. White (Eds.), *Portraits of pioneers in psychology.* Hillsdale, NJ: Erlbaum.

Beilin, H. (1992a). Piaget's enduring contribution to developmental psychology. *Developmental Psychology, 28*, 191–204.

Beilin, H. (1992b). Piaget's new theory. In H. Beilin & P. B. Pufall (Eds.), *Piaget's theory: Prospects and possibilities.* Hillsdale, NJ: Erlbaum.

Bell, A. H., Hadj-Bouziane, F., Frihauf, J. B., Tootell, R. B. H., & Ungerleider, L. G. (2009). Object representations in the temporal cortex of monkeys and humans as revealed by functional magnetic resonance imaging. *Journal of Neurophysiology, 101*, 688–700.

Bell, A. P., Weinberg, M. S., & Hammersmith, S. K. (1981). *Sexual preference: Its development in men and women.* Bloomington, IN: Indiana University Press.

Bell, J. H. & Bromnick, R. D. (2003). The social reality of the imaginary audience: A grounded theory approach. *Adolescence, 38*, 205–219.

Bell, M. A. & Fox, N. A. (1996). Crawling experience is related to changes in cortical organization during infancy: Evidence from EEG coherence. *Developmental Psychobiology, 29*, 551–561.

Bell, M. A. & Fox, N.A. (1992). The relations between frontal brain electrical activity and cognitive development during infancy. *Child Development, 63*, 1142–1163.

Bell, M. A., Wolfe, C. D., & Adkins, D. R. (2007). Frontal lobe development during infancy and childhood. In D. Coch, G. Dawson, & K. W. Fisher (Eds.), *Human behavior, learning and the developing brain: Typical development* (pp. 247–276). New York: Guilford.

Bell, R. Q. (1968). A reinterpretation of the direction of effects of socialization. *Psychological Review, 75*, 81–95.

Bellinger, D. C. & Adams, H. F. (2001). Environmental pollutant exposures and children's cognitive abilities. In R. J. Sternberg & E. L. Grigorenko (Eds.), *Environmental effects on cognitive abilities.* Mahwah, NJ: Erlbaum.

Bellinger, D. C., Leviton, A., Needleman, H. L., Waternaux, C., & Rabinowitz, M. (1986). Low-level lead exposure and infant development in the first year. *Neurobehavioral Toxicology and Teratology, 8*, 151–161.

Belsky, J. (1988). The "effects" of infant day care reconsidered. *Early Childhood Research Quarterly, 3*, 235–272.

Belsky, J. (2006). Determinants and consequences of infant-parent attachment. In L. Balter & C. Tamis-LeMonda (Eds.), *Child psychology: A handbook of contemporary issues* (2nd ed.) (pp. 53–77). New York: Psychology Press.

Belsky, J. & Fearon, R. M. P. (2008). Precursors of attachment security. In J. Cassidy & P. R. Shaver (Eds.), *Handbook of attachment: Theory, research, and clinical applications (2nd edition)* (pp. 295–316). New York, NY: Guilford.

Belsky, J., Fish, M., & Isabella, R. (1991). Continuity and discontinuity in infant negative and positive emotionality: Family antecedents and attachment consequences. *Developmental Psychology, 27*, 421–431.

Belsky, J. & Rovine, M. (1988). Nonmaternal care in the first year of life and infant-parent attachment security. *Child Development, 59*, 157–167.

Bem, D. J. (2000). Exotic becomes erotic: Interpreting the biological correlates of sexual orientation. *Archives of Sexual Behavior, 29*, 531–548.

Bem, D. J. (2001). Exotic becomes erotic: Integrating biological and experiential antecedents of sexual orientation. In A. R. D'Augelli & C. J. Patterson (Eds.), *Lesbian, gay, and bisexual identities and youth: Psychological perspectives.* New York: Oxford University Press.

Bem, S. L. (1981). Gender schema theory: A cognitive account of sex typing. *Psychological Review, 88*, 354–364.

Bem, S. L. (1989). Genital knowledge and gender constancy in preschool children. *Child Development, 60*, 649–662.

Benasich, A. A. & Brooks-Gunn, J. (1996). Maternal attitudes and knowledge of child-rearing: Associations with family and child outcomes. *Child Development, 67*, 1186–1205.

Benderly, B. L. (2007). Experimental drugs on trial. *Scientific American, 297(4)*, 92–99.

Benenson, J. F. & Dweck, C. S. (1986). The development of trait explanations and self-evaluations in the academic and social domains. *Child Development, 57*, 1179–1187.

Benenson, J. F., Markovits, H., Roy, R., & Denko, P. (2003). Behavioural rules underlying learning to share: Effects of development and context. *International Journal of Behavioral Development, 27*, 116–121.

Benes, F. M. (2001). The development of the prefrontal cortex: The maturation of neurotransmitter systems and their interaction. In C. A. Nelson & M. Luciana (Eds.), *Handbook of developmental cognitive neuroscience* (pp. 79–92). Cambridge, MA: MIT Press.

Bennett, I. J., Motes, M. A., Rao, N. K., & Rypma, B. (2011). White matter integrity predicts visual search performance in young and older adults. *Neurobiology of Aging, 33*, e21–e31.

Benoit, D. (1993). Failure to thrive and feeding disorders. In C. H. Zeanah Jr. (Ed.), *Handbook of infant mental development.* New York: Guilford.

Benson, J. B. (1990). The significance and development of crawling in human infancy. In J. E. Clark & J. H. Humphrey (Eds.), *Advances in motor development research* (Vol. 3). New York: AMS Press.

Benson, J. B. & Uzgiris, I. C. (1985). Effects of self-initiated locomotion on infant search activity. *Developmental Psychology, 21*, 923–931.

Beran, T. N., Ramirez-Serrano, A., Kuzyk, R., Fior, M., & Nugent, S. (2011). Understanding how children understand robots: Perceived animism in child-robot interaction. *International Journal of Human-Computer Studies, 69*, 539–550.

Berenbaum, S. A., Martin, C. L., & Ruble, D. N. (2008). Gender development. In W. Damon & R. M. Lerner (Eds.), *Child and adolescent development: An advanced course* (pp. 647–695). Hoboken, NJ: John Wiley & Sons.

Berenbaum, S. A., Martin, C. L., Hanish, L. D., Briggs, P. T., & Fabes, R. A. (2008). Sex differences in children's play. In J. B. Becker, K. J. Berkley, N. Geary, E. Hampson, J. Herman, & E. Young (Eds.) *Sex differences in the brain: From genes to behavior* (pp. 275–290). New York, NY: Oxford University Press.

Berenbaum, S. A. & Snyder, E. (1995). Early hormonal influences on childhood sex-typed activity and playmate preferences: Implications for the development of sexual orientation. *Developmental Psychology, 31*, 31–42.

Berg, D. H. (2008). Working memory and arithmetic calculation in children: The contributory roles of processing speed, short-term memory, and reading. *Journal of Experimental Child Psychology, 99*, 288–308.

Berg, W. K. & Berg, K. M. (1987). Psychophysiological development in infancy. In J. Osofsky (Ed.), *Handbook of infant development* (2nd ed.). New York: Wiley.

Berger, S. E. (2010). Locomotor expertise predicts infants' perseverative errors. *Developmental Psychology, 46*, 326–336.

Berk, L. E. (1994). Why children talk to themselves. *Scientific American, 271*, 78–83.

Berk, L. E. & Garvin, R. A. (1984). Development of private speech among low-income Appalachian children. *Developmental Psychology, 20* (2), 271–286.

Berk, L. E. & Landau, S. (1993). Private speech of learning disabled and normally achieving children in classroom academic and laboratory contexts. *Child Development, 64*, 556–571.

Berko, J. (1958). The child's learning of English morphology. *Word, 14*, 150–177.

Berkowitz, M. W., Gibbs, J. C., & Broughton, J. M. (1980). The relation of moral judgment stage disparity to developmental effects of peer dialogues. *Merrill-Palmer Quarterly, 26*, 341–357.

Berlin, L. J., Brooks-Gunn, J., McCarton, C., & McCormick, M. C. (1998). The effectiveness of early intervention: Examining risk factors and pathways to enhanced development. *Preventive Medicine, 27*, 238–245.

Berlin, L. J., Cassidy, J., & Appleyard, K. (2008). The influence of early attachments on other relationships. In J. Cassidy & P. R. Shaver (Eds.), *Handbook of attachment: Theory, research, and clinical applications (2nd edition)* (pp. 333–347). New York, NY: Guilford.

Berndt, T. J. (1979). Developmental changes in conformity to peers and parents. *Developmental Psychology, 15*, 608–616.

Berndt, T. J. (1981). Age changes and changes over time in prosocial intentions and behavior between friends. *Developmental Psychology, 17*, 408–416.

Berndt, T. J. (1986). Sharing between friends: Contexts and consequences. In E. C. Mueller & C. R. Cooper (Eds.), *Process and outcome in peer relationships.* New York: Academic Press.

Berndt, T. J. (1988). The nature and significance of children's friendships. In R. Vasta (Ed.), *Annals of child development* (Vol. 5). Greenwich, CT: JAI Press.

Berndt, T. J. (1989). Friendships in childhood and adolescence. In W. Damon (Ed.), *Child development today and tomorrow.* San Francisco: Jossey-Bass.

Berndt, T. J. (2002). Friendship quality and social development. *Current Directions in Psychological Science, 11*, 7–10.

Berndt, T. J. & Heller, K. A. (1986). Gender stereotypes and social inferences: A developmental study. *Journal of Personality and Social Psychology, 50*, 889–898.

Berndt, T. J. & Keefe, K. (1995). Friends' influence on adolescents' adjustment to school. *Child Development, 66*, 1312–1329.

Berndt, T. J., Miller, K. E., & Park, K. (1989). Adolescents' perceptions of friends' and parents' influence on aspects of their school adjustment. *Journal of Early Adolescence, 9*, 419–435.

Berndt, T. J. & Perry, T. B. (1990). Distinctive features and effects of adolescent friendships. In R. Montemayor, G. R. Adams, & T. P. Gullotta (Eds.), *From childhood to adolescence: A transitional period?* London: Sage.

Bernier, A. & Meins, E. (2008). A threshold approach to understanding the origins of attachment disorganization. *Developmental Psychology, 44,* 969–982.

Bernier, J. G. & Siegel, D. H. (1994). Attention-deficit hyperactivity disorder: A family ecological systems perspective. *Families in Society, 75,* 142–150.

Berridge, K. C. (2000). Measuring hedonic impact in animals and infants: microstructure of affective taste reactivity patterns. *Neuroscience & Biobehavioral Reviews, 24,* 173–198.

Berry, J. W. (1966). Temme and Eskimo perceptual skills. *International Journal of Psychology, 1,* 207–229.

Berry, J. W. (2002). *Cross-cultural psychology: Research and applications.* New York, NY: Cambridge University Press.

Berry, J. W. (2007). Acculturation. In J. Grusec & P. Hastings (Eds.), *Handbook of socialization: Theory and research* (pp. 543–558). New York: Guilford.

Bertenthal, B. I. (1996). Origins and early development of perception, action, and representation. *Annual Review of Psychology, 47,* 431–459.

Bertenthal, B. I. & Bai, D. L. (1989). Infants' sensitivity to optical flow for controlling posture. *Developmental Psychology, 25,* 936–945.

Bertenthal, B. I., Campos, J. J., & Barrett, K. (1984). Self-produced locomotion: An organizer of emotional, cognitive, and social development in infancy. In R. Emde & R. Harmon (Eds.), *Continuities and discontinuities in development.* New York: Plenum.

Bertenthal, B. I., Campos, J. J., & Haith, M. M. (1980). Development of visual organization: The perception of subjective contours. *Child Development, 51,* 1072–1080.

Bertenthal, B. I., Campos, J. J., & Kermoian, R. (1994). An epigenetic perspective on the development of self-produced locomotion and its consequences. *Current Directions in Psychological Science, 3,* 140–145.

Bertenthal, B. I. & Clifton, R. K. (1998). Perception and action. In W. Damon (Series Ed.) & D. Kuhn & R. S. Siegler (Vol. Eds.), *Handbook of child psychology: Vol. 2. Cognition, perception, and language* (5th ed.). New York: Wiley.

Bertenthal, B. I., Longo, M. R., & Kenny, S. (2007). Phenomenal permanence and the development of predictive tracking in infancy. *Child Development, 78,* 350–363.

Bertin, E. & Bhatt, R. S. (2006). Three-month-olds' sensitivity to orientation cues in the three-dimensional depth plane. *Journal of Experimental Child Psychology, 93,* 45–62.

Bertin, E. & Striano, T. (2006). The still-face response in newborn, 1.5-, and 3-month-old infants. *Infant Behavior and Development, 29,* 294–297.

Best, C. T. (1995). Learning to perceive the sound pattern of English. In C. K. Rovee-Collier & L. P. Lipsitt (Eds.), *Advances in infancy research* (Vol. 9). Norwood, NJ: Ablex.

Best, D. L. (2001). Cross-cultural gender roles. In J. Worell (Ed.), *Encyclopedia of women and gender* (Vol. 1). San Diego, CA: Academic Press.

Best, D. L. (2010). Gender. In M. H. Borstein (Ed.), *Handbook of cultural developmental science* (pp. 209–222). New York, NY: Psychology Press.

Betrán, A.P., Merialdi, M., Lauer, J.A., Bing-Shun, W., Thomas, J., Van Look, P., & Wagner, M. (2007). Rates of cesarean section: Analysis of global, regional and national estimates. *Paediatric and Perinatal Epidemiology, 21,* 98–113.

Bever, T. G. (Ed.). (1982). *Regressions in mental development: Basic phenomena and theories.* Hillsdale, NJ: Erlbaum.

Bhatt, R. S. & Rovee-Collier, C. (1994). Perception and 24-hour retention of feature relations in infancy. *Developmental Psychology, 30,* 142–150.

Bhavnagri, N. & Parke, R. D. (1991). Parents as direct facilitators of children's peer relationships: Effects of age of child and sex of parent. *Journal of Social and Personal Relationships, 8,* 423–440.

Bialystok, E. (2001). *Bilingualism in development: Language, literacy, and cognition.* New York: Cambridge University Press.

Bialystok, E. (2007). Cognitive effects of bilingualism: How linguistic experience leads to cognitive change. *International Journal of Bilingual Education and Bilingualism, 10,* 210–223.

Bickerton, D. (1984). The language bioprogram hypothesis. *Behavioral and Brain Sciences, 7,* 173–187.

Bienert, H. & Schneider, B. (1995). Deficit-specific social skills training with peer-nominated aggressive-disruptive and sensitive-isolated preadolescents. *Journal of Clinical Child Psychology, 24,* 287–299.

Bierman, K. L. & Powers, C. J. (2009). Social skills training to improve peer relations. In K. H. Rubin, W. M. Bukowski, & B. Laursen (Eds.), *Handbook of peer interactions, relationships, and groups* (pp. 603–621). New York: Guilford.

Biernat, M. (1991). A multicomponent, developmental analysis of sex typing. *Sex Roles, 24,* 567–586.

Bigelow, A. E. (1981). The correspondence between self- and image movement as a cue to self-recognition for young children. *Journal of Genetic Psychology, 139,* 11–26.

Bigelow, A. E., MacLean, K., & Proctor, J. (2004). The role of joint attention in the development of infants' play with objects. *Developmental Science, 7,* 518–526.

Bigler, R. S., Brown, C. S., & Markell, M. (2001). When groups are not created equal: Effects of group status on the formation of intergroup attitudes in children. *Child Development, 72,* 1151–1162.

Bigler, R. S. & Liben, L. S. (1990). The role of attitudes and interventions in gender-schematic processing. *Child Development, 61,* 1440–1452.

Bigler, R. S. & Liben, L. S. (1993). A cognitive-developmental approach to social stereotyping and reconstructive memory in Euro-American children. *Child Development, 64,* 1507–1518.

Biological systems. (1988, June 10). *Science, 240,* 1383.

Birch, S. A. J. & Bloom, P. (2007). The curse of knowledge in reasoning about false beliefs. *Psychological Science, 18,* 382–386.

Birnholz, J. C. & Benacerraf, B. R. (1983). The development of human fetal hearing. *Science, 222,* 516–518.

Biro, F. M., McMahon, R. P., Striegel-Moore, R., Crawford, P. B., Obarzanek, E., Morrison, J. A., et al. (2001). Impact of timing of pubertal maturation on growth in black and white female adolescents: The National Heart, Lung, and Blood Institute Growth and Health Study. *Journal of Pediatrics, 138,* 636–643.

Bisanz, J. & Lefevre, J. (1990). Strategic and nonstrategic processing in the development of mathematical cognition. In D. F. Bjorklund (Ed.), *Children's strategies: Contemporary views of cognitive development* (pp. 213–244). Hillsdale, NJ: Erlbaum.

Bishop, E. G., Cherny, S. S., Corley, R., Plomin, R., DeFries, J. C., & Hewitt, J. K. (2003). Developmental genetic analysis of general cognitive ability from 1 to 12 years in a sample of adoptees, biological siblings, and twins. *Intelligence, 31,* 31–49.

Bjorklund, D. F. (1997). The role of immaturity in human development. *Psychological Bulletin, 122,* 153–169.

Bjorklund, D. F. (2000a). *Children's thinking* (3rd ed.). Belmont, CA: Wadsworth.

Bjorklund, D. F. (Ed.). (2000b). *False-memory creation in children and adults: Theory, research, and implications.* Mahwah, NJ: Erlbaum.

Bjorklund, D. F. (2006). Mother knows best: Epigenetic inheritance, maternal effects, and the evolution of human intelligence. *Developmental Review, 26,* 213–242.

Bjorklund, D. F., Dukes, C., & Brown, R. D. (2009). The development of memory strategies. In M.L. Courage & N. Cowan (Eds.), *The development of memory in infancy and childhood* (pp. 145–175). Hove, U.K.: Psychology Press.

Bjorklund, D. F., Muir-Broaddus, J. E., & Schneider, W. (1990). The role of knowledge in the development of strategies. In D. F. Bjorklund (Ed.), *Children's strategies: Contemporary views of cognitive development.* Hillsdale, NJ: Erlbaum.

Bjorklund, D. F. & Pellegrini, A. D. (2000). Child development and evolutionary psychology. *Child Development, 71,* 1687–1708.

Bjorklund, D. F. & Pellegrini, A. D. (2002a). Evolutionary perspectives on social development. In P. K. Smith & C. H. Hart (Eds.), *Blackwell handbook of childhood social development.* Madden, MA: Blackwell Publishers.

Bjorklund, D. F. & Pellegrini, A. D. (2002b). *The origins of human nature: Evolutionary developmental psychology.* Washington, DC: American Psychological Association.

Bjorklund, D. F. & Pellegrini, A, D. (2011). Evolutionary perspectives on social development. In P.K.Smith & K.H.Hart (Eds.). *The Wiley-Blackwell handbook of childhood social development, 2nd edition* (pp. 64–81). Hoboken, NJ: Wiley.

Bjorklund, D. F. & Rosenblum, K. E. (2002). Context effects in children's selection and use of simple arithmetic strategies. *Journal of Cognition and Development, 3,* 225–242.

Bjorklund, D. F. & Schneider, W. (1996) The interaction of knowledge, aptitude, and strategies in children's memory performance. In H. W. Reese (Ed.), *Advances in child development and behavior* (Vol. 26). San Diego, CA: Academic Press.

Bjorklund, D. F., Younger, J. L., & Pellegrini, A. D. (2002). The evolution of parenting and evolutionary approaches to childrearing. In M. H. Bornstein (Ed.), *Handbook of parenting* (2nd ed., Vol. 2). Mahwah, NJ: Erlbaum.

Blachford, S. (2002). *The Gale encyclopedia of genetic disorders.* Detroit, MI: Gale Group.

Blachman, D. R. (2005). Predictors of peer rejection, acceptance, and victimization among girls with and without ADHD. *Dissertation Abstracts International: Section B: The Sciences and Engineering, 65,* 4817.

Black, J. E., Jones, T. A., Nelson, C. A., & Greenough, W. T. (1998). Neuronal plasticity and the developing brain. In N. E. Alessi, J. T. Coyle, S. I. Harrison, & S. Eth (Eds.), *Handbook of child and adolescent psychiatry. Vol. 6: Basic psychiatric science and treatment.* New York, NY: Wiley.

Blackwell, L. S., Trzesniewski, K. H., & Dweck, C. S. (2007). Implicit theories of intelligence predict achievement across an adolescent transition: a longitudinal study and an intervention. *Child Development, 78,* 246–263.

Blaga, O. M. & Colombo, J. (2006). Visual processing and infant ocular latencies in the overlap paradigm. *Developmental Psychology, 42,* 1069–1076.

Blair, M. & Somerville, S. C. (2009). The importance of differentiation in young children's acquisition of expertise. *Cognition, 112*(2), 259–280.

Blake, J. (2000). *Routes to child language.* New York: Cambridge University Press.

Blakemore, S. J. & Frith, U. (2005). The learning brain: Lessons for education: A précis. *Developmental Science, 8,* 459–465.

Blanchard, R. (2004). Quantitative and theoretical analyses of the relation between older brothers and homosexuality in men. *Journal of Theoretical Biology, 230,* 173–187.

Blanchard, R. & Lippa, R. A. (2007). Birth order, sibling sex ratio, handedness, and sexual orientation of male and female participants in a BBC Internet research project. *Archives of Sexual Behavior, 36,* 163–176.

Blanchard, R., Zucker, K. J., Cavacas, A., Allin, S., Bradley, S. J., & Schachter, D. C. (2002). Fraternal birth order and birth weight in probably prehomosexual feminine boys. *Hormones and Behavior, 41,* 321–327.

Blasi, A. (1980). Bridging moral cognition and moral action: A critical review of the literature. *Psychological Bulletin, 88,* 1–45.

Blasi, A. (1983). Moral cognition and moral action: A theoretical perspective. *Developmental Review, 3,* 178–210.

Blass, E. M. & Camp, C. A. (2003). Changing determinants of crying termination in 6- to 12-week-old human infants. *Developmental Psychobiology, 42,* 312–316.

Blass, E. M., Ganchrow, J. R., & Steiner, J. E. (1984). Classical conditioning in newborn humans 2–48 hours of age. *Infant Behavior and Development, 7,* 223–235.

Blass, E. M. & Smith, B. A. (1992). Differential effects of sucrose, fructose, glucose, and lactose. *Developmental Psychology, 28,* 804–810.

Blatchford, P., Baines, E., & Pellegrini, A. (2003). The social context of school playground games: Sex and ethnic differences, and changes over time after entry to junior school. *British Journal of Developmental Psychology, 21,* 481–505.

Bloom, L. (1973). *One word at a time.* The Hague, Netherlands: Mouton.

Bloom, L. (1993, Winter). Word learning. *SRCD Newsletter,* 1–13.

Bloom, L. (1998). Language acquisition in developmental contexts. In W. Damon (Series Ed.) & D. Kuhn & R. S. Siegler (Vol. Eds.), *Handbook of child psychology: Vol. 2. Cognition, perception, and language* (5th ed.). New York: Wiley.

Bloom, L., Hood, L., & Lightbrown, N. P. (1974). Imitation in language development: If, when, and why. *Cognitive Psychology, 6,* 380–420.

Bloom, L., Lightbrown, P., & Hood, L. (1975). Structure and variation in child language. *Monographs of the Society for Research in Child Development, 40* (2, Serial No. 160).

Bloom, L., Margulis, C., Tinker, E., & Fujita, N. (1996). Early conversations and word learning: Contributions from child and adult. *Child Development, 67,* 3154–3175.

Bloom, P. (1996). Controversies in language acquisition: Word learning and the part of speech. In R. Gelman & T. Au (Eds.), *Perceptual and cognitive development.* San Diego, CA: Academic Press.

Bloom, P. (2000). *How children learn the meanings of words.* Cambridge, MA: MIT Press.

Bloom, P. & Markson, L. (1998). Intention and analogy in children's naming of pictorial representations. *Psychological Science, 9,* 200–204.

Blount, B. G. (1982). The ontogeny of emotions and their vocal expression in infants. In S. A. Kuczaj (Ed.), *Language development* (Vol. 2). Hillsdale, NJ: Erlbaum.

Blumenfeld, R. S. & Ranganath, C. (2007). Prefrontal cortex and long-term memory encoding: An integrative review of findings from neuropsychology and neuroimaging. *The Neuroscientist, 13,* 280–291.

Bobier, W. R., Guinta, A., Kurtz, S., & Howland, H. C. (2000). Prism induced accommodation in infants 3 to 6 months of age. *Vision Research, 40,* 529–537.

Boccia, M. & Campos, J. J. (1989). Maternal emotional signals, social referencing, and infants' reactions to strangers. In N. Eisenberg (Ed.), *New directions for child development: No. 44. Empathy and related emotional responses.* San Francisco: Jossey-Bass.

Boer, F. & Westenberg, P. M. (1994). The factor structure of the Buss and Plomin EAS Temperament Survey (Parental Ratings) in a Dutch sample of elementary school children. *Journal of Personality Assessment, 62,* 537–551.

Bogartz, R., Shinskey, J. L., & Schilling, T. H. (2000). Object permanence in five-and-a-half-month-old infants? *Infancy, 1,* 403–428.

Bohannon, J. N. III, Padgett, R. J., Nelson, K. E., & Mark, M. (1996). Useful evidence on negative evidence. *Developmental Psychology, 32,* 551–555.

Bohannon, J. N. III & Stanowicz, L. (1988). The issue of negative evidence: Adult responses to children's language errors. *Developmental Psychology, 24,* 684–689.

Boivin, M. & Hymel, S. (1997). Peer experiences and social self-perceptions: A sequential model. *Developmental Psychology, 33,* 135–145.

Boivin, M., Hymel, S., & Hodges, E. (2001). Toward a process view of peer rejection and harassment. In J. Juvonen & S. Graham (Eds.), *Peer harassment in school: The plight of the vulnerable and victimized* (pp. 265–289). New York: Guilford.

Boldizar, J. P., Perry, D. G., & Perry, L. C. (1989). Outcome values and aggression. *Child Development, 60,* 571–579.

Bolger, K. E. & Patterson, C. J. (2001). Developmental pathways from child maltreatment to peer rejection. *Child Development, 72,* 549–568.

Bollinger, J., Rubens, M. T., Zanto, T. P., & Gazzaley, A. (2010). Expectation-driven changes in cortical functional connectivity influence working memory and long-term memory performance. *The Journal of Neuroscience, 27,* 14399–14410.

Bonvillian, J. D. (1999). Sign language development. In M. Barrett (Ed.), *The Development of Language* (pp. 277–311). Hove, U.K.: Psychology Press.

Booth, A., Granger, D. A., Mazur, A., & Kivlighan, K. T. (2006). Testosterone and social behavior. *Social Forces, 85,* 167–191.

Booth-Laforce, C. & Kerns, K. A. (2008). Child-parent attachment relationships, peer relationships, and peer-group functioning. In K. H. Rubin, W. M. Bukowski, & B Laursen (Eds.), *Handbook of peer interactions, relationships, and groups* (pp. 490–507). New York, NY: Guilford.

Booth-LaForce, C., Oh, W., Kim, A. H., Rubin, K. H., Rose-Krasnor, L., & Burgess, K. (2006). Attachment, self-worth, and peer-group functioning in middle childhood. *Attachment and Human Development, 8,* 309–325.

Booth-LaForce, C., Rubin, K. H., Rose-Krasnor, L., & Burgess, K. (2004). Attachment and friendship predictors of psychosocial functioning in middle childhood and the mediating roles of social support and self-worth. In K. Kerns & R. Richardson (Eds.), *Attachment in Middle Childhood* (pp. 161–188). New York: Guilford.

Borenstein, M., Hedges, L. V., Higgins, J. P. T., & Rothstein, H. R. (2009). Introduction to meta-analysis. Chichester, UK: John Wiley & Sons.

Borke, H. (1975). Piaget's mountains revisited: Changes in the egocentric landscape. *Developmental Psychology, 11,* 240–243.

Bornstein, M. H. (2002). Parenting infants. In M. H. Bornstein (Ed.), *Handbook of parenting (2nd edition). Volume 1: Children and parenting.* (pp. 3–44). Mahwah, NJ: Erlbaum.

Bornstein, M. H. & Arterberry, M. E. (1999). Perceptual development. In M. H. Bornstein & M. E. Lamb (Eds.), *Developmental psychology: An advanced textbook* (4th ed.) Mahwah, NJ: Erlbaum.

Bornstein, M. H. & Arterberry, M. E. (2003). Recognition, categorization, and apperception of the facial expression of smiling by 5-month-old infants. *Developmental Science, 6,* 585–599.

Bornstein, M. H., DiPietro, J. A., Hahn, C., Painter, K., Haynes, O. M., & Costigan, K. A. (2002). Prenatal cardiac function and postnatal cognitive development: An exploratory study. *Infancy, 3,* 475–494.

Bornstein, M. H., Hahn, C. S., Bell, C., Haynes, O. M., Slater, A., Golding, J., Wolke, D., et al. (2006). Stability in cognition across early childhood: A developmental cascade. *Psychological Science, 17,* 151–158.

Bornstein, M. H., Haynes, O. M., Pascual, L., Painter, K. M., & Galperin, C. (1999). Play in two societies: Pervasiveness of process, specificity of structure. *Child Development, 70,* 317–331.

Bornstein, M. H. & Sigman, M. D. (1986). Continuity in mental development from infancy. *Child Development, 57,* 251–274.

Bornstein, M. H. & Tamis-LaMonda, C. S. (1990). Activities and interactions of mothers and their firstborn infants in the first six months of life: Covariation, stability, continuity, correspondence, and prediction. *Child Development, 61,* 1206–1217.

Bornstein, M. H., Tamis-LeMonda, C. S. Hahn, C., & Haynes, O. M. (2008). Maternal responsiveness to young children at three ages: Longitudinal analysis of a multidimensional, modular, and specific parenting construct. *Developmental Psychology, 44,* 867–874.

Bosacki, S. & Astington, J. W. (1999). Theory of mind in preadolescence: Relations between social understanding and social competence. *Social Development, 8,* 237–255.

Bosacki, S. L., Marini, Z. A., & Dane, A. V. (2006). Voices from the classroom: Pictorial and narrative representations of children's bullying experiences. *Journal of Moral Education, 35,* 231–245.

Bosch, L. & Sebastian-Galles, N. (2001). Evidence of early language discrimination abilities in infants from bilingual environments. *Infancy, 2,* 29–50.

Boston, M. B. & Levy, G. D. (1991). Changes and differences in preschoolers' understanding of gender scripts. *Cognitive Psychology, 6,* 417–432.

Bottoms, B. L. & Goodman, G. S. (Eds.). (1996). *International perspectives on child abuse and children's testimony: Psychological research and law.* Thousand Oaks, CA: Sage.

Bottoms, B. L., Goodman, G. S., Schwartz-Kenney, B. M., Sachsenmaier, T., & Thomas, S. (1990, March). *Keeping secrets: Implications for children's testimony.* Paper presented at the American Psychology and Law Society Meeting, Williamsburg, VA.

Bouchard, T. J. (1997). IQ similarity in twins reared apart: Findings and responses to critics. In R. J.

Sternberg & E. L. Grigorenko (Eds.), *Intelligence, heredity, and environment.* New York: Cambridge University Press.

Bouchard, T. J. (2004). Genetic influence on human psychological traits: A survey. *Current Directions in Psychological Science, 13,* 148–151.

Bouchard, T. J. (2008). Genes and human psychological traits. In P. Carruthers, S. Laurence, & S. Stich (Eds.), *The innate mind Volume 3: Foundations and the future* (pp. 69–89). New York, NY: Oxford University Press.

Bouchard, T. J., Lykken, D. T., McGue, M., Segal, N. L., & Tellegen, A. (1990). Sources of human psychological differences: The Minnesota Study of Twins Reared Apart. *Science, 250,* 223–228.

Bouchard, T. J. & McGue, M. (1981). Familial studies of intelligence: A review. *Science, 212,* 1055–1059.

Bouchard, T. & McGue, M. (2003). Genetic and environmental influences on human psychological differences. *Journal of Neurobiology, 54,* 4–45.

Bourne, V. J. & Gray, D. L. (2009). Hormone exposure and functional lateralisation: Examining the contributions of prenatal and later life hormonal exposure. *Psychoneuroendocrinology, 34,* 1214–1221.

Bourne, V. J. & Maxwell, A. M. (2009). Examining the sex difference in lateralisation for processing facial emotion: Does biological sex or psychological gender identity matter? *Neuropsychologia, 48,* 1289–1294.

Bouvier, S. E., & Engel, S. A. (2011). Delayed effects of attention in visual cortex as measured with fMRI. *NeuroImage, 57,* 1177–1183.

Bowering, E. R., Maurer, D., Lewis, T. L., & Brent, H. P. (1997). Constriction of the visual field of children after early visual deprivation. *Journal of Pediatric Ophthalmology and Strabismus, 34,* 347–356.

Bowerman, M. (1975). Cross-linguistic similarities at two stages of syntactic development. In E. H. Lenneberg & E. E. Lenneberg (Eds.), *Foundations of language: A multidisciplinary approach.* New York: Academic Press.

Bowerman, M. (1976). Semantic factors in the acquisition of rules for word use and sentence construction. In D. M. Morehead & A. E. Morehead (Eds.), *Normal and deficient child language.* Baltimore: University Park Press.

Bowerman, M. (1982). Reorganizational processes in lexical and syntactic development. In E. Wanner & L. R. Gleitman (Eds.), *Language acquisition: The state of the art.* New York: Cambridge University Press.

Bowlby, J. (1969). *Attachment and loss: Vol. 1. Attachment.* New York: Basic Books.

Bowlby, J. (1973). *Attachment and loss: Vol. 2. Separation.* New York: Basic Books.

Bowlby, J. (1980). *Attachment and loss: Vol. 3. Loss.* New York: Basic Books.

Bowlby, J. (1982). *Attachment and loss: Vol. 1. Attachment* (2nd ed.). New York: Basic Books. (Original work published 1969)

Bowlby, J. (1988). *A secure base: Parent-child attachment and healthy human development.* New York: Basic Books.

Boyce, W. F., Doherty-Poirier, M., MacKinnon, D., Fortin, C., Saab, H., King, M., & Gallupe, O. (2006). Sexual health of Canadian youth: Findings from the *Canadian Youth, Sexual Health, and HIV/AIDS Study. Canadian Journal of Human Sexuality, 15,* 59–68.

Boyes, M. C. & Allen, S. G. (1993). Styles of parent-child interaction and moral reasoning in adolescence. *Merrill-Palmer Quarterly, 39,* 551–570.

Boysson-Bardies, B. (1999). *How language comes to children.* Cambridge, MA: MIT Press.

Brackbill, Y., Adams, G., Crowell, D. H., & Gray, M. L. (1966). Arousal level in neonates and preschool children under continuous auditory stimulation. *Journal of Experimental Child Psychology, 4,* 178–188.

Braddick, O. J. (1993). Segmentation versus integration in visual motion processing. *Trends in Neurosciences, 16,* 263–268.

Braddick, O. J., Atkinson, J., & Wattam-Bell, J. (2003). Normal and anomalous development of visual motion processing: Motion coherence and dorsal-stream vulnerability. *Neuropsychologia, 41,* 1769–1784.

Braddick, O. J., Wattam-Bell, J., & Atkinson, J. (1986). Orientation-specific cortical responses develop in early infancy. *Nature, 320,* 617–619.

Bradley, C. B., McMurray, R. G., Harrell, J. S., & Deng, S. (2000). Changes in common activities of 3rd though 10th graders: The CHIC study. *Medicine and Science in Sports and Exercise, 32,* 2071–2078.

Bradley, R. H. (1994). The HOME inventory: Review and reflections. In H. W. Reese (Ed.), *Advances in child development and behavior* (Vol. 25). San Diego, CA: Academic Press.

Bradley, R. H. (1999). The home environment. In S. L. Friedman & T. D. Wachs (Eds.), *Measuring environment across the life span: Emerging methods and concepts.* Washington, DC: APA.

Bradley, R. H. & Caldwell, B. M. (1984a). 174 children: A study of the relationship between home environment and cognitive development during the first 5 years. In A. W. Gottfried (Ed.), *Home environment and early cognitive development.* New York: Academic Press.

Bradley, R. H. & Caldwell, B. M. (1984b). The relation of infants' home environments to achievement test performance in first grade: A follow-up study. *Child Development, 55,* 803–809.

Bradley, R. H. & Corwyn, R. F. (2002). Socioeconomic status and child development. *Annual Review of Psychology, 53,* 371–399.

Bradley, R. H., Corwyn, R. F., Caldwell, B. M., Whiteside-Mansell, L., Wasserman, G. A., & Mink, I. T. (2000). Measuring the home environments of children in early adolescence. *Journal of Research on Adolescence, 10,* 247–288.

Bradley, R. H., Mundfrom, D. J., Whiteside, L., Casey, P. H., & Barrett, K. (1994). A factor analytic study of the Infant-Toddler and Early Childhood versions of the HOME inventory administered to White, Black, and Hispanic American parents of children born preterm. *Child Development, 65,* 880–888.

Brain Development Cooperative Group & Evans, A. C. (2006). The NIH MRI study of normal brain development. *NeuroImage, 30,* 184–202.

Braine, M. D. S. (1976). Children's first word combinations. *Monographs of the Society for Research in Child Development, 41(1,* Serial No. 164).

Braine, M. D. S. & Rumain, B. (1983). Logical reasoning. In P. H. Mussen (Series Ed.) & J. H. Flavell & E. M. Markman (Vol. Eds.), *Handbook of child psychology: Vol. 3. Cognitive development* (4th ed.). New York: Wiley.

Bramham, J., Morris, R. G., Hornak, J., Bullock, P., & Polkey, C. E. (2009). Social and emotional functioning following bilateral and unilateral neurosurgical prefontal cortex lesions. *Journal of Neuropsychology, 3,* 125–143.

Branigan, G. (1979). Some reasons why successive single word utterances are not. *Journal of Child Language,* 6, 411–421.

Brannon, E. M., Abbott, S., & Lutz, D. J. (2004). Number bias for the discrimination of large visual sets in infancy. *Cognition, 93,* B59-B68.

Braskie, M. N., Landau, S. M., Wilcox, C. E., Taylor, S. D., O'Neill, J. P., Baker, S. L., Madison, C. M., & Jagust, W. J. (2011). Correlations of striatal dopamine synthesis with default network deactivations during working memory in younger adults. *Human Brain Mapping, 32,* 947–961.

Brauer, J., Anwander, A., & Friederici, A. D. (2011). Neuroanatomical prerequisites for language functions in the maturing brain. *Cerebral Cortex, 21,* 459–466.

Braungart, J. M., Fulker, D. W., & Plomin, R. (1992a). Genetic mediation of the home environment during infancy: A sibling adoption study of the HOME. *Developmental Psychology, 28,* 1048–1055.

Braungart, J. M., Plomin, R., DeFries, J. C., & Fulker, D. W. (1992b). Genetic influence on tester-rated infant temperament as assessed by Bayley's Infant Behavior Record: Non-adoptive and adoptive siblings and twins. *Developmental Psychology, 28,* 40–47.

Brazelton, T. B. (1982). Joint regulation of neonate-parent behavior. In E. Z. Tronick (Ed.), *Social interchange in infancy: Affect, cognition, and communication.* Baltimore: University Park Press.

Brazelton, T. B. & Nugent, J. K. (2011). *Neonatal Behavioral Assessment Scale* (4th ed.). London: Mac Keith Press.

Brazelton, T. B. & Yogman, M. W. (Eds.). (1986). *Affective development in infancy.* Norwood, NJ: Ablex.

Breiner, S. J. (1990). *Slaughter of the innocents: Child abuse through the ages.* New York, NY: Plenum.

Breslau, N., Paneth, N., Lucia, V., & Paneth-Pollak, R., (2005). Maternal smoking during pregnancy and offspring IQ, *International Journal of Epidemiology 34,* 1047–1053.

Bretherton, I. (1988). How to do things with one word: The ontogenesis of intentional message making in infancy. In M. D. Smith & J. L. Locke (Eds.), *The emergent lexicon.* San Diego, CA: Academic Press.

Bretherton, I. (1995). The origins of attachment theory: John Bowlby and Mary Ainsworth. In S. Goldberg, R. Muir, & J. Kerr (Eds.), *Attachment theory: Social, developmental, and clinical perspectives.* Hillsdale, NJ: Analytic Press.

Bretherton, I. & Beeghly, M. (1982). Talking about internal states: The acquisition of an explicit theory of mind. *Developmental Psychology, 18,* 906–921.

Bretherton, I. & Munholland, K. A. (2008). Internal working models in attachment relationships: Elaborating a central construct in attachment theory. In J. Cassidy & P. R. Shaver (Eds.) *Handbook of attachment: Theory, research, and clinical applications (2nd edition)* (pp. 102–127). New York, NY: Guilford.

Breton, J.-J., Bergeron, L., Valla, J.-P., Berthiaume, C., Gaudet, N., Lambert, J., St-Georges, M., Houde, L., & Lépine, S. (1999). Quebec Child Mental Health Survey: Prevalency of DSM-III-R mental health disorders. *Journal of Child Psychology and Psychiatry, 40,* 375–384.

Briggs, G. G., Freeman, R. K., & Yaffe, S. J. (2008). *Drugs in pregnancy and lactation,* 8th edition. Philadelphia, PA: Lippincott Williams & Wilkins.

Bright-Paul, A. & Jarrold, C. (2009). A temporal discriminability account of children's eyewitness suggestibility. *Developmental Science, 12*(4), 647–661.

Bringman, J. J. & Phillips, O. P. (2006). Pharmacological therapy. In J. M. Vugt. & L.

P. Schulman (Eds.), *Prenatal medicine* (pp. 399–417). New York, NY: Taylor and Francis.

Brisk, M. (1998). Bilingual education: From compensatory to quality schooling. Mahwah, NJ: Erlbaum.

Broberg, A., Lamb, M. E., & Hwang, P. (1990). Inhibition: Its stability and correlates in sixteen- to forty-month-old children. *Child Development, 61,* 1153–1163.

Broderick, P. C. & Korteland, C. (2002). Coping style and depression in early adolescence: Relationships to gender, gender role, and implicit beliefs. *Sex Roles, 46,* 201–213.

Brodmann, K., (1912). Neue Ergebnisse über die vergleichende histologische Lokalisation der Grosshirnrinde mit besonderer Berücksichtigung des Stirnhirns. *Anat. Anz. (Suppl.), 41,* 157–216.

Brody, G. H. (Ed.). (1996). *Sibling relationships: Their causes and consequences.* Norwood, NJ: Ablex.

Brody, G. H. (1998). Sibling relationship quality: Its causes and consequences. *Annual Review of Psychology, 49,* 1–24.

Brody, G. H. & Flor, D. L. (1998). Maternal resources, parenting practices, and child competence in rural single-parent African American families. *Child Development, 69,* 803–816.

Brody, G. H., Stoneman, Z., & McCoy, J. K. (1994). Forecasting sibling relationships in early adolescence from child temperament and family processes in middle childhood. *Child Development, 65,* 771–778.

Brody, L. R. & Hall, J. A. (2010). Gender, emotion, and socialization. In J. Chrisler & D. R. McCreary (Eds.) *Handbook of gender research in psychology: Vol. 1: Gender research in general and experimental psychology* (pp. 429–454). New York, NY: Springer.

Brody, N. (1997). Intelligence, schooling, and society. *American Psychologist, 52,* 1046–1050.

Brodzinsky, D. M. & Pinderhughes, E. (2002). Parenting and child development in adoptive families. In M. H. Bornstein (Ed.), *Handbook of parenting* (2nd ed., Vol. 1). Mahwah, NJ: Erlbaum.

Bronfenbrenner, U. (1979). *The ecology of human development: Experiments by nature and design.* Cambridge, MA: Harvard University Press.

Bronfenbrenner, U. (1986). Recent advances in research on human development. In R. K. Silbereisen, K. Eyferth, & G. Rudinger (Eds.), *Development as action in context: Problem behavior and normal youth development.* New York: Springer-Verlag.

Bronfenbrenner, U. (1992). Ecological systems theory. In R. Vasta (Ed.), *Six theories of child development: Revised formulations and current issues.* London: Kingsley.

Bronfenbrenner, U. (1993). The ecology of cognitive development: Research models and fugitive findings. In R. H. Wozniak & K. W. Fischer (Eds.), *Development in context.* Hillsdale, NJ: Erlbaum.

Bronfenbrenner, U. (1999). Environments in developmental perspective: Theoretical and operational models. In S. L. Friedman & T. D. Wachs (Eds.), *Measuring environment across the life span: Emerging methods and concepts.* Washington, DC: American Psychological Association.

Bronfenbrenner, U. & Ceci, S. J. (1994). Nature-nurture reconceptualized in developmental perspective: A bioecological model. *Psychological Review, 101,* 568–586.

Bronfenbrenner, U. & Morris, P. A. (2006). The bioecological model of human development. In W. Damon & R. M. Lerner (Series Ed.) & R. M. Lerner (Vol. Ed.), *Handbook of child psychology: Vol. 1. Theoretical models of human development* (6th ed., pp. 793–828). Hoboken, NJ: Wiley.

Brooke, J. (1991, June 15). Signs of life in Brazil's industrial valley of death. *New York Times International,* p. 2.

Brooks-Gunn, J. (1987). Pubertal processes and girls' psychological adaptation. In R. M. Lerner & T. L. Foch (Eds.), *Biological psychosocial interactions in early adolescence.* Hillsdale, NJ: Erlbaum.

Brooks-Gunn, J. (1991). Maturational timing variations in adolescent girls, consequences of. In R. M. Lerner, A. C. Petersen, & J. Brooks-Gunn (Eds.), *Encyclopedia of adolescence* (Vol. 2). New York: Garland.

Brooks-Gunn, J. (2003). Do you believe in magic? What we can expect from early childhood intervention programs. *Society for Research in Child Development Social Policy Report, 17*(1).

Brooks-Gunn, J., Duncan, G., & Aber, J. L. (Eds.). (1997). *Neighborhood poverty: Vol. 1. Context and consequences for children.* New York: Russell Sage Foundation.

Brooks-Gunn, J., Han, W., & Waldfogel, J. (2002). Maternal employment and child cognitive outcomes in the first three years of life: The NICHD Study of Early Child Care. *Child Development, 73,* 1052–1072.

Brooks-Gunn, J. & Markman, L. B. (2005). The contribution of parenting to racial and ethnic gaps in school readiness, *The Future of Children, 15,* 139–168.

Brooks-Gunn, J. & Reiter, E. O. (1990). The role of pubertal processes. In S. S. Feldman & G. R. Elliott (Eds.), *At the threshold: The developing adolescent.* Cambridge, MA: Harvard University Press.

Brosnan, S. F. (2006). Nonhuman species' reactions to inequity and their implications for fairness. *Social Justice Research, 19,* 153–185.

Brown, A. L. (1997). Transforming schools into communities of thinking and learning about serious matters. *American Psychologist, 52,* 399–413.

Brown, A. L. & Campione, J. C. (1990). Communities of learning and thinking, or a context by any other name. In D. Kuhn (Ed.), *Developmental perspectives on teaching and learning thinking skills.* Basel, Switzerland: Karger.

Brown, A. L., Kane, M. J., & Echols, C. (1986). Young children's mental models determine analogical transfer across problems with a common goal structure. *Cognitive Development, 1,* 103–121.

Brown, A. L. & Palincsar, A. S. (1989). Guided cooperative learning and individual knowledge acquisition. In L. B. Resnick (Ed.), *Cognition and instruction: Issues and agendas.* Hillsdale, NJ: Erlbaum.

Brown, A. M., Adusumilli, V., & Lindsey, D. T. (2005). Detection of vernier and contrast-modulated stimuli with equal Fourier energy spectra by infants and adults. *Journal of Vision, 5,* 230–243.

Brown, B. (1999). Optimizing expression of the common human genome for child development. *Current Directions in Psychological Science, 8,* 37–41.

Brown, B. B. (1990). Peer groups and peer cultures. In S. S. Feldman & G. R. Elliott (Eds.), *At the threshold: The developing adolescent.* Cambridge, MA: Harvard University Press.

Brown, J. S., Collins, A., & Duguid, P. (1989). Situated cognition and the culture of learning. *Educational Researcher, 18,* 32–42.

Brown, K. W. & Gottfried, A. W. (1986). Development of cross-modal transfer in early infancy. In L. P. Lipsitt & C. K. Rovee-Collier (Eds.), *Advances in infancy research* (Vol. 4). Norwood, NJ: Ablex.

Brown, M., Keynes, R., & Lumsden, A. (2001). *The developing brain.* New York: Oxford University Press.

Brown, R. (1958a). How shall a thing be called? *Psychological Review, 65,* 14–21.

Brown, R. (1958b). *Words and things.* Glencoe, IL: Free Press.

Brown, R. (1973). *A first language: The early stages.* Cambridge, MA: Harvard University Press.

Brown, R. & Hanlon, C. (1970). Derivational complexity and order of acquisition in child speech. In J. R. Hayes (Ed.), *Cognition and the development of language.* New York: Wiley.

Browne, C. A. & Woolley, J. D. (2001). Theory of mind in children's naming of drawings. *Journal of Cognition and Development, 2,* 389–411.

Brownell, C. A. & Carriger, M. S. (1990). Changes in cooperation and self-other differentiation during the second year. *Child Development, 61,* 1164–1174.

Brownell, C. A. & Strauss, M. A. (1984). Infant stimulation and development: Conceptual and empirical considerations. *Journal of Children in Contemporary Society, 6,* 109–130.

Browning, S. & Bray, J. H. (2009). Treating stepfamilies: A subsystems-based approach. In J. H. Bray & M. Stanton (Eds.). *The Wiley-Blackwell handbook of family psychology* (pp. 487–498). Hoboken, NJ: Wiley.

Brum, G. D. & McKane, L. K. (1989). *Biology: Exploring life.* New York: Wiley.

Bruner, J. (1983). *Child's talk: Learning to use language.* New York: Norton.

Bruner, J. (1999). The intentionality of referring. In P. D. Zelazo, J. W. Astington, & D. R. Olson (Eds.), *Developing theories of intention.* Mahwah, NJ: Erlbaum.

Bruner, J., Roy, C., & Ratner, N. (1982). The beginnings of request. In K. E. Nelson (Ed.), *Children's language* (Vol. 3). Hillsdale, NJ: Erlbaum.

Buckingham, D. & Shultz, T. R. (2000). The developmental course of distance, time, and velocity concepts: A generative connectionist model. *Journal of Cognition and Development, 1,* 305–345.

Bugental, D. B. & Grusec, J. E. (2006). Socialization processes. In W. Damon & R. M. Lerner (Series Eds.) & N. Eisenberg (Vol. Ed.), *Handbook of child psychology: Vol. 3. Social, emotional, and personality development* (6th ed.) (pp. 366–428). Hoboken, NJ: Wiley.

Bugental, D. B. & Happaney, K. (2002). Parental attributions. In M. H. Bornstein (Ed.), *Handbook of parenting* (2nd ed., Vol. 3). Mahwah, NJ: Erlbaum.

Buhrmester, D. (1990). Intimacy of friendship, interpersonal competence, and adjustment during preadolescence and adolescence. *Child Development, 61,* 1101–1111.

Buhrmester, D. (1992). The developmental courses of sibling and peer relationships. In F. Boer & J. Dunn (Eds.), *Children's sibling relationships: Developmental and clinical issues.* Hillsdale, NJ: Erlbaum.

Buhrmester, D. & Furman, W. (1990). Perceptions of sibling relationships during middle childhood and adolescence. *Child Development, 61,* 1387–1398.

Buhrmester, D. & Prager, K. (1995). Patterns and functions of self-disclosure during childhood and adolescence. In K. J. Rotenberg (Ed.), *Disclosure processes in children and adolescents.* New York: Cambridge University Press.

Bukowski, W. M., Brendgen, M., & Vitaro, F. (2007). Peers and socialization: Effects on externalizing and internalizing problems. In J. Grusec & P. Hastings (Eds.), *Handbook of socialization: Theory and research* (pp. 355–381). New York: Guilford.

Bukowski, W. M. & Hoza, B. (1989). Popularity and friendship: Issues in theory, measurement, and outcome. In T. J. Berndt & G. W. Ladd (Eds.), *Peer relationships in child development.* New York: Wiley.

Bukowski, W. M., Motzoi, C., & Meyer, F. (2009). Friendship as process, function, & outcome. In K.H. Rubin, W. M. Bukowski, & B. Laursen (Eds.) *Handbook of peer interactions, relationships, and groups* (pp. 217–231). New York: Guilford.

Bullock, M. & Lutkenhaus, P. (1988). The development of volitional behavior in the toddler years. *Child Development, 59,* 664–674.

Bullock, M. & Lutkenhaus, P. (1990). Who am I? Self-understanding in toddlers. *Merrill-Palmer Quarterly, 36,* 217–238.

Burchinal, M. R., Bryant, D. M., Lee, M. W., & Ramey C. T. (1992). Early day care, infant-mother attachment, and maternal responsiveness in the infant's first year. *Early Childhood Research Quarterly, 7,* 383–396.

Burchinal, M. R., Peisner-Feinberg, E., Pianta, R., & Howes, C. (2002). Development of academic skills from preschool through second grade: Family and classroom predictors of developmental trajectories. *Journal of School Psychology, 40,* 415–436.

Burchinal, M. R., Roberts, J. E., Hooper, S., & Zeisel, S. A. (2000). Cumulative risk and early cognitive development: A comparison of statistical risk models. *Developmental Psychology, 36,* 793–807.

Burgess, K. B. & Younger, A. J. (2006). Self-schemas, anxiety, somatic and depressive symptoms in socially withdrawn children and adolescents. *Journal of Research in Childhood Education, 20,* 175–187.

Burkhalter, A., Bernardo, K. L., & Charles, V. (1993). Development of local circuits in human visual cortex. *Journal of Neuroscience, 13,* 1916–1931.

Burns, T. C., Yoshida, K. A., Hill, K., Werker, J. F. (2007). Bilingual and monolingual infant phonetic development. *Applied Psycholinguistics, 28*(3), 455–474.

Busch, N. A., Dubois, J., & VanRullen, R. (2009). The phase of ongoing EEG oscillations predicts visual perception. *The Journal of Neuroscience, 29,* 7869–7876.

Busch, N. A. & VanRullen, R. (2010). Spontaneous EEG oscillations reveal periodic sampling of visual attention. *Proceedings of the National Academy of Science, 107,* 16048–16053.

Bushman, B. J. & Anderson, C. A. (2009). Comfortably numb: Desensitizing effects of violent media on helping others. *Psychological Science, 21,* 273–277.

Bushman, B. J. & Huesmann, L. R. (2010). Aggression. In S. T. Fiske, D.T. Gilbert, & G. Lindzey (Eds.). *Handbook of social psychology* (Vol. 2), (pp. 833–863). Hoboken, NJ: John Wiley & Sons.

Bushnell, E. W. (1982). Visual-tactual knowledge in 8-, 9-, and 11-month-old infants. *Infant Behavior and Development, 5,* 63–75.

Bushnell, E. W. (1994). A dual-processing approach to cross-modal matching: Implications for development. In D. J. Lewkowicz & R. Lickliter (Eds.), *The development of intersensory perception: Comparative perspectives.* Hillsdale, NJ: Erlbaum.

Bushnell, I. W. R. (2001). Mother's face recognition in newborn infants: Learning and memory. *Infant and Child Development, 10, 67–74.*

Bushnell, I. W. R., Sai, F., & Mullin, J. T. (1989). Neonatal recognition of the mother's face. *British Journal of Developmental Psychology, 7,* 3–15.

Buss, A. H. & Plomin, R. (1984). *Temperament: Early developing personality traits.* Hillsdale, NJ: Erlbaum.

Buss, A. H. & Plomin, R. (1986). The EAS approach to temperament. In R. Plomin & J. Dunn (Eds.), *The study of temperament: Changes, continuities and challenges.* Hillsdale, NJ: Erlbaum.

Buss, D. M. (1999). *Evolutionary psychology: The new science of the mind.* Boston: Allyn and Bacon.

Buss, D. M. & Kenrick, D. T. (1998). Evolutionary social psychology. In D. T. Gilbert, S. T. Fiske, & G. Lindzey (Eds.), *The handbook of social psychology* (4th ed., Vol. 2). Boston: McGraw-Hill.

Bussey, K. & Bandura, A. (1984). Gender constancy, social power, and sex-linked modeling. *Journal of Personality and Social Psychology, 47,* 1292–1302.

Bussey, K. & Bandura, A. (1992). Self-regulatory mechanisms governing gender development. *Child Development, 63,* 1236–1250.

Bussey, K. & Bandura, A. (1999). Social-cognitive theory of gender development and differentiation. *Psychological Review, 106,* 676–713.

Bussey, K. & Bandura, A. (2004). Social cognitive theory of gender development and functioning. In A. H. Eagly, A. E. Beall, & R. J. Sternberg (Eds.), *The psychology of gender* (2nd ed., pp. 92–119). New York: Guilford.

Bussey, K. & Perry, D. G. (1982). Same-sex imitation: The avoidance of cross-sex models or the acceptance of same-sex models? *Sex Roles, 8,* 773–784.

Bussière, P., Cartwright, F., Crocker, R., Ma, X., Oderkirk, J., & Zhang, Y. (2001). *Measuring up: The performance of Canada's youth in reading. mathematics, and science.* Statistics Canada, catalogue no. 81-590-XIE.

Bussière, P., Cartwright, F., & Knighton, T. (2004). Measuring Up: Canadian Results of the OECD PISA study. The Performance of Canada's Youth in Mathematics, Reading, and Problem-Solving: 2003 First Findings for Canadians Aged 15. Statistics Canada, Catalogue no. 81-590-XPE – No. 2.

Bussière, P., Knighton, T., & Pennock, D. (2007). Measuring Up: Canadian Results of the OECD PISA study. The Performance of Canada's Youth in Mathematics, Reading, and Problem-Solving: 2003 First Findings for Canadians Aged 15. Statistics Canada, Catalogue no. 81-590-XPE- No. 3.

Butler, R. (1990). The effects of mastery and competitive conditions on self-assessment at different ages. *Child Development, 61,* 201–210.

Butler, R. (1992). What young people want to know when: The effects of mastery and ability on social information seeking. *Journal of Personality and Social Psychology, 62,* 934–943.

Butler, R. (1996). Effects of age and achievement goals on children's motives for attending to peer's work. *British Journal of Developmental Psychology, 14,* 1–18.

Butler, R. & Ruzany, N. (1993). Age and socialization effects on the development of social comparison motives and normative ability assessment in kibbutz and urban children. *Child Development, 64,* 532–543.

Butovskaya, M., Verbeek, P., Ljungberg, T., & Lunardini, A. (2000). A multicultural view of peace-making among young children. In F. Aureli & F. B. M. de Waal (Eds.), *Natural conflict resolution.* Berkeley, CA: University of California Press.

Butterworth, G. (1995). The self as an object of consciousness in infancy. In P. Rochat (Ed.), *The self in infancy: Theory and research.* Amsterdam: Elsevier.

Buunk, B. P., Kuyper, H., & van der Zee, Y. (2005). Affective response to social comparison in the classroom. *Basic and Applied Social Psychology, 27,* 229–237.

Buunk, B. P., Zurriaga, R., Peiro, J. M., Nauta, A., & Gosalvez, I. (2005). Social comparisons at work as related to a cooperative social climate and to individual differences in social comparison orientation. *Applied Psychology: An International Review, 54,* 61–80.

Byers-Heinlein, K., Burns, T. F., & Werker, J. F. (2010). The roots of bilingualism in newborns. *Psychological Science, 21*(3), 343–348.

Byrne, B. M. (1996). *Measuring self-concept across the life span: Issues and instrumentation.* Washington, DC: American Psychological Association.

Byrnes, J. P. (1988). Formal operations: A systematic reformulation. *Developmental Review, 8,* 66–87.

Byrnes, J. P., Miller, D. C., & Schafer, W. D. (1999). Gender differences in risk taking: A meta-analysis. *Psychological Bulletin, 125,* 367–383.

Bystrom, I., Blakemore, C., & Rakic, P. (2008). Development of the human cerebral cortex: Boulder Committee revisited. *Nature Review: Neuroscience, 9,* 110–22.

C

Cachón-González, M. B., Wang, S. Z., Lynch, A., Ziegler, R., Cheng, S. H. & Cox, T. M. (2006). Effective gene therapy in an authentic model of Tay-Sachs-related diseases. *Proceedings of the National Academy of Sciences of the United States of America, 103,* 10373–10378.

Cadinu, M., Maass, A., Rosabianca, A., & Kiesner, J. (2005). Why do women underperform under stereotype threat? Evidence for the role of negative thinking. *Psychological Science, 16,* 572–578.

Caetano, G., Jousmäki, V., & Hari, R. (2007). Actor's and observer's primary motor cortices stabilize similarly after seen or heard motor actions. *Proceedings of the National Academy of Science, 104,* 9058–9062.

Cain, K. M. & Dweck, C. S. (1995). The relation between motivational patterns and achievement cognitions through the elementary years. *Merrill-Palmer Quarterly, 41,* 25–52.

Cairns, R. B. & Cairns, B. D. (2006). The making of developmental psychology. In W. Damon & R. M. Lerner (Series Ed.), & R. M. Lerner (Vol. Ed.), *Handbook of child psychology: Vol. 1. Theoretical models of human development* (6th ed., pp. 89–65). Hoboken, NJ: Wiley.

Cairns, R. B., Cairns, B. D., Neckerman, H. J., Ferguson, L. L., & Gariepy, J. (1989). Growth and aggression: I. Childhood to early adolescence. *Developmental Psychology, 25,* 320–330.

Cairns, R. B., Cairns, B. D., Neckerman, H. J., Gest, S. D., & Gariepy, J. (1988). Social networks and aggressive behavior: Peer support or peer rejection? *Developmental Psychology, 24,* 815–823.

Caldwell, B. M. & Bradley, R. (1984). *The Home Observation for Measurement of the Environment (HOME) Inventory.* Little Rock, AR: University of Arkansas at Little Rock.

Calkins, S. D., Dedmon, S. E., Gill, K. L., Lomax, L. E., & Johnson, L. M. (2002). Frustration in infancy: Implications for emotion regulation, physiological processes, and temperament. *Infancy, 3,* 175–197.

Calkins, S. D. & Fox, N. A. (1992). The relations among infant temperament, security of attachment, and behavioral inhibition at twenty-four months. *Child Development, 63,* 1456–1472.

Callanan, M. A. (1985). How parents label objects for young children: The role of input in the acquisition of category hierarchies. *Child Development, 56,* 508–523.

Calvete, E., Orue, I., Estevez, A., Villardon, L., & Padilla, P. (2010). Cyberbullying in adolescents: Modalities and aggressors' profile. *Computers in Human Behavior, 26,* 1128–1135.

Camarata, S. & Leonard, L. B. (1986). Young children pronounce object words more accurately than action words. *Journal of Child Language, 13,* 51–65.

Campbell, A. (2008). Attachment, aggression and affiliation: The role of oxytocin in female social behavior. *Biological Psychology, 77,* 1–10.

Campbell, A., Shirley, L., & Caygill, L. (2002). Sex-typed preferences in three domains: Do two-year-olds need cognitive variables? *British Journal of Psychology, 93,* 203–217.

Campbell, D. & Eaton, W. O. (1999). Sex differences in the activity level of infants. *Infant and Child Development, 8,* 1–17.

Campbell, F. A., Pungello, E. P., Miller-Johnson, S., Burchinall, M., & Ramey, C. T. (2001). The development of cognitive and academic abilities: Growth curves from an early childhood educational experiment. *Developmental Psychology, 37*(23), 1–242.

Campbell, S. B. (2000). Attention-deficit/hyper activity disorder: A developmental view. In A. Sameroff, M. Lewis, & S. M. Miller (Eds.), *Handbook of developmental psychopathology* (2nd ed.). New York: Plenum.

Campos, J., Frankel, C., & Camras, l. (2004). On the nature of emotion regulation. *Child Development, 75,* 377–394.

Campos, J. J., Anderson, D. I., Barbu-Roth, M. A., Hubbard, E. M., Hertenstein, M. J., & Witherington, D. (2000). Travel broadens the mind. *Infancy, 1,* 149–220.

Campos, J. J., Bertenthal, B. I., & Kermoian, R. (1992). Early experience and emotional development: The emergence of wariness of heights. *Psychological Science, 3,* 61–64.

Campos, J. J., Hiatt, S., Ramsay, D., Henderson, C., & Svejda, M. (1978). The emergence of fear on the visual cliff. In M. Lewis & L. Rosenblum (Eds.), *The origins of affect.* New York: Plenum.

Campos, R. G. (1989). Soothing pain-elicited distress in infants with swaddling and pacifiers. *Child Development, 60,* 781–792.

Camras, L. A. & Fatani, S. S. (2008). The development of facial expressions. In M. Lewis, J. M. Haviland-Jones, & L. M. Barrett (Eds.), *Handbook of emotions,* 3rd edition (pp. 291–303). New York: Guilford.

Canadian Council on Animal Care (2005). Guidelines for the treatment of animals in behavioural research and teaching. *Animal Behavior, 69*(1), i–vi.

Canadian Council on Learning. (2007). *Lessons in Learning: French Immersion Education in Canada, May 17, 2007.* Available at: search.ccl-cca.ca/CCL/Templates/LessonsInLearning.aspx?NRMODE=Published&NRORIGINALURL=%2fCCL%2fReports%2fLessonsInLearning%2fLinL20070517_French_Immersion_programs%2ehtm&NRNODEGUID=%7bD7BE5D44-98F3-4327-90F2-87ACDEC8CD05%7d&NRCACHEHINT=NoModifyGuest#_edn20

Canadian Paediatric Society (2010). *Getting ready to bring your baby home.* Downloaded September 22, 2010 from http://www.caringforkids.cps.ca/pregnancybabies/babyhome.htm

Canadian Paediatric Society. (2007). *Fetal alcohol spectrum disorder: What you should know about drinking during pregnancy.* Available at: www.caringforkids.cps.ca/babies/FASpregnancy.htm#alcohol.

Canadian Parents for French (2008). *Enrolment trends 2006-2007.* Ottawa, ON: Author. Retrieved from http://www.cpf.ca/eng/resources-reports-enrolment-0607.html December 23, 2010.

Canadian Psychological Association. (2001). *Canadian code of ethics for psychologists* (3rd ed.). Ottawa: Canadian Psychological Association.

Cantin, S. & Boivin, M. (2004). Change and stability in children's social network and self-perceptions during transition from elementary to junior high school. *International Journal of Behavioral Development, 28,* 561–570.

Caplan, M., Vespo, J. E., Pedersen, J., & Hay, D. F. (1991). Conflict and its resolution in small groups of one- and two-year-olds. *Child Development, 62,* 1513–1524.

CARE Study Group (2008). Maternal caffeine intake during pregnancy and risk of fetal growth restriction: A large prospective observational study. *British Medical Journal, 337,* a2332.

Carey, S. (1977). The child as word learner. In M. Halle, J. Bresnan, & G. A. Miller (Eds.), *Linguistic theory and psychological reality.* Cambridge, MA: MIT Press.

Carey, S. (2000). The origin of concepts. *Journal of Cognition and Development, 1,* 37–41.

Carey, W. B. & McDevitt, S. C. (1978). Revision of the Infant Temperament Questionnaire. *Pediatrics, 61,* 735–739.

Carlson, V., Cicchetti, D., Barnett, D., & Braunwald, K. G. (1989). Finding order in disorganization: Lessons from research on maltreated infants' attachments to their caregivers. In D. Cicchetti & V. Carlson (Eds.), *Child maltreatment: Theory and research on the causes and consequences of child abuse and neglect.* New York: Cambridge University Press.

Carmichael, S. L. & Shaw, G. M. (2000). Maternal life event stress and congenital anomalies. *Epidemiology, 11,* 30–35.

Carnagey, N. L., Anderson, C. A., & Bushman, B. J. (2007). The effect of video game violence on physiological desensitization to real-life violence. *Journal of Experimental Social Psychology, 43,* 489–496.

Caron, A. J., Caron, R. F., & MacLean, D. J. (1988). Infant discrimination of naturalistic emotional expressions: The role of face and voice. *Child Development, 59,* 604–616.

Carpendale, J. I. M. & Krebs, D. L. (1995). Variations in moral judgment as a function of type of dilemma and moral choice. *Journal of Personality, 63,* 289–313.

Carr, M. & Jessup, D. L. (1997). Gender differences in first grade mathematics strategy use: Social and metacognitive influences. *Journal of Educational Psychology, 98,* 318–328.

Carr, M., Jessup, D. L., & Fuller, D. (1999). Gender differences in first-grade mathematics strategy use: Parent and teacher contributions. *Journal for Research in Mathematics Education, 30,* 20–46.

Carson, G., Cox, L. V., Crane, J., Croteau, P., Graves, L., Kluka., S., Koren, G., Martel., M-J., Midmer, D., Nulman, I., Poole, N., Senikas, V., Wood, R. (2010). Alcohol use and pregnancy consensus clinical guidelines. *Journal of Obstetrics and Gynaecology in Canada,* 32 (Supplement 3), S1–S33.

Carver, L. J. & Bauer, P. J. (2001). The dawning of a past: The emergence of long-term explicit memory in infancy. *Journal of Experimental Psychology: General, 130,* 726–745.

Case, R. & Okamoto, Y. (1996). The role of central conceptual structures in the development of children's thought. *Monographs of the Society for Research in Child Development, 61* (1–2, Serial No. 246).

Casey, B. J. & de Haan, M. (2002). Introduction: New methods in developmental science. *Developmental Science, 5,* 265–267.

Casey, B. J., Tottenham, N., Liston, C., & Durston, S. (2005). Imaging the developing brain: What have we learned about cognitive development? *Trends in Cognitive Science, 9,* 104–110.

Cashon, C. H. & Cohen, L. B. (2000). Eight-month-old infants' perception of possible and impossible events. *Infancy, 1(4),* 429–446.

Caspi, A., Henry, B., McGee, R. O., Moffitt, T. E., & Silva, P. A. (1995). Temperamental origins of child and adolescent behavior problems: From age 3 to age 15. *Child Development, 66,* 55–68.

Caspi, A., Moffitt, T. E., Newman, D. L., & Silva, P. A. (1996). Behavioral observations at age 3 predict adult psychiatric disorders: Longitudinal evidence from a birth cohort. *Archives of General Psychiatry, 53,* 1033–1039.

Caspi, A. & Shiner, R. L. (2006). Personality development. In N. Eisenberg (Ed.), *Handbook of child psychology: Vol. 3. Social, emotional, and personality development* (6th edition, pp. 300–365). Hoboken, NJ: Wiley.

Cassia, V. M., Simion, F., & Umilta, C. (2001). Face preference at birth: The role of an orienting mechanism. *Developmental Science, 4,* 101–108.

Cassidy, J. (2008). The nature of the child's ties. In J. Cassidy & P. R. Shaver (Eds.), *Handbook of attachment: Theory, research, and clinical applications* (2nd edition) (pp. 3–22). New York, NY: Guilford.

Cassidy, W., Jackson, M., & Brown, K. N. (2009). Sticks and stones can break my bones, but how can pixels hurt me? Students' experiences with cyber-bullying. *School Psychology International, 30*(4), 383–402.

Catherine, N. L., Ko, J. J., & Barr, R. G. (2008). Getting the word out: advice on crying and colic in popular parenting magazines. *Journal of Developmental and Behavioral Pediatrics, 29,* 508–511.

Catron, T. F. & Masters, J. C. (1993). Mothers' and children's conceptualizations of corporal punishment. *Child Development, 64,* 1815–1828.

Caudill, W. & Schooler, C. (1973). Child behavior and child rearing in Japan and the United States: An interim report. *Journal of Nervous and Mental Disease, 157,* 323–338.

Caudill, W. & Weinstein, H. (1969). Maternal care and infant behavior in Japan and America. *Psychiatry: Journal for the Study of Interpersonal Processes, 32,* 12–43.

Caughy, M. O. (1996). Health and environmental effects on the academic readiness of school-age children. *Developmental Psychology, 32,* 515–522.

Cavallotti, D., Casilla, G., Piantelli, G., Verrotti, C., Fieni, S., & Gramellini, D. (2004). Early complications of prenatal invasive diagnostics: Perspective analysis. *Acta Biomedica, 75 Suppl 1,* 23–26.

Cavanagh, S. E., Riegle-Crumb, C., & Crosnoe, R. (2007). Puberty and the education of girls. *Social Psychology Quarterly, 70,* 186–198.

Cavanaugh, J. C. & Perlmutter, M. (1982). Metamemory: A critical examination. *Child Development, 53,* 11–28.

CBC Archives (2006). Thalidomide: bitter pills, broken promises. Available at: http://archives.cbc.ca/IDD-1-75-88/science_technology/thalidomide/

CBC News (2005). Cyber-bullying. Available at: www.cbc.ca/news/background/bullying/cyber_bullying.html. Accessed March 8, 2011.

Americans and European Americans. *Child Development, 72,* 1832–1843.

CBC News (2007). 11 Ontario students suspended for "cyber-bullying." Available at: www.cbc.ca/news/canada/story/2007/02/12/school-facebook.html. Accessed March 8, 2011.

Ceci, S. J. (1996). *On intelligence: A bioecological treatise on intellectual development* (expanded ed.). Cambridge, MA: Harvard University Press.

Ceci, S. J., & Bruck, M. (1995). *Jeopardy in the courtroom: A scientific analysis of children's testimony.* Washington, DC: American Psychological Association.

Ceci, S. J. & Bruck, M. (1998). Children's testimony. In W. Damon (Series Ed.) & I. E. Sigel & K. A. Renninger (Vol. Eds.), *Handbook of child psychology: Vol. 4. Child psychology in practice* (5th ed.). New York: Wiley.

Ceci, S. J. & Williams, W. M. (1997). Schooling, intelligence, and income. *American Psychologist, 52,* 1051–1058.

Ceci, S. J. & Williams, W. M. (2007). Little g: Prospects and constraints. *European Journal of Personality, 21,* 716–718.

Cervone, D., Mor, N., Orom, H., Shadel, W. G., & Scott, W. D. (2004). Self-efficacy beliefs on the architecture of personality: On knowledge, appraisal, and self-regulation. In R. Baumeister & K. Vohs (Eds.), *Handbook of self-regulation: Research, theory, and applications* (pp. 188–210). New York: Guilford.

Chaiklin, S. (2011). Social scientific research and societal practice: Action research and cultural-historical research in methodological light. In K. Lewin & L. S. Vygotsky, *Mind Culture and Activity, 18*(2), pp. 129–147.

Chamberlain, P. & Patterson, G. R. (1995). Discipline and child compliance in parenting. In M. H. Bornstein (Ed.), *Handbook of parenting: Vol. 4. Applied and practical parenting.* Mahwah, NJ: Erlbaum.

Chambers, C. T., Cassidy, K. L., McGrath, P. J., Gilbert, C. A., & Craig, K. D. (1996). *Child facial coding system: Revised manual.* Halifax, NS: Dalhousie University/Vancouver: University of British Columbia.

Chandler, M. J. (1973). Egocentrism and antisocial behavior: The assessment and training of social perspective-taking skills. *Developmental Psychology, 9,* 326–332.

Chandler, M. J., Greenspan, S., & Barenboim, C. (1973). Judgments of intentionality in response to videotaped and verbally presented moral dilemmas: The medium is the message. *Child Development, 44,* 315–320.

Chandler, M. J. & Lalonde, C. (1996). Shifting to an interpretive theory of mind: 5- to 7-year-olds' changing conceptions of mental life. In A. J. Sameroff & M. M. Haith (Eds.), *The five to seven year shift: The age of reason and responsibility.* Chicago: University of Chicago Press.

Chandler, M. J., Lalonde, C. E., Sokol, B. W., & Hallett, D. (2003). Personal persistence, identity development, and suicide: A study of native and non-native North American adolescents. *Monographs of the Society for Research in Child Development, Serial No., 273, 68.* Boston: Blackwell Publishing.

Chandler, M. J. & Proulx, T. (2006). Changing selves in changing worlds: Youth suicide on the fault-lines of colliding cultures. *Archives of Suicide Research, 10,* 125–140.

Chang, R. K. R., Keens, T. G., Rodriguez, S., & Chen, A. Y. (2008). Sudden Infant Death Syndrome: Changing Epidemiologic Patterns in California 1989-2004. *The Journal of Pediatrics, 153,* 498–502.

Chao, R. (2001). Extending the research on the consequences of parenting style for Chinese

Chao, R. & Tseng, V. (2002). Parenting of Asians. In M. H. Bornstein (Ed.), *Handbook of parenting* (2nd ed., Vol. 3). Mahwah, NJ: Erlbaum.

Chapman, M. (1988). *Constructive evolution: Origins and development of Piaget's thought.* Cambridge: Cambridge University Press.

Chapman, M. (1992). Equilibration and the dialectics of organization. In H. Beilin & P. B. Pufall (Eds.), *Piaget's theory: Prospects and possibilities.* Hillsdale, NJ: Erlbaum.

Chapman, R. S., Streim, N. W., Crais, E. R., Salmon, D., Strand, E. A., & Negri, N. A. (1992). Child talk: Assumptions of a developmental process model for early language learning. In R. A. Chapman (Ed.), *Processes in language acquisition and disorders.* St. Louis, MO: Mosby Year Book.

Charach, A., Pepler, D., & Ziegler, S. (1995). Bullying at school. *Education Canada, 37,* 12–18.

Charlesworth, R. & Hartup, W. W. (1967). Positive social reinforcement in the nursery school peer group. *Child Development, 38,* 993–1002.

Charlesworth, W. R. & Dzur, C. (1987). Gender comparisons of preschoolers' behavior and resource utilization in group problem solving. *Child Development, 58,* 191–200.

Charlton, R. A., Barrick, T. R., Markus, H. S., & Morris, R. G. (2010). The relationship between episodic long-term memory and white matter integrity in normal aging. *Neuropsychologia, 48,* 114–122.

Chase, W. G. & Simon, H. A. (1973). The mind's eye in chess. In W. G. Chase (Ed.), *Visual information processing.* New York: Academic Press.

Chavajay, P. & Rogoff, B. (1999). Cultural variation in management of attention by children and their caregivers. *Developmental Psychology, 35,* 1079–1090.

Chen, C. & Stevenson, H. W. (1995). Motivation and mathematics achievement: A comparative study of Asian-American, Caucasian-American, and East Asian high school students. *Child Development, 66,* 1215–1234.

Chen, C. P., Kuhn, P., Advis, J. P., & Sarkar, D. K. (2006). Prenatal ethanol exposure alters the expression of period genes governing the circadian function of β-endorphin neurons in the hypothalamus. *Journal of Neurochemistry, 97,* 1026–1033.

Chen, H. (2006). *Atlas of genetic diagnosis and counseling.* Totowa, NJ: Humana Press.

Chen, J. & Gardner, H. (1997). Alternative assessment from a multiple intelligences theoretical perspective. In D. P. Flanagan, J. L. Genshaft, & P. L. Harrison (Eds.), *Contemporary intellectual assessment.* New York: Guilford.

Chen, L. & Woo, S. (2007). Correction in female PKU mice by repeated administration of mPAH cDNA Using phiBT1 integration system. *Molecular Therapy, 15,* 1789–1795.

Chen, X. (2002). Peer relationships and networks and socio-emotional adjustment: A Chinese perspective. In B. Cairns & T. Farmer (Eds.), *Social networks from a developmental perspective.* New York: Cambridge University Press.

Chen, X., Chung, J., Lechcier-Kimmel, R., & French, D. (2011). Culture and social development. In P. K.Smith & K. H. Hart (Eds.), *The Wiley-Blackwell handbook of childhood social development, 2nd edition* (pp. 141–160). Hoboken, NJ. Wiley.

Chen, X. & French, D. C. (2008). Children's social competence in cultural context. *Annual Review of Psychology, 59,* 591–616.

Chen, X., Rubin, K. H., & Li, Z. (1995). Social functioning and adjustment in Chinese children: A longitudinal study. *Developmental Psychology, 31,* 531–539.

Chen, X., Rubin, K. H., & Sun, Y. (1992). Social reputation and peer relationships in Chinese and Canadian children: A cross-cultural study. *Child Development, 63,* 1336–1343.

Chen, X., Striano, T., & Rakoczy, H. (2004). Auditory-oral matching behavior in newborns. *Developmental Science, 7,* 42–47.

Chen, Z., Sanchez, R. P., & Campbell, T. (1997). From beyond to within their grasp: The rudiments of analogical problem solving in 10- and 13-month-olds. *Developmental Psychology, 33,* 790–801.

Chen, Z. & Siegler, R. S. (2000). Across the great divide: Bridging the gap between understanding of toddlers' and older children's thinking. *Monographs of the Society for Research in Child Development, 65(2),* Serial No. 261.

Cherny, S. S. (1994). Home environmental influences on general cognitive ability. In J. C. DeFries, R. Plomin, & D. W. Fulker (Eds.), *Nature and nurture during middle childhood.* Cambridge, MA: Blackwell.

Cherny, S. S. & Cardon, L. R. (1994). General cognitive ability. In J. C. DeFries, R. Plomin, & D. W. Fulker (Eds.), *Nature and nurture during middle childhood.* Oxford, England: Blackwell.

Cherny, S. S., Fulker, D. W., Corley, R. P., Plomin, R., & DeFries, J. C. (1994a). Continuity and change in infant shyness from 14 to 20 months. *Behavior Genetics, 24,* 365–379.

Cherny, S. S., Fulker, D. W., Emde, R. N., Robinson, J., Corley, R. P., Reznick, J. S., et al. (1994b). A developmental-genetic analysis of continuity and change in the Bayley mental development index from 14 to 24 months: The MacArthur Longitudinal Twin Study. *Psychological Science, 5,* 354–360.

Cherny, S. S., Saudino, K., Fulker, D., Plomin, R., Corley, R., & DeFries, J. (2001). The development of observed shyness from 14 to 20 months: Shyness in context. In R. Emde & J. Hewitt (Eds.), *Infancy to early childhood: Genetic and environmental influences on developmental change* (pp. 269–282). New York: Oxford University Press.

Chess, S. (2005). Wisdom from teachers. *Journal of the American Academy of Child and Adolescent Psychiatry, 44,* 623–624.

Chess, S. & Thomas, A. (1987). *Origins and evolution of behavior disorders: From infancy to early adult life.* Cambridge, MA: Harvard University Press.

Chess, S. & Thomas, A. (1996). *Temperament, Theory and Practice.* New York: Brunner/Mazel.

Chi, M. T. H. (1978). Knowledge structures and memory development. In R. S. Siegler (Ed.), *Children's thinking: What develops?* Hillsdale, NJ: Erlbaum.

Chi, M. T. H., Glaser, R., & Farr, M. J. (Eds.). (1988). *The nature of expertise.* Hillsdale, NJ: Erlbaum.

Chi, M. T. H. & Koeske, R. D. (1983). Network representation of a child's dinosaur knowledge. *Developmental Psychology, 19,* 29–39.

Choi, S. (1997). Language-specific input and early semantic development: Evidence from children learning Korean. In D. I. Slobin (Ed.), *The crosslinguisitic study of language acquisition: Vol. 5. Expanding the contexts.* Mahwah, NJ: Erlbaum.

Choi, S. (2000). Caregiver input in English and Korean: Use of nouns and verbs in book-reading and toy-play contexts. *Journal of Child Language, 27,* 69–96.

Chomsky, N. (1959). A review of B. F. Skinner's *Verbal Behavior. Language, 35,* 26–58.

Chomsky, N. (1965). *Aspects of the theory of syntax.* Cambridge, MA: MIT Press.

Chouinard, M. M. & Clark, E. V. (2003). Adult reformulations of child errors as negative evidence. *Journal of Child Language, 30*(3), 637–669.

Christenson, S. L. & Sheridan, S. M. (2001). *School and families.* New York: Guilford.

Christian, K., Bachnan, H. J., & Morrison, F. J. (2001). Schooling and cognitive development. In R. J. Sternberg & E. L. Grigorenko (Eds.), *Environmental effects on cognitive abilities.* Mahwah, NJ: Erlbaum.

Christophe, A., Nespor, M., Guasti, M. T., and Van Ooyen, B. (2003). Prosodic structure and syntactic acquisition: The case of the head-direction parameter. *Developmental Science, 6,* 211–220.

Chudley, A., Conry, J., Cook, J., Loock, C., Rosales, T., & Leblanc, N. (2005). Fetal alcohol spectrum disorder: Canadian guidelines for diagnosis. *Canadian Medical Association Journal, 172(5 supp),* S3-S21.

Chugani, H. T. (1998). A critical period of brain development: Studies of cerebral glucose utilization with PET. *Preventive Medicine, 27,* 184–188.

Chugani, H. T., Phelps, M. E., & Mazziotta, J. C. (1987). Positron Emission Tomography study of human brain functional development. *Annals of Neurology, 22,* 487–497.

Cicchetti, D. (2010). Developmental psychopathology. In R. Lerner (Ed.), *Handbook of lifespan development, Vol. 2 Social and emotional development* (pp. 511–589). Hoboken, NJ: Wiley.

Cicchetti, D. & Carlson, V. (Eds.). (1989). *Child maltreatment: Theory and research on the causes and consequences of child abuse and neglect.* New York: Cambridge University Press.

Cicchetti, D. & Rogosch, F. A. (2001). Diverse patterns of neuroendocrine activity in maltreated children. *Development and Psychopathology, 13,* 677–694.

Cicchetti, D. & Valentino, K. (2006). An ecological–transactional perspective on child maltreatment: Failure of the average expectable environment and its influence on child development. In D. Cicchetti & D. J. Cohen (Eds.), *Developmental psychopathology: Vol. 3. Risk, disorder, and adaptation* (2nd ed., pp. 129–201). Hoboken, NJ: Wiley.

Cillessen, A. H. N., Bukowski, W. M., & Haselager, G. J. T. (2000). Stability of sociometric categories. In A. H. N. Cillessen & W. M. Burkowski (Eds.), *New directions for child and adolescent development: No. 88. Recent advances in the measurement of acceptance and rejection in the peer system.* San Francisco: Jossey-Bass.

Cillessen, A. H. N. & Mayeux, L. (2004). Sociometric status and peer group behavior: Previous findings and current directions. In J. B. Kupersmidt & K. A. Dodge (Eds.), *Children's peer relations: From development to intervention* (pp. 3–20). Washington, DC: American Psychological Association.

Cillessen, A. H. N., Van IJzendoorn, H. W., Van Lishout, C. F. M., & Hartup, W. W. (1992). Heterogeneity among peer-rejected boys: Subtypes and stabilities. *Child Development, 63,* 893–905.

Cillessin, A. (2009). Sociometric methods. In K.H. Rubin, W. M. Bukowski, & B. Laursen (Eds.) *Handbook of peer interactions, relationships, and groups* (pp. 82–99). New York: Guilford.

Clark, E. V. (1987). The principle of contrast: A constraint on language acquisition. In B. MacWhinney (Ed.), *Mechanisms of language acquisition.* Hillsdale, NJ: Erlbaum.

Clark, E. V. (1993). *The lexicon in acquisition.* New York: Cambridge University Press.

Clark, E. V. (1995). Later lexical development and word learning. In P. Fletcher & B. MacWhinney (Eds.), *The handbook of child language.* Cambridge, MA: Blackwell.

Clarke, A. M. & Clarke, A. D. B. (1976). *Early experience: Myth and evidence.* London: Open Books Publishing.

Clarke-Stewart, K. A. (1989). Infant day care: Maligned or malignant? *American Psychologist, 44,* 266–273.

Clearfield, M. W. (2004). The role of crawling and walking experience in infant spatial memory, *Journal of Experimental Child Psychology, 89,* 214–241.

Clearfield, M. W. & Mix, K. S. (2001). Amount versus number: Infants' use of area and contour length to discriminate small sets. *Journal of Cognition and Development, 2,* 243–260.

Clements, A. M., Rimrodt, S. L., Abel, J. R., Blankner, J. G., Mostofsky, S. H., Pekar, J. J., Denckia, M. B., & Cutting, L. E. (2006). Sex differences in cerebral laterality of language and visuospatial processing. *Brain and Language, 98,* 150–158.

Cleveland, H. H., Jacobson, K. C., Lipinski, J. J., & Rowe, D. C. (2000). Genetic and shared environmental contributions to the relationship between the HOME environment and adolescent achievement. *Intelligence, 28,* 69–86.

Cleveland, H. H. & Wiebe, R. P. (2003). The moderation of adolescent-to-peer similarity in tobacco and alcohol use by school levels of substance use. *Child Development, 74,* 279–291.

Clifton, R. K., Gwiazda, J., Bauer, J. A., Clarkson, M. G., & Held, R. M. (1988). Growth in head size during infancy: Implications for sound localization. *Developmental Psychology, 24,* 477–483.

Clohessy, A. B. & Posner, M. I. (1991). The development of inhibition of return in early infancy. *Journal of Cognitive Neuroscience, 3*(4), 345–350.

Clumeck, H. V. (1980). The acquisition of tone. In G. H. Yeni-Komshian, J. Kavanagh, & C. A. Ferguson (Eds.), *Child phonology: Vol. 1. Production.* New York: Academic Press.

Coch, D., Skendzel, W., Grossi, G., & Neville, H. (2005). Motion and color processing in school-age children and adults: An ERP study. *Developmental Science, 8,* 372–386.

Cochran, M. & Niego, S. (2002). Parenting and social networks. In M. H. Bornstein (Ed.), *Handbook of parenting* (2nd ed., Vol. 4). Mahwah, NJ: Erlbaum.

Cohen, D. (1979). *J. B. Watson: The founder of behaviorism.* London: Routledge & Kegan Paul.

Cohen, D. & Strayer, J. (1996). Empathy in conduct-disordered and comparison youth. *Developmental Psychology, 32,* 988–998.

Cohen, L. B. (1998). An information-processing approach to infant perception and cognition. In F. Simion & G. Butterworth (Eds.), *The development of sensory, motor and cognitive capacities in early infancy: From perception to cognition.* Hove, UK: Psychology Press.

Cohen, L. B. (2006). The role of three-dimensional ultrasound in prenatal diagnosis. In J. M. Vugt. & L. P. Schulman (Eds.), *Prenatal medicine* (pp. 353–368). New York, NY: Taylor and Francis.

Cohen, L. B. & Amsel, G. (1998). Precursors to infants' perception of the causality of a simple event. *Infant Behavior and Development, 21,* 713–731.

Cohen, L. B. & Marks, K. S. (2002). How infants process addition and subtraction events. *Developmental Science, 5,* 186–212.

Cohen, L. B. & Strauss, M. S. (1979). Concept acquisition in the human infant. *Child Development, 50,* 419–424.

Cohen, N. R., Cross, E. S., Tunik, E., Grafton, S. T., & Culham, J. C. (2009). Ventral and dorsal stream contributions to the online control of immediate and delayed grasping: A TMS approach. *Neuropsychologia, 47,* 1553–1562.

Cohen, S. E. (1974). Developmental differences in infants' attentional responses to face-voice incongruity of mother and stranger. *Child Development, 45,* 1155–1158.

Cohen-Bendahan, C. C., van de Beek, C., & Berenbaum, S. A. (2005). Prenatal sex hormone effects on child and adult sex-typed behavior: Methods and findings. *Neuroscience & Biobehavioral Reviews, 29,* 353–384.

Cohen-Kadosh, K., & Johnson, M. H. (2007). Developing a cortex specialized for face perception. *Trends in Cognitive Sciences, 11,* 367–369.

Coie, J. D. (2004). The impact of negative social experience on the development of antisocial behavior. In J. Kupersmidt & K. A. Dodge (Eds.), *Peer relations in childhood: From development to intervention to public policy.* Washington, DC: American Psychological Association.

Coie, J. D. & Dodge, K. A. (1998). Aggression and antisocial behavior. In W. Damon (Series Ed.) & N. Eisenberg (Vol. Ed.), *Handbook of child psychology: Vol. 3. Social, emotional, and personality development* (5th ed.). New York: Wiley.

Coie, J. D. & Krehbiel, G. (1984). Effects of academic tutoring on the social status of low-achieving, socially rejected children. *Child Development, 55,* 1465–1478.

Coie, J. D. & Kupersmidt, J. (1983). A behavioral analysis of emerging social status in boys' groups. *Child Development, 54,* 1400–1416.

Colapinto, J. (2000). *As nature made him.* New York: HarperCollins.

Colby, A. & Kohlberg, L. (1987). *The measurement of moral judgment* (Vols. 1–2). New York: Cambridge University Press.

Colby A., Kohlberg, L., Gibbs, J. C., & Lieberman, M. (1983). A longitudinal study of moral judgment. *Monographs of the Society for Research in Child Development, 48* (1–2, Serial No. 200).

Cole, M. (1996). *Cultural psychology: A once and future discipline.* Cambridge, MA: Harvard University Press.

Cole, M. (1999). Culture in development. In M. H. Bornstein & M. E. Lamb (Eds.), *Developmental psychology: An advanced textbook* (4th ed.). Mahwah, NJ: Erlbaum.

Cole, M. (2006). Culture and cognitive development in phylogenetic, historical, and ontogenetic perspective. In W. Damon & R. M. Lerner (Series Eds.) & K. Dunn & R. S. Siegler (Volume Eds.), *Handbook of child psychology* (6th ed., Vol. 2, pp. 636–683). Hoboken, NJ: Wiley.

Cole, M. & Packer, M. (2010). Culture in development. In M. H. Bornstein & M. E. Lamb (Eds.), *Developmental science: An advanced textbook* (6th ed.). London: Psychology Press.

Cole, P. M. (1986). Children's spontaneous control of facial expression. *Child Development, 57,* 1309–1321.

Coleman, E. B. (1998). Using explanatory knowledge during collaborative problem solving in science. *Journal of the Learning Sciences, 7,* 387–427.

Collins, R. L. (2011). Content analysis of gender roles in the media: Where are we now and where should we go? *Sex Roles, 64,* 290–298.

Collins, W. A., Maccoby, E. E., Steinberg, L., Hetherington, E. M., & Bornstein, M. H. (2000). Contemporary research on parenting: The case for nature *and* nurture. *American Psychologist, 55,* 218–232.

Collins, W. A. & Russell, G. (1991). Mother-child and father-child relationships in middle childhood and adolescence: A developmental analysis. *Developmental Review, 11,* 99–136.

Collis, G. M. (1985). On the origins of turn-taking: Alternation and meaning. In M. D. Barrett (Ed.), *Children's single-word speech.* New York: Wiley.

Colombo, J. (2001). The development of visual attention in infancy. *Annual Review of Psychology, 52,* 337–367.

Colombo, J., & Bundy, R. S. (1981). A method for the measurement of infant auditory selectivity. *Infant Behavior and Development, 4,* 219–223.

Colombo, J. & Mitchell, D. W. (2009). Infant visual habituation. *Neurobiology of Learning and Memory, 92,* 225–234.

Colombo, J., Shaddy, D. J., Richman, W. A., Maikranz, J. M., & Blaga, O. M. (2004). The developmental course of habituation in infancy and preschool outcome. *Infancy, 5,* 1–38.

Colpin, H. (2002). Parenting and psychosocial development of IVF children: Review of the research literature. *Developmental Review, 22,* 644–673.

Colvin, M. K., Funnell, M. G., & Gazzaniga, M. S. (2005). Numerical processing in the two hemispheres: Studies of a split-brain patient. *Brain and Cognition, 57,* 43–52.

Comer, R. & Gould, E. (2011). *Psychology around us.* Hoboken, NJ: Wiley.

Compas, B. R., Conner-Smith, J. J., Saaltzman, H., Thomsen, A. H., & Wadsworth, M. E. (2001). Coping with stress during childhood and adolescence: Problems, progress, and potential in theory and development. *Psychological Bulletin, 127,* 87–127.

Comstock, G. & Scharrer, E. (2006). Media and popular culture. In K. A. Renninger, I. E. Sigel, W. E. Damon, & R. M. Lerner (Eds.), *Handbook of child psychology: Vol 4, Child psychology in practice* (6th ed., pp. 817–863). Hoboken, NJ: Wiley.

Condry, K. F., Smith, W. C., & Spelke, E. S. (2001). Development of perceptual organization. In F. Lacerda, C. von Hofsten, & M. Heimann (Eds.), *Emerging cognitive abilities in early infancy.* Mahwah, NJ: Erlbaum.

Conduct Problems Prevention Research Group (CPPRG). (1992). A developmental and clinical model for the prevention of conduct disorder: The FAST Track Program. *Development and Psychopathology 4,* 509–527.

Conduct Problems Prevention Research Group (CPPRG). (1999). Initial impact of the Fast Track prevention trial for conduct problems: I. The high-risk sample. *Journal of Consulting and Clinical Psychology, 67,* 631–647.

Conduct Problems Prevention Research Group (CPPRG). (2002). Evaluation of the first 3 years of the Fast Track prevention trial with children at high risk for adolescent conduct problems. *Journal of Abnormal Child Psychology, 30,* 19–35.

Conduct Problems Prevention Research Group (CPPRG). (2004). The effects of the fast track program on serious problem outcomes at the end of elementary school. *Journal of Clinical Child and Adolescent Psychology, 33,* 650–661.

Conduct Problems Prevention Research Group (CPPRG). (2007). Fast track randomized controlled trial to prevent externalizing psychiatric disorders: Findings from grades 3 to 9. *Journal of the American Academy of Child & Adolescent Psychiatry, 46,* 1250–1262.

Conel, J. L. (1939–1967). *The postnatal development of the human cerebral cortex,* Vols. I - VIII. Cambridge, MA: Harvard University Press.

Conger, R. D. & Donnellan, M. B. (2007). An interactionist perspective on the socioeconomic context of human development. *Annual Review of Psychology, 58,* 175–199.

Connell, J. P. & Ilardi, B. C. (1987.) Self-system concomitants of discrepancies between children's and teachers' evaluations of academic competence. *Child Development, 58,* 1297–1307.

Connellan, J., Baron-Cohen, S., Wheelwright, S., Batki, A., & Ahluwalia, J. (2000). Sex differences in human neonatal social perception. *Infant Behavior and Development, 23,* 113–118.

Constanzo, P. R. (1970). Conformity development as a function of self-blame. *Journal of Personality and Social Psychology, 14,* 366–374.

Conti, D. J. & Camras, L. A. (1984). Children's understanding of conversational principles. *Journal of Experimental Child Psychology, 38,* 456–463.

Cooley, C. H. (1902). *Human nature and the social order.* New York: Charles Scribner's Sons.

Cooper, R. P. & Aslin, R. N. (1990). Preference for infant-directed speech in the first month after birth. *Child Development, 61,* 1584–1595.

Cooper, R. P. & Aslin, R. N. (1994). Developmental differences in infant attention to the spectral properties of infant-directed speech. *Child Development, 65,* 1663–1677.

Coplan, R. J. & Arbeau, K. A. (2009). Peer interactions and play in early childhood. In K.H. Rubin, W. M. Bukowski, & B. Laursen (Eds.), *Handbook of peer interactions, Relationships, and groups* (pp. 143–161). New York: Guilford.

Coplan, R. J., Girardi, A., Findlay, L. C., & Frohlick, S. L. (2007). Understanding solitude: Young children's attitudes and responses toward hypothetical socially withdrawn peers. *Social Development, 16,* 390–409.

Coplan, R., Prakash, K., O'Neil, K., & Armer, M. (2004). Do you "want" to play? Distinguishing between conflicted shyness and social disinterest in early childhood. *Developmental Psychology, 40,* 244–258.

Coppola, M. & Newport, E. L. (2005). Grammatical subjects in home sign: Abstract linguistic structure in adult primary gesture systems without linguistic input. *Proceedings of the National Academy of Sciences of the United States of America, 102,* 19249–19253.

Copreni, E., Penzo, M., Carrabino, S., & Conese, M. (2004). Lentivirus-mediated gene transfer to the respiratory epithelium: a promising approach to gene therapy of cystic fibrosis. *Gene Therapy, 11,* S67–S75.

Corbetta, M. & Shulman, G. L. (1998). Human cortical mechanisms of visual attention during orienting and search. *Philosophical Transaction of the Royal Society London Series B, 353,* 1352–1362.

Cordes, S. & Brannon, E. M. (2008). The difficulties of representing continuous extent in infancy: Using number is just easier. *Child development, 79*(2), 476–489.

Corina, D. P., Vaid, J., & Bellugi, U. (1992). The linguistic basis of left hemisphere specialization. *Science, 255,* 1258–1260.

Cornelius, M. D. & Day, N. L. (2000). The effects of tobacco use during and after pregnancy on exposed children. *Alcohol Research and Health, 24,* 242–249.

Cornelius, M. D., Ryan, C. M., Day, N. L., Goldschmidt, L., & Willford, J. A. (2001). Prenatal tobacco effects on neuropsychological outcomes among preadolescents. *Journal of Developmental and Behavioral Pediatrics, 22,* 217–225.

Cornelius, M. D., Taylor, P., Geva, D., & Day, N. (1995). Prenatal tobacco exposure and marijuana use among adolescents: Effects on offspring gestational age, growth, and morphology. *Pediatrics, 95,* 738–743.

Corwyn, R. F. & Bradley, R. H. (1999). Determinants of paternal and maternal investment in children. *Infant Mental Health, 20,* 238–256.

Cosmides, L. & Tooby, J. (2001). Unraveling the enigma of human intelligence: Evolutionary psychology and the multimodular mind. In R. J. Sternberg & J. C. Kaufman (Eds.), *The evolution of intelligence.* Mahwah, NJ: Erlbaum.

Cossette, L., Pomerleau, A., Malcuit, F., & Kaczorowski, J. (1996). Emotional expressions of female and male infants in a social and nonsocial context. *Sex Roles, 35,* 693–710.

Coster, W. J., Gersten, M. S., Beeghly, M., & Cicchetti, D. (1989). Communicative functioning in maltreated toddlers. *Developmental Psychology, 25,* 1020–1029.

Costigan, C. L. & Dokis, D. P. (2006). Relations between parent-child acculturation differences and adjustment within immigrant Chinese families. *Child Development, 77,* 1252–1267.

Costigan, C., Su, T. F., & Hua, J. M. (2009). Ethnic identity among Chinese Canadian youth: A review of the Canadian literature. *Canadian Psychology, 50,* 261–272.

Costin, S. E. & Jones, D. C. (1992). Friendship as a facilitator of emotional responsiveness and prosocial interventions among young children. *Developmental Psychology, 28,* 941–947.

Cote, L. R. & Bornstein, M. H. (2009). Child and mother play in three U.S. cultural groups: Comparisons and associations. *Journal of Family Psychology, 23,* 355–363.

Coté, S. M., Vaillancourt, T. , Barker, E. D., Nagin, D., & Tremblay, R. E. (2007). The joint development of physical and indirect aggression: Predictors of continuity and change during childhood. *Development and Psychopathology, 19,* 37–55.

Coté, S. M., Vaillancourt, T., LeBlanc, J. C., Nagin, D., & Tremblay, R. E. (2006). The development of physical aggression from toddlerhood to preadolescence: A nation-wide longitudinal study of Canadian children. *Journal of Abnormal Child Psychology, 34,* 71–85.

Courage, M. L., Edison, S. C., & Howe, M. L. (2004). Variability in the early development of visual self-recognition. *Infant Behaviour & Development, 27,* 509–532.

Courage, M. L. & Howe, M. L. (2002). From infant to child: The dynamics of cognitive change in the second year of life. *Psychological Bulletin, 128,* 250–277.

Cowan, P. A. (1978). *Piaget with feeling.* New York: Holt, Rinehart & Winston.

Cowan P. A., Cohn, D. A., Cowan, C. P., & Pearson, J. L. (1996). Parents' attachment histories and children's externalizing and internalizing behaviors: Exploring family systems models of linkage. *Journal of Consulting and Clinical Psychology, 64,* 53–63.

Cowan, P. A. & Cowan, C. P. (2002). What an intervention design reveals about how parents affect their children's academic achievement and behavior problems. In J. G. Borkowski, S. L. Ramey, & M. Bristol-Power (Eds.), *Parenting and the child's world: Influences on academic, intellectual, and social-emotional development.* Mahwah, NJ: Erlbaum.

Cowperthwaite, B., Hains, S. M., & Kisilevsky, B. S. (2007). Fetal behavior in smoking compared to non-smoking pregnant women. *Infant Behavior and Development, 30,* 422–430.

Cox, B. D. & Lightfoot, C. (Eds.). (1997). *Sociogenetic perspectives on internalization.* Mahwah, NJ: Erlbaum.

Coyle, T. R. (2001). Factor analysis of variability measures in eight independent samples of children and adults. *Journal of Experimental Child Psychology, 78,* 330–358.

Coyle, T. R. & Bjorklund, D. F. (1997). Age differences in, and consequences of, multiple- and variable-strategy use on a multitrial sort-recall task. *Developmental Psychology, 33,* 372–380.

Coyne, S. M., Nelson, D. A., & Underwood, M. (2011). Aggression in children. In P. K. Smith & K. H. Hart (Eds.). *The Wiley-Blackwell handbook of childhood social development,* 2nd edition (pp. 491–509). Hoboken, NJ. Wiley.

Cragg, L., Kovacevic, N., McIntosh, A. R., Poulsen, C., Martinu, K., Leonard, G., & Paus, T. (2011). Maturation of EEG power spectra in early adolescence: A longitudinal study. *Developmental Science, 14,* 935–943.

Crago, M. B. (1988). *Cultural context in the communicative interaction of young Inuit children.* Unpublished doctoral dissertation. McGill University.

Craig, C. M. & Lee, D. N. (1999). Neonatal control of sucking pressure: Evidence for an intrinsic tau-guide. *Experimental Brain Research, 124,* 371–382.

Craig, K. D., Grunau, R. V. E., & Aquan-Assee, J. (1988) Judgment of pain in newborns: Facial activity and cry as determinants. *Canadian Journal of Behavioral Science, 20,* 442–451.

Craig, W. & Harel, Y. (2004) Bullying and fighting. In C. Currie et al. (Eds.), *Young people's health in context: International report from the HBSC 2001/02 survey.* WHO Policy Series: Health policy for children and adolescents Issue 4, WHO Regional Office for Europe, Copenhagen. World Health International Report, World Health Organization.

Craig, W. & Pepler, D. (1995). Peer processes in bullying and victimization: An observational study. *Exceptionality Education Canada, 5,* 81–95.

Craig, W. & Pepler, D. (2003). Identifying and targeting risk for involvement in bullying and victimization. *Canadian Journal of Psychiatry, 48,* 577–582.

Craig, W. & Pepler, D. (2007). Understanding bullying: From research to practice. *Canadian Psychology, 48,* 86–93.

Craig, W., Pepler, D., & Blais, J. (2007). Responding to bullying: What works. *School Psychology International, 28,* 465–477.

Crain, W. (2011). *Theories of development: Concepts and applications* (6th edition). Upper Saddle River, NJ: Pearson.

Crawford, N. (2002). Science-based program curbs violence in kids. *Monitor on Psychology, 33,* 38.

Creasey, G. L. & Koblewski, P. J. (1991). Adolescent grandchildren's relationships with maternal and paternal grandmothers and grandfathers. *Journal of Adolescence, 14,* 373–387.

Crick, N. R. & Dodge, K. A. (1994). A review and reformulation of social information-processing mechanisms in children's social adjustment. *Psychological Bulletin, 115,* 74–101.

Crick, N. R., Ostrov, J. M., & Yawabata, Y. (2007). Relational aggression and gender: An overview. In D. J. Flannery, A. T. Vazsonyi, & I. D. Waldman (Eds.), *The Cambridge handbook of violent behavior and aggression* (pp. 245–259). New York, NY: Cambridge University Press.

Crick, N. R. & Werner, N. (1998). Response decision processes in relational and overt aggression. *Child Development, 69,* 1630–1639.

Criss, M. M., Pettit, G. S., Bates, J. E., Dodge, K. A., & Lapp, A. L. (2002). Family adversity, positive peer relationships, and children's externalizing behavior: A longitudinal perspective on risk and resilience. *Child Development, 73,* 1220–1237.

Crittenden, P. M. & Ainsworth, M. D. S. (1989). Child maltreatment and attachment theory. In D. Cicchetti & V. Carlson (Eds.), *Child maltreatment: Theory and research on the causes and consequences of child abuse and neglect.* New York: Cambridge University Press.

Crockenberg, S. B. (1986). Are temperamental differences in babies associated with predictable differences in care giving? In J. V. Lerner & R. M. Lerner (Eds.), *New directions for child development: No. 31. Temperament and social interaction during infancy and childhood.* San Francisco: Jossey-Bass.

Crockett, L. J. & Petersen, A. C. (1987). Pubertal status and psychosocial development: Findings from the early adolescence study. In R. M. Lerner & T. L. Foch (Eds.), *Biological psychosocial interactions in early adolescence.* Hillsdale, NJ: Erlbaum.

Croen, L., Najjar, D., Fireman, B., & Grether, J. (2007). Maternal and paternal age and risk of autism spectrum disorders. *Archives of Pediatrics & Adolescent Medicine, 161,* 334–340.

Crompton, L. (2003). *Homosexuality and civilization.* Cambridge, MA: Belknap Press.

Crone, E. A. & van der Molen, M. W. (2008). Neurocognitive development of performance monitoring and decision making. In C.A. Nelson & M. Luciana (Eds.), *Handbook of developmental cognitive neuroscience* (2nd ed., pp. 883–896). Cambridge, MA: MIT Press.

Crone, E. A. & Westenberg, P. M. (2009). A brain-based account of developmental changes in social decision making. In M. de Haan & M. R. Gunnar (Eds.), *Handbook of developmental social neuroscience* (pp. 378–398). New York: Guilford Press.

Crone, E. A., Zanolie, K., Van Leijenhorst, L., Westenberg, P. M., & Rombouts, A. R. B. (2008). Neural mechanisms supporting flexible performance adjustment during development. *Cognitive, Affective, and Behavioral Neuroscience, 8,* 165–177.

Crook, C. K. (1979). The organization and control of infant sucking. In H. W. Reese & L. P. Lipsitt (Eds.), *Advances in child development and behavior* (Vol. 14). New York: Academic Press.

Cross, S. E. & Gore, J. S. (2003). Cultural models of the self. In M. R. Leary & J. P. Tangney (Eds.), *Handbook of self and identity.* New York: Guilford.

Crouchman, M. (1985). What mothers know about their newborns' visual skills. *Developmental Medicine and Child Neurology, 27,* 455–460.

Crow, T. J. (2004). Cerebral asymmetry and the lateralization of language: Core deficits in schizophrenia as pointers to the gene. *Current Opinion in Psychiatry, 17,* 97–106.

Crowell, J. A. & Feldman, S. S. (1991). Mothers' working models of attachment relationships and mother and child behavior during separation and reunion. *Developmental Psychology, 27,* 597–605.

Crowell, J. A., Fraley, C., & Shaver, P. R. (2008). Measurement of individual differences in adolescent and adult attachment, In J. Cassidy & P. R. Shaver (Eds.), *Handbook of attachment: Theory, research, and clinical applications (2nd edition)* (pp. 599–634). New York, NY: Guilford.

Cummings, E. M. & Cummings, J. S. (2002). Parenting and attachment. In M. H. Bornstein (Ed.), *Handbook of parenting* Vol. 5 (2nd ed.). Mahwah, NJ: Erlbaum.

Cunningham, F. G., Leveno, K. L., Bloom, S., Hauth, J. C., Rouse, D. J., & Spong, C. Y. (2010). *Williams obstetrics, 23rd edition,* New York, NY: McGraw-Hill Medical.

Curtiss, S. (1977). *Genie: A psycholinguistic study of a modern day "wild child."* New York: Academic Press.

Cutting, A. L. & Dunn, J. (2006). Conversations with siblings and with friends: Links between relationship quality and social understanding. *British Journal of Developmental Psychology, 24,* 73–87.

Czernochowski, D., Mecklinger, A., & Johansson, M. (2009). Age-related changes in the control of episodic retrieval: An ERP study of recognition memory in children and adults. *Developmental Science, 12,* 1026–1040.

Czeschlik, T. & Rost, D. H. (1995). Sociometric types and children's intelligence. *British Journal of Developmental Psychology, 13,* 177–189.

D

Damon, W. (1983). *Social and personality development.* New York: Norton.

Damon, W. (1984). Peer education: The untapped potential. *Journal of Applied Developmental Psychology, 5,* 331–343.

Daneman, M. & Case, R. (1981). Syntactic form, semantic complexity, and short-term memory: Influences on children's acquisition of new linguistic structures. *Developmental Psychology, 17,* 367–378.

Dannemiller, J. L. (1985). The early phase of dark adaptation in human infants. *Vision Research, 25,* 207–212.

Dannemiller, J. L. & Hanko, S. A. (1987). A test of color constancy in 4-month-old infants. *Journal of Experimental Child Psychology, 44,* 255–267.

Dannemiller, J. L. & Stephens, B. R. (1988). A critical test of infant pattern preference models. *Child Development, 59,* 210–216.

Danner, F. W. & Day, M. C. (1977). Eliciting formal operations. *Child Development, 48,* 1600–1606.

Darwin, C. (1859). *The origin of species.* London: Murray.

Darwin, C. (1871/1896). *Descent of man.* New York: Appleton.

Darwin, C. (1872). *The expression of emotions in man and animals.* London: Murray.

Darwin, C. (1877). A biographical sketch of an infant. *Mind, 2,* 285–294.

Dasen, P. R. (1975a). Concrete operational development in Canadian Eskimos. *International Journal of Psychology, 10,* 165–180.

Dasen, P. R. (1975b). Concrete operational development in three cultures. *Journal of Cross-Cultural Psychology, 6,* 156–172.

David, A. L. & Rodeck, C. H. (2006). Gene therapy. In J. M. Vugt. & L. P. Schulman (Eds.), *Prenatal medicine* (pp. 535–564). New York, NY: Taylor and Francis.

David, C. F. & Kistner, J. A. (2000). Do positive self-perceptions have a "dark side"? Examination of the link between perceptual bias and aggression. *Journal of Abnormal Child Psychology, 28,* 327–337.

Davidson, D., Cameron, P., & Jergovic, D. (1995). The effects of children's stereotypes on their memory for elderly individuals. *Merrill-Palmer Quarterly Journal of Developmental Psychology, 41,* 70–90.

Davidson, D., Jergovic, D., Imami, Z., & Theodos, V. (1997). Monolingual and bilingual children's use of the mutual exclusivity constraint. *Journal of Child Language, 24,* 3–24.

Davidson, D. & Tell, D. (2005). Monolingual and bilingual children's use of mutual exclusivity in the naming of whole objects. *Journal of Experimental Child Psychology,* 92(1), 25–45.

Davies, W., Isles, A. R., & Wilkinson, L. S. (2001). Imprinted genes and mental dysfunction. *Annals of Medicine, 13,* 428–436.

Davis, T. L. (1995). Gender differences in masking negative emotions: Ability or motivation? *Developmental Psychology, 31,* 660–667.

Davison, G., Blankstein, K., Flett, G., & Neale, J., (2008). *Abnormal psychology* (Third Canadian Edition). Etobicoke, ON: Wiley.

Davison, K. K. & Birch, L. L. (2002). Processes linking weight status and self-concept among girls from ages 5 to 7 years. *Developmental Psychology, 38,* 735–748.

Dawkins, R. (1976). *The selfish gene.* New York: Oxford University Press.

Dawood, K., Bailey, M., & Martin, N. G. (2009). Genetic and environmental influences on sexual orientation. In Y. K. Kim (Ed.), *Handbook of behavior genetics* (pp. 269–279), New York, NY: Springer.

Day, M. C. (1975). Developmental trends in visual scanning. In H. W. Reese (Ed.), *Advances in child development and behavior* (Vol. 10). New York: Academic Press.

Day, N. L., Richardson, G. A., Goldschmidt, L., & Cornelius, M. D. (2000). Effects of prenatal tobacco exposure on preschoolers' behavior. *Journal of Developmental and Behavioral Pediatrics, 21,* 180–188.

Day, R. H. (1987). Visual size constancy in infancy. In B. E. McKenzie & R. H. Day (Eds.), *Perceptual development in early infancy: Problems and issues.* Hillsdale, NJ: Erlbaum.

De Civita, M., Pagani, L., Vitaro, F., & Tremblay, R. E. (2004). The role of maternal educational aspirations in mediating the risk of income source on academic failure in children from persistently poor families. *Children and Youth Services Review, 26,* 749–769.

De Civita, M., Pagani, L., Vitaro, F., & Tremblay, R. E. (2007). Does maternal supervision mediate the impact of income source on behavioral adjustment in children from persistently poor families? *Journal of Early Adolescence, 27,* 40–66.

De Genna, N. M., Stack, D. M., Serbin, L. A., Ledingham, J. E., & Schwartzman, A. E. (2007). Maternal and child health problems: The inter-generational consequences of early maternal aggression and withdrawal. *Social Science & Medicine, 64,* 2417–2426.

de Haan, M. (2001). The neuropsychology of face processing in infancy. In C. A. Nelson & M. Luciana (Eds.), *Handbook of developmental cognitive neuro-science.* Cambridge, MA: MIT Press.

de Haan, M. (2007). *Infant EEG and event-related potentials: Studies in developmental psychology.* New York, NY: Psychology Press.

de Haan, M. (2008). Neurocognitive mechanisms for the development of face processing. In C.A. Nelson & M. Luciana (Eds.), *Handbook of developmental cognitive neuroscience* (2nd ed., pp. 509–522). Cambridge, MA: MIT Press.

de Haan, M. & Nelson, C. A. (1998). Discrimination and categorisation of facial expressions of emotions during infancy. In A. Slater (Ed.), *Perceptual development: Visual, auditory, and speech perception in infancy.* Hove, UK: Psychology Press.

de Haan, M. & Nelson, C. A. (1999). Brain activity differentiates face and object processing in 6-month-old infants. *Developmental Psychology, 35,* 1113–1121.

de Jager, B., Jansen, M., & Reezigt, G. (2005). The development of metacognition in primary school learning environments. *School Effectiveness and School Improvement, 16,* 179–196.

De Lisi, R. & Goldbeck, S. L. (1999). Implications of Piagetian theory for peer learning. In A. M. O'Donnell & A. King (Eds.), *Cognitive perspectives on peer learning.* Mahwah, NJ: Erlbaum.

De Lisi, R. & Staudt, J. (1980). Individual differences in college students' performance on formal operations tasks. *Journal of Applied Developmental Psychology, 1,* 201–208.

De Lisi, R. & Wolford, J. (2002). Improving children's mental rotation accuracy with computer game playing. *Journal of Genetic Psychology, 163,* 272–283.

De Ribaupierre, A., Rieben, L., & Lautrey, J. (1991). Developmental change and individual differences: A longitudinal study using Piagetian tasks. *Genetic, Social, and General Psychology Monographs, 117,* 285–311.

de Veer, M. W., Gallup, G. G. J., Theall, L. A., van den Bos, R., & Povinelli, D. J. (2003). An 8-year longitudinal study of mirror self-recognition in chimpanzees (Pan troglodytes). *Neuropsychologia, 41,* 229–234.

de Villiers, J. G. (1980). The process of rule learning in child speech: A new look. In K. E. Nelson (Ed.), *Children's language* (Vol. 2). New York: Gardner.

de Villiers, J. G. & de Villiers, P. A. (1999). Language development. In M. H. Bornstein & M. E. Lamb (Eds.), *Developmental psychology: An advanced textbook* (4th ed.). Mahwah, NJ: Erlbaum.

de Waal, F. B. M. (1993). Reconciliation among primates: A review of empirical evidence and unresolved issues. In W. A. Mason & S. Mendoza (Eds.), *Primate social conflict.* Albany, NY: State University of New York Press.

de Waal, F. B. M. (1996). *Good natured: The origins of right and wrong in humans and other animals.* Cambridge, MA: Harvard University Press.

de Waal, F. B. M. (1997). Food transfers through mesh in brown capuchins. *Journal of Comparative Psychology, 111,* 370–378.

de Waal, F. B. M. (2000). Primates—a natural heritage of conflict resolution. *Science, 289,* 586–590.

de Waal, F. B. M. (2005). A century of getting to know the chimpanzee. *Nature, 437,* 56–59.

de Waal, F. B. M. (2008). Putting the altruism back into altruism: The evolution of empathy. *Annual Review of Psychology, 59,* 279–300.

De Wolff, M. S. & van IJzendoorn, M. H. (1997). Sensitivity and attachment: A meta-analysis on parental antecedents of infant attachment. *Child Development, 68,* 571–591.

Deák, G. O. (2000). Hunting the fox of word learning: Why "constraints" fail to capture it. *Developmental Review, 20,* 29–80.

Deák, G. O., Ray, S. D., & Brenneman, K. (2003). Children's perseverative appearance-reality errors are related to emerging language skills, *Child Development, 74,* 944–964.

DeBaryshe, B. D., Patterson, G. R., & Capaldi, D. M. (1993). Performance model for academic achievement in early adolescent boys. *Developmental Psychology, 29,* 795–804.

Decaluwe, V. & Braet, C. (2003). Prevalence of binge-eating disorder in obese children and adolescents seeking weight-loss treatment. *International Journal of Obesity, 27,* 404–409.

DeCasper, A. J. & Fifer, W. P. (1980). Of human bonding: Newborns prefer their mothers' voices. *Science, 208,* 1174–1176.

DeCasper, A. J., Lecanuet, J.-P., Busnel, M.-C., Granier-Deferre, C., & Mau-Geais, R. (1994). Fetal reactions to recurrent maternal speech. *Infant Behavior and Development, 17,* 159–164.

DeCasper, A. J. & Prescott, P. A. (1984). Human newborns' perception of male voices: Preference, discrimination, and reinforcing value. *Developmental Psychobiology, 17,* 481–491.

DeCasper, A. J. & Spence, M. J. (1986). Newborns prefer a familiar story over an unfamiliar one. *Infant Behavior and Development, 9,* 133–150.

DeCasper, A. J. & Spence, M. J. (1991). Auditory mediated behavior during the perinatal period: A cognitive view. In M. J. S. Weiss & P. R. Zelazo (Eds.), *Newborn attention: Biological constraints and the influence of experience.* Norwood, NJ: Ablex.

DeFries, J. C., Plomin, R., & Fulker, D. W. (Eds.). (1994). *Nature and nurture during middle childhood.* Oxford, England: Blackwell.

Dehaene-Lambertz, G. & Dahaene, S. (1994). Speed and cerebral correlates of syllable discrimination in infants. *Nature, 370,* 292–295.

Dehaene-Lambertz, G., Dehaene, S., & Hertz-Pannier, L. (2002). Functional neuroimaging of speech perception in infants. *Science, 298,* 2013–2015.

Dejin-Karlsson, E., Hanson, B. S., Estergen, P., Sjoeberg, N., & Marshal, K. (1998). Does passive smoking in early pregnancy increase the risk of small-for-gestational age infants? *American Journal of Public Health, 88,* 1523–1527.

Del Carmen, R., Pedersen, F. A., Huffman, L. C., & Bryan, Y. E. (1993). Dyadic distress management predicts subsequent security of attachment. *Infant Behavior and Development, 16,* 131–147.

Delhanty, J. D. A. (2006). Human cytogenetics. In P. Ferretti, A. Copp, C. Tickle, & G. Moore (Eds.) *Embryos, genes, and birth defects* (2nd edition) (pp. 33–49). Hoboken, NJ: Wiley.

DeLoache, J. S. (2000). Dual representation and young children's use of scale models. *Child Development, 71,* 329–338.

DeLoache, J. S. (2011). Early development of the understanding and use of symbolic artifacts. In U. Goswami (Ed.), *The Wiley-Blackwell handbook of childhood cognitive development, second edition* (pp. 312–336). Chichester, UK: Blackwell Publishing Ltd.

DeLoache, J. S., Miller, K. F., & Pierretsoukas, S. L. (1998). Reasoning and problem solving. In W. Damon (Series Ed.) & D. Kuhn & R. S. Siegler (Vol. Eds.), *Handbook of child psychology: Vol. 2. Cognition, perception, and language* (5th ed.). New York: Wiley.

DeLoache, J. S., Pierroutsakos, S. L., & Troseth, G. L. (1996). The three "R's" of pictorial competence. In R. Vasta (Ed.), *Annals of child development* (Vol. 12). London: Jessica Kingsley Publishers.

DeMarie, D. & Ferron, J. (2003). Capacity, strategies, and metamemory: Tests of a three-factor model of memory development. *Journal of Experimental Child Psychology, 84,* 167–193.

Demetras, M. J., Post, K. N., & Snow, C. E. (1986). Feedback to first language learners: The role of repetitions and clarification questions. *Journal of Child Language, 13,* 275–292.

Demetrick, A., Mouyl, A. & Spanoudis, G. (2010). The development of mental processing. In W. F. Overton (Ed.), *The Handbook of lifespan development: Volume 1: Cognition, biology, and methods* (pp. 306–345). Hoboken, NJ: John Wiley & Sons, Inc..

Denenberg, V. & Thoman, E. (1981). Evidence for a functional role for active (REM) sleep in infancy. *Sleep, 4,* 185–191.

Denham, S. A. (1998). *Emotional development in young children.* New York: Guilford.

Denham, S. A., Bassett, H. H., & Wyatt, T. (2007). The socialization of emotional competence. In J. E. Grusec & P. D. Hastings (Eds.), *Handbook of socialization: Theory and research* (pp. 614–637). New York, NY: Guilford.

Denham, S. A. & Couchoud, E. A. (1991). Social-emotional predictors of preschoolers' responses to adult negative emotion. *Journal of Child Psychology and Psychiatry and Allied Disciplines, 32,* 595–608.

Denham, S. A. & McKinley, M. (1993). Sociometric nominations of preschoolers: A psychometric analysis. *Early Education and Development, 4,* 109–122.

Dennis, W. (1960). Causes of retardation among institutional children: Iran. *Journal of Genetic Psychology, 96,* 47–59.

Dennis, W. & Najarian, P. (1957). Infant development under environmental handicap. *Psychological Monographs, 71* (7, Whole No. 436).

Denton, K. & Zarbatany, L. (1996). Age differences in support processes in conversations between friends. *Child Development, 67,* 1360–1373.

Deprest, J., Lewi, L., Jani, J., et al. (2006). Fetoscopic instrumentation and techniques. In J. M. Vugt & L. P. Schulman (Eds.), *Prenatal medicine* (pp. 473–491). New York, NY: Taylor and Francis.

DeRosier, M. E. & Thomas, J. M. (2003). Strengthening sociometric prediction: Scientific advances in the assessment of children's peer relations. *Child Development, 74,* 1379–1392.

Deruelle, C. & de Schonen, S. (1998). Do the right and left hemispheres attend to the same visuospatial information within a face in infancy? *Developmental Neuropsychology, 14,* 535–554.

Dettling, A. C., Gunnar, M. R., & Donzella, B. (1999). Cortisol levels of young children in full-day child-care centers: Relations with age and temperament. *Psychoneuroendocrinology, 24,* 519–536.

Deutsch, F. M., Servis, L. J., & Payne, J. D. (2001). Paternal participation in child care and its effects on children's self-esteem and attitudes toward gendered roles. *Journal of Family Issues, 22,* 1000–1024.

DeVries, M. W. & Sameroff, A. J. (1984). Culture and temperament: Influences on infant temperament in three East African societies. *American Journal of Orthopsychiatry, 54,* 83–96.

DeVries, R. & Zan, B. (1994). *Moral classrooms, moral children: Creating a constructivist atmosphere in early education.* New York: Teachers College Press.

Diamond, A. (1990a). The development and neural bases of memory functions, as indexed by the A-not-B and delayed response tasks, in human infants and infant monkeys. *Annals of the New York Academy of Sciences, 608,* 267–317.

Diamond, A. (1990b). Developmental time course in human infants and infant monkeys, and the neural bases, of inhibitory control in reaching. *Annals of the New York Academy of Sciences, 608,* 637–676.

Diamond, A. (2000). Close interrelation of motor development and cognitive development and of the cerebellum and prefrontal cortex. *Child Development, 71,* 44–56.

Diamond, A. (2001). A model system for studying the role of dopamine in the prefrontal cortex during early development in humans: Early and continuously treated phenylketonuria. In C.A. Nelson & M. Luciana (Eds.), *Handbook of developmental cognitive neuroscience* (pp. 433–472). Cambridge, MA: MIT Press.

Diamond, A. (2002). Normal development of prefrontal cortex from birth to young adulthood: cognitive functions, anatomy, and biochemistry. In D. T. Stuss & R. T. Knight (Eds.), *Principles of Frontal Lobe Function* (pp. 466–503). New York: Oxford University Press.

Diamond, A. (2005). Attention-deficit disorder (attention-deficit/hyperactivity disorder without hyperactivity): A neurobiologically and behaviorally distinct disorder from attention-deficit/hyperactivity disorder (with hyperactivity). *Development and Psychopathology, 17,* 807–825.

Diamond, A. (2006a). Bootstrapping conceptual deduction using physical connection: Rethinking frontal cortex. *Trends in Cognitive Science, 10,* 212–218.

Diamond, A. (2006b). The early development of executive functions. In E. Bialystok & F. Craik (Eds.), *Lifespan cognition: Mechanisms of change* (pp. 70–95). Oxford: Oxford University Press.

Diamond, A. & Goldman-Rakic, P. S. (1989). Comparison of human infants and rhesus monkeys on Piaget's AB task: Evidence for dependence on dorsolateral prefrontal cortex. *Experimental Brain Research, 74,* 24–40.

Diamond, A., Prevor, M. B., Callender, G., & Druin, D. (1997). Prefrontal cortex cognitive deficits in children treated early and continuously for PKU. *Monographs of the Society for Research in Child Development, 62* (4, Serial No. 252), 1–208.

Diamond, L. M., Savin-Williams, R. C., & Dubé, E. M. (1999). Sex, dating, passionate friendships, and romance: Intimate peer relations among lesbian, gay, and bisexual adolescents. In W. Furman, B. B. Brown, & C. Feiring (Eds.), *The development of romantic relationships in adolescence.* Cambridge: Cambridge University Press.

Diamond, M. (1993). Homosexuality and bisexuality in different populations. *Archives of Sexual Behavior, 22,* 291–310.

Diamond, M. & Sigmundson, H. K. (1997). Sex reassignment at birth. Long-term review and clinical implications. *Archives of Pediatric Adolescent Medicine, 151,* 298–304.

Dick, D. M., Rose, R. J., Viken, R. J., & Kaprio, J. (2000). Pubertal timing and substance use: Associations between and within families across adolescence. *Developmental Psychology, 36,* 180–189.

Dickens, W. T. & Flynn, J. R. (2001). Heritability estimates versus large environmental effects: The IQ paradox resolved. *Psychological Review, 108,* 346–369.

Dickens, W. T. & Flynn, J. R. (2006). Black Americans reduce the racial IQ gap: Evidence from standardization samples. *Psychological Science, 17,* 913–920.

Dick-Read, G. (1933). *Natural childbirth.* New York: Dell.

Dick-Read, G. (1944). *Childbirth without fear.* New York: Dell.

Dien, D. S. F. (1982). A Chinese perspective on Kohlberg's theory of moral development. *Developmental Review, 2,* 331–341.

Diener, M. L., Goldstein, L. H., & Mangelsdorf, S. C. (1995). The role of prenatal expectations in parents' reports of infant temperament. *Merrill-Palmer Quarterly, 41,* 172–190.

Diesendruck, G. & Bloom, P. (2003). How specific is the shape bias? *Child Development, 74,* 168–178.

Dietrich, K. N. (1999). Environmental toxicants and child development. In H. Tager-Flusberg (Ed.), *Neurodevelopmental disorders.* Boston: MIT Press.

Dietz, P. M., England, L. J., Shapiro-Mendoza, C. K., Tong, V. T., Farr, S. L., & Callaghan, W. M. (2010). Infant morbidity and mortality attributable to prenatal smoking in the U.S. *American Journal of Preventive Medicine, 39,* 45–52.

DiLalla, L. F. (2002). Behavior genetics of aggression in children: Review and future directions. *Developmental Review, 22,* 593–622.

Dingemans, A. E., Bruna, M. J., and van Furth, E. F. (2002). Binge eating disorder: A review. *International Journal of Obesity, 26,* 299–307.

Dinges, M. M. & Oetting, E. R. (1993). Similarity in drug use patterns between adolescents and their friends. *Adolescence, 28,* 253–266.

Dionne, G. (2005). Language development and aggressive behavior. In R. E. Tremblay, W. W. Hartup, & J. Archer (Eds.), *Developmental origins of aggression* (pp. 330–352). New York: Guilford.

Dionne, G., Tremblay, R., Boivin, M., Laplante, D., & Perusse, D. (2003). Physical aggression and expressive vocabulary in 19-month-old twins. *Developmental Psychology, 39,* 261–273.

DiPietro, J. (2004). The role of prenatal maternal stress in child development. *Current Directions in Psychological Science, 13,* 71–74.

DiPietro, J. (2005). Neurobehavioral assessment before birth. *Mental Retardation and Developmental Disabilities Research Reviews, 11,* 4–13.

DiPietro, J. A., Bornstein, M. H., Costigan, K. A., Pressman, E. K., Hahn, C., Painter, K., et al. (2002). What does fetal movement predict about behavior during the first two years of life? *Developmental Psychobiology 40,* 358–371.

DiPietro, J. A., Hodgson, D. M., Costigan, K. A., Hilton, S. C., & Johnson, T. R. B. (1996a). Fetal neurobehavioral development. *Child Development, 67,* 2553–2567.

DiPietro, J. A., Hodgson, D. M., Costigan, K. A., Hilton, S. C., & Johnson, T. R. B. (1996b). Fetal antecedent of infant temperament. *Child Development, 67,* 2568–2583.

DiPietro, J. A., Novak, M., Costigan, K., Atella, L., & Reusing, S. (2006). Maternal psychological distress during pregnancy in relation to child development at age two. *Child Development, 77,* 573–587.

DiPietro, J. A., Suess, P. E., Wheeler, J. S., Smouse, P. H., & Newlin, D. B. (1995). Reactivity and regulation in cocaine-exposed neonates. *Infant Behavior and Development, 18,* 407–414.

Dishion, T. J. & Bullock, B. M. (2002). Parenting and adolescent problem behavior: An ecological analysis of the nurturance hypothesis. In J. G. Borkowski, S. L. Ramey & M. Bristol-Power (Eds.), *Parenting and the child's world: Influences on academic, intellectual, and social-emotional development.* Mahwah, NJ: Erlbaum.

Dishion, T. J. & Piehler, T. F. (2009). Deviant by design: Peer contagion in development, interventions, and schools. In K. H. Rubin, W. M. Bukowski, & B. Laursen (Eds.) *Handbook of peer interactions, relationships, and groups* (pp. 589–602). New York: Guilford.

Dixon, R. A. & Lerner, R. M. (1999). History and systems in developmental psychology. In M. H. Bornstein & M. E. Lamb (Eds.), *Developmental psychology: An advanced textbook* (4th ed.). Mahwah, NJ: Erlbaum.

Dobkins, K. R. (2005). Enhanced Red/Green Color Input to Motion Processing in Infancy: Evidence for Increasing Dissociation of Color and Motion Information during Development. In Y. Munakata & M. Johnson (Eds.), *Attention and Performance XXI* (pp. 401–423). Oxford: Oxford University Press.

Dodge, K. A. (1986). A social information processing model of social competence in children. In M. Perlmutter (Ed.), *Minnesota symposia on child psychology: Vol. 18. Cognitive perspectives on children's social and behavioral development.* Hillsdale, NJ: Erlbaum.

Dodge, K. A., Coie, J. D., & Lynam, D. (2006). Aggression and antisocial behavior in youth. In N. Eisenberg, W. Damon, & R. M. Lerner (Eds.), *Handbook of child psychology Vol. 3: Social, emotional, and personality development* (6th ed., pp. 719–788). Hoboken, NJ: Wiley.

Dodge, K. A. & Crick, N. R. (1990). Social-information processing bases of aggressive behavior in children. *Personality and Social Psychology Bulletin, 16,* 8–22.

Dodge, K. A. & Feldman, E. (1990). Issues in social cognition and sociometric status. In S. R. Asher & J. D. Coie, (Eds.), *Peer rejection in childhood.* New York: Cambridge University Press.

Dodge, K. A., Lansford, J. E., Burks, V. S., Bates, J. E., Pettit, G. S., Fontaine, R. & Price, J. M. (2003).

Peer rejection and social information-processing factors in the development of aggressive behavior problems in children. *Child Development, 74,* 374–393.

Dodge, K. A., Murphy, R. R., & Buchsbaum, K. (1984). The assessment of intention-cue detection skills in children: Implications for developmental psychopathology. *Child Development, 55,* 163–173.

Dodge, K. A. & Pettit, G. S. (2003). A biopsychosocial model of the development of chronic conduct problems in adolescence. *Developmental Psychology, 39,* 349–371.

Doise, W. & Mugny, G. (1984). *The social development of the intellect.* Oxford: Pergamon.

Dolan, B. (1999). From the field: Cognitive profiles of First Nations and Caucasian children referred for psychoeducational assessment. *Canadian Journal of School Psychology, 15,* 63–71.

Domsch, H., Lohaus, A., & Thomas, H. (2009). Prediction of childhood cognitive abilities from a set of early indicators of information processing capabilities. *Infant Behavior and Development, 32,* 91–102.

Donaldson, M. (1982). Conservation: What is the question? *British Journal of Psychology, 73,* 199–207.

Dontigny, L., Arsenault, M-Y. & Martel, M-J. (2008). Rubella in pregnancy. *Journal of Obstetrics and Gynaecology in Canada, 30,* 152–158.

Dore, J. (1976). Children's illocutionary acts. In R. Freedle (Ed.), *Comprehension and production.* Hillsdale, NJ: Erlbaum.

Dore, J. (1985). Holophrases revisited: Their "logical" development during dialog. In M. D. Barrett (Ed.), *Children's single-word speech.* New York: Wiley.

Dornbusch, S. M. (1994, February). *Off the track.* Presidential address presented at the meeting of the Society for Research in Adolescence, San Diego, CA.

Dougherty, T. & Haith, M. M. (1993, March). *Processing speed in infants and children: A component of IQ?* Paper presented at the meeting of the Society for Research in Child Development, New Orleans.

Dowling, M. & Bendell, D. (1988). Characteristics of small-for-gestational-age infants. *Infant Behavior and Development,* 11, 77.

Dozier, M. & Rutter, M. (2008). Challenges to the development of attachment relationships faced by young children in foster and adoptive care. In J. Cassidy & P. R. Shaver (Eds.), *Handbook of attachment: Theory, research, and clinical applications (2nd edition)* (pp. 698–717). New York, NY: Guilford.

Dreeban, R. & Barr, R. (1988). Classroom composition and the design of instruction. *Sociology of Education, 61,* 129–142.

Dronkers, N. F., Redfern, B. B., & Knight, R. T. (2000). The neural architecture of language disorders. In M. Gazzaniga (Ed.), *The New Cognitive Neurosciences* (2nd ed., pp. 949–958). Cambridge, MA: MIT Press.

Drotar, D. K., Eckerle, D., Satola, J., Pallotta, J., & Wyatt, B. (1990). Maternal interactional behavior with nonorganic failure-to-thrive infants: A case comparison study. *Child Abuse and Neglect, 14,* 41–51.

Dryburgh, H. (2000). Teenage pregnancy. *Health Reports, 12,* Statistics Canada, Catalogue 82–003.

Duckworth, E. (1987). *The having of wonderful ideas and other essays on teaching and learning.* New York: Teachers College Press.

Duffy, F. H., Als, H., & McAnulty, G. B. (1990). Behavioral and electrophysiological evidence for gestational age effects in healthy preterm and full-term infants studied two weeks after expected due date. *Child Development, 61,* 1271–1286.

Dufresne, A. & Kobasigawa, A. (1989). Children's spontaneous allocation of study time: Differential and sufficient aspects. *Journal of Experimental Child Psychology, 47,* 274–296.

Duncan, G. J. & Brooks-Gunn, J. (1997). *Consequences of growing up poor.* New York: Russell Sage Foundation.

Duncan, G. J. & Brooks-Gunn, J. (2000). Family poverty, welfare reform, and child development. *Child Development, 71,* 188–196.

Duncan, J. R., Randall L. L., Belliveau, R. A., Trachtenberg, F. L., Randall, B., Habbe, D., Mandell, F., Welty, T.K., Iyasu, S., & Kinney, H. C. (2008).The effect of maternal smoking and drinking during pregnancy upon nicotine receptor brainstem binding in infants dying of the Sudden Infant Death Syndrome: Initial observations in a high risk population. *Brain Pathology, 18*(1), 21–31.

Duncan, R. M. & Pratt, M. W. (1997). Microgenetic change in the quantity and quality of preschoolers' private speech. *International Journal of Behavioral Development, 20,* 367–383.

Dunn, J. (1988). *The beginnings of social understanding.* Cambridge, MA: Harvard University Press.

Dunn, J. (1992). Sisters and brothers: Current issues in developmental research. In F. Boer & J. Dunn (Eds.), *Children's sibling relationships: Developmental and clinical issues.* Hillsdale, NJ: Erlbaum.

Dunn, J. (1993). *Young children's close relationships.* Newbury Park, CA: Sage.

Dunn, J. (1999). Siblings, friends, and the development of social understanding. In W. A. Collins & B. Laursen (Eds.), *Minnesota symposia on child psychology: Vol. 30. Relationships as developmental contexts.* Mahwah, NJ: Erlbaum.

Dunn, J. (2002). Sibling relationships. In P. K. Smith & C. H. Hart (Eds.), *Blackwell handbook of childhood social development.* Madden, MA: Blackwell Publishers.

Dunn, J. (2004). *Children's friendships: The beginnings of intimacy.* Malden, MA: Blackwell.

Dunn, J. (2006). Moral development in early childhood and social interaction in the family. In M. Killen & J. G. Smetana (Eds.), *Handbook of moral development* (pp. 331–350). Mahwah, NJ: Erlbaum.

Dunn, J. (2007). Siblings and socialization. In J. E. Grusec & P. D. Hastings (Eds.), *Handbook of socialization: Theory and research* (pp. 309–327). New York: Guilford.

Dunn, J., Cutting, A. L., & Demetriou, H. (2000). Moral sensibility, understanding others, and children's friendship interactions in the preschool period. *British Journal of Developmental Psychology, 18,* 159–177.

Dunn, J. & Herrera, C. (1997). Conflict resolution with friends, siblings, and mothers: A developmental perspective. *Aggressive Behavior, 23,* 343–357.

Dunn, J. & Kendrick, J. (1982). The speech of two- and three-year-olds to infant siblings: "Baby talk" and the context of communication. *Journal of Child Language, 9,* 579–595.

Dunn, J. & McGuire, S. (1992). Sibling and peer relationships in childhood. *Journal of Child Psychology and Psychiatry and Allied Disciplines, 33,* 67–105.

Dunn, J. & Munn, P. (1986). Siblings and the development of prosocial behaviors. *International Journal of Behavioral Development, 9,* 265–284.

Durston, S. & Casey, B. J. (2006). What have we learned about cognitive development from neuroimaging. *Neuropsychologia, 44,* 2149–2157.

Dweck, C. S. (1999). *Self-theories: Their role in motivation, personality, and development.* Philadelphia: Psychology Press.

Dweck, C. S. (2002a). The development of ability conceptions. In A. Wigfield & J. S. Eccles (Eds.), *Development of achievement motivation* (pp. 57–88). San Diego, CA: Academic Press.

Dweck, C. S. (2007). Is math a gift? Beliefs that put females at risk. In S. Ceci & W. Williams (Eds.), *Why aren't more women in science: Top researchers debate the evidence* (pp. 47–55). Washington, DC: American Psychological Association.

Dweck, C. S. & London, B. (2004). The role of mental representation in social development. *Merrill-Palmer Quarterly, 50,* 428–444.

Dweck, C. S. & Molden, D. C. (2005). Self-Theories: Their impact on competence motivation and acquisition. In A. Elliot & C. S. Dweck (Eds.), *Handbook of competence and motivation.* New York: Guilford.

E

Eagly, A. H. & Crowley, M. (1986). Gender and helping behavior: A meta-analytic review of the social psychological literature. *Psychological Bulletin, 100,* 283–308.

Eagly, A. H., Wood, W., & Diekman, A. B. (2000). Social role theory of sex differences and similarities: A current appraisal. In T. Eckes & H. M. Trautner (Eds.), *The developmental social psychology of gender.* Mahwah, NJ: Erlbaum.

East, P. L. & Rook, K. S. (1992). Compensatory patterns of support among children's peer relationships: A test using school friends, nonschool friends, and siblings. *Developmental Psychology, 28,* 163–172.

Eaton, W. O. (1994). Temperament, development, and the Five-Factor Model: Lessons from activity level. In C. F. Halverson Jr., G. A. Kohnstamm, & R. P. Martin (Eds.), *The developed structure of temperament and personality from infancy to adulthood.* Hillsdale, NJ: Erlbaum.

Eaton, W. O. & Enns, L. R. (1986). Sex differences in human motor activity level. *Psychological Bulletin, 100,* 19–28.

Eaton, W. O. & Saudino, K. J. (1992). Prenatal activity level as a temperament dimension? Individual differences and the developmental functions in fetal movement. *Infant Behavior and Development, 15,* 57–70.

Eccles, J. S. (2007). Families, schools, and developing achievement-related motivations and engagement. In J. Grusec & P. Hastings (Eds.), *Handbook of socialization: Theory and research* (pp. 665–691). New York: Guilford.

Eccles, J. S., Arbreton, A., Buchanan, C., Jacobs, J., Flanagan, C., Harold, R., et al. (1993). School and family effects on the ontogeny of children's interests, self-perceptions, and activity choice. In J. Jacobs (Ed.), *Nebraska symposium on motivation: Vol. 40. Developmental perspectives on motivation.* Lincoln, NE: University of Nebraska Press.

Eccles, J. S., Freedman-Doan, C., Frome, P., Jacobs, J., & Yoon, K. S. (2000). Gender-role socialization in the family: A longitudinal approach. In T. Eckes & H. M. Trautner (Eds.), *The developmental social psychology of gender.* Mahwah, NJ: Erlbaum.

Eccles, J. S., Jacobs, J. E., Harold, R. D., Yoon, K. S., Arbreton, A., & Freedman-Doan, C. (1993). Parents and gender-role socialization during the middle childhood and adolescent years. In S. Oskamp & M. Costanzo (Eds.), *Gender issues in contemporary society.* Thousand Oaks, CA: Sage.

Eccles, J. S., Lord, S., & Roeser, R. W (1996). Round holes, square pegs, rocky roads, and sore feet: The impact of stage/environment fit on young adolescents' experiences in schools and families. In D. Cicchetti & S. L. Toth (Eds.), *Rochester symposium on developmental psychopathology: Vol. 8. Adolescence: Opportunities and challenges.* Rochester, NY: University of Rochester Press.

Eccles, J. S., Lord, S., Roeser, R. W., Barber, B. L., & Jozefowicz, D. M. H. (1997). The association of school transitions in early adolescence with developmental trajectories through high school. In J. Schulenberg, J. Maggs, & K. Hurrelmann (Eds.), *Health risks and developmental transitions during adolescence.* New York: Cambridge University Press.

Eccles, J. S. & Roeser, R. W. (1999). School and community influences on human development. In M. H. Bornstein & M. E. Lamb (Eds.), *Developmental psychology: An advanced textbook* (4th ed.). Mahwah, NJ: Erlbaum.

Eccles, J. S., Roeser, R., Vida, M., Fredricks, J., & Wigfield, A. (2006). Motivational and achievement pathways through middle childhood. In L. Balter & C. Tamis-LeMonda (Eds.), *Child psychology: A handbook of contemporary issues* (2nd ed., pp. 325–355). New York: Psychology Press.

Eckel, L. A., Arnold, A. P., Hampson, E., Becker, J. P., Blaustein, J. D., & Herman, J. P. (2008). Research and methodological issues in the study of sex differences and hormone-behavior relations. In J. B. Becker, K. J. Berkley, N. Geary, E. Hampson, J. Herman, & E. Young (Eds.), *Sex differences in the brain: From genes to behavior* (pp. 36–61). New York, NY: Oxford University Press.

Eckerman, C. O., Hsu, H., Molitor, A., Leung, E. H. L., & Goldstein, R. F. (1999). Infant arousal in the en-face exchange with a new partner: Effects of prematurity and perinatal biological risk. *Developmental Psychology, 35,* 282–293.

Eckstein, S. & Shemesh, M. (1992). The rate of acquisition of formal operational schemata in adolescence: A secondary analysis. *Journal of Research in Science Teaching 29,* 441–451.

Edelman, G. M. (1993). Neural Darwinism: Selection and reentrant signaling in higher brain function. *Neuron, 10,* 115–125.

Edelman, G. M. (2003). Proceedings from the National Academy of Sciences: *Naturalizing consciousness: A theoretical framework. USA, 100,* 5520–5524.

Eder, R. A. (1989). The emergent personologist: The structure and content of 3 1/2-, 5 1/2-, and 7 1/2-year olds' concepts of themselves and others. *Child Development, 60,* 1218–1228.

Eder, R. A. (1990). Uncovering young children's psychological selves: Individual and developmental differences. *Child Development, 61,* 849–863.

Egeland, B. & Farber, E. (1984). Infant-mother attachment: Factors related to its development and changes over time. *Child Development, 55,* 753–771.

Egeland, B. & Heister, M. (1995). The long-term consequences of infant day-care and mother-infant attachment. *Child Development, 66,* 474–485.

Eichenbaum, H., Yonelinas, A. R., & Ranganath, C. (2007). The medial temporal lobe and recognition memory. *Annual Review of Neuroscience, 30,* 123–152.

Eichstedt, J. A., Serbin, L. A., Poulin-Dubois, D., & Sen, M. G. (2002). Of bears and men: Infants' knowledge of conventional and metaphorical gender stereotypes. *Infant Behavior and Development, 25,* 296–310.

Eigsti, I. M., Zayas, V., Mischel, W., Shoda, Y., Ayduk, O., Dadlani, M. B., et al. (2006). Predicting cognitive control from preschool to late adolescence and young adulthood. *Psychological Science, 17,* 478–484.

Eilers, R. E. & Oller, D. K. (1988). Precursors to speech: What is innate and what is acquired? In R. Vasta (Ed.), *Annals of child development* (Vol. 5). Greenwich, CT: JAI Press.

Eimas, P. D. (1975). Auditory and phonetic coding of the cues for speech: Discrimination of the [r-l] distinction by young infants. *Perception and Psychophysics, 18,* 341–347.

Eimas, P. D., Siqueland, E. R., Jusczyk, P., & Vigorito, J. (1971). Speech perception in infants. *Science, 171,* 303–306.

Eisen, A. & Kearney, C. (1995). *Practitioner's guide to treating fear and anxiety in children and adolescents.* Northvale, NJ: Jason Aronson, Inc.

Eisen, M. L., Quas, J. A., & Goodman, G. S. (Eds.). (2002). *Memory and suggestibility in the forensic interview.* Mahwah, NJ: Erlbaum.

Eisenberg, N. (1982). The development of reasoning regarding prosocial behavior. In N. Eisenberg (Ed.), *The development of prosocial behavior.* New York: Academic Press.

Eisenberg, N. (1986). *Altruistic emotion, cognition, and behavior.* Hillsdale, NJ: Erlbaum.

Eisenberg, N. (1987). The relation of altruism and other moral behaviors to moral cognition: Methodological and conceptual issues. In N. Eisenberg & J. Strayer (Eds.), *Empathy and its development.* New York: Cambridge University Press.

Eisenberg, N. (2010). Empathy-related responding: Links with self-regulation, moral judgment, and moral behavior. In M. Mikulincer & P. R. Shaver (Eds.), *Prosocial motives, emotions, and behavior: The better angels of our nature* (pp. 129–148). Washington, DC: American Psychological Association.

Eisenberg, N., Cameron, E., Tryon, K., & Dodez, R. (1981). Socialization of prosocial behavior in the preschool classroom. *Developmental Psychology, 17,* 773–782.

Eisenberg, N., Carlo, G., Murphy, B., & Van Court, P. (1995). Prosocial development in late adolescence: A longitudinal study. *Child Development, 66,* 1179–1197.

Eisenberg, N. & Fabes, R. A. (1998). Prosocial development. In W. Damon (Series Ed.) & N. Eisenberg (Vol. Ed.), *Handbook of child psychology: Vol. 3. Social, emotional, and personality development* (5th ed.). New York: Wiley.

Eisenberg, N., Fabes, R. A., & Murphy, B. C. (1996). Parents' reactions to children's negative emotions: Relations to children's social competence and comforting behavior. *Child Development, 67,* 2227–2247.

Eisenberg, N., Fabes, R. A., & Spinrad, T. L. (2006). Prosocial development. In N. Eisenberg, W. Damon, & R. M. Lerner (Eds.), *Handbook of child psychology Vol. 3: Social, emotional, and personality development* (6th ed., pp. 646–718). Hoboken, NJ: Wiley.

Eisenberg, N., Fabes, R. A., Carlo, G., & Troyer, D. (1992). The relations of maternal practices and characteristics to children's vicarious emotional responsiveness. *Child Development, 63,* 583–602.

Eisenberg, N. & Murphy, B. (1995). Parenting and children's moral development. In M. H. Bornstein (Ed.), *Handbook of parenting: Vol. 4. Applied and practical parenting.* Mahwah, NJ: Erlbaum.

Eisenberg, N., Pidada, S., & Liew, J. (2001). The relations of regulation and negative emotionality to Indonesian children's social functioning. *Child Development, 72,* 1747–1763.

Eisenberg, N., Spinrad, T., & Sadovsky, A. (2006). Empathy-related responding in children. In M. Killen & J. G. Smetana (Eds.), *Handbook of moral development* (pp. 517–550). Mahwah, NJ: Lawrence Erlbaum.

Eisenberg, N., Zhou, Q., Spinrad, T. L., Valiente, C., Fabes, R. A., & Liew, J. (2005). Relations among positive parenting, children's effortful control, and externalizing problems : A three-wave longitudinal study. *Child Development, 76*(5), 1055–1071.

Eisenberg, R. B. (1976). *Auditory competence in early life.* Baltimore: University Park Press.

Ekman, P. (1993). Facial expression and emotion. *American Psychologist, 48,* 384–392.

El Abd, S., Turk, J., & Hill, P. (1995). Annotation: Psychological characteristics of Turner syndrome. *Journal of Child Psychology and Psychiatry, 36,* 1109–1125.

Elder, G. H. & Caspi, A. (1988). Human development and social change: An emerging perspective on the life course. In N. Bolger, A. Caspi, G. Downey, & M. Moorehouse (Eds.), *Persons in context: Developmental processes.* New York: Cambridge University Press.

Elder, G. H. & Conger, R. D. (2000). *Children of the land.* Chicago: University of Chicago Press.

Elias, M. J., Parker, S., & Rosenblatt, J. L. (2005). Building Educational Opportunity. In S. Goldstein & R. B. Brooks (Eds.), *Handbook of resilience in children* (pp. 315–336). New York: Springer Publications.

Elkind, D. (2007). *The hurried child.* Cambridge, MA: De Capro Press.

Ellenberg, D., Lewis, T. L., Maurer, D., Brar, S., & Brent, H. P. (2002). Better perception of global motion after monocular than after binocular deprivation. *Vision Research, 42,* 169–179.

Elliott, R. & Vasta, R. (1970). The modeling of sharing: Effects associated with vicarious reinforcement, symbolization, age, and generalization. *Journal of Experimental Child Psychology, 10,* 8–15.

Ellis, B. J. & Bjorklund, D. F. (Eds.). (2005). *Origins of the social mind: Evolutionary psychology and child development.* New York: Guilford.

Ellis, B. J. & Garber, J. (2000). Psychosocial antecedents of variations in girls' pubertal timing: Maternal depression, stepfather presence, and marital and family stress. *Child Development, 71,* 485–501.

Ellis, S. (1997). Strategy choice in sociocultural context. *Developmental Review, 17,* 490–524.

Ellis, S., Rogoff, B., & Cromer, C. C. (1981). Age segregation in children's social interactions. *Developmental Psychology, 17,* 399–407.

Ellis, S. & Siegler, R. S. (1994). Development of problem solving. In R. J. Siegler (Ed.), *Handbook of perception and cognition: Vol. 12. Thinking and problem solving.* New York: Academic Press.

Elman, J., Bates, E., Johnson, M., Karmiloff-Smith, A., Parisi, D., & Plunkett, K. (1996). *Rethinking innateness.* Cambridge, MA: MIT Press.

Elmer, S., Hänggi, J., Meyer, M., & Jäncke, L. (2010). Differential language expertise related to white matter architecture in regions subserving sensory-motor coupling, articulation, and interhemispheric transfer. *Human Brain Mapping, 32,* 2064–2074.

Emde, R. N. (1992). Individual meaning and increasing complexity: Contributions of Sigmund Freud and René Spitz to developmental psychology. *American Psychologist, 28,* 347–359.

Emde, R. N., Biringen, Z., Clyman, R. B., & Oppenheim, D. (1991). The moral sense of infancy: Affective core and procedural knowledge. *Developmental Review, 11,* 251–270.

Emde, R. N. & Harmon, R. J. (Eds.). (1984). *Continuities and discontinuities in development.* New York: Plenum.

Emde, R. N., Plomin, R., Robinson, J., Corley, R., DeFries, J., Fulker, D. W., et al. (1992). Temperament, emotion, and cognition at fourteen months: The MacArthur Longitudinal Twin Study. *Child Development, 63,* 1437–1455.

Emery, R. E. (2004) *The truth about children and divorce.* New York, NY: Viking Press.

Emery, R. E. & Laumann-Billings, L. (1998). An overview of the nature, causes, and consequences of abusive family relationships: Toward differentiating maltreatment and violence. *American Psychologist, 53(2),* 121–135.

England, D. E., Descartes, L., & Collier-Meek, M. A. (2011). Gender role portrayal and the Disney princesses. *Sex Roles, 64,* 555–567.

Ennis, R. H. (1976). An alternative to Piaget's conceptualization of logical competence. *Child Development, 47,* 903–919.

Ennouri, K. & Bloch, H. (1996). Visual control of hand approach movements in newborns. *British Journal of Developmental Psychology, 14,* 327–338.

Enright, R. D. & Satterfield, S. J. (1980). An ecological validation of social cognitive development. *Child Development, 51,* 156–161.

Entwisle, D. R. & Alexander, K. L. (2000). Diversity in family structure: Effects on schooling. In D. H. Demo, K. R. Allen, & M. A. Fine (Eds.), *Handbook of family diversity.* New York: Oxford University Press.

Environment Canada. (2003). *Polychlorinated iphenyls.* Available at: www.ec.gc/pcb/eng/index_e.htm

Epstein, J. L. (1983). Selections of friends in differently organized schools and classrooms. In J. L. Epstein & M. Karweit (Eds.), *Friends in school.* New York: Academic Press.

Epstein, J. L. (1986). Friendship selection: Developmental and environmental influences. In E. C. Mueller & C. R. Cooper (Eds.), *Process and outcome in peer relationships.* New York: Academic Press.

Epstein, J. L. (1989). The selection of friends: Changes across the grades and in different school environments. In T. J. Berndt & G. W. Ladd (Eds.), *Peer relationships in child development.* New York: Wiley.

Epstein, J. L. (2002). *School, family, and community partnerships: Your handbook for action* (2nd ed.). Thousand Oaks, CA: Corwin Press.

Erdlen, R. J. & Rickrode, M. R. (2007). Social skills groups with youth: A cognitive-behavioral perspective. In R. W. Christner, J. L. Stewart, & A. Freeman (Eds.), *Handbook of cognitive-behavior group therapy with children and adolescents* (pp. 485–506). New York: Routledge/Taylor & Francis.

Erdley, C. & Asher, S. (1998). Linkages between children's beliefs about the legitimacy of aggression and their behavior. *Social Development, 7,* 321–339.

Eron, L. D. & Huesmann, L. R. (1986). The role of television in the development of prosocial and antisocial behavior. In D. Olweus, J. Block, & M. Radke-Yarrow (Eds.), *Development of antisocial and prosocial behavior.* Orlando, FL: Academic Press.

Eron, L. D., Huesmann, L. R., Dubow, E., Romanoff, R., & Yarmel, R. W. (1987). Aggression and its correlates over 22 years. In D. H. Crowell, I. M. Evans, & C. R. O'Donnell (Eds.), *Childhood aggression and violence: Source of influence, prevention, and control.* New York: Plenum.

Ervin, S. M. (1964). Imitation and structural change in children's language. In E. H. Lenneberg (Ed.), *New directions in the study of language.* Cambridge, MA: MIT Press.

Eskenazi, B., Prehn, A. W., & Christianson, R. E. (1995). Passive and active maternal smoking as measured by serum cotinine: The effect on birthweight. *American Journal of Public Health, 85,* 395–398.

Espelage, D. L., Holt, M. K., & Henkel, R. R. (2003). Examination of peer-group contextual effects on aggression during early adolescence. *Child Development, 74,* 205–220.

Espy, K. A., Molfese, V. J., & DiLalla, L. F. (2001). Effects of environmental measures on intelligence in young children: Growth curve modeling of longitudinal data. *Merrill-Palmer Quarterly, 47,* 42–73.

Etzel, B. C. & Gewirtz, J. L. (1967). Experimental modification of caretaker-maintained high rate operant crying in a 6- and a 20-week old infant *(Infans tyrannotearus):* Extinction of crying with reinforcement of eye contact and smiling. *Journal of Experimental Child Psychology, 5,* 303–317.

Evans, E. M., Schweingruber, H., & Stevenson, H. W. (2002). Gender differences in interest and knowledge acquisition: The United States, Taiwan, and Japan. *Sex Roles, 47,* 153–167.

Evans, M. A. (2010). Language performance, academic performance, and signs of shyness: A comprehensive review. In K. H. Rubin & R. J. Coplan (Eds.), *The development of shyness and social withdrawal* (pp. 179–212). New York: Guilford.

Evelyth, P. B. (1986). Population differences in growth. In F. Falkner & J. M. Tanner (Eds.), experiential correlates in three-month-old infants. *Child Development, 57,* 1054–1061.

F

Fabes, R. A., Eisenberg, N., Karbon, M., Troyer, D., & Switzer, G. (1994). The relations of children's emotion regulation to their vicarious emotional responses and comforting behavior. *Child Development, 65,* 1678–1693.

Fabes, R. A., Martin, C. L., & Hanish, L. D. (2003). Young children's play qualities in same-, other-, or mixed-sex peer groups. *Child Development, 74,* 921–932.

Fabes, R. A., Martin, C. L., & Hanish, L. D. (2009). Children's behaviors and interactions with peers. In K. H. Rubin, W. M. Bukowski, & B. Laursen (Eds.), *Handbook of peer interactions, relationships, and groups* (pp. 45–62). New York: Guilford.

Fabricius, W. V. & Steffe, L. (1989, April). *Considering all possible combinations: The early beginnings of a formal operational skill.* Paper presented at the meeting of the Society for Research in Child Development, Kansas City, MO.

Fagan, J. F. III. (1973). Infants' delayed recognition memory and forgetting. *Journal of Experimental Child Psychology, 16,* 424–450.

Fagan, J. F. III. (2005). *The Fagan Test of Infant Intelligence: Manual.* Cleveland, OH: Case Western Reserve University. Available at http://infantest.com/ftii.pdf.

Fagan, J. F. III & Detterman, D. H. (1992). The Fagan Test of Infant Intelligence: A technical summary. *Journal of Applied Developmental Psychology, 13,* 173–193.

Fagan, J. F., Holland, C. R., & Wheeler, K. (2007). The prediction, from infancy, of adult IQ and achievement. *Intelligence, 35,* 225–232.

Fagan, J. F. III, Shepherd, P., & Knevel, C. (1991, April). *Predictive validity of the Fagan Test of Infant Intelligence.* Meeting of the Society for Research in Child Development, Seattle, WA.

Fagot, B. I. (1977). Consequences of moderate cross-gender behavior in preschool children. *Child Development, 48,* 902–907.

Fagot, B. I. (1985). Beyond the reinforcement principle: Another step toward understanding sex role development. *Developmental Psychology, 21,* 1097–1104.

Fagot, B. I. & Gauvain, M. (1997). Mother-child problem solving: Continuity through the early childhood years. *Developmental Psychology, 33,* 480–488.

Fagot, B. I., Leinbach, M. D., & Hagan, R. (1986). Gender labeling and the adoption of sex-typed behaviors. *Developmental Psychology, 22,* 440–443.

Fagot, B. I., Rodgers, C. S., & Leinbach, M. D. (2000). Theories of gender socialization. In T. Eckes & H. M. Trautner (Eds.), *The developmental social psychology of gender.* Mahwah, NJ: Erlbaum.

Fairburn, C. G. & Brownell, K. D. (Eds.). (2002). *Eating disorders and obesity: A comprehensive handbook* (2nd ed.). New York: Guilford.

Faith, M. S. (2010). Development of child taste and food preferences: The role of exposure. In W.S. Agras (Ed.), *The Oxford handbook of eating disorders* (pp. 137–147). Oxford University Press, New York.

Fantuzzo, J. W., McDermott, P. A., Manz, P. H., Hampton, V. R., & Burdick, N. A. (1996). The Pictorial Scale of Perceived Competence and Social Acceptance: Does it work with low-income urban children? *Child Development, 67,* 1071–1084.

Fantz, R. L. (1961). The origin of form perception. *Scientific American, 204,* 66–72.

Fantz, R. L. (1963). Pattern vision in newborn infants. *Science, 140,* 296–297.

Faraone, S. V. & Biedermann, J. (2000). Nature, nurture, and attention deficit hyperactivity disorder. *Developmental Review, 20,* 568–581.

Farrar, M. J. (1990). Discourse and the acquisition of grammatical morphemes. *Journal of Child Language, 17,* 607–624.

Farrar, M. J. (1992). Negative evidence and grammatical morpheme acquisition. *Developmental Psychology, 28,* 90–98.

Farrell, A. D. & Vulin-Reynolds, M. (2007). Violent behavior and the science of prevention. In D. J. Flannery, A. T. Vazsonyi, & I. D. Waldman (Eds.), *The Cambridge handbook of violent behavior and aggression* (pp. 767–786). New York, NY: Cambridge University Press.

Farver, J. M. (1993). Cultural differences in scaffolding pretend play: A comparison of American and Mexican mother-child and sibling-child pairs. In K. MacDonald (Ed.), *Parent-child play: Descriptions and implications.* Albany, NY: State University of New York Press.

Farver, J. M. (1999). Activity setting analysis: A model for examining the role of culture in development. In A. Göncü (Ed.), *Children's engagement in the world: Sociocultural perspectives.* Cambridge: Cambridge University Press.

Farver, J. M. & Branstetter, W. H. (1994). Preschoolers' prosocial responses to their peers' distress. *Developmental Psychology, 30,* 334–341.

Farver, J. M. & Wimbarti, S. (1995). Indonesian children's play with their mothers and older siblings. *Child Development, 66,* 1493–1503.

Feigenson, L., Carey, S., & Spelke, E. (2002). Infants' discrimination of number vs. continuous event. *Cognitive Psychology, 44,* 33–66.

Feinman, S., Roberts, D., Hsieh, K., Sawyer, D., & Swanson, D. (1992). A critical review of social referencing in infancy. In S. Feinman (Ed.), *Social referencing and the social construction of reality in infancy.* New York: Plenum.

Feiring, C. (1996). Concepts of romance in 15-year-old adolescents. *Journal of Research on Adolescence, 6,* 181–200.

Feldman, D. H. (1986). *Nature's gambit: Child prodigies and the development of human potential.* New York: Basic Books.

Feldman, D. H. (2004). Piaget's stages: the unfinished symphony of cognitive development. *New Ideas in Psychology, 22,* 175–231.

Feldman, P. J., Dunkel-Schetter, C., Sandman, C. A., & Wadhwa, P. D. (2000). Maternal social support predicts birth weight and fetal growth in human pregnancy. *Psychosomatic Medicine, 62,* 715–725.

Feldman, R. (2007). Parent–infant synchrony and the construction of shared timing; physiological precursors, developmental outcomes, and risk conditions. *Journal of Child Psychology and Psychiatry, 48,* 329–354.

Feng, J., Spence, I., & Pratt, J. (2007). Playing an action video game reduces gender differences in spatial cognition. *Psychological Science, 18,* 850–855.

Fennell, C. T., Byers-Heinlein, K., & Werker, J. F. (2007). Using speech sounds to guide word learning: The case of bilingual infants. *Child Development, 78*(5), 1510–1525.

Fennell, C. T. & Waxman, S. R. (2010). What paradox? Referential cues allow for infant use of phonetic detail in word learning. *Child Development, 81*(5), 1376–1383.

Fennell, C. T. & Werker, J. F. (2003). Early word learners' ability to access phonetic detail in well-known words. *Language & Speech, 46(2),* 245–264.

Fennema, E., Carpenter, T. P., Jacobs, V. R., Franke, M. L., & Levi, L. W. (1998). A longitudinal study of gender differences in young children's mathematical thinking. *Educational Researcher, 27,* 6–11.

Fenson, L., Dale, P. S., Reznick, J. S., Bates E., Thal, D. J., & Pethick, S. J. (1994). Variability in early communicative development. *Monographs of the Society for Research in Child Development, 59(5,* Serial No. 242)

Ferguson, C. A. (1983). Reduplication in child phonology. *Journal of Child Language, 10,* 239–243.

Fernald, A. (1993). Approval and disapproval: Infant responsiveness to vocal affect in familiar and unfamiliar languages. *Child Development, 64,* 657–674.

Fernald, A. & Hurtado, N. (2006). Names in frames: Infants interpret words in sentence frames faster than words in isolation. *Developmental Science, 9*(3), F33–F40.

Fernald, A. & O'Neill, D. K. (1993). Peekaboo across cultures: How mothers and infants play with voices, faces, and expectations. In K. MacDonald (Ed.), *Parent-child play.* Albany, NY: State University of New York Press.

Fernald, A., Perfors, A., & Marchman, V. A. (2006). Picking up speed in understanding: Speech processing efficiency and vocabulary growth across the second year. *Developmental Psychology, 42,* 98–116.

Fernald, A., Taeschner, T., Dunn, J., Papousek, M., Boysson-Bardies, B., & Fukui, I. (1989). A cross-language study of prosodic modifications in mothers' and fathers' speech to preverbal infants. *Journal of Child Language, 16,* 477–501.

Ferrier, S., Dunham, P., & Dunham, F. (2000). The confused robot: Two-year-olds' responses to breakdowns in conversation. *Social Development, 9,* 337–347.

Ferriera, A. J. (1969). *Prenatal environment.* Springfield, IL: Charles C. Thomas.

Ferry, A., Hespos, S., & Waxman, S. (2010). Categorization in 3- and 4-Month-Old Infants: An Advantage of Words Over Tones. *Child Development, 81*(2), 472–479.

Feshbach, S. & Singer, R. D. (1971). *Television and aggression: An experimental field study.* San Francisco: Jossey-Bass.

Feuerstein, R., Rand, Y., Haywood, H. C., Kyram, L., & Hoffman, M. B. (1995). *Learning Propensity Assessment Device-manual.* Jerusalem: International Center for the Enhancement of Learning Potential.

Field, T. M. (1987). Affective and interactive disturbances in infants. In J. D. Osofsky (Ed.), *Handbook of infant development* (2nd ed.). New York: Wiley.

Field, T. M. (2001). *Touch.* Cambridge, MA: MIT Press.

Field, T., Diego, M., & Hernandez-Reif, M. (2010). Preterm infant massage therapy research: A review. *Infant Behavior and Development, 33,* 115–124.

Field, T. M. & Walden, T. A. (1982). Production and perception of facial expressions in infancy and early childhood. In H. W. Reese & L. P. Lipsitt (Eds.), *Advances in child development and behavior* (Vol. 16). New York: Academic Press.

Fields, J. & Casper, L. M. (2001). *America's families and living arrangements: March 2000.* Washington, DC: U.S. Census Bureau.

Fields, S. A. & McNamara, J. R. (2003). The prevention of child and adolescent violence. A review. *Aggression and Violent Behavior, 8,* 61–91.

Fifer, W. P. & Moon, C. M. (1995). The effects of fetal experience with sound. In J.-P. Lecanuet, W. P. Fifer, N. A. Krasnegor, & W. P. Smotherman (Eds.), *Fetal development: A psychobiological perspective.* Hillsdale, NJ: Erlbaum.

Finch, A., Spirito, A., Imm. P., & Ott, E. (1993). Cognitive self-instruction for impulse control in children. In A. Finch, W. Nelson, & E. Ott (Eds.), *Cognitive-behavioral procedures with children and adolescents* (pp. 233–256). Boston, MA: Allyn and Bacon.

Fine, G. A. (1987). *With the boys: Little League baseball and preadolescent culture.* Chicago: University of Chicago Press.

Fink, B., Manning, J. T., Neave, N., Tan, U. (2004). Second to fourth digit ratio and hand skill in Austrian children. *Biological Psychology, 67,* 375–384.

Finn, J. D., Gerber, S. B., Achilles, C. M., & Boyd-Zaharias, J. (2001). The enduring effects of small classes. *Teachers College Record, 103,* 145–183.

Finn, J. D., Gerber, S. B., Boyd-Zaharias, J. (2005). Small classes in the early grades, academic achievement, and graduating from high school. *Journal of Educational Psychology, 97, 214–223.*

Finnegan, L. P. & Fehr, K. O. (1980). The effects of opiates, sedative-hypnotics, amphetamines, cannabis, and other psychoactive drugs on the fetus and newborn. In O. J. Kalant (Ed.), *Research advances in alcohol and drug problems: Vol. 5. Alcohol and drug problems in women.* New York: Plenum.

Fischer, K. W. & Bidell, T. R. (1998). Dynamic development of psychological structures in action and thought. In W. Damon (Series Ed.) & R. M. Lerner (Vol. Ed.), *Handbook of child psychology: Vol. 1. Theoretical models of human development* (5th ed.). New York: Wiley.

Fish, M. (2001). Attachment in low-SES rural Appalachian infants: Contextual, infant, and maternal interaction risk and protective factors. *Infant Mental Health Journal, 22,* 641–664.

Fisher, C. B. & Tryon, W. W. (Eds.). (1990). *Ethics in applied developmental psychology: Emerging issues in an emerging field.* Norwood, NJ: Ablex.

Fisher, D., Serbin, L. A., Stack, D. M., Ruttle, P. L., Ledingham, J. E., & Schwartzman, A. E. (2007). Intergenerational predictors of diurnal cortisol secretion in early childhood. *Infant and Child Development, 16,* 151–170.

Fisher, J. O. & Birch, L. L. (2001). Early experience with food and eating: Implications for the development of eating disorders. In J. K. Thompson & L. Smolak (Eds.), *Body image, eating disorders, and obesity in youth: Assessment, prevention, and treatment.* Washington, DC: APA.

Fivush, R. (2007). Maternal reminiscing style and children's understanding of self and emotion. *Clinical Social Work Journal, 35,* 37–46.

Fivush, R. & Buckner, J. P. (2000). Gender, sadness, and depression: The development of emotional focus through gendered discourse. In A. H. Fischer (Ed.), *Gender and emotion: Social psychological perspectives.* New York: Cambridge University Press.

Fivush, R., Sales, J. M., Goldberg, A., Bahrick, L., & Parker, J. (2004). Weathering the storm: Children's long-term recall of Hurricane Andrew. *Memory, 12,* 104–118.

Flack, J. C. & de Waal, F. B. M. (2000). 'Any animal whatever': Darwinian building blocks of morality in monkeys and apes. In L. D. Katz (Ed.), *Evolutionary origins of morality: Cross disciplinary perspectives.* Thorveton, UK: Imprint Academic.

Flannery, D. J., Singer, M. I., van Dulman, M., Kretschmar, J. M., & Belliston, L. M. (2007). Exposure to violence, mental health, and violent behavior. In D. J. Flannery, A. T. Vazsonyi, & I. D. Waldman (Eds.), *The Cambridge handbook of violent behavior and aggression* (pp. 306–321). New York, NY: Cambridge University Press.

Flannery, D. J., Vazsonyi, A. T., Liau, A. K., Guo, S., Powell, K. E., Atha, H., et al. (2003). Initial behavior outcomes for the PeaceBuilders universal school-based violence prevention program. *Developmental Psychology, 39,* 292–308.

Flavell, J. H. (1963). *The developmental psychology of Jean Piaget.* Princeton, NJ: Van Nostrand.

Flavell, J. H. (1970). Developmental studies of mediated memory. In H. W. Reese & L. P. Lipsitt (Eds.), *Advances in child development and behavior* (Vol. 5). New York: Academic Press.

Flavell, J. H. (1971). First discussant's comments. What is memory development the development of? *Human Development, 14,* 272–278.

Flavell, J. H. (1985). *Cognitive development* (2nd ed.). Englewood Cliffs, NJ: Prentice Hall.

Flavell, J. H. (1986). Development of children's knowledge about the appearance-reality distinction. *American Psychologist, 41,* 418–425.

Flavell, J. H., Flavell, E. R., & Green, F. L. (1983). Development of the appearance-reality distinction. *Cognitive Psychology, 15,* 95–120.

Flavell, J. H., Friedrichs, A., & Hoyt, J. (1970). Developmental changes in memorization processes. *Cognitive Psychology, 1,* 324–340.

Flavell, J. H., Green, F. L., & Flavell, E. R. (1989). Young children's ability to differentiate appearance-reality and level 2 perspective taking in the tactile modality. *Child Development, 60,* 201–213.

Flavell, J. H., Miller, P. H., & Miller, S. A. (2002). *Cognitive development* (4th ed.). Upper Saddle River, NJ: Prentice Hall.

Flavell, J. H., Shipstead, S. G., & Croft, K. (1980). What young children think you see when their eyes are closed. *Cognition, 8,* 369–387.

Fletcher, A. C., Darling, N. E., Steinberg, L., & Dornbusch, S. (1995). The company they keep: Relation of adolescents' adjustment and behavior to their friends' perceptions of authoritative parenting in the social network. *Developmental Psychology, 31,* 300–310.

Fletcher, A. C., Elder, G. H., & Mekos, D. (2000). Parental influences on adolescent involvement in community activities. *Journal of Research on Adolescence, 10,* 29–48.

Fletcher, P. (1999). Specific language impairment. In M. Barrett (Ed.), *The development of language*. Hove, UK: Psychology Press.

Flicker, S., Flynn, S., Larkin, J., Travers, R., Guta, A., Pole, J., & Layne, C. (2009). *Sexpress: The Toronto Teen Survey Report*. Planned Parenthood Toronto. Toronto, ON.

Flieller, A. (1999). Comparison of the development of formal thought in adolescent cohorts aged 10 to 15 years (1967–1999 and 1972–1993). *Developmental Psychology, 35,* 1048–1058.

Floden, D., Alexander, M. P., Kubu, C. S., Katz, D., & Stuss, D. T. (2008). Impulsivity and risk-taking behavior in focal frontal lobe lesions. *Neuropsychologia, 46,* 213–223.

Floor, P. & Akhtar, N. (2006). Can 18-month-old infants learn words by listening in on conversations? *Infancy, 9*(3), 327–339.

Flynn, E., Pine, K., & Lewis, C. (2007). Using the microgenetic method to investigate cognitive development: An introduction. *Infant and Child Development, 16,* 1–6.

Flynn, E. & Siegler, R. (2007). Measuring change: Current trends and future directions in microgenetic *research. Infant and Child Development, 16,* 135–149.

Flynn, J. R. (1998). IQ gains over time: Toward finding the causes. In U. Neisser (Ed.), *The rising curve: Longterm gains in IQ and related measures*. Washington, DC: APA.

Flynn, J. R. (2006). Tethering the elephant: Capital cases, IQ, and the Flynn Effect. *Psychology, Public Policy, and Law, 12,* 170–189.

Flynn, J. R. (2007). *What is intelligence? Beyond the Flynn effect*. New York: Cambridge University Press.

Fogel, A., Nelson-Goens, G. C., Hsu, H., & Shapiro, A. F. (2000). Do different infant smiles reflect different positive emotions? *Social Development 9,* 497–520.

Fogel, A., Stevenson, M. B., & Messigner, D. (1992). A comparison of the parent-child relationship in Japan and the United States. In J. L. Roopnarine & D. B. Carter (Eds.), *Annual advances in applied developmental psychology: Vol. 5. Parent-child socialization in diverse cultures*. Norwood, NJ: Ablex.

Fogel, A. & Thelen, E. (1987). Development of early expressive and communicative action: Reinterpreting the evidence from a dynamic systems perspective. *Developmental Psychology, 23,* 747–761.

Folling-Albers, M., & Hartinger, A. (1998). Interest of boys and girls in elementary school. In L. Hoffman, A. Krap, K. A. Renninger, & J. Baumert (Eds.), *Interest and learning*. Kiel, Germany: Institute for Science Education.

Fontaine, R. G., Tanha, M., Yang, C., Dodge, K. A., Bates, J. E., & Pettit, G. S. (2010). Does response evaluation and decision (RED) mediate the relation between hostile attribution style and antisocial behavior in adolescence? *Journal of Abnormal Child Psychology, 38,* 615–626.

Forehand, R. & Kotchick, B. A. (2002). Behavioral parent training: Current challenges and potential solutions. *Journal of Child and Family Studies, 11,* 377–384.

Forman, E. A. & Ansell, E. (2002). Orchestrating the multiple voices and inscriptions of a mathematics classroom. *Journal of the Learning Sciences, 11,* 251–274.

Forman, E. A. & Cazden, C. B. (1985). Exploring Vygotskian perspectives in education: The cognitive value of peer interaction. In J. V. Wertsch (Ed.), *Culture, communication, and cognition: Vygotskian perspectives*. Cambridge: Cambridge University Press.

Forman, E. A. & McPhail, J. (1993). Vygotskian perspective in children's collaborative problem solving activity. In E. A. Forman, N. Minick, & C. A. Stone (Eds.), *Contexts for learning: Sociocultural dynamics in children's development*. Oxford: Oxford University Press.

Fox, N. & Hane, A. A. (2008). Studying the biology of human attachment. In J. Cassidy & P. R. Shaver (Eds.), *Handbook of attachment: Theory, research, and clinical applications (2nd edition)* (pp. 217–240). New York, NY: Guilford.

Franchin, L., Donati, C., Benelli, B., Zobec, F., Berchialla, P., Cemin, M., & Gregori, D. (2011). Interaction of children with toys to be assembled: A way to promote development of cognition and manual skills. *The Ergonomics Open Journal, 4,* 55–60.

Francis, P. L., Self, P. A., & Horowitz, F. D. (1987). The behavioral assessment of the neonate: An overview. In J. D. Osofsky (Ed.), *Handbook of infant development* (2nd ed.). New York: Wiley.

Franco, P., Seret, N., Van Hees, J. N., Scaillet, S., Groswasser, J., & Kahn, A. (2005). Influence of swaddling on sleep and arousal characteristics of healthy infants. *Pediatrics, 115,* 1307–1311.

Frank, D., Augustyn, M., Grant-Knight, W., et al. (2001). Growth, development, and behavior in early childhood following cocaine exposure. *Journal of the American Medical Association, 285,* 1613.

Frankel, F. & Feinberg, D. (2002). Social problems associated with ADHD vs. ODD in children referred for friendship problems. *Child Psychiatry and Human Development, 33,* 125–146.

Frawley, T. J. (2008). Gender schema and prejudicial recall: How children misremember, fabricate, and distort gendered picture book information. *Journal of Research in Childhood Education, 22,* 291–303.

Fredricks, J. A. & Eccles, J. S. (2005). Family socialization, gender, and sport motivation and involvement. *Journal of Sport & Exercise Psychology, 27,* 3–31.

Freedland, R. L. & Bertenthal, B. I. (1994). Developmental stages in interlimb coordination: Transition to hands-and-knees crawling. *Psychological Science, 5,* 26–32.

French, R. M., Mareschal, D., Mermillod, M., & Quinn, P. (2004). The role of bottom-up processing in perceptual categorization by 3- to 4-month old infants: Simulations and data. *Journal of Experiential Psychology: General, 133,* 382–397.

Fried, P. (1989). Postnatal consequences of maternal marijuana use in humans. *Annals of the New York Academy of Sciences, 562,* 123–132.

Fried, P. (2002a). Adolescents prenatally exposed to marijuana: Examination of facets of complex behaviours and comparisons with the influence of *in utero* cigarettes. *Journal of Clinical Pharmacology, 42(11* Suppl), 97S–102S.

Fried, P. (2002b). Pregnancy and effects on offspring from birth through adolescence. In F. Grotenhermen & E. Russo (Eds.) *Cannabis and cannabinoids: Pharmacology, toxicology, and therapeutic potential* (pp. 269–278). New York: Haworth Press.

Fried, P., Watkinson, B., & Gray, R. (2003) Differential effects on cognitive functioning in 13- to 16-year-olds prenatally exposed to cigarettes and marijuana. *Neurotoxicology and Teratology, 25,* 427–436.

Fried, P.A., O'Connell, C. M., & Watkinson, M. A. (1992). Sixty- and 72-month follow-up of children prenatally exposed to marijuana, cigarettes, and alcohol: Cognitive and language assessment. *Developmental and Behavioral Pediatrics, 13,* 383–391.

Friedberg, R. & McClure, J. (2002). *Clinical practice of cognitive therapy with children and adolescents*, New York: Guilford.

Friedman, J. M. (1981). Genetic disease in the offspring of older fathers. *Obstetrics and Gynecology 57,* 745–749.

Friedman, S. L. & Boyle, D. E. (2008). Attachment in U.S. children experiencing nonmaternal care in the early 1990s. *Attachment and Human Development, 10,* 225–261.

Friendly, M. & Beach, J. (2005). *Early childhood education and care in Canada 2004*. Toronto: Childcare Resource and Research Unit. Available at: http://action.web.ca/home/crru/rsrcs_crru_full.shtml?x=78309

Frisch, H. L. (1977). Sex stereotypes in adult-infant play. *Child Development, 48,* 1671–1675.

Frith, U. (1989). *Autism: Explaining the enigma*. Oxford, England: Basil Blackwell.

Frodi, A. M., Lamb, M. E., Leavitt, L. A., & Donovan, W. L. (1978). Fathers' and mothers' responses to infant smiles and cries. *Infant Behavior and Development, 1,* 187–198.

Fromkin, V. & Rodman, R. (1988). *An introduction to language* (4th ed.). New York: Holt, Rinehart, and Winston.

Fuentemilla, L., Càmara, E., Münte, T., Krämer, U. M., Cunillera, T., Marco-Pallarés, Tempelmann, C., & Rodriguez-Fornells, A. (2009). Individual differences in true and false memory retrieval are related to white matter brain microstructure. *The Journal of Neuroscience, 29,* 8698–8703.

Fujisawa, K. K., Kutsukake, N., & Hasegawa, T. (2006). Peacemaking and consolation in Japanese preschoolers witnessing peer aggression. *Journal of Comparative Psychology, 120,* 48–57.

Fukahara, H., Shimura, Y., & Yamanouchi, I. (1988, November). *The transmission of ambient noise and self-produced sound into the human body*. Poster presented at the second joint meeting of the Acoustical Society of America and the Acoustical Society of Japan, Honolulu.

Fuligni, A. J., Eccles, J. S., & Barber, B. L. (1995). The long-term effects of seventh-grade ability grouping in mathematics. *Journal of Early Adolescence, 15,* 58–89.

Fullard, W., McDevitt, S. C., & Carey, W. B. (1984). Assessing temperament in one to three year old children. *Journal of Pediatric Psychology, 9,* 205–217.

Fullard, W. & Reiling, A. M. (1976). An investigation of Lorenz's "babyness. " *Child Development, 47,* 1191–1193.

Funk, J. B., Baldacci, H. B., Pasold, T., & Baumgardner, J. (2004). Violence exposure in real-life, video games, television, movies, and the internet: Is there desensitization? *Journal of Adolescence, 27,* 23–39.

Furman, W. & Gavin, L. A. (1989). Peers' influence on adjustment and development. In T. J. Berndt & G. W. Ladd (Eds.), *Peer relationships in child development*. New York: Wiley.

Furman, W. & Lanthier, R. (2002). Parenting siblings. In M. H. Bornstein (Ed.), *Handbook of parenting* (2nd ed., Vol. 1). Mahwah, NJ: Erlbaum.

Furman, W., Rahe, D., & Hartup, W. (1979). Rehabilitation of socially withdrawn preschool children through mixed-age and same-age socialization. *Child Development, 50,* 915–922.

Furrow, D., Nelson, K., & Benedict, H. (1979). Mothers' speech to children and syntactic development: Some simple relationships. *Journal of Child Language, 6,* 423–442.

Furstenberg, F. F. (1993). How families manage risk and opportunity in dangerous neighborhoods. In W. J. Wilson (Ed.), *Sociology and the public agenda*. Newbury Park, CA: Sage.

G

Gabbe, S. G., Niebyl, J. R., & Simpson, J. L. (2007). *Obstetrics: Normal and problem pregnancies.* Philadelphia, PA: Elsevier.

Gagnon, M., Gosselin, P., der Buhs, I. H., Larocque, K., & Milliard, K. (2010). Children's recognition and discrimination of fear and disgust facial expressions. *Journal of Nonverbal Behavior, 34,* 27–42.

Galazios, G., Tripsianis, G., Tsikouras, P., Koutlaki, N., & Liberis, V. (2010). Fetal distress evaluation using and analyzing the variables of antepartum computerized cardiotocography. *Archives of Gynecology and Obstetrics, 281*(2), 229–233.

Galen, B. R. & Underwood, M. K. (1997). A developmental investigation of social aggression among children. *Developmental Psychology, 33,* 589–600.

Gallagher, A. M. & De Lisi, R. (1994). Gender differences in Scholastic Aptitude Test-mathematics problem solving among high-ability students. *Journal of Educational Psychology, 86,* 204–211.

Gallagher, A. M., De Lisi, R., Holst, P. C., McGillicuddy-De Lisi, A. V., Morely, M., & Cahalan, C. (2000). Gender differences in advanced mathematical problem solving. *Journal of Experimental Child Psychology, 75,* 165–190.

Gallagher, K. C. (2002). Does child temperament moderate the influence of parenting on adjustment? *Developmental Review, 22,* 623–643.

Gallahue, D. L. & Ozmun, J. C. (1995). *Understanding motor development: Infants, children, adolescents, adults* (3rd ed.). Madison, WI: Brown & Benchmark.

Gallistel, C. R. & Gelman, R. (1992). Preverbal and verbal counting and computation. *Cognition, 44,* 43–74.

Gallup, G. G. Jr. (1970). Chimpanzees: Self-recognition. *Science, 167,* 86–87.

Gallup, G. G. Jr., Anderson, J. R., & Shillito, D. J. (2002). The mirror test. In M. Bekoff, C. Allen, & G. M. Burghardt (Eds.), *The cognitive animal: Empirical and theoretical perspectives on animal cognition.* Cambridge, MA: MIT Press.

Gally, M. (2002, January 23). Research: Boys to men. *Education Week.* Retrieved February 9, 2003 from www.edweek.org/ew/newstory.cfm?slug519boys.h21.

Galsworthy, M. J., Dionne, G., Dale, P. S., & Plomin, R. (2000). Sex differences in early verbal and non-verbal cognitive development. *Developmental Science, 3,* 206–215.

Ganea, P. A., Allen, M. L., Butler, L., Carey, S., & DeLoache, J. S. (2009). Toddlers' referential understanding of pictures, *Journal of Experimental Child Psychology, 104,* 283–295.

Ganis, G., Thompson, W. L., Mast, F. W., & Kosslyn, S. M. (2003). Visual imagery in cerebral visual dysfunction. *Neurologic Clinics, 21,* 631 646.

Garai, J. E. & Scheinfeld, A. (1968). Sex differences in mental and behavioral traits. *Genetic Psychology Monographs, 7,* 169–299.

Garbarino, J. & deLara, E. (2004). Coping with the consequences of school violence. In J. C. Conoley & A. P. Goldstein (Eds.), *School violence intervention: A practical handbook* (2nd ed., pp. 400–415). New York: Guilford.

Garcia-Rill, E., Kobayashi, T., & Good, C. (2003). The developmental decrease in REM sleep. *Thalamus & Related Systems, 2,* 115–131.

Gardner, H. (1983). *Frames of mind: The theory of multiple intelligences.* New York: Basic Books.

Gardner, H. (1993). *Frames of mind: The theory of multiple intelligences* (10th anniversary ed.). New York: Basic Books.

Gardner, H. (1999). *Intelligence reframed: Multiple intelligence in the 21st century.* New York: Basic Books.

Gardner, R. J. M. & Sutherland, G. R. (2004). *Chromosome abnormalities and genetic counselling* (3rd ed.). New York: Oxford.

Garner, P. W., Jones, D. C., & Miner, J. L. (1994). Social competence among low-income preschoolers: Emotion socialization practices and social cognitive correlates. *Child Development, 65,* 622–637.

Garrison, W. T. & Earls, F. J. (1987). *Temperament and child psychopathology.* Newbury Park, CA: Sage.

Garton, A. (1992). *Social interaction and the development of language and cognition.* Hillsdale, NJ: Erlbaum.

Gartrell, N., Deck, A., Rodas, C., Peyser, H., & Banks, A. (2005). The national lesbian family study: Interviews with the 10-year-old children. *American Journal of Orthopsychiatry, 75,* 518–524.

Garvey, C. (1986). Peer relations and the growth of communication. In E. C. Mueller & C. R. Cooper (Eds.), *Process and outcome in peer relationships.* New York: Academic Press.

Garvey, C. (1990). *Play.* Cambridge, MA: Harvard University Press.

Gaskins, S. (1999). Children's daily lives in a Mayan village: A case study of culturally constructed roles and activities. In A. Göncü (Ed.), *Children's engagement in the world: Sociocultural perspectives.* New York: Cambridge.

Gaudet, S. & Clément, R. (2005). Identity maintenance and loss: Concurrent processes among the Fransaskois. *Canadian Journal of Behavioural Science, 37,* 110–122.

Gauvain, M., Beebe, H., & Zhao, S. (2011). Applying the cultural approach to cognitive development. *Journal of Cognition and Development, 12,* 121–133.

Gauvain, M. & Fagot, B. I. (1995). Child temperament as a mediator of mother-toddler problem solving. *Social Development, 4,* 257–278.

Gava, L., Valenza, E., & Turati, C. (2009). Newborns' perception of left-right spatial relations. *Child Development, 80*(6), 1797–1810.

Gazelle, H. & Ladd, G. W. (2003). Anxious solitude and peer exclusion: A diathesis-stress model of internalizing trajectories in childhood. *Child Development, 74,* 257–278.

Ge, X., Conger, R. D., Cadoret, R. J., Neiderhiser, J. M., Yates, W., Troughton, E., & Stewart, M. A. (1996). The developmental interface between nature and nurture: A mutual influence model of child antisocial behavior and parents' behaviors. *Developmental Psychology, 32,* 574–589.

Ge, X., Conger, R. D., & Elder, G. H. Jr. (2001a). Pubertal transition, stressful life events, and the emergence of gender differences in adolescent depressive symptoms. *Developmental Psychology, 37,* 404–417.

Ge, X., Conger, R. D., & Elder, G. H. Jr. (2001b). The relation between puberty and psychological distress in adolescent boys. *Journal of Research on Adolescence, 11,* 49–70.

Geary, D. C. (1995b). Reflections of evolution and culture in children's cognition: Implications for mathematical development and instruction. *American Psychologist, 50,* 24–37.

Geary, D. C. (1996). International differences in mathematical achievement: Their nature, courses, and consequences. *Current Directions in Psychological Science, 5,* 133–137.

Geary, D. C. (1998). *Male, female: The evolution of human sex differences.* Washington, DC: American Psychological Association.

Geary, D. C. (2002). Principles of evolutionary educational psychology. *Learning and Individual Differences, 12,* 317–345.

Geary, D. C. (2005). The motivation to control and the origin of mind: Exploring the life-mind joint point in the tree of knowledge system. *Journal of Clinical Psychology, 61,* 21–46.

Geary, D. C. & Bjorklund, D. F. (2000). Evolutionary developmental psychology. *Child Development, 71,* 57–65.

Geary, D. C., Saults, S. J., Liu, F., & Hoard, M. K. (2000). Sex differences in spatial cognition, computational fluency, and arithmetical reasoning. *Journal of Experimental Child Psychology, 77,* 337–353.

Gelman, R. (1972). Logical capacity of very young children: Number invariance rules. *Child Development, 43,* 75–90.

Gelman, R. (1982). Basic numerical abilities. In R. J. Sternberg (Ed.), *Advances in the psychology of human intelligence* (Vol. 1). Hillsdale, NJ: Erlbaum.

Gelman, R. (1991). Epigenetic foundations of knowledge structures: Initial and transcendent constructions. In S. Carey & R. Gelman (Eds.), *The epigenesis of mind.* Hillsdale, NJ: Erlbaum.

Gelman, R. & Gallistel, C. R. (1978). *The child's understanding of number.* Cambridge, MA: Harvard University Press.

Gelman, S. A. (2000). The role of essentialism in children's concepts. In H. W Reese (Ed.), *Advances in child development and behavior* (Vol. 27). San Diego, CA: Academic Press.

Gelman, S. A. (2003). *The essential child: Origins of essentialism in everyday thought.* New York: Oxford University Press.

Gelman, S. A. & Bloom, P. (2007). Developmental changes in the understanding of generics. *Cognition, 105,* 166–83.

Gelman, S. A. & Coley, J. D. (1990). The importance of knowing a dodo is a bird: Categories and induction in 2-year-old children. *Developmental Psychology, 26,* 796–804.

Gelman, S. A., Heyman, G. D., & Legare, C. H. (2007). Developmental changes in the coherence of essentialist beliefs about psychological characteristics. *Child Development, 78,* 757–74.

Gelman, S. A. & Markman, E. M. (1986). Categories and induction in young children. *Cognition, 23,* 183–209.

Gelman, S. A., Wilcox, S. A., & Clark, E. V (1989). Conceptual and lexical hierarchies in young children. *Cognitive Development, 4,* 309–326.

Genesee, F. (1987). *Learning through two languages: Studies of immersion and bilingual education.* Cambridge, MA: Newbury House.

Genesee, F. (Ed.). (1994). *Educating second language children.* New York: Cambridge University Press.

Genesee, F. & Gandara, P. (1999). Bilingual education programs: A cross-national perspective. *Journal of Social Issues, 55,* 665–685.

Genesee, F., Nicoladis, E., & Paradis, J. (1995). Language differentiation in early bilingual development. *Journal of Child Language, 22,* 611–631.

Genesee, F., Paradis, J., & Crago, M. B. (2004). *Dual language development & disorders: A handbook on bilingualism and second language learning, Vol. 11.* Baltimore: Paul H. Brookes Publishing.

Gentile, D. A., Lynch, P. J., Linder, J. R., & Walsh, D. A. (2004). The effects of violent video game habits on adolescent hostility, aggressive behaviors, and school performance. *Journal of Adolescence, 27,* 5–22.

Gentner, D. (1982). Why nouns are learned before verbs: Linguistic relativity versus natural partitioning. In S. A. Kuczaj (Ed.), *Language development* (Vol. 2). Hillsdale, NJ: Erlbaum.

George, C. & Solomon, J. (1989). Internal working models of parenting and security of attachment at age six. *Infant Mental Health Journal, 10,* 222–237.

George, C. & Solomon, J. (2008). The caregiving system: A behavioral systems approach to parenting. In J. Cassidy & P. R. Shaver (Eds.), *Handbook of attachment: Theory, research, and clinical applications (2nd edition)* (pp. 833–856). New York, NY: Guilford.

Gerken, L. A., Wilson, R., & Lewis, W. (2005). 17-month-olds can use distributional cues to form syntactic categories. *Journal of Child Language, 32,* 249–268.

Germo, G. R., Chang, E. S., Keller, M. A., & Goldberg, W. A. (2007). Child sleep arrangements and family life: Perspectives from mothers and fathers. *Infant and Child Development, 16,* 433–456.

Gerry, D., Faux, A., & Trainor, L. (2010). Effects of Kindermusik training on infants' rhythmic enculturation. *Developmental Science, 13*(3), 545–551.

Gershkoff-Stowe, L. (2001). The course of children's naming errors in early word learning. *Journal of Cognition and Development, 2,* 131–155.

Gershkoff-Stowe, L. & Hahn, E. R. (2007). Fast mapping skills in the developing lexicon. *Journal of Speech, Language, and Hearing Research, 50,* 682–697.

Gerson, H., Sorby, S.A., Wysocki, A., & Baartmans, B.J. (2001). The development and assessment of multimedia software for improving 3-D spatial visualization skills. *Computer Applications in Engineering Education, 9,* 105–113.

Gertner, Y., Fisher, C., & Eisengart, J. (2006). Learning words and rules: Abstract knowledge of word order in early sentence comprehension. *Psychological Science, 17,* 684–691.

Geschwind, N. & Galaburda, A. (1987). *Cerebral lateralization.* Cambridge, MA: MIT Press.

Gesell, A. (1925). *The mental growth of the preschool child.* New York: Macmillan.

Gesell, A. & Thompson, H. (1929). Learning and growth in identical infant twins: An experimental study by the method of co-twin control. *Genetic Psychological Monographs, 6,* 1–24.

Gesell, A. & Thompson, H. (1938). *The psychology of early growth.* New York: Macmillan.

Gest, S. D., Sesma, A., Masten, A. S., & Tellegen, A. (2006). Childhood peer reputation as a predictor of competence and symptoms 10 years later. *Journal of Abnormal Child Psychology, 34,* 509–526.

Gewirtz, J. L. & Boyd, E. F. (1976). Mother-infant interaction and its study. In H. W Reese (Ed.), *Advances in child development and behavior* (Vol. 11). New York: Academic Press.

Gewirtz, J. L. & Boyd, E. F. (1977). Experiments on mother-infant interaction underlying mutual attachment acquisition: The infant conditions the mother. In T. Alloway, P. Pliner, & L. Kramer (Eds.), *Advances in the study of communication and affect: Vol. 3. Attachment behavior.* New York: Plenum.

Gewirtz, J. L. & Pelaez-Nogueras, M. (1991a). The attachment metaphor and the conditioning of infant separation protests. In J. L. Gewirtz & W. M. Kurtines (Eds.), *Intersections with attachment.* Hillsdale, NJ: Erlbaum.

Gewirtz, J. L. & Pelaez-Nogueras, M. (1991b). Proximal mechanisms underlying the acquisition of moral behavior patterns. In W. M. Kurtines & J. L. Gewirtz (Eds.), *Handbook of moral behavior and development: Vol. 1.* Hillsdale, NJ: Erlbaum.

Gewirtz, J. L. & Pelaez-Nogueras, M. (1992a). B. F. Skinner's legacy to human infant behavior and development. *American Psychologist, 47,* 1411–1422.

Gewirtz, J. L. & Pelaez-Nogueras, M. (1992b). Social referencing as a learned process. In S. Feinman (Ed.), *Social referencing and the social construction of reality in infancy.* New York: Plenum.

Ghaderi, A. (2006). The foundation of the self and the assessment of self-esteem. In A. Columbus (Ed.), *Advances in psychology research* (pp. 69–86). Hauppauge, NY: Nova Science Publishers.

Ghatala, E. S., Levin, J. R., Pressley, M., & Lodice, M. G. (1985). Training cognitive strategy monitoring in children. *American Educational Research Journal, 22,* 199–216.

Gianino, A. & Tronick, E. Z. (1988). The mutual regulation model: The infant's self and interactive regulation coping and defense. In T. Field, P. McCabe, & N. Schneiderman (Eds.), *Stress and coping.* Hillsdale, NJ: Erlbaum.

Giardino, J., Gonzalez, A., Steiner, M., & Fleming, A.S. (2008). Effects of motherhood on physiological and subjective responses to infant cries in teenage mothers: A comparison with non-mothers and adult mothers. *Hormones and Behavior, 53,* 149–158.

Gibbons, J. L. (2000). Gender development in cross-cultural perspective. In T. Eckes & H. M. Trautner (Eds.), *The developmental social psychology of gender.* Mahwah, NJ: Erlbaum.

Gibbs, J. C. (2003). *Moral development and reality: Beyond the theories of Kohlberg and Hoffman.* Thousand Oaks, CA: Sage.

Gibbs, J. C. (2010). *Moral development and reality: Beyond the theories of Kohlberg and Hoffman* (2nd edition). Boston, MA: Pearson Allyn & Bacon.

Gibson, E. J. (1969). *Principles of perceptual learning and development.* New York: Appleton-Century-Crofts.

Gibson, E. J. (1988). Exploratory behavior in the development of perceiving, acting, and the acquiring of knowledge. *Annual Review of Psychology, 39,* 1–41.

Gibson, E. J. (1993). Ontogenesis of the perceived self. In A. T. Neisser (Ed.), *The perceived self: Ecological and interpersonal sources of self-knowledge.* Cambridge, MA: Cambridge University Press.

Gibson, E. J. & Pick, A. D. (2000a). *Perceptual learning and development: An ecological view.* New York: Oxford University Press.

Gibson, E. J. & Pick, A. D. (2000b). *An ecological approach to perceptual learning and development.* New York: Oxford University Press.

Gibson, E. J. & Walk, R. D. (1960). The "visual cliff. " *Scientific American, 202,* 64–71.

Gibson, E. J. & Walker, A. (1984). Development of knowledge of visual-tactual affordances of substance. *Child Development, 55,* 453–460.

Gibson, J. J. (1966). *The senses considered as perceptual systems.* Boston: Houghton Mifflin.

Giedd, J. N. & Rapoport, J. L. (2010). Structural MRI of pediatric brain development: What have we learned and where are we going? *Neuron, 67,* 728–734.

Gifford-Smith, M. E. & Rabiner, D. (2004). Social information processing and children's social adjustment. In J. B. Kupersmidt & K. A. Dodge (Eds.), *Children's Peer Relations: From Development to Intervention* (pp. 61–79). Washington, DC: American Psychological Association.

Gilbert, C. A., Lilley, C. M., Craig, K. D., McGrath, P. J., Court, C. A., Bennett, S. M., & Montgomery, C. J. (1999). Postoperative pain expression in preschool children: Validation of the Child Facial, Coding System. *Clinical Journal of Pain, 15,* 192–200.

Gilbert, W. M., Nesbitt, T. S., & Danielsen, B. (1999). Childbearing beyond age 40: Pregnancy outcomes in 24,032 cases. *Obstetrics and Gynecology, 93,* 9–14.

Gilligan, C. (1982). *In a different voice: Psychological theory and women's development.* Cambridge, MA: Harvard University Press.

Gilmore, R. O. & Johnson, M. H. (1997). Egocentric action in early infancy: Spatial frames of reference for saccades. *Psychological Science, 8,* 224–230.

Ginsberg, N. (2006). Preimplantation genetic diagnosis. In J. M. Vugt. & L. P. Schulman (Eds.), *Prenatal medicine* (pp. 282–315). New York, NY: Taylor and Francis.

Ginsburg, H. & Opper, S. (1988). *Piaget's theory of intellectual development* (3rd ed.). Englewood Cliffs, NJ: Prentice Hall.

Giudicelli, M. D., Serazin, V., Le Sciellour, C., Albert, M., Selva, J., & Giudicelli, Y. (2008). Increased achondroplasia mutation frequency with advanced age and evidence for G1138A mosaicism in human testis biopsies. *Fertility and Sterility, 89,* 1651–1656.

Giusti, R. M., Iwamoto, K., & Hatch, E. E. (1995). Diethylstilbestrol revisited: A review of the long-term health effects. *Annals of Internal Medicine, 122,* 778–788.

Glasgow, K. L., Dornbusch, S. M., Troyer, L., Steinberg, L., & Ritter, P. I. (1997). Parenting style, adolescents' attributions, and educational outcomes in nine heterogeneous high schools. *Child Development, 68,* 507–529.

Glassman, M. (1994). All things being equal: The two roads of Piaget and Vygotsky. *Developmental Review, 14,* 186–214.

Gleason, J. B. & Ely, R. (2002). Gender differences in language development. In A. McGillicuddy-De Lisi & R. De Lisi (Eds.), *Advances in applied developmental psychology: Vol. 21. Biology, society, and behavior: The development of sex differences in cognition.* Westport, CT: Ablex.

Gleason, J. B. & Weintraub, S. (1978). Input and the acquisition of communicative competence. In K. E. Nelson (Ed.), *Children's language* (Vol. 1). New York: Gardner.

Gleitman, L. R. & Gillette, J. (1999). The role of syntax in verb learning. In W. C. Ritchie & T. K. Bhatia (Eds.), *Handbook of child language acquisition.* San Diego, CA: Academic Press.

Glenn, S. M., Cunningham, C. C., & Joyce, P. F. (1981). A study of auditory preferences in nonhandicapped infants and infants with Down's syndrome. *Child Development, 52,* 1303–1307.

Glick, B. & Gibbs, J. C. (2011). *Aggression replacement training: A comprehensive intervention for aggressive youth* (3rd ed.). Champaign, IL: Research Press.

Goh, Y I., Bollano, E., Einarson, T. R., & Koren, G. (2006). Prenatal multivitamin supplementation and rates of congenital anomalies: A meta-analysis. *Journal of Obstetrics and Gynaecology Canada, Aug,* 680–689.

Goldberg, J. D. & Musci, T. J. (2006). Invasive prenatal diagnostic techniques. In J. M. Vugt & L. P. Schulman (Eds.), *Prenatal medicine* (pp. 189–204). New York, NY: Taylor and Francis.

Goldberg, M. E., Bisley, J. W., Powell, K. D., & Gottlieb, J. (2006). Saccades, salience and attention: The role of the lateral intraparietal area in visual behavior. *Progress in Brain Research, 155,* 157–175.

Goldberg, S. & DiVitto, B. (2002). Parenting children born preterm. In M. H. Borstein (Ed.), *Handbook of parenting (2nd edition). Volume 1: Children and parenting* (pp. 329–354). Mahwah, NJ: Erlbaum.

Goldberg, W. A. & Keller, M. A. (2007). Parent-infant co-sleeping: Why the interest and concern? *Infant and Child Development, 16,* 331–339.

Goldenberg, R. L. (1995). Small for gestational age infants. In B. P. Sachs, R. Beard, E. Papiernik, & C. Russell (Eds.), *Reproductive health care for women and babies.* New York: Oxford University Press.

Goldfield, B. A. (2000). Nouns before verbs in comprehension vs. production: The view from pragmatics. *Journal of Child Language, 27,* 501–520.

Goldfield, B. A. & Reznick, J. S. (1990). Early lexical acquisition: Rate, content, and the vocabulary spurt. *Journal of Child Language, 17,* 171–183.

Goldfield, B. A. & Snow, C. E. (2001). Individual differences: Implications for the study of language acquisition. In J. B. Gleason (Ed.), *The development of language* (5th ed.). Boston: Allyn and Bacon.

Goldin-Meadow, S. (2003). *The resilience of language: What gesture creation in deaf children can tell us about how all children learn language.* New York: Psychology Press.

Goldin-Meadow, S. (2007). Pointing sets the stage for learning language — and creating language. *Child Development, 78,* 741–745.

Goldman, A. S. (1980). Critical periods of prenatal toxic insults. In R. H. Schwartz & S. J. Yaffe (Eds.), *Drug and chemical risks to the fetus and newborn.* New York: Alan R. Liss.

Goldsmith, H. H., Aksan, N., Essex, M., & Vandells, D. L. (2001). Temperament and socioemotional adjustment to kindergarten: A multi-informant perspective. In T. D. Wachs & G. A. Kohnstamm (Eds.), *Temperament in context.* Mahwah, NJ: Erlbaum.

Goldsmith, H. H., Buss, K. A., & Lemery, K. S. (1997). Toddler and childhood temperament: Expanded content, stronger genetic evidence, new evidence for the importance of environment. *Developmental Psychology, 33,* 891–905.

Goldsmith, H. H., Buss, A. H., Plomin, R., Rothbart, M. K., Thomas, A., Chess, S., et al. (1987). Roundtable: What is temperament. Four approaches. *Child Development, 58,* 505–529.

Goldsmith, H. H. & Harman, C. (1994). Temperament and attachment: Individuals and relationships. *Current Directions in Psychological Science, 3,* 53–57.

Goldsmith, H. H. & Rothbart, M. K. (1991). Contemporary instruments for assessing early temperament by questionnaire and in the laboratory. In J. Strelau & A. Angleitner (Eds.), *Explorations in temperament: International perspectives on theory and measurement.* New York: Plenum.

Goldstein, A. P. (2004a). Art and beyond: The prepare curriculum. In A. Goldstein, R. Nensen, B. Daleflod, & M. Kalt (Eds.), *New perspectives on aggression replacement training* (pp. 154–170). Chichester, UK: Wiley.

Goldstein, A. P. (2004b). Evaluations of effectiveness. In A. Goldstein, R. Nensen, B. Daleflod, & M. Kalt (Eds.), *New perspectives on aggression replacement training* (pp. 230–244). Chichester, UK: Wiley.

Goldstein, A. P. (2004c). Skillstreaming: The behavioral component. In A. Goldstein, R. Nensen, B. Daleflod, & M. Kalt (Eds.), *New perspectives on aggression replacement training* (pp. 23–50). Chichtester, UK: Wiley.

Golinkoff, R. M. & Hirsh-Pasek, K. (Eds.) (1999). *How babies talk: The magic and mystery of language in the first three years.* New York: Dutton/Penguin Press.

Golombok, S. (2006). New family forms. In A. Clarke-Stewart & J. Dunn (Eds.), *Families count: Effects on child and adolescent development* (pp. 273–298). New York: Cambridge University Press.

Golombok, S., Cook, R., Bish, A., & Murray, C. (1995). Families created by the new reproductive technologies: Quality of parenting and social and emotional development of the children. *Child Development, 66,* 285–298.

Golombok, S., MacCallum, F., & Goodman, E. (2001). The "test-tube" generation: Parent-child relationships and the psychological well-being of in vitro fertilization children at adolescence. *Child Development, 72,* 599–608.

Golombok, S. & Tasker, F. (2010). Gay fathers. In M. E. Lamb (Ed.) *The role of the father in child development* (5th edition, pp. 319–340). Hoboken, NJ: Wiley.

Gomez, R. L. (2002). Variability and detection of invariant structure. *Psychological Science, 13,* 431–436.

Göncü, A., Mistry, J., & Mosier, C. (2000). Cultural variations in the play of toddlers. *International Journal of Behavioral Development, 24,* 321–329.

Good, T. L. & Brophy, J. E. (2000). *Looking in classrooms* (8th ed.). New York: Longman.

Goodman, G. S., Hirschmann, J. E., Hepps, D., & Rudy L. (1991). Children's memory for stressful events. *Merrill-Palmer Quarterly, 37,* 109–158.

Goodman, G. S., Pyle Taub, S., Jones, D. P. H., England, P., Port, L. K., Rudy, L., et al. (1992). Testifying in criminal court. *Monographs of the Society for Research in Child Development, 57*(5, Serial No. 229).

Goodman, R. & Stevenson, J. (1989). A twin study of hyperactivity: II. The aetiological role of genes, family relationships, and perinatal adversity. *Journal of Child Psychology and Psychiatry, 30,* 691–709.

Goodnow, J. J. (1990). The socialization of cognition: What's involved? In J. W Stigler, R. A. Shweder, & G. Herdt (Eds.), *Cultural psychology: Essays on comparative human development.* New York: Cambridge University Press.

Goodnow, J. J. (1996). Acceptable ignorance, negotiable disagreement: Alternative views of learning. In D. R. Olson & N. Torrance (Eds.), *The handbook of education and human development: New models of learning, teaching, and schooling.* Cambridge, MA: Blackwell.

Goodnow, J. J. (2002). Parents' knowledge and expectations: Using what we know. In M. H. Bornstein (Ed.), *Handbook of parenting* (2nd ed., Vol. 3). Mahwah, NJ: Erlbaum.

Goodwin, C. J. (2011). *Research in psychology: Methods and design* (6th edition). Hoboken, NJ: John Wiley & Sons.

Goodwyn, S. L., Acredolo, L. P., & Brown, C. A. (2000). Impact of symbolic gesturing on early language development. *Journal of Nonverbal Behavior, 24,* 81–103.

Goodz, N. S. (1989). Parental language mixing in bilingual families. *Journal of Infant Mental Health, 10,* 25–34.

Gopnik, A. (2001). Theories, language and culture: Whorf without wincing. In M. Bowerman and S. Levinson (eds.), *Conceptual development and language acquisition.* New York: Cambridge University Press.

Gopnik, A. (2009). *The philosophical baby.* New York, NY: Picador.

Gopnik, A. & Meltzoff, A. N. (1987). Early semantic developments and their relationship to object permanence, means-ends understanding and categorization. In K. Nelson & A. VanKleek (Eds.), *Children's language* (Vol. 6). Hillsdale, NJ: Erlbaum.

Gopnik, A. & Meltzoff, A. N. (1996). *Words, thoughts, and theories.* Cambridge, MA: MIT Press.

Gorman, K. S. & Pollitt, E. (1992). Relationship between weight and body proportionality at birth, growth during the first year of life, and cognitive development at 36, 48, and 60 months. *Infant Behavior and Development, 15, 279–296.*

Gosselin, P. (2005). Le décodage de l'expression faciales des émotions au cours de l'enfance. *Psychologie canadienne, 46,* 126–138.

Gosselin, P. & Larocque, C. (2000). Facial morphology and children's categorization of facial expressions of emotions: A comparison between Asian and Caucasian faces. *The Journal of Genetic Psychology, 161,* 346–358.

Gosselin, P. & Pélissier, D. (1996). Effet de l'intensité sur la catégorisation des prototypes émotionnels faciaux chez l'enfant et l'adulte. *Journal International de Psychologie, 31,* 225–234.

Gosselin, P. & Simard, J. (1999). Children's knowledge of facial features: distinguishing fear and surprise. *Journal of Genetic Psychology, 160,* 181–193.

Goswami, U. (1992). *Analogical reasoning in children.* Hove, UK: Erlbaum.

Goswami, U. (1995). Transitive relational mappings in three- and four-year-olds: The analogy of Goldilocks and the three bears. *Child Development, 66,* 877–892.

Goswami, U. (1996). Analogical reasoning and cognitive development. In H. W Reese (Ed.), *Advances in child development and behavior* (Vol. 26). New York: Academic Press.

Goswami, U. & Brown, A. L. (1990). Higher-order structure and relational reasoning: Contrasting analogical and thematic relations. *Cognition, 36,* 207–226.

Gotlieb, S. J., Baisini, F. J., & Bray, N. W (1988). Visual recognition memory in IVGR and normal birth-weight infants. *Infant Behavior and Development, 11,* 223–228.

Gottesman, I. I. (1974). Developmental genetics and ontogenetic psychology: Overdue détente and propositions from a matchmaker. In A. Pick (Ed.), *Minnesota symposia on child psychology* (Vol. 8). Minneapolis, MN: University of Minnesota Press.

Gottfried, A. W., Gottfried, A. E., Bathurst, K., & Guerin, D. W. (1994). *Gifted IQ: Early developmental aspects.* New York: Plenum Press.

Gottlieb, G. (1998). Normally occurring environmental and behavioral influences on gene activity: From central dogma to probabilistic epigenesis. *Psychological Review, 105,* 792–802.

Gottman, J. M. (1983). How children become friends. *Monographs of the Society for Research in Child Development, 48* (3, Serial No. 201).

Gottman, J. M., Gonso, J., & Rasmussen, B. (1975). Social interaction, social competence, and friendship in children. *Child Development, 46,* 709–718.

Goudena, P. P. (1987). The social nature of private speech of preschoolers during problem solving. *International Journal of Behavioral Development, 10,* 187–206.

Gouvela, P. A. R., Brucki, S. M. D., Malheiros, S. M. F., & Bueno, O. F. A. (2007). Disorders in planning and strategy application in frontal lobe lesion patients. *Brain and Cognition, 63,* 240–246.

Graber, J. A., Brooks-Gunn, J., Paikoff, R. L., & Warren, M. P. (1994). Prediction of eating problems: An 8-year study of adolescent girls. *Developmental Psychology, 30,* 823–834.

Graber, J. A., Brooks-Gunn, J., & Petersen, A. C. (Eds.). (1996). *Transitions through adolescence: Interpersonal domains and context.* Mahwah, NJ: Erlbaum.

Graber, J. A., Seeley, J. R., Brooks-Gunn, J., & Lewinsohn, P. M. (2004). Is pubertal timing associated with psychopathology in young adulthood? *Child and Adolescent Psychiatry, 43,* 718–726.

Graham, F. K. & Clifton, R. K. (1966). Heart-rate change as a component of the orienting response. *Psychological Bulletin, 65,* 305–320.

Graham, S. & Hoehn, S. (1995). Children's understanding of aggression and withdrawal as social stigmas: An attributional analysis. *Child Development, 66,* 1143–1161.

Graham, S., Hudley, C., & Williams, E. (1992). Attributional and emotional determinants of aggression among African-American and Latino young adolescents. *Developmental Psychology, 28,* 731–740.

Graham, S. & Juvonen, J. (1998a). Self-blame and peer victimization in middle school: An attributional analysis. *Developmental Psychology, 34,* 587–599.

Graham, S. & Juvonen, J. (1998b). A social cognitive perspective on peer aggression and victimization. In R. Vasta (Ed.), *Annals of child development* (Vol. 13). London: Kingsley.

Graham, S., Taylor, A. Z., & Ho, A. Y. (2009). Race and ethnicity in peer relations research. In K.H. Rubin, W. M. Bukowski, & B. Laursen (Eds.), *Handbook of peer interactions, relationships, and groups* (pp. 394–413). New York: Guilford.

Gralinski, J. H. & Kopp, C. B. (1993). Everyday rules for behavior: Mothers' requests to young children. *Developmental Psychology, 29,* 573–584.

Granrud, C. (2006). Size constancy in infants: 4-month-olds' responses to physical versus retinal image size. *Journal of Experimental Psychology: Human Perception and Performance, 32,* 1398–1404.

Grant, H. & Dweck, C. S. E. (2003). Clarifying achievement goals and their impact. *Journal of Personality and Social Psychology, 85,* 541–553.

Grantham-McGregor, S., Ani, C., & Fernald, L. (2001). The role of nutrition in intellectual development. In R. J. Sternberg & E. L. Grigorenko (Eds.), *Environmental effects on cognitive abilities.* Mahwah, NJ: Erlbaum.

Graziano, W. G. (1987). Lost in thought at the choice point: Cognition, context, and equity. In J. C. Masters & W. P. Smith (Eds.), *Social comparison, social justice, and relative deprivation.* Hillsdale, NJ: Erlbaum.

Green, K. D., Forehand, R., Beck, S. J., & Vosk, B. (1980). An assessment of the relationship among measures of children's social competence and children's academic achievement. *Child Development, 51,* 1149–1156.

Greenberg, M. T., Domitrovich, C., & Bumbarger, B. (2001). The prevention of mental disorders in school-age children: Current state of the field. *Prevention and Treatment, 4,* Article 001a. Online article available at: http://journals.apa.org/prevention/volume4/pre004001a.html.

Greenberger, E. & Chen, C. (1996). Perceived family relationships and depressed mood in early and late adolescence: A comparison of European and Asian Americans. *Developmental Psychology, 32,* 707–716.

Greene, J. P. (1998). *A meta-analysis of the effectiveness of bilingual education.* Claremont, CA: Tomas Rivera Policy Institute.

Greenfield, P. M. (1966). On culture and conservation. In J. S. Bruner, R. R. Oliver, & P. M. Greenfield (Eds.), *Studies in cognitive growth.* New York: Wiley.

Greenough, W. T. & Black, J. E. (1999). Experience, neural plasticity, and psychological development. In N. Fox, L. A. Leavitt, & J. G. Warhol (Eds.), *The role of early experience in infant development* (pp. 29–40). Pompton Plains, NJ: Johnson and Johnson Pediatric Institute.

Gregory, A. M., Ball, H. A., & Button, T. M. (2011) Behavioral genetics. In P. K. Smith & K. H. Hart (Eds.), *The Wiley-Blackwell handbook of childhood social development, 2nd edition.* Hoboken, NJ: Wiley.

Grèzes, J. & Decety, J. (2002). Does visual perception of object afford action? Evidence from a neuroimaging study. *Neuropsychologia, 40,* 212–222.

Grigorenko, E. L. (2000). Heritability and intelligence. In R. J. Sternberg (Ed.), *Handbook of intelligence.* New York: Cambridge University Press.

Grolnick, W. & Beiswenger, K. L. (2006). Facilitating children's self-esteem: The role of parents and teachers. In M. Kernis (Ed.), *Self-esteem: issues and answers: A sourcebook of current perspectives* (pp. 230–237). New York: Psychology Press.

Grolnick, W., Bridges, L. J., & Connell, J. P. (1996). Emotion-regulation in two-year-olds: Strategies and emotional expression in four contexts. *Child Development, 67,* 928–941.

Gronau, R. C. & Waas, G. A. (1997). Delay of gratification and cue utilization: An examination of children's social information processing. *Merrill-Palmer Quarterly, 43,* 305–322.

Groome, L. J., Mooney, D. M., Holland, S. B., Smith, L. A., Atterbury J. L., & Dykman, R. A. (1999). Behavioral state affects heart rate response to low-intensity sound in human fetuses. *Early Human Development, 54,* 39–54.

Groome, L. J., Swiber, M. J., Atterbury, J. L., Bentz, L. S., & Holland, S. B. (1997). Similarities and differences in behavioral state organization during sleep periods in the perinatal infant before and after birth. *Child Development, 68,* 1–11.

Gross, A. L. & Ballif, B. (1991). Children's understanding of emotion from facial expressions and situations: A review. *Developmental Review, 11,* 368–398.

Grossmann, K. E. & Grossmann, K. (1990). The wider concept of attachment in cross-cultural research. *Human Development, 33,* 31–47.

Grossmann, K., Grossman, K. E., Kindler, H., & Zimmermann, P. (2008). A wider view of attachment and exploration: The influence of mothers and fathers on the development of psychological security from infancy to young adulthood. In J. Cassidy & P. R. Shaver (Eds.), *Handbook of attachment: Theory, research, and clinical applications (2nd edition)* (pp. 857–879). New York, NY: Guilford.

Grossmann, K., Grossmann, K. E., Spangler, G., Suess, G., & Unzner, L. (1985). Maternal sensitivity and newborns' orientation responses as related to quality of attachment in northern Germany. In I. Bretherton & E. Waters (Eds.), Growing points of attachment theory and research. *Monographs of the Society for Research in Child Development, 50(1–2,* Serial No. 209).

Grossmann, T., Gliga, T., Johnson, M. H., & Mareschal, D. (2009). The neural basis of perceptual category learning in human infants. *Journal of Cognitive Neuroscience, 21*(12), 2276–2286.

Grotuss, J., Bjorklund, D. F., & Csinady, A. (2007). Evolutionary developmental psychology: Developing human nature. *Acta Psychologica Sinica, 39,* 439–453.

Grunau, R. E., Holsti, L., Jeroen, W. B., & Peters, J. W. B. (2006). Long-term consequences of pain in human neonates. *Seminars in Fetal and Neonatal Medicine, 11,* 268–275.

Grusec, J. E. (2006). The development of moral behavior and conscience from a socialization perspective. In M. Killen & J. Smetana (Eds.), *Handbook of moral development* (pp. 243–266). Mahwah, NJ: Erlbaum.

Grusec, J. E. & Abramovitch, R. (1982). Imitation of peers and adults in a natural setting: A functional analysis. *Child Development, 53,* 636–642.

Grusec, J. E. & Davidov, M. (2007). Socialization in the family: The roles of parents. In J. E. Grusec & P. D. Hastings (Eds.), *Handbook of socialization: Theory and research* (pp. 284–308). New York: Guilford.

Grusec, J. E., Goodnow, J. J., & Cohen, L. (1996). Household work and the development of concern for others. *Developmental Psychology, 32,* 999–1007.

Grusec, J. E., Kuczynski, L., Rushton, J. P., & Simutis, Z. M. (1979). Learning resistance to temptation through observation. *Developmental Psychology, 15,* 233–240.

Grusec, J. E. & Lytton, H. (1988). *Social development: History, theory, and research.* New York: Springer-Verlag.

Guerin, D. W. & Gottfried, A. W. (1994). Developmental stability and change in parent reports of temperament: A ten-year longitudinal investigation from infancy through preadolescence. *Merrill-Palmer Quarterly, 40,* 334–355.

Guilford, J. P. (1985). The structure-of-intellect model. In B. B. Wolman (Ed.), *Handbook of intelligence.* New York: Wiley.

Guilford, J. P. (1988). Some changes in the structure-of-the-intellect model. *Educational and Psychological Measurement, 48,* 1–4.

Gulya, M., Rovee-Collier, C., Galluccio, L., & Wilk, A. (1998). Memory processing of a serial list by very young infants. *Psychological Science, 9,* 303–307.

Gunn, A., Cory, E., Atkinson, J., Braddick, O., Wattam-Bell, J., Guzzetta, A., & Cioni, G. (2002). Dorsal and ventral stream sensitivity in normal development and hemiplegia. *Neuroreport, 13,* 843–847.

Gunnar, M. R., Brodersen, L., Krueger, K., & Rigatuso, J. (1996). Dampening of adrenocortical responses during infancy: Normative changes and individual differences. *Child Development, 67,* 877–889.

Gunnar, M. R., Fisch, R. O., & Malone, S. (1984). The effects of a pacifying stimulus on behavioral and adrenocortical responses to circumcision in the newborn. *Journal of the American Academy of Child Psychiatry, 23,* 34–38.

Gunnar, M. R., Larson, M. C., Hertsgaard, L., & Harris, M. L. (1992). The stressfulness of separation among nine-month-old infants: Effects of social context variables and infant temperament. *Child Development, 63,* 290–303.

Gunnar, M. R., Malone, S., Vance, G., & Fisch, R. O. (1985). Coping with aversive stimulation in the neonatal period: Quiet sleep and plasma cortisol levels during recovery from circumcision. *Child Development, 56,* 824–834.

Gunnar, M. R., Mangelsdorf, S., Larson, M., & Hertsgaard, L. (1989). Attachment, temperament, and adrenocortical activity in infancy: A study of psychoendocrine regulation. *Developmental Psychology, 25,* 355–363.

Gunnar, M. R. & Quevedo, K. (2007). The neurobiology of stress and development. *Annual Review of Psychology, 58,* 145–173.

Gunnar, M. R., Tout, K., de Haan, M., & Pierce, S. (1997). Temperament, social competence, and adrenocortical activity in preschoolers. *Developmental Psychobiology, 31,* 65–85.

Gurucharri, C. & Selman, R. L. (1982). The development of interpersonal understanding during childhood, preadolescence, and adolescence: A longitudinal follow-up study. *Child Development, 53,* 924–927.

Gustafson, G. E., Wood, R. M., & Green, J. A. (2000). Can we hear the causes of infants' crying?

In R. G. Barr, B. Hopkins, & J. A. Green (Eds.), *Crying as a sign, a symptom, and a signal: Clinical, emotional, and developmental aspects of infant and toddler crying.* New York: Cambridge University Press.

Gutman, L. M. & Eccles, J. S. (2007). Stage-environment fit during adolescence: Trajectories of family relations and adolescent outcomes. *Developmental Psychology, 43,* 522–537.

Guttentag, R. E., Ornstein, P. A., & Siemens, L. (1987). Children's spontaneous rehearsal: Transitions in strategy acquisition. *Cognitive Development, 2,* 307–326.

H

Hack, M., Klein, N. K., & Taylor, H. G. (1995). Long-term developmental outcomes of low birth weight infants. *The future of children* (Vol. 5, No. 1). Los Angeles: Packard Foundation.

Hadad, B., Maurer, D., & Lewis, T. (2010). The effects of spatial proximity and collinearity on contour integration in adults and children. *Vision Research, 50*(8), 772–778.

Haeckel, E. (1977). Last words on evolution. In D. N. Robinson (Ed.), *Significant contributions to the history of psychology: 1750–1920.* Washington, DC: University Publications of America. (Original work published 1906).

Hagen, J. W. & Hale, G. A. (1973). The development of attention in children. In A. D. Pick (Ed.), *Minnesota symposia on child psychology* (Vol. 7). Minneapolis, MN: University of Minnesota Press.

Hagerman, R. J. (1996). Biomedical advances in developmental psychology: The case of Fragile X syndrome. *Developmental Psychology, 32,* 416–424.

Hahn, C. S. & DiPietro, J. A. (2001). In-vitro fertilization and the family: Quality of parenting, family functioning, and child psychosocial adjustment. *Developmental Psychology, 37,* 37–48.

Haight, W. L., Parke, R. D., & Black, J. E. (1997). Mothers' and fathers' beliefs about and spontaneous participation in their toddlers' pretend play. *Merrill-Palmer Quarterly, 43*(2), 271–290.

Hainline, L. (1998). The development of basic visual abilities. In A. Slater (Ed.), *Perceptual development: Visual, auditory, and speech perception in infancy.* Hove, UK: Psychology Press.

Hainline, L. & Abramov, I. (1992). Assessing visual development: Is infant vision good enough? In C. Rovee-Collier & L. P. Lipsitt (Eds.), *Advances in infancy research* (Vol. 7). Norwood, NJ: Ablex.

Haith, M. M. (1966). The response of the human newborn to visual movement. *Journal of Experimental Child Psychology, 3,* 235–243.

Haith, M. M. (1980). *Rules that babies look by.* Hillsdale, NJ: Erlbaum.

Haith, M. M. (1986). Sensory and perceptual processes in early infancy. *Journal of Pediatrics, 109,* 158–171.

Haith, M. M. (1990). Progress in the understanding of sensory and perceptual processes in early infancy. *Merrill-Palmer Quarterly,* 36, 1–26.

Haith, M. M. (1991). Gratuity, perception-action integration and future orientation in infant vision. In F. Kessel, A. Sameroff, & M. Bornstein (Eds.), *The past as prologue in developmental psychology: Essays in honor of William Kessen.* Hillsdale, NJ: Erlbaum.

Haith, M. M. (1994). Visual expectations as the first step toward the development of future-oriented processes. In M. M. Haith, J. B. Benson, R. J. Roberts Jr., & B. F. Pennington (Eds.), *The development of future-oriented processes.* Chicago: University of Chicago Press.

Haith, M. M. (1998). Who put the cog in infant cognition? *Infant Behavior and Development, 21,* 161–179.

Haith, M. M. & Benson, J. B. (1998). Infant cognition. In W. Damon (Series Ed.) & D. Kuhn & R. S. Siegler (Vol. Eds.), *Handbook of child psychology: Vol. 2. Cognition, perception, and language* (5th ed.). New York: Wiley.

Haith, M. M., Benson, J. B., Roberts, R. J. Jr., & Pennington, B. F. (Eds.). (1994). *The development of future-oriented processes.* Chicago: University of Chicago Press.

Haith, M. M., Wentworth, N., & Canfield, R. L. (1993). The formation of expectations in early infancy. In C. Rovee-Collier & L. P. Lipsitt (Eds.), *Advances in infancy research* (Vol. 8). Norwood, NJ: Ablex.

Hakuta, K. (1999). The debate on bilingual education. *Journal of Developmental and Behavioral Pediatrics, 20,* 36–37.

Halbfinger, D. M. (2003, Feb. 9). For students on a week at a fantasy space camp, the mission continues. *New York Times,* p. 23.

Hales, J. B. & Brewer, J. B. (2011). The timing of associative memory formation: Frontal lobe and anterior medial temporal lobe activity at associative binding predicts memory. *Journal of Neurophysiology, 105,* 1454–1463.

Halford, G. S. & Boyle, F. M. (1985). Do young children understand conservation of number? *Child Development, 56,* 165–176.

Halim, M. L. & Ruble, D. (2010). Gender identity and stereotyping in early and middle childhood. *Handbook of gender research in psychology: Vol. 1: Gender research in general and experimental psychology* (pp. 495–525). New York, NY: Springer.

Halit, H., de Haan, M., & Johnson, M. H. (2003). Cortical specialisation for face processing: face-sensitive event-related potential components in 3- and 12-month-old infants. *NeuroImage, 19,* 1180–1193.

Hall, D., Lee, S., & Bélanger, J. (2001). Young children's use of syntactic cues to learn proper names and count nouns. *Developmental Psychology, 37,* 298–307.

Hallett, D., Chandler, M. J., & Lalonde, C. E. (2007). Aboriginal language knowledge and youth suicide. *Cognitive Development, 22,* 392–399.

Hallinan, M. T. & Kubitschek, W. N. (1999). Curriculum differentiation and high school achievement. *Social Psychology of Education, 3,* 41–62.

Halpern, C. T., Udry, J. R., Campbell, B., & Suchindraw, C. (1994). Relationships between aggression and pubertal increases in testosterone: A panel analysis of adolescent males. *Social Biology 40,* 8–24.

Halpern, D. F. (2012). *Sex differences in cognitive abilities* (4th ed.). New York, NY: Psychology Press.

Halpern, D. F., Benbow, C. P., Geary, D. C., Gur, R. C., Hyde, J. S., & Gernsbacher, M. A. (2007). The science of sex differences in science and mathematics. *Psychological Science in the Public Interest, 8,* 1–51.

Halpern, D. F., Straight, C. A., & Stephenson, C. L. (2011). Beliefs about cognitive gender differences: Accurate for direction, underestimated for size. *Sex Roles, 64,* 336–347.

Halpern, L. F., MacLean, W. E. Jr., & Baumeister, A. A. (1995). Infant sleep-wake characteristics: Relation to neurological status and the prediction of developmental outcome. *Developmental Review, 15,* 255–291.

Halverson, C. F. & Deal, J. E. (2001). Temperamental change, parenting, and the family context. In T. D. Wachs & G. A. Kohnstamm (Eds.), *Temperament in context.* Mahwah, NJ: Erlbaum.

Hammen, C. & Zupan, B. A. (1984). Self-schemas, depression, and the processing of personal information in children. *Journal of Experimental Child Psychology, 37,* 598–608.

Hammerness, P. G. (2009). *ADHD.* Westport, CT: Greenwood Press.

Hammersly, M. (2006). Ethnography: problems and prospects. *Ethnography and Education, 1,* 3–14.

Hampson, I. & Nelson, K. (1993). The relation of maternal language to variation in rate and style of language acquisition. *Journal of Child Language, 20,* 313–342.

Hampton, E. (2008) Endocrine contributions to sex differences in visuospacial perception and cognition. In J. B. Becker, K. J. Berkley, N. Geary, E. Hampson, J. Herman, & E. Young (Eds.), *Sex differences in the brain: From genes to behavior* (pp. 311–326). New York, NY: Oxford University Press.

Hamre, B. & Pianta, R. C. (2000). Early teacher-child relationships and children's social and academic outcomes through eighth grade. *Child Development, 72,* 625–638.

Hangya, B., Tihanyi, B. T., Entz, L., Fabó, D., Eróss, L., Wittner, L., Jakus, R., Varga, V., Freund, T. F., & Ulbert, I. (2011). Complex propagation patterns characterize human cortical activity during slow-wave sleep. *The Journal of Neuroscience, 31,* 8770–8779.

Hans, S. L. (1992). Maternal opioid use and child development. In I. S. Zagon & T. A. Slotkin (Eds.), *Maternal substance abuse and the developing nervous system.* San Diego, CA: Academic Press.

Hansen, M. B. & Markman, E. M. (2005). Appearance questions can be misleading: A discourse-based account of the appearance-reality problem. *Cognitive Psychology, 50,* 233–263.

Harasty, J. M., Double, K. L., Halliday, G. M., Kril, J. J., & McRitchie, D. A. (1997). Language-associated cortical regions are proportionally larger in the female brain. *Archives of Neurology, 54,* 171–176.

Harel, J., Eshel, Y., Ganor, O., & Scher, A. (2002). Antecedents of mirror self-recognition of toddlers: Emotional availability, birth order and gender. *Infant Mental Health Journal, 23,* 293–309.

Harkness, S., Raeff, C., & Super, C. M. (Eds.). (2000). *New directions for child and adolescent development: No. 87. Variability in the social construction of the child.* San Francisco: Jossey-Bass.

Harkness, S. & Super, C. M. (2002). Culture and parenting. In M. H. Bornstein (Ed.), *Handbook of parenting: Vol. 2: Biology and ecology of parenting* (2nd ed., pp. 253–380). Mahwah, NJ: Erlbaum.

Harlow, H. F. & Harlow, M. K. (1966). Learning to love. *American Scientist, 54,* 244–272.

Harper, L. V. & Kraft, R. H. (1986). Lateralization of receptive language in preschoolers: Test-retest reliability in a dichotic listening task. *Developmental Psychology, 22,* 553–556.

Harris, J. R. (1995). Where is the child's environment? A group socialization theory of development. *Psychological Review, 102,* 458–489.

Harris, J. R. (1998). *The nurture assumption.* New York: Free Press.

Harris, L. (1997). *The Metropolitan Life survey of the American teacher 1997: Examining gender issues in public schools.* New York: Louis Harris and Associates.

Harris, M., Jones, D., & Grant, J. (1983). The nonverbal context of mothers' speech to infants. *First Language, 4,* 21–30.

Harris, N. G. S., Bellugi, U., Bates, E., Jones, W., & Rossen, M. (1997). Contrasting profiles of language development in children with Williams and Down syndromes. *Developmental Neuropsychology, 13,* 345–370.

Harris, P. (2006). Social cognition. In W. Damon & R. M. Lerner (Series Eds.) & D. Kuhn & R. S. Siegler (Vol. Eds.), *Handbook of child psychology: Vol. 2. Cognition, perception, and language* (6th ed.) (pp. 811–858). Hoboken, NJ: Wiley.

Harris, P. L. (1989). Object permanence in infancy. In A. Slater & G. Bremner (Eds.), *Infant development.* Hillsdale, NJ: Erlbaum.

Harris, P. L. (2000). On not falling down to earth: Children's metaphysical questions. In K. S. Rosengren, C. N. Johnson, & P. L Harris (Eds.), *Imagining the impossible.* New York: Cambridge University Press.

Harris, P. L. (2008). Children's understanding of emotion. In M. Lewis, J. M. Haviland-Jones, & L. M. Barrett (Eds.), *Handbook of emotions*, 3rd edition (pp. 320–331). New York: Guilford.

Hart, C. H., Yang, C., Nelson, L., Robinson, C., Olsen, J., Nelson, D., Porter, C., Jin, S., Olsen, S., & Wu, P. (2000). Peer acceptance in early childhood and subtypes of socially withdrawn behaviour in China, Russia, and the United States. *International Journal of Behavioral Development, 24,* 73–81.

Hart, D. (1988b). A longitudinal study of adolescents' socialization and identification as predictors of adult moral judgment development. *Merrill-Palmer Quarterly, 34,* 245–260.

Hart, D., Atkins, R., & Donnelly, T. M. (2006). Community service and moral development. In M. Killen & J. Smetana (Eds.), *Handbook of moral development* (pp. 633–656). Mahwah, NJ: Erlbaum.

Hart, D., Matsuba, M. K., & Atkins, R. (2008). The moral and civic effects of learning to serve. In L. P. Nucci & D. Narvaez (Eds.), *Handbook of moral and character education* (pp. 484–499). New York, NY: Routledge.

Harter, S. (1985a). Competence as a dimension of self-evaluation: Toward a comprehensive model of self-worth. In R. L. Leahy (Ed.), *The development of the self.* Orlando, FL: Academic Press.

Harter, S. (1985b). *The Self-Perception Profile for Children.* Denver, CO: University of Denver.

Harter, S. (1986). Processes underlying the construction, maintenance, and enhancement of the self-concept in children. In J. Suls & A. Greenwald (Eds.), *Psychological perspectives on the self (Vol.* 3). Hillsdale, NJ: Erlbaum.

Harter, S. (1988). *The Self-Perception Profile for Adolescents.* Unpublished manual, University of Denver, Denver, CO.

Harter, S. (1999). *The construction of the self: A developmental perspective.* New York: Guilford.

Harter, S. (2003). The development of self-representations during childhood and adolescence. In M. Leary & J. Tangney (Eds.), *Handbook of self and identity* (pp. 610–642). New York: Guilford.

Harter, S. (2006a). The development of self-esteem. In M. Kernis (Ed.), *Self-esteem: issues and answers: A sourcebook of current perspectives* (pp. 144–150). New York: Psychology Press.

Harter, S. (2006b). The self. In N. Eisenberg, W. Damon, & R. Lerner *(Eds.), Handbook of child psychology: Vol 3, Social, emotional, and personality development* (3rd ed., pp. 505–570). Hoboken, NJ: Wiley.

Harter, S. (2008). The developing self. In W. Damon & R. M. Lerner (Eds.), *Child and adolescent development: An advanced course* (pp. 216–260). Hoboken, NJ: Wiley.

Harter, S. & Pike, R. (1984). The Pictorial Scale of Perceived Competence and Social Acceptance for Young Children. *Child Development, 55,* 1969–1982.

Harter, S. & Whitesell, N. R. (2003). Beyond the debate: Why some adolescents report stable self-worth over time and situation, whereas others report changes in self-worth. *Journal of Personality, 71,* 1027–1058.

Hartig, M. & Kanfer, F. H. (1973). The role of verbal self-instructions in children's resistance to temptation. *Journal of Personality and Social Psychology, 25,* 259–267.

Hartshorn, K. (2003). Reinstatement maintains a memory in human infants for 1½ years. *Developmental Psychobiology, 42,* 269–282.

Hartung, C. M. & Widiger, T A. (1998). Gender differences in the diagnosis of mental disorders: Conclusions and controversies of the DSM-IV *Psychological Bulletin, 123,* 260–278.

Hartup, W. W. (1983). Peer relations. In P. H. Mussen (Series Ed.) & E. M. Hetherington (Vol. Ed.), *Handbook of child psychology: Vol 4. Socialization, personality, and social development* (4th ed.). New York: Wiley.

Hartup, W. W. (1992). Conflict and friendship relations. In C. U. Shantz & W. W Hartup (Eds.), *Conflict in child and adolescent development.* Cambridge: Cambridge University Press.

Hartup, W. W. (1993). Adolescents and their friends. In B. Laursen (Ed.), *New directions for child development: No. 60. Close friendships in adolescence.* San Francisco: Jossey-Bass.

Hartup, W. W. & Abecassis, M. (2002). Friends and enemies. In P. K. Smith & C. H. Hart (Eds.), *Blackwell handbook of childhood social development.* Madden, MA: Blackwell Publishers.

Hartup, W. W., French, D. C., Laursen, B., Johnson, M. K., & Ogawa, J. R. (1993). Conflict and friendship relations in middle childhood: Behavior in a closed-field situation. *Child Development, 64,* 445–454.

Hasselhorn, M. (1992). Task dependency and the role of category typicality and metamemory in the development of an organizational strategy. *Child Development, 63, 202–214.*

Hassett, J. M., Siebert, E. R., & Wallen, K. (2008). Sex differences in rhesus monkey toy preferences parallel those of children. *Hormones and Behavior, 54,* 359–364.

Hastings, P. D., Utendale, W. T., & Sullivan, C. (2007). The socialization of prosocial development. In J. E. Grusec & P. D. Hastings (Eds.), *Handbook of socialization: Theory and research* (pp. 638–664). New York: Guilford.

Hastings, P. D., Zahn-Waxler, C., & McShane, K. (2006). We are, by nature, moral creatures: Biological bases of concern for others. In M. Killen & J. Smetana (Eds.), *Handbook of moral development* (pp. 483–516). Mahwah, NJ: Erlbaum.

Hatano, G. & Inagaki, K. (1991). Sharing cognition through collective comprehension activity. In L. B. Resnick, J. M. Levine, & S. D. Teasley (Eds.), *Perspectives on socially shared cognition.* Washington, DC: American Psychological Association.

Hatano, G. & Inagaki, K. (1998). Cultural contexts of schooling revisited: A review of *The Learning Gap* from a cultural psychology perspective. In S. G. Paris & H. M. Wellman (Eds.), *Global prospects for education: Development, culture, and schooling.* Washington, DC: American Psychological Association.

Haviland, J. M. & Lelwica, M. (1987). The induced affect response: 10-week-old infants' response to three emotion expressions. *Developmental Psychology, 23,* 97–104.

Hawk, C. K. & Holden, G. W. (2006). Meta-parenting: An initial investigation into a new parental social cognition construct. *Parenting, 6,* 321–342.

Hawkins, D. L., Pepler, D. J., & Craig, W. M. (2001). Naturalistic observations of peer interventions in bullying. *Social Development, 10,* 512–527.

Hay, D. F. (1985). Learning to form relationships in infancy: Parallel attainments with parents and peers. *Developmental Review, 5,* 122–161.

Hay, D. F. (1986). Learning to be social: Some comments on Schaffer's "The child's entry into a social world." *Developmental Review, 6,* 107–114.

Hay, D. F., Caplan, M., & Nash, A. (2009). The beginnings of peer relations. In K. H. Rubin, W. M. Bukowski, & B. Laursen (Eds.), *Handbook of peer interactions, relationships, and groups* (pp. 121–142). New York: Guilford.

Hay, D. F., Castle, J., Stimsom, C., & Davies, L. (1995). The social construction of character in toddlerhood. In M. Killen & D. Hart (Eds.), *Morality in everyday life: Developmental perspectives* (pp. 23–51). Cambridge: Cambridge University Press.

Hay, D. F. & Murray, P. (1982). Giving and requesting: Social facilitation of infants' offers to adults. *Infant Behavior and Development, 5,* 301–310.

Hayne, H. (1996). Categorization in infancy. In C. Rovee Collier & L. P. Lipsitt (Eds.), *Advances in infancy research* (Vol. 10). Norwood, NJ: Ablex.

Hayne, H. (2004). Infant memory development: Implications for childhood amnesia. *Developmental Review, 24,* 33–73.

Hayne, H., Rovee-Collier, C., & Perris, E. E. (1987). Categorization and memory retrieval by three-month-olds. *Child Development, 58*(3), 750–767.

Haynes, H., White, B. L., & Held, R. (1965). Visual accommodation in human infants. *Science, 148,* 528–530.

He, C. & Trainor, L. J. (2009). Finding the pitch of the missing fundamental in infants. *Journal of Neuroscience, 29,* 7718–7722.

Health Canada (2002). *Congenital abnormalities in Canada—A perinatal health report.* Ottawa: Minister of Public Works and Government Services Canada. Cat. No. H39–641/2002E.

Health Canada (2003). *Canadian perinatal health report.* Ottawa: Minister of Public Works and Government Services Canada. Cat. No. H49–142/2003E.

Health Canada (2005). *Gene therapy.* Downloaded on September 27, 2010 from http://www.hc-sc.gc.ca/sr-sr/biotech/about-apropos/gen_therap-eng.php

Health Canada (2007). *Canadian tobacco use monitoring survey. Table 7. Smoking and pregnancy, women age 20-44 years.* Available at http://www.hc-sc.gc.ca/hc-ps/tobac-tabac/research-recherche/stat/_ctums-esutc_2007/ann-table7-eng.php

Health Canada, (2011). *Canadian tobacco use monitoring survey (CTUMS): CTUMS 2010 Wave 1 survey results.* Accessed September 8, 2011 from http://www.hc-sc.gc.ca/hc-ps/tobac-tabac/research-recherche/stat/_ctums-esutc_2010/w-p-1_sum-som-eng.php

Heath, S. B. (1983). *Ways with words: Language, life and work in communities and classrooms.* Cambridge, England: Cambridge University Press.

Heath, S. B. (1989). Oral and literate traditions among black Americans living in poverty. *American Psychologist, 44,* 367–373.

Hebb, D. O. (1949). *The organization of behavior.* New York: Wiley.

Heine, A., Thaler, V., Tamm, S., Hawelka, S., Schneider, M., Torbeyns, J., De Smedt, B., Verschaffel, L., Stern, E., & Jacobs, A. M. (2010). What the eyes already 'know': using eye movement measurement to tap into children's implicit numerical magnitude representations. *Infant and Child Development*, *19,* 175–186.

Helwig, C. C., Hildebrandt, C., & Turiel, E. (1995). Children's judgments about psychological harm in social context. *Child Development, 66,* 1680–1693.

Helwig, C. C., Zelazo, P. D., & Wilson, M. (2001). Children's judgments of psychological harm in normal and noncanonical situations. *Child Development, 72,* 66–81.

Helwig, R., Anderson, L., & Tindal, G. (2001). Influence of elementary student gender on teachers' perceptions of mathematics achievement. *Journal of Educational Research, 95,* 93–102.

Hemker, L., Granrud, C. E., Yonas, A., & Kavšek, M. (2010). Infant perception of surface texture and relative height as distance information: A Preferential-reaching study. *Infancy, 15*(1), 6–27.

Herbenick, D., Reece, M., Schick, V., Sanders, S. S., Dodge, B., & Fortenberry, J. D. (2010). Sexual behavior in the United States: Results from a national probability sample of men and women ages 14-94. *Journal of Sexual Medicine, 7,* 255–265.

Herdt, G. & Boxer, A. M. (1993). *Children of Horizons: How gay and lesbian teens are leading a new way out of the closet.* Boston: Beacon.

Herdt, G. & McClintock, M. (2000). The magical age of 10. *Archives of Sexual Behavior, 29,* 587–606.

Herek, G. M. (2006). Legal recognition of same-sex relationships in the United States: A social science perspective. *American Psychologist. 61,* 607–621.

Herman, J. P. & Young, E. (Eds.) (2008). *Sex differences in the brain: From genes to behavior* (pp. 291–309). New York, NY: Oxford University Press.

Herman, L. M. (2002). Exploring the cognitive world of the bottlenosed dolphin. In M. Bekoff, C. Allen, & G. M. Burghardt (Eds.), *The cognitive animal: Empirical and theoretical perspectives on animal cognition.* Cambridge, MA: MIT Press.

Herrera, C. & Dunn, J. (1997). Early experiences with family conflict: Implications for arguments with a close friend. *Developmental Psychology, 33,* 869–881.

Herrnstein, R. J. (1971, September). I. Q. *Atlantic Monthly,* pp. 43–64.

Herrnstein, R. J. & Murray, C. (1994). *The bell curve: Intelligence and class structure in American life.* New York: Free Press.

Hershberger, S. L. (2001). Biological factors in the development of sexual orientation. In A. R. D'Augelli & C. J. Patterson (Eds.), *Lesbian, gay, and bisexual identities and youth: Psychological perspectives.* New York: Oxford University Press.

Herzog, D. B., Greenwood, D. N., Dorer, D. J., Flores, A. T., Ekeblad, E. R., Richards, A., et al. (2000). Mortality in eating disorders: A descriptive study. *International Journal of Eating Disorders, 28,* 20–26.

Heschel, A. & Burkart, J. (2006). A new mark test for mirror self-recognition in non-human primates. *Primates, 47,* 187–198.

Hesse, E. (2008). The adult attachment interview: Protocol, method of analysis, and empirical studies. In J. Cassidy & P. R. Shaver (Eds.) *Handbook of attachment: Theory, research, and clinical applications (2nd edition)* (pp. 552–598). New York, NY: Guilford.

Hesse, E. & Main, M. (2000). Disorganized infant, child, and adult attachment: Collapse in behavioral and attentional strategies. *Journal of the American Psychoanalytic Association, 48,* 1097–1127.

Hetherington, E. M. (2006). The influence of conflict, marital problem solving, and parenting on children's adjustment in nondivorced, divorced, and remarried families. In A. Clarke-Stewart & J. Dunn (Eds.), *Families Count: Effects on Child and Adolescent Development* (pp. 203–237). New York: Cambridge University Press.

Hetherington, E. M. & Clingempeel, W. G. (1992). Coping with marital transitions: A family systems perspective. *Monographs of the Society for Research in Child Development, 57* (Serial No. 227).

Hetherington, E. M. & Kelly, J. (2002). *For better or worse: Divorce reconsidered.* New York: Norton.

Hetherington, E. M. & Parke, R. D. (1979). *Child psychology: A contemporary viewpoint.* New York: McGraw-Hill.

Hetherington, E. M. & Stanley-Hagan, M. (1999). The adjustment of children with divorced parents: A risk and resiliency perspective. *Journal of Child Psychology and Psychiatry, 40,* 129–140.

Hetherington, E. M. & Stanley-Hagan, M. S. (2002). Parenting in divorced and remarried families. In M. Bornstein (Ed.), *Handbook of parenting* (2nd ed., Vol. 3). Mahwah, NJ: Erlbaum.

Hewlett, B. S., Fouts, H. N., Boyette, A. H., & Hewlett, B. L. (2011). Social learning among Congo Basin hunter-gatherers. *Philosophical Transactions of the Royal Society B, 366,* 1168–1178.

Hewlett, B. S., Lamb, M. E., Leyendecker, B., & Scholmerich, A. (2000). Internal working models, trust, and sharing among foragers. *Current Anthropology, 41,* 287–297.

Heyes, C. & Huber, L. (Eds.). (2000). *The evolution of cognition.* Cambridge, MA: MIT Press.

Heyman, G. (2001). Children's interpretation of ambiguous behavior: Evidence for a 'boys are bad' bias. *Social Development, 10,* 230–247.

Heyman, G. D., Dweck, C. S., & Cain, K. M. (1992). Young children's vulnerability to self-blame and helplessness: Relationship to beliefs about goodness. *Child Development, 63,* 401–415.

Hicks, D. (1996). *Discourse, learning, and schooling.* New York: Cambridge University Press.

Hilborn, R. (2010). Canadians adopted 2,122 children from abroad in 2009. *Family Helper,* October 22, 2010. Downloaded on January 27, 2011 from www.familyhelper.net/news/101025stats.html.

Hildreth, K. & Rovee-Collier, C. (2002). Forgetting functions of reactivated memories over the first year of life. *Developmental Psychobiology, 41,* 277–288.

Hilgard, E. R. (1987). *Psychology in America: A historical survey.* San Diego, CA: Harcourt Brace Jovanovich.

Hinds, P. & Kiesler, S. (2002). *Distributed work.* Cambridge, MA: MIT Press.

Hinduja, S. & Patchin, J. W. (2010). Bullying, Cyberbullying, and Suicide. *Archives of Suicide Research, 14,* 206–221.

Hines, M. (2009). Gonadal hormones and sexual differentiation of human brain and behavior. In R. T. Rubin & D. W. Pfaff (Eds.), *Hormone/behavior relations of clinical importance: Endocrine systems interacting with brain and behavior* (pp. 207–247). New York: NY: Academic/Elsevier.

Hines, M. (2010). Gendered behavior across the lifespan. In M. Lamb & A. Freund (Eds.), *Handbook of life-span development (Vol. 2: Social and emotional development,* pp. 341–378). Hoboken, NJ: John Wiley & Sons.

Hines, M. & Kaufman, F. R. (1994). Androgen and the development of human sex-typical behavior: Rough-and-tumble and sex of preferred playmates in children with congenital adrenal hyperplasia (CAH). *Child Development, 65,* 1042–1053.

Hinshaw, S. (2000). Attention-deficit/hyperactivity disorder: The search for viable treatments. In P. Kendall (Ed.), *Child and Adolescent Therapy* (pp. 88–128). New York: Guilford.

Hirsch, B. J. & Renders, R. J. (1986). The challenge of adolescent friendships: A study of Lisa and her friends. In S. E. Hobfolk (Ed.), *Stress, social support, and women.* Washington, DC: Hemisphere.

Hirsh-Pasek, K. & Golinkoff, R. M. (1996). *The origins of grammar: Evidence from early language comprehension.* Cambridge, MA: MIT Press.

Hirsh-Pasek, K., Treiman, R., & Schneiderman, M. (1984). Brown and Hanlon revisited: Mothers' sensitivity to ungrammatical forms. *Journal of Child Language, 11,* 81–88.

Hittelman, J. H. & Dickes, R. (1979). Sex differences in neonatal eye contact time. *Merrill-Palmer Quarterly, 25,* 171–184.

Hmelo-Silver, C. E. & Pfeffer, M. G. (2004). Comparing expert and novice understanding of a complex system from the perspective of structures, behaviors and functions. *Cognitive Science, 28,* 127–138.

Ho, D. Y. F. (1995). Selfhood and identity in Confucianism, Taoism, Buddhism, and Hinduism: Contrasts with the West. *Journal for the Theory of Social Behavior, 25,* 115–139.

Hocksbergen, R. C. (1999). The importance of adoption for nurturing and enhancing the emotional and intellectual potential of children. *Adoption Quarterly, 1,* 29–42.

Hoek, D., Ingram, D., & Gibson, D. (1986). Some possible causes of children's early word overextensions. *Journal of Child Language, 13,* 477–494.

Hoff, E. (2006). How social contexts support and shape language development. *Developmental Review, 26,* 55–88.

Hoff, E. & Naigles, L. (2002). How children use speech to acquire a lexicon. *Child Development, 73,* 418–433.

Hoff, T. (1992). Psychology in Canada one hundred years ago: James Mark Baldwin at the University of Toronto. *Canadian Psychology, 33,* 683–694.

Hoff-Ginsberg, E. (1990). Maternal speech and the child's development of syntax: A further look. *Journal of Child Language, 17,* 85–99.

Hoff-Ginsberg, E. & Shatz, M. (1982). Linguistic input and the child's acquisition of language. *Psychological Bulletin, 92,* 3–26.

Hoffman, L. W. & Youngblade, L. M. (1999). *Mothers at work: Effects on children's well being.* New York: Cambridge University Press.

Hoffman, M. L. (1970). Moral development. In P. H. Mussen (Ed.), *Carmichael's manual of child psychology* (3rd ed., Vol. 2). New York: Wiley.

Hoffman, M. L. (1975). Altruistic behavior and the parent-child relationship. *Journal of Personality and Social Psychology, 31,* 937–943.

Hoffman, M. L. (1984). Empathy, its limitations, and its role in a comprehensive moral theory. In J. L. Gewirtz & W. Kurtines (Eds*.), Morality, moral development, and moral behavior.* New York: Wiley.

Hoffman, M. L. (1994). Discipline and internalization. *Developmental Psychology, 30,* 26–28.

Hoffman, M. L. (2000). *Empathy and moral development.* New York: Wiley.

Hoffman, M. L. (2008). Empathy and prosocial behavior. In M. Lewis, J. M. Haviland-Jones, & L. M. Barrett (Eds.), *Handbook of emotions,* 3rd edition (pp. 440–455). New York: Guilford.

Hogan, D. & Tudge, J. R. H. (1999). Implications of Vygotsky's theory for peer learning. In A. M. O'Donnell & A. King (Eds.), *Cognitive perspectives on peer learning.* Mahwah, NJ: Erlbaum.

Hogan, M. J. & Strasburger, V. C. (2008). Media and prosocial behavior in children and adolescents. In

L. Nucci & D. Narvaez (Eds.), *Handbook of moral and character education* (pp. 537–553). New York, NY: Taylor and Francis.

Hogge, W. A. (1990). Teratology. In I. R. Merkatz & J. E. Thompson (Eds.), *New perspectives on prenatal care.* New York: Elsevier.

Hoglund, W. L. & Leadbeater, B. J. (2004). The effects of family, school, and classroom ecologies on changes in children's social competence and emotional and behavioral problems in first grade. *Developmental Psychology, 40,* 533–544.

Holditch-Davis, D. (2005). Sleeping behaviour of preterm infants and its impact on psychosocial child development. In R. E. Tremblay R. G. Barr, & R. D. Peters (Eds.), *Encyclopedia on early childhood development* [online] (pp. 1–10). Montreal, Quebec: Centre of Excellence for Early Childhood Development. Available at: www.excellence-earlychildhood.ca/documents/Holditch-DavisANGxp_rev.pdf.

Holditch-Davis, D., Belyea, M., & Edwards, L. J. (2005). Prediction of 3-year developmental outcomes from sleep development over the preterm period. *Infant Behavior and Development, 28,* 118–131.

Holditch-Davis, D., Scher, M., Schwartz, T., & Hudson-Barr, D. (2004). Sleeping and waking state development in preterm infants. *Early Human Development, 80,* 43–64.

Holekamp, K. E. & Engh, A. L. (2002). Field studies of social cognition in spotted hyenas. In M. Bekoff, C. Allen, & G. M. Burghardt (Eds.), *The cognitive animal: Empirical and theoretical perspectives on animal cognition.* Cambridge, MA: MIT Press.

Hollich, G. J., Hirsh-Pasek, K., & Golinkoff, R. M. (2000). Breaking the language barrier: An emergentist coalition model of word learning. *Monographs of the Society for Research in Child Development, 65* (3, Serial No. 262).

Holmes, J. (1995). "Something there is that doesn't love a wall": John Bowlby, attachment theory, and psychoanalysis. In S. Goldberg, R. Muir, & J. Kerr (Eds.), *Attachment theory: Social, developmental, and clinical perspectives.* Hillsdale, NJ: Analytic Press.

Holmes-Lonergan, H. A. (2003). Preschool children's collaborative problem solving interactions: The role of gender, pair type, and task. *Sex Roles, 48,* 505–517.

Hood, B. M. (1993). Inhibition of return produced by covert shifts of visual attention in 6-month-old infants. *Infant Behavior and Development, 16,* 245–254.

Hood, B. M. & Atkinson, J. (1993). Disengaging visual attention in the infant and adult. *Infant Behavior and Development, 16,* 405–422.

Hooker, K., Nesselroade, D. W., Nesselroade, J. R., & Lerner, R. M. (1987). The structure of intraindividual temperament in the context of mother-child dyads: P-technique factor analyses of short-term change. *Developmental Psychology, 23,* 332–346.

Hopkins, B. (1991). Facilitating early motor development: An intracultural study of West Indian mothers and their infants living in Britain. In J. K. Nugent, B. M. Lester, & T. B. Brazelton (Eds.), *The cultural context of infancy: Vol 2. Multicultural and interdisciplinary approaches to parent-infant relations.* Norwood, NJ: Ablex.

Hopkins, K. B., McGillicuddy-De Lisi, A. V., & De Lisi, R. (1997). Student gender and teaching methods as sources of variability in children's computational arithmetic performance. *Journal of Genetic Psychology, 158,* 333–345.

Horn, S. (2003). Adolescents' reasoning about exclusion from social groups. *Developmental Psychology, 39,* 11–84.

Horn, S. (2006). Group status, group bias, and adolescents' reasoning about the treatment of others in school contexts. *International Journal of Behavioral Development, 30,* 208–218.

Horn, S. S., Daddis, C., & Killen, M. (2008). Peer relationships and social groups: Implications for moral education. In L. Nucci & D. Narvaez (Eds.), *Handbook of moral and character education* (pp. 267–287). New York, NY: Taylor and Francis.

Horne, R. S. C., Franco, P., Adamson, T. M., Groswasser, J., & Kahn, A. (2004). Influences of maternal cigarette smoking on infant arousability. *Early Human Development, 79,* 49–58.

Horowitz, F. D. (1992). John B. Watson's legacy: Learning and environment. *Developmental Psychology, 28,* 360–367.

Howe, M. L. (2000). *The fate of early memories.* Washington, DC: American Psychological Association.

Howe, N. & Recchia, H. (2008). Siblings and sibling rivalry. In M. Haith & J. Benson (Eds.), *Encyclopaedia of infant and early childhood development* (pp. 154–164). Oxford: Elsevier.

Howe, N., Ross, H. S., & Recchia, H. (2011). Sibling relations in early and middle childhood. In P. K. Smith & K. H. Hart (Eds.), *The Wiley-Blackwell handbook of childhood social development, 2nd edition* (pp. 356–372). Hoboken, NJ. Wiley.

Howes, C. (1987). Social competence with peers in young children: Developmental sequences. *Developmental Review, 7,* 252–272.

Howes, C. (2009). Friendship in early childhood. In K. H. Rubin, W. M. Bukowski, & B. Laursen (Eds.), *Handbook of peer interactions, relationships, and groups* (pp. 180–194). New York: Guilford.

Howes, C. (2011). Children's social development within the socialization context of child care and early childhood education. In P. Smith & K. Hart (Eds.), *The Wiley-Blackwell handbook of childhood social development, 2nd edition* (pp. 246–262). Hoboken, NJ. Wiley.

Howes, C., Galinsky, E., & Kontos, S. (1998). Child care caregiver sensitivity and attachment. *Social Development, 7,* 25–36.

Howes, C. & Hamilton, C. E. (1992). Children's relationships with caregivers: Mothers and child care teachers. *Child Development, 63,* 859–866.

Howes, C., Hamilton, C. E., & Philipsen, L. C. (1998). Stability and continuity of caregiver and child-peer relationships. *Child Development, 69, 418–426.*

Howes, C. & James, J. (2002). Children's social development within the socialization context of childcare and early childhood education. In P. K. Smith & C. H. Hart (Eds.), *Blackwell handbook of childhood social development.* Madden, MA: Blackwell Publishers.

Howes, C. & Lee, L. (2006). Peer relations in young children. In L. Balter & C. S. Tamis-LeMonda (Eds.), *Child psychology: A handbook of contemporary issues* (2nd ed., pp. 135–151). New York: Psychology Press.

Howes, C. & Ritchie, S. (1999). Attachment organizations in children with difficult life circumstances. *Development and Psychopathology, 11,* 251–268.

Howes, C. & Ritchie, S. (2002). *A matter of trust: Connecting teachers and learners in the early childhood classroom.* New York: Teachers College Press.

Howes, C. & Spieker, S. (2008). Attachment relationships in the context of multiple caregivers. In J. Cassidy & P. R. Shaver (Eds.), *Handbook of attachment: Theory, research, and clinical applications (2nd edition)* (pp. 317–332). New York, NY: Guilford.

Howes, C., Unger, O. A., & Matheson, C. C. (1992). *The collaborative construction of pretend: Social pretend play functions.* Albany, NY: State University of New York Press.

Howes, C., Unger, O., & Seidner, L. B. (1989). Social pretend play in toddlers. Parallels with social play and with solitary pretend. *Child Development, 60,* 77–84.

Hoy, E. A., Bill, J. M., & Sykes, D. H. (1988). Very low birthweight: A long-term developmental impairment? *International Journal of Behavioral Development, 11,* 37–67.

Hubbard, J. A. (2001). Emotion expression processes in children's peer interaction: The role of peer rejection, aggression, and gender. *Child Development, 72,* 1426–1438.

Hudley, C. & Graham, S. (1993). An attributional intervention to reduce peer-directed aggression among African-American boys. *Child Development, 64,* 124–138.

Hudson, J. A. & Mayhew, E. M. (2009). The development of memory for recurring events. In M. Courage and N. Cowan (Eds.), *The development of memory in infancy and childhood* (pp. 69–92). New York, NY: Psychology Press.

Hudson, J. I., Hiripi, E., Pope, H. G., & Kessler, R. C. (2007). The prevalence and correlates of eating disorders in the National Comorbidity Survey replication. *Biological Psychiatry, 61,* 348–358.

Huesmann, L. R. & Kirwil, L. (2007). Why observing violence increases the risk of violent behavior by the observer. In D. J. Flannery, A. T. Vazsonyi, & I. D. Waldman (Eds.), *The Cambridge handbook of violent behavior and aggression* (pp. 545–570). New York, NY: Cambridge University Press.

Huesmann, L. R. & Miller, L. S. (1994). Long-term effects of repeated exposure to media violence in childhood. In L. R. Huesmann (Ed.), *Aggressive behavior: Current perspectives.* New York: Plenum.

Huesmann, L. R., Lagerspetz, K., & Eron, L. D. (1984). Intervening variables in the television violence-aggression relation: Evidence from two countries. *Developmental Psychology, 20,* 746–775.

Huesmann, L. R., Moise-Titus, J., Podolski, C.-L., & Eron, L. D. (2003). Longitudinal relations between children's exposure to TV violence and their aggressive and violent behavior in young adulthood: 1977–1992. *Developmental Psychology, 39,* 201–221.

Hughes, C. (2002). Executive functions and development: Emerging themes. *Infant and Child Development, 11,* 201–209.

Hughes, C. & Dunn, J. (2002). 'When I say a naughty word'. A longitudinal study of young children's accounts of anger and sadness in themselves and close others. *British Journal of Developmental Psychology 20,* 515–535.

Hughes, C., White, A., Sharpen, J., & Dunn, J. (2000). Antisocial, angry, and unsympathetic: "Hard-to-manage" preschoolers' peer problems and possible cognitive influences. *Journal of Child Psychology and Psychiatry and Allied Disciplines, 41,* 169–179.

Hughes, F. P. (2009). *Children, play, and development.* Thousand Oaks, CA: Sage Publications, Inc.

Hughes, M. B., Shults, J., McGrath, J., & Medoff-Cooper, B. (2002). Temperament characteristics of premature infants in the first year of life. *Journal of Development & Behavioral Pediatrics, 23,* 430–435.

Huijbregts, S., Séguin, J., Zelazo, P., Parent, S., Japel, C., & Tremblay, R. (2006). Interrelations between maternal smoking during pregnancy, birth weight and sociodemographic factors in the prediction of early cognitive abilities. *Infant and Child Development, 15,* 593–607.

Hunt, C. E. & Hauck, F. R. (2006). Sudden infant death syndrome. *Canadian Medical Association Journal, 174,* 1861–1869.

Hunter, J. E., & Hunter, R. F. (1984). Validity and utility of alternative predictors of job performance. *Psychological Bulletin, 96,* 72–98.

Huot, M., Bisson, N., Davidovic, L., Mazroui, R., Labelle, Y., Moss, T., & Khandjian, E. (2005). The RNA-binding protein fragile X-related 1 regulates somite formation in Xenopus laevis. *Molecular Biology of the Cell, 16,* 4350–4361.

Hurley, J. C. & Underwood, M. K. (2002). Children's understanding of their research rights before and after debriefing: Informed assent, confidentiality and stopping participation. *Child Development, 73,* 132–143.

Huston, A. C. & Wright, J. C. (1998). Mass media and children's development. In W. Damon (Series Ed.) & I. E. Sigel & K. A. Renninger (Vol. Eds.), *Handbook of child psychology: Vol. 4. Child psychology in practice* (5th ed.). New York: Wiley.

Hutchins, E. (1983). Understanding Micronesian navigation. In D. Gentner & A. Stevens (Eds.), *Mental models.* Hillsdale, NJ: Erlbaum.

Huttenlocher, J., Haight, W., Bryk, A., Seltzer, M., & Lyons, T. (1991). Early vocabulary growth: Relation to language input and gender. *Developmental Psychology, 27,* 236–248.

Huttenlocher, J., Smiley, P., & Charney, R. (1983). Emergence of action categories in the child: Evidence from verb meanings. *Psychological Review, 90,* 72–93.

Huttenlocher, P. R. (1990). Morphometric study of human cerebral cortex development. *Neuropsychologia, 28,* 517–527.

Huttenlocher, P. R. (2002). *Neural plasticity: The effects of environment on the development of the cerebral cortex.* Cambridge, MA: Harvard University Press.

Huttenlocher, P. R. & Dabholkar, A. S. (1997). Regional differences in synaptogenesis in human cerebral cortex. *Journal of Comparative Neurology, 387,* 167–78.

Huttenlocher, P. R., de Courten, C., Garey, L. J., & Van Der Loos, H. (1982). Synaptogenesis in human visual cortex—evidence for synapse elimination during normal development. *Neuroscience Letters, 33,* 247–252.

Hymel, S., Closson, L. M., Caravita, S. C. S., & Vaillancourt, T. (2011). Sociometric status among peers: From sociometric attraction, to peer acceptance, to perceived popularity. In P. K. Smith & K. H. Hart (Eds.), *The Wiley-Blackwell handbook of childhood social development, 2nd edition* (pp. 375–392). Hoboken, NJ. Wiley.

Hymel, S., Vaillancourt, T., McDougall, P., & Renshaw, P. D. (2002). Acceptance and rejection by the peer group. In P. Smith & C. Hart (Eds.), *Blackwell handbook of childhood social development* (pp. 265–284). London: Blackwell Publishers.

Hymel, S., Woody, E., & Bowker, A., (1993). Social withdrawal in childhood: Considering the child's perspective. In K. Rubin & J. Asendorpf (Eds.), *Social withdrawal, inhibition, and shyness in childhood* (pp. 237–262). Hillsdale NJ: Erlbaum.

I

Iannotti, R. (1978). Effect of role-taking experiences on role taking, empathy, altruism, and aggression. *Developmental Psychology, 14,* 119–124.

Ide, J. K., Parkerson, J., Haertel, G. D., & Walberg, H. J. (1981). Peer group influence on educational outcomes: A quantitative synthesis. *Journal of Educational Psychology, 73,* 472–484.

Ike, N. (2000). Current thinking on XYY syndrome. *Psychiatric Annals, 30*(2), 91–95.

Iliescu, B. F. & Dannemiller, J. L. (2008). Brain–behavior relationships in early visual development. In C. A. Nelson & M. Luciana (Eds.), *Developmental cognitive neuroscience* (pp. 127–146). Cambridge, MA: MIT Press.

Imada, T., Zhang, Y., Cheour, M., Taulu, S., Ahonen, A., & Kuhl, P. K. (2006). Infant speech perception activates Broca's area: A developmental magnetoencephalography study. *NeuroReport, 17,* 957–962.

Inagaki, K. (1981). Facilitation of knowledge integration through classroom discussion. *Quarterly Newsletter of the Laboratory of Comparative Human Cognition, 3,* 26–28.

Inagaki, K. & Hatano, G. (2006). Young children's conception of the biological world. *Current Directions in Psychological Science, 15,* 177–181.

Inagaki, K., Hatano, G., & Morita, F. (1998). Construction of mathematical knowledge through whole-class discussion. *Learning and Instruction, 8,* 503–526.

Indersmitten, T. & Gur, R.C. (2003). Emotion processing in chimeric faces: Hemispheric asymmetries in expression and recognition of emotions. *The Journal of Neuroscience, 23,* 3820–3825.

Indian and Northern Affairs Canada. (1996). *The Royal Commission on Aboriginal Peoples.* Available: www.ainc-inac.gc.ca/ch/rcap/sg/sgmm_e.html

Inhelder, B. & Piaget, J. (1958). *The growth of logical thinking from childhood to adolescence.* New York: Basic Books.

International Human Genome Sequencing Consortium. (2004). Finishing the euchromatic sequence of the human genome. *Nature, 431,* 931–945.

Isabella, R. A. (1993). Origins of attachment: Maternal interactive behavior across the first year. *Child Development, 64,* 605–621.

Isabella, R. A. (1994). The origins of infant–mother attachment: Maternal behavior and infant development. In R. Vasta (Ed.), *Annals of child development* (Vol. 10). London: Kingsley.

Isabella, R. A. & Belsky, J. (1991). Interactional synchrony and the origins of infant-mother attachment: A replication study. *Child Development, 62,* 373–384.

Ischebeck, A., Schocke, M., & Delazer, M. (2009). The processing and representation of fractions within the brain: An fMRI investigation. *NeuroImage, 47,* 403–413.

Isley, S. L., O'Neil, R., Clatfelter, D., & Parke, R. (1999). Parent and child expressed affect and children's social competence: Modeling direct and indirect pathways. *Developmental Psychology, 35,* 547–560.

Iverson, J. M. & Goldin-Meadow, S. (2005). Gesture paves the way for language development. *Psychological Science, 16,* 367–371.

Iyasu, S., Randall, L. L., Welty, T. K., Hsia, J., Kinney, H. C., Mandell, F., McClain, M., Randall, B., Habbe, D., Wilson, H., & Willinger, M. (2002). Risk factors for sudden infant death syndrome among northern plains Indians. *Journal of the American Medical Association, 288,* 2717–2723.

Izard, C. (1995). Innate and universal facial expressions: Evidence from developmental and cross-cultural research. *Psychological Bulletin, 115,* 288–299.

J

Jacklin, C. N. (1989). Female and male: Issues of gender. *American Psychologist, 44,* 127–133.

Jackson, W. & Verberg, N. (2007). *Methods: Doing social research* (4th ed.). Toronto: Pearson.

Jacobs, B., Schall, M., & Scheibel, A. B. (1993). A quantitative dendritic analysis of Wernicke's area in human. I. Gender, hemispheric, and environmental factors. *The Journal of Comparative Neurology, 327,* 97–111.

Jacobsen, T. & Hofmann, V. (1997). Children's attachment representations: Longitudinal relations to school behavior and academic competency in middle childhood and adolescence. *Developmental Psychology, 33,* 703–710.

Jacobson, J. L. & Jacobson, S. W. (1988). New methodologies for assessing the effects of prenatal toxic exposure on cognitive functioning in humans. In M. Evans (Ed.), *Toxic contaminants and ecosystem health: A Great Lakes focus.* New York: Wiley.

Jacobson, J. L., Jacobson, S. W., Padgett, R. J., Brimitt, G. A., & Billings, R. L. (1992). Effects of prenatal PCB exposure on cognitive processing efficiency and sustained attention. *Developmental Psychology, 28,* 297–306.

Jacobvitz, D. & Sroufe, L. A. (1987). The early caregiver-child relationship and attention-deficit disorder with hyperactivity in kindergarten: A prospective study. *Child Development, 58,* 1496–1504.

Jacques, S. & Zelazo, P. D. (2001). The Flexible Item Selection Task (FIST): A measure of executive function in preschoolers. *Developmental Neuropsychology, 20,* 573–591.

Jadva, V., Badger, S., Morrissette, M., & Golombok, S. (2009). 'Mom by choice, single by life's circumstance. . .' Findings from a large scale survey of the experiences of single mothers by choice. *Human Fertility, 12,* 175–184.

Jaffe, J., Beebe, B., Feldstein, S., Crown, C. L., & Jasnow, M. D. (2001). Rhythms of dialogue in infancy: Coordinated timing in development. *Monographs of the Society for Research in Child Development, 66,* 1–131.

Jaffee, S. & Hyde, J. S. (2000). Gender differences in moral orientation: A meta-analysis. *Psychological Bulletin, 126,* 703–726.

Jaffee, S. R., Caspi, A., Moffitt, T. E., Dodge, K. A., Rutter, M., Taylor, A. & Tully, L. A. (2005). Nature x nurture: Genetic vulnerabilities interact with physical maltreatment to promote conduct problems. *Development and Psychopathology, 17,* 67–84.

Jahoda, G. (1993). *Crossroads between culture and mind: Continuities and changes in theories of human nature.* Cambridge, MA: Harvard University Press.

James, W. (1890). *Principles of psychology.* New York: Holt.

James, W. (1892). *Psychology: The briefer course.* New York: Holt.

Jamison, W. (1977). Developmental inter-relationships among concrete operational tasks: An investigation of Piaget's stage concept. *Journal of Experimental Child Psychology, 24,* 235–253.

Jansson, L. M., DiPietro, J. A., Elko, A., & Velez, M. (2010). Infant autonomic functioning and neonatal abstinence syndrome. *Drug and Alcohol Dependence, 109,* 198–204.

Jaswal, V. K. & Hansen, M. B. (2006). Learning words: Children disregard some pragmatic information that conflicts with mutual exclusivity. *Developmental Science, 9*(2), 158–165.

Jencks, C. (1972). *Inequality.* New York: Basic Books.

Jennings, K. D. (1975). People versus object orientation, social behavior, and intellectual abilities in preschool children. *Developmental Psychology, 11,* 511–519.

Jensen, A. R. (1981). *Straight talk about mental tests.* New York: Free Press.

Jobe, A. H. (2004). Postnatal corticosteroids for preterm infants—Do what we say, not what we do. *New England Journal of Medicine, 350,* 1349–1351.

Joh, A., Sweeney, B., & Rovee-Collier, C. (2002). Minimum duration of reactivation at 3 months of age. *Developmental Psychobiology, 40,* 23–32A.

John, A. E., Rowe, M. L. & Mervis, C. B. (2009). Referential communication skills of children with Williams Syndrome: Understanding when messages are not adequate. *American Journal on Intellectual and Developmental Disabilities, 114*(2), 85–99.

Johnson, A. (2007). The maternal experience of kangaroo holding. *Journal of Obstetric, Gynecology, and Neonatal Nursing, 36,* 568–573.

Johnson, C. D. & Davidson, B. L. (2010). Huntington's disease: progress toward effective disease-modifying treatments as a cure. *Human Molecular Genetics, 19,* R98–R102.

Johnson, J. S. & Newport, E. L. (1989). Critical period effects in second language learning: The influence of maturational state on the acquisition of English as a second language. *Cognitive Psychology, 21,* 60–99.

Johnson, M. H. (1990). Cortical maturation and the development of visual attention in early infancy. *Journal of Cognitive Neuroscience, 2,* 81–95.

Johnson, M. H. (1997). *Developmental Cognitive Neuroscience* (Building a brain, Ch. 2). Oxford: Blackwell.

Johnson, M. H. (2001). Functional brain development during infancy. In G. Bremner & A. Fogel (Eds.), *Blackwell handbook of infant development.* Malden, MA: Blackwell Publishers.

Johnson, M. H. (2007). The social brain in infancy: A developmental cognitive neuroscience approach. In D. Coch, K. W. Fischer, & G. Dawson (Eds.), *Human behavior, learning, and the developing brain: Typical development* (pp. 115–137). New York, NY: Guilford Press.

Johnson, M. H. & de Haan, M. (2011). *Developmental cognitive neuroscience (Third edition).* Oxford, UK: Wiley-Blackwell.

Johnson, M. H., Dziurawiec, S., Ellis, H., & Morton, J. (1991). Newborns' preferential tracking of facelike stimuli and its subsequent decline. *Cognition, 40,* 1–19.

Johnson, M. H., Mareschal, D., & Csibra, G. (2008). The development and integration of dorsal and ventral visual pathways in object processing. In C. Nelson & M. Luciana (Eds.), *Handbook of developmental cognitive neuroscience* (2nd ed., pp. 467–478). Cambridge: MIT Press.

Johnson, S. P., Amso, D., & Slemmer, J. A. (2003). Development of object concepts in infancy: Evidence for early learning in an eye-tracking paradigm. *Proceedings of the National Academy of Sciences, 100,* 10568–10573.

Johnson, S. P. & Aslin, R. N. (1995). Perception of object unity in 2-month-old infants. *Developmental Psychology, 31,* 739–745.

Johnson, W., Bouchard, T. J., McGue, M., Segal, N. L., Tellegen, A., Keyes, M., & Gottesman, I. I. (2007). Genetic and environmental influences on the Verbal-Perceptual-Image Rotation (VPR) model of the structure of mental abilities in the Minnesota study of twins reared apart. *Intelligence, 35,* 542–562.

Johnston, J. C., Durieux-Smith, A. & Bloom, K. (2005). Teaching gestural signs to infants to advance child development: A review of the evidence. *First Language, 25*(2), 235–251.

Jones, C. & Adamson, L. B. (1987). Language use in mother-child and mother-child-sibling interactions. *Child Development, 58,* 356–366.

Jones, D. C. (1985). Persuasive appeals and responses to appeals among friends and acquaintances. *Child Development, 56,* 757–763.

Jones, E. F. & Thomson, N. R. (2001). Action perception and outcome valence: Effects on children's inferences of intentionality and moral and liking judgments. *Journal of Genetic Psychology, 162,* 154–166.

Jones, K. L., Smith, D. W., Ulleland, C. N., & Streissguth, A. P. (1973). Pattern of malformation in offspring of chronic alcoholic mothers. *Lancet, 1,* 1267–1271.

Jones, M. C. (1924). A laboratory study of fear: The case of Peter. *Pedagogical Seminary, 31,* 308–315.

Jones, M. C. (1965). Psychological correlates of somatic development. *Child Development, 36,* 899–911.

Jones, S. S. (2009). The development of imitation in infancy. *Philosophical Transactions of the Royal Society B, 364,* 2325–2335.

Joos, S. K., Pollitt, E., Mueller, W. H., & Albright, D. L. (1983). The Bacon Chow study: Maternal nutritional supplementation and infant behavioral development. *Child Development, 54,* 669–676.

Jordan, A. B., Schmitt, K. L., & Woodard, E. H. (2001). Developmental implications of commercial broadcasters' educational offerings. *Journal of Applied Developmental Psychology, 22,* 87–101.

Jordan, H. E. & Kindred, J. E. (1948). *Textbook of embryology* (5th ed.). New York: Apple-Century Crofts.

Joseph, J. (2000). Not in their genes: A critical view of the genetics of attention-deficit hyperactivity disorder. *Developmental Review, 20,* 539–567.

Josse, G., Mazoyer, B., Crivello, F., & Tzourio-Mazoyer, N. (2003). Left planum temporale: An anatomical marker of left hemispheric specialization for language comprehension. *Cognitive Brain Research, 18,* 1–14.

Joy, L. A., Kimball, M. M., & Zabrack, M. L. (1986). Television and children's aggressive behavior. In T. M. Williams (Ed.), *The impact of television: A natural experiment in three communities* (pp. 303–360). New York: Academic Press.

Juby, H., Billette, J. M., Laplante, B., & Le Bourdais, C. (2007). Nonresident fathers and children: Parents' new unions and frequency of contact. *Journal of Family Issues, 28,* 1220–1245.

Juby, H., Le Bourdais, C., & Marcil-Gratton, N. (2005). *Moving on: The expansion of the family network after parents separate* (Research Report 2004-FCY-9E, Phase 3). Ottawa: Department of Justice Canada, Family, Children and Youth Section.

Jung, V., Short, R., Letourneau, N., & Andrews, D. (2007). Interventions with depressed mothers and their infants: Modifying interactive behaviours. *Journal of Affective Disorders, 98,* 199–205.

Jusczyk, P. (1985). The high amplitude sucking technique as a methodological tool in speech perception research. In G. Gottlieb & N. A. Krasnegor (Eds.), *Measurement of audition and vision in the first year of postnatal life: A methodological overview.* Norwood, NJ: Ablex.

Jusczyk, P. W. (1997). *The discovery of spoken language.* Cambridge, MA: MIT Press.

Jusczyk, P. W., Cutler, A., & Redanz, N. J. (1993). Infants' preference for the predominant stress patterns of English words. *Child Development, 64,* 675–687.

Jusczyk, P. W., Houston, D. M., & Newsome, M. (1999). The beginnings of word segmentation in English-learning infants. *Cognitive Psychology, 38,* 159–207.

Jusczyk, P. W., Pisoni, D. B., & Mullennix, J. (1992). Some consequences of stimulus variability on speech processing by 2-month-old infants. *Cognition, 43,* 253–291.

Juvonen, J. & Galván, A. (2008). Peer influence in involuntary social groups: Lessons from research on bullying. In M. Prinstein & K. Dodge (Eds.), *Understanding peer influence in children and adolescents* (pp. 225–244). New York: Guilford Press.

Juvonen, J. & Gross, E. F. (2008). Extending the school grounds? Bullying experiences in cyberspace. *Journal of School Health, 78*(9), 496–505.

K

Kadosh, K. C. & Johnson, M. H. (2007). Developing a cortex specialized for face perception. *Trends in Cognitive Sciences, 11*(9), 367–369.

Kagan, J. (1991). The theoretical utility of constructs for self. *Developmental Review, 11,* 244–250.

Kagan, J. (1994). *Galen's prophecy.* New York: Basic Books.

Kagan, J. (1997). Temperament and the reactions to unfamiliarity. *Child Development, 68,* 139–143.

Kagan, J. (1998). Is there a self in infancy? In M. D. Ferrari & R. J. Sternberg (Eds.), *Self-awareness: Its nature and development.* New York: Guilford.

Kagan, J. (2002). *Surprise, uncertainty, and mental structures.* Cambridge, MA: Harvard University Press.

Kagan, J. & Fox, N. A. (2006) Biology, culture, and temperamental biases. In W. Damon & R. M. Lerner (Series Eds.) & N. Eisenberg (Vol. Ed.), *Handbook of child psychology: Vol. 3. Social, emotional, and personality development* (6th ed., pp. 167–225). Hoboken, NJ: Wiley.

Kagan, J. & Snidman, N. (2004). *The long shadow of temperament.* Cambridge, MA: Harvard University Press.

Kagan, J., Reznick, J. S., & Gibbons, J. (1989). Inhibited and uninhibited types of children. *Child Development, 60,* 838–845.

Kagan, J., Reznick, J. S., & Snidman, N. (1987). The physiology and psychology of behavioral inhibition. *Child Development, 58,* 1459–1473.

Kagan, J., Reznick, J. S., & Snidman, N. (1988). Biological bases of childhood shyness. *Science, 240,* 167–171.

Kagan, J., Snidman, N., & Arcus, D. M. (1992). Initial reactions to unfamiliarity. *Current Directions in Psychological Science, 1,* 171–174.

Kagan, J., Reznick, J. S., Snidman, N., Gibbons, J., & Johnson, M. O. (1988). Childhood derivatives of inhibition and lack of inhibition to the unfamiliar. *Child Development, 59,* 1580–1589.

Kahana-Kalman, R. & Walker-Andrews, A. (2001). The role of person familiarity in young infants' perception of emotional expressions. *Child Development, 72,* 352–369.

Kail, R. V. & Miller, C. A. (2006). Developmental change in processing speed: Domain specificity and stability during childhood and adolescence. *Journal of Cognition and Development, 7,* 119–137.

Kaitz, M., Good, A., Rokem, A. M., & Eidelman, A. I. (1987). Mothers' recognition of their newborns by olfactory cues. *Developmental Psychology, 20,* 587–591.

Kaitz, M., Lapidot, P., Bronner, R., & Eidelman, A. I. (1992). Parturient women can recognize their infants by touch. *Developmental Psychology, 28,* 35–39.

Kaitz, M., Meirov, H., Landman, I., & Eidelman, A. I. (1993). Infant recognition by tactile cues. *Infant Behavior and Development, 16,* 333–341.

Kaler, S. R. & Kopp, C. B. (1990). Compliance and comprehension in very young toddlers. *Child Development, 61,* 1997–2003.

Kamii, C. & DeVries, R. (1993). *Physical knowledge in preschool education: Implications of Piaget's theory* (rev. ed.). New York: Teachers College Press.

Kamins, M. L. & Dweck, C. S. (1999). Person versus process praise and criticism: Implications for contingent self-worth and coping. *Developmental Psychology, 35,* 835–847.

Kamptner, L., Kraft, R. H., & Harper, L. V. (1984). Lateral specialization and social-verbal development in preschool children. *Brain and Cognition, 3,* 42–50.

Kandel, E. R. & O'Dell, T. J. (1992). Are adult mechanisms also used for development? *Science,* 258, 243–245.

Kane, E. W. (2006). No way my boys are going to be like that! *Gender and Society, 20,*149–176.

Karmel, B. Z. & Maisel, E. B. (1975). A neuronal activity model for infant visual attention. In L. B. Cohen & P. Salapatek (Eds.), *Infant perception: From sensation to cognition: Vol. 1. Basic visual processes.* New York: Academic Press.

Karmiloff, K. & Karmiloff-Smith, A. (2001). *Pathways to language.* Cambridge, MA: Harvard University Press.

Karniol, R. & Miller, D. T. (1981). The development of self-control in children. In S. S. Brehm, S. M. Kassin, & F. X. Gibbons (Eds.), *Developmental social psychology: Theory and research.* New York: Oxford University Press.

Karp, H. (2002). *The happiest baby on the block: The new way to calm crying and help your newborn baby sleep longer.* New York: Bantam Books.

Karp, H. (2007). Swaddling and excessive crying. *The Journal of Pediatrics,* 151, e2–e3.

Karzon, R. G. (1985). Discrimination of polysyllabic sequences by one- to four-month-old infants. *Journal of Experimental Child Psychology, 39,* 326–342.

Kasprian, G., Langs, G., Brugger, P.C., Bittner, M., Weber, M., Arantes, M., & Prayer, D. (2011). The prenatal origin of hemispheric asymmetry: An in utero neuroimaging study. *Cerebral Cortex, 21,* 1076–1083.

Katz, D. L. & Friedman, R. S. (2008). *Nutrition in clinical practice: A comprehensive, evidence-based manual for the practitioner.* Philadelphia, PA: Lippincott Williams & Wilkins.

Katz, P. A. & Ksansnak, K. R. (1994). Developmental aspects of gender role flexibility and traditionality in middle childhood and adolescence. *Developmental Psychology, 30,* 272–282.

Kaufman, A. S. & Kaufman, N. L. (1983). *Kaufman Assessment Battery for Children.* Circle Pines, MN: American Guidance Service.

Kaufman, A. S. & Kaufman, N. L. (2004). *Kaufman Assessment Battery for Children—Second edition, technical manual.* Circle Pines, MN: American Guidance Service.

Kaufman, J., Csibra, G., & Johnson, M. H. (2003). Representing occluded objects in the human infant brain. *Proceedings of The Royal Society B: Biological Sciences, 270,* S140–S143.

Kaufman, J., Csibra, G., & Johnson, M. H. (2005). Oscillatory activity in the infant brain reflects object maintenance. *Proceedings of the National Academy of Sciences, 102,* 15271–15274.

Kavanaugh, R. D. (2006). Pretend play and theory of mind. In L. Balter & C. S. Tamis-LeMonda (Eds.), *Child psychology: A Handbook of contemporary issues* (2nd ed., pp. 153–166). New York: Psychology Press.

Kavsek, M. J. (2002). The perception of static subjective contours in infancy. *Child Development, 73,* 331–344.

Kavsek, M. J. (2004). Predicting later IQ from infant visual habituation and dishabituation: A meta-analysis. *Applied Developmental Psychology, 25,* 369–393.

Kawabata, H., Gyoba, J., Inoue, H., & Ohtsubo, H. (1999). Visual completion of partly occluded grating in infants under one month of age. *Vision Research, 39,* 3586–3591.

Kawasaki, C., Nugent, J. K., Miyashita, H., Miyahara, H., & Brazelton, T. B. (1994). The cultural organization of infants' sleep. *Children's Environments, 11,* 135–141.

Kay, D. A. & Anglin, J. M. (1982). Overextension and underextension in the child's expressive and receptive speech. *Journal of Child Language, 9,* 83–98.

Kazanina, N., Phillips, C., & Idsardi, W. (2006). The influence of meaning on the perception of speech sounds. *Proceedings of the National Academy of Sciences, 103,* 11381–11386.

Kazdin, A. E. (2003). Problem-solving skills training and parent management training for conduct disorder. In A. E. Kazdin & J. R. Weisz (Eds.) *Evidence-based psychotherapies for children and adolescents* (pp. 241–262). New York: Guilford.

Kazdin, A. E. (2005). Child, parent, and family-based treatment of aggressive and antisocial child behavior. In E. D. Hibbs & P. S. Jensen (Eds.), *Psychosocial treatments for child and adolescent disorders: Empirically based strategies for clinical practice* (2nd ed., pp. 445–476). Washington, DC: American Psychological Association.

Keating, D. P. (1988). Byrnes' reformulation of Piaget's formal operations: Is what's left what's right? *Developmental Review, 8,* 376–384.

Kee, D. W. & Guttentag, R. (1994). Resource requirements of knowledge access and recall benefits of associative strategies. *Journal of Experimental Child Psychology, 57,* 211–223.

Keefe, K. & Berndt, T. J. (1996). Relations of friendship quality to self-esteem in early adolescence. *Journal of Early Adolescence, 16,* 110–129.

Keefe, M. R. (1987). Comparison of neonatal nighttime sleep-wake patterns in nursery versus rooming-in environments. *Nursing Research, 36,* 140–144.

Keenan, J. P., Wheeler, M. A., & Ewers, M. (2003). The neural correlates of self-awareness and self recognition. In T. Kircher & A. David (Eds.). The self in neuroscience and psychiatry (pp. 166–179). New York: Cambridge University Press.

Keenan, K., & Shaw, D. (1997). Developmental and social influences on young girls' early problem behavior. *Psychological Bulletin, 121,* 95–113.

Keenan, T. (2000). Mind, memory, and metacognition: The role of memory span in children's developing understanding of the mind. In J. W. Astington (Ed.), *Minds in the making: Essays in honor of David R. Olson.* Malden, MA: Blackwell Publishers.

Keil, F. C. (2006). Cognitive science and cognitive development. In D. Kuhn & R. S. Siegler (Eds.), *Handbook of child psychology 6th edition: Vol 2: Cognition, perception, and language (pp. 609–635).* Hoboken, NJ: Wiley.

Keith, L. K. & Bracken, B. A. (1996). Self-concept instrumentation: A historical and evaluative review. In B. A. Bracken (Ed.), *Handbook of self-concept: Developmental, social, and clinical considerations.* New York: Wiley.

Kellman, P. J. (1996). The origins of object perception. In R. Gelman & T. Au (Eds.), *Perceptual and cognitive development.* San Diego, CA: Academic Press.

Kellman, P. J. & Banks, M. (1998). Infant visual perception. In W. Damon (Series Ed.) & D. Kuhn & R. S. Siegler (Vol. Eds.), *Handbook of child psychology: Vol. 2. Cognition, perception, and language* (5th ed.). New York: Wiley.

Kellman, P. J., & Spelke, E. S. (1983). Perception of partly occluded objects in infancy. *Cognitive Psychology, 15,* 483–524.

Kelly, E. B. (2007). *Gene therapy: Health and medical issues today.* Wesport, CT: Greenwood Publishing Group.

Kemler Nelson, D. G., Hirsh-Pasek, K., Jusczyk, P., & Cassidy, K. W. (1989). How the prosodic cues in motherese might assist language learning. *Journal of Child Language, 16,* 55–68.

Kendall, P. C. & Choudhury, M. S. (2003). Children and adolescents in cognitive-behavioral therapy: Some past efforts and current advances, and the challenges in our future. *Cognitive Therapy and Research, 27,* 89–104.

Kennell, J. (2002). On becoming a family: Bonding and the changing patterns in baby and family behavior. In J. Gomes-Pedro, K. Nugent, J. Young, & T. B. Brazelton (Eds.), *The infant and family in the twenty-first century* (pp. 31–43). New York: Brunner-Routledge.

Kenrick, D. T. & Luce, C. L. (2000). An evolutionary life-history model of gender differences and similarities. In T. Eckes & H. M. Trautner (Eds.), *The developmental social psychology of gender.* Mahwah, NJ: Erlbaum.

Kent, R. D. & Bauer, H. R. (1985). Vocalizations of one-year-olds. *Journal of Child Language, 12,* 491–526.

Kerestes, M., Youniss, J., & Metz, E. (2004). Longitudinal patterns of religious perspective and civic integration. *Applied Developmental Science, 8,* 39–46.

Kerns, K. A. (2008). Attachment in middle childhood. In J. Cassidy & P. R. Shaver (Eds.) *Handbook of attachment: Theory, research, and clinical applications (2nd edition)* (pp. 366–382). New York, NY: Guilford.

Kerr, A. & Zelazó, P. D. (2004). Development of "hot" executive function: The children's gambling task. *Brain and Cognition, 55,* 148–157.

Kerr, M., Lambert, W. W., & Bem, D. J. (1996). Life course sequelae of childhood shyness in Sweden: Comparison with the United States. *Developmental Psychology, 32,* 1100–1105.

Kerr, M., Lambert, W. W., Stattin, H., & Klackenberg Larsson, I. (1994). Stability of inhibition in a Swedish longitudinal sample. *Child Development, 65,* 138–146.

Kerzerho, S., Gentaz, E., & Streri, A. (2009). Factors influencing manual discrimination of orientations in 5-month-old infants. *Perception, 38*(1), 44–51.

Key, A. P., Ferguson, M., Molfese, D. L., Peach, K., Lehman, C., & Molfese, V. J. (2007). Smoking during pregnancy affects speech processing ability in newborns. *Environmental Health Perspectives, 115,* 623–629.

Kienbaum, J. & Wilkening, F. (2009). Children's and adolescents' intuitive judgements about distributive justice: Integrating need, effort, and luck. *European Journal of Developmental Psychology, 6,* 481–498.

Killen, M. & Rutland, A. (2011). *Children and* social *exclusion: Morality, prejudice, and group identity.* Chichester, UK: Wiley-Blackwell.

Killen, M., Lee-Kim, J., McGlothin, H., & Stangor, C. (2002). How children and adolescents evaluate gender and racial exclusion. *Monographs of the Society for Research in Child Development, 67*(4), (Serial No. 271).

Killen, M., Rutland, A., & Jampol, N. S. (2009). Social exclusion in childhood and adolescence. In K. H. Rubin, W. M. Bukowski, & B. Laursen (Eds.), *Handbook of peer interactions, relationships, and groups* (pp. 249–266). New York: Guilford.

Kihlstrom, J. F., Beer, J. S., & Klein, S. B. (2003). Self and identity as memory. In M. Leary & J. Tangney (Eds.), *Handbook of self and identity* (pp. 68–90). New York, NY: Guilford Press.

Kim, H. & Chung, R. H. (2003). Relationship of recalled parenting style to self-perception in

Korean American college students. *Journal of Genetic Psychology, 164,* 481–492.

Kim, M., McGregor, K. K., & Thompson, C. K. (2000). Early lexical development in English- and Korean-speaking children: Language-general and language specific patterns. *Journal of Child Language, 27,* 225–254.

Kimball, M. M. (1986). Television and sex-role attitudes. In T. M. Williams (Ed.), *The impact of television: A natural experiment in three communities* (pp. 265–302). New York: Academic Press.

Kimmelman, J. (2008). The ethics of human gene transfer. *Nature Reviews—Genetics, 9,* 239–244.

Kimura, D. (2002). Sex hormones influence human cognitive pattern. *Neuroendrocrinology, 23,* 67–77.

Kimura, D. (2004). Human sex differences in cognition: Fact, not predicament. *Sexualities, Evolution, and Gender, 6,* 45–53.

Kimura, D. & Clarke, P. G. (2002). Women's advantage on verbal memory is not restricted to concrete words. *Psychological Reports, 91,* 1137–1142.

King, S. & Laplante, D. (2005). The effects of prenatal maternal stress on children's cognitive development: Project Ice Storm. *Stress: The International Journal on the Biology of Stress, 8,* 35–45.

Kingsbury, M. A., & Finlay, B. L. (2001). The cortex in multidimensional space: Where do cortical areas come from? *Developmental Science, 4,* 125–142.

Kinsbourne, M. (1989). A model of adaptive behavior related to cerebral participation in emotional control. In G. Gainotti & C. Caltagirone (Eds.), *Emotions and the dual brain* (pp. 248–260). New York: Springer-Verlag.

Kircher, T. J., Senior, C., Philips, M. L., Rabe-Hesketh, S., Benson, P. J., Bullmore, E. T., et al. (2001). Recognizing one's own face. *Cognition, 78,* B1–B15.

Kiriakidis, S. P. & Kavoura, A. (2010). Cyberbullying: A review of the literature on harassment through the internet and other electronic means. *Family and Community Health, 33*(2), 82–93.

Kirkham, N. Z., Cruess, L., & Diamond, A. (2003). Helping children apply their knowledge to their behavior on a dimension-switching task. *Developmental Science, 6,* 449–467.

Kisilevsky, B. S., Hains, S. M. J., Brown, C. A., Lee, C. T., Cowperthwaite, B., Stutzman, S. S., et al. (2009). Fetal sensitivity to properties of maternal speech and language. *Infant Behavior and Development, 32*(1), 59–71.

Kisilevsky, B. S. & Muir, D. W. (1984). Neonatal habituation and dishabituation to tactile stimulation during sleep. *Developmental Psychology, 20,* 367–373.

Kisilivesky B., Hains, S., Lee, K., Xie, X., Huang, H., Ye, H., Zang, K., & Wang, Z. (2003). Effects of experience on fetal voice recognition. *Psychological Science, 14,* 220–224.

Klahr, D. & MacWhinney, B. (1998). Information processing. In W. Damon (Editor-in-Chief), K. Dunn, & R. S. Siegler (Eds.), *Handbook of child psychology* (5th ed., Vol. 2, pp. 631–678). New York: Wiley.

Klaus, M. H. & Kennell, J. H. (1976). *Maternal-infant bonding.* St. Louis, MO: Mosby.

Klaus, M. H., Kennell, J. H., & Klaus, P. H. (1995). *Bonding: Building the foundations of secure attachment and independence.* Reading, MA: Addison-Wesley

Kleeman, W. J., Schlaud, M., Fieguth, A., Hiller, A. S., Rothamel, T., & Troger, H. D. (1999). Body and head position, covering of the head by bedding, and risk of sudden infant death syndrome (SIDS). *International Journal of Legal Medicine, 112,* 22–26.

Klein, M. C. (2005). Obstetrician's fear of childbirth: How did it happen? *Birth: Issues in Perinatal Care, 32,* 207–209.

Kleinfeld, J. S. (1996). The surprising ease of changing the belief that the schools shortchange girls. In R. J. Simon (Ed.), *From data to public policy: Affirmative action, sexual harassment, domestic violence and social welfare.* Lanham, MD: University Press of America.

Kleinspehn-Ammerlahn, A., Riediger, M., Schmiedek, F., von Oertzen, T., Li, S., & Lindenberger, U. (2011). Dyadic drumming across the lifespan reveals a zone of proximal development in children. *Developmental Psychology, 47,* 632–644.

Klimes-Dougan, B. & Kistner, J. (1990). Physically abused pre-schoolers' responses to peers' distress. *Developmental Psychology, 26,* 599–602.

Klingberg, T. (2006). Development of a superior frontal-intraparietal network for visuo-spatial working memory. *Neuropsychologia, 44,* 2171–2177.

Klinberg, T., Hedehus, M., Temple, E., Salz, T., Gabrieli, J. D., Moseley, M. E., & Poldrack, R. A. (2000). Microstructure of temporo-parietal white matter as a basis for reading ability: Evidence from diffusion tensor magnetic resonance imaging. *Neuron, 25,* 493–500.

Klingman, A. (2006). Children and war trauma. In K. A. Renninger, I. E. Sigel, W. Damon, & R. M. Lerner (Eds.), *Handbook of child psychology: Vol 4, Child psychology in practice* (6th ed., pp. 619–652). Hoboken, NJ: Wiley.

Klinnert, M. D., Sorce, J. F., Emde, R. N., Stenberg, C., & Gaensbaurer, T. (1984). Continuities and change in early emotional life: Maternal perceptions of surprise, fear, and anger. In R. N. Emde & R. J. Harmon (Eds.), *Continuities and discontinuities in development.* New York: Plenum.

Knafo, A. & Israel, S. (2010). Genetic and environmental influences on prosocial behavior. In M. Mikulincer & P. R. Shaver (Eds.), *Prosocial motives, emotions, and behavior: The better angels of our nature* (pp. 149–167). Washington, DC: American Psychological Association.

Knafo, A. & Plomin, R. (2006). Prosocial behavior from early to middle childhood: Genetic and environmental influences on stability and change. *Developmental Psychology, 42,* 771–786.

Knafo, A., Zahn-Waxler, C., Davidov, M., Van Hulle, C., Robinson, J., & Rhee, S. H. (2009). Empathy in early childhood: Genetic, environmental and affective contributions. *Annals of the New York Academy of Sciences, 1167,* 103–114.

Knickmeyer, R. C., Gouttard, S., Kang, C., Evans, D., Wilber, K., Smith, J. K., Hamer, R. M., Lin, W., Gerig, G., & Gilmore, J. H. (2008). A structural MRI study of human brain development from birth to 2 years. *The Journal of Neuroscience, 28,* 12176–12182.

Knops, N. B. B., Sneeuw, K. C. A., Brand, R., Hille, E. T. M., Ouden, A. L., Wit, J.-M., & Verloove-Vanhorick, S. P. (2005). Catch-up growth up to ten years of age in children born very preterm or with very low birth weight. *BMC Pediatrics, 5,* 26–35.

Knudsen, E. I. (2004). Sensitive periods in the development of the brain and behavior. *Journal of Cognitive Neuroscience, 16,* 1412–1425.

Kochanska, G. (1997a). Multiple pathways to conscience for children with different temperaments: From toddlerhood to age 5. *Developmental Psychology, 33,* 228–240.

Kochanska, G. (1997b). Mutually responsive orientation between mothers and their young children: Implications for early socialization. *Child Development, 68,* 94–112.

Kochanska, G. (2002). Committed compliance, moral self, and internalization: A mediational model. *Developmental Psychology, 38,* 339–351.

Kochanska, G. & Aksan, N. (1995). Mother-child mutually positive affect, the quality of child compliance to requests and prohibitions, and maternal control as correlates of early internalization. *Child Development, 66,* 236–254.

Kochanska, G., Aksan, N., & Joy, M. E. (2007). Children's fearfulness as a moderator of parenting in early socialization: two longitudinal studies. *Developmental Psychology, 43,* 222–237.

Kochanska, G., Coy, K. C., & Murray, K. T. (2001). The development of self-regulation in the first four years of life. *Child Development, 72,* 1091–1111.

Kochanska, G., Murray, K., Jacques, T. Y., Koenig, A. L., & Vandergeest, K. A. (1996). Inhibitory control in young children and its role in emerging internalization. *Child Development, 67,* 490–507.

Kodish, E. (2005). *Ethics and research with children: A case-based approach.* New York: Oxford University Press.

Koenigsknecht, R. A. & Friedman, P. (1976). Syntax development in boys and girls. *Child Development, 47,* 1109–1115.

Kogan, C. S., Boutet, I., Cornish, K., Graham, G. E., Berry-Kravis, E., Drouin, A., Milgram, N. W. (2009). A comparative neuropsychological test battery differentiates cognitive signatures of Fragile X and Down syndrome. *Journal of Intellectual Disability Research, 53,* 125–142.

Kohlberg, L. (1964). Development of moral character and moral behavior. In L. W. Hoffman & M. L. Hoffman (Eds.), *Review of child development research* (Vol. 1). New York, NY: Sage.

Kohlberg, L. (1966). A cognitive-developmental analysis of children's sex role concepts and attitudes. In E. E. Maccoby (Ed.), *The development of sex differences.* Stanford, CA: Stanford University Press.

Kohlberg, L. (1969). Stage and sequence: The cognitive-developmental approach to socialization. In D. A. Goslin (Ed.), *Handbook of socialization theory and research.* Chicago: Rand McNally.

Kohlberg, L. (1976). Moral stages and moralization: The cognitive-developmental approach. In T. Likona (Ed.), *Moral development and behavior: Theory, research, and social issues.* New York: Holt, Rinehart and Winston.

Kohlberg, L. (1981). *Essays on moral development: Vol. 1. The philosophy of moral development.* New York: Harper & Row.

Kohlberg, L. (1984). *The psychology of moral development: The nature and validity of moral stages.* San Francisco: Harper & Row.

Kohlberg, L. (1987). The development of moral judgment and moral action. In L. Kohlberg (Ed.), *Child psychology and childhood education: A cognitive-developmental view.* New York: Longman.

Kohlberg, L. & Candee, D. (1984). The relationship of moral judgment to moral action. In W. M. Kurtines & J. L. Gewirtz (Eds.), *Morality, moral behavior, and moral development.* New York: Wiley.

Kohlberg, L. & Kramer, R. (1969). Continuities and discontinuities in childhood and adult moral development. *Human Development, 12,* 93–120.

Kohlberg, L., Levine, C., & Hewer, A. (1983). *Moral stages: A current formulation and a response to critics.* Basel, Switzerland: Karger.

Kohlberg, L., Yaeger, J., & Hjertholm, E. (1968). Private speech: Four studies and a review of theories. *Child Development, 39,* 817–826.

Kolb, B. (1989). Brain development, plasticity, and behavior. *American Psychologist, 44,* 1203–1212.

Kolb, B. & Whishaw, I. Q. (2009). *Fundamentals of human neuropsychology (6th edition).* New York, NY: Worth.

Konner, M. (1972). Aspects of the developmental ethology of a foraging people. In N. Blurton-Jones (Ed.), *Ethological studies of child behavior.* Cambridge, MA: Cambridge University Press.

Konner, M. J. (1976). Maternal care, infant behavior and development among the Kung. In R. B. Lee & I. DeVore (Eds.), *Kalahari hunter-gatherers.* Cambridge, MA: Harvard University Press.

Kontos, S., Howes, C., Galinsky, E. (1996). Does training make a difference to quality in family child care? *Early Childhood Research Quarterly, 11,* 427–445.

Kopp, C. B. (1982). Antecedents of self-regulation: A developmental perspective. *Developmental Psychology, 18,* 199–214.

Koren, G., Fantus, E., & Nulman, I. (2010). Managing fetal alcohol spectrum disorder in the public school system: A needs assessment pilot. *Journal of Population Therapeutics and Clinical Pharmacology, 17,* e78–e89.

Korn, S. J. (1984). Continuities and discontinuities in difficult/easy temperament: Infancy to young adulthood. *Merrill-Palmer Quarterly, 30,* 189–199.

Korner, A. F. & Thoman, E. (1970). Visual alertness in neonates as evoked by maternal care. *Journal of Experimental Child Psychology, 10,* 67–78.

Kornhaber, M. (1994). *The theory of multiple intelligences: Why and how schools use it.* Cambridge, MA: Harvard Graduate School of Education.

Kosslyn, S. M., Pascual-Leone, A., Felician, O., Camposano, S., Keenan, J. P., Thompson, W. L., Ganis, G., Sukel, K. E., & Alpert, N. M. (1999). The role of area 17 in visual imagery: Convergent evidence from PET and rTMS. *Science, 284,* 167–170.

Kostelny, K. & Garbarino, J. (1994). Coping with the consequences of living in danger: The case of Palestinian children and youth. *International Journal of Behavioral Development, 17,* 595–611.

Kotz, S. A. (2009). A critical review of ERP and fMRI evidence on L2 syntactic processing. *Brain and Language, 109,* 68–74.

Kovacs, D. M., Parker, J. G., & Hoffman, L. W. (1996). Behavioral, affective, and social correlates of involvement in cross-sex friendship. *Child Development, 67,* 2269–2286.

Kovács, I. (1996). Gestalten of today: Early processing of visual contours and surfaces. *Behavioural Brain Research, 82,* 1–11.

Kovács, I., Kozma, P., Fehér, Á., & Benedek, G. (1999). Late maturation of visual spatial integration in humans. *Proceedings of the National Academy of Science, 96,* 12204–12209.

Kovács, I., Polat, U., Norcia, A. M., Pennefather, P. M., & Chandna, A. (2000). A new test of contour integration deficits in patients with a history of disrupted binocular experience during visual development. *Vision Research, 40,* 1775–1783.

Kowal, A. & Kramer, L. (1997). Children's understanding of parental differential treatment. *Child Development, 68,* 113–126.

Kowal, A., Kramer, L., Krull, J. L., & Crick, N. R. (2002). Children's perceptions of the fairness of parental preferential treatment and their socioemotional well-being. *Journal of Family Psychology, 16,* 297–306.

Kowalski, R. M. & Limber, S. P. (2007). Electronic bullying among middle school students. *Journal of Adolescent Health, 41,* S22–S30.

Kowalski, R. M., Limber, S. P., & Agatston, P. W. (2008). *Cyber bullying: In the digital age.* Hoboken, NJ: Wiley.

Kozulin, A. (1990). *Vygotsky's psychology.* Cambridge, MA: Harvard University Press.

Kraft, R. H. (1984). Lateral specialization and verbal/spatial ability in preschool children: Age, sex and familial handedness differences. *Neuropsychologia, 22,* 319–335.

Krauzlis, R. (2009). A priority map for movement and perception in the primate superior colliculus. *Journal of Vision, 9,* 10.

Krebs, D. L. & Van Hesteren, F. (1994). The development of altruism: Toward an integrative model. *Developmental Review, 14,* 103–158.

Kreitler, S. & Kreitler, H. (1989). Horizontal decalage: A problem and its solution. *Cognitive Development, 4,* 89–119.

Kreutzer, M. A., Leonard, C., & Flavell, J. H. (1975). An interview study of children's knowledge about memory. *Monographs of the Society for Research in Child Development, 40* (1, Serial No. 159).

Kroger, J. K., Nystrom, L. E., Cohen, J. D., & Johnson-Laird, P. N. (2008). Distinct neural substrates for deductive and mathematical processing. *Brain Research, 1243,* 86–103.

Kropp, J. P. & Haynes, O. M. (1987). Abusive and nonabusive mothers' ability to identify general and specific emotion signals of infants. *Child Development, 58,* 187–190.

Kruger, A. C. (1992). The effect of peer and adult-child transactive discussions on moral reasoning. *Merrill-Palmer Quarterly, 38,* 191–211.

Kruger, A. C. & Tomasello, M. (1986). Transactive discussions with peers and adults. *Developmental Psychology, 22,* 681–685.

Kruk, E. (2008). *Child custody, access, and parental responsibility: The search for a just and equitable standard.* Guelph, ON: Father Involvement Research Alliance. Downloaded on January 15, 2011 from http://www.fira.ca/resources.php.

Kuchuk, A., Vibbert, M., & Bornstein, M. H. (1986). The perception of smiling and its experiential correlates in three-month-old infants. *Child Development, 57,* 1054–1061.

Kuczaj, S. A. (1982). Language play and language acquisition. In H. W Reese (Ed.), *Advances in child development and behavior* (Vol. 17). New York: Academic Press.

Kuczynski, L. & Kochanska, G. (1990). Development of children's noncompliance strategies from toddlerhood to age 5. *Developmental Psychology, 26,* 398–408.

Kuczynski, L. & Kochanska, G. (1995). Function and content of maternal demands: Developmental significance of early demands for competent action. *Child Development, 66,* 616–628.

Kuhl, P. K. (1991). Perception, cognition, and the ontogenetic and phylogenetic emergence of human speech. In S. Brauth, W. Hall, & R. Dooling (Eds.), *Plasticity of development.* Cambridge, MA: MIT Press/Bradford Books.

Kuhl, P. K. (2001). Speech, language, and developmental change. In F. Lacerda, C. von Hofsten, & M. Heimann (Eds.), *Emerging cognitive abilities in early infancy.* Mahwah, NJ: Erlbaum.

Kuhl, P. K. & Meltzoff, A. N. (1982). The bimodal perception of speech in infancy. *Science, 218,* 1138–1141.

Kuhl, P. K. & Meltzoff, A. N. (1984). The intermodal representation of speech in infants. *Infant Behavior and Development, 7,* 361–381.

Kuhl, P. K. & Meltzoff, A. N. (1988). Speech as an inter-modal object of perception. In A. Yonas (Ed.), *Minnesota symposia on child psychology: Vol. 20. Perceptual development in infancy.* Hillsdale, NJ: Erlbaum.

Kuhl, P. K., Stevens, E., Hayashi, A., Deguchi, T., Kiritani, S., & Iverson, P. (2006). Infants show a facilitation effect for native language phonetic perception between 6 and 12 months. *Developmental Science, 9,* F1-F9.

Kuhn, D. & Franklin, S. (2006). The second decade: What develops (and how)? In W. Damon & R. Lerner (Series Eds.), D. Kuhn & R. Siegler (Vol. Eds.), *Handbook of child psychology: Vol. 2. Cognition, perception, and language (6th ed.).* Hoboken, NJ: Wiley.

Kuhn, D., Ho, V., & Adams, C. (1979). Formal reasoning among pre- and late-adolescents. *Child Development, 50,* 1128–1135.

Kulin, H. E. (1991). Puberty, hypothalamic-pituitary changes of. In R. M. Lerner, A. C. Peterson, & J. Brooks-Gunn (Eds.), *Encyclopedia of adolescence* (Vol. 2). New York: Garland.

Kulynych, J. J., Vladar, K., Jones, D. W., & Weinberger, D. R. (1994). Gender differences in the normal lateralization of the supratemporal cortex: MRI surface-rendering morphometry of Heschl's gyrus and the planum temporale. *Cerebral Cortex, 4,* 107–118.

Kumar, R., Macey, P. M., Woo, M. A., Alger, J. R., & Harper, R. M. (2008). Diffusion tensor imaging demonstrates brainstem and cerebellar abnormalities in congenital central hypoventilation syndrome. *Pediatric Research, 64,* 275–280.

Kupersmidt, J. B. & Trejos, S. L. (1987, April). *Behavioral correlates of sociometric status among Costa Rican children.* Paper presented at the meeting of the Society for Research in Child Development, Baltimore.

Kurdek, L. A. (1980). Developmental relations among children's perspective taking, moral judgment, and parent-rated behaviors. *Merrill-Palmer Quarterly, 26,* 103–121.

Kurtz, B. E. & Borkowski, J. G. (1987). Development of strategic skills in impulsive and reflective children: A longitudinal study of metacognition. *Journal of Experimental Child Psychology, 43,* 129–148.

Kushnerenko, E., Winkler, I., Horvath, J., Naatanen, R., Pavlov, I., Fellman, V., & Huotilainen, M. (2007). Processing acoustic change and novelty in newborn infants. *European Journal of Neuroscience, 26,* 265–274.

Kylliäinen, A., Braeutigam, S., Hietanen, J. K., Swithenby, S. J., & Bailey, A. J. (2006). Face and gaze processing in normally developing children: A magnetoencephalographic study. *European Journal of Neuroscience, 23,* 801–810.

Kyratzis, A., Marx, T., & Wade, E. (2001). Preschoolers communicative competence: register shift in the marking of power in different contexts of friendship group talk. *First Language, 21,* 387–429.

L

Laberge A.-M., Michaud, J., Richter, A., Lemyre, E., Lambert, M., Brais, B., Mitchell, G. A. (2005). Population history and its impact on medical genetics in Quebec. *Clinical Genetics, 68,* 287–301.

Laboratory of Comparative Human Cognition. (1983). Culture and cognitive development. In P. H. Mussen (Series Ed.) & W. Kessen (Vol. Ed.), *Handbook of child psychology: Vol. 1. History, theory, and methods* (4th ed.). New York: Wiley.

Ladd, B. K. & Ladd, G. W. (2001). Variations in peer victimization: Relations to children's maladjustment. In J. Juvonen & S. Graham (Eds.), *Peer harassment in school: The plight of the vulnerable and victimized.* New York: Guilford.

Ladd, G. W. (2005). *Peer relationships and social competence of children and adolescents.* New Haven, CT: Yale University Press.

Ladd, G. W., Buhs, E. S., & Troop, W. (2002). Children's interpersonal skills and relationships in school settings: Adaptive significance and implications for school-based prevention and intervention programs. In P. K. Smith & C. H. Hart (Eds.), *Blackwell handbook of childhood social development.* Madden, MA: Blackwell Publishers.

Ladd, G. W. & Hart, C. H. (1992). Creating informal play opportunities: Are parents' and preschoolers' initiations related to children's competence with peers? *Developmental Psychology, 28,* 1179–1187.

Ladd, G. W., Kochenderfer-Ladd, B., & Rydell, A.-M. (2011). Children's interpersonal skills and school-based relationships. In P. K. Smith & K. H. Hart (Eds.). *The Wiley-Blackwell handbook of childhood social development, 2nd edition* (pp. 181–206). Hoboken, NJ. Wiley.

Ladd, G. W. & Pettit, G. (2002). Parents' and children's peer relationships. In M. H. Bornstein (Ed.), *Handbook of parenting* (2nd ed., Vol. 5). Mahwah, NJ: Erlbaum.

LaFrance, M., Hecht, M. A., & Paluck, E. L. (2003). The contingent smile: A meta-analysis of sex differences in smiling. *Psychological Bulletin, 129,* 305–334.

LaFreniere, P., Masataka, N., Butovskaya, M., Chen, Q., Dessen, M. A., Atwanger, K., et al. (2002). Cross-cultural analysis of social competence and behavior problems in preschoolers. *Early Education and Development, 13,* 201–219.

Lagattuta, K. H. (2005). When you shouldn't do what you want to do: young children's understanding of desires, rules, and emotions. *Child Development, 76,* 713–733.

Lahey, B. B., Gordon, R. A., Loeber, R., Stouthamer Loeber, M., & Farrington, D. P. (1999). *Journal of Abnormal Child Psychology, 27,* 247–260.

Laible, D. J. & Thompson, R. A. (1998). Attachment and emotional understanding in preschool children. *Developmental Psychology, 34,* 1038–1045.

Laible, D. J. & Thompson, R. A. (2007). Early socialization: A relationship perspective. In J. E. Grusec & P. D. Hastings (Eds.), *Handbook of socialization: Theory and research* (pp. 181–207). New York: Guilford.

Laing, E., Butterworth, G., Ansari, D., Gsodl, M., Longhi, E., Panagiotaki, G., Peterson, S., et al. (2002). Atypical development of language and social communication in toddlers with Williams syndrome. *Developmental Science, 5,* 233–246.

Laing, G. J. & Logan, S. (1999). Patterns of unintentional injury in childhood and their relation to socio-economic factors. *Public Health, 113,* 291–294.

Lamaze, F. (1970). *Painless childbirth: Psychoprophylactic method.* Chicago: Henry Regnery.

Lamb, M. E. (2010). How *do* fathers influence children's development? Let me count the ways. In M. E. Lamb (Ed.), *The role of the father in child development* (5th edition, pp. 1–26). Hoboken, NJ: Wiley.

Lamb, M. E. & Lewis, C. (2010). The development and significance of father-child relationships in two-parent families. In M. E. Lamb (Ed.), *The role of the father in child development* (5th edition, pp. 94–153). Hoboken, NJ: Wiley.

Lamb, M. E. & Poole, D. A. (1998). *Investigative interviews of children: A guide for helping professionals.* Washington, DC: American Psychological Association.

Lamb, M. E., Sternberg, K., & Prodromidis, M. (1992). Nonmaternal care and the security of infant-mother attachment: A reanalysis of the data. *Infant Behavior and Development, 15,* 71–83.

Lamb, M. E., Thompson, R. A., & Frodi, A. M. (1982). Early social development. In R. Vasta (Ed.), *Strategies and techniques of child study.* New York: Academic Press.

Lamborn, S. D., Dornbusch, S. M., & Steinberg, L. (1996). Ethnicity and community context as moderators of the relation between family decision making and adolescent adjustment. *Child Development, 67,* 283–301.

LaMontagne, P. J. & Habib, R. (2010). Stimulus-driven incidental episodic retrieval involves activation of the left posterior parietal cortex. *Neuropsychologia, 48,* 3317–3322.

Lancy, D. F. (1996). *Playing on the mother ground: Cultural routines for children's development.* New York: Guilford.

Langer, O. (1990). Critical issues in diabetes and pregnancy. In I. R. Merkatz & J. E. Thompson (Eds.), *New perspectives on prenatal care.* New York: Elsevier.

Langer, W. L. (1974). Infanticide: A historical survey. *History of Childhood Quarterly, 1,* 353–365.

Langlois, J. H. & Downs, A. C. (1979). Peer relations as a function of physical attractiveness: The eye of the beholder or behavioral reality? *Child Development, 50,* 409–418.

Langlois, J. H., Kalakanis, L., Rubenstein, A. J., Larson, A., Hallam, M., & Smoot, M. (2000). Maxims or myths of beauty: A meta-analytic and theoretical review. *Psychological Bulletin, 126,* 390–423.

Langlois, J. H., Ritter, J. M., Casey, R. J., & Sawin, D. B. (1995). Infant attractiveness predicts maternal behaviors and attitudes. *Developmental Psychology, 31,* 464–472.

Langlois, J. H., Roggmana, L. A., Casey, R. J., Ritter, J. M., Reiser-Danner, L. A., & Jenkins, V. Y. (1987). Infant preference for attractive faces: Rudiments of a stereotype? *Developmental Psychology, 23,* 363–369.

Lanyon, L. J., Giaschi, D., Young, S. A., Fitzpatrick, K., Diao, L., Bjornson, B., & Barton, J. J. S. (2009). Combined function MRI and diffusion tensor imaging analysis of visual motion pathways. *Journal of Neuro-Ophthalmology, 29,* 96–103.

Lanza, E. (1997). *Language mixing in infant bilingualism: A sociolinguistic perspective.* Oxford: Oxford University Press.

Laplante, D. P., Barr, R. G., Brunet, A., Galbaud du Fort, G., Meaney, M., Saucier, J.-F., Zelazo, P., & King, S. (2004). Stress during pregnancy affects intellectual and linguistic functioning in human toddlers. *Pediatric Research, 56,* 400–410.

Lapsley, D. K. (2006). Moral stage theory. In M. Killen & J. G. Smetana (Eds.), *Handbook of moral development* (pp. 37–66). Mahwah, NJ: Lawrence Erlbaum.

Laranjo, J., Bernier, A., Meins, E., & Carlson, S. M. (2010). Early manifestations of children's theory of mind: The roles of maternal mind-mindedness and infant security of attachment. *Infancy, 15,* 300–323.

Largo, R. H., Molinari, L., Weber, M., Pinto, L. C., & Duc, G. (1985). Early development of locomotion: Significance of prematurity, cerebral palsy and sex. *Developmental Medicine and Child Neurology, 27,* 183–191.

Larson, R. W. & Verma, S. (1999). How children and adolescents spend time across the world: Work, play and developmental opportunities. *Psychological Bulletin, 125,* 701–736.

Laupta, M. & Turiel, E. (1993). Children's concepts of authority and social contexts. *Journal of Educational Psychology, 85,* 191–197.

Laursen, B., Finkelstein, B. D., & Betts, N. T. (2001). A developmental meta-analysis of peer conflict resolution. *Developmental Review, 21,* 423–449.

Laursen, B., Hartup, W. W., & Koplas, A. L. (1996). Towards understanding peer conflict. *Merrill-Palmer Quarterly, 42,* 76–102.

Laursen, B. & Purcell, G. (2009). Conflict in peer relationships. In K. H. Rubin, W. M. Bukowski, & B. Laursen (Eds.) *Handbook of peer interactions, relationships, and groups* (pp. 267–286). New York: Guilford.

Lave, J. & Wenger, E. (1991). *Situated learning: Legitimate peripheral participation.* New York: Cambridge University Press.

Lavelli, M. & Fogel, A. (2002). Developmental changes in mother-infant face-to-face communication: Birth to 3 months. *Developmental Psychology, 38,* 288–305.

Lavin, T. A., Hall, D. G., & Waxman, S. R. (2006). East and west: A role for culture in the acquisition of nouns and verbs. In K. Hirsch-Pasek & R. M. Golinkoff (Eds.), *Action meets word: How children learn verbs.* New York: Oxford University Press.

Le Grand, R., Mondloch, C. J., Maurer, D., & Brent, H. P. (2003). Expert face processing requires visual input to the right hemisphere during infancy. *Nature Neuroscience, 6,* 1108–1112.

Le Grand, R., Mondloch, C. J., Maurer, D., & Brent, H. P. (2004). Impairment in holistic face processing following early visual deprivation. *Psychological Science, 15,* 762–768.

Leadbeater, B. (2008). Engaging community champions in the prevention of bullying. In D. Pepler & W. Craig, (Eds.), *Understanding and addressing bullying: An international perspective,* PREVNet Series (Vol 1, pp.166–183). Bloomington, IN: AuthorHouse.

Leadbeater, B. (2010). The fickle fates of push and pull in the dissemination of mental health programs for children. *Canadian Psychology, 51,* 221–230.

Leadbeater, B. & Hoglund, W. (2006). Changing the social contexts of peer victimization. *Journal of the Canadian Academy of Child and Adolescent Psychiatry, 15,* 21–26.

Leadbeater, B. J. & Way, N. (2001). *Growing up fast: Transitions to early adulthood of inner-city adolescent mothers.* Mahwah, NJ: Erlbaum.

Leaper, C. (2002). Parenting girls and boys. In M. H. Bornstein (Ed.), *Handbook of parenting* (2nd ed., Vol. 1). Mahwah, NJ: Erlbaum.

Leaper, C., Anderson, K. J., & Sanders, P. (1998). Moderators of gender effects on parents' talk to their children: A meta-analysis. *Developmental Psychology, 34,* 3–27.

Leaper, C., Breed, L., Hoffman, L., & Perlman, C. A. (2002). Variations in the gender-stereotyped content of children's television cartoons across genres. *Journal of Applied Social Psychology, 32,* 1653–1662.

Leaper, C. & Friedman, C. K. (2007). The socialization of gender. In J. Grusec & P. Hastings (Eds.), *Handbook of socialization: Theory and research* (pp. 561–587). New York: Guilford.

Leaper, C. & Smith, T. E. (2004). A meta-analytic review of gender variations in children's language use: Talkativeness, affiliative speech, and assertive speech. *Developmental Psychology, 40,* 993–1027.

Lebra, T. S. (1976). *Japanese patterns of behavior.* Honolulu: University Press of Hawaii.

Lebra, T. S. (1994). Mother and child in Japanese socialization: A Japan-U.S. comparison. In P. M. Greenfield & R. R. Cocking (Eds.), *Cross-cultural roots of minority child development.* Hillsdale, NJ: Erlbaum.

Lecanuet, J.-P. (1998). Fetal responses to auditory and speech stimuli. In A. Slater (Ed.), *Perceptual development: Visual, auditory, and speech perception in infancy.* Hove, UK: Psychology Press.

Ledingham, J. E. (1981). Developmental patterns of aggressive and withdrawn behaviour in childhood: A possible method for identifying preschizophrenics. *Journal of Abnormal Child Psychology, 9,* 1–22.

Ledingham, J. E., Younger, A., Schwartzman, A., & Bergeron, G. (1982). Agreement among teacher, peer, and self rating of children's aggression, withdrawal, and likeability. *Journal of Abnormal Child Psychology, 10,* 363–372.

Lee, C., Barr, R. G., Catherine, N., & Wicks, A. (2007). Age-related incidence of publicly reported shaken baby syndrome cases: is crying a trigger for shaking? *Journal of Developmental and Behavioral Pediatrics, 28,* 288–293.

Lee, C. & Bates, J. E. (1985). Mother-child interaction at the age of two years and perceived difficult temperament. *Child Development, 56,* 1314–1325.

Lee, C. T., Brown, C. A., Hains, S. M. J., & Kisilevsky, B. S. (2007). Fetal development: Voice processing in normotensive and hypertensive pregnancies. *Biological Research for Nursing, 8,* 272–282.

Lee, D. N. & Aronson, E. (1974). Visual proprioceptive control of standing in human infants. *Perception and Psychophysics, 15,* 529–532.

Lee, V. E., Brooks-Gunn, J., Schnur, E., & Liaw, F.-R. (1990). Are Head Start effects sustained? A longitudinal follow-up comparison of disadvantaged children attending Head Start, no preschool, and other preschool programs. *Child Development, 61,* 495–507.

Lee, V. E., & Burkam, D. T. (2002). *Inequality at the starting gate: Social background differences in achievement as children begin school.* Washington, DC: Economic Policy Institute.

Leger, D. W., Thompson, R. A., Merritt, J. A., & Benz, J. J. (1996). Adult perception of emotion intensity in human infant cries: Effects of infant age and cry acoustics. *Child Development, 67,* 3238–3249.

Legerstee, M. (1991). The role of person and object in eliciting early imitation. *Journal of Experimental Child Psychology, 51,* 423–433.

Legerstee, M. (1994). Patterns of 4-month-old infant responses to hidden silent and sounding people and objects. *Early Development and Parenting 3,* 71–80.

Legerstee, M. (2005). Infants' sense of people: Precursors to a Theory of Mind. New York: Cambridge University Press.

Legerstee, M. & Markova, G. (2007). Intentions make a difference: Infant responses to still-face and modified still-face conditions. *Infant Behavior and Development, 30,* 232–250.

Legerstee, M., Markova, G., & Fisher, T. (2007). The role of maternal affect attunement in dyadic and triadic communication. *Infant Behavior and Development, 2,* 296–306.

Legerstee, M., Pasic, N., Barillas, Y & Fahy L. (2004). Social emotional development: The basis for mentalism. In S. Gallagher, S. Watson, P. LeBrun, & P. Romanski (Eds.), *Ipseity and alterity: Interdisciplinary approaches to intersubjectivity* (pp. 33–46). Rouen, France: Publications de l'Université de Rouen.

Legerstee, M. & Varghese, J. (2001). The role of maternal affect mirroring on social expectancies in three-month-old infants. *Child Development, 72,* 1301–1313.

Leiderman, P. H. & Seashore, M. J. (1975). Mother-infant separation: Some delayed consequences. In *Parent-infant interaction* (CIBA Foundation Symposium No. 33). New York: Elsevier.

Leinbach, M. D., Hort, B. E., & Fagot, B. I. (1997). Bears are for boys: Metaphorical associations in young children's gender stereotypes. *Cognitive Development, 12,* 107–130.

Leiter, M. P. (1977). A study of reciprocity in preschool play groups. *Child Development, 48,* 1288–1295.

Lemaire, P. & Callies, S. (2009). Children's strategies in complex arithmetic. *Journal of Experimental Child Psychology, 103,* 49–65.

Lemerise, E. A. & Dodge, K. A. (2008). The development of anger and hostile interactions. In M. Lewis, J. M. Haviland-Jones, & L. M. Barrett (Eds.), *Handbook of emotions,* 3rd edition (pp. 730–741). New York: Guilford.

Lemery, K. & Goldsmith, H. H. (1999). Genetically informative designs in the study of behavioral development. *International Journal of Behavioral Development, 23,* 293–317.

Lenneberg, E. H. (1967). *Biological foundations of language.* New York: Wiley.

Lenroot, R. K. & Giedd, J. N. (2006). Brain development in children and adolescents: Insights from anatomical magnetic resonance imaging. *Neuroscience and Biobehavioral Reviews, 30,* 718–29.

Leon, G. R. (1991). Bulimia nervosa in adolescence. In R. M. Lerner, A. C. Petersen, & J. Brooks-Gunn (Eds.), *Encyclopedia of adolescence.* New York: Garland.

Leppänen, J. M., Moulson, M. C., Vogel-Farley, V. K., & Nelson, C. A. (2007). An ERP study of emotional face processing in the adult and infant brain. *Child Development, 78*(1), 232–245.

Lepper, M. R., Greene, D., & Nisbett, R. E. (1973). Undermining children's intrinsic interest with extrinsic reward: A test of the "overjustification" hypothesis. *Journal of Personality and Social Psychology, 28,* 129–137.

Lerner, R. M. (1982). Children and adolescents as producers of their own development. *Developmental Review, 2,* 342–370.

Lerner, R. M., & Von Eye, A. (1992). Sociobiology and human development: Arguments and evidence. *Human Development, 35,* 12–33.

Lesko, N. (Ed.). (2000). *Masculinities at school.* London: Sage.

Lester, B. M. (1984). A biosocial model of infant crying. In L. P. Lipsitt (Ed.), *Advances in infancy research* (Vol. 3). Norwood, NJ: Ablex.

Lester, B. M. (2000). Prenatal cocaine exposure and child outcome: A model for the study of the infant at risk. *Israel Journal of Psychiatry and Related Sciences, 37,* 223–235.

Lester, B. M., Hoffman, J., & Brazelton, T. B. (1985). The rhythmic structure of mother-infant interaction in term and preterm infants. *Child Development, 56,* 15–27.

Lester, B. M. & Tronick, E. Z. (2001). Behavioral assessment scales: The NICU Network Neurobehavioral Scale, the Neonatal Behavioral Assessment Scale, and the Assessment of the Preterm Infant's Behavior. In L. T. Singer & P. S. Zeskind (Eds.), *Biobehavioralal assessment of the infant.* New York: Guilford.

Leung, E. H. L. & Rheingold, H. L. (1981). Development of pointing as a social gesture. *Developmental Psychology, 17,* 215–220.

Levin, I. & Druyan, S. (1993). When sociocognitive transaction among peers fails: The case of misconceptions in science. *Child Development, 63,* 1571–1591.

LeVine, R. A. (1988). Human parental care: Universal goals, cultural strategies, individual behavior. In R. A. LeVine, P. M. Miller, & M. M. West (Eds.), *New directions for child development: No. 40. Parental behavior in diverse societies.* San Francisco: Jossey-Bass.

LeVine, R. A., Dixon, S., LeVine, S., Richman, A., Leiderman, P. H., Keefer, C. H., et al. (1994). *Child care and culture: Lessons from Africa.* Cambridge: Cambridge University Press.

Levine, S. C., Huttenlocher, J., Taylor, A., & Langrock, A. (1999). Early sex differences in spatial skill. *Developmental Psychology, 35,* 940–949.

Levitt, M. J., Weber, R. A., Clark, M. C., & McDonnell, P. (1985). Reciprocity of exchange in toddler sharing behavior. *Developmental Psychology, 21,* 122–123.

Levitt, P. (2003). Structural and functional maturation of the developing primate brain. *Journal of Pediatrics, 143,* S35–S45.

Levy, G. D. & Fivush, R. (1993). Scripts and gender: A new approach for examining gender-role development. *Developmental Psychology, 13,* 126–146.

Lewis, C. C. (1995). *Educating hearts and minds: Reflections on Japanese preschool and elementary education.* Cambridge: Cambridge University Press.

Lewis, M. (1993a). Early socioemotional predictors of cognitive competence at 4 years. *Developmental Psychology, 29,* 1036–1045.

Lewis, M. (2000). The promise of dynamic systems approaches for an integrated account of human development. *Child Development, 71,* 36–43.

Lewis, M. (2008a). Self-conscious emotions: Embarrassment, pride, shame, and guilt. In M. Lewis, J. M. Haviland-Jones, & L. M. Barrett (Eds.), *Handbook of emotions,* 3rd edition (pp. 742–756). New York: Guilford.

Lewis, M. (2008b). The emergence of human emotions. In M. Lewis, J. M. Haviland-Jones, & L. M. Barrett (Eds.), *Handbook of emotions,* 3rd edition (pp. 304–319). New York: Guilford.

Lewis, M. (2011). The origins and uses of self-awarenesss or the mental representation of me. *Consciousness and Cognition, 20,* 120–129.

Lewis, M., Alessandri, S. M., & Sullivan, M. W. (1990). Violation of expectancy, loss of control, and anger expression in young infants. *Developmental Psychology, 26,* 745–751.

Lewis, M. & Michaelson, L. (1985). Faces as signs and symbols. In G. Zivin (Ed.), *Development of expressive behavior: Biological-environmental interaction.* New York: Academic Press.

Lewis, M. & Ramsey, D. S. (1997). Stress reactivity and self-recognition. *Child Development, 68,* 621–629.

Lewis, M. & Ramsay, D. S. (2004). Development of self-recognition, personal pronoun use, and pretend play during the 2nd year. *Child Development, 75,* 1821–1831.

Lewis, M. & Sullivan, M. (2005). The development of self-conscious emotions. In A. Elliot & C. Dweck (Eds.), *Handbook of competence and motivation* (pp. 185–201). New York: Guilford.

Lewis, T. L., Ellemberg, D., Maurer, D., Wilkinson, F., Wilson, H. R., Dirks, M., & Brent, H. P. (2002). Sensitivity to global form in glass patterns after early visual deprivation in humans. *Vision Research, 42,* 939–948.

Lewis, T. L., Maurer, D., & Brent, H. P. (1995). The development of grating acuity in children treated for unilateral or bilateral congenital cataract. *Investigative Ophtalmology & Visual Science, 36,* 2080–2095.

Lewkowicz, D. J. (2000). The development of temporal intersensory perception: An epigenetic systems/ limitations view. *Psychological Bulletin, 126,* 281–308.

Lewkowicz, D. J. (2010). Infant perception of audio-visual speech synchrony. *Developmental Psychology, 46*(1), 66–77.

Lewkowicz, D. J. & Turkewitz, G. (1981). Intersensory interaction in newborns: Modification of visual preferences following exposure to sound. *Child Development, 52,* 827–832.

Lewontin, R. (2000). *It ain't necessarily so: The dream of the human genome and other illusions.* New York: New York Review of Books.

Li, Q. (1999). Teachers' beliefs and gender differences in mathematics: A review. *Educational Research, 41,* 63–76.

Li, Q. (2007). New bottle but old wine: A research of cyberbullying in schools. *Computers in Human Behavior, 23,* 1777–1791.

Li, T. Q. & Wahlund, L. O. (2011). The search for neuroimaging biomarkers of Alzheimer's disease with advanced MRI techniques. *Acta Radiologica, 52,* 211–222.

Liben, L. S. (2006). Education for spatial thinking. In K. A. Renninger, I. E. Sigel, W. E. Damon, & R. M. Lerner (Eds.), *Handbook of child psychology Vol. 4: Child Psychology in Practice* (6th ed., pp. 197–247). Hoboken, NJ: Wiley.

Liben, L. S. & Bigler, R. (2002). The developmental course of gender differentiation: Conceptualizing, measuring, and evaluating constructs and pathways. *Monographs of the Society for Research in Child Development, 67* (2, Serial No. 269).

Liben, L. S. & Christensen, A. E. (2010). Spatial development. In U. Goswani (Ed.), *The Wiley-Blackwell handbook of childhood cognitive development* (pp. 446–472). Oxford, U.K.: Wiley-Blackwell.

Liben, L. S. & Signorella, M. L. (1993). Gender-schematic processing in children: The role of initial interpretations of stimuli. *Developmental Psychology, 29,* 141–149.

Lidz, C. & Elliott, J. G. (Eds.). (2000). *Dynamic assessment: Prevailing models and application.* New York: JAI Press.

Lidz, J. (2007). The abstract nature of syntactic representations: Consequences for a theory of learning. In E. Hoff & M. Shatz (Eds.), *Handbook of language development.* Blackwell: Oxford.

Lidz, J. (2010). Language learning and language universals. *Biolinguistics 4,* 201–217.

Liebert, R. M. (1984). What develops in moral development? In W. M. Kurtines & J. L. Gewirtz (Eds.), *Morality, moral behavior, and moral development.* New York: Wiley.

Liederman, J., Kantrowitz, L., & Flannery, K. (2008). Male vulnerability to reading disability is not likely to be a myth: A call for new data. *Journal of Learning Disabilities, 38,* 109–129.

Lillard, A., Pinkham, A. M., & Smith, E. (2011). Pretend play and cognitive development. In U. Goswami (Ed.), *The Wiley-Blackwell handbook of childhood cognitive development, second edition* (pp. 285–311). Chichester, UK: Blackwell Publishing Ltd.

Lindberg, M. A. (1980). Is knowledge base development a necessary and sufficient condition for memory development? *Journal of Experimental Child Psychology, 30,* 401–410.

Lindsey, E. W. & Mize, J. (2001). Contextual differences in parent-child play: Implications for children's gender role development. *Sex Roles, 44,* 155–176.

Lindsey, E. W., Mize, J., & Pettit, G. S. (1997). Differential play patterns of mothers and fathers of sons and daughters: Implications for children's gender role development. *Sex Roles, 37,* 643–661.

Linver, M. R., Martin, A., & Brooks-Gunn, J. (2004). Measuring infants' home environment: The IT-HOME for infants between birth and 12 months in four national data sets. *Parenting: Science and Practice, 4,* 115–137.

Lippé, S., Roy M. S., Perchet C., & Lassonde M. (2007). Electrophysiological markers of visuocortical development. *Cerebral Cortex, 17,* 100–107.

Lipscomb, T. J., McAllister, H. A., & Bregman, N. J. (1985). A developmental inquiry into the effects of multiple models on children's generosity. *Merrill-Palmer Quarterly, 31,* 335–344.

Lipsitt, L. P. (1990). Learning and memory in infants. *Merrill-Palmer Quarterly, 36,* 53–66.

Lipsitt, L. P. (1992). Discussion: The Bayley Scales of Infant Development: Issues of prediction and outcome revisited. In C. K. Rovee-Collier & L. P. Lipsitt (Eds.), *Advances in infancy research* (Vol. 7). Norwood, NJ: Ablex.

Lipsitt, L. P., Engen, T., & Kaye, H. (1963). Developmental changes in the olfactory threshold of the neonate. *Child Development, 34,* 371–376.

Lisonkova, S., Janssen, P. A., Sheps, S. B., Lee, S. K., & Dahlgren, L. (2010). The effect of maternal age on adverse birth outcomes: Does parity matter? *Journal of Obstetrics and Gynaecology in Canada, 32,* 541–548.

Liu, D., Sabbagh, M. A., Gehring, W. J. & Wellman, H. M. (2009) Neural correlates of children's theory of mind development. *Child Development, 80,* 318–326.

Liu, H. M., Kuhl, P. K., & Tsao, F. M. (2003). An association between mothers' speech clarity and infants' speech discrimination skills. *Developmental Science, 6,* F1-F10.

Liu, J. S. (2011). Molecular genetics of neuronal migration disorders. *Current Neurology and Neuroscience Reports, 11,* 171–178.

Lobel, M., Dunkel-Schetter, C., & Scrimshaw, S. C. M. (1992). Prenatal maternal stress and prematurity: A prospective study of socioeconomically disadvantaged women. *Health Psychology, 11*(1), 32–40.

Lochman, J. E. (2006). Translation of research into interventions. *International Journal of Behavioral Development, 30,* 31–38.

Lochman, J. E., Powell, N., Boxmeyer, C., Deming, A. M., & Young, L. (2007). Cognitive-behavior group therapy for angry and aggressive youth. In R. W. Christner, J. L. Stewart, & A. Freeman (Eds.), *Handbook of cognitive-behavior group therapy with children and adolescents: Specific settings and presenting problems* (pp. 333–348). New York: Routledge/Taylor & Francis.

Lochman, J. E., Powell, H. M. W., & Fitzgerald, D. P. (2006). Aggressive children: Cognitive-behavioral assessment and treatment. In P. C. Kendall (Ed.), *Child and Adolescent Therapy: Cognitive-Behavioral Procedures* (3rd ed., pp. 33–81). New York: Guilford.

Lochman, J. E. & Wells, K. C. (2004). The Coping Power Program for preadolescent aggressive boys and their parents: Outcome effects at the 1-year follow-up. *Journal of Consulting and Clinical Psychology, 72,* 571–578.

Locke, J. L. (1989). Babbling and early speech: Continuity and individual differences. *First Language, 9,* 191–206.

Locke, J. L. (1993). *The child 's path to spoken language.* Cambridge, MA: Harvard University Press.

Locke, J. L. & Pearson, D. M. (1990). Linguistic significance of babbling: Evidence from a tracheostomized infant. *Journal of Child Language, 17,* 1–16.

Lockman, J. J. & Adams, C. D. (2001). Going around transparent and grid-like barriers: Detour ability as a perception-action skill. *Developmental Science, 4,* 463–471.

Lockman, J. J. & McHale, J. P. (1989). Object manipulation in infancy: Developmental and contextual determinants. In J. J. Lockman & N. L. Hazen (Eds.), *Action in social context: Perspectives on early development.* New York: Plenum.

Loehlin, J. C. (1992). *Genes and environment in personality development.* Newbury Park, CA: Sage.

Loehlin, J. C. (2000). Group differences in intelligence. In R. J. Sternberg (Ed.), *Handbook of intelligence.* New York: Cambridge University Press.

Loenneker, T., Klaver, P., Bucher, K., Lichtensteiger, J., Imfeld, A., & Martin, E. (2011). Microstructural development: Organizational differences of the fiber architecture between children and adults in dorsal and ventral visual streams. *Human Brain Mapping, 32,* 935–946.

Lohmann, H., Tomasello, M., & Meyer, S. (2005). Linguistic communication and social understanding. In J. Wilde Astington & J. Baird (Eds.), *Why language matters for theory of mind* (pp. 245–265). New York: Oxford University Press.

Long, T. (2004). *Excessive crying in infancy.* London, UK: Whurr Publishers.

Lorenz, K. Z. (1937). The companion in the bird's world. *Auk, 54,* 245–273.

Lorenz, K. Z. (1950). Innate behaviour patterns. *Symposia for the Study of Experimental Biology, 4,* 211–268.

Lotem, A. & Winklerb, D. (2004) Can reinforcement learning explain variation in early infant crying? *Behavioral and Brain Sciences, 27,* 468.

Lott, B. & Maluso, D. (2001). Gender development: Social learning. In J. Worell (Ed.), *Encyclopedia of women and gender* (Vol. 1). San Diego, CA: Academic Press.

Lourenco, O. & Machado, A. (1996). In defense of Piaget's theory: A reply to 10 common criticisms. *Psychological Review, 103,* 143–164.

Luciana, M. & Nelson, C.A. (1998). The functional emergence of prefrontally-guided working memory systems in four- to eight-year-old children. *Neuropsychologia, 36,* 273–293.

Ludemann, P. M. (1991). Generalized discrimination of positive facial expressions by seven- and ten-month-old infants. *Child Development, 62,* 55–67.

Lundqvist, C. & Sabel, K.-G. (2000). Brief report: The Brazelton Neonatal Behavioral Assessment Scale detects differences among newborn infants of optimal health. *Journal of Pediatric Psychology, 25,* 577–582.

Luster, T. & Denbow, E. (1992). Home environment and maternal intelligence as predictors of verbal intelligence: A comparison of preschool and school-age children. *Merrill-Palmer Quarterly, 38,* 151–175.

Luthar, S. S., Cicchetti, D., & Becker, B. (2000). The construct of resilience: A critical evaluation and guidelines for future work. *Child Development, 71,* 543–562.

Lyon, T. D. & Flavell, J. H. (1993). Young children's understanding of forgetting over time. *Child Development, 64,* 789–800.

Lyons-Ruth, K., Bronfman, E., & Parsons, E. (1999). Maternal frightened, frightening, or atypical behavior and disorganized infant attachment patterns. In J. I. Vondra & D. Barnett (Eds.), Atypical attachment in infancy and early childhood among children at developmental risk. *Monographs of the Society for Research in Child Development, 64* (3, Serial No. 258).

Lyons-Ruth, K. & Jacobvitz, D. (2008). Attachment disorganization: Genetic factors, parenting contexts, and developmental transformation from infancy to adulthood. In J. Cassidy & P. R. Shaver (Eds.), *Handbook of attachment: Theory, research, and clinical applications (2nd edition)* (pp. 666–697). New York, NY: Guilford.

Lytton, H. (1977). Do parents create, or respond to, differences in twins? *Developmental Psychology, 13,* 456–459.

Lytton, H. (1980). *Parent-child interaction: The socialization process observed in twin and singleton families.* New York: Plenum.

Lytton, H. (2000). Toward a model of family-environmental and child-biological influences on development. *Developmental Review, 20,* 150–179.

M

MacCallum, F., Golombok, S., & Brinsden, P. (2007). Parenting and child development in families with a child conceived through embryo donation. *Journal of Family Psychology, 21,* 287–287.

Maccoby, E. E. (1998). *The two sexes: Growing up apart, coming together.* Cambridge, MA: Harvard University Press.

Maccoby, E. E. (2000a). Parenting and its effects on children: On reading and misreading behavior genetics. *Annual Review of Psychology, 51,* 1–27.

Maccoby, E. E. (2000b). Perspectives on gender development. *International Journal of Behavioral Development, 24,* 398–406.

Maccoby, E. E. (2002). Parenting effects: Issues and controversies. In J. G. Borkowski, S. L. Ramey, & M. Bristol-Power (Eds.), *Parenting and the child's world: Influences on academic, intellectual, and social-emotional development.* Mahwah, NJ: Erlbaum.

Maccoby, E. E. (2007). Historical overview of socialization research and theory. In J. E. Grusec & P. D. Hastings (Eds.), *Handbook of socialization: Theory and research* (pp. 13–41). New York: Guilford.

Maccoby, E. E. & Martin, J. A. (1983). Socialization in the context of the family: Parent-child interaction. In P. H. Mussen (Series Ed.) & E. M. Hetherington (Vol. Ed.), *Handbook of child psychology: Vol. 4. Socialization, personality, and social development* (4th ed.). New York: Wiley.

MacDonald, K. & Parke, R. D. (1986). Parent-child physical play: The effects of sex and age of children and parents. *Sex Roles, 15,* 367–378.

MacFarlane, A. (1975). Olfaction in the development of social preferences in the human neonate. In *Parent-infant interaction* (CIBA Foundation Symposium No. 33). Amsterdam: Elsevier.

Machado-Aranda, D., Adir, Y., Young, J. L., Briva, A,, Budinger, G. R., Yeldandi, A. V., Sznajder, J. I., Dean, D. A. (2005). Gene transfer of the Na+,K+-ATPase beta1 subunit using electroporation increases lung liquid clearance. *American Journal of Respiratory Critical Care Medicine, 171,* 204–211.

MacKay, D. F., Smith, G. C. S., Dobbie, R., & Pell, J. P. (2010). Gestational age at delivery and special educational need: Retrospective cohort study of 407,503 schoolchildren. *Proceedings of the Library of Science: Medicine, 7*(6): e1000289. doi:10.1371/journal.pmed.1000289

Macrae, K. A. (2003). Attachment in blind infants: A systematic investigation using Ainsworth's Strange Situation. *Dissertation Abstracts International: Section B: The Sciences and Engineering, 63,* 6121.

MacWhinney, B. (1987). The competition model. In B. MacWhinney (Ed.), *Mechanisms of language acquisition.* Hillsdale, NJ: Erlbaum.

MacWhinney, B. (2004). A multiple process solution to the logical problem of language acquisition. *Journal of Child Language, 31*(4), 883–914.

MacWhinney, B. & Bates, E. (1993). *The crosslinguistic study of sentence processing.* Cambridge: Cambridge University Press.

MacWhinney, B. & Chang, F. (1995). Connectionism and language learning. In C. A. Nelson (Ed.), *Minnesota symposia on child psychology: Vol. 28. Basic and applied perspectives on learning cognition, and development.* Mahwah, NJ: Erlbaum.

MacWhinney, B. & Leinbach, J. (1991). Implementations are not conceptualizations: Revising the verb learning model. *Cognition, 40,* 121–157.

Maddux, J. E. & Gosselin, J. T. (2003). Self-efficacy. In M. Leary & J. Tangney (Eds.), *Handbook of self and identity* (pp. 218–238). New York: Guilford.

Magnusson, D., Bergman, L. R., Rudiger, G., & Torestada, B. (Eds.). (1994). *Problems and methods in longitudinal research: Stability and change.* New York: Cambridge University Press.

Main, M. & Goldwyn, R. (1998). Adult attachment rating and classification systems. In M. Main (Ed.), *Assessing attachment through discourse, drawings, and reunion situations.* New York: Cambridge University Press.

Main, M. & Hesse, E. (1990). Parents' unresolved traumatic experiences are related to infant disorganized attachment status: Is frightened and/or frightening behavior the linking mechanism? In M. T. Greenberg & D. Cicchetti (Eds.), *Attachment in the preschool years.* Chicago: University of Chicago Press.

Main, M., Hesse, E., & Kaplan, M. (2005). Predictability of attachment behavior and representational processes at 1, 6, and 19 years of age. In K. E. Grossmann, K. Grossmann, & E. Waters (Eds.) *Attachment from infancy to adulthood: The major longitudinal studies.* New York: Guilford.

Main M., Kaplan, N., & Cassidy, J. (1985). Security in infancy, childhood and adulthood: A move to the level of representation. In I. Bretherton & E. Waters (Eds.), Growing points of attachment theory and research. *Monographs of the Society for Research in Child Development, 50* (1–2, Serial No. 209).

Majeres, R. L. (1999). Sex differences in phonological processes: Speeded matching and word reading. *Memory and Cognition, 27,* 246–253.

Malacova, E., Li, J., Blair, E., Mattes, E., de Klerk, N., & Stanley, F. (2009). Neighbourhood socioeconomic status and maternal factors at birth as moderators of the association between birth characteristics and school attainment: A population study of children attending government schools in Western Australia. *Journal of Epidemiology and Community Health, 63,* 842–849.

Malatesta, C. Z., Culver, C., Tesman, J. R., & Shepard, B. (1989). The development of emotion expression during the first two years of life. *Monographs of the Society for Research in Child Development, 54(1–2,* Serial No. 219).

Malatesta, C. Z., Grigoryev, P., Lamb, C., Albin, M., & Culver, C. (1986). Emotion socialization and expressive development in preterm and full term infants. *Child Development, 57,* 316–330.

Malina, R. M. (1990). Physical growth and performance during the transitional years (9–16). In R. Montemayor, G. R. Adams, & T. Gullotta (Eds.), *From childhood to adolescence: Vol. 2. Advances in adolescent development.* London: Sage.

Mandel, D., Kemler Nelson, D. G., & Jusczyk, P. W. (1996). Infants remember the order of words in a spoken sentence. *Cognitive Development, 11,* 181–196.

Mandler, J. M. (1998). Representation. In W. Damon (Series Ed.) & D. Kuhn & R. S. Siegler (Vol. Eds.), *Handbook of child psychology: Vol. 2. Cognition, perception, and language* (5th ed.). New York: Wiley.

Mandler, J. M. (2000). Perceptual and conceptual processes in infancy. *Journal of Cognition and Development, 1,* 3–36.

Mandler, J. M. (2004). *The foundations of mind: Origins of conceptual thought.* New York: Oxford University Press.

Mandoki, M. W., Summer, G. S., Hoffman, R. P., & Riconda, D. L. (1991). A review of Klinefelter's syndrome in children and adolescents. *Journal of the American Academy of Child and Adolescent Psychiatry, 30,* 167–172.

Mangelsdorf, S. C., Plunkett, J. W., Dedrick, C. F., Berlin, M., Meisels, S. J., McHale, J. L., et al. (1996). Attachment security in very low birth weight infants. *Developmental Psychology, 32,* 914–920.

Manke, B., Saudino, K. J., & Grant, J. D. (2001). Extreme analyses of observed temperament dimensions. In R. N. Emde & J. K. Hewitt (Eds.), *Infancy to early childhood.* New York: Oxford University Press.

Manning, J. T., Churchill, A. J. G., & Peters, M. (2007). The effects of sex, ethnicity, and sexual orientation on self-measured digit ratio (2D:4D). *Archives of Sexual Behaviour, 36,* 223–233.

Mannino, D. M., Moorman, J. E., Kingsley, B., Rose, D., & Repace, J. (2001). Health effects related to environmental tobacco smoke exposure in the United States. *Archives of Pediatric and Adolescent Medicine, 155,* 36–41.

Mannle, S. & Tomasello, M. (1987). Fathers, siblings, and the Bridge Hypothesis. In K. E. Nelson & A. VanKleeck (Eds.), *Children's language* (Vol. 6). Hillsdale, NJ: Erlbaum.

Mar, R. A., Tackett, J. L., & Moore, C. (2010). Exposure to media and theory-of-mind development in preschoolers. *Cognitive Development, 25,* 69–78.

Maratsos, M. (1976). *Language development: The acquisition of language structure.* Morristown, NJ: General Learning Press.

Maratsos, M. (1983). Some current issues in the study of the acquisition of grammar. In P. H. Mussen (Series Ed.) & J. H. Flavell & E. M. Markman (Vol. Eds.), *Handbook of child psychology: Vol. 3. Cognitive development* (4th ed.). New York: Wiley.

Maratsos, M. (1988). The acquisition of formal word classes. In Y. Levy, I. M. Schlesinger, & M. D. S. Braine (Eds.), *Categories and processes in language acquisition.* Hillsdale, NJ: Erlbaum.

Maratsos, M. (1998). The acquisition of grammar. In W. Damon (Series Ed.) & D. Kuhn & R. S. Siegler (Vol. Eds.), *Handbook of child psychology: Vol. 2. Cognition, perception, and language* (5th ed.). New York: Wiley.

Marcotte, D., Fortin, L., Potvin, P., & Papillon, M. (2002). Gender differences in depressive symptoms during adolescence: Role of gender-typed characteristics, self-esteem, body image, stressful life events, and pubertal status. *Journal of Emotional and Behavioral Disorders, 10,* 29–42.

Marcus, D. M. & Snodgrass, W. R. (2005). Do no harm: Avoidance of herbal medicines during pregnancy. *Obstetrics and Gynecolology, 105,* 1119–1922.

Marcus, G. F. (1996). Why do children say "breaked"? *Current Directions in Psychological Science, 5,* 81–85.

Marcus, G. F. (2001). *The algebraic mind: Integrating connectionism and cognitive science.* Cambridge, MA: MIT Press.

Marcus, G. F., Pinker, S., Ullman, M., Hollander, M., Rosen, T. J., & Xu, F. (1992). Over regularization in language acquisition. *Monographs of the Society for Research in Child Development, 57*(4, Serial No. 228).

Marcus, G. F., Vijayan, S., Bandi Rao, S., & Vishton, P. M. (1999). Rule-learning in seven-month-old infants. *Science, 283,* 77–80.

Mares, M. L., & Woodard, E. (2005). Positive effects of television on children's social interactions: A metaanalysis. *Media Psychology, 7,* 301–322.

Mareschal, D. (2010). Computational perspectives on cognitive development. WIREs: Cognitive Science, 1, 696–708.

Mareschal, D. & Johnson, S. P. (2002). Learning to perceive object unity: A connectionist account. *Developmental Science, 5,* 151–185.

Marino, R. A., Rodgers, C. K., Levy, R., & Munoz, D. P. (2008). Spatial relationships of visuomotor transformations in the superior colliculus map. *Journal of Neurophysiology, 100,* 2564–2576.

Marino, S., Ciurleo, R., Bramanti, P., Federico, A., & De Stefano, N. (2011). H-MR spectroscopy in traumatic brain injury. *Neurocritical Care, 14,* 127–133.

Markham, J. A. & Greenough, W. T. (2004). Experience-driven brain plasticity: Beyond the synapse. *Neuron Glia Biology, 1,* 351–363.

Markman, E. M. (1989). *Categorization and naming in children: Problems of induction.* Cambridge, MA: MIT Press.

Markman, E. M. (1991). The whole object, taxonomic, and mutual exclusivity assumptions as initial constraints on word meanings. In S. A. Gelman & J. P. Byrnes (Eds.), *Perspectives on language and thought: Interrelations in development.* Cambridge: Cambridge University Press.

Markman, E. M. & Wachtel, G. F. (1988). Children's use of mutual exclusivity to constrain the meanings of words. *Cognitive Psychology, 20,* 121–157.

Markus, H. R. & Kitayama, S. (1991). Culture and the self: Implications for cognition, emotion, and motivation. *Psychological Review, 98,* 224–253.

Markus, H. R. & Kitayama, S. (1994). A collective fear of the collective: Implications for selves and theories of selves. *Personality and Social Psychology Bulletin, 20,* 568–579.

Marlier, L. & Schaal, B. (2005). Human newborns prefer human milk: Conspecific milk odor is attractive without postnatal exposure. *Child Development, 76,* 155–168.

Marlier, L., Schaal, B., & Soussignan, R. (1998). Neonatal responsiveness to the odor of amniotic and lacteal fluids: A test of perinatal chemosensory continuity. *Child Development, 69,* 611–623.

Marsh, H. W., Barnes, J., Cairns, L., & Tidman, M. (1984). Self-Description Questionnaire: Age and sex effects in the structure and level of self-concept for preadolescent children. *Journal of Educational Psychology, 76,* 940–956.

Marsh, H. W., Craven, R. G., & Martin, A. J. (2006). What is the nature of self-esteem? Unidimensional and multidimensional perspectives. In M. Kernis (Ed.), *Self-esteem issues and answers: A sourcebook of current perspectives* (pp. 16–24). New York: Psychology Press.

Marsh, H. W., Ellis, L. A., & Craven, R. G. (2002). How do preschool children feel about themselves? Unraveling measurement and multidimensional self-concept structure. *Developmental Psychology, 38,* 376–393.

Marsh, H. W., Ellis, L. A., Parada, R. H., Richards, G., & Heubeck, B. G. (2005). A short version of the self description questionnaire II: Operationalizing criteria for short-form evaluation with new applications of confirmatory factor analyses. *Psychological Assessment, 17,* 81–102.

Marshall, K. (2006). *Converging gender roles.* Ottawa, ON: Statistics Canada — Catalogue no. 75-001-XIE.

Marsiglio, W., Amato, P., Day, R. D., & Lamb, M. E. (2000). Scholarship on fatherhood in the 1990s and beyond. *Journal of Marriage and the Family, 62,* 1173–1191.

Martin, C. L. (1989). Children's use of gender-related information in making social judgments. *Developmental Psychology, 25,* 80–88.

Martin, C. L., Ruble, D. N., & Szkrybalo, J. (2002). Cognitive theories of early gender development. *Psychological Bulletin, 128,* 903–933.

Martin, C. L. & Halverson, C. E. (1983). The effects of sex-typing schemas on young children's memory. *Child Development, 54,* 563–574.

Martin, C. L. & Little, J. K. (1990). The relation of gender understanding to children's sex-typed preferences and gender stereotypes. *Child Development, 61,* 1427–1439.

Martin, G. B. & Clark, R. D. (1982). Distress crying in neonates: Species and peer specificity. *Developmental Psychology, 18,* 3–9.

Martin, J. A., Park, M. M., & Sutton, P. D. (2002). Births: Preliminary data for 2001. *Centers for Disease Control: National Vital Statistics Reports, 50* (10).

Martino, S., Marconi, P., Tancini, B., Dolcetta, D., De Angelis, M.G., Montanucci, P., Bregola, G., Sandhoff, K., Bordignon, C., Emiliani, C., Manservigi, R., & Orlacchio, A. (2005). A direct gene transfer strategy via brain internal capsule reverses the biochemical defect in Tay-Sachs disease. *Human Molecular Genetics, 14,* 2113–2123.

Martorano, S. C. (1977). A developmental analysis of performance on Piaget's formal operational tasks. *Developmental Psychology, 13,* 666–672.

Martorell, R. (1984). Genetics, environment, and growth: Issues in the assessment of nutritional status. In A. Velasquez & H. Bourges (Eds.), *Genetic factors in nutrition.* Orlando, FL: Academic Press.

Marvin, R. S. & Britner, P. A. (2008). Normative development: The ontogeny of attachment. In J. Cassidy & P. R. Shaver (Eds.), *Handbook of attachment: Theory, research, and clinical applications (2nd edition)* (pp. 269–294). New York, NY: Guilford.

Masataka, N. (1993). Effects of contingent and noncontingent maternal stimulation on the social behavior of three- to four-month-old Japanese infants. *Journal of Child Language, 20,* 303–312.

Masataka, N. (1996). Perception of motherese in a signed language by 6-month-old deaf infants. *Developmental Psychology, 32,* 874–879.

Masataka, N. (1998). Perception of motherese in Japanese sign language by 6-month-old hearing infants. *Developmental Psychology, 34,* 241–246.

Masataka, N. (1999). Preference for infant-directed singing in 2-day-old infants of deaf parents. *Developmental Psychology, 35,* 1001–1005.

Massey, C. M. & Gelman, R. (1988). Preschoolers' ability to decide whether a photographed unfamiliar object can move itself. *Developmental Psychology 24,* 307–317.

Masten, A. S., Hubbard, J. J., Gest, S. D., Tellegen, A., Garmezy, N., & Ramiriez, M. (1999). Competence in the context of adversity: Pathways to resilience and maladaptation from childhood to late adolescence. *Development and Psychopathology, 11,* 143–169.

Masters, J. C. (1979). Modeling and labeling as integrated determinants of children's sex-typed imitative behavior. *Child Development, 50,* 364–371.

Masters, J. C. & Furman, W. (1981). Popularity, individual friendship selection, and specific peer interaction among children. *Developmental Psychology, 17,* 344–350.

Matheny, A. P. Jr. (1986). Stability and change of infant temperament: Contributions from infant, mother, and family environment. In G. Kohnstamm (Ed.), *Temperament discussed.* Berwyn, PA: Swets North America.

Matheny, A. P. Jr. (1989). Children's behavioral inhibition over age and across situations: Genetic similarity for a trait during change. *Journal of Personality, 57* (special issue), 215–235.

Mathews, G. (1996). The stuff of dreams, fading: Ikigai and "the Japanese self. " *Ethos, 24,* 718–747.

Mathews, T. J. & MacDorman, M. F. (2006) Infant mortality statistics from the 2003 period linked birth/infant death data set. *National Vital Statistics Report, 54,* 1–29.

Mathews, T. J., Menacker, F., & MacDorman, M. F. (2004). Infant mortality statistics from the 2002 period: Linked birth/infant death data set. *National Vital Statistics Reports, 53,* No. 10.

Mathiesen, K. S. & Tambs, K. (1999). The EAS Temperament Questionnaire-factor structure, age trends, reliability, and stability in a Norwegian sample. *Journal of Child Psychology and Psychiatry and Allied Disciplines, 40,* 431–439.

Maticka-Tyndale, E. (2001). Sexual health and Canadian youth: How do we measure up? *Canadian Journal of Human Sexuality, 10,* 1–17.

Matuga, J. M. (2003). Children's private speech during algorithmic and heuristic drawing tasks. *Contemporary Educational Psychology, 28,* 552–572.

Maurer, D. (1985). Infants' perception of facedness. In T. M. Field & N. A. Fox (Eds.), *Social perception in infants.* Norwood, NJ: Ablex.

Maurer, D., Ellemberg, D., & Lewis, T. L. (2006). Repeated measures of contrast sensitivity reveal limits to visual plasticity after early binocular deprivation in humans. *Neuropsychologica, 44,* 2104–2112.

Maurer, D. & Lewis, T. L. (2001). Visual acuity and spatial contrast sensitivity: Normal development and underlying mechanisms. In C. A. Nelson & M. Luciana (Eds.), *Handbook of developmental cognitive neuroscience.* Cambridge, MA: MIT Press.

Maurer, D., Lewis, T. L., & Mondloch, C. J. (2005). Missing sights: Consequences for visual cognitive development. *Trends in Cognitive Sciences, 9,* 144–151.

Maurer, D., Mondloch, C. J., & Lewis, T. L. (2007). Sleeper effects. *Developmental Science, 10,* 40–47.

Maurer, D. & Salapatek, P. (1976). Developmental changes in the scanning of faces by young infants. *Child Development, 47,* 523–527.

Maurer, D., Stager, C. L., & Mondloch, C. J. (1999). Cross-modal transfer of shape is difficult to demonstrate in one-month-olds. *Child Development, 70,* 1047–1057.

Maxson, S. C. & Canastar, A. (2007). The genetics of aggression in mice. In D. J. Flannery, A. T. Vazsonyi, & I. D. Waldman (Eds.), *The Cambridge handbook of violent behavior and aggression* (pp. 91–110). New York, NY: Cambridge University Press.

Mayer, N. K. & Tronick, E. Z. (1985). Mothers' turn-giving signals and infant turn-taking in mother-infant interaction. In T. M. Field & N. A. Fox (Eds.), *Social perception in infants.* Norwood, NJ: Ablex.

Mayes, L. C. & Fahy, T. (2001). Prenatal drug exposure and cognitive development. In R. J. Sternberg & E. L. Grigorenko (Eds.), *Environmental effects on cognitive abilities.* Mahwah, NJ: Erlbaum.

Maynard Smith, J. (1976). Group selection. *Quarterly Review of Biology, 51,* 277–283.

Mazroui, R., Huot, M. E., Tremblay, S., Filion, C., Labelle, Y., & Khandjian, E. (2002). Trapping of messenger RNA by Fragile X Mental Retardation protein into cytoplasmic granules induces translation repression. *Human Molecular Genetics, 11,* 3007–3017.

McCabe, A. E. (1989). Differential language learning styles in young children: The importance of context. *Developmental Review, 9,* 1–20.

McCall, R. B. (1981). Early predictors of later IQ: The search continues. *Intelligence, 5,* 141–148.

McCall, R. B., Applebaum, M. I., & Hogarty, P. S. (1973). Developmental changes in mental performance. *Monographs of the Society for Research in Child Development, 38* (3, Serial No. 150).

McCartney, K. (Ed.). (1990). *New directions for child development: No. 49. Child care and maternal employment: A social ecology approach.* San Francisco: Jossey-Bass.

McClelland, J. L. & Siegler, R. S. (Eds.). (2001). *Mechanisms of cognitive development.* Mahwah, NJ: Erlbaum.

McClelland, M. M., Ponitz, C. C., Messersmith, E. E., & Tominey, S. (2010). Self-regulation: Integration of cognition and emotion. In R. Lerner (Ed.) *Handbook of lifespan development, Vol.1 Cognition, biology, and methods,* (pp. 509–553). Hoboken, NJ: Wiley.

McCrae, R. R., Costa, P. T. Jr., Terracciano, A., Parker, W. D., Mills, C. J., De Fruyt, F., et al. (2002). Personality trait development from age 12 to age 18: Longitudinal, cross-sectional and cross-cultural analyses. *Journal of Personality and Social Psychology, 83,* 1456–1468.

McCune-Nicolich, L. (1981). The cognitive bases of relational words in the single word period. *Journal of Child Language, 8,* 15–34.

McDaniel, D., McKee, C., & Cairns, H. S. (Eds.). (1997). *Methods for assessing children's syntax.* Cambridge, MA: MIT Press.

McDougall, P., Hymel, S., Vaillancourt, T., & Mercer, L. (2001). The consequences of early peer rejection. In M. Leary (Ed.), *Interpersonal Rejection* (pp. 231–247). New York: Oxford University Press.

McDowell, D. J., O'Neil, R., & Parke, R. D. (2000). Display rule application in a disappointing situation and children's emotional reactivity. *Merrill-Palmer Quarterly, 46,* 306–324.

McElwain, N. L. & Volling, B. L. (2005). Preschool children's interactions with friends and older siblings: Relationship specificity and joint contributions to problem behavior. *Journal of Family Psychology, 19,* 486–496.

McFayden-Ketchum, S. A., Bates, J. E., Dodge, K. A., & Pettit, G. S. (1996). Patterns of change in early childhood aggressive-disruptive behavior: Gender differences in predictions from early coercive and affectionate mother-child interactions. *Child Development, 67,* 2417–2433.

McGillicuddy-De Lisi, A. V., Watkins, C., & Vinchur, A. J. (1994). The effect of relationship on children's distributive justice reasoning. *Child Development, 65,* 1694–1700.

McGraw, M. B. (1935). *Growth: A study of Johnny and Jimmy.* New York: Applet on Century-Crofts.

McGraw, M. B. (1940). Suspension grasp behavior of the human infant. *American Journal of the Disabled Child, 60,* 799–811.

McGue, M., Bouchard, T. J. Jr., Iacono, W. G., & Lykken, D. T (1993). Behavior genetics of cognitive ability: A life-span perspective. In R. Plomin & G. E. McClearn (Eds.), *Nature, nurture, and psychology.* Washington, DC: American Psychological Association.

McGue, M. & Lykken, D. T (1992). Genetic influences on risk of divorce. *Psychological Science, 3,* 368–373.

McGuiness, D. & Morley, C. (1991). Sex differences in the development of visuo-spatial ability in preschool children. *Journal of Mental Imagery, 15,* 143–150.

McHale, S. M., Crouter, A. C., & Whiteman, S. D. (2003). The family contexts of gender development in childhood and adolescence. *Social Development, 12,* 125–148.

McHale, S. M., Updegraff, K. A., Helms-Erikson, H., & Crouter, A. C. (2001). Sibling influences on gender development in middle childhood and early adolescence: A longitudinal study. *Developmental Psychology, 37,* 115–125.

McKenna, J. J. & Volpe, L. E. (2007). Sleeping with baby: An internet-based sampling of parental experiences, choices, perceptions, and interpretations in a Western industrialized context. *Infant and Child Development, 16,* 359–385.

McKenzie, M. J. & McDonough, S. C. (2009). Transactions between perception and reality: Maternal beliefs and infant regulatory behavior. In A. Sameroff (Ed.), *The transactional model of development: How children and contexts shape each other* (pp. 35–54). Washington, DC: American Psychological Association.

McKinnon, D. H., McLeod, S., & Reilly, S. (2007). The prevalence of stuttering, voice, and speech-sound disorders in primary school students in Australia. *Language, Speech, and Hearing Services in Schools, 38,* 5–15.

McLaughlin, B., White, D., McDevitt, T., & Raskin, R. (1983). Mothers' and fathers' speech to their young children: Similar or different? *Journal of Child Language, 10,* 245–252.

McLoyd, V. C., Aikens, N. L., & Burton, L. M. (2006). Childhood poverty, policy, and practice. In K. A. Reninger and I. E. Sigel (Eds.), *Handbook of child psychology,* 6th Edition, Volume 4: Child Psychology in Practice (pp. 700–775). Hoboken, NJ: John Wiley & Sons, Inc.

McManus, I. C. & Bryden, M. P. (1991). Geschwind's theory of cerebral lateralization: Developing a formal, causal model. *Psychological Bulletin, 110,* 237–253.

McNeill, D. (1992). *Hand and mind: What gestures reveal about thought.* Chicago: University of Chicago Press.

McPherson, S. L. & Thomas, J. R. (1989). Relation of knowledge and performance in boys' tennis: Age and expertise. *Journal of Experimental Child Psychology, 48,* 190–211.

Meadow, W., Lee, G., Lin, K., & Lantos, J. (2004). Changes in mortality for extremely low birth weight infants in the 1990s: Implications for treatment decisions and resource use. *Pediatrics, 113,* 1223–1229.

Mebert, C. J. (1989). Stability and change in parents' perceptions of infant temperament: Early pregnancy to 13.5 months postpartum. *Infant Behavior and Development, 2,* 237–244.

Mebert, C. J. (1991). Dimensions of subjectivity in parents' ratings of infant temperament. *Child Development, 62,* 352–361.

Medendorp, W. P., Goltz, H. C., Vilis, T., & Crawford, J. D. (2003). Gaze-centered updating of visual space in human parietal cortex. *The Journal of Neuroscience, 23,* 6209–6214.

Media Awareness Network (2005). *Young Canadians in a wired world-Phase II* (2005). Available at: www.media-awareness.ca/english/research/YCWW/phaseII/

Medoff-Cooper, B., Carey, W. B., & McDevitt, S. C. (1993). The Early Infancy Temperament Questionnaire. *Journal of Developmental and Behavioral Pediatrics, 14,* 230–235.

Medrich, E. A., Roizen, J. A., Rubin, V., & Buckley, S. (1982). *The serious business of growing up: A study of children's lives outside school.* Berkeley: University of California Press.

Meeuwissen, , E. B., Takashima, A., Fernandez, G., & Jensen, O. (2011). Evidence for human fronto-central gamma activity during long-term memory encoding of word sequences. *PLoS One, 6,* e21356.

Mehler, J., Bertoncine, J., Barriere, M., & Jassik Gershenfeld, D. (1978). Infant recognition of mother's voice. *Perception, 7,* 491–497.

Mehler, J., Jusczyk, P. W., Lambertz, G., Halsted, N., Bertoncini, J., & Amiel-Tison, C. (1988). A precursor of language acquisition in young infants. *Cognition, 29,* 143–178.

Meichenbaum, D. (1977). *Cognitive-behavior modification.* New York, NY: Plenum.

Meichenbaum, D. & Goodman, J. (1971). Training impulsive children to talk to themselves: A means of developing self-control. *Journal of Abnormal Psychology, 77,* 115–126.

Meichenbaum, D. & Goodman, S. (1979). Clinical use of private speech and critical questions about its study in natural settings. In G. Zivin (Ed.), *The development of self-regulation through private speech.* New York: Wiley.

Meins, E. (1997). Security of attachment and maternal tutoring strategies: Interaction within the zone of proximal development. *British Journal of Developmental Psychology, 15,* 129–144.

Meins, E., Fernyhough, C., Fradley, E., & Tuckey, M. (2001). Rethinking maternal sensitivity: Mothers' comments on infants' mental processes predict security of attachment at 12 months. *Journal of Child Psychology and Psychiatry, 42,* 637–648.

Meins, E., Fernyhough, C., Wainwright, R., Clark-Carter, D., Gupta, M., Fradley, E., & Tuckey, M. (2003). Pathways to understanding mind: Construct validity and predictive validity of maternal mind-mindedness. *Child Development, 74,* 1194–1211.

Meltzoff, A. N. (1995). Infants' understanding of people and things: From body imitation to folk psychology. In J. Bermudez, A. J. Marcel, & N. Eilan (Eds.), *The body and the self.* Cambridge, MA: MIT Press.

Meltzoff, A. N. (2002). Elements of a developmental theory of imitation. In A. N. Meltzoff and W. Prinz, *The imitative mind: Development, evolution, and brain bases, Cambridge studies in cognitive perceptual development* (pp. 19–41). New York: Cambridge University Press.

Meltzoff, A. N. (2011). Social cognition, and the origins of imitation, empathy, and theory of mind. In U. Goswami (Ed.), *The Wiley-Blackwell handbook of childhood cognitive development, second edition* (pp. 49–75). Chichester, UK: Blackwell Publishing Ltd.

Meltzoff, A. N. & Borton, R. W. (1979). Intermodal matching by human neonates. *Nature, 282,* 403–404.

Meltzoff, A. N. & Moore, M. K. (1977). Imitation of facial and manual gestures by human neonates. *Science, 198,* 75–78.

Meltzoff, A. N. & Moore, M. K. (1983). Newborn infants imitate adult facial gestures. *Child Development, 54,* 702–709.

Meltzoff, A. N. & Moore, M. K. (1989). Imitation in newborn infants: Exploring the range of gestures imitated and the underlying mechanisms. *Developmental Psychology, 25,* 954–962.

Meltzoff, A. N. & Moore, M. K. (1994). Imitation, memory, and the representation of persons. *Infant Behavior and Development, 17,* 83–99.

Meltzoff, A. N. & Moore, M. K. (1995). A theory of the role of imitation in the emergence of self. In P. Rochat (Ed.), *The self in infancy: Theory and research.* Amsterdam: Elsevier.

Meltzoff, A. N. & Moore, M. K. (1999a). A new foundation for cognitive development in infancy: The birth of the representational infant. In E. K.

Scholnick, K. Nelson, S. A. Gelman, & P. H. Miller (Eds.), *Conceptual development: Piaget's legacy.* Mahwah, NJ: Erlbaum.

Meltzoff, A. N. & Moore, M. K. (1999b). Persons and representation: Why infant imitation is important for theories of human development. In J. Nadel & G. Butterworth (Eds.), *Imitation in infancy.* Cambridge: Cambridge University Press.

Menacker, F., Declercq, E., and MacDorman, M. F. (2006). Cesarean delivery: Background, trends, and epidemiology. *Seminars in Perinatology, 30,* 235–241.

Menard, S. (2002). *Longitudinal research (2nd edition).* Newbury Park, CA: Sage.

Mendle, J., Harden, K.P., Brooks-Gunn, J., & Graber, J.A. (2010). Development's tortoise and hare: Pubertal timing, pubertal tempo, and depressive symptoms in boys and girls. *Developmental Psychology, 465,* 1341–1353.

Menella, J. A., Forestell, C. A., Morgan, L. K., & Beauchamp, G. K. (2009). Early milk feeding influences taste acceptance and liking during infancy. *The American Journal of Clinical Nutrition, 90,* 780S–788S.

Menig-Peterson, C. L. (1975). The modification of communicative behaviors in preschool-aged children as a function of the listener's perspective. *Child Development, 46,* 1015–1018.

Menn, L. & Ratner, N. B. (Eds.). (2000). *Methods for studying language production.* Mahwah, NJ: Erlbaum.

Mennella, J. A., Jagnow, C. P., & Beauchamp, G. K. (2001). Prenatal and postnatal flavor learning by human infants. *Pediatrics, 107,* 88–94.

Meredith, H. V. (1963). Change in the stature and body weight of North American boys during the last 80 years. In L. P. Lipsitt & C. C. Spiker (Eds.), *Advances in child development and behavior* (Vol. 1). New York: Academic Press.

Merriman, J., Rovee-Collier, C., & Wilk, A. (1997). Exemplar spacing and infants' memory for category information. *Infant Behavior and Development,* 20, 219–232.

Merriman, W. E. (1997). CALLED: A model of early word learning. In R. Vasta (Ed.), *Annals of child development* (Vol. 13). London: Kingsley.

Mervis, C. B. (1987). Child-basic object categories and early lexical development. In U. Neisser (Ed.), *Concepts and conceptual development: Ecological and intellectual factors in categorization.* New York: Cambridge University Press.

Mervis, C. B., Morris, C. A., Bertrand, J., & Robinson, B. F. (1999). Williams syndrome: Findings from an integrated program of research. In H. Tager-Flusberg (Ed.), *Neuro developmental disorders.* Cambridge, MA: MIT Press.

Meyer-Bahlburg, H. F. L., Ehrhardt, A. A., Rosen, L. R., Gruen, R. S., Veridiano, N. P., Vann, F. H., et al. (1995). Prenatal estrogens and the development of homosexual orientation. *Developmental Psychology, 31,* 12–21.

Meyer-Bahlburg, H. F., Dolezal, C., Baker, S. W., & New, M. I. (2008). Sexual orientation in women with classical or non-classical congenital adrenal hyperplasia as a function of degree of prenatal androgen excess. *Archives of Sexual Behavior, 37,* 85–99.

Michael, A. & Eccles, J. S. (2003). When coming of age means coming undone: Links between puberty and psychosocial adjustment among European American and African American girls. In C. Hayward (Ed.), *Gender differences at puberty* (pp. 277–303). New York: Cambridge University Press.

Midgett, J., Ryan, B. A., Adams, G. R., & Corville-Smith, J. (2002). Complicating achievement and self-esteem: Considering the joint effects of child characteristics and parent-child interactions. *Contemporary Educational Psychology, 27,* 132–143.

Mikulincer, M. & Shaver, P. R. (2007). *Attachment in adulthood: Structure, dynamics, & change.* New York: Guilford.

Mikulincer, M. & Shaver, P. R. (2010). Does gratitude promote prosocial behavior? The moderating role of attachment security. In M. Mikulincer & P. R. Shaver (Eds.), *Prosocial motives, emotions, and behavior: The better angels of our nature* (pp. 267–284). Washington, DC: American Psychological Association.

Miller, C. F., Trautner, H. M., & Ruble, D. N. (2006). The role of gender stereotypes in children's preferences and behavior. In L. Balter, & C. S. Tamis-LeMonda (Eds.), *Child psychology: A handbook of contemporary issues* (2nd ed., pp. 293–323). New York: Psychology Press.

Miller, J. G. (2006). Insights into moral development from cultural psychology. In M. Killen & J. G. Smetana (Eds.), *Handbook of moral development* (pp. 375–398). Mahwah, NJ: Erlbaum.

Miller, M. W. (1986). Effects of alcohol on the generation and migration of cerebral cortical neurons. *Science, 233,* 1308–1311.

Miller, P. H. (1990). The development of strategies of selective attention. In D. F. Bjorklund (Ed.), *Children's strategies: Contemporary views of cognitive development.* Hillsdale, NJ: Erlbaum.

Miller, P. H. (2000). How best to utilize a deficiency: A commentary on Waters' "Memory strategy development." *Child Development, 71,* 1013–1017.

Miller, P. H. (2001). *Theories of developmental psychology* (4th ed.). New York: Worth.

Miller, P. H. (2011). Piaget's theory: Past, present, and future. In U. Goswami (Ed.), *The Wiley-Blackwell handbook of childhood cognitive development, second edition* (pp. 649–672). Chichester, UK: Blackwell Publishing Ltd.

Miller, P. H., Blessing, J. S., & Schwartz, S. (2006). Gender differences in high-school students' views about science. *International Journal of Science Education, 28,* 363–381.

Miller, S. A. (1976). Nonverbal assessment of Piagetian concepts. *Psychological Bulletin, 83,* 405–430.

Miller, S. A. (1982). Cognitive development: A Piagetian perspective. In R. Vasta (Ed.), *Strategies and techniques of child study.* New York: Academic Press.

Miller, S. A. (1986). Certainty and necessity in the understanding of Piagetian concepts. *Developmental Psychology, 22,* 3–18.

Miller, S. A. (2000). Children's understanding of preexisting differences in knowledge and belief. *Developmental Review, 20,* 227–282.

Miller, S. A. (2007). *Developmental research methods* (3rd ed.). Thousand Oaks, CA: Sage.

Miller, S. A. & Brownell, CA. (1975). Peers, persuasion, and Piaget: Dyadic interaction between conservers and nonconservers. *Child Development, 46,* 992–997.

Miller, S. A. & Davis, T. L. (1992). Beliefs about children: A comparative study of mothers, teachers, peers, and self. *Child Development, 63,* 1251–1265.

Miller, S. A., Hardin, C. A., & Montgomery, D. E. (2003). Young children's understanding of the conditions for knowledge acquisition. *Journal of Cognition and Development, 4,* 325–356.

Mills, R. S. L. & Grusec, J. E. (1988). Socialization from the perspective of the parent-child relationship. In S. Duck (Ed.), *Handbook of personal relationships.* Chichester, England: Wiley.

Mills, R. S. L. & Grusec, J. E. (1989). Cognitive, affective, and behavioral consequences of praising altruism. *Merrill-Palmer Quarterly, 35,* 299–326.

Milner, A. D. & Goodale, M. A. (2008). Two visual systems re-viewed. *Neuropsychologia, 46,* 774–785.

Minde, K. (1993). Prematurity and illness in infancy: Implications for development and intervention. In C. H. Zeanah Jr. (Ed.), *Handbook of infant mental development.* New York: Guilford.

Minde, K. (2000). Prematurity and serious medical conditions in infancy: Implications for development, behavior, and intervention. In C. H. Zeanah Jr. (Ed.), *Handbook of infant mental health* (2nd ed.). New York: Guilford.

Mintz, T. H. (2003). Frequent frames as a cue for grammatical categories in child directed speech. *Cognition, 90(1),* 91–117.

Mirmiran, M., Maas, Y. G. H., and Ariagno, R. L. (2003). Development of fetal and neonatal sleep and circadian rhythms. *Sleep Medicine Reviews, 7,* 321–334.

Mischel, W. & Ayduk, O. (2004). Willpower in a cognitive-affective processing system: The dynamics of delay of gratification. In R. Baumeister & K. Vohs (Eds.), *Handbook of self-regulation: Research, theory, and applications* (pp. 99–129). New York: Guilford.

Mischel, W., Shoda, Y., & Peake, P. K. (1988). The nature of adolescent competencies predicted by preschool delay of gratification. *Journal of Personality and Social Psychology, 54,* 687–696.

Mischel, W., Shoda, Y., & Rodriguez, M. L. (1989). Delay of gratification in children. *Science, 244,* 933–938.

Mishna, F. & MacFadden, R. (2008). *Cyber bullying survey.* Unpublished research report, University of Toronto, Toronto, ON. Available at: http://www.governmentevents.ca/ypo2008/presentations/634.pdf. Accessed March 8, 2011.

Mishna, F., Saini, M., & Solomon, S. (2009). Ongoing and online: Children and youth's perceptions of cyber bullying. *Children and Youth Services Review, 31,* 1222–1228.

Mitchell, E. A. & Milerad, J. (2006). Smoking and sudden infant death syndrome. *Reviews on Environmental Health, 21,* 81–103.

Mitchell, J. J., Capua, A., Clow, C., & Scriver, C. R. (1996). Twenty-year outcome analysis of genetic screening programs for Tay-Sachs and β-thalassemia disease carriers in high schools. *American Journal of Human Genetics, 59,* 793–798.

Mitchell, R. W. (2003). Subjectivity and self-recognition in animals. In M. R. Leary & J. P. Tangney (Eds.), *Handbook of self and identity.* New York: Guilford.

Mitzenheim, P. (1985). The importance of Rousseau's developmental thinking for child psychology. In G. Eckardt, W. G. Bringman, & L. Sprung (Eds.), *Contributions to a history of developmental psychology.* Berlin: Mouton.

Mix, K., Huttenlocher, J., & Levine, S. C. (2002). Multiple cues for quantification in infancy: Is number one of them? *Psychological Bulletin, 128,* 278–294.

Miyake, K., Campos, J., Bradshaw, D., & Kagan, J. (1986). Issues in sociocemotional development. In H. Stevenson, H. Azuma, & K. Hakuta (Eds.), *Child development and education in Japan.* New York: Freeman.

Miyashita-Lin, E. M., Hevner, R., Wassarman, K. M., Martinez, S., & Rubenstein, J. L. R. (1999). Early neocortical regionalization in the absence of thalamic innervation. *Science, 285,* 906–909.

Miyawaki, K., Strange, W., Verbrugge, R., Liberman, A. M., Jenkins, J. J., & Fujimura, O. (1975). An effect of linguistic experience: The discrimination of the [r] and [l] by native speakers of Japanese and English. *Perception and Psychophysics, 18,* 331–340.

Mizokawa, A. & Koyasu, M. (2007). Young children's understanding of another's apparent crying and its relationship to theory of mind. *Psychologia, 50,* 291–307.

Modgil, S. & Modgil, C. (1976). *Piagetian research: Compilation and commentary* (Vols. 1–8). Windsor, England: NFER.

Moen, P., Elder, G. H., & Luscher, K. (Eds.). (1995). *Examining lives in context: Perspectives on the ecology of human development.* Washington, DC: American Psychological Association.

Moerk, E. L. (1996). Input and learning processes in first language acquisition. In H. W Reese (Ed.), *Advances in child development and behavior* (Vol. 26). San Diego, CA: Academic Press.

Moerk, E. L. (2000). *The guided acquisition of first language skills.* Stamford, CT: Ablex.

Moffitt, A. R. (1973). Intensity discrimination and cardiac reaction in young infants. *Developmental Psychology, 8,* 357–359.

Moffitt, T. E. (2005). The new look of behavioral genetics in developmental psychopathology: Gene-environment interplay in antisocial behaviors. *Psychological Bulletin, 131,* 533–554.

Moffitt, T. E. (2007). A review of research on the taxonomy of life-course persistent versus adolescence-limited antisocial behavior. In D. J. Flannery, A. T. Vazsonyi, & I. D. Waldman (Eds.), *The Cambridge handbook of violent behavior and aggression* (pp. 49–74). New York, NY: Cambridge University Press.

Molfese, D. L. & Molfese, V. J. (1979). Hemispheric and stimulus differences as reflected in the cortical responses of newborn infants to speech stimuli. *Developmental Psychology, 15,* 505–511.

Moll, H. & Tomasello, M. (2006). Level 1 perspective-taking at 24 months of age. *British Journal of Developmental Psychology, 24,* 603–613.

Moller, L. & Serbin, L. A. (1996). Antecedents of toddler gender segregation: Cognitive consonance, gender-typed toy preferences and behavioral compatibility. *Sex Roles, 35,* 445–460.

Mondloch, C. J., Le Grand, R., & Maurer, D. (2002). Configural face processing develops more slowly than featural face processing. *Perception, 31,* 553–566.

Mondloch, C. J., Le Grand, R., & Maurer, D. (2003). Early visual experience is necessary for the development of some – but not all – aspects of face processing. In O. Pascalis & A. Slater (Eds.), *The development of face processing in infancy and early childhood: Current perspectives* (pp. 99–117). New York: Nova Science Publishers.

Mondloch, C. J., Lewis, T. L., Budreau, D. R., Maurer, D., Dannemiller, J. L., Stephens, B. R., & Kleiner-Gathercoal, K. A. (1999). Face perception during early infancy. *Psychological Science, 10, 419–422.*

Mondschein, E. R., Adolph, K. E., & Tamis-LeMonda, C. S. (2000). Gender bias in mothers' expectations about infant crawling. *Journal of Experimental Child Psychology, 77,* 304–316.

Money, D. & Steben, M. (2008). Guidelines for the management of herpes simplex virus in pregnancy. *Journal of Obstetrics and Gynaecology in Canada, 30,* 514–519.

Money, J. C. (1975). Ablatio penis: Normal male infant sex-reassigned as a girl. *Archives of Sexual Behavior, 4,* 65–71.

Money, J. C. & Annecillo, C. (1987). Crucial period effect in psychoendocrinology: Two syndromes, abuse dwarfism and female (CVAH) hermaphroditism. In M. H. Bornstein (Ed.), *Sensitive periods in development: Interdisciplinary perspectives.* Hillsdale, NJ: Erlbaum.

Money, J. C. & Ehrhardt, A. A. (1972). *Man and woman, boy and girl.* Baltimore: Johns Hopkins University Press.

Montgomery, D. E. (1993). Young children's understanding of interpretive diversity between different-age listeners. *Developmental Psychology, 29,* 337–345.

Monzo, L. & Rueda, R. (2006). A sociocultural perspective on acculturation: Latino immigrant families negotiating diverse discipline practices. *Education and Urban Society, 38,* 188–203.

Moon, C., Cooper, R. P., & Fifer, W. P. (1993). Two-day-olds prefer their native language. *Infant Behavior and Development, 16,* 495–500.

Moore, B. S. & Eisenberg, N. (1984). The development of altruism. In G. J. Whitehurst (Ed.), *Annals of child development* (Vol. 1). Greenwich, CT: JAI Press.

Moore, C. & Corkum, V. (1994). Social understanding at the end of the first year of life. *Developmental Review, 14,* 349–372.

Moore, C. & Lemmon, K. (Eds.). (2001). *The self in time: Developmental perspectives.* Mahwah, NJ: Erlbaum.

Moore, D. S. & Johnson, S. P. (2008). Mental rotation in human infants: A sex difference. *Psychological Science, 19,* 1063–1066.

Moore, K. L. (1989). *Before we are born* (Third Edition). Philadelphia: Saunders.

Moore, M. R. & Brooks-Gunn, J. (2002). Adolescent parenthood. In M.Bornstein (Ed.), *Handbook of parenting: Vol. 3: Being and becoming a parent* (2nd ed., pp. 173–214). Mahwah, NJ: Lawrence Erlbaum.

Moore, R. R. (2011). *Mothers' responses to children's negative emotions and their effects on emotion regulation.* Unpublished doctoral dissertation, School of Psychology, University of Ottawa. Ottawa, ON.

Moran, S. & Gardner, H. (2006). Extraordinary achievements: A developmental and systems analysis. In W. Damon & R. M. Lerner (Series Eds.) & D. Kuhn & R. S. Siegler (Vol. Eds.), *Handbook of child psychology: Vol. 2. Cognition, perception, and language* (6th ed.) (pp. 906–949). Hoboken, NJ: Wiley.

Morell, V. (1993). The puzzle of the triple repeats. *Science, 260,* 1422–1423.

Morelli, G., Rogoff, B., Oppenheim, D., & Goldsmith, D. (1992). Cultural variations in infants' sleeping arrangements: Questions of independence. *Developmental Psychology, 28,* 604–613.

Morgan, J. L., Bonamo, K. M., & Travis, L. L. (1995). Negative evidence on negative evidence. *Developmental Psychology, 31,* 180–197.

Morgan, M. (2005). *The midbrain.* Infobase Publishing.

Morgane, P. J., Austin-LaFrance, R., Bronzino, J., Tonkiss, J., Diaz-Cintra, S., Cintra, L., et al. (1993). Prenatal malnutrition and development of the brain. *Neuroscience and Biobehavioral Reviews, 17,* 91–128.

Morin, A. (2004). A neurocognitive and socioecological model of self-awareness. *Genetic, Social, & General Psychology Monographs, 130,* 197–202.

Moro, E. (1918). Daserste Trimenon. *Munch. med. Wschr, 65,* 1147–1150.

Morra, S., Gobbo, C., Marini, Z., & Sheese, R. (2008). Cognitive development: Neo-Piagetian perspectives. New York, NY: Taylor & Francis Group/Lawrence Erlbaum Associates.

Morrison, F. J., Griffith, E. M., & Alberts, D. M. (1997). Nature-nurture in the classroom: Entrance age, school readiness, and learning in children. *Developmental Psychology, 33,* 254–262.

Morrison, F. J., Smith, L., & Dow-Ehrensberger, M. (1995). Education and cognitive development. A natural experiment. *Developmental Psychology, 31,* 789–799.

Morrone, M. C., Burr, D. C., & Florentini, A. (1993). Development of infant contrast sensitivity to chromatic stimuli. *Vision Research, 33,* 2535–2552.

Morrongiello, B. A. (1988). Infants' localization of sounds along two spatial dimensions: Horizontal and vertical *axes. Infant Behavior and Development, 11,* 127–143.

Morrongiello, B. A. (1994). Effects of colocation on auditory-visual interactions and cross-modal perception in infants. In D. J. Lewkowicz & R. Lickliter (Eds.), *The development of intersensory perception: Comparative perspectives.* Hillsdale, NJ: Erlbaum.

Morrongiello, B. A., Fenwick, K. D., Hiller, L., & Chance, G. (1994a). Sound localization in newborn human infants. *Developmental Psychobiology, 27,* 519–538.

Morrongiello, B. A., Humphrey, G. K., Timney, B., & Choi, J. (1994b). Tactual object exploration and recognition in blind and sighted children. *Perception, 23,* 833–848.

Moses, P., Roe, K., Buxton, R., Wong, E., Frank, L., & Stiles, J. (2002). Functional MRI of global and local processing in children. *NeuroImage, 16,* 415–424.

Moshman, D. (1998). Cognitive development beyond childhood. In D. Kuhn & R. S. Siegler (Vol. Eds.) & W. Damon (Series Ed.), *Handbook of child psychology: Vol. 2. Cognition, perception, and language* (5th ed.). New York: Wiley.

Moskowitz, D. S. & Schwartzman, A. E. (1989). Painting group portraits: Studying life outcomes for aggressive and withdrawn children. *Journal of Personality, 57,* 723–746.

Moss, E., Bureau, J., Cyr, C., & Dubois-Comtois, K. (2006). Is the maternal Q-Set a valid measure of preschool child attachment behavior? *International Journal of Behavioral Development, 30,* 488–497.

Moss, E., Bureau, J.-F., St-Laurent, D., & Tarabulsy, G. (2011). Understanding disorganized attachment at preschool and school age: Examining divergent pathways of disorganized and controlling children. In J. Solomon, J. & C. George (Eds.), *Disorganized attachment and caregiving* (in press). New York, NY: Guilford.

Moss, E., Cyr, C., & Dubois-Comtois, K. (2004). Attachment in early school-age and developmental risk: Examining family contexts and behavior problems of controlling-caregiving, controlling-punitive and behaviorally-disorganized children. *Developmental Psychology,40,* 519–532.

Moss, E., Smolla, N., Cyr, C., Dubois-Comtois, K., Mazzarello, T., & Berthiaume, C. (2006). Attachment and behavior problems in middle childhood as reported by adult and child informants. *Development and Psychopathology, 18,* 425–444.

Moss, E. & St-Laurent, D. (2001). Attachment at school age and academic performance. *Developmental Psychology, 37,* 863–874.

Mounteer, C. A. (1987). Roman childhood, 200 B.C. to A.D. 600. *Journal of Psychohistory, 14,* 233–254.

Mounts, N. S. & Steinberg, L. (1995). An ecological analysis of peer influence on adolescent grade point average and drug use. *Developmental Psychology, 31,* 915–922.

Mrzljak, L., Uylings, H. B., van Eden, C. G., & Judas, M. (1990). Neuronal development in human prefrontal cortex in prenatal and postnatal stages. *Progress in Brain Research, 85,* 185–222.

Mueller, C. (1996). Multidisciplinary research of multimodal stimulation of premature infants: An integrative review of the literature. *Maternal-Child Nursing Journal, 24,* 18–31.

Mueller, W. H. (1986). The genetics of size and shape in children and adults. In F. Falkner & J. M. Tanner (Eds.), *Human growth: A comprehensive treatise* (2nd ed., Vol. 3). New York: Plenum.

Muir, D. & Clifton, R. K. (1985). Infants' orientation to the location of sound sources. In G. Gottlieb & N. A. Krasnegor (Eds.), *Measurement of audition and vision in the first year of postnatal life: A methodological overview.* Norwood, NJ: Ablex.

Muir, D. & Hains, S. (2004). The U-shaped developmental function for auditory localization. *Journal of Cognition and Development, 5,* 123–130.

Müller, U., Carpendale, J. I. M., & Smith, L. (2009). *The Cambridge companion to Piaget.* New York, NY: Cambridge University Press.

Müller, U., Jacques, S., Brocki, K., & Zelazo, P. D. (2009). The executive functions of language in preschool children. In A. Winsler, C. Fernyhough, & I. Montero (Eds.), *Private speech, executive functioning, and the development of verbal self-regulation* (pp. 1–41). New York, NY: Cambridge University Press.

Mumme, D. L., Fernald, A., & Herrera, C. (1996). Infants' responses to facial and vocal emotional signals in a social referencing paradigm. *Child Development, 67,* 3219–3237.

Munakata, Y. (1998). Infant perseveration and implications for object permanence theories: A PDP model of the AB task. *Developmental Science, 1,* 161–184.

Munakata, Y. (2006). Information processing approaches to development. In W. Damon & R. M. Lerner (Series Eds.) & K. Dunn & R. S. Siegler (Volume Eds.), *Handbook of child psychology* (6th ed., Vol. 2, pp. 426–463). Hoboken, NJ: Wiley.

Munakata, Y., McClelland, J. L., Johnson, M. H., & Siegler, R. S. (1997). Rethinking infant knowledge: Toward an adaptive process account of successes and failures in object permanence tasks. *Psychological Review, 104,* 686–713.

Mundy, P., Block, J., Delgado, C., Pomares, Y., Van Hecke, A. V. & Parlade, M. V. (2007). Individual differences and the development of infant joint attention. *Child Development, 78,* 938–954.

Munroe, R. H., Shimmin, H. S., & Munroe, R. L. (1984). Gender understanding and sex role preference in four cultures. *Developmental Psychology, 20,* 673–682.

Murata, A., Gallese, V., Luppino, G., Kaseda, M., & Sakata, H. (2000). Selectivity for the shape, size, and orientation of objects for grasping in neurons of monkey parietal area AIP. *Journal of Neurophysiology, 83,* 2580–2601.

Murata, P. J., McGlynn, E. A., Siu, A. L., & Brook, R. H. (1992). *Prenatal care.* Santa Monica, CA: Rand.

Murphey, D. A. (1992). Constructing the child: Relations between parents' beliefs and child outcomes. *Developmental Review, 12,* 199–232.

Murphy, K., McKone, E., & Slee, J. (2003). Dissociations between implicit and explicit memory in children: The role of strategic processing and the knowledge base. *Journal of Experimental Child Psychology,* 84, 124–165.

Murray, A. D., Johnson, J., & Peters, J. (1990). Fine-tuning of utterance length to preverbal infants: Effects on later language development. *Journal of Child Language, 17,* 511–525.

Murray, C. & Golombok, S. (2005). Solo mothers and their donor insemination infants: Follow-up at age 2 years. *Human Reproduction, 20,* 1655–1660.

Murray, F. B. (1982). Learning and development through social interaction and conflict: A challenge to social learning theory. In L. Liben (Ed.), *Piaget and the foundation of knowledge.* Hillsdale, NJ: Erlbaum.

Murray-Close, D., Ostrov, J. M., & Crick, N. R. (2007). A short-term longitudinal study of growth of relational aggression during middle childhood: Associations with gender, friendship intimacy, and internalizing problems. *Development and Psychopathology 19,* 187–203.

N

Nader, R., Job, E., Badali, M., & Craig, K. (2004). Infant crying in context. *Behavioral and Brain Sciences, 27,* 469–470.

Naeye, R. L., Diener, M. M., & Dellinger, W. S. (1969). Urban poverty: Effects on prenatal nutrition. *Science, 166,* 1026.

Nagy, E. & Molnar, P. (2004). Homo imitans or homo provocans? Human imprinting model of neonatal imitation. *Infant Behavior and Development, 27,* 54–63.

Naigles, L. G. & Gelman, S. A. (1995). Overextensions in comprehension and production revisited: Preferential-looking in a study of dog, cat, and cow. *Journal of Child Language, 22,* 19–46.

Namy, L. L. & Waxman, S. R. (1998). Words and gestures: Infants' interpretations of different forms of symbolic reference. *Child Development, 69,* 295–308.

National Center for Biotechnology Information (2003). *Human genome project information.* Downloaded on September 28, 2010 from http://www.ornl.gov/sci/techresources/Human_Genome/posters/chromosome/faqs.shtml

National Center for Education Statistics. (1997). *Digest of education statistics 1997* (NCES 98–015). Washington, DC: U.S. Department of Education.

National Research Council (2001). *Eager to learn: Educating our preschoolers.* Committee on Early Childhood Pedagogy, B. T. Bowman, M. S. Donovan, & M. S. Burns (Eds.). Commission on Behavioral and Social Sciences and Education. Washington, DC: National Academy Press.

National Research Council, and Institute of Medicine. (2000). *From neurons to neighborhoods: The science of early childhood development.* J. P. Shonkoff & D. A. Phillips (Eds.). Washington, DC: National Academy Press.

Nazzi, T. (2005). Use of phonetic specificity during the acquisition of new words: Differences between consonants and vowels. *Cognition, 98(1),* 13–30.

Nazzi, T. & Ramus, F. (2003). Perception and acquisition of linguistic rhythm by infants. *Speech Communication 41*(1–2), 233–243.

Needham, A., Dueker, G., & Lockhead, G. (2005). Infants' formation and use of categories to segregate objects. *Cognition, 94,* 215–240.

Needham, J. (1959). *A history of embryology.* Cambridge: Cambridge University Press.

Needleman, H. L., Schell, A. S., Bellinger, D., Leviton, A., & Alldred, E. N. (1990). The long-term effects of exposure to low doses of lead in childhood: An 11-year follow-up report. *New England Journal of Medicine, 322,* 83.

Neiderhiser, J. M., Reiss, D., Hetherington, E. M., & Plomin, R. (1999). Relationships between parenting and adolescent adjustment over time: Genetic and environmental contributions. *Developmental Psychology, 35,* 680–692.

Neilsen, M. & Dissanayake, C. (2004). Pretend play mirror self-recognition and imitation: A longitudinal investigation through the second year. *Infant Behavior & Development, 27,* 342–365.

Neisser, U., Boodoo, G., Bouchard, T. J. Jr., Boykin, A. W., Brody, N., Ceci, S. J., et al. (1996). Intelligence: Knowns and unknowns. *American Psychologist, 51,* 77–101.

Nelson, C. A. (1987). The recognition of facial expressions in the first two years of life: Mechanisms of development. *Child Development, 58,* 889–909.

Nelson, C. A. (2006). Neural bases of cognitive development. In D. Kuhn and R. S. Siegler (Eds.), *Handbook of child psychology,* 6th ed., Volume 2: Cognition perception, and language (pp. 3–57). Hoboken, NJ: Wiley.

Nelson, C. A. & Luciana, M. (2008). *Handbook of developmental cognitive neuroscience (2nd ed.).* Cambridge, MA: MIT Press.

Nelson, C. A., Thomas, K. M., & de Haan, M. (2006). Neural bases of cognitive development. In W. Damon, R. Lerner, D. Kuhn, & R. Siegler (Vol. Eds.), *Handbook of child psychology: Vol. 2. Cognition, perception, and language* (6th. ed., pp. 3–57). New York: Wiley.

Nelson, E. A. S., Schiefenhoevel, W., & Haimerl, F. (2000). Child care practices in nonindustrialized societies. *Pediatrics, 105,* e75.

Nelson, K. (1973). Structure and strategy in learning to talk. *Monographs of the Society for Research in Child Development, 38(1–2,* Serial No. 149).

Nelson, K. (1985). *Making sense: The acquisition of shared meaning.* Orlando, FL: Academic Press.

Nelson, K., Hampson, J., & Shaw, L. K. (1993). Nouns in early lexicons: Evidence, explanations, and implications. *Journal of Child Language, 20,* 61–84.

Nelson, M. & Finch, A. (2000). Managing anger in youth: A cognitive-behavioral intervention approach. In P. Kendall (Ed.), *Child and Adolescent Therapy* (pp. 129–170). New York: Guilford.

Nelson, S. A. (1980). Factors influencing young children's use of motives and outcomes as moral criteria. *Child Development, 51,* 823–829.

Nelson, W. M., Finch, A. J., & Cash, A. G. (2006). Anger management with children and adolescents: Cognitive-behavioral therapy. In P. C. Kendall (Ed.), *Child and Adolescent Therapy: Cognitive-Behavioral Procedures* (3rd ed., pp. 114–165). New York: Guilford.

Nesdale, D. & Flesser, D. (2001). Social identity and the development of children's group attitudes. *Child Development, 72,* 506–517.

Neves, G., Cooke, S. F., & Bliss, T. V. P. (2008). Synaptic plasticity, memory and the hippocampus: A neural network approach to causality. *Nature Reviews Neuroscience, 9,* 65–75.

Neville, H. (2007). *Experience shapes human brain development and function.* Invited Address at the Biennial Meeting of the Society for Research in Child Development, Boston, MA.

Newcomb, A. F. & Bagwell, C. L. (1995). Children's friendship relations: A meta-analytic review. *Psychological Bulletin, 117,* 306–347.

Newcomb, A. F., Bukowski, W. M., & Pattee, L. (1993). Children's peer relations: A meta-analytic review of popular, rejected, neglected, controversial, and average sociometric status. *Psychological Bulletin, 113,* 99–128.

Newcombe, N. S. (2002). The nativist-empiricist controversy in the context of recent research on spatial and quantitative development. *Psychological Science, 13,* 395–402.

Newcombe, N. S., Drummey, A. B., Fox, N. A., Lie, E., & Ottinger-Alberts, W. (2000). Remembering early childhood: How much, how, and why (or why not). *Current Directions in Psychological Science, 9,* 55–58.

Newcombe, N. S., Mathason, L., & Terlecki, M. (2002). Maximization of spatial competence: More important than finding the cause of sex differences. In A. V. McGillicuddy-De Lisi & R. De Lisi (Eds.), *Biology, society, and behavior: The development of sex differences in cognition.* Greenwich, CT: Ablex.

Newman, D. L., Caspi, A., Moffitt, T. E., & Silva, P. A. (1997). Antecedents of adult interpersonal functioning: Effects of individual differences in age 3 temperament. *Developmental Psychology, 33,* 206–217.

Newman, G. E., Choi, H., Wynn, K., & Scholl, B. J. (2008). The origins of causal perception: Evidence from postdictive processing in infancy. *Cognitive Psychology, 57,* 262–291.

Newman, P. R. (1982). The peer group. In B. B. Wolman (Ed.), *Handbook of developmental psychology.* Engelwood Cliffs, NJ: Prentice Hall.

Newport, E. L. (1990). Maturational constraints on language learning. *Cognitive Science, 14,* 11–28.

Newport, E. L. (1991). Contrasting concepts of the critical period for language. In S. Carey & R. Gelman (Eds.), *The epigenesis of mind: Essays on biology and cognition.* Hillsdale, NJ: Erlbaum.

Nguyen, H.-H. D. & Ryan, A. M. (2008). Does stereotype threat affect test performance of minorities and women? A meta-analysis of experimental evidence. *Journal of Applied Psychology, 93,* 1314–1334.

Niccols, A. (2007). Fetal alcohol syndrome and the developing socio-emotional brain. *Brain and Cognition, 65,* 135–142.

NICHD Early Child Care Research Network. (1999). Child care and mother-child interaction in the first three years of life. *Developmental Psychology, 35,* 1399–1413.

NICHD Early Child Care Research Network. (2001). Child care and children's peer interaction at 24 and 36 months: The NICHD Study of Early Child Care. *Child Development, 72,* 1478–1500.

NICHD Early Child Care Research Network. (2002). Early child care and children's development prior to school entry: Results from the NICHD Study of Early Child Care. *American Educational Research Journal, 39,* 133–164.

NICHD Early Child Care Research Network. (2003). Does amount of time spent in child care predict socioemotional adjustment during the transition to kindergarten? *Child Development, 74,* 976–1005.

Nicholls, J. G. & Hazzard, S. P. (1993). *Education as adventure: Lessons from second grade.* New York: Teachers College Press.

Nielsen, M., & Dissanayake, C. (2004). Pretend play, mirror self-recognition and imitation: A longitudinal investigation through the second year. *Infant Behavior & Development, 27,* 342–365.

Nielsen, M., Dissanayake, C., & Kashima, Y. (2003). A longitudinal investigation of self–other discrimination and the emergence of mirror self-recognition. *Infant Behavior and Development, 26,* 213–226.

Nienhuis, A. W. (2008). Development of gene therapy for blood disorders. *Blood, 111,* 4431-4444.

Nigro, C. J. (2007). Formal operational thinking with adults: Testing the Piagetian model (Jean Piaget). Dissertation Abstracts International: Section B. *The Sciences and Engineering, 67,* 5446.

Ninio, A. & Snow, C. E. (1988). Language acquisition through language use: The functional sources of children's early utterances. In Y. Levy, I. M. Schlesinger, & M. D. S. Braine (Eds.), *Categories and processes in language acquisition.* Hillsdale, NJ: Erlbaum.

Ninio, A. & Snow, C. E. (1996). *Pragmatic development.* Boulder, CO: Westview Press.

Ninio, A. & Snow, C. E. (1999). The development of pragmatics: Learning to use language appropriately. In W. C. Ritchie & T. K. Bhatia (Eds.), *Handbook of child language acquisition.* San Diego, CA: Academic Press.

Nisan, M. (1984). Distributive justice and social norms. *Child Development, 55,* 1020–1029.

Noble, C. & Bradford, W. (2000). *Getting it right for boys... and girls.* London: Routledge.

North, A. S. & Noyes, J. M. (2002). Gender influences on children's computer attitudes and cognition. *Computers in Human Behavior, 18,* 135–150.

Novitski, N., Houtilainin, M., Tervaniemi, M., Näätänen, R., & Fellman, V. (2007). Neonatal frequency discrimination in 250-4000-Hz range: Electrophysiological evidence. *Clinical Neurophysiology, 118,* 412–419.

Nowakowski, R. S. (1987). Basic concepts of CNS development. *Child Development, 58,* 568–595.

Nowakowski, R. S. (2006). Stable neuron numbers from cradle to grave. *Proceedings of the National Academy of Sciences, 103,* 12219–12220.

Nowakowski, R. S. & Hayes, N. L. (2005). General principles of CNS development. In M. H. Johnson, Y. Munakata, & R. O. Gilmore (Eds.), *Brain development and cognition: A reader, 2nd ed.* Oxford: Blackwell.

Nucci, L. P. (1997). Culture, universals, and the personal. In H. D. Saltzstein (Ed.), *New directions for child development: No. 76. Culture as a context for moral development: New perspectives on the particular and the universal.* San Francisco: Jossey-Bass.

Nucci, L. P. (2008). Social cognitive domain theory and moral education. In L. P. Nucci & D. Narvaez (Eds.), *Handbook of moral and character education* (pp. 291–309). New York, NY: Routledge.

Nugent, K. J., Petrauskas, B. J., & Brazelton, T. B. (2009). *The newborn as a person: Enabling healthy infant development worldwide.* Hoboken, NJ: John Wiley & Sons Inc.

Nuñez, S. C., Dapretto, M., Katzir, T., Starr, A. Bramen, J., Dan, E., Bookheimer, S., & Sowell, E. R. (2011). fMRI of syntactic processing in typically developing children: Structural correlates in the inferior frontal gyrus. *Developmental Cognitive Neuroscience, 1,* 313–323.

Nunnally, J. C. (1982). The study of human change: Measurement, research strategies, and methods of analysis. In B. B. Wolman (Ed.), *Handbook of developmental psychology.* Englewood Cliffs, NJ: Prentice Hall.

Nuttall, R. L. & Pezaris, E. (2001). Spatial-mechanical reasoning skills versus mathematical self-confidence as mediators of gender differences on mathematics sub-tests using cross-national gender-based items. *Journal for Research in Mathematics Education, 32,* 28–57.

Nye, B., Hedges, L. V., & Konstantopoulos, S. (2001). Are effects of small classes cumulative? Evidence from a Tennessee experiment. *Journal of Educational Research, 94,* 336–345.

Nyiti, R. M. (1982). The validity of "cultural differences explanations" for cross-cultural variation in the rate of Piagetian cognitive development. In D. A. Wagner & H. W. Stevenson (Eds.), *Cultural perspectives on child development.* San Francisco: W. H. Freeman.

O

O'Brien, M. & Huston, A. C. (1985). Development of sex-typed play behavior in toddlers. *Developmental Psychology, 21,* 866–871.

O'Connor, D. B., Archer, J., & Wu, F. C. (2004). Effects of testosterone on mood, aggression, and sexual behavior in young men: A double-blind, placebo-controlled, cross-over study. *Journal of Clinical Endocrinology and Metabolism, 89,* 2837–2845.

O'Connor, M. C. (1996). Managing the intermental: Classroom group discussion and the social context of learning. In D. I. Slobin, J. Gerhardt, A. Kyratzis, & J. Guo (Eds.), *Social interaction, social context, and language: Essays in honor of Susan Ervin-Tripp.* Mahwah, NJ: Erlbaum.

O'Connor, R. D. (1972). Relative efficacy of modeling, shaping, and the combined procedures for modification of social withdrawal. *Journal of Abnormal Psychology, 79,* 327–334.

O'Connor, T. G., Deater-Deckard, K., Fulker, D., Rutter, M., & Plomin, R. (1998). Genotype-environment correlations in late childhood and early adolescence: Antisocial behavioral problems and coercive parenting. *Developmental Psychology 34,* 970–981.

O'Connor, T. G., Heron, J., Golding, J., Beveridge, M., & Glover, V. (2002). Maternal antenatal anxiety and children's behavioural/emotional problems at 4 years. *British Journal of Psychiatry, 180,* 502–508.

O'Donnell, A. M. & King, A. (Eds.). (1999). *Cognitive perspectives on peer learning.* Mahwah, NJ: Erlbaum.

O'Leary, D. D. M. (2005). Do cortical areas emerge from a protocortex? In M. H. Johnson, Y. Munakata, & R. O. Gilmore (Eds.), *Brain development and cognition: A reader, 2nd ed.* Oxford: Blackwell.

O'Neill, D. K. (2005). Talking about "new" information: The given/new distinction and children's developing theory of mind. In J. W. Astington and J. A. Baird (Eds.), *Why language matters for theory of mind* (pp. 84–105). New York: Oxford University Press.

O'Neill, D. K., Astington, J. W., & Flavell, J. H. (1992). Young children's understanding of the role that sensory experiences play in knowledge acquisition. *Child Development, 63,* 474–490.

O'Neill, D. K. & Chong, S. C. F. (2001). Preschool children's difficulty understanding the types of information obtained through the five senses. *Child Development, 72,* 803–815.

O'Sullivan, L. F., Graber, J. A., & Brooks-Gunn, J. (2001). Adolescent gender development. In J. Worell (Ed.), *Encyclopedia of women and gender* (Vol. 1). San Diego, CA: Academic Press.

Oakes, J., Gamoran, A. & Page, R. N. (1992). Curriculum differentiation: Opportunities, outcomes, and meanings. In P. Jackson (Ed.), *Handbook of research on curriculum.* New York: Macmillan.

Oakes, L. M., Coppage, D. J., & Dingel, A. (1997). By land or by sea: The role of perceptual similarity in infants' categorization of animals. *Developmental Psychology, 33,* 396–407.

Odd, D. E., Rasmussen, F., Gunnell, D., Lewis, G., & Whitelaw A. (2008). A cohort study of low Apgar scores and cognitive outcomes. *Archives of disease in childhood, 93,* 115–120.

Odom, S. L. & Strain, P. S. (1984). Peer-mediated approaches to promoting children's social interaction: A review. *American Journal of Orthopsychiatry, 54,* 544–557.

Oehler, J. M. & Eckerman, C. D. (1988). Regulatory effects of human speech and touch in premature infants prior to term age. *Infant Behavior and Development, 11,* 249.

Ohring, R., Graber, J. A., & Brooks-Gunn, J. (2002). Girls' recurrent and concurrent body dissatisfaction: Correlates and consequences over 8 years. *International Journal of Eating Disorders, 31,* 404–415.

Oishi, K., Mori, S., Donohue, P. K., Ernst, T., Anderson, L., Buchthal, S., Faria, A., Jiang, H., Li, X., Miller, M. I., van Ziji, P. C. M., & Chang, L. (2011). Multi-contrast human neonatal brain atlas: Application to normal neonate development analysis. *NeuroImage, 56,* 8–20.

Oliner, S. P. & Oliner, P. M. (1988). *The altruistic personality: Rescuers of Jews in Nazi Europe.* New York: Free Press.

Oller, D. K. (2000). *The emergence of the speech capacity.* Mahwah, NJ: Erlbaum.

Oller, D. K. & Eilers, R. E. (1988). The role of audition in infant babbling. *Child Development, 59*, 441–449.

Oller, D. K. & Pearson, B. Z. (2002). Assessing the effects of bilingualism. In D. K. Oller (Ed.), *Language and literacy in bilingual children.* Clevedon, UK: Multilingual Matters.

Olofsson, J. K., Nordin, S., Sequeira, H., & Polich, J. (2008). Affective picture processing: An integrative review of ERP findings. *Biological Psychology, 77*, 247–265.

Olson, G. M. & Sherman, T. (1983). Attention, learning, and memory in infants. In P. H. Mussen (Series Ed.) & M. M. Haith & J. J. Campos (Vol. Eds.), *Handbook of child psychology: Vol. 2. Infancy and developmental psychobiology* (4th ed.). New York: Wiley.

Olson, S. L. & Kashiwagi, K. (2000). Teacher ratings of behavioral self-regulation in preschool children: A Japanese/U.S. comparison. *Journal of Applied Developmental Psychology, 21*, 609–617.

Olson, S. L., Bates, J. E., & Kaskie, B. (1992). Caregiver-infant interaction antecedents of children's school-age cognitive ability. *Merrill-Palmer Quarterly, 38*, 309–330.

Olson, S. L., Bates, J. E., Sandy, J. M., & Lanthier, R. (2000). Early developmental precursors of externalizing behavior in middle childhood and adolescence. *Journal of Abnormal Child Psychology, 28*, 119–133.

Olweus, D. (1997). Bully/victim problems in school: Facts and intervention. *European Journal of Psychology of Education, 12*, 495–510.

Olweus, D. (2001). Peer harassment: A critical analysis and some important issues. In J. Juvonen & S. Graham (Eds.), *Peer harassment in school: The plight of the vulnerable and victimized.* New York: Guilford.

Olweus, D. (2004). The Olweus Bullying Prevention Programme: Design and implementation issues and a new national initiative in Norway. In P. K. Smith, D. Pepler, & K. Rigby (Eds.), *Bullying in schools: How successful can interventions be?* (pp. 13–36). New York: Cambridge University Press.

Oppenheim, R. W. & Johnson, J. (2003). Programmed cell death and neurotrophic factors. In L. R. Squire, F. E. Bloom, S. K. McConnell, J. L. Roberts, N. C. Spitzer, & M. J. Zigmond (Eds.), *Fundamental neuroscience* (pp. 499–532). New York: Elsevier.

Ornstein, P. A., Baker-Ward, L., Gordon, B. N., Pelphrey, K. A., Tyler, C. S., & Gramzow, E. (2006). The influence of prior knowledge and repeated questioning on children's long-term retention of the details of a pediatric examination. *Developmental Psychology, 42*, 332–344.

Ornstein, P. A. & Haden, C. A. (2001). Memory development or the development of memory? *Current Directions in Psychological Science, 10*, 202–205.

Ornstein, P. A. & Light, L. L. (2010). Memory development across the lifespan. In W. F. Overton (Ed.), *The Handbook of lifespan development: Volume 1: Cognition, biology, and methods* (pp. 259–305). Hoboken, NJ: John Wiley & Sons, Inc.

Ornstein, P. A., Naus, M. J., & Liberty, C. (1975). Rehearsal and organizational processes in children's memory. *Child Development, 56*, 818–830.

Osadchy, A., Kazmin, A., & Koren, G. (2009). Nicotine replacement therapy during pregnancy: Recommended or not. *Journal of Obstetrics and Gynaecology in Canada, 31*, 744–747.

Osofsky, J. D. (2004). *Younger children and trauma: Intervention and treatment.* New York, NY: Guilford.

Ostby, Y., Tamnes, C. K., Fjell, A. M., Westlye, L. T., Due- Tonnessen, P., & Walhovd, K. B. (2009). Heterogeneity in subcortical brain development: A structural magnetic resonance imaging study of brain maturation from 8 to 30 years. *The Journal of Neuroscience, 29*, 11772–11782.

Oster, H. (2005). The repertoire of infant facial expressions: an ontogenetic perspective. In J. Nadel & D. Muir (Eds.), *Emotional Development* (pp. 261–292). New York: Oxford University Press.

Ostrov, J. M. & Crick, N. R. (2007). Forms and functions of aggression during early childhood: A short-term longitudinal study. *School Psychology Review, 36*, 22–43.

Ostrov, J. M. & Keating, C. F. (2004). Gender differences in preschool aggression during free play and structured interactions: An observational study, *Social Development, 13*, 255–277.

Overton, W. F. (2010). Life-span development: Concepts and issues. In W. F. Overton (Ed.), *The Handbook of lifespan development: Volume 1: Cognition, biology, and methods* (pp. 1–29). Hoboken, NJ: John Wiley & Sons, Inc.

Owen, D. R. (1979). Psychological studies in XYY men. In H. L. Vallet & I. H. Porter (Eds.), *Genetic mechanisms of sexual development.* New York: Academic Press.

Owen, L. & Golombok, S. (2009) Families created by assisted reproduction: Parent-child relationships in late adolescence. *Journal of Adolescence, 32*, 835–848.

Oyama, S. (2000). *Evolutions eye: A systems view of the biology-culture divide.* Durham, NC: Duke University Press.

Özçaliskan, S. & Goldin-Meadow, S. (2005). Gesture is at the cutting edge of early language development. *Cognition, 96*, B101–113.

Özçaliskan, S. & Goldin-Meadow, S. (2010). Sex differences in language first appear in gesture. *Developmental Science, 13*(5), 752–760.

P

Paarlberg, K. M., Vingerhoets, A., Passchier, J., & Dekker, G. A. (1995). Psychosocial factors and pregnancy outcome: A review with emphasis on methodological issues. *Journal of Psychosomatic Research, 39*, 563–595.

Pacey, M. (2009). *Fetal alcohol syndrome and fetal alcohol spectrum disorder among aboriginal peoples.* Prince George, BC: National Collaborating Centre for Aboriginal Health.

Paikoff, R. L. & Brooks-Gunn, J. (1990). Physiological processes: What role do they play during the transition to adolescence? In R. Montemayor, G. R. Adams, & T. Gullotta (Eds.), *From childhood to adolescence: Vol. 2. Advances in adolescent development.* London: Sage.

Palincsar, A. S. & Herrenkohl, L. R. (1999). Designing collaborative contexts: Lessons from three research programs. In A. M. O'Donnell & A. King (Eds.), *Cognitive perspectives on peer learning.* Mahwah, NJ: Erlbaum.

Pallas, A. M., Entwisle, D. R., Alexander, K. L., & Stluka, M. F. (1994). Ability-group effects: Instructional, social, or institutional? *Sociology of Education, 67*, 27–46.

Pancsofar, N., Vernon-Feagans, L., & the Family Life Project Investigators (2010). Fathers' early contributions to children's language development in families from low-income rural communities. *Early Childhood Research Quarterly, 25*, 450–463.

Panigrahy, A., Filiano, J. J., Sleeper, L. A., et al. (1997). Decreased kainite binding in the arcuate nucleous of the sudden infant death syndrome. *Journal of Neuropathological Experimental Neurology, 56*, 1253–1261.

Paquet, C. & Steben, M. (2010). Prevention of and screening for herpes simplex: A survey of Quebec physicians. *Journal of Obstetrics and Gynaecology in Canada, 32*, 126–131.

Paradis, J., Nicoladis, E., & Genesee, F. (2000). Early emergence of structural constraints on code-mixing: Evidence from French-English bilingual children. *Bilingualism: Language and Cognition, 3*(3), 245–261.

Parekh, V. C., Pherwani, A., Udani, P. M., & Mukkerjie, S. (1970). Brain weight and head circumference in fetus, infant, and children of different nutritional and socioeconomic groups. *Indian Pediatrics, 7*, 347–358.

Paris, S. G. & Oka, E. R. (1986). Children's reading strategies, meta-cognition, and motivation. *Developmental Review, 6*, 25–56.

Parke, R. D. (1977). Some effects of punishment on children's behavior—revisited. In E. M. Hetherington & R. D. Parke (Eds.), *Contemporary readings in child psychology.* New York: McGraw-Hill.

Parke, R. D. & Buriel, R. (2006). Socialization and the family: Ethnic and ecological perspectives. In N. E. Eisenberg, W. Damon, & R. M. Lerner (Eds.), *Handbook of child psychology Vol. 3: Social, emotional, and personality development* (6th ed., pp. 429–504). Hoboken, NJ: Wiley.

Parke, R. D. & Clarke-Stewart, A. (2011). *Social development.* Hoboken, NJ: Wiley & Sons, Inc.

Parker, J. G. & Asher, S. R. (1987). Peer relations and later personal adjustment: Are low-accepted children at risk? *Psychological Bulletin, 102*, 357–389.

Parkkonen, L., Andersson, J., Hämäläinen, M., & Hari, R. (2008). Early visual brain areas reflect the percept of an ambiguous scene. *Proceedings of the National Academy of Sciences, 105*, 20500–20504.

Parmelee, A. H. & Sigman, M. D. (1983). Perinatal brain development and behavior. In P. H. Mussen (Series Ed.) & M. M. Haith & J. J. Campos (Vol. Eds.), *Handbook of child psychology: Vol. 2. Infancy and developmental psychobiology* (4th ed.). New York: Wiley.

Parten, M. B. (1932). Social participation among preschool children. *Journal of Abnormal and Social Psychology, 27*, 243–269.

Parvizi, J. & Damasio, A.R. (2003). Neuroanatomical correlates of brainstem coma. *Brain, 126*, 1524–1536.

Pascalis, O., de Haan, M., Nelson, C. A., & de Schonen, S. (1998). Long-term recognition memory for faces assessed by visual paired comparison in 3- and 6-month-old infants. *Journal of Experimental Psychology: Learning, Memory, and Cognition, 24*, 249–260.

Pascalis, O., De Schonen, S., Morton, J., & Deruelle, C. (1995). Mother's face recognition by neonates: A replication and an extension. *Infant Behavior and Development, 18*, 79–85.

Pascual-Leone, J. (1987). Organismic processes for neo-Piagetian theories: A dialectical causal account of cognitive development. *International Journal of Psychology, 22*, 531–570.

Pascual-Leone, J. & Johnson, J. (1999). A dialectical constructivist view of representation: Role of mental attention, executives, and symbols. In I. E. Sigel (Ed.), *Development of mental representation: Theories and applications* (pp. 169–200). Mahwah, NJ: Erlbaum.

Passarge, E. (2007). *Color atlas of genetics, 3rd edition.* New York, NY: Thieme Medical Publishers.

Passarotti, M., Paul, B. M., Bussiere, J. R., Buxton, R. B., Wong, E. C., & Stiles, J. (2003). The development of face and location processing: An fMRI study. *Developmental Science, 6,* 100–117.

Patchin, J. W. & Hinduja, S. (2006). Bullies move beyond the schoolyard: A preliminary look at cyber-bullying. *Youth Violence and Juvenile Justice, 4,* 148–169.

Paterson, S., Brown, J. H., Gsodl, M., Johnson, M. H., & Karmiloff-Smith, A. (1999). Cognitive modularity and genetic disorders. *Science, 286,* 2355–2358.

Patterson, C. J. (1982). Self-control and self-regulation in childhood. In T. M. Field, A. Huston, H. C. Quay, L. Troll, & G. E. Finley (Eds.), *Review of human development.* New York: Wiley.

Patterson, C. J. & Hastings, P. D. (2007). Socialization in the context of family diversity. In J. E. Grusec & P. D. Hastings (Eds.), *Handbook of socialization: Theory and research* (pp. 328–351). New York: Guilford.

Patterson, G. R. (1982). *Coercive family process.* Eugene, OR: Castalia.

Patterson, G. R. (2005). Coercive cycles in families. In G. Sugai & R. Horner (Eds.), *Encyclopedia of behavior modification and cognitive behavior therapy: Vol 3. Educational applications* (pp. 1224–1226). Thousand Oaks, CA: Sage Publications.

Patterson, G. R., Reid, J. B., & Dishion, T. J. (1992). *Antisocial boys.* Eugene, OR: Castalia.

Patterson, M. L. & Werker, J. F. (2002). Infants' ability to match dynamic phonetic and gender information in the face and voice. *Journal of Experimental Child Psychology, 81,* 93–115.

Paus, T., Collins, D. L., Evans, A. C., Leonard, G., Pike, B., & Zijdenbos, A. (2001). Maturation of white matter in the human brain: A review of magnetic resonance studies. *Brain Research Bulletin, 54,* 255–266.

Pea, R. D. (2004). The social and technological dimensions of scaffolding and related theoretical concepts for learning, education, and human activity. *The Journal of Learning Sciences, 134,* 423–451.

Peake, P. K., Hebl, M., & Mischel, W. (2002). Strategic attention deployment for delay of gratification in working and waiting situations. *Developmental Psychology, 38,* 313–326.

Pecheux, M., Lepecq, J., & Salzarulo, P. (1988). Oral activity and exploration in 1-2-month-old infants. *British Journal of Developmental Psychology, 6,* 245–256.

Pedersen, P. M., Jorgensen, H. S., Nakayama, H., Raaschou, H. O., & Olsen, T. S. (1995). Aphasia in acute stroke: Incidence, determinants, and recovery. *Annals of Neurology, 38,* 659–666.

Pederson, D. R. & Moran, G. (1996). Expressions of the attachment relationship outside of the Strange Situation. *Child Development, 67,* 915–927.

Pederson, D. R. & Ter Vrugt, D. (1973). The influence of amplitude and frequency of vestibular stimulation on the activity of two-month-old infants. *Child Development, 44,* 122–128.

Pedlow, R., Sanson, A., Prior, M., & Oberklaid, F. (1993). Stability of maternally reported temperament from infancy to 8 years. *Developmental Psychology, 29,* 998–1007.

Pegg, J. E., Werker, J. F., & McLeod, P. J. (1992). Preference for infant-directed over adult-directed speech: Evidence from 7-week-old infants. *Infant Behavior and Development, 15,* 325–345.

Peiper, A. (1963). *Cerebral function in infancy and adulthood.* New York: Consultants Bureau.

Peirano, P., Algarin, C., & Uauy, R. (2003). Sleep-wake states and their regulatory mechanisms throughout human development. *The Journal of Pediatrics, 143,* 70–79.

Peisner-Feinberg, E. S., Burchinal, M. R., Clifford, R. M., Culkin, M. L., Howes, C., Kagan, S. L., et al. (2001). The relation of preschool child-care quality to children's cognitive and social developmental trajectories through second grade. *Child Development, 72,* 1534–1553.

Pelaez-Nogueras, M., Field, T., Cigales, M., Gonzalez, A., & Clasky, S. (1994). Infants of depressed mothers show less "depressed" behavior with their nursery teachers. *Infant Mental Health Journal, 15,* 358–367.

Pelham, W. E. & Hinshaw, S. P. (1992). Behavior intervention for attention-deficit hyperactivity disorder. In S. M. Turner, K. S. Calhoun, & H. E. Adams (Eds.), *Handbook of clinical behavior therapy* (2nd ed.). New York: Wiley.

Pellegrini, A. D., Roseth, C., Mliner, S., Bohn, C., van Ryzin, M., Vance, N., et al. (2007). Social dominance in preschool classrooms. *Journal of Comparative Psychology, 121,* 54–64.

Penner, S. G. (1987). Parental responses to grammatical and ungrammatical child utterances. *Child Development, 58,* 376–384.

Pennington, B. F. (2001). Genetic methods. In C. A. Nelson & M. Lucian. (Eds.), *Handbook of developmental cognitive neuroscience.* Cambridge, MA: MIT Press.

Perner, J., Ruffman, T. K., & Leekam, S. R. (1994). Theory of mind is contagious: You catch it from your sibs. *Child Development, 65,* 1228–1238.

Perron, M. & Gosselin, P. (2004). Le développement de l'évocation des emotions, *Enfance, 56,* 133–147.

Perrson, G. E. B. (2005). Young children's prosocial and aggressive behaviors and their experiences of being targeted for similar behaviors by peers. *Social Development, 14,* 206–228.

Perry, D. G. & Bussey, K. (1979). The social learning theory of sex differences: Imitation is alive and well. *Journal of Personality and Social Psychology, 37,* 1699–1712.

Perry, D. G. & Perry, L. C. (1983). Social learning, causal attribution, and moral internalization. In J. Bizanz, G. L. Bizanz, & R. Kail (Eds.), *Learning in children: Progress in cognitive development research.* New York: Springer-Verlag.

Perry, D. G., Perry, L. C., & Weiss, R. J. (1989). Sex differences in the consequences that children anticipate for aggression. *Developmental Psychology, 25,* 312–319.

Peters, B. R., Atkins, M. S., & McKay, M. M. (1999). Adopted children's behavior problems: A review of five explanatory models. *Clinical Psychology Review, 19,* 297–328.

Peters, D. P. (1991). The influence of stress and arousal on the child witness. In J. Doris (Ed.), *The suggestibility of children's recollections.* Washington, DC: American Psychological Association.

Peters, R. DeV. (2005). A community-based approach to promoting resilience in young children, their families, and their neighbourhoods. In R. Peters, B. Leadbeater, & R. McMahon (Eds.), *Resilience in children, families and communities: Linking context to practice and policy* (pp. 157–176). New York: Springer.

Peters, R. DeV., Petrunka, K., & Arnold, R. (2003). The better beginnings, better futures project: A universal, comprehensive, community-based approach for primary preschool children and their families. *Journal of Clinical Child and Adolescent Psychology 32,* 215–227.

Petersen, A. C. (1987). The nature of biological-psychosocial interactions: The sample case of early adolescence. In R. M. Lerner & T. L. Foch (Eds.), *Biological psychosocial interactions in early adolescence.* Hillsdale, NJ: Erlbaum.

Peterson, C. C. & Biggs, M. (2001). "I was really, really really mad!" Children's use of evaluative devices in narratives about emotional events. *Sex Roles, 45,* 801–825.

Peterson, C. C. (2000). Kindred spirits: Influences on siblings' perspectives on theory of mind. *Cognitive Development, 15,* 435–455.

Peterson, C. C., Pardy, L., Tizzard-Drover, T., & Warren, K. L. (2005). When initial interviews are delayed a year: Effect on children's 2-year recall. *Law and Human Behavior, 29,* 527–541.

Peterson, C. C., & Parsons, B. (2005). Interviewing former 1- and 2-year olds about medical emergencies 5 years later. *Law and Human Behavior, 29,* 743–754.

Peterson, C. C. & Siegal, M. (2002). Mindreading and moral awareness in popular and rejected preschoolers. *British Journal of Developmental Psychology, 20,* 205–224.

Peterson, L. (1983a). Influence of age, task competence, and responsibility focus on children's altruism. *Developmental Psychology, 19(14),* 1–148.

Peterson, L. (1983b). Role of donor competence, donor age, and peer presence on helping in an emergency. *Developmental Psychology, 19,* 873–880.

Petitto, L. A. (2000). On the biological foundations of human language. In K. Emmorey & H. Lane (Eds.), *The signs of language revisited: An anthology to honor Ursula Bellugi and Edward Klima* (pp. 449–473). Mahwah, NJ: Lawrence Erlbaum Associates.

Petitto, L. A., Holowka, S., Sergio, L. E., Levy, B., & Ostry, D. J. (2004). Baby hands that move to the rhythm of language: Hearing babies acquiring sign languages babble silently on the hands. *Cognition, 93,* 43–73.

Petitto, L. A. & Marentette, P. F. (1991). Babbling in the manual mode: Evidence for the ontogeny of language. *Science, 251,* 1493–1496.

Petrill, S. A., Lipton, P. A., Hewitt, J. K., Plomin, R., Cherny, S. S., Corley, R., DeFries, J. C. (2004). Genetic and environmental contributions to general cognitive ability through the first 16 years of life. *Developmental Psychology, 40,* 805–812.

Petrill, S. A., Plomin, R., DeFries, J. C., & Hewitt, J. K. (Eds.) (2003). *Nature, nurture, and the transition to adolescence.* New York: Oxford University Press.

Pettit, G. S., Laird, R. D., Dodge, K. A., Bates, J. E., & Criss, M. M. (2001). Antecedents and behavior-problem outcomes of parental monitoring and psychological control in early adolescence. *Child Development, 72,* 583–598.

Pettit, G. S. & Mize, J. (2007). Social-cognitive processes in the development of antisocial and violent behavior. In D. J. Flannery, A. T. Vazsonyi, & I. D. Waldman (Eds.), *The Cambridge handbook of violent behavior and aggression* (pp. 322–343). New York, NY: Cambridge University Press.

Phares, V. (2008). *Understanding abnormal child psychology* (2nd ed.). Hoboken, NJ: Wiley.

Phillips, D. A. (1984). The illusion of incompetence among academically competent children. *Child Development, 55,* 2000–2016.

Phillips, D. A. (1987). Socialization of perceived academic competence among highly competent children. *Child Development, 58,* 1308–1320.

Phillips, D. A. & Zimmerman, M. (1990). The developmental course of perceived competence and incompetence among competent children. In R. J. Sternberg & J. Kolligian (Eds.), *Competence considered.* New Haven, CT: Yale University Press.

Phillips, R. B., Sharma, R., Premachandra, B. R., Vaughn, A. J., & Reyes-Lee, M. (1996). Intrauterine exposure to cocaine: Effect on neurobehavior of neonates. *Infant Behavior and Development, 19,* 71–81.

Phinney, J. S. (1993). A three stage model of ethnic identity development in adolescence. In M. E. Bernal & G. P. Knight (Eds.), *Ethnic identity: Formation and transmission among Hispanics and other minorities.* Albany, NY: SUNY Press.

Phinney, J. S. & Kohatsu, E. L. (1997). Ethnic and racial development and mental health. In J. Schulenberg, J. L. Maggs, & K. Hurrelmann (Eds.), *Health risks and developmental transitions during adolescence.* Cambridge: Cambridge University Press.

Piaget, J. (1926). *The language and thought of the child.* New York: Harcourt Brace.

Piaget, J. (1932). *The moral judgment of the child.* London: Routledge and Kegan Paul.

Piaget, J. (1951). *Play, dreams, and imitation in childhood.* New York: Norton.

Piaget, J. (1952). *The origins of intelligence in children.* New York: International Universities Press.

Piaget, J. (1954). *The construction of reality in the child.* New York: Basic Books.

Piaget, J. (1957). Logique et equilibre dans les comportements du sujet. In L. Apostel, B. Mandelbrot, & J. Piaget (Eds.), *Etudes d'épistémologie génétique* (Vol. 2). Paris: Presses Universitaires de France.

Piaget, J. (1964). Development and learning. In R. E. Ripple & V. N. Rockcastle (Eds.), *Piaget rediscovered.* Ithaca, NY: Cornell University Press.

Piaget, J. (1968). *On the development of memory and identity.* Barre, MA: Clark University Press and Barre Publishers.

Piaget, J. (1969). *The child's conception of time.* London: Routledge & Kegan Paul.

Piaget, J. (1970). *The child's conception of movement and speed.* London: Routledge & Kegan Paul.

Piaget, J. (1971). *Science of education and the psychology of the child.* New York: Viking.

Piaget, J. (1972). Intellectual evolution from adolescence to adulthood. *Human Development, 15,* 1–12.

Piaget, J. (1976). *To understand is to invent: The future of education.* New York: Penguin.

Piaget, J. (1977). *The development of thought: Equilibration of cognitive structures.* New York: Wiley.

Piaget, J. (1979). Correspondence and transformation. In F. B. Murray (Ed.), *The impact of Piagetian theory.* Baltimore: University Park Press.

Piaget, J. (1980). Recent studies in genetic epistemology. *Cahiers Foundation Archives, Jean Piaget,* No. 1.

Piaget, J. (1983). Piaget's theory. In P. H. Mussen (Series Ed.) & W. Kessen (Vol. Ed.), *Handbook of child psychology: Vol. 1. History, theory, and methods* (4th ed.). New York: Wiley.

Piaget, J. & Inhelder, B. (1956). *The child's conception of space.* London: Routledge & Kegan Paul.

Piaget, J. & Inhelder, B. (1974). *The child's construction of quantities.* London: Routledge & Kegan Paul.

Piaget, J., Inhelder, B., & Szeminska, A. (1960). *The child's conception of geometry.* New York: Basic Books.

Piaget, J. & Szeminska, A. (1952). *The child's conception of number.* New York: Basic Books.

Pianta, R. C. (1999). *Enhancing relationships between children and teachers.* Washington, DC: American Psychological Association.

Pick, H. L. Jr. (1992). Eleanor J. Gibson: Learning to perceive and perceiving to learn. *Developmental Psychology, 28,* 787–794.

Picton, T. W. (2007). Audiometry using auditory steady-state responses. In R. Burkard, M. Don, & J. J. Eggermont, (Eds.), *Auditory evoked potentials* (pp. 441–462). Baltimore: Lippincott, Williams & Wilkins.

Picton, T. W. & Taylor, M. J. (2007). Electrophysiological evaluation of human brain development. *Developmental Neuropsychology, 31,* 249–278.

Pierce, S. H. & Lange, G. (2000). Relationships among metamemory, motivation and memory performance in young school-age children. *British Journal of Developmental Psychology,* 18, 121–135.

Pierroutsakos, S. L. & DeLoache, J. S. (2003). Infants' manual exploration of pictured objects varying in realism. *Infancy, 4,* 141–156.

Pine, J. M., Lieven, E. V. M., & Rowland, C. F. (1997). Stylistic variation at the "single-word stage": Relations between maternal speech characteristics and children's vocabulary composition and usage. *Child Development, 68,* 807–819.

Pinker, S. (1987). The bootstrapping problem in language acquisition. In B. MacWhinney (Ed.), *Mechanisms of language acquisition.* Hillsdale, NJ: Erlbaum.

Pinker, S. (1994). *The language instinct: How the mind creates language.* New York: William Morrow.

Pinker, S. (1999). *Words and rules.* New York: HarperCollins.

Pinker, S. & Jackendoff, R. (2005). The faculty of language: What's special about it? *Cognition, 95,* 201–236.

Pinto, A., Folkers, E., & Sines, J. O. (1991). Dimensions of behavior and home environment in school-age children: India and the United States. *Journal of Cross-Cultural Psychology, 22,* 491–508.

Pipe, M. E. & Salmon, K. (2009). Memory development and the forensic context. In M. Courage and N. Cowan (Eds.), *The development of memory in infancy and childhood* (pp. 241–282). New York, NY: Psychology Press.

Pipp, S., Easterbrooks, M. A., & Harmon, R. J. (1992). The relation between attachment and knowledge of self and mother in one- to three-year-old infants. *Child Development, 63,* 738–750.

Pipp, S., Fischer, K. W., & Jennings, S. (1987). Acquisition of self- and mother knowledge in infancy. *Developmental Psychology, 23,* 86–96.

Pipp-Siegel, S. & Foltz, C. (1997). Toddlers' acquisition of self/other knowledge: Ecological and interpersonal aspects of self and other. *Child Development, 68,* 69–79.

Pisella, L. Sergio, L., Blangero, A., Torchin, H., Vighetto, A., & Rossetti, Y. (2009). Optic ataxia and the function of the dorsal stream: Contributions to perception and action. *Neuropsychologia, 47,* 3033–3044.

Pitcher, D., Walsh, V., & Duchaine, B. (2011). The role of the occipital face area in the cortical face perception network. *Experimental Brain Research, 209,* 481–493.

Plantinga, J. & Trainor, L. J. (2009). Melody recognition by two-month-old infants. *The Journal of the Acoustical Society of America, 125,* EL58–EL62.

Pleck, J. H. (2010). Paternal involvement: Revised conceptualization and theorerical linkages with child outcomes. In M. E. Lamb (Ed.), *The role of the father in child development* (5th edition, pp. 58–93). Hoboken, NJ: Wiley.

Plomin, R. (1990). *Nature and nurture.* Belmont, CA: Wadsworth.

Plomin, R. (2000). Behavioral genetics. In M. Bennett (Ed.), *Developmental psychology: Achievements and prospects.* Philadelphia: Psychology Press.

Plomin, R. (2004). Genetics and developmental psychology. *Merrill-Palmer Quarterly, 50,* 341–352.

Plomin, R. & Asbury, K. (2005). Nature and nurture: Genetic and environmental influences on behavior. *Annals of the American Academy of Political and Social Science, 600,* 86–94.

Plomin, R., Asbury, K., & Dunn, J. F. (2001). Why are children in the same family so different? Nonshared environment a decade later. *Canadian Journal of Psychiatry, 46,* 225–233.

Plomin, R., DeFries, J. C., McClearn, G. E., & McGuffin, P. (2008). *Behavioral Genetics.* (5th Edition). New York: Worth Publishers.

Plomin, R., DeFries, J. C., McClearn, G. E., & Rutter, M. (1997). *Behavioral genetics* (3rd ed.). New York: W. H. Freeman.

Plomin, R., Emde, R. N., Braungart, J. M., Campos, J., Corley, R., Fulker, D. W., et al. (1993). Genetic change and continuity from fourteen to twenty months: The MacArthur Longitudinal Twin Study. *Child Development, 64,* 1354–1376.

Plomin, R., Fulker, D. W., Corley, R., & DeFries, J. C. (1997b). Nature, nurture, and cognitive development from 1 to 16 years: A parent-offspring adoption study. *Psychological Science, 8,* 442–447.

Plomin, R. & McGuffin, P. (2003). Psychopathology in the postgenomic era. *Annual Review of Psychology, 54,* 205–228.

Plomin, R., Reiss, D., Hetherington, E. M., & Howe, G. W. (1994). Nature and nurture: Genetic contributions to measures of the family environment. *Developmental Psychology, 30,* 32–43.

Plomin, R. & Rutter, M. (1998). Child development, molecular genetics, and what to do with genes once they are found. *Child Development, 69,* 1223–1242.

Plomin, R. & Spinath, F. M. (2004). Intelligence: Genetics, genes, and genomics. *Journal of Personality and Social Psychology, 86,* 112–129.

Polivy, J. & Herman, C. P. (2002). Causes of eating disorders. *Annual Review of Psychology, 53,* 187–213.

Polka, L., Colontonio, C., & Sundara, M. (2001). A cross-language comparison of /d/-/O/ perception: Evidence for a new developmental pattern. *Journal of the Acoustical Society of America, 109,* 190–220.

Pollitt, E., Golub, M., Gorman, K., Grantham-McGregor, S., Levitsky, D., Schurch, B., et al. (1996). A reconceptualization of the effects of undernutrition on children's biological, psychosocial, and behavioral development. *Social Policy Report: Society for Research in Child Development, 10,* 1–31.

Pollitt, E., Gorman, K., Engle, P., Martorell, R., & Rivera, J. (1993). Early supplementary feeding and cognition: Effects over two decades. *Monographs of the Society for Research in Child Development, 58* (6, Serial No. 235).

Polman, H., Orobio de Castro, B., & van Aken, M. (2008). Experimental study of the differential effects of playing versus watching violent video games on children's aggressive behavior. *Aggressive Behavior, 34,* 256–264.

Pomerantz, E. M., Grolnick, W. S., & Price, C. E. (2005). The role of parents in how children approach achievement: A dynamic process perspective. In A. J. Elliot & C. S. Dweck (Eds.), *Handbook of competence and motivation* (pp. 229–278). New York: Guilford.

Pomerantz, E. M., Ruble, D. N., Frey K. S., & Greulich, F. (1995). Meeting goals and confronting conflict: Children's changing perceptions of social comparison. *Child Development, 66,* 723–738.

Pomerleau, A., Bolduc, D., Malcuit, G., & Cossette, L. (1990). Pink or blue: Environmental gender stereotypes in the first two years of life. *Sex Roles, 22,* 359–367.

Pomerleau, A., Malcuit, G., & Sabatier, C. (1991). Child-rearing practices and parental beliefs in three cultural groups of Montreal: Québécois, Vietnamese, Haitian. In M. H. Bornstein (Ed.), *Cultural approaches to parenting.* Hillsdale, NJ: Erlbaum.

Poole, D. A. & Lindsay, D. S. (2002). Children's suggestibility in the forensic context. In M. L. Eisen, J. A. Quas, & G. S. Goodman (Eds.), *Memory and suggestibility in the forensic context.* Mahwah, NJ: Erlbaum.

Porath, A. & Fried, P. (2005). Effects of prenatal cigarette and marijuana exposure on drug use among offspring. *Neurotoxicology and Teratology, 27,* 267–277.

Portail Québécois des Maladies Génétiques Orphelines (2010). Downloaded June 3, 2010 from http://www.pqmgo.org/.

Porter, R. H., Balogh, R. D., & Makin, J. W. (1988). Olfactory influences on mother-infant interaction. In C. Rovee-Collier & L. P. Lipsitt (Eds.), *Advances in infancy research* (Vol. 5). Norwood, NJ: Ablex.

Porter, R. H., Raimbault, C., Henrot, A., & Saliba, E. (2008). Responses of Pre-term Infants to the Odour of Mother's Milk. In J. L. Hurst, R. J. Beynon, S. C. Roberts, & T. D. Wyatt (Eds.), *Chemical Signals in Vertebrates 11* (pp. 337–342). Springer New York.

Posada, G., Waters, E., Crowell, J. A., & Lay, K. (1995). Is it easier to use a secure mother as a secure base? Attachment Q-sort correlates of the Adult Attachment Interview. In E. Waters, B. E. Vaughn, G. Posada, & K. Kondo-Ikemura (Eds.), Caregiving, cultural, and cognitive perspectives on secure-base behavior and working models. *Monographs of the Society for Research in Child Development, 60(2–3,* Serial No. 244).

Postma, A., Kessels, R. P. C., & van Asselen, M. (2008). How the brain remembers and forgets where things are: The neurocognition of object-location memory. *Neuroscience & Biobehavioral Reviews, 32,* 1339–1345.

Pougnet, E., Serbin, L. A., Stack, D. M., & Schwartzman, A. E. (2011). Fathers' influence on children's cognitive and behavioural functioning: A longitudinal study of Canadian families. *Canadian Journal of Behavioural Science, 43,* 173–182.

Poulin-Dubois, D., Graham, S., & Sippola, L. (1995). Early lexical development: The contribution of parental labeling and infants' categorization abilities. *Journal of Child Language, 22,* 325–343.

Poulin-Dubois, D. & Serbin, L. A. (2006). La connaissance des catégories de genre et des stéréotypes sexués chez le jeune enfant. *Enfance, 58,* 283–310.

Poulin-Dubois, D., Serbin, L. A., Eichstedt, J. A., Sen, M. G., & Beissel, C. F. (2002). Men don't put on makeup: Toddlers' knowledge of the gender stereotyping of household activities. *Social Development, 11,* 166–181.

Poulson, C. L. & Nunes, L. R. P. (1988). The infant vocal-conditioning literature: A theoretical and methodological review. *Journal of Experimental Child Psychology, 46,* 438–450.

Povinelli, D. J. (1995). The unduplicated self. In P. Rochat (Ed.), *The self in infancy. Theory and research.* Amsterdam: Elsevier.

Povinelli, D. J. (2001). The self: Elevated in consciousness and extended in time. In C. Moore & K. Lemmon (Eds.), *The self in time: Developmental perspectives.* Mahwah, NJ: Erlbaum.

Povinelli, D. J. & Bering, J. M. (2002). The mentality of apes revisited. *Current Directions in Psychological Science, 11,* 115–119.

Powell, G. F., Brasel, J. A., & Blizzard, R. M. (1967). Emotional deprivation and growth retardation simulating ideopathic hypopituitarism: I. Clinical evaluation of the syndrome. *New England Journal of Medicine, 276,* 1271–1278.

Power, T. G. (2000). *Play and exploration in children and animals.* Mahwah, NJ: Erlbaum.

Powlishta, K. K. (1995). Intergroup processes in childhood: Social categorization and sex role development. *Developmental Psychology, 31*(78), 1–788.

Powlishta, K. K., Sen, M. G., Serbin, L. A., Poulin-DuBois, D., & Eichstedt, J. A. (2001). From infancy through middle childhood: The role of social and cognitive factors in becoming gendered. In R. K. Unger (Ed.), *Handbook of the psychology of women and gender.* New York: Wiley.

Pozdnyakova, I. & Regan, L. (2005). New insights into fragile X syndrome. *FEBS Journal 272,* 872–878.

Prader, A., Tanner, J. M., & Von Harnack, G. A. (1963). Catch up growth following illness or starvation. *Journal of Pediatrics, 62,* 646–659.

Pratt, M. W., Arnold, M. L., Pratt, A. T., & Diessner, R. (1999). Predicting adolescent moral reasoning from family climate: A longitudinal study. *Journal of Early Adolescence, 19,* 148–175.

Pratt, M. W., Kerig, P., Cowan, P. A., & Cowan, C. P. (1988). Mothers and fathers teaching 3-year-olds: Authoritative parenting and adult scaffolding of young children's learning. *Developmental Psychology, 24,* 832–839.

Prayer, D., Kasprian, G., Krampl, E., Ulm, B., Witzani, L., Prayer, L., & Brugger, P.C. (2006). MRI of normal fetal brain development. *European Journal of Radiology, 57,* 199–216.

Pressley, M., Borkowski, J. G., & O'Sullivan, J. (1985). Children's metamemory and the teaching of memory strategies. In D. L. Forrest-Pressley, G. E. MacKinnon, & T. G. Waller (Eds.), *Metacognition, cognition, and human performance: Vol. 1. Theoretical perspectives.* New York: Academic Press.

Pressley, M., Forrest-Pressley, D., & Elliot-Faust, D. J. (1988). What is strategy instructional enrichment and how to study it: Illustrations from research on children's prose memory and comprehension. In F. E. Weinert & M. Perlmutter (Eds.), *Memory development: Universal changes and individual differences.* Hillsdale, NJ: Erlbaum.

Pressley, M., Levin, J. R., & Bryant, S. L. (1983). Memory and strategy instruction during adolescence: When is explicit instruction needed? In M. Pressley & J. R. Levin (Eds.), *Cognitive strategy research: Psychological foundations.* New York: Springer-Verlag.

Previc, F. H. (1994). Assessing the legacy of the G–B–G model. *Brain and Cognition, 26,* 174–180.

PREVNet. (2010). *Promoting relationships and eliminating violence.* Available at: www.prevnet.ca. Accessed March 8, 2011.

Price, J. M. (1996). Friendship of maltreated children and adolescents: Contexts for expressing and modifying relationship history. In M. Bukowski, A. F. Newcomb, & W. H. Hartup (Eds.), *The company they keep.* New York: Cambridge University Press.

Price-Williams, D., Gordon, W., & Ramirez, M. (1969). Skill and conservation: A study of pottery-making children. *Developmental Psychology, 1,* 769.

Priess, H. A. & Hyde, J. S. (2010). Gender and academic abilities and preferences. In J. Chrisler & D. R. McCreary (Eds.), *Handbook of gender research in psychology: Vol. 1: Gender research in general and experimental psychology* (pp. 297–316). New York, NY: Springer.

Prifitera, A., Weiss, L. G., Saklofske, D. H., & Rolphus, E. (2005). The WISC-IV in the clinical assessment context. In A. Prifitera, D. H. Saklofske, & L. G. Weiss (Eds.), *WISC-IV: Clinical Use and Interpretation* (pp. 3–32). Burlington, MA: Elsevier.

Prior, M., Smart, M. A., Sanson, A., & Oberklaid, F. (1993). Sex differences in psychological adjustment from infancy to 8 years. *Journal of the Academy of Child and Adolescent Psychiatry, 32,* 291–304.

Provenzale, J. M., Isaacson, J., Chen, S., Stinnett, S., & Liu, C. (2010). Correlation of apparent diffusion coefficient and fractional anisotropy values in the developing infant brain. *American Journal of Roentgenology, 195,* W456–W462.

Pruett, M. K. & Barker, R. (2009). Children of divorce: New trends and ongoing dilemmas. In J. H. Bray & M. Stanton (Eds.), *The Wiley-Blackwell handbook of family psychology* (pp. 463–474). Hoboken, NJ: Wiley.

Public Health Agency of Canada (2003). *Perinatal transmission of HIV.* Downloaded on October 1, 2010 from http://www.phac-aspc.gc.ca/publicat/cig-gci/index-eng.php

Public Health Agency of Canada (2004b). *Fetal alcohol spectrum disorder: Knowledge and attitudes of health care professionals about fetal alcohol syndrome.* Accessed October 2010 at http://www.phac-aspc.gc.ca/publicat/fasd-surv-etcaf-enquete/index-eng.php

Public Health Agency of Canada (2006b). *Canadian immunization guide: Seventh Edition – 2006.* Cat: HP40-3/2006E ISBN: 0-660-19392-2. Downloaded on October 1, 2010 from http://www.phac-aspc.gc.ca/publicat/cig-gci/index-eng.php

Public Health Agency of Canada (2008). *Healthy pregnancy.* Accessed October 2010 from http://www.phac-aspc.gc.ca/hp-gs/know-savoir/smoke-fumer-eng.php

Public Health Agency of Canada (2009). *What mothers say: The Canadian Maternity Experiences Survey.* Accessed on October 7, 2010 from http://www.phac-aspc.gc.ca/rhs-ssg/pdf/survey-eng.pdf

Public Health Agency of Canada. (2004a). *Aboriginal Head Start in urban and northern communities.* Available at: www.phac-aspc.gc.ca/dca-dea/programsmes/ahs_main_e.html

Public Health Agency of Canada. (2005). *Canada Prenatal Nutrition Program.* Retrieved March 10, 2005, from www.phac-aspc.gc.ca/dca-dea/programs-mes/cpnp_goals_e.html

Public Health Agency of Canada. (2006a). *Alcohol use during pregnancy and awareness of fetal alcohol syndrome and fetal alcohol spectrum disorder: Results of a national survey.* Available at: www.phac-aspc.gc.ca/publicat/fas-saf-natsurv-2006/index.html

Pullybank, J., Bisanz, J., Scott, C., & Champion, M. A. (1985). Developmental invariance in the effects of functional self-knowledge on memory. *Child Development, 56,* 1447–1454.

Putallaz, M. & Wasserman, A. (1990). Children's entry behavior. In S. R. Asher & J. D. Coie (Eds.), *Peer rejection in childhood.* New York: Cambridge University Press.

Putnam, S. P., Sanson, A. V., & Rothbart, M. K. (2002). Child temperament and parenting. In M. H. Bornstein (Ed.), *Handbook of parenting* (2nd ed., Vol. 1). Mahwah, NJ: Erlbaum.

Putzar, L., Hötting, K., Rösler, F., & Röder, B. (2007). The development of visual feature binding processes after visual deprivation in early infancy. *Vision Research, 47,* 2616–2626.

Q

Quaiser-Pohl, C., Geiser, C., & Lehmann, W. (2006). The relationship between computer-game preference, gender, and mental-rotation ability. *Personality and Individual Differences, 40,* 609–619.

Quas, J. A., Goodman, G. S., Bidrose, S., Pipe, M., Craw, S., & Ablin, D. S. (1999). Emotion and memory: Children's long-term remembering, forgetting, and suggestibility. *Journal of Experimental Child Psychology, 72,* 235–270.

Quinn, P. C. (1999). Development of recognition and categorization of objects and their spatial relations in young infants. In L. Balter & C. S. Tamis-Monda (Eds.), *Child psychology: A handbook of contemporary issues.* Philadelphia: Psychology Press.

Quinn, P. C. & Eimas, P. D. (1996). Perceptual organization and categorization in young infants. In C. K. Rovee-Collier & L. P. Lipsitt (Eds.), *Advances in infancy research* (Vol. 10). Norwood, NJ: Ablex.

Quinn, P. C. & Liben, L. S. (2008). A sex difference in mental rotation in young infants. *Psychological Science, 19,* 1067–1070.

Quinn, P. C., Yahr, J., Kuhn, A., Slater, A. M., & Pascalis, O. (2002). Representation of the gender of human faces by infants: A preference for female. *Perception, 31,* 1109–1121.

R

Raboud, J., Li, M., Blitz, S., D'Aquila, A., Sterling, S., & Walmsley, S. (2010) Factors associated with HIV-positive women carrying pregnancies to term. *Journal of Obstetrics and Gynaecology in Canada, 32,* 756–762.

Radford, A. (1990). *Syntactic theory and the acquisition of English syntax: The nature of early child grammars of English.* Oxford, England: Blackwell.

Radke, S., de Lange, F. P., Ullsperger, M., & de Bruijn, E. R. A. (2011). Mistakes that affect others: An fMRI study on processing of own errors in a social context. *Experimental Brain Research, 211,* 405–413.

Radke-Yarrow, M., McCann, K., DeMulder, E., & Belmont, B. (1995). Attachment in the context of high-risk conditions. *Development and Psychopathology, 7,* 247–265.

Radke-Yarrow, M. & Zahn-Waxler, C. (1986). The role of familial factors in the development of prosocial behavior: Research findings and questions. In D. Olweus, J. Block, & M. Radke-Yarrow (Eds.), *Development of antisocial and prosocial behavior.* Orlando, FL: Academic Press.

Rados, M., Judas, M., & Kostovic, I. (2006). In vitro MRI of brain development. *European Journal of Radiology, 57,* 187–198.

Radziszewska, B. & Rogoff, B. (1988). Influence of adult and peer collaborators on children's planning skills. *Developmental Psychology, 24,* 840–848.

Rakic, P. (1988). Specifications of cerebral cortical areas. *Science, 241,* 170–176.

Rakic, P. (2005). Less is more: progenitor death and cortical size. *Nature Neuroscience, 8,* 981–982.

Rakoczy, H., Tomasello, M., & Striano, T. (2005). On tools and toys: How children learn to act on and pretend with 'virgin objects'. *Developmental Science, 8,* 57–73.

Ramey, C. T., Campbell, F. A., Burchinal, M., Skinner, M. L., Gardner, D. M., & Ramey, S. L. (2000). Persistent effects of early childhood education on high-risk children and their mothers. *Applied Developmental Psychology, 4,* 2–14.

Ramey, C. T. & Ramey, S. L. (1998). Early intervention and early experience. *American Psychologist, 53,* 109–120.

Ramey, C. T., Ramey, S. L., & Lanzi, R. G. (2001). Intelligence and experience. In R. J. Sternberg & E. L. Grigorenko (Eds.), *Environmental effects on cognitive abilities.* Mahwah, NJ: Erlbaum.

Ramsay, C. & Lewis, M. (2001). Temperament, stress, and soothing. In T. D. Wachs & G. A. Kohnstamm (Eds.), *Temperament in context.* Mahwah, NJ: Erlbaum.

Ramsey, J. L. & Langlois, J. H. (2002). Effects of the "beauty is good" stereotype on children's information processing. *Journal of Experimental Child Psychology, 81,* 320–340.

Ramsey, J. L., Langlois, J. H., Hoss, R. A., Rubenstein, A. J., & Griffin, A. G. (2004). Origins of a stereotype: Categorization of facial attractiveness by 6-month-old infants. *Developmental Science, 7,* 201–211.

Rankin, J. L., Lane, D. J., Gibbons, F. X., & Gerrard, M. (2004). Adolescent self-consciousness: Longitudinal age changes and gender differences in two cohorts. *Journal of Research on Adolescence, 14,* 1–21.

Rapoport, J. L., Buchsbaum, M. S., Zahn, T. P., Weingartner, H., Ludlow, D., & Mikkelson, E. J. (1978). Dextroamphetamine: Cognitive and behavioral effects in normal prepubertal boys. *Science, 199*(4328), 560–563.

Raskauskas, J. & Stoltz, A. D. (2007). Involvement in traditional and electronic bullying among adolescents. *Developmental Psychology, 43,* 564–575.

Raskin, P. A. & Israel, A. C. (1981). Sex-role imitation in children: Effects of sex of child, sex of model, and sex-role appropriateness of modeled behavior. *Sex Roles, 7,* 1067–1077.

Ratner, N. B. (1988). Patterns of parental vocabulary selection in speech to very young children. *Journal of Child Language, 15,* 481–492.

Raver, C. C. (1996). Relations between social contingency in mother-child interaction and 2-year-olds' social competence. *Developmental Psychology, 32,* 850–859.

Rawlins, W. K. (1992). *Friendship matters: Communication, dialectics, and the life course.* New York: Aldine de Gruyter.

Recht, D. R. & Leslie, L. (1988). Effect of prior knowledge on good and poor readers' memory of text. *Journal of Educational Psychology, 80,* 16–20.

Reddy, L. & Kanwisher, N. (2006). Coding of visual objects in the ventral stream. *Current Opinion in Neurobiology, 16,* 408–414.

Reddy, V. (1999). Prelinguistic communication. In M. Barrett (Ed.), *The development of language.* Hove, UK: Psychology Press.

Redlinger, W. E. & Park, T. (1980). Language mixing in young bilinguals. *Journal of Child Language, 7,* 337–352.

Reich, S. M. & Vandell, D. L. (2011). The interplay between parents and peers as socializing influences in children's development. In P. K. Smith & K. H. Hart (Eds.), *The Wiley-Blackwell handbook of childhood social development, 2nd edition* (pp. 263–280). Hoboken, NJ: Wiley.

Reichenberg, A., Gross, R., Weiser., M., Bresnahan, M., Silverman, J., Harpal., S., Rabinowitz, J., Shulman, C., Malaspina, D., Lubin, G. Knobler, H. Davidson, M., & Susser, E. (2006). Advancing paternal age and autism. *Archives of General Psychiatry, 63,* 1026–1032.

Reid, J. B., Patterson, G. R., & Snyder, J. J. (2002). *Antisocial behavior in children and adolescents: A developmental analysis and model for intervention.* Washington, DC: American Psychological Association.

Reid, M., Landesman, S., Treder, R., & Jaccard, J. (1989). "My Family and Friends": Six- to twelve-year-old children's perceptions of social support. *Child Development, 60,* 896–910.

Reinders, H. & Youniss, J. (2006). School-based required community service and civic development in adolescents. *Applied Developmental Science, 10,* 2–12.

Reinisch, J. M. & Sanders, S. A. (1992). Prenatal hormonal contributions to sex differences in human cognitive and personality development. In A. A. Gerall & H. Moltz (Eds.), *Sexual differentiation. Handbook of behavioral neurobiology* (Vol. 11). New York: Plenum Press.

Reinisch, J. M., Ziemba-Davis, M., & Sanders, S. A. (1991). Hormonal contributions to sexual dimorphic behavioral development in humans. *Psychoneuroendocrinology, 16,* 213–278.

Reisman, J. E. (1987). Touch, motion and perception. In P. Salapatek & L. Cohen (Eds.), *Handbook of infant perception: Vol. 1. From sensation to perception.* New York: Academic Press.

Reiss, D., Neiderhiser, J. M., Hetherington, E. M., & Plomin, R. (2000). *The relationship code: Deciphering genetic and social patterns in adolescent development.* Cambridge, MA: Harvard University Press.

Reissing, E. D., Andruff, H. L., & Wentland, J. J. (2012). Looking back: The experience of first sexual intercourse and current sexual adjustment in young heterosexual adults. *Journal of Sex Research, 49,* 27–35.

Rennie, D. A. C., Bull, R., & Diamond, A. (2004). Executive functioning in preschoolers: Reducing the inhibitory demands of the dimensional change card sort task. *Developmental Neuropsychology, 26,* 423–443.

Repacholi, B. M. (1998). Infants'use of attentional cues to identify the referent of another person's emotional expression. *Developmental Psychology, 34,* 1017–1025.

Repetti, R. L. (1996). The effects of perceived daily social and academic failure experiences on school-age children's subsequent interactions with parents. *Child Development, 67,* 1467–1482.

Resches, M. & Perez Pereira, M. (2007). Referential communication abilities and Theory of Mind development in preschool children. *Journal of Child Language, 34*(1), 21–52.

Rescorla, L. A. (1980). Overextension in early language development. *Journal of Child Language, 7,* 321–335.

Rescorla, L. A. (1981). Category development in early language. *Journal of Child Language, 8,* 225–238.

Rest, J., Narvaez, D., Bebeau, M. J., & Thoma, S. J. (1999). *Postconventional moral thinking: A neo-Kohlbergian approach.* Mahwah, NJ: Erlbaum.

Restle, F., Shiffrin, R., Castellan J., Lindman, H. & Pisoni, D. (Eds.). (1975). "Integration and Inference in Children's Comprehension and Memory" by S. G. Paris. In F. Restle, R. Shiffrin, J. Castellan, H. Lindman, & D. Pisoni (Eds.), *Cognitive Theory,* Vol. 1, Mahwah, NJ: Erlbaum.

Retica, A. (2006, Dec. 10). Homophily. *New York Times Magazine.* Downloaded on January 24, 2011 from http://www.nytimes.com/2006/12/10/magazine/10Section2a.t-4.html.

Reznick, J. S., Gibbons, J. L., Johnson, M. O., & Mcdonough, P. M. (1989). Behavioral inhibition in a normative sample. In J. S. Reznick (Ed.), *Perspectives on behavioral inhibition.* Chicago: University of Chicago Press.

Reznick, J. S., Kagan, J., Snidman, N., Gersten, M., Baak, K., & Rosenberg, A. (1986). Inhibited and uninhibited behavior: A follow-up study. *Child Development, 51,* 660–680.

Rhee, S. H. & Waldman, I. D. (2002). Genetic and environmental influences on antisocial behavior: A meta-analysis of twin and adoption studies. *Psychological Bulletin, 128,* 490–529.

Rhee, S. H. & Waldman, I. D. (2007). Behavior-genetics of criminality and aggression. In D. J. Flannery, A. T. Vazsonyi, & I. D. Waldman (Eds.), *The Cambridge handbook of violent behavior and aggression* (pp. 77–90). New York, NY: Cambridge University Press.

Rhee, S. H. & Waldman, I. D. (2011). Genetic and environmental influences on aggression. In P. R. Shaver & M. Mikulincer (Eds.), *Human aggression and violence: Causes, manifestations, and consequences* (pp. 143–163). Washington, DC: American Psychological Association.

Rheingold, H. L. (1982). Little children's participation in the work of adults, a nascent prosocial behavior. *Child Development, 53,* 114–125.

Rhen, T. & Crews, D. (2008). Why are there two sexes? In J. B. Becker, K. J. Berkley, N. Geary, E. Hampson, J. Herman, & E. Young (Eds.), *Sex differences in the brain: From genes to behavior* (pp. 3–14). New York, NY: Oxford University Press.

Rhodes, M. & Brickman, D. (2008). Preschoolers' responses to social comparisons involving relative failure. *Psychological Science, 19,* 968–972.

Rholes, W. S. & Lane, J. W. (1985). Consistency between cognitions and behavior: Cause and consequence of cognitive moral development. In J. B. Pryor & J. D. Day (Eds.), *The development of social cognition.* New York: Springer-Verlag.

Ricciuti, H. N. (1993). Nutrition and mental development. *Current Directions in Psychological Science, 2,* 43–46.

Rice, M. L. & Woodsmall, L. (1988). Lessons from television: Children's word learning when viewing. *Child Development, 59,* 420–429.

Richards, D. S., Frentzen, B., Gerhardt, K. J., McCann, M. E., & Abrams, R. M. (1992). Sound levels in the human uterus. *Obstetrics and Gynecology, 80,* 186–190.

Richards, J. E. (2001). Cortical indexes of saccade planning following covert orienting in 20-week-old infants. *Infancy, 2,* 135–158.

Rickard, T. C., Romero, S. G., Basso, G., Wharton, C., Flitman, S., & Grafman, J. (2000). The calculating brain: An fMRI study. *Neuropsychology, 38,* 325–335.

Rieger, G., Linsemeier, J. A., Gigax, L., & Bailey, J. M. (2008). Sexual orientation and childhood gender nonconformity: Evidence from home videos. *Developmental Psychology, 44,* 46–58.

Riese, M. L. (1987). Temperament stability between the neonatal period and 24 months. *Developmental Psychology, 23,* 216–222.

Rieser, J., Yonas, A., & Wikner, K. (1976). Radial localization of odors by human newborns. *Child Development, 47,* 856–859.

Riesman, P. (1992). *First find your child a good mother.* New Brunswick, NJ: Rutgers University Press.

Rigby, K. (2008). Children and bullying. Malden, MA: Blackwell Publishing.

Rigby, K., & Slee, P. (1993). Children's attitudes toward victims. In D. Tattum (Ed.), *Understanding and managing bullying.* Oxford: Heinemann School Management.

Ritts, V., Patterson, M. L., & Tubbs, M. E. (1992). Expectations, impressions, and judgments of physically attractive students: A review. *Review of Educational Research, 62,* 413–426.

Rivkees, S. A. (2007). The development of circadian rhythms: From animals to humans. *Sleep Medicine Clinics, 2,* 331–341.

Robbins, W. J., Brady, S., Hogan, A. G., Jackson, C. M., & Greene, C. W. (1928). *Growth.* New Haven, CT: Yale University Press.

Roberts, D. & Foehr, U. (2004). *Kids and media in America.* Cambridge: Cambridge University Press.

Robins, R. W. & Trzesniewski, K. H. (2005). Self-esteem development across the lifespan. *Current Directions in Psychological Science, 14,* 158–162.

Robinson, E. J. (1981). The child's understanding of inadequate messages and communication failure: A problem of ignorance or egocentrism? In W. P. Dickson (Ed.), *Children's oral communication skills.* New York: Academic Press.

Robinson, G., Conry, J., & Conry, R. (1987). Clinical profile and prevalence of fetal alcohol syndrome in an isolated community in British Columbia. *Canadian Medical Association Journal, 137,* 203–207.

Robinson, J. L., Reznick, J. S., Kagan, J., & Corley, R. (1992). The heritability of inhibited and uninhibited behavior: A twin study. *Developmental Psychology, 28,* 1030–1037.

Robson, S. J., Tan, W. S., Adeyemi, A., & Dear, K. B. G. (2009). Estimating the rate of cesarean section by maternal request: Anonymous survey of obstetricians in Australia. *Birth, 36,* 208–212.

Roca, M., Parr, A., Thompson, R., Woolgar, A., Torraiva, T., Antoun, N., Manes, F., & Duncan, J. (2010). Executive function and fluid intelligence after frontal lobe lesions. *Brain, 133,* 234–247.

Rochat, P. (1989). Object manipulation and exploration in 2- to 5-month-old infants. *Developmental Psychology, 25,* 871–884.

Rochat, P. (1993). Hand-mouth coordination in the newborn: Morphology, determinants, and early development of a basic act. In G. J. P. Savelsbergh, (Ed.), *The development of coordination in infancy.* London: Elsevier.

Rochat, P. (2001). *The infant's world.* Cambridge, MA: Harvard University Press.

Rochat, P. (2003). Five levels of self-awareness as they unfold early in life. *Consciousness and Cognition: An International Journal, 12,* 717–731.

Rochat, P. (2011). The self as phenotype. *Consciousness and Cognition, 20,* 109–119.

Rochat, P., Dias, M. D., Liping, G., Broesch, T., Passos-Ferreira, C., Winning, A., & Berg, B. (2009). Fairness in distributive justice by 3- and 5-year-olds across seven cultures. *Journal of Cross-Cultural Psychology, 40,* 416–442.

Rochat, P. & Striano, T. (2002). Who's in the mirror? Self-other discrimination in specular images by four- and nine-month-old infants. *Child Development, 73,* 35–46.

Rode, S., Chang, P., Fisch, R., & Sroufe, L. A. (1981). Attachment patterns of infants separated at birth. *Developmental Psychology, 17,* 188–191.

Rodman, H. R., Skelly, J. P., & Gross, C. G. (1991). Stimulus selectivity and state dependence of activity in inferior temporal cortex in infant monkeys. *Proceedings of the National Academy of Sciences, 88,* 7572–7575.

Roelants, M., Hauspie, R., & Hoppenbrouwers, K. (2009). References for growth and pubertal development from birth to 21 years in Flanders, Belgium. *Annals of Human Biology, 36,* 680–694.

Roeser, R. W., Eccles, J. S., & Sameroff, A. J. (2000). School as a context for early adolescents' academic and social-emotional adjustment: A summary of research findings. *Elementary School Journal, 100,* 443–471.

Roggman, L. A., Langlois, J. H., Hubbs-Tait, L., & Rieser-Danner, L. A. (1994). Infant daycare, attachment, and the "file drawer problem." *Child Development, 65,* 1429–1443.

Rogoff, B. (1981). Schooling and the development of cognitive skills. In H. C. Triandis & A. Heron (Eds.), *Handbook of cross-cultural psychology: Vol. 4. Developmental psychology.* Boston: Allyn & Bacon.

Rogoff, B. (1990). *Apprenticeship in thinking.* New York: Oxford University Press.

Rogoff, B. (1998). Cognition as a collaborative process. In W. Damon (Series Ed.) & D. Kuhn & R. S. Siegler (Vol. Eds.), *Handbook of child psychology: Vol. 2. Cognition, perception, and language* (5th ed.). New York: Wiley.

Rogoff, B. (2003). *The cultural nature of human development.* New York: Oxford University Press.

Rogoff, B. & Chavajay, P. (1995). What's become of research on the cultural basis of cognitive development? *American Psychologist, 50,* 859–887.

Rogoff, B., Mistry, J., Goncu, A., & Mosier, C. (1993). Guided participation in cultural activity by toddlers and caregivers. *Monographs of the Society for Research in Child Development, 58* (Serial No. 236).

Rogosch, F. A., Cicchetti, D., Shields, A., & Toth, S. L. (1995). Parenting dysfunction in child maltreatment. In M. H. Bornstein (Ed.), *Handbook of parenting: Vol. 4. Applied and practical parenting.* Mahwah, NJ: Erlbaum.

Roid, G. (2003). *Stanford-Binet Intelligence Scales* (5th ed.). Chicago: Riverside Publishing.

Roid, G. & Pomplun, M. (2005) Interpreting the Stanford-Binet Intelligence Scales, Fifth Edition. In Flanagan, D. & Harrison, P. (Eds.), *Contemporary Intellectual Assessment: Theories, Tests, and Issues* (pp. 325–343). New York: Guilford.

Roisman, G. I., Collins, W. A., Sroufe, L. A., & Egeland, B. (2005). Predictors of young adults' representations of and behavior in their current romantic relationships: Prospective tests of the prototype hypothesis. *Attachment & Human Development, 7,* 105–121.

Roisman, G. I., Madsen, S. D., Hennighausen, K. H., & Collins, W. A. (2001). The coherence of dyadic behavior across parent-child and romantic relationships as mediated by the internalized representation of experience. *Attachment and Human Development, 3,* 156–172.

Roland, A. (1988). *In search of self in India and Japan.* Princeton, NJ: Princeton University Press.

Romano, E., Tremblay, R. E., Boulerice, B., & Swisher, R. (2005). Multilevel correlates of childhood physical aggression and prosocial behavior. *Journal of Abnormal Child Psychology, 33,* 565–578.

Rommetveit, R. (1979). On the architecture of inter-subjectivity. In R. Rommetveit & R. M. Blakar (Eds.), *Studies of language, thought, and verbal communication.* New York: Academic Press.

Rosander, K. & von Hofsten, C. (2004). Infants' emerging ability to represent occluded object motion. *Cognition, 91,* 1–22.

Rose, A. J. & Rudolph, K. D. (2006). A review of sex differences in peer relationship processes: Potential tradeoffs for the emotional development of girls and boys. *Psychological Bulletin, 132,* 98–131.

Rose, A. J. & Smith, R. L. (2009). Sex differences in peer relationships. In K.H. Rubin, W. M. Bukowski, & B. Laursen (Eds.), *Handbook of peer interactions, relationships, and groups* (pp. 379–393). New York: Guilford.

Rose, S. A. (1994). From hand to eye: Findings and issues in infant cross-modal transfer. In D. J. Lewkowicz & R. Lickliter (Eds.), *The development of intersensory perception: Comparative prespectives.* Hillsdale, NJ: Erlbaum.

Rose, S. A., Gottfried, A. W., & Bridger, W. H. (1981). Cross-modal transfer and information processing by the sense of touch in infancy. *Developmental Psychology, 17,* 90–98.

Rose, S. A. & Orlian, E. K. (1991). Asymmetries in cross-modal transfer. *Child Development, 62,* 706–718.

Rose, S. A. & Ruff, H. A. (1987). Cross-modal abilities in human infants. In J. D. Osofsky (Ed.),

Handbook of infant development (2nd ed.). New York: Wiley.

Rose-Krasnor, L. & Denham, S. (2009). Social-emotional competence in early childhood. In K. H. Rubin, W. M. Bukowski, & B. Laursen (Eds.), *Handbook of peer interactions, relationships, and groups* (pp. 162–179). New York: Guilford.

Rosen, G. D., Galaburda, A. M., & Sherman, G. F. (1990). The ontogeny of anatomic asymmetry: Constraints derived from basic mechanisms. In A. B. Scheibel & A. F. Wechsler (Eds.), *Neurobiology of higher cognitive function.* New York: Guilford.

Rosen, T. S. & Johnson, H. L. (1988). Drug-addicted mothers, their infants, and SIDS. *Annals of the New York Academy of Sciences, 533,* 89–95.

Rosenbaum, J. F., Biederman, J., Bolduc-Murphy, E. A., & Faraone, S. V. (1993). Behavioral inhibition in childhood: A risk factor for anxiety disorders. *Harvard Review of Psychiatry, 1*(1), 2–16.

Rosenberg, M. (1986b). Self-concept from middle childhood through adolescence. In J. Suls (Ed.), *Psychological perspectives on the self (Vol. 3).* Hillsdale, NJ: Erlbaum.

Rosengren, K. S. & Braswell, G. (2001). Variability in children's reasoning. In H. W. Reese & R. Kail (Eds.), *Advances in child development and behavior* (Vol. 28). San Diego, CA: Academic Press.

Rosengren, K. S., Gelman, S. A., Kalish, C. W., & McCormick, M. (1991). As time goes by: Children's early understanding of growth in animals. *Child Development, 62,* 1302–1320.

Rosenstein, D. & Oster, H. (1997). Differential facial responses to four basic tastes in newborns. In P. Ekman & E. L. Rosenberg (Eds.), *What the face reveals: Basic and applied studies of spontaneous expression using the Facial Action Coding System (FACS). Series in affective science.* New York: Oxford University Press.

Rosenthal, C. & Gladstone, J. (2000). *Grandparenthood in Canada.* Ottawa, ON: The Vanier Institute of the Family. Retrieved on January 24, 2011 from www.vifamily.ca/media/node/411/attachments/grandparenthood_canada.pdf.

Ross, H. & Howe, N. (2009). Family influences on children's peer relationships. In K. H. Rubin, W. M. Bukowski, & B. Laursen (Eds.), *Handbook of peer interactions, relationships, and groups* (pp. 508–527). New York: Guilford.

Ross, H. S. & Lollis, S. P. (1987). Communication within infant social games. *Developmental Psychology, 16,* 391–396.

Ross, J. B. & McLaughlin, M. M. (Eds.). (1949). *The portable medieval reader.* New York: Viking Press.

Ross, J., Zinn, A., & McCauley, E. (2000). Neurodevelopmental and psychosocial aspects of Turner syndrome. *Mental Retardation and Developmental Disabilities Research Review, 6,* 135–141.

Ross, S. A. (1971). A test of the generality of the effects of deviant preschool models. *Developmental Psychology, 4,* 262–267.

Rossignol, M., Philippot, P., Douilliez, C., Crommelinck, M., & Campanella, S. (2005). The perception of fearful and happy facial expression is modulated by anxiety: An event-related potential study. *Neuroscience Letters, 377,* 115–120.

Rosso, P. (1990). *Nutrition and metabolism in pregnancy.* New York: Oxford University Press.

Rothbart, M. K. (1989). Behavioral approach and inhibition. In J. S. Reznick (Ed.), *Perspectives on behavioral inhibition.* Chicago: The University of Chicago Press.

Rothbart, M. K., Ahadi, S. A., & Evans, D. E. (2000). Temperament and personality: Origins and outcomes. *Journal of Personality and Social Psychology, 78,* 122–135.

Rothbart, M. K., Ahadi, S. A., & Hershey, K. L. (1994). Temperament and social behavior in childhood. *Merrill-Palmer Quarterly, 40,* 21–39.

Rothbart, M. K. & Bates, J. E. (2006). Temperament. In W. Damon & R. M. Lerner (Series Eds.) & N. Eisenberg (Vol. Ed.), *Handbook of child psychology: Vol. 3. Social, emotional, and personality development* (6th ed., pp. 99–166). Hoboken, NJ: Wiley.

Rothbart, M. K. & Bates, J. E. (2008). Temperament. In W. Damon & R. M. Lerner (Eds.), *Child and adolescent development: An advanced course* (pp. 54–92). Hoboken, NJ: Wiley.

Rothbart, M. K., Derryberry, D., & Hershey, K. (2000). Stability of temperament in childhood: Laboratory infant assessment to parent report at seven years. In V. J. Molfese & D. L. Molfese (Eds.), *Temperament and personality development across the life span.* Mahwah, NJ: Erlbaum.

Rothbart, M. K. & Hwang, J. (2005). Temperament and the development of competence and motivation. In A. Elliot & C. Dweck (Eds.), *Handbook of competence and motivation* (pp. 167–184). New York: Guilford.

Rothbart, M. K. & Posner, M. I. (1985). Temperament and the development of self-regulation. In L. C. Hartledge & C. F. Telzrow (Eds.), *The neuropsychology of individual differences: A developmental perspective.* New York: Plenum.

Rothbart, M. K., Posner, M.I., & Hershey, K. L. (1995). Temperament, attention, and developmental psychopathology. In D. Cicchetti & D. J. Cohen (Eds.), *Manual of developmental psychopathology* (Vol. 1). New York: Wiley.

Rothbaum, F., Kakinuma, M., Kagaoka, R., & Azuma, H. (2007). Attachment and amae: Parent–child closeness in the United States and Japan. *Journal of Cross-Cultural Psychology, 38,* 465–486.

Rovee-Collier, C. K. (1999). The development of infant memory. *Current Directions in Psychological Science, 8,* 80–85.

Rovee-Collier, C. K. (2001). Information pick-up by infants: What is it, and how can we tell? *Journal of Experimental Child Psychology, 78,* 35–49.

Rovee-Collier, C. K., Hartshorn, K., & DiRubbo, M. (1999). Long-term maintenance of infant memory *Developmental Psychobiology, 35,* 91–102.

Rovee Collier, C. K. & Hayne, H. (1987). Reactivation of infant memory: Implications for cognitive development. In H. W. Reese (Ed.), *Advances in child development and behavior* (Vol. 20). New York: Academic Press.

Rovee-Collier, C. K. & Shyi, G. (1992). A functional and cognitive analysis of infant long-term retention. In M. L. Howe, C. J. Brainerd, & V. F. Reyna (Eds.), *Development of long-term retention.* New York: SpringerVerlag.

Rowe, R., Maughan, B., Worthman, C. M., Costello, E. J., & Angold, A. (2004). Testosterone, antisocial behavior, and social dominance in boys: Pubertal development and biosocial interaction. *Biological Psychiatry, 55,* 546–552.

Royer, J. M., Tronsky, L. N., Chan, Y., Jackson, S. J., & Marchant, H. III (1999). Math-fact retrieval and the cognitive mechanism underlying gender differences in math test performance. *Contemporary Educational Psychology, 24,* 181–266.

Rubenstein, A. J., Kalakanis, L., & Langlois, J. H. (1999). Infant preferences for attractive faces: A cognitive explanation. *Developmental Psychology 35,* 848–855.

Rubenstein, J. & Howes, C. (1976). The effect of peers on toddler interaction with mother and toys. *Child Development, 47,* 597–605.

Rubin, J. Z., Provenzano, F. J., & Luria, Z. (1974). The eye of the beholder: Parents' views on sex of newborns. *American Journal of Orthopsychiatry, 44,* 512–519.

Rubin, K. H. (1988). *The Social Problem-Solving Test—revised.* Waterloo, ON: University of Waterloo Press.

Rubin, K. H. (1989). *The Play Observation Scale (POS).* Unpublished manuscript. University of Waterloo, Waterloo, ON.

Rubin, K. H. (1993). The Waterloo Longitudinal Project: Correlates and consequences of social withdrawal from childhood to adolescence. In K. H. Rubin & J. B. Asendorpf (Eds.), *Social withdrawal, inhibition, and shyness in childhood.* Hillsdale, NJ: Erlbaum.

Rubin, K. H. & Asendorpf, J. B. (Eds.). (1993). *Social withdrawal, inhibition, and shyness in childhood.* Hillsdale, NJ: Erlbaum.

Rubin, K. H., Bream, L., & Rose-Krasnor, L. (1991). Social problem solving and aggression in childhood. In D. J. Pepler & K. H. Rubin (Eds.), *The development and treatment of childhood aggression.* Hillsdale, NJ: Erlbaum.

Rubin, K. H., Bukowski., W. M., & Parker, J. G. (2006). Peer interactions, relationships, and groups. In N. E. Eisenberg, W. Damon, & R. M. Lerner (Eds.), *Handbook of child psychology Vol. 3: Social, emotional, and personality development* (6th ed., pp. 571–645). Hoboken, NJ: Wiley.

Rubin, K. H. & Burgess, K. B. (2002). Parents of aggressive and withdrawn children. In M. Bornstein (Ed.), *Handbook of parenting: Vol. 1: Children and parenting (2nd ed., pp.* 383–418). Mahwah, NJ: Erlbaum.

Rubin, K. H., Burgess, K. B., & Coplan, R. J. (2002). Social withdrawal and shyness. In P. K. Smith & C. H. Hart (Eds.), *Blackwell handbook of childhood social development.* Madden, MA: Blackwell Publishers.

Rubin, K. H., Burgess, K. B., Dwyer, K. M., & Hastings, P. D. (2003). Predicting preschoolers' externalizing behaviors from toddler temperament, conflict, and maternal negativity. *Developmental Psychology, 39,* 164–176.

Rubin, K. H. & Coplan, R. J. (2007). Paying attention to and not neglecting social withdrawal and social isolation. In G. W. Ladd (Ed.), *Appraising the human developmental sciences: Essays in honor of Merrill-Palmer Quarterly* (pp. 156–185). Detroit, MI: Wayne State University Press.

Rubin, K. H., Coplan, R. J., & Bowker, J. (2009). Social withdrawal and shyness in childhood and adolescence. *Annual Review of Psychology, 60,* 11.1–11.31.

Rubin, K. H., Coplan, R. J., Bowker, J. C., & Menza, M. (2011). Social withdrawal and shyness. In P. K. Smith & K. H. Hart (Eds.), *The Wiley-Blackwell handbook of childhood social development, 2nd edition* (pp. 434–452). Hoboken, NJ: Wiley.

Rubin, K. H., Dwyer, K., Booth-LaForce, C., Kim, A., Burgess, K., & Rose-Krasnor, L. (2004). Attachment, friendship, and psychosocial functioning in early adolescent. *Journal of Early Adolescence, 24,* 326–356.

Rubin, K. H., Fein, G. G., & Vandenberg, B. (1983). Play. In P. H. Mussen (Series Ed.) & E. M. Hetherington (Vol. Ed.), *Handbook of child psychology: Vol. 4. Socialization, personality, and social development* (4th ed.). New York: Wiley.

Rubin, K. H. & Krasnor, L. R. (1986). Social-cognitive and social behavioral perspectives on problem solving. In M. Perlmutter (Ed.), *Minnesota symposia on child psychology: Vol. 19. Cognitive perspectives on children's social and behavioral development.* Hillsdale, NJ: Erlbaum.

Rubin, K. H. & Maioni, T. L. (1975). Play preference and its relationship to egocentrism, popularity and classification skills in preschoolers. *Merrill-Palmer Quarterly, 21,* 171–179.

Rubin, K. H. & Rose-Krasnor, L. (1992). Interpersonal problem solving and social competence in children. In W. B. Van Hasselt & M. Hersen (Eds.), *Handbook of social development.* New York: Plenum.

Rubin, K. H., Stewart, S. L., & Chen, X. (1995). Parents of aggressive and withdrawn children. In M. H. Bornstein (Ed.), *Handbook of parenting. Vol 1. Children and parenting.* Mahwah, NJ: Erlbaum.

Rubin, K. H., Watson, K. S., & Jambor, T. W. (1978). Free-play behaviors in preschool and kindergarten children. *Child Development, 49,* 534–536.

Rubin, Z. (1980). *Children's friendships.* Cambridge, MA: Harvard University Press.

Ruble, D. N. & Dweck, C. S. (1995). Self-perceptions, person conceptions, and their development. In N. Eisenberg (Ed.), *Review of personality and social psychology: Vol. 15. Development and social psychology: The interface.* Thousand Oaks, CA: Sage.

Ruble, D. N. & Flett, G. L. (1988). Conflicting goals in self-evaluative information seeking: Developmental and ability level analyses. *Child Development, 59,* 97–106.

Ruble, D. N. & Frey, K. S. (1987). Social comparison and outcome evaluation in group contexts. In J. C. Masters & W. P. Smith (Eds.), *Social comparison, social justice, and relative deprivation.* Hillsdale, NJ: Erlbaum.

Ruble, D. N. & Frey, K. S. (1991). Changing patterns of behavior as skills are acquired: A functional model of self-evaluation. In J. Suls & T. A. Wills (Eds.), *Social comparison: Contemporary theory and research.* Hillsdale, NJ: Erlbaum.

Ruble, D. N., Martin, C. L., & Berenbaum, S. A. (2006). Gender development. In N. Eisenberg, W. Damon, & R. Lerner (Eds.), *Handbook of child psychology: Vol. 3, Social, emotional, and personality development* (6th ed., pp. 858–932). Hoboken, NJ: Wiley.

Ruble, D. N., Taylor, L. J., Cyphers, L., Greulich, F. K., Lurye, L. E., & Shrout, P. E. (2007). The role of gender constancy in early gender development. *Child Development, 78,* 1121–1136.

Ruddy, M. G. (1993). Attention shifting and temperament at 5 months. *Infant Behavior and Development, 16,* 255–259.

Rudolph, K. D., Lambert, S. F., Clark, A. G., & Kurlakowsky K. D. (2001). Negotiating the transition to middle school: The role of self-regulatory processes. *Child Development, 71,* 929–946.

Ruff, H. A., Capozzoli, M., & Weissberg, R. (1998). Age, individuality, and contexts as factors in sustained visual attention during the preschool years. *Developmental Psychology, 34,* 454–464.

Ruff, H. A. & Kohler, E. C. J. (1978). Tactual-visual transfer in six-month-old infants. *Infant Behavior and Development, 1,* 259–264.

Ruff, H. A. & Rothbart, M. K. (1996). *Attention in early development.* New York: Oxford University Press.

Ruffman, T., Perner, J., Naito, M., Parkin, L., & Clements, W. A. (1998). Older (but not younger) siblings facilitate false belief understanding. *Developmental Psychology, 34,* 161–174.

Rushton, J. P. & Jensen, A. R. (2005). Thirty years of research on race differences in cognitive ability. *Psychology, Public Policy, and Law, 11,* 235–294.

Russell, J. A. & Bullock, M. (1985). Multidimensional scaling of emotional facial expressions: Similarities from preschoolers to adults. *Journal of Personality and Social Psychology, 48,* 1290–1298.

Russell, A. (2011). Parent-child relationships and influences. In P. K. Smith & K. H. Hart (Eds.), *The Wiley-Blackwell handbook of childhood social development, 2nd edition* (pp. 337–355). Hoboken, NJ. Wiley.

Russell, A., Mize, J., & Bissaker, K. (2002). Parent-child relationships. In P. K. Smith & C. H. Hart (Eds.), *Blackwell handbook of childhood social development.* Madden, MA: Blackwell Publishers.

Russell, G. & Russell, A. (1987). Mother-child and father-child relationships in middle childhood. *Child Development, 58,* 1573–1585.

Russell, S. T. (2006). Substance use and abuse and mental health among sexual-minority youths: Evidence from Add Health. In A. M. Omoto & H. S. Kurtzman (Eds.), *Sexual orientation and mental health: examining identity and development in lesbian, gay, and bisexual people.* Washington, DC: American Psychological Association.

Rust, J., Golombok, S., Hines, M., & Johnston, K. (2000). The role of brothers and sisters in the gender development of preschool children. *Journal of Experimental Child Psychology, 77,* 292–303.

Rutter, M. (1983). School effects on pupil progress: Research findings and policy implications. *Child Development, 54,* 1–29.

Rutter, M. (1987). Continuities and discontinuities from infancy. In J. D. Osofsky (Ed.), *Handbook of infant development* (2nd ed.). New York: Wiley.

Rutter, M. (2002). Nature, nurture, and development: From evangelism through science toward policy and practice. *Child Development, 73,* 1–21.

Rutter, M., & Caesar, P. (Eds.). (1991). *Biological risk factors for psychosocial disorders.* Cambridge: Cambridge University Press.

Rutter, M., MacDonald, H., Lecouteur, A., Harrington, R., Bolton, P., & Bailey, A. (1990). Genetic factors in child psychiatric disorders: II. Empirical findings. *Journal of Child Psychology and Psychiatry, 31,* 39–84.

Ruys, J. H., de Jonge, G. A., Brand, R., Engelberts, A. C., Semmekrot, B. A. (2007). Bed-sharing in the first four months of life: A risk factor for sudden infant death. *Acta, 96,* 1399–1403.

Rvachew, S., Alhaidary, A., Mattock, K., & Polka, L. (2008). Emergence of the corner vowels in the babble produced by infants exposed to Canadian English or Canadian French. *Journal of Phonetics, 36*(4), 564–577.

Ryan, A. M. (2001). The peer group as a context for the development of young adolescent motivation and achievement. *Child Development, 72,* 1135–1150.

Rymer, R. (1994). *Genie: A scientific tragedy.* New York: Harper Collins.

S

Saarni, C., Campos, J. J., Camras, L. A., & Witherington, D. (2008). Principles of emotion and emotional competence. In W. Damon & R. M. Lerner (Eds.), *Child and adolescent development: an advanced course* (pp. 361–405). Hoboken, NJ: Wiley.

Sabbagh, M. A., Xu, F., Carlson, S. M., Moses, L. G., & Lee, K. (2006). The development of executive function and theory of mind: A comparison of Chinese and U.S. preschoolers. *Psychological Science, 17,* 74–81.

Sachs, J. (2001). Communication development in infancy. In J. B. Gleason (Ed.), *The development of language* (5th ed.). Boston: Allyn and Bacon.

Sachs, J. & Devin, J. (1976). Young children's use of age-appropriate speech styles in social interaction and role-playing. *Journal of Child Language, 3*(8), 1–98.

Sack, G. (2008). *USMLE Road Map: Genetics.* New York, NY: McGraw-Hill Medical.

Saewyc, E. (2011). Research on adolescent sexual orientation: Development, health disparities, stigma, and resilience. *Journal of Research on Adolescence, 21,* 256–272.

Saffran, J. R. (2003). Statistical language learning: Mechanisms and constraints. *Current Directions in Psychological Science, 12,* 110–114.

Saffran, J. R., Aslin, R. N., & Newport, E. L. (1996). Statistical learning by 8-month-old infants. *Science, 274,* 1926–1928.

Saffran, J. R., Werker, J. F., & Werner, L. A. (2006). The infant's auditory world: Hearing, speech, and the beginnings of language. In D. Kuhn and R. S. Siegler (Eds.), *Handbook of child psychology* (Vol. 2, Cognition, perception, and language, pp. 58–108). Hoboken, NJ: Wiley.

Sage, N. A. & Kindermann, T. A. (1999). Peer networks, behavior contingencies, and children's engagement in the classroom. *Merrill-Palmer Quarterly, 45,* 143–171.

Sagi, A. & Hoffman, M. L. (1976). Empathic distress in the newborn. *Developmental Psychology, 12,* 175–176.

Sagi, A., Lamb, M. E., Shoham, R., Dvir, R., & Lewkowicz, K. S. (1985). Parent-infant interaction in families on Israeli kibbutzim. *International Journal of Behavioral Development, 8,* 273–284.

Sagi, A., van IJzendoorn, M. H., Aviezer, O., Donnell, F., Koren-Karie, N., Joels, T., et al. (1995). Attachments in multiple-caregiver and multiple-infant environments: The case of the Israeli kibbutzim. In E. Waters, B. E. Vaughn, G. Posada, & K. Kondo-Ikemura (Eds.), Care-giving, cultural, and cognitive perspectives on secure-base behavior and working models. *Monographs of the Society for Research in Child Development, 60* (2–3, Serial No. 244).

Saigal S. (2004). Behavioural and emotional functioning in preterm infants. In R. E. Tremblay, R.G. Barr, R. De V. Peters (Eds.), *Encyclopedia on early childhood development* [online]. Montreal, Quebec: Centre of Excellence for Early Childhood Development, 1–7.

Saigal, S., Hoult, L. A., Streiner, L. L., Stoskopf, F. L., & Rosenbaum, P. L. (2000). School difficulties in adolescence in a regional cohort of children who were extremely low birth weight. *Pediatrics, 105,* 325–331.

Saklofske, D. H., Weiss, L. G., Beal, A. L., & Coalson, D. (2003). The Wechsler scales for assessing children's intelligence: Past to present. In J. Georgas, L. Weiss, F. van de Vijver, & D. Saklofske (Eds.), *Culture and children's intelligence* (pp. 3–21). New York: Academic Press.

Salapatek, P. (1968). Visual scanning of geometric figures by the human newborn. *Journal of Comparative Physiology and Psychology, 66,* 247–258.

Salapatek, P. & Kessen, W. (1973). Prolonged investigation of a plane geometric triangle by the human newborn. *Journal of Experimental Child Psychology, 15,* 22–29.

Saleh, M., Lazonder, A. W., & De Jong, T. (2005). Effects of within-class ability grouping on social interaction, achievement, and motivation. *Instructional Science, 33,* 105–119.

Saleh, M., Lazonder, A. W., & De Jong, T. (2007). Structuring collaboration in mixed-ability groups to promote verbal interaction, learning, and motivation of average-ability students. *Contemporary Educational Psychology, 32,* 314–331.

Salmivalli, C., Peets, K., & Hodges, E. V. (2011). Bullying. In P. K. Smith & K. H. Hart (Eds.), *The Wiley-Blackwell handbook of childhood social development*, 2nd edition (pp. 510–528). Hoboken, NJ: Wiley.

Salois, K. (1999). A comparative study of the Wechsler Intelligence Scale for Children-Third Edition (WISC-III) test performance: Northern Cheyenne and Blackfeet reservation Indian children with the standardization sample. *Dissertation Abstracts International: Section B: The Sciences and Engineering, 60(4-B)*, pp. 1909.

Saltzstein, H. D., Weiner, A. S., Munk, J. J., Suppraner, A., Blank, R., & Schwartz, R. P. (1987). Comparison between children's own moral judgments and those they attribute to adults. *Merrill-Palmer Quarterly, 33,* 33–51.

Sameroff, A. J., Seifer, R., Baldwin, A., & Baldwin, C. (1993). Stability of intelligence from preschool to adolescence: The influence of social and family risk factors. *Child Development, 64,* 80–97.

Samuels, C. A. (1986). Bases for the infant's developing self-awareness. *Human Development, 29,* 36–48.

Sander, L. W., Snyder, P. A., Rosett, H. L., Lee, A., Gould, J. B., & Ouellette, E. (1977). Effects of alcohol intake during pregnancy on newborn state regulation: A progress report. *Alcoholism: Clinical and Experimental Research, 1,* 233–241.

Sanders, J. L. & Buck, G. (2010). A long journey: Biological and non-biological parents' experiences raising children with FASD. *Journal of Population Therapeutics and Clinical Pharmacology, 17,* e308–e322.

Sanson, A., Hemphill, S. A., & Smart, D. (2002). Temperament in social development. In P. K. Smith & C. H. Hart (Eds.), *Blackwell handbook of childhood social development.* Malden, MA: Blackwell Publishers.

Sanson, A., Prior, M., & Kyrios, M. (1990). Contamination of measures in temperament research. *Merrill-Palmer Quarterly, 36,* 179–192.

Sanson, A. & Rothbart, M. K. (1995). Child temperament and parenting. In M. H. Bornstein (Ed.), *Handbook of parenting: Vol. 4. Applied and practical parenting.* Mahwah, NJ: Erlbaum.

Santens, S., Roggeman, C., Fias, W., & Verguts, T. (2010). Number processing pathways in human parietal cortex. *Cerebral Cortex, 20,* 77–88.

Sarafino, E. P. (2008). *Health psychology: Biopsychosocial interactions (6th edition).* Hoboken, NJ: Wiley.

Sartario, A., Lafrotuna, C. L., Poglaghi, S., & Trecate, L. (2002). The impact of gender, body dimension, and body composition in hand-grip strength in healthy children. *Journal of Endocrinological Investigation. 25,* 431–435.

Sattler, J. M. (1988). *Assessment of children* (3rd ed.). San Diego, CA: Jerome M. Sattler Publisher, Inc.

Sattler, J. M. (2001). *Assessment of children: Cognitive applications* (4th ed.). San Diego, CA: Jerome M. Sattler Publisher, Inc.

Sattler, J. M. & Hoge, R. D. (2006). *Assessment of children: Behavioral, social, and clinical foundations* (5th ed.). San Diego, CA: Jerome M. Sattler Publisher, Inc.

Saucier, D. & Ehresman, C. (2010). The physiology of sex differences. In J. Chrisler & D. R. McCreary (Eds.), *Handbook of gender research in psychology: Vol. 1: Gender research in general and experimental psychology* (pp. 215–233). New York, NY: Springer.

Savin-Williams, R. C. (1987). *Adolescence: An ethological perspective.* New York: Springer-Verlag.

Savin-Williams, R. C. (1998) *…and then I became gay: Young men's stories.* New York: Routledge.

Saxton, M. (1997). The Contrast Theory of negative input. *Journal of Child Language, 24*(1), 139–161.

Saxton, M. (2000). Negative evidence and negative feedback: Immediate effects on the grammaticality of child speech. *First Language, 20,* 221–252.

Sayegh, Y. & Dennis, W (1965). The effect of supplementary experiences upon the behavioral development of infants in institutions. *Child Development, 36,* 81–90.

Scalf, P. E., Dux, P. E., & Marois, R. (2011). Working memory encoding delays top-down attention to visual cortex. *Journal of Cognitive Neuroscience, 23,* 2593–2604.

Scarborough, H. & Wyckoff, J. (1986). Mother, I'd still rather do it myself: Some further non-effects of "motherese." *Journal of Child Language, 13,* 431–437.

Scarr, S. (1992). Developmental theories for the 1990s: Development and individual differences. *Child Development, 63,* 1–19.

Scarr, S. (1993). Biological and cultural diversity: The legacy of Darwin for development. *Child Development, 64,* 1333–1353.

Scarr, S. (1998). American child care today. *American Psychologist, 53,* 95–108.

Scarr, S. & Kidd, K. K. (1983). Developmental behavior genetics. In P. H. Mussen (Series Ed.) & M. M. Haith & J. J. Campos (Vol. Eds.), *Handbook of child psychology: Vol. 2. Infancy and developmental psychobiology* (4th ed.). New York: Wiley.

Scarr, S. & McCartney, K. (1983). How people make their own environments: A theory of genotype-environment effects. *Child Development, 54,* 424–435.

Scarr-Salapatek, S. (1975). Genetics and the development of intelligence. In F. Horowitz (Ed.), *Review of child development research* (Vol. 4). Chicago: University of Chicago Press.

Schacter, F. F., Shore, E., Hodapp, R., Chalfin, S., & Bundy, C. (1978). Do girls talk earlier? Mean length of utterance in toddlers. *Developmental Psychology, 14,* 388–392.

Schaffer, C. E. & Blatt, S. J. (1990). Interpersonal relationships and the experience of perceived efficacy. In R. J. Sternberg & J. Kolligian (Eds.), *Competence considered.* New Haven, CT: Yale University Press.

Schaffer, H. R. (1986). Some thoughts of an ordinologist. *Developmental Review, 6,* 115–121.

Schaffer, H. R. (1996). *Social Development.* Malden, MA: Blackwell Publishing.

Schaffer, H. R. & Emerson, P. E. (1964). The development of social attachments in infancy. *Monographs of the Society for Research in Child Development, 29* (3, Serial No. 94).

Scheers, N. J., Rutherford, G. W., & Kemp, J. S. (2003). Where should infants sleep? A comparison of risk for suffocation of infants sleeping in cribs, adult beds, and other sleeping locations. *Pediatrics, 112,* 883–889.

Scher, A., Epstein, R., & Tirosh, E. (2004). Stability and changes in sleep regulation: A longitudinal study from 3 months to 3 years. *International Journal of Behavioral Development, 28,* 268–274.

Schilling, T. H. (2000). Infants' looking at possible and impossible screen rotations: The role of familiarization. *Infancy, 1(4),* 389–402.

Schlesinger, I. M. (1988). The origin of relational categories. In Y. Levy, I. M. Schlesinger, & M. D. S. Braine (Eds.), *Categories and processes in language acquisition.* Hillsdale, NJ: Erlbaum.

Schmidt, L. A. & Fox, N. A. (1997). The development and outcomes of childhood shyness: A multiple psychophysiologic measure approach. In R. Vasta (Ed.), *Annals of child development* (Vol. 13). London: Kingsley.

Schmidt, L. A. & Fox, N. A. (1998). Fear-potentiated startle responses in temperamentally different human infants. *Developmental Psychobiology, 32,* 113–120.

Schmidt, L. A., Fox, N. A., Rubin, K. H., & Sternberg, E. M. (1997). Behavioral and neuroendocrine responses in shy children. *Developmental Psychobiology, 30,* 127–140.

Schmidt, L. A., Fox, N. A., Schulkin, J., & Gold, P. W. (1999). Behavioral and psychophysiological correlates of self-presentation in temperamentally shy children. *Developmental Psychobiology, 35,* 119–135.

Schmidt, U. (2000). Eating disorders. In D. Kohen (Ed.), *Women and mental health.* London: Routledge.

Schmithorst, V. J., Wilke, M., Dardzinski, B. J., & Holland, S. K. (2005). Cognitive functions correlate with white matter architecture in a normal pediatric population: A diffusion tensor MRI study. *Human Brain Mapping, 26*(2), 139–147.

Schmuckler, M. A. (1995). Self-knowledge of body position: Integration of perceptual and action system information. In P. Rochat (Ed.), *The self in infancy: Theory and research.* Amsterdam: Elsevier.

Schmuckler, M. A. & Fairhall, J. L. (2001).Visual-proprioceptive intermodal perception using point light displays. *Child Development, 72,* 949–962.

Schmuckler, M. A. & Jewell, D. T. (2007). Infants' visual-proprioceptive intermodal perception with imperfect contingency information. *Developmental Psychobiology, 49,* 387–398.

Schmuckler, M. A. & Tsang-Tong, H. Y. (2000). The role of visual and body movement information in infant search. *Developmental Psychology, 36*(4), 499–510.

Schneider, B. H., Atkinson, L., & Tardif, C. (2001). Child-parent attachment and children's peer relations: A quantitative review. *Developmental Psychology, 37,* 86–100.

Schneider, B. H., Benenson, J., Fulop, F., Berkics, M., & Sandor, M. (2011). Cooperation and competition. In P. K. Smith & K. H. Hart (Eds.), *The Wiley-Blackwell handbook of childhood social development, 2nd edition* (pp. 472–490). Hoboken, NJ. Wiley.

Schneider, B. H. & Byrne, B. M. (1985). Children's social skills training: A meta-analysis. In B. H. Schneider, K. H. Rubin, & J. E. Ledingham (Eds.), *Children's peer relations: Issues in assessment and intervention.* New York: Springer-Verlag.

Schneider, B. H., Rubin, K. H., & Ledingham, J. E. (Eds.). (1985). *Children's peer relations: Issues in assessment and intervention.* New York: Springer-Verlag.

Schneider, W. (1999). The development of metamemory in children. In D. Gopher & A. Kuriat (Eds.), *Attention and performance: XVII. Cognitive regulation of performance: Interaction of theory and application.* Cambridge, MA: MIT Press.

Schneider, W. & Bjorklund, D. F. (1998). Memory. In W. Damon (Series Ed.) & D. Kuhn & R. S. Siegler (Vol. Eds.), *Handbook of child psychology: Vol. 2. Cognition, perception, and language* (5th ed.). New York: Wiley.

Schneider, W., Gruber, H., Gold, A., & Opwis, K. (1993). Chess expertise and memory for chess positions in children and adults. *Journal of Experimental Child Psychology, 56,* 328–349.

Schneider, W., Korkel, J., & Weinert, F. E. (1987). *The knowledge base and memory performance: A comparison of academically successful and unsuccessful learners.* Paper presented at the meeting of the American Educational Research Association, Washington, DC.

Schneider, W., Kron-Sperl, V., & Hunnerkopf, M. (2009). The development of young children's memory strategies: Evidence from the Wurzburg Longitudinal Memory Study. *European Journal of Developmental Psychology, 6,* 70–99.

Schneider, W. & Pressley, M. (1997). *Memory development between 2 and 20* (2nd ed.) Mahwah, NJ: Erlbaum.

Schonert-Reichl, K. A. (1999). Relations of peer acceptance, friendship adjustment, and social behavior to moral reasoning during early adolescence. *Journal of Early Adolescence, 19,* 249–279.

Schonfeld, A. M., Mattson, S. N., Lang, A., Delis, D. C., & Riley, E. P. (2001). Verbal and nonverbal fluency in children with heavy prenatal alcohol exposure. *Journal of Studies on Alcohol, 62,* 239–246.

Schroeder, J. A. (2010). Sex and gender in sensation and perception. In J. Chrisler & D. R. McCreary (Eds.), *Handbook of gender research in psychology: Vol. 1: Gender research in general and experimental psychology* (pp. 235–257). New York, NY: Springer.

Schuengel, C., Bakermans-Kranenburg, M., van IJzen-doorn, M. H., & Blom, M. (1999). Unresolved loss and infant disorganization: Links to frightening maternal behavior. In J. Solomon & C. George (Eds.), *Attachment disorganization.* New York: Guilford.

Schultz, T. R. & Darley J. M. (1991). An information-processing model of retributive moral judgments based on "legal reasoning." In W. M. Kurtines & J. L. Gewirtz (Eds.), *Handbook of moral behavior and development: Vol. 2. Research.* Hillsdale, NJ: Erlbaum.

Schultz, T. R. & Wright, K. (1985). Concepts of negligence and intention in the assignment of moral responsibility. *Canadian Journal of Behavioural Science, 17,* 97–108.

Schultz, T. R., Wright, K., & Schleifer, M. (1986). Assignment of moral responsibility and punishment. *Child Development, 57,* 177–184.

Schwartz, C. E., Snidman, N., & Kagan, J. (1999). Adolescent social anxiety and outcome of inhibited temperament in childhood. *Journal of the American Academy of Child and Adolescent Psychiatry, 28,* 1008–1015.

Schwartz, C. E., Wright, C. I., Shin, L. M., Kagan, J., & Rauch, S. L. (2003). Inhibited and uninhibited infants "grown up": Adult amygdalar response to novelty. *Science, 300,* 1952–1953.

Schwartz, D., Dodge, K. A., Pettit, G. S., & Bates, J. E. (1997). The early socialization of aggressive victims of bullying. *Child Development, 68,* 665–675.

Schwartz, G., Kim, R. M., Kolundzija, A. B., Rieger, G., & Sanders, A. R. (2010). Biodemographic and physical correlates of sexual orientation of men. *Archives of Sexual Behavior, 39,* 93–109.

Schwartz, P. D., Maynard, A. M., & Uzelac, S. M. (2008). Adolescent egocentrism: A contemporary view. *Adolescence, 43,* 441–448.

Schwartz, R. G. & Camarata, S. (1985). Examining relationships between input and language development: Some statistical issues. *Journal of Child Language, 12,* 199–207.

Schwartz, R. G., Leonard, L. B., Frome-Loeb, D. M., & Swanson, L. A. (1987). Attempted sounds are sometimes not: An expanded view of phonological selection and avoidance. *Journal of Child Language, 14,* 411–418.

Schwartzman, A. E., Ledingham, J. E., & Serbin, L. A. (1985). Identification of children at risk for adult schizophrenia: A longitudinal study. *International Review of Applied Psychology, 34,* 363–380.

Schwenck, C., Bjorklund, D. F., & Schneider, W. (2007). Factors influencing the incidence of utilization deficiencies and other patterns of recall/strategy-use relations in a strategic memory task. *Child Development, 78*(6), 1771–1787.

Schwenck, C., Bjorklund, D. F., & Schneider, W. (2009). Developmental and individual differences in young children's use and maintenance of a selective memory strategy. *Developmental Psychology, 45*(4), 1034–1050.

Schyns, P. G., Jentzsch, I., Johnson, M., Schweinberger, S. R., & Gosselin, F. (2003). A principled method for determining the functionality of brain responses. *Neuroreport, 14,* 1665–1669.

Scott, F., Peters, H., Boogert, T., Robertson, R., Anderson, J., McLennan, A., Kesby, G., Edelman, D. (2002). The loss rates for invasive prenatal testing in a specialised obstetric ultrasound practice. *The Australian and New Zealand Journal of Obstetrics and Gynaecology, 42,* 55–58.

Scott, S. K. & Wise, R. J. S. (2003). PET and fMRI studies of the neural basis of speech perception. *Speech Communication, 41,* 23–34.

Scriver, C. R. (2001). Not preventing – yet, just avoiding Tay-Sachs disease. *Advances in Genetics, 44,* 267–274.

Seashore, M. J., Leifer, A. D., Barnett, C. R., & Leiderman, P. H. (1973). The effects of denial of early mother-infant interaction on maternal self-confidence. *Journal of Personality and Social Psychology, 26,* 369–378.

Sebald, H. (1989). Adolescent peer orientation: Changes in the support system during the last three decades. *Adolescence, 24,* 937–945.

Seem, S. R. & Clark, M. D. (2006). Healthy women, healthy men, and healthy adults: An evaluation of gender-role stereotypes in the twenty-first century. *Sex Roles, 55,* 247–258.

Segal, N. L. (1999). *Entwined lives.* New York: Penguin Putnam.

Seginer, R. (1998). Adolescents' perceptions of relationships with older sibling in the context of other close relationships. *Journal of Research on Adolescence, 8,* 287–308.

Seidman, E., Allen, L., Aber, J. L., Mitchell, C., & Feinman, J. (1994). The impact of school transition in early adolescence on the self-system and perceived social context of poor urban youth. *Child Development, 65,* 507–522.

Seifer, R. (2000). Temperament and goodness of fit: Implications for developmental psychopathology. In A. J. Sameroff & M. Lewis (Eds.), *Handbook of developmental psychopathology* (2nd ed.). Dordrecht, Netherlands: Kluwer Academic Publishers.

Seifer, R., & Schiller, M. (1995). The role of parenting sensitivity, infant temperament, and dyadic interaction in attachment theory and assessment. In E. Waters, B. E. Vaughn, G. Posada, & K. Kondo-Ikemura (Eds.), Caregiving, cultural, and cognitive perspectives on secure-base behavior and working models. *Monographs of the Society for Research in Child Development, 60* (2–3, Serial No. 244).

Selman, R. L. (1980). *The growth of interpersonal understanding: Development and clinical analyses.* New York: Academic Press.

Semendeferi, K. (1999). The frontal lobes of the great apes with a focus on the gorilla and the orangutan. In S. T. Parker, R. W. Mitchell, & H. L. Miles (Eds.), *The mentalities of gorillas and organgutans.* Cambridge: Cambridge University Press.

Semendeferi, K., Lu, A., Schenker, N., & Damasio, H. (2002). Humans and great apes share a large frontal cortex. *Nature Neuroscience, 5,* 272–276.

Sénéchal, M. (2006). Testing the home literacy model: parent involvement in kindergarten is differentially related to grade 4 reading comprehension, fluency spelling, and reading for pleasure. *Scientific Studies of Reading 10,* 59–87.

Sénéchal, M., & LeFevre, J.-A. (2002). Parental involvement in the development of children's reading skill: A five-year longitudinal study. *Child Development, 73,* 445–460.

Senghas, A., Kita, S., & Özyürek, A. (2004). Children creating core properties of language: Evidence from an emerging sign language in Nicaragua. *Science, 305,* 1779–1782.

Serbin, L. A., Peters, P. L., McAffer, V. J., & Schwartzman, A. E. (1991). Childhood aggression and withdrawal as predictors of adolescent pregnancy, early parenthood, and environmental risk for the next generation. *Canadian Journal of Behavioural Science, 23,* 318–331.

Serbin, L. A., Poulin-Dubois, D., & Eichstedt, J. (2002). Infants' responses to gender-inconsistent events. *Infancy, 3,* 531–542.

Serbin, L. A., Poulin-Dubois, D., Colburne, K. A., Sen, M. G., & Eichstedt, J. A. (2001). Gender stereotyping in infancy: Visual preferences for and knowledge of gender-stereotyped toys in the second year. *International Journal of Behavioral Development, 25,* 7–15.

Serbin, L. A., Powlishta, K. K., & Gulko, J. (1993). The development of sex-typing in middle childhood. *Monographs of the Society for Research in Child Development, 58*(Serial No. 232).

Serbin, L. A. & Sprafkin, C. (1986). The salience of gender and the process of sex-typing in three- to seven-year-old children. *Child Development, 57,* 1188–1199.

Seress, L. & Abraham, H. (2008). Pre- and postnatal morphological development of the human hippocampal formation. In C. A. Nelson & M. Luciana (Eds.), *Handbook of developmental cognitive neuroscience* (2nd ed., pp. 187–212). Cambridge, MA: MIT Press.

Seress, L. (2001). Morphological changes of the human hippocampal formation from midgestation to early childhood. In C. A. Nelson & M. Luciana (Eds.), *Handbook of developmental cognitive neuroscience* (pp. 45–58). Cambridge, MA: MIT Press.

Seth, A. K. & Baars, B. J. (2005). Neural Darwinism and consciousness. *Consciousness and Cognition,* 14, 140–168.

Sethi, A., Mischel, W., Aber, J. L., Shoda, Y., & Rodriguez, M. L. (2000). The role of strategic attention deployment in development of self-regulation: Predicting preschoolers' delay of gratification from mother-toddler interactions. *Developmental Psychology, 36,* 767–777.

Shah, T., Sullivan, K., & Carter, J. (2006). Sudden infant death syndrome and reported maternal smoking during pregnancy. *American Journal of Public Health, 96,* 1757–1759.

Shah, V.S. & Ohlsson, A. (2007). Venepuncture versus heel lance for blood sampling in term neonates. *Cochrane Database of Systematic Reviews, 4,* CD001452.

Shantz, C. U. & Hartup, W. W. (Eds.). (1995). *Conflict in child and adolescent development.* New York: Cambridge University Press.

Sharpe, R. M. & Skakkebaek, N. E. (1993). Are oestrogens involved in falling sperm counts and disorders of the male reproductive tract? *Lancet, 341,* 1392–1395.

Shatz, M. (1983). On transition, continuity, and coupling: An alternative approach to communicative development. In R. M. Golinkoff (Ed.), *The transition from prelinguistic to linguistic communication.* Hillsdale, NJ: Erlbaum.

Shatz, M. & Gelman, R. (1973). The development of communication skills: Modifications in the speech of young children as a function of the listener. *Monographs of the Society for Research in Child Development, 38* (5, Serial No. 152).

Shatz, M. & McCloskey, L. (1984). Answering appropriately: A developmental perspective on conversational knowledge. In S. A. Kuczaj (Ed.), *Discourse development: Progress in cognitive developmental research.* New York: Springer-Verlag.

Shayer, M., Ginsburg, D., & Coe, R. (2007). Thirty years on – a large anti-Flynn effect? The Piagetian test *Volume & Heaviness* norms 1975–2003. *British Journal of Educational Psychology, 77,* 25–41.

Shayer, M. & Wylam, H. (1978). The distribution of Piagetian stages of thinking in British middle and secondary school children: II. 14 to 16 year old and sex differentials. *British Journal of Educational Psychology, 48,* 62–70.

She, H.-C. (2000). The interplay of a biology teacher's beliefs, teaching practices and gender-based student-teacher classroom interaction. *Educational Research, 42,* 100–111.

Shea, D. L., Lubinski, D., & Benbow, C. P. (2001). Importance of assessing spatial ability in intellectually talented young adolescents: A 20-year longitudinal study. *Journal of Educational Psychology, 93,* 604–614.

Sheehan, M. J. & Watson, M. (2008). Reciprocal influences between maternal discipline techniques and aggression in children and adolescents. *Aggressive Behavior, 34,* 245–255.

Shen, K. & Paré, M. (2007). Neuronal activity in superior colliculus signals both stimulus identity and saccade goals during visual conjunction search. *Journal of Vision, 7*(5):15, 1–13.

Shepard, T. H. (1986). Human teratogenicity. *Advances in Pediatrics, 33,* 225–268.

Sheridan, C., Draganova, R., Ware, M., Murphy, P., Govindan, R., Siegel, E. R. et al. (2010). Early development of brain responses to rapidly presented auditory stimulation: A magnetoencephalographic study. *Brain and Development, 32*(8), 642–657.

Sheridan, C. J., Matuz, T., Draganova, R., Eswaran, H., & Preissi, H. (2010). Fetal magnetoencephalography – Achievements and challenges in the study of prenatal and early postnatal brain responses: A review. *Infant and Child Development, 19,* 80–93.

Sherif, M., Harvey, O. J., White, B. J., Hood, W. R., & Sherif, C. W. (1988). *Intergroup conflict and cooperation: The Robbers Cave experiment.* Norman, OK: University of Oklahoma Press.

Shi, R. & Gauthier, B. (2005). Recognition of function words in 8-month-old French-learning infants. *Journal of the Acoustical Society of America, 117,* 2426.

Shi, R., Morgan, J. L., & Allopenna, P. (1998). Phonological and acoustic bases for earliest grammatical category assignment: A cross-linguistic perspective. *Journal of Child Language, 25,* 169–201.

Shi, R., Werker, J., & Morgan, J. (1999). Newborn infants' sensitivity to perceptual cues to lexical and grammatical words. *Cognition, 72,* B11–21.

Shields, D. L. & Bredemeier, B. L. (2008). Sport and the development of character. In L. P. Nucci & D. Narvaez (Eds.), *Handbook of moral and character education* (pp. 500–519). New York, NY: Routledge.

Shigetomi, C. C., Hartmann, D. P., & Gelfand, D. M. (1981). Sex differences in children's altruistic behavior and reputations for helpfulness. *Developmental Psychology, 17,* 434–437.

Shirley, M. M. (1933). *The first two years; a study of twenty-five babies.* Minneapolis, MN: University of Minnesota Press.

Shirpak, K. R., Maticka-Tyndale, E., & Chinichian, M. (2007). Iranian immigrants' perceptions of sexuality in Canada: A symbolic interactionist approach. *Canadian Journal of Human Sexuality, 16,* 113–128.

Shoda, Y., Mischel, W., & Peake, P. K. (1990). Predicting adolescent cognitive and self-regulatory competencies from preschool delay of gratification: Identifying diagnostic conditions. *Developmental Psychology, 26,* 978–986.

Shonkoff, J. P. & Phillips, D. A. (2000). *From neurons to neighborhoods: The science of early childhood development.* Washington, DC: National Academy Press.

Shore, C. M. (1995). *Individual differences in language development.* Thousand Oaks, CA: Sage.

Shu, S. (1999). *Grandparents, parents, and children: A study of three-generation family structure and intergenerational relationships in contemporary China.* Unpublished doctoral dissertation, University of London.

Shucard, J. L. & Shucard, D. W. (1990). Auditory evoked potentials and hand preference in 6-month-old infants: Possible gender-related differences in cerebral organization. *Developmental Psychology, 26,* 923–930.

Shucard, J. L., Shucard, D. W., Cummins, K. R., & Campos, J. J. (1981). Auditory evoked potentials and sex-related differences in brain development. *Brain and Language, 13,* 91–102.

Shulman, S. & Collins, W. A. (Eds.). (1997). *New directions for child development: No. 78. Romantic relationships in adolescence: Developmental perspectives.* San Francisco: Jossey-Bass.

Shultz, T. R. (2003). *Computational Developmental Psychology*. Cambridge, MA: MIT Press.

Shure, M. B. & Spivack, G. (1980). Interpersonal problem-solving as a mediator of behavioral adjustment in preschool and kindergarten children. *Journal of Applied Developmental Psychology, 1,* 29–44.

Shwe, H. I. & Markman, E. M. (1997). Young children's appreciation of the mental impact of their communicative signals. *Developmental Psychology, 33,* 630–636.

Shweder, R. A., Goodnow, J. J., Hatano, G., LeVine, R. A., Markus, H. R., & Miller, P. J. (2006). *The Cultural psychology of development: One mind, many mentalities.* In W. Damon & R. M. Lerner (Series Eds.) & R. M. Lerner (Vol. Ed.), *Handbook of child psychology: Vol. 1. Theoretical models of human development* (6th ed., pp. 716–792). Hoboken, NJ: Wiley.

Shweder, R. A., Mahapatra, M., & Miller, J. (1987). Culture and moral development. In J. Kagan & S. Lamb (Eds.), *The emergence of morality in young children.* Chicago: University of Chicago Press.

Shweder, R. A. & Much, M. C. (1987). Determinations of meaning: Discourse and moral socialization. In W. M. Kurtines & J. L. Gewirtz (Eds.), *Moral development through social interaction.* New York: Wiley.

Sieber, J. E. (1992). *Planning ethically responsible research: A guide for students and internal review boards.* Newbury Park, CA: Sage.

Siegel, L. S. (1984). Home environment influences on cognitive development in preterm and full-term children during the first 5 years. In A. W. Gottfried (Ed.), *Home environment and early cognitive development.* New York: Academic Press.

Siegel, L. S. (1989). A reconceptualization of prediction from infant test scores. In M. H. Bornstein & N. Krasnegor (Eds.), *Stability and continuity in mental development.* Hillsdale, NJ: Erlbaum.

Siegel, L. S. (1992). Infant motor, cognitive, and language behaviors as predictors of achievement at school age. In C. K. Rovee-Collier & L. P. Lipsitt (Eds.), *Advances in infancy research* (Vol. 7). Norwood, NJ: Ablex.

Siegler, R. S. (1991). *Children's thinking (2nd* ed.). Englewood Cliffs, NJ: Prentice Hall.

Siegler, R. S. (1996). *Emerging minds: The process of change in children's thinking.* New York: Oxford University Press.

Siegler, R. S. (1998). *Children's thinking* (3rd ed.). Upper Saddle River, NJ: Prentice Hall.

Siegler, R. S. (2000). The rebirth of children's learning. *Child Development, 71,* 26–35.

Siegler, R. S. (2005). Children's learning, American Psychologist, *60,* 769–778.

Siegler, R. S. (2006). Microgenetic analyses of learning. In W. Damon & R. Lerner (Eds.) *Handbook of child psychology: Vol. 2 Cognition, perception, and language,* pp. 464–510. Hoboken, NJ: Wiley.

Siegler, R. S. & Alibali, M. (2005). Sociocultural theories of development. In *Children's thinking* (pp. 107–140). Upper Saddle River, NJ: Prentice Hall.

Siegler, R. S. & Jenkins, E. (1989). *How children discover new strategies.* Hillsdale, NJ: Erlbaum.

Siegler, R. S. & Shipley, C. (1995). Variation, selection, and cognitive change. In T. J. Simon & G. S. Halford (Eds.), *Developing cognitive competence: New approaches to process modeling.* Hillsdale, NJ: Erlbaum.

Siegler, R. S. & Svetina, M. (2006). What Leads Children to Adopt New Strategies? A Microgenetic/Cross-Sectional Study of Class Inclusion. *Child Development, 77,* 997–1015.

Siervogel, R. M., Waynard, L. M., Wisemandle, W. A., Roche, A. F., Guo, S. S., Chumlea, W. C., et al. (2000). Annual changes in total body fat and fat-free mass in children from 8 to 18 years in relation to changes in body mass index: The Fels Longitudinal Study. *Annals of the New York Academy of Science, 904,* 420–423.

Sigel, I. E. (1986). Reflections on the belief-behavior connection: Lessons learned from a research program on parental belief systems and teaching strategies. In W. K. Ashmore & D. M. Brodzinsky (Eds.), *Thinking about the family: Views of parents and children.* Hillsdale, NJ: Erlbaum.

Sigel, I. E. & McGillicuddy-De Lisi (2002). Parental beliefs are cognitions: The dynamic belief systems model. In M. H. Bornstein (Ed.), *Handbook of parenting* (2nd ed., Vol. 3). Mahwah, NJ: Erlbaum.

Sigman, M. (1995). Nutrition and child development: More food for thought. *Current Directions in Psychological Science, 4,* 52–55.

Silver, L. B. (1999). *Attention-deficit hyperactivity disorder* (2nd ed.). Washington, DC: American Psychiatric Press.

Simmerman, K. & Christner, R. W. (2007). Cognitive-behavior group therapy with children who are ostracized or socially isolated. In R. W. Christner, J. L. Stewart, & A. Freeman (Eds.), *Handbook of cognitive-behavior group therapy with Children and Adolescents* (pp. 409–426). New York: Routledge/Taylor & Francis.

Simmons, R. G., Carlton-Ford, S. L., & Blyth, D. A. (1987). Predicting how a child will cope with the transition to junior high school. In R. M. Lerner & T. M. Foch (Eds.), *Biological-psychosocial interactions in early adolescence.* Hillsdale, NJ: Erlbaum.

Simpson, J. A. & Beckes, L. (2010). Evolutionary perspectives on prosocial behavior. In M. Mikulincer & P. R. Shaver (Eds.), *Prosocial motives, emotions, and behavior: The better angels of our nature* (pp. 35–53). Washington, DC: American Psychological Association.

Simpson, J. A. & Belsky, J. (2008). Attachment theory within a modern evolutionary framework. In J. Cassidy & P. R. Shaver (Eds.) *Handbook of attachment: Theory, research, and clinical applications (2nd edition)* (pp. 131–157). New York, NY: Guilford.

Singer, W. (2007). Binding by synchrony. *Scholarpedia, 2,* 1657.

Singh, L., Nestor, S., Parikh, C. & Yull, A. (2009). Influences of infant-directed speech on early word recognition. *Infancy, 14*(6), 654–666.

Single Mothers by Choice (2009). Downloaded on January 15, 2011 from http://singlemothersbychoice.com/index.html.

Skelton, C. (2001). *Schooling the boys: Masculinities and primary education.* Buckingham, UK: Open University Press.

Skinner, B. F. (1953). *Science and human behavior.* New York: Macmillan.

Skinner, B. F. (1957). *Verbal behavior.* New York: Appleton-Century-Crofts.

Skoczenski, A. M. & Norcia, A. M. (2002). Late maturation of visual hyperacuity. *Psychological Science, 13,* 537–541.

Skowronski, J. J., Betz, A. L., Thompson, C. P., & Larsen, S. F. (1995). Long-term performance in autobiographical event dating: Patterns of accuracy and error across a two-and-a-half year time span. In A. L. Healy & L. B. Bourne (Eds.), *Acquisition and long term retention of knowledge and skills: The durability and specificity of cognitive procedures.* Newbury Park, CA: Sage.

Slaby, R. G. & Frey, K. S. (1975). Development of gender constancy and selective attention to same-sex models. *Child Development, 46,* 849–856.

Slade, A. (1987). Quality of attachment and early symbolic play. *Developmental Psychology, 23,* 78–85.

Slater, A. (1995). Visual perception and memory at birth. In C. K. Rovee-Collier & L. P. Lipsitt (Eds.), *Advances in infancy research* (Vol. 9). Norwood, NJ: Ablex.

Slater, A., Johnson, S. P., Brown, E., & Badenoch, M. (1996). Newborn infants' perception of partly occluded objects. *Infant Behavior and Development, 19,* 145–148.

Slater, A., Johnson, S. P., Kellman, P. J., & Spelke, E. S. (1994). The role of three-dimensional depth cues in infants' perception of partly occluded objects. *Early Development and Parenting, 3,* 187–191.

Slater, A., Mattock, A., & Brown, E. (1990). Size constancy at birth: Newborn infant's responses to retinal and real size. *Journal of Experimental Child Psychology, 49,* 314–322.

Slater, A., Mattock, A., Brown, E., & Bremner, J. G. (1991). Form perception at birth: Cohen and Younger (1984) revisited. *Journal of Experimental Child Psychology, 51,* 395–406.

Slaughter-DeFoe, D. T., Nakagawa, K., Takanishi, R., & Johnson, D. J. (1990). Toward cultural/ecological perspectives on schooling and achievement in African- and Asian-American children. *Child Development, 61,* 363–383.

Slobin, D. I. (1982). Universal and particular in the acquisition of language. In E. Wanner & L. R. Gleitman (Eds.), *Language acquisition: The state of the art.* Cambridge: Cambridge University Press.

Slobin, D. I. (1985a). evidence for the language-making capacity. In D. I. Slobin (Ed.), *The crosslinguistic study of language acquisition: Vol. 2. Theoretical issues.* Hillsdale, NJ: Erlbaum.

Slobin, D. I. (Ed.). (1985b). *The crosslinguistic study of language acquisition: Vol. 2. Theoretical issues.* Hillsdale, NJ: Erlbaum.

Slomkowski, C. L. & Dunn, J. (1993, March). *Conflict in close relationships.* Paper presented at the meeting of the Society for Research in Child Development, New Orleans.

Slomkowski, C. L. & Killen, M. (1992). Young children's conceptions of transgressions with friends and non-friends. *International Journal of Behavioral Development, 15,* 247–258.

Smetana, J. G. (2006). Social-cognitive domain theory: Consistencies and variations in children's moral and social judgments. In M. Killen & J. G. Smetana (Eds.), *Handbook of moral development* (pp. 119–154). Mahwah, NJ: Lawrence Erlbaum.

Smetana, J. G. & Braeges, J. L. (1990). The development of toddlers' moral and conventional judgments. *Merrill-Palmer Quarterly, 36,* 329–346.

Smetana, J. G., Schlagman, N., & Adams, P. (1993). Preschoolers' judgments about hypothetical and actual transgressions. *Child Development, 64,* 202–214.

Smilansky, S. (1968). *The effects of sociodramatic play on disadvantaged preschool children.* New York: Wiley.

Smiley, P. A. & Dweck, C. S. (1994). Individual differences in achievement goals among young children. *Child Development, 65,* 1723–1743.

Smith, A., Fried, P., Hogan, M., & Cameron, I. (2004). Effects of prenatal marijuana on response inhibition: An fMRI study of young adults. *Neurotoxicology and Teratology, 26,* 533–542.

Smith, A., Fried, P., Hogan, M., & Cameron, I. (2006). Effects of prenatal marijuana on visuospatial working memory: An fMRI study in young adults. *Neurotoxicology and Teratology, 28,* 286–295.

Smith, A., Stewart, D., Peled, M., Poon, C., & Saewyc, E. (2009). *A Picture of health: Highlights from the 2008 BC Adolescent Health Survey.* Vancouver, BC: McCreary Centre Society.

Smith, B. A. & Blass, E. M. (1996). Taste-mediated calming in premature, preterm, and full-term human infants. *Developmental Psychology, 32,* 1084–1089.

Smith, E. & Udry J. (1985). Coital and non-coital sexual behaviors of white and black adolescents. *American Journal of Public Health, 75,* 1200–1203.

Smith, P. K. & Drew, L. M. (2002). Grandparenthood. In M. H. Bornstein (Ed.), *Handbook of parenting* (2nd ed., Vol. 3). Mahwah, NJ: Erlbaum.

Smith, R. (1999). The timing of birth. *Scientific American, 280,* 68–75.

Smolin, L. A. & Grosvenor, M. B. (2010). *Nutrition: Science and applications (2nd edition).* Hoboken, NJ: Wiley.

Snarey, J. R. (1985). Cross-cultural universality of social-moral development: A critical review of Kohlbergian research. *Psychological Bulletin, 97,* 202–232.

Snow, C. E. (1983). Saying it again: The role of expanded and deferred imitations in language acquisition. In K. E. Nelson (Ed.), *Children's language* (Vol. 4). Hillsdale, NJ: Erlbaum.

Snow, C. E. (1999). Social perspectives on the emergence of language. In B. MacWhinney (Ed.), *The emergence of language.* Mahwah, NJ: Erlbaum.

Snow, C. E. & Goldfield, B. A. (1983). Turn the page please: Situation-specific language acquisition. *Journal of Child Language, 10,* 551–569.

Snow, C. E., Pan, B. E., Imbens-Bailey, A., & Herman, J. (1996). Learning how to say what one means: A longitudinal study of children's speech act use. *Social Development, 5,* 56–84.

Snow, C. E., Perlman, R., & Nathan, D. (1987). Why routines are different: Toward a multiple-factors model of the relation between input and language acquisition. In K. E. Nelson & A. VanKleeck (Eds.), *Children's language* (Vol. 6). Hillsdale, NJ: Erlbaum.

Snustad, D. P. & Simmons, M. J. (2009). *Principles of genetics (5th edition).* Hoboken, NJ: Wiley.

Snyder, J. J. & Patterson, G. R. (1995). Individual differences in social aggression: A test of a reinforcement model of socialization in the natural environment. *Behavior Therapy, 26,* 371–391.

Snyder, J. J., Reid, J., & Patterson, G. R. (2003). A social learning model of child and adolescent antisocial behavior. In B. B. Lahey, T. E. Moffitt, & A. Capsi (Eds.), *Causes of conduct disorder and juvenile delinquency* (pp. 27–48). New York: Guilford.

Snyder, J., Schrepferman, L., McEachern, A., Barner, S., Johnson, K., & Provines, J. (2008). Peer deviancy training and peer coercion: Dual processes associated with early-onset conduct problems. *Child Development, 79,* 252–268.

Snyder, J., Schrepferman, L., Oeser, J., Patterson, G., Stoolmiller, M., Johnson, K., & Snyder, A. (2005). Deviancy training and association with deviant peers in young children: Occurrence and contribution to early-onset conduct problems. *Development and Psychopathology, 17,* 397–413.

Snyder, J., West, L., Stockemer, V., & Gibbons, S. (1996). A social learning model of peer choice in the natural environment. *Journal of Applied Developmental Psychology, 17,* 215–237.

Society for Research in Child Development (2007). *Ethical standards for research with children.* Downloaded August 23, 2010 from http://www.srcd.org/index.php?option=com_content&task=view&id=68&Itemid=499

Soderstrom, M., Conwell, E., Feldman, N., & Morgan, J.L. (2009). Statistical learning in language acquisition: Beyond demonstrations, towards a theory. *Developmental Science, 12,* 409–411.

Soderstrom, M., White, K. S., Conwell, E., & Morgan, J. L. (2007). Receptive grammatical knowledge of familiar content words and inflection in 16-month-olds. *Infancy, 12*(1), 1–29.

Sohlberg, M. E. & Olweus, D. (2003). Prevalence estimation of school bullying with the Olweus bully/victim questionnaire. *Aggressive Behavior, 29,* 239–268.

Sokolov, E. N. (1960). *Perception and the conditioned reflex.* New York: Macmillan.

Solomon, G. E. A., Johnson, S. C., Zaitchik, D., & Carey, S. (1996). Like father, like son: Young children's understanding of how and why offspring resemble their parents. *Child Development, 67,* 151–171.

Solomon, J. & George, C. (2008). The measurement of attachment security and related constructs in infancy and early childhood. In J. Cassidy & P. R. Shaver (Eds.), *Handbook of attachment: Theory, research, and clinical applications (2nd edition)* (pp. 283–416). New York, NY: Guilford.

Solomon, J. & George, C. (2011). *Disorganized attachment and caregiving.* New York, NY: Guilford.

Soltis J. (2004). The signal functions of early infant crying. *Behavioral and Brain Sciences, 27,* 443–90.

Somary, K. & Stricker, G. (1998). Becoming a grandparent: A longitudinal study of expectations and early experiences as a function of sex and lineage. *Gerontologist, 38,* 53–61.

Sommerville, J. (1982). *The rise and fall of childhood.* Beverly Hills, CA: Sage.

Sonnenschein, S. (1988). The development of referential communication: Speaking to different listeners. *Child Development, 59,* 694–702.

Sophian, C. (1995). Representation and reasoning in early numerical development: Counting, conservation, and comparison between sets. *Child Development, 66,* 559–577.

Sophian, C. (1998). A developmental perspective on children's counting. In C. Donlan (Ed.), *The development of mathematical skills: Studies in developmental psychology.* Hove, UK: Psychology Press.

Sorce, J. F., Emde, R. N., Campos, J. J., & Klinnert, M. D. (1985). Maternal emotional signaling: Its effect on the visual cliff behavior of 1-year-olds. *Developmental Psychology, 21,* 195–200.

Soska, K. C., Adolph, K. E., & Johnson, S. P. (2010). Systems in development: Motor skill acquisition facilitates three-dimensional object completion. *Developmental Psychology*, *46*, 129–138.

Southgate, V., Csibra, G., Kaufman, J., & Johnson, M. H. (2008). Distinct processing of objects and faces in the infant brain. *Journal of Cognitive Neuroscience, 20,* 741–749.

Southwell, A. L., Ko, K., & Patterson, P. H. (2009). Intrabody gene therapy ameliorates motor, cognitive, and neuropathological symptoms in multiple mouse models of Huntington's disease. *Journal of Neuroscience, 29,* 13589–13602.

Spangler, G. & Grossmann, K. E. (1993). Biobehavioral organization in securely and insecurely attached infants. *Child Development, 64,* 1439–1450.

Spearman, C. (1927). *The abilities of man.* New York: Macmillan.

Speer, J. R. & Flavell, J. H. (1979). Young children's knowledge of the relative difficulty of recognition and recall memory tasks. *Developmental Psychology, 15,* 214–217.

Spelek, E. S. & Newport, E. L. (1998). Nativism, empiricism, and the development of knowledge. In W. Damon (Series Ed.) & R. M. Lerner (Vol. Ed.), *Handbook of child psychology: Vol. 1. Theoretical models of human development* (5th ed.). New York: Wiley.

Spelke, E. S. (1976). Infants' intermodal perception of events. *Cognitive Psychology, 8,* 533–560.

Spelke, E. S. (1985). Perception of unity, persistence, and identity: Thoughts on infants' conceptions of objects. In J. Mehler & R. Fox (Eds.), *Neonate cognition: Beyond the blooming buzzing confusion.* Hillsdale, NJ: Erlbaum.

Spelke, E. S. (1988). Where perceiving ends and thinking begins: The apprehension of objects in infancy. In A. Yonas (Ed.), *Minnesota symposia on child psychology: Vol. 20. Perceptual development in infancy.* Hillsdale, NJ: Erlbaum.

Spelke, E. S. (1991). Physical knowledge in infancy: Reflections on Piaget's theory. In S. Carey & R. Gelman (Eds.), *The epigenesis of mind.* Hillsdale, NJ: Erlbaum.

Spelke, E. S., Breinlinger, K., Macomber, J., & Jacobson, K. (1992). Origins of knowledge. *Psychological Review, 99,* 605–632.

Spelke, E. S. & Cortelyou, A. (1981). Perceptual aspects of social learning: Looking and listening in infancy. In M. E. Lamb & L. R. Sherrod (Eds.), *Infant social cognition: Empirical and theoretical considerations.* Hillsdale, NJ: Erlbaum.

Spelke, E. S. & Hermer, L. (1996). Early cognitive development: Objects and space. In R. Gelman & T. Au (Eds.), *Perceptual and cognitive development.* San Diego, CA: Academic Press.

Spelke, E. S. & Kinzler, K. D. (2007). Core knowledge. *Developmental Science, 10,* 89–96.

Spelke, E. S. & Owsley, C. J. (1979). Intermodal exploration and knowledge in infancy. *Infant Behavior and Development, 2,* 13–28.

Spelke, E. S., Phillips, A., & Woodward, A. L. (1995). Infants' knowledge of object motion and human action. In D. Sperber, D. Premack, & A. J. Premack (Eds.), *Causal cognition.* Oxford, England: Clarendon Press.

Spelke, E. S. & von Hofsten, C. (2001). Predictive reaching for occluded objects by 6-month-old infants. *Journal of Cognition and Development, 2,* 261–281.

Spencer, J. P., Vereijken, B., Diedrich, F. J., & Thelen, E. (2000). Posture and the mergence of manual skills. *Developmental Science, 3,* 216–233.

Spencer, M. B. & Markstrom-Adams, C. (1990). Identity processes among racial and ethnic minority children in America. *Child Development, 61,* 290–310.

Spielmann, R. (2002). *'You're so fat!' Exploring Ojibwe discourse.* Toronto: University of Toronto Press.

Spinath, B. & Spinath, F. M. (2005). Development of self-perceived ability in elementary school: The role of parents' perceptions, teacher evaluations, and intelligence. *Cognitive Development, 20,* 190–204.

Spinath, B., Spinath, F. M., Harlaar, N., & Plomin, R. (2006). Predicting school achievement from general cognitive ability, self-perceived ability, and intrinsic value. *Intelligence, 34,* 363–374.

Squire, L. R. (2009). Memory and brain systems: 1969-2009. *The Journal of Neuroscience*, *29*, 12711–12716.

Squire, L. R. & Schachter, D. L. (2002). *Neuropsychology of Memory*. New York: Guilford Press.

Sroufe, L. A. (1986). Bowlby's contribution to psychoanalytic theory and developmental psychology: Attachment, separation, loss. *Journal of Child Psychology and Psychiatry, 27,* 841–849.

Sroufe, L. A. (1990). An organizational perspective on the self. In D. Cicchetti & M. Beeghly (Eds.), *The self in transition: Infancy to childhood.* Chicago: University of Chicago Press.

Sroufe, L. A. (1996). *Emotional development.* New York: Cambridge University Press.

Sroufe, L. A. (2005). Attachment and development: A prospective, longitudinal study from birth to adulthood. *Attachment & Human Development, 7,* 349–367.

Sroufe, L. A., Bennett, C., Englund, M., Urban, J., & Shulman, S. (1993). The significance of gender boundaries in preadolescence: Contemporary correlates and antecedents of boundary relations and maintenance. *Child Development, 64, 455–466.*

Sroufe, L. A., Egeland, B., Carlson, E. A., & Collins, W A. (2005). *The development of the person: The Minnesota study of risk and adaptation from birth to adulthood.* New York: Guilford.

Stacey, J. & Biblarz, T (2001). (How) does the sexual orientation of parents matter? *American Sociological Review, 66,* 159–183.

Stack, D. M. & Muir, D. W (1992). Adult tactile stimulation during face-to-face interactions modulates five month-olds' affect and attention. *Child Development, 63,* 1509–1525.

Stack, D. M., Serbin, L. A., Enns, L. N., Ruttle, P. L., & Barrieau, L. (2010). Parental effects on children's emotional development over time and across generations. *Infants & Young Children, 23,* 52–69.

Stack, D. M., Serbin, L. A., Schwartzman, A. E., & Ledingham, J. E. (2005). Girls' aggression across the life course: Long-term outcomes and intergenerational risk. In D. Pepler, K. Madsen, C. Webster, & K. Levene (Eds.), *Development and treatment of girlhood aggression.* Mahwah, NJ: Erlbaum.

Stade, B. C., Stevens, B., Ungar, W. J., Beyene, J., & Koren, G. (2006). Health-related quality of life of Canadian children and youth prenatally exposed to alcohol. *Health and Quality of Life Outcomes, 4*:81 doi:10.1186/1477-7525-4-81.

Stager, C. L. & Werker, J. F. (1997). Infants listen for more phonetic detail in speech perception than in word-learning tasks. *Nature, 388,* 381–382.

Stanovich, K. E. (1993). Does reading make you smarter? Literacy and the development of verbal intelligence. In H. W. Reese (Ed.), *Advances in child development and behavior* (Vol. 24). San Diego, CA: Academic Press.

Stanwood, G. D. & Levitt, P. (2001). The effects of cocaine on the developing nervous system. In C. A. Nelson & M. Luciana (Eds.), *Handbook of developmental cognitive neuroscience.* Cambridge, MA: MIT Press.

Starkey, P. & Cooper, R. (1980). Perception of numbers by human infants. *Science, 210,* 1033–1034.

Statistics Canada (2003). The Daily, Tuesday December 9, 2003: *Parents and grandchildren.* Available at: www.statcan.ca/Daily/English/031209/d031209b.htm

Statistics Canada (2005). The Daily, Wednesday, March 9, 2005: *Divorces.* Available at: www.statcan.ca/Daily/English/050309/d050309b.htm.

Statistics Canada (2006). The Daily, Monday, July 31, 2006: *Births.* Available at: www.statcan.ca/Daily/English/060731/d060731b.htm.

Statistics Canada (2007a). The Daily, Wednesday September 12, 2007: *2006 Census: Families, marital status, households and dwelling characteristics.* Available at: www.statcan.ca/Daily/English/070912/td070912.htm

Statistics Canada (2007b). *Births: 2005.* Catalogue no. 84F0210XIE. Ottawa: Ministry of Industry.

Statistics Canada (2008). Trends in teen sexual behaviour and condom use. *Health Reports, 19,* no. 3, catalogue no. 82-003-XPE.

Staub, E. (1971). Helping a person in distress: The influence of implicit and explicit rules of conduct on children and adults. *Journal of Personality and Social Psychology, 17,* 137–145.

Staunton, H. (2005). Mammalian sleep. *Naturwissenschaften, 35,* 15.

Steben, M. & Sacks, S. L. (1997). Genital herpes: The etiology and control of a common sexually transmitted disease. *The Canadian Journal of Human Sexuality, 6,* 127–150.

Steele, H., Steele, M., & Fonagy, P. (1996). Associations among attachment classifications of mothers, fathers, and their infants. *Child Development, 67,* 541–555.

Steffens, M. C. & Jelenek, P. (2011). Separating implicit gender stereotypes regarding math and language: Stereotypes are self-serving for boys and men, but not for girls and women. *Sex Roles, 64,* 324–335.

Steinberg, L. (2001). We know some things: Parent–adolescent relationships in retrospect and prospect. *Journal of Research on Adolescence, 11,* 1–19.

Steinberg, L., Mounts, N. S., Lamborn, S. D., & Dornbusch, S. M. (1991). Authoritative parenting and adolescent adjustment across varied ecological niches. *Journal of Research on Adolescence, 1,* 19–36.

Steiner, J. E. (1979). Human facial expressions in response to taste and smell stimulation. In H. W. Reese & L. P. Lipsitt (Eds.), *Advances in child development and behavior* (Vol. 13). New York: Academic Press.

Stephens, B. E. & Vohr, B. R. (2009). Neurodevelopmental outcome of the premature infant. *Pediatric Clinics of North America, 56,* 631–646.

Stern, M., Karraker, K., McIntosh, B., Moritzen, S., and Olexa, M. (2006). Prematurity stereotyping and mothers' interactions with their premature and full-term infants during the first year. *Journal of Pediatric Psychology, 31,* 597–607.

Sternberg, R. J. & Grigorenko, E. J. (2002a). *Dynamic testing: The nature and measurement of learning potential.* New York: Cambridge University Press.

Sternberg, R. J. (2004). Culture and intelligence. *American Psychologist, 59,* 325–338.

Sternberg, R. J. (2009a). Sketch of a componential subtheory of human intelligence. In J. C.

Kaufman, E. L. & Grigorenko (Eds.), *The essential Sternberg: Essays on intelligence, psychology, and education* (pp. 3–32). New York, NY: Springer Publishing Co.

Sternberg, R. J. (2009b). The nature of creativity. In J. C. Kaufman, E. L. & Grigorenko (Eds.), *The essential Sternberg: Essays on intelligence, psychology, and education* (pp. 103–118). New York, NY: Springer Publishing Co.

Sternberg, R. J. (2009c). The theory of successful intelligence. In J. C. Kaufman, E. L. & Grigorenko (Eds), *The essential Sternberg: Essays on intelligence, psychology, and education* (pp. 71–100). New York, NY: Springer Publishing Co.

Sternberg, R. J. & Grigorenko, E. J. (Eds.). (2002b). *The general factor of intelligence: How general is it?* Mahwah, NJ: Erlbaum.

Sternberg, R. J., Grigorenko, E. L., & Bundy, D. A. (2001). The predictive value of IQ. *Merrill-Palmer Quarterly, 47,* 1–41.

Sternberg, R. J., Grigorenko, E. L., & Kidd, K. C. (2005). Intelligence, race, and genetics. *American Psychologist, 60,* 46–59.

Sternberg, R. J. & Lubart, T. I. (1996). Investing in creativity. *American Psychologist, 51,* 677–688.

Stevens, J. H. Jr. (1984). Black grandmothers' and black adolescent mothers' knowledge about parenting. *Developmental Psychology, 20*(6), 1017–1025.

Stevens, M., Golombok, S., Beveridge, M., & Study Team, ALSPAC (2002). Does father absence influence children's gender development? Findings from a general population study of preschool children. *Parenting: Science and Practice, 2,* 47–60

Stevenson, H. W., Chen, C., & Lee, S. Y. (1993). Mathematics achievement of Chinese, Japanese, and American children: Ten years later. *Science, 259,* 53–58.

Stevenson, H. W., Lee, S. Y., & Stigler, J. W. (1986). Mathematics achievement of Chinese, Japanese, and American children. *Science, 231,* 693–699.

Stevenson, H. W., Lee, S., Chen, C., Stigler, J. W., Hsu, C., & Kitamura, S. (1990). Contexts of achievement: A study of American, Chinese, and Japanese children. *Monographs of the Society for Research in Child Development, 55* (1–2, Serial No. 221).

Stice, E., Presnell, K., & Bearman, S. K. (2001). Relation of early menarche to depression, eating disorders, substance abuse, and comorbid psychopathology among adolescent girls. *Developmental Psychology, 37,* 608–619.

Stifter, C. A. & Braungart, J. M. (1995). The regulation of negative reactivity in infancy: Function and development. *Developmental Psychology, 31,* 448–455.

Stifter, C. A., Coulehan, C. M., & Fish, M. (1993). Linking employment to attachment: The mediating effects of maternal separation anxiety and interactive behavior. *Child Development, 64,* 1451–1460.

Stifter, C. A. & Fox, N. A. (1990). Infant reactivity: Physiological correlates of newborn and 5-month temperament. *Developmental Psychology, 26,* 582–588.

Stigler, J. W., Fernandez, C., & Yoshida, M. (1996). Traditions of school mathematics in Japanese and American classrooms. In L. P. Steffe & P. Nesher (Eds.), *Theories of mathematical learning.* Mahwah, NJ: Erlbaum.

Stipek, D. J. & MacIver, D. (1989). Developmental change in children's assessment of intellectual competence. *Child Development, 60,* 521–538.

Stipek, D. J. (1992). The child at school. In M. E. Lamb & M. H. Bornstein (Eds.), *Developmental psychology: An advanced textbook* (3rd ed.). Hillsdale, NJ: Erlbaum.

Stipek, D. J. (2002). *Motivation to learn: Integrating theory and practice* (4th ed.). Boston: Allyn & Bacon.

Stipek, D. J., Recchia, S., & McClintic, S. (1992). Self-evaluation in young children. *Monographs of the Society for Research in Child Development, 57*(1, Serial No. 226).

Stipek, D. J. & Tannatt, L. (1984). Children's judgments of their own and their peers' academic competence. *Journal of Educational Psychology, 76,* 75–84.

Stocker, C. M. & Dunn, J. (1990). Sibling relationships in childhood: Links with friendships and peer relationships. *British Journal of Developmental Psychology, 8,* 227–244.

Stocker, C. M. & Mantz-Simmons, L. M. (1993). *Children's friendship and peer status: Links with family relationships, temperament, and social skills.* Unpublished manuscript.

Stormshak, E. A., Bierman, K. L., McMahon, R. J., Lengua, L. J., & Conduct Problems Prevention Research Group (2000). Parenting practices and child disruptive behavior problems in early elementary school. *Journal of Clinical Child Psychology, 29,* 17–29.

Strapp, C. M. (1999). Mothers', fathers', and siblings' responses to children's language errors: Comparing sources of negative evidence. *Journal of Child Language, 26,* 373–391.

Strathearn, L. (2003). Long-term cognitive function in very low-birth-weight infants. *JAMA: Journal of the American Medical Association, 289,* 2209.

Straube, S. & Fahle, M. (2011). Visual detection and identification are not the same: Evidence from psychophysics and fMRI. *Brain and Cognition, 75,* 29–38.

Straughan, R. (1986). Why act on Kohlberg's moral judgments? (Or how to reach Stage 6 and remain a bastard). In S. Modgil & C. Modgil (Eds.), *Lawrence Kohlberg: Consensus and controversy.* Philadelphia: Falmer.

Strayer, J. & Roberts, W. (1989). Children's empathy and role playing: Child and parental factors, and relations to prosocial behaviour. *Journal of Applied Developmental Psychology, 10,* 227–239.

Strayer, J. & Roberts, W. (2004). Children's anger, emotional expressiveness and empathy: Relations with parents' empathy, emotional expressiveness, and parenting practices. *Social Development, 13,* 229–254.

Streissguth, A. P. & Connor, P. D. (2001). Fetal alcohol syndrome and other effects of prenatal alcohol: Developmental cognitive neuroscience implications. In C. A. Nelson & M. Luciana (Eds.), *Handbook of developmental cognitive neuroscience.* Cambridge, MA: MIT Press.

Streri, A. (2003). Cross-modal recognition of shape from hand to eyes in human newborns. *Somatosensory and Motor Research, 20,* 13–18.

Streri, A. & Féron, J. (2005). The development of haptic abilities in very young infants: From perception to cognition. *Infant Behavior and Cognition, 28,* 290–304.

Streri, A. & Gentaz, E. (2004). Cross-modal recognition of shape from hand to eyes and handedness in human newborns. *Neuropsychologia, 42,* 1365–1369.

Striano, T. & Rochat, P. (2000). Emergence of selective social referencing in infancy. *Infancy 1,* 253–264.

Subrahmanyam, K. & Greenfield, P. M. (1996). Effect of video game practice on spatial skills in girls and boys. In P. M. Greenfield & R. R. Cocking (Eds.), *Interacting with video* (pp. 95–114). Norwood, NJ: Ablex.

Subrahmanyam, K., Greenfield, P. M., Kraut, R., & Gross, E. (2001). The impact of computer use on children's and adolescents' development. *Applied Developmental Psychology, 22,* 7–30.

Suddendorf, T., Simcock, G., & Nielsen, M. (2007). Visual self-recognition in mirrors and live videos: Evidence for a developmental asynchrony. *Cognitive Development, 22,* 185–196.

Sue, S. & Ozaki, S. (1990). Asian-American educational achievements: A phenomenon in search of an explanation. *American Psychologist, 45,* 913–920.

Sullivan, M. W., Lewis, M., & Alessandri, S. M. (1992). Cross-age stability in emotional expressions: During learning and extinction. *Developmental Psychology, 28,* 58–63.

Sundara, M., Polka, L., & Genesee, F. (2006). Language-experience facilitates discrimination of /d-/ in monolingual and bilingual acquisition of English. *Cognition, 100(2),* 369–388.

Super, C. M. (1981). Cross-cultural research on infancy. In H. C Triandis & A. Heron (Eds.), *Handbook of cross-cultural psychology: Vol. 4. Developmental psychology.* Boston: Allyn & Bacon.

Super, C. M. & Harkness, S. (1986). The developmental niche: A conceptualization at the interface of child and culture. *International Journal of Behavioral Development* (Special Issue: Cross-cultural human development) *9,* 545–569.

Super, C. M. & Harkness, S. (1997). The cultural structuring of child development. In J. W. Berry, P. R. Dasen, & T. S. Saraswathi (Eds.), *Handbook of cross-cultural psychology: Vol. 2. Basic processes and human development.* Boston: Allyn and Bacon.

Super, C. M. & Harkness, S. (2002). Culture structures the environment for development. *Human Development, 45,* 270–274.

Susman-Stillman, A., Kalkose, M., Englund, B., & Waldman, I. (1996). Infant temperament and maternal sensitivity as predictors of attachment security. *Infant Behavior and Development, 19,* 33–47.

Suttle, C. M., Banks, M. S., & Graf, E. W. (2002). FPL and sweep VEP to tritan stimuli in young human infants. *Vision Research, 42,* 2879–2891.

Sutton-Smith, B. & Roberts, J. M. (1973). The cross-cultural and psychological study of games. In B. Sutton-Smith (Ed.), *The folk games of children.* Austin, TX: University of Texas Press.

Suzuki, L. A. & Valencia, R. (1997). Race-ethnicity and measured intelligence. *American Psychologist, 52,* 1103–1114.

Swain, I. U., Zelazo, P. R., & Clifton, R. K. (1993). Newborn infants' memory for speech sounds retained over 24 hours. *Developmental Psychology, 29,* 313–323.

Sweeney, L. & Rapee, R. (2001) Social phobia in children and adolescents: Psychological treatments. In W. R. Crozier & L. E. Alden (Eds.), *International handbook of social anxiety* (pp. 525–537). New York: Wiley.

Swingler, M. M., Willoughby, M. T., & Calkins, S. D. (2011). EEG power and coherence during preschoolers' performance of an executive function battery. *Developmental Psychology, 53,* 771–784.

Swingley, D. & Aslin, R. N. (2002). Lexical neighbourhoods and the word-form representations of 14-month-olds. *Psychological Science, 13,* 480–484.

T

Taddio, A., Katz, J., Bersich, A. L., Goren, K. (1997). Effect of neonatal circumcision on pain response during subsequent routine vaccination. *Lancet, 349,* 599–603.

Taddio, A., Shah, V., Gilbert-MacLeod, C., & Katz, J. (2002). Conditioning and hyperalgesia in newborns exposed to repeated heel lances. *Journal of the American Medical Association, 288,* 857–861.

Tager-Flusberg, H. & Calkins, S. (1990). Does imitation facilitate the acquisition of grammar? Evidence from a study of autistic, Down's syndrome and normal children. *Journal of Child Language, 17,* 591–606.

Takahashi, K. (1986). Examining the Strange Situation procedure with Japanese mothers and 12-month-old infants. *Developmental Psychology, 22,* 265–270.

Takahashi, K. (1990). Are the key assumptions of the "Strange Situation" procedure universal? A view from Japanese research. *Human Development, 33,* 23–30.

Tamis-LeMonda, C. S. & Bornstein, M. H. (1991). Individual variation, correspondence, stability, and change in mother and toddler play. *Infant Behavior and Development, 14,* 143–162.

Tamis-Lemonda, C. S. & Bornstein, M. H. (1994). Specificity in mother-toddler language-play relations across the second year. *Developmental Psychology, 30,* 283–292.

Tamis-LeMonda, C. S., Uzgiris, I. C., & Bornstein, M. H. (2002). Play in parent-child interactions. In M. H. Bornstein (Ed.), *Handbook of parenting* (2nd ed., Vol. 5). Mahwah, NJ: Erlbaum.

Tamres, L. K., Janicki, D., & Helgeson, V. S. (2002). Sex differences in coping behavior: A meta-analytic review and an examination of relative coping. *Personality and Social Psychology Review, 6,* 2–30.

Tangney, J. P., Stuewig, J., & Mashek, D. J. (2007). Moral emotions and moral behavior. *Annual Review of Psychology, 58,* 345–372.

Tanner, J. M. (1987). Issues and advances in adolescent growth and development. *Journal of Adolescent Health Care, 8,* 470–478.

Tanner, J. M. (1990). *Fetus into man: Physical growth from conception to maturity* (2nd ed.). Cambridge, MA: Harvard University Press.

Tanner, J. M. (1992). Growth as a measure of the nutritional and hygienic status of a population. *Hormone Research, 38*(1), 106–121.

Tappan, M. B. (1997). Language, culture, and moral development: A Vygotskian perspective. *Developmental Review, 17,* 78–100.

Tappan, M. B. (2006). Mediated moralities: Sociocultural approaches to moral development. In M. Killen & J. G. Smetana (Eds.), *Handbook of moral development.* (pp. 351–374). Mahwah, NJ: Lawrence Erlbaum.

Tarabulsy, G. M., Pascuzzo, K., Moss, E., St-Laurent, D., Bernier, A., Cyr, C., & Dubois-Comtois, K. (2008). Attachment-based intervention for maltreating families. *American Journal of Orthopsychiatry, 78,* 322–332.

Tardif, T. (2006). But are they really verbs? Chinese words for action. In K. Hirsh-Pasek & R. M. Golinkoff (Eds.), *Action meets word: How children learn verbs* (pp. 477–498). New York: Oxford University Press.

Tardif, T., Gelman, S. A., & Xu, F. (1999). Putting the "noun bias" in context: A comparison of English and Mandarin. *Child Development, 70,* 620–635.

Taylor, H. G., Klein, N., Minich, N. M., & Hack, M. (2000). Middle-school-age outcomes in children with very low birthweight. *Child Development, 71,* 1495–1511.

Taylor, J., Iacono, W. G., & McGue, M. (2001). Evidence for a genetic etiology of early-onset delinquency. *Journal of Abnormal Behavior, 109,* 634–643.

Taylor, L. & Ingram, R. E. (1999). Cognitive reactivity and despressotypic information processing in children of depressed mothers. *Journal of Abnormal Psychology, 108,* 202–210.

Taylor, M. G. (1996). The development of children's beliefs about social and biological aspects of gender differences. *Child Development, 67,* 1555–1571.

Taylor, M., Cartwright, B. S., & Bowden, T. (1991). Perspective taking and theory of mind: Do children predict interpretive diversity as a function of differences in observers' knowledge? *Child Development, 62,* 1334–1351.

Taylor, M., Esbensen, B. M., & Bennett, R. T. (1994). Children's understanding of knowledge acquisition: The tendency for children to report that they have always known what they have just learned. *Child Development, 65,* 1581–1604.

Taylor, R. D., Casten, R., & Flickinger, S. M. (1993). Influence of kinship social support on the parenting experiences and psychosocial adjustment of African-American adolescents. *Developmental Psychology, 29,* 382–388.

Taylor, S. D. (2004). Predictive genetic test decisions for Huntington's disease: Context, appraisal and new moral imperatives. *Social Science & Medicine, 58,* 137–149.

Taylor, S. D. (2005). Predictive genetic test decisions for Huntington's disease: Elucidating the test/no-test dichotomy. *Journal of Health Psychology, 10,* 597–612.

Teller, D. Y. & Bornstein, M. H. (1987). Infant color vision and color perception. In P. Salapatek & L. Cohen (Eds.), *Handbook of infant perception: Vol. 1. From sensation to perception.* New York: Academic Press.

Temcheff, C. E., Serbin, L. A, Martin-Storey, A., Stack, D. M., Hodgins, S., Ledingham, J. E., & Schwartzman, A. E. (2008). Continuity and pathways from aggression in childhood to family violence in adulthood: A 30-year longitudinal study. *Journal of Family Violence, 23,* 231–242.

Tenenbaum, H. R. & Leaper, C. (2003). Parent-child conversations about science: The socialization of gender inequities? *Developmental Psychology, 39,* 34–47.

Teo, T., Becker, G., & Edelstein, W. (1995). Variability in structured wholeness: Context factors in L. Kohlberg's data on the development of moral judgment. *Merrill-Palmer Quarterly, 41,* 381–393.

Terlecki, M. S. & Newcombe, N. S. (2005). How important is the digital divide? The relation of computer and videogame usage to gender differences in mental rotation ability. *Sex Roles, 53,* 433–441.

Terwogt, M. M. (2002). Emotional states in self and others as motives for helping in 10-year-old children. *British Journal of Developmental Psychology, 20,* 131–147.

Tessier, R., Charpak, N., Giron, M., Cristo, M., de Calume, Z. F., & Ruiz-Pelaez, J. G. (2009). Kangaroo Mother Care, home environment and father involvement in the first year of life: a randomized controlled study. *Acta Paediatrica, 98,* 144–150.

Tessier, R., Cristo M., Velez S., Giron M., de Calume Z. F., & Ruiz- Palaez, J. G. (1998). Kangaroo mother care and the bonding hypothesis. *Pediatrics, 102,* 1–7.

Tessier, R., Cristo, M., Velez, S., Giron, M., Nadeau, L., & Charpak, N. (2003). Kangaroo Mother Care: a method of protecting high-risk premature infants against developmental delay. *Infant Behavior and Development, 26,* 36–38.

Tessier-Lavigne, M. & Goodman, C. S. (1996). The molecular biology of axon guidance. *Science, 274,* 1123–1133.

Teti, D. M. (1992). Sibling interaction. In V. B. Van Hasselt & M. Hersen (Eds.), *Handbook of social development.* New York: Plenum.

Teuber, H. L. (2009). The riddle of frontal lobe function in man. *Neuropsychology Review, 19,* 25–46.

Thalidomide Victims' Association of Canada. (2006). *Thalidomide Victims' Association of Canada.* Available at: www.thalidomide.ca/en/index.html

Thanh, N. X. & Jonsson, E. (2010). Drinking alcohol during pregnancy: Evidence from Canadian community health survey 2007/2008. *Journal of Population Therapeutics and Clinical Pharmacology, 17,* e302–e307.

Tharp, R. G. (1989). Psychocultural variables and constants: Effects on teaching and learning in schools. *American Psychologist, 44,* 349–359.

Thelen, E. (1994). Three-month-old infants can learn task-specific patterns of interlimb coordination. *Psychological Science, 5,* 280–285.

Thelen, E. (2000). Motor development as foundation and future of developmental psychology. *International Journal of Behavioral Development, 24,* 385–397.

Thelen, E. & Adolph, K. E. (1992). Arnold L. Gesell: The paradox of nature and nurture. *Developmental Psychology, 28,* 368–380.

Thelen, E. & Corbetta, D. (2002). Microdevelopment and dynamic systems: Applications to infant motor development. In N. Granott and J. Parziale (Eds.), *Microdevelopment: Transition processes in development and learning Cambridge studies in cognitive perceptual development* (pp. 59–79). New York: Cambridge University Press.

Thelen, E., Corbetta, D., & Spencer, J. (1996). The development of reaching during the first year: The role of movement speed. *Journal of Experimental Psychology: Human Perception and Performance, 22,* 1059–1076.

Thelen, E. & Fisher, D. M. (1983). The organization of spontaneous leg movements in newborn infants. *Journal of Motor Behavior, 15,* 353–377.

Thelen, E., Fisher, D. M., & Ridley-Johnson, R. (2002). The relationship between physical growth and a newborn reflex. *Infant Behavior and Development, 25,* 72–85.

Thelen, E. & Smith, L. B. (2006). Dynamic systems theories. In W. Damon & R. M. Lerner (Series Ed.) & R. M. Lerner (Vol. Ed.), *Handbook of child psychology: Vol. 1. Theoretical models of human development* (6th ed., pp. 258–312). Hoboken, NJ: Wiley.

Thiessen, E. D., Hill, E., & Saffran, J. R. (2005). Infant-directed speech facilitates word segmentation. *Infancy, 7,* 53–71.

Thoman, E. B. (1990). Sleeping and waking states in infants: A functional perspective. *Neuroscience and Biobehavioral Reviews, 14,* 93–107.

Thoman, E. B. (1993). Obligation and option in the premature nursery. *Developmental Review, 13,* 1–30.

Thomas, A. & Chess, S. (1977). *Temperament and development.* New York: Bruner/Mazel.

Thomas, A. & Chess, S. (1984). Genesis and evaluation of behavioral disorder: From infancy to early adult life. *American Journal of Psychiatry, 141,* 1–9.

Thomas, A. & Chess, S. (1986). The New York Longitudinal Study: From infancy to early adult life. In R. Plomin & J. Dunn (Eds.), *The study of temperament: Changes, continuities and challenges.* Hillsdale, NJ: Erlbaum.

Thomas, A., Chess, S., & Birch, H. G. (1968). *Temperament and behavior disorders in children.* New York: New York University Press.

Thomas, E. (2004). *Aggressive behaviour outcome for young children: Change in parenting environment predicts change in behaviour.* Statistics Canada, Catalogue no. 89-599-MIE-No. 001.

Thomas, M. S. C. & Johnson, M. H. (2008). New advances in understanding sensitive periods in brain development. *Current Directions in Psychological Science, 17,* 1–5.

Thompson, R. A. (1990). Vulnerability in research: A developmental perspective on research risk. *Child Development, 61,* 1–16.

Thompson, R. A. (2000). The legacy of early attachments. *Child Development, 71,* 145–152.

Thompson, R. A. (2006). The development of the person: Social understanding, relationships, conscience, self. In W. Damon & R. M. Lerner (Series Eds.) & N. Eisenberg (Vol. Ed.), *Handbook of child psychology: Vol. 3. Social, emotional, and personality development (6th ed.,* pp. 25–98). Hoboken, NJ: Wiley.

Thompson, R. A. (2008). Early attachment and later development: Familiar questions, new answers. In J. Cassidy & P. R. Shaver (Eds.), *Handbook of attachment: Theory, research, and clinical applications (2nd edition)* (pp. 348–365). New York, NY: Guilford.

Thompson, R. A., Connell, J. P., & Bridges, L. J. (1988). Temperament, emotion, and social interactive behavior in the Strange Situation: A component process analysis of attachment system functioning. *Child Development, 59,* 1102–1110.

Thompson, R. A., Flood, M. F., & Lundquist, L. (1995). Emotion regulation: Its relations to attachment and developmental psychopathology. In D. Cicchetti & S. L. Toth (Eds.), *Emotion, cognition, and representation. Rochester Symposium on Developmental Psychopathology (Vol. 6).* Rochester, NY: University of Rochester Press.

Thompson, R. A., Lamb, M. E., & Estes, D. (1982). Stability of infant-mother attachment and its relationship to changing life circumstances in an unselected middle-class sample. *Child Development, 53,* 144–148.

Thompson, R. A. & Meyer, S. (2007). The socialization of emotion regulation in the family. In J. Gross (Ed.), *Handbook of emotion regulation* (pp. 249–268). New York: Guilford Press.

Thompson, R. H., Cotnoir-Bichelman, N. M., McKerchar, P. M., Tate, T. L., & Dancho, K. A. (2007). Enhancing early communication through infant sign training. *Journal of Applied Behavior Analysis, 40,* 15–23.

Thorne, B. (1993). *Gender play: Girls and boys in school.* New Brunswick, NJ: Rutgers University Press.

Thurstone, L. L. (1938). *Primary mental abilities.* Chicago: University of Chicago Press.

Thurstone, L. L. & Thurstone, T. G. (1962). *SRA primary mental abilities.* Chicago: Science Research Associates.

Tibbetts, J. (2010). Legal experts debate jail for fetal alcohol offenders. *Ottawa Citizen,* August 17, 2010.

Tiedemann, J. (2000). Parents' gender stereotypes and teachers' beliefs as predictors of children's concept of their mathematical ability in elementary school. *Journal of Educational Psychology, 92,* 144–151.

Tieszen, H. R. (1979). Children's social behavior in a Korean preschool. *Journal of Korean Home Economics Association, 17,* 71–84.

Tinbergen, N. (1973). *The animal in its world: Explorations of an ethologist, 1932–1972 (Vols. 1 & 2).* Cambridge, MA: Harvard University Press.

Tincoff, R. & Jusczyk, P. W. (1999). Some beginnings of word comprehension in six-month-olds. *Psychological Science, 10,* 172–175.

Tisak, M. S. & Turiel, E. (1988). Variation in seriousness of transgressions and children's immoral and conventional concepts. *Developmental Psychology 24,* 352–357.

Tobey, A. E. & Goodman, G. S. (1992). Children's eyewitness memory: Effects of participation and forensic context. *Child Abuse and Neglect, 16,* 779–796.

Tomasello, M. (1999). Having intentions, understanding intentions, and understanding communicative intentions. In P. D. Zelazo, J. W. Astington, & D. R. Olson (Eds.), *Developing theories of intention.* Mahwah, NJ: Erlbaum.

Tomasello, M. (2003). *Constructing a language: A usage-based theory of language acquisition.* Cambridge, MA: Harvard University Press.

Tomasello, M. (2006). Acquiring linguistic constructions. In D. Kuhn, R. S. Siegler, W. Damon, & R. M. Lerner (Eds.), *Handbook of child psychology: Vol 2, Cognition, perception, and language (6th ed.).* (pp. 255–298) Hoboken, NJ: John Wiley & Sons Inc.

Tomasello, M. (2009). Universal grammar is dead. *Behavioral and Brain Sciences, 32*(5), 470–471.

Tomasello, M., Carpenter, M., & Liszkowski, U. (2007). A new look at infant pointing. *Child Development, 78*(3), 705–722.

Tomasello, M., Conti-Ramsden, G., & Ewert, B. (1990). Young children's conversations with their mothers and fathers: Differences in breakdown and repair. *Journal of Child Language, 17,* 115–130.

Tomasello, M. & Farrar, M. J. (1986). Joint attention and early language. *Child Development, 57,* 1454–1463.

Tomasello, M. & Merriman, W. E. (Eds.). (1995). *Beyond names for things: Young children's acquisition of verbs.* Hillsdale, NJ: Erlbaum.

Tomassini, V., Jbabdi, S., Kincses, Z. T., Bosnell, R., Douaud, G., Pozzilli, C., Matthews, P. M., & Johansen-Berg, H. (2011). Structural and functional bases for individual differences in motor learning. *Human Brain Mapping, 32,* 494–508.

Torkildsen, J., Sannerud, T., Syversen, G., Thormodsen, R., Simonsen, H. G., Moen, I., Smith, L., & Lindgren, M. (2006). Semantic organization of basic-level words in 20-month-olds: An ERP study *Journal of Neurolinguistics, 19(6),* 431–454.

Tortora, G. J. & Derrickson, B. (2009). *Anatomy and Physiology*, 12th Edition. Hoboken, NJ: John Wiley & Sons, Inc.

Touchette, N. (1990). Evolutions: Fertilization. *Journal of NIH Research, 2,* 94–97.

Tout, K., de Haan, M., Campbell, E. K., & Gunnar, M. R. (1998). Social behavior correlates of cortisol activity in child care: Gender differences and time-of-day effects. *Child Development, 69,* 1247–1262.

Tracy, R. L. & Ainsworth, M. D. S. (1981). Maternal affectionate behavior and infant-mother attachment patterns. *Child Development, 52,* 1341–1343.

Trainor, L. J. (2005). Are there critical periods for musical development? *Developmental Psychobiology*, *46*, 262–278.

Trainor, L. J., Shahin, A., & Roberts, L. E. (2003). Effects of musical training on the auditory cortex in children. *Annals of the New York Academy of Sciences*, *999*, 506–513.

Trainor, L. J., Tsang, C. D., & Cheung, V. H. W. (2002). Preference for sensory consonance in 2- and 4-month-old infants. *Musical Perception, 20,* 187–194.

Trautner, H. M., Ruble, D. N., Cyphers, L., Kirsten, B., Behrendt, R., & Hartmann, P. (2005). Rigidity and flexibility of gender stereotypes in childhood: Developmental or differential? *Infant and Child Development, 14,* 365–381.

Travis, K. E., Leonard, M. K., Brown, T. T., Hagler, D. J., Curran, M., Dale, A. M., Elman, J. L., & Halgren, E. (2011). Spatiotemporal neural dynamics of word understanding in 12- to 18-month-old infants. *Cerebral Cortex, 21,* 1832–1839.

Trehub, S. E. (1976). The discrimination of foreign speech contrasts by infants and adults. *Child Development, 47,* 466–472.

Trehub, S. E. (2000). Human processing predispositions and musical universals. In N. L. Wallin, B. Merker, & S. Brown (Eds.), *The origins of music* (pp. 427–448). Cambridge, MA: MIT Press.

Trehub, S. E. (2003). The developmental origins of musicality. *Nature Neuroscience, 6,* 669–673.

Trehub, S. E. & Henderson, J. (1994, July). *Caregivers' songs and their effect on infant listeners.* Proceedings of the Meeting of the International Conference for Music Perception and Cognition. Liege, Belgium.

Trehub, S. E. & Schellenberg, E. G. (1995). Music: Its relevance to infants. In R. Vasta (Ed.), *Annals of child development* (Vol. 11). London: Kingsley.

Trehub, S. E. & Schneider, B. A. (1983). Recent advances in the behavioral study of infant audition. In S. E. Gerber & G. T. Mencher (Eds.), *Development of auditory behavior.* New York: Grune & Stratton.

Trehub, S. E., Schneider, B. A., Morrongiello, B. A., & Thorpe, L. A. (1988). Auditory sensitivity in school-age children. *Journal of Experimental Child Psychology, 46,* 273–285.

Trehub, S. E., Thorpe, L. A., & Cohen, A. J. (1991, April). *Infants auditory processing of numerical information.* Paper presented at the meeting of the Society for Research in Child Development, Seattle, WA.

Tremblay, R. E. & Nagin, D. S. (2005). The developmental origins of physical aggression in humans. In R. E. Tremblay, W. W. Hartup, & J. Archer (Eds.), *Developmental origins of aggression* (pp. 83–106). New York: Guilford Press.

Tremblay, R. E., Pihl, R. O., Vitaro, F., Dobkin, P. L. (1994). Predicting early onset of male antisocial behavior from preschool behavior. *Archives of General Psychiatry, 51,* 732–739.

Trevathen, W. R. (1987). *Human birth: An evolutionary perspective.* New York: Aldine de Gruyter.

Trexler, R. C. (1973). The foundlings of Florence, 1395–1455. *History of Childhood Quarterly, 1,* 259–284.

Trick, L. M., Audet, D., & Dales, L. (2003). Age differences in enumerating things that move: Implications for the development of multiple-object tracking. *Memory and Cognition, 31,* 1229–1237.

Trick, L. M., Jaspers-Fayer, F., & Sethi, N. (2005). Multiple-object tracking in children: The "Catch the Spies" task. *Cognitive Development, 20,* 373–387.

Trickett, P. K. & McBride-Chang, C. (1995). The developmental impact of different forms of child abuse and neglect. *Developmental Review, 15,* 311–337.

Trivers, R. L. (1971). The evolution of reciprocal altruism. *Quarterly Review of Biology, 46,* 35–57.

Trivers, R. L. (1972). Parental investment and sexual selection. In B. Campbell (Ed.), *Sexual selection and the descent of man 1871–1971.* New York: Aldine de Gruyter.

Trivers, R. L. (1983). The evolution of cooperation. In D. L. Bridgeman (Ed.), *The nature of prosocial development.* New York: Academic Press.

Trocmé, N., MacLaurin, B., Fallon, B., Daciuk, J., Billingsley, D., Tourigny, M., et al. (2001). *Canadian incidence study of reported child abuse and neglect: Final report.* Ottawa: Minister of Public Works and Government Services Canada.

Tronick, E. (2005). Why is connection with others so critical? The formation of dyadic states of consciousness and the expansion of the individuals' states of consciousness: coherence governed by selection and the co-creation of meaning out of messy meaning making. In J. Nadel & D. Muir (Eds.), *Emotional Development* (pp. 293–315). New York: Oxford University Press.

Tronick, E. (2008). Social interaction. In J. B. Benson & M. M. Haith (Eds.), *Social and emotional development in infancy and early childhood* (pp. 429–436). New York: Academic Press.

Tronick, E. Z. (1989). Emotions and emotional communication in infants. *American Psychologist, 44,* 112–119.

Tronick, E. Z., Morelli, G. A. Ivey, P. K. (1992). The Efe forager infant and toddler's pattern of social relationships: Multiple and simultaneous. *Developmental Psychology, 28,* 568–577.

Troseth, G. L., Pickard, M. E. B., & DeLoache, J. S. (2007). Young children's use of scale models: Testing an alternative representational insight. *Developmental Science, 10,* 763–769.

Tsui, L. & Nicoladis, E. (2004). Losing it: Similarities and differences in first intercourse experiences of men and women. *Canadian Journal of Human Sexuality, 13,* 95–107.

Tsujimoto, S. (2008). The prefrontal cortex: Functional neural development during early childhood. *The Neuroscientist, 14,* 345–358.

Tsujimoto, S., Yamamoto, T., Kawaguchi, H., Koizumi, H., & Sawaguchi, T. (2004). Prefrontal cortical activation associated with working memory in adults and preschool children: an event-related optical topography study. *Cerebral Cortex, 14,* 703–712.

Tu, W. (1994). Embodying in the universe: A note on Confucian self-realization. In R. T. Ames, W. Dissanayake, & T. P. Kasulis (Eds.), *Self as person in Asian theory and practice.* Albany, NY: State University of New York Press.

Tubman, J. G., Lerner, R. M., Lerner, J. V., & Von Eye, A. (1992). Temperament and adjustment in young adult-hood: A 15-year longitudinal analysis. *American Journal of Orthopsychiatry, 62,* 564–574.

Tucker, C. J., McHale, S. M., & Crouter, A. C. (2001). Conditions of sibling support in adolescence. *Journal of Family Psychology, 15,* 254–271.

Tudge, J. R. H. (1989). When collaboration leads to regression: Some negative consequences of socio-cognitive conflict. *European Journal of Social Psychology, 19,* 123–138.

Tudge, J. R. H. (1992). Processes and consequences of peer collaboration: A Vygotskian analysis. *Child Development, 63,* 1364–1379.

Tudge, J. R. H. & Rogoff, B. (1989). Peer influences on cognitive development: Piagetian and Vygotskian perspectives. In M. H. Bornstein & J. Bruner (Eds.), *Interaction in human development.* Hillsdale, NJ: Erlbaum.

Tuladhar, R., Harding, R., Adamson, T. M., & Horne, R. S. C. (2005). Comparison of postnatal development of heart rate responses to trigeminal stimulation in sleeping preterm and term infants. *Journal of Sleep Research, 14,* 29–36.

Turati, C., Cassia, V. M., Simion, F., & Leo, I. (2006). Newborns' face recognition: Role of inner and outer facial features. *Child Development, 77,* 297–311.

Turiel, E. (2002). *The culture of morality.* New York: Cambridge University Press.

Turiel, E. (2006). The development of morality. In N. E. Eisenberg, W. E. Damon, & R. M. Lerner (Eds.), *Handbook of child psychology Vol. 3: Social, emotional, and personality development* (6th ed., pp. 789–857). Hoboken, NJ: Wiley.

Turiel, E., Killen, M., & Helwig, C. C. (1987). Morality: Its structure, functions, and vagaries. In J. Kagan & S. Lamb (Eds.), *The emergence of moral concepts in young children.* Chicago: University of Chicago Press.

Turkheimer, E. (2000). Three laws of behavior genetics and what they mean. *Current Directions in Psychological Science, 9,* 160–164.

Turkheimer, E. & Waldron, M. (2000). Nonshared environment: A theoretical, methodological, and quantitative review. *Psychological Bulletin, 126,* 78–108.

Turkheimer, E., Haley, A., Waldron, M., D'Onofrio, B., & Gottesman, I. I. (2003). Socioeconomic status modifies heritability of IQ in young children. *Psychological Science, 14,* 623–628.

Twenge, J. M. & Campbell, W. K. (2001). Age and birth cohort differences in self-esteem: A cross-temporal meta-analysis. *Personality and Social Psychology Review, 5,* 321–344.

Tzourio-Mazoyer, N., Landeau, B., Papathanassiou, D., Crivello, F., Etard, O., Delcroix, N., Mazoyer, B., & Joliot, M. (2002). Automated anatomical labeling of activations in SPM using a macroscopic anatomical parcellation of the MNI MRI single-subject brain. *NeuroImage, 15,* 273–289.

Tzuriel, D. (2001). *Dynamic assessment of young children.* New York: Kluwer Academic Publishers.

Tzuriel, D. & Egozi, G. (2010). Gender differences in spatial ability of young children: The effects of training and processing strategies. *Child Development, 81,* 1417–1430.

U

U.S. Department of Education (2001). *Digest of education statistics 2000.* Washington, DC: U.S. Government Printing Office.

U.S. Department of Justice (2007). *Crime in the United States, Table 33: Ten year arrest trends by sex, 1997–2006.* Available at: www.fbi.gov/ucr/cius2006/data/table_33.html

Ullman, M. T., Miranda, R. A., & Travers, M. L. (2008). Sex differences in the neurocognition of language. In J. B. Becker, K. J. Berkley, N. Geary, et al. (Eds.), *Sex on the brain: From genes to behavior* (pp. 291–309). New York, NY: Oxford University Press.

Underwood, M. K. (2003). *Social aggression among girls.* New York: Guilford.

Underwood, M. K. (2004). Gender and peer relations: Are the two gender cultures really all that different? In J. B. Kupersmidt & K. A. Dodge (Eds.), *Children's peer relations: From development to intervention* (pp. 21–36). Washington, DC: American Psychological Association.

Underwood, M. K. & Buhrmester, D. (2007). Friendship features and social exclusion: An observational study examining gender and social context. *Merrill-Palmer Quarterly, 53,* 412–438.

Underwood, M. K., Mayeux, L., & Galperin, M. (2006). Peer relations during middle childhood: Gender, emotions, and aggression. In L. Balter & C. S. Tamis-LeMonda (Eds.), *child psychology: A handbook of contemporary issues* (2nd ed., pp. 241–261). New York: Psychology Press.

Urberg, K. A. (1999). Introduction: Some thoughts about studying the influence of peers on children and adolescents. *Merrill-Palmer Quarterly, 45,* 1–12.

Urberg, K. A., Degirmencioglu, S. M., & Pilgrim, C. (1997). Close friend and group influence on adolescent cigarette smoking and alcohol use. *Developmental Psychology, 33,* 834–844.

Uttal, D. H. (2000). Seeing the big picture: Map use and the development of spatial cognition. *Developmental Science, 3,* 247–286.

V

Vaden, K. I., Piquado, T., & Hickok, G. (2011). Sublexical properties of spoken words modulate activity in Broca's area but not superior temporal cortex: Implications for models of speech recognition. *Journal of Cognitive Neuroscience, 23,* 2665–2674.

Vaillancourt, T. & Hymel, S. (2006). Aggression, social status and the moderating role of sex and peer-valued characteristics. *Aggressive Behavior, 32,* 396–408.

Vaillancourt, T., Hymel, S., & McDougall, P. (2003). Bullying is power: Implications for school-based intervention strategies. *Journal of Applied School Psychology, 19,* 157–176.

Valenza, E., Simion, F., Cassia, V. M., & Umiltà, C. (1996). Face preference at birth. *Journal of Experimental Psychology: Human Perception and Performance, 22,* 892–903.

Valian, V. (1996). *Parental replies: Linguistic status and didactic role.* Cambridge, MA: MIT Press.

Valian, V. (1999). Input and language acquisition. In W. C. Ritchie & T. K. Bhatia (Eds.), *Handbook of child language acquisition.* San Diego, CA: Academic Press.

Van Allen, M. I., McCourt, C., Lee, N. S. (2002). *Preconception health: folic acid for the primary prevention of neural tube defects. A resource document for health professionals, 2002.* Ottawa: Minister of Public Works and Government Services Canada. (Cat. Number H39-607/2002E).

van Bakel, H. J. A., & Riksen-Walraven, J. M. (2002). Parenting and development of one-year-olds: Links with parental, contextual, and child characteristics. *Child Development, 73,* 256–273.

Van Balen, F. (1998). Development of IVF children. *Developmental Review, 18,* 30–46.

Van Den Bergh, B. R. H. (1992). Maternal emotions during pregnancy and fetal and neonatal behavior. In J. G. Nijhuis (Ed.), *Fetal behavior: Developmental and perinatal aspects.* New York: Oxford University Press.

van den Boom, D. C. (1994). The influence of temperament and mothering on attachment and exploration: An experimental manipulation of sensitive responsiveness among lower-class mothers with irritable infants. *Child Development, 65,* 1457–1477.

van den Boom, D. C. & Hoeksma, J. B. (1994). The effect of infant irritability on mother-infant interaction: A growth-curve analysis. *Developmental Psychology, 30,* 581–590.

van der Meer, A. L. H., van der Weel, F. R., & Lee, D. N. (1996). Lifting weights in neonates: Developing visual control of reaching. *Scandinavian Journal of Psychology, 37,* 424–436.

Van der Veer, R. & Valsiner, J. (1988). Lev Vygotsky and Pierre Janet: On the origin of the concept of sociogenesis. *Developmental Review, 8,* 52–65.

Van Giffen, K. & Haith, M. M. (1984). Infant visual response to gestalt geometric forms. *Infant Behavior and Development, 7,* 335–346.

van IJzendoorn, M. H., Goldberg, S., Kroonenberg, P. M., & Frenkel, O. J. (1992). The relative effects of maternal and child problems on the quality of attachment: A meta-analysis of attachment in clinical samples. *Child Development, 63,* 840–858.

van IJzendoorn, M. H., Juffer, F., & Duyvesteyn, M. G. C. (1995). Breaking the intergenerational cycle of insecure attachment: A review of the effects of attachment-based interventions on maternal sensitivity and infant security. *Journal of Child Psychology and Psychiatry and Allied Disciplines, 36,* 225–248.

van IJzendoorn, M. H., Juffer, F., Poelhuis, C. W. (2005). Adoption and cognitive development: A meta-analytic comparison of adopted and non-adopted children's IQ and school performance. *Psychological Bulletin, 131,* 301–316.

van IJzendoorn, M. H. & Sagi, A. (1999). Cross-cultural patterns of attachment: Universal and contextual dimensions. In J. Cassidy & P. Shaver (Eds.), *Handbook of attachment* (pp. 713–734). New York: Guilford.

van IJzendoorn, M. H. & Sagi-Schwartz, A. (2008). Cross-cultural patterns of attachment: Universal and contextual dimensions. In J. Cassidy & P. R. Shaver (Eds.), *Handbook of attachment: Theory, research, and clinical applications (2nd edition)* (pp. 880–905). New York, NY: Guilford.

van IJzendoorn, M. H., Vereijken, C. M. J. L., Bakermans-Kranenburg, M. J., & Riksen-Walraven, J. M. (2004). Assessing attachment security with the Attachment Q Sort: Meta-analytic evidence for the validity of the observer AQS. *Child Development, 75,* 1188–1213.

Vandell, D. L. (2000). Parents, peer groups, and other socializing influences. *Developmental Psychology, 36,* 699–710.

Vandell, D. L., Minnet, A. M., Johnson, B. S., & Santrock, J. W. (1990). *Siblings and friends: Experiences of school-aged children.* Unpublished manuscript, University of Texas at Dallas.

Vasilyeva, M. & Huttenlocher, J. (2004). Early development of scaling ability. *Developmental Psychology, 40,* 682–690.

Vass, E. (2007). Exploring processes of collaborative creativity—The role of emotions in children's joint creative writing. *Thinking Skills and Creativity, 2,* 107–117.

Vasta, R. & Liben, L. S. (1996). The water-level task: An intriguing puzzle. *Current Directions in Psychological Science, 5,* 171–177.

Vasta, R., Rosenberg, D., Knott, J. A., & Gaze, C. E. (1997). Experience and the water-level task revisited: Does expertise exact a price? *Psychological Science, 8,* 336–339.

Vaughn, B. E., Bost, K. K., & van IJzendoorn, M. H. (2008). Attachment and temperament: Additive and interactive influences on behavior, affect, and cognition during infancy and early childhood. In J. Cassidy & P. R. Shaver (Eds.), *Handbook of attachment: Theory, research, and clinical applications (2nd edition)* (pp. 192–216). New York, NY: Guilford.

Vaughn, B. E., Bradley, C. F., Joffe, L. S., Seifer, R., & Barglow, P. (1987). Maternal characteristics measured prenatally are predictive of ratings of temperamental "difficulty" on the Carey Infant Temperament Questionnaire. *Developmental Psychology, 23,* 152–161.

Vaughn, B. E., Kopp, C. B., & Krakow, J. B. (1984). The emergence and consolidation of self-control from eighteen to thirty months of age: Normative trends and individual differences. *Child Development, 55,* 990–1004.

Vaughn, B. E. & Waters, E. (1990). Attachment behavior at home and in the laboratory: Q-sort observations and Strange Situation classifications of one-year-olds. *Child Development, 61,* 1965–1990.

Vennemann, M., Bajanowski, T., Brinkmann, B., Jorch, G., & Sauerland, & C., & Mitchell, E. (2009). Sleep environment risk factors for SIDS: the German SIDS study. *Pediatrics, 123,* 1162–1170.

Venter, J. C., Adams, M. D., Myers, E. W., et al. (2001). The sequence of the human genome. *Science, 291,* 1304–1351.

Verbeek, P. (2006). Everybody's monkey: Primate moral roots. In M. Killen & J. G. Smetana (Eds.), *Handbook of moral development* (pp. 423–460). Mahwah, NJ: Lawrence Erlbaum.

Verbeek, P., Hartup, W. W., & Collins, W. A. (2000). Conflict management in children and adolescents. In F. Aureli & F. B. M. de Waal (Eds.), *Natural conflict resolution.* Berkeley, CA: University of California Press.

Verschueren, K., Marcoen, A., & Schoefs, V. (1996). The internal working model of the self, attachment, and competence in five-year-olds. *Child Development, 67,* 2493–2511.

Vierikko, E., Pulkkinen, L., Kaprio, J., Viken, R., & Rose, R. J. (2003). Sex differences in genetic and environmental effects on aggression. *Aggressive Behavior, 29,* 55–68.

Vietze, P. M. & Vaughan, H. G. (1988). *Early identification of infants with developmental disabilities.* Philadelphia: Grune & Stratton.

Vihman, M. M. (1985). Language differentiation by the bilingual infant. *Journal of Child Language, 12,* 297–324.

Vihman, M. M. & Miller, R. (1988). Words and babble at the threshold of language acquisition. In M. D. Smith & J. L. Locke (Eds.), *The emergent lexicon.* Orlando, FL: Academic Press.

Vitaro, F., Boivin, M., & Bukowski, W. M. (2009). The role of friendship in child and adolescent psychosocial development. In K.H. Rubin, W. M. Bukowski, & B. Laursen (Eds.), *Handbook of peer interactions, relationships, and groups* (pp. 568–585). New York: Guilford.

Vitaro, F., Brendgen, M., & Tremblay, R. E. (2001). Preventive intervention: Assessing its effects on the trajectories of delinquency and testing for mediational processes. *Applied Developmental Science, 5,* 201–213.

Vogel, E. (1963/1991). *Japan's new middle class.* Berkeley, CA: University of California Press.

Volbrecht, M. M., Lemery-Chalfant, K., Aksan, N., Zahn-Waxler, C , & Goldsmith,H. H. (2007). Examining the familial link between positive affect and empathy development in the second year. *Journal of Genetic Psychology, 168,*105–129.

Volpe, J. J. (2000). Overview: normal and abnormal human brain development. *Mental Retardation and Developmental Disabilities Research Review, 6,* 1–5.

Volterra, V. & Taeschner, T. (1978). The acquisition and development of language by bilingual children. *Journal of Child Language, 5,* 311–326.

von Hofsten, C. (1982). Eye-hand coordination in newborns. *Developmental Psychology, 18,* 450–461.

von Hofsten, C., Kellman, P., & Putaansuu, J. (1992). Young infants' sensitivity to motion parallax. *Infant Behavior and Development, 15,* 245–264.

von Hofsten, C. & Siddiqui, A. (1993). Using the mother's actions as a reference for object exploration in 6- and 12-month-old infants. *British Journal of Developmental Psychology,* 11, 61–74.

Vondra, J. I., Hommerding, K. D., & Shaw, D. S. (1999). Stability and change in infant attachment style in a low-income sample. *Monographs of the Society for Research in Child Development, 64(3),* 119–144.

Vouloumanos, A. & Werker, J. F. (2007). Listening to language at birth: Evidence for a bias for speech in neonates. *Developmental Science, 10,* 159–164.

Voyer, D., Voyer, S., & Bryden, M. P. (1995). Magnitude of sex differences in spatial abilities: A meta-analysis and consideration of critical variables. *Psychological Bulletin, 117,* 250–270.

Vuchinich, S., Bank, L., & Patterson, G. R. (1992). Parenting, peers, and the stability of antisocial behavior in preadolescent boys. *Developmental Psychology, 28,* 510–521.

Vurpillot, E. (1968). The development of scanning strategies and their relation to visual differentiation. *Journal of Experimental Child Psychology, 6,* 632–650.

Vurpillot, E. & Ball, W A. (1979). The concept of identity and children's selective attention. In G. A. Hale & M. Lewis (Eds.), *Attention and cognitive development.* New York: Plenum.

Vygotsky, L. S. (1934/1962). *Thought and language.* Cambridge, MA: MIT Press.

Vygotsky, L. S. (1981). The genesis of higher mental functions. In J. V Wertsch (Ed.), *The concept of activity in Soviet psychology.* Armonk, NY: M. E. Sharpe.

W

Wachs, T. D. (1988). Relevance of physical environment influences for toddler temperament. *Infant Behavior and Development, 11,* 431–445.

Wachs, T. D. (1992). *The nature of nurture.* Newbury Park, CA: Sage.

Wachs, T. D. (1994). Fit, context, and the transition between temperament and personality. In C. F. Halverson Jr., G. A. Kohnstamm, & R. P. Martin (Eds.), *The developing structure of temperament and personality from infancy to adulthood.* Hillsdale, NJ: Erlbaum.

Wadsworth, S. J., Corley, R. P., Hewitt, J. K., & DeFries, J. C. (2001). Stability of genetic and environmental influences on reading performance at 7, 12, and 16 years of age in the Colorado Adoption Project. *Behavior Genetics, 31,* 353–359.

Wadsworth, S. J., Corley, R. P., Hewitt, J. K., Plomin, R., & DeFries, J. C. (2002). Parent-offspring resemblance for reading performance at 7, 12 and 16 years of age in the Colorado Adoption Project. *Journal of Child Psychology and Psychiatry and Allied Disciplines, 43,* 769–774.

Wadsworth, S. J., Corley, R. P., Plomin, R., Hewitt, J. K., & DeFries, J. C. (2006). Genetic and environment influences on continuity and change in reading achievement in the Colorado Adoption Project. In A. C. Huston & M. N. Ripke (Eds.), *Developmental contexts in middle childhood* (pp. 87–106). New York: Cambridge University Press.

Wagner, B. M. & Phillips, D. A. (1992). Beyond beliefs: Parent and child behaviors and children's perceived academic competence. *Child Development, 63,* 1380–1391.

Wailoo, K. & Pemberton, S. (2006). *The troubled dream of genetic medicine.* Baltimore: The Johns Hopkins University Press.

Wainryb, C. (2000). Values and truths: The making and judging of moral decisions. In M. Laupa (Ed.), *New directions for child and adolescent development: No. 89. Rights and wrongs: How children and young adults evaluate the world.* San Francisco: Jossey-Bass.

Wainryb, C. (2006). Moral development in culture: Diversity, tolerance, & justice. In M. Killen & J. G. Smetana (Eds.), *Handbook of moral development* (pp. 211–240). Mahwah, NJ: Lawrence Erlbaum.

Walker, H. M., Colvin, G., & Ramsey, E. (1995). *Antisocial behavior in school: Strategies and best practices.* Pacific Grove, CA: Brooks/Cole.

Walker, L. J. (1989). A longitudinal study of moral reasoning. *Child Development, 60,* 157–166.

Walker, L. J. (1991). Sex differences in moral reasoning. In W. M. Kurtines & J. L. Gewirtz (Eds.), *Handbook of moral behavior and development: Vol. 2. Research.* Hillsdale, NJ: Erlbaum.

Walker, L. J. (2006). Gender and morality. In M. Killen & J. G. Smetana (Eds.), *Handbook of moral development* (pp. 93–115). Mahwah, NJ: Erlbaum.

Walker, L. J. & Hennig, K. H. (1999). Parenting style and the development of moral reasoning. *Journal of Moral Education, 28,* 359–374.

Walker, L. J., DeVries, B., & Trevarthen, S. D. (1987). Moral stages and moral orientations in real-life and hypothetical dilemmas. *Child Development, 58,* 842–858.

Walker, L. J., Hennig, K. H., & Krettenauer, T. (2000). Parent and peer contexts for children's moral reasoning development. *Child Development, 71,* 1033–1048.

Walker, L. J. & Taylor, J. H. (1991). Family interactions and the development of moral reasoning. *Child Development, 62,* 264–283.

Walker, S. P., Wachs, T. D., Gardner, J. M., Lozoff, B., Wasserman, G. A., Pollitt, E., & Carter, J. A. (2007). Child development: risk factors for adverse outcomes in developing countries. *The Lancet, 369,* 145–157.

Walker-Andrews, A. S. (1997). Infants' perception of expressive behaviors: Differentiation of multimodal information. *Psychological Bulletin, 121,* 437–456.

Walker-Andrews, A. S., Bahrick, L. E., Raglioni, S. S., & Diaz, I. (1991). Infants' bimodal perception of gender. *Ecological Psychology, 3,* 55–75.

Wallach, M. A. & Kogan, N. (1966). *Modes of thinking in young children.* New York: Holt, Rinehart, and Winston.

Wallen, K. (2005). Hormonal influences on sexually differentiated behavior in nonhuman primates. *Frontiers in Neuroendocrinology, 26,* 7–26.

Waller, N. G., Kojetin, B. A., Bouchard, T. J. Jr., Lykken, D. T., & Tellegen, A. (1990). Genetic and environmental influences on religious interests, attitudes, and values: A study of twins reared apart and together. *Psychological Science, 1,* 138–142.

Wallerstein, J. (2008). Divorce. In J. Benson & M. Haith (Eds.), *Social and emotional development in infancy and early childhood* (pp. 108–118). New York: Academic Press.

Wallerstein, J. S., Lewis, J. M., & Blakeslee, S. (2000). *The unexpected legacy of divorce: A 25 year landmark study.* New York: Hyperion.

Wallis, C. (2011). Performing gender: A content analysis of gender display in music videos. *Sex Roles, 64,* 160–172.

Walton, G. E., Bower, N. J., & Bower, T. G. (1992). Recognition of familiar faces by newborns. *Infant Behavior and Development, 15,* 265–269.

Wanzek, J., Vaughn, S., Kim, A., & Cavanaugh, C. L. (2006). The effects of reading interventions on social outcomes for elementary students with reading disabilities: A synthesis. *Reading and Writing Quarterly, 22,* 121–138.

Ward, M. J. & Carlson, E. A. (1995). Associations among adult attachment representations, maternal sensitivity, and infant-mother attachment in a sample of adolescent mothers. *Child Development, 66,* 69–79.

Wark, G. R. & Krebs, D. L. (1996). Gender and dilemma differences in real-life moral judgment. *Developmental Psychology, 32,* 220–230.

Warkany, J. (1977). History of teratology. In J. G. Wilson & F. C. Fraser (Eds.), *Handbook of teratology: Vol 1. General principles and etiology.* New York: Plenum.

Warkany, J. (1981). Prevention of congenital malformations. *Teratology, 23,* 175–189.

Warren, A. R. & McCloskey, L. A. (1997). Language acquisition in social contexts. In J. B. Gleason (Ed.), *The development of language* (4th ed.). Boston: Allyn and Bacon.

Wasserman, G. A., Liu, X., Pine, D. S., & Graziano, J. H. (2000). Contribution of maternal smoking during pregnancy and lead exposure to early child behavior problems. *Neurotoxicology and Teratology, 23,* 13–21.

Wasz-Hockert, O., Michelsson, K., & Lind, J. (1985). Twenty-five years of Scandinavian cry research. In B. M. Lester & C. Z. Boukydis (Eds.), *Infant crying: Theoretical and research perspectives.* New York. Plenum.

Waters, E. (1987). Attachment Q-set (Version 3). Retrieved February 14, 2011 from www.psychology.sunysb.edu/attachment/measures/content/aqs_items.pdf

Waters, E. (1995). The Attachment Q-Set (Version 3. 0) (Appendix A). In E. Waters, B. E. Vaughn, G. Posada, & K. Kondo-Ikemura (Eds.), Caregiving, cultural, and cognitive perspectives on secure-base behavior and working models. *Monographs of the Society for Research in Child Development, 60* (2–3, Serial No. 244).

Waters, H. S. (2000). Memory strategy development: Do we need yet another deficiency? *Child Development, 71,* 1004–1012.

Watkins, K. & Paus, T. (2004). Modulation of motor excitability during speech perception: The role of Broca's area. *Journal of Cognitive Neuroscience, 16,* 978–987.

Watson, J. B. (1928). *Psychological care of infant and child.* New York: Norton.

Watson, J. B. & Rayner, R. (1920). Conditioned emotional reactions. *Journal of Experimental Psychology 3,* 1–14.

Watson, J. D. (1968). *The double helix: A personal account of the discovery of the structure of DNA.* New York: Atheneum.

Watson, J. D. & Crick, F. H. C. (1953). Molecular structure of nucleic acid: A structure for deoxyribose nucleic acid. *Nature, 171,* 737–738.

Watt, H. M. G. (2010). Gender and occupational choice. *Handbook of gender research in psychology: Vol. 2: Gender research in social and applied psychology* (pp. 379–400). New York, NY: Springer.

Wattendorf, D. J. & Muenke, M. (2005). Fetal Alcohol Spectrum Disorders. *American Family Physician, 72*(2), 279–285. http://www.aafp.org/afp/2005/0715/p279.html

Waxman, S. R. (1990). Linguistic biases and the establishment of conceptual hierarchies. *Cognitive Development, 5,* 123–150.

Waxman, S. R. (2004). Everything had a name, and each name gave birth to a new thought: Links between early word-learning and conceptual organization. In D. G. Hall & S. R. Waxman (Eds.), *Weaving a lexicon.* Cambridge: MIT Press.

Waxman, S. R. & Booth, A. E. (2001). Seeing pink elephants: Fourteen-month-olds' interpretations of novel nouns and adjectives. *Cognitive Psychology, 43(3),* 217–242.

Waxman, S. R. & Booth, A. E. (2003). The origins and evolution of links between word learning and conceptual organization: New evidence from 11-month-olds. *Developmental Science, 6(2),* 130–137.

Waxman, S. R. & Lidz, J. (2006). Early word learning. In D. Kuhn & R. Siegler (Eds.), *Handbook of child psychology, 6th edition, Volume 2* (pp. 299–335). Hoboken NJ: Wiley.

Waxman, S. R. & Markow, D. B. (1995). Words as invitations to form categories: Evidence from 12- to 13-month-old infants. *Cognitive Psychology, 29,* 257–302.

Way, N. (2004). Intimacy, desire, and distrust in the friendships of adolescent boys. In N. Way & J. Y. Chu (Eds.), *Adolescent boys: Exploring diverse cultures of boyhood* (pp. 167–196). New York, NY: New York University Press.

Webb, N. M. & Palincsar, A. S. (1996). Group processes in the classroom. In D. C. Berliner & R. C. Calfee (Eds.), *Handbook of educational psychology.* New York: Simon & Schuster Macmillan.

Webb, S. J., Monk, C. S., & Nelson, C. A. (2001). Mechanisms of postnatal neurobiological development: Implications for human development. *Developmental Neuropsychology, 19,* 147–171.

Wechsler, D. (2002). *Weschsler Preschool and Primary Scales of Intelligence: Third edition.* San Antonio, TX: Psychological Corporation.

Wechsler, D. (2003). *Weschsler Intelligence Scale for Children: Fourth edition,* San Antonio, TX: Psychological Corporation.

Wegiel, J., Kuchna, I., Nowicki, K., Imaki, H., Wegiel, J., Marchi, E., Ma, S. Y., Chauhan, A., Chauhan, V., Bobrowicz, T. W., de Leon, M., Saint Louis, L. W., Cohen, I. L., London, E., Brown, W. T., & Wisniewski, T. (2010). The neuropathology of autism: Defects of neurogenesis and neuronal migration, and dysplastic changes. *Acta Neuropathologica, 119,* 755–770.

Weinberg, M. K., Tronick, E. Z., Cohn, J. F., & Olson, K. L. (1999). Gender differences in emotional expressivity and self-regulation during early infancy. *Developmental Psychology, 35,* 175–188.

Weinfield, N. S., Sroufe, L. A., & Egeland, B. (2000). Attachment from infancy to early adulthood in a high-risk sample: Continuity, discontinuity, and their correlates. *Child Development, 71,* 695–702.

Weinfield, N. S., Sroufe, L. A., Egeland, B., & Carlson, E. (2008). Individual differences in infant-caregiver attachment: Conceptual and empirical aspects of security. In J. Cassidy & P. R. Shaver (Eds.) *Handbook of attachment: Theory, research, and clinical applications (2nd edition)* (pp. 78–101). New York, NY: Guilford.

Weinraub, M., Clemens, L. P., Sockloff, A., Ethridge, T., Gracely, E., & Myers, B. (1984). The development of sex role stereotypes in the third year: Relationships to gender labeling, gender identity, sex-typed toy preference, and family characteristics. *Child Development, 55,* 1493–1503.

Weinraub, M., Horvath, D. L., & Gringlas, M. B. (2002). Single parenthood. In M. H. Bornstein (Ed.), *Handbook of parenting: Vol. 3: Being and becoming a parent* (2nd ed., pp. 109–140). Mahwah, NJ: Erlbaum.

Weisleder, A. & Waxman, S. R. (2010). What's in the input? Frequent frames in child-directed speech offer distributional cues to grammatical categories in Spanish and English. *Journal of Child Language, 37,* 1089–1108.

Weisner, T. S. (1996). The 5 to 7 transition as an ecocultural project. In A. Sameroff & M. M. Haith (Eds.), *The five to seven year shift: The age of reason and responsibility.* Chicago: University of Chicago Press.

Weisner, T. S., Garnier, H., & Loucky, J. (1994). Domestic tasks, gender egalitarian values and children's gender typing in conventional and nonconventional families. *Sex Roles, 30,* 23–54.

Weiss, B., Dodge, K. A., Bates, J. E., & Pettit, G. S. (1992). Some consequences of early harsh discipline: Child aggression and a maladaptive social information processing style. *Child Development, 63,* 1321–1335.

Weissberg, R. P. (1985). Designing effective social problem-solving programs for the classroom. In B. H. Schneider, K. H. Rubin, & J. E. Ledingham (Eds.), *Children's peer relations: Issues in assessment and intervention.* New York: Springer-Verlag.

Wekselman, K., Spiering, K., Hetterberg, C., Kenner, C., & Flandermeyer, A. (1995). Fetal alcohol syndrome from infancy to childhood: A review of the literature. *Journal of Pediatric Nursing, 10,* 296–303.

Wellman, H. M. (1977). Preschoolers' understanding of memory-relevant variables. *Child Development, 48,* 1720–1723.

Wellman, H. M. (1988). The early development of memory strategies. In F. E. Weinert & M. Perlmutter (Eds.), *Memory development: Universal changes and individual differences.* Hillsdale, NJ: Erlbaum.

Wellman, H. M. (2011). Developing a theory of mind. In U. Goswami (Ed.), *The Wiley-Blackwell handbook of childhood cognitive development, second edition* (pp. 259–284). Chichester, UK: Blackwell Publishing Ltd.

Wellman, H. M., Ritter, K., & Flavell, J. H. (1975). Deliberate memory behavior in the delayed reactions of very young children. *Developmental Psychology, 11,* 780–787.

Wender, P. (2000). *ADHD: Attention-deficit hyperactivity disorder in children and adults.* New York, NY: Oxford University Press.

Weng, X., Odouli, R., & De-Kun, L. (2008). Maternal caffeine consumption during pregnancy and the risk of miscarriage: A prospective cohort study. *American Journal of Obstetrics and Gynecology, 198,* 279.e1-279.e8.

Wentworth, N., Benson, J. B., & Haith, M. M. (2000). The development of infants' reaches for stationary and moving targets. *Child Development, 71,* 576–601.

Wentworth, N., Haith, M. M., & Hood, R. (2002). Spatiotemporal regularity and interevent contingencies as information for infants' visual expectations. *Infancy, 3,* 303–322.

Wentzel, K. R. & Erdley, C. A. (1993). Strategies for making friends: Relations to social behavior and peer acceptance in early adolescence. *Developmental Psychology, 29,* 819–826.

Werker, J. F., Fennell, C. T., Corcoran, K. M., & Stager, C. L. (2002). Infants' ability to learn phonetically similar words: Effects of age and vocabulary. *Infancy, 3,* 1–30.

Werker, J. F., Pons, F., Dietrich, C., Kajikawa, S., Fais, L., & Amano, S. (2007). Infant-directed speech supports phonetic category learning in English and Japanese. *Cognition, 103(1),* 147–162.

Werker, J. F. & Tees, R. C. (1999). Influences on infant speech processing: Toward a new synthesis. *Annual Review of Psychology, 50,* 509–535.

Werker, J. F. & Tees, R. C. (2002). Cross-language speech perception: Evidence for perceptual reorganization during the first year of life. *Infant Behavior and Development, 25,* 121–133.

Werker, J. F. & Tees, R. C. (2005). Speech perception as a window for understanding plasticity and commitment in language systems of the brain. *Developmental Psychobiology, 46,* 233–251.

Werker, J. F. & Vouloumanos, A. (2001). Speech and language processing in infancy: A neurocognitive approach. In C. A. Nelson & M. Luciana (Eds.), *Handbook of developmental cognitive neuroscience* (pp. 269–280). Cambridge, MA: MIT Press.

Werler, M. M., Mitchell, A. A., Hernandez-Diaz, S., & Honein, M. A. (2005). Use of over-the-counter medications during pregnancy. *American Journal of Obstetrics and Gynecology, 193,* 771–777.

Werner, E. & Smith, R. (1982). *Vulnerable but invincible: A study of resilient children.* New York: McGraw Hill.

Werner, L. A. & Bargones, J. Y. (1992). Psychoacoustic development of human infants. In C. Rovee-Collier & L. P. Lipsitt (Eds.), *Advances in infancy research* (Vol. 7). Norwood, NJ: Ablex.

Werth, L. H. (1984). Synchrony of cueing modalities. Communicative competence between the mother and blind infant. *Early child development and care, 18,* 53–60.

Wertheimer, M. (1961). Psychomotor coordination of auditory-visual space at birth. *Science, 134,* 1692.

Wertheimer, M. (1985). The evolution of the concept of development in the history of psychology. In G. Eckardt, W. G. Bringmann, & L. Sprung (Eds.), *Contributions to a history of developmental psychology.* Berlin: Mouton.

Wertsch, J. (1985). *Vygotsky and the social formation of mind.* Cambridge, MA: Harvard University Press.

Wertsch, J. V. & Tulviste, P. (1992). J. S. Vygotsky and contemporary developmental psychology. *Developmental Psychology, 28,* 548–557.

Westermann, G., Sirois, S., Shultz, T.R., & Mareschal, D. (2006). Modeling developmental cognitive neuroscience. *Trends in Cognitive Science, 10,* 287–232.

Wettersten, K. B., Guilmino, A., Herrick, C. G., Hunter, P. J., Kim, G. Y., Jagow, D., et al. (2005). Predicting educational and vocational attitudes among rural high school students. *Journal of Counseling Psychology, 52,* 658–663.

Whalen, D. H., Levitt, A. G., & Goldstein, L. M. (2007). VOT in the babbling of French- and English-learning infants. *Journal of Phonetics, 35*(3), 341–352.

Wheaton, L. A., Nolte, G., Bohlhalter, S., Fridman, E., & Hallett, M. (2005). Synchronization of parietal and premotor areas during preparation and execution of praxis hand movements. *Clinical Neurophysiology, 116,* 1382–1390.

Wheeler, L. & Suls, J. (2005). Social comparison and self-evaluations of competence. In A. Elliot & C. Dweck (Eds.), *Handbook of competence and motivation* (pp. 566–578). New York: Guilford.

White, B. L., Castle, P., & Held, R. (1964). Observations on the development of visually directed reaching. *Child Development, 35,* 349–364.

White, S. & Tharp, R. G. (1988, April). *Questioning and wait-time: A cross-cultural analysis.* Paper presented at the meeting of the American Educational Research Association, New Orleans, LA.

White, T. G. (1982). Naming practices, typicality, and under extension in child language. *Journal of Experimental Child Psychology, 33,* 324–346.

White, T. L., Leichtman, M. D., & Ceci, S. J. (1997). The good, the bad, and the ugly: Accuracy, inaccuracy and elaboration in preschoolers' reports about a past event. *Applied Cognitive Psychology, 11,* S37-S54.

White, T., & Hilgetag, C. C. (2008). Gyrification of the human brain. In C. A. Nelson & M. Luciana (Eds.), *Developmental cognitive neuroscience.* Cambridge, MA: MIT Press.

Whitehurst, G. J. & DeBaryshe, B. D. (1989). Observational learning and language acquisition: Principles of learning, systems, and tasks. In G. E. Speidel & K. E. Nelson (Eds.), *The many faces of imitation in language learning.* New York: Springer-Verlag.

Whitehurst, G. J. & Novak, G. (1973). Modeling, imitation training, and the acquisition of sentence phrases. *Journal of Experimental Child Psychology, 16,* 332–345.

Whitehurst, G. J. & Sonnenschein, S. (1985). The development of communication: A functional analysis. In G. J. Whitehurst (Ed.), *Annals of child development* (Vol. 2). Greenwich, CT: JAI Press.

Whiteside, M. F. & Becker, B. J. (2000). Parental factors and the young child's post-divorce adjustment: A meta-analysis with implications for parenting arrangements. *Journal of Family Psychology, 14,* 5–26.

Whiting, B. B. & Edwards, C. P. (1988). *Children of different worlds: The formation of social behavior.* Cambridge, MA: Harvard University Press.

Whiting, B. B. & Whiting, J. W. M. (1975). *Children of six cultures: A psycho-cultural analysis.* Cambridge, MA: Harvard University Press.

Whitley, R. & Goldenberg, R. (1990). Infectious disease in the prenatal period and the recommendations for screening. In I. R. Merkatz & J. E. Thompson (Eds.), *New perspectives on prenatal care.* New York: Elsevier.

Whitney, E. N. & Rolfes, S. R. (2011). *Understanding nutrition (12th edition).* Belmont, CA: Thompson.

Widen, S. C. & Russell, J. A. (2003). A closer look at preschoolers' freely produced labels for facial expressions. *Developmental Psychology, 39,* 114–128.

Widen, S. C. & Russell, J. A. (2008) Young children's understanding of others' emotions. In M. Lewis, J. M. Haviland-Jones, & L. M. Barrett (Eds.), *Handbook of emotions, 3rd edition* (pp. 348–363). New York: Guilford.

Wigfield, A., Battle, A., Keller, L. B., & Eccles, J. S. (2002). Sex differences in motivation, self-concept, career aspiration and career choice: Implications for cognitive development. In A. V. McGillicuddy-De Lisi & R. De Lisi (Eds.), *Biology, society, and behavior: The development of sex differences in cognition.* Greenwich, CT: Ablex.

Wigfield, A., Eccles, J. S., Yoon, K. S., Harold, R. D., Arbreton, A., Freedman-Doan, K., et al. (1997). Changes in children's competence beliefs and subjective task values across the elementary school years: A three-year-study. *Journal of Educational Psychology, 89,* 451–469.

Wilcke, J.C., O'Shea, R. P., & Watts, R. (2009). Frontoparietal activity and its structural connectivity in binocular rivalry. *Brain Research, 1305,* 96–107.

Wilcox, A. J., Baird, D. D., Weinberg, C. R., Hornsby, P. P., & Herbst, A. L. (1995). Fertility in men exposed prenatally to diethylstilbestrol. *New England Journal of Medicine, 332,* 1411–1416.

Wilcox, T., Bortfeld, H., Armstrong, J., Woods, R., & Boas, D. (2009). Hemodynamic response to featural and spatiotemporal information in the infant brain. *Neuropsychologia, 47,* 657–662.

Wilcox, T., Haslup, J. A., & Boas, D. A. (2010). Dissociation of processing of featural and spatiotemporal information in the infant cortex. *NeuroImage, 53,* 1256–1263.

Wiley, A. R., Rose, A. J., Burger, L. K., & Miller, P. J. (1998). Constructing autonomous selves through narrative practices: A comparative study of working-class and middle-class families. *Child Development, 69,* 833–847.

Wilk, A. E., Klein, L., & Rovee-Collier, C. (2001). Visual-preference and operant measures of infant memory. *Developmental Psychobiology, 39,* 301–312.

Willard, N. E. (2007). An educator´s guide to cyberbullying and cyberthreats. Available from http://www.cyberbully.org/cyberbully/docs/cbcteducator.pdf. Accessed March 4, 2011.

Willis, M. L., Palermo, R., Burke, D., Atkinson, C. M., & McArthur, G. (2010). Switching associations between facial identity and emotional expression: A behavioural and ERP study. *NeuroImage, 50,* 329–339.

Wilson, M. (Ed.). (1995). *African American family life: Its structural and ecological aspects.* San Francisco: Jossey-Bass.

Wilson, R. D. (2007). Principles of human teratology: Drug, chemical, and infectious exposure. *Journal of Obstetrics and Gynaecolology in Canada, 29,* 911–917.

Wilson, R. S. (1983). The Louisville Twin Study: Developmental synchronies in behavior. *Child Development, 54,* 298–316.

Wilson, R. S. (1986). Growth and development of human twins. In F. Falkner & J. M. Tanner (Eds.), *Human growth: A comprehensive treatise.* New York: Plenum.

Wilson, S. M., Corley, R. P., Fulker, D. W., & Reznick, S. J. (2001). Experimental assessment of specific cognitive abilities during the second year of life. In R. N. Emde & J. K. Hewitt (Eds.),

Infancy to early childhood. New York: Oxford University Press.

Wilson-Costello, D., Friedman, H., Minich, N., Siner, B., Taylor, G., Schluchter, M., & Hack, M. (2007). Improved neurodevelopmental outcomes for extremely low birth weight infants in 2000–2002. *Pediatrics, 119,* 37–45.

Windle, M. & Lerner, R. M. (1986). The "goodness-of-fit" model of temperament-context relations: Interaction or correlation? In J. V. Lerner & R. M. Lerner (Eds.), *New directions for child development: No. 31. Temperament and social interaction in infants and children.* San Francisco: Jossey-Bass.

Windsor, J. (1993). The functions of novel word compounds. *Journal of Child Language, 20,* 119–138.

Winner, E. (1996). *Gifted children.* New York: Basic Books.

Winner, E. (2000). The origins and ends of giftedness. *American Psychologist, 55,* 159–169.

Winsler, A. (2009). Still talking to ourselves after all these years: A review of current research on private speech. In A. Winsler, C. Fernyhough, & I. Montero (Eds.), *Private speech, executive functioning, and the development of verbal self-regulation* (pp. 1–41). New York, NY: Cambridge University Press.

Winsler, A., Manfra, L., & Diaz, R. M. (2007). "Should I let them talk?": Private speech and task performance among preschool children with and without behavior problems. *Early Childhood Research Quarterly, 22,* 215–231.

Witelson, S. F. (1976). Sex and the single hemisphere: Specialization of the right hemisphere for spatial processing. *Science, 193,* 425–427.

Witherington, D. C., Campos, J. J., Anderson, D. I., Lejeune, L., & Seah, E. (2005). Avoidance of heights on the visual cliff in newly walking infants. *Infancy, 7,* 285–298.

Wodrich, D. (2006). Sex chromosome anomalies. In L. Phelps (Ed.), *Chronic health-related disorders in children.* Washington, DC: American Psychological Association.

Wolchik, S. A., Wilcox, K. L., Tein, J., & Sandler, I. N. (2000). Maternal acceptance and consistency of discipline as buffers of divorce stressors on children's psychological adjustment problems. *Journal of Abnormal Child Psychology, 28,* 87–102.

Woldorff, M. G., Fox, P. T., Matzke, M., Lancaster, J. L., Veeraswamy, S., Zamarripa, F. Seabolt, M., Glass, T., Gao, J. H., Martin, C. C., & Jerabek, P. (1997). Retinotopic organization of early visual spatial attention effects as revealed by PET and ERPs. *Human Brain Mapping, 5,* 280–286.

Wolf, U., Rapoport, M. J., & Schweizer, T. A. (2009). Evaluating the affective component of the cerebellar cognitive affective syndrome. *The Journal of Neuropsychiatry and Clinical Neurosciences, 21,* 245–253.

Wolff, P. H. (1959). Observations on newborn infants. *Psychosomatic Medicine, 21,* 110–118.

Wolff, P. H. (1966). The causes, controls and organization of behavior in the neonate. *Psychological Issues, 5*(17), 1–105.

Wolff, P. H. (1969). The natural history of crying and other vocalizations in early infancy. In B. Foss (Ed.), *Determinants of infant behavior* (Vol. 4). London: Methuen.

Wood, E., Desmarais, S., & Gugula, S. (2002). The impact of parenting experience on gender stereotyped toy play of children. *Sex Roles, 47,* 39–49.

Wood, W. & Eagly, A. H. (2002). A cross-cultural analysis of the behavior of women and men: Implications for the origins of sex differences. *Psychological Bulletin, 128,* 699–727.

Wood, W. & Eagly, A. H. (2010). Gender. In S. T. Fiske, D.T. Gilbert, & G. Lindzey (Eds.), *Handbook of social psychology (Vol. 2)* (pp. 629-667). Hoboken, NJ: John Wiley & Sons.

Woods, T., Coyle, K., Hoglund, W., & Leadbeater, B. (2007). Changing the contexts of peer victimization: The effects of a primary prevention program on school and classroom levels of victimization. In J. E. Zins, M. J. Elias, & C. A. Maher (Eds.), *Bullying, victimization, and peer harassment: A handbook of prevention and intervention* (pp. 369–388). New York: Haworth Press.

Woodward, A. L. (2000). Constraining the problem space in early word learning. In R. Golinkoff, K. Hirsh-Pasek, L. Bloom, G. Hollich, L. Smith, A. Woodward, N. Akhtar, M. Tomasello, & G. Hollich (Eds.), *Becoming a word learner: A debate on lexical acquisition* (pp. 81–114). New York: Oxford University Press.

Woody-Dorning, J. & Miller, P. H. (2001). Children's individual differences in capacity: Effects on strategy production and utilization. *British Journal of Developmental Psychology, 19,* 543–557.

World Health Organization (2010). *Trends in maternal mortality: 1990 to 2008.* Geneva, Switzerland: WHO Press.

Worobey J. & Blajda, V. M. (1989). Temperament ratings at 2 weeks, 2 months, and 1 year: Differential stability of activity and emotionality. *Developmental Psychology, 25,* 257–263.

Wright, J. C., Huston, A. C., Vandewater, E. A., Bickham, D. S., Scantlin, R. M., Kotler, J. A., et al. (2001). American children's use of electronic media in 1997: A national survey. *Applied Developmental Psychology, 22,* 31–47.

Wright, M. (1999). The history of developmental psychology in Canada. *The Canadian Journal of Research in Early Childhood Education, 8,* 31–36.

Wright, M. (2002). Flashbacks in the history of psychology in Canada: Some early "headline" makers. *Canadian Psychology, 43,* 21–34.

Wu, W. X., Ma, X. H., Zhang, Q., Chakrabarty, K., & Nathanielsz, P. W. (2003). Characterization of two labor-induced genes, DSCR1 and TCTE1L, in the pregnant ovine myometrium. *Journal of Endocrinology, 178,* 117–126

Wu, X., Hart, C. H., Draper, T. W., & Olsen, J. A. (2001). Peer and teacher sociometrics for preschool children: Cross-information concordance, temporal stability, and reliability. *Merrill-Palmer Quarterly, 47,* 416–443.

Wu, Z. & Schimmele, C. (2009). Divorce and repartnering. In M. Baker (Ed.), *Families: Changing trends in Canada.* Toronto, ON: McGraw-Hill Ryerson.

Wynn, K. (1992). Addition and subtraction by human infants. *Nature, 358,* 749–750.

Wynn, K. (1995). Origins of numerical knowledge. *Mathematical Cognition, 1,* 36–60.

Wynn, K. (1998). Numerical competence in infants. In C. Donlan (Ed.), *The development of mathematical skills: Studies in developmental psychology.* Hove, UK: Psychology Press.

X

Xu, F. & Arriaga, R. I. (2007). Number discrimination in 10-month-old infants. *British Journal of Developmental Psychology, 25,* 103–108.

Xu, F., Cote, M., & Baker, A. (2005). Labeling guides object individuation in 12-month-old infants. *Psychological Science, 16(5),* 372–377.

Y

Yankowitz, J. (1996). Surgical fetal therapy. In J. A. Kuller, N. C. Cheschier, & R. C. Cefalo (Eds.), *Prenatal diagnosis and reproductive genetics.* St. Louis, MO: Mosby.

Yates, G. C. R., Yates, S. M., & Beasley, C. J. (1987). Young children's knowledge of strategies in delay of gratification. *Merrill-Palmer Quarterly, 33,* 159–169.

Yinon, Y., Farine, D., & Yudin, M. H. (2010). Cytomegalovirus infection in pregnancy. *Journal of Obstetrics and Gynaecology in Canada, 32,* 348–354.

Yonas, A. (1981). Infants' responses to optical information for collision. In R. N. Aslin, J. R. Alberts, & M. R. Peterson (Eds.), *Development of perception: Psychobiological perspectives: Vol. 2. The visual system.* New York: Academic Press.

Yonas, A. & Granrud, C. E. (1985). Development of visual space perception in young infants. In J. Mehler & R. Fox (Eds.), *Neonate cognition.* Hillsdale, NJ: Erlbaum.

Yonas, A. & Owsley, C. (1987). Development of visual space perception. In P. Salapatek & L. Cohen (Eds.), *Handbook of infant perception: Vol. 2. From perception to cognition.* New York: Academic Press.

Young, S. K., Fox, N. A., & Zahn-Waxler, C. (1999). The relations between temperament and empathy in 2-year-olds. *Developmental Psychology, 35,* 1189–1197.

Younger, A. J., Gentile, C., & Burgess., K. (1993). Children's perceptions of social withdrawal: Changes across age. In K. Rubin & J. Asendorpf (Eds.), *Social withdrawal, inhibition, and shyness in childhood* (pp. 215–236). Hillsdale, NJ: Erlbaum.

Younger, A. J., Schneider, B. H., & Guirguis-Younger, M. (2008). How children describe their shy/withdrawn peers. *Infant and Child Development, 17,* [in press].

Younger, A. J., Schneider, B., Wadeson, R., Guirguis, M., & Bergeron, B. (2000). A behaviour-based, peer-nomination measure of social withdrawal in children. *Social Development, 9,* 544–564.

Youniss, J. & Volpe, J. (1978). A relational analysis of children's friendship. In W. Damon (Ed.), *New directions for child development: No. 1. Social cognition.* San Francisco: Jossey-Bass.

Yussen, S. R. & Levy, Y. M. (1975). Developmental changes in predicting one's own span of short-term memory. *Journal of Experimental Child Psychology, 19,* 502–508.

Z

Zahn-Waxler, C., Friedman, R. J., Cole, P. M., & Mizuta, I. (1996). Japanese and United States preschool children's responses to conflict and distress. *Child Development, 67,* 2462–2477.

Zahn-Waxler, C. & Radke-Yarrow, M. (1982). The development of altruism: Alternative research strategies. In N. Eisenberg (Ed.), *The development of prosocial behavior.* San Diego, CA: Academic Press.

Zahn-Waxler, C., Radke-Yarrow, M., Wagner, E., & Chapman, M. (1992). Development of concern for others. *Developmental Psychology, 28,* 126–136.

Zahn-Waxler, C., Robinson, J. L., & Emde, R. N. (1992). The development of empathy in twins. *Developmental Psychology, 28,* 1038–1047.

Zahn-Waxler, C., Schiro, K., Robinson, J., Emde, R. N., & Schmitz, S. (2001). Empathy and prosocial patterns in young MZ and DZ twins: Development and genetic and environmental influences. In R. N Emde & J. K. Hewitt (Eds.), *Infancy to early childhood: Genetic and environmental influences on developmental change.* Oxford: Oxford University Press.

Zametkin, A. J., Nordahl, T. E., Gross, M., King, A. C., Semple, W. E., Rumsey, J., et al. (1990). Cerebral glucose metabolism in adults with hyperactivity of childhood onset. *New England Journal of Medicine, 20,* 1361–1366.

Zarbatany, L., McDougall, P., & Hymel, S. (2000). Gender-differentiated experience in the peer culture: Links to intimacy in preadolescence. *Social Development, 9,* 62–79.

Zeifman, D. M. (2001). An ethological analysis of human infant crying: Answering Tinbergen's four questions. *Developmental Psychobiology, 39,* 265–285.

Zeifman, D. M. & Hazan, C. (2008). Pair bonds as attachments: Reevaluating the evidence. In J. Cassidy & P. R. Shaver (Eds.), *Handbook of attachment: Theory, research, and clinical applications (2nd edition)* (pp. 436–455). New York, NY: Guilford.

Zelazo, P. D. (1999). Language, levels of consciousness, and the development of intentional action. In P. D. Zelazo, J. W. Astington, & D. R. Olson (Eds.), *Developing theories of intention.* Mahwah, NJ: Erlbaum.

Zelazo, P. D., Carlson, S. M., & Kesek, A. (2008). The development of executive function in childhood. In C. Nelson & M. Luciana (Eds.), *Handbook of developmental cognitive neuroscience* (2nd ed., pp. 553–574). Cambridge, MA: MIT Press.

Zelazo, P. D. & Frye, D. (1998). Cognitive complexity and control: II. The development of executive function in childhood. *Current Directions in Psychological Science, 7,* 121–126.

Zelazo, P. D. & Müller, U. (2011). Executive function in typical and atypical development. In U. Goswani (Ed.), *The Wiley-Blackwell handbook on childhood cognitive development* (2nd Edition, pp. 574–603). West Sussex, UK: Wiley-Blackwell Publishing.

Zelazo, N. A., Zelazo, P. R., Cohen, K. M., & Zelazo, P. D. (1993). Specificity of practice effects on elementary neuromotor patterns. *Developmental Psychology, 29,* 686–691.

Zelazo, P. R. (1971). Smiling to social stimuli: Eliciting and conditioning effects. *Developmental Psychology, 4,* 32–42.

Zelazo, P. R., Weiss, M. J. S., & Tarquino, N. (1991). Habituation and recovery of neonatal orienting to auditory stimuli. In M. J. S. Weiss & P. R. Zelazo (Eds.), *Newborn attention: Biological constraints and the influence of experience.* Norwood, NJ: Ablex.

Zempsky, W. T. & Cravero, J. P. (2004). Committee on Pediatric Emergency Medicine, and secondary relief of pain and anxiety in pediatric patients in emergency medical systems. *Pediatrics, 114,* 1348–1356.

Zentner, M. R. & Kagan, J. (1998). Infants' perception of consonance and dissonance in music. *Infant Behavior and Development, 21,* 483–492.

Zeskind, P. S. & Lester, B. M. (2001). Analysis of infant crying. In L. T. Singer & P. S. Zeskind (Eds.), *Biobehavioral assessment of the infant.* New York: Guilford.

Zeskind, P. S. & Marshall, T. R. (1988). The relation between variations in pitch and maternal perceptions of infant crying. *Child Development, 59,* 193–196.

Zeskind, P. S. & Ramey, C. T. (1981). Preventing intellectual and interactional sequelae of fetal malnutrition: A longitudinal, transactional and synergistic approach to development. *Child Development, 52,* 213–218.

Zhang, W. & Luck, S. J. (2008). Discrete fixed-resolution representations in visual working memory. *Nature, 453,* 233–235.

Zigler, E. F. & Finn-Stevenson, M. (1999). Applied developmental psychology. In M. H. Bornstein & M. E. Lamb (Eds.), *Developmental psychology: An advanced textbook* (4th ed.). Mahwah, NJ: Erlbaum.

Zigler, E. F. & Styfco, S. J. (Eds.). (1993). *Head Start and beyond: A national plan for extended childhood intervention.* New Haven, CT: Yale University Press.

Zimbardo, P. G. & Radl, S. L. (1999). *The shy child: A guide to preventing and overcoming shyness from infancy to adulthood.* Cambridge, MA: Malor Books.

Zimmerman, B. J. (1983). Social learning theory: A contextualist account of cognitive functioning. In C. J. Brainerd (Ed.), *Recent advances in cognitive-developmental theory: Progress in cognitive development research.* New York: Springer-Verlag.

Zimmerman, B. J. & Blom, D. E. (1983). Toward an empirical test of the role of cognitive conflict in learning. *Developmental Review, 3,* 18–38.

Zoccolillo, M., Romano, E., Joubert, D., Mazzarello, T., Côté, S., Boivin, M. Pérusse, D., & Tremblay R. E. (2005). The intergenerational transmission of aggression and antisocial behavior. In R. E. Tremblay, W. W. Hartup, & J. Archer (Eds.), *Developmental origins of aggression* (pp. 335–375). New York: Guilford.

Zucker, K. J. (2001). Biological influences on psycho-sexual differentiation. In R. Unger (Ed.), *Handbook of the psychology of women and gender.* New York: Wiley.

Zucker, K. J., Bradley, S. J., Oliver, G., Blake, J., Fleming, S., & Hood, J. (1996). Psychosexual development of women with congenital adrenal hyperplasia. *Hormones and Behavior, 30,* 300–318.

Zukow-Goldring, P. (2002). Sibling caregiving. In M. H. Bornstein (Ed.), *Handbook of parenting* (2nd ed., Vol. 3). Mahwah, NJ: Erlbaum.

Zupan, B. A., Hammen, C., & Jaenicke, C. (1987). The effects of current mood and prior depressive history on self-schematic processing in children. *Journal of Experimental Child Psychology, 43,* 149–158.

NAME INDEX

C

G

K

X

Y

Z

SUBJECT INDEX

J

O

P